Motion Picture Studio Directory
and
Trade Annual
1920

A Page-by-Page Reproduction

Silver
 Creek
  Press

2019

ISBN 978-1-945307-15-7

Where Paramount Artcraft Pictures Are Made

THE Famous-Players Lasky studio in Hollywood, California, known all over the world as the Lasky studios. Here are found the huge sky-light buildings for interiors, enormous laboratories, costume and research departments, acres of out-door locations, whole cities built for sets and, all in all, the most completely organized producing unit in the world.

Airplane view of the Lasky Studios

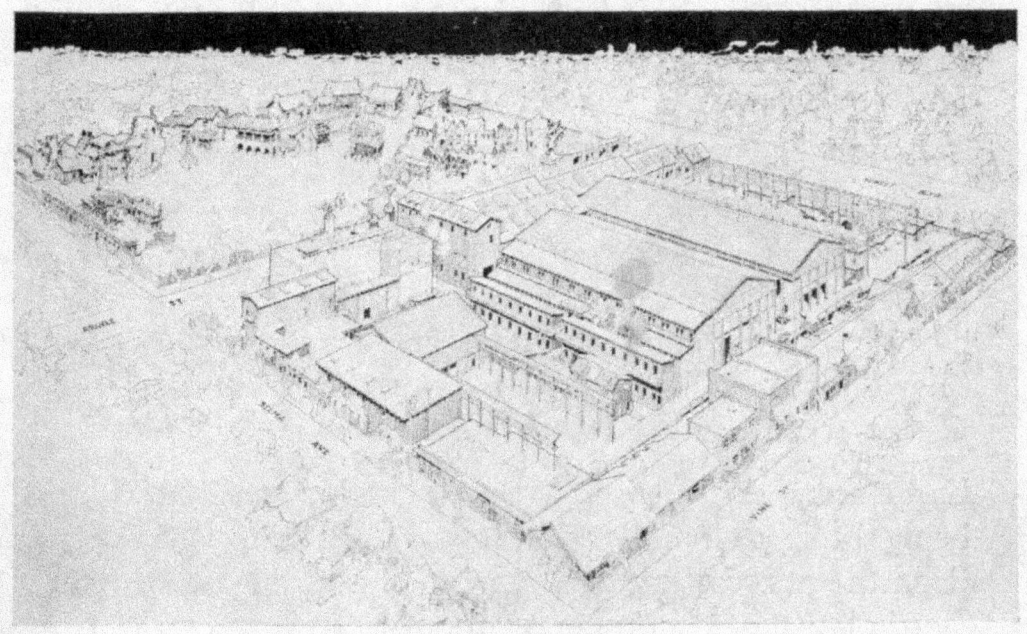

Drawing showing buildings and out-door sets

Famous Players-Lasky

Model of Studio as it will appear when completed

THE most complete and up-to-date institution of its kind in the world is now nearing completion in Long Island City.

A reinforced-concrete, fire-proof studio building and laboratories wherein all the eastern producing activities of Paramount Artcraft will be housed, covering over 140,000 square feet of ground area.

The studio will contain elaborate dressing-room facilities equipped with shower baths, lounging rooms and all the latest conveniences for the artists. Elaborate suites will be provided for stars, directors and their assistants and each director will be furnished with an individual projection room equipped with every modern facility.

Large scene docks equipped with modern machinery are being built to handle all sets mechanically. Scenario departments, casting department, modeling department, wardrobe rooms, property rooms, and a completely

New $2,000,000 Studio

equipped modern theatre are part of the enormous plans for this huge institution.

An up-to-date restaurant for the exclusive use of artists, a refrigerating plant, a sanitary barber shop, hair dressing parlors, libraries, reading rooms, locker rooms, Turkish baths, green room, club rooms and gymnasium are other units provided in this new Famous Players studio.

The studio building is being equipped with the most modern sprinkler system, and elevators for the quick handling of scenes and sets will be provided. Modern ventilating and air-cooling systems are being installed beneath the enormous glass roof. Every improved invention known to modern science will be employed. On the block adjoining there will be erected a three-story building devoted exclusively to laboratory purposes. It is now practically completed.

View of ground of new Studio on May 16, 1919

IF these walls could speak they would tell wonder-tales of the filming of some of the most pretentious, the most artistic and the most financially successful moving pictures ever made.

For this is the noted "56th St." studio, long the home of moving picture art in New York City.

The famous "56th St." Studio

The only big company studio situated in the very heart of New York City at 130 West 56th St., this studio has become as famous as any theatre on Broadway. For here the very greatest artists and stars of the speaking stage and the screen have acted before the camera, and the greatest directors of the entire industry have all at one time or another been within its portals.

Other of the enormous production activities of Famous Players in the east have been carried out in the huge Fort Lee studio and in various other studios in the outlying districts of the city.

With the completion of the new $2,000,000 studio all these activities will be concentrated in the new Long Island City studio.

The Place Where the Slap-stick was Born

NO outsider is allowed within these sacred portals. For here is an institution as famous as Plymouth Rock and a million times as jazzy.

"Mack Sennett Studios"—what a wealth of beautiful imagery those words produce! A peep into the working home of such laugh-producers as Ben Turpin, Charlie Murray, Ford Sterling, Kala Pasha, and of the king of them all, Mack Sennett himself, would be an event worth recording in history.

From the Bathing Beauties to the intricately-planned thrills of the incomparable Paramount-Sennett Comedies, there is room in this huge studio plant for them all. Here the best brains of the moving picture comedy world are working for the delight of millions, for it is here that the Sennett Comedy Features are provided for a comedy-hungry public.

No comedy studios on earth can approach this hallowed spot in the wealth of its traditions, just as no comedy pictures on earth can hope to come up to the high standard set by Mack Sennett, the father of picture comedy and the leader of them all!

Where Thomas H. Ince

Headquarters Building, Thomas H. Ince Studios

THE enormous producing activities of Thomas H. Ince take place in a studio plant that occupies eleven acres of ground at Culver City, Cal. These new studios have become one of the show places of southern California, because of their architectural beauty and their vast size.

The "mansion," or administration building, houses all the executive offices of the Ince Company. This stately building, set back on a tree-studded lawn, faces the boulevard. The working buildings are hidden in the rear, and include two huge glass stages, dressing rooms, scene docks, shops,

Outside the dressing-rooms

Productions are Made

property rooms and wardrobe buildings, all in separate units. A new laboratory and a duplicate lighting plant to be used in case the original plant is ever out of commission, are two additional units to the grounds.

In these new and beautiful studios the Thomas H. Ince productions take

A corner of the art-title department

form. Mr. Ince's technical and producing staff is world-famed. His stars, Charles Ray, Dorothy Dalton, Enid Bennett, Douglas MacLean and Doris May are the most popular in filmdom.

The new Thomas H. Ince studios provide a fitting home for such artists, and assure exhibitors and public of the finest motion picture work that modern invention and artistic genius can supply.

A floor interior of one of the studios

Fatty Arbuckle Studio

Fatty Arbuckle Studio

AND this is where "The Garage" was made—the funniest Fatty Arbuckle Comedy ever produced—in fact, the funniest two-reel comedy that has graced the screen in a year or two of holidays. The man, woman or child who won't laugh from the beginning to the end of "The Garage" doesn't exist. It's the biggest hit in picture comedy history

And here is where it was made. Such a location deserves immortal fame for that reason alone. But beside that reason for historic notoriety, consider the fact that here is where "Back Stage," "The Hayseed," "A Desert Hero," "Out West," "The Sheriff," "The Bell Boy," and all the other world-famed Arbuckle comedies were born and bred and had their being.

But what matter the studio, even if it were a cinema palace. Give the world Fatty Arbuckle, some picture film and a motion picture camera and there's joy enough for all the world, even if he had to produce in a barn.

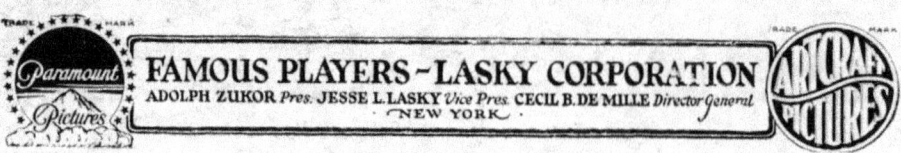

Katherine MacDonald
Starred in

"THE THUNDERBOLT"
By J. Grubb Alexander and D. F. Whitcomb

"THE TURNING POINT"
By Robert W. Chambers

"THE BEAUTY MARKET"
By Marjory Land May

"THE GUESTS OF HERCULES"
By C. N. and A. N. Williams

First National Release
Management Sam E. Rork

NORMA TALMADGE

Starring in

First National Attractions

NORMA TALMADGE FILM CO.

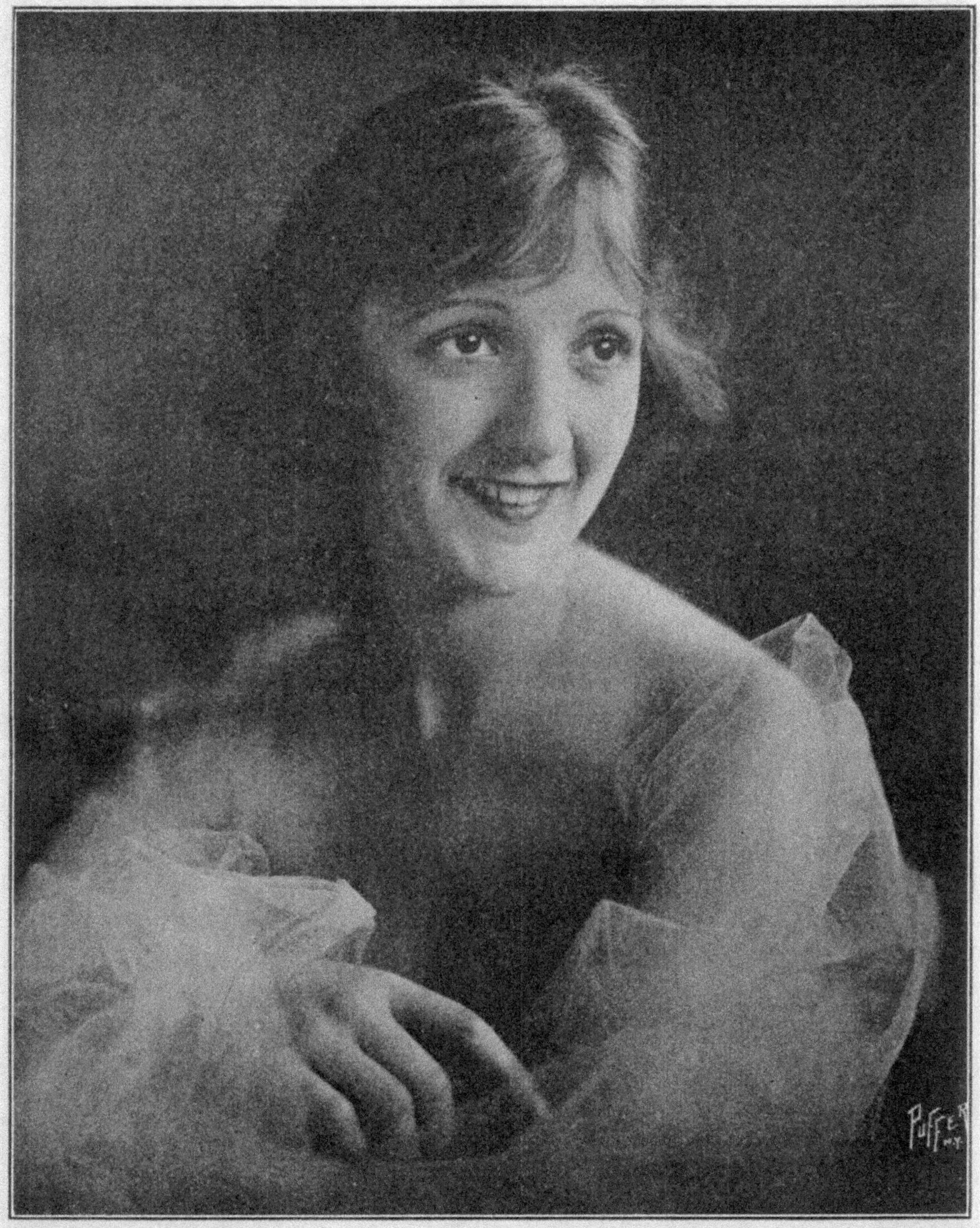

CONSTANCE TALMADGE

Starring in

First National Attractions

CONSTANCE TALMADGE FILM CO.

Anita Stewart

Cosmopolitan Productions

are selected for the screen from stories appearing in the pages of the great chain of Hearst Magazines and Newspapers.

Advertising

Outside of the pre-advertising these pictures receive when they are read in the magazines, they are advertised with display space in The Atlanta Georgian, The Chicago American, The Chicago Herald and Examiner, The Boston American, The Boston Advertiser, The San Francisco Examiner, The Los Angeles Examiner, The New York American, The New York Evening Journal, The Washington Times, The Wisconsin News, and other newspapers of large circulation.

Production

A studio in the heart of New York City covering an entire block. A staff of writers, directors and technical experts make Cosmopolitan Productions entertainment features of superior quality.

International Film Service Co., Inc.

729 Seventh Avenue
New York City

Alfred Cheney Johnston

MARION DAVIES

STARRING in Cosmopolitan Productions and the entrancing heroine of Robert W. Chambers' "Restless Sex"

ROGER LYTTON

142 East 18th Street, N. Y. C.

Stuyvesant 433

SYLVIA BREAMER

CATHERINE CALVERT
MANAGEMENT EDWARD SMALL

MAUD HILL

The Company Goldwyn Keeps

The canny exhibitor who has kept stride for stride with the amazing advance in modern picture production knows that Goldwyn Pictures attract a following of their own—the solid, steady, profit-building element in every community.

You know that Goldwyn means better business and more of it. Are you getting your share of the company Goldwyn keeps?

GOLDWYN PICTURES CORPORATION
Samnel Goldwyn, *President*

The dramatic flame that is Farrar—the melting smile of Tom Moore—the thrilling emotional fervor of Pauline Frederick—Jack Pickford's fresh and youthful charm—the rollicking comedy of Mabel Normand—the infectious humor of Will Rogers—the sparkling sprightliness of Madge Kennedy—Goldwyn stars ripple the histrionic scale!

From staccato comedy to gripping drama, from chuckles to tears. It's the Goldwyn interpretation of variety. It's giving your patrons what they want!

GOLDWYN PICTURES CORPORATION
Samuel Goldwyn, *President*

Pauline FREDERICK

Jack PICKFORD

Madge KENNEDY

Geraldine Farrar

Mabel Normand

Tom Moore

Will Rogers

Pauline Frederick

Madge Kennedy

Jack Pickford

Booth Tarkington

Booth Tarkington's Edgar Comedies

Two Reel Features

"The Adventures and Emotions of Master Edgar Pomeroy, Aged about Eleven, and *not* the Best Boy in Town—nor the Worst."

In Booth Tarkington's own words, there is the kernel of the Edgar Comedies. Another "Penrod," brought to life on the screen with all the delicious humor that has made this the most popular character in fiction.

GOLDWYN PICTURES CORPORATION
Samuel Goldwyn, *President*

Rex BEACH Mary Roberts RINEHART Gouverneur MORRIS

Rupert HUGHES

These great names have a permanent place in the hearts of the American public. Millions are held in the thrall of their magic pens—millions more throng to the presentation of their creations upon the screen.

Ride the crest of this mighty wave of popular approval. Link your theatre to the finest achievement in modern screen production!

GOLDWYN PICTURES CORPORATION
Samuel Goldwyn, *President*

Gertrude ATHERTON   **Leroy SCOTT**   **Basil KING**

Rex Beach

Rupert Hughes

Gertrude Atherton

Mary Roberts Rinehart

Basil King

Leroy Scott

Gouverneur Morris

Goldwyn-Bray Pictographs

Ford Educational Weekly

One-reel features that throw a dazzling highlight on any picture programme.

Uproariously funny animated cartoons, exquisite scenic bits and short snappy educationals — blended with the characteristic Goldwyn *flaire* for effect.

GOLDWYN PICTURES CORPORATION
Samuel Goldwyn, *President*

Goldwyn Service Sells!

It sells the exhibitor because it's the kind of advertising that sells his patrons.

From a two column newspaper ad to a smashing twenty four sheet poster, Goldwyn advertising pulsates with a dynamic spirit of salesmanship.

Get behind every Goldwyn Picture you show—and push! We're here to help you, with the kind of help that registers success!

GOLDWYN PICTURES CORPORATION

Samuel Goldwyn, *President*

WILLIAM DUNCAN

EDITH JOHNSON

JOSEPH ROCK — VITAGRAPH

Samuelson Films

Starring

MADGE TITHERADGE
PEGGY HYLAND
ISOBEL ELSOM
MAUDIE DUNHAM
DAISY BURRELL

C. M. HALLARD
CAMPBELL GULLAN
TOM REYNOLDS
JAMES LINDSAY

and

OWEN NARES

G. B. SAMUELSON
UNIVERSAL CITY
CALIFORNIA

THE SAMUELSON FILM MFG. CO., LTD.
WORTON HALL
ISLEWORTH
ENGLAND

C. M. Hallard
with
G. B. SAMUELSON

DOLORES CASSINELLI

"The Cameo Girl"

Star of "The Virtuous Model," "The Right to Lie" and "A Web of Deceit"

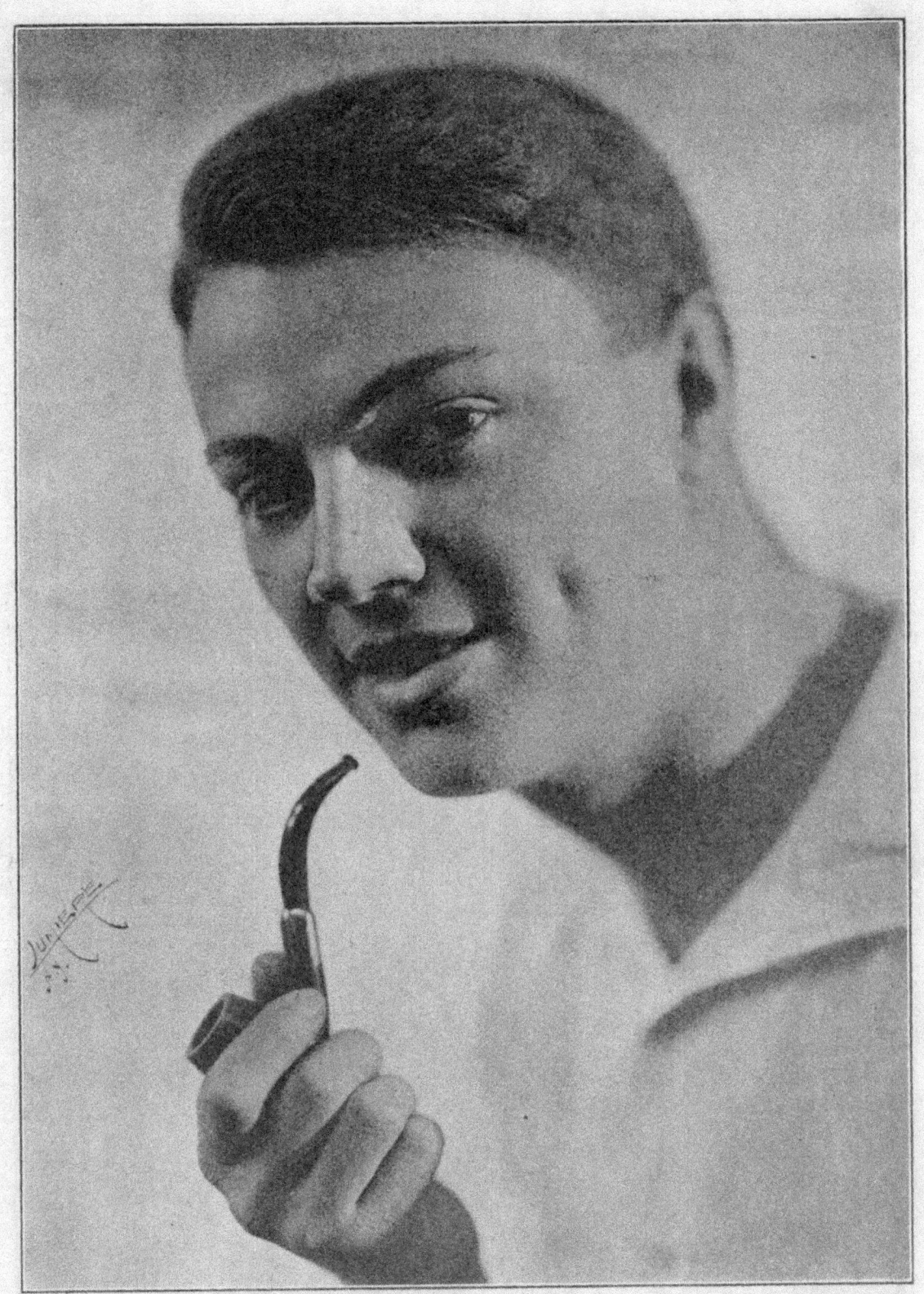

ROBERT GORDON

Featured in Blackton Productions
Released by Pathe

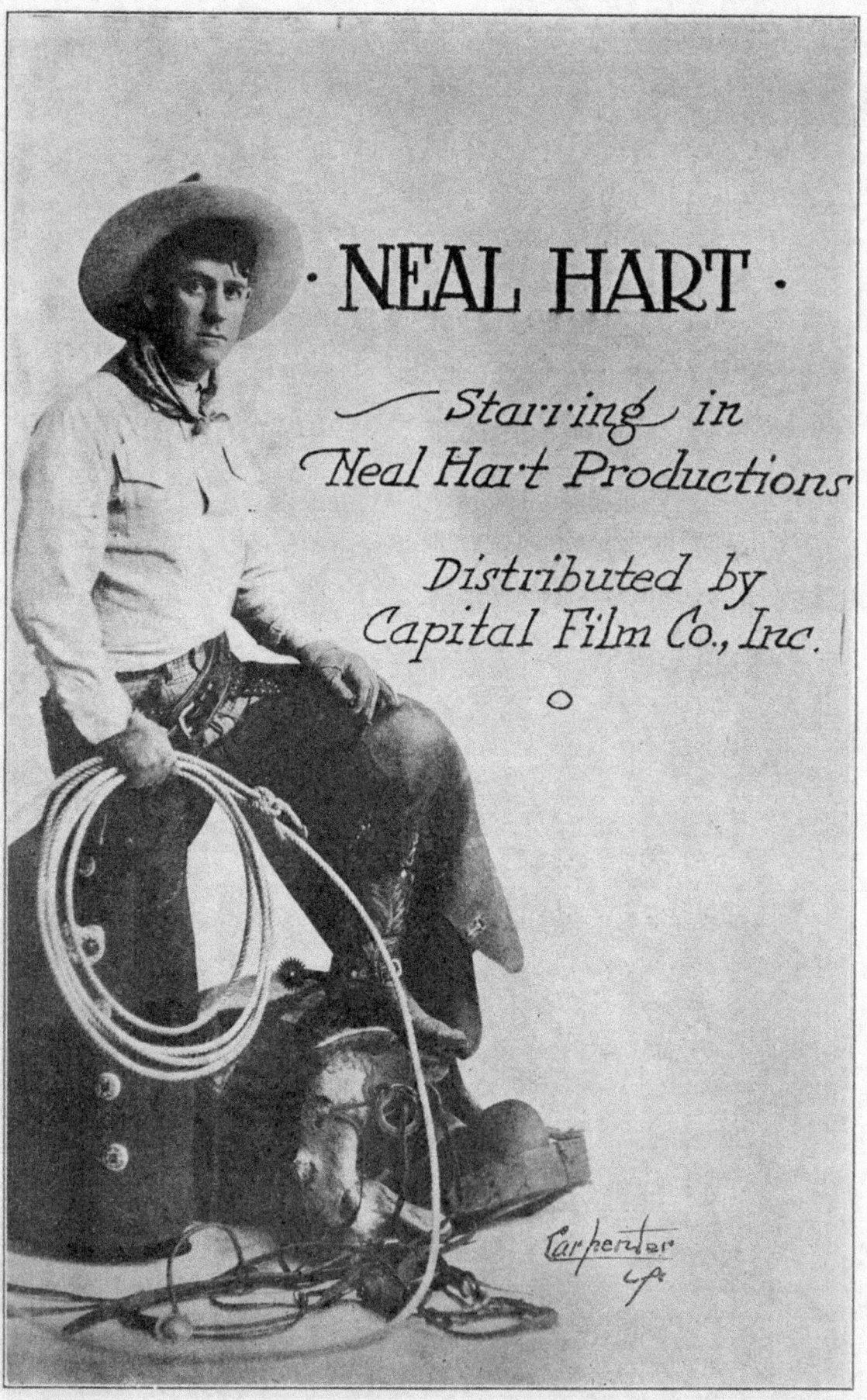

CORINNE BARKER

MANAGEMENT
EDWARD SMALL

EDW. THAYER MONROE

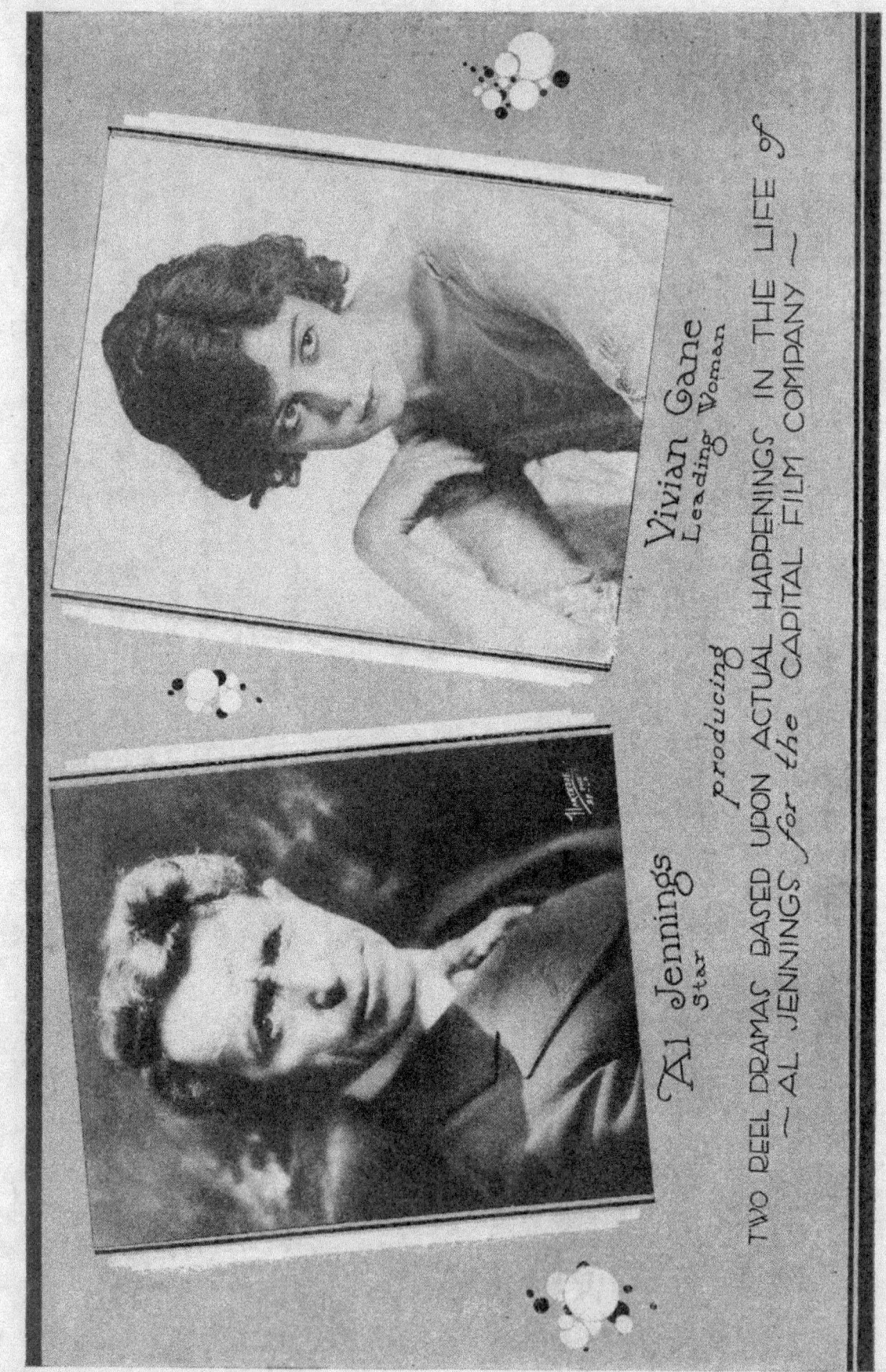

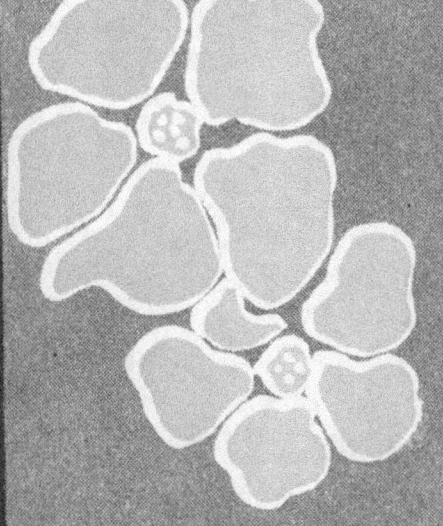

ROBERTSON-COLE

THE independent producer, the man of ideals, the man with a vision and the ability to put it over is the man responsible for the success of production.

The destruction of the independent, the suppression of ideals, is akin to the standardization of Art. The standardization of Art is the death of the industry.

From the beginning Robertson-Cole has backed the independent producer. We have invited the best efforts of all with a guarantee of adequate return.

We will continue to place our resources back of the men of big ideals, the men of broad instinct, the independent producers.

ROBERTSON-COLE COMPANY
Division of Films
EXECUTIVE OFFICES NEW YORK CITY

ROBERTSON-COLE

THE future of the exhibitor lies entirely in the preservation of his complete independence.

His right to select is his most sacred and valuable right. To destroy it means the destruction of progress in the making of pictures.

Robertson-Cole stands for progress and INDEPENDENCE. In a word, we stand with the exhibitor.

His success is our success and we are pledged to make our success his success. Our joint success is the greatest guarantee of the future of the industry.

Business methods, the fair deal and fair price, and mutual co-operation, is our pledge to the exhibitor.

ROBERTSON-COLE DISTRIBUTING
CORPORATION

A. S. KIRKPATRICK
Vice President and General Manager.

JANE JENNINGS

STUART HOLMES

Management Edward Small

EDMUND LOWE

MANAGEMENT EDWARD SMALL

Morris R. Schlank

Producing
Hank Mann two reel Comedies
released through Arrow.

IRENE TAMS
PERSONAL MANAGEMENT
of
ARTHUR H. JACOBS

Lloyd (Ham) Hamilton

Featured in HENRY LEHRMAN COMEDIES

Initial Release "The TWILIGHT BABY"
FIRST NATIONAL

Gene Pollar

Playing Tarzan in

"The Return of Tarzan"

Numa Pictures Corporation

1476 Broadway, New York City

Walter Miller

Featured in productions for

Artclass Pictures Corporation

Released by Robertson-Cole

MOTION PICTURE ART DIRECTORS ASSOCIATION

An educational and co-operative organization for the furtherance of the artistic development of motion pictures, holding meetings at regular intervals for the exchange of ideas, securing lecturers whose discourses will promote discussion of subjects pertaining to the work of members, and for the establishment and maintenance of a library on art, architecture and kindred subjects, beneficial to the members and their employers, the producers.

ALFRED W. ALLEY, *President*
1632½ Winona Blvd.
Holly. 3062

ESDRAS C. HARTLEY, *Sec'y.*
1221 W. 7th St.
60121

R. E. SIBLEY, *Vice-Pres.*
2138 Marathon St.
Wil. 2469

SIDNEY M. ULLMAN, *Treas.*
1557 Gordon St.
Holly. 42

FRANK S. BROWN — *South 5473*
142 W. 37th Place

BEN CARRE
6732 Hollywood Blvd.

DAVID B. EDWARDS
335 N. Vendome St. — *53770*

ROBT. J. ELLIS — *59287*
1827 N. Vermont Ave.

CHAS. I. FARBER — *Holly 3230*
5738 Waring Ave.

LEWIS GEIB — *Holly 992*
4426 Russell Ave.

FRED GABOURIE
5164 Argyle St.

EDWARD J. HAAS — *597613*
7726 Walnut Drive

AL HERMAN — *Holly 2131*

W. S. HINSHELWOOD
5663 Santa Monica Blvd. — *Holly 4080-4*

C. TRACY HOAG — *Wilt 2245*
1143 Logan St.

JOHN K. HOLDEN — *Holly 1130*
745 Cahuenga Ave.

G. A. HOLLICKER — *Bway 4949*
1312 Maryland St.

CHAS. D. HULL — *Holly 2371*
4555 Prospect Ave.

J. I. JACKMAN
1429 Logan St.

CHAS. H. KEYSON — *Holly 3056*
7266 Sunset Blvd.

EDWARD M. LANGLEY
3105½ Kenwood Ave. — *7327*

ROY HEWITT McCRAY
1537 N. Alexandria St. — *Holly 2131*

MILTON T. MENASCO
6511½ Hollywood Blvd. — *577337*

AMOS J. MYERS
1422 Gordon St.

CHAS. ODDS — *67103*
123 N. Grand Ave.

JACK OKEY — *560695*
537 N. Ardmore Ave.

EARLE F. OLIN — *Holly 2890*
5417 Sunset Blvd.

FRANK D. ORMSTON
Hotel Glidden, Hollywood

MAX PARKER — *West 1279*
919 W. 35th Place

A. R. RITTER — *Wilt 3480*
1742 Kane St.

J. H. ROGERS — *Holly 1131*
5536 Delongpre St.

ALLEN RUOFF — *Wilt 5621*
1442 McCullum St.

ELMER E. SHEELEY
1601 Edgemont St.

W. E. SHEPHERD — *South 5633 J*
347 E. 33rd St.

E. J. SHULTER — *Holly 4485*
Hollywood Apts.

WILSON SILSBY — *Pico 350*
223 S. Flower

FIELDER C. SLINGLUFF
Universal City

M. P. STAULCUP — *57476*
1905 N. Wilcox

A. B. STURGES — *568183*
4561 W. 2nd St.

TOM F. WARRILLOW
1546 N. Western Ave. — *599122*

REX D. WESTON — *12881*
Gibson Apts., 4th & Hope

GEO. H. WILLIAMS
6664 Franklin Ave.

JOHN VOSHEELE
C. K. Young Studio

MOTION PICTURE
DIRECTORS ASSOCIATION

New York Lodge
234 W. 55th St.—Circle 1844

Los Angeles Lodge
6372 Hollywood Blvd.

Adolphi, John
Arbuckle, Roscoe G.
Archainbaud, Geo.
August, Edwin
Barker, Reginald
Beal, Frank
Beaudine, Wm.
Beaumont, Harry
Bertram, Wm.
Blystone, John G.
Borzage, Frank
Brooke, Van Dyke
Buel, Kenean
Campbell, Colin
Carleton, Lloyd B.
Carewe, Edwin
Chaudet, Louis Wm.
Chautard, Emile
Christie, Al. E.
Clements, Roy
Cline, E. F.
Conway, Jack
Crane, Frank H.
Crisp, Donald W.
Daly, Wm. Robt.
Dawley, J. Searle
DeGrasse, Joseph
Dillon, J. F.
Duncan, Wm.
Eagle, Oscar
Edwards, J. Gordon
Edwards, Walter
Fishbach, Fred
Fitzmaurice, George
Fleming, Carroll
Ford, Francis
French, Chas. K.
Gasnier, Louis J.

Gerrard, Douglas
Giblyn, Charles
Gordon, James
Haddock, Wm. F.
Harvey, John J.
Heffron, Thomas N.
Henderson, Dell
Henley, Hobart
Herman, Victor
Holubar, Allen J.
Hopper, E. Mason
Hunt, Jay
Ince, John C.
Ince, Ralph
Ingraham, Lloyd
Irving, George
Jaccard, Jacques
Kelsey, Fred A.
King, Henry
Kirkland, David
Knoles, Harley
LeSaint, Ed. J.
Lessey, George A.
Lloyd, Frank
Lund, O. A. C.
MacGregor, Norval
MacQuarrie, Murdock J.
Marshall, George
McGill, Lawrence B.
Melford, George
Middleton, Edwin
Millarde, Harry
Miller, Ashley
Miller, Chas. A.
Morgan, George
Neill, Roy
O'Brien, John
Olcott, Sidney

Otto, Henry W.
Payton, Stuart
Perret, Leonce
Powers, Francis J.
Reynolds, Lynn F.
Ricketts, Thomas
Robertson, John S.
Ruggles, Wesley
Sargent, George L.
Scardon, Paul
Schertzirger, Victor
Seitz, George B.
Sidney, E. Scott
Siegman, George A.
Sloman, Edward
Smalley, Phillips
Stanton, Richard
Swim, Capt. O. H.
Taylor, S. E. V.
Taylor, Wm. Desmond
Terriss, Tom
Thomson, Fred. A.
Tourneur, Maurice
Vale, Travers
Van, Wally
Vekroff, Perry N.
Vignola, Robert G.
Vincent, James
Walsh, Raoul A.
Ward, Ernest
Webb, Kenneth
West, Raymond B.
Williams, C. Jay
Wilson, Ben
Withey, Chet
Worsley, Wallace
Worthington, Wm.
Wright, Fred E.
Young, James

LILLIAN R. GALE—*N. Y. Press Representative*

CHET WITHEY

Associated with D. W. Griffith

"The Hun Within"
"The New Moon"—Norma Talmadge
"The Teeth of the Tiger"—Paramount-Artcraft
"She Loves and Lies"—Norma Talmadge

"ROMANCE," with Doris Keane

GEO. D. BAKER
DIRECTOR

Some Past Releases

A Night Out
MAY ROBSON

Tarantula
ANTONIO MORENO
EDITH STOREY

The Shell Game
EMMY WEHLAN

His Father's Son
LIONEL BARRYMORE

Peggy Does Her Darndest
MAY ALLISON

The Lion's Den
BERT LYTELL

The Wager
EMILY STEVENS

The White Raven
ETHEL BARRYMORE

Revelation
NAZIMOVA

The Cinema Murder
MARION DAVIES

The Man Who Lost Himself
WM. FAVERSHAM

Address 130 West 44th Street
New York City

William D. Taylor

PARAMOUNT ARTCRAFT SPECIALS
Current Release
HUCKLEBERRY FINN

Jerome Storm
DIRECTOR
of
Charles Ray Productions
— during the past year.

Rex Ingram
DIRECTOR
METRO PICTURES CORP.

First Release since return from the Royal Flying Corps: "CAPTAIN COURAGE"
(Universal Special)
Coming: "SHORE-ACRES" (Metro) —
Walter Mayo, Assistant Director.

KENNETH WEBB
M. P. D. A.

Director—Famous Players-Lasky Corporation

ROY WEBB
Assistant Director

GEORGE FOLSEY
Cinematographer

TOM TERRISS
Director

RECENT RELEASES

"The Lion and the Mouse"   "The Vengeance of Durant"
"The Third Degree"   "The Fortune Hunter"
"The Climbers"

VICTOR FLEMING
Now directing
DOUGLAS FAIRBANKS

First Release:

"WHEN THE CLOUDS ROLL BY"

Next Production:

"TRAILIN'"

Victor Fleming
Fairbanks Studio
Hollywood, Calif.

WILLIAM PARKER

AUTHOR AND ADAPTER OF SCREEN STORIES

Associated with
KING W. VIDOR

A CREED AND A PLEDGE

I BELIEVE in the motion picture that carries a message to humanity.

I BELIEVE in the picture that will help humanity to free itself from the shackles of fear and suffering that have so long bound it with iron chains.

I WILL NOT knowingly produce a picture that contains anything I do not believe to be absolutely true to human nature, anything that could injure anyone, nor anything unclean in thought or action.

NOR WILL I deliberately portray anything to cause fright, suggest fear, glorify mischief, condone cruelty or extenuate malice.

I WILL NEVER picture evil or wrong, except to prove the fallacy of its lure.

SO LONG AS I direct pictures, I will make only those founded upon the principle of right and I will endeavor to draw upon the inexhaustible source of Good for my stories, my guidance, and my inspiration.

King W. Vidor

FORTHCOMING
A Series of Special Productions for First National

JAMES A. FITZPATRICK
PRIZMA

ARTHUR ROSSON

Director

of

Douglas Fairbanks *in* "Headin' South"—*Artcraft*

Louise Glaum *in* "Sahara"—*J. Parker Reed*

Tom Mix *in* "Rough Riding Romance"—*Fox*

Mildred Harris Chaplin *in* "A Splendid Hazard"—*Realart*

	Address:	
DICK ROSSON	L. A. A. C.	HAROLD ROSSON
Associate	Los Angeles, Cal.	Photographer

Sherwood Macdonald

Director –

John Emerson   Anita Loos

EMERSON-LOOS PRODUCTIONS

For CONSTANCE TALMADGE
A Temperamental Wife
The Virtuous Vamp———In Search of a Sinner

For NORMA TALMADGE
The Social Secretary

For PARAMOUNT-ARTCRAFT
Come on In———Oh, You Women!

For DOUGLAS FAIRBANKS
Reaching for the Moon———Down to Earth
In Again, Out Again———Wild and Woolly
His Picture in the Paper———The Americano

Address: 130 West 44th Street, New York

Robert T. Thornby

directing

Blanche Sweet

for

Jesse D. Hampton Productions

shortly to produce
Thornby Special Features

Presented by
Jesse D Hampton
Studio: Hollywood · Cal

ERNEST C. WARDE

Directing

J. WARREN KERRIGAN CO.

Frank L. Geraghty, Asst.   Arthur L. Todd, Cinematographer

Robert Brunton Studios, Hollywood

JOHN STAHL
Director

MANAGEMENT EDWARD SMALL

HAROLD J. BINNEY
Producer-Director

LATEST PRODUCTIONS

"The Boarder Legion" — by Zane Grey ..... Starring Blanche Bates & Hobart Bosworth Released by Goldwyn

"Desert Gold" by Zane Grey Released by Hodkinson

"The Cup of Fury" by Rupert Hughes ... A Goldwyn Special

IN PREPARATION

"Earthbound" by Basil King A Goldwyn Special

Directed by
T. Hayes Hunter
means
A Special with Box Office Attractions

R. WILLIAM NEILL

(Management Edward Small)

Who Will Direct a Series of R. William Neill Productions to Be Made in England and to Be Released Through First National

HOBART HENLEY
Personally Supervising and Directing
HOBART HENLEY PRODUCTIONS
363 West 125th Street New York City

George Brackett Seitz
M. P. D. A.

Star, Director and Producer of his
Greatest Serial

"BOUND AND GAGGED"
By Frank Leon Smith

Previous Successes:

"THE FATAL RING" "THE LIGHTNING RAIDER"
"THE HOUSE OF HATE" (Pathe) "THE BLACK SECRET"

WILFRID NORTH
DIRECTOR
GUY EMPEY PRODUCTIONS

LEONCE PERRET
Director General, Perret Pictures, Inc.
Author—Producer—Director
CURRENT PRODUCTIONS:
"THIRTEENTH CHAIR"   "A. B. C. OF LOVE"
"TWIN PAWNS"   "A MODERN SALOME"

EDWIN CAREWE ANNOUNCES

The Following Productions for 1920

"RIO GRANDE"..................................By Augustus Thomas
"QUEEN OF THE MOULIN ROUGE".........By Paul M. Potter
"WHAT MAN CALLS LOVE"...............By Augustus Thomas
"HABIT"...By Tom Barry

PAST ACHIEVEMENTS

"THE RIGHT TO LIE"...........................Dolores Cassinelli
"THE WEB OF LIES".............................Dolores Cassinelli

"The Soul of a Woman"...........................Emily Stevens
"The Snowbird"....................................Mabel Taliaferro
"The House of Tears".............................Emily Stevens
"The Splendid Sinner"...........................Mary Garden
"Her Great Price"................................Mabel Taliaferro
"The Voice of Conscience,"
               Francis X. Bushman and Beverly Bayne
"God's Half Acre"................................Mabel Taliaferro
"Pals First".......................................Harold Lockwood
"The Trail to Yesterday"..........................Bert Lytell
"The Way of the Strong".......................Anna Q. Nilsson

MR. CAREWE'S PAST ACHIEVEMENTS WILL MERIT THE CLOSE
ATTENTION OF EXHIBITORS TO HIS FUTURE PRODUCTIONS

DISTRIBUTED BY
PATHÉ

EDWIN CAREWE PRODUCTIONS, Inc.

Suite 809 Brokaw Bldg.   1457 Broadway

HARRY CAHANE, *Treasurer*

FRANK REICHER
Producer of Important Feature Films
Who Directed
"EMPTY ARMS"

BEN WILSON PRODUCTIONS
Producing Serials
Current Release: "The Trail of the Octopus"

In Production: "The Screaming Shadow," Released February 1, 1920
Through
HALLMARK PICTURES CORP.
Frank Hall, *President*
Address: Universal City, Calif.

J. GORDON COOPER

Director

Management Edward Small

Directed Herbert Rawlinson in
W. J. FLYNN SERIES

Now Directing for
HALLMARK PRODUCTIONS

PERRY VEKROFF

Director

Latest Release " THE ISLE OF JEWELS," Serial Starring Stuart Holmes

MANAGEMENT EDWARD SMALL

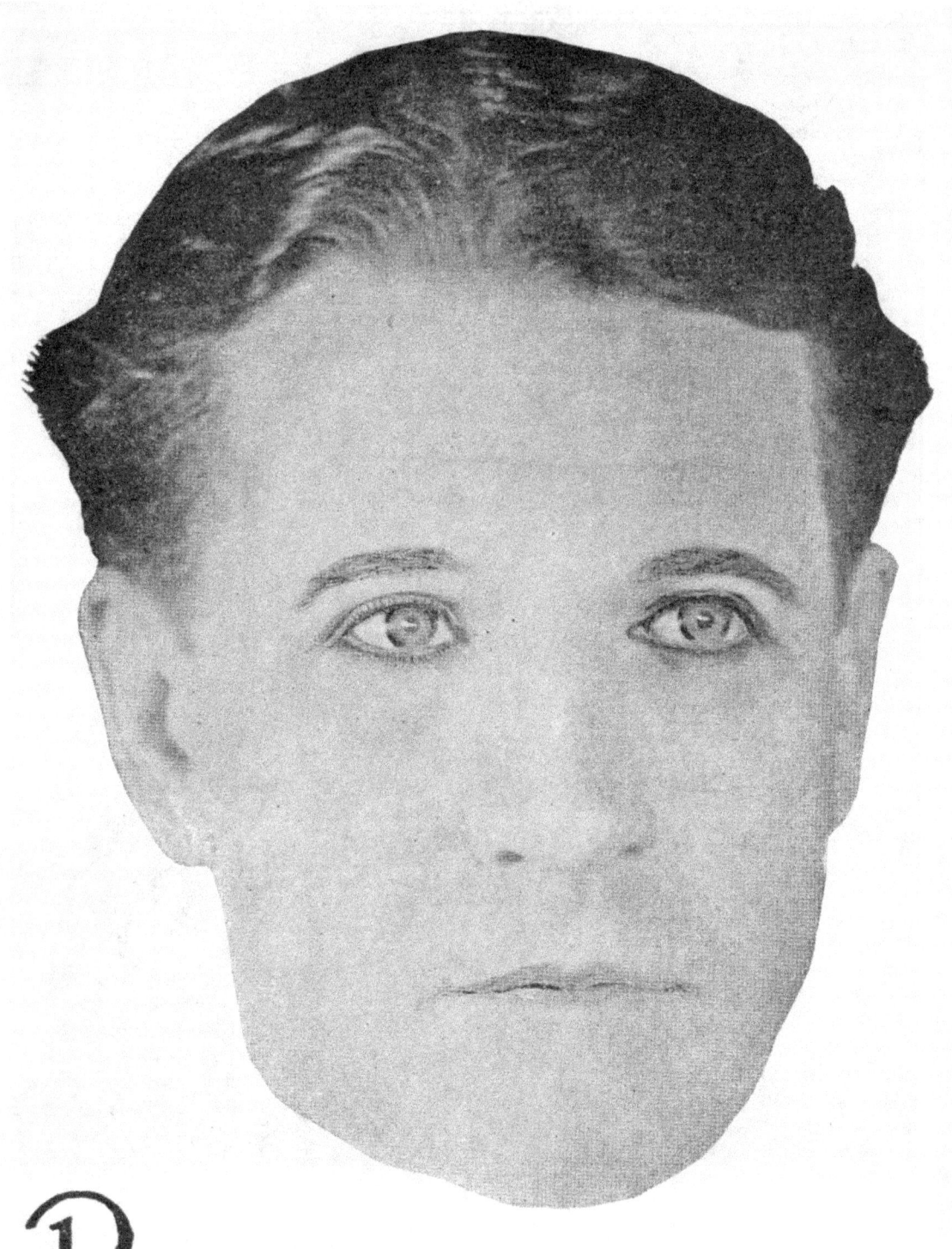

Romaine Fielding

THE BLACHÉS

Directors

Producers

Manufacturers

HERBERT BLACHÉ

MADAME BLACHÉ

DIRECTED

Nazimova
Viola Dana
May Allison
Florence Reed
Petrova
Mary Miles Minter
Edmund Breese
Holbrook Blinn
Frank Keenan
Bessie Love
Emily Stevens
Ethel Barrymore
King Baggot

MIDNIGHT PATROL

ZEPPELINS LAST RAID

THE GUILTY MAN

CALL OF THE NORTH
CHAS. RAY

DAUGHTER OF THE WOLF
LILA LEE

FALSE FACES

THE GRIM GAME
HOUDINI

BEHIND THE DOOR
BOSWORTH

Irvin Willat Master Director

WILLAT PRODUCTIONS, INC.
LOS ANGELES   NEW YORK

FRANCIS FORD
INDEPENDENT PRODUCER

Serials — Features — Comedies

1919 PRODUCTIONS

"Silent Mystery"
"Mystery of 13" | SERIALS
"Gates of Doom"

"Crimson Shoals" — Feature

CORRESPONDENCE SOLICITED

FRANCIS FORD – SOLE OWNER

HARRY ELLIS DEAN
GEN'L MANAGER

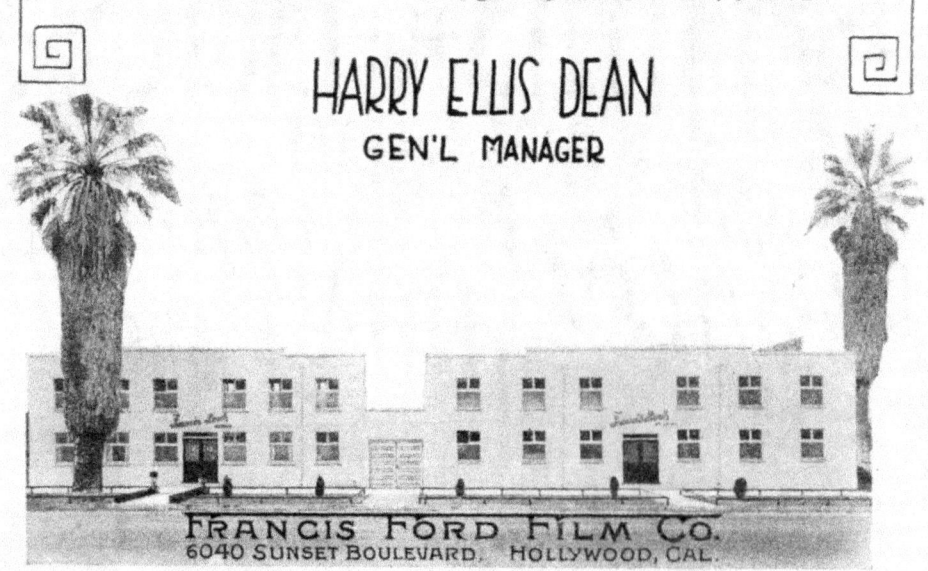

Francis Ford Film Co.
6040 Sunset Boulevard, Hollywood, Cal.

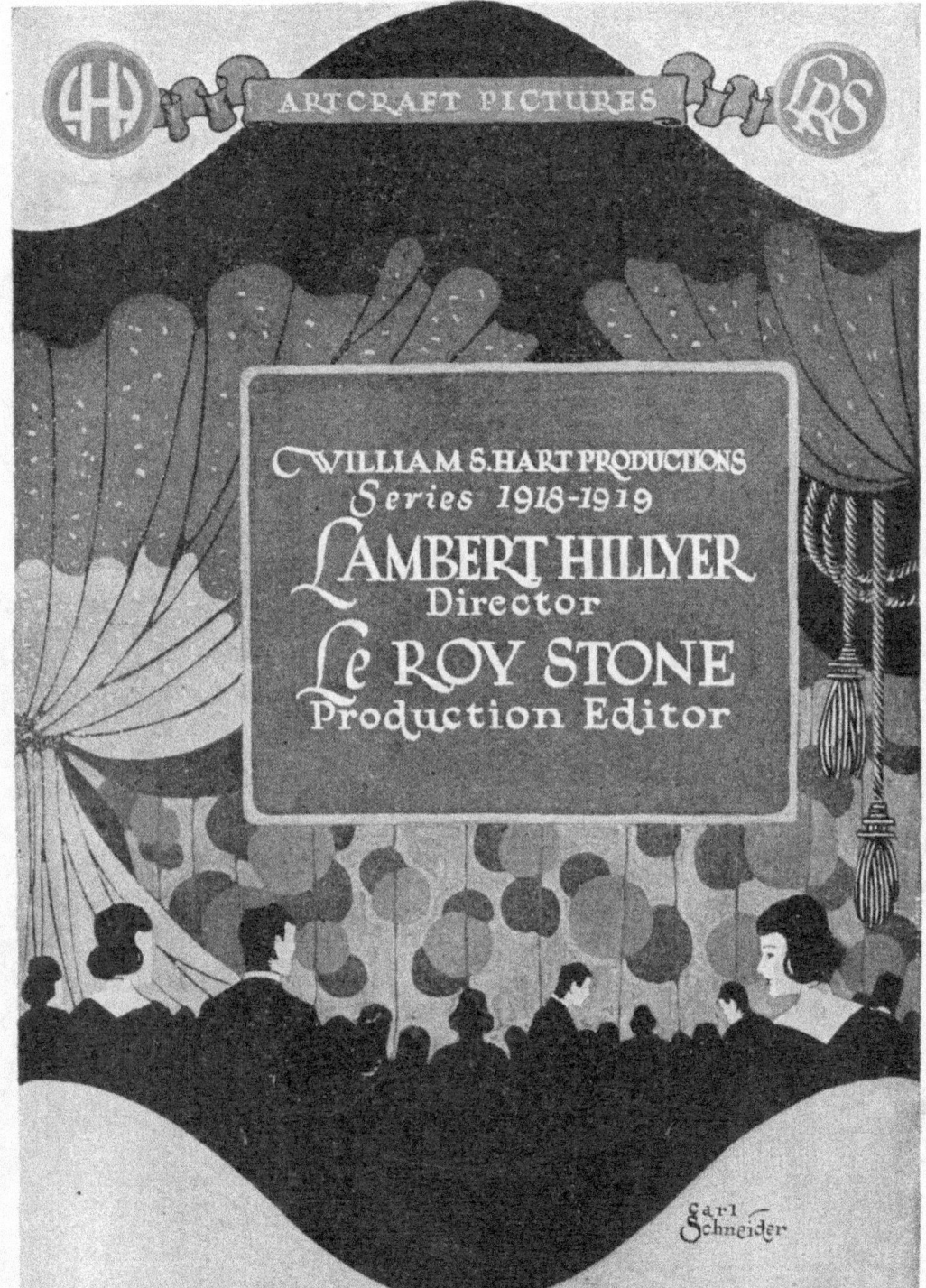

HARRY O. HOYT

"The director of motion pictures must be first of all a story teller—he must have the gifts of the novelist and the playwright or he cannot reach the heights. The author brings to picture direction an appreciation of story values—he has read and studied in preparation for his production and as a result intelligence marks the picture."

Author of several hundred original stories and scenarios.

Directed Montague Love, Dorothy Green, Arthur Ashley, Virginia Hammond and others in "A Broadway Saint," "Forest Rivals," "Through the Toils," etc., for World Film Corporation.

Now Directing
Miss Catherine Calvert in
"That Woman"

Engaged until
January First
Nineteen Twenty-one

FINIS FOX
METRO SCENARIO STAFF
(SEE BIOGRAPHY)

EVE UNSELL
Scenarios

272 Lincoln Road　　　　　　　　　　　　Brooklyn, N. Y.

TOM J. GERAGHTY

*Scenario Writer
and
Editor of Production*

with

DOUGLAS FAIRBANKS

"When the Clouds Roll By"
"Turn to the Right"—and maybe more

At the tender age of seven when I wrote my first magic lantern show entitled "Murder Is Awful."

Cable Address
Kwas-Nujol

T. J. G.
Hollywood, Calif.

WALTER RICHARD HALL
Director and Author

SERIALS

"THE FATAL FORTUNE"

"A WOMAN IN GREY"

"THE MAN WITHOUT A FACE"

AND "THE STEEL MASK"

FEATURES

"HATE"

"SOULS OF MEN"

"THE LEECH"

"BUCKING THE TIGER," ETC.

Continuity That Reaches the Screen as It Is Written

ADDRESS
1203 Candler Building, N. Y. C.

'PHONE
Bryant 8440

Edmund Goulding

MANAGEMENT
EDWARD SMALL

TELEPHONE
VANDERBILT 2500

MY RECORD:

1916—Successful short-story writer.

1917—Editor-in-Chief of a big magazine.

1918—Soldier of Uncle Sam.

1919—Continuity writer at VITAGRAPH (East Coast) and author of original screen stories for Louise Huff and others.

1920—Picturizing big plays and novels at METRO (West Coast) and writing originals for leading stars.

1921—Past performance is the best guarantee of future success. I look ahead confidently, with a solid background of practical experience behind me.

H. THOMPSON RICH

Frances Guihan

Specializing in Adapting Stories for the Screen

— 1920 RELEASES —

"Broadway Bab"
"Ruth Roland – Pathe Serial"
by Johnston McCulley.
Louis Mayer Production
Starring Anita Stewart.

"Sherry"
by George Barr McCutcheon,
for Edgar Lewis
Three Frohman Productions
Starring Texas Guinan

Address: 1717 So. Flower St., — Los Angeles

STUDIO
GRANTWOOD, N. J.

Copyright 1919

COST OF PRODUCTION
$500,000.00

THE PHOTOPLAY DE LUXE

ENTITLED

TEN PARTS "DETERMINATION" TEN PARTS

CAPT. F. F. STOLL, AUTHOR

SHOWING

Scotland Yard Activity
Whitechapel Rabble Characters
Chinese Dope Den
Women of the Street
Dive Scene
The Fagin School
The Fence
The Great Bank Robbery
The Good Samaritan
The Master Mind of Crooks

CAST—
ALL STAR

SHOWING

The International Sport
The International Beauty
Four International Sporting Events
The Horse Race
The Auto Race
The Aviation Meet
The Boxing Contest
The Great Gambling Scene
The Mission of Humanity

CAST—
ALL STAR

Unanimous Opinion: The Greatest Human Interest Story Ever Written

ESTIMATED TIME FOR PRODUCTION, EIGHT MONTHS

Producers:

United States Photoplay Corporation

WASHINGTON, D. C.

AMERICAN SOCIETY OF CINEMATOGRAPHERS

OUR MOTTO: LOYALTY! PROGRESS! ART!

OUR IDEAL: That membership in this Society may become a mark of honor and distinction based on merit.

This organization has been formed for the purpose of bringing into the closest confederation all—but only—those leaders in the cinematographic science whose attainments in their chosen field entitle them to membership in this Society, for the purpose of maintaining the high standard set for themselves—and at the same time promote the interest and welfare and protect the rights of all who shall be so fortunate as to be called to membership.

At this date our membership consists of the following cinematographers:

Philip E. Rosen, Pres.   Charles G. Rosher, Vice-Pres.   Victor Milner, Sec'y
Wm. C. Foster, Treas.

Joe August	H. Lyman Broening	Chester A. Lyons
L. D. Clawson	Henry Cronjager	Reggie Lyons
Eugene Gaudio	Ernest S. Depew	Hugh C. McClung
Frank B. Good	Arthur Edeson	Ira H. Morgan
King D. Gray	William Fildew	Ernest S. Palmer
Walter L. Griffin	Ross G. Fisher	Paul P. Perry
J. D. Jennings	Gaetone G. Gaudio	G. C. Peterson
Roy H. Klaffki	Fred Le Roy Granville	Sol Polito
Robert S. Newhard	Albert G. Heimerl	George Rizard
Stephen S. Norton	F. W. Jackman	A. Scholtz
L. Guy Wilky	Charles E. Kaufman	Homer A. Scott
	H. F. Koenekamp	John F. Seitz
John Arnold	Edward Kull	R. H. Totheroh
Friend F. Baker	Robert B. Kurrle	J. C. Van Trees
William J. Beckway	Sam Landers	Gilbert Warrenton
R. J. Bergquist	Walter Lundin	Philip H. Whitman

Membership is by invitation only, each man being judged solely upon his record and ability as a cinematographer and his personal fitness as a man.

Address:

325 Markham Building, 6372 Hollywood Blvd.

Hollywood, California

DAL CLAWSON SOLVES LIGHTING PROBLEMS, MAKING POSSIBLE ADDITIONAL REALISM FOR INTERIOR SCENES

"After many others have failed in an attempt to use natural interior settings for scenes in films, Dal Clawson with his assistant, Pete Harrod, has worked out appliances that make possible photography of all kinds of settings with artificial light.

"This is indeed a step in the advancement of motion picture plays, for it makes possible a material decrease in the cost of production and at the same time assures absolute realism. It is by using interiors actually erected for a given purpose and used for that purpose a number of months or years. It is assured that the correct atmosphere will be secured and that such settings have a great advantage over those built at the studios especially for the making of film scenes. The studio created set is so apt to be incorrect, it is a very easy matter for the technical men to overlook the little details that mean so much in the scene. Then, too, the actual marks made by wear and tear are hard to duplicate. All of these are to be had in a film if actual interiors are used and this applies to residences and public buildings of all kinds.

"The photography work has been most successfully carried out by Dal Clawson in a number of photoplays he has photographed for Lois

Weber. Included in this list of screen plays photographed entirely in the homes of the elite are, "For Husbands Only," "Forbidden," "A Midnight Romance," "Mary Regan," and the one he is now finishing which will be Miss Weber's initial release through Famous Players-Lasky Corporation. In "The Midnight Romance" all of the interior scenes with the exception of one were made in residences and public buildings, the two being filmed at the studio where a special set was erected.

"The special contrivances necessary for this kind of work, created by Mr. Clawson, are now being patented and it is probable they will shortly be placed on the market. In the making of these appliances, the inventive genius of both Mr. Clawson and his assistant, Pete Harrod, has brought to the film industry articles of merit that will make possible economic measures for the film industry."

Frank D. Williams

Photographing Motion Pictures Since 1905

Four and one-half years head cameraman Mack Sennett Studios.

Photographer for Charles Chaplin first eighteen months of his screen career.

Photographing Sessue Hayakawa for Haworth Company.

Current Releases:

The Dragon Painter	The Tong Man
The Man Beneath	The Beggar Prince
The Grey Horizon	The Undertow

Previous Releases:

MABEL NORMAND in "Mickey."
ANNETTE KELLERMAN in "Queen of the Seas"

Inventor and patentee of tank method making possible undersea photography used in the filming of "Queen of the Seas," and now in use by the Annette Kellermann Company; and of method of substituting any background in motion pictures or photographs after negatives of action or subjects have been made. Both methods for lease.

Address Haworth Pictures Corp., 4500 Sunset Blvd.
Hollywood, California

PALMER PHOTOPLAY
"STORY HEADQUARTERS"

ADVISORY COUNCIL
1. CECIL B. DeMILLE
   Director-General Famous Players
   -Lasky- Corporation
2. THOMAS H. INCE
   Head of the
   Thomas H. Ince Studios
3. LOIS WEBER
   Lois Weber Productions
   Noted Director, Author
4. ROB WAGNER
   Special Saturday Evening Post
   Writer and Screen Authority

CONTRIBUTORS
1. Frank Lloyd
2. Jeanie MacPherson
3. Clarence Badger
4. Denison Clift
5. Al E. Christie
6. Jasper Ewing Brady
7. George Beban
8. Kate Corbaley
9. Hugh McClung
10. Rob Wagner
11. Eric Howard
12. Adeline Alvord

Department of Education

Somewhere in America this year scores of new photoplay writers will be developed.

Many—perhaps a majority—of these new writers will be trained and developed through the Palmer course and service. Some of them will be the famous photoplaywrights of the future.

The day of the untrained amateur scenario writer is passed. The era of the writer trained in screencraft is here—now!

A genuine opportunity awaits men and women of creative impulse who are willing to train themselves intensively in the new art of photoplay writing.

Now approaching our third year of educational work, we can point with gratification to the development of many new photoplaywrights. Most of them came to us without either experience or previous success. A number of our more successful students have taken staff scenario positions in Los Angeles studios. Others are doing splendid free-lance work.

The Palmer Course makes it possible for anyone to secure this training by correspondence instruction in his own home during his spare time, at nominal cost.

The educational policy of the Department of Education is supervised by an Advisory Council comprising a group of the industry's leading men and women. Our Director of Education is Frederick Palmer, an able and experienced scenario writer, editor and teacher. Assisting Mr. Palmer in guiding students along the right paths are twelve able men and women who are directly connected with the motion picture industry and who are leaders in their respective fields of endeavor.

To those interested in learning the details of the Palmer course and service, we will be glad to send a copy of our general catalog, and the booklet, "Proof Positive," which has been especially prepared for skeptics. A post card will bring both of these interesting and informative books to you post paid.

Palmer Photoplay Corporation
565-592 I. W. Hellman Building
Los Angeles, Cal.

CORPORATION

Los Angeles—"Film Capital of the World"

TO PRODUCERS: The Palmer Photoplay Corporation offers a complete story service—carefully-selected *good* originals, short stories, books and plays; continuities that are backed by a guarantee of satisfaction; research work of the highest class.

Each of these departments is directed by *experienced* specialists whose services are at the disposal of producers at any time upon request.

Studios that do not maintain continuity or research departments are invited to investigate the economic advantages of Palmer Service. A letter or 'phone call will bring full information. A private branch exchange connects all departments.

PALMER PHOTOPLAY CORPORATION
Bess Meredyth Exchange, Affiliated
Los Angeles

EXECUTIVE OFFICES
1. Office of the President.
3. Office of the Secretary-Treasurer.
5. Office of Head of Photoplay Sales Department.

EXECUTIVE OFFICES
2. Office of the Vice-President.
4. Office of the General Manager.
6. Office of Director of the Research and Technical Department.
7. Office of Head of the Continuity Department.

DEPARTMENTAL OFFICES
1. Reception Room.
3. Correspondence Department.
5. Addressograph Department.
7. Entrance to all Departments.

DEPARTMENTAL OFFICES
2. Office of the Presidents Assistant.
4. Accounting Department.
6. Multigraph Department.

Willis and Inglis, Inc.

Motion Picture and Theatrical Enterprises

Los Angeles and New York

EDWARD SMALL

Representing

Stars—Directors—Authors Producers

Specialist in the Exploitation of Screen Personalities

Artists Represented Only Under Written Contract of Management

---

1493 Broadway   **New York City**

(Putnam Building)   Tel.: 2389 Bryant

JOHN J. LIVINGSTON

1440 BROADWAY
HOLLAND BUILDING
NEW YORK

STARS

Directors   MOTION PICTURE REPRESENTATIVE AND MANAGER   *Scenarios*

Principals

Phone: BRYANT
3805—6243—6244

SIGN OF SERVICE

Chamberlain Brown
1482 Broadway   New York

Phone Bryant 9130

M O T I O N   P I C T U R E S

Exclusive manager for—
ROBERT EDESON
FRITZI SCHEFF
VERA MICHELENA
CREIGHTON HALE
BESSIE McCOY DAVIS
LUCILLE MANION
MARTHA MAYO
ARTHUR ASHLEY
FLORENCE MILLS
HARRY FOX
JACK NORWORTH
JULIA KELETY
CARL HYSON AND DOROTHY DICKSON
DONALD GALLAHER
MONA KINGSLEY
EARLE FOXE
VALESKA SURATT
WILLIAM ROSELLE
HELEN LOWELL
CHARLES RUGGLES
ZELDA SEARS
EDMOND LOWE
BARRY BAXTER
RICHARD PYLE

Casting directors for players in all branches of the picture field and scenarios suited to well known stars

MOTION PICTURE DEPARTMENT

Under the Supervision of

EDITH ROSE

SIGN OF SERVICE

San Francisco Film Exchange Board of Trade

Organized and Perpetuated that Dealings between Exhibitors and Exchanges be Fair and Equitable, thereby Bringing about a Closer Relationship of these Important Divisions for the General Betterment of Conditions of the Film Industry in Northern California and Nevada.

H. L. KNAPPEN,
President.

CHAS. ROSENTHAL, Jr.,
Vice-President.

R. B. QUIVE,
Sec'y and Treas.

MILTON A. NATHAN,
Attorney.

LOUIS HYMAN
All Star Feature Distributors, Inc.
191 Golden Gate avenue
Market 292

E. B. MAYER
AND
CHARLES ROSENTHAL, Jr.
M. & R. Feature Film Exchange
107 Golden Gate avenue
Park 178

A. M. BOWLES
American Film Mfg. Company
985 Market street
Garfield 323

H. J. HENRIOLLE,
Pathe Exchange, Inc.
985 Market street
Garfield 323

M. H. KOHN
Consolidated Film Corporation
116 Golden Gate avenue
Prospect 2634

R. B. QUIVE
Realart Pictures Corporation
995 Market street
Douglas 5450

C. A. WHITNEY
Community Motion Picture Bureau
821 Market street
Sutter 2591

FLOYD ST. JOHN
Republic Distributing Corporation
104 Golden Gate avenue
Prospect 3132

J. BREHANY
Equity Pictures Corporation
995 Market street
Douglas 4958

H. L. KNAPPEN,
Select Pictures Corporation
985 Market street
Sutter 2466

H. G. ROSEBAUM
Famous Players-Lasky Corporation
Pacific Building
Sutter 4572

S. Y. EDWARDS
Turner & Dahnken
134 Golden Gate avenue
Prospect 2500

W. A. CRANK
Robertson-Cole Company
177 Golden Gate avenue
Market 2975

M. L. MARKOWITZ
Universal Film Exchanges, Inc.
121 Golden Gate avenue
Market 248

F. W. VOIGT
Metro Pictures Corporation
55 Jones street
Market 906

FRANK C. BURHANS
Vitagraph, Incorporated
985 Market street
Sutter 2974

Milton A. Nathan, Attorney, 521 Chronicle Building

BRUNTON SERVICE

Insures the highest quality of production in the minimum of time!

The Robert Brunton Studios have made it possible for any one to produce motion pictures without having to own a studio.

Some of the screen triumphs made at this perfectly equipped plant:

"The Miracle Man"	"Heart of the Hills"	"The Dwelling Place of Light"
"Desert Gold"	"The Illustrious Prince"	"Soldiers of Fortune"
"The Westerners"	"The Woman Michael Married"	"The Temple of Dusk"
"Just a Wife"	"The Beloved Cheater"	"Desert of Wheat"
"Luck of the Irish"	"Upstairs and Down"	"The Joyous Liar"
"The Better Wife"	"A White Man's Chance"	"The Lord Loves the Irish"
"The Dragon Painter"	"Bill Apperson's Boy"	"When Bearcat Went Dry"
"The Heart of Rachael"	"Billy Jim"	"The World Aflame"
"Live Sparks"	"The Bells"	"A Man's Country"
"That Something"	"Beckoning Roads"	"The House of Intrigue"
"Back to God's Country"	"Rio Grande"	"The Heart of a Fool"
"The Wolf"	"Dare-Devil Jack"	"When the Clouds Roll By"
"Blind Youth"	"His Majesty, the American"	"Carmen of the Klondike"
"The Splendid Hazard"	"The Sage Brusher"	
"One Week End"		
"The Hoodlum"		
"The Spite Bride"		
"Pollyanna"		

The Robert Brunton Studios, Inc.

5301 to 5601 Melrose Avenue   Los Angeles, Cal.

THE
HAL BENEDICT STUDIOS, INC.

Offers

To the Motion Picture Producer

working space in one of *the largest and most completely equipped studios in Greater New York, located at College Point.*

Two connecting stages, 100 x 70 ft. and 60 x 50 ft., respectively. Latest type Wohl, Kligel and Cooper-Hewitt lighting, with a 56 switch, double throw 4 panel Metropolitan Board. Capacity 15,000 amperes.

Complete scenic equipment with expert crew. Offices, dressing-rooms, projection and loading rooms, shops, etc.

For detailed information and terms, telephone

HAL BENEDICT
FLUSHING 3000

BURSTON FILMS
(INC.)

GUARANTEES
for
1920

The same wide advancement
in quality of productions

by

LOUIS BURSTON

Which made the super-serials—
THE HAWK'S TRAIL
THE MYSTERY OF "13"
THE SILENT MYSTERY

PRE-EMINENT IN THEIR FIELD

BURSTON FILMS, INC.	LOUIS BURSTON, Pres't
Longacre Building	6050 Sunset Boulevard
New York City	Los Angeles, Calif.

SOL LESSER—Distributor
—POLICY FOR 1920—

Sol Lesser, creator of innovations in the distribution of shadow plays, presented in a distinctive and unique manner.

In the exploitation of **Mack Sennett's Comedy "Yankee Doodle In Berlin",** with the Sennett Bathing Girls, Mr. Lesser established a precedent in silver screen presentation, that proved to be a popularity riot. This was the verdict of the exhibitor and public alike. The Bathing Girls went over with a bang. They were new.

He created the personal appearance in conjunction with the shadow drama.

He now offers—

George Beban Production with the personal appearance of Mr. Beban in his famous characterization of the big hearted Italian, immortalized by his famous stage play **"The Sign of the Rose."**

Also—

Annette Kellerman, with her feminine form divine, fresh as the morning's dew in Springtime,—with the personal appearance of Miss Kellerman.

Great plays, with great players, presented with exquisite perfection.—Beautiful in production.—Perfect in presentation.

Mr. Lesser gained an enviable record in film presentation and exploitation, by the distribution of such well known plays of the silver sheet as—"Hearts of The World"—"Intolerance"—"Cabiria"—"The Spoilers"—"The Ne'er Do Well"—"Mickey", etc.

SOL LESSER, Distributor
IRVING M. LESSER, Manager

OFFICES

418 Longacre Bldg., New York
514 W. 8th Street, Los Angeles

Branch Offices in all large cities thruout America

Affiliations in Europe, So. America and the Far East

THE FROHMAN AMUSEMENT CORPORATION

ANNOUNCES FOR THE YEAR 1920

"THE INVISIBLE RAY"

Starring RUTH CLIFFORD and JACK SHERRILL supported by an unparalleled serial cast.

The greatest serial the world has even seen
Written by Mr. Guy McConnell

A startling innovation, a staggering dramatic production in fifteen episodes.

Four super-features with stars of international renown

Two extraordinary seven reel productions adapted from two of the most popular novels of the year, each with its own female star.

Twenty-six two reel Western Dramatic Productions starring MYNA CUNARD, popularly known as

"*The Girl of the Great Divide.*"

Original creative features in two reel lengths.

Twenty-six two reel Comedies with a star comedian of positive box office drawing power.

These attractions will be produced along the lines of the usual Frohman standard which means the last word in photoplay art.

THE FROHMAN AMUSEMENT CORPORATION
WILLIAM L. SHERRILL, *President*

Executive Offices   310 Times Building   New York City

Announcing

A Series of Eight Reel Western Melodramas

Sylvanite Productions

Picturing the West as it was

Each of the eight five reel productions will have as its star performers, the most daring and accomplished cowboys and cowgirls whose names have appeared in all western made pictures from the west in the past several years, and who have won a majority of the prizes at all big Western Rodeos.

"OUTLAWED"

The first subject will be released about March 1st

SYLVANITE PRODUCTIONS

Studio Address: Long Beach, Calif.

FINDING The MARKET

Most important of all phases of motion picture manufacture is the market.

Experience is of prime importance. Trustworthiness is vital.

We are in constant and intimate touch with the market. We know where your picture will sell for the most money. We'll get the biggest price for your negative from both domestic and foreign distribution.

Fair dealing and honest relations with producers and distributors have built for us an established and select clientelle.

The next time you have a picture for the market consult us. Let us show you where the money is—and get it for you.

C. B. PRICE CO., Inc.

Motion Pictures

IMPORT — DOMESTIC — EXPORT

Times Building, New York City

HAL ROACH

for five years producer of comedies

for

PATHE

exclusively

The Harold Lloyd Special Two Reel Comedies

Acknowledged generally to be the best comedies of their length ever made

The Rolin One Reel Comedies

Featuring "Snub" Pollard and Little "Sunshine Sammy"

All productions produced under Mr. Roach's personal supervision

HAROLD ROACH, President
ROLIN FILM COMPANY
406 COURT STREET
LOS ANGELES, CAL.

PATHÉ

A World Organization, Justly Proud of Its Sanity and Strength

Pathe Exchange Inc. is a distributing organization, highly specialized, with thirty two exchanges located in the logical distributing centres of the United States.

Pathe has left to others the production of film, believing that the maximum of success comes with concentration. Pathe has concentrated upon selling. Pathe has built up an unsurpassed marketing organization, highly trained in all its branches, and one that attains the widest possible distribution.

FEATURES: Pathe distributes the productions of **Edgar Lewis, Hobart Henley, Frank Keenan, Jesse D. Hampton, Edwin Carewe, J. Stuart Blackton, Leonce Perret** and **Albert Capellani.**

SERIALS: Pathe distributes serials produced by **George B. Seitz, Inc., Ruth Roland Serials, Inc., Arthur Beck, Louis J. Gasnier,** and **Robert Brunton.**

COMEDIES: Pathe distributes the **Harold Lloyd Special Two Reel Comedies** produced by **Hal E. Roach**; the Rolin One Reel Comedies with **Snub Pollard**; the Mrs. Sidney Drew Two Reel Comedies with **John Cumberland**; the "Bringing Up Father" Two Reel Comedies for the International.

SHORT SUBJECTS: **Pathe News,** the famous news weekly, issued twice a week, and **Pathe Review,** the film magazine, issued once a week, are standards of quality everywhere.

PATHÉ, WITH ITS UNIQUE RECORD OF 25 SUCCESSFUL YEARS IN THE MOTION PICTURE BUSINESS, PRESENTS THE BEST EXAMPLE IN THE BUSINESS OF A HIGHLY SPECIALIZED AND EFFICIENT DISTRIBUTING ORGANIZATION

IN 1620 a ship called *Mayflower* arrived on America's shore and thereby established a milestone in history. In 1920, three hundred years later, history repeated itself. A motion picture company called MAYFLOWER established, through the photoplays it presented, a new standard for the Screen. That this standard will continue to rise is assured by the fact that MAYFLOWER presents the productions of George Loane Tucker, Emile Chautard, Allan Dwan, R. A. Walsh, Charles Miller and Sidney A. Franklin.

MAYFLOWER PHOTOPLAY CORPORATION

ISAAC WOLPER, President
1465 Broadway, New York

Either You or Your Competitor

will soon own a

First National Franchise

Competing exhibitors in the same town cannot own franchises

MOTION PICTURE STUDIO DIRECTORY

AND TRADE ANNUAL

PUBLISHED BY

MOTION PICTURE NEWS

INCORPORATED

WM. A. JOHNSTON
President

HARRY F. SEWALL
Vice-President

E. KENDALL GILLETT
Secretary and Treasurer

MARGUERITE JONES
Editor

HOME OFFICE

729 - 7th Avenue, New York, N. Y.
Phone: Bryant 9360

REPRESENTATIVES

J. C. JESSEN, Mgr.
205 Baker Detwiller Building, 412 West 6th Street, Los Angeles, California
Phone: Pico 780

1920

L. H. MASON
220 S. State St.
Chicago, Ill.
Phone: Harrison 7667

1920

Copyright, 1920, by Motion Picture News, Inc.

"The sign of a masterpiece in color"

A practical achievement of practical color motion photography for practical exhibitors who want practical results combined with the highest artistic qualities in the subjects they use.

PRIZMA MASTER PICTURES, photographed in Nature's colors, represent the supreme achievement of 1919 in the motion picture industry.

Used by all leading theatres to build prestige and profits.

*ARE YOU
SHOWING PRIZMA?*

PRIZMA, INCORPORATED
71 West 23rd Street, New York, N. Y.

Motion Picture Studio Directory

and

Trade Annual

1920—SIXTH EDITION

Table of Contents

Art Gallery of Film Personages	11-202
Actors' Biographies	203
Actresses	257
Child Players	286
Film Producers	289
Directors	294
Scenario Writers	317
Cinematographers	329
Motion Picture Organizations	339
Who's at the Helm	341
Directory of Film Companies	350
Foreign Market	363
Seventh Motion Picture News Chart of Film Trade Conditions	368
List of 1919 Film Releases	370
Directory of Newspapers and Motion Picture Theatres	487
List of Studios	516

A Complete Index can be found at the Back

Pauline Frederick

Motion Picture Studio Directory
and
Trade Annual

ACTORS

— A —

ABBE, Jack Yutaka; b. Japan, educ. Japan, Sendai, coll. and high schl.; stage career, 2 yrs.; screen career, Essanay ("The Curse of Iku"), Triangle ("Her American Husband," "Who's to Blame," "Mystic Faces"), Metro (Empress in "Red Lantern"), Hampton ("Pagan God"), Hayakawa ("Henchman"), Metro ("The Willow Tree"). Plays leads opposite Tsuru Oaki for Universal. Hght., 5, 4½; wght., 125; black har, brown eyes. Ad., 1904 Argyle Av., Hollywood, Cal. Phone 579087.

ABRAHAM, Jake; b. N. Y. C., 1854; educ. San Francisco; stage career, Rainer & Bird's Minstrels; screen career, Paralta, Lasky, Brunton, etc. ("By the World Forgot," "The Gentleman from Indiana," "The Only Way"), Jack Pickford ("In Wrong"), Goldwyn ("Girl from Outside"), Selig ("The Lost City"), American ("Social Briars"), Vitagraph ("The Girl in the House," "A Gentleman's Agreement," "The Dawn of Understanding"). Hght., 5, 4; wght., 150; gray hair and eyes. Ad., 231 S. Hill St., Los Angeles, Cal.

ACKER, Eugene; b. Stockholm, Sweden, May 13, 1889; educ. there; stage career, European prods.; screen career, Palm M. P. Co., Selig, Essanay ("Dignified Family," George Ade's Fables, "Prisoner at the Bar"), Metro ("Sylvia on a Spree," "My Four Years in Germany," "Men"). Hght., 5, 1; wght., 156; light complexion, light hair, blue eyes; Member Green Room Club. Ad., home, 334 W. 56th st., N. Y. C.—Col. 9799. Studio, Metro, Hollywood, Cal.

ACORD, Art.; b. Stillwater, Okla., 1890; early career, cowboy and ranchman; stage career, Dick Stanley Wild West Show, 1919, with Buffalo Bill, 1911, rode second at Pendleton, Ore. Cheyenne and Salt Lake roundups, won championship in broncho riding at Klamath Falls, 1912; screen career, starred in Chas. E. Van Loan stories, ("Buck Parvin in the Movies"), Fox ("Cleopatra"), 18 mos. in service, Universal ("Out West," "Behind the Fighting Line," "The Cow Boy and the Kid"), now being featured in Western serial. Hght., 6, 1; wght., 185; light hair, blue eyes. Ad., Universal Studio.

ADAMS, Lionel; educ. pub. schls.; stage career, leading man in "The Hour," "Paid in Full," "The Christian," "The Spendthrift," "Ben Hur," with Julia Marlowe, Anne Russell, Wm. Gillette; screen career, Vitagraph ("Mystery of Mary," "Lady of the Lighthouse"), Paragon ("The Closed Road"), Shomer-Ross ("The Sacred Flame"). Hght., 5, 11; wght., 155; dark hair, dark blue eyes. Ad., 340 W. 56th st., N. Y. Circle 7281, or Lambs Club, N. Y.

AINSWORTH, Charles Sydney; b. Manchester, Eng., 1886; educ. Madison, Wis.; stage career, with Maude Adams in "Little Minister," played Denton in "Arizona," with Montgomery and Stone in "Wizard of Oz," with Robert Edeson in "Fortune Hunter"; screen career, Essanay 1913 ("On Trial"), Selig ("Brown of Harvard"), Goldwyn ("One Week of Life," "The Crimson Gardenia," "A Man and His Money," "Heartsease," "Girl From Outside," "The Gay Lord Quex"). Hght., 5, 11½; wght., 156; fair complexion, brown hair. Ad., Goldwyn studio, Culver City, Calif.

AITKEN, Spottiswoode; b. Edinburgh, Scotland; educ. there; stage career, with Augustin Daly and many others, in all-star company mgmt. Brady; 27 yrs. in legitimate; screen career, Reliance ("The Birth of a Nation"), Fine Arts American Tourneur ("The White Heather"), Paramount ("Jane Goes A-Wooing," "Hay-Foot, Straw-Foot"), Hodkinson ("Fighting Thru"), Universal ("The Wicked Darling"), Fox ("Evangeline," "Broken Commandments"), Hampton-Pathe ("Woman of Pleasure"), First Nat'l ("The Thunderbolt").

ALBERTSON, Arthur; b. Waycross, Ga., 1892; educ., Univ. of Florida, Wash. and Lee Univ.; stage career, mgmt. Klaw & Erlanger, Wm. A. Brady stck.; screen career, Red Feather-Universal ("It Happened in Honolulu"), Kalem ("The Missing Heiress"), Selznick ("The Argyle Case"). Hght., 5, 9; wght., 160; medium complexion, brown hair, dark gray eyes.

ALBERTSON, E. Cort; b. Reading, Pa.; educ. Penn. Univ.; stage career, "Madam Sherry," "Girl From Rector's"; starred in "Stubborn Cinderella," "The Dance Dream" screen career, Kalem ("Masked Dancer"), Fox ("Freedom"), serial "The Carter Case," lead with Edith Taliaferro in "Whose Your Brother," Lillian Walker in serial "One Million Dollars Reward," Margaret Marsh in "Wits Against Wits." Hght., 5, 11½; wght., 170; light complexion, brown hair and eyes. Ad., Green Room Club, N. Y. studio ad., Grossman Pictures, Inc., Ithaca, N. Y.

ALEXANDER, Clifford; b. San Jose, Cal. 1891; educ. there; stage career, 6 yrs. in stk., now in stk. Alcazar theatre, San Francisco, Cal.; screen career, Paralta ("Madame Who," "Turn of a Card," "Patriotism," "Intelligence," "With Hoops of Steel," "Maid o' the Storm," "Heart of Rachel"), Pathe ("The Silver Girl"). Hght., 6; wght., 155; light hair, blue eyes.

ALEXANDER, Edward; b. Ogdensburg, N. Y.; educ. there; stage career, several years in stock and rep.; screen career, Universal, Horsley, Fox ("The Arm of the Law," "The Tale of Two Cities," "North of Fifty-Three"), Glendale Films (Dir. "The Lone Bandit"), Metro ("No Man's Land," "In Judgment Of," "The Island of Intrigue"), Paramount ("Heart of Youth"). Hght., 5, 11; wght., 155; black hair, dark gray eyes.

ALEXANDER, Frank D.; b. Olympia, Wash., 1882; educ. pub. and high schls., Ore.; early career, cowboy and stage driver; screen career, 1½ yrs. with Keystone Vitagraph ("Huns and Hyphens," "Bears and Bad Men," "Humbugs and Husbands," "Pluck and Plotters"). Ad., 4311 Prospect ave., Hollywood, Cal.; studio, Vitagraph.

ALEXANDER, Gus; educ., N. Y.; stage career, "Wildfire," "The Whirl of the Town," stage and pictures for 24 years; screen career, Biograph, Mutt and Jeff, Universal-Christie, Lloyd, Blackton ("Life's Greatest Problem"), Fox ("Les Miserables"). Hght., 4, 4; wght., 118; brown hair, blue eyes. Ad., Betts & Fowler, 1482 Bway., N. Y. Bryant 5664.

ALLARDT, Arthur; b. N. Y.; educ. N. Y. Phila. schls., stage career, 10 yrs. legit., vaud. Pacific Coast, N. Y., Phila.; screen career, Majestic, Thanhouser, Frontier, Corona ("The Curse of Eve"), Paralta ("One Dollar Bid," "Patriotism," "Intelligence"), Pathe ("The Midnight Stage"), Paramount ("Louisiana"). Hght., 6; wght., 165; complexion, fair; brown hair. Sings. Ad., 5519 A. Sierra Vista st., Hollywool, Cal., Holly 1473.

ALLEN, Alfred; b. Alfred, N. Y., 1886; screen career, 3 yrs. with Universal, Bluebird, Lois Weber Prods. ("The Whim," "Price of a Good Time"), Universal ("Wolves of the North," "Riders of Vengeance," "The Sleeping Lion," "Loot," "His Divorced Wife"), Robertson-Cole ("The Other Half"). Hght., 6; wght., 195; light hair, gray eyes. Ad., University Club, L. A.

AMADOR, Charles Edward; also scenario writer; b. Oakland, Calif.; educ. there; screen career, Bulls-Eye ("Bone Dry," "A Rural Romance," "One $1,000.00 Short," "Hot Dogs"), Vitagraph-Larry Semon comedy ("Well, I'll be ——," "His Home, Sweet Home," "Scamps and Scandals"). Hght., 5, 6; wght., 135; dark brown hair, brown eyes. Ad., Jack White Comedies, Los Angeles, Cal., phone 61464.

ANDERSON, Robert; b. Denmark, 1890; educ. Denmark; screen career, Fine Arts ("Intolerance"), Metro ("Draft 258"), D. W. Griffith ("Hearts of the World"), Universal ("Heart of Humanity"), Lasky ("Fires of Faith"), Universal ("Petal on the Current," "Right to Happiness," "Common Property"). Now in Denmark. Hght., 5, 10; wght, 180; medium hair, blue eyes. Ad., home, 1752½ No. Vermont ave., Los Angeles, Cal.

ANDREWS, Frank; educ. Boston; stage career, over 30 yrs. exper., playing everything from children to old men. Shakespeare, "East Lynne," N. Y. prods. with Belasco, Frohman, Brady, Cort, Cohen & Harris, etc.; screen career, Vitagraph, Famous Players, Goldwyn, Fox, Metro, World, etc., "For France," "Children of Shelto," "Capt. Swift," "The Nightingale," "When My Ship Comes In," "Sport of Kings," "Poor Little Rich Girl," "The Road Between," etc. Hght., 6; wght., 175; white hair, dark brown eyes. Permanent ad., Actor's Equity, N. Y.

ANKER, William; b. France, 1860; educ. Lycee Imperial of Rouen, France; early exper., professor of languages; screen career, 10 yrs., playing for following cos.: Universal, Thanhouser, Fox, Biograph, Gaumont, Metro, World, Kleine (as the father in "Wild Oats"; as the professor in "The Green Cloak," etc.), International ("The Cinema Murder"), Edgar Lewis ("Another Man's Shoe"), Numa ("Return of Tarzan"), Selznick ("Memory"). Hght., 5, 7; white hair and beard, gray-blue eyes. Ad., 339 W. 58th st., N. Y. Phone, Col. 9998.

AOYAMA, Yukio; b. Nagoya City, Japan, 1888; stage career, leading man, Cherry Blossom Players, Los Angeles; screen career, Lasky ("The Bravest Way"), Pathe ("Japanese Nightingale"); featured in ("Harikari"), Cal. M. P. Corp., Metro ("The Red Lantern") Fox ("Thieves"). Hght., 5, 5; wght., 130; black hair, black eyes. Ad., home, 229½ N. San Pedro st., Los Angeles.

ARBUCKLE, Andrew; b. Galveston, 1884; educ. St. Louis; stage career, vaud. playing Western characters; screen career, Metro ("Big Tremaine"), Ince-Triangle ("Happiness"), Artcraft ("Romance of Happy Valley"), Brunton ("A White Man's Chance"), Hart ("John Petticoats"), Mary Pickford ("The Hoodlum"), United ("Square Shootin' Dan"), Goldwyn ("Pinto"), Hampton (with Blanche Sweet). Hght., 5, 10; wght., 235; auburn hair, blue eyes. Ad., Hulburt Apts., Los Angeles, Cal.

ARBUCKLE, Maclyn; also scenario writer; b. San Antonio, Texas; educ. Glasgow, Scotland, and Boston, Mass.; stage career, since 1888, in "The Emigrant," later in Charles Frohman Cos., Frawley Stk. Co., San Francisco; in "Why Smith Left Home," "The County Chairman," also in vaud.; screen career, Pallas ("The Reform Candidate"), Famous Players ("The County Chairman"), San Antonio Pictures ("Mr. Potter of Texas," "Mr. Bingle," "Squire Phin"). Hght., 5, 9; wght., 235; brown hair, blue eyes. Ad., P. O. Box 872, San Antonio, Texas.

ARBUCKLE, Roscoe, also producing-director; b. Kansas, 1887; stage career, on tour in drama and stock repertoire; managed own company for two yrs.; screen career, began with Keystone, 1913, as extra man at $3 per day; advanced to regular parts; later played leads and became director; directing and acting for nearly 3 yrs., Keystone, Paramount ("His Wedding Night," "Fatty in Coney Island"), Arbuckle-Paramount ("The Bell Boy," "Out West," "Good Night. Nurse," "The Cook," "The Sheriff," "Camping Out," "Love," "A Desert Hero," "Back Stage," "The Hayseed," "The Garage") Ad. Comique Film Co., Long Beach, Cal.

ARDIZONI, John; b. 1882; stage career, mus. com., drama, opera, in "Twin Beds," "Pierrot, the Prodigal," Geo. Arliss "Hamilton," "The Melting Pot"; screen career, Vitagraph ("The Man of Mystery,") with E. H. Sothern ("The Glory of Yolande"), World ("Phil for Short"), Fox ("A Woman There Was"), World ("The American Way"), Faversham ("Man Who Lost Himself"), Wm. Collier prods. Hght., 5, 11; wght., 190; dark complexion. Ad. 33 W. 84th st., N. Y. Schuyler 9949.

AREY, Wayne; b. Rock Falls, Ill., April 12, 1880; educ. there; stage career, stock in Minneapolis, Brooklyn, Atlanta, Toronto and Lawrence, Mass., in N. Y. prods. mgmt. Liebler, Belasco, Chas. Frohman, etc.; screen career, Thanhouser (late pictures, "Hinton's Double," "The Heiress," "The Woman in White," "It Happened to Adele"), Pathe ("War and the Woman"). Hght., 6; wght., 185; brown hair, blue eyes. Home ad., 37 North ave., New Rochelle, N. Y.

ARLING, Charles; b. Toronto, Canada; educ. there; stage career, with Francis Wilson, Henry W. Savage, Blanche Walsh, Shuberts, 3 yrs.; screen career, Anita Stewart ("In Old Kentucky"), Curwood-Carver ("Back to God's Country"), Fox ("Snares of Paris," "Vagabond Luck"), Wm. S. Hart ("Wagon Tracks"). Hght., 6; wght., 190; dark brown hair, blue-gray eyes. Ad., 1835 Argyle ave., Hollywood, Cal. Phone 579596.

ARNOLD, Edward; b. N. Y.; educ. pub. schls. and Columbia Univ.; stage career, with Robert B. Mantell, Ethel Barrymore, John Drew, Maxine Elliott, James K. Hackett; stock in St. Paul, Philadelphia; screen career, Essanay, 1915 ("When the Man Speaks"), Emerald Film Co. ("A Slacker's Heart"), World ("Phil for Short," "A Broadway Saint"). Hght., 5, 11; wght., 155; light brown hair, blue eyes.

ASHER, Max; Universal; b. Oakland, Cal., 1879; educ. pub. schls.; stage career, People's stock, Oakland, with Louis and Kale in musical comedy for 4 yrs.; screen career, Keystone, 1912, Universal-Joker, Universal ("Max Comes from the West"), Vitagraph ("Counts and Noaccounts," "Bonds and Banners," "Laws and Outlaws"), Vitagraph ("A Yankee Princess"). Hght., 5, 9; wght., 205; dark hair, eyes and complexion. Ad., Vitagraph Studio, L. A., Cal.

ASHLEY, Arthur H.; also director; b. and educ. N. Y.; stage career, stock with Payton, Spooner, Poli, Baker, Davis; in "Brewster's Millions"; screen career, Vitagraph 3½ yrs., Thanhouser 1 yr., World (late pictures, "The Iron Ring," "Rasputin, the Black Monk," "Shall We Forgive Her?" "A Creole's Revenge," "Broken Ties"), Goldwyn ("Be Careful, Mary"), World ("The American Way," "The Praise Agent," "Forest Rivals").

ATWILL, Lionel; b. London, Eng.; educ. Eng.; stage career, featured in "The Lodger" (Maxine Elliott theatre), "Another Man's Shoes" (39th St. theatre), leading man Belasco theatre in "Tiger, Tiger"); screen career, F.-P.-Lasky Corp. (opp. Elsie Ferguson, "For Sale"). Hght., 5, 10; wght., 160; brown hair, gray eyes. Ad., Lotus Club, N. Y.

AUBREY, James; b. Liverpool, Eng.; educ. Liverpool; stage career, Fred Karno's "Night in English music hall," doing the Terrible Turk (orig.), vaud. and mus. com., Gus Hill's "Around the Clock"; screen career, Mittenthal's Starlight Pathe comedies, playing Heinie in "Heinie and Louie" comedies, "A Merry Chase," "Monkey Shines"), Vitagraph ("Rah, Rah, Rah," "Maid and Muslin," "Dames and Dentists"). Hght., 5, 6; wght., 165; blue eyes, brown hair. Ad., Green Room Club, N. Y.; studio, Vitagraph, Los Angeles, Cal.

AUCKER, William; stage career, with Irene Fenwick in "Wild Oats"; screen career, Pathe, Thanhouser, Universal, Solax, Kleine, Metro ("The Turmoil"). Hght., 5, 7; fair complexion, white hair.

AUGUST, Edwin (Phillipe von der Butz), also director and author; b. St. Louis, Mo.; educ. Christian Bros. Coll., St. Louis, Mo.; stage career, with Otis Skinner, Mrs. Leslie Carter, Digby Bell; screen career, Edison, Biograph, Vita., Univ., Edwin August Feature Films, Kleine-Edison (author and director "Bondwoman"), Bluebird ("City of Tears"), ("Broadway Scandal"), Univ. ("Mortgaged Wife"), World ("The Poison Pen"), Artcolor ("A Tale of Two Nations"). Hght., 5, 11; wght., 155. Member M. P. D. A. and Friars Club, N. Y.

AUSTEN, Leslie; b. London, 1888; educ. Cambridge Univ.; stage career, with Elsie Ferguson, Gertrude Kingston, Jane Cowl, in "Joseph and His Brethren"; screen career, Metro, Fox, Lubin, Art Drama ("A Man and a Woman"), Fox ("Two Little Imps," "Caught in the Act"), Famous Players ("Mrs. Dane's Defense," Pauline Frederick), ("Woman of Impulse," Lina Cavaliere), Fox ("My Little Sister"), Select ("Marie, Ltd."). Hght., 6; wght., 165; brunette, blue eyes. Ad., home, 220 Wadsworth ave., N. Y., St. Nich. 2828.

AUSTIN, Albert; b. Birmingham, Eng., 1885; educ. Birmingham; stage career first came to this country with Charles Chaplin in "A Night in an English Music Hall," stock in Denver, Colo., for 2 yrs.; screen career, Lone Star Film ("The Floorwalker," "The Fireman," "The Vagabond," "One A. M.," "A Dog's Life," Shoulder Arms," "Sunnyside,"

ACTORS

"The Count"), Chaplin ("A Dog's Life," "Shoulder Arms"). Hght., 5, 11; wght., 160; brown hair and eyes. Sect. to Charlie Chaplin.

AUSTIN, Jere; also director; b. Minneapolis; educ. Rensselaer Polytech. and Univ. of Minn. Stage career, several years Western Stock Cos. Ralph Stuart, Dan'l Frawley, etc.; screen career, Famous Players ("Resurrection," "Fedora"), Goldwyn ("All Woman," "Hidden Fires," "A Perfect Lady," "Day Dreams," "Woman on Index"), Screencraft ("The Tap"), United ("The Eternal Mother"), Realart ("Barna Vetta"). Hght., 6, 1; wght., 195; dark hair and eyes. Ad., Green Room Club, N. Y.

AVERY, J. Ray; b. San Diego, Calif.; educ. there and San Francisco; stage career, 1905, in stk., rep., mus., com., vaud. and one-piece; screen career, juvenile and light comedy with Goldwyn, Ince, Griffith, Brunton and American studios, Universal ("Ambition," "The Woman in the Plot," "The Phantom Melody"), Goldwyn ("The Tower of Ivory," "The Blooming Angel"). Hght., 5, 7; wght., 140; dark brown hair, dark blue eyes. Home ad., Alpin Hotel, Los Angeles, Calif. Bway. 317.

— B —

BACON, Lloyd Francis; b. San Jose, Cal., 1889; educ. Santa Clara Coll., Cal.; screen career, Keystone ("Pearls and Perils"), Artcraft ("Square Deal Sanderson," "Wagon Tracks"), Robertson-Cole ("House of Intrigue"), Fox ("Vagabond Love," "The Feud"). Hght., 5, 10; wght., 150; brown hair and blue eyes. Ad., home, Camerford Apts., 5716 Camerford ave., Los Angeles.

BAGGOT, King; also director; b. St. Louis, Mo.; educ. Christian Bros. College, St. Louis; stage career, stk. cos. and under mgmt. Frohman, Liebler & Co., Shuberts, etc., star in "The Violation"; screen career, Universal ("Ivanhoe," "Dr. Jekyl and Mr. Hyde," "Absinthe," "Shadows"), Metro ("Kildare of the Storm," "Man Who Stayed at Home"), Burston Films ("The Hawk's Trail" serial), B. B. Hampton ("The Dwelling Place of Light"), played in over 300 pictures. Hght., 6; wght., 185; brown hair, blue eyes. Ad., Lambs Club, N. Y. C., or Hollywood Hotel, Hollywood, Calif.

BAILEY, Bill; b. Omaha, Neb.; educ. Milwaukee, Wis.; stage career, 15 yrs., many prods.; mngt. K. & E., Pabst Eng. Stock Co., Milwaukee; screen career, Essanay, Mutual, World, etc.; Dir. comedies for Universal; Rolfe-Metro ("A Million a Minute"), Wharton ("The Eagle's Eye"), Fox ("Bonnie Annie Laurie"), Blackton ("The Common Cause"), Metro ("Shadows of Suspicion"), Goldwyn ("Speedy Meade"). Triangle ("Three Black Eyes").

BAINBRIDGE, William Herbert; b. England, 1853; educ. England; early career, mining engineer; screen career, National, Ince ("False Faces"), Brunton studio with Kitty Gordon, Helen Kellar, Bessie Barriscale; Universal ("The Desire of a Moth," "Broadway Scandal," "The Kaiser, the Beast of Berlin"), Hampton-Hodkinson ("Desert Gold"), First National ("Heart of the Hills"). Hght., 5,11½; wght., 200; medium complexion, brown hair, blue eyes. Home ad., 6778 Hollywood Blvd., Los Angeles.

BAIRD, Stewart; b. Boston; educ. Harvard; stage career, New Theatre Co., N. Y., "All for the Ladies"; leads in "Sybil," "The Kiss Burglar," Frohman; screen career, Famous Players ("Moth and the Flame," "Incorrigible Dukan"), Kalem ("The Runaway Wife"), Metro. Hght., 6; wght., 168; dark complexion, brown hair, brown eyes. Ad., 15 Central Park West, N. Y. Col. 4509. Studio ad., Shubert office, N. Y.

BAKER, Edwin King (Eddie Baker); b. Washington, D. C., Nov. 17, 1896; educ. Washington, D. C., and Calif.; stage career, with Baker stk. in repertoire thru Eastern States; screen career, began with Universal, before entering army was with Joker Comedy, late work doing heavies with Gale Henry, 12 picture ("Poor Fish," "Pant," "Kids," etc.); now with Al Christie. Hght., 6, 1; wght., 190; fair complexion, brown hair, blue eyes. Home ad., Jean Hotel, Los Angeles, Cal. Pico 3035; studio ad., Christie Studio, Hollywood, Cal.

BANKS, Perry; b. Victoria, B. C., 1877; educ. Pierce Christian Coll., Cal.; stage career, 15 yrs. stock and rep., with Robt. Downing in rep.; vaud. and circus; did Griffith's sketch, "In Washington's Time"; screen career, American (best pictures "Other Side of the Door," "Overalls," "The Overcoat," "Faith," "Melissa of the Hills," "The Sea Master," "A Sporting Chance," "Six Feet Four," "Eve in Exile").

BARKER, Bradley; b. Hempstead, L. I., 1885; educ. N. Y.; stage career, 5 yrs. dramatic stck.; screen career, 7 yrs., Famous Players ("Come Out of the Kitchen," "Wanted a Husband"), Realart ("Erstwhile Susan," "Fear Market"), Acme, Chas. Miller Co. ("Heart of a Gypsy"). Hght., 5, 11; wght., 180; dark complexion, dark brown hair, hazel eyes; writes scenarios. Ad., Southhold Apts., 150th st. and Broadway, N. Y., and Green Room Club.

BARNETT, Chester; b. Piedmont, Mo.; educ. St. Benedict's Coll., Atchison, Kan.; stage career, Belasco 2 yrs., "The Climax" (Weber); screen career, Crystal, Peerless, Warner Features, Equitable (appearing in "Trilby," "The Wishing Ring," "Marrying Money," "Heart of the Blue Ridge," "Little Miss Brown," "The Pit," "Old Dutch," "The Gentleman from Mississippi," "La Vie de Boheme"), Selznick ("The Law of Compensation"), Submarine Film ("The Submarine Eye"), Select ("Break the News to Mother"), Submarine Film ("Girl of the Sea"). Hght., 5, 9½; wght., 155; dark hair, brown eyes. Ad., 555 West 171st st., N. Y.

BARRIE, Nigel; b. Calcutta, India; educ. Haileyburg Coll., England; stage career, with Sir Frank Benson, Sir Herbert Tree, Fred Terry and Julia Neilson, John Drew, Grace George, leads in "Count of Luxemburg," "Gypsy Love," "The Laughing Husband," Professional dancer in vaud. with Joan Sawyer; screen career, Famous Players ("Bab" series, "Widow By Proxy"), Select ("The Marionettes," "The Better Wife"), Robertson-Cole ("Joselyn's Wife," "Tangled Threads"), Paramount ("Cinema Murder"), First National ("The Turning Point"), American ("The Honey Bee"). Hght., 6, 1; wght., 175; black hair, brown eyes. Home ad., 1919 N. Van Ness ave., Hollywood, Cal. Phone 599891.

BARRINGTON, Herbert; b. England; educ. Cincinnati; stage career, with Mansfield in Shakespeare, 1899, with Wyndham in London, 1900, in "Florodora," N. Y., in stock and on tour, starred in "When We Were Twenty-One"; screen career, from 1911, Edison, then Solax, Thanhouser, Pilot, Biograph, Universal, World ("Maternity," "Shall We Forgive Her?" "A Self-Made Widow").

BARROWS, Harry A.; b. Saco, Me., 1875; educ. Thornton Acad., Saco; stage career, in mus. com. with Elsie Janis, Lew Fields, Henry W. Savage, Frohman and Dillingham; also in rep.; screen career, Famous Players, Biograph, Fox, Howarth ("Temple of Dusk"), Jewel ("Kaiser, the Beast of Berlin"), Universal ("The Right to Happiness," "The Trembling Hour"), Brentwood ("Come Again, Smith"), American ("Hobbs in a Hurry"), Lois Weber Co. ("For Husbands Only"), Astra ("Common Clay"), Ince ("In the Claws of the Hun"). Hght., 6; wght., 200; light complexion, dark hair, blue eyes. Ad., 1552 Hudson ave., Los Angeles, Cal.

BARRY, Eddie; b. Phila., Pa., 1887; stage career, comedian in Madame Sherry Co., in "The Red Rose," "A Knight for a Day," "Comin' Thru the Rye," "A Stubborn Cinderella"; stk. at Keith and Proctor's, N. Y. C., Poli's, Springfield, Mass., etc.; screen career, Christie ("Working His Way," "A Lucky Slip," "Vamping Reuben's Millions," "His Cut-Up Life," specials, "Rowdy Ann," "Dangerous Dan McGrew," "Shades of Shakespeare," "Wild and Western"). Hght., 5, 10; wght., 137; auburn hair and brown eyes. Home ad., 6424 Dix st., Hollywood, Cal.; studio ad., Christie studio, Hollywood, Cal.

BARRYMORE, John; b. 1882; stage career, since 1903, appeared as Max in "Magda," starred in "Toddles," "The Fortune Hunter," "A Slice of Life," "The Affairs of Anatol," "A Thief for a Night," "Justice," "Peter Ibbetson," "Redemption," "The Jest"; screen career, Famous Players (featured in "The Dictator," "Nearly a King," "The Red Widow," "The Lost Bridegroom"), L. Lawrence Weber Prod. ("Raffles, the Amateur Cracksman"), Famous Players ("On the Quiet," "Here Comes the Bride," "The Test of Honor," "Dr. Jekyll and Mr. Hyde." Ad., Lambs Club, N. Y.

BARRYMORE, Lionel; stage career, with Nance O'Neil, James Herne, John Drew, in "The Best of Friends," "Pantaloon," "Fires of Fate," toured vaud. in "The Still Voice"; "The Copperhead," "The Jest"; screen career, Biograph, Pathe, "Exploits of Elaine"; Metro, starred in comedy and dramatic parts, "The Yellow Streak," "Great Green Eye," "The Millionaire's Double"), Famous Players ("The Copperhead"). Ad., Famous Players, N. Y.

BARTHELMESS, Richard; b. N. Y. City, 1895; educ. Trinity College, Hartford, Conn.; screen career, Herbert Brenon productions ("War Brides"), Famous Players ("Bab's Burglar," "Bab's Diary," "The Seven Swans," "Rich Man, Poor Man," "Three Men and a Girl"), Goldwyn ("Nearly Married"), D. W. Griffith ("The Hope Chest," "Boots," "Broken Blossoms," "Scarlet Days," "Girl Who Stayed at Home"), Dorothy Gish Co. ("Peppy Polly," "I'll Get Him Yet"). Hght., 5, 7; wght., 135; dark complexion, dark hair, brown eyes. Ad., Lambs Club, N. Y. or L. A. A. C., Los Angeles, Cal.

BARTLETT, Harry; b. Pittsburg, Pa.; educ. there; stage career, began 1882, chiefly vaud.; "Mutt" in Mutt and Jeff, on road and with own company; screen career, 3 yrs., Famous Players ("Anne of Green Gables," "The Copperhead"), with Leah Baird in "The Volcano." Hght., 6, ½; wght., 170; gray hair, blue eyes. Ad., 2297 Eighth ave., N. Y. Phone Mngsd. 2597.

BEAMISH, Frank; b. Memphis, Tenn., 1881; educ. Christian Brothers Coll.; stage career, with Chas. Frohman, E. H. Sothern, Rose Stahl; screen career, Equitable-World, Peerless-World ("The Revolt"), Fox ("Putting One Over," "Checkers"). Hght., 6; wght., 165; complexion fair, light brown hair, blue eyes.

BEBAN, George; stage career, since 8 yrs. old, singing in Reed and Emerson's minstrels, stk. in San Francisco, mus. com., "Nancy Brown," with Weber and Fields, comedy lead in "Fantana" and "The American Idea," starred in "The Sign of the Rose"; screen career NYMP ("An Alien"), Morosco ("Lost in Transit," "The Land of the Free," "Jules of the Strong Heart," "One More American"), Independent Prod. ("Hearts of Men"), Sol Lesser ("One in a Million"). Ad., Friars Club, N. Y. Home ad., 7018 Hawthorne st., Hollywood, Cal., Holly 3851; studio ad., 904 Girard st., Los Angeles.

BECHTEL, Wm. A.; stage career, 30 yrs., Europe and America; screen career, Peerless, Edison, Ivan, Graphic ("Echo of Youth"), Vitagraph ("Vengeance of Durand," "Gray Tower Mystery"), Wistaria Corp. ("The Lurking Peril"). Hght., 5, 9; wght., 160; dark hair and eyes. Ad., home, 173 W. 79th st., N. Y. C.; Schuyler 1661.

BEERY, Noah, Jr.; b. Kansas City, Mo., 1884; stage career, with Mansfield, Cohan and Harris, H. B. Harris, Klaw and Erlanger; screen career, Artcraft ("Believe Me, Xantippe," "The Whispering Chorus," "The Squaw Man"), loaned to Metro for "The Red Lantern," with Nazimova, Lasky ("The Sea Wolf"), B. B. Hampton ("The Sagebrusher"), Louis B. Mayer ("The Fighting Shepherdess"). Hght., 6, 1; wght., 212; dark hair and eyes. Ad., home, 6421 Ivarene st., Hollywood, Cal.; studio, Lasky.

BELASCO, Jay; b. Brooklyn, N. Y.; educ. England, Bedford; stage career, dram. and vaud. throughout Europe, Africa, Australia and U. S.; screen career since 1915, 2 yrs. dir. and star of Christie Comedies; 1 yr. Blue Bird Features, Universal, 2 pictures with Frank Keenan ("Enter a Vagabound," "Out of the Ashes"). Hght., 5, 10; wght., 152; dark hair and eyes. Ad., Hotel Glidden, Hollywood, Cal. Holly 3910.

BELMONT, Joseph (Baldy); b. St. Clair, Mich.; educ. Catholic Acad., Port Huron; stage career, stk., rep., vaud., etc. in "Trilby," "Oliver Twist," "The Girl of the Golden West," etc., mgmt. David Belasco, B. F. Keith, Poli Stock, etc.; screen career, Crystal (wrote, directed and played leads in more than 40 "Baldy" Belmont comedies), Griffith's Reliance-Majestic (directed 1 and 2 reel dramas), Fine Arts, Keystone since Dec., 1915 ("Skidding Hearts," "Oriental Love," "Won by a Fowl," "Never Too Old," "Star Boarder," "No Mother to Guide Her"). Hght., 5, 6½; wght., 155; dark hair, brown eyes. Home ad., 1712 Allesandro, Los Angeles, Cal.; studio ad., Sennett, L. A. Cal.

BENEDICT, Kingsley, also scenario writer; b. Buffalo, N. Y., Nov. 14, 1882; educ. Columbia Coll.; stage career, with Charles Frohman, Klaw & Erlanger, William A. Brady, Shuberts, etc.; screen career, Universal ("The Water Spy," "The Human Target," etc.); author of several plays, "The Niche in the Wall," "The Coward," "A Woman's Law," "The Craven," Bluebird ("Who Will Marry Me?"). Hght., 5, 7; wght., 150; brown hair and blue eyes. Ad., Universal, Universal City.

BENHAM, Harry; b. Valparaiso, Ind., Feb. 26, 1886; educ. Chicago and Goshen, Ind.; stage career, "Madame Sherry," "Sultan of Sulu," "Pinafore," "Florodora," etc.; screen career, World (opp. Alice Brady in "The Dancer's Peril"), Ed. Warren Prod. ("Warfare of the Flesh"), Apollo ("When You and I Were Young"), Metro ("The Outsider"), Pathe ("The Frame-Up," "Convict 993"). Hght., 5, 11; wght., 170; brown hair and eyes. Ad., Green Room Club, N. Y.

BENNER, Yale Despine; b. N. Y., 1875; educ. Brooklyn; stage career, in "The Stolen Story," "Zira," "Leah Kleschna," "The Three Twins," vaud., leading man with Hope Booth; screen career, Edison, 5 yrs. (playing leads, straights, character comedy, heavies), Thanhouser ("The Pillory"), Metro ("A Wife by Proxy").

BENNETT, Joseph; b. Los Angeles, Cal.; screen career, Alkire Prod. ("An Ace in a Hole"), Fox ("The Feud"), American ("Rose of Hell"), Lewis Stone Co. ("Man's Desire"), Triangle ("Golden Fleece," "Crown Jewels," "Marked Cards," "Limousine Life," "Indiscreet Corrine"). Hght., 5, 10½; wght., 153; dark brown hair, blue eyes. Home ad., Baker Apts., Los Angeles, Cal. Bdwy. 940.

BENNETT, Richard; b. Bennetts Switch, Ind., 1873; educ. Kokomo, Logansport, Ind.; stage career, from 1891, covering period of 15 yrs. leading man and star mgmt. Chas. Frohman, Empire theatre, N. Y., and on tour; prod. as star personally, "Damaged Goods," "The Unknown Purple," "For the Defense"; screen career, American-Mutual (star in screen version of "Damaged Goods," late pictures, "And the Law Says," "Gilded Youth"). Hght., 5, 10; wght., 160; dark brown hair, dark gray eyes.

BENNISON, Louis; b. Oakland, Cal.; educ. Univ. of Cal.; stage career, 15 yrs. stk. in West; supported Richard Bennett in "Damaged Goods," Emily Stevens, "Unchastened Woman," starred 2 yrs. in "Johnny Get Your Gun"; screen career, Goldwyn ("Oh, Johnny"), Betzwood ("High Pockets," "Road Called Straight," "Misfit Earl," "Sandy Burke," "Speedy Meade"). Hght., 6, 1; wght., 165; dark hair, gray eyes. Ad., Lambs Club, N. Y.

BENSON, Clyde; b. Marshalltown, Iowa; early career, 15 yrs. on legit. stage, "Everywoman" 4 seasons, "The Climax" 2 seasons, "Unbroken Road" 1 season; screen career, Universal, Select ("The Savage Woman"), with Priscilla Dean in "The Virgin of Stamboul," Ince-Paramount ("The Sheriff's Son," "Green Eyes," "Maggie Pepper"), Hodkinson ("The Best Man"), with J. Warren Kerrigan in "Live Sparks," now playing in Jack Dempsey serial. Hght., 6; wght., 170; brown hair, fair complexion. Ad., Balboa Hotel, 1221 West 7th st., Los Angeles, Cal. Phone 60121; studio, Brunton.

BENTON, Curtis; b. Toledo, O., 1885; educ. Vanderbilt Univ.; stage career, from 1903, with Robert Hilliard in "A Fool There Was," 2 seasons with Cohan and Harris in "The Fortune Hunter," "Broadway Jones," etc., writer of vaud. acts and short stories; screen career, Imp-Universal ("Pursuit Eternal," "Conscience"—author—"Lady High and Mighty," "Everygirl," juv. in "Twenty Thousand Leagues Under the Sea"), Fox ("Jealousy," "The Siren"). Hght., 5, 10; wght., 180; dark hair, blue eyes. Home ad., 520 W. 130th st., N. Y. C. Ad., Green Room Club, N. Y. C.

BERGEN, Thurlow; stage career, stk, "De Luxe Anne", screen career, Pathe ("The Stain," "The Boundary Rider," "A Prince of India," "The Fireman and the Girl," "A Change of Heart," "A Woman's Fight," "The Stolen Birthright"), Unity ("The Lottery Man"), Fox "The Love Auction," "The Lure of Ambition"). Ad., care Edward Small, Inc., N. Y.

BERGMAN, Henry; Chaplin First Natl. ("A Dog's Life," "Shoulder Arms," "Sunnyside"), Chaplin ("A Day's Pleasure"). Ad., Boulevard Apts., Hollywood, Cal. Chaplin Studio, Hollywood, Cal.

BERRELL, George; b. Philadelphia, 1849; educ. St. Mary's Coll., Wilmington, Del.; stage career, 44 yrs. in drama, with Booth, Barrett,

ACTORS

McCullough, Mary Anderson; screen career, Lubin, Lasky, Bosworth, Metro ("As the Sun Went Down," "In for Thirty Days"), Universal ("The Three Godfathers"), Lasky ("Love Insurance"), Fred Stone ("The Duke of Chimney Butte"), Mary Pickford ("Pollyanna"). Hght., 6; wght., 175; gray eyes and hair. Home ad., 1532 Vista st., Los Angeles, Cal.

BEVAN, Billy; b. Orange, New South Wales, Australia, 1887; educ. Sydney, Australia; stage career, 8 yrs. with Pollard's Australian Opera Co., "Mikado," "Belle of New York," "Geisha," "Floradora," "Sergeant Bone"; screen career, L-Ko, Lehrman, Fox, Christie, etc., "Somebody's Widow," "What Did Father Say," "Their Little Kid," "His Smashing Career," Mack Sennett ("Salome versus Shenandoah," "A Lady's Tailor"). Hght., 5, 8; wght., 185; auburn hair, brown eyes. Ad., Mack Sennett Comedies, Edendale, Calif.

BLACK, W. W.; b. Irvington, N. Y., 1871; stage career, in K. & E., Savage, Lederer prods.; screen career, Metro ("The Greatest Power"), Goldwyn ("The Hell Cat"), Norma Talmadge Co. ("Secret of the Storm Country"), Fox ("The Prussian Cur"), Popular Players ("Raffles"), Goldwyn ("High Pockets"), "The Floor Below"), J. Vincent Corp. ("The Spirit of Lafayette"), International ("The Hidden Truth"), S. K. Krellberg ("The Fatal Fortune," serial). Ad., 111 Manhattan st., N. Y. Morningside 8145.

BLACKWELL, Carlyle; b. Troy, Pa., 1888; educ. Syracuse; stage career, in Broadway successes, including "Brown of Harvard" and "Right of Way"; Keith and Proctor stock co.; screen career, Lasky, International, World, "The Beloved Blackmailer," "Road to France," "The Allies," "Hit or Miss," "Love in a Hurry," "Courage for Two," "Three Green Eyes." Has written, produced and acted his own stories. Hght., 5, 11; wght., 155; dark complexion, eyes and hair. Ad., Lambs Club, N. Y.

BLINN, Holbrook; b. San Francisco; educ. San Francisco and Stanford Univ.; stage career, 27 yrs. acting, starring, and managing, famous producer of 1-act plays at Princess theatre, N. Y.; screen career, World ("The Butterfly on the Wheel," "The Unpardonable Sin," "Husband and Wife," "The Hidden Scar"), Pathe ("The Empress"), McClure ("Pride"), World ("The Boss," "McTeague"), World-Tourneur ("The Ivory Snuff-Box"), Steger ("Prima Donna's Husband"). Ad., Journey's End, Croton-on-Hudson, N. Y.

BLOOMER, Raymond; b. Rochester, N. Y.; stage career, 10 yrs. stock, with Belasco, "A Good Little Devil," "Fair and Warmer," "Squab Farm," also Comic Opera; screen career, Famous Players ("Out of a Clear Sky"), Screencraft ("The Prodigal Wife"), Marion Davies Film Co. ("The Belle of N. Y."). Hght., 6 ft.; wght., 168; dark complexion, eyes, hair. Ad., 683 West End ave., N. Y. River 9944.

BLUE, Monte; b. Indianapolis, 1890; educ. Purdue Univ.; stage career, 2 yrs. vaud.; screen career, Griffith, Pathe, Triangle, Douglas Fairbanks ("Wild and Wooly," "Man From Painted Post"), Mary Pickford ("M'Liss," "Johanna Enlists"), Lasky ("Squaw Man," "Rustling a Bride," "Told in the Hills," "In Missouri," "Everywoman," "Thirteenth Commandment," "Too Much Johnson"). Hght., 6, 2; wght., 185; brown hair and eyes. Ad., Lasky Film Corp., Vine st., Hollywood, Calif.

BOLAND, Eddie "Bo"; b. San Francisco, Calif., 1885; educ. St. Charles Academy, San Francisco; stage career, 6 yrs.; screen career, since 1912, Universal ("Lady Raffles series, "Lucille Love" serial, "Peg o' Ring" serial, featured 14 mos. with Ernie Shield in one reel "Joker" comedies), now featured with Harry Pollard in one reel Rolin Comedies (Pathe), "All at Sea," "Call for Mr. Caveman," "Order in the Court," "Giving Away the Bride," etc. Hght., 5, 7½; wght., 135; fair complexion, brown hair, blue eyes. Home ad., 208 S. Figueroa st., Los Angeles. Phone 62570; studio ad., Rolin.

BOLDER, Robert; b. London, England; educ. Christ's Hospital, The Blue Coat School; stage career, 37 years on stage; screen career, 7 yrs., 2 yrs. stk. Essanay, Astra ("Japanese Butterfly"), Vitagraph ("Diplomatic Mission"), Fox ("Fame & Fortune"), Fairbanks ("Arizona"), Goldwyn ("Strictly Confidential," "Upstairs"), Haworth ("The Beggar and the Prince"). Hght., 5, 2; wght., 185; silver grey hair, blue eyes. Home ad., 1394 N. Vermont ave., Los Angeles. Phone 597690; studio ad., Haworth Co., Brunton Studios.

BOSWORTH, Hobart Van Zandt; b. Marietta, Ohio; educ. there; stage career, since 1885; 10 yrs. at Daly's theatre, New York, supporting Mrs. Fiske, Marlowe, Crossman, Amelia Bingham, as leading man, starred by Harrison Fiske, stage director Belasco theatre, Los Angeles, up to 1909; screen career, played lead in first picture made in Los Angeles, Selig ("Monte Cristo," and 112 others), Bosworth, Inc. ("The Sea Wolf," "Buckshot John," "Pursuit of the Phantom"), Lasky ("Joan the Woman," "Oliver Twist," "Little American," "Woman God Forgot"), Universal ("Two Men of Sandy Bar," "Way of the World"), T. Hays Hunter Special ("Border Legion"), featured in two pictures with Ince and one yr. with J. Parker Read. Home ad., 236 S. Rampart Blvd., Los Angeles, Calif. Wilshire 17.

BOTELER, Wade; b. Santa Ana, Calif.; educ. Los Angeles; stage career, 3 yrs. acting in stk., 2 yrs. dir. stk., 1 season with Otis Skinner; screen career, Famous Players ("Very Good Young Man"), Ince ("Crooked Straight," "23½ Hours Leave"), Goldwyn ("Hard Proposition," "Cup of Fury"). Hght., 6; wght., 180; red hair, blue eyes. Home ad., 1910 West 42nd Place, Los Angeles, Calif.; Vermont 5361; studio, Thomas H. Ince.

BOTTER, Henry P.; educ. Boston, Mass.; stage career, actor and director in stock and productions, also vaudeville; screen career with Edison, Biograph, Kalem, Essanay and Monmouth Film Co. Ad., 216 W. 51st St., N. Y.

BOWERS, John; b. Indiana; stage career, with Donald Robertson, Beulah Poynter, in "The Family Cupboard," "Things That Count," screen career, Griffith, World Metro, Famous Players, Thanhouser, World ("The Divorce Game," "Betsy Ross," "Joan of the Woods," "Day Dreams," "Sis Hopkins," "Daughter of Mine," "The Pest"), Goldwyn ("Thru the Wrong Door," "Strictly Confidential," "Tower of Ivory," "Woman in Room 13"). Hght., 6; wght., 180; dark hair and eyes. Ad., c/o Goldwyn Pict. Corp., N. Y. C.

BOWES, Clifford W.; b. Pueblo, Colo.; educ. Los Angeles, Calif.; screen career, entered picture industry in 1915; 2½ yrs. with Mack Sennett, 6 mos. with Fox, attained rank of warrant flyer when discharged from navy April, 1919. Hght., 5, 5; wght., 140; dark brown hair, blue eyes. Home ad., 3011 Lake st., Ocean Park, Cal., phone 4033.

BRACY, Sidney; b. Melbourne, Australia, 1882; educ. Melbourne Univ.; stage career, 6 yrs. with late J. C. Williamson in Australia, with Kyrle Bellew, supported Viola Allen, with Nazimova, Nat Goodwin, in revival of "Robin Hood" and "Rob Roy," in N. Y.; screen career, Thanhouser ("Million Dollar Mystery," "The Miser's Reversion"), Fox ("Merely Mary Ann," "Sporting Blood"), Universal ("Elusive Isabel," "Temptation and the Man," etc.), Arrow ("Crime and Punishment," "The Deemster"), Famous ("The Long Trail"). Hght., 5, 8; wght., 148; brown hair and eyes.

BRADBURY, Ronald; b. Walla Walla, Wash., 1886; educ. Baker Sch., Walla Walla, and Chicago; stage career, Baker Stock Co., Portland, Ore., 7 yrs featured over Orpheum and Pantages circuits; own companies; screen career, Universal ("Colorado," "Big Bill Brent"), Lasky ("To Have and to Hold"), Kalem ("The Harvest of Gold," "On the Brink of War," "The False Prophet," "The Resurrection of Gold Bar"). Ad., Vitagraph Studios, Hollywood, Cal.

BRADY, Edwin J.; b. N. Y., 1889; educ. pub. sch. and Coll. City of N. Y.; stage career, mus. com., vaud. and dram. stk.; screen career, Selig, Universal, Nestor; joined Balboa 1915 ("Who Pays?" series, "Neal of the Navy"), Selig ("Out of the Shadows," "Hedge of Heart's Desire," "The Fount of Courage), Pathe-Keenan ("The False Code"), Goldwyn "Almost a Husband"), World-Macauley ("When Bearcat Went Dry"). Wght., 165; hght., 5, 10½; brown hair, brown eyes.

BRAMMALL, John Gardiner; b. Rochdale, Eng.; educ. Christ Church, Eng.; stage career with Maxine Elliott, Mabel Taliaferro, Lillian Russell; screen career, Biograph, Fine Arts, Lasky, Fox ("House on the Land," "Confession," "The Girl Who Came Back"), Pathe ("The Master Man"), Metro ("Her Inspiration"), American ("Six Feet Four"). Hght., 5, 7; wght., 135; light hair, gray eyes. Ad., 1630½ Morton ave., Los Angeles, Cal., phone 53603.

BREESE, Edmund; b. Brooklyn, N. Y., 1871; educ. there; 20 yrs. on legitimate stage; featured 4 yrs. in "Lion and the Mouse," lead in "Today," "The Fear Market"; 2 yrs. "Why Marry?"; screen career, Lasky ("The Master Mind"), Fox ("Walls of Jericho"), Metro ("Shooting of Dan McGrew," "Song of Wage Slave," "Spell of Yukon," "Lure of Heart's Desire," "Weakness of Strength"), Ivan Abramson ("Someone Must Pay"), Gaumont ("A Temporary Wife"). Hght., 5, 9½; wght., 152; brown hair, blue eyes. Ad., home, Edmund Breese Farm, Norwalk, Conn.

BRINLEY, Charles E.; b. Yuman, Ariz.; educ. there; screen career, 8 yrs. with Universal ("The Lone Hand," "Tempest Cody," "Down But Not Out," "Tray of Hearts," "Liberty," "Red Ace"), Pathe ("Patra"). Hght., 5, 11½; wght., 160; gray hair, brown eyes. Home ad., 1646 Lake Shore ave., Los Angeles, Cal., phone 51702.

BROOKS, Joe; b. St. Louis, Mo.; educ. Rock Church Sch., St. Louis; stage career, Odan Stock Co., 1 yr.; screen career, Biograph ("Judith," "The Battle of Truth"), Sawyer ("Love's Cross Roads"), Fairbanks ("Reaching for the Moon," "Mr. Fix-It"). Hght., 6; wght., 185; black hair, brown eyes. Home ad., 1109 W. 10th St., Los Angeles, Cal., phone 556470.

BROOKS, Sam; b. Brooklyn, N. Y., 1891; educ. Brooklyn; stage career, 7 yrs. on stage; screen career, Rolin Pathe, Lonesome Luke Series, Snub Pollard Comedies, Harold Lloyd Comedies. Hght., 4; wght., 100; fair complexion, brown hair, blue eyes. Home ad., 215 W. 50th St., Los Angeles, Cal., phone 288218; studio ad., Rolin Co., Culver City, Cal.

BROUGHTON, Lewis; educ. England and Paris; stage career, 20 yrs. on legit. stage; screen career, Premier ("The Greater Will"), Selznick lead in "The Woman's Game"). Hght., 6; wght., 140; light hair, blue eyes. Ad., 50 W. 94th St., N. Y. C., Riverside 516.

BROWN, J. Edwin; b. Boston, Mass.; educ. Boston; stage career, 42 yrs. on legit. stage as stage director; screen career, Universal ("The Isle of Life," "The Black Box," "For Her Mother's Sake," "The Cry of Conscience," "A Romany Rose," "The Birth of Patriotism," "The House of Gloom," "The Scarlet Shadow"). Hght., 5, 8; wght., 130; brown hair and blue eyes.

BROWN, William H.; b. Northampton, Mass.; stage career, with Dorothy Morton Opera Co., stock at Castle Square, Boston, La Salle stock, Chicago, with "Messenger Boy" Co.; screen career, Yankee Film and other feature cos., Reliance-Majestic, Fine Arts ("Casey at the Bat," "The Rummy," "The Wharf Rat," "The House Built Upon Sands," "The Bad Boy"), Paramount-Artcraft ("The Valley of the Giants," "In Mizzoura").

BROWNE, Bothwell, Female Impersonator; b. Denmark; stage career, 20 yrs., Shubert, vaud.; originated Gibson Girl and Cleopatra in "Serpent of the Nile"; screen career, Paramount-Sennett, starred in "Miss Jack"; Lesser-Sennett "Yankee Doodle in Berlin"). Hght., 5, 11; wght., 165; blond hair, blue eyes. Ad., Sherwood Apts., 4th and Grand ave., Los Angeles, Cal.

BRUNTON, William, b. Canada; educ. Canada; stage career, road shows Canada and United States, played stk. and rep., with own show, over Western circuit and vaud.; screen career, joined Kalem 1912, with Universal, Signal, in "The Girl and the Game," "The Lost Express," Metro ("As the Sun Went Down"), Lasky ("Cruise of the Make Believes," "The Squaw Man"), Metro ("As the Sun Went Down"), Para.-Artcraft ("Valley of the Giants"). Hght., 5, 7; wght., 140; light hair, brown eyes, fair complexion. Home ad., 819 Mariposa st., Glendale, Cal., Glendale 531-W.

BRYANT, Charles; b. Hartford, Eng., 1887; educ. Ardingly College; stage career, 21 yrs., 10 yrs. in America with Ethel Barrymore, Mrs. Patrick Campbell, Chas. Frohman, Mme. Nazimova; screen career, Brenon-Selznick ("War Brides"), Metro ("Revelation," "Toys of Fate," "Eye for Eye," "Out of the Fog," "The Brat," "Stronger Than Death"). Hght., 6, 3; wght., 190; brown hair, blue eyes. Ad., care of Metro, Hollywood, Cal.

BUCKLEY, Floyd Thomas, characters; b. Floresville, Tex., 1882; educ. Syracuse Univ. and Am. Acad. Drama; stage career, mus. com., vaud., stk., drama; screen career, Famous ("Nanette of the Wilds"), International ("The Flower of Faith"), Rolfe ("Master Mystery," "Scream in the Night"), McManus ("Lost Battalion"). Now with Helen Holmes in the serial, "The Fatal Fortune," S. L. K. Serial Corp. Hght., 5, 11½; wght., 187; light complexion, dark hair, blue eyes. Ad., home, 251 W. 39th St., or Green Room Club, N. Y.

BUCKLEY, William; b. Chicago, Ill., 1891; educ. there; stage career, stk., Denver, Chicago, vaud., "Brown of Harvard," "Strongheart"; screen career, Majestic, Universal, Famous Players, Essanay, Thos. H. Ince, Goldwyn, Metro, Vitagraph. Hght., 6, 1; wght., 169; medium complexion, brown hair, dark eyes. Home ad., Biltmore Apts., 330 So. Grand ave., Los Angeles, Cal., Main 4104.

BUNKER, Ralph; educ. Harvard Univ.; stage career, featured in "The Very Idea," comedy lead with Arthur Hopkins, "Good Gracious Annabelle," "Plots and Playwrights," Comedy theatre, N. Y., "Hobohemia"; screen career, with Constance Talmadge in "In Search of a Sinner," Films, Inc. ("That Woman," with Catherine Calvert), "Gloria's Romance," with Billie Burke. Hght., 5, 7½; wght., 135; black hair, dark eyes. Ad., Harvard Club, 27 W. 44th st., N. Y. C.

BUNNY, George; b. N. Y., 1867; educ. Brooklyn; stage career, actor in various prod. for 25 yrs.; screen career, Eastern Film Corp. ("Capt. Eric," and a number of one-reel comedies); Fox ("A Camouflaged Kiss"), Goldwyn ("Friend Husband"), Fox ("Caught in the Act"), World ("A Broadway Saint," "The Poison Pen"), Selznick ("Piccadilly Jim"). Hght., 5, 8; wght., 200; gray hair, blue eyes. Ad., home, 31 Trinity st., New Britain, Conn.

BURKE, Joseph; b. N. Y. C.; educ. England; stage career, since a boy in mus. com. and vaud.; screen career, with Pathe, Famous Players, Fox, Geo. Kleine, Ivan, Rolfe; recent pictures, Norma Talmadge ("De Luxe Annie"), Famous Players ("Come On In," "Good Bye, Bill," "Oh, You Women"), Town and Country ("Independence, By Gosh"), Edison ("A Fool's Paradise"), Fox ("Help! Help! Police!"), Screencraft ("The Trap"), Vitagraph ("The Winchester Woman," "Green God"), Selznick ("The Country Cousin"), Briggs, Oh, Man Series. Hght., 5, 9; wght., 135; gray hair, dark blue eyes. Home ad., 310 W. 14th st., N. Y. C., Chelsea 10365.

BURNS, Ed. J.; b. Phila., 1892; educ. Catholic schools Penna.; stage career, Orpheum Stock Co., Phila., 1 yr.; screen career, Fox, Vitagraph, Famous Players, World, with Kitty Gordon in "Her Hour"; leads with Elsie Ferguson, Alice Brady, Pauline Frederick, Corinne Griffith, Gladys Leslie, Hodkinson ("Made in America"), Keeney-Sherry ("A Marriage for Convenience"), Fox ("Miss Adventure"), Para.-Artcraft ("The Love Burglar," "Male and Female"). Hght., 5, 11½; wght., 135; dark complexion, eyes, hair. Home ad., 547 Riverside Dr. N. Y., Mngsde 3753; studio ad., Universal.

BURNS, Fred; b. Ft. Keogh, Mont., 1878; early career, ranching, breaking horses, later with Buffalo Bill's Wild West, 101 Ranch, gave rope throwing and riding exhibitions throughout U. S. and Europe; screen career, Selig, Reliance-Majestic, Pallas, Fine Arts ("Birth of a Nation," "Ben Blair"), Clune ("Eyes of the World"), Artcraft ("Fancy Jim Sherwood"), Vitagraph ("Sunlight's Last Raid," "The Fighting Trail"), Artcraft ("Bound in Morocco"). Has been assisting Douglas Fairbanks and Ruth Roland for past year.

BURNS, Neal; b. Bristol, Pa.; educ. Atlantic City, N. J.; stage career, "Just Out of College," "The Girl in the Taxi," "The Sporting Deacon," "A Winsome Widow," "A Stubborn Cinderella," "The Girl of My Dreams," "Yankee Prince," Morosco Theatre Stk., Los Angeles; screen career, Christie ("He Married His Wife," "Rough and Western"), Goldwyn ("Darn That Stocking," "A Dollar Down"). Hght., 5, 6; wght., 141; brown hair and eyes. Ad., 6424 Dix st., Hollywood, Cal., phone 929; studio ad., National Studios.

BURNS, Robert Paul (Bobby Burns); b. Philadelphia., Pa., 1878; stage career, 5 yrs. in vaud., 6 seasons mus. comedies, "Babes in Toyland," "Wizard of Oz"; screen career, 10 years with Selig, Lubin, Reliance, World, Vim and

ACTORS

Jaxon Comedies, Mr. Pokes of Pokes & Jabes Series, Cuckoo Comedies. Studio ad., 750 Riverside ave., Jacksonville, Fla., or Photo Products, Commercial Trust Bldg., 41st & Bway., N. Y. C.

BURNS, Sammy; b. N. Y., 1888; became acrobat with Hassan-Ben Ali troupe at six yrs. old, toured world; appeared in Europe with Sylvester Schaefer Family; in vaud. in Europe and U. S.; mus. com. "Tick Tock Man of Oz," etc.; screen career, 15 com. with Vogue, L-Ko, wrote, dir. and starred "Bombs aand Bandits," "A Mexican Muddle," "Rural Rogues," "A Doggone Dog"; in tech. and scen. depts. of Keystone; wrote, dir. and acted in several Black Diamond com.; now star King Cole Comedies. Ad., Motion Picture Producing Co. of America, 398 Fifth ave., N. Y. C. Studio, Dongan Hills, S. I., N. Y.

BURRESS, William; b. New Cornerstown, O., 1867; educ. Uhrichsville, O.; early career, worked for Penn. Railroad; stage career, Chas. Frohman, Klaw and Erlanger, Shuberts, various vaud. and stk. cos.; screen career, Fox "End of the Trail," "Man from Bitter Roots," "Fires of Conscience," "Island of Desire," "The Spy," "The Forbidden Room"), Universal ("Broadway Love," "Paid in Advance"), Goldwyn ("Heartsease," "Lord and Lady Algy"). Studio ad., Garson Studios, Los Angeles.

BURTON, Clarence; b. Windsor, Mo.; stage career, stk. at Curtis theatre, Denver, for 3 yrs., 2 seasons at Miles theatre, Minneapolis, Minn., etc., toured Orpheum Circuit and other vaud. circuits in several acts, most of which were written by himself; screen career, 1913, Famous Players ("Hawthorne of the U. S. A.," "The Six Best Cellars," "Thou Art the Man!"), now with Lasky Stock Co. Hght., 5, 11; wght., 176; brown hair and eyes. Ad., Lasky Studio, Hollywood, Cal.

BURTON, Ned; b. U. S.; educ. Harvard Univ.; stage career, 18 yrs. in vaud. as senior member of Burton and Brookes, 2 seasons with Julian Eltinge Co., 1 season in original "Potash and Perlmutter" Co.; screen career, Peerless ("The Man of the Hour"), Herbert Brenon ("War Brides," with Nazimova), Artcraft ("The Poor Little Rich Girl"), Goldwyn ("The Auction Block"), World ("The Moral Deadline"), Fox ("Thou Shalt Not"), Hodkinson ("Thunderbolts of Fate"). Hght., 6; wght., 245; white hair, blue eyes. Ad., home, 214 W. 92d st., N. Y. Riverside 2709.

BUSHMAN, Francis Xavier; b. Norfolk, Va., Jan. 10, 1885; educ. Ammendale Coll., Maryland; early career, wrestler, bicycle racer, artist's model, student of sculpture; stage career, at 9 appeared in "The Lady of Lyons," in "Queen of the Moulin Rouge," "Going Some," also in stk., rep., etc.; screen career, from 1911, Essanay ("Graustark," "The Master Thief"), March, 1915, joined Metro (first serial, "The Great Secret," "Romeo and Juliet," "The Voice of Conscience," "Red, White and Blue Blood," "Social Quicksands," "A Pair of Cupids," "The Poor Rich Man"), Vitagraph ("Daring Hearts"). Member Friars Club. Hght., 5, 11; wght., 186; complexion, light, brown hair, blue eyes.

BUTLER, David Wyngate b. San Francisco, Cal., 1895; educ. Leland Stanford, Jr., Univ.; stage career, Alcazar Stk. Co. 3 yrs. at Morosco theatre, Los Angeles, stage mgr. for Oliver Morosco's "Upstairs and Down," "Lombardi, Ltd.," "Sadie Love"; screen career, Griffith ("The Greatest Thing in Life," "Girl Who Stayed at Home"), Selznick ("Upstairs and Down"), Brentwood ("Better Times," "The Other Half"), Dorothy Gish ("Nugget Nell"), Universal ("The Unpainted Woman," "The Petal on the Current," "Bonnie, Bonnie Lassie"), Tourneur ("The County Fair"). Hght., 6; wght., 185; dark complexion, black hair. blue eyes. Home ad., 972 Arapahoe st., Los Angeles. Phone 52998.

BUTT, Lawson W.; b. 1883; stage career, leads, "The Wanderer," "Merry Wives of Windsor," "Taming of the Shrew"; screen career, Metro, Selig, Paralta ("Shackled," "The One Woman"), Pathe ("Her Man"), G. L. Tucker ("Miracle Man"), United ("Playthings of Passion"), Goldwyn ("The World and Its Woman"), Hampton-Hod. ("Desert Gold"), Tyrad ("It Happened in Paris"), "Tower of Ivory," "Dangerous Days," "The One Woman"). Hght., 6, 2; complexion dark. Studio ad., Goldwyn, Culver City, Cal.

BUTTERWORTH, Ernest; b. England; educ. there; early career, military profession; screen career, Griffith ("Intolerance," "Broken Blossoms," "Greatest Thing in Life"), Fairbanks ("Arizona," "Say, Young Fellow," "Knickerbocker Buckaroo"), own company ("The Little Cripple," "Children of the Mission"). Hght., 5, 7½; wght., 170; slightly gray hair, brown eyes. Home ad., 6100 Elinor av., Los Angeles. Holly 3110.

BYRAM, Ronald; b. Brisbane, Australia; educ. Sidney Univ., Aust.; stage career, 5 yrs. with J. C. Williamson, Ltd., Aust., in "Shirley Kaye," "Lord and Lady Algy," with Wm. Faversham and Maxine Elliott; screen career, Famous Players, "Out of the Shadows," with Pauline Frederick, Vitagraph ("A Gentleman of Quality"). Hght., 6 ft.; wght., 168; dark complexion, brown eyes, dark hair. Home ad., 116 W. 71st st., N. Y. C. and L. A. Athletic Club, L. A., Cal.

— C —

CAIN, Robert; b. 1882; stage career, "The Misleading Lady," "The Deep Purple," "The Blue Mouse," "The Man of the Hour"; screen career, Famous Players, Bacon-Backer ("Men"), Select ("The Death Dance"), Paramount ("Secret Service," "Paid in Full," "In Mizzoura"), Fox ("Eastward Ho!"), Para-Artcraft ("Male and Female"). Hght., 5, 10; medium complexion.

CAMERON, Rudolph W. B.; b. Washington, D. C., 1892; educ. Georgetown Univ.; stage exper. in Geo. Broadhurst's "Rich Man, Poor Man"; screen career, Vitagraph ("The More Excellent Way," "Clover's Rebellion"), Vice-President and Gen. Mgr. of Anita Steward Prod., Inc. Ad., 6 West 48th st., N. Y. C.; studio, Anita Stewart Prods., 3800 Mission Road, Los Angeles, Cal.

CAMERON, Tom; educ. Derby, England; stage career, 3 seasons circus-singing clown, 3 seasons comic opera and musical comedy, 4 seasons dramatic rep., 12 yrs. vaud.; screen career, 4 yrs. Fox ("Child of the Wild," "Blue Streak"), Pathe ("Hillcrest Mystery"), Abramson ("The Window Opposite"), Warner ("The Other Man's Wife"), Dalton ("The White Rook"), Ince ("Black is White"), Constance Talmadge ("At the Barn"). Hght., 5, 10½; wght., 165; light brown hair, gray eyes. Ad., 512 W. 146th st., N. Y., Audubon 47.

CAMPEAU, Frank; b. Detroit, Mich.; educ. Notre Dame, Ind.; with Louis Morrison in "Faust," Frank Mayo in "Pudd'nhead Wilson," "Arizona," "The Virginian," "Kindling," "Ghost Breaker," "Believe Me, Xantippe," "Within the Law"; screen career, Griffith ("Jordan is a Hard Road"), C. K. Young ("Cheating Cheaters"), Fairbanks ("Man From Painted Post," "Reaching of the Moon," "Heading South," "Mr. Fixit," "Say, Young Fellow," "His Majesty, the American," "When the Clouds Roll By"). Hght., 5, 10; wght., 155; dark hair, dark gray eyes. Home ad., Angeles Hotel, Los Angeles, Cal.; Main 8890; studio, Douglas Fairbanks Studio.

CANNON, Pomeroy; b. Kentucky; educ. there and New York; stage career, Belasco, Frohman, minstrel, vaud., opera; screen career, Fairbanks ("Good Bad Man"), Morosco-Pallas ("Parson of Paramint"), Fox ("Honor System," "A Camouflage"), Goldwyn ("When Doctors Disagree," "Flame of the Desert," "Cup of Fury"). Hght., 6, 2; wght., 225; dark hair and eyes. Home ad., 4407 Clayton ave., Los Angeles, Cal., phone 599213.

CAREY, Harry; b. N. Y., 1880; educ. N. Y. Univ.; early career, actor, playwright, prospector and cowboy; stage career, starred in his own plays, "Montana," "Heart of Alaska," stock; screen career, Biograph, Universal ("Riders of Vengeance," "Roped," "Outcasts of Poker Flat," "Fight for Love," "Bare Fists," "Riders of the Law," "Gun Fightin' Gentleman," "Marked Men," "Man Who Wouldn't Shoot"). Hght., 6; wght., 180; blonde hair. Studio, Universal City.

CARLETON, William T.; b. 1859; educ. London, Eng.; stage career, 40 years leading operatic baritone, proprietor and star of Carleton Opera Co. 15 yrs., with Liebler Bros.; screen career, Famous Players, Pathe, Mutual, Goldwyn, Peerless, Metro ("Eye for Eye," "The Danger Mark," World ("Home Wanted," "His Father's Wife," "Me and Capt. Kidd"), Artcraft ("A Society Exile"). Hght., 6; wght., 190; ruddy complexion, dark hair, gray eyes. Ad., The Lotus Club, 10 W. 57th st., N. Y. C.

CARLYLE, J. Montgomery; b. N. Y. C.; educ. Cornell Univ. '02; stage career, "Charlie's Aunt," Chas. Frohman Co., 2 seasons; "Duchess of Danzig," Alf Hayman Co., 1 season; Owen Davis Stk. Co., 2 yrs.; Belasco stk., 3 yrs.; screen career, Baby Marie Osborne Co. ("Marie's Trip West"), Universal ("Midnight Man," "Just Bill"), Sherrill Co. ("Spirit Cabin Mine"), Goldwyn ("Flame of the Desert"), Fox ("Girl in Bohemia"), American ("Hands Up"), Hght., 6; wght., 201; light brown hair, dark blue eyes. Home ad., Iris Apts., 1220 Olive st., Los Angeles, Cal.

CARLYLE, Richard; educ. Little Rock, Ark.; stage career, 14 yrs., including 6 N. Y. prod., "Under Cover," "Pays to Advertise," "The Torches," "Upstairs & Down"; screen career, Marion Leonard ("The Vow"), Knickerbocker ("Bridge of Sighs," "The Purple Knight"), Lubin ("Those Who Toil"), Grandin ("Stolen Will"), Goldwyn ("Spotlight Sadie"), Famous Players ("The Copperhead"). Hght., 5, 9; wght., 145; brown hair, dark blue eyes. Ad., Green Room Club, N. Y.

CARRIGAN, Thomas Jay; b. and educ. Lapeer, Mich.; stage career, with Belasco, Schubert, Lew Fields, Castle Sq. Stk. of Boston, College Stk. of Chicago, Baker Stk. Co. of Portland, Ore., W. S. Harkins Co., in Eastern Canada and So. America, "Mother Carey's Chicken"; screen career, "The Copperhead," with Lionel Barrymore, Selig ("The Two Orphans," "Cinderella," "The Royal Box"), Fox ("Checkers"), World ("Dust of Desire"), Camera Art ("Somewhere in Love"), Capellani ("Little Mother Hubbard"). Hght., 5, 11; wght., 168; brown hair, gray eyes. Ad., Lambs Club, N. Y.

CARROLL, William Arthur; b. N. Y. C.; educ. there; stage career, 1889, with Rice & Dixey, with Jos. & W. Jefferson, in "The Henrietta"; screen career, since 1910, 2 yrs. with Gaston Melies, 3½ yrs. Biograph, 2½ yrs. American, Ince ("Bill Henry"), National ("Blue Bonnett," "The Confession"), Metro ("One Thing at a Time O' Day"). Hght., 5, 10½; wght., 145; brown hair, blue eyes. Home ad., 7028 Hollywood blvd., Los Angeles, phone 577116, or Actor's Assn., Hollywood 1946.

CARTER, Harry; b. Louisville, 1879; educ. Hobart Coll.; stage career, rep. with Mrs. Fiske, "Excuse Me," stage director for Charles Dillingham, "The Red Mill"; screen career, Universal ("The Mystery of the Gray Ghost," "The Circus of Life," "One Clear Call," "Beloved Jim," "The Bride's Awakening," "The Marriage Life," "The Kaiser, the Beast of Berlin," "A Kentucky Cinderella," "Beans"); Metro ("After His Own Heart." Hght., 6; wght., 190; brown hair, blue eyes. Ad., Universal City, Calif.

CARUSO, Enrico; b. Naples, Italy; educ. Italy; opera singer; screen career, Famous Players ("My Cousin" and "Prince Ubaldo"). Hght., 5, 6; dark complexion, dark eyes, chestnut hair. Ad., Knickerbocker Hotel, N. Y. C.

CAVENDER, Glen, also director; b. Tucson, Ariz., 1887; stage career, vaud., musical team, Buffalo Bill; screen career, St. Louis M. P. Co., Albuquerque, Universal, NYMP, Keystone (dir-14 mon.; played in "The Surf Girl," dir. "Lion and the Girl," "A Dog Catcher's Love"), Sennett-Paramount, "Are Waitresses Safe?" "The Kitchen Lady"), Lehrman ("His Musical Sneeze"), Sunshine "High Life in Jail"), director, Arbuckle ("The Sheriff," "The Cook"). Awarded medal of Legion of Honor of France for bravery in Boxer Rebellion. Hght., 5, 9½; wght., 175; light brown hair, blue eyes. Ad., 5718 Carlton Way, L. A., Cal.; studio, Fox Sunshine.

CECIL, Edward; b. San Francisco, Calif.; educ. there; stage career, several years in stk. vaud. rep. and prod.; screen career, co-lead with Jim Corbett in "Burglar and Lady," Priscilla Dean in "Wild Cat of Paris," Madeleine Travers in "Danger Zone," Peggy Hyland in "The Lost Princess," Eleanor Fiar in "The Girl of Bohemia," Grace Cunard in "After the War," Betty Blythe in "Third Generation." Hght. 5, 11; wght., 165; brown hair, hazel eyes. Ad., Brentwood Film Corp., Fountain Ave., Los Angeles, Calif.

CHANDLER, Warren; b. Bklyn., N. Y., 1881; stage career, stock cos. California; screen career. Famous Players, Ivan, Frohman Amusement Co., Vitagraph ("The Birth of a Race," "The Adventure Shop," "Grey Towers Mystery"), Pathe ("My Husband's Other Wife"). Hght.. 6½ ft.; wght., 185; fair complexion, brown hair, blue eyes. Ad., 885 Bushwick ave., Brooklyn, N. Y. Bush 6513.

CHANEY, Lon; b. and educ. Colorado Springs; stage career, directed and produced "Pop" Fischer and Kolb and Dill attractions, dancing comedian; screen career, Universal ("Fires of Rebellion," "Broadway Love," "Anything Once," "A Broadway Scandal," "That Devil, Bateese" "The Wicked Darling," "Paid in Advance"), Para-Artcraft ("The False Faces," "The Miracle Man," "Victory"), Ex.-Mutual ("A Man's Country"), World-Macauley ("When Bearcat Went Dry").Ad., Goldwyn Studio, Culver City, Calif.; home ad., 1575 Edgemont, Hollywood, Calif.; Holly 1111.

CHAPLIN, Charles Spencer, also producing-director; b. Paris, 1889; stage career, in London theatres, "Rags and Riches," "Billy" in "Sherlock Holmes," came to America with "Night in an English Music Hall"; screen career, in Keystone, Essanay, Lone Star-Mutual ("The Rink," "Easy Street," "Tillie's Punctured Romance"), Mutual ("The Immigrant," "The Adventurer"). Now starring with First Exhibitors Circuit, a company of his own formation. Chaplin-First Natl. ("A Dog's Life," "Shoulder Arms," "A Day's Pleasure," "Sunnyside"). Hght., 5, 4; wght, 125; brown hair, blue eyes. Ad., home, Los Angeles Athletic Club; studio, Charlie Chaplin Film Co., 1416 La Brea ave., L. A., Cal.

CHAPLIN, Sydney, also director; b. Cape Town, So. Africa; educ. London; stage career, with Chas. Froham, Fred Karno "A Night in an English Music Hall"; screen career, "Submarine Pirate" and others for Keystone; bus. mgr. for brother, Chas. Chaplin, for 3 yrs.; Sydney Chaplin Prod. ("One Hundred Million"). Hght., 5, 7½; wght., 165; black hair, dark brown eyes. Ad., Sydney Chaplin Prod., 6642 Santa Monica Blvd., Los Angeles, Calif.

CHASE, Colin; b. Lewiston, Idaho, Apr. 13, 1888; educ. Chicago and Newport, R. I.; early career, staff artist on Chicago papers; stage career, 2 seasons stk., 1 season in "Sam Houston," vaud.; screen career, Essanay, Colorado, Universal, Morosco, Ince-Triangle ("A Strange Transgressor"), Fox ("Conscience," "The Awakening," "A Branded Soul," "The Moral Law," "Eastward Ho!"). Expert horseback rider. Hght., 5, 11; wght., 165; complexion dark, brown hair, gray eyes.

CHESEBORO, George; screen career, Texas Guinan two-reelers, Frohman Corp. ("The She-Wolf") Selig ("The Lost City" serial).

CHRISTMAN, Pat. (Ora N.); b. Meadville, Mo., 1882; educ. Chillicothe, Mo.; early career, cow puncher, horse breaker 4 yrs.; screen career, Lubin, Pathe, Reliance, Selig ("The Pony Express," "The Canbyhill Outlaw," "When Cupid Slipped"), Fox ("Western Blood," "Six Shooter Andy," "Ace High," "Rough Riding Romance"). Held bucking horse championship in Dallas, Tex., 1906. Ad., studio, Fox, L. A., Cal.

CLAPHAM, Leonard T.; b. Louisville, Ky.; educ. there; early career, locomotive engineer; screen career, Universal ("Heart of Humanity," "Liberty" serial, "Great Air Robbery," "Cyclone Smith" series, "Lion Man" serial), Goldwyn ("Leave it to Susan"), Fox ("Lone Star Range," "Last of the Duanes"). Hght., 6, 1½; wght., 187; light hair, blue eyes. Home ad., 1535 Edgemont ave., Los Angeles, Calif. Holly 635.

CLARK, Frank M.; b. Cincinnati, Ohio; educ. there; stage career, 1874, own cos. in Australia, theatrical mgr.; screen career, 10 yrs. with Selig Polyscope Co. ("The Spoilers," "Dextry," "Ne'er Do Well," "The Rosary," "The Still Alarm," "The Lost City" serial), Fox ("The Price of Silence"). Hght., 5, 9; wght., 170; fair complexion, grey hair and eyes. Home ad., 231 Parkside, Los Angeles, Calif. East 2898; studio, 3800 Mission Road, Los Angeles. East 33.

CLARK, Harvey, b. Boston, 1886; educ. Mass. Coll., Cambridge; stage career, with Otis Skinner, Robert Hilliard, own act in vaud.; screen career, NYMP, American ("The Gentle Intruders," "The Frame-up," "Melissa of the Hills," "A Sporting Chance," "Six Feet Four"), Triangle ("Restless Souls," "Prudence on

SELZNICK PICTURES

The New Home of Selznick Pictures

The Selznick Pictures Studio is now under construction in Long Island City. It will be the largest as well as the most completely equipped studio building in the world.

The first two National Pictures produced for distribution through Select Pictures Corporation are:

"JUST A WIFE"

Adapted from one of Eugene Walter's most successful stage plays.

Direction – Howard Hickman
Scenario by Katherine Reed

❦ ❦ ❦

"BLIND YOUTH"

A picturization of the famous play by Lou Tellegen and Willard Mack

Direction—Al Green
Scenario by Katherine Reed

NATIONAL PICTURE THEATRES, INC.
SELECT PICTURES CORPORATION

Lewis J. Selznick
President

THE SYMBOL OF SUCCESS!

PERFORMANCE counts in every phase of Big Business!

Behind the new symbol—REPUBLIC PICTURES—lies the performance and progress that has stood the test of time and comparison.

A symbol of broadened leadership and perfect organization in which you get the dollars-and-cents profits that *must* come from proved box-office attractions and "live-wire" exploitation.

As SELECT has merited your confidence and esteem, so will Republic.

New in name—but old in the experience and understanding of the needs of those who have gained by mutual trust

Lewis J. Selznick

REPUBLIC DISTRIBUTING CORPORATION
LEWIS J. SELZNICK, Advisory Director — **BRITON N. BUSCH**, President
130 West 46th Street   New York City

PICTURES

R. CECIL SMITH

Now writing exclusively for Selznick

The most prolific writer of today for the screen

(Product of the past two years)

Price Mark .... Dalton	Maternal Spark .... Sedgwick	Free and Equal ..... All Star
Love Letters ...... Dalton	The Busher .... Ray	Trail of Yukon . Bosworth
Tyrant Fear .... Dalton	Playing the Game ...... Ray	Madcap Madge .... Thomas
Green Eyes .... Dalton	Son of Snows .... Ray	Out the Night .... Thomas
Mating Marcella .... Dalton	Claws of the Hun ..... Ray	Wife's Money ...... O'Brien
Extravagance ...... Dalton	Straight and Narrow ... Ray	Country Cousin .. H'm'rst'n
Hard Boiled .... Dalton	Wedding Ring ..... Bennett	Rosalie Byrnes .... H'm'rst'n
Homebreaker ...... Dalton	Coals of Fire ...... Bennett	Who's Who .... Moore
L'Apache .... Dalton	Flying Colors .... Desmond	Bond of Fear ... Roy Stuart
Wife's Friend ...... Dalton	Master of Home .. Desmond	What's Your Husband
Her Bit .... Dalton	Sudden Gentleman Desmond	Doing ..... Maclean-May
	Little Reformer ...... Love	

EDWARD J. MONTAGNE

Screen Dramatist

ABOUT 200 ORIGINALS

ABOUT 100 FEATURE ADAPTATIONS

RELEASES OF 1919

THE COMBAT	(Anita Stewart)
OUT YONDER	(Olive Thomas)
THE LION AND THE MOUSE	(Alice Joyce)
A STITCH IN TIME	(Gladys Leslie)
BEATING THE ODDS	(Harry Morey)
THE MAN WHO WON	(Harry Morey)
A GENTLEMAN OF QUALITY	(Earle Williams)
CUPID FORECLOSES	(Bessie Love)
TOO MANY CROOKS	(Gladys Leslie)
SUE, OF BOLINAS PLAINS	(Bessie Love)
THE GIRL-WOMAN	(Gladys Leslie)
HIS DARKEST HOUR	(Harry Morey)
FIGHTING DESTINY	(Harry Morey)
HUMAN DESIRE	(Anita Stewart)
BEAUTY-PROOF	(Harry Morey)

NOW WRITING FOR SELZNICK

Green Room Club, N. Y. City

Writing *Continuity

George D. Proctor

My Pledge: I will not accept for adaptation any story in which I can not see the foundation of a good feature production.

FOR REFERENCES SEE THE SCREEN

Coming Adaptations

"THE FORTUNE TELLER"—An Albert Capellani production starring Marjorie Rambeau.

"OTHER MEN'S SHOES"—An Edgar Lewis production.

"IN WALKED MARY"—Capellani production. Directed by George Archainbaud. Starring June Caprice.

NOW A STAFF WRITER OF SELZNICK PICTURES

Permanent Address

Green Room Club, 139 West 47th Street, New York City. Bryant 407

★ *Meaning: Translation of drama into terms of the screen.*

ROBERT ELLIS

Management of Myron Selznick

MERLE JOHNSON

writing

Originals and Continuity

for

Selznick Pictures

Latest Works:
"Red Pepper"
"She Held Her Husband"
"Hard Luck O'Day"

ACTORS

Broadway"), Pathe ("This Hero Stuff"), Amer. Pathe ("Eve in Exile"). Hght., 5, 9; wght., 158; brown hair and eyes. Ad., American Studio, Santa Barbara, Calif.

CLARY, Charles; b. Charleston, Ills.; screen career, 9 yrs., Fox ("Wolves of the Night," "The Splendid Sin"), Goldwyn ("Street Called Straight," "Woman in Room 13"), Morosco ("Girl Named Mary"), Universal ("Under Suspicion") Hght., 6; wght., 190; dark iron grey hair, hazel eyes. Home ad., 1774 N. Vine St., Hollywood, Calif. Phone 577025, or Actor's Assn., 6412 Holly Blvd., Los Angeles.

CLIFFE, Henry Cooper; b. Oxford, England; educ. England; stage career, in many productions as leading man and star; screen career, Fox ("Gold and the Woman," etc.), Rolfe-Metro ("An Enemy to Society," "Final Judgment," etc.), Astra-Pathe ("Arms and the Woman"), Selznick ("The Argyle Case"), Metro "Raffles"), Plays and Players ("Soul of a Magdalene"). Hght., 5, 11½; wght., 176; dark complexion, dark hair, brown eyes. Home ad., Whitestone Landing, L. I., N. Y.

CLIFFORD, William; b. New Orleans, 1878; educ. Toronto Conservatory of Music; stage career, 18 yrs., Mantell, Whiteside and own co.; screen career, Universal, Mutual, Fox ("Sins of a Parent," "Tale of Two Cities"), Metro ("Under Handicap," "Paradise Garden," "Square Deceiver," "A Man of Honor"), Fox ("Gambling in Souls"), National ("Long Arm of Mannister"). Home ad., 6669 Sunset Blvd., Hollywood, Cal.

COBB, EDMUND F.; b. Albuquerque, New Mexico, 1892; stage career, stk.; screen career, Lubin, Essanay and others, at present Art-O-Graf, latest feature releases, "Wolves of the Street," "The Desert Scorpion." Hght., 6, ½; wght., 165; hair, brown; eyes, brown. Ad., Art-O-Graf, 305 Guardian Trust Bldg., Denver, Col.

CODY, Albert R.; b. Portland, Oreg.; educ. Bishop Scott's Mil. Acad.; stage career, 3 yrs. in Opera in Milan, Italy, Grand Opera in England for 1 yr.; screen career, with Charles Ray in "The Hon. Lord Algy," J. Warren Kerrigan in "Turn of a Card," "Joyous Liar," Frank Keenan, "The Bells," Bessie Barriscale, "Two Gun Betty," "All of a Sudden Norma," "Kitty Kelly, M. D.," Dorothy Dalton, "Flame of the Yukon," now playing in Jack Dempsey serial. Hght., 5, 9; wght., 165; black hair, blue eyes. Home ad., 1212 So. Grand, Los Angeles, Cal., Bway 6349.

CODY, Lewis J.; b. Waterville, Me., 1885; educ., McGill Univ., Montreal; stage career, stock, rep. leads in "Via Wireless," Frohman prod., 2 seasons at N. Y. Winter Garden, with own co.; screen career, Fox ("A Branded Soul"), Metro, ("Treasure of the Sea," "The Demon"), Lois Weber ("For Husbands Only"), Artcraft ("Don't Change Your Husband"), Lew Cody Films Corp. ("The Beloved Cheater," "The Butterfly Man"). Ad., 1979 Grace ave., Los Angeles, Cal.

COGLEY, Nick, also director; b. N. Y., 1869; educ. St. Francis Xavier Coll., N. Y.; stage career, started at Lyceum theatre in light opera, Lillian Russell, Della Fox; screen career, Selig, Keystone ("Saved by Wireless," "Oriental Love," "Hearts and Sparks"), Paralta ("Maid o' the Storm"), Goldwyn ("Sis Hopkins," "Toby's Vow"). Has written several scenarios. Hght., 5, 7½; wght., 195; blond hair, blue eyes.

COHILL, William Wright; educ. Univ. of Pa.; stage career, Al Woods, "Business Before Pleasure," chorus lady, Poli Co's, starred in vaud.; screen career, World, Pathe, Famous Players, Metro ("Eye for Eye," "Five Thousand an Hour"), S. L. Pictures ("Virtuous Men"), 2 yrs. stk.). Hght., 5, 8; wght., 150; dark hair and eyes. Ad. 56 Farrington st., Flushing, L. I., N. Y. Flushing 64-J.

COLEMAN, Frank; b. Newburg, N. Y.; educ. Waterbury, Conn.; stage career, Garden City Quartette, Bennett-Molton stk.; screen career, with L-Ko. Rolin, Essanay, Chaplin and Lone Star ("Carmen," "Police," "The Floorwalker"), Lehrman-Sunshine ("A High Diver's Kiss"), Fox-Sunshine ("Dabbling in Society," "Wild Waves and Women"). Hght., 5, 11; wght., 287; brown hair, grey eyes. Ad., 1670 N. st., Andrews pl., Los Angeles, Cal.

COLEMAN, Vincent; educ. N. P. pub. schls. and private tutors; stage career, began at age of 12; Cecil Spooner Stk. Co., Corse Payton Stk. Co., with Arnold Daly in "Beau Brummel," etc.; screen career, Fox ("Should a Husband Forgive?"), Fischer ("Law of Nature"), Creation ("Freedom of Ireland"), Goldwyn ("Partners of the Night"), Moss ("The Scarlet Trail"). Hght., 6; wght., 178; brown hair, blue eyes. Ad., Green Room Club, N. Y.

COLESON, Robert; b. West Point, Miss., 1892; educ. So. Christian Col. and Mississippi Univ.; stage career, 2 yrs. stk.; screen career, Hodkinson ("Made in America," serial), McManus ("Lost Battalion"), W. H. Prod. ("Everybody's Business"), Wistaria ("Lurking Peril" serial). Served in war as Lieut. of Infantry. Hght., 6; wght., 172; dark hair, blue eyes. Ad., Green Room Club, N. Y.

CONKLIN, Charles J.; b. San Francisco, Cal.; educ. there; stage career, 15 yrs. musical comedy, dram. stk., vaud. Keith and Orpheum circuits; screen career, Mack Sennett ("Two Tough Tenderfeet," "The Battle Royal," "East Lynn with Variations," "Uncle Tom Without the Cabin," "Salome vs. Shenandoah"). Hght., 5, 6; wght., 160; black hair, dark brown eyes. Home ad., 5135 Sunset blvd., Los Angeles, Cal.; studio, Mack Sennett studios.

CONKLIN, Chester; b. Oskaloosa, Iowa; educ. there; early career, circus clown, stock and road comedian; screen career, Majestic, Keystone for 3 yrs., Sennett-Paramount, Fox-Sunshine Comedies ("Back to Nature Girls," "Her Private Husband," "The Great Nickel Robbery," "Those Dangerous Eyes." Hght., 5, 5; wght., 140; brown hair, blue eyes. Home ad., 1235 West 41st st., Los Angeles, Cal. Vermont 2760.

CONKLIN, William; b. Brooklyn, N. Y.; educ. Brooklyn Polytechnic; stage career, "The Virginian," "Paid in Full," "Over Night," "The Round-Up," leading man in number of stock cos.; screen career, Paralta, American, Ince ("The Price Mark," "Flare-Up Sal," "Love Letters," "The Virtuous Thief," "Woman in the Suit Case," "Red Hot Dollars," "Sex"). Hght., 6, 1; wght., 183; black hair, dark gray eyes. Home ad., 1766 La Brea ave., Los Angeles, Cal.; phone 579008; studio, Thos. H. Ince.

CONLEY, Effie; b. Norwich, Conn., 1857; educ. Boston, Mass.; stage career, Daly's theatre, N. Y. C., with Julia Marlowe, Viola Allen, Henrietta Crossman, Margaret Anglin, Edwin Booth, in "Poor Little Rich Girl," "'Way Down East," "Deep Purple," Daniel Frohman Stk. Co.; screen career, Vitagraph, Triangle, Metro, Lasky, Goldwyn "The Wager," "Toys of Fate," "Peggie Does Her Darndest," "It Pays to Advertise," "Revelation," "Blind Man's Eyes." Hght., 5, 11¾; wght., 180; dark complexion, dark gray hair. Home ad., 5419 Harold Way, Hollywood, Cal. Studio ad., Metro Pictures Corp., Los Angeles, Holly 4485.

CONNELLY, Edward J.; b. N. Y. C.; stage career, 5 yrs. with James A. Herne's "Shore Acres" Co., with Fritzi Scheff in "Babette," "The Bird Center," "Higgledy-Piggledy"; screen career, N. Y. Motion Pict. Co., Thomas Ince Prod., Serial Producing Co., Pathe, Astra, manoffs," "Toys of Fate," with Nazimova, The Metro, Herbert Brenon; "Fall of the Ro-Devil," "Rasputin," "The Willow Tree," "Shore Acres." Hght., 6; wght., 150; dark complexion, brown hair, and eyes. Ad., Lambs Club, N. Y., and Metro Studio, Hollywood, Cal.

CONNESS, Robert; b. Ill.; educ. St. Mary's Kan.; stage career, leading man with Blanche Walsh, Mary Mannering, Francis Wilson, stk., Louis Mann, "Julie Bonbon"; screen career, Edison, Frohman ("The Witching Hour"), Art Dramas ("The Rainbow"), Paramount ("The Martyrdom of Philip Strong"), K-E-S-E ("A Message to Garcia," "The Master Passion," "The Ghost of Old Morro"), Van Dyke ("A Song of Sixpence"). Hght., 5, 11½; wght., 175; dark hair, blue eyes.

CONNOLLY, Jack; b. Denver, Colo.; educ. there; stage career, 10 yrs. vaud., mus. com. and dram. stk.; screen career, Diando Pathe ("The Saw Dust Trail," "Dolly's Vacation," "Milady of the Beanstalk," "The Little Patriot," "The Voice of Destiny," "The Little Diplomat"), Ince ("The Egg Crate Wallop"), Wyan Mack ("Bubbles"), Leon T. Osborne ("One Way Trail"), now playing in "The Lincoln Highwayman." Hght., 5, 11; wght., 172; dark brown hair, dark green eyes. Home ad., 971 Virgil ave., Los Angeles; Wilshire 584.

COOK, Warren; b. Boston, 1870; educ. Boston; stage career, with Phoebe Davis in "Way Down East," in "The Conspiracy," 3 yrs. with Castle Square stk., Boston and stk. in other cities; screen career, Edison, Vitagraph, Kalem, Faversham & Elliot ("Man Who Lost Himself"), Ince-Paramount ("The White Book"), Artcraft ("Pride of the Clan," "Seven Keys to Baldplate"), Art Drama ("Infidelity"), Pathe serial ("The Great Gamble"), Marion Davies ("April Folly"), Chas. Miller ("A Dangerous Game"), Capellani ("The Right to Lie"), Tourneur ("My Lady's Garter," "Woman"). Hght., 6; wght., 175; gray hair, blue eyes. Ad., Green Room Club, N. Y.

COOLEY, Hallam; b. N. Y., 1888; educ. Univ. of Minn.; stage career, stock, in "The Man from Mexico"; screen career, Selig, American, Universal, Keystone; Universal ("Brass Bullet"), Pickford ("Daddy Long Legs"), Goldwyn ("One of the Finest," "Upstairs," "Girl From Outside"), Paramount ("Happy Tho Married," "Girl Dodger," "More Deadly Than the Male"), National ("Long Arm of Mannister"). Hght., 6; brown hair, blue eyes.

COOMBS, Guy, also director; b. Wash., D. C., 1882; stage career, Mrs. Fiske in "Becky Sharp," "The White Horse Tavern," "The Rivals," with Joseph Jefferson; screen career, with Edison, Kalem (Alice Joyce series), later directing, leads with Metro, Kleine, Ivan ("The Promise," "Two Men and a Woman"), Famous ("Bab's Diary," "Bab's Burglar"), Metro ("Flower of the Dusk").

COOPER, Claude Hamilton; b. London, Eng.; stage career, 23 yrs. stk., rep., 3 seasons with Russ Whytal, 3 yrs. with F. F. Proctor, stk.; screen career, dir. Gaumont talking pictures, made first 12 pictures for Solax, acted for Famous Players, All-Star, Kinemacolor, Reliance, with Ethel Barrymore in "The Nightingale," with Jane Cowl and Mary Pickford, Universal ("Her Friend the Burglar"); directed and played lead in one-reel comedies for 18 months; at present with "Boys Will Be Boys" at Belmont Theatre. Hght., 5, 6; wght., 137; dark hair, blue eyes. Ad., 23 Main St., Yonkers, N. Y.

COOPER, George (George Healy); b. Newark, 1891; educ. N. Y.; stage career, Newark Stock Co., Blaney Stock Co., Fiske O'Hara, vaud.; screen career, with Vitagraph, specializing in Italian, Spanish, French types ("Mills of the Gods," "A Night Out," "Hunted Woman," "The Suspect," "Her Secret"), Goldwyn ("The Auction Block"), Paramount ("The Dark Star").

COOPER, Jack; b. Manchester, Eng., 1880; educ. there; stage career, vaud. 3 yrs.; screen career, Mack Sennett ("Beware of Boarders," "Her Screen Idol," "Her First Beau"), Fox Sunshine ("Money Talks," "Virtuous Husbands," "Merry Jail Birds," "Yellow Dog Catcher," "Footlight Maids," "Hungry Lions and Tender Hearts," "The Heart Snatcher"). Hght., 5, 7; wght., 135; dark hair, blue eyes. Home ad., 5666 Fernwood Ave., Hollywood, Cal.; studio, Fox Sunshine, Hollywood.

CORBETT, James J.; b. San Francisco, 1868; educ. Sacred Heart College, Frisco; stage career, with Wm. A. Brady, Henry Frazer, H. B. Harris, "Naval Cadet," "Pals," "Facing the Music," "Burglar and the Lady," etc.; screen career, "Burglar and the Lady," "The Midnight Man," "Riders of Vengeance." Hght., 6, 1½; wght., 190; dark hair, gray eyes. Home ad., Bayside, L. I., Hotel Alexandria, L. A.; studio, Universal City, Cal.

COREY, Eugene; b. Florence, Italy; educ. there; screen career, 1 yr. stk. with D. W. Griffith, 6 mos. Universal, "Law of the North West," "Evidence," "Velvet Hand," "Sleeping Lion," 2 reel specials for Christie. Hght., 5, 11; wght., 172; brown hair and eyes. Home ad., 333 Olive St., Los Angeles, Cal.; phone 62257; studio, Christie.

CORTES, Armand; b. Nimes, France, 1885; educ. City Col., N. Y. C.; stage career, with James T. Powers, Fritzi Scheff, Sam Bernard, Lenore Ulric in "Tiger Rose," etc.; screen career, "House of Bondage," featured in "Yellow Menace," serial, Famous Players, heavy with Mae Murray, Pauline Fredericks, Geo M. Cohan in "Seven Keys," etc., leads in "Hearts of the Northland," heavy in Gaumont's first release, "A Temporary Wife," and with Wm. Collier in "Taking the Count," now playing Rockoff in "The Return of Tarzan." Good violinist. Hght., 5, 11; wght., 155; dark brown hair; brown eyes. Ad., Friars Club, N. Y. C.

COSSAR, John Hay; b. London, England; educ. N. Y. C. Col.; stage career, 30 yrs. exp.; screen career, National ("Strong Arm of Mannister," "Masks and Hearts"), Lois Weber ("Home"), Fox ("The Feud"), Astra ("Common Clay"), Vitagraph ("Highest Trump"), Lasky ("Love Insurance"). Hght., 5, 10; wght., 168; iron gray hair, dark brown eyes. Home ad., 1606 N. Alexandria Ave., Los Angeles. Phone 597686.

COSTELLO, Maurice; b. Pittsburgh; educ. there; stage career, 18 yrs.; screen career, 7 yrs. with Vitagraph ("A Tale of Two Cities," "Mr. Barnes of N. Y.," "The Man Who Couldn't Beat God," "The Crown Prince's Double"), Erbograph ("The Crimson Stain Mystery"), Vitagraph ("The Captain's Captain," "Man Who Won," "Cambric Mask," "Girl Woman"). Hght., 5, 10; wght., 160; brown hair, blue-gray eyes. Ad., Bayside, L. I., N. Y.

COWELL, George; b. Auburn, N. Y.; educ. Stockton; stage career, 2 yrs. in stock, rep. and vaud.; screen career, Alkire ("An Ace in the Hole"), Ince ("Borrowed Plumage," "Wooden Shoes"), Lasky ("Years of the Locust," Grim Game"). Hght., 5, 10; wght., 145; light brown hair, brown eyes. Home ad., 610 S. Carondelet St., Los Angeles; Wilshire 2970; studio, Alkire Productions.

COXEN Edward; educ. San Francisco and Berkeley, Cal.; stage exp., stk.; screen career, Solaxart ("Carmen of the Klondike"), Paralta ("A Law Unto Herself," "Within the Cup," "Heart of Rachael"), United ("Crime of the Hour"), Goldwyn ("Go West, Young Man"), Hampton-Hod. ("Desert Gold"), First Natl. ("In Old Kentucky"). Hght., 5, 11; wght., 168; brown hair, blue eyes. Ad., 2520 W. 7th St., Los Angeles, Cal.; Wil. 2060; studio, care of Willis & Inglis.

CRAIG, Charles; screen career, Artcraft ("Poor Little Rich Girl"), Brenon ("The Fall of the Romanoffs"), Fox (late pictures, "Royal Romance," "A Rich Man's Plaything," "Should a Husband Forgive?"), Vitagraph ("Gray Towers Mystery"). Ad., 639 Hudson Ave., West New York, N. Y.

CRANE, James L.; b. Rantoul, Ill.; educ. Williams College; stage schooling, repertoire and stk.; plays "The Price," "Guilty Man," "American Ace," "The Pawn," "Under Orders"; screen career, "His Bridal Night," "Sinners," as leading man supporting Alice Brady; "Misleading Widow," "Sadie Love," "Wanted: A Husband," as leading man supporting Billie Burke. Hght., 5, 11; wght., 155; dark complexion, black hair, grey eyes. Member Lambs and N. Y. Athletic Clubs.

CRANE, Ogden; b. N. Y., educ. there and prep. sch. Newburgh, N. Y.; stage career, with Mrs. Patrick Campbell in "The Sorceress," Louis Mann in "The Man Who Stood Still," under mgmt. Chas. Frohman, Wm. Brady, Klaw & Erlanger, etc.; screen career, Goldwyn ("Jinks"), Vitagraph ("The Hornet's Nest," "Light of Western Stars"), Mayflower ("Soldiers of Fortune"), Federal ("The Dwelling Place of Light"), Haworth ("The Greater Profit"), Lasky ("The Valley of the Giants"). Hght., 6; wght., 176; grey hair, blue eyes. Home ad., Actors Assn. of Hollywood, Cal.

CRANE, Ward; b. Albany, N. Y.; educ. there; screen career, Marion Davies ("The Dark Star"), Alan Dwan ("Soldiers of Fortune," "Luck of the Irish," "Heart of a Fool"). Hght., 5, 11; wght., 175; dark hair, brown eyes. Home ad., 2101 Canyon Drive, Hollywood, Cal. Phone 277965; Studio, Alan Dwan Studio.

CRIMANS, W. W.; b. 1877; stage career, 20 yrs., prods., stk., with Geo. Fawcett, J. K. Hackett, Amelia Bingham, Dick Bennett, Geo. Beban, leads in "Kick In," "At Bay," "Maternity"; screen career, with Clara Kimball Young in "Light." Hght., 5, 11; complexion, med.

CRIMMINS, Daniel; b. Liverpool, Eng.; educ. Bishop Sch., Detroit; stage career, toured for many seasons in vaud., headline act, starred with own mus. com. co., "Wizzard of Oz"; screen career, Vitagraph, 10 mos. with Pathe, Reliance, Kleine (1 yr. in "Musty Suffer" series), Artcraft ("Johnny Get Your Gun," "Under the Top"), Wallace Reid ("You're Fired"), Dorothy Phillips ("Ambition"), Fatty Arbuckle ("The Garage"). W. S. Campbell Co. (Joe Martin, 5 reels). Hght., 5, 3; brown hair, blue eyes. Has written and prod. several one and two act comedies. Home ad., 201 Lake Shore Terrace, Los Angeles, Cal.

CRITTENDEN, Dwight; b. Oakland, Calif.; educ. England, Germany, U. S.; traveled in all of northern Europe, So. Africa, Panama, etc.; stage career, with Savage in grand and light opera, Ben Greet, Brady; screen career, Famous Players ("The Veiled Adventure"), Lois Weber ("Home"), Geo. Loane Tucker ("Miracle Man"), Mary Pickford ("The Hoodlum"), Goldwyn ("Cup of Fury", "Pinto," "Little Shepherd of Kingdom Come"). Hght., 6; wght., 175; gray hair and eyes. Home ad., 5406 Lexington, Hollywood, Calif. Phone 599241.

CUMMINGS, Irving; b. N. Y., 1888; educ. there; stage career, Davidson Stock, "The Man of the Hour," "The Great Divide," "In Search of a Sinner," with Henry Miller, Lillian Russell; screen career, since 1910, World ("Rasputin, the Black Monk"), Fox ("The Woman Who Gave"), DeMille ("Don't Change Your Husband"), World ("Mandarin's Gold," "Unveiling Hand"), Paramount ("Men, Women & Money," "Secret Service," "What Every Woman Learns," "Everywoman"), United ("Her Code of Honor"), Select ("The Better Wife"). Hght., 5, 11; wght., 170; black hair, brown eyes. Ad., Lasky Studio, Hollywood, Calif.; Home ad., 1837 Morgan Pl., Hollywood.

CUMMINGS, Robert; heavies; b. Richmond, Va., 1867; educ. there; stage career, from 1883, stk. rep., etc., appeared with Fanny Davenport, and in orig. casts of "The Great Divide," "One Parole," "The Bluebird," 1919, "His Honor, Abe Potash"; prop. and mgr., Cummings Stk. Co., 6 yrs.; screen career, with Biograph, Famous Players, World, Metro ("The Awakening of Hela Richie," "Romeo and Juliet," Fox ("A Rich Man's Plaything"), S. L. Pictures ("Virtuous Men"), Vitigraph with Gladys Leslie and others. Hght., 6; wght., 200; brown hair and eyes. Home ad., 56 S. 17th st., Flushing, L. I., N. Y.

CUNEO, Lester; b. Indian Territory, 1888; educ. Northwestern Univ.; stage career, stock rep., "The House Next Door"; screen career, Selig (dir.), Essanay (Geo. Ade comedies, Prince Gabriel in "Graustark"), Metro ("Mister 44," "Big Tremaine," "Pidgin Island," "The Haunted Pajamas," "Under Handicap," "Paradise Garden," "Love Me for Myself Alone"). Hght, 6, 1½; wght, 180; black hair, gray eyes; 18 mos. in U. S. service. Returned to Los Angeles in December, 1919. Ad. 90 Willis & Inglis, L. A., Calif.

CURRAN, Thomas A.; b. Australia, 1879; educ. Australia; stage career, 17 yrs. in stk. and legit. prod., with "Excuse Me," "Oh, Oh, Delphine," etc.; screen career, Universal ("Earl of Pawtucket"), Metro ("Greater Love Hath No Man," "Her Great Match"), Thanhouser ("Silas Marner," "The Nymph," "Brothers Equal," "The World and the Woman," "The Vicar of Wakefield," "A Modern Monte Cristo," "The Candy Girl," "The Heart of Ezra Greer"). Hght, 5, 10; wght. 160; gray hair, dark blue eyes.

CURRIER, Frank; b. Norwich, Conn., 1857; educ. Boston; stage career, call boy at 10, played with Julia Marlowe, Viola Allen, Nat Goodwin, etc., "Way Down East" 5 yrs.; toured Europe and Australia; screen career, 6 yrs. Vitagraph, Metro ("Revelation," "Toys of Fate," "The Red Lantern," "Peggy Does Her Darndest"), Nazimova ("The Brat"), Anita Stewart ("Kingdom of Dreams"), "Easy to Make Money," "It Pays to Advertise," "Should a Woman Tell?" "The Right of Way." Hght., 5, 11; wght., 180; gray hair, hazel eyes. Ad., 6665 Selma ave., Hollywood, Cal.

CURTIS, Jack; b. San Francisco; educ. there; stage career, 1898, stk., rep., musical & dram., also road shows and directed own shows, vaud. Orpheum; screen career, Humanity ("The Gift Supreme"), Fox ("The Hell Ship"), "Man's Desire"; Universal ("Brute Breaker"), Goldwyn ("The Pest"), H. O. Davis ("The Servant in the House"), Triangle ("Until They Get Me," "Little Red Decides"). Hght., 6; wght., 200; dark hair and eyes. Home ad., 7146 Watseka, Culver City, Calif. Phone 70314.

— D —

D'ALBROOK, Sidney, b. Chicago; educ. Northwestern Military Acad.; stage career, in "The Wolf," "Virginian," "The Telephone Girl"; screen career, Artcraft ("Heart of the Wilds," "Three Men and a Girl"), Blackton ("The Common Cause"), MacManus ("The Lost Battalion," "Bruised Humanity"), Rolfe ("A Scream in the Night"), Helen Holmes serial ("The Fatal Fortune"), Blackton ("Life's Great Problem"). Hght., 5, 10½; wght., 155; fair complexion, black hair and eyes. Ad., Green Room Club, N. Y.

DALY, Arnold; b. Brooklyn, 1875; educ. Acad. of the Sacred Heart, and St. Patrick's, Brooklyn; stage career, first success in "Pudd'nhead Wilson," "Secret Service," "When We Were Twenty-one," produced and appeared in many successes, including "Mrs. Warren's Profession," "Arms and the Man," also with dramatic sketch in vaud.; screen career, Pathe ("Exploits of Elaine," serial; "The House of Fear," played or dir. several others); Frohman ("A Man Without a Country").

DANIELS, Frank b. Dayton, O.; educ. Boston and N. E. Conservatory of Music; stage career, Boston Opera co., under mgmt. of John Norris, original "Bad Boy" in "Peck's Bad Boy," under W. H. Harris five years; star own mgmt., "Little Puck," under Charles B. Dillingham in "The Office Boy," "Omar Khayyam," and others; screen career, Vitagraph (in "Crooky Scruggs," "Mr. Jack" series, "Captain Jinks" series. Ad., Studio, Vitagraph, Brooklyn.

DARCLAY, Louis; b. Belgium, 1895; educ. there and Paris; stage exper., 2½ yrs. in London and France; screen career, Universal, Harold Bell Wright Story Pict. Corp., Eclair, Film Art, Paris; 1918 America, Metro ("The Parisian Tigress"), Para.-Artcraft ("L'Apache"). Hght., 5, 11; wght., 143; blond hair, dark blue eyes. Ad., 1825 Morgan Pl., Hollywood, Cal.

DAVIDSON, John; b. N. Y. 1886; educ. Columbia Univ.; stage career, with Mrs. Fiske in "Madame Sand," also in "Penrod," "Young Man's Fancy"; screen career, Quality-Metro ("The Wall Between," "A Million a Minute"), Kleine ("Green Cloak," "Sentimental Lady," "Caravan," "Danger Signal"), World ("Pawn of Fate," "The Genius Pierre," "Black Circle," "Forest Rivals," "Through the Toils"), Goldwyn ("The Stronger Vow"). Ad., 4 West 108th st., N. Y. C.

DAVIDSON, Max; b. Berlin, educ. Berlin and U. S.; stage career, from 1897, melodrama, vaud., in "Fighting Fate," "The Bowery Newsgirl," "Billy the Kid," "Alias Jimmy Valentine"; screen career, since 1913, Biograph, Reliance-Majestic, Fine Arts (as "Izzy" in the Izzy series of comedies, in "Puppets," "The Doll Shop"), First Nat'l ("The Hoodlum"). Hght., 5, 4; wght., 130; black hair, blue eyes.

DAVIDSON, William Beatman; b. Dobbs Ferry, N. Y., 1888; educ. Columbia Univ.; early career, law and banking; screen career, Goldwyn ("Friend Husband," "Our Little Wife"), Fox ("Why I Would Not Marry," "La Belle Russe," "A Woman There Was"), Metro ("The White Raven," "The Greatest Power"), Pathe ("The Capitol," "Impossible Catherine"), Mayfair ("Persuasive Peggy"). Hght., 6, 1; wght., 195; dark hair, blue eyes. Home ad., Green Room Club, N. Y. C.

DAVIES, Howard; b. Liverpool; educ. Cambridge Univ., Eng.; stage career, with Wilson Barrett in revival "Lights of London," title role in Lewis Morrison's "Faust"; toured West in 'Lady Audley's Secret," in Liebler's revival of "Faust," 5 yrs. in vaud., etc.; screen career, with Vitagraph, first leading man for Melies in U. S.; Universal, Majestic, leading man Oz. Co., in "Sapho," Morosco-Pallas, Haworth ("His Birthright"), Metro ("Boston Blackie's Little Pal"), Triangle ("It's a Bear"), Paramount ("A Sporting Chance"), Brunton-Hodkinson ("A White Man's Chance"). Hght., 5, 10½; wght., 190; dark complexion, brown hair. Ad. 6852 Boltom rd., Hollywood, Cal.; Holly 1400.

DAVIS, Edwards; b. Santa Clara, Calif., 1873; educ. Kentucky Univ. (M. A.); stage career, debut in "The Cherry Pickers," N. Y. C., 1900; headliner in vaud. for 12 yrs. in own plays "The Unmasking," "All Rivers Meet at Sea," "The Picture of Dorian Gray," "The Kingdom of Destiny"; screen career, Famous ("Daughter of MacGregor," "The Knife"), Vitagraph (" The Question," "The Transgression"), Goldwyn ("Dodging a Million"), Select ("De Luxe Annie"), Capellani ("The Love Cheat"), McManus ("The Gray Brother"); latest dramatic engagement, David Belasco's "Daddies"; Pres. of Green Room Club, N. Y. C., 3 yrs.; now Pres. of National Vaudeville Artist's Club, 229 West 46th st., N. Y. C.

DAVIS, J. Gunnis; b. Sunderland, Eng.; educ. London; stage career, 20 yrs. under mgmts. W.

S. Penley, Oscar Barrett, Frank Curzon, James Welch, Fisher & Ripley, Chas. Frohman, Dan Frohman, J. K. Hackett, Henry W. Savage, Proctor's stk.; screen career, Eclair stk. 2 yrs. ("13 at Table," "Going for Father," "Adventures in Diplomacy," World ("Little Duchess," "Stolen Orders"), Famous, Goldwyn, Solax, Gaumont stk. 1 yr., Pathe, at present leading comedian with Cissy Fitzgerald. Hght., 5, 7; wght., 109; fair hair, blue eyes. Home ad., 2704 Ocean Front, Los Angeles, Calif., or Actors Equity, N. Y.

DAWSON, Ivo; b. Rutlandshire, Eng.; educ. Uppingham Pub. Schl., Eng.; stage career, 16 yrs. with Sir George Alexander, 7 yrs. with Sir John Hare, London, and American Tours, with Sir Herbert Tree, and Chas. Frohman, London and America, also with Geo. Tyler, late Henry Harry, late Chas. Klein, and Margaret Anglin; screen career, State Picture Co., London ("The Keeper of the Door"), International ("Miracle of Love"), Selznick ("Out of the Night"). Hght., 6; wght., 173; dark brown hair and eyes. Ad., management of Edward Small, 1493 Broadway, N. Y. C., or 215 W. 70th st., N. Y. C., Columbus 5588.

DEAN, Jack; b. Wash., 1880; educ. Stamford Mil. Acad. and Yale; stage career, with Jas. A. Herne, Eleanor Robson, in Shakespearean rep., with Lawrence D'Orsey, William Collier, leading man with Fannie Ward; screen career, Lasky ("Betty to the Rescue," "Her Strange Wedding," "Unconquered," "The Crystal Gazer"), Pathe ("The Yellow Ticket"), Selznick ("Sealed Hearts"). Hght, 5, 11; wght., 170; brown hair and eyes.

DEAN, Louis; b. Wilmington, Del.; educ. Washburn Coll., Topeka; stage career, dir. Mme. Modjeska, Henrietta Crossman, Wilton Lackaye; stk., starred in "Sherlock Holmes," "The Bells," etc.; screen career, Fox (The Kaiser in "My Four Years in Germany"), Blackton prod. (Capt. Bach in "The Common Cause," "Blood Barrier," "Moonshine Trail"), Sim Photo Plays ("Unconditional Surrender," "The Destroyer of Humanity," "Birth of a Race"), Selznick ("Sealed Hearts"). Hght., 5, 10½; wght., 180; fair complexion, dark hair, blue eyes. Home ad., 1808 Marmion ave., N. Y. C., Tremont 6581.

DEARHOLT, Ashton; b. Milwaukee, Wis.; educ. Culver Mil. Acad.; screen career, over 3 yrs., with American (in "Van Loan" series, "Her Country's Call," "Peggy Leads the Way"), Universal ("The Bride's Awakening," "The Brass Bullet"), Fox ("Pitfalls of a Big City"), Goldwyn ("The Tower of Ivory"), with Bessie Barriscale in B. B. Features, Universal ("Cabaret Girl," "The Girl in the Dark"). Hght., 6; wght., 170; dark hair and eyes. Home ad., 6735 Hollywood blvd., Los Angeles, Cal.

DE CONDE, Syn. M., b. Brazil; educ. Paris; screen career, featured lead in pictures made in Paris for 3 yrs., Nazimova-Metro ("Revelation"), Fox ("The Crystal Fate"), Paramount ("Out of the Shadow"), Artcraft ("Girl Who Stayed at Home"), Goldwyn ("Flame of the Desert"), Universal ("Rouge and Riches"). Hght., 5, 8; wght., 138; black hair and eyes. Ad., 215 W. 88th, St., N. Y.

DE CORDOBA, Pedro; b. and educ. N. Y.; stage career, "If I Were King," with Sothern 2 seasons, Sothern and Marlowe, "Merely Mary Ann," in "The Blue Bird," "Sister Beatrice," "Sadie Love," "Tiger Rose," "Where Poppies Bloom," "The Light of the World"; screen career, with Lasky ("Carmen," "Temptation," "Maria Rose"), Artcraft ("Barbary Sheep"), Select ("The New Moon"), Famous Players ("Girl of the South"), Thos. Ince ("The Dark Mirror"). Ad., 64 E. 86th st., N. Y. C.

DE CORDOVA, Leander; educ. Collegiate School and Private Tutors, Kingston, Jamaica, and B. W. Indes; stage career, starred in "The Shadow Behind the Throne," "Wireless the Loop-Hole," "Your Flag and Mine," with Klaw and Erlanger, etc.; screen career, Rolfe ("Scream in the Night"); McManus Corp. ("Lost Battalion"), Metro. Ad., Edward Small, 1493 Broadway, N. Y. C.

DE GRASSE, Samuel Alfred; b. Bathhurst, New Brunswick; early career practiced dentistry; screen career, Griffith ("Birth of a Nation," "Intolerance," "Diana of the Follies"), Douglas Fairbanks ("Good, Bad Man," "Half Breed," "Wild and Wooly"), Mary Pickford ("Heart of the Hills"), Universal ("Silk Lined Burglar," "Blind Husbands"). Hght., 5, 10½; wght., 150; black hair, dark brown eyes. Home ad., 1729 Winona blvd., Hollywood, Cal., Holly 2216.

DeHAVEN, Carter; b. Chicago, 1886; educ. there; stage career, vaud., head of Carter De Haven Vaud. and Farce Comedy Co., De Haven trio, Weber and Fields, "Girl in the Taxi," "Hanky Panky"; screen career, Universal ("The Losing Winner," "The College Orphan," "From B'way to a Throne," "Youth of Fortune"); engaged by National Film Corp. to play in series of 13 pictures; Goldwyn ("In a Pinch," "Why Divorce"), now with Paramount. Home ad., 7237 Franklin ave., L. A., Cal; studio, National.

DE LACY, John V.; educ., N. Y. C.; stage career, 7 yrs. vaud. and 7 yrs. legit. prod.; screen career, "Broadway Jones," "Wanted—For Murder," "Queen of the Seas," "Retribution," "The Cavell Case," "The Auction Block," "Prunella," "Doll's House," "Rose of No Man's Land," "Small Town Girl," "The Unpardonable Sin," Craig Kennedy Serial, "The Carter Case," "Price of Malice," "Patsy," "Peg of the Pirates," "The Love Net," "Hash-House Heiress" Hght., 5, 8; wght., 145; dark brown hair, blue eyes. Home ad., 167 E. 61st st., Plaza 6719; Friars Club and Green Room Club.

DELANEY, Bert.; b. Minneapolis, 1891; educ. Notre Dame; stage career, with Lewis Waller in "Henry the Fifth," "The Five Frankfurters," vaud. in "At Bay"; screen career, Edison, Thanhouses (juv. leads in "The Road to Fame," "His Profession," "The Net"). Hght., 5, 10; dark complexion, dark eyes.

DELANEY, Leo; educ. Manhattan Coll. and N. Y. Law Schl.; stage career, "Brown of Harvard," "The Virginian"; screen career, 7 yrs. with Vitagraph and other companies. Hght., 5, 9½; wght., 155; dark hair and eyes. Ad., Green Room Club, N. Y.

DENT, Vernon; b. San Jose, Cal.; educ. there and Oakland, Cal.; screen career, Hank Mann Comedies ("A Harem Hero," "An Eye for Figures," "Broken Bubbles," "A Depot Romance," "A Gas Attack") Hght., 5, 9; wght., 215; dark brown hair, dark blue eyes. Home ad., Rutland Apts., Los Angeles, Cal., South 106; studio, Hank Mann Comedies, Francis Ford Studio.

DEPP, Harry; b. St. Louis, Mo.; educ. St. Louis Univ.; stage career, with Elsie Janis in "The Fair Co-Ed," K. & E. 8 yrs., "The Pink Lady," "The Little Cafe," numerous stock cos.; screen career, Universal, Triangle, Keystone, leads in numerous comedies, Fox, Mutual-Strand ("Dan Cupid, M. D.," "The Girl in the Box," "Their Baby"), Christie ("Mixed Drinks," "Good Night, Judge," "Are Honeymoons Happy," "Their Little Wife," etc). Hght., 5, 4; wght., 139; light hair and complexion, blue eyes. Home ad., 1912 Kent st., L. A., Wilshire 4623; studio, Christie Film Co., Hollywood, L. A, Cal.

DESMOND, William; b. Dublin, Ireland; educ. N. Y.; stage career, "Quo Vadis," Burbank Stock, starred in "The Judge and the Jury," "The Bird of Paradise"; screen career, Triangle ("Beyond the Shadow," "A Sudden Gentleman"), Hampton Prod. "Life's a Funny Proposition," "The Prodigal Liar"), Ex-Mutual ("Mints of Hell"), Ro-Cole ("Bare-Fisted Gallagher," "Whitewashed Walls," "A Sage Brush Hamlet," "Dangerous Water," "The Blue Bandanna"), United ("Her Code of Honor"), Pathe ("The Prince and Betty"). Author of 3 vaud. sketches. Hght., 5, 11; wght., 170; black hair, blue eyes. Ad., L. A. Athletic Club, L. A., Cal.; studio, J. D. Hampton Studio, Hollywood Cal.

DE VAULL, Wm. P.; b. 1870, San Francisco; educ. there; stage career, over 20 yrs. prod. stk. and road cos.; screen career, 3½ yrs. Griffith studios, Universal ("Blind Husbands"), King Vidor ("Better Times"), Brentwood ("Poor Relations"). Hght., 5, 7; wght., 168; gray hair and eyes. Ad., 4472 Sunset blvd., Los Angeles, Cal., phone 59427.

DEVERE, Harry T.; b. N. Y.; educ. there; stage career, from age of 5, with Fanny Davenport, Mrs. Fiske, "Ben Hur," "Madame X.," vaud.; screen career, American, Selig ("The Journey's End," "The Ne'er Do Well"), Morosco, Bosworth ("The Code of Marcia Gray"), Pallas ("Davy Crockett"), Fox ("The End of the Trail"), Ro-Cole ("The Lamb and the Lion"), Fox ("Last of the Duanes," "Wings of the Morning"). Hght., 6; wght., 190; gray hair, blue eyes.

DEXTER, Elliott; b. Houston, Texas; stage career, stk. leads for Marie Doro, etc.; screen career, Paramount, leads for Alice Brady, Mary Pickford, etc.; Cecil De Mille, ("We Can't Have

Everything," "The Whispering Chorus," "The Girl Who Came Back," "The Squaw Man," "Old Wives for New"), Paramount ("Maggie Pepper"), Artcraft ("Don't Change Your Husband," "For Better, for Worse"). Ad., care Artcraft, Hollywood, Cal.

DILLION, John Webb; educ. New Haven, Conn. and Phila. Dental Coll.; stage career, with Viola Allen in Shakespeare, with James O'Neil in romantic drama, dramatic stock cos. in Minneapolis, Chicago, Milwaukee, Omaha, etc.; screen career, Fox ("Why I Would Not Marry"), B. A. Rolfe Co. ("Scream in the Night"), Goldwyn ("Joan of Plattsburg"), Pathe ("House of Hate" serial), A. F. Beck Prods. ("Isle of Jewels" serial). Hght., 6; wght., 175; dark hair and eyes. Ad., Green Room Club, N. Y. C.

DONALDSON, Arthur; b. Norsholm, Sweden, 1875; educ. Sweden; stage career, since 7 yrs. old, Duff Opera Co., Augustin Daly, Henry W. Savage; original prince in "Prince of Pilsen," sang role in 1,345 performances; screen career, Famous, Pathe, World ("Hearts of Men"), Vitagraph ("For France"); man of mystery in "Runaway Jane," "Her American Prince," Vitagraph ("Over the Top," "The Captain's Captain," "Miss Dulcie From Dixie," "Fighting Destiny," "Daring Hearts"), World ("Coax Me"), Select ("The Undercurrent"), First Nat'l ("Mind the Paint Girl"), Ferret-Pathe ("The A B C of Love"). Hght., 6; wght., 195; brown hair, blue eyes. Ad., 75 Sherman ave., N. Y., St. Nich 9186.

DONNELLY, James A.; b. Boston, Mass.; educ. Boston; stage career, for thirty years in opera and musical comedy; screen career, Edison, Keystone, Vitagraph ("Pluck and Plotters," "Cupid Forecloses"). Hght., 5, 8; wght., 200; dark hair, gray eyes. Ad., Mason Hotel, Los Angeles, Cal.

DOOLEY, Johnny; educ. Oxford; stage career, circus acrobat, vaud., dramatic stk. and musical comedy; screen career, Johnny Dooley Film Comedies ("Bobby the Office Boy," "Private Preserves," "Pep"). Hght., 5, 6; wght., 140; blond hair and blue eyes. Ad., Lambs Club, N. Y. C.

DORETY, Charlie; b. San Francisco, educ. L. A.; stage exper., vaud. and dancing; screen career, Fox, Sunshine, L-Ko ("Roaring Lions and Wedding Bells," "Tight Squeeze," "Mongrels," "A Neighbor's Keyhole"), Bull's Eye Film Corp. ("Haunted Hearts"). Hght., 5, 4; wght., 126; black hair and eyes. Ad., 1270 Rose Courts, St. Andrew Pl., Hollywood, Cal.; studio, Lehrman, Culver City, Cal.

DORIAN, Charles W.; b. Santa Monica, 1891; educ. there; stage career, vaud.; screen career, National, Universal ("She Couldn't Resist Him," "Onda of the Orient," "Lone Larry," Triangle ("Hell's End"), Bluebird ("The Sealed Envelope"). Hght., 5, 11; wght., 175; brown hair, blue eyes. Ad., home, Edmunds Hotel, Ocean Park, Cal.; studio, Universal City.

DOWLING, Joseph; b. Pittsburg, 1850; educ. there; stage career, 5 yrs. in Grand opera stock co., in "Henry the Fifth," starred in "The Red Spider"; screen career, from 1914, Ince, Mastercraft, Paralta ("A Law Unto Herself," "Intelligence," "With Hoops of Steel," "Maid o' the Storm"), Solaxart ("Carmen of the Klondike"), Frank Keenan ("More Trouble," "Tidebrook"), J. Warren Kerrigan ("The Joyous Liar," "Live Sparks"), "Midnight Stages," "The Bells," "Desert of Wheat," Geo. Loane Tucker ("The Miracle Man"). Hght., 6, 1; wght., 185; white hair, blue eyes. Ad., 5302 Virginia Ave., Hollywood, Cal.

DRUCE, Hubert; b. 1870, Richmond, England; educ. London Univ.; stage career, with Richard Mansfield in repertory, 3 seasons leading comedian with John Drew, 2 seasons with Grace George, 1 season with Laurette Taylor, produced "Mr. Hopkinson," "The Night of the Party"; screen career, Empire All Star Mutual ("Please Help Emily," "My Wife"), last season with John Barrymore in "Redemption," this season produced "The Master of Ballantrae," Goldwyn ("Dodging a Million"). Ad., home, 62 Sherman Ave., Lincoln Ave., Lincoln Park, Yonkers, N. Y. Yonkers 279-J.

DRUMIER, Jack; b. Phila., 1864; educ. Univ. of Penn.; early career, practiced law; stage career, leading man for 20 yrs., appearing in "Captain Swift," "The Gilded Fool"; screen career, World ("The Beloved Blackmailer," "Just Sylvia," "The Snug Harbor," "An Amateur Widow," "Phil for Short," "Courage for Two," "Home Wanted," "The Quickening Flame," "Three Green Eyes," "The Praise Agent," "Forest Rivals"), Hght., 5, 11; wght., 190; brown hair, blue eyes. Ad., 1783 Marmion Ave., N. Y. C. Tremont 3470.

DRYDEN, Wheeler; b. Brixton, London, Eng., 1892; educ. Clapham Coll. and Streatham Hill Coll., London; stage career, 4 yrs. principal comedian of Charles Hewitt and A. Phillips' Dramatic and Comedy Co., touring far East in rep. of 70 plays; screen career Sunrise Film Co. ("A Dream of the Orient"), Stage Womens' War Relief, prod. by Universal ("Tom's Little Star"), Universal ("Hard Lines!"). Hght., 5, 8½, wght., 155; dark brown hair and eyes. Ad., c/o Actor's Equity Assn., N. Y. C.

DUCROW, Tote G.; b. Barcelona, Spain; stage career, 35 years exp. in all branches of profession, legitimate, vaud., circus; screen career, Fine Arts ("The Americano"), Vitagraph ("Fighting Trail," "Perils of Thunder Mountain"), Metro ("Red Lantern"), Lasky ("Rim Rock Jones"), Astra ("Corsican Bros."), Reliance ("Celestial Code"), American ("Betty and the Buccaneers"), Universal ("Fighting Gringo," now in stk. for serial). Ad., 4618 Fountain Ave., Los Angeles, Cal. Phone 59470.

DUDLEY, Charles; b. Ft. Grant, Ariz., 1883; stage career, comic op.; screen career, Balboa (Joe Welcher in "Neal of the Navy," "Who Pays?" series), Knick. Star ("Twin Souls"), Balboa-Mutual ("A Bit of Kindling," "The Secret of Black Mountain"). Hght., 6; wght., 160; blond hair, blue eyes. Home ad., 1435 Wilcox Ave., Hollywood, Cal.

DUFFY, Jack; b. Pawtucket, R. I., 1879; educ. there; stage career, vaud. and musical comedy; screen career, Vitagraph, Universal ("Peg of the Ring," "The Purple Mask," "Farmers and Framers," "Misfits and Matrimony"). Hght., 5, 8; wght., 132; has written "Destiny of the Sea," "Both Rivals Win," "A Woman More Beautiful Than I," Metro ("Blackie's Redemption"). Ad., home, 4607 Fountain Ave., Hollywood, Cal.; Holly 3970; studio Vitagraph.

DUMONT, Gordon; b. Milwaukee, Wis.; educ. there and St. Francis Solannus Coll., Quincy, Ill.; screen career, Ince, De Mille, in "Heart of a Fool," with Alan Dwan. Hght., 5, 10; wght., 160; dark complexion, dark hair, brown eyes. Home ad., 1322 Curson Ave., Hollywood, Cal. Phone 579809.

DUNBAR, Robert N; b. Beaver, Pa.; educ. Phila.; stage career, grand opera, leading tenor in "Gypsy Baron"; screen career, Lubin ("Third Degree"), Lasky ("The Goose Girl"), Morosco ("The Yankee Girl"), McClure ("Eyes of the World"), Triangle ("Broadway Arizona"), Fox ("The Forbidden Room," "Fighting For Gold"). Hght., 6; wght., 180; brown hair and gray eyes.

DUNCAN, Albert Edward ("Bud"), also author; b. Brooklyn, 1886; educ. Berkeley Military Sch., N. Y.; stage career, vaud. with Kolb and Dill; screen career, as Jeff in "Mutt and Jeff," Kalem ("The Fatal Violin," "A Managerie Mix-Up," "The Onion Magnate's Revenge," "Seaside Romeos," "Rival Romeos," "Twin Caddies"). Clever Comedies, Paramount "Maggie Pepper"). Hght., 4, 11; wght., 122; fair complexion, blond hair, blue eyes.

DUNCAN, H. William, also director; b. Stocland; educ. America; early career, instructor in McFadden's Physical Culture School, established own school; stage career, vaud. with Sandow, the wrestler; leads in Forepaugh stock, formed own co.; wrote "The Fifth Generation," "The Sporting Editor"; screen career, Selig, leads and director; Vitagraph "Dead Shot Baker," "The Fighting Trail," "Wolfville," "The Tenderfoot," "The Last Man," "Vengeance and the Woman," "A Fight for Millions," "The Man of Might," "Smashing Barriers"). Member M. P. D. A. Hght., 5, 10; wght., 180; dark brown hair, dark blue eyes. Ad., Vitagraph, Los Angeles, Cal., or L. A. Athletic Club, Los Angeles, Cal.

DUNKINSON, Harry Leopold; b. N. Y., 1876; educ. there; stage career, since 9 yrs. old, with Denman Thompson in "Old Homestead," Augustin Daly, Horace McVicker; screen career, Essanay, since 1914 ("The Misleading Lady," "Mary Page," "The Beach Comber"), Universal ("The Edge of the Law," "Barter"), Artcraft ("Selfish Yates"), Fox ("The Forbidden Room," "The Rebellious Bride," "Love is Love," "Chasing Rainbows"). Universal

("Rouge and Riches"). Hght., 5, 11; wght., 217; brown hair, blue eyes. Studio ad., Universal.

DUNN, Bobby; b. Milwaukee, Wis., 1891; educ. St. John's Mil. Acad.; champion high diver of the World, with Dr. Carver's diving horses; screen career, Sennett Comedies, Fox Sunshine Comedies. Studio ad., Fox Sunshine Comedies.

DUNN, Edward Frank; stage career, 2 yrs. in Musical Comedies on Broadway, 3 yrs. in stock cos.; screen career, Blackton ("Moonshine Trail," "Dawn," "The Blood Barrier"), Vitagraph feature comedies 1 yr. Hght., 6, 1½; wght., 187; brown hair and eyes. Ad., 241 Linden Ave., Brooklyn, N. Y., Flatbush 6287.

DUNN, J. Malcolm; educ. England; stage career, lead in several London theatres, Australia and So. Africa, "Sweet Kitty Bellairs" with David Belasco, Orlando in "As You Like It" with Henrietta Crosman, lead in "The House Next Door" Cohan and Harris, "Seven Sisters" with Laurette Taylor, "Mons. Beaucaire," "Butterfly on the Wheel," "Arms and the Girl" with Wm. Harris, Jr.; screen career, Edison ("The Magic Skin"), Vitagraph ("The Scarlet Runner"), several pictures for Biograph, Famous-Lasky ("Arms and the Girl," "Dr. Jekyll and Mr. Hyde"). Hght. 5, 11; wght., 165; blond hair, grey eyes. Ad., The Boulevard, Beechhurst, L. I., N. Y. Flushing 2439 or Lambs Club, N. Y.

DUNN, William R.; b. Astoria, L. I., 1884; educ. Brooklyn; stage career, in Payton Stock, Brooklyn, Mrs. Leslie Carter, Nance O'Neil, vaud.; screen career, Vitagraph ("Man Behind the Curtain," "The Secret Kingdom," "Clover's Rebellion," "The Princess of Park Row," "I Will Repay," "Mary Jane's Pa"), Fox ("I Want to Forget," "Woman, Woman"), Select ("The Undercurrent"). Ad., 241 Linden Ave., Bklyn., N. Y. Flatbush 6287.

DUPREE, George; b. Cincinnati, O., 1874; educ. N. Y.; 25 yrs. stage exper., screen career, Famous Players, Goldwyn, Fox, Pathe ("Woman the Germans Shot," "Dance of Death"), Acme ("Thirteenth Chair"), Tourneur ("The Whip"), Famous ("The Avalanche"), American Cinema ("Inner Voice"), Selznick ("Great Lover"), Craig Kennedy Serial. Ad., 316 W. 47th St., N. Y. C. Bryant 8094.

DURHAM, Lewis; b. New Oxford, Pa.; educ. Georgetown; early career, professional ball player on Brooklyn Natl., Wash. Amer. and N. Y. Natl.; screen career, NYMP, Horsley ("The Conscience of John David"), Triangle ("An Even Break," "One Shot Ross"), Goldwyn ("Flame of the Desert"). Hght., 5, 10½; wght., 183; brown hair, blue eyes. Ad., home, 504 Hull St., Ocean Park, Cal.; studio, Goldwyn.

DURNING, Bernard J.; b. N. Y. C.; educ. Fordham Univ., stage career, stage manager several seasons; screen career, Biograph 2 yrs., Edison 6 yrs., directed Shirley Mason productions, also O. Henry pictures, with John Collins, "In The Fog," "Blackjack Bargainer," "Weaver of Dreams"; Metro (Played in "Blackie's Redemption"), World ("When Bearcat Went Dry").

— E —

EARLE, Edward; b. Toronto, Can.; educ. Toronto; stage career, in many prods., including "The Bishop's Carriage," "Sweet Kitty Bellairs," "Glorious Betsy," "The Shepherd King," "The Blue Moon" with James T. Powers, "The Matinee Idol" with De Wolf Hopper, "The Quaker Girl," etc.; screen career, Famous Players, Edison, Metro, Vitagraph ("For France," "The Blind Adventure," "One Thousand Dollars," "Transients in Arcadia," "Buried Treasure"), Select ("His Bridal Night"), Para-Artcraft ("Miracle of Love"). Hght., 5, 11½; wght., 160. Ad., Lambs Club, N. Y.

EDESON, Robert; b. New Orleans, La.; educ. Brooklyn; stage career, 25 yrs. starring in many prods.; screen career, Lasky ("The Call of the North"), NYMP, Mutual ("The Absentees"), Vitagraph ("Mortmain," "The Cave Man"), Pathe ("The Light That Failed," "Big Jim Garrity"), Raver-Art Dramas ("The Public Defender"), Selznick ("Sealed Hearts"). Ad., Lambs Club, N. Y.

EDWARDS, Chas., b. N. Y., 1887; educ. N. Y.; stage career, with Frohman, Rich and Harris, Frank McKee, Sydney Rosenfield, vaud.; screen career, Metro Sidney Drew Comedies, Select, Metro ("The Man Who Stayed at Home," "Wilson or the Kaiser"), Perret ("Lafayette, We Come"), Select ("The Woman the Germans Shot"), World ("The Clouded Name"). Hght., 5, 11; wght., 171; medium complexion, gray hair, dark blue eyes. Ad., 139 West 47th st., N. Y.

ELDRIDGE, Charles; b. Saratoga Springs, N. Y.; educ. Lanesboro, Mass.; stage career, Variety Theatre, Buffalo, stk. comedian, prods. under Frohman, Mansfield; screen career, Vitagraph 4½ yrs. ("Love vs. Law"), Metro ("The Pretenders," "Eye for Eye"), Famous ("Sunshine Nan"), Tourneur ("Sporting Life"), Arden ("The Challenge"), Famous ("Red Head"), Vitagraph ("Man Who Might Have Been"), Selznick. Hght., 5, 5; wght., 157; white hair and blue eyes. Ad., 102 Riverside Drive, N. Y. C. Schuyler 9487. Member Green Room Club, N. Y. C.

ELKAS, Edward; b. N. Y. 1862; educ. there; stage career, director for Lulu Glaser and Alice Nielsen, Aborn Opera Co. and mus. com.; screen career, Vitagraph ("Mortmain"), Selznick ("Foolish Virgin"), Metro ("Lifted Veil"), Birth of Race Co. ("Birth of a Race"), Fox ("Les Miserables"), Tourneur ("Woman," "Blue Bird," "Prunella"), Vitagraph ("Locked Door," "The Goddess"), Goldwyn ("Joan From Plattsburg," "Venus Model"). Hght., 5, 6; wght., 179; fair complexion, gray hair, blue eyes. Ad., 2155 86th st., Brooklyn, N. Y. Bath Beach 1428. Member Green Room Club, N. Y.

ELLIOTT, Frank; b. Cheshire, England; educ. Liverpool Univ.; stage career, leading man in Drury Lane prods., member Drury Lane Fund, and therefore, a Rayol player; screen career, 6 yrs. as leading man and heavy, in about 150 pictures, Fox ("Wings of the Morning"), Universal ("The Gorgeous Butterfly"), Metro ("The Hope"). Hght., 6; brown hair, blue eyes. Ad., 1735 Highland ave., Hollywood, Calif., phone 577876.

ELLIOTT, Robert; b. Ireland; stage career, leads in "Seven Keys to Baldpate," "Country Girl," repertoire Forbes-Robertson, lead with Margaret Illington "Within the Law," "The Lie"; screen career, Metro, McClure, Goldwyn, Betzwood, Sunset, World; supported Ethel Barrymore, Alice Brade, Nance O'Neil, Marjorie Rambeau, Pauline Frederick, Dorothy Dalton, Gail Kane, Irene Fenwick, Dolores Cassinelli, Theda Bara, Virginia Pearson, Mabel Normand; Famous ("Resurrection"), Fox ("Checkers"), Ince ("L'Apache"), Powell—Mutual ("Mary Moreland"), U. S. Govt. ("Spirit of Lafayette"), Perret ("Unknown Love"). Hght. 6, 1½; wght., 185; dark brown hair, blue eyes. Ad., 130 W. 44th st., N. Y. C.

ELMER, William; b. Council Bluffs, Iowa, 1872; educ. Pacific Univ.; stage career, rep. with Frederick Warde and Louis James, stock; screen career, Biograph, Selig, Lasky, Lasky-Paramount ("The Countess Charming"), Ince-Para, Para ("Firefly of France," "Playing the Game," "Coals of Fire," "Wolves of the Rail"), Fox ("Married in Haste," "Cheating Herself"), Paramount ("The Dub," "Maggie Pepper," "Alias, Mike Moran"). Hght., 5, 10½; wght., 165; brown hair, blue eyes. Ad., home, 212 E. 23rd st., Los Angeles, Cal.; studio, Goldwyn.

ELTINGE, Julian; b. 1883, educ. Boston, Mass.; stage career, "Mr. Wicks of Wickham," mngt. Ed. E. Rice; vaud., with Harry Lauder, "Fascinating Widow," "Crinoline Girl," "Cousin Lucy"; screen career, Over the Rhine Co. & Lasky ("Over the Rhine," "Countess Charming," "Clever Mrs. Carfax," "The Widow's Might"), Republic ("An Adventuress"). Hght., 5, 8½; wght., 165; brown hair; gray eyes. Ad., c/o Fred J. Balshofer, Hollywood, Calif.

ENTWISTLE, Harold; b. London, Eng.; educ. Heidelburg, Lycee Vitry, Paris, and Eng.; stage career, 25 yrs., Chas. Frohman, 6 yrs., Henry Irving, Wilson Barrett, Mrs. Patrick Campbell, Mrs. Langtry, Forbes-Robertson; screen career, Famous Players, Metro, Perret, Goldwyn, Ince ("Too Fat to Fight," "In the Hollow of Her Hand," "The Divorcee," "A Soul Adrift"). Hght., 5, 11; wght., 175; white hair, blue eyes. Ad., 251 West 88th st., N. Y. Riverside 5576.

EVANS, Herbert D.; b. London, Eng.; educ. there; stage career, Beerbohm Tree, His Majes-

ACTORS

ty's theatre, "Quinney's," "The Great Adventure" (Winthrop Ames), "Potash and Perlmutter"; screen career, leads opposite Mme. Petrova, Virginia Pearson, Edna Goodrich, Eva Tanguay, Barbara Castleton; Vitagraph ("The Third Degree"). Hght., 6, 2; wght., 190; dark hair, dark eyes. Ad., Friars Club, N. Y.

—F—

FAIRBANKS, Douglas; b. Denver, 1883; educ. Mil. Acad. and Colorado Schl. of Mines, Harvard; stage career, rep., vaud., under dir. Wm. A. Brady in "The Pit," "Two Little Soldier Boys"; featured in "Frenzied Finance," "A Gentleman from Mississippi"; co-starred with W. H. Crane in the "New Henrietta"; screen career, Fine Arts ("The Americano"), Artcraft ("In Again, Out Again," "Wild and Woolly," "Reaching for the Moon," "A Modern Musketeer," "Headin' South," "Mr. Fix-It," "Bound in Morocco," "Say, Young Fellow," "He Comes Up Smiling," "Arizona," "Down to Earth," "The Knickerbocker Buckaroo"), United Artists ("His Majesty, the American," "When the Clouds Roll By"). Ad., Douglas Fairbanks Co., Hollywood, Cal.

FARLEY, James Lee; b. Waldron, Ark., 1882; educ. Univ., Mo.; early career, Govt. & railroad service; stage career, rep. & stk.; screen career, Selig, Fox, Univ. ("Brute Force", American ("For the Family Name," "The Bride's Silence"), Bluebird ("Sue of the South"). Hght., 5, 11; wght., 185; brown eyes and hair.

FARNUM, Dustin; b. Hampton Beach, N. H., 1874; stage career, with Ethel Tucker Co., Chauncey Olcott, starred in "The Virginian," "The Ranger," "The Squaw Man," "Cameo Kirby," "Littlest Rebel"; screen career, Lasky ("The Squaw Man," "The Virginian," Pallas-Paramount ("A Gentleman from Indiana," "David Garrick," "Parson of Paniment," "Ben Blair," "A Son of Erin"), Fox ("The Scarlet Pimpernell," "The Spy"), "Durand of the Bad Lands," "North of 53"), United ("The Light of Western States," "The Man in the Open," "A Man's Fight," "The Corsican Brothers"). Studio ad., United Farnum Prod., Glendale, Calif.

FARNUM, Franklyn; b. Boston, Mass., June 5, 1883; educ. Boston, Mass.; stage career, 12 yrs., leading man for Chas Frohman, Henry W. Savage, George Lederer, Nixon & Zimmerman, Jos. Webber; screen career, Universal ("The Clock," "Fighting Grin," "Anything Once"), Metro ("In Judgment Of"), seria! for Selig now releasing through Canyon Films, 130 W. 46 st., N. Y. Hght., 5, 11; wght., 168; dark complexion, dark hair, brown eyes. Home ad., 4845 Elmwood ave., Los Angeles, Calif., Holly 3257.

FARNUM, William; b. Boston, 1876; educ. Bucksport, Me.; stage career, from age of 15, in "Prince of India," "Virginius," starred 5 yrs. in "Ben Hur," leading man with Olga Nethersole, starred with Dustin Farnum 2 seasons in "The Littlest Rebel," 10 yrs. a legit. star; screen career, Selig ("The Spoilers"), Fox ("A Tale of Two Cities," "Les Miserables," "Riders of the Purple Sage," "Lone Star Ranger," "Wolves of the Night," "Last of the Duanes," "Wings of the Morning," "If I Were King"). Hght., 5, 10½; brown hair, blue eyes. Ad., Fox Film Corp., N. Y. C.

FAULKNER, Ralph C.; b. and educ. San Antonio, Tex.; early career, cartoonist and reported in Mexico, Los Angeles, San Francisco; monologist in vaud.; screen career, Albuquerque Film, Thanhouser ("War and the Woman"), impersonating Woodrow Wilson, specializes in cowboys and Indians; Fox ("The Prussian Cur"). Hght., 5, 10; wght., 175; brown eyes and hair. Ad., N. V. A. Club, 229 W. 46th st., N. Y.

FAVERSHAM, William; b. and educ. England; stage career; star under own management in "The Squaw Man," "The World and His Wife," "Herod," "Julius Ceasar," "Othello," "Romeo and Juliet," "The Fawn," "The Hawk," "Lord and Lady Algy. Screen career; Famous Players, ("The Silver King," "The Man Who Found Himself"). Ad., 116 W. 39th st., N. Y. C. Greeley 3376, or Lambs' Club, N. Y.

FAWCETT, George; b. Virginia; educ. Univ. of Virginia; stage career, extensive experience in United States and England; screen career, Universal, Fine Arts, Selig ("The Crisis"), Select, Selznick ("Panthea"), Artcraft ("The Great Love," "Romance of Happy. Valley," "Hearts of the World," "Cinderella Man," "The Hun Within"), Paramount ("The Hope Chest," "I'll Get im Yet," "Out of Luck," "Turning the Tables"), Artcraft ("Girl Who Stayed at Home"), Griffith ("Scarlet Days"), First Nat'l ("The Greatest Question). Ad., Griffith Studio, Mamaroneck, N. Y.

FAY, Hugh; b. N. Y.; educ. N. Y.; stage career, with Barry and Fay, Lillian Russell in "The Grand Duchess," "Coming Through the Rye," "Three Twins," "Belle of New York"; screen career, with Keystone ("Village Vampire"), Sunshine ("Roaring Lions on a Midnight Express," "A Neighbor's Keyhole," "My Husband's Wife"), Metro ("Almost Married," "A Favor to a Friend," "Please Get Married"), Rob-Cole ("Better Times"). Hght., 6; wght., 135; light hair, brown eyes. Home ad., 1775 Las Palmas, Los Angeles; studio, Lehrman, Cal.

FELLOWES, Rockcliffe; b. Ottawa, Can., 1885; educ. Bishop's Coll. Schl., Lennoxville; stage career, with Ethel Barrymore, Cyril Scott, "Within the Law," "Under Cover"; screen career, Fox ("Where Love Leads," "The Bondage of Fear," "The House Cat," "The Web of Desire"), Selznick ("The Easiest Way"), Goldwyn ("Cup of Fury"). Hght., 5, 11; wght., 175; brown hair and eyes. Home ad., 450 Madison ave., N. Y. C.; studio, Goldwyn.

FENTON, Mark; b. Crestline, O., Nov. 11, 1866; stage career, Charles Frohman's "All the Comforts of Home" and "The Sporting Duchess," in Shakespearian drama with Booth and Barrett, in cos. of Otis Skinner, Madame Modjeska, in stk. many yrs.; screen career, Biograph, Pathe and Universal ("The Car of Chance," "Flirting with Death," "The Man Trap," "Saving the Last Mail"), Universal ("A Fight for Love," "Molly and I"), Jewell ("The Kaiser, the Beast of Berlin"). Hght., 5, 10; wght., 190; complexion fair, brown hair, gray eyes. Home ad., 518 W. 47th st., N. Y.; studio, Francis Ford.

FERGUSON, Casson; b. Alexandria, La., 1891; educ. there and Paris; stage career, 10 yrs. Shakespeare and mus. com. in America; revue, mus. com. and concert in London, Grand Opera in Paris; screen career, Morosco, Lasky, Ince, Universal, Triangle, Hampton ("How Could You, Jean?" "The Only Road"), Paramount ("Jane Goes A-Wooing," "Secret Service"), Artcraft ("Johnny Get Your Gun"), Goldwyn ("Flame of the Desert"). Hght., 5, 11; wght., 150; brown hair, blue gray eyes. Home ad., 1522 Manhattan pl., L. A.; Holly 2107; studio, Lasky, Hollywood, Cal.

FIELD, George; b. San Francisco; educ. Chicago; stage career, 10 yrs. in mus. com., stock and vaud.; screen career, American ("The Key"), Selig ("Beware of Strangers"), Metro ("The Testing of Mildred Vane"), Rob-Cole ("A Trick of Fate," "A Sage Brush Hamlet"), Hodkinson ("End of the Game"). Studio ad., Universal City, Cal.

FILLMORE, Clyde; educ. Univ. of Oregon, Johns Hopkins Univ.; stage career, 4 yrs. under mngmt. Cohan & Harris in "It Pays to Advertise," "House of Glass," "He and She," "The Little Teacher"), Anderson & Weber in "The Very Idea," "Civilian Clothes," at Morosco Theatre, Los Angeles; screen career, Universal ("Millionaire Pirate," "Fire Flingers," "Sundown Trail," "His Great Success"), Fox ("When Fate Decides"). Hght., 6, 2; wght., 195; brown hair, gray eyes. Home ad., 1715a Wilcox ave., Hollywood, Cal.; phone 579059.

FISHER, George; b. Republic, Mich.; educ. Milwaukee, Wis.; stage career, 6 yrs., began in 1907; screen career, started in 1914 with Thos. H. Ince, Paralta ('Within the Cup," "Maid of the Storm"), Selznick ("Mrs. Leffingwell's Boots"), Universal ("Fires of Youth"), Pathe ("Gates of Brass"), Hall Prod. Co. ("The Awakening"). Hght., 5, 11; wght., 170; light brown hair, brown eyes. Home ad., 1133 So. Hoover st., Los Angeles, Cal.; phone 54006.

FITZROY, Louis; b. Fort Brady, Mich.; educ. Ohio Univ.; stage career began in 1886, dram. stk., Columbus, Ohio; screen career, began in 1911 with Cameraphone, N. Y., Fox ("A Bird of Prey"), Metro ("The Four-Flusher," "The Devil's Deputy"). Hght., 5, 11; wght., 150; gray hair, dark blue eyes. Home ad., 1322 McCadden place, Hollywood, Cal.; Holly 1834.

FLANAGAN, D. J.; b. Ireland, 1876; stage career,

mgmt. Brady and Ziegfeld, com. opera, mus. com., played with Alice Nielson, Grace Van Studdiford, Anna Held, Julian Eltinge, etc.; screen career, World ("Trilby," "La Boheme"), Selznick ("The Common Law"), McClure ("Sloth"), M. H. Hoffman ("One Hour"). Hght., 5, 10½; wght., 180; brown hair, blue eyes. Home ad., 523 W. 134th st., N. Y.

FOOTE, Courtenay; b. Yorkshire, Eng.; educ. Oxford; early career, studied civil engineering; stage career, with Beerbohm Tree, in rep.; America, all star cast of "Oliver Twist"; mgmt. Chas. Frohman, Belasco, Liebler, etc.; screen career, Vitagraph, Bosworth, Fine Art Films, Morosco ("Cross Currents," "An International Marriage"), Famous Players, Mutual ("Love's Law"), Artcraft ("His Parisian Wife"), Paramount ("The Two Brides"). Ad., 66 W. 38th st., N. Y. C.

FORD, Harrison; b. Kansas City, Mo.; educ. there and Los Angeles; stage career, stk. in Baltimore, Md.; in 1914, Syracuse, N. Y., 1913 and 1915; Famous Players ("Unclaimed Goods," "Girls," "The Third Kiss," "The Lottery Man"). Hght., 5, 10; wght., 160; brown hair and eyes. Ad., Lasky Studio, Lasky, Hollywood, Cal.

FORMAN, Tom; b. Mitchell Co., Tex.; stage career, Belasco stock, Los Angeles, toured west at head of own rep. co.; screen career, Kalem, Lubin, Lasky ("The American Consul," "Her Strange Wedding," "The Jaguar's Claw," "Forbidden Paths"), Pallas-Paramount ("A Kiss for Susie," "Hashamura Togo," "The Trouble Buster"), Artcraft ("For Better, For Worse"), Paramount ("Heart of Youth," "Told in the Hills"), Famous Players ("The Tree of Knowledge," "The Round-Up"). Blond hair, blue eyes. Ad., Lasky Studio, Hollywood, Cal.

FORMES, Carl, Jr.; b. London, Eng., 1848; stage educ. Meiningen Theat., under Duke of Meiningen and Baron von Chroneck; stage career, engagements in Berlin, Dresden, Vienna, Amsterdam, Stanton Opera Co.'s world tour; screen career, Kalem, Fine Arts ("Old Heidelberg," "Macbeth," etc.), Select ("Up the Road with Sallie"), Vitagraph ("A Rogue's Romance"). Hght., 5, 10½; wght., 148; brown hair, blue eyes.

FORREST, Allan; b. Brooklyn, N. Y.; educ. Univ. Sch., Cleveland, Ohio; stage career, stk. in Cleveland and Baltimore, Md.; screen career, 3 yrs. American Film Co., Santa Barbara, Cal., leading man for Mary Miles Minter. Hght., 6; wght., 160; dark hair and eyes. Ad., Los Angeles Athletic Club.

FORTH, George J.; b. Philadelphia; early exper. gentleman farmer; screen career, Vitagraph ("A Municipal Report"), Thanhouser, Edison, Pathe ("The Sixteenth Wife," "The Heart of Ezra Greer," "Bobby's Bravery," "The Girl from the Sea"), Goldwyn ("Our Little Wife"). Hght., 5, 11; wght., 170; brown hair and eyes. Home ad., Green Room Club, 139 W. 47th St., N. Y.

FOSHAY, Harold; b. and educ. Brooklyn; stage career, vaudeville and stock; screen career, Metro, Biograph, Harry Raph, Vitagraph ("The Girl Problem"), Edgar Lewis Prod. ("Other Men's Shoes"). Hght., 5, 9; wght., 145; light hair, blue eyes. Ad., 34 Jefferson Ave., Brooklyn, N. Y.

FOSS, Darrell Burton; b. 1893, So. Wisconsin; educ., Chicago & So. Cal.; screen career, Kalem, Ince, Triangle ("Without Honor"), Metro ("Return of Mary," "Testing of Mildred Vane," with May Allison, "The Red Lantern" with Nazimova.), Nazimova ("The Brat"), May Allison ("The Walk Offs"), Lasky ("Rose o'the River"), Universal special (featured in "Loot"). Hght., 6; wght., 160; dark complexion, brown hair and eyes. Home ad., 103 Rose Ave., Venice, Cal.; or, 5527 Fernwood Ave., Hollywood, Cal. Holly 2098.

FOSTER, J. Morris; b. Foxberg, Pa.; educ. Stamford Univ.; stage career, with Henrietta Crossman, Olive Windham, in "The Christian Pilgrim," "The Sixth Commendment," "What Happened to Mary," Harry David Stk. Co.; screen career, Thanhouser, Famous Players, Universal, American, Hampton; "The Innocent Lie," "High Speed," "The Secret Man," "Overland Red," "The Parish Priest," 5 Pathe releases. Hght., 5, 10½; wght., 150; medium brown hair, blue eyes. Home ad., 1572 La Baig Ave., Hollywood, Cal.

FOXE, Earle A.; b. Oxford, O., 1888; educ. Ohio State Univ.; stage career, Chicago stk., in "The Deserters," "The Stranger," "The Cub," with Douglas Fairbanks; screen career, Griffith ("The Escape," "The Man Upstairs"), Lasky ("The Trail of the Lonesome Pine"), Triangle ("From Two to Six"), Select ("The Honeymoon"), Metro ("Outwitted"), Pathe ("The Fatal Ring" serial), Goldwyn ("Peck's Bad Girl"). Hght., 6, 1; wght., 178; light complexion, light brown hair, blue eyes.

FRANCIS, Alec Budd; b. London, Eng.; educ. Uppingham Coll.; stage career, with various prods. in England, India, South Africa and United States; screen career, Vitagraph, Eclair, World, Goldwyn ("The Face in the Dark," "The Glorious Adventure," "The Venus Model"), C. K. Young-Select ("The Marionettes"), Goldwyn ("Day Dreams," "Crimson Gardenia," "City of Comrades," "Heartsease," "World and Its Woman," "Lord and Lady Algy," "Flame of the Desert"), United ("Her Code of Honor"), Select ("Probation Wife"). Hght., 5, 11; wght., 157; light hair, gray eyes; ad., Goldwyn Studio, Culver City, Cal.

FRANCK, John L.; b. Louisville, Ky., 1850; educ. Louisville; early career, as clown and in minstrels; screen career, entered pictures when they were first installed on the Coast, with Bison, Kalem, Fine Arts, Famous Players, Fox, Universal ("Virgin of Stamboul"), Mary Pickford ("Pollyanna"), Metro, C. K. Young ("Eyes of Youth"), Goldwyn ("Flame of the Desert"), Vitagraph, Selig ("Auction of Souls"). Ad., 1811 Sunset Blvd., Los Angeles, Cal.

FRANK, J. Herbert; stage career, 10 yrs. Wm. A. Brady, vaudeville, stock; screen career, Vitagraph, 2 yrs., World, Metro, Talmadge; "Tempered Steel," Petrova co.; "Good Bye, Bill," Famous; "Freedom," Fox; "Dodging a Million," Goldwyn; Fox ("For Freedom"), Photoplay Libraries ("Empty Arms"). Hght., 5, 11; wght., 180; dark complexion, hair and eyes. Ad., home, 152 W. 49th St., N. Y. C.; Bryant, 8116 and 5217.

FRAUNHOLZ, Fraunie French; b. and educ. Balto., Md.; 15 yrs. stage exper., stk. and own act in vaud.; screen career, Solax, Metro, Famous Players, Thanhouser, Universal, with Petrova, Florence Reed, Edmund Breese, Gail Kane, Mary Miles Minter; Perret ("Lafayette We Come," "Stars of Glory," "Thirteenth Chair"). Hght., 5, 8; wght., 140; brown hair, gray eyes. Ad., Fort Lee, N. J.

FRENCH, Chas. K.; b. Columbus, Ohio; educ. there; stage career, variety, minstrel and dram., song and dance man, banjoist comedian, character actor; screen career, Nazimova ("Hermit Doctor of Garja"), "Law of the North" with Chas. Ray, with Dorothy Dalton in "The Weaker Sex," Tom Mix "High Speed," Wm. S. Hart ("Tiger Man"), Wm. Russell "That Hero Stuff." Hght., 5, 11½; wght., 190; brown gray hair, blue eyes. Ad., 2217 Ewing St., Los Angeles, Cal. Wilshire 2847.

FRENCH, George B.; Storm Lake, Iowa; stage career, for 15 yrs. in dram. stk., on road, and in vaud.; with Louis James "Parsifal," etc.; screen career, National ("Tarzan of the Apes," "Back to Nature"), Christie ("In and Out," "500 or Bust," "Sally's Blighted Career," "His Pajama Girl"). Hght., 5, 10; wght., 140; dark hair and eyes. Home ad., 1636 Argyle Ave., Hollywood, Cal.; studio ad., Christie, Hollywood.

FUREY, Jas. A.; b. and educ. Brooklyn; stage career, 38 yrs.; screen career, Pathe ("The Awakening of Helena Ritchie," "Destruction" with Theda Bara), Fox ("Her Sister," "Queen of Hearts"), Peerless ("Phil"), Blackton ("Dawn"), Vitagraph ("Climbers"), Famous ("On With the Dance"), Selznick ("Love"). Hght., 5, 9; wght., 150; white hair, blue eyes. Ad., 454 Classon Ave., Brooklyn, N. Y. Prospect 7128.

— G —

GADEN, Alexander; b. Montreal, Canada, Feb. 20, 1880; educ. there; stage career, stock, throughout U. S., etc., playing over 500 parts; also with Savage's prod., "Madame X"; screen career, Famous, Universal, Vitagraph, Gaumont ("The Hidden Face," "The Gates of Divorce," "The Toll of War") Hodkinson ("The Bandbox"), Artco ("The Capitol"). Hght., 5, 9½; wght., 175; fair complexion, dark brown hair, brown eyes; has written several successful playlets and photoplays.

GAILLARD, Robert; b. Adrian, Mich.; educ. Wisconsin University; stage career, 15 yrs.

leading man, manager, director; screen career, 8 yrs. with Vitagraph Co. ("In the Balance," "A Girl of the Times," "The Clutch of Circumstance," "Beauty Proof," "The Adventure Shop," "Silent Strength," "The Man Who Won," "Beating the Odds," "In Honor's Web"). Hght., 6 ft.; wght., 186; brown hair, brown eyes. Home, 3718 ave. J, Bklyn, N. Y.

GALLAGHER, Raymond; b. San Francisco, 1889; educ. Sacred Heart Coll.; screen career, 10 yrs. exp., stk. and road shows, leading man in "The Wolf," "Mrs. Temple's Telegram," "The Girl of the Golden West," Alcazar Stk. Co.; screen career, Melies, Lubin, Universal ("His Divorced Wife," "The Phantom Melody"). Hght., 5, 9; wght., 160; dark complexion, brown hair and eyes. Ad., Sherwood Apts., Los Angeles. Pico 3202.

GAMBLE, Warburton; educ. England; stage career, London, under Sir Herbert Tree, Forbes Robertson, Chas. Frohman, with Tree in "Colonel Newcomb"; in New York, "The Outcast" with Elsie Ferguson, the aviator in Shaw's "Misalliance," "Margaret Schiller" with Miss Ferguson, "Milestones"; screen career, Paramount ("The Outcast," "Silver King," "A Society Exile," "The Invisible Bond," "Two Brides"), Goldwyn ("Thirty a Week," "The Palliser Case"), Raver ("As a Man Thinks," "La Belle Russe"). Hght., 5, 11½; wght., 165; dark hair, dark gray eyes. Ad., Whitestone, L. I., N. Y. Flushing 1324-R.

GELDART, Clarence H.; b. St. John, N. B.; educ. Collins Coll., Boston; stage career, 15 yrs., with Mansfield, Neil Burgess, Russ Whytal, Lewis & Tilbury and stk. cos.; screen career, Fine Arts, Griffith ("Intolerence"), Nat. Drama (Gen. Arnold in "The Fall of a Nation"), Lasky stk. co. ("Hidden Pearls," "Gypsy Trail," "The Way of a Man with a Maid," "Secret Garden," "The Goat"). Hght., 5 ft. 11 in.; Wght., 180 lbs.; light complexion, brown hair, gray eyes. Home ad., 1765 G. No. Bronson ave., Hollywood, Cal. Phone 577811. Studio ad., Lasky, Hollywood, Cal.

GERALD, Pete; b. Piacenza, Italy, 1864; stage career, 35 yrs. vaud., circus, drama, from contortionist to leading man; screen career, L-Ko ("Born to the Purple," "Phantom Island," "The Eye of Fear"), Universal ("The Purple Mask"), Bluebird ("The Craving"), Monopol (Crimson Shoals"); acrobat and athletic contortionist. Hght., 5, 9; wght., 140; black hair, brown eyes. Ad., home, 1442 Union ave., Los Angeles, Calif.

GERARD, Charles; b. Carlow, Ireland, 1887; educ. Castleknock and Dublin Univ.; stage career, in London, "The Country Girl," with George Edwardes, "The Gay Gordons"; screen career, Famous Players, Paramount ("Little Miss Optimist"), Universal ("The Double Standard"), Select ("The New Moon," "The Isle of Conquest"), Paramount ("Pettigrew's Girl," "Something to Do"), Artcraft ("The Counterfeit," "The Teeth of the Tiger"). Ad., Hotel Algonquin, N. Y.

GIBBS, Robert Paton, b. Pa.; educ. Univ. of Va.; stage career, "The Flame," "Trilby," "Madam X," "Ghosts"; screen career, Savage (title role in "Robinson Crusoe"), Pathe, Kalem ("Grip of the Charlatan"), World ("The Beloved Adventuress"), Metro ("Man Who Stayed at Home"), Fox ("Lure of Ambition"), World ("The Beloved Adventuress"). Hght., 5, 8; wght., 155; dark complexion, gray hair, black eyes. Ad., 16 Gramercy Park, N. Y.

GIBSON, Ed ("Hoot"); b. Tekamah, Nebr. 1892; early career, cowboy, with Bud Atkin's circus to Australia; screen career, since 1911, Selig, Kalem ("Hazards of Helen"), Universal ("A Knight of the Range," "The Crow," "The Voice on the Wire," "Shameless Salvason," "The Trail of the Holdup Men," "The Lone Hand," "The Double Holdup," "The Sheriff's Oath," "The Jay Bird," "Harmony Ranch," "Roaring Dan"). Hght., 5, 10; wght., 160; Light hair and blue eyes. Studio, Universal City, Calif.

GILBERT, Jack; b. Logan, Utah, 1895; educ. Hitchcock Mil. Acad., San Rafael, Calif.; stage career, Baker Stk. Co. in Portland, Ore. and Seattle, Wash., Forepaugh Stk. Co., Cincinati, road shows; screen career, Ince ("Princess of the Dark," "Golden Rule," "Millionaire Vagrant"), Mary Pickford ("Heart of the Hills"), Geo. Loane Tucker ("Ladies Must Live"), Maurice Tourneur ("White Heather," "Glory of Love"). Home ad., L. A. Athletic Club, Los Angeles, Calif. Studio, Maurice Tourneur Co., Goldwyn studio, Culver City, Calif.

GILES, Corliss; b. Providence, R. I.; educ. there; stage career, with Lou Tellegen, "King of Nowhere," "The Ware Case," "The Iron Dove," John Cort (stock in large cities); screen career, Clara K. Young ("Shirley Kaye," "The Marionettes," "The House of Glass"), Miller-Hallmark ("Love, Honor and ?"), Hallmark ("Heart of a Gypsy"). Hght., 5, 11½; wght., 170; dark hair and eyes. Home ad., Lambs Club, N. Y. C.

GIRARD, Jos. W.; b. Williamsport, Pa.; educ. Phila., Pa.; stage career, 20 yrs. exp.; screen career, 1 yr. with Edison, 4 yrs. with Universal ("Two Souled Women," "Beast of Berlin," "Loot," "Paid in Advance," "Midnight Man" serial), Payton Pictures, Inc. ("Sign of the Rat"). Hght., 6; wght., 185; gray hair, brown eyes. Home ad., 1757 Orange Drive, Hollywood, Calif. phone 577320.

GLASS, Gaston; b. 1895 and educ. Paris, France; stage career, 5 yrs. with Sarah Bernhardt in France and U. S.; screen career, Pathe Freres, Gaumont, Paris; Famous Players-Lasky ("Oh, You Women," "Honeymoon for Three," "Let's Elope"), Warner ("Open Your Eyes"), McManus ("Lost Battalion"), World ("Women of Lies", Ed. Jose Prod. ("Mothers of Men"). Hght., 5, 10½; wght., 156; dark hair, brown eyes. Ad., 48 W. 49th St., N. Y. C.

GLENDON, J. Frank; b. Choteau, Mont., 1885; educ. Montana Wesleyan Univ.; stage career, 9 yrs.; screen career, Vitagraph (O. Henry stories and "Woman in the Web," "The Changing Woman," "By the World Forgot," "Dawn of Understanding," "Wishing Ring Man," "The Enchanted Barn"). Hght., 6; wght., 175; gray eyes, brown hair. Ad., 5925 Yucca st., Hollywood, Cal.; studio, Vitagraph, L. A., Cal.

GOLDSMITH, Frank; b. 1881; stage career, 8 yrs. mgmt. of Chas. Frohman, with Shubert, Brady, Winthrop Ames, "Truth" with Grace George; screen career, Wartons, Peerless, Paragon, World Film ("The Page Mystery"), Mutual ("Reputation"), Artcraft ("The Rise of Janice Cushing"), Goldwyn ("Oh, Johnny"), Fox ("Woman, Woman"). Hght., 5, 10½; dark complexion.

GOLDSWORTHY, John Heath; educ. privately in England; stage career, 17 yrs. in England and America with George Edwardes, Shubert, Frohman, and at present with "The Royal Vagabond," Cohan and Harris; screen career, Metro ("The Better Man," "The Yellow Streak," "Debt of Honor," "Corner in Cotton," "The Divorcee"), Fox ("The Second Wife"), Famous Players ("The Red Widow," "Career of Katherine Bush"), Vitagraph ("The Sporting Duchess"). Hght, 6, 1½; wght., 175; brown hair, blue eyes. Ad., Cohan & Harris Theatre, N. Y. C.

GOODWINS, Fred.; b. London, Eng. 1891; educ. Grocer's Co. Coll., London; stage career, with Sir George Alexander, John Drew, Chas. Frohman, etc.; screen career, Edison, Essanay, Christie, Select ("Mrs. Leffington's Boots"), Lois Webber ("For Husbands Only"), Metro ("The Testing of Mildred Vane," "Making Good", Paramount ("Way of a Man With a Maid"), Pathe ("Common Clay"), Jewel-Universal ("Forbidden"). Hght., 5, 10; wght., 150; blond hair and blue eyes.

GORDON, Harris; b. Glenside, Pa.; educ. Cheltenham Acad.; stage career, with Louis Mann; screen career, Reliance, Solax, Famous, Thanhouser ("The Picture of Dorian Gray," "God's Witness," "The Price of Her Silence," "The Girl Who Wanted to Live," "The Image Maker"), Famous Players ("Doublecrossed"), Select Pictures ("The Honeymoon"), Screencraft ("The Prodigal Wife," "Suspense"). Hght., 6; wght., 156; light hair, blue eyes.

GORDON, Huntley; b. Montreal, Can., educ. Bannister Court School, England; screen career, Vitagraph, leads for Ralph Ince, Metro ("The Million Dollar Dollies," "Our Mrs. McChesney"), Blackton ("The Common Cause"), Vitagraph ("Too Many Crooks," "The Unknown Quantity"), Selznick ("The Glorious Lady," "Out Yonder"). Hght., 6; wght., 170; fair complexion, light hair, blue eyes. Add., Bayshore, L. I., N. Y. Bayshore 527.

GORDON James; b. Pittsburgh, Pa.; 10 yrs stage; screen career, Edison, Famous Players, Pathe, Wharton, Paramount ("The Final Close-Up"), Select ("Jacques of the Silver North"), First National ("The Thunderbolt"), directed "The Great Wide Trail," played in "The Girl from Outside," "Behind the Door," "Are You Married?" "Mary's Ankle," "The Sea Wolf," "Experimental Marriage." Member M. P. D. A. Home ad., 4520 Fountain Ave., Los Angeles, Cal., phone 59584.

GORDON, Robert; educ. Polytechnic Junior College; stage career, one season with Hollywood Community Players; screen career, Lasky ("Tom Sawyer," "Huck and Tom," "The Varmint," "Cap'n Kidd, Jr."), Blackton ("Missing," "The Moonshine Trail," "Dawn," "The Blood Barrier"). Hght., 5, 11; wght., 160; light brown hair, dark brown eyes. Ad., 25 W. 45th st., N. Y.

GOWLAND, Gibson; b. England; educ. private schls. Eng.; stage career, legitimate; screen career, Paramount ("White Heather," "Ladies Must Live"), Universal ("Blind Husbands"), Metro ("The Right of Way"), First National ("The Fighting Shepherdess"). Hght., 6; wght., 190; brown hair, blue eyes. Home ad., 1401 El Molino, Los Angeles, Cal.

GRANBY, Joseph; b. Boston, 1885; educ. there; stage career, Castle Sq. and Boston stk., in "Fine Feathers," vaud. for two seasons with Valeska Suratt; screen career, Universal ("Man From Nowhere"), Fox ("Jealousy," "The Victim"), World ("Rasputin, the Black Monk"), Metro ("The Great Romance"), Ince-Paramount ("Black Is White"), Hallmark-Fitzgerald Prod. Hght., 5, 10½; wght., 155; dark complexion, dark hair, brown eyes. Home ad., 518 W. 134th st., Mngsde. 9798, or Green Room Club, N. Y.

GRANT, Edwin J.; b. Cambridge, Mass., 1893; stage career, stock, "Seven Days' Leave," "Getting Together," Ziegfeld Midnight Frolic; screen career, World, Petrova Co., Talmadge Co., Goldwyn, Famous, Fox ("The Panther Woman," "The Safety Curtain," "Private Peat," "Why America Will Win"). In U. S. Service; played in "Atta Boy" and stage mgr. for Frank Tinney, the blackface comedian, now forming dramatic stk. co. of own at Somerville, Mass. Hght., 5, 8; wght., 160; black hair, blue eyes. Ad., 21 Webster ave., Somerville, Mass., and Film Players, 138 W. 46th st., N. Y. C.

GRASSBY, Bertram; b. Lincolnshire, Eng., 1880; educ. U. S.; stage career, rep, stk.; screen career, Selig, Universal, Fox ("Blindness of Divorce"), Griffith ("Romance of Happy Valley"), Para-Gish ("Battling Jane," "The Hope Chest"), Rob-Cole ("Hoopla," "What Every Woman Wants," "The Gray Horizon," "The Illustrious Prince"), Fox ("Cowardice Court"), Amer.-Pathe ("Yvonne from Paris"), Hodkinson ("The Lone Wolf's Daughter"). Hght., 6; wght., 175; black hair and eyes. Ad., 1632 Vista st., Hollywood, and care Willis & Inglis, L. A., Cal.

GRATTAN, Stephen; screen career, Fox ("The Ruling Passion," "The Spider and the Fly," "A Tortured Heart," "The Family Stain," "Should a Mother Tell?"), Brennon Selznick ("The Lone Wolf"), Select ("A Scream in the Night"). Home ad., Hotel Van Courtlandt, N. Y.

GRAVES, Ralph; b. Cleveland, O.; screen career, 2 yrs. Essanay, Univ., World ("Tinsel"), Tourney ("Sporting Life," "The White Heather"), Paramount ("I'll Get Him Yet," "The Home Town Girl," "Out of Luck"), Universal ("The Scarlet Shadow," "What Am I Bid?"), Griffith ("Scarlet Days"), First National ("The Greatest Question"). Hght., 6, 1; wght., 170; brown hair, blue eyes. Ad., L. A. A. Club, Los Angeles, Cal., and Griffith Studio, Mamaroneck, N.Y.

GRAY, Clifford B.; educ. St. Luke's Schl., Wayne, Pa., Lake Forest Acad., Cornell Univ.; stage career, with Lew Fields, Musical Comedy, stock in Chicago, vaud.; screen career, Pathe ("Beulah," opposite H. B. Walthall), Famous Players ("The Crucible," "The Cost"), World ("Nathan Hale," "Daughter of the Sea"), Metro ("Strength of the Weak"). Hght., 5, 8; wght., 150; dark hair, blue eyes. Ad., Friars Club, N. Y.

GREENE, Kempton; b. Shreveport, La., 1890; educ. Friends' Sch., Phila.; stage career, "Checkers"; screen career, Lubin ("A Question of Right," "The Man from the Sea"), Selig ("Brown of Harvard"), Goldwyn ("Our Little Wife"), Oliver Film Corp. ("Craig Kennedy Serial"), Arrow ("A Fool's Gold"), Vitagraph ("Fortune's Child"), Fox ("My Little Sister"), World ("Crook of Dreams," "Forest Rivals"). Hght., 5, 9; wght., 148; blond complexion.

GREENLEAF, Chas. L.; b. Evanston, Ill., 1890; educ. Lake View H. S., Chicago, and Univ. of Minnesota; stage career, legitimate, covering period of 4 yrs., Sari, comedy and Forbes-Robertson Shakespearian plays; screen career, Essanay ("Little Girl Next Door"), 5 characters in "Love's Sweet Dream," Portray Films ("For Her Lover's Sake"). Hght., 5, 11; wght., 165; dark brown hair, blue eyes. Home ad., 4358 Fountain ave., Los Angeles, Cal.; phone 597120.

GRIBBON, Harry; b. 1888 and educ. N. Y. C.; stage career, 15 yrs.; Ziegfeld Follies, Louise Gunning, Shuberts, K. & E., etc.; screen career, Keystone, Fox, Sennett - Paramount ("His Smothered Love," "Ladies First"), Mack Sennett Rural Comedies ("Down on the Farm"), 5-reel comedy for Gt. Western Prod. Co. Home ad., 1337 N. Alvarado, Los Angeles, Cal.; phone 55174.

GRIMWOOD, Herbert; b. Essex, England; educ. Forest School, Eng.; stage career, F. R. Benson Shakespearean Co., heavy leads with Sir H. Beerbohm Tree and for 8 yrs. to Oscar Asche and Lily Brayton; screen career, Douglas Fairbanks Co. ("When the Clouds Roll By"), 2 productions for Jesse Hampton Co. Hght., 5, 8½; wght., 156; iron gray hair, hazel eyes. Home ad., 1825 Argyle ave., Los Angeles, Cal.; phone 579575.

GRISEL, Louis R.; b. N. Y., 1849; educ. Phila.; stage career, "The Lion and the Mouse," "Such a Little Queen," stage mgr. for McVicker's theatre, Chicago; screen career, Pathe (one and two-reel features), Reliance ("Solomon and Son"), Eclair, World ("Broken Chains," "The Crimson Door"), Goldwyn ("The Cinderella Man"), World ("Love in a Hurry," "The Bluffer," "The Moral Deadline"), Artcraft ("His Parisian Wife"), Realart ("Mystery of the Yellow Room").

GROSSMITH, Lawrence b. London, 1877; educ. St. Paul's Coll., London Univ. Sch. and Shrewsbury; stage career, in London, 1896-1915; in U. S. Played Freddy Popple in "Nobody Home"; screen career, J. S. Blackton ("The Common Cause"), Lawrence Grossmith Comedy, 1 reel ("Making Good with Mother"). Ad., Booth theatre, N. Y.

GUISE, Thomas Sheldon; b. Detroit; educ. there; stage career, 35 yrs. with De Wolf Hopper, Francis Wilson, Lillian Russell; screen career, Famous, Savage, Ince, Triangle ("Broadway Arizona," "The Clodhopper," "The Wolf Woman," "The Idolaters," "The Tar Heel Warrior," "The Stainless Barrier"), Rob-Cole ("Josselyn's Wife," "Hearts Asleep," "Woman Michael Married"), Pathe ("The Forbidden Room"), Paramount ("23½ Hours' Leave"). Hght., 5, 10; wght., 175; gray hair and eyes.

— H —

HACKATHORN, George, Juveniles and leads; b. Pendleton, Ore.; educ. there; stage career, "Devil's Auction," "Girl I Left Behind Me"; first exp. at age of 9, stk. and vaud. as singer; screen career, Universal ("Sue of the South," "Heart of Humanity"), Barriscale Features ("Josselyn's Wife"), Lasky ("Too Much Johnson"), Paralta ("A Law Unto Herself"), now with Lois Weber in her first Paramount-Artcraft special with all-star cast, also with Fox and Harold Bell Wright Pictures Corp. Hght., 5, 7; wght., 120; dark brown hair, brown eyes. Ad., Lois Weber Studios.

HACKETT, Albert; educ. private tutorage and Professional Children's School, N. Y. C.; stage career, melodrama, "Traveling Salesman," "Writing on the Wall," with Olga Nethersole, "Just a Woman," with Walter Hampden and Josephine Victor; screen career, Pathe ("Poor Jimmy"), Lubin ("Four Years"), Gaumont ("The House Party"), Edison ("Boy Who Cried Wolf," "The Grail"), Metro ("Dope"), World ("Ginger"), Famous Players ("Come Out of the Kitchen," "Anne of Green Gables"). Hght., 5, 9; wght., 139; brown hair and eyes. Ad., 10 W. 64th St., N. Y. C. Columbus 3875.

HAINES, Robert Terrell; b. Muncie, Ind.; educ. Kansas City pub. schls. and Univ. of Missouri; stage career, starred in "The Darling of the Gods," "Once Upon a Time," "The Spendthrift"; in vaud.; also leading man for Mrs. Fiske, Viola Allen, Olga Nethersole, Grace George; stock star in N. Y., Cleveland, Baltimore, Syracuse; screen career, leads in Equitable, Gaumont, Erbograph ("The Victim"), Art ("The Capitol"). Hght., 5, 10; wght., 174; dark complexion, dark hair and eyes. Ad., Lambs' Club, N. Y.

ACTORS

HALE, Alan; b. Wash., D. C., 1892; educ. Phila.; stage career, stk., vaud., "Rainbow Girl," "Rock-a-Bye Baby," "Friendly Enemies"; screen career, Famous, Peerless ("Scarlet Oath"), Fox ("The Lone Thief"), Selznick ("The Price She Paid"), Metro ("The Whirlpool"), M. H. Hoffman ("One Hour"), Graphic ("Moral Suicide"). Hght., 6; wght., 195; blond hair, blue eyes. Ad., home, 630 W. 135th st., N. Y.; Mngsde 5060.

HALE, Creighton; b. Cork, Ireland; educ. Dublin and London; coming of theatrical family; stage career, from early age, in various London prods.; came to America with Gertrude Elliott's "Dawn of a To-morrow"; appeared in Broadway prods. with John Mason, Holbrook Blinn, Edmund Breeze, in leading roles; screen career, Metro ("Woman the Germans Shot," "Wilson or the Kaiser," "The Thirteenth Chair"), Capellani ("Oh, Boy," "The Love Cheat," "A Damsel in Distress"), World ("The Black Circle"), Griffith production, not yet released. Ad., Great Neck Station, L. I., N. Y.

HALL, Al.; stage career, stk. co., Poli Stk., Payton Stk.; screen career, Arrow ("Deemster"), "Twenty Million Dollar Mystery," H. H. Prod. ("His Way Back"), Fox ("Doing Their Bit," "Miss U. S. A."). Hght., 5, 8; wght., 150; blond hair, brown eyes. Ad., Green Room Club, N. Y.

HALL, Ben; b. & educ. Brooklyn, N. Y.; screen career; 6 yrs. with Imp, Universal, Herbert Brenon; lyr. stage manager for Herbert Brenon; hght., 5, 9; wght. 129; light hair, blue eyes. Now with British & Colonial Kinematograph Co., Ltd., 35 Endell St., Longacre, W. C. 2, London, England.

HALL, Donald; b. Murree, North West Province, East India, Aug. 14, 1878; educ. London, Eng.; stage career, baritone lead in "Florodora" and "The Girl Behind the Counter," played with Anna Held, Fritzi Scheff and other stars in the United States; screen career, Perfection-Kleine ("The Awakening of Ruth"), Metro ("Alias Mrs. Jessup"), Universal ("The Raggedy Queen"), Goldwyn ("The Face in the Dark"), Oliver ("Craig Kennedy Serial") World ("Love and the Woman"), Emory Film Corp. ("The Chosen Path"), Selznick ("The Broken Melody"). Played society and character parts. Hght., 5, 9; wght., 170; light complexion, dark hair, gray eyes. Ad., Green Room Club, N. Y.

HALL, Howard, also scenario writer; b. Evanston, Ill., 1878; educ. State Normal Schl.; stage career, 30 yrs. starred 12 yrs. in own plays; screen career, Pathe, Vitagraph, Equitable, Gaumont ("According to Law"), Beach ("The Barrier"), Metro ("Alias Mrs. Jessup"), Warren Prod. ("Weavers of Life"), France Film Co. ("The Natural Law"), Metro ("The Gold Cure"). Hght., 6, 1½; wght., 185; medium complexion, dark hair, dark eyes. Ad., home, Decatur, Mich., and Green Room Club, N. L.

HALL, Thurston; b. Boston; educ. Winchester, Mass.; stage career, Ben Hur in "Ben Hur," supported Lillian Russell in "Wildfire," Marguerite Clark, Charlotte Walker, Amelia Bingham, "The Only Girl," "Love of Mike," "Have a Heart"; screen career, Fox (Marc Antony in Theda Bara prod., "Cleopatra"), leads in Thos. Ince prod., Paralta, Famous ("Tyrant Fear," "We Can't Have Everything"), C. DeMille ("The Squaw Man"), Universal ("The Weaker Vessel," "The Unpainted Woman"), lead with Gail Kane in "Empty Arms." Now with "Civilian Clothes" at Morosco Theatre, N. Y. Hght., 6; wght., 200; fair complexion, brown hair, gray-blue eyes. Ad., Morosco Theatre, N. Y.

HALL, Winter; b. Christchurch, New Zealand; educ. there; stage career, 15 yrs. in Australia and New Zealand under J. C. Williamson, Ltd., and Brough Fleming Comedy Co.; screen career Lasky ("The Primrose Ring," "The House of Silence," "Till I Come Back to You," "Capt. Kidd, Jr.," "City of Dim Faces," "The Tree of Knowledge"), Metro ("The Red Lantern"), W. S. Hart ("The Money Corral"), Katherine MacDonald ("The Bleeders"). Hght., 6; wght., 185; gray hair, blue eyes. Home ad., 1963 Beachwood Drive, Hollywood, Cal., Holly 3943.

HALLAM, Henry; b. London, 1867; educ. London; stage career, with Frank Wilson, Pauline Hall, own sketch, with Lillian Russell; screen career, Kleine ("Gloria's Romance"), Vitagraph ("Lion and the Mouse," "The Climbers"), Fox "Help, Help, Police," "Never Say Quit," "Kathleen Mavourneen"). Hght., 5, 11½; wght., 179; gray hair, blue eyes. Home ad., 4 W. 109th st., N. Y. Academy 4878.

HALLARD, C. M.; b. Edinburgh, Scotland; educ. Edinburgh Acad. and Univ.; stage career, 30 yrs. with Sir Frank Benson, Sir Herbert Tree, Sir John Hare, Charles Frohman, 3 yrs. doing lead at Drury Lane, "Sealed Orders," "Best o' Luck"; screen career, Samuelson ("The Elder Miss Blossom," "Gamblers All," "The Husband Hunter," "The Edge of Beyond," "The Bridal Chair," "Faith, Hope and Charity"). Hght., 5, 10; wght., 182; gray hair, blue eyes. Home ad., Alvarado Hotel, Los Angeles, Cal.; studio, G. B. Samuelson, Universal City.

HAM, Harry; b. Napanee, Ont.; educ. Yale Univ.; screen career, Famous, Bosworth (supported Elsie Janis), Metro ("Father and the Boys"), Christie ("Tramp, Tramp, Tramp," "A Gay Deceiver," "His Wedded Wife," "Kidding Sister," "He Fell on the Beach," "Down by the Sea," "Crazy by Proxy," "The Honeymooners," "Skirts." Ad., home, Los Angeles Athletic Club. Studio ad., Christie Studio.

HAMER, Fred; b. Lancashire, England; educ. Manchester, Eng.; early career, 10 yrs. in British Army; stage career, 7 yrs. in stk. and as stage mgr., Belasco Theatre and Morosco Theatre, Los Angeles, played in orig. prod. of "Bird of Paradise"; screen career, Majestic ("His Little Pal," "Texas Bill's Last Ride," "Blue Pete's Escape," "Bank Burglar's Fate," "Broken Nose Bailey"), Fine Arts ("Stage Struck," "Man and His Mate"), Griffith "Hearts of the World," "Broken Blossoms"), "The Great Radium Mystery," serial. Ad., Great Western Serial Co., L-Ko Studio, Hollywood, Cal.; home ad., 4412 Sunset Drive, Los Angeles. Holly 971.

HAMILTON, Hale; b. Ft. Madison, Iowa; educ. Shattuck Military Academy and Univ. of Michigan; stage career, Shakespearian repertoire; in Wilton Lackaye's "The Pit," "The Ne'er Do Well," Drury Lane Theatre, London, "Sealed Orders," "A Pair of Sixes"; screen career, Metro ("The Winning of Beatrice," "After His Own Heart," "Full of Pep," "That's Good," "In His Brother's Place," "The Four-Flusher," "Five Thousand an Hour," "Johnny on the Spot"). Hght., 6; wght., 175; light hair, blue eyes. Ad., L. A. Athletic Club.

HAMILTON, Mahlon; b. Baltimore, Md.; educ. there and Maryland Agriculture Coll.; stage career, "The Great Question," "Israel" (Chas. Frohman), "The Chaperon" (Maxine Eliott), etc.; screen career, Pathe, co-star in serial ("The Hidden Hand"), Artcraft ("The Danger Mark"), Select ("The Death Dance"), Kitty Gordon Prod., Mary Pickford ("Daddy Longlegs"), Anita Stewart ("Kingdom of Dreams," "In Old Kentucky," "Ladies Must Live"), Blanche Sweet ("The Deadlier Sex"), Brentwood Films ("The Third Generation"). Hght., 6; wght., 185; light brown hair, blue eyes.

HANNA, Franklyn; b. 1875; stage career, Senator Murphy in "Potash and Perlmutter," lead in "Under Cover," vaud.; screen career, Thanhouser, Edison, Metro, Vitagraph ("The Message of the Mouse," "Richard the Brazen"), M. H. Hoffman ("One Hour"), Metro ("The Gold Cure," "The Great Romance"), World ("The American Way"), Pathe ("The Web of Deceit"). Hght., 6, 2; complexion, dark; blue eyes.

HARDIN, Neil C.; b. Louisiana, Mo.; educ. Univ. of Michigan; early career, lawyer; stage career, 2 yrs. under direction Allan Damaby; screen career, Universal, Pathe ("The Neglected Wife"), Metro ("Johnny on the Spot"), National ("Modern Husbands"), American ("The Dangerous Talent"). Hght., 5, 10½; wght., 150; dark brown hair, dark blue eyes. Ad., c/o Willis and Ingliss, Los Angeles, Cal.

HARE, Francis Lumsden; b. Ireland, 1875; educ. St. Dunstan's, London; stage career, 20 yrs. leading man, Ethel Barrymore, Maude Adams, Billie Burke, John Drew, Gertrude Elliott; screen career, World ("Love's Crucible"), Pathe ("Arms and the Woman"), Famous Players ("The Avalanche"), Films Specials ("Mothers of Men"), Selznick ("The Country Cousin"), L. Weber ("The Blue Pearl"), Crest ("No Children Allowed"). Hght., 6; wght., 175; brown hair. Member Lambs', Players', Dunwoodie Country and Malba Field Clubs, and Green Room Club, London. Ad., home, Ballingarry, Whitestone Landing, L. I., N. Y.

HARKNESS, Carter B.; b. 1888; stage career, 3 yrs. stk.; screen career, Biograph, Edison, Fox ("Gold and the Woman," "Her People"), Thanhouser 2 yrs., Edison ("The Battle of Tapoli"), Rador ("The Spirit of 1917"). Hght., 5, 11; medium complexion. Ad., 118 W. 64th st., N. Y. Col. 8665.

HARLAN, Kenneth; b. N. Y. C., 1895; educ. N. Y. C.; stage career, followed T. Roy Barnes in "See My Lawyer," lead with Gertrude Hoffman, played in "The Fortune Hunter," "Boys of Company B," "The Lottery Man," "The Country Boy"; screen career, Famous Players, Metro, Ince Lois Weber prod. ("The Whim"), Paralta ("A Man's Man"), Bluebird ("The Wine Girl," "Bread," "The Model's Confession," "Midnight Madness," "The Turning Point"). Hght., 5, 11; wght., 165; dark complexion, dark hair, black eyes. Studio ad., Katherine MacDonald Film Corp.

HARLAM, Macey; b. N. Y.; educ. N. Y.; stage career, Frohman, Harris, Klaw and Erlanger, Fiske, Woods, "Yellow Ticket," "Inside the Lines," Otis Skinner, "Eyes of Youth"; screen career, Famous Players, Douglas Fairbanks, World, Triangle ("Nannette of the Wilds," "The Sorceress"), Goldwyn ("Flame of the Desert," "The Woman and the Fool," "Toby's Bow"). Hght., 5, 9½; wght., 155; black hair, brown eyes. Ad., Lambs' Club, N. Y.

HARLAN, Otis; b. Zanesville, O.; educ. Kenyon College, Gambier, O.; became member Chas. Hoyt's Co., "A Black Sheep," producing manager, "The Vanderbilt Cup," "The Parisian Model"; screen career, Selig (plays adapted from Hoyt comedies, "A Black Sheep," "A Stranger in New York," "A Milk White Flag," "A Temperance Town"), Edison ("Regeneration of Sam Packard," "Everybody Loves a Fat Man"), Otis Harlan Co. ("Welcome Home"). Ad., The Otis Harlan Co., Georgia & Gerard ave., Los Angeles, Cal.

HARMON, "Pat"; b. Lewistown, Ill.; educ. there; stage career, 8 yrs. in stk., rep. and circus; screen career, began in 1914, Kinemacolor, Fox, Griffith, Ince, L-Ko, Universal, "Speed Maniac" with Tom Mix, "The Busher" with Charles Ray. Hght., 6; wght., 210; brown hair and eyes. Home ad., 516 W. 42nd Place, Los Angeles, Cal. Phone 28375.

HARRISON, James ("Jimmie"); b. Milwaukee, Wis.; educ. there and Chicago; screen career, stk. for 1 season in Chicago, "Bird of Paradise" Morosco, with Lenore Ulrich, 30 mos.; 1 season vaud. in sketch, with James T. Powers in "Somebody's Luggage"; screen career, Griffith ("The Bad Boy," "Madame Bo-Peep"), Christie Comedies for one year; army 20 mos., 7 mos. in France; with Christie since April 1919 ("Kids and Kidlets," "Reno, All Change," "Nearly Newlyweds," and 14 others. Hght., 5, 9; wght., 140; dark complexion, black hair, brown eyes. Home ad., 1618 Hudson st., Hollywood, Cal., Holly 2728; studio, Christie.

HARRON, Robert; b. N. Y., 1894; left school at 14 to become errand boy in Biograph studios; screen career, from 1908, Biograph, Reliance-Majestic, Fine Arts; in "The Birth of a Nation," "Intolerance," "Near to Earth," Goldwyn ("Sunshine Alley"), Griffith ("Hearts of the World," "The Great Love," "The Greatest Thing in Life," "True Heart Susie," "Romance of Happy Valley," "Girl Who Stayed at Home," "The Greatest Question"). Ad., Griffith Studio, Mamaroneck, N. Y.

HART, Albert; stage career, with Richard Mansfield, and many Broadway successes; screen career, "Big Foot Ben," "Man Hunt," "Sickening Flame," "Driving Power," "Page Mystery," "A Woman of Redemption," "Allies," World ("The Roughneck," "The Little Intruder," "The Quickening Flame," "Miss Crusoe," "The Oakdale Affair"), Independent ("The Challenge of Chance").

HART, Neal, also director; b. Richmond, N. Y.; educ. Bucknell Univ., Lewisburg, Pa.; early career, served as deputy sheriff and marshal in Wyoming, mgr. several large ranches in Wyoming; screen career, in pictures 5 yrs., featured in 2, 3 and 5-reel subjects, Universal ("Man From Montana," "Lion's Claw" serial), Circle H. Film Co. ("When the Desert Smiled"), Capital ("A Knight of Western Land," "The Dead Line," "The Square Shooter," "Sands of the Desert," "Bare Knuckled Gallagher," "The Element of Might"). Hght., 5, 9; wght., 170; dark brown hair, dark blue eyes. Home ad., 6258 Yucca ave., Hollywood, Calif. Phone 57413; studio, Capital Film Co., Inc.

HART, William S.; b. Newburgh, N. Y.; stage career, debut at 19 with Daniel B. Bandmann, supported Modjeska; screen career, Ince, Hart-Artcraft ("Wolves of the Trail," "Blue Blazes Rawden," "The Tiger Man," "Selfish Yates," "Shark Monroe," "Riddle Gawne," "The Border Wireless," "Branding Broadway," "The Breed of Men," "The Poppy Girl's Husband," "The Money Corral," "Square Deal Sanderson," "Wagon Tracks," "John Petticoats"), William S. Hart Co., organized Sept., 1919, Famous Players ("Sand," "The Toll Gate"). Hght., 6, 1; wght., 190; brown hair, blue eyes. Ad., Wm. S. Hart Co., Bates and Effie sts., Hollywood, Calif.

HARVEY, Lew; b. Wisconsin; educ. Portland; stage career, 3 yrs. legitimate; screen career, Texas Guinan Co. ("Not Guilty," "The Lady of the Law," "Bob White"). Hght., 5, 11; wght., 160; black hair, brown eyes. Home ad., 630 W. 4th st., Los Angeles, Calif.; phone 16439.

HATCH, Wm. Riley; b. & educ. Cleveland, O.; studied art for 3 yrs. in Paris; stage career, 35 yrs., opera & mus. com.; with Augustus Daly; "Squaw Man" with Louis Waller in London, "Paid in Full" 2 seasons N. Y., with Wm. Gillett in "Secret Service," "Sherlock Holmes," etc., Wm. Collier "Nothing but Lies"; screen career, with Pauline Frederick, Petrova, Famous Players, "Teeth of the Tiger"; E. K. Lincoln, "The Inner Voice"; Dorothy Gish, "Her Majesty." Hgt., 6; wght. 209; dark brown hair, black eyes. Member Lambs Club. Ad., Bayside, L. I., N. Y.; Bayside 676.

HATTERAS, Richard; educ. Harrow, England; stage career, produced Shaw's "Pygmalion" and "The Second Mrs. Tanqueray" for Mrs. Patrick Campbell, was leading man for Margaret Illington in "The Lie" for a year's tour; screen career, Frohman ("John Gladyde's Honor"), Empire All Star ("The Outcast"), Rapf ("The Struggle Everlasting"), Famous Players ("The Fear Market"). Hght., 6; wght., 140; dark brown hair, hazel eyes. Ad., Hotel Majestic, N. Y.

HATTON, Edward; b. Kentucky; screen career, began in 1915, Vitagraph ("Rose of Wolfville"), Tex. Guinan ("Bob White"), Doubleday ("God's Children"), Bill Farnum ("The Last of the Duanes," "In the Heart of a Fool"). Hght., 5, 9½; wght., 155; blond hair, blue eyes. Home ad., 924 West 6th st., Los Angeles, Calif.

HATTON, Raymond; b. Red Oak, Iowa; educ. there; stage career, played in all the foremost produs. of the day, portraying mostly character roles; screen career, Famous Players, "The Whispering Chorus," "We Can't Have Everything," "Arizona," "Male and Female," "Everywoman," "The Sea Wolf," "Young Mrs. Winthrop," "The Dancing Fool"). Hght., 5, 7; wght., 140; brown hair, blue eyes. Ad., Lasky Studio, Hollywood, Calif.

HAYAKAWA, Sessue; b. Tokio, Japan, 1889; educ. college in Japan and Univ. of Chicago; stage career, 6 yrs. of stage experience in Japan; screen career, Paramount ("City of Dim Faces"), Haworth-Mutual ("His Birthright," "Temple of Dusk"), Haworth-Robertson-Cole ("Bonds of Honor," "A Heart in Pawn," "Courageous Coward," "The Debt," "The Grey Horizon"), Rob-Cole ("The Man Beneath," "The Mysterious Prince," "The Dragon Painter," "The Tong Man," "His Highness—the Beggar"). Hght., 5, 7½; wght., 157; black hair and black eyes. Ad., Haworth Pict. Corp., Brunton Studio, Los Angeles, Cal.

HAYES, Frank; b. San Francisco, 1871; educ. San Francisco; stage career, mus. com., vaud., stock, tour; screen career, Keystone ("Fatty and Mabel Adrift," "Stolen Magic," and over 40 other Keystones), Sunshine Comedies, Vitagraph ("Cupid Forecloses"), Metro ("After His Own Heart"). Ad., 1417 N. Alvarado, L. A., Cal.

HAYS, Wm. T.; educ. Wentworth Military Acad., Lexington, Mo.; stage career, 30 yrs.; screen career, Fox ("Troublemakers," "American Buds," "Eastward Ho!"), Edison ("Awakening of Ruth"), Metro ("The Brass Check"), Selznick ("Sealed Hearts," "Piccadilly Jim"), International ("Miracle of Love"), Mayflower ("Scrap of Paper"). Hght., 5, 11; wght., 160, Gray hair, blue eyes. Ad., 331 W. 45th st., N. Y.; Bryant 2533.

HEARN, Edward; b. Dayton, Wash., 1888; educ. Whitman Coll.; screen career, from 1915, Universal ("Her Bitter Cup," "The Seekers," "The Undercurrent," "Idle Wives," "Treason"), Fox ("Patsy"), Signal Film ("The Lost Express"),

ACTORS

Bluebird ("Lure of Luxury," "The Last of His People"), Bradbury Prods. ("Into the Night"), now with Jack Dempsey in Pathe serial "Daredevil Durant." Hght., 6; wght., 190; brown hair, brown eyes. Home ad., 5807 Lexington, Hollywood, Cal.

HEBERT, Henry J.; b. Providence, R. I.; educ. there and St. Lawrence Univ., Canton, N. Y.; stage career, 12 yrs., "The City," "Brewster's Millions," "Batchelor's Baby," etc., 5 yrs. in Keith's stk.; screen career, Norma Talmadge ("Ghosts of Yesterday"), Famous ("La Tosca"), Doris Kenyon ("Wild Honey"), Fox (supported Wm. Farnum for 2 yrs., "When Fate Decided," "Rose of the West," "Last of the Duanes"), Mary Pickford ("Heart of the Hills"), Fox ("Lost Money," "Sergt. Tim Rierdon"). Hght., 5, 11; wght., 175; dark hair, brown eyes. Home ad., 2208 Fargo st., Los Angeles, Calif. Wilt. 2623; studio, Fox.

HENRY, George; educ. St. Louis Hall, Montreal, Can.; stage career, 25 yrs., started as trick and straight pony rider, with Jas. Melville Family, Wood's Museum, Madison Square theatre; screen career, Fox ("A Fool There Was"), World, Famous Players, Biograph, Vitagraph, ("Grain of Dust," "When It Strikes Home," etc. Hght., 5, 9; wght., 172; mixed gray hair, dark gray eyes. Permanent ad., 229 W. 46th st., N. Y. C.; Bryant 4020.

HERBERT, A. J.; b. Melbourne, Aus.; educ. there, Scotch College; stage exper., came from England with Chas. Frohman, supported Doris Keane in "Romance," Mrs. Pat Campbell in "Pygmalion," Nat Goodwin, Mrs. Fiske, "Fair and Warmer," "The Melting of Molly"; screen career, Famous Players, Metro, Vitagraph, Selig ("In the Hollow of Her Hand," "The Man Who Stayed at Home"), Hodkinson ("As a Man Thinks," "Coax Me"). Selznick ("Country Cousin"), Gaumont ("Making Her His Wife"). Hght., 5, 10; wght., 140; dark brown hair, dark blue eyes. Ad., Green Room Club, N. Y.

HERBERT, Holmes Edward; b. Dublin, Ire., 1882; educ. Rugby, Eng.; stage career, 7 yrs. in U. S., with Billie Burke, Grace George, Ethel Barrymore, Blanche Bates, Elsie Ferguson, in England at Drury Lane, Adelphia, Duke of York's, etc.; screen career, Famous Players ("A Doll's House," "His House in Order"), Tourneur ("My Lady's Garter," "White Heather"), Ince ("Other Men's Wives," "Market of Souls," "Black Is White"), Perrett ("A, B, C of Love"). Hght., 6; wght., 176; fair complexion, light hair, gray eyes. Ad., 36 28th st., Beechhurst, L. I., N. Y. Flushing 3878 J.

HERNANDEZ, George F.; b. Placerville, Cal., 1863; educ. Oakland, Calif.; stage career, 26 yrs., including 4 yrs. in stk.; screen career, Selig, Metro, Lasky, Universal ("The Girl of Lost Lake," "God's Crucible," "The Greater Law," "Cherries Are Ripe," "Be a Little Sport"), Keenan ("The Silver Girl"), Triangle ("Up and Down," "Broadway Arizona"), Lois Weber (Anita Stewart in "Mary Regan"), Haworth-Hayakawa ("Courageous Coward"), Ince-Paramount ("Watch Out, William"), Blackwell, Inc. ("East or West"). ght., 5, 5; wght., 196; dark complexion, brown hair and eyes. Home ad., 2228 Duane st., Los Angeles, Calif.; Wilshire 2647.

HERSHOLT, Jean, also director; b. Copenhagen, Denmark; educ. Jesuit Coll., Copenhagen; stage career, 12 yrs. in Denmark, Sweden and Norway; screen career, NYMP and Universal, 2 yrs.; Triangle one yr. ("The Servant in the House"), First National ("Whom the Gods Would Destroy"), American-Lifeograph ("The Golden Trail," "Men of Today and Tomorrow"). Hght., 5, 11; wght., 180; brown hair, dark blue eyes. Ad., American Lifeograph Co., Portland, Ore.

HEYES, Herbert; b. Little Falls, Wash.; educ. Hill's Mil. Acad., Portland, Ore.; stage career, 12 yrs. in prods. and stk. as leading man and stage director; star of "Truxton King," "The Man on the Box," in tour "Girl of the Golden West"; screen career, leading man with Helen Keller in "Deliverance"; co. star Rex Beach's "Heart of the Sunset"), Ro-Cole ("The Heart of Rachael"); leading man with Theda Bara, Constance Talmadge, May Allison, Emmy Wehlen, Ethel Clayton, etc. Hght., 6, 1½; wght., 190; dark complexion, dark brown hair, hazel eyes. Home ad., Hotel Hollywood, Los Angeles, Calif. Holly 4101.

HICKMAN, Alfred, also scenario writer; stage career, Sir Henry Irving, Augustin Daly, original Little Billy in "Trilby," Frohman, "Man and Superman," David Belasco's "The Lily"; screen career, "The Witch," "Fall of the Romanoffs," "Lone Wolf," Famous Players ("Pursuit of Polly," "Make Believe Wife," "Barnabetta," "Fear Market," "Little Miss Hoover," "Here Comes the Bride"). Hght., 5, 8; wght., 160; brown hair, blue eyes. Ad., 105 W. 55th st., N. Y. C., Lambs Club or N. Y. Athletic Club.

HICKS, Henry C.; b. England; 4 yrs. war service in Belgium and France, 18th Royal Fusiliers and 1st Cavalry Division; screen career, Lasky ("Thou Art the Man," "The Dancing Fool"). Hght., 5, 10; wght., 150; brown hair, blue eyes. Home ad., 2440 W. Pico st., Los Angeles, Calif.; West 1680.

HIERS, Walter; b. Cordele, Ga.; educ. Savannah and Peekskill Mil. Acad.; stage career, vaud. in sketches; screen career, Lasky ("It Pays to Advertise"), Ince ("What's Your Husband Doing?" "Hard Boiled"), Goldwyn ("When Doctors Disagree," "The Fear Woman," "Spotlight Sadie"), Select ("An Experimental Marriage"), First National ("The Turning Point"), Ince ("Bill Henry"). Hght., 5, 10½; wght., 230. Home ad., Engstrum Apts., 623 W. 5th st., Los Angeles, Calif. Main 7374.

HIGBY, Wilbur; b. Churchill, Miss., Aug. 21, 1869; educ. Michigan and Hillsdale Coll.; stage career, 20 yrs., in stk and on road with Otis Skinner, Wilton Lackaye, Marguerite Clark, stk. star at Garrick Theatre, St. Louis, etc.; screen career, Fine Arts ("Intolerance," "Diane of the Follies"), D. W. Griffith ("Broken Blossoms," "True Heart Susie," "I'll Get Him Yet"), American ("Brass Buttons"), Ince ("Homer Comes Home"). Hght., 5, 10½; wght., 180; brown hair, gray eyes. Home ad., 1805 Wilcox ave., Hollywood, Calif.

HILL, Rollo Lee; b. Minneapolis, Minn.; educ. Univ. of M.; stage career, theatre mgr. road, Broadhurst & Currie, stock cos., Minneapolis, leads in stock, Louisville, Ky., Minneapolis; screen career, Thos. H. Ince ("The Idolator"), Triangle ("Station Content," "Lonely Woman"), special prods. ("Old Wives for New," "Men of Today and Tomorrow"), Paramount ("Girls," "The Crystal Globe"), Universal ("The Sign of the Four"). Hght., 5, 11; wght., 165; dark hair and eyes. Ad., P. O. Box 205, Glendale, Calif.; Wil. 172., or Actors' Assn., Hollywood, Calif.

HILLIARD, Harry S.; b. Cincinnati, O.; educ. Cincinnati High and Miami Medical Coll.; stage career, with Wilton Lackaye, Blanche Ring, Florence Reed, Marie Dressler, also in special production of "Mrs. Temple's Telegram"; screen career, Universal, Fox ("Every Girl's Dream"), Metro ("The Successful Adventure"), Universal ("A Romance of Rome"), Fox ("The Sneak," "Cheating Herself"), Bluebird ("Little White Savage"), Triangle ("The Little Rowdy"), Jewel-Univ. ("Destiny"). Member of Lambs Club. Hght., 5, 11; wght., 170; brown hair and eyes. Home ad., 1903 Wilcox ave., Hollywood, Cal.; phone 577939.

HINES, John; b. Golden, Colo., July 25, 1895; educ. Pittsburgh and C. C. of N. Y.; 8 yrs. on stage; screen career. Peerless-World ("Miss Petticoats," opp. Marie Dressler in "Tillie Wakes Up," "Alias Jimmy Valentine"), World ("A Scrap of Paper," "Neighbors," "The Little Intruder," "Heart of Gold," "Three Green Eyes"), Fox ("Eastward Ho!"). Hght., 5, 9; wght., 150; dark hair, brown eyes. Ad., 548 W. 164th st., N. Y. C.

HOFFMAN, Otto F.; b. N. Y. C.; educ. there; stage career, 20 yrs., with Elsie Ferguson in "The Strange Woman," "Spring Main," Louis Mann in "The Cheater," Selwyn's "Coming Home to Roost"; screen career, Ince ("Sheriff's Son," "String Beans," "Nine O'clock Town," "Home Town," "Egg Crate Wallop," "The Busher," "23½ Hours' Leave," "Paris Green"), Goldwyn ("City of Comrades"). Hght., 5, 7½; wght., 130; dark brown hair, dark eyes. Ad., Box 55, Culver City, Calif.; studio, Ince.

HOLDING, Thomas; b. Black Heath, Kent, England; educ. Rugby; stage career, 12 yrs., Edward Terry, Forbes-Robertson, Maxine Elliot, Nazimova; screen career, Famous Players, Morosco (dir. "The Redeeming Love"), Petrova Pictures ("Daughters of Destiny"), Universal ("Vanity Pool"), Fox ("The Danger Zone"), Paramount ("The Lady of Red Butte"), Ro-Cole ("Tangled Threads," "Beckoning Roads"), Goldwyn ("Peace of Roaring River"), Hodkinson ("Lone Wolf's Daughter"). Hght., 6; wght., 172; dark hair, blue eyes. Ad., 1476 Morgan Place, L. A., Cal. Phone 597397.

HOLLAND, Cecil C.; stage career, 5 yrs. legitimate stock and rep.; screen career, 1912, Selig Co., 2 yrs. in army, Morosco ("His Sweetheart," "Pals"), Lasky ("Each to His Kind," "The Bottle Imp"), Selig ("The Crisis," "Garden of Allah," "Gentleman Adventurer," "In Tune With the Wild," "Bloom Center" serial). Ad., instructor at National Acad. of Photoplay Arts, Los Angeles, Calif. Home ad., 2626 W. 9th st., Los Angeles; phone 51036.

HOLLINGSWORTH, Alfred; also scenario writer; b. Nebraska; educ. Pueblo, Colo.; stage career, 14 yrs., Richard Mansfield, E. H. Sothern, Leslie Carter, David Belasco, Daniel Frohman, Klaw & Erlanger, etc.; screen career, Goldwyn ("The Strange Boarder," "Leave It to Susan," "The One Way Trail"), Ince ("23½ Hours' Leave"), Metro ("The Uplifters"), American ("Fair Enough"), Vitagraph ("Adventures of Simple Harry," "The Trail of the Hawk" serial), Metro ("Please Get Married"). Hght., 6; wght., 200; dark brown hair, dark blue eyes. Home ad., 5408 Hollywood blvd., Los Angeles, Calif.; phone 597538.

HOLMES, Stuart; b. Chicago, 1887; educ. Art Inst.; stage career, with Henry E. Dixey in "Mary Jane's Pa"; screen career, Selznick ("The Wild Girl," "The Ghosts of Yesterday," "Poor Rich Man," "When Men Betray," "Sins of the Children"), Norma Talmadge ("The New Moon," "Way of a Woman"), Hallmark ("The Other Man's Wife," "A Dangerous Affair," "Love, Honor and ?"), World ("Dust of Desire," "Little Intruder"), Pathe ("Isle of Jewels," " 15 episode serial). Hght., 6; wght., 182; gray eyes, reddish hair. Ad., care Edward Small, Inc., 1493 Bway, N. Y.

HOLMES, Taylor; b. Newark, N. J.; stage career, "His Majesty Bunker Bean," "The Commuters," "The Third Party," "The Million"; screen career, Essanay ("The Small Town Guy," "Ruggles of the Red Gap," "A Pair of Sixes," "The Rainbow Chaser," "Uneasy Money"), Triangle ("Upside Down," "Taxi," "A Regular Fellow," "Three Black Eyes," "It's a Bear"), Taylor Holmes Prod. ("Nothing But the Truth," "The Very Idea"). Hght., 5, 8½; wght., 150; dark hair, brown eyes. Ad., Friars Club, N. Y. C.

HOLT, Jack; b. Winchester, Va.; educ. V. M. I.; stage exper., 4 seasons stk.; screen career, Universal, Select, Paramount ("The Honor of His House"), Ince-Para. ("A Desert Wooing," "The Marriage Ring"), Select ("Cheating Cheaters"), Paramount ("The Life Line," "Victory"), First National ("A Midnight Romance"), Rob-Cole ("Kitty Kelly, M. D."), Artcraft ("For Better, For Worse"). Hght., 6; wght., 173; dark brown hair and eyes. Ad., Lasky studios, Hollywood, Calif.

HOOSE, Ralph R.; juveniles; b. Mishawaka, Ind., 1900; screen career, Castle studios, Chicago, Comedy Co., "Do the Dead Talk?" Specialty Feature Films ("Within Our Gates"), Micheaux Films. Hght., 5, 3; wght, 122; brown hair and eyes. Ad., Castle Studios, 2232 N. California ave., Chicago, Ill.

HORNE, W. T.; b. Chicago; educ. Conn.; stage career, since 1885; screen career, Vitagraph ("The Enchanted Barn"), the Judge in all Judge Brown's pictures for 2 yrs; ("Surprising Carlotta"), National ("Boys Will Be Boys"), Capitol ("Bare Knuckies"), Universal ("Graft." "Who was the Other Man?," "A Social Buccaneer"), Signal ("The Knotted Cord"). Hght., 5, 10½; wght., 198; grayish brown hair, blue eyes. Ad., 2004 Cahuenga ave., Los Angeles, Calif.; Holly 2780.

HOUDINI, Harry; b. Appleton, Wis.; stage career, since 1883; legitimate, circus, vaud.; screen career, Octogen Film Corp. ("The Master Mystery"), Lasky ("The Grim Game," "Deep Sea Loot"), Cinema Lux., Paris ("Adventures of Houdini in Paris"). Hght., 5, 7; wght., 179; black gray hair; steel blue eyes. Ad., Lasky Studio.

HOUSMAN, Arthur; b. N. Y., 1890; educ. N. Y.; stage career, vaud. comedy parts in N. Y.; screen career, 5 yrs. with Edison, featured for a yr. in 8 comedies, Selig ("Brown of Harvard"), Metro ("Red, White and Blue Blood"), about 1 yr. with Goldwyn ("All Woman," "Bondage of Barbara," "Back to the Woods," "The Gay Lord Quex," "Toby's Bow," "The Blooming Angle"), Tourneur ("The County Fair"). Ad., 395 E. 197th st., N. Y. C.

HOWARD, Charles Ray; b. San Diego, Calif.; educ. there and N. Y. C.; stage career, 3 yrs. stk., rep. and prod., Guy Bates Post in "Omar, the Tentmaker"; screen career, 2 yrs. with Biograph and Edison, Fox ("Every Mother's Son"), H. & H. Prod. ("Soul of a Nation"), World ("Neighbors"), Government Films ("America Was Right"), Herbert Brenon ("Eternal Sin"). Hght., 5, 10; wght., 150; brown hair, light brown eyes. Home ad., 902 Gratton st., Los Angeles, Calif. Bway 140.

HOWARD, George; b. and educ. Philadelphia; stage career, 20 yrs., under Chas. Frohman, Empire Theatre stk., leading man for Ethel Barrymore, Mrs. Leslie Carter, Blanche Walsh; with Faversham & Elliott in "Lord and Lady Algy"; screen career, "The Cup of Chance," with Alice Brady; "Out of the Dark," Vitagraph; "Piccadilly Jim," Selznick. Hght., 6; wght., 170; brown hair, blue eyes. Member Lambs Club. Home ad., 654 St. Nicholas ave., N. Y.; Audubon 6460.

HOXIE, Hart; Lasky ("Blue Blazes Rawden," "Nan of Music Mountain," "Johnny Get Your Gun"), Vitagraph serials ("The Iron Test," "Fight for Millions"), Paramount-Artcraft ("Valley of the Giants," "Told in the Hills"). Ad., 1041 Verdugo Rd., Los Angeles.

HOXIE, Jack; b. Oklahoma; early career, raised on cattle ranch, was cowboy, won several championships as trick and fancy rider of horses; screen career, Lasky, now starring in "Lightning Bryce" serial with National Film Corp., 1116 Lodi st., Los Angeles, Calif. Home ad., 1325 N. Hobart blvd., Hollywood, Calif.; Holly 1213.

HOYT, Arthur; b. Georgetown, Colo.; stage career, 16 yrs. Liebler, H. W. Savage, Hunter Bradford Players, etc.; screen career, Lasky, Universal, Triangle ("The Lash," "Little Partner," "Man Who Took a Chance," "The Showdown," "Broadway Arizona," "Bringing Home Father," "Polly Ann"), "In the Heart of a Fool" with Allan Dwan for Mayflower Photoplay Corp. Ad., Los Angeles Athletic Club, Los Angeles, Calif.

HOYT, Edward N.; b. Auburn, N. Y., 1859; educ. Brooklyn, N. Y.; stage career, many prods., with Joseph Proctor, 1883, MacVickar stk., Chicago, Robert Mantell, Walker Whiteside, "Quo Vadis," many Shakespearean prods., two seasons starring as "Hamlet"; screen career, Edison, Universal, Biograph, Pathe, Metro, Selznick (clergyman in "The Foolish Virgin"), World Film ("The Crimson Dove"), Harry Rapf ("The Struggle Everlasting"), past 15 mos. war work. Hght., 5, 9; wght., 152; gray hair, bald, brown eyes. Home ad., 1793 Montgomery ave., N. Y. C.

HUGHES, Gareth; b. Llanelly, Wales, 1897; educ. there and Paris; stage career, starred in "Everyman," featured in "Salome," "Moloch," "The Guilty Man," "Margaret Schiller," Benjamin in "Joseph and His Brethren"; screen career, C. K. Young ("Eyes of Youth"), Marguerite Clark ("Mrs. Wiggs of the Cabbage Patch"), Florence Reed ("Woman Under Oath"), Norma Talmadge ("The Isle of Conquest"), now with Harry Garson. Hght., 5, 5; wght., 125; fair complexion; brown hair, blue eyes. Home ad., 223 W. 12th st., N. Y. C.; Chelsea 8713; studio, Garson Studios, Los Angeles, Calif.; Wilshire 81.

HUGHES, Lloyd; b. Bisbee, Ariz., 1899; educ. Polytechnic, L. A.; screen career, Paramount ("The Haunted Bedroom"), Jewel ("The Heart of Humanity"), Select ("The Indestructible Wife"), Metro ("Satan, Junior"), Rob.-Cole ("Turn in the Road"), Ince-Para. ("The Virtuous Thief"). Ad., Ince Studio, Culver City, Cal.

HUMAN, Billy; b. Ft. Worth, Tex., 1890; educ. Peacock Mil. Acad., Univ. of Texas; screen career, Universal ("Behind the Lines," "One Wild Night"), Hodkinson ("The Forfeit"), Triangle ("The Unbroken Promise"). Hght., 6; wght., 185; brown hair and eyes.

HUNT, Leslie M.; b. Lafayette, Ind., 1885; educ. Hyde Park, High Schl. and Univ. of Ill.; stage career, "The Squaw Man," "My Lady's Garter," "Penrod," etc.; screen career, Metro ("Life's Whirlpool"), Edison ("Cy Whittaker's Ward," "The Unbeliever"), Goldwyn ("Peck's Bad Girl"), Cummins ("Some Wild Oats"), Realart ("Erstwhile Susan"). With Marie Dressler in "Tilly's Nightmare." Hght., 6; wght., 150; dark hair, blue eyes. Ad., Green Room Club, N. Y.

HUNTLEY, Hugh; educ. Paris and Shrewsbury Schl., Eng.; stage career, with Geo. Edwardes' Co., Daly theatre, London, Juvenile lead for Marie Tempest, juvenile leads in Australia with J. C. Williamson, Ltd., 5 yrs.; screen career, Australian Famous Players ("The Monk and

ACTORS

the Woman"), Famous Players ("His Official Fiancee"), Vitagraph ("The Climbers"). Now with "The Lost Leader" at Greenwich Village theatre. Hght., 5, 10; wght., 160; dark brown hair, brown eyes. Ad., 15 E. Boulevard, Whitestone, L. I., N. Y. Flushing 79-W.

HUNTLY, Fred W.; b. London, 1863 and educ. there; stage career, 1879, Covent Garden theatre, Gilbert & Sullivan, Carleton Opera cos.; Spanish and Philippine wars; screen career, Metro, Morosco ("Johanna Enlists," "Wetona"), Mary Pickford ("Heart of the Hills"), First National ("Kingdom of Dreams," "Daddy Long Legs"), Lasky ("Love's Insurance," "The Sea Wolf"). Hght., 5, 10½; wght., 160; gray hair, hazel eyes. Ad., 2017 Ivanhoe ave., Los Angeles, Cal.

HUTCHINSON, Chas. A.; b. Pittsburgh; educ. Western Univ.; stage career, several Bway successes and vaud. for 8 yrs.; screen career, Triumph, Crystal, Brenon, Solax, Vitagraph, Pathe ("Wolves of Kultur"), Western ("Great Gamble"), All Good ("The Whirlwind"). Hght., 5, 10; wght., 160; dark complexion, hair and eyes. Ad., 2 Arden st., N. Y. C. St. Nich. 3616.

—I—

IRWIN, Boyd; b. Brighton, England; educ. Belfast, Ireland; stage career, 17 yrs. in England and Australia in rep.; screen career, began in 1915 in Australia, with J. C. Williamson Prods., Southern Cross Feature Film Co., Haymarket Picture Corp., all of Australia, as leading man, came to Los Angeles in 1919, lead in "The Sign of the Rat" serial. Hght., 6; wght. 170; brown hair, blue eyes. Home ad., 400 Washington ave., Santa Monica, Calif.; studio, with Bessie Barriscale, Brunton Studios, Los Angeles, Calif.

—J—

JAMEISON, William Edward (Bud); b. Vallejo, Calif., 1894; educ. San Francisco; early career, performer and cafe entertainer; stage career, 4 yrs. in vaud., stk., and on road; screen career, Essanay, Rolin-Pathe ("Lonesome Luke" series), 3 yrs. with Harold Lloyd, 1 yr. with L-Ko. Hght., 6; wght., 270; light complexion, brown hair, blue eyes. Ad., 132 North Hill, Los Angeles, Calif.

JAMES, Gladden; b. Zanesville, O.; educ. Columbus, O.; stage career, child actor at age of 6, later in many prods., "Under the Greenwood Tree," "Way Down East," "The Third Degree," "Officer 666," etc.; screen career, Ivan ("Babbling Tongues"), Select ("Scandal"), Fine Arts ("The Social Secretary"), Pathe ("Mystery of the Double Cross," "Hearts of Love"), Select ("Heart of Wetona"), Vitagraph ("The Midnight Bride"), Curtiss Pict. ("Who's Your Brother"). Hght., 5, 11; wght., 160; light hair, blue eyes. Ad., 1767 Bedford ave., Brooklyn, N. Y.; Flatbush 10335.

JAMES, James Wharton; b. Richmond, Ky.; educ. Wm. Jewell Coll., Mo.; stage exper., stk., instructor Dramatic Art, "Volunteer Players" at Camp Kearney, entertainer for Y. M. C. A. overseas; screen career, Artcraft ("Wild and Wooly"), Universal ("Man Who Dared Goď"), featured in 3 Judge Brown stories, "The Preacher's Son," "Marrying Off Dad," "The Accusing Foe"), Metro ("Almost Married"). Hght., 6; wght. 160; dark brown hair, dark gray eyes. Studio ad., Pickford Co., 5341 Melrose ave., Los Angeles, Cal.

JASMINE, Arthur; b. St. Paul, Minn.; educ. there; stage career, 3 yrs. legitimate; screen career, Essanay ("Broncho Billie's Parents"), Universal ("Man in the Moonlight," "Common Property," "Lasca"). Hght., 5, 7½; wght., 144; dark brown hair, brown eyes. Home ad., 560 N. Hill st., Los Angeles, Calif.; Pico 3337.

JEFFERSON, Thomas; b. N. Y. C.; educ. here and abroad; stage career, many years on stage; screen career, Pathe ("Hands Up"), Metro ("The Spenders"), Goldwyn ("Sis Hopkins"), National ("Tarson of the Apes," "Romance of Tarzan"), Universal ("Beloved Liar"), Fine Arts ("The Fencing Master"), Metro ("Lombardi, Ltd."), Alan Dwan ("Splendid Hazard"). Ad., 2652 Beachwood Drive, Los Angeles, Calif.; phone 577729.

JEFFERY, Hugh S.; b. Belfast, Ireland; educ. Queens Coll., Belfast, Ireland; stage career, 15 yrs., with Robt. Mantell, Robt. Edeson, May Irwin, and in "The Littlest Rebel"; screen career, World, Metro ("Out of the Fog"), S-L Pictures ("Virtuous Men"). Hght., 5, 9½; wght., 160; dark complexion, dark hair, blue eyes. Ad., Green Room Club, N. Y.

JENNINGS, Al; b. Virginia, 1863; educ. Virginia Univ.; early career, lengthy career as outlaw, elected Governor of Oklahoma, later practised law; screen career, began in 1914, now engaged in production of 24 two-reel pictures based upon personal experiences, under contract with the Capital Film Co. Hght., 5, 5; wght., 145; auburn hair, gray eyes. Home ad., 2733 Kenwood ave., Hollywood, Calif.

JOBSON, Edward; b. Phila., Pa., 1864; educ. San Francisco; stage career, with Evans and Hoey, Frank Daniels, Paul Dresser and many others; screen career, Essanay, Balboa, Rob-Cole ("The Mints of Hell"), Fox ("Cheating Herself," "The Merry-Go-Round"), Paramount ("The Egg Crate Wallop"). Hght., 5, 9¾; wght., 245; gray hair, gray eyes. Ad., home, 1626 Vine st., Hollywood, Calif.

JOBY, Hans, also assist. director; b. Kronstadt, Hungary, 1884; educ. Leipsig Conservatory; stage career, 10 yrs. opera singer; screen career, in Denmark and Berlin, Universal, L-Ko. Hght., 5, 6; wght., 180; brown hair and eyes. Home ad., Oak Log Cabin, Laurel Canyon, Hollywood, Calif.; Holly 3662; studio, Century Comedies.

JOHNSON, Emory; b. San Francisco, 1894; educ. Univ. of Cal.; screen career, Essanay, Pathe, Universal ("The Devil's Bondwoman," "The Right to Be Happy," "The Mystery of the Gray Ghost," "My Little Boy," "Green Magic"), Universal ("A Mother's Secret"), Ince-Para ("Green Eyes"), Paramount ("Woman Next Door," "Alias Mike Moran"), American ("Trixie from Broadway," "Put Up Your Hands," "The Tiger Lily," "The Hellon"). Hght., 6, 2; wght., 185; brown hair, blue eyes. Ad., home, 1834 El Cerrita pla., Hollywood, Cal.

JOHNSON, Noble; b. Colorado Springs, Colo.; early career, ranching, stock raising, horse training in Colo., amateur athlete, boxer and endurance runner in N. Y.; screen carer, Universal ("Love Aflame," "Last of Night Riders," "The Human Tiger," "Red Ace," "Bull's Eye," "Lure of the Circus," "Midnight Man," "Beach Comber"), National Film ("Lightning Brice"). Hght., 6, 2; wght., 215; dark hair and eyes. Ad., P. O. Box 31, Universal City, Calif.; Wilshire 6557.

JOHNSTON, J. W.; b. Ireland; educ. N. Y. and Dublin; stage career, Sothern, Frohman, "The Squaw Man," "The Waif," stock; screen career, Pathe, Lasky, Famous ("Destiny's Toy"), Metro ("God's Half Acre," "The Adopted Son," "The Eternal Mother"), Fine Arts ("Fifty-Fifty"), Paramount ("The Test of Honor"), Goldwyn ("Speedy Meade"), World ("The Praise Agent"), Pathe ("Twin Pawns"). Hght., 6; wght., 175; dark hair, dark eyes. Ad., 356 Wadsworth ave., N. Y.

JONES, Buck; b. Vincennes, Ind.; educ. Indianapolis; screen career, Fox ("True Blue," "Riders of the Purple Sage," "Rainbow Trail," "Speed Maniac," "Western Blood," "Square Shooter," "Last Straw"), with Charles Ray in "Sheriff's Son." Hght., 5, 11¾; wght., 173; brown hair, gray eyes. Home ad., 2210 Clifford ave., Los Angeles, Calif.; studio, Fox.

JORDAN, Sid.; b. Muskogee, Okla., 1888; educ. Cherokee Indian sch., Vanita, Okla.; stage career, 101 Ranch Show, Parker Amus. Co.; screen career, Selig ("The Pony Express," "A Mistake in Rustlers," "The Sheriff's Blunder"), Fox ("The Wilderness Trail," "Fighting for Gold," "Rough Riding Romance"). Hght., 5, 10; wght., 170; dark complexion, brown hair and eyes.

JOY, Ernest C.; b. Minneapolis, Minn., 1880; educ. Minnesota Univ.; stage career, 10 yrs. in stock, 5 yrs. under Liebler and Co.; with Wilton Lackaye, Margaret Anglin; screen career, Eclair, Kinemacolor, Thanhouser, Majestic, Lasky-Paramount ("Freckles," "Little Miss Optimist," "The Call of the East," "The White Man's Law," "One More American"), Artcraft ("Johnny Get Your Gun"). Writes scenarios and short stories. Hght., 6; wght. 190; brown hair and blue eyes. Ad., home, 4335 Kingswell ave., Hollywood; studio, Lasky, Hollywood, Cal.

JOYNER, Francis; educ. Houston, Texas; stage career, dramatic stk., road tours with Willard Mack, Shakespeare with Ben Greet; screen career, "The Auction Block," Metro ("Daybreak," "The Brass Check"), Famous Players

("Less Than Dust," "The Copperhead"). Hght., 5, 9; wght., 130; brown hair and eyes. Ad., Green Room Club, N. Y.

— K —

KANN, Marvin; educ. prep. school, 2 yrs. Univ. Washington & Lee; screen career, 1 yr. stk. Bishop Stk. Co., Pittsburgh, Pa.; screen career, Selznick ("Piccadilly Jim," "Red Robin Hood"), etc. Hght., 6; wght., 180; brown hair, gray eyes. Ad., 101 W. 126th st., N. Y.; Morningside 4367.

KARNS, Roscoe; b. San Bernardino, Calif.; educ. Univ. Calif.; stage exper.; stk. in Calif., with Marjorie Rambeau; screen career, Brentwood ("Poor Relations"), now with King Vidor. Hght., 5, 10; wght., 165; brown hair and eyes. Home ad., Seminole Apts., Hollywood, Calif.; studio, King Vidor Productions.

KARR, Hilliard Sinclair; b. and educ. Houston, Texas, 1899; screen career, Master Pict. Co. ("Nathan Busts Into the Movies"), Florida Film ("Hot Sands and Cold Feet"), Sunbeam Comedies ("Work and Win 'Em," "His Conscience His Guide," "A Traveling Man's Temptations," "A Trial by Jury"), Cuckoo Comedies ("Starting Out in Life"). Hght., 5, 10; wght., 318; red hair, blue eyes. Ad., home 3501 Burlington ave., Houston, Texas.

KEATON, "Buster"; b. Kansas; stage career, vaud., 16 yrs. with "The Three Keatons"; screen career, Arbuckle-Paramount ("The Butcher Boy," "A Reckless Romeo," "Rough House," "His Wedding Night," "Fatty at Coney Island," "A Country Hero," "The Bell Boy," "Moonshine," "Good Night, Nurse"). Hght., 5, 6; wght., 140; dark complexion, black hair, brown eyes. Home ad., Long Beach, Cal. Ad., Arbuckle Co., Lehrman Studios, Culver City, Calif.

KEELING, Robert Lee; stage career, with Robert Mantell and Robert Hilliard; screen career, Famous Players ("The Counterfeit"), Vitagraph ("Mind-the-Paint Girl," "Over the Top"), "La Belle Russe," "Wives of Men," "Her Husband's Honor," Fox ("Putting One Over"), Screen Classics ("Shadows of Suspicion"), Selznick ("Out of the Night"). Hght., 5, 11; wght., 140; light brown hair, hazel eyes. Ad., 135 E. 34th st., N. Y.; Murray Hill 1074.

KEENAN, Frank; b. Dubuque, Ia.; educ. Boston Coll.; stage career, stk., rep., vaud.; with Joseph Proctor, Boston Museum Co., Charles Hoyt, succeeded James A. Herne in "Hearts of Oak," David Belasco; screen career, Ince ("The Thoroughbred"), Universal, Pathe ("Loaded Dice," "More Trouble," "The Night Stage," "Tod of the Times," "Statesright Raver," "The Defender"), Keenan-Pathe ("Gates of Brass," "The Silver Girl," "World Aflame," "The False Code," "Brothers Divided"). Hght., 6, 1½; wght., 170; light hair, blue eyes. Ad., Frank Keenan Prod., Inc., Brunton Studios, Hollywood, Cal.

KELLARD, Ralph; b. N. Y. C.; educ. there; stage career, 3 seasons mngt. David Belasco, with David Warfield in "Music Master," in orig. prod. of "The Warrens of Virginia," 3 seasons owner and star of Ralph Kellard Stk. Co., leading man in orig. N. Y. prods. of "Rebecca of Sunnybrook Farm," "Eyes of Youth," "Nancy Lee," "Over Here," "A Stitch in Time"; screen career, Pathe ("The Shielding Shadow," "Pearl of the Army," "The Hillcrest Mystery"), Select ("Scream in the Night"), Hallmark, Famous Players ("The Cost"). Hght., 6; wght., 155; light complexion, red-brown hair, brown eyes. Home ad., Post Road, Rye, N. Y.

KELLY, Paul; b. Brooklyn, N. Y., 1899; educ. private schls. and tutors; stage career, child actor with David Warfield in "Grand Army Man," with Robert Mantell Co. in "The Confession," "Mother," "Ninety and Nine," in Belasco's "A Good Little Devil," in "Seventeen," "Penrod," "Golden Age"; screen career, Vitagraph ("Jarr Family" series and "Buddy" series), Edison ("Star Spangled Banner," "Knights of the Square Table"), Artcraft (("Anne of Green Gables"), Government ("Fit to Fight"). Now with H. Savage in "Shavings." Hght., 5, 11; light brown hair, dark eyes. Ad., 82 Schermerhorn st., Brooklyn, N. Y.

KENNEDY, Ed.; b. Monterey Co., Cal., 1890; stage career, 2 in vaud., 2 yrs. in mus. com. with "A Stubborn Cinderella," "The Alaskan"; screen career, Keystone ("A Game Old Knight," "Oriental Love," "The Lost Baby"). Hght., 6, 1; wght., 210. Studio ad., Fox Sunshine Studio, Hollywood, Calif.

KENNY, Colin; b. Dublin; educ. Rugby, England; stage career, 10 yrs. legit.; screen career, Lois Weber ("Price of a Good Time"), Metro ("Unexpected Places"), National ("Tarzan of the Apes," "Return of Tarzan"), Goldwyn ("Girl from Outside," "Toby's Bow"), Selznick ("Blind Youth"). Hght., 5, 11; wght., 170; dark brown hair, dark green eyes. Home ad., Melrose Hotel, Los Angeles, Calif., Pico 1121.

KENT, Charles; b. London, Eng., 1852; educ. Dulwich Coll.; stage career, from 1875 to 1906; screen career, Vitagraph ("Scarlet Runner," "The Enemy," "Whom the Gods Destroy," "Soldiers of Chance," "Miss Dulcie from Dixie," "The Gamblers," "Kennedy Square," "Daniel," "Duplicity of Hargraves"). Ad., 92 Remson st., Brooklyn, N. Y.

KENT, Cranfurd; b. London; educ. there; stage career, mus. com., "Deep Purple," etc.; screen career, Goldwyn ("Thais"); Famous Players ("The Danger Mark," "Ordeal of Rosetta," "Prince Cosmo," "Good Gracious, Annabelle," "Broadway Jones," "Career of Katherine Bush," "Come Out of the Kitchen"), Metro ("Kildare of Storm"), Edgar Lewis ("Other Men's Shoes"), Fox ("Thou Shalt Not"), Realart ("Sinners"). Hght., 5, 10; wght., 156; dark brown hair, dark gray eyes. Ad., Lambs Club, N. Y.

KEPLER, Edward; educ. Austria and Switzerland; stage career, Vienna, Amsterdam, Holland, Petrograd, Berlin, Irving Place Theater, N. Y.; screen career, Herbert Brenon ("Empty Pockets"), Metro ("Poor Rich Man"), Deitrich-Beck ("The Bandbox"), American Cinema ("The Inner Voice"), Norma Talmadge ("Woman That Gives"). Hght., 5, 9; wght., 134; brown hair, dark gray eyes. Ad., 200 W. 52nd st., N. Y.; Circle 3660.

KERRIGAN, Jack Warren; b. Louisville, Ky., 1889; educ. Chicago Univ.; stage career, Klaw & Erlanger prods. "The Road to Yesterday," "Brown of Harvard"; screen career, Essanay, American (leads for 3 yrs.), Universal ("Rory o' the Bogs," "Terrence O'Rourke," "The Dollar Bid," "Prisoner of the Pines," "Live Sparks," "$30,000," now with own company producing at Brunton Studios ("The Joyous Liar," "The Dream Cheater," "One Week End." Hght., 6, 1; wght., 190; black hair, hazel eyes. Home ad., 1743 Cahanga ave., Hollywood, Calif.

KERRY, Norman; b. N. Y.; educ. St. John's Military Acad., Annapolis, Md.; screen career, Paramount-Artcraft, "The Little Princess," "Amarilly of Clothesline Alley"; Select, "Up the Road With Sally," "Good Night, Paul"; Allan Dwan for Mayflower, "Soldiers of Fortune," "A Splendid Hazard." Hght., 6, 2; wght., 180; dark hair, hazel eyes. Ad., 1745 McCadden place, Los Angeles, Calif.; Brunton Studio.

KILGOUR, Joseph; b. Ayr, Ont., Canada; educ. Canada and England; stage career, 20 yrs., leading man with Henrietta Crossman, Mrs. Fiske and others, "Arizona," "The Easiest Way," "Ready Money," etc.; screen career, Vitagraph, "Thou Art the Man," "The Writing on the Wall"; Select, "The Easiest Way"; Metro, "The Divorcee," etc. Hght., 5, 11; wght., 200; dark brown hair, dark gray eyes. Permanent ad., Garden Court Aprts., Hollywood, Calif.; Holly 3420.

KIM, Sam; b. China; educ. China, Korea, Japan and America; early career, general in Chinese army; stage career, "Daughter of Heaven," etc.; screen career, Chinese Ambassador in "Woman Who Gave," double of Houdini in Houdini serial, "Lightning Raider," serial with Pearl White, "Spirit of Poppies," "Lost Battalion," "Isle of Jewels" serial, "Faith and Fortune," lead with Helen Holmes, "Green God," "Two American Buds," "Inner Voice." Plays Hindoo and Indian parts. Hght., 5, 8; wght., 165. Ad., 170 W. 126th st., N. Y. C.; Mngside 5639.

KIMBALL, Edward Marshall; b. Keokuk, Ia., 1859; educ. Collegiate Inst., Baraboo, Wis.; 40 yrs. on legit. stage, stk., operatic and vaud. exper., "The Stranger," "A Girl From Rector's," etc.; screen career, Select, "The Common Law," "Magda"; Vitagraph, "The Christian," "David Garrick"; World, "The Hidden Fear"; to be featured in "Old Jed Prouty." Hght., 5, 10; wght., 225; gray hair and eyes. Home ad., 1515 Cerro Gordo st., or 2425 S. Western ave., L. A., Calif.

ACTORS

KING, Emmett C.; b. Griffin, Ga.; educ. So. Georgia Coll.; stage career, James O'Neil in "Monte Cristo," Frank Mayo in "Puddin' Head," leading man with Mrs. Patrick Campbell, appeared in "Everywoman," "Experience," with George Arliss in "Alexander Hamilton"; screen career, with Madge Kennedy in "The Fair Pretender"; Metro ('In His Brother's Place," "Please Get Married"), Goldwyn ("The Fear Woman"), with J. Warren Kerrigan in "In One Week End," B. B. Features ("Beckoning Roads"), Allan Dwan Prod. ("In the Heart of a Fool"). Hght., 6; wght., 185; gray hair; blue eyes. Ad., Hotel Rosslyn, L. A., Calif.

KIRKLAND, Hardee; b. Savannah, Ga.; educ. West Point; stage exper., McKee-Rankin stk., "Innocence," with Pauline Frederick, "The Woman," Belasco; screen career, Fox, "Les Miserables"; Mayflower, "The Splendid Hazard"; Geo. Loane Tucker, "Ladies Must Live," with Hazel Dawn in "The Feud Girl." Hght., 5, 11; wght., 175; dark hair, tinged with gray; dark blue eyes. Home ad., 5553 Hollywood blvd., Hollywood, Calif.; phone 597139.

KIRKWOOD, James; b. Grand Rapids, Mich.; educ. there; stage exper., 18 yrs.; screen career, Biograph, Reliance, Universal, Mutual, American, Keeney, "Marriage of the Underworld"; Fox & Famous Players 1918; "The Struggle Everlasting," "Eve's Daughter"; First National, directed Jack Pickford in "In Wrong"; Allan Dwan for Mayflower, "The Luck of the Irish," "In the Heart of a Fool." Hght., 6; wght., 180; sandy hair, blue eyes. Home ad., 725 Rodea ave., Beverly Hills, Los Angeles, Calif.

KLEIN, Robert; b. Paris, 1882; educ. Charlemagne Coll., Paris; stage career, dancing; screen career, American ("Lure of the Mask," "The Idol," "Secretary of Frivolous Affairs," "The Bride's Silence," "Charity Castle," "Southern Pride"), Mutual ("Whose Wife?" "Annie for Spite," "For the Family Name," "Souls in Pawn"), Fox ("Married in Haste").

KOLKER, Henry; also director; educ. Quincy, Ill.; stage career, 20 yrs., 15 yrs. annual appearing in N. Y. as leading man in B'way prods.; screen career, Kleine ("Gloria's Romance"), "The Shell Game," "Social Hypocrites," "House of Glass," "Wilson or the Kaiser"), Metro (played in "The Parisian Tigress," "Blackie's Redemption," with Nazimova in "The Red Lantern"), Rob-Cole (directed "Woman Michael Married," played in "Her Purchase Price"), directed "The Third Generation." Home ad., 1764 N. Sycamore, L. A., Calif.

KORTMAN, Robert; b. Phila.; educ. England & Germany; early career, in U. S. Cavalry; screen career, Ince, "Cash Parrish's Pal," "Shooting-Iron Parson," "The Waifs," "The No-Good Guy," "Captive God"; Para-Artcraft, "The Narrow Trail," "Square Deal Sanderson," "Radial Mystery"; with A. E. F. until discharged in March, 1919. Home ad., Marine Apts., Ocean Park, Calif.; phone 5055.

KOUPAL, T. Morse; b. N. Y., 1890; educ. City Coll.; stage career, with Mrs. Louis James; Edith Wynne Matthison, Charlotte Walker; screen career, Knickerbocker ("Tides of Time"), Gaumont ("Capital Punishment," "Unsuspected Isles"), Charter Features, Metro ("Out of the Fog"). Hght., 6; wght., 185; light complexion, sandy hair, blue eyes. Ad., 240 W. 122d st., N. Y. C.

— L —

LA CROIX, Emile; b. Alsace, France; stage career, 35 yrs. on legitimate stage, 3 yrs. stk.; screen career, (Richelieu in "The Three Guardsmen," "Runaway Princess," Pharaoh in "Joseph and His Brethren," "Yellow Menace"), Peerless-World ("Brand of Satan"), World ("A Broadway Saint"). Hght., 5, 11; wght., 170; white hair, gray eyes. Home ad., 251 W. 48th st., N. Y. C.

LAIDLAW, Roy; b. Canada; educ. there; stage career, 12 yrs. stk. and road cos.; screen career, Ince, Paralta ("His Robe of Honor," "Honor's Cross," "With Hoops of Steel"), Curwood-Carver ("Back to God's Country"), J. Warren Kerrigan ("Live Sparks"), J. D. Hampton ("The Weaker Sex"). Hght., 5, 10; wght., 160; gray hair, dark blue eyes. Home ad., R. F. D. 7, Box 733, Los Angeles, Calif.; phone 70004.

LANDIS, Cullen; screen career, Universal ("The Outcasts of Poker Flat"), American ("Where the West Begins"), Goldwyn ("Upstairs," "Jinx," "Almost a Husband," "Girl From Outside").

LANE, Charles; educ. high and prep. schools; stage career, 25 yrs. under mgmt. Chas. Frohman, David Belasco, Klaw & Erlanger, Arthur Hopkins, Shuberts, etc.; screen career, Essanay ("Ruggles of Red Gap"), Famous Players ("Mrs. Black Is Back," "Man From Mexico," "Wanted—A Husband," "Dr. Jekyl and Mr. Hyde"), Cosmopolitan, "The Restless Sex." Hght., 6, 1; wght., 180; gray hair, brown eyes. Ad., 130 W. 44th st., N. Y.

LANNING, Frank; b. Marion, Iowa; educ. Marion and Cedar Rapids; stage career, with Blanche Bates in "Girl of the Golden West," J. D. Hampton ("The Prodigal Liar," "The Mints of Hell," "Bare Fisted Gallagher," "Betty and the Prince," "The Blue Bandanna," "A Sage Brush Hamlet," "House of a Thousand Candles"), Morosco ("Huckleberry Finn"), B. B. Hampton ("Desert Gold"), Carlyle Blackwell ("The Half Breed"). Ad., 1135 N. Madison, Los Angeles, Calif.; phone 597532.

LANOE, J. Jiquel; b. Britanny, France; stage career, with George M. Cohan, Leslie Carter, Alcazar stk. in San Francisco; screen career, 5 yrs. with D. W. Griffith, Famous Players ("The Eternal City"), Allan Dwan ("A Splendid Hazard"). Hght., 5, 8; wght., 160; dark hair, brown eyes. Home ad., New Hollywood Apts., Hollywood, Calif.

LA RENO, Dick; b. Ireland; educ. N. Y. C.; stage career, 15 yrs. on legit. stage, 10 yrs. vaud., 5 yrs. with circus; screen career, Lasky ("Squaw Man," "Cameo Kirby"), Fox ("The Hell Ship," "Camouflaged"), Universal ("The Beach Combers"), Hampton ("The Blue Bandanna"), Frank Keenan ("The World Aflame"), J. Warren Kerrigan ("A White Man's Chance"), Dustin Farnum ("A Man's Fight"), known as the Sheriff of the Movies. Hght., 6; wght., 218; iron gray hair, dark brown eyes. Home ad., 1411 Gordon st., Hollywood, Calif.; Holly 4019.

LARKIN, George; b. N. Y., 1890; educ. privately; stage career, circus, vaud., stk.; screen career, Diano Film Co. ("Wolf Face" serial, "Coming of the Law," "Zongar"), Astra serial ("Hands Up"), Wistaria ("Lurking Peril"), Pathe ("Tiger's Trail," "Terror of the Range," "Border Raiders"). Hght., 5, 8½; wght., 165; dark hair and eyes. Ad., care Ed. Small, 1493 Bway, N. Y. C.

LA ROCQUE, Rod; b. Chicago; educ. Nebraska; stage career, stk., legitimate, vaud.; screen career, Essanay, Goldwyn ("The Venus Model," "A Perfect 36," "Hidden Fires"), Mutual ("The Kaiser Bride"), Famous Players ("Easy to Get"), American Cinema ("Greater Than Love"). Hght., 6; wght., 175; dark hair and eyes. Ad., Green Room Club, N. Y.

LARSON, Oscar M.; also asst. director; b. Stockholm, Sweden; educ. there and Chicago, Ill.; stage career, with Lincoln J. Carter and Lorin J. Howard Stk. Co., Chicago, Ill.; screen career, Universal ("Bedford's Hope"), Rolin-Pathe ("Kicking the Germ Out of Germany"), W. H. Clifford Co. ("Democracy"), Biograph ("The Battle of Truth"), Universal ("From Dawn to Dark"). Hght., 5, 7; wght., 160; light brown hair, dark blue eyes. Home ad., 406 Court st., Los Angeles, Calif.; Pico 680.

LAW, Burton; b. Ouray, Colo., 1880; educ. Stern's Acad., Chicago; stage career, burlesque and comedy, stock; screen career, Thanhouser, Universal ("Broken Coin," "Sign of the Crescent," "The Sea Lily," written by himself, "A Mountain Tragedy," "Treason," "Like Wildfire"), Bluebird ("Who Will Marry Me?"), Fox ("Cowardice Court"). Hght., 5, 10; wght., 170; dark complexion, black hair, brown eyes.

LAW, Walter; b. Dayton, Ohio, 1878; educ. Ohio State Univ.; stage career, original cast of "Quo Vadis," starred for 5 yrs. in "The Sign of the Cross," 10 yrs. vaud.; screen career, Fox ("The Darling of Paris," "Camille," "The Heart of a Lion," "The Greatest Love," starred in "War Bride's Secret"), Goldwyn ("A Perfect Lady"), Acme ("The Thirteenth Chair"), Fox ("If I Were King"). Hght., 6, 1; wght., 220. Ad., Green Room Club, N. Y.

LAWRENCE, W. E.; b. Brooklyn, 1893; educ. there; artist's model for Christy, Leyendecker; screen career, Reliance-Majestic ("The Battle of the Sexes"), Fine Arts ("Old Folks at Home," "Intolerance"), Artcraft ("The Little Princess"), Triangle ("The Passion Flower"), Sunshine ("Damaged No-Goods"), Para. ("Mile-a-Minute Kendall"), Vitagraph ("The

Girl Woman"). Hght., 5, 10½; wght., 180; black hair, blue eyes.

LEDERER, Otto; b. Prague, Bohemia; educ. Vienna; stage career, opera in Vienna, Irving Place theatre; screen career, Selig, Vitagraph ("Mr. Aladdin of Broadway," "The Lady Sheriff," "Red Prince," "Dead Shot Baker," "The Flaming Omen," "The Woman in the Web," "The Diplomat of Wolfville," "Cupid Forecloses," "Over the Garden Wall"), now in Japan. Hght., 6; wght., 170½; dark eyes, black hair. Ad., 1852 Hillcrest ave., Hollywood, Cal.

LEE, Harry; b. Richmond, Va., June 1, 1872; educ. private and parochial schl.; stage career, 1893 with Fred Bryton in "Forgiven"; screen career, Famous Players ("Lady Eileen"), Goldwyn ("Friend Husband," "Hell Cat"), De Luxe ("Twilight"), Keeney ("Romance of the Underworld"), Triangle ("Upside Down"), Empey ("The Undercurrent"), Buffalo M. P. Corp. ("Spirit of Kings"), now with Guy Empey Pict. Hght., 5, 10½; wght., 171; fair complexion, dark brown hair, blue eyes. Home ad., 145 W. 12th st., N. Y.; Chelsea 5774.

LE GUERE, George; b. New Orleans, La.; educ. Georgetown Univ., Wash., D. C.; stage career, with Forbes-Robertson, Margaret Anglin, Charlotte Walker, Wm. Hodge, Jane Cowl, David Warfield, etc., in "The Man From Home," etc.; screen career, Essanay, Metro, Famous, Pathe, Brenon ("Third Floor Back," with Forbes-Robertson), Select ("Cecelia of the Pink Roses," "The Way of a Woman"), World ("The Hand Invisible"), Ind. ("Sun Up"). Hght., 5, 9; wght., 135; blond complexion. Home ad., 8 W. 107th st., N. Y.; Acad. 1445.

LEIBER, Fritz; stage career, in People's Stock, Chicago, with Julia Marlowe, Robt. B. Mantell, David Warfield, Mme. Petrova; screen career, Metro, Fox ("Cleopatra," "If I Were King"). Home ad., Atlantic Highlands, N. J.

LEVERING, James; b. Bristol, Eng., 1861; educ. Belgrave Coll., Bristol, and Oxford Univ.; stage career, with Sir Henry Irving, also in "Silver King," "Dr. Jekyll and Mr. Hyde," "Private Secretary," etc., and several yrs. in stk.; screen career, with Edison, Pathe, Lubin, Norma Talmadge, Florence Reed, Gaumont ("Rain of Death," "Dead Alive"), Solax ("Pit and Pendulum," "Brennan of the Moor"), Frohman Amuse. ("My Own United States"). Hght., 5, 6; wght., 145. Home ad., 132 Manhattan ave., Jersey City, N. J.

LEWIS, B. A.; screen career, Mary Pickford ("The Heart of the Hills," "The Hoodlum"), Anita Stewart ("The Fighting Shepherdess"), Universal ("The Unique Crook"), C. K. Young ("Eyes of Youth"). Ad., Union League Club, Los Angeles, Calif.

LEWIS, Mitchell; b. Syracuse, N. Y.; educ. Syracuse Univ. and Naval Acad.; 6 yrs. in U. S. Navy; stage career, "The Two Orphans," with Wm. Faversham 3 yrs., "The Squaw Man" in Eng., "Chinese Honeymoon," "Everywoman," with Nazimova in "'Ception Shoals"; screen career, first Metro pictures of Harold Lockwood and Viola Dana, Rex Beach ("The Barrier"), Select ("Children of Banishment," "Code of the Yukon"), Screen Classics ("Burning Daylight," "A Daughter of the Snows," "Smoke Bellew"). Hght., 6, 1; wght., 195; black hair, brown eyes. Ad., 418 Mason Bldg., Los Angeles, Calif.

LEWIS, Ralph; b. Englewood, Ill.; educ. Northwestern Univ.; stage career, rep., mus. com., with Wilton Lackaye, Jas. K. Hackett, Julia Marlowe, 4 yrs. vaud.; screen career, Fine Arts, Fox ("Jack and the Beanstock," "Talk of the Town"), Mary Pickford ("The Hoodlum"), C. K. Young ("Eyes of Youth"), Douglas Fairbanks ("Till the Clouds Roll By"), starring in "Common Sense." Hght., 5, 10; wght., 180. Home ad., 6267 Yucca, Los Angeles, Calif.

LEWIS, Sheldon; b. Phila., Pa.; stage career, 20 yrs. in stk., starring; leading man for Mrs. Fiske, Ada Rehan, Blanche Walsh, and with Wm. Brady's prod. "Life"; screen career, Pathe ("The Clutching Hand," in "The Exploits of Elaine," "The Iron Claw," "The Hidden Hand," "Wolves of Kultur"), Virginia Pearson Photoplays, 1919-20. Home ad., 464 Riverside Drive, N. Y. C.

LEWIS, Walter P.; b. Albany, N. Y., June, 1871; educ. Albany; stage career, Zieke Pettingill with "Quincy Adams Sawyer," "Quo Vadis," "David Harum"; vaud.; screen career, "Seven Pearls," "Out of a Clear Sky," "Pals First," "To Hell With the Kaiser," "The Avenging Trial," Vitagraph ("Man Who Might Have Been"), First National ("A Woman Under Oath"), Willat & Shurtliff ("The Star Rover"). Hght., 6, 1; wght., 180; light hair, blue eyes. Home ad., 237 W. 107th st., N. Y.; Acad. 490.

LINCOLN, E. K.; b. Johnstown, Pa.; stage career, stk. 4 yrs.; also "The College Widow," "Strongheart," "The Squaw Man," "The Virginians," "The Woman"; screen career, World, Goldwyn, Perret Prod. ("For the Freedom of the World," "Lafayette, We Come," "Stars of Glory"), Hodkinson ("Fighting Through," "Desert Gold"), S. L. Pict. ("Virtuous Men" and "The Inner Voice"), Western, society and character roles. Hght., 6; wght., 185; black hair and hazel eyes. Owns modern m. p. studios at Grantwood, N. J., and Blandford, Mass. Ad., 110 W. 40th st., N. Y.

LINCOLN, Elmo (Otto Elmo Linkenhelt); b. Rochester, Ind., Feb. 6, 1889; educ. there; stage career, Holden Stk. Co., 2 seasons; screen career, in D. W. Griffith's "Birth of a Nation," "Intolerance," Fox ("Treasure Island"), National ("Tarzan of the Apes," "The Romance of Tarzan," "The Kaiser, the Beast of Berlin"), "Elmo the Mighty," "Beachcomber," "Fighting Through." Hght., 5, 11½; wght., 200; brown hair, blue eyes. Home ad., 2719 Sunset blvd., Los Angeles, Calif.; studio, Universal.

LINDER, Max; b. Bordeaux, France; educ. there and Paris; stage career, stk. in Europe; screen career, Pathe (Max comedies), Essanay (wrote, dir. and starred in "Max Comes Across," "Max in a Taxi," "Max, the Heartbreaker," "Max Plays Detective," "Max Wants a Divorce"); fought in war, wounded at Aisne; proposed for Knight of Legion of Honor Cross for services rendered his country; has just returned to America. Hght., 5, 4; wght., 125; dark complexion, black hair, brown eyes. Ad., Beverly Hills, Los Angeles, Calif., and 229 W. 42d st., N. Y.

LINGHAM, Thomas; b. Indianapolis, Ind., 1874; stage career, with James O'Neill, E. H. Sothern, Robert Mantell; screen career, Kalem ("Stingaree" series), Signal ("Medicine Bend," "Manager of B. & A.," "A Lass of the Lumberlands," "The Lost Express"); ice skater. Hght., 6; wght., 185; complexion brunette, green eyes, dark brown hair. Ad., 201 E. Acacia st., Tropico, Calif.; studio ad., Ruth Roland Co., Horsley Studio.

LITTLEFIELD, Lucien L.; b. Richmond, Va.; educ. Staunton Mil. Acad., Staunton, Va.; studied at dramatic schl. in N. Y.; stage career, stk. in San Antonio, Tex., in various sketches; screen career, Imp, Rex, Lasky ("Joan of Arc," "The Miser," "The Gutter Magdalene," "The Golden Fetter"), Lasky-Paramount ("The Hostage"), Paramount-Artcraft ("Everywoman"). Hght., 5, 11; wght., 145; blond hair and green eyes.

LIVINGSTON, Jack; b. St. Albans, Vt.; educ. Chicago, Ill.; stage career, six yrs. legit.; screen career, in addition to having been featured, has played leads opposite Vivian Martin, Dorothy Dalton, Peggy Hyland, Bessie Barriscale, Jane Novak and others; 6 yrs. in pictures. Hght., 6; wght., 175; dark brown hair, dark blue eyes. Home ad., 1230 Gardner st., Los Angeles, Calif.; phone 577810.

LLOYD, Harold C.; b. Nebraska, 1893; educ. Denver, Omaha and San Diego; stage career, began at age of 12; stk. and road shows; screen career, Universal, Edison, Keystone, was original Lonesome Luke in those series; Pathe, 52 one-reel Lloyd comedies, 2-reel comedies ("Bumping Into Broadway," "Capt. Kidd's Kids," "His Royal Slyness," "From Hand to Mouth"). Hght., 5, 9; wght., 150; black hair, blue eyes, light complexion. Home ad., 369 South Hoover st., Los Angeles, Calif.; studio ad., Rolin Film Co., Court and Hill sts., Los Angeles.

LOCKNEY, J. P.; b. Philadelphia; educ. there; stage career, stk., with John McCullough; wrote "The Hidden Crime" and "The Girl With the Taking Way" (vaud. sketch), in which he toured; screen career, 5 yrs. with Ince-Paramount ("The Silent Man," "String Beans"), Paramount ("Hay-foot, Straw-foot," "The Sheriff's Son," "Greased Lightning," "The Egg Crate Wallop"). Hght., 5, 10; wght., 190; dark hair, brown eyes. Studio ad., Ince, Los Angeles.

LONG, Captain Walter; b. Milford, N. H., 1884; educ. Nashua, N. H.; stage career, stk. rep. and vaud., with Holbrook Blinn, H. B. Warner, under mgmt. of Shubert and Frohman; screen career, Essanay, Reliance, Lasky ("Years of the Locust," "The Golden Fetter," "Hashimura Togo"), Fine Arts ("Intolerance"), Arteraft ("The Poppy Girl's Husband"), Fox ("Chasing Rainbows"), Hampton-Hod. ("Desert Gold"), Griffith ("Scarlet Days"). Hght., 5, 11; wght., 175; brown hair, gray eyes. Ad., 4406 Sunset Drive, Los Angeles, Cal.

LONSDALE, Harry G.; b. Worcester, Eng.; educ. Worcester Cathedral; stage career, with Mansfield in "Beau Brummel," with E. S. Willard in repertoire, with Nat C. Goodwin, 2 seasons at the old Boston Museum stk.; screen career, Selig ("The Brand of Cain," "Beware of Strangers"), Fox ("Conscience"), Rob-Cole ("The Illustrious Prince"), Select ("The Last of His People"). Hght., 5, 10; wght., 160.

LOSEE, Frank; b. and educ. Bklyn.; 25 yrs. with Belasco, Frohman, K. & E., the Shuberts, John Cort; screen career, Famous Players ("The Eternal City," "Old Homestead," "La Tosca," "Helene of the North," "The Spider," "Bab's Stories," "Paid in Full," "Here Comes the Bride," "His Parisian Wife," "The Firing Line," "Good Gracious, Annabelle," "Marie, Ltd"). Ad., Famous Players, N. Y.

LOUIS, Willard; b. San Francisco, Cal., 1882; stage career, with Edward Harrigan, appeared in many Broadway prods., played lead 2 yrs. in "Seven Days"; screen career, Fox ("The Merry-go-Round"), Goldwyn ("Letty," "Jubilo," "Going Some"), Universal ("Unpainted Woman," "The Scarlet Strain," "The Highest Bidder"). Ad., 2124 Beachwood Drive, Los Angeles, Calif.

LOVE, Montagu; b. Calcutta, India, 1877; educ. England; stage career, mgmt. Belasco, Joseph Brooks, Shuberts, W. A. Brady, Cyril Maude (in London); screen career, Pathe, Metro ("The Cross Bearer," "Rasputin," "Brand of Satan," "The Awakening"), World ("The Rough Neck," "The Hand Invisible," "The Quickening Flame," "Three Green Eyes," "A Broadway Saint," "The Steel King"). Hght., 6, 1; wght., 195; fair complexion, red hair, blue eyes.

LOWELL, John; b. Pleasant Grove, Iowa; educ. Iowa and S. D.; early career, cowboy, surveyor; screen career, star of recent World release "The Clouded Name"; playing leads in Blazed Trail Prods., "When Bad Dan Rides," "The Hidden Pit," "The Danger Patrol," "Across the Line," "Tell Tale Tracks," "Where Peril Lurks," "Code of the North." Hght., 6, 2; wght.,185; dark hair and eyes. Ad., Blazed Trail Prod., care Arrow Film Corp., 220 W. 42d st., N. Y. C.

LUCAS, Wilfred; b. Canada; educ. Montreal high schl. and McGill Univ.; stage career, light and grand opera abroad and in America, 2 seasons in "Quo Vadis"; screen career, Fine Arts ("His Excellency, the Governor," "Food Gamblers"), Paramount ("The Judgment House"), Universal ("The Wild Cat"), Metro ("The Return of Mary"), Allan Dwan for Mayflower ("Soldiers of Fortune"), now in Australia.

LUCY, Arnold; stage career, character actor of 25 yrs. exper. in comedy and drama in London and New York, in "Fanny's First Play," Wm. Knox, "Nothing but the Truth," "The Bishop," "Eternal Magdalene," "Roads of Destiny"; screen career, "The Devil's Toy," Edison ("Vanity Fair"), Fairbanks ("In Again, Out Again"), Vitagraph ("Nymph of the Foothills"), Famous Players ("The Cost"). Hght., 5, 7; wght., 140; light brown hair, gray eyes. Ad., Westover Court, 210 W. 44th st., N. Y. C.; Bryant 5860.

LYON, Ben; b. Atlanta, Ga., 1899; educ. Baltimore Park School and Balto. City College, Md.; stage career, "Seventeen," "Milestones," "Kick In," "Kismet," "Nothing But the Truth," "Too Many Cooks," "Fair and Warmer," "Piccadilly Jim," "The Gibson Upright"; screen career, featured with Faire Binney in "Open Your Eyes," Violet Mersereau's leading man in "Morgan's Raiders," co-star with Marian Swayne in "The Transgressor," leads in Edison's "Conquest Series." Complexion brunette, dark brown hair, dark blue eyes. Ad., Stuart Walker Co., 304 Carnegie Hall Bldg., N. Y.

LYONS, Eddie, also director; b. Beardstown, Ill., 1886; stage career, rep., Marlowe stk., Chicago, "Mrs. Wiggs of Cabbage Patch," mgmt. Liebler, vaud., "Beverly of Graustark" rd. co.; screen career, Biograph, Imp, Nestor ("The Rushin' Dancers," "Dolls and Dollars," "Too Much Women," "Bad News," "A Fire Escape Finish," "There and Back," "A Hasty Hazing," "His Wife's Relatives"), co-starred with Lee Moran in Star Comedies, making 52 single-reel comedies past year for Universal, now producing feature comedy dramas for Universal ("Everything But the Truth"). Hght., 5, 8; wght., 143; gray eyes, dark brown hair. Ad., Universal City, Calif.

LYTELL, Bert; b. and educ. N. Y. C.; stage career, stock, many Broadway prod., lead with Irene Fenwick, "Mary's Ankle"; screen career, Brenon ("The Lone Wolf"), Metro ("The Spender," "Faith," "One-Thing-at-a-Time-O'Day"), Metro-Screen Classics ("Lombardi, Ltd.," "The Right of Way," "Alias Jimmy Valentine"). Hght., 5, 10½; wght., 155; brown hair, hazel eyes. Studio, Metro, Hollywood, Cal.

LYTELL, Wilfred; b. N. Y. C.; stage exper. "The Country Boy," "His Brother's Keeper," "Captain Kidd, Jr.," "Business Before Pleasure"; screen career, Ince-Vitagraph, "The Destroyer," "The Conflict," "The 90 and 9," "The Lily and the Rose," Warren prod. with House Peters; Metro ("Our Mrs. McChesney"), Arthur F. Beck, Inc. ("Isle of Jewels" serial). Hght., 5, 10; wght., 155; dark hair and eyes. Home ad. 5 Jackson st., Bayside, L. I., N. Y.

LYTTON, Roger; b. New Orleans, La.; educ. Dresden, London, Paris, Columbia Univ.; stage career, E. H. Sothern's leading man in "The Proud Prince"; 20 yrs. on stage; screen career, member of old Vitagraph Co. ("Vengeance of Durant," "Battle Cry of Peace," "Panthea," "Lest We Forget," "Burden of Proof," "The Forbidden City," "The Third Degree"), Selznick ("A Regular Girl"), Hallmark-Miller ("High Speed"). Hght., 5, 11; wght., 180; dark complexion, iron gray hair, brown eyes. Member Columbia Univ. Club, N. Y. Ad., 142 East 18th st., N. Y.; Stuyvesant 433.

— M —

MacDERMOTT, Marc; b. London, Eng.; educ Australia; stage career, 7 yrs. with Geo. Ringold's Co. in Australia, with Mrs. Patrick Campbell in U. S. and England, with Richard Mansfield, mgmt. Charles Frohman, etc.; screen career, Edison, 6 yrs., twice sent around world by Edison as their star; Vitagraph ("The Green God," "An Alabaster Box"), Fox ("Buchanan's Wife," "Kathleen Mavourneen"), Norma Talmadge ("The New Moon"), Perret ("13th Chair"), Rolfe-Fischer ("The Amazing Lover," "The Red Virgin"). Hght., 6; wght., 175; auburn hair, brown eyes. Ad., 546 W. 113th St., N. Y. C.; Cathedral 7483.

MacDONALD, Donald; screen career, Paramount ("The Law of Men," "Extravagance," "The Market of Souls"), Select ("Who Cares?"), Pathe ("The Silver Girl"), Rob-Cole ("The House of Intrigue").

MacDONALD, Wallace; b. Mulgrave, Nova Scotia, Canada; educ. Sydney, N. S.; stage career, stock cos. at Vancouver, B. C., and San Francisco, Calif., Phoenix, Ariz., and El Paso, Tex.; screen career, co-star on Triangle and Vitagraph programs, leading man for Pauline Frederick, Mae Marsh, Mabel Normand, Marguerite Clark, Mary Miles Minter, Olive Thomas, Anita Stewart. Hght., 5, 10; wght., 142; dark brown hair and eyes. Ad., L. A. Athletic Club, Los Angeles, Calif.

MacDOWELL, Melbourne; b. Little Washington, N. J.; educ. N. Y.; stage career, 25 yrs., husband of Fanny Davenport, appeared in Sardou repertory, starred in stock several seasons, "Tosca," "Theodora," "Fedora," "Gismonda"; screen career, Ince-Para. ("Tyrant Fear," "Claws of the Hun," "Coals of Fire"), National "The Lamb and the Lion," "Passions Three," "Wolves of the Rail"), with Allan Dwan for Mayflower ("Soldiers of Fortune"). Hght., 6; wght., 210; dark complexion, gray hair and eyes. Home ad., 1047 Everett St., Los Angeles, Cal.

MACK, Hayward; b. Albany, N. Y.; educ. Iowa Coll.; early career, civil engineer and newspaper man; stage career, 7 yrs. in stock, vaud. and prods.; screen career, since 1910. Imp, Majestic, Famous Players, Biograph, Universal ("The Spindle of Life"), Amer. Mutual ("Impossible Susan"), Hodkinson ("Fighting Through"), American ("Some Liar," "Put Up Your Eyes"), Fox ("Love Is Love," "The Speed Maniac," "Thieves"). Hght., 6; wght., 185; dark hair, blue eyes.

MACK, Joseph P.; educ. Rome, Italy; stage career, 12 yrs. legitimate, 12 yrs. vaud.; screen career, 6 yrs., Detrich Co. ("Wild Honey"), Metro ("Brass Check," "Under Suspicion"), E.

V. B. ("Little, But Oh My!"), Fox ("Never Say Quit," "Shark Rawley), Hallmark ("Chain of Evidence"), Raver ("Golden God"), Porter ("Train-Wreckers"). Hght., 5, 11; wght., 200; dark hair and eyes. Ad., 301 W. 46th St., N. Y.; Bryant 4578.

MACKAY, Charles; educ. N. Y. College; stage career, N. Y. prods. with Wm. A. Brady, Mrs. Henry Harris, George Tyler, Charles Frohman, Klaw and Erlanger; screen career, Tourneur ("The Velvet Paw"), World-Peerless ("The Unpardonable Sin," "That Oakdale Affair," "The Woman of Lies," "Me and Capt. Kidd," "The Poison Pen," "The Steel King"). Hght., 5, 10; wght., 170; gray eyes. Ad. Coytesville, N. J.; Fort Lee 38 W.

MACKAY, Edward; stage career, leading man with Mrs. Fiske, Henrietta Crosman, Grace George, Nethersole; stock star, Washington, D. C., Brooklyn, N. Y., Chicago, Toronto, etc.; screen career, Famous Players ("Port of Missing Men," "Clothes," "The Clue," "The Secret Orchard"), Ivan ("Man and His Angel," "The Faded Flower," "The Window Opposite"). Now with Oliver Morosco. Hght., 5, 10; wght., 155; light hair, dark eyes. Ad., home, Coytesville, N. J.

MacLEAN, Douglas; b. Phila.; educ. Northwestern Univ., Pres. Sch., and Lewis Inst. Tech.; stage career, juvenile in stock cos., also with Maude Adams in "Peter Pan" and other Barrie plays, other Broadway appearances; screen career, Artcraft ("The Hun Within," "Johanna Enlists," "Capt. Kidd, Jr."), Ince-Para. ("Fuss and Feathers"), now starring for Thomas H. Ince ("23½ Hours Leave," "What's Your Husband Doing," "Mary's Ankle"). Hght., 5, 9½; wght., 145; brown hair and eyes. Ad., 406 S. Alvarado St., Los Angeles, Calif; studio, Thos. H. Ince.

MacLEAN, R. D.; b. New Orleans, La.; educ. Washington & Lee Univ., Lexington, Va.; stage career, starred for several yrs. in classic rep., "Brutus and Othello," with Wm. Faversham Co.; screen career, Goldwyn ("The Silver Horde," "Little Shepherd of Kingdom Come"), also with Jack Pickford. Hght., 5, 11; wght., 190; iron gray hair, brown eyes. Home ad., 1764 Sycamore ave., Los Angeles, Calif.; phone 579793; studio, Goldwyn.

MAC QUARRIE, Frank; b. San Francisco, Cal.; educ. there; stage career, 19 yrs. with Nance O'Neill, stk. with Henry Miller and 5 yrs. stk. Vancouver, B. C.; one season "The Spoilers"; screen career, Universal 3 yrs. ("The Flash of Fate," "The Man Trap"), Triangle ("Praig" in Black Box serial, "Broadway to the Throne," "Two Men from Sandy Bar"), National ("Girl of My Dreams"), Rob-Cole ("Whitewashed Walls"), Universal ("Loot," "Under Suspicion"). Hght., 5, 8; wght., 140; brown hair, blue eyes. Ad., Oakwoods Hotel, Los Angeles, Calif.

MAILES, Charles Hill; b. Halifax, N. S.; 1870; stage career, since 24 yrs. old, in vaud., concert work, Shakespearian roles, also in "The Squaw Man," "The Clansman," "The Oath"; screen career, over 5 yrs. with Biograph, Universal ("A Young Patriot," "Bitter Sweet," "The Lair of the Wolf," "The Dynast," "The Spotted Lily," "The Power," "The Girl Who Won Out," "Beloved Jim," "Talk of the Town"), Metro ("Full of Pep"), Pathe ("Our Better Selves"), Fox ("The Speed Maniac"), Para-Artcraft ("Red Hot Dollars"). Iron gray hair.

MALATESTA, Frederic M., also director; b. Naples, Italy; educ. there and Rome; stage career, Italy and South America; screen career, Pathe ("The Wolf-faced Man" serial, "The Devil's Trail"), Griffith ("The Greatest Thing in Life"), American ("The Other Side of Eden"), Metro ("The Legion of Death," "The Demon," "Full of Pep," "The Four-Flusher"). Directed Max Linder for the Essanay Co. Hght., 6; wght., 185; dark hair and eyes. Ad. 4520 Russell Ave., Los Angeles, Calif.; phone 599062.

MALONEY, Leo. D.; b. San Jose, Cal., 1888; educ. Santa Clara Coll., Cal.; early career, on ranch until young man; screen career, Pathe, Signal ("The Girl and the Game," "Whispering Smith," "Medicine Bend," "Judith of the Cumberlands," "Manager of B. and A.," "A Lass of the Lumberlands," "The Overland Disaster," "The Lost Express"), Vitagraph ("A Fight for Millions"), Universal ("The Spitfire of Seville"), World ("The Arizona Catclaw"). Hght., 5, 11; wght., 170.

MANN, Hank, also director; b. N. Y. C.; educ. Morris High School; stage career, vaud.; screen career, Mack Sennett ("The Village Blacksmith," "His Bread and Butter"), Fox ("Bon Bon Riot," "His First Blow Out"), Hank Mann Comedies ("Messenger," "Harem Hero," "Eye for Figures"). Hght., 5, 8; wght., 165; light brown hair, brown eyes. Home ad., 1021 Lake Shore Ave., Los Angeles, Calif; Wilshire 1262; studio, Hank Mann Comedies Co., Francis Ford Studio, Los Angeles.

MARBURGH, Bertram; b. 1875; stage career, with John Drew in "Much Ado About Nothing," with Wm. Faversham in "The Squaw Man," with Maude Adams in "Chanticler," with Robert Hilliard in "Argyle Case"; screen career, Wharton ("The Eagle's Eye"), Fox ("Checkers"), World ("Social Pirates"), Powell ("You Never Know Your Luck"). Height, 5, 10½; complexion, dark. Ad., Lambs Club, N. Y.

MARCUS, James A.; stage career, from 1881, in "The Lights of London," stage director for the Fay Templeton Opera Co., "The Cub," "The Sign of the Cross"; screen career, Fox ("Carmen," "Regeneration," "Honor System," "Betrayed," "This Is the Life," "The Conqueror," "Evangeline," "Should a Husband Forgive?").

MARKS, Willis; b. Rochester, Minn.; educ. there; stage career, began in 1888 in St. Paul, Minn., member of Morosco, Burbank Theatre, Los Angeles, for 9 yrs.; screen career, 5 yrs., Lasky ("Man from Funeral Range"), "The Dancing Fool"), Vitagraph ("The Wishing Ring Man," "Over the Garden Wall"), Ince ("Greased Lightning"), Universal ("The Trembling Hour"), Haworth ("The Greater Profit"). Hght., 5, 8; wght., 140; gray hair and eyes. Home ad., 1341½ Toberman St., Los Angeles, Calif.; West 4046.

MARMONT, Percy; educ. St. Anne's, Redhill, Surrey, England; stage career, in England, with Sir Herbert Tree, Sir Geo. Alexander, Cyril Maude, etc.; in U. S., with Anne Murdock, Ethel Barrymore, Belasco, and in "The Invisible Foe"; screen career, Paramount ("Rose of the World," "The Lie"), Goldwyn ("Turn of the Wheel"), Famous Players ("Three Men and a Girl"), Select ("In the Hollow of Her Hand"), Vitagraph ("Vengeance of Durand," "The Winchester Woman," "The Climbers," "Pride," "The Sporting Duchess"). Hght., 6; wght., 150; blond hair, blue-gray eyes. Ad., Lambs Club, N. Y.

MARQUIS, Joseph Philip; b. N. Y. C.; educ. there; stage career, stk. co. one year; screen career, Biograph ("Midnight Girl," "Oh, Louise," "My Girl Suzanne"), Universal ("Lonora," "A Matter of Taste"), MacManus ("Bruised Humanity"). Hght., 6; wght., 175; blond hair, blue eyes. Ad., 75 W. 94th st., N. Y.; Riverside 2989.

MARR, Gordon; b. London, Ont. Canada, 1891; educ. Toronto Univ.; 5 yrs. stage exper., stk., etc.; screen career, Wash. M. P. Corp., Fox ("The Coming of the Law," "The Greater Law"). Enlisted 1915 with Canadians, overseas 18 mos., honorably discharged. Metro ("Fools and Their Money," "The Island of Intrigue"). Hght., 5, 7½; wght., 138; dark complexion, eyes, hair. Ad., Glidden Hotel, Hollywood, Cal.

MARSHALL, Tully; b. Nevada City, Calif; educ. private sch. and Santa Clara Coll., Calif.; screen career, All Star, Fine Arts, D. W. Griffith ("The Girl Who Stayed at Home"), Famous Players-Lasky, Goldwyn, Thos. Ince, Maurice Tourneur ("Life Line"), Paramount-Artcraft ("Everywoman"), Rex Beach ("The Crimson Gardenia"), etc. Hght., 5 10½; wght., 140; brown-gray hair, brown eyes. Ad., 128 Ridgewood Place, Los Angeles, Calif; studio, Lasky.

MASON, "Smiling" Billy, also director; educ. Chicago, Univ. of Michigan, Copenhagen, Denmark; stage career, circus clown, in "Shepherd King"; screen career, Pathe, Essanay, World Film, Universal ("A Box of Tricks"), Christie ("Their Seaside Tangle," "Help! Help! Police!" "One Good Turn," "Whose Wife"), Bluebird ("A Taste of Life"), Vitagraph ("The Wolf"). Hght., 5, 11; wght., 156; blond hair, dark blue eyes. Ad., home, 1608 N. Alexandria Ave., Hollywood.

MASON, Charles E.; b. Warren County, Ky.; educ. Bowling Green, Ky.; stage career, stk. co. in Portland, Oreg.; screen career, Metro ("The Yellow Dove"), Astor Co., Fox. North West Motion Pict., etc. Hght., 6; wght., 190; dark brown hair, blue eyes. Ad., home, 1750½ Western Ave., Hollywood, Calif.; 'phone, 597681; studio ad., Lew Cody Co., Hollywood, Calif.

MASON, Dan; b. Syracuse, N. Y., 1857; educ. Syracuse; stage career, Washburn stk., with Wm. Collier in "The Man from Mexico," "Why Smith Left Home," in "Naughty Anthony," "The Prince of Pilsen," "Miss Patsy"; screen career, Edison stk., Fox ("The Scarlet Letter," "The Slave," "The Broadway Sport," "Every Girl's Dream," "Thou Shalt Not Steal"), Fox

ACTORS

("The Lure of Ambition"). Hght., 5, 9; wght., 175; black hair, black eyes.

MASON, Sidney L.; b. Paterson, N. J., 1886; educ. there; stage career, Manhattan Opera House Co., N. Y.; mgmt. Cohan and Harris, "Stop Thief"; screen career, Bluebird ("Honor of Mary Blake"), Fox ("Painted Madonna," "The Fallen Idol"), Frank Powell ("The Promise"), Fox ("Bonnie Annie Laurie," "The Forbidden Path"), Universal ("The Trap"), Perret ("A Modern Salome", McCord Pict. ("The Wild Faun"). Hght., 5, 11; wght., 163; dark complexion, dark hair, brown eyes. Ad., 3657 Broadway, N. Y. C., or Green Room Club.

MAYALL, Herschel; b. Bowling Green, Ky.; educ. Farmington, Me., and Univ. of Minn.; stage career, 25 yrs. 14 yrs. leading man in stk. cos. in New York, Cincinnati, etc.; screen career, Ince ("Civilization"), Morosco (with Leonore Ulrich), Brunton ("Carmen of the Klondyke"), Bessie Barriscale ("The Heart of Rachael"), Wm. Farnum ("Wings of the Morning"), Alaskan Prod. Co. ("The Seal of Death"). Hght., 5, 10; wght., 185; dark brown hair, dark gray eyes. Home ad., 1486 Allison Ave., Los Angeles, Calif.

MAYO, Frank; b. N. Y., 1886; educ. Peekskill Mil. Acad.; stage career, with grandfather in "Davy Crockett," "Woman in the Case," "The Squaw Man," 3 yrs. with Arthur Boucher and Herbert Sleath, Eng., mgr. own sketch, Eng.; screen career, featured in "Power and the Glory," etc.; leads with Alice Brady, Ethel Clayton, June Elvidge, Louise Huff, Kitty Gordon, Lois Weber prod. ("Mary Regan"), Universal ("The Peddlar," "Burnt Wings," "Lasca," "The Brute Breaker," "A Little Brother of the Rich." Hght., 5, 11½; wght., 165; brown hair, gray eyes. Ad., 7018 Franklin Ave., Los Angeles, Cal.

McCALL, Billy; b. 1870, and educ. Peoria, Ill.; 25 yrs. stage exper., vaud., etc.; screen career, Ince, Marie Dressler, Horsley, Fox, Vitagraph ("Bears and Bad Men," "Huns and Hyphens," "Fight for Millions," "Smashing Barriers"). Hght., 5, 9½; wght., 175; dark hair, blue eyes. Ad., 447½ S. Flower St., Los Angeles, Calif.

McCARTHY, Myles; b. Montreal, Can.; educ. McGill Univ., Montreal; stage career, under mgmt. of Frohmans, E. E. Rice, W. E. Nankeville, Chas. B. Dillingham, George Broadhurst, etc., also headliner in vaud.; screen career, with Selig, Gaumont, Thanhouser, National, Vitagraph ("The Highest Trump"), United ("A Man's Fight"), Keenan-Pathe ("The False Code"), Universal ("Twisted Souls"), Metro ("Silence Sellers"). Hght., 5, 11½; wght., 163; iron gray hair and blue eyes.

McCOY, Harry H., also director; b. 1895 and educ. Phila., Pa.; stage experi., vaud. and legit. in N. Y.; screen career, Mack Sennett 5½ years, American, Selig, featured with Coleen Moore, "The Hoosier Romance," directing and playing own comedy leads 2 yrs. with Margarita Fisher in "Fair Enough," "His Wife's Friend," Lehrman ("Twilight Baby"), Arbuckle ("The Garage"). Hght., 5, 8½; wght., 155; light hair, brown eyes. Home ad., 1627 S. Union ave., L. A., Cal.

McCULLOUGH, Philo; b. San Brendo, Cal.; educ. there and Los Angeles; screen career, Selig, Mutual, Kalem, Metro, Bluebird ("The Dream Lady," "Rich Man's Darling"), Allan Dwan Prods. ("Soldiers of Fortune," "The Splendid Hazard," "Heart of a Fool"). Hght., 5, 11½; wght., 175; light complexion, light brown hair, dark blue eyes. Studio, Allan Dwan at Brunton Studios, Los Angeles, Cal. Holly 4080.

McDANIEL, George; b. Georgia; educ. Georgia Tech., Atlanta Coll. of Physicians; stage career, 5 yrs. operatic and concert work, 2 seasons with Victor Herbert prods. as principal baritone, Pythias in 1915 revival of "Damon and Pythias," 2 seasons Morosco stk., etc.; screen career, Lasky ("The Little Princess"), Bluebird ("The Door Between"), Select ("The Shuttle"), Fox ("The She Devil," "Lost Money," "What Would You Do?"), H. B. Wright ("The Shepherd of the Hills"), Universal ("The Woman Under Cover"), Metro ("Lombardi, Ltd."). Featured in own prods. at Art Unit Studios, Glendale, Cal.; home ad., Actors' Assn. of Los Angeles. Holly 1946.

McDONALD, Francis J.; b. Bowling Green, Ky., 1891; educ. St. Xavier Coll., Cincinnati; stage career, since 1905, 1 season leading man at Spokane, 7 mos. on Orpheum Circuit; screen career, 2 yrs. with Universal, then to Fine Arts for 15 mos., and then back to Universal ("The Black Orchid," "The Mansard Mystery," "O'Connor's Mag"), Triangle ("The Passion Flower," "The Confession," "Hearts and Masks," "The Kentucky Colonel"). Hght., 5, 9; wght, 155; black hair, brown eyes. Studio ad., National Film Corp., 1116 Lodi st., Los Angeles; home ad., Glidden Hotel, Holly Blvd., Hollywood, Cal.

McDOWELL, Nelson; b. Greenfield, Mo.; educ. North Western Univ., Chicago; stage career, 2 yrs. stock co., Chicago, 4 yrs. lecture platform; screen career, Paramount ("Romance of the Redwoods"), Vitagraph ("A Diplomatic Mission," "The Home Trail," "The Flaming Omen"), Universal ("The Charmer," "The Sundown Trail"), Fox ("Sadie," "One Touch of Sin," "Bruce of the Circle A"), Mitchell Lews Co. ("Jaques of the Silver North"), Byron Powers Co. ("The Planters"), B. B. Hampton ("Desert of Wheat"), Rex Beach-Goldwyn ("Going Some"). Hght., 6, 2; wght., 189; light complexion, brown hair, blue-gray eyes. Ad., 1802 N. Van Ness ave., Hollywood, Cal., or Willis & Inglis, Los Angeles, Cal.

McEWEN, Walter; b. 1865; stage career, 20 yrs. with Geo. Edwards, Gaiety theatre, London, also with Winthrop Ames; screen career, Peerless, Fox, Famous Players, Kalem, Vitagraph (with E. H. Sothern in "The Chattel"), Select ("The Probation Wife"), Hodkinson ("The Bandbox"). Hght., 5, 8.

McGARRY, Garry; b. Franklin, Pa., Oct. 17, 1889; educ. Sacred Heart Acad., Franklin, and Canisus Coll., Buffalo; stage career, in "The Soul Kiss," "The Waltz Dream," "The Confession," 2 seasons with Tom Terriss, a season each with Frank Keenan and Madame Dore in vaud.; screen career, Vitagraph ("The Daughter of Israel," "A Question of Clothes," "The Wrong Girl," "The Tigress," "Prince in a Pawnshop"), Paramount-Artcraft ("False Faces"). Hght., 5, 7; wght., 129; fair complexion, brown hair and eyes. Ad., Lambs Club, N. Y. C.

McGOWAN, John W. (Jack); b. and educ., Muskegon, Mich., 1894; stage career, "The Time, Place and Girl," "My Wife's Family," "Her Soldier Boy," "My Girl from Brazil," "Oh, Boy," Ziegfeld Follies, Ziegfeld Midnight Frolic, Century Review; screen career, Metro ("Flower of the Dusk," "Oh, Annice," "The Gold Cure"). Hght., 5, 9; wght, 160; light hair, blue eyes.

McGRAIL, Walter; b. and educ. Bklyn, N. Y., 1889; stage career, 2 yrs. comic opera, 3 yrs. vaud.; screen career, Vitagraph, 5 yrs ("Within the Law," "Womanhood," "Business of Life," "Miss Ambition"), Pathe ("The Black Secret"), Selznick ("Country Cousin," "Greater than Fame"). Hght., 6; wght., 175; dark complexion, black hair, blue eyes. Ad., 105 Berkeley place, Brooklyn, N. Y., or Lambs Club.

McGREGOR, Gordon; b. Scotland, 1885; educ. Watts Coll., Edinburgh; stage career, from 1895; toured New England in "Evangeline"; screen career, from 1911, Selig, Lasky ("Brewster's Millions," "The Squaw Man"), Horsley (Mina and Cub comedies), Metro ("A Man of Honor"). Hght., 5, 11; wght., 175; blue eyes, black hair.

McINTOSH, Burr; b. Wellesville, O., 1862; educ. Lafayette Coll. and Princeton Univ.; reported for Phila. News; stage career, in "Trilby," "The Man of the Hour," on tour in "The Gentleman from Mississippi"; screen career, played Wallingford in Pathe "Wallingford" serial, Mutual ("My Partner"). Ad., Lotos Club, N. Y.

McKEE, Raymond; b. Chicago, 1892; stage career, lead in "Grit, the Newsboy," with Robert Hilliard in "A Fool There Was," "The Phantom Legion," mus. com., "The Golden Girl," stk. in Atlanta and Chicago; screen career, Edison ("Heart of the Hill"), Metro ("The Sunbeam"), Conquest-Forum Films ("Kidnapped," "Lady of the Photograph"), Kleine ("The Unbeliever), Fox ("Kathleen Mavourneen"), World ("Capt. Kidd"), A. E. F. 1st sgt. 18 mos. Hght., 5, 7½; wght., 130; gray eyes, brown hair. Home ad., 587 Riverside Drive, N. Y.; or Friars Club., N. Y. C.

McKIM, Robert; b. San Jacinto, Cal., 1887; educ. San Francisco; stage career, stk. with Alcazar, San Francisco, 3 seasons over Orpheum circuit with Mrs. Langtry; screen career, Ince-Paramount ("The Silent Man," "Son of His Father," "Love Me," "The Marriage Ring," "The Vamp", "Green Eyes," "Law of the North"), Goldwyn ("The Silver Horde," "Woman in Room 13"). Hght., 6; wght., 175; black hair, brown eyes. Home ad., 708 Crescent Drive, Beverly Hills, Cal.; studio, Goldwyn, Culver City, Cal.

McLEAN, Jack; b. 1893 and educ. Brookline, Mass.; stage career, "Mary's Ankle," "Watch Your Step"; screen career, Goldwyn, Graphic, Fox ("Blue Eyed Mary"), Famous Players ("Mrs. Wiggs of the Cabbage Patch"), Vitagraph ("Thin Ice," "The Unknown Quantity"), Graphic ("The Echo of Youth"), World ("His Father's Wife"), W. H. Prod. ("The Lost Battalion"). Hght., 5, 8½; wght., 140; brown hair, blue eyes. Permanent ad., 35 Walter ave., Brookline, Mass.

McQUARRIE, Albert; b. San Francisco, 1882; stage career, began at Alcazar theatre in 1904, on dram. stage until 1913; screen career, started with David Horsley, with Universal 3 yrs., 2 pictures with Bryant Washburn for Pathe, Douglas Fairbanks ("Bound in Morocco," "He Comes Up Smiling," "Arizona," "Knickerbocker Buckeroo," "His Majesty, the American," "When the Clouds Roll By"). Hght., 5, 9; wght., 160; brown hair, gray eyes. Home ad., 1624 Hudson ave., Los Angeles, Cal.; Holly 2737.

MEIGHAN, Thomas; b. Pittsburgh, Pa.; educ. there; stage career, played a season with Grace George, 2 yrs. in Pittsburgh Stk. Co., leading man in London engagement of "The College Widow," 3 yrs. with David Warfield in "The Return of Peter Grimm," also in "On Trial"; screen career, Paramount-Artcraft ("M'liss," "Out of a Clear Sky," "The Heart of Wetona," "Male and Female," "Don't Change Your Wife," "The Miracle Man"). Hght., 6; wght., 170; black hair, brown eyes. Ad., L. A. Athletic Club; studio, Lasky, Hollywood, Cal.

MERLO, Anthony; b. Italy; educ. N. Y.; screen career, Fox, Famous Players, World, Brenon-Selznick, Universal, Metro, Maurice Tourneur ("A Daughter of France," "Human Driftwood," "Maid of Belgium," "The Cross Bearer," "The Awakening," "The Sea Waif," "The Heart of Gold," "Woman," "Sporting Life"), World ("Phil for Short," "Mandarin's Gold," "The Unveiling Hand"). Hght., 5, 10; wght., 165; dark complexion, brown hair, brown eyes. Ad., care of Fox, N. Y.

MESTAYER, Harry; b. San Francisco; educ. N. Y. and Boston Latin; stage career, with Holbrook Blinn, Helen Ware, E. H. Sothern, James K. Hackett, "The Son-Daughter"; screen career, George Kleine's ("Stop Thief"), Selig ("The Millionaire Baby," "The House of a Thousand Candles," "The Gold Ship"), Triangle ("High Tide," "Wife or Country"). Ad., Lambs Club, N. Y.

METCALFE, Earl Keeney; b. Newport, Ky., 1889; educ. Cincinnati, O.; stage career, 7 yrs. in stk. and N. Y. prods.; vaud.; screen career, Lubin, 4 yrs. ("The Phantom Happiness"), Select ("World to Live In"), World ("The Battler," "Coax Me," "Woman of Lies," "Poison Pen"), Vitagraph ("The Fortune Hunter"), Shomer ("The Great Mystery"). Directed Jas. Montgomery Flagg comedies; 19 mos. in U. S. Army as 2nd Lieut. with 69th N. Y. Inf., 1 yr. in France. Hght., 5, 11; wght., 170; brown hair, blue eyes. Ad., Lambs Club, N. Y.

MILASH, Robert E.; b. N. Y. C., Apr. 18, 1885; educ. N. Y. C.; stage career, under Frohman in "The Girl I Left Behind Me," with James K. Hackett in "The Prisoner of Zenda"; screen career, Edison, Biograph, Pathe, Crystal, Universal ("Timothy Dobbs, That's Me" series), World ("The Roughneck"), Paramount ("Mrs. Wiggs of the Cabbage Patch," "The Two Brides"), Pathe ("The Moonshine Trail"). Hght., 6, 7; wght., 122; gray hair, blue eyes, dark complexion. Home ad., 512 W. 151st st., N. Y. C.

MILLER, Harold Atchison; b. Redondo Beach, Cal.; educ. Los Angeles; screen career, Selznick ("Upstairs and Down"), Frank Keenan Co. ("World of Flame"), Universal ("The Peddler"), Allan Dwan ("Heart of a Fool"). Hght., 6, 1; wght., 160; brown hair and eyes. Home ad., 4520 W. 18th st., Los Angeles, Cal.; phone 72469.

MILLER, Walter; b. Atlanta, Ga.; educ. there and Brooklyn, N. Y.; stage career, Roe Stock, Stanley Stk., Hall Stk., Jersey City, Lyceum Stk., Brooklyn, N. Y.; screen career, Metro ("The Slacker," "Miss Robinson Crusoe," "Draft 258"), Ralph Ince ("11th Commandment"), Vitagraph ("Thin Ice," "A Girl at Bay," "The Friendly Call"), Artclass ("The Open Door"). Hght, 5, 11; wght., 165; dark brown hair, brown eyes. Home ad., 235 West 107th st., N. Y. C.; Acad. 1106; and offices Artclass Pict., Longacre Bldg., N. Y.

MILLETT, Arthur Nelson; b. Maine, 1874; educ. Coll. of Sacred Heart, Denver, and European sch. of music; stage career, 14 yrs., with Patta Roso for a yr.; screen career, Triangle ("Ship of Doom," "Sea Panther"), Fox ("The Framer"), "King Spruce" with Mitchell Lewis, "Out of Count," "Sparks" with Jack Warren Kerrigan, "23½ Hours Leave," "Egg-Crate Wallop" with Charles Ray, "Count of the Times" with Frank Keenan. Hght., 6, ¾; wght., 196; brown hair, dark eyes. Ad., 2707 S. Normandie, Los Angeles, Cal.

MILLS, Frank; b. Kalamazoo, Mich.; educ. Univ. of Mich.; stage career, Chas. Frohman, Belasco, Daniel Frohman, prods.; "Sue," 5 yrs. with Sir Herbert Tree, Mrs. Pat Campbell, Sir J. Forbes-Robertson, etc.; in America, leads with Olga Nethersole, Elsie Ferguson, Mary Mannering, etc.; in "Bought and Paid For"; screen career, Select ("De Luxe Annie"), De Luxe ("Wild Honey," "Twilight"), Famous Players ("Let's Elope," "The Misleading Widow"), First National ("Wives of Men"), Pathe ("The Bramble Bush"), "Actors' Equity Strike," by the Assn., Capellani ("The Right to Lie"), American Cinema ("Women Men Forget"). Hght., 5, 11; wght., 172; dark hair, blue eyes. Home ad., 264 W. 57th st., N. Y. Circle 1561.

MIX, Tom, also writer and director; early career, rode the plains as a cowboy, was a member of the Rough Riders during Spanish-American War; screen career, with Selig, Fox ("Cupid's Round Up," "Western Blood," "Ace High," "Hell's Roaring Reform," "Treat 'Em Rough," "Fame and Fortune," "Mr. Logan, U. S. A.," "Wilderness Trail," "Fighting for Gold," "Dare Devil," "Rough Riding Romance," "Three Gold Coins"). Member M. P. D. A. of Los Angeles. Ad., Fox studios, Los Angeles. Home ad., 5841 Carlton Way, Hollywood.

MONG, William V., also scenario writer; b. Chambersburg, Pa., 1875; stage career, with Newton Beers in "Lost in London," vaud. in own play, "The Clay Baker," in "The House Next Door," "The Light in the Window," etc.; screen career, Essanay, Selig, scenario editor, acting and directing for Universal, Crest Picture Co.; Tour- ("The County Fair"), Geo. Loane Tucker ("Ladies Must Live"), Katherine MacDonald ("The Turning Point"), Bessie Barriscale ("Luck of Geraldine Laird"). Hght., 5, 9; wght., 140; dark hair, dark brown eyes. Ad., home, RR No. 2, Whittier, Cal. Studio ad., Brunton. Whittier 5151.

MONTAGUE, Frederick; b. London, England; educ. Richmond; stage career, with Augustin Daly, E. H. Sothern, leading man 2 yrs. with Mme. Modjeska; screen career, Vitagraph, Thanhouser, Lasky, Universal ("A Prince for a Day," "Little Marian's Triumph," "His Robe of Honor," "Lure of the Circus," "The Rough Lover"), Rob-Cole ("His Debt"), Hampton-Hodkinson ("The Best Man"). Hght., 5, 8½; wght., 165; gray hair, brown eyes. Ad., 133 W. 21st St., Los Angeles, Cal.

MONTGOMERY, Earl Triplett; b. Santa Cruz Co., Cal., 1893; educ. Nome, Alaska; stage career, 2 seasons mus. com.; screen career, L-Ko, American, 4 yrs. with Vitagraph ("Bums and Boarders," "Chumps and Cops," "Farms and Fumbles," "Love and Lather," "Damsels and Dandies," "Zip and Zest," "Harems and Hokum," "Vamps and Variety," "Caves and Croquettes," "Rubes and Robbers"). Hght., 5, 8; wght., 180; light brown hair, hazel eyes. Ad., 204 S. Dillen St., Los Angeles, Calif.; phone 51648; studio, Vitagraph.

MOORE, Matt; b. Ireland, 1888; educ. Toledo, O.; screen career, Artcraft ("Pride of the Clan"), Universal ("20,000 Leagues Under the Sea"), Ardsley Film Corp. ("Runaway Romany"), Neilan Prod. ("Unpardonable Sin"), J. Parker Reid ("Sahara"), Buffalo M. P. Co. ("Sport of Kings"), Artcraft ("Heart of the Wilds"), Selznick ("A Regular Fellow," "The Glorious Lady"), Marion Davies ("The Dark Star," "Getting Mary Married"). Ad., 110 W. 48th St., N. Y.

MOORE, Owen, b. Ireland; came to U. S. when 11 yrs. old; educ. Toledo, O.; stage career, from twentieth yr., juvenile leads in several road

ACTORS

attractions; screen career, since 1909, Biograph, Reliance-Majestic, Fine Arts, Famous Players ("A Coney Island Princess," "A Girl Like That," "The Little Boy Scout"), Beach-Goldwyn ("The Crimson Gardenia"), Selznick ("Piccadilly Jim," "Who's Who"). Hght., 5, 10; wght., 140; dark hair and eyes. Ad. C/o Selznick Pict. Corp., N. Y.

MOORE, Tom; b. County Meath, Ire.; educ. there and Toledo, O.; stage exper., 7 yrs. stk.; screen career, 6 yrs. Kalem, Lubin, Lasky, Select, Selig ("Brown of Harvard"), Goldwin; starred in "Thirty a Week," "Go West Young Man," "A Man and His Money," "One of the Finest," "Lord and Lady Algy," "The Gay Lord Quex," "City of Comrades," "Toby's Bow," "Duds"). Hght., 5, 10½; wght, 142; light brown hair, blue eyes. Ad., 1919 Van Ness ave., Los Angeles; studio, Goldwyn, Culver City, Cal.

MOORE, Victor; b. Hammonton, N. J.; stage career, with John Drew in "Rosemary," in Klaw and Erlanger's "Jack and the Beanstalk," chorus man in "Change Your Act or Back to the Woods," etc.; several yrs. in "45 Minutes from Broadway," "The Talk of New York," etc.; screen career, Lasky ("Snobs," "Chimmie Fadden" series, "The Race," "The Clown"), Klever Komedies ("The Moneyless Honeymoon," "The Cinderella Husband," "Camping," "Home Defence," "The Sleepwalker," etc. Hght., 5, 7½; wght., 200; dark complexion, brown hair and eyes. Home ad., 139 Harrison ave., Baldwin, L. I., N. Y.

MORAN, Lee; also director and scenario writer; b. Chicago, Ill.; educ. St. Ignatius Coll., Chicago; stage career, musical comedy, vaud.; screen career, from 1912, Lyons & Moran comedies ("Duck Out of Water," "Camping Out," "Bullsheviks," "Dog-Gone Shame"). Hght., 5, 10; wght., 135; brown hair, blue-gray eyes. Ad., 131 Ridgewood Place, Los Angeles, Calif., Holly 4340; studio, Lyons-Moran Co., Universal Studio.

MORAN, William F.; b. New Orleans, La.; educ. there; stage career, stock, rep. and prod.; screen career, 1 yr. stock with Diamond Film Co. of New Orleans, John Ince ("Please Get Married"), Rex Beach-Goldwyn ("Cup of Fury," with Helen Chadwick), Bradbury Prods., Inc. ("Angel of the Hollyhocks," "The Dawning Light"). Hght., 5, 11; wght., 140; dark hair, brown eyes. Home ad., Bonnie Brier Hotel, Hollywood, Calif., Holly 2744; studio ad., Brunton.

MORANTI, Milburn; b. San Francisco, Calif.; stage career, several yrs. circus and dram. cos., starring in own legit. prods.; screen career, Universal, Triangle, Keystone, first 15 of the Gale Henry comedies for Model Comedy Co., now appearing in own Mercury Comedies as character comedian. Hght., 6, 8; wght., 150; black hair, dark eyes. Ad., Mercury Comedies, Balboa, Calif.

MORDANT, Edwin; stage career, prominent all over U. S., Canada and Mexico; starred in "The Prisoner of Zenda," "Faust," "Oliver Twist," leading roles in "Secret Service," "Sherlock Holmes," "The Tempest," "Midsummer Night's Dream," "Business Before Pleasure," 1919, "His Honor, Abe Potash"; screen career, Famous Players ("Moth and the Flame," "Seven Sisters," "Molly-Make-Believe," "Poor Little Peppina," "The Undying Flame," "The Cost"). Member Lambs Club, N. Y. Southern Society, Councilman Actor's Equity Assn., Actors and Artistes Assn. of America. Ad., 305 W. 45th st., N. Y. Bryant 7730.

MORENO, Antonio Garrido Monteagudo; b. Madrid, 1888; educ. Madrid, Catholic Sisters Schl. and pub. schls., New York City; came to U. S. at age of 14; stage career, with Mrs. Leslie Carter, with Tyrone Power, Constance Collier, Wilton Lackaye; screen career, went to Vitagraph in 1914, playing leads ("The First Law," "The Mark of Cain"), starred in the "Naulahka," "The Angel Factory," "The Iron Test," "Perils of Thunder Mountain," "The Unforseen Hand," and feature subjects. Ad., L. A. Athletic Club, studio, Vitagraph, Hollywood, Cal.

MOREY, Harry T.; b. Michigan; stage career, associated with many well-known stars and attractions; screen career, since 1909 with Vitagraph ("The Golden Goal," "The Green God," "All Man," "Playing with Fate," "Silent Strength," "The Man Who Won," "Fighting Destiny," "The Gamble," "Beating the Odds," "The Darkest Hour," "In Honor's Web." Ad., studio, Vitagraph, Brooklyn, N. Y.

MORGAN, Frank; b. N. Y., 1890; educ. Cornell Univ.; stage career, stk., "A Full House," "In Cold Type"; screen career, Vitagraph, Edison, McClure, Fox ("A Modern Cinderella"), K. E. S. E. ("Sight in Darkness"), Goldwyn ("Baby Mine"), Master D. Feat ("Who's Your Neighbor?"), Select ("At the Mercy of Men"), Vitagraph ("Gray Tower Myster." "The Golden Shower"). Hght., 5, 11; wght., 166; light complexion, brown hair, dark eyes. Ad., 310 W. 79th st., N. Y. C.

MORLEY, Jay; b. Port Orange, Fla.; educ. Columbus, Ohio; stage career, 5 yrs. dram. stock; screen career, Selig, Universal, Warner Features, Lubin, Fox, Paralta, Doraldina ("The Cave Women"), Vitagraph ("Over the Garden Wall," "The Roads We Take," "The Little Boss," "Telamacus Friend," "A Fighting Colleen"). Hght., 5, 10; wght., 183; brown hair, dark eyes. Ad., 1520 Hudson ave., Hollywood, Calif.; phone 57683; studio, Vitagraph.

MORRISON, Arthur; b. St. Louis, Mo., 1880; educ. there; stage career, Hopkins stk., Chicago, with Richard Mansfield, mus. com., 6 yrs. vaud.; screen career, Pathe, Triangle ("The Feud Girl"), Ray Comedies ("Casey, the Fireman"), Superlative Pictures ("Between Men"), Overland Film ("A Man's Law"), Hampton-Hodkinson ("Desert Gold," "The Sage Brusher"). Hght., 5, 11½; wght., 183; dark brown hair, blue eyes; medium complexion. Home ad., 905 E. 173d st., N. Y. C.; studio, Zane Grey Pictures, Inc., Brunton Studio, Los Angeles, Calif.

MORRISON, James Woods; b. Matoon, Ill., 1888; educ. Univ. of Chicago; stage career, vaud. stk.; screen career, Vitagraph, 6 yrs. Ivan ("Enlighten Thy Daughter," "One Law for Both," "Two Men and a Woman," "Babbling Tongues," "Sins of Ambition," "Life Against Honor"), Vitagraph ("Over the Top," "Miss Dulcie from Dixie," "The Midnight Marriage"), Fox ("Sacred Silence"), Selznick ("The Woman Game"). Hght., 5, 8; wght., 135; brown hair and eyes. Ad., 327 W. 56th st., N. Y. Col. 3019.

MORTIMER, Henry; b. Toronto, Ont.; educ. St. Michael's Coll., Toronto, St. Catherine's Coll. Inst.; stage career, with Mrs. Fiske, Elsie Ferguson, Louis Mann, John Barrymore; screen career, Metro ("Her Great Price," "Their Compact"), Unity ("The Pursuing Vengeance"), Betzwood ("The Road Called Straight"), Ince ("His Wife's Friend"), Realart ("The Fear Market"). Hght., 5, 11; wght., 170; dark brown hair, dark blue eyes. Ad., Lambs Club, N. Y., or Bryant 3968.

MOWER, Jack; b. Honolulu, 1890; educ. Punahou Coll., Honolulu; stage career, 6 mos. stock, 2 yrs. mus. com., vaud.; screen career, Vitagraph, Selig ("The Primitive Woman," "Money Isn't Everything"), American ("Molly of the Follies," "Mantle of Charity"), Metro ("Island of Intrigue"), Cody ("The Beloved Cheater"), Pathe "The Third Eye" serial). (Pacific Coast champion swimmer for 4 yrs.). Hght., 6; wght., 180; medium complexion, brown hair, gray eyes. Home ad., Elk's Club, Glendale, Calif.; studio, Astra, Glendale, Calif.

MULHALL, Jack; b. N. Y.; educ. N. Y. Columbia Univ.; stage career, 2 yrs. with West End Stk., N. Y., on Orpheum Circuit, with James K. Hackett in "The Grain of Dust"; screen career, Biograph (played leads for 4 yrs.), Universal ("Safe," "Sirens of the Sea," "High Speed," "Three Women of France," "The Midnight Man," "Boss of Powderville," "Madame Spy"), Para., Blackton ("Wild Youth"), Universal ("The Brass Bullet"), Metro ("Should a Woman Tell?" "The Hope"). Hght., 5, 11; wght., 159. Home ad., 5557 Harold Way, Hollywood, Calif; studio. Metro, Hollywood.

MULLEN, Gordon Douglass; b. Winnipeg, 1889; educ. Wesley Coll.; stage career, vaud., stk. in Winnipeg and Toronto; screen career, 1914-15 with NYMP, Horsley ("Could a Man Do More?") Paramount ("Crooked Straight"). Hght., 5, 9½; wght., 162; brown hair and eyes.

MURRAY, Charles; b. Laurel, Ind., 1872; educ. Cincinnati; stage career, 20 yrs. with Ollie Mack as Murray and Mack; screen career, 2 yrs with Biograph, Keystone, Sennett-Para. ("Her Blighted Love," "Never Too Old," "Reilly's Wash Day," "Trying to Get Along," "The Dentist," "Up in Alf's Place," "The Speak-Easy"). Hght., 6; wgh., 200; red hair, light gray eyes. Ad., studio, Mack Sennett Comedies, 1712 Allesandro st., L. A., Calif. Home ad., 422 S. Hoover st., Los Angeles, phone 53466.

MUSGRAVE, Billy; b. Toledo, O., 1890; educ. Toledo and Chicago, Ill.; stage career, associated with well known stock and road attractions as child actor and juvenile; screen career, Rolin, Powers, Universal ("The Hero of Bunko Hill," "The Blood of Gladness"), Triangle

("Crown Jewels"), Select ("The Midnight Patrol"), Metro ("Blackie's Redemption"). Hght., 5, 8½; wght, 140; brown hair and eyes. Ad., home, Armondale Hotel, Los Angeles.

MUSSETT, Charles; b. 1876; stage career, 18 yrs. with Chas. Frohman, Wilson Barrett, Cyril Maude, mus. com., "Blue Pearl" Co., "East Is West"; screen career, Edison, Peerless, Vitagraph, Paragron, Triangle. Hght., 6; fair complexion. Ad., Lambs Club, N. Y.

— N —

NAGEL, Conrad; b. Des Moines, Iowa, 1896; educ. Highland Park College, Des Moines; stage exper., "Experience," "Man Who Came Back," "Forever After"; screen career, Wm. A. Brady, ("Little Women"), Vitagraph ("Lion and the Mouse," Alice Joyce), Famous Players-Lasky with Alice Brady. Hght., 6; wght., 165; blond hair, blue eyes. Home ad., Lambs Club, N. Y.

NEILL, James; b. Savannah, Ga., educ. Carolina Mil. Inst. and Univ. of Georgia; stage career, leading man in "Mr. Barnes of N. Y.," leading man for Mrs. Fiske, member all-star cast in "Held by the Enemy"; screen career, Universal (dis. J. Warren Kerrigan, Cleo Madison), Kalem (dir.), Lasky, Para. ("Say, Young Fellow," "The Girl Who Came Back," "Men, Women and Money," "The Rescuing Angel," "His Official Fiancee," "Everywoman"), Artcraft ("Don't Change Your Husband"), Select ("Romance and Arabella"). Ad., Goldwyn Studio, Culver City, Cal.

NEILL, Richard R.; b. Phila., educ. there; stage career, 6 yrs. mgmt. Chas. Frohman, with E. H. Sothern, "The Other Girl," "Girls of Gottenberg," with Margaret Anglin, W. H. Thompson, etc.; screen career, Fox, Metro, World, Ince ("The Broken Law," "The Road to France," "Pals First," "The Great Gamble," "The White Rock"). Author of several scenarios. Hght., 6; wght., 180; dark brown hair. Ad., Lambs Club, N. Y. Ad., home, 2676 Decatur ave., N. Y. C. Tremont 3766.

NELSON, Jack; b. Memphis, Tenn., 1882; educ. Mil. Acad., Sweetwater, Tenn.; stage career, for 12 yrs., Belasco Stock, with Henry Miller in "Mice and Men," own stock co. in Springfield, Mo., for 2 yrs; screen career, Selig, Ince, Universal ("The Flash of Fate," "The Man Trap"), Bluebird ("Winner Takes All," "The Long Chance"), Paramount ("The Girl Dodger," "23½ Hours Leave"), Fox ("The Wilderness Trail," "Rose of the West," "Rough Riding Romance"). Hght., 5, 10; wght., 150; brown hair, gray eyes.

NICHOLS, George O.; b. Rockford, Ill., 1864; stage career, stock in San Francisco and Chicago 14 yrs., with road cos. 5 yrs.; screen career, with Edison as actor, then as assistant to Griffith at Biograph for 3 yrs., director for Thanhouser 1 yr., Lubin 1 yr., Keystone 1 yr., then Universal, Ince-Paramount ("The Son of His Father," "Keys to the Righteous"). Artcraft ("Battling Jane," "The Romance of Happy Valley"), Goldwyn ("Mickey," "When Doctors Disagree," "Pinto"), Griffith ("The Greatest Question"), First National ("Bill Apperson's Boy"). Member of M. P. D. A. Home ad., 1442 Alvarado Terrace, Los Angeles, Cal.

NORCROSS, Frank M.; b. Boston; stage career, 20 yrs., actor, manager, Frohman, and own co.; screen career, Biograph, Griffith, Universal, Kalem, World, Metro, 1918-19 with Vitagraph; in "The Highest Bidder," "The Spark Divine," "The Girl Woman," "The Fortune Hunter," "The Undercurrent," "Beware," "From Bankers to Bums." Hght., 5, 10; wght., 250; fair complexion, grayish hair, gray eyes. Ad., 50 Warburton ave., Yonkers, N. Y. Yonkers 2789.

NORTHRUP, Harry S.; b. Paris, France; educ. San Francisco and Univ. of Calif.; stage career, stock in San Francisco, heavies with E. H. Sothern, Henry Miller Wm. Faversham, Mary Mannering, Mrs. Leslie Carter; screen career, Douglas Fairbanks ("Arizona"), Harry Garson ("The Hushed Hour"), Metro ("Way of the Strong"), Universal ("The Brute Breaker"), Allan Dwan ("Luck of the Irish"). Hght., 6; wght., 175; brown hair and eyes. Home ad., Hotel Clark, Los Angeles, Calif.

NOWELL WEDGWOOD, also musical director; b. Porsmouth, N. H.; educ. Univ. of Pa.; stage career, Klaw & Erlanger's "Ben Hur," supported Blanche Bates, Amelia Bingham, William Faversham, etc.; screen career, United ("The Corsican Brothers," "A Man's Fight," "Adele"), Brunton ("The Dream Cheater," "The Lord Loves the Irish"), B. B. Features ("Kitty Kelly, M. D.," "Her Purchase Price"), J. D. Hampton ("Man Who Turned White"), First Nat'l ("The Beauty Market"), Haworth ("The Man Beneath"). Hght., 5, 11; wght., 165; dark brown hair and eyes. Member Actors' Equity Assn., Friars Club. Ad., care Actors' Assn. of Los Angeles, 6412 Hollywood blvd., Los Angeles, Calif.; Holly 1946.

NYE, G. Raymond; b. Tamaqua, Pa.; educ. Wilmington, Del., Phila., Pa., and Univ. of Penn.; stage career, 5 yrs. road shows, vaud. and stock; screen career, Fox ("When a Man Sees Red" "Salome" "Rainbow Trail," "Last of the Duanes," "Lone Star Ranger," "Wolves of the Night"), Hart ("Dan Kurrie's Inning"). Hght., 5, 11½; wght., 215; dark brown hair and eyes. Home ad., Roberts Apts. 1042 Sanborn ave., Los Angeles, Calif.; Wilshire 5327.

— O —

OAKER, John; b. Ottawa, 1893; educ. Isaac Woodbury Comm. Coll., Los Angeles; stage career, 2 yrs. in stock, Burbank theatre, Los Angeles; screen career, Bosworth ("Majesty of the Law"), Horsley in 1915 ("Haunting Symphony"), Centaur-Mutual ("The Single Code"), Vogue ("A Vanquished Flirt"), Marine Film Co. ("Lorelei of the Sea"), Fox ("The Sneak"). Hght., 5, 5; wght., 155; black hair and eyes.

OAKMAN, WHEELER; b. Washington, D. C.; educ. there; stage career, "Under Southern Skies," "Strongheart," "Checkers," also rep.; screen career, Selig, Fox, Universal, Triangle, Keystone ("Mickey"), Blanche Sweet ("Woman of Pleasure"), S. C. Photo Co. ("Back to God's Country"), Charlotte Walker ("Eve in Exile"), Priscilla Dean ("Virgin of Stamboul"). Hght., 5, 11; wght., 170; brown hair and eyes. Home ad., 5611 Hollywood blvd., Los Angeles, Calif.

O'BRIEN, Eugene; b. Colo., 1884; educ. Univ. of Colo.; stage career, mus. com., Frohmans, Elsie Janis, Ethel Barrymore, Margaret Illington, Ann Murdock, Fritzi Scheff; screen career, Artcraft ("Rebecca of Sunnybrook Farm"), Select ("The Ghosts of Yesterday"), Keeney ("A Romance of the Underworld"), Select ("By Right of Purchase," "De Luxe Annie"), Para ("Little Miss Hoover," "Come Out of the Kitchen"), F. P.-Lasky ("Fires of Faith"), Selznick ("The Perfect Lover," "Sealed Hearts," "The Broken Melody," "His Wife's Money," "A Fool and His Money"). Hght., 6; wght., 160; light brown hair, blue eyes. Ad., Players' Club, N. Y.; studio, care Selznick Pict. Corp., N. Y.

O'CONNOR, Edward; b. Dublin, Ireland, Feb. 20, 1862; stage career, 34 yrs., com. and char. parts in support of Al. Leach, Andrew Mack, Kathryn Kidder, William Courtleigh, Rogers Bros., "Old Lady 31"; vaud.; screen career, Edison 6 yrs., Pathe ("Hazel Kirke," "Get Rich Quick Wallingford"), World ("Man Who Stood Still"), Mirror, K. E. S. E. ("One Touch of Nature"), Fox ("Kathleen Mavourneen"). Now in "The Lost Leader" at Greenwich Village theatre. Ad., 15 Filmore ave., Corona, L. I., N. Y.; Newtown 1253-R.

O'CONNOR, Harry M.; b. Chicago, Ill., 1873; educ. Seattle, Wash.; stage career, stk. and vaud.; screen career, Fox, Paralta, National etc., Lasky ("The Girl of My Dreams," "Blindfolded," "The Dub," "Have Another," "The Haunted House"), Paramount ("The Dub"), Rob-Cole ("The Long Lane's Turning"). Hght., 6; wght., 195; medium complexion, brown eyes, brown hair. Ad., 1316 Tamarind ave., Hollywood, Cal. Holly 2566.

O'CONNOR, Louis J.; b. Providence, R. I., 1880; stage career, Western Stk., also with Shubert Prods.; screen career, Selznick ("Glorious Lady"), Goldwyn ("Woman in the Index," "Partners of the Night"), Pathe ("The Fatal Ring"). Hght., 5, 11; wght., 210; slightly gray hair, hazel eyes. Ad., Green Room Club, N. Y.

OGLE, Charles; b. Morgan Co., Ohio; educ. Chicago, Ill. Coll. of Law; stage career, 20 yrs., 3 yrs. with Klaw & Erlanger, 3 yrs. Shuberts, 2 yrs. Dan Frohman, 3 yrs. Chauncey Olcott, etc.; screen career, 7 yrs. with Edison, 4 yrs. with Famous Players ("Valley of the Giants," "Told in the Hills," "Capt. Hawthorne of the U. S. A.," "Treasure Island," "Jack Straw"). Hght., 6, 2½; wght., 200; dark brown hair and eyes. Ad., Lasky Studio, Hollywood, Calif.

OLAND, Warner; b. Sweden, 1880; educ. Boston; stage career, with Viola Allen in "The Christian," "Eternal City," "Twelfth Night," "Winter's Tale," with Sothern and Marlowe in "A Fool There Was," "Yellow Ticket," etc.; screen career, Wharton-International ("Patria"), Astra ("The Cigarette Girl," "The Naulahka"), World ("Mandarin Gold"), Famous Players ("The Avalanche," "Witness for the Defense"), Pathe ("Twin Pawns"), Translator of Strindberg's plays; scenario writer and producer. Hght., 5, 11; wght., 180; brown hair and eyes. Home ad., 257 W. 86th st., N. Y., or Hollywood Hotel, Hollywood, Calif.

OLIVER, Guy; b. Chicago, 1880; educ. Logan sch., Lamar, Mo.; stage career, vaud. 4 seasons, stk. and road; screen career, from 1911, Lubin 2 yrs., Kinemacolor 1 season, Eclair 1 yr., Selig, Artcraft ("The Little American," "M'liss," "Rimrock Jones," "The Whispering Chorus," "Less Than Kin," "Under the Top"), Paramount ("The Roaring Road," "The Valley of the Giants," "The Heart of Youth," "Told in the Hills," "It Pays to Advertise," "Hawthorne of the U. S. A." "Male and Female"). Hght., 5, 11; wght., 176; brown hair, gray eyes. Home addr 6063 Selma ave., Los Angeles, Cal.; studio, Lasky, Hollywood, Cal.

OLIVO, Valerio; b. Mexico City; educ. abroad; stage career, 3 yrs. abroad and So. America; screen career, Francis Ford ("The Silent Mystery," "Mystery of 13," "Gates of Doom"). Home ad., Bachelor's Lodge, Hollywood, Cal.; phone 577177; studio, Francis Ford.

O'MALLEY, Patrick H.; b. 1892, Dublin, Ireland; educ. Forest City, Pa.; stage career, stk. in British Isles, France and Germany, with Olcott Co. 3 yrs.; screen career, Kalem, Gauntier, Edison, Famous Players, Universal ("Breath of the Gods"), Metro ("False Evidence"), Goldwyn ("Blooming Angel"). Hght., 5, 11; wght., 168; brown hair, blue eyes. Home add., 5610 Franklin ave., Hollywood, Calif.; studio, Universal City.

O'NEILL, James; b. Phila., Pa.; educ. Univ. of Penn.; stage career, 20 yrs. as singer and actor, playing in many prods. and starring in "The Burglar"; screen career, 4 yrs. with Solax playing characters in over 200 pictures for the Blaches, with U. S. Amusement Corp., Famous Players ("The Traveling Salesman"), Bluebird ("The Honor of Mary Blake," "Little Miss Nobody," "The Ragged Queen"). White hair and blue eyes. Ad., Green Room Club, N. Y.

O'REILLY, J. Francis; educ. St. John's College, Brooklyn, N. Y.; stage career, 25 yrs.; screen career, straight and characters, Famous Players, World, Metro, Fox, Doris Kenyon Co., Mirror Films, Tourneur, Capellani, Vitagraph, etc; 1919-20 with Morosco's "Civilian Clothes" co. Hght., 5, 10; wght., 160; gray hair, blue eyes. Ad., 23 Martin ave., Glendale, Brooklyn, N. Y.; Rich Hill 769.

ORMONDE, Eugene; b. Boston; educ. there, England and France; stage career, Augustin Dalys, David Belasco, Mrs. Fiske, Margaret Anglin, etc.; screen career, Famous Players, Triangle, Fox ("Dancing Girl," "Morals of Marcus," "Bella Donna," "The Woman Who Gave," "The Light"). Hght., 6; wght., 180; dark complexion, hair, eyes. Ad., 16 Gramercy Park, N. Y.

OVERTON, Evart Emerson; b. Osborne, O.; educ. Osborne and Ohio State Univ.; early career, newspaper man; stage career, in mus. comedy and vaud., appeared with Raymond Hitchcock and other stars; screen career, Vitagraph ("Lost on Dress Parade," "The Bottom of the Well," "The Enchanted Profile," "Heredity," "The Purple Dress"). Hght., 6, 2; wght., 186; brown hair, blue eyes. Ad., Vitagraph, Brooklyn, N. Y.

OVEY, George; b. Grunty Co., Mo.; educ. Kansas City, Mo.; stage career, starred in "A Knight for a Day" 2 seasons, starred one season in "The Runaways," star stk. engagement at Portland, Me.; screen career, Horsley, Gaiety comedies ("Dropped Into Scandal," "Are Flirts Foolish?," "Dark and Cloudy," "Hits and Misses," "Cursed by His Cleverness"). Hght., 5, 4; wght., 130; brown hair and eyes. Ad., 1501 Gower st., Los Angeles, Calif.; Holly 3100; studio, Gaiety Comedies, Inc.

— P —

PAGET, Alfred; b. England; early career, British Army in Boer war; stage career, from 1907, Belasco Stk. Co., with Julia Marlowe in "The Goddess of Reason," and Guy Bates Post in "The Bridge"; screen career, since 1910, Biograph, Reliance-Majestic, Fine Arts, in a number of photoplays under Griffith's supervision, including "Intolerance," "Nina the Flower Girl"), Morosco ("Big Timber"), Fox, ("Alladin and the Wonderful Lamp"), Jewel ("When a Girl Loves").

PAISLEY, G. Chas.; b. Glasgow, Scotland; educ. Univ. of Glasgow; stage career, 1910 tour of G. B. with Cinderella pantomime, 1911 Alladin pantomime, headed own act over the Beresford tour, with Harry Lauder's rep., etc.; screen career, 1912, London Film Co. ("Lady of the Lake," "Merchant of Venice," wrote and made 39 two-reel comedies with Jack Purves, English woman impersonator). Hght., 5, 9; wght., 143; auburn hair, blue eyes. Ad., Hotel Glidden, Hollywood, Calif.

PALLETTE, Eugene; b. Winfield, Kan.; educ. Culver Mil. Acad.; stage career, 12 yrs. in "Alias Jimmy Valentine"; screen career, Universal, American, Majestic, Selig, Fine Arts ("Hell-to-Pay Austin," "Intolerance"), Morosco-Paramount ("The Marcellini Millions," "The World Apart," "The Heir of the Ages"), Paralta ("A Man's Man," "Turn of a Card"), Famous Players ("The Ghost House"), National Film Corp. ("Tarzan of the Apes"), Houdini ("Under Sea Loot"), Metro ("Amateur Adventuress," "Fair and Warmer," "Jimmy Valentine," "Parlor, Bedroom and Bath," "Twin Beds"). Hght., 5, 9½; wght., 155; dark brown hair, blue eyes. Home ad., Gates Hotel, Los Angeles, Calif.

PAPE, Edward Lionel; educ. Eton and Trinity College, Oxford, England; stage career, "Fanny's First Play," "General John Regan," etc.; screen career, several pictures before the war, ("The Sporting Duchess") for Vitagraph. Hght., 5, 9; wght., 170; brown hair, blue gray eyes. Ad., Friars Club, N. Y.

PARKE, William, Jr.; b. Phila., Pa.; educ. Phila. pub. schls. and by tutors; stage career, 2 yrs. dram. stk. mgmt. Brady, A. H. Woods, with Andrew Mack, Arnold Daly, etc.; screen career, Famous Players, Thanhouser ("Vicar of Wakefield," "Her New York," "The Candy Girl"), Astra-Pathe ("The Cigarette Gorl," "Streets of Illusion," "The Last of the Carnaby's," "A Crooked Romance"). Hght., 5, 8; wght., 130; brown hair, hazel eyes. Captain in R. F. C. in France. Ad., 514 W. 184th st., N. Y.

PATTEE, Herbert Horton, also scenario writer; b. Ft. Fairfield, Me.; educ. Wash., D. C.; stage career, Boston stk., with Booth, Barrett, Modjeska, Henry Miller, Walker Whiteside, vaud.; screen career, Edison ("A Royal Pauper"), Metro ("The Millionaire's Double"), Veritas ("And the Children Pay"), Goldwyn ("For the Freedom of the East"), Vitagraph ("The Cambric Mask," "The Vengeance of Durand," "The Fortune Hunter," "In Honor's Web," "Silent Strength") Hght., 5, 10; wght., 170; brown hair, blue eyes. Ad., 2339 Morris ave., N. Y.; Fordham 2250.

PAUNCEFORT, George; b. San Francisco; educ. Boston and Da Voe College; stage career, with Frohman, Shubert, John Drew, "Gay Lord Quex," Chas. Hopkinson; screen career, Blackton, Metro, Pathe Jimmy Dale serial Educational "The Purple Lady," "Her Great Price," "Marriage," "The Key to Power." Hght., 5, 10½; wght., 160; brown hair, blue eyes. Ad., 177 W. 79th, N. Y.

PEARCE, George C.; b. N. Y.; educ. Trinity Schl.; stage career, with Henry E. Dixey's summer opera co., leading tenor in rep opera, 6 yrs. a member Empire Theatre Stk. Co., mgmt. Charles Frohman, with Henry Miller; screen career, Biograph 2 yrs., Triangle, Culver City ("Intolerance"), Universal ("The Masked Woman"), Bluebird ("Treason," "The Black Mantilla," "The Pointed Finger," "The Woman With the Parakeets"), Triangle ("Crown Jewels"), Vitagraph ("A Gentleman of Quality"). Studio ad., Triangle, Culver City, Cal. Permanent ad., The Players, 16 Gramercy Park, N. Y. C.

PEGG, Vester; b. Ponca City, Okla., 1889; early career, spent on ranch, toured with 101 Ranch Wild West Show; screen career, NYMP, Bison, Kalem, Vitagraph, Reliance-Majestic, Fine

Arts ("The Birth of a Nation"), Fox ("Blue Blood and Red"), Universal ("The Texas Sphinx," "The Range War," "The Secret Man," "The Marked Man," "A Woman's Fool," "Hell Bent," "Ace of the Saddle," "Bare Fists," "Riders of the Law"). Studio ad., Selig, Los Angeles, Calif.

PEIL, Edward; b. Racine, Wis.; educ. Univ. of Notre Dame, South Bend, Ind.; stage career, with Mme. Modjeska, in road cos. of "The Witching Hour," "Brewster's Millions," mus. com., "The Century Girl," leads in stk. 5 yrs.; screen career, American, Lubin, Selig, Pathe, D. W. Griffith ("Eyes of the World," "Borrowed Clothes," "Greatest Thing in Life," "Broken Blossoms"), Jesse Hampton ("Cressy," "Pagan God," "House of Thousand Candles," "The Dragon Painter"). Home ad., 1729 Sunset blvd., Hollywood, Calif.; Wilshire 3774.

PENILL, Richard; b. Jersey City, N. J.; educ. N. Y.; 5 yrs. stk. in England; screen career, Ince, Universal, Lois Weber, Brunton, Vitagraph, Lasky, "American Ace," "Doctor and the Woman," "Home," Paramount ("The Silver King"). Hght., 5, 10; wght., 161; brown hair, blue eyes. Ad., Yorkshire Hotel, L. A., Cal.

PERCYVAL, T. Wigney; b. Yorkshire, England; stage career, with Wilson Barrett, Herbert Tree, in England; with Ethel Barrymore, Dillingham, K. and E. Frohman, Belasco, Ames, in America; screen career, Fox ("Bilall in 'She"), Famous Players. Home ad., 56 W. 11th st., N. Y.

PERIOLAT, George E.; b. Chicago, Ill.; educ. there; stage career, 17 yrs. with Otis Skinner, Julia Arthur, "Arizona," Adelaide Thurston Co., stk.; screen career, 1 yr. Selig, 2 yrs. Universal, 8 yrs. American ("Mate of the Sally Ann," "The Hellium," "Tiger Lily"). Hght., 5, 10; wght., 187; brown-gray hair, blue-gray eyes. Home ad., Engstrum Apts., Los Angeles, Cal.; Main 7374.

PERRY, Walter; screen career, Rob-Cole ("A Sage Brush Hamlet," "The Pagan God," "Dangerous Waters," "A Fugitive From Matrimony"), Hampton-Pathe ("Fighting Cressy," "Prince and Betty").

PETTIE, Graham; b. Edinburgh, Scotland; educ. King's Coll., London, Trinity Coll., Cambridge; stage career, 18 yrs., supported Richard Mansfield, Forbes-Robertson, Margaret Anglin, Charles Coghlan; screen career, Triangle ("Heirs for a Day," "Honest Man"), Hampton ("The Westerners"), Metro ("The Right of Way," "Old Lady 31"). Hght., 5, 8; wght., 156; brown hair, dark blue eyes. Home ad., 1597 W. 21st st., Los Angeles, Calif.; phone 72891.

PHILLIPS, Augustus; b. Rensselaer, Ind.; educ. Univ. of Ind.; stage career, stock San Francisco and N. Y., "The Wolf," "Small Town Girl," "Lady Betty"; screen career, Edison, Vitagraph, Universal, Metro ("The Gates of Eden," "Threads of Fate," "Aladdin's Other Lamp," "Blue Jeans," "The Lion's Den," "Peggy Does Her Darndest"), Para-Artcraft ("The Grim Game"), Goldwyn ("Toby's Bow"). Hght., 5, 10; wght., 169; dark complexion, dark brown hair, gray eyes.

PICKFORD, Jack; b. Toronto, Can. 1896; educ. St. Francis Mil. Acad., N. Y.; stage career, "Peg Robin," "The Three of Us"; screen career since 1909, Biograph, 1 yr., Famous Players ("Great Expectations," "Freckles," "The Girl at Home," "The Varmint," "What Money Can't Buy," "The Ghost House," "Tom Sawyer," "Jack and Jill," "Huckleberry Finn," "The Spirit of '17"; own co. ("Sandy," "In Wrong"), Goldwyn ("Little Shepherd of Kingdom Come," "The Double Dyed Deceiver"). Ad., studio, Goldwyn, Culver City, Calif.

PIERCE, Ben; stage career, juvenile and character roles in light comedy and comedy productions; associated with American and Atlantic Amuse. Co.; screen career, Jester and Screencraft Comedies; to appear in series of comedies with Sammy Burns, Motion Picture Producing Co. of America; also write continuities. Hght., 5, 11½; wght., 180; brown hair, blue eyes. Ad., 321 21st st., Brooklyn, N. Y.

PIERSON, Leo; b. Abilene, Kan., 1890; educ. St. Vincent's Coll., Los Angeles; stage career, Belasco stk. and Burbank theatre, Los Angeles; screen career, helped make pictures 12 foreign countries, the Orient and South Seas; Universal ("The Birth of Patriotism," "A Soldier of the Legion"), Selig ("The Fount of Courage"), Hart ("Poppy Girl's Husband," "Wagon Tracks"), New Art Films ("Sins of Parents"), Pasograf ("Spreading Evil"), Beban ("Hearts of Men"). Hght., 5, 11; wght., 160; dark hair, hazel eyes. Ad., 3048 W. 12th st., Los Angeles, Calif.

PIKE, William; b. Salt Lake City; stage career, 12 yrs.; screen career, Cal. M. P. Corp., Fox, Rolfe "Salvation Nell," "The Unwritten Law," "Faust," "The Master Mystery"), Oliver Films ("The Carter Case" serial), Grossman Pictures ("One Million Dollars Reward" serial). Hght., 5, 8½; wght., 155; dark hair and eyes. Ad., St. Margaret Hotel, W. 47th st., N. Y.

PLAYTER, Wellington; b. England, 1883; educ. N. Y. State Normal Sch.; stage career, stock leads in Denver, Salt Lake, Rochester, on road with Playter players; screen career, Edison, Famous Players, Metro, directed Wharton's "Eagle Eye Serial," lead, Universal, National ("The Search for Arcadia"), Goldwyn (opp. Mae Marsh), Ex. Mutual ("In Search of Arcady"), Arrow ("Fool's Gold"), First National ("Back to God's Country"). Hght., 6, 1½; wght., 232; light hair, blue eyes, athletic build. Ad., 5553 Hollywood Blvd., Los Angeles, Calif.

POLLAR, Gene; b. N. Y. C.; screen career, Numa Pictures Corp. (lead in "The Return of Tarzan"). Hght., 6, 2; wght., 215; black hair, brown eyes. Ad., Numa Pictures Corp., 1476 Broadway, N. Y.

POLLARD, Harry ("Snub"); b. Melbourne, Aus.; educ. there; stage career, 6 yrs. with Pollard Juvenile Opera Co.; screen career, since 1915, Morosco, Ferris Hartman, Essanay, now with Rolin making 2-reel (Harry Pollard Co.) comedies ("All at Sea," "Start Something," "How Dry I Am"). Hght., 5, 6½; wght., 148; brown hair and eyes. Home ad., 406 Court st., Los Angeles, Calif.; Pico 680; studio, Rolin.

POLO, Eddy; b. San Francisco; educ. continent; stage career, variety shows, musical comedies and circus; screen career, leads in "The Broken Coin," "Liberty," "Ouda of the Orient," "Gray Ghost," "Bull's Eye," "Lure of the Circus," "Money Madness." Hght., 5, 8½; wght., 175; black hair and eyes. Home ad., 6629 Hollywood Blvd., Los Angeles, Calif., phone 577763; studio, Universal.

POTEL, Victor; b. Lafayette, Ind., 1889; early career, business in Chicago and Memphis, Tenn.; screen career, was engaged by G. M. Anderson because of physique, first picture with Essanay (lead in "Slippery Slim" series), with Universal, 1915, Keystone, Mary Pickford ("Capt. Kidd, Jr."), Metro ("Amateur Adventuress," "Full of Pep," "The Heart of a Child"), Paramount-Artcraft ("In Mizzoura"), Thos. H. Ince ("Mary's Ankle"), Universal ("Petal of the Current"), Goldwyn ("Billy Fortune Series"). Hght., 6, 1; wght., 130; light brown hair, blue eyes. Home ad., 5742 Virginia ave., Hollywood, Calif.

POWELL, David; b. Scotland; stage career, with Sir H. B. Tree in London, Ellen Terry, Forbes-Robertson; screen career, World, Famous Players, Selznick, Empire ("The Unforeseen," "The Beautiful Adventure," "The Girl and the Judge," "The Better Half," "The Make Believe Wife," "Under the Greenwood Tree"), Artcraft ("His Parisian Wife"), United ("The Woman Under Oath"), Paramount ("The Firing Line," "Teeth of the Tiger"). Hght., 5, 10; wght., 160; dark hair and eyes. Ad., Famous Players, N. Y.

POWELL, Russ; b. Indianapolis, 1875; stage career, 9 yrs., vaud., Orpheum circuit, "Madcap Duchess," "Chocolate Soldiers," 2 seasons as basso San Francisco Opero Co.; screen career, Biograph, National, with Vogue since its organization ("Morning After," "Missing Heiress"), Pathe ("Brothers Divided"). Hght., 5, 11; wght., 295. Studio ad., Keenan Prod., Inc., Brunton Studios, Los Angeles.

PRIOR, Herbert; b. Oxford, Eng.; educ. Oxford; stage career, 15 yrs.; screen career, Biograph, Majestic, Edison, Famous ("Mrs. George Washington"), Artcraft ("Poor Little Rich Girl," "The Model's Confession," "A Burglar for a Night," "Great Expectations"), Nazimova "Stronger Than Death"), Mary Pickford ("Pollyanna"). Hght., 6; wght., 180; dark hair, gray eyes. Ad., 6519a DeLongpre ave., Hollywood, Calif.

PURVES, Jack H.; b. Edinburgh, Scot.; educ. Heriot Watt Coll., Edinburgh; stage career, 1½ yrs. legit. stage, juvenile leads and leads in "Peter Pan" tour; screen career, London Film Co. ("Dick Whittington," "House Temperly"), 39 successful comedies high-class, also a female impersonator. Hght., 5, 7; wght., 136; black hair, blue eyes. Home ad., Glidden Hotel, Los Angeles, Calif., Holly 3910.

— R —

RANDALL, Bernard; b. Odessa, Russia, 1884; educ. N. Y. and W. Jersey Military Acad.; stage career, actor and stage mgr. in many N. Y. successes, in dram. and vaud. houses throughout country in past 14 yrs.; screen career, Rex Beach ("The Auction Block"), Blackton ("Safe for Democracy," "Life's Greatest Problem"), Vitagraph ("The Clarion Call," "Within the Law"), H & H Prods. ("The Collar Line"), Vitagraph ("The Song of the Soul"), Bluebird ("Together"), Grossman ("Million Dollars Reward"), Benny Leonard Serial, "The Evil Eye." Hght., 5, 11; wght., 160; dark hair, gray eyes. Ad., Green Room Club, N. Y.

RANDOLF, Anders; b. 1875, Denmark; stage career, stk. in Columbus, Cleveland, Buffalo; also with Wm. Farnum's all-star co., Henrietta Crossman, etc.; screen career, 4 yrs. Vitagraph, leading and title part in "413"; Master Drama "Who's Your Neighbor?", Olcott Players, Inc. ("The Belgian"), Buffalo M. P. Corp. ("The Price of Virtue"), Goldwyn ("Splendid Sinner"), Vitagraph ("Lion and the Mouse"), Famous Players ("Erstwhile Susan"), International ("Cinema Murder"), Griffith ("The Black Beach"). Ad., Lambs Club, N. Y., and 15 W. 67th st., N. Y.

RATTENBERRY, Harry L.; b. Sacramento, Calif., 1858; stage career, from 1879, 27 yrs. of operatic work in all principal cities, 1 season in "The Chorus Lady"; screen career, Powers, Keystone, Mutual, Rolin, 3 yrs. with Christie, Lasky ("Oliver Twist"), Universal ("High Speed"), Ince-Para. ("Playing the Game"), Mary Pickford ("M'Liss"), Selznick ("Indiscreet Corinne"), George Beban ("Hearts of Men"). Hght., 5, 11; wght., 295; brown hair and eyes. Ad., 1554 N. Alexandria ave., Los Angeles.

RAWLINSON, Herbert; b. Brighton, Eng., 1885; educ. Eng. and France; stage career, repertoire and stk.; screen career, Selig, Bosworth, Universal ("Florting with Death," "The Flash of Hate," "The Man Trap," "Come Through," "Smashing Through"), Goldwyn ("The Turn of the Wheel"), Famous Players ("Good Gracious, Annabelle"), Blackton ("The Common Cause," "House Divided"), Oliver (Craig Kennedy serial; Chief Flynn Secret Service series), Blackton Prod. ("Passers-By"). Hght., 6; wght., 165; brown hair, blue eyes. Ad., Lambs Club, N. Y.

RAY, Albert; b. New Rochelle, N. Y., 1893; educ. N. Y.; stage career, "Buster Brown" at 7 yrs., mus. com., vaud., stk.; screen career, Pathe, Vitagraph, Fox, Loie Weber, Ince, Universal, etc. "Home," "Bluebird," "When Do We Eat," "Married in Haste," "Love Is Love," "Bet a Little Sport," "The Lost Princess," "Tin Pan Alley," "The Honey Bee," "Vagabond Luck"). Hght., 6 ft.; wght., 160; brown hair, dark blue eyes. Ad., L. A. A. Club, Los Angeles, Calif.; studio, Fox.

RAY, Charles; b. Jacksonville, Ill., 1891; educ. Illinois and Los Angeles Polytech. Schl.; stage career, 4½ yrs. in mus. and dram. stk., vaud., etc.; screen career, Ince-Para. ("String Beans," "The Sheriff's Son," "The Coward," "The Busher," "The Girl Dodger," "The Egg-Crate Wallop," "Greased Lightning," "Bill Henry," "Crooked Straight," "Red Hot Dollars," "Paris Green"). Hght., 6, ½; wght., 170; dark brown hair, brown eyes. Ad., Charles Ray Prods., 615 Wright and Callendar Bldg., Los Angeles, Calif.

RAYMOND, Dean; stage career, stk., vaud. and prods.; screen career, Bluebird ("The Boy Girl," "Little Miss Nobody"), Photo Drama ("Warning"), Goldwyn ("Cinderella Man"), General ("For Freedom of the World"), Eva Tanguay ("The Wild Girl"), Ivan ("Conquered Hearts"), Metro ("Winning of Beatrice"). Hght., 5, 9; wght., 170; light gray hair, dark gray eyes. Ad., Green Room Club, N. Y.

RAYMOND, Pete; stage career, 2 seasons with Belasco "The Woman," Morosco "Mile-a-Minute Kendall," Cohan & Harris "Tailor Made Man"; 15 yrs. in stk. Chicago, St. Louis, Kansas City, Minneapolis, etc.; screen career, Ivan-Abramson ("Some One Must Pay"), Selznick ("Sealed Hearts," "The Imp"), Famous Players ("On With the Dance"), Democracy Co. (Democracy"). Hght., 6; wght. 200; brown hair and eyes. Ad., Elks Club, 116 W. 43d st., N. Y.

REEVES, Bob; b. Marlin, Texas; educ. there and A. & M. Coll., Texas; early career, cowboy; screen career, Universal ("To the Tune of Bullets"), Pacific Prod. Co. ("Elmo the Mighty," "The Radium Mystery"). Hght., 6, 2½; wght., 200; brown hair, gray eyes. Home ad., 223 S. Flower, Los Angeles, Calif., B'way, 2120.

REID, Wallace; b. St. Louis, Mo.; educ. N. Y. and New Jersey Mil. Acad.; early career; held position on editorial staff of Motor Magazine; stage career, appeared in a vaud. sketch by his father, Hal Reid; screen career, Vitagraph, Universal (wrote, acted and directed), with D. W. Griffith in "Birth of a Nation," Lasky (leading man for Geraldine Farrar in "Carmen," "Joan the Woman," etc., Famous Players ("Believe Me, Xantippe," "The Roaring Road," "You're Fired," "The Love Burglar," "Valley of the Giants," "Hawthorne of the U. S. A.," "Double Speed," "Excuse My Dust," "The Dancin' Fool"). Hght., 6, 1; wght., 170; light brown hair, blue eyes. Ad., Lasky Studio, Hollywood, Calif.

RENE, Alex W.; b. Prague (Bohemia); educ. Prague, Vienna, Canada, Southern France; stage career, operatic stage, also dramatic since early childhood, abroad, Canada and stk. cos. Chicago; screen career, World ("Dangerous Ground," "Dark Silence"), Independent ("The Blood Stain"), Edison ("Barnaby Lee"), Otto ("Scouting for Washington"), Bloxbee ("Young America"), Camo Art Film ("Somewhere in Love"); famous fencing expert. Hght., 5, 11; wght., 153; light brown hair, dark eyes. Ad., Actors Equity Assn., N. Y.

RENFROE, James L.; b. Denison, Texas; educ. there; stage career, in vaud.; screen career, Cuckoo Comedies, Sunbeam Comedies ("Hot Sands and Cold Feet," "His Concrete Dome," "His Conscience His Guide," "A Traveling Saleman's Temptations," "Work and Win 'em," "A Trial by Jury."). Hght., 5, 4½; wght., 120; dark complexion, black hair, blue eyes. Ad., 436 E. 3d st., Jacksonville, Fla.

RICH, Charles G.; b. N. Y. C.; educ. N. Y. Univ.; early career, dramatic critic and writer; screen career, Vitagraph ("The Iron Test" serial. "Perils of Thunder Mountain" serial, "The Invisible Hand" serial, "The Fighting Coleen"). Hght., 5, 11; wght., 155; brown hair, blue eyes. Ad., 4356 Kingswell ave., Los Angeles, Calif.; studio, Vitagraph.

RICHARDSON, Jack H.; b. London, Eng.; educ. Lindisfarm Coll., West Cliff-on-Sea, England; stage career, Geo. Edwards Co., Gaiety theatre, London, London Music Halls, stk. Vancouver, B. C.; screen career, Chaplin Co., Henry Lehrman ("Milk Fed Vamp," "Roaring Lions and Wedding Bells," etc.), Diando Films ("Old Maid's Baby," etc.), Paton Film Co. ("The Sign of the Rat"). Hght., 5, 7; wght., 150; dark hair and eyes. Home ad., 2905 Washington Blvd., Ocean Park, Calif.

RICHMAN, Charles; b. Chicago; educ. Chicago Coll. of Law; stage career, with Ada Rehan in London and America, Blanche Bates, Mary Mannering, starred under mgmt. of the Shuberts, Wm. A. Brady and David Belasco; screen career, Lasky, Fox, Vitagraph ("The Secret Kingdom," "The More Excellent Way"), Public Rights Film ("The Public Be Damned"), Richman P. Corp. ("Over There"), Select ("The Hidden Truth"), Graphic ("The Echo of Youth"). Hght., 6, 1; wght., 196; brown hair and hazel eyes. Home ad., 65 Northfield rd., West Orange, N. J., and Lambs Club, N. Y.

RICHMOND, Warner Paul; b. Culpeper, Va.; educ. Univ. of Va.; stage career, leads in "Eyes of Youth," "Trail of the Lonesome Pine," "Misleading Lady," "As a Man Thinks," "Indian Summer," "Little Miss Brown"; screen career, Triangle, Selig, Tourneur prods. ("Sporting Life," "Woman," "My Lady's Garter"), Vitagraph ("Gray Towers Mystery"). Hght., 5, 11; wght., 165; fair complexion, brown hair, blue eyes. Ad., Green Room Club, N. Y.

RIDGWAY, John H. ("Jack"); b. Phila., Pa., 1866; educ. pub. schls., Phila.; early career, 2 yrs. in Forepaugh's Stock, Phila., and 2 yrs. with Forepaugh's circus; screen career, 5 yrs. with Lubin ("The Third Degree," "The Lion and the Mouse," "The Gamblers," etc), Famous Players ("Poor Little Peppina"), 4 yrs. with Universal ("Under Southern Skies," played all characters with King Baggot), Vitagraph ("The Unknown Quantity"). Has played Western and society roles. Hght., 5, 10; wght., 200; light complexion, gray hair and blue eyes. Home ad., 360 West 42d st., N. Y. C.

RIESNER, C. Francis ("Chuck"); b. Minneapolis, Minn.; educ. there; stage career, 10 yrs. in Keith and Orpheum circuits in vaud., starred in Dillingham's "Stop! Look! Listen!" and "Queen of the Movies"; screen career, scenario dept. at the Keystone ("His First False Step," "His Lying Heart"), with C. Chaplin ("A Dog's Life"), Rothackers-Chicago. Hght., 5, 11; wght., 178; brown hair and eyes. Ad., 6122 De Longpre ave., Hollywood, Calif.

RITCHIE, Billie; b. Glasgow, Scotland, 1877; stage career, vaud. com., mus. com., played in "A Night in an English Music Hall," also in "A Night on Broadway," "Vanity Fair," "Around the Clock," over Orpheum Circuit; screen career, L-Ko., playing in many one, two and three-reel farce-comedies "Where Is My Wife?"), Fox ("The House of Terrible Scandals"), Sunshine Comedies ("The Twilight Baby"). Hght., 5, 7½; wght., 140. Home ad., Laurel Canyon, Hollywood, Calif.; studio, Lehrman Studio, Culver City, Calif.

ROACH, Bert; b. Washington, D. C.; educ. there; stage career, 3 yrs. with Henry B. Harris, in "Louisiana Lou," "The Commuters"; screen career, Reliance, Majestic, Keystone ("Fatty's Magic Pants"), Universal ("Cactus and Kale," "Soapsuds and Sirens"), L-Ko. ("Dirty's Daring Dash"), Sennett ("Yankee Doodle in Berlin"). Hght., 5, 11; wght., 195; light hair and light eyes.

ROBBINS, Marc; b. 1870; early career, ranching; stage career, with Fanny Davenport, in Shakespearean roles in N. Y., stk. dir. 5 yrs. in St. Louis; screen career, with Universal, 1914, playing character leads with Kerrigan, Joe de Grasse and Frank Lloyd, late Universal pictures ("The Mainspring," "Her Soul's Inspiration"), Fox ("American Methods," "The Heart of a Lion," "True Blue," "Riders of the Purple Sage," "For Freedom," "The Man Hunter"). Ad., Zane Grey Pict., Inc., Brunton Studio.

ROBERTS, Theodore; b. San Francisco, Calif.; educ. there; stage career, played first leads with Robson and Crane, Fanny Davenport, played Svengali in "Trilby," Simon Legree in "Uncle Tom's Cabin," "The Squaw Man," "The Barrier," vaud.; screen career, Famous Players ("Old Wives for New," "M'liss," "Believe Me, Xantippe," "The Roaring Road," "Male and Female," "Hawthorne of the U. S. A."). Hght., 6; wght., 195; gray hair, blue eyes. Ad., Lasky Studio, Hollywood, Calif.

ROBSON, Andrew; b. Hamilton, Can., 1868; 25 yrs. on stage; starred 12 seasons "Royal Box," "Richard Carvel," etc.; screen career, Fox ("The Devil's Wheel"), Bluebird ("A Broadway Scandal," "That Devil Bateese," "Which Woman?"), W. S. Hart Co. ("Branding Broadway"), Ince-Paramount ("Alarm Clock Andy," "A Virtuous Thief," "Law of Men"), United ("The Corsican Brothers"), Rob-Cole ("The Beloved Cheater," "The Butterfly Man"). Hght., 5, 10; wght., 190; gray hair, brown eyes. Ad., Hotel Rosslyn, Los Angeles, Cal.

ROCK, Charles; b. Velore, E. Indies, 1866; educ. Brighton Coll., Eng.; stage career, Sir J. Hare; screen career (Scrooge in "A Christmas Carol," Hardcastle in "She Stoops to Conquer," Colonel Sapt in "Prisoner of Zenda," also leads in "Sons of Satan," "Rupert of Hentzau"), Vitagraph ("Firm of Girdlestone"), Cosmofotofilm ("I Believe"), World ("The Better 'Ole"). Ad., St. Margaret's, Middlesex, Eng.

ROCK, Joseph P.; b. N. Y. C., 1892; educ. N. Y. Normal and Chautauqua Normal; early career, teacher of dancing, physical culture, director of carnival; screen career, Vitagraph 4 yrs., Rock and Montgomery in Big V Comedies ("Bumbs and Boarders," "Chumps and Cops," "Farms and Fumbles," "Love and Lather," "Damsels and Dandies," "Zip and Zest," "Harems and Hokum," "Vamps and Variety," "Caves and Croquettes," "Rubes and Robbers"). Hght., 5, 5; wght., 145; black hair, dark blue eyes. Home ad., 1450 N. Normandie, Los Angeles, Calif.; phone 599052; studio, Vitagraph.

RODNEY, Earl; b. Toronto, Can.; educ. Notre Dame Univ.; stage career, vaud., stk. and on road; screen career, Griffith, Keystone, Bluebird ("City of Tears"), Ince. Para. ("Biggest Show on Earth," "Naughty, Naughty," "Keys of the Righteous"), Christie ("Two A. M.," "The Looney Honeymoon," " 'Twas Midnight," "Furs and Folly," "Ducks," "Monkey Shines"). Hght., 5, 11; wght., 167; dark complexion, eyes, hair. Ad., 2754 W. 14th st., Los Angeles, Cal. Studio, Christie, Hollywood, Cal.

ROGERS, Will; b. near Claremore, Indian Territory; stage career, 1905, vaud., fancy roper, Hammerstein's Roof, 8 yrs. vaud., 5 yrs. Follies and Midnight Frolics; screen career, Goldwyn ("Bill Hyde"), "Almost a Husband," "Jubilo," "The Strange Boarder"; author of "The Peace Conference" and "Prohibition." Hght., 5, 11; wght., 170; dark hair, gray eyes. Home ad., Culver City, Calif.; phone 56664.

ROONEY, Gilbert; educ. Univ. of Penn.; stage career, with Robt. Hilliard in "The Fool There Was," Edward Abeles in "Brewster's Millions," "Ready Money," "Pom Pom"; screen career, World ("Woman in 47"), Universal ("Parentage"), Selznick ("Country Cousin"), Erbograph ("Burning Question"), Lasky ("Framed Up"), International ("Adventures of Dorothy Dare" serial), Edward Warren ("Weavers of Life"), Vitagraph ("Blind Adventure"), Norma Talmadge ("Daughter of Two Worlds"); 2 yrs. in service, Tank Corps. Hght., 5, 10; wght., 155; brown hair and eyes. Ad., Green Room Club, N. Y.

ROSCOE, Albert; b. Nashville, Tenn., 1887; educ. Vanderbilt Univ., Nashville; 15 yrs. on stage as leading man and director; screen career, Famous Players, Leonce Perret, Fox ("The Siren's Song"), "Evangeline"), Ex. Mutual ("A Man's Country"), Goldwyn ("The City of Comrades"), Rob-Cole ("Her Purchase Price"). Hght., 6; wght., 175; brown eyes, black hair. Ad., Lambs' Club N. Y.

ROSEMAN, Ed. F.; b. Terre Haute, Ind., 1875; stage career, 6 yrs. with Lincoln J. Carter, Wright Lorimer, in "The Shepherd King"; screen career, supporting Mary Pickford, Robert Warwick; Edgar Lewis Prods. ("The Barrier," "Calibre 38"), Betzwood ("High Pockets"), World ("The Red Woman"), Virginia Pearson Co. ("Impossible Katherine"), Fox ("13th Bride" serial). Hght., 6; wght., 185; dark hair and eyes. Ad., Green Room Club, N. Y.

ROSS, D. George; educ. Washington, D. C., and N. Y.; stage career, vaud., "Romance of the Underworld," with "Way Down East," "The Holdup," with Will Hart stk.; screen career, Donovan Prods., Pathe, Selznick, "Bullin' the Bullsheviki"; served in France 18 mos. Hght., 5, 5; wght., 125; gray hair, blue eyes. Ad., Hotel Princeton, N. Y.; Bryant 3582.

ROSS, Milton; b. California; educ. Univ. of the Pacific for ministry; stage career, Mary Mannering in "Janice Meredith," Melbourne McDowell, James O'Neil, vaud.; screen career, Ince ("Truthful Tulliver"), Triangle, Artcraft-Paramount ("The Narrow Trail," "The Silent Man," "Riddle Gawne"), Universal ("Pretty Smooth," "The Exquisite Thief"), Hodkinson ("The End of the Game"), Goldwyn ("Flame of the Desert"), Hampton-Pathe ("A Woman of Pleasure"). Hght., 5, 10; wght., 190; dark hair and eyes. Ad., Goldwyn Studio, Culver City, Calif.

RUSSELL, William; educ. Fordham Univ.; stage career from age of 8, Ethel Barrymore in "Cousin Kate," David Higgins, Chauncey Olcott, Blanche Bates, Poli stk., starred in "St. Elmo," vaud.; screen career, Biograph, Thanhouser, Famous, Pathe ("The Midnight Trail," "Hearts or Diamonds," "Up Romance Road," "Hobbs in a Hurry"), Amer.-Pathe ("A Sporting Chance," "Where the West Begins," "Brass Buttons," "Six Feet Four," "This Hero Stuff"), Fox ("Sacred Silence," "Eastward Ho," "The Lincoln Highwayman"). Hght.,6, 2; wght., 203; dark hair and eyes. Member M.P.D.A. Ad., Fox Studio, Hollywood, Calif.

— S —

SACK, Nathaniel; b. & educ. Russia; stage career, 10 yrs. with Leonard Rayne Dramatic Co., toured extensively the Orient, British Colonies and So. Africa; in U. S. A. since 1912 with Mme. Nazimova, Fannie Ward, Walker Whiteside, Frank Keenan, "The Big Chance," with Mary Nash; screen career, Kalem ("Glory of Youth"), Famous Players ("Man From Mexico," "Mistress Nell"), Artcraft ("Less Than Dust"), Pathe ("Innocent"), Metro ("Will o' the Wisp"). Specialty, Oriental characters. Hght., 5, 7; wght., 145; dark brown hair and eyes. Home ad., 126 W. 119th st., N. Y. C.; Morningside 1963.

SACKVILLE, Gordon; b. Petersborough, Ontario, 1880; educ. Kalamazoo Coll., studied voice culture in London and Paris; stage career, "Circus Girl," "Chinese Honeymoon," with Richard Mansfield, N. Y. Hippodrome; screen career, Edison, Rex, Universal, Selig ("The Cherry Pickers"), Bosworth ("An Odyssey of the North"), Balboa ("The Grip of Evil," "The Girl Angle," "Glad Glory"), Falcon-General ("The Best Man"), Pioneer ("The Boomerang"), World ("The Arizona Cat Claw"). Hght., 6, 1; wght., 210; brown hair and eyes.

SAGE, Stuart; b. Sioux Falls, S. D., 1893; educ. Todd Seminary, Neb. Military Acad.; stage career, 2 yrs. vaud., "Help Wanted," "Argyle Case," "Baby Mine," with Emma Dunn in "Old Lady 31," stk., mus. com.; screen career, Fox ("The War Bride's Secret," "Two Little Imps," "Trouble Makers"), Lasky ("Brewster's Millions"); original "Argonne Players." Hght., 5, 9; wght., 140; fair complexion, light hair, blue eyes. Ad., c/o Melville Rosenow, New Amsterdam Theatre Bldg., N. Y.

SALISBURY, Monroe; b. N. Y.; studied art and music; stage career, from 1898; rep. with Richard Mansfield, Mrs. Fiske, John Drew, Nance O'Neil, etc., followed Wm. Farnum in "The Prince of India," under Chas. Frohman, K. & E., stk. at Castle Square, Boston, etc.; screen career, since 1913; Fine Arts, Lasky ("The Goose Girl"), Clune (Allesandro in "Ramona," "Eyes of the World"), Universal ("The Devil Between," "The Sleeping Lion," "The Phantom Melody"). Home ad., 5956 Hollywood Blvd., Los Angeles, Calif.

SANFORD, Philip; b. N. Y. C.; stage career, with Chas. Frohman, David Belasco, Cyril Maude, "Sherlock Holmes," "Secret Service"; screen career, Metro, Vitagraph ("The Sign Invisible," "The White Raven," "Strength of Men"), Hodkinson ("Made in America"), Zion ("Broken Barrier"), Community ("Home Keeping of Jim"), Adolph Phillip ("Midnight Girl"), Edgar Lewis ("Other Men's Shoes"), Betzwood ("Sandy Burke of U-Bar-U"); specializes in Western heavies. Hght., 6; wght., 200; light complexion, brown hair and eyes. Home ad., 637 Bedford ave., Brooklyn, N. Y., or Green Room Club, N. Y.

SANTSCHI, Thomas; b. Kokomo, Ind.; stage career, stock; screen career, Selig ("The Crisis," "The Garden of Allah," "The City of Purple Dreams," "The Still Alarm," "Little Orphant Annie"), Farrar-Goldwyn ("Shadows," "The Stronger Vow"), First National ("Her Kingdom of Dreams"), Universal ("Hugon, the Mighty"). Hght., 6, 2; sandy hair, blue eyes. Home ad., 1523 Micheltorena st., Los Angeles, Calif; Wilshire, 755.

SARNO, Hector V.; b. Naples, Italy, 1880; educ. there; stage career, Eimete Novelli Co. 5 yrs., Italy; screen career, Vitagraph, Universal, Fox, Goldwyn, Pathe, Metro ("Isle of Intrigue"), Rex Beach ("Silver Horde"), Dorothy Phillips ("Right to Happiness"), Ed. Carewe ("Rio Grande"), Romaine Film Co. ("Give and Take"), and several heavies opposite H. B. Warner. Hght., 5, 10; wght., 175; black hair, dark brown eyes. Ad., 4344 Fountain ave., Los Angeles, Calif.

SAWYER, Donald; b. Dundee, N. Y., 1894; educ. Rochester, N. Y.; stage career, played Joe Blake in "A Man's Home," with Geo. Nash, Hyperion Buncombe in Henry Savage's "Toot, Toot," Cyril Kinney in "The Country Cousin," with Alexandria Carlyle; screen career, Metro Goldwyn, Famous Players, Pathe, Drew comedies, "His Bonded Wife," etc. Hght., 5, 10½; wght., 140; brown hair, blue eyes. Ad., 241 W. 45th st., N. Y. C.; Bryant 7098.

SAXE, Templer (Templer William Edward Ederein); b. Redhill, England; educ. Bonn and Brussels Univs.; stage career, leading baritone Carl Rosa Opera Co. (London), "An English Daisy," "Piff, Paff, Pouff"; screen career, Vitagraph ("Strength of the Weak," "Mind the Paint Girl," "Lion and the Mouse," "Miss Ambition," "Pride"), Paramount-Artcraft ("The Teeth of the Tiger"), Constance Talmadge ("At the Barn"), Vitagraph ("One Thousand Dollars"). Hght., 5, 10; wght., 170; dark brown hair, gray-blue eyes. Ad., Green Room Club, N. Y.

SAXON, Hugh; b. New Orleans, La.; educ. Vanderbilt Univ., Nashville, Tenn.; stage career, with Thomas W. Keene, Henry Dixey, Maud Granger, Marie Wainwright; Charles Hoyt's comedies, Belasco Stk., Geary Stk., Ferris Stk. and own cos., also travelled over world in vaud. and circus clown; screen career, Wm. S. Hart ("Dan Kurrie's Inning"), Brentwood ("The Other Half"), Ince ("Alarm Clock Andy"). Hght., 5, 9½; wght., 165; silver gray hair, dark blue eyes. Home ad., 2610 Juliet, Los Angeles, Calif; phone 72540.

SCHABLE, Robert, also director; stage career, with Ethel Barrymore, John Drew, Marie Doro, Annie Russell, George Fawcett, Nazimova, "Everywoman," etc.; screen career, Famous Players-Lasky ("The Marriage Price," "World to Live In," "Red Head," "Test of Honor," "Firing Line," "Sinners," "On with the Dance"), Hght., 5, 7; wght., 145; light hair, blue eyes. Ad., Lambs Club, N. Y. C.

SCHENCK, Earl; b. Columbus, O.; educ. Ohio State Univ.; stage career, Stubbs Wilson Stk. Co., lead in Wm. A. Brady's "Way Down East," with Jas. K. Hackett, also vaud.; screen career, Pathe, World, Metro ("My Four Years in Germany," "The Spirit of Lafayette," "Ruling Passions," "Sacred Flame," "Blue Pearl," featured in Vitagraph O. Henry stories. Ad., Green Room Club, N. Y., or care Edward Small, Inc.

SCHUMM, Harry W.; b. Chicago, Ill.; educ. Chicago Univ.; stage career, 18 yrs. leading and heavy man, Hopkins Stock Co., Chicago, 1917 with Klaw & Erlanger, Morosco, 9 mos. Musical Stock, Camp Kearny; screen career, 6 yrs with Universal exclusive direction Francis Ford, now direction Phil Rosen and Al Santell. Hght., 5, 11½; wght., 175; dark brown hair and eyes. Home ad., 1727 Kent st., Los Angeles, Calif; Wilshire 4855; Walter Farnum, personal rep., Grant Bldg., Los Angeles.

SCOTT, William; b. 1893; educ. N. Y.; stage career, with Maude Adams, Joseph Jefferson, Kelcey and Shannon; screen career, Artcraft ("Amarilly of Clothesline Alley"), Fox ("Riders of the Purple Sage," "True Blue," "Kultur," "The Forbidden Room," "Pitfalls of a Big City," "Chasing Rainbows," "Broken Commandments," "Thieves," "Flames of the Flesh"). Hght., 5, 11; wght., 168; light complexion. Ad., home, 1923 Kent st., L. A., Cal.

SEARS, Allan; b. San Antonio; educ. Knox Coll.; concert work; stage career, stock, com opera; screen career, Reliance-Majestic ("The Birth of a Nation"), Fine Arts ("The Little Yank," "Children of the Feud," "Girl of the Timberlands"), Triangle ("Madame Bo-Beep"), Bluebird ("The Red, Red Heart"), Jewel ("Kaiser, the Beast of Berlin"), Metro ("Kate of Kentucky," "The Amateur Adventuress," "Her Inspiration"), Universal ("Destiny"). Ad., 4618 Russell st., Hollywood, Cal.

SEDGWICK, Edward, also scenario writer; educ. St. Mary's Univ., Texas Univ.; stage career, actor and stage dir., 10 yrs. in vaud. and mus. com., also dram. stk. and rep. ex; screen career, Lubin, Universal, American, Metro ("Haunted Pajamas"), Famous Players ("The Varmint"), Fox ("Yankee Way," "Checkers"); has written original stories as follows: "The Yankee Way," "Cheating the Public," "Stolen Honor," "Rough and Ready," "The Winning Stroke," "The Sea Beast," with continuities also, for Fox; also new Fox serial, "Bride No. 13." Hght., 6; wght., 245; brown hair, blue eyes. Ad., 245 W. 51st st., N. Y.; Circle 1730.

SEDLEY, Henry; b. N. Y.; educ. St. Paul's School, Andover Acad., Yale Univ.; stage career, 6 yrs.; screen career, 5 yrs., ("The Daredevil," "Thunderbolts of Fate," "The Kaiser Bride," "Embarrassment of Riches," "Marriage of Convenience," "Stranger Within the Gates," "The Clouded Name," "Corruption," "The Hidden Hand" Pathe serial, "Taxi"). Hght., 5, 11; wght., 155; fair complexion. Home ad., 114 W. 79th st., N. Y. C., or Green Room Club, N. Y.

SEIGMANN, George; b. N. Y.; educ. Boston Univ., La Salle Acad.; stage career, with Chas. Frohman, Harry Doel Parker; screen career, Fine Arts ("Intolerance," "The Little Yank"), Crystal ("Mother Love and the Law"), Griffith ("Birth of a Nation," "Hearts of the World," "The Great Love"), Dwan ("The Grafters"). Hght., 6, 2; wght., 230; brown hair and eyes. Home ad., 4518 Fountain ave., Los Angeles, Calif; phone 597529.

SELBY, Norman ("Kid McCoy"); b. Rushville, Ind.; early career, professional boxer; screen career, Feature Film ("The Great Diamond Robbery"), Fine Arts (the Rube in "Betty of Grey Stone"), Griffith ("Broken Blossoms"). Hght., 6; wght., 200; dark hair and eyes. Studio ad., Garson.

SELL, Henry G.; b. Los Angeles, 1889; stage career, stk. cos., Laurie in "Little Women," also with Arnold Daly, Lily Langtry, Julia Dean, etc.; screen career, Crystal, Astra, World ("Fine Feathers," "The Fatal Ring," "Lightning Raider"), Argus ("House Without Children"), Vitagraph ("Thin Ice"), Perret ("Twin

Pawn"), Serico ("Jeweled Hand" serial). Hght., 5, 10; wght., 155; brown hair and eyes. Ad., Green Room Club, N. Y.

SHAW, Brinsley; b. N. Y. C.; educ. Coll. City N. Y.; stage career, co-star with Margaret Wycherley in "The 13th Chair," E. H. Sothern Co., J. C. Williamson mgmt., Australia, Richard Mansfield, "The Squaw Man" orig. prod.; screen career, Anita Stewart ("Mary Regan"), Vitagraph ("The Wolf," "The Hornet's Nest," "The Invisible Hand"). Hght., 6; wght., 160; brown hair, gray eyes. Ad., 16 Gramercy Park, N. Y. C.

SHEER, William A.; b. Birmingham, Eng.; educ. Eng.; premier jockey for 3 yrs.; stage career, vaud. alone and with Isabelle De Armond; mus. com., "Isle of Spice," etc., produced "Oh, Look!" Orpheum, 1 season; screen career, Keystone-Mack Sennett, 1 yr., Fox ("Regeneration," "Within the Law"), World, general casting director, Universal ("The Cabaret Girl," "Sealed Envelope"), Norma Talmadge ("A Daughter of Two Worlds," character lead). Hght., 5, 10; wght., 140; brown hair, blue eyes. Ad., 1600 Broadway, N. Y. C., or 1627½ N. Kingsley Drive, Los Angeles, Calif.; Holly 4452.

SHERIDAN, Frank; b. Boston, Mass.; educ. Boston; stage career, featured actor in "Paid in Full," "Fine Feathers," "The Unwritten Law," "Blackmail," "The Next of Kin," "Three Faces East"; screen career, Kleine ("The Money Master"), Pathe ("At Bay," "Ruler of the Road"), Equitable ("The Man Higher Up"), World ("The Struggle"), Ivan "Enlighten Thy Daughter"), Universal ("His Woman"), Norma Talmadge ("Daughter of Two Worlds"). Ad., 1531 Broadway, N. Y.

SHERRILL, Jack; b. Atlanta, Ga., April 14, 1898; educ. Berkeley School, N. Y. C.; stage career, stock, vaud.; screen career, Frohman ("Just Out of College," "The Witching Hour"), Art Dramas ("The Rainbow," "Once to Every Man"), Authors Film Co.-Mutual ("The Silent Witness"), Frohman ("Once to Every Man," "The Invisible Ray"). Hght., 5, 9½; wght., 135; light complexion, brown hair, blue eyes. Ad., 166 W. 72nd st., N. Y., and c/o Frohman Amuse. Corp., Times Bldg., N. Y.

SHERRY, J. Barney; b. Germantown, Pa.; educ. private schls., Phila., and Catholic College, Germantown; screen career, Thos. H. Ince ("Civilization"), Universal ("Little Brother of the Rich," "Breath of the Gods"), Marshall Neilan ("The River's End"), Universal ("The Forged Bride"). Hght., 6, ¾; wght., 200; iron gray hair, gray eyes. Home ad., 224 San Vincente, Santa Monica, Calif; phone 508.

SHIELDS, Earnest W.; b. 1884; educ. Chicago and Grand Rapids; stage career, "Soldiers of Fortune," stock, stage mgr. for Shubert, vaud.; screen career, Kalem, Edison, Universal ("The Broken Coin," "Birth of Patriotism"), Bluebird ("Wanted—A Home," "Good Morning, Judge"), Fox ("The Speed Maniac," "The Square Shooter"), Vitagraph ("For Love and Honor" serial with William Duncan); 29 mos. active service, vice-pres. Hollywood post, American Legion. Hght., 5, 9; wght., 140; brown hair and eyes. Home ad., 7 Carver Court, Los Angeles, Calif.; phone 577112.

SHIELDS, Wilbert; educ. Hoboken, N. J.; stage exper., stk. and vaud.; screen career, Jester, Thanhauser ("The Recruit," "Man Without a Country"). Hght., 5, 8; wght., 148; black hair, blue eyes. Ad., 800 Bloomfield st., Hoboken, N. J.; Hoboken 578.

SHIRLEY, Arthur; b. Sydney, Australia; stage career, 8 yrs.; screen career, Australian Films. Ltd., Kalem, Universal, National Drama (lead in "The Fall of a Nation"), Selig (John Valiant in "The Valiants of Virginia"), Ince ("Bawbs o' Blue Ridge"), Balboa ("Betty Be Good," "The Wildcat," "Bab the Fixer," "Petticoats and Pants"), Universal ("Roped"). Hght., 6; wght., 185; brown hair, blue eyes. Ad., home 1201 Fielding ave., Hollywood.

SHORT, Antrim; b. Cincinnati, Ohio; educ. private tutor; stage career, 7 yrs. legit. stage; screen career, Bluebird, American, Pathe, Universal ("Jewel in Pawn," "The Yellow Dog"), Metro ("Please Get Married," "The Right of Way"), Hampton "Cressy"), Famous Players ("Romance and Arabella"). Hght., 5, 7½; wght., 135; medium brown hair, blue eyes. Ad., 1771 Cahuenga ave., Los Angeles, Calif.; Holly 1713.

SHUMWAY, Leonard C.; b. Salt Lake City, 1884; educ. Univ. of Salt Lake; stake career, stk.; screen career, Universal, Kalem, Selig, Lubin. Universal ("The Phantom's Secret," "Helen Grayson's Strategy"). Fox ("Bride of Fear," "Bird of Prey," "The Scarlet Road," "The Siren's Song," "The Speed Maniac," "A Girl in Bohemia"), Hodkinson ("The Love Hunger"), Amer.-Pathe ("Eve in Exile"). Hght., 6; wght., 180.

SIEGEL, Bernard; b. Lemberg, Austria; educ. Vienna Univ.; stage career, stk. for many yrs. in Austria, also stk. in U. S. at N. Y., St. Louis, Phila.; screen career, with Lubin and Vitagraph, in "Souls in Bondage," "Within the Law," "The Glory of Yolande," "The Maelstrom," "The Green God," "The Cambric Mask," "Beauty Proof," "Dan La Roche," "Fighting Destiny." Hght., 5, 9; wght., 145; brown hair and eyes. Ad., 2573 E. 14th st., Brooklyn, N. Y. Coney Island 1122 W.

SILLS, Milton; b. Chicago, Ill.; educ. Univ. of Chicago; stage career, 8 yrs. as leading man, Belasco, Shubert, Brady, Frohman; screen career, Goldwyn, Select, Fox, World, Universal ("The Claw," "The Savage Woman," "The Yellow Ticket," "The Mysterious Client," "The Other Woman"); late pictures, "The Stronger Vow," "Woman Thou Gavest Me," "The Fear Woman," "What Every Woman Learns," "Street Called Straight," "Eyes of Youth." Hght., 6; wght., 180; light hair, gray eyes. Home ad., 1816 Argyle st., Hollywood, Cal.

SIMPSON, Allan Hart; educ. N. Y. C., Columbia Univ.; stage career, 1 yr. with Corse Payton Stk. Co., boy parts; screen career, Paramount-Flagg comedies ("The Last Battle"), stock with Goldwyn, Famous Players ("Career of Catherine Bush"); posed for Arrow Collars, Chesterfield Cigarette heads and Liberty Loan posters by James Montgomery Flagg and J. C. Leyendecker. Hght., 5, 11; wght., 160; light hair, dark eyes. Ad., 530 Riverside Dr., N. Y. Morningside 2842.

SIMPSON, Russell; b. San Francisco, 1880; educ. there; stage career, 12 yrs. stk., road shows, B'way prods. with Belasco, Savage, K. & E.; screen career, 7 yrs. Famous Players, Metro, First National, Goldwyn, World, in Rex-Beach-Goldwyn "The Brand," "The Barrier," "Blue Jeans," "Our Teddy," "Cressy," "Out of the Dust," "Bill Apperson's Boy." Hght., 6; wght., 175; medium brown hair, gray eyes. Ad., 5158 Hollywood blvd., Los Angeles, Cal., phone 597051.

SINGLETON, Joseph E.; b. Melbourne, Australia, 1881; educ. there; stage career, 12 yrs. stock, vaud.; screen career, Universal, Fine Arts ("Girl of the Timber Claims"), American, Keystone, author vaud. acts and scenarios, "The Skull of Life," "He Drew the Line," "The Cross Roads," "The Booster," "The Perfect Woman"), Fox ("Aladdin and the Wonderful Lamp"), Artcraft ("Shark Monroe"), Al. Jennings prod. ("The Lady of the Dugout"), Vitagraph ("The Enchanted Barn"). Hght., 6, 1; wght., 195; dark hair, dark eyes.

SMILEY, Joseph W.; b. Boston, 1875; educ. there; stage career, Hanlon Brothers, Fanny Davenport, rep. Klaw and Erlanger; screen, Imp., director of Lubin and for Jules Brulatour, Artcraft, World, Goldwyn, Fox, etc.; recent pictures, Elsie Ferguson ("Hearts of the Wild"), Virginia Pearson ("Queen of Hearts"), Select ("Break the News to Mother," "The Isle of Conquest"), Fox ("Luck and Pluck," "Never Say Quit"), World ("The Moral Deadline," "The Poisoned Pen"). Ad., Friars Club, N. Y.

SMILEY, Robert W.; b. Washington, D. C.; stage career, T. Boggs Johns in "Pair of Sixes," E. H. Sothern, "Everyman," "Common Clay," Grace George, Otis Skinner; screen career, Edison, Imp ("Prince and Pauper," "Aunt Maria's Substitute," "Ruling Passions." Hght., 5, 9; wght., 175; dark complexion, brown hair, blue gray eyes. Ad., St. Paul Hotel, N. Y.

SOMERVILLE, George J. ("Slim"); b. Albuquerque, N. M., 1892; educ. Chatham, Can.; stage career, mus. com., vaud., rep., stk.; screen career, Keystone ("Their Social Splash," "His Bread and Butter," "A Dog Catcher's Love," "His Precious Life," "The Winning Punch"), Paramount ("Roping Her Romeo," "Are Waitresses Safe?"), Sennett-Para. ("It Pays to Exercise," "The Kitchen Lady"), Sunshine ("High Diver's Last Kiss"). Hght., 6, 2; wght., 164. Ad., home, 520 S. Flower st., Los Angeles.

SOTHERN, Sam; b. London, England; educ. there; stage career, legit;; screen career, Douglas Fairbanks ("His Majesty, the American"), Garson ("Eyes of Youth"). Ad., Lowe's Exchange, 1123 Broadway, N. Y.; studio, Garson.

SPERE, Charles; b. Omaha, Neb.; educ. Neb. Univ. and Northwestern Univ., Chicago; stage career, 1 season vaud.; screen career, Ince ("A Desert Wooing"), Vitagraph ("A Fighting Colleen," "Pegeen," "Man Who Wouldn't Tell"), American ("A Bachelor's Wife," "The Hellion"), New Art Films ("The Solitary Sin"), Brunton ("What Every Mother Knows"), National ("The Lamb and the Lion"). Hght., 5, 10½; wght., 150; brown hair and eyes. Ad., 408 S. Alvarado st., Los Angeles, Cal.

SPINGLER, Harry; b. Buffalo, N. Y.; educ. there; stage career, vaud., 1908-1912, with Al H. Wilson Co.; screen career, Reliance, Life Photo ("Northern Lights," "The Ordeal"), Fox ("Samson," "The Plunderer," "The Bondman"), Ivan ("Her Surrender"), Ocean ("Driftwood"), Universal ("Cheaters," "Woman Under Cover"), Fox ("Flames of the Flesh"). Hght., 5, 9; wght., 155; fair complexion, blond hair, gray eyes.

SPOTTSWOOD, James Carlisle; educ. Gonzaga Coll., St. John's College; Georgetown Univ., Washington, D. C.; stage career, Mary Mannering, featured in Shubert's "Going Some," "Midnight Sons," Julian Eltinge's "Fascinating Widow" and "Crinoline Girl," 8 seasons leading juvenile with A. H. Woods prods., "Mary's Ankle," "Parlor, Bedroom and Bath," "His Honor, Abe Potash"; screen career, Thanhouser ("Weighed in the Balance"), Vitagraph ("The Climbers"). Hght., 5, 7; wght., 145; light brown hair, blue eyes. Ad., Lambs Club, N. Y.

SPROTTE, Bert; b. Huisum, Schleswig-Holstein; educ. Halle, S. Saxony; stage career, 15 yrs., 8 yrs. in Europe, 7 yrs. Milwaukee and Chicago; screen career, W. S. Hart ("Selfish Yates," "Shark Monroe," "Breed of Men"), F. Keenan ("The World Aflame"), Harold Bell Wright Co. ("Shepherd of the Hills"), Goldwyn ("Girl from Outside"), Universal ("Brute Breaker"), Amer. Lifeograph Co. ("The Golden Trail," "Men of Today and Tomorrow"). Hght., 6, 1; wght., 200; iron gray hair, gray eyes. Home ad., 2025 W. 7th ave., Los Angeles, Cal. Holly 1964.

STANDING, Gordon H.; b. London, Eng., 1889; educ. Upper Latimer and St. Paul's, London, Eng.; stage career, with Leonard Rayne in S. Africa; 2 yrs. student McGill, Montreal; 3 yrs. Canadian Mounted Rifles; with Paul Armstrong in vaud.; "A Full House," H. H. Frazee, Shuberts, A. H. Woods; screen career, Triangle ("Three Black Eyes"), Independent ("Up and Down"), Rolfe ("Red Virgin"), Famous Players, Pathe, World; 2 yrs. A. E. F., 21 mos. actual service. Hght., 6; wght., 185; chestnut brown hair, brown eyes. Add., care Arthur H. Jacobs, Inc., 145 W. 45th st., N. Y. C.

STANDING, Herbert; stage career, with Sir Henry Irving, Sir Charles Wyndham, 23 yrs. Criterion theatre, London; screen career, Para-Artcraft ("How Could You, Jean," "He Comes Up Smiling"), Metro ("In Judgment Of"), Goldwyn ("The Wrong Door," "Strictly Confidential," "Almost Married," "Lord and Lady Algy," "Cup of Fury"). Ad., 615 So. Catalina st., Los Angeles, Cal.

STANDING, Herbert, Jr.; b. London, Eng., 1887; educ. St. Paul's Schl., London; stage career, leads with Amelia Bingham, Nance O'Neil, George Edwards, Sir Beerbohm Tree; screen career, Betzwood ("Misfit Earl"), Carl Carleton ("En L'Air"), Vitagraph ("Jewels"), Famous Players, Pathe, World, Goldwyn. Hght., 6; wght., 185; dark brown hair and eyes. Ad., Sterling Apts., 126 W. 49th st., N. Y. Bryant 5138.

STANDING, Wyndham; b. London, Eng., 1880; educ. St. Paul's Coll.; stage career, 1899, sir Henry Irving, Mr. and Mrs. Kendal, Miss Fortescue, Comstock and Gest, Wm. A. Brady, Shubert, Lyceum theatre, London; screen career, Triangle-Ince, Famous Players, Goldwyn, International, Maurice Tourneur Prods., "Rose of the World," "Paid in Full," "Eyes of the Soul," "Miracle of Love," "Witness for the Defense," "Earth Bound." Hght., 6, 1; wght., 180; brown hair, gray eyes. Ad., Goldwyn Studio, Culver City, Cal.

STANLEY, Edwin; b. Chicago; stage career, dram. stk., vaud.; screen career, "King Lear," "Divorce and the Daughter," "Law of Compensation," "Justt a Woman," "Marriages Are Made," "Every Mother's Son," "An Honest Thief," "The Love Auction." Ad., Green Room Club, N. Y.

STANLEY, Forrest; stage career, stk., rep.; screen career, Morosco ("Kilmeny," "Mme. La Presidente," "Making of Maddalena," etc.), Pallas ("Reform Candidate," "The Heart of Paula"), Bosworth ("Rug Maker's Daughter"), Morosco ("His Official Fiancee"), Universal ("Under Suspicion," "The Triflers"), First National ("The Thunderbolt"). Home ad., 207 S. Ardmore ave., Los Angeles, Cal.; phone 560597.

STARKEY, Bert; educ. Fall River, Mass.; stage career, with H. W. Savage for 4 yrs.; vaud. with own act and others; over the United Time for about 5 yrs.; screen career, Pathe ("Fatal Ring,' serial), World ("The Boss"), "Jimmy Valentine," "Deep Purple"), Metro ("Broadway Bill," "The Come Back"), 4 yrs. in stk. with World Motion Picture Co.; now with Dorothy Dalton. Hght., 5, 6; wght., 127; dark hair and eyes. Ad., 300 W. 17th st., care Condon, N. Y. Chelsea 7084.

STARR, Frederic; b. San Francisco; educ. there; stage career, 15 yrs., with Nance O'Neil and stk.; screen career, Brunton ("Jack Dempsey serial), Fox ("Camouflage"), Jesse Hampton ("A Woman of Pleasure"), Universal ("The Beach Combers," "The Sea Flower"), Hart ("The Poppy Girl's Husband"), Ince ("Vive La France"), Goldwyn, B. B. Hampton ("A Desert of Wheat"). Hght., 6, 2; wght., 225; dark brown hair and eyes. Home ad., 6056 Carlton Way, Los Angeles, Cal. Holly 387.

STEARNS, Louis; b. N. Y. C., 1867 educ. Columbia Coll., N. Y. C.; stage career, 20 yrs., "Business Before Pleasure," with A. H. Woods; screen career, Fox ("Painted Madonna"), Universal ("Great Problem"), Metro ("Great Romance"), Rolfe ("Scream in the Night"), Norma Talmadge ("Her Only Way"), B. S. Moss ("Break the News to Mother"), Adanac Co. ("The World Shadow"). Hght., 5, 10½; wght., 185. Ad., Green Room Club, N. Y.

STEEL, Vernon; b. Santiago, Chile; educ. England; stage career, leading man with Phyliss Neilson Terry, Oscar Asche and Lily Brayton, Forbes-Robertson, George Alexander, etc.; screen career, Goldwyn, Vitagraph, Famous Players ("Firing Line," "Witness for the Defense"), Atlas ("Phantom Honeymoon"). Now playing in "Declassee" with Ethel Barrymore at Empire theatre. Hght., 6; wght., 155; brown hair, hazel eyes. Ad., 56 W. 11th st., N. Y. C. Chelsea 9494.

STEERS, Larry; b. Chicago; educ. there; stage career, Bush Temple Stock, Chicago, Robert Edeson, "Strongheart," stock at St. Louis, Mo.; screen career, Lasky ("City of Dim Faces"), Morosco ("Little Comrade"), Goldwyn ("Heartsease"), Metro ("Right of Way"), Keenan ("Out of the Dust"). Hght., 6; wght., 175; dark hair, brown eyes. Home ad., 3700 Sunset, Los Angeles, Cal.; phone 597263.

STEPPLING, John; b. 1869; educ. Univ. Penn.; stage career, Frohman, Sothern in "Prisoner of Zenda," Olga Nethersole, "Sappho," Wm. Gillette, "Secret Service"; screen career, Essanay, Famous ("The Bishop's Carriage," "Tess of the D'Urbervilles," "Johanna Enlists"), Fox ("The Divorce Trap"), Rob.-Cole ("Life's a Funny Proposition"), Paramount ("The Rescuing Angel"), Metro ("Lombardi, Ltd."), First National ("The Inferior Sex"). Ad., 2017 Argyle ave., Hollywood, Cal.

STERLING, Ford; screen career, Mack Sennett Comedies ("Yankee Doodle in Berlin," "The Little Widow," "Hearts and Flowers," "Among Those Present," "Uncle Tom Without the Cabin," "His Last False Step," "A Lady's Tailor"). Ad., 5638 Carlton Way, Hollywood, Cal.

STEVENS, Edwin; b. California; educ. Univ. of Cal.; early career, banking, mining and scouting; stage career, since 1883, "The School for Scandal," "The Devil"; screen career, directed for Universal, played in World ("The Devil's Toy"), Artcraft ("The Squaw Man"), Metro ("Faith"), Select ("Cheating Cheaters"), Pathe ("The Profiteers"), Goldwyn ("The Crimson Gardenia"), Para-Artcraft ("Hawthorne of the U. S. A."), Hodkinson ("The Lone Wolf's Daughter"). Hght.; 6; wght., 200; brown hair, blue eyes. Ad., Lambs Club, N. Y.

STEVENS, George; b. and educ. London; came to U. S. with Mrs. Langtry, with A. M. Palmer Stk. Co.; screen career, 5 yrs. with Vitagraph, C. K. Young, Metro, Famous Players, Paramount ("Come Out of the Kitchen"). Hght., 5, 9; wght., 159; gray hair, blue eyes. Ad., 295 Monroe st., Brooklyn, N. Y. Bedford 7044.

STEVENSON, Chas. E.; b. Sacramento, Cal.; educ. there; screen career, Harold Lloyd

("Bumping Into Broadway," "Capt. Kidd's Kids," "From Hand to Mouth," "His Royal Shyness"). Hght., 5, 11; wght., 185; brown hair and eyes. Home ad., 1636 Magnolia ave., Los Angeles, Cal., W 1796; studio, Rolin.

STEWART, Roy; b. San Diego, Cal.; educ. Univ. of Cal.; stage career, traveling stock cos. on West Coast, with Florodora Co. on tour, etc.; screen career, Majestic, American, Universal, Triangle ("Wolves of the Border," "The Silent Rider"), Fine Arts ("The House Built Upon Sand," "The Doll Shop," "The Fugitive"), B. B. Hampton ("The Westerners," "The Sagebrusher," "Desert of Wheat"), Selznick ("Just a Wife"). Hght., 6, 2; wght., 190; black hair and brown eyes. Studio ad., Roy Stewart Feature Films, 641 N. Hobart Blvd., Los Angeles, Calif.

STEWART, Victor A.; b. London, Eng.; educ. Wimbleton College, Eng.; stage career, vaud.; screen career, Vitagraph, Lubin ("Within the Law," "Everybody's Girl," "Find the Woman," "Adventure Shop"). Hght., 5, 10½; wght., 180; chestnut hair, gray eyes. Ad., 2200 Coney Island ave., N. Y.

ST. JOHN, Al; b. Santa Ana, Calif.; educ. there; screen career, Keystone-Triangle ("Fatty and Mabel Adrift," "He Did and He didn't," "The Bright Lights," "His Wife's Mistake," "The Moonshiners"), Arbuckle ("The Butcher-Boy," "A Reckless Romeo," "His Wedding Night"), Warner Bros. ("Speed"), will appear in 2-reel comedy every month, released by Paramount. Hght., 5, 6½; wgh., 150; light complexion, blond hair, blue eyes. Home ad., 4411 Victoria Park Place, Los Angeles; phone 75477; studio ad., Astra Studio, Glendale, Calif.; Glendale 902.

STOCKDALE, Carl; b. Worthington, Minn., 1874; educ. Univ. of North Dakota; stage career, stock and vaud.; screen career, Fine Arts ("Intolerance," "Atta Boy's Last Race"), American ("A Night in New York," "Peggy Leads the Way"), Al Jennings prod. ("The Lady of the Dugout"), Griffith ("The Greatest Question"), J. Warren Kerrigan ("After Hours"), "The Trembling Hour" with Mary MacLaren, "The Fatal 30" serial with Jack Dempsey, "Brass Buttons" with William Russell. Hght., 5, 11; wght., 155; brown hair, blue eyes. Ad., home 1627 Winona Blvd., Los Angeles, Cal. Holly 2913.

STONE, Lewis; screen career, "The River's End" with Marshall Neilan, "Man's Desire," Lasky ("Held by the Enemy). Home ad., 226 S. Rampart blvd., Los Angeles, Calif.; phone 52449; studio, Neilan Prods.

STOWE, Leslie; b. Louisiana; educ. Georgetown Univ., Texas; stage career, Augustin Daly Stk. Co., "Ben Hur," "Shore Acres," etc.; screen career, Metro, Fox, World ("Social Quicksands," "The Closed Road," "The Impostors"), Famous Players ("The Copperhead"), Mayflower ("Bolshevism on Trial"), Metro ("The Adopted Son"), Paragon ("La Boheme"), Arnold ("The Carter Case"). Hght., 5, 10½; wght., 210; gray hair, blue eyes. Ad., Green Room Club, N. Y.

STOWELL, William H.; b. Boston, Mass., March 13, 1885; educ. Boston H. S.; stage career, 2 seasons in mus. com. in Chicago, leading man at Whitney Opera House, 3 seasons lead in road cos. touring the East; screen career, since 1909, Selig, Universal ("The Doll's House," "Bondage," "Man of God," "Broadway Love"), Lois Weber Prod. ("The Man Who Dared God," etc.), Jewel ("The Tale of the Town," "Heart of Humanity," "When a Girl Loves," "Destiny," "Right to Happiness"). Home ad., 1729 N. Normande ave., Los Angeles, Calif. Studio, Universal, Universal City.

STRONG, Eugene; educ. Univ. of Chicago; stage career, 15 yrs.; screen career, Metro ("Lady Frederick," "The Border Legion," "Safe for Democracy," "The Divorcee"), Vitagraph ("A Stitch in Time," "Vengeance of Durand"), Burton King ("Power of Woman"), Empey-Select ("The Undercurrent"), Hallmark ("Wit Wins"). Hght., 6, 2; wght., 185; dark complexion, dark hair, blue eyes. Ad., c/o Edward Small, Inc., N. Y.

SULLIVAN, Danny; b. Newark, N. J., 1885; educ. there; stage career, minstrels, "Babes in Toyland," 5 yrs. with "The Wizard of Oz"; screen career, Biograph, 3 yrs. in comedies, Fox (the Gambler in "The Blue Streak," "Wife Number Two," "Thou Shalt Not Steal"), Frank Hall ("The Other Man's Wife"). Ad., home, 206 W. 109th st., N. Y.

SULLIVAN, William A.; educ. N. Y.; stage career, 15 yrs. legit. stage; screen career, Thanhouser ("Million Dollar Mystery"), Pathe 2 yrs. ("Honest Thief," "Getaway Kate," "Cigarette Girl," "Lightning Raider"). Hght. 5, 7½; wght., 145; brown hair, blue eyes. Ad., 340 W. 56th st., N. Y.; Circle 6784.

SUTHERLAND, John; b. Scotland; educ. there; screen career, Famous Players ("Silver King," "The Lie," "His House in Order," "Test of Honor," "Uncle Tom's Cabin"), Biograph ("The Imp"), Crest ("Grain of Dust"), Goldwyn ("Dodging a Million"). Hght., 5, 10; wght., 168; fair complexion, gray hair, dark eyes. Ad., 340a Ninth st., Brooklyn, N. Y.

SUTHERLAND, Victor; b. Paducah, Ky., 1889; educ. Ky.; stage career, Morgan Stock Co.; screen career, Victor ("The Dancer and the King"), Fox ("Daredevil Kate"), Rex Beach ("The Barrier"), Ed. Lewis Prod. ("The Bar Sinister," "The Sign Invisible," "Calibre 38"), Fox ("Her Price"). Ad., Green Room Club, N. Y.

SWAIN, Mack; b. Salt Lake City, 1876; educ. there; early career, own company, vaud., mus. com., drama, stock; screen career, Keystone (comedy leads in "The Schemers," "Safety First Ambrose"), Sennett-Paramount ("The Pullman Bride"), L-Ko ("Ambrose and the Lion Hearted"). Hght., 6, 2; wght., 240. Studio, Sunset, Los Angeles, Calif.

SWICKARD, Charles; stage career, s'k; screen career, Universal-Bluebird, Metro, Fox ("Light of Western Stars"), Metro ("The Spender," "Faith," "Almost Married"), Thos. H. Ince ("The Toast of Death," "The Beckoning Flame"), Para-Artcraft. ("Hell's Hinges," "Captive God"), H. B. Warner ("Beggar of Cawnpoor"). Ad., 1533 Arlington ave., Los Angeles, Calif.

SWICKARD, Josef; stage career, 25 yrs. Dramatic and vaud., America, So. Africa and Europe; screen career, Thanhouser, Majestic, Keystone, Fox ("Tale of Two Cities"), Metro, Ince ("Keys of the Righteous"), Mitchel Lewis "Last of His People"), Bessie Barriscale ("Trick of Fate"), Brentwood ("The Third Generation"). Hght., 5, 10½ wght., 155; iron gray hair, dark blue eyes. Home ad., 1533 Arlington ave., Los Angeles, Calif., West 4263.

— T —

TABER, Richard; b. N. J.; educ. there; stage career, "Coat Tales," "The Willow Tree," "Little Miss Brown"; screen career, Pathe ("At Bay," "Kick In"), Essanay ("Eyes That See Not," "When My Lady Smiles," "Caught"), World ("Miss Crusoe"). Hght., 5, 6½; wght., 140; dark hair, dark eyes. Ad., Lambs Club, N. Y.

TEAD, Phillips; b. Somerville, Mass.; educ. Amherst Coll., '15; stage career, "Oh, Lady, Lady," "The King," with Leo Ditrichstein, "Our Mrs. McChesney"; screen career, Norma Talmadge ("She Loves and Lies"), Selznick ("The Woman's Game"), Famous Players ("The Lost Paradise"). Hght., 5, 8½; wght., 134; brown hair, dark blue eyes. Ad., 136 W. 44th st., N. Y. C.; Bryant 2592.

TEARLE, Conway; b. N. Y., 1850; stage career, Sir Charles Wyndham, Ellen Terry, Billie Burke, Ethel Barrymore, Viola Allen, stk. with Grace George; screen career, Brenon ("The Fall of the Romanoffs"), Paramount ("Stella Maris"), Select ("The Reason Why"), First National ("Virtuous Wives," "A Virtuous Vamp," "Mind the Paint Girl," "Two Weeks"), Select ("Way of a Woman," ("She Loves and Lies"), United ("Her Game"). Hght., 5, 11; wght., 180; dark hair and eyes. Ad., Friars' Club, N. Y.

TELLEGEN, Lou; b. Athens, Greece, Nov. 26, 1881; stage career, leading man with Sarah Bernhardt in Paris and on tour, director and star on London and American stages; screen career, Pathe, Lasky ("The Unknown," "The Victory of Conscience," "The Victoria Cross"), Lasky-Paramount ("The Long Trail," "What Money Can't Buy," "The Thing We Love," "Blind Youth"), Goldwyn ("World and its Woman," "Flame of the Desert"). Hght., 6; wght., 175; dark hair, gray eyes. Ad., c/o Goldwyn, N. Y.

THOMAS, Al Franklyn; b. and educ. N. Y. C.; stage career, 15 yrs.; screen career, Metro, Kalem, Fox, Famous Players, Davenport ("Rule of Reason"), Moss ("In the Hands of the Law"), Garrick ("The Eternal Law," "Where is My Father?"), Oliver ("Carter Case"), Bloxbee ("The Manicure Man"), Gaumont ("Temporary Wife"), Creation ("For the Freedom of Ireland"), Francis Grandon ("Conquered Hearts"). Hght., 5, 9½; wght., 168; dark hair and eyes. Ad., Green Room Club, N. Y.

THOMPSON, Hugh; b. St. Louis, Mo., 1887; educ. there; stage career, 8 yrs. stk.; screen career, Metro ("Secret Strings"), United ("Woman Under Oath"), Rothapfel ("False Gods"), World ("Phil for Short"), Hallmark ("Wit Wins"), Graphic ("Someone Must Pay"), Gaumont ("Making Her His Wife"), Gibraltar ("Cynthia of the Minute.") Hght., 6, 2; wght., 180; dark complexion, brown hair and eyes. Ad., Green Room Club, N. Y. Press representative, Lillian Gale, 234 W. 55th st., N. Y.

TILTON, Edwin Booth; b. Chicago, Ill.; educ. N. Y. and Providence, R. I.; stage career, first prof. appearance "Lights O' London," season 1885-86, under mgnt. K. & E., Henry Savage, Shuberts, Frohman, etc.; screen career, Lubin, Fox ("Under the Yoke," "Merrie-Go-Round," "Right After Brown," "Words and Music," "Auld Lang Syne," "Heritage of Eden"), Keenan ("Gates of Brass," "World Aflame"), Constance Talmadge ("The Shuttle"). Hght., 5, 11½; wght., 180; dark gray hair, hazel eyes. Home ad., 1731 N. Normandie ave., Los Angeles, Calif.; phone 59230.

TODD, Harry; b. Alleghany, Pa., 1865; stage career, at age of 14; screen career, Essanay ("Pete's Pants"), Selig (Mustang Pete, "Snakeville" comedies), Rolin, Metro ("Thirty Days," "The Baby Devil"), Bluebird ("Taste of Love"), Metro ("A Favor to a Friend," "Please Get Married). Hght., 5, 9; wght., 160; brown hair, blue eyes, dark complexion. Ad., home, 5736 Santa Monica Blvd., Hollywood, Cal.

TOOKER, William H.; b. N. Y. C., Sept. 2, 1875; educ. pub. schls., N. Y. C.; stage career, first part in "A Hole in the Ground"; stock engagements, also important roles with John Mason, Emma Dunn, Lionel Barrymore, etc.; screen career, Fox (featured in "A Fool's Revenge"), Metro ("Draft 258," "Red, White and Blue Blood"), Fox ("Woman, Woman"), Select ("The Woman the Germans Shot"). Hght., 5, 11; wght., 187; light complexion, light hair, blue eyes. Home ad., 25 St. Nicholas Terrace, N. Y. C. Morningside 8420.

TOWER, Halsey; b. Buffalo, N. Y.; educ. there; stage career, "Mary Jane's Pa," also vaud.; screen career, High Life Comedy Co. ("The Wedding Punch," "Her Rough Knight," "The Girl Betwixt," "Bosom Enemies"). Hght., 5, 8; wght., 150; brown hair, blue eyes. Ad., 1004 Wright-Callender Bldg.; phone 13924.

TRAVERS, Richard C.; b. Can.; educ. St. Andrew's Coll., Can.; early career, practiced medicine and in army; screen career, Essanay pictures, "Lost, Twenty-four Hours," "Borrowed Sunshine," "The Egg," "The Phantom Buccaneer," "Among Those Present," "The Hoodooed Story"), State Rights ("House Without Children"), Fox ("The White Moll"). Hght., 6, 1; wght., 207; black hair, brown eyes; 3 yrs. in U. S. service. Ad., Bayshore, L. I., N. Y.

TRENTON, Pell; b. N. Y. C.; educ. Columbia Univ., stage career, supported Julia Marlowe, Maxine Elliott, Laurette Taylor, Marie Doro, King Love in "Everywoman," with Fannie Ward on vaud. tour, Sir Herbert Tree; screen career, C. K. Young ("House of Glass"), Metro ("The Uplifters," "Fair and Warmer," "The Willow Tree"), with Edith Storey in "The Better Profit," Blanche Sweet ("Cressy"). Hght., 6; wght., 175; black hair, dark blue eyes. Home ad., 1722 La Brea ave., Los Angeles, Calif.; Holly 5797.

TRIMBLE, George S.; b. N. Y., Oct. 10, 1874; educ. N. Y.; stage career, 25 yrs., stk. and mus. com. with Frohman, Mantell, etc., screen career, Lubin ("The House Next Door"), Famous Players ("Silks and Satins," "Arms and the Girl"), World ("The Man Who Stood Still"), Pathe ("Wallingford" series), Capellani ("Damsel in Distress"), Chautard ("Liza Ann"). Hght., 5, 11½; wght., 265; dark hair, brown eyes. Home ad., Green Room Club, N. Y.

TRUESDELL, Fred C.; b. Coldwater, Mich.; educ. Michigan; stage career, stk., vaud. and comic opera, including "Suwanee River," "The Pink Lady," "Easiest Way," "La Bohema," "Alias Jimmie Valentine," with E. H. Sothern; screen career, Metro ("Wilson and the Kaiser," as President Wilson), Perret ("Lafayette, We Come"); played in stk. co. of U. S. soldiers in Paris and thru France during the past year. Hght., 5, 10½; wght., 170; gray hair, green eyes. Ad., 230 W. 107th st., N. Y. Acad. 2757; or Green Room Club, N. Y.

TRUEX, Ernest; b. Kansas City; educ. Whittier School, Denver, Colo.; stage career, 20 yrs., created leads in "A Good Little Devil," "Over Night," "Very Good Eddie," "The Very Idea"; screen career, Famous Players ("Come On In," "Goodbye, Bill," "Oh, You Women," "Stick Around," "Knight of the Dub," "Too Good to Be True"). Hght., 5, 2½; wght., 120; light hair, blue eyes. Ad., Great Neck, L. I., N. Y. Great Neck 411 R.

TURNER, Bowd M. (Smoke); b. Cumberland, Md.; stage exper., 20 yrs. stk. touring; screen career, Essanay ("Little Shoes," "Phantom Buccaneer"), Fox ("Mr. Logan, U. S. A.," "Treat 'Em Rough," "Coming of the Law," "Hell Roarin' Reform," "Married in Haste"). Hght., 5, 8½; wght., 140; black hair, blue eyes. Home ad., 5502 Santa Monica Blvd., Los Angeles, Cal.; phone 597125.

TURNER, F. A.; b. Boston, 1866; stage career, "The Black Crook," with Blanche Bates, Henry Miller, Robert Edeson and Edgar Selwyn; screen career, Imp, Biograph, Reliance-Majestic, Fine Arts ("Atta Boy's Last Race," "Children of the Feud," "Intolerance"), Triangle ("Madame Bo-Peep"), Bluebird ("Playthings," "The Love Swindle"), Metro ("As the Sun Went Down"), Select ("Heart of Wetona"), Para-Art ("The Miracle Man").

TURNER, William H.; b. Ireland; stage career, 25 yrs., "David Harum," "Father and the Boys"; screen career, Lubin ("The Nation's Peril," "The Gods of Faith," "Gods of Fate"), Monmouth ("Jimmy Dale"), Art Dramas ("Her Good Name"), Vitagraph ("Church with Overshot Wheel"), O. Henry's "The Sporting Duchess"). Hght., 5, 8; wght., 165; gray hair, dark eyes. Ad., Green Room Club, N. Y.

TURPIN, Ben; b. 1874, New Orleans; stage career, Sam T. Jack's Burlesque Co., Chicago, "Busy Izzy," 11 yrs. vaud.; screen career, Essanay 2½ yrs.; first slapstick comedian in pictures, 1 yr. with Charlie Chaplin, "A Night Out," "His New Job," Vogue Comedies, Paramount ("A Clever Dummy," "Roping a Romeo"), Mack Sennett ("East Lynne with Variations," "Yankee Doodle in Berlin," "Uncle Tom without the Cabin," "Salome vs. Shenandoah"). Hght., 5, 4; wght., 120; dark complexion, black hair, cock eyes. Ad., home, 5560 Santa Monica Blvd., Los Angeles, Cal.; phone 599383; studio ad., Mack Sennett Comedies, L. A., Cal.

— V —

VALENTINO, Rudolph; b. Taranto, Italy; educ. Mil. and Agricultural Coll. in Italy; stage career, 3 yrs. vaud. with Bonnie Glass and Joan Sawyer, 2 seasons mus. comedy; screen career, Mae Murray specials ("The Big Little Person," "Delicious Little Devil"), Universal ("Society Sensation," "All Night"), Dorothy Gish ("Out of Luck"), C. K. Young ("Eyes of Youth"), Dorothy Phillips ("Ambition"). Hght., 5, 11; wght., 154; black hair, dark brown eyes. Ad., 692 Valencia st., Los Angeles, Cal., Wilshire 476.

VAN DYKE, Truman; b. Natchez, Miss., 1897; educ., Miss. A. & M. Coll. and Marion Inst. Alabama; stage career, dramatic club at college doing amateur work all through Southern States; screen career, 6 mos. stk. with Triangle, Vitagraph ("Wishing Ring Man," "Over the Garden Wall"), Universal ("The Red Glove," "Betty Reforms," "The Peddler"). Hght., 5, 11; wght., 155; dark red hair, gray-brown eyes. Ad., Gen. Delivery, Culver City, Cal.; phone 70304.

VANE, Denton; b. Brooklyn, 1886; educ. Jacksonville, Fla.; stage career, several seasons in vaud., with Maude Odell, stock in Portland, Seattle, San Francisco and Los Angeles in mus. com., played in support of Ethel Barrymore, Blanche Bates, etc.; screen career, Selig, Kalem (leads opp. Irene Boyle), joined Vitagraph in 1914 ("The Stolen Treaty," "Soldiers of Chance," "The Hillman," "Love Watches," "The Golden Goal," "Playing with Fate," "Beauty Proof," "Fortune's Child," "A Girl at Bay," "Man Who Won"). Hght., 5, 8; wght., 160; dark hair, brown eyes. Home ad.,

422 State st., Brooklyn, and Green Room Club, N. Y.

VAN LOAN, Philip; b. Amsterdam, Holland, 1884; educ. there; stage career, played Christ in Oberammergau Passion Play, played Ibsen, Sudermann, Hauptmann in Germany, Holland, Belgium; screen career, Fox ("Queen of the Sea"), Famous (Christ in "The Sign of the Cross"), Blackton ("The Common Cause"), also directed for 4 yrs. with Great Northern Film Co., Copenhagen, Denmark; International Film Co., Beatrice Fairfax Series; Bloxbe Film Co., Young American series. Hght., 5, 11½; wght., 175; dark hair, dark eyes. Ad., 335 E. 79th st., N. Y.; Lenox 10007.

VAN METER, Harry L.; b. Malta Bend, Mo.; early career, physical culture teacher, Denver; stage career, from 1895, in stk., Denver, with Henry Kolker, Blanche Bates, Orrin Johnson; screen career, leads with Nestor, American 3 yrs. ("Beloved Rogues"), Paralta ("A Man's Man"), Universal ("Princess Virtue," "Broadway Love"), with Dustin Farnum in "A Man's Fight," Frank Keenan ("Out of the Ashes"), Metro ("Judah"), Universal ("Beach Combers," "The Day She Paid"). Ad., Metro Studios, Hollywood, Calif.

VERNON, Bobbie; b. Chicago, 1897; educ. there; stage career, with Kolb and Dill, mus. com., vaud.; screen career, Universal, Keystone, Christie ("Pearls in a Peach," "Bobby Comes Marching Home," "Fair, but False," "Watch Your Step, Mother," "Why Wild Men Go Wild," "Papa by Proxy," "Oh, Doctor, Doctor," and 20 other Christie Comedies). Now working in Christie's Specials. Hght., 5, 2½; wght., 145; light hair, blue eyes; 4 mos. in U. S. Navy. Ad., 1756 N. Western ave., Hollywood; studio, Christie, L. A., Cal.

VIVIAN, Robert; b. London, Eng., 1867; educ. London, France and Germany; stage career 15 years in London with Sir Henry Irving, "A Good Little Devil," with David Belasco, Maude Adams in "A Kiss for Cinderella"; screen career, Famous Players ("Under the Greenwood Tree," "The Counterfeit"), Tourneur ("Law of the Land"), Selznick ("Piccadilly Jim," "The Spite Bride"), Norma Talmadge ("Mr. Butler Buttles"), Fox ("La Belle Russe"); now engaged in A. H. Wood's "A Room at the Ritz." Hght., 5, 11; wght., 171; fair complexion, brown hair, blue eyes. Ad., 156 W. 46th st., N. Y.; Bryant 7811.

— W —

WADE, John P.; b. Ohio; educ. Mt. St. Mary's College, St. Francis Xavier's Jesuit College; stage career, stk., wrote, starred in and directed vaud. acts, with T. Daniel Frawley Stk. in tour of the Far East; screen career, Biograph, Edison, Famous Players, Vitagraph ("The Third Degree"), S.-L. Pict. ("Virtuous Men"), Rob.-Cole ("The Open Door"). Hght., 5, 10½; wght., 165; iron gray hair, dark eyes. Ad., 507 W. 112th st., N. Y. C.; Mngde. 7582.

WALKER, Robert Donald; b. Bethlehem, Pa., 1888; educ. Horace Mann School, N. Y.; stage career, in musical comedies; screen career, Edison, Fox, Metro ("Aladdin's Other Lamp," "God's Law and Man's," "Lady Barnacle," "The Girl Without a Soul," "Blue Jeans"), Select ("The Whirlpool"), Fox ("The Light"), Goldwyn ("City of Comrades"), First National ("Burglar by Proxy"), Fox ("The Merry-Go-Round"), Universal ("Rouge and Riches"). Hght., 6; wght., 160; dark brown hair, blue eyes.

WALLOCK, Edwin N.; b. Council Bluffs, Ia., 1878; educ. Benedictine Univ., Atchison, Kan.; stage career, for 18 yrs. with Thomas Keene, Richard Mansfield, Frederick Warde, head of own co., and also in stk. in East; screen career, with Selig, in many jungle zoo pictures, Universal ("Behind the Line," "Even as You and I"), Ince-Paramount ("The Price Mark"), Hampton-Hodkinson ("The Sage Brusher"). Hght., 5, 11; wght., 185; black hair, gray eyes. Home ad., 3522 N. Broadway, Los Angeles.

WALPOLE, Stanley; b. Melbourne, Australia, 1886; educ. Carlton, Aust.; stage career, on stage since 17 yrs. old, played in rep. and prod. under mgmt. J. C. Williamson, "Monsieur Beaucaire," "Prisoner of Zenda"; screen career, Universal ("Moira," "Dollar Mark," "Unconventional Girl," "Seeds of Redemption," "Crimson Trail"), Vitagraph ("Fortune's Child"), McClure ("Yellow Eel"). "Caloola" (Australia), Capellani prod. Hght., 5, 10½; wght., 165; brown hair, gray eyes. Ad., Green Room Club, N. Y.

WALSH, George; b. N. Y., 1892; educ. N. Y. High Schl. of Commerce, studied law at Fordham and Georgetown Univs.; screen career, Fox ("The Book Agent," "Some Boy," "The Kid Is Clever," "The Yankee Way," "This Is the Life," "The Pride of N. Y.," "Jack Spurlock, Prodigal," "Brave and Bold," "I'll say So," "Luck and Pluck," "Putting One Over," "Never Say Quit," "The Winning Stroke," "Help, Help, Police"). Hght., 5, 11; wght., 180; dark hair and eyes. Ad., Fox, N. Y.

WALTEMEYER, Jack; b. Salida, Col., 1884; educ. Col.; stage career, 18 yrs. stk. in Spokane, Portland, Del., Sacramento, Seattle, Roanoke, Va.; screen career, Universal, L-Ko, Kalem, Vitagraph ("The Iron Test"), Paralta ("Carmen of the Klondike"), Triangle ("The Gun Women"). Hght., 5, 10½; wght., 170; brown hair, blue eyes. Home ad., 1232 Tamarind ave., Los Angeles, Cal.

WALTHALL, Henry B.; b. Shelby Co., Ala.; stage career, played through East; screen career, from 1910, Griffith ("Birth of a Nation," "Great Love"), Ince ("False Faces"), National, Ex-Mutual ("And a Still Small Voice," "The Come Back," "A Long Lane's Turning"), Mayflower ("A Splendid Hazard"). Hght., 5, 6; wght., 135; dark complexion, dark brown hair, brown eyes. Home ad., 25 Arcadia Terrace, Santa Monica, Los Angeles, Calif.; S. M. 277-J.

WARD, Chance E.; b. Dayton, O., 1878; screen career, Universal, 1912, as actor and asst. dir., later as actor and dir.; asst. dir. Kalem, then dir., producing Ham and Bud comedies 9 months; with American, 1915, directing with James Douglass, made "Johnnie's Birthday," Metro, played in "Island of Intrigue." Ad., Hollywood, Cal.

WARD, Freddie Fay; b. San Francisco, 1907; screen career, Universal, Triangle, Brunton, Fox; Village Boy, Italian and French parts. Hght., 4, 9; wght., 81; dark brown hair, dark blue eyes. Ad., 434 N. Alvarado st., Los Angeles, Cal.; Wils. 6169.

WARD, Hap H.; b. Santa Ana, Cal.; educ. Los Angeles; stage career, 7 yrs., Keith, Wm. Morris, and Orpheum Circuits of vaud., Western Wheel Burlesque, 3 yrs., mus. com. 10 yrs.; screen career, began with Gale Henry in 1918; later Francis Ford throughout the "Silent Mystery"; back with Gale Henry for past year. Hght., 5, 7; wght., 135; brown hair and eyes. Home ad., 1416 N. Kenmore, Hollywood, Calif.; 599273 Phone. Studio ad., Gale Henry Comedies, Bulls Eye Studio, Hollywood, Calif.

WARDE, Frederick B.; b. Wardington, Oxfordshire, England, 1851; stage career, started in 1867 when he appeared as second murderer in "Macbeth," is noted chiefly for his many interpretations of Shakespearean roles, both in this country and abroad; other plays in which he has appeared are "Brunhilde," "Mary Stuart"; screen career, Thanhouser ("King Lear," "Vicar of Wakefield," "Hinton's Double," "Fires of Youth," "Under False Colors," "The Heart of Ezra Greer"), World ("The Unveiling Hand," "Silas Marner"). Ad., 1720 Ditmas av., B'klyn, N. Y.; Flatbush 3378-J.

WARNER, H. B.; b. St. John's Woods, London, Eng.; educ. Bedford, Eng., and Univ. Coll., London, Eng.; stage career, with Sir Charles Wyndham, Sir Herbert Tree, Marie Tempest, in England, came to America in 1905 to play opposite Eleanor Robson; screen career, Ince ("The Ghost Breaker," "The Vagabond Prince"), McClure, Frohman ("God's Man"), Jesse D. Hampton ("Man Who Turned White," "Pagan God," "For a Woman's Honor," "Grey Wolf's Ghost," "Fugitive From Matrimony," "House of a Thousand Candles"). Hght., 6, ½; wght., 167; fair hair, blue eyes. Permanent ad., Hollywood Hotel, Hollywood, Calif.; studio, Hampton.

WARREN, Fred H.; b. Rock Island, Ill.; stage career, Warren & Conley, vaud.; screen career, Metro ("Kildare of Storm," "Sylvia on a Spree," played in "Johnny on the Spot," "A Favor to a Friend," "Turning the Tables"), First National ("Heart o' the Hills."

WARWICK, Major Robert; b. Sacramento, Calif.; educ. San Francisco; stage career, played in stk. at Valencia theatre, San Francisco, "The Dollar Mark" at Wallach's, N. Y.; Screen career, World ("Man of the Hour"),

Selznick ("The Argyle Case," "A Modern Othello," "The Mad Lover"), Famous Players ("Secret Service," "Told in the Hills," "In Mizzoura," "Tree of Knowledge," "Thou Art the Man!" Enlisted and served as Captain on Gen. Pershing's staff, later given Major's commission. Hght., 6; wght., 175; brown hair and eyes. Ad., Lasky Studio, Hollywood, Calif.

WASHBURN, Bryant; b. Chicago, 1889; educ. there; stage career, from 1907, with George Fawcett in several successes, starred in "The Fighter"; screen career, Essanay, 6 yrs., Pathe, Artcraft ("Till I Come Back to You," "The Way of a Man with a Maid"), Famous Players ("A Very Good Young Man," "Love Insurance," "Why Smith Left Home," "Too Much Johnson," "It Pays to Advertise," "Six Best Cellars," "Sick-a-Bed"). Hght., 6; wght., 155; dark complexion, dark brown hair, brown eyes. Ad., 7003 Hawthorne ave., Hollywood, Calif.; studio, Lasky.

WEBB, George; b. Indianapolis, Ind.; educ. Minneapolis and Los Angeles; stage career, 8 yrs. leading man in stock cos., Minneapolis, Los Angeles, Seattle, San Francisco, etc., own co. 3 trips to Hawaiian Islands; screen career, 4 yrs., American, Universal, Triangle, Thos. H. Ince ("John Petticoats" with Wm. S. Hart, "Alarm Clock Andy" with Chas. Ray, "Below the Surface" with Hobart Bosworth, Fox ("Miss Adventure"). Hght., 5, 11; wght., 160; dark brown hair, blue eyes. Home ad., 1218 No. Bronson ave., Los Angeles, Calif.; phone 579820.

WEIGEL, Paul; b. Halle, Saxony; educ. Germany; stage career, since 1885; screen career, since 1916, Lasky, Metro ("The She Devil," "Dubarry," "The Light," "Smiles"), Fox ("Evangeline"), Famous Players ("Luck in Pawn"), Universal ("The Beachcombers," "Breath of the Gods"). Hght., 5, 8; wght., 145; dark gray hair, gray eyes. Home ad., 6806 Hollywood Blvd., Los Angeles, Calif.; Holly 2744.

WELCH, Niles; b. Hartford, Conn.; educ. St. Paul's School, Yale Univ., Columbia Univ.; stage career, 4 yrs. legit., stock; screen career, World, Universal, Pathe, Goldwyn, Technicolor ("The Gulf Between," first picture prod. in colors), Norma Talmadge ("Secret of the Storm Country"), Famous Players ("Miss George Washington"), Metro ("Her Boy," "One of Many"), Ince ("The Law of Men," "The Virtuous Thief," "Stepping Out"), Bessie Barriscale ("Beckoning Roads," "Luck of Geraldine Laird"). Hght., 6; wght., 165; medium brown hair, dark blue eyes. Home ad., 6650 Leland Way, Los Angeles, Calif.; Holly 316.

WELDEN, Jess C.; b. Keine Valley, N. Y.; educ. there; stage career, 3 yrs. as circus clown; screen career, Hehrman Comedies ("Milk-Fed Vamp," "Roaring Lions and Wedding Bells"), Chas. Chaplin ("The Count"), "Broken Bubble." Hght., 4, 8; wght., 185; dark hair, blue eyes. Home ad., 334 So. Figueroa st., Los Angeles, Calif.; phone 13404.

WELSH, William J.; b. Phila.; stage career, opera, dramatic, with Belasco in "Under Two Flags," managed Joseph Santley on tour; screen career, with Universal (playing heavies in "Traffic in Souls," "Neptune's Daughter," "Peg of the Wilds," characters in "Lords of High Decision," "Elusive Isabel," "In the Heart of New York"), Selznick ("The Foolish Virgin"), Frank Seng "Parentage"), Pathe ("The Little Diplomat").

WEST, Billy; b. Russia; educ. Chicago; stage career, prods. and vaud.; screen career, King Bee Billy West's comedies ("Cupid's Rival," "The Pest," "Back Stage," "The Slave," "The Hero," "Candy Kid," "The Stranger," "The Rogue," "A Scrapper," "Playmates," "Bright and Early," "Straight and Narrow," "The Messenger," "The Orderly"). Making 2-reel comedies for Cropper Dist. Corp., 207 Wabash ave., Chicago, Ill.; studio, Emerald, 1717 No. Wells st., Chicago.

WEST, Charles H.; b. Pittsburgh, 1886; educ. Western Univ. of Pa.; stage career, from 1904, stage mgr., stock rep., with J. K. Hackett; screen career, since 1910, with Biograph until 1915, Fine Arts, Lasky, Selig, Universal ("The Little Pirate"), Paramount ("White Man's Law," "The Girl Who Came Back"), Universal ("Flask of Fate," "His Divorced Wife," "The Phantom Melody"). Hght., 5, 11; wght., 150; light complexion, light brown hair, dark brown eyes. Ad., 1437 So. Bonnie Brae, Los Angeles, Calif.

WHEATCROFT, Stanhope; b. N. Y., 1888; educ. Columbia Univ.; stage career, from prod. of "Nancy Stair" at Criterion theatre, N. Y.; screen career, Fox ("East Lynne," "Under Two Flags," "A Modern Cinderella"), World, Universal ("The Right to Happiness," "The Amazing Wife," "The Breath of the Gods," "Harmony Ranch"), National ("The Blue Bonnet"), Morosco ("The Veiled Adventure," "The Old Town Girl"). Hght., 5, 11; wght., 145; dark hair, brown eyes. Ad., Hotel Hollywood, Hollywood, Calif.

WHITCOMB, Barry; b. Australia, 1872; educ. Australia and City of London Coll.; stage career, 25 yrs. with leading Eng. mgmts., Irving, Tree, Frohman, Mrs. Langtry, Willard, etc.; screen career, Fox ("The Serpent," "Hypocrites"), Famous Players ("The Undying Flame"), Arrow ("The Deemster"), C. K. Young ("Common Law"), Nazimova ("Eye for Eye," "'Ception Shoals"), Mayflower ("Bolshevism on Trial"), World-Peerless ("The Battler"). Hght., 5, 10; wght., 178; brown hair, brown eyes. Home ad., West Fort Lee, N. J. Fort Lee 41-R.

WHITE, Billy; b. Sacramento, Calif.; educ. there and San Francisco; stage career, stage mgr. Silver King Co., minstrel, etc.; screen career, Keystone, Ince, Kerrigan, Christie, C. K. Young, Fairbanks ("American Ace," "Brewster's Millions"), Fox ("Tale of Two Cities"), Charlie Chaplin ("A Dog's Life"), Selig ("The Spoilers"), Universal ("The Broken Coin," "Lucille Love"), Burston ("The Hawk's Trail"). Hght., 5, 4; wght., 175; light hair, blue eyes. Home ad., 416 Madison ave., Los Angeles, Calif., Wilshire 5395.

WHITE, George; b. and educ. Washington, D. C.; stage career, "Kismet," "Man Higher Up," "Putting It Over," stk. in Balto.; screen career, Goldwyn ("All Woman"), Metro ("The Slacker"), Hobart Henley ("Gay Old Dog"). Hght., 5, 5; wght., 132; brown hair. Ad., Green Room Club, N. Y.

WHITLOCK, T. Lloyd; b. Springfield, Mo.; educ. Missouri Univ.; early career, civil engineer; stage career, stock; screen career, Biograph, Klein, Kalem, Universal ("A Gentle Ill Wind," "The Edge of the Law," "Lasca," "Rouge and Riches"), National ("The Boomerang," "The Love Call," "Rose Marie"), Beban ("One Man in a Million"). Hght., 6, 1½; wght., 175; brown hair and eyes. Ad., 3 Carver Court, Hollywood, Calif., phone 579388.

WHITMAN, Alfred; b. Chicago, 1890; educ. Lewis Inst., Chicago; stage career, with Estelle Allen in "Barriers Burned Away"; screen career, 2 yrs. with NYMPH, Morosco, American, Universal, Vitagraph ("The Eighth Great-Grand-Parent," "Cavanaugh of the Forest Ranges," "The Home Trail," "The Girl from Beyond," "A Gentleman's Agreement," "Tongues of Flame," "Days of Forty-Nine," "Trick of Fate"), Hodkinson ("End of the Game," "The Best Man"). Hght., 6, 1.; wght., 195; dark brown hair and eyes. Ad., 4500 Franklin ave., Los Angeles, Calif.

WHITMAN, Walt; screen career, Jewell ("Heart of Humanity"), Pathe ("Cry of the Weak"), Universal ("Destiny"), World-Macauley ("When Bearcat Went Dry"), Para-Arteraft ("John Petticoats").

WHITSON, Frank; b. N. Y. C., 1876; educ. Peekskill Mil. Acad., 1 yr. at medical coll.; stage career, 15 yrs., stk. in N. Y., Chicago, in "Sporting Life," 6 yrs. in vaud.; screen career, Metro, Fox, Universal, Ince-Triangle ("The Son of a Gun," "The Tigress," "Send Him Away With a Smile," "Social Briers"), Artcraft ("Square Deal Sanderson"), Rob-Cole ("Trick of Fate," "Hearts Asleep"), Select ("Faith of the Strong"). Hght., 5, 11; wght., 180; brown hair and dark brown eyes. Ad., home, 1136 Gordon st., Los Angeles, Cal.

WILBUR, Crane, also co-director; b. Athens, N. Y., Nov. 17, 1889; educ. pub. schls.; stage career, from age of 15, rep., stock, etc., 7 yrs. with Mrs. Fiske; screen career, Pathe ("The Perils of Pauline" series), Horsley ("The Spite Husband," "The Painted Lie," "Unlucky Jim," "The Morals of Men," "The Eye of Envy," "Heirs of Hate," "The Blood of His Fathers," "Unto the End"), Triangle ("Devil M'Care," "Breezy Jim"), Victor Kremer ("Stripped for a Million," author and actor). Hght., 5, 9; wght., 169; brown hair, gray eyes. Ad., c/o N. T. Granlund, 1493 B'way, N. Y.

WILLIAMS, Earle Rafael; b. Sacramento, Calif., Feb. 28, 1880; educ. pub. and hgh. schls. Oakland, Polytech., Coll. of Calif.; stage career, with Baldwin-Melville stock co., New Orleans, 1901; with Frederick Belasco co., San Francisco and Portland; with James Neill stock co.,

Henry Dixey, Rose Stahl, Mary Mannering, Helen Ware, Geo. Beban; screen career, with Vitagraph, leads and heavies, in ("The Grell Mystery," "The Hillman," "The Seal of Silence," "The Girl in His House," "An American Live Wire," "A Diplomatic Mission," "The Man Who Wouldn't Tell," "The Highest Trump," "A Gentleman of Quality," "The Usurper," "A Rogue's Romance," "The Hornet's Nest," "The Wolf," "The Black Gate"). Hght., 5, 11; wght., 176; dark complexion, black hair, blue eyes. Studio ad., Vitagraph, B'klyn, N. Y.

WILSON, Ben, also director; b. Corning, Iowa; educ. there and Centerville, Iowa; stage career, 12 yrs. stock and prods.; screen career, Edison (lead in "Who Will Marry Mary" serial), Universal (lead in "Voice on the Wire," "The Mystery Ship," directed "The Brass Bullet" serials), Hallmark (lead in "Trail of the Octopus," "The Screaming Shadow" serials), starred in various features. Hght., 5, 11¼; wght., 176; dark hair, brown eyes. Home ad., 219 So. Harvard Blvd., Los Angeles, Calif., phone 560661; studio, Ben Wilson Prods.

WILSON, Hal; b. N. Y. C.; educ. Coll. of City of N. Y.; stage career, 20 yrs. Harrigan and Hart, Frohman, A. H. Woods, Murray Stk. Co. under H. V. Donnelly's mgmt.; screen career, from 1907, 3 yrs. dir. Eclair, Fine Arts (appeared in "Casey at the Bat," "The Little Yank"), Griffith ("Intolerance"), Universal comedies, Vitagraph ("Clowns Best Performers," "The Blind Miner," "Tale of Two Cities"), Metro ("Easy to Make Money"). Hght., 5, 8; wght., 160; gray hair, brown eyes. Home ad., 5142 De Longpre ave., Los Angeles, Calif., Holly 639; studio, Lois Weber Prods.

WILSON, Tom; b. Helena, Mont., 1880; early career, soldier, professional boxer, trained Fitzsimmons for fight with Corbett; stage career, with Fitzsimmons in "A Fight for Love," with Eva Tanguay in vaud.; screen career, Reliance-Majestic, Fine Arts ("Atta Boy's Last Race," "The Americano," "Wild and Wooly," "Amarilly of Clothesline Alley"), Chaplin ("A Dog's Life," "Shoulder Arms," "Sunnyside," "A Day's Pleasure"). Hght., 6, 2; wght., 220; dark brown hair, dark gray eyes. Ad., 1352 Spaulding ave., Los Angeles, Calif.

WINDERMER, Fred C.; b. Muscatine, Iowa; educ. there; screen career, directed Essanay Snakeville series, Essanay-Chaplin ("A Night Out," "The Champion", "Work," "The Tramp"), Hank Mann ("The Messenger," "The Gas Attack," "His Waiting Career," "Hopping the Bells," "A Rural Romeo"). Home ad., 5800 Franklyn ave., Hollywood, Calif.; studio, Hank Mann Co.

WING, Ward; b. Springfield, Mo.; educ. Kansas City, Mo.; stage career, Geo. Ade's "The Mayor and the Manicure," over U. B. O. time 2 yrs., Lyric Stock Co., Woodward Stock Co., Martin Stock Co., Rush Stock Co.; screen career, Lasky, Universal ("The Eagle," "A Mother's Sacrifice," "The Camera Man," "The Monkey Bus," "Loot"), Christie ("Her Helping Hand"), Metro ("In His Brother's Place"), New Art ("The Solitary Sin"), Selig ("Cupid's Thumb Print"). Hght., 5, 8; wght., 140; dark brown hair, dark blue eyes. Ad., Actor's Assn. of Los Angeles, Calif., Holly 1946.

WISE, Harry; b. N. Y.; educ. N. Y.; stage career, vaud., light opera; screen career, Metro ("Out of the Fog"), Famous Players ("Fifi," "The Avalanche"), Universal ("Shot in the Dark," "Servant of the Slums"), Selznick with Elsie Janis. Hght., 5, 5; wght., 148; dark hair, brown eyes. Ad., 269 W. 45th st., N. Y., Bryant 2257.

WOODWARD, Henry F.; b Charleston, West Va.; educ. M. D. degree at Univ. of Md., B. A. degree at Univ. of W. Va.; early career, 1st Lieut. in Philippine Islands, 2 yrs. in U. S. Engineers; screen career, Fox ("Lawless Love"), Lois Weber ("Forbid"), Brunton ("Hearts Asleep"), Lasky, (3 yrs. stock, "The Mystery Girl," "Your Fired"), Garson ("Road Through the Dark"), Brentwood ("Where There's a Will"), Brunton ("Are You Legally Married?"), Para.-Artcraft ("Male and Female"). Hght., 6; wght., 180, brown hair, blue eyes. Home ad., 1953 Ivar st., Hollywood, Calif.; Holly 3188.

WYNNE, Hugh; b. N. Y. C., 1868; educ. St. Mark's, Southboro, Mass., and Exeter, N. H.; stage career, Wilton Lackaye Players, H. B. Warner Co., Henrietta Crossman, "Polly of the Circus," etc.; screen career, Metro ("American Widow," "Their Funny Affair"), Vitagraph ("One Thousand Dollars," "Tangled Lives"), etc. Hght., 5, 8; wght., 135; gray hair, blue eyes. Home ad., Huntington, L. I., N. Y.

— Y —

YOUNG, Tammany; b. N. Y. C.; stage career, with Nat Goodwin, Holbrook Blinn, William Farnum, Beatrice Forbes-Robertson, David Belasco, Cohan & Harris, Klaw & Erlanger, "Alias Jimmy Valentine," "Bought and Paid For," "The Man Inside," A. H. Woods, "The Big Chance," "Kick In"; screen career, Fox ("Checkers"), MacManus ("Lost Battalion"), Goldwyn ("The Service Star," "The Racing Strain," with Mae Marsh, "The Woman on the Index"), Selznick (with Elsie Janis in "A Regular Girl," "The Imp"), Famous Players ("The Amazons"), Thomas Mott Osborne's "Our Gray Brothers." Ad., 150 W. 36th st., N. Y., Greeley 2082.

The industry's reference book.

Motion Picture Studio Directory and Trade Annual.

ACTRESSES

—A—

ADAMS, Claire; b. Winnipeg, Can.; educ. Canada and England; screen career, Red Cross ("Spirit of the Red Cross"), Educational ("Key to Power"), Government ("Richard Bennett"), Betzwood ("End of the Road," "Lord Jim"), Famous-Players ("Invisible Bond"), Zane Grey Pict. ("Desert of Wheat"), with H. B. Warner in Jesse D. Hampton prod. Ad., care Federal Photoplays, Brunton Studios, Los Angeles, Calif.

ADAMS, Dora Mills; screen career, Vitagraph, Famous, 2 yrs., Pathe, Metro ("The Square Deceiver"), Brenon ("Passing of the Third Floor Back"), Perret-Pathe ("Twin Pawns"), John Dooley comedy; Pathe ("The Black Hawk"), Selznick ("Piccadilly Jim"). Hght., 5, 10; wght., 118; dark complexion, brown hair and eyes. Home ad., 485 Rugby Road, Brooklyn, N. Y.

ADAMS, Kathryn; b. St. Louis, Mo., 1897; educ. St. Louis; stage career, musical comedy, 1 yr.; screen career, Metro, World, Famous Players, Thanhouser ("Vicar of Wakefield"), Pathe, ("Streets of Illusion," "The Silver Girl"), Goldwyn ("Baby Mine"), Vitagraph ("A Rogue's Romance," "A Gentleman of Quality"), Triangle ("Restless Souls"), Fox ("Cowardice Court"), Universal ("Little Brother of the Rich," "The Brute Breaker"). Hght., 5, 7; wght., 130; blond hair, dark gray eyes. Ad., 1553 N. Mariposa, Los Angeles, Calif.; phone 59476.

AIKEN, Alma; b. Chicago; educ. Notre Dame Acad., Boston Highlands; stage career with Fanny Davenport and Marie Wainwright; screen career, Reliance, Biograph, Famous Players ("The Test of Honor"). Hght., 5, 6; wght., 168; gray hair, gray eyes. Ad., 258 W. 52nd st., N. Y. Circle 1080.

ALDEN, Mary; b. New Orleans; educ. Art Students' League, N. Y.; stage career, Baldwin-Melville, Hunter-Bradford stk. cos.; with Mrs. Fiske, with Phillips Smalley in "The Wolf"; screen career, Fox, Pathe, Biograph, Reliance-Majestic, Fine Arts, Artcraft, Selznick ("The Argyle Case"), Famous Players ("The Land of Promise," "The Straight Path," "Common Clay"), Blanche Sweet Co. ("The Unpardonable Sin"), Robertson-Cole ("The Broken Butterfly"), Realart ("Erstwhile Susan"). Ad., Rex Arms, 945 Orange st., Los Angeles, Cal.

ALEXANDER, Claire; b. N. Y., 1897; educ. N. Y. pub. schs. and Portland, Ore., high sch.; screen career, Fine Arts, Famous Players, joined Horsley, 1916 (in Cub comedies, "Jerry's Big Mystery," "Jerry's Picnic," "Jerry's Jam," "Jerry's Soft Snap"), Keystone-Triangle ("His Disgusted Passion"), Triangle ("Child of M'sieu"). Hght., 4, 10; wght., 101; dark brown hair, hazel eyes.

ALEXANDER, Sara; b. Wheeling, W. Va.; early career, in stock in Salt Lake City 6 yrs., then with Barrett-McCullough Co.; has appeared at various times with Lydia Thompson, John T. Raymond, Kyrle Bellew; screen career, Fox ("Caprice of the Mountains," "Little Miss Happiness," "The Jungle Trail").

ALLEN, Beatrice; stage career of 12 yrs.; 4 yrs. with Nazimova, Jas. K. Hackett, Fannie Ward, Wm. Farnum; Jewish Girl in "Riddle Woman," "Kyrle Bellew," 2 yrs., with "Bunty Pulls the Strings"; screen career, Famous Players ("Anne of Green Gables"). Now with Mary Ryan in "A Room at the Ritz," management of A. H. Woods. Hght., small; wght., 115; dark eyes, dark hair. Ad., home, Bayside, L. I.; phone Bayside 949-W.

ALLEN, Diana; b. Gotland, Sweden; educ. New Haven, Conn.; stage career, "Follies," 1917-18; "The Frolic," 1919, "Miss 1917"; screen career, Rolfe-Fisher ("The Red Virgin"), Triangle ("Three Black Eyes"), Tourneur ("Woman"), Diamond Film Co., Breed-Howell. Hght., 5, 3; wght., 115; blond hair, blue eyes. Ad., care Betts & Fowler, 1482 Broadway, N. Y. Bryant 5664.

ALLEN, Phyllis; b. Staten Island, N. Y.; stage career, vaud. and mus. com., with Kate Castleton in "The Dazzler," 1893; screen career, Selig, Keystone Comedies 2½ yrs.; characters, Sunshine Comedies, Vitagraph, etc. Hght., 5, 8; wght., 180; red hair, blue eyes. Home ad., 230 S. Beaudry ave., Los Angeles, Calif. Phone Broad 7422.

ALLEN, Ray; educ. San Francisco, Calif.; stage exper. for good many years; screen career, Perret-Pathe ("Lafayette, We Come"), Pathe, ("The Right to Lie," "Innocence"), Community ("The Home Coming of Jim"). Hght., 5, 8; wght., 155; grey hair, dark eyes. Ad., 2569 Bedford ave., Brooklyn, N. Y. Flatbush 6030-R.

ALLEN, Ricca; b. Victoria, B. C.; educ. Calif.; stage career, America, England, Australia, So. Africa and Egypt; screen career, character leads with D. W. Griffith, Metro, Frohman, World, Louis Dennison, Herbert Brenon, Apex. Hght., 5, 10; brunette, dark eyes. Home ad., 360 W. 55th st., N. Y.

ALLISON, May; b. Georgia; educ. Birmingham and Centenary Female Coll., Cleveland, Tenn.; first stage appearance as Beauty in "Everywoman," title role in "Quaker Girl," with W. H. Crane in "David Harum"; screen career, from 1915, Famous Players ("Governor's Lady"), Metro ("The Winning of Beatrice," "In for Thirty Days," "Peggy Does Her Darndest," "Isle of Intrigue," "Almost Married," "The Uplifters"). Metro-Screen Classics ("Fair and Warmer," "The Walk-Offs"). Hght., 5, 5; wght., 125; fair complexion, golden hair, blue eyes. Ad., Metro, Hollywood, Calif.

ALTER, Lottie; b. La Cross, Wis.; educ. St. Mary's, Wis.; stage career, "The Girl I Left Behind Me," 2 yrs. with Joseph Jefferson, Sr., in U. S., England and Australia, "Excuse Me," Lovely Mary in "Mrs. Wiggs of the Cabbage Patch"; screen career, Pathe ("An Arizona Romance"), Famous ("The Eternal City"), Savage ("Excuse Me," "See Saw"), Wharton ("Exploits of Elaine," "The Lottery Man"), Morosco, "Cappy Ricks"). Ad., home, Bayside, L. I.; phone Bayside 941-R.

ANDERSON, Claire; b. and educ. Detroit, Mich.; screen career, Fine Arts, Triangle-Keystone ("The Answer," "Mlle. Paulette," "The Prince of Applause"), Triangle ("Crown Jewels"), Select ("Who Cares"), Universal ("Spitfire of Seville," "Rider of the Law"); playing comedienne leads. Hght., 5, 5; wght., 132; fair complexion, light hair, brown eyes. Ad., home, 3524 White House pl., Los Angeles, Cal.

ANDERSON, Helen Relyea ("Mother"); b. N. Y. C., June, 1874; educ. Canadian Convent; early career, school teacher; stage career, concert work; screen career, Vitagraph ("Over the Top," "Kitty Mackay," "Anselo Lee"), World ("Blood of the Trevor"), Fox ("The Soul of Buddha"), Tourneur ("The Life Line"), Mary Pickford ("The Hoodlum"), Metro ("Castles in the Air," "Lion's Den," "Should a Girl Tell"), Vitagraph Comedies. Hght., 5, 3; wght., 148; fair complexion, brown hair, grey eyes. Ad., 1527 Third st., Santa Monica, Calif. Phone 217-J. Personal rep., Rose Mullaney, Security Bldg.

ANDERSON, Mary; b. Brooklyn, June 28, 1897; educ. Brooklyn, Erasmus Hall, Holy Cross Schl; early career, amateur Grecian dancing for charity; screen career, 5 yrs. Select ("The Hushed Hour"), Artcraft ("Johnny Get Your Gun," "False Faces"), Metro ("The Spender"), Super Art ("Bubbles"), Morgan Features ("Reforming a Reformer"), Selig ("The Haunted Ranch"). Now featured in Selig Serial. Hght., 4, 11; wgh., 105; golden hair, blue eyes. Home ad., 1532 Third st., Santa Monica, Calif. Phone 217-J.

ANDERSON, Mignon; b. Baltimore, Md.; educ. N. Y. C.; early experience; stage career, with Richard Mansfield, Julia Marlowe, etc., as a child actress; screen career, Thanhouser, Universal ("A Wife on Trial," "The Get-a-way," "The Master Spy"), Metro, ("The Claim," "Blind Man's Eyes"), Keenan-Pathe ("The Midnight Stage"), Robertson-Cole ("The House of Intrigue"), Mitchell Lewis ("King Spruce"), also lead in "Hell Fire"). Hght., 5; wght., 94; fair complexion, blond hair. Studio ad., 7572 La Baig ave., Hollywood, Calif.

AOKI, Tsuru; b. Tokio, Japan, Sept. 9, 1892; educ. Japan and convent in this country; stage career, since 8 yrs. old with aunt and uncle; screen career, Lasky-Paramount ("The Call of the East"), Essanay ("The Curse of Iku"), Lasky ("The Bravest Way"), Haworth ("His Birthright," "Bonds of Honor," "Heart in Pawn," "The Grey Horizon"), Robertson-Cole ("The Courageous Coward," "The Dragon Painter," "The Breath of the Gods," "Locked Lips," "The Tokio Siren"). Hght., 5, 1; wght., 120; black hair and eyes.

ARTHUR, Julia; b. Hamilton, Ont., Can.; educ. Canada; stage career, began at 12 yrs. Palmers Co., stk., Henry Irving Co., star in "Lady of Quality," "More Than Queen," Shakespearian roles, "Eternal Magdalene" with Selwyn; produced "Romeo and Juliet," "As You Like It," "Seremonda," etc.; screen career, Blackton ("The Common Cause"), Plunkett & Carroll ("The Woman the Germans Shot"). Hght., 5, 4½ wght., 125; dark hair and eyes. Ad., Hotel Biltmore, N. Y. C.

ASHTON, Iris; b. El Paso, Texas; educ. San Francisco; stage career, studied in San Francisco under Madame Ferrier and Maude Ott, drama and aesthetic ballroom dancing; screen career, Rainbow ("How Can I Earn a Living"), Triangle ("You Can't Believe Everything," "False Ambition," "Prudence on Broadway"), stock one year with Ince; Maurice Tourneur ("Glory of Love"). Hght., 5, 7½; wght., 138; dark brown hair and eyes. Maurice Tourneur Productions, Goldwyn Studio; home ad., 7116 Tecumseh st., Culver City, Calif. Phone 70304.

ASHTON, Sylvia; b. in mid-ocean of American parents; stage career, 15 yrs. in stk. and en tour; screen career, 10 yrs., C. B. DeMille ("Old Wives for New," "Don't Change Your Husband," "Why Change Your Wife?"), Famous Players ("Jack Straw," "Thou Art the Man!"). Hght., 5, 6; wght., 140; blond hair, blue eyes. Ad., Lasky Studio, Hollywood, Calif.

AYRES, Agnes; b. Chicago; educ. there; screen career, Essanay, Vitagraph ("Richard the Brazen"), O. Henry-General ("The Defeat of the City," "The Girl and the Graft," "The Enchanted Profile," "The Purple Dress," "One Thousand Dollars"), Fox ("Sacred Silence"), American Cinema ("The Inner Voice"). Ad., New York City.

— B —

BAILEY, Mildred E.; b. West Haven, Conn., Nov. 12, 1898; educ. prep. schl. at Deep River, Conn., and New Haven Coll. for Girls; stage career, 12 mos. with Poli stk. at New Haven; screen career, Metro ("Extravagance"), Niagara ("Perils of the Girl Reporters," "Up Romance Road"), Mutual ("Hearts or Diamonds"), Petrova ("The Black Butterfly"). Hght., 5, 2; wght., 134; brown hair, gray-brown eyes. Home ad., 1808 Marmion ave., N. Y.

BAIRD, Leah; b. Chicago, Ill.; educ. there; screen career, "Hearts of the First Empire," "Absinthe," "Neptune's Daughter," "People vs. John Doe," "One Law for Both," International ("Echo of Youth"), Hodkinson ("As a Man Thinks," "The Capitol," "Cynthia of the Minute"), author of many scenarios. Dark hair and brown eyes. Ad., W. W. Hodkinson Corp., N. Y., and care A. F. Beck, 135 W. 44th st., N. Y.

BALLIN, Mabel; b. and educ. Philadelphia; stage exper., 3½ yrs.; screen career, Famous Players, Vitagraph, Triangle, Goldwyn, Tourneur, World ("The White Heather"), ("The Quickening Flame"), Goldwyn ("Lord and Lady Algy"), Rob.-Cole ("The Illustrious Prince"). Hght., 5, 3; wght., 122; light brown hair, brown eyes. Home ad., Lincroft, Saugatuck, Conn.; 2021 Beachwood Drive, Los Angeles, Cal.

BANKS, Mrs. Estar; b. Boston, Mass.; educ. there; on speaking stage 36 years; screen career, Edison, Universal, Famous Players ("At First Sight," "Hit the Trail Halliday," "Woman of Impulse"), Vitagraph ("Love versus Mammon"), Rapf ("Sins of the Children"); now with "La La Lucille." Hght., 5, 3½; wght., 116; gray hair, brown eyes. Ad., Bijou Fernandez office, 42d st., West, New Amsterdam Thea. Bldg., N. Y.

BARA, Theda; b. 1890; screen career, Fox ("A Fool There Was," "Carmen," "Her Double Life," "The Vixen," "The Price of Silence," "The Tiger Woman," "Cleopatra," "Her Greatest Love," "Heart and Soul," "Camille," "The Rose of Blood," "Du Barry," "The Forbidden Path," "Salome," "The Soul of Buddah," "The Clemenceau Case," "When a Woman Sins," "The She-Devil," "The Siren's Song," "The Light," "A Woman There Was," "La Belle Russe," "Kathleen Mavourneen," "The Lure of Ambition." Hght., 5, 6; wght., 135; dark brown hair and eyes. 1920, A. H. Wood's "The Blue Flame."

BARKER, Corinne; educ. Acad. of Sacred Heart, Salem, Ore.; stage career, "The Crinoline Girl" with Julian Eltinge, "Potash and Perlemutter," "The Squab Farm," "Sirley Kaye" with Elsie Ferguson, "On With the Dance," with John Mason and Julia Dean, "Remnant" with Florence Nash; screen career, Goldwyn ("Money Mad," "Peck's Bad Girl," "One Week of Life," "Peace of Roaring River"), Fox ("Why I Would Not Marry"), Vitagraph ("The Climbers," "The Golden Shower"), Selznick ("The Broken Melody"), International ("The Restless Sex"). Hght., 5, 8; wght., 138; dark brown hair, hazel eyes. Ad., 1 West 30th st., N. Y.; Mad. Sq. 3770.

BARNEY, Marion; educ. Univ. of Calif.; stage career, Frohman, Klaw & Erlanger, David Belasco, John Cort, stk. leads; screen career, World-Peerless ("Heart of Gold," "Love and the Woman," "Dust of Desire," "His Father's Wife," "Poison Pen," "Steel King"), James Vincent ("The Spirit of Lafayette"). Hght., 5, 6; wght., 145; blond hair, blue-gray eyes. Ad., 312 Manhattan ave., N. Y. C.; Cathedral 8208.

BARRISCALE, Bessie; b. N. Y.; stage career, starred in "The Rose of the Rancho," "Bird of Paradise" and "We Are Seven"; screen career, Paralta ("Within the Cup," "Patriotism," "The Heart of Rachael," "Two Gun Betty"), B. B. Features ("Trick of Fate," "Josselyn's Wife," "Tangled Threads," "Woman Michael Married," "Her Purchase Price," "Beckoning Roads"). Hght., 5, 2; wght., 123; blond hair, brown eyes. Studio ad., Brunton Studios, 5341 Melrose ave., Los Angeles, Calif.

BARRYMORE Ethel; b. Phila., Pa., 1879; stage career, since 1894, as Kate Fennell in "The Bauble Shop" with her uncle, John Drew; English debut in 1897 as Miss Kittridge in "Secret Service" with Gillette, on tour in "The Bells" with Irving; starred in "The Twelve-Pound Look," "Our Mrs. McChesney"; 1919, "Delcasse"; screen career, All Star ("The Nightingale"), Metro ("Awakening of Helena Richie," "The White Raven," "The Lifted Veil," "The Whirlpool," "An American Widow," "The Eternal Mother," "Lady Frederick," "Our Mrs. McChesney," "The Divorcee"). Ad., 130 East 65th st., N. Y.

BARTON, Grace; stage career, mus. com., "Broadway Jones," "Over Night"; screen career, Famous Players, Fox, Kleine, Universal ("The Raggedy Queen"), World ("Heart of Gold"). Hght., 5, 7½; complexion medium.

BAXTER, Thuma Jadee; b. Milton, Ky., 1897; educ. Bowling Green, Ky., Ward-Bellmont, Nashville, Tenn.; stage career, Follies 1918, Shuberts, Monte Cristo, stk.; screen career, Hallmark Prod. ("The Heart of a Gypsy"), Curtis Special ("Who Is Your Brother?"), Jester Comedies ("Shime"), World ("His Father's Wife"). Hght., 5, 3; wght., 115; fair complexion, black hair, dark brown eyes. Ad., 520 N. Meridian st., Apt. 26, Indianapolis, Ind.

BAYNE, Beverly; b. Minneapolis, Minn., 1895; educ. Minneapolis, Phila., and Hyde Park High Sch., Chicago; screen career, Essanay ("Under Royal Patronage," "Graustark," "Dear Old Girl," etc.), Metro ("Romeo and Juliet," "The Great Secret," "Their Compact," "God's Outlaw," "The Voice of Conscience," "The Adopted Son," "The Red, White and Blue Blood," "Social Quicksands," "A Pair of Cupids," "The Poor Rich Man"), Vitagraph ("Daring Hearts"); has appeared in more than 500 photoplays. Hght., 5, 2; wght., 125; dark brown hair, brown eyes.

BECK, Lillian; b. Cincinnati; educ. St. Joseph's Convent; stage career, "Never Say Die," With Wm. Collier, mus. com.; screen career, 7 yrs. Kleine ("Gloria's Romance"), Metro ("Nothing But the Truth"), King Cole Comedies. Hght., 5, 6; wght., 150; light brown hair, blue eyes. Permanent ad., 709 W. 170th st., N. Y. C.; Wadsworth 4480.

BELMORE Daisy; b. 1889; stage career, "The Fawn," "Our Mrs. Gibbs," "In Half an Hour"; screen career, Famous Players ("The Better

Man"), Select ("His Bridal Night"). Hght., 5, 8.

BENNETT, Belle; b. near Dublin, Ireland; began stage career five weeks later in father's road show, continuing until 1915; screen career, Universal ("In the Fires of Rebellions," "The Charmer"), Triangle ("The Bond of Fear," "The Hell Cat of Alaska," "Ashes of Hope," "Fuel of Life," "Because of the Woman," "The Devil Dodger," "The Lonely Woman," "The Mayor of Filbert"). Hght., 5, 2; wght., 125; light complexion, Roman gold hair, gray eyes.

BENNETT, Enid; b. York, Western Australia; educ. Perth, W. Australia; stage career, in America and abroad in support of Fred Niblo, Otis Skinner, etc.; screen career, starring dramatic ingenue, Thos. E. Ince ("Fuss and Feathers," "The Vamp," "Biggest Show on Earth," "Law of Men," "Haunted Bedroom," "Virtuous Thief," "Stepping Out," "What Every Woman Learns," "Woman in the Suit-Case"). Hght., 5, 3; wght., 102; golden brown hair, hazel eyes. Ad., Ince Studio, Culver City, Calif.

BERKELEY, Gertrude; educ. College Hill, Poughkeepsie, N. Y.; stage exper., with Chas. Frohman, Henry Miller, Mme. Nazimova, Maxine Elliott, etc.; screen career, Fox, Brenon, Pathe, Famous, World ("Song of Songs," "Just Sylvia," "War Brides"), Select ("Break the News to Mother," "The Way of a Woman"). Hght., 5, 5; wght., 155; brown hair, hazel eyes. Ad., Ridgewood, N. J.; Ridgewood 669 or 265.

BERNARD, Dorothy; b. Port Elizabeth, S. Africa, 1890; educ. Australia and Marlborough Schl. Los Angeles, Cal.; stage career, from age of 2, child parts in U. S., Australia, New Zealand, England, leads in many stk. cos. in U. S., under mgmt. Shuberts, Selwyn & Co., etc.; screen career, Biograph, 2 yrs., Kalem, Lubin, Famous Players, with Fox 18 mos. (in "Little Gypsy," "Sporting Blood," "Fine Feathers," "Les Miserables"), Brady ("Little Women"), C. P. R. and Canadian Government ("The World Shadow"). Hght., 5, 5; wght., 124; olive complexion, brown hair, brown eyes. Ad., 112 23d st., Elmhurst, L. I., N. Y.

BESSERER, Eugenie; b. Marseilles, France; educ. Convent of Notre Dame, Ottawa, Canada; stage career, since early childhood with McKee Rankin, Wilton Lackaye, Frank Keenan, various stk. cos., under mgmt. J. C. Williamson in Australia; screen career, Selig ("Crises," "Carpet From Bagdad"), "Little Orphant Annie," "Auction of Souls"), D. W. Griffith ("Scarlet Days"), Humanity Film ("The Gift Supreme"). Home ad., 2215 Baxter st., Los Angeles, Calif.; Wilshire 2994.

BIALA, Sara; educ. Drake Univ., Des Moines, Iowa, Chicago Musical Coll.; stage career, Shakespearean rep., stk. cos., "Baby Mine" with Marguerite Clark, "The Ghost Breaker" with H. B. Warner, "Romance," Nazimova's role in second "War Brides" Co., with George Arliss in "Paganini," London and N. Y. prods. of "Some Baby," "The Torches," "The Weaker One," vaud.; screen career, Hallmark ("Heart of a Gypsy"), Famous Players ("The Fear Market"), Italian, French, Spanish and Oriental types and emotional roles. Hght., 5, 5; wght., 118; dark brown hair, brown eyes. Ad., Rehearsal Club, 220 West 46th st., N. Y. C.

BILLINGS, Florence B.; educ. private schl., N. Y.; screen career, Vitagraph, 2½ yrs., Hallmark ("Wit Wins," "Heart of a Gypsy", "Dangerous Affair"), Laurence Weber ("The Blue Pearl"), Selznick ("Woman Game"). Ad., Actors Equity, N. Y.; home, 601 W. 139th st., N. Y.

BILLINGTON, Francelia; b. Dallas, Texas, Feb. 1, 1897; educ. Sacred Heart Convent, Los Angeles, Calif.; screen career, Griffith, Reliance, Majestic, American, Universal ("Blind Husbands," "The Day She Paid"). Hght., 5, 6; wght., 135; light complexion, light brown hair, dark gray eyes. Studio ad., Universal Film Co.; home ad., 127 W. Chestnut st., Glendale, Calif. Glendale 2177-R.

BINNEY, Constance; b. N. Y.; educ. Brearly Schl. in Westover, Conn., French Convent, Paris, France; took part in the Booth Pageant in Detroit; placed under contract with Winthrop Ames, associated with Comstock & Elliott as dancer in "Oh! Lady, Lady"; appeared in Maurice Tourneur's "Sporting Life" and played opposite John Barrymore in "Test of Honor" and "Here Comes the Bride"; starred in Rachael Crothers' "39 East"; starred in Realart picture, "Erstwhile Susan." Ad., c/o Realart Pictures Corp., 469 Fifth ave., N. Y.

BINNEY, Faire; b. N. Y. C., 1901; educ. Concord, Mass.; screen career, Maurice Tourneur ("Sporting Life," "Woman"), Famous Players ("Here Comes the Bride," with John Barrymore), Republic ("The Blue Pearl"). Hght., 5, 1; wght., 106; brown hair, hazel eyes. Ad., 212 E. 62nd st., N. Y., Plaza 4767.

BIRON, Lillian; b. Independence, Kans.; educ. California; stage career, 1 yr. stock; screen career, 3 yrs. in pictures, 2 yrs. in Mack Sennett Comedies, Vitagraph ("Roop and Riots," "Ministers and Matrimony"). Hght., 5, 4; wght., 120; blond hair, blue eyes. Home ad., 7810 Fountain ave., Hollywood, Calif; studio, Gayety Comedies, 1501 Gower st., Hollywood.

BLACK, Fritzie; b. Galveston, Texas; educ. N. Y.; stage career, 10 yrs. in stk, rep. and prod. and vaud.; screen career, National ("Wolf on Wall Street"), Anita Stewart ("Fighting Shepherdess"), Universal, 3 yrs. ("We Are French"). Hght., 5, 2; wght., 127; auburn hair, brown eyes. Ad., Broadway Hotel, Los Angeles, Calif., Pico 875.

BLACKWELL, Irene; b. B'klyn, N. Y., educ. Penna.; screen career: Fox, "Why I Would Not Marry," "Miss Innocence," "Caught in the Act"; Metro, "His Bonded Wife"; Hallmark, "High Speed"; Supreme, "The Mystery Mind"; Photoplay Libraries, "Empty Arms." Hght., 5, 5½; wght., 135; black hair; green eyes. Ad., 340 West 86th St., N. Y. Schuyler 4481.

BLINN, Genevieve; b. San Francisco, Calif.; educ. Sacred Heart Convent, Oakland, Calif.; stage career, stk. in Los Angeles, Indianapolis, Winnipeg, Salt Lake City, with Madame Kalich in N. Y.; screen career, Fox (Daughter of the Gods," "American Methods," "Conscience," "Du Barry," "Cleopatra," "When Fate Decides," "Last of the Duanes"). Hght., 5, 6; wght., 132; fair complexion, blond, dark blue eyes.

BLYTHE, Betty; b. 1893, Los Angeles; educ. Univ. of Calif. and Paris; stage career, Morosco 1 yr., Comstock & Gest, 2 yrs., "So Long Letty," "Nobody Home," "Experience"; screen career, Vitagraph ("Over the Top," with Harry Morey for 1 yr. in "His Own People," "Tangled Lives," "The Green God"), World ("Dust of Desire"), Selznick ("Undercurrent"), Goldwyn ("Silver Horde"), Brentwood ("Third Generation"), Curwood-Carver Prod. ("The Yellowback"). Hght., 5, 8; wght., 145; dark hair and complexion, blue eyes. Ad., Goldwyn Studios, Los Angeles, Calif.

BOLAND, Mary; b. Phila., Pa.; educ. Detroit; stage career, with Virginia Harned, supported Robert Edeson in "Strongheart," yr. in London, Dustin Farnum, Francis Wilson, 4 yrs. leading woman for John Drew, "Clarence"; screen career, NYMP ("The Stepping Stone"), World ("Price of Happiness"), Pathe ("Big Jim Garrity"), Bacon-Backer ("A Woman's Experience"), Selznick ("The Perfect Lover"), Gaumont ("The Contrary Wife"). Hght., 5, 6; wght., 127; blond hair, blue eyes. Ad., 21 W. 58th st., N. Y., Plaza 9379.

BOOKER, Beula; b. Silverton, Colo.; educ. in Denver, Colo., and Notre Dame, Paris; 3 yrs. on the stage on Western and Eastern coasts and in Denver; 3 yrs. in picture, most recent picture being "The Dwelling Place of Light," with Federal Photoplays. Hght., 5, 2; wght., 105; brown hair and eyes. Ad., Actors Assn. 6412 Hollywood Blvd., Hollywood, Calif.

BOONE, Dell; b. Springfield, Mo., 1894; educ. New Orleans; stage experience, Southern stock cos.; screen career, World Film, Pathe, Duplex ("Shame," "The Girl and the Horses"), Paramount ("Other Men's Wives"), "The Honey Bee," with Rupert Julian, now with Fox; has traveled extensively and ridden through Panama jungle. Hght., 5, 6½; blond hair, blue eyes. Home ad., 6650 Leland Way, Hollywood, Calif., Holly 316.

BOUTON, Betty; educ. Univ. of Penn.; stage career, trained at Sargeant Sch. of Dram. Art., in stock, with Nat Goodwin in "The Merchant of Venice," with Bertha Kalich, "The Riddle Woman"; screen career, with Marguerite Clark, Shirley Mason, Dustin Farnum, Mary Pickford, etc.; "Three Men and a Girl," "The Final Close Up," "A Man's Fight," "Daddy Long Legs," "Heart of the Hills," "The Hellship." Ad., Marshall Neilan Studio.

BOYLE, Irene; b. N. Y., 1896; educ. N. Y. and Washington; screen career, Kalem multiple reel pictures, Edgar Lewis Prod. ("Other Men's Shoes"), Bloxby ("Young America" series), Rex Beach ("Heart of the Sunset"), Jack London ("The Star Rover"). Hght., 5, 2½; wght., 112; dark brown hair, grey eyes. Ad., 617 W. 135th st., N. Y., Mngside 8306.

BRADY, Alice; b. N. Y. C.; educ. convent, N. J.; studied in Boston for grand opera; stage career, "The Balkan Princess," at Herald Square theatree, singing and comedy roles for 3 yrs. Gilbert & Sullivan opera, "Sinners," "Family Cupboard," "Forever After"; screen career, World, Select ("The Whirlpool," "The Death Dance," "The Better Half," "Her Great Chance," "His Bridal Night"), Realart ("Sinners," "Fear Market"). Hght., 5, 7; wght., 198; dark complexion, dark hair and eyes. Ad., Realart, N. Y.

BREAMER, Sylvia; b. Sydney, Australia; educ. there; stage career, 5 yrs. in American successes in Australia, with Grace George in N. Y., "The Argyle Case," "Bought and Paid For," etc.; screen career, Triangle-Ince, Tourneur ("My Lady's Garter"), Artcraft ("The Family Skeleton," "We Can't Have Everything"), J. S. Blackton ("Missing," "The Common Cause," "A House Divided," "The Moonshine Trail," "Dawn," "My Husband's Other Wife"). Hght., 5, 7; wght., 135; dark brown hair and eyes. Ad., c/o Mayflower Photoplay Corp., 1465 Broadway, N. Y.

BRENT, Evelyn; b. Tampa, Fla., 1899; educ. Normal Coll., N. Y.; screen career, Metro ("The Lure of Heart's Desire," "The Soul Market," "The Spell of the Yukon," "The Iron Woman," "The Millionaire's Double"), Master Drama ("Who's Your Neighbor?"), Arrow ("Fool's Gold"), Frank Hall ("The Other Man's Wife"), Fox ("Help, Help, Police"), Selznick ("The Glorious Lady").

BROCKWELL, Gladys; b. Brooklyn, N. Y., 1894; educ. privately; stage career, since childhood, stk., rep., vaud.; with Willard Mack; screen career, Lubin, NYMP, Reliance-Majestic, Fine Arts, Universal, Fox ("Call of the Soul," "The Divorce Trap," "The Sneak," "The Forbidden Room," "Pitfalls of a Big City," "Chasing Rainbows," "Broken Commandments," "Thieves," "Flames of the Flesh," "The Devil's Wheel," "The Strange Woman"). Studio, Fox, 1401 N. Western ave., Los Angeles, Calif.

BRODY, Anne G.; educ. N. Y. C.; stage career, stock and vaud.; screen career, Vitagraph for 5 yrs ("Girl at Bay," "Princess of Puck Row," "The Suspect," O. Henry Prod.), Universal, Kalem, Pathe ("The Yellow Ticket"), Fox, Reliance, Famous Players ("Mrs. Wiggs of the Cabbage Patch"), Selznick ("The Perfect Lover"), Curtiss ("Who's Your Brother?"), Serico Prod. ("The Jewelled Hand" serial). Hght., 5; wght., 160; black hair, brown eyes. Ad., 92 St. Nicholas ave., N. Y.; Cathedral 9240.

BROOKE, Myra; educ. Sacred Heart, Philadelphia, Pa.; stage career, with Rankin 2 yrs., Mansfield 4 yrs., Winthrop Ames, Little Theatre, Harry Corson Clark, many mus. com.; screen career, Metro 2½ yrs., Reliance, Edison, Gaumont, Briggs Comedies, Mrs. Sidney Drew. Hght., 5, 4½; wght., 200; brown hair, dark blue eyes. Ad., 111 W. 125th st., N. Y. C. Mngsde. 4590.

BROWN, Anita; b. New Haven, Conn.; educ. there; stage career, burlesque, comedy, Poli Stock Co.; screen career, Metro ("Eye for Eye"), Famous ("Mrs. Wiggs Cabbage Patch"), Fox ("Fallen Idol"), Pathe ("Lightning Raider, 12th Episode"), Briggs Comedies, Gaumont ("Making Her His Wife"), Pathe ("Sunshine Annie"), Cuckoo Comedies. Hght., 5, 7½; wght., 270; fair complexion, dark brown hair and eyes. Home ad., 201 E. 66th st., N. Y. C., or 750 Riverside ave., Jacksonville, Fla.

BROWN, Iva; b. London, England; educ. Los Angeles, Calif.; screen career, Paramount-Al St. John Comedies; worked in "Cleaning Up" and "Ship Ahoy!" Hght., 5, 6; wght., 115; dark complexion, black hair, brown eyes. Home ad., Monroe Apts., Los Angeles, Calif. Phone 558140.

BRUCE, Beverly; b. Montreal, Can.; stage career, leads in stk. in Phila. and Montreal, "Within the Law," "Under Cover," "Bought and Paid For," "Tess of the Storm Country"; screen career ("Evangeline"), Continental ("David Copperfield," "Cricket on the Hearth"), London Film Co. ("Little Dorritt," "The Decoy"), Hepworth, Fleur de Lys ("Empty Arms," "The Street"), Willard King Bradley ("This Is the Life," "Babette of the Moulin Rouge"). Ad., care of Willard King Bradley, 1552 Broadway, N. Y. C.

BRUCE, Kate; character woman, was with the original Biograph Co. under D. W. Griffith, has appeared in nearly all Griffith productions, recent ones: "A Romance of Happy Valley," "The Girl Who Stayed at Home," "Scarlet Days." Ad., Griffith Studio, Mamaroneck, N. Y.

BRUNDAGE, Mrs. Mathilde; b. Louisville, Ky.; screen career, Pioneer ("Wives of Men," "Her Game"), Norma Talmadge ("New Moon"), Famous Players ("Career of Catherine Bush"), Chas. Miller ("Heart of a Gypsy"), Faversham & Elliott ("The Man Who Lost Himself"). Hght., 5, 6; wght., 148; silver gray hair and brown eyes. Ad., home, 100 Hillcrest ave., Park, Yonkers, N. Y. Yonkers 3305-R.

BRUNETTE, Florence (Fritzi); b. Savannah, Ga., 1894; screen career, Yankee Film, Universal 5 yrs., last 2 yrs. with Selig, Lasky, Selig, Bluebird ("Playthings," "The Velvet Hand," "Sealed Orders"), National ("The Still Small Voice"), Select ("Jacques of the Silver North"), Paramount ("Woman Thou Gavest Me"), Pathe-Amer. ("A Sporting Chance"), Robt.-Cole ("Whitewashed Walls"), Universal ("Woman Under Cover"), Brunton-Hodkinson ("The Lord Loves the Irish"). Hght., 5, 3; wght., 117; olive complexion, black hair, gray-blue eyes. Ad., Brunton Studio, Hollywood; home ad., Hollywood Hotel, Hollywood, Calif.

BURKE, Billie (Mrs. Florenz Ziegfeld); b. Washington, D. C., 1886; educ. there and in France; first appeared on the stage singing in the principal mus. halls in Austria, Germany, Russia, France, won success at the Pavilion, London, supporting Edna May in "The School Girl" at the Prince of Wales Theatre, London; N. Y. debut made under mgmt. Frohman, playing opposite John Drew in "My Wife" at the Empire, later success "The Pink Pajama Girl"; screen career, Kleine ("Gloria's Romance"), Famous Players-Para. ("The Mysterious Miss Terry," "The Land of Promise," "Arms and the Girl," "Good Gracious, Annabel," "The Make Believe Wife," "The Misleading Widow," "Sadie Love," "Wanted, a Husband"). Ad., Famous Players, 485 Fifth ave., N. Y. C.

BURKE, Olive; b. Boston; educ. private schls., N. Y. and Paris; screen career, Frank P. Donovan's Prods., Vitagraph, Selznick, World, "Bullin' the Bullsheviki," "Pardon Me," "Neptune's Stepdaughter," "Double Trouble." Hght., 5, 4; wght., 120; blond hair, brown eyes. Ad., Frank P. Donovan's Prods., Inc., 118 W. 45th st., N. Y.

BURNHAM, Beatrice; b. Galveston, Tex., Feb. 10, 1902; screen career, Morosco, Fox, Ince, Clune ("Eyes of the World"), Metro ("Hidden Children"), Goldwyn ("Upstairs"), Universal ("Burnt Feathers"). Hght., 5; wght., 110; olive complexion, black hair and eyes. Ad., 5614 Franklin ave., Hollywood, Calif. Phone 597785.

BUSCH, Mae; b. Melbourne, Austr.; educ. convent, Madison, N. J.; stage career, leads with Eddie Foy; screen career, Keystone, with Eddie Foy, Weber and Fields ("Wife and Auto Trouble," "Better Late Than Never"), Para-Artcraft ("The Grim Game"), "The Devil's Pass Key." Hght., 5, 5; wght., 125; black hair, gray eyes. Studio ad., Universal City, Calif.

BUTLER, "Babs"; b. Ogdensburg, N. Y., 1902; educ. there and N. Y.; screen career, World, Famous Players, Pathe; at present playing lead in Translantic Boarding School Girls comedies; daughter of Major H. B. Butler, D. C.; fair hair, blue eyes; hght., 5, 2. Ad., West Fort Lee, N. J.; studio ad., Transatlantic Film Co. of America, 729 Seventh ave., N. Y. C.

BYRON, Nina; b. New Zealand, 1900; screen talent discovered by Nicholas Dunaew; screen career, Ince-Triangle ("Truthful Tulliver"), Pallas-Paramount ("The Heir of the Ages"), Lasky ("The Source," "The Dub," with Wallace Reid, "Johnny Get Your Gun," with Fred Stone, Pioneer ("The Boomerang"). Hght., 5, 3; wght., 110; light brown hair, brown eyes. Ad., Lasky Studio, Hollywood, Cal.

— C —

CALDWELL, Virginia; b. Peoria, Ill.; educ. Windmoore Hall Convent, Kansas City, Mo.; stage career, with Raymond Hitchcock in "Hitchy-Koo," also in Florenz Ziegfeld's Follies; screen career, Lasky ("Secret Service" with Robt. Warwick), Metro ("Lombardi, Ltd." and "The Right of Way" with Bert Lytell). Hght., 5, 7; wght., 129; brown hair, green eyes. Home ad., Blackstone Apts., Los Angeles, Calif.; Main 244.

CALHOUN, Alice B.; b. Cleveland, Ohio; educ. there and private tuition; screen career, Acme ("The Thirteenth Chair"), W. H. Prods.

ACTRESSES

("Everybody's Business"), Vitagraph ("A Bride in Bond"). Home ad., 736 Riverside Drive, N. Y. C.

CALHOUN, Jean; screen career, Universal ("The Exquisite Thief"), Fox ("The Splendid Sin," "Thieves," "The Feud"), Keenan-Pathe ("The False Code").

CALVERT, Catherine (Mrs. Paul Armstrong); b. Baltimore, Md.; stage career, leading roles in "Brown of Harvard," "Deep Purple," "Romance of the Underworld," "The Escape"; screen career, Keeney Pic. Corp. ("A Romance of the Underworld," "Marriage," "Out of the Night," "A Marriage of Convenience"), Famous-Lasky ("Fires of Faith," "Career of Katherine Bush"). Hght., 5, 6; wght., 125; complexion brunette, dark brown hair and eyes. Home ad., 124 W. 55th st., N. Y. C.; Circle 461. Office, Films, Inc., 1482 Broadway, N. Y.

CAPRICE, June; b. Arlington, Mass., 1899; educ. Boston; screen career, Fox ("Caprice of the Mountains," "A Modern Cinderella," "The Ragged Princess," "A Child of the Wild," "Every Girl's Dream," "Miss U. S. A.," "Sunshine Maid," "A Camouflaged Kiss," "Blue Eyed Mary"), Albert Capellani ("Oh, Boy!"), Pathe ("The Love Cheat," "A Damsel in Distress"). Hght., 5, 2; wght., 105; light complexion, light hair, blue eyes. Ad., c/o Capellani Prods., 1457 Broadway, N. Y.

CAREW, Ora; b. Salt Lake City, Utah; educ. Reland Hall Seminary and private tutor; stage career, vaud., mus. com. and dram. stk.; screen career, Goldwyn, "Go West, Young Man"; Para, "Too Many Millions"; Universal ("Love's Protege," "Loot," "Under Suspicion," "The Peddler of Lies"). Hght., 5, 3; wght., 120; dark brown hair, brown eyes. Home add., 5517 Carlton Way, Los Angeles, Calif.; Holly 788; studio, Universal Film Co.

CARMEN, Jewel; educ. St. Mary's Acad., Portland, Oreg.; screen career, "The Half-Breed" with Doug. Fairbanks, Fox ("Tale of Two Cities," "Les Miserables," "The Bride of Fear," "The Confession," "You Can't Get Away With It"). Hght., 5, 5; wght., 115; light brown hair, dark blue eyes. Ad., care Roland West, 260 W. 42d st., N. Y. C; Bryant 2564.

CARRINGTON, Evelyn Carter; stage career, 20 yrs., with Chas. & Daniel Frohman, Wm. Brady, Chas. Dillingham, Henry Savage, played parts ranging from Shakespeare to musical comedy, grand dames; screen career, with Constance Talmadge in "In Search of a Sinner," character part. Hght., 5, 10; wght., 200; dark brown hair, blue eyes. Ad., 484 Hawthorne ave., Yonkers, N. Y.; phone 6363-M.

CARROLL, Marcelle; b. Biarritz, France; educ. Sacred Heart Convent, Paris, and Boston; stage exper., with Fritzi Scheff in "Pretty Mrs. Smith," with Wm. Gillette in "Successful Calamity"; screen career, Herbert Brenon, J. S. Blackton ("The Marble Heart," "Daughter of the Gods," "Fall of the Romanoffs," "The Common Cause," "Moonshine and Shadows," "Somewhere in Love"), with Taylor Holmes in "Nothing But the Truth." Hght., 5; wght., 104; black hair, brown eyes, fair complexion. Ad., Starlit Bungalow, roof of Godfrey Bldg., 729 Seventh ave., N. Y. C.

CASSINELLI, Dolores; b. N. Y.; educ. Holy Name Convent, Chicago; screen career, Essanay ("When Soul Meets Soul," "Do Dreams Come True," "The Greek Singer"), Perret ("Lafayette, We Come," "Stars of Glory," "A Soul Adrift"), Capellani ("The Virtuous Model"), Carew prod. ("The Right to Lie," "The Web of Lies"); known on the screen as the Cameo Girl. Hght., 5, 7; wght., 135; black hair, hazel eyes. Personal representative, Harry Cahane, Room 809, 1457 Broadway, N. Y.

CASSITY, Ellen L.; b. Jackson, Tenn.; educ. Louisville, Ky.; stage career, Follies; screen career, Fox ("Checkers"), World ("Through the Toils") Frank Hall ("Other Men's Wives"), Carl Harbaugh ("Love Honor and "). Hght., 5, 6½; wght., 135; blond hair, dark gray eyes. Ad., Betts & Fowler, N. Y.; Bryant 5664.

CASTLE, Irene; b. New Rochelle, 1893; educ. N. Y.; stage career, vaud., mus. com., last appearance in "Watch Your Step"; screen career, International ("Patria"), Astra-Pathe ("Sylvia of the Secret Service," "The Girl From Bohemia," "Stranded in Arcady," "The Mark of Cain," "The Hillcrest Mystery," "The First Law," "The Mysterious Client," "Convict 993"), Famous Players-Lasky ("The Firing Line"). Hght., 5, 7; wght., 115; brown hair, gray eyes. Ad., care Famous Players, 486 Fifth Ave., N. Y.

CASTLETON, Barbara; b. Little Rock, Ark., 1896; educ. "The Castle," New Rochelle; screen career, Ivan ("Sins of Ambition"), Essanay ("On Trial"), World ("Heart of a Girl," "Just Sylvia"), Famous Players "The Silver King" opp. Wm. Faversham, "Peg o' My Heart"), Ince ("Americanism"), Eminent Authors-Goldwyn ("The Tower of Ivory," "Dangerous Days"), Hampton ("The Man Who Turned White" opp. H. B. Warner). Hght., 5, 5; wght., 128; brown hair and eyes. Ad., 19 W. 69th st., N. Y. C.

CAVALIERI, Lina; b. Rome, Italy, 1874; educ. for grand opera under Mme. Mariani-Mase; stage career, operatic debut Lisbon, Portugal, 1900, first American appearance with Hammerstein Man. Opera House, N. Y., 1906; screen career, Paramount ("The Temptress," "The Two Brides"). Studio ad., Paramount, 485 Fifth ave.

CECIL, Nora; b. England, 1879; educ. London stage career, played in many English prods., yrs. with Klaw & Erlanger; screen career, Universal, World ("Miss Crusoe"), Fox ("Woman Woman"), Selznick ("Picadilly Jim"). Hght. 5, 8; wght., 145; light complexion, brown hair brown eyes. Home ad., Lake st., Englewood N. J. Englewood 1746.

CHADWICK, Helene; b. Chadwick, N. Y.; educ there; screen career, Astra-Pathe, Paramount ("Girls"), Pathe ("Go Get 'Em, Garringer"), Goldwyn ("Heartsease"), National ("Long Arm of Mannister"), Goldwyn ("The Cup of Fury," "Scratch My Back"). Hght., 5, 7; wght., 130; light hair, brown eyes, light complexion. Ad., Goldwyn Studio, Culver City, Calif.; home ad., 4428 Sunset Blvd., Los Angeles, Holly 3049.

CHAMBERS, Marie; b. Phila.; educ. Paris; stage career, under Woods, Brady, Fiske, stk., leading woman for Lou-Tellegen in "Blind Youth"; screen career, Famous Players ("The Woman in the Case"), Triangle ("Fifty-Fifty"), World ("Maternity"), Capellani ("The Virtuous Model"). Now playing in " Nightie Night" at Princess theatre. Hght., 5, 5; wght., 122; fair complexion, blond hair, dark eyes. Ad., 145 E. 35th st., N. Y. Murray Hill 3123.

CHAPMAN, Audrey Emily; b. Phila., 1899; educ. there and Los Angeles; screen career, Triangle ("Marriage"), Morosco ("Her Country First"), Vitagraph ("The Usurper"), Pickford ("Daddy Long Legs"), Vitagraph ("The Luck of Geraldine Laird," "The Mormon Trail"). Hght., 5, 3; wght., 124; blond hair, blue eyes. Ad., 4887 Melrose ave., Hollywood, Calif.

CHAPMAN, Edythe; screen career, Metro ("Faith"), Artcraft ("The Knickerbocker Buckaroo"), Paramount ("The Home Town Girl," "Secret Service," "The Winning Girl," "Alias Mike Moran," "The Rescuing Angel"), Goldwyn ("Flame of the Desert"), Select ("Experimental Marriage"), Para-Art. ("Everywoman").

CHARLESON, Mary; b. Dungonon, Ireland, May 18, 1893; educ. convent in Los Angeles, Calif.; stage career, ingenue with grand opera co. on Pacific Coast; screen career, Vitagraph, Selig ("The Prince Chap," "The Country That God Forgot"), Essanay ("The Truant Soul," "Little Shoes," "The Saint's Adventure"), Paralta ("His Robe of Honor," "Humdrum Brown," "With Hoops of Steel"), Natl. Ex., Mutual ("A Long Lane's Turning"), Select ("Upstairs and Down"). Hght., 5, 2; wght., 110; brunette, dark brown hair, gray eyes.

CHILDERS, Naomi; b. Penn.; educ. Maryville Convent, St. Louis, Mo.; stage career, "Madam X," "Ready Money," "Among Those Present," with H. B. Warner; screen career, Vitagraph, Metro ("The Yellow Dove," "Blind Man's Eyes," "Shadows of Suspicion," with Harold Lockwood), Goldwyn ("Lord and Lady Algy," "Gay Lord Quex," "Street Called Straight," "Duds"). Hght., 5, 6½; wght., 135; dark brown hair, blue eyes. Home ad., 1824 Highland ave., Hollywood, Calif., Holly 2002; studio, Goldwyn, Culver City, Calif.

CLAIRE, Gertrude; b. Boston; stage career, rep., managed own stk. co.; screen career, Biograph ("Ramona"), Imp, Rex, Nestor, NYMPH, Ince-Triangle ("Golden Rule Kate"), Ince-Paramount ("A Nine o'Clock Town"), Select ("Romance and Arabella"), Goldwyn ("Crimson Gardenias," "Jinx"), Paramount ("Hard Boiled," "Little Comrade," "Stepping Out," "Widow by

Proxy"), Metro ("Blind Man's Eyes"), Pathe ("Brothers Divided"). Hght., 5, 2; gray hair, blue eyes. Home ad., 1233 Trenton st., Los Angeles, Calif., Main 7834.

CLARK, Marguerite; b. Cincinnati, 1887; educ. Ursuline convent; stage career, since 1899, with De Wolf Hopper for several seasons, "Baby Mine"; screen career, Famous Players ("Bab's Burglar," "Bab's Matinee Idol," "Bab's Diary," "Still Waters," "The Seven Swans," "Prunella," "Rich Man, Poor Man," "The Golden Bird," "A Honeymoon for Three," "Mrs. Wiggs of the Cabbage Patch," Three Men and a Girl," "Let's Elope"), Paramount ("Little Miss Hoover," "Girls," "Widow by Proxy"). Hght., 4, 10; wght., 90; fair complexion, brown hair, hazel eyes. Ad., home, 50 Central Pk. West; studio, Famous, N. Y.

CLARKE, Betty Ross; b. Langdon, N. D.; educ. Stanley Hall, Minn.; stage career, lead in "Fair and Warmer," 1st road co.; stk. in Halifax, Pittsburg, Haverhill, Mass., Des Moines and Staten Island; screen career, Fox ("If I Were King"), Taylor Holmes ("The Very Idea"), D. W. Griffith ("Romance"). Hght., 5, 6; wght., 134; light brown hair, dark gray eyes. Ad., 245 W. 51st st., N. Y. C., Circle 1730.

CLAY, Velma Louise; b. San Antonio, 1898; educ. Univ. of Texas; stage exper., stk. and vaud.; screen career, Diando, American, Universal, Pathe ("The Little Diplomat"). Hght., 5, 6; wght., 125; blond hair, brown eyes. Ad., 1407 Bond st., Los Angeles, Calif., phone 20853.

CLAYTON, Ethel; b. Champaign, Ill.; educ. St. Elizabeth's Convent, Chicago; stage career, T. D. Frawley Stock Co., "The Devil," with Edwin Stevens, "The Country Boy"; screen career, Lubin ("The Lion and the Mouse," "The Great Divide," "The Blessed Miracle," "The Fortune Hunter," "Dollars and the Woman"), World ("The Stolen Paradise," "The Soul Without Windows"), Famous Players ("Pettigrew's Girl," "Woman's Weapons," "Maggie Pepper," "Men, Women and Money," "A Sporting Chance," "More Deadly Than the Male," "The Thirteenth Commandment," "Young Mrs. Winthrop"). Hght., 5, 5; wght., 130; red gold hair, gray eyes. Ad., Lasky Studios, Hollywood.

CLAYTON, Marguerite; b. Salt Lake City, 1896; educ. St. Mary's Acad., Salt Lake; screen career, Essanay, ("The Long Green Trail," "Stardust"), Famous Players ("Hit-the-Trail Holliday," with Geo. Cohan), Essanay ("Prince of Graustark"), World ("The Bronze Man," "Inside the Lines"), Eff & Eff ("Bolshevist Burlesque"), Select ("The New Moon"), Fox, Richard Stanton Prod. Hght., 5, 4; wght., 120; fair complexion, blond hair, blue eyes. Ad., Hotel Ansonia, B'way and 72nd st., N. Y.

CLEMENT, Eloise May; b. New Orleans, La., 1892; educ. private tutors and Wellesley Coll.; stage career, leading woman with Jas. O'Neil in "Monte Cristo," and Shakespearean rep. at 16, stk. and rd.; screen career, World ("Just Sylvia," "The Love Defender"), Marion Davies ("The Burden of Proof"). Hght., 5, 7; wght., 138; red hair, dark blue eyes.

CLIFFORD, Kathleen; b. Charlottesville, Va.; educ. Brighton, England; stage career, vaud., Winter Garden with Gaby Deslys, starred in "The Winsome Widow," A. H. Wood's "The Heart of a Child," H. H. Frazee's "Business Before Pleasure"; screen career, made debut with Balboa in serial "Who Is Number One?" also in "The Law that Divides," "The Angel Child," with Douglas Fairbanks in "When the Clouds Roll By." Home ad., Virginia Hotel, Long Beach, Calif.

CLIFFORD, Ruth; b. Rhode Island, Feb. 17, 1900; educ. St. Mary's Seminary, Bayview, R. I.; screen career, Edison, Universal, Jewel ("The Kaiser—the Beast of Berlin"), Bluebird ("Fires of Youth," "The Lure of Luxury," "The Game Is Up," "The Millionaire Pirate"), Republic ("The Amazing Woman"), Vitagraph ("The Black Gate"). Frohman Amuse. Corp. ("The Invisible Ray"). Hght., 5, 5½; wght., 123; light complexion, light brown hair, dark blue eyes. Home ad., 1802 Cherokee st., Los Angeles, Cal.

COLLINS, May; b. N. Y.; educ. there; stage career, "The Betrothal," "At 9.45," "She Would and She Did," with Grace George; screen career, Universal ("A Matter of Taste," "The Winning Shot"), Maple Leaf ("Hearts of the North Land"). Hght., 5, 3½; wght., 120; brown hair, gray eyes. Ad., 119 Forley st., Elmhurst, L. I., N. Y. Newtown 1096.

COLWELL, Goldie; b. Edinburgh, Scotland, 1893; educ. Immaculate Heart Convent, Los Angeles; stage career, from 1911, dramatic leads in rep. co., Kansas City; screen career, 1912, Selig, featured with Tom Mix in Westerners, Horsley, first in Cub comedies ("Jerry's Gentle Nursing"), then in dramatic leads ("When Avarice Rules"), Fox ("Vengeance is Mine"), with Mitchell Lewis in "The Code of the Yukon," has been writing scenarios and short stories during past year. Hght., 5, 6; wght., 137; light hair, brown eyes. Home ad., 1028 Overton st., Los Angeles, Calif.

COMPSON, Betty; b. Salt Lake City; stage career, vaud.; screen career, Christie ("Those Wedding Bells," "Down by the Sea," "The Honeymooners," "As in Days of Old," "A Blessed Blunder," "Their Seaside Tangle"), Pathe ("The Terror of the Range," "The Little Diplomat"), World ("The Devil's Trail"), Robt.-Cole ("Prodigal Liar"), Universal ("Light of Victory"), Para.-Art. ("Miracle Man"). Blue eyes, light hair. Now with Geo. Loane Tucker, Brunton Studios, Los Angeles, Calif.; home ad., 3526 Winslow Drive, Los Angeles, Calif.; phone 597220.

CONCORD, Lillian; b. Omaha, Neb.; educ. Univ. of Cal., Univ. of Wis., also studied voice culture in Paris; stage career, "The Kingdom of Destiny," "The Red Widow," "The Midnight Girl," and vaud.; screen career, Frohman ("The Woman in 47"), Universal ("The Ivy and the Oak," "Heritage of Hate"), Fox ("The Troublemaker," "The Girl from Rectors"). Now with "The Boomerang," by David Belasco. Hght., 5, 8; wght., 140; blond hair, blue eyes. Ad., home, 340 W. 85th st., N. Y.

COOLING, Maud; stage career, vaud. and productions; screen career, important parts with Bluebird, Goldwyn, Pathe. Hght., 5, 4½; wght., 128; dark brown hair, brown eyes. Ad., Packard Exchange, N. Y.

COOPER, Edna Mae; b. Baltimore, Md.; educ. there; screen career, Lasky ("Men, Women and Money," "Old Wives for New," "The Things We Love," "Rimrock Jones," "The Village Cut-Up," "You Never Saw Such a Girl," "Whispering Chorus"), Morosco ("The Third Kiss"), Brunton ("The Scoffer"). Hght., 5, 6; wght., 135; brown hair, hazel eyes. Home ad., 4424 Sunset Drive, Los Angeles, Calif. Holly 1502.

COOPER, Miriam; b. Baltimore; educ. there and N. Y. Art School; screen career, Reliance-Majestic ("The Birth of a Nation"), Fine Arts ("When Fate Frowned," "Intolerance"), Fox ("The Honor System," "The Silent Lie," "The Innocent Sinner," "Betrayed," "The Prussian Cur," "Evangeline," "Should a Husband Forgive?"). Brown eyes, dark hair. Ad., c/o R. A. Walsh, Mayflower Photoplay Corp., N. Y.

CORNWALL, Anne; b. Brooklyn, Jan. 17, 1897; educ. Catskill, N. Y.; stage career, mus. com.; screen career, Select ("The Knife," "The Hollow of Her Hand"), Artcraft ("Prunella"), Special ("Quest of the Big 'Un"), Famous Players ("Indestructible Wife," "World to Live In," "Copperhead"), Artcraft Special ("Firing Line"). Hght., 4, 11; wght., 102; dark brown hair and dark eyes. Studio ad., Famous Players Studio, N. Y.

COTTON, Lucy; b. Houston, Texas; educ. studied in Houston under Mrs. Alma McDonell and Theodora Ursula Irvine at Carnegie Hall and Anton Diehl Conservatoire Music, Houston; stage career, understudied Ina Claire in "Quaker Girl," played in "Little Women," "Polygamy," "Up in Mabel's Room"; screen career, co-starred with Boland in "The Prodigal Wife," starred in "Blind Love," featured in Artcraft-Cosmopolitan Special "The Miracle of Love," Selznick ("The Broken Melody"), Mayflower-Chautard ("The Invisible Foe"); now with International. Hght., 5, 6; wght., 125; light brown hair, dark brown eyes. Ad., The Nevada, 70th st. and Broadway, N. Y.; Col. 1570.

COURTOT, Marguerite Gabrielle; b. Summit, N. J., Aug. 20, 1897; educ. N. Y. and Switzerland; early career, posing for Harrison Fisher; screen career, Kalem, 3 yrs., Famous Players ("Rolling Stones"), France Film Co. ("The Natural Law," "The Unbeliever"), Selznick ("The Perfect Lover"), Artcraft Special ("Teeth of the Tiger"), Pathe serials ("Bound and Gagged," "Pirate Gold"). Hght., 5, 2½; wght., 110; light clear complexion, golden brown hair, greenish blue eyes. Home ad., 19 Hudson pl., Weehawken, N. J.; Union 1795.

CRAIG, Blanche; educ. Boston, Mass.; stage exper., vaud. and legit.; screen career, Famous Players ("Come On In"), Goldwyn, World, Fox

ACTRESSES

("I Want to Forget"). Ad., 323 W. 70th st., N. Y.

CRONK, Olga; b. Cawker City, Kansas; educ. Topeka; screen career, Dwan ("Luck of the Irish," "The Heart of a Fool"). Hght., 5, 5; wght., 125; auburn hair, blue eyes. Home ad., 694 S. Burlington, Los Angeles, Calif.

CROWELL, Josephine Bonaparte; b. Canada; educ. Canada and Boston; early career, public reader in Boston; stage career, with Robert Hilliard, Frank Keenan, mgmt. Harrison Grey Fiske, toured 2 seasons in "The County Fair," mgmt. K. & E.; screen career, Fine Arts ("The Birth of a Nation," "Intolerance"), Artcraft ("Rebecca of Sunnybrook Farm," "Hearts of the World"), Robertson-Cole ("Josselyn's Wife," "House of Intrigue"), Paramount ("Puppy Love," "Peppy Polly"), Fox ("Flames of the Flesh"), First Nat'l ("Greatest Question"). Hght., 5, 5; wght., 140; brown hair, brown eyes.

CRUTE, Sally; b. 1893, Chattanooga, Tenn.; educ. Huntsville, Ala.;; stage career, lead in 'The Deep Purple," "Within the Law," with Douglas Fairbanks in "Officer 666"; screen career, Edison, Lubin, Metro ("The Light of the Dusk," "A Wife by Proxy," "Blue Jeans," "The Awakening of Ruth"), Sidney Olcott Players ("The Belgian"), Metro ("The Poor Rich Man"), De Luxe ("Twilight"), World ("A Broadway Saint"), Select ("The Undercurrent"). Hght., 5, 5½; wght., 130; fair complexion, blond hair, blue eyes. Home ad., Palisade st., Ft. Lee, N. J.

CULLINGTON, Margaret; b. New Rochelle, N. Y.; educ. N. Y.; born and reared on legitimate stage under father's stage direction; screen career, Pathe ("Caroline of the Corners"), 9 pictures with Baby Marie Osborne, Fox ("Camouflage" with Buck Jones). Hght., 5, 9¾; wght., 136; brown hair, dark blue eyes. Now with Tom Mix at Fox Studio. Home ad., 1322 McCadden place, Hollywood, Calif.; Holly 1834.

CUMMING, Dorothy; b. Burrows, Australia; educ. Sidney, Australia; stage career, 4 yrs. leading woman to J. C. Williamson, Ltd., Australia, in "Milestones," with Cyril Maude in "Grumpy," "Caste," "School for Scandal," lead at Belasco theatre, N. Y., 9 mos. in "Tiger, Tiger"; screen career, George Loane Tucker ("Ladies Must Live"), Goldwyn ("Woman and the Puppet"), Bessie Barriscale ("Woman Who Understood"). Hght., 5, 7; wght., 125; brown hair and eyes. Ad., 2047 Cahuenga ave., Los Angeles, Calif.; phone 1943.

CURLEY, Pauline; b. Holyoke, Mass.; educ. private tutor; stage career, at age of 5 entered stk., vaud. coast to coast tour, "A Daddy by Express," scored hit in "Polygamy" 1914-15; screen career, Brenon ("The Fall of the Romanoffs"), Artcraft ("Bound in Morocco"), Brentwood ("The Turn in the Road"), Haworth-Robertson-Cole ("The Man Beneath"), Independent ("The Solitary Sin"), Alkire-Robertson-Cole ("Love Apple"), Vitagraph ("The Unforeseen Hand"). Hght., 5, 4; wght., 115; light complexion, blond hair, hazel eyes. Home ad., 806 Waterloo st., Los Angeles; Calif.; Wilshire 4801.

— D —

DALTON, Dorothy; b. Chicago, Ill., Sept. 22, 1893; educ. Sacred Heart Acad., Chicago; stage career, several seasons in stk. on B. F. Keith's and Orpheum circuits in vaud.; "Aphrodite"; screen career, Triangle-Ince ("Wild Winship's Widow," "The Flame of the Yukon"), Ince ("Vive la France," "Quicksand," "Market of Souls," "L'Apache," "His Friend's Wife," "Black Is White," "Dark Mirror," "Other Men's Wives"), Famous Players ("Half an Hour"). Hght., 5, 3; wght., 127; dark brown hair, gray eyes. Ad., Hotel Des Artistes, 1 West 67th st., N. Y. C., or 805 Crescent Drive, Beverly Hills, Cal.

DALY, Hazel; screen career, Essanay ("Skinner's Dress Suit," "Skinner's Bubble," "Filling His Own Shoes," "A Corner in Smiths"), Selig ("Tub Brown of Harvard"), Triangle ("The Little Rowdy"), Goldwyn ("The Gay Lord Quex").

DANA, Margaret; b. Charleston, S. C., 1895; educ. Convent Lady of the Woods, Terre Haute, Ind.; screen career, Essanay, Arrow, playing parts of every description. Hght., 5, 7½; wght., 138; brown eyes, brunette. Home ad., 254 W. 76th st., N. Y. C.

DANA, Viola; b. Brooklyn, 1898; educ. New York; stage career, 11 yrs., appeared in "Rip Van Winkle," "The Littlest Rebel," "The Poor Little Rich Girl"; screen career, Edison ("The Stoning"), Metro ("Blue Jeans," "A Weaver of Dreams," "The Night Rider," "Flower of the Dusk," "Oh, Annice," "The Gold Cure," "The Baby Devil," "Diana Ardway," "Jeanne of the Gutter," "False Evidence," "Some Bride," "Satan Junior," "Parisian Tigress," "The Microbe," "Please Get Married," "The Willow Tree"). Home ad., 7070 Franklin ave., Los Angeles, Cal.; studio, Metro, Hollywood.

DANIELS, Bebe; b. Dallas, Texas, 1901; educ. convent in Los Angeles; stage career, played child parts with Burbank and Belasco Stk. cos. in L. A., Valencia Stk. co., San Francisco; screen career, 2 yrs. leading parts Rolin-Pathe Comedies, Famous Players ("Why Change Your Wife?" "Everywoman," "The Dancin' Fool"). Hght., 5, 4; wght., 123; black hair and eyes. Ad., Lasky Studio, Hollywood, Cal.

DARLING, Grace; b. N. Y., 1896; educ. N. Y.; early career, newspaper writer; screen career, International ("Beatrice Fairfax"), S. L. Prod. ("Virtuous Men"), Rothapfel ("False Gods"), Rolfe ("Amazing Lovers"). Hght., 5, 6; wght., 127; blond hair, blue eyes. Ad., 25 East 64th st., N. Y. C.

DARLING, Helen; stage career, classical dancing for four yrs.; screen career, past nine mos. with Al. Christie. Hght., 5, 5; wght., 120; auburn hair, blue eyes. Home ad., 6019 Yucca st., Los Angeles, Cal.; Holly 3158; studio, Christie.

DARLING, Ida; b. and educ. N. Y. C.; stage exper., 15 yrs.; screen career, Famous, Vitagraph, World, Fox, Norma Talmadge, etc. ("The Make Believe Wife," "Marriage," "Broadway Jones"), Metro ("Man Who Stayed at Home"), Rothapfel ("False Gods"), International ("Miracle of Love"), Norma Talmadge ("Two Women"), Grossmith ("Making Good with Mother"). Gray hair, brown eyes. Ad., Cumberland Hotel, 54th st. and Bway, N. Y. C.

DARMOND, Grace; stage career, several seasons in stock, leading role in "A Texas Steer," "House of a Thousand Candles," "A Black Sheep"; screen career, Technicolor ("The Gulf Between"), Vitagraph ("The Seal of Silence," "The Girl in His House," "A Diplomatic Mission," "A Gentleman of Quality"), J. D. Hampton, Vitagraph ("The Highest Trump"), Rob.-Cole ("What Every Woman Wants"), Para.-Artcraft ("Valley of the Giants"), Burston Films serial, "The Hawk's Trail." Hght., 5, 3½; wght., 129; blond hair, dark eyes. Home ad., 7216 Franklin ave., Hollywood, Cal.

DAVENPORT, Alice; b. N. Y. C., 1864; educ. Miss Irving's Sch., N. Y.; stage career, from age of 5, played over 800 parts in 25 yrs. in stk., on tour and in rep. with noted actors; screen career, 4 mos. Nestor, Horsley, one of orig. six who made first Keystone, Sunshine Comedies, played characters for Fox. Hght., 5, 2; wght., 140; ruddy complexion, gray hair, hazel eyes. Ad., 1748 N. Western ave., Hollywood, Cal.

DAVENPORT, Blanche; b. London, Eng.; educ. Alpaugh Coll., London; stage career, Aborn Opera Co.; screen career, Pathe, Thanhouser ("The Woman, the Saint and the Devil"), Triangle ("American—That's All"), Keeney ("Marriage for Convenience"), Metro ("God's Highway"), McManus ("Lost Battalion"), Marion Davies ("Miracle of Love"), Edison ("The Unbeliever"), Sidney Olcott ("The Belgian"), Fox ("Life of General Pershing"). Hght., 5, 3; wght., 139; fair complexion, blond hair, blue eyes. Home ad., 100 Convent ave., N. Y.; Mngside 3887.

DAVIES, Marion; b. Brooklyn, 1898; educ. N. Y.; stage career, "Betty," "Oh, Boy"; screen career, Select ("The Belle of New York"), International Film Co., Cosmopolitan Prod. ("The Dark Star," "April Folly," "The Cinema Murder," "The Restless Sex," "Superman," "Getting Mary Married"). Hght., 5, 4½; wght., 123; golden hair, blue eyes. Ad., International Film Co., 729 Seventh ave., N. Y. C.

DAVIS, Mildred; b. Philadelphia, Pa.; educ. Friend's School, Phila.; screen career, Metro ("Weaver of Dreams"), Pathe ("All Wrong," Pathe comedies), leads in Mutual comedies, now co-starring with Harold Lloyd. Hght., 5; wght., 100; blond hair, blue eyes. Ad., Rolin Film Co., Los Angeles, Cal. Home ad., 5947 Carlton Way, Hollywood, Cal.; phone 579227.

DAVISON, Grace; b. Oceanside, L. I.; educ. N. Y.; Long Island society girl, organized own company and made "Wives of Men," starring Florence Reed, Miss Davison playing second lead; starring in "Atonement" with Conway Tearle, "A Convert of Revenge" with Montague Love, and Selznick Prod. Hght., 5, 6½; wght., 135; dark hair and eyes. Ad., 1465 Broadway, N. Y.

DAW, Marjorie; b. Colorado Springs, Colo., 1902; educ. Westlake Sch.; screen career, Universal, Lasky ("Joan the Woman"), Artcraft ("Rebecca of Sunnybrook Farm," "Arizona," "He Comes Up Smiling," "Bound in Morocco," "Mr. Fix-It," "Say, Young Fellow"), Fairbanks ("Knickerbocker Buckaroo," "His Majesty, the American"), Marshall Neilan ("The River's End"). Hght., 5, 2½; wght., 104; light brown hair, hazel eyes. Home ad., 6609 St. Frances Court, Los Angeles. Holly 3709; studio, Marshall Neilan Prod.

DAWN, Hazel; b. Ogden City, Utah; educ. Roundwood, Cal., and London, Eng.; stage career, yr. mus. com. in London, 4 yrs. with K. and E. in "The Pink Lady," starred in "The Debutante," etc.; screen career, Famous Players ("The Heart of Jennifer," "The Masqueraders," "The Saleslady," "Under Cover," etc., Herbert Brenon ("The Lone Wolf"). Hght., 5, 4½; wght., 135; blond hair, hazel eyes. Ad., home, Amityville, L. I., N. Y.

DEAN, Julia; b. St. Paul, 1880; educ. Salt Lake City; stage career, with stk. cos. in West from 1899-1902, supported Nat. Goodwin, Eleanor Robson, "Paid in Full," "Bought and Paid For," etc.; screen career, Triangle ("Matrimony"), Universal ("Judge Not"), Triumph ("The Ransom"), LoKugel ("How Molly Made Good"), World ("Rasputin"), Schomer ("Ruling Passions"), S. W. W. Relief ("An Honorable Cad"), Famous Players ("Society Exile"). Ad., 320 W. 51st st., N. Y. C.

DEAN, Priscilla; b. N. Y. C.; educ. private tutors; stage career, 15 yrs. in stk., rep., vaud., prod.; screen career, from 1911, Biograph, Pathe, World, now with Universal ("Exquisite Thief," "Virgin of Stamboul," "Pretty Smooth," "Kiss or Kill," "Wicked Darling," "Wildcat of Paris," "Two-Souled Woman," "Brazen Beauty," "Beautiful Beggar"). Hght., 5, 4; wght., 125; dark brown hair, brown eyes. Ad., Universal Studio, Universal City, Cal.

DEANE, Hazel; b. Perth, Australia; educ. San Francisco, Cal.; stage career, 8 yrs. in vaud.; screen career, Balboa ("Soft Soap"), Fox ("Money Talks"), National ("That Darned Stocking," "Matrimoniacs"). Hght., 5, 2½; wght., 120; blond hair, gray eyes. Home ad., 5817 Virginia ave., Hollywood, Cal.; Holly 2677; studio, Vitagraph.

DEARING, Ann; educ. High School, N. Y. C.; screen career, World ("Tinsel"), Independent Sales ("My Four Years in Germany"), Famous Players ("Marie, Ltd.," "Career of Catherine Bush"). Hght., 5, 5; wght., 119; dark brown hair, blue eyes. Ad., 2 W. 111th st., N. Y. C.; Univ. 5719.

De CORDOBA, Mercedes; b. N. Y. C.; educ. there; studied 5 yrs. in Europe; stage career, with Wm. Faversham in "The Hawk," French theatre in "Les Lumineuses," "The Wanderer," "Chu-Chin-Chow," also Shakespearean roles; screen career, Edison, Famous Players ("Out of a Clear Sky"), with Marguerite Clark; Universal, with Violet Mercereau. Hght., 5, 6; wght., 125; black hair and eyes. Ad., 77 East 89th st., N. Y. C.

DE FOREST, Patsey; b. Port Penn, Del.; educ. Philadelphia and private sch.; stage career, small parts as a child, played with Francis Bushman in stock, child parts; screen career, Lubin, leads with O. Henry Stories ("Her Secret," "Hugs and Hubbubs," "A Night in New Arabia," "Lost in Dress Parade," "The Guilty Party," "The Last Leaf"), Vitagraph ("The Love Doctor," "Alabaster Box"), 2 yrs. with Larry Semon. Hght., 5; wght., 107; auburn hair, dark brown eyes. Home ad., 446 N. Virgil ave., Los Angeles, Cal.; Wil. 1171.

De HAVEN, Flora Parker (Mrs. Carter De Haven); b. Perth Amboy, N. J.; stage exper., stk. in New Orleans, leading woman for Nat Goodwin, vaud., queen in "Queen of the Moulin Rouge"; screen career, Universal ("The Mad Cap," "Youth of Fortune," "College Orphan"), 13 two-reel comedies for National, now with Paramount. Home ad., 7237 Franklin ave., Los Angeles, Cal.

DE LACY, May E.; educ. N. Y. C.; stage career, 3 yrs. vaud.; screen career, World ("Human Driftwood," "Tillie Makes Up," "Price of Pride," "Stolen Paradise," "Wanted—A Mother"), Fox ("Romeo and Juliet," "Les Miserables"), Metro ("Duchess of Doubt"), Famous ("Arms and the Girl"). Hght., 5, 6; wght., 130; light brown hair, blue eyes. Ad., 167 E. 61st st., N. Y. C.; Plaza 6719.

De La MOTTE, Marguerite; b. Duluth, Minn.; educ. San Diego, Cal.; screen career, H. B. Warner ("The Pagan God," "For a Woman's Honor"), Jesse D. Hampton ("A Sagebrush Hamlet," "Dangerous Waters"), B. B. Hampton ("The Sagebrusher"), Jack Pickford ("In Wrong"). Hght., 5, 2; wght., 105; fair hair, hazel eyes. Home ad., 1918 Pinehurst Road, Los Angeles, Cal.; phone 577912.

DELARO, Hattie; b. Brooklyn, N. Y.; educ. Packard Institute, Bklyn.; stage career, with Augustin Daly, Nat Goodwin and many mus. coms.; orig. soubrette in Gilbert and Sullivan's operas; also vaud.; screen career, Famous Players ("Old Homestead"), Metro ("Blindness of Love," "Awakening of Helena Richie," etc.), O. Henry series for Vitagraph ("Mind the Paint Girl," "Marriage"), Rothapfel ("False Gods"), International ("April Follies"), grand dames and "mother" roles. Hght., 5, 5; dark hair, dark gray eyes. Home ad., 541 W. 124th st., Apt. 15, N. Y. C.; Mngsde 2669.

DEMPSTER, Carol; b. California; early career, studied under Ruth St. Denis and toured as one of Denishawn dancers; screen career, D. W. Griffith prods. ("Romance of Happy Valley," "The Girl Who Stayed at Home," "Scarlet Days"). Ad., Griffith Studio, Mamaroneck, N. Y.

DE REMER, Rubye; b. Denver, Colo.; stage career, Ziegfeld Girl, "Midnight Frolic"; screen career, Rex Beach ("The Auction Block"), Ivan ("Enlighten Thy Daughter"), Metro ("Pals First" and "The Great Romance," with Harold Lockwood), Blackton ("Safe for Democracy"), Famous Players ("Fires of Faith"), Hodkinson ("His Temporary Wife"). Hght., 5, 6; wght., 122; fair complexion, blond hair, blue eyes. Ad., 33 W. 67th st., N. Y.

DESHON, Florence; b. Tacoma, Wash.; educ. N. Y.; stage career, Belasco, "Seven Chances"; screen career, Goldwyn ("The Auction Block"), Vitagraph ("The Other Man," "The Desire of Women," "A Bachelor's Children," "Love Watches," "The Cambric Mask"), Goldwyn ("Cup of Fury," "Dangerous Days"). Hght., 5, 7; wght., 142; dark hair, brown eyes. Home ad., 6229 DeLongpre ave., Los Angeles, Cal.; studio, Goldwyn, Culver City, Cal.

De VORE, Dorothy; b. Fort Worth; educ. there and Los Angeles; stage exper., 1 season vaud.; screen career, 15 comedies Lyons & Moran, Christie ("Know Thy Wife," "Oh, Baby," "Anybody's Widow," "Two A. M.," "A Looney Honeymoon," "Nearly Newlyweds," "Should Husbands Dance," "Twas Midnight"). Hght., 5, 2; wght., 115; brown hair and eyes. Ad., 4560 Hollywood Blvd., Los Angeles, Cal.; studio, Christie, Hollywood, Cal.

DOMINQUEZ, Beatrice; b. San Bernardino, Cal.; educ. Sacred Heart Convent; stage career, Spanish dancer under name of La Bella Sevilla; 2 yrs. at P. O. I. Exposition and San Diego Exposition; 6 mos. with "The Land of Joy Review"; 1 yr. on tour with own co.; screen career, Douglas Fairbanks ("Bound in Morocco"), Universal ("Light of Victory," "The Sundown Trail," "The Beach Comber"). Hght., 5, 4; wght., 122; black hair and eyes. Ad., 4011 University ave., Los Angeles, Cal.

DORO, Marie; b. Duncannon, Pa., 1885; educ. Peebles and Thompson Sch. and Miss Bronson's Sch., N. Y.; stage career, 1901, "Sherlock Holmes" with Gillette, "Richest Girl," "Oliver Twist," "Diplomacy," "Butterfly on the Wheel"; screen career, Famous, Lasky ("Oliver Twist," "The Lash," "Lost and Won"), Lasky-Paramount ("Heart's Desire"), Republic ("Twelve-Ten"). Hght., 5, 4; wght., 115; brown hair and eyes. Home ad., 615 Fifth ave., N. Y.

DRESSLER, Marie; b. Coburg, Canada, Nov. 9, 1871; educ. Canada; stage career, began 1886 in "Under Two Flags," with Lew Fields Travesty Co. vaud. in U. S. and London, "What Happened to Jones"; screen career, Kalem, Lasky ("The Blacklist," "The Leach"), with Charlie Chaplin in "Tillie's Punctured Romance," "Burlesque on Carmen"). Hght., 5, 5; wght., 128; brown hair and blue-gray eyes. 1920, legitimate prod.

DREW, CORA; b. America; educ. there; stage career, from babyhood to age of 22; screen career, last six yrs., scenario and magazine articles, newspaper fashion stuff; Weber-Smalley ("Where Are My Children?"), Maclyn Arbuckle ("It's No Laughing Matter"), Fox ("When a

ACTRESSES

Man Sees Red"), 2 yrs. stk. with Griffith, Universal ("Prince of Ave. A"), with Mildred Harris in Meyer Co. Hght., 5, 5; wght, 123; brown-gray hair, hazel eyes. Ad., Actors' Assn., Los Angeles, Cal.

DREW, Mrs. Sidney (Lucille McVey); b. Sedalia, Mo., 1890; educ. Sedalia Coll. of Music, Nebraska Sch. of Expression; stage career, entertainer for Redpath Lyceum, U. S. and Europe; screen career, Vitagraph (playing comedies directed by Sidney Drew in "The Story of the Glove"), Metro ("Reliable Henry," "One of the Family," "Her First Game," "Henry's Ancestors," "The Patriot," "The Rebellion of Mr. Minor," "A Close Resemblance," "As Others See Us," "The Spirit of Merry Christmas"), Famous Players ("Once a Mason," "The Amateur Liar," "Harold, the Last of the Saxons," "Bunkered," "A Sisterly Scheme"), Pathe ("After Thirty"). Studio ad., 363 W. 125th st., N. Y. C.

DUBREY, Clare; b. N. Y., 1893; educ. in convents; stage career, stk.; screen career, Universal, Fox ("When Fate Decides"), Rob-Cole ("Modern Husbands," "What Every Woman Wants"), World ("The Devil's Trail"), Pathe ("The Old Maid's Baby," "The Sawdust Doll," "The World Aflame"), Vitagraph ("The Wishing Ring Man"), Selznick ("The Spite Bride"), Ince ("Americanism"), Metro ("The Walkoffs"), ("Heart of a Child"). Hght., 5, 7; wght., 130; auburn hair, brown eyes. Ad., Metro Studio.

DUNBAR, Helen; b. N. Y.; educ. Eden Hall, Pa.; stage career, 16 yrs. in comic opera, Weber and Fields, own rep. co., "The Little Minister"; screen career, Essanay, Metro, Lasky-Paramount ("The Squaw Man"), Paralta ("Maid o' the Storm"), Metro ("Making Good"), Pathe ("All Wrong," "Common Clay"), Rob-Cole ("Josselyn's Wife"), Paramount ("Jane Goes A-Wooing," "Venus in the East," "Men, Women and Money," "The Winning Girl," "Puppy Love"), Hodkinson ("Fighting Through"). Hght., 5, 6; auburn hair, brown eyes. Studio ad., Universal City, Cal.

DUNHAM, Mandie; b. Essex, England; educ. Holmwood Coll., Westcliffe-on-Sea, England; stage career, 5 yrs. musical comedy at Gaiety Theatre with George Grossmith and Leslie Henson in "To-night's the Night" and "Theodore and Co." at Adelphi with W. H. Berry in "The Boy"; screen career, Samuelson (London) ("Lads of the Village"), Barker (London) ("The Beetle"), Samuelson (Cal.) ("Temporary Gentlemen"). Hght., 5, 2; wght., 105; blond hair, brown eyes. Home ad., 1265 Third ave., Los Angeles, Cal.; phone 747-89; studio, Samuelson, Universal City, Cal.

DUPRE, Louise; b. Atlanta, 1897; educ. convent; stage career, 10 yrs., "Paid in Full," "The Wolf," "Hanky Panky"; screen career, Pathe ("Perils of Pauline"), Vitagraph, Famous Players, World, Mary Pickford as her understudy in "Pollyanna." Home ad., Hotel Glidden, Hollywood, Cal.; Holly 3910.

DURFEE, Minta (Mrs. Roscoe Arbuckle); b. Los Angeles, 1897; early career in mus. com. and vaud.; screen career, Keystone since 1913 as comedienne ("His Wife's Mistake," "Mickey"). Wght., 130; red hair, blue eyes. Ad., Truart Pictures, 1457 B'way, N. Y.

DWYER, Ruth; educ. Brooklyn; stage career, musical comedy 2 yrs.; screen career, 1 yr. with Universal, Wistaria ("The Lurking Peril"), Hallmark ("The Evil Eye"). Hght., 5, 2; wght., 109; blond hair, brown eyes. Ad., 1533 West 3rd st., Brooklyn, N. Y.

— E —

EDDY, Helen Jerome; b. N. Y. C.; educ. Los Angeles; screen career, Morosco ("His Sweetheart," "Lost in Transit"), Lasky ("One More American"), Universal ("The Blinding Trail"), Brentwood ("The Turn in the Road"), Haworth ("The Man Beneath," "The Tong Man"), Tourneur ("The County Fair"), Mary Pickford ("Pollyanna"). Hght., 5, 7; wght., 135; dark hair and eyes. Home ad., 1911 N. Van Ness ave., Los Angeles, Cal.; Holly 3326.

EDGINGTON, Ida; educ. Fogg School, Nashville, Tenn.; screen career, series of Beauty Pictures for the Screen Magazine of the Universal Film Co., "The Burning Question," Catholic Art Assn. Hght., 5, 4½; wght., 128; light brown hair and dark eyes. Ad., 235 W. 76th st., N. Y.; Schuyler 1759.

ELVIDGE, June C.; b. St. Paul, Minn., June 30, 1893; educ. Penn. Coll.; early career, concert singer; stage career, Winter Garden, "Passing Show of 1914"; screen career, World ("Stolen Orders," "The Quickening Flame," "The Love Defender"), World ("The Moran Deadline," "Three Green Eyes," "Coax Me," "His Father's Wife," "The Woman of Lies," "Poison Pen," "The Steel King"), Mayflower-Miller prod. ("The Call of the Yukon"). Hght., 5, 9; wght., 135; brown hair and eyes. Ad., Bayside, L. I., N. Y.

ESMONDE, Merceita (Mrs. Harry Northrup); b. Phila., educ. N. Y. C.; stage career, 5 yrs. with Chas. Frohman; screen career, Empire All Star Corp., Famous Players ("Less Than the Dust," "Beautiful Adventure," "Oh, You Women"). Wght., 135; brown hair and eyes. Ad., 419 W. 119th st., N. Y. C.

EYTON, Bessie; b. Santa Barbara, Cal.; educ. there; screen career, Selig ("The Crisis," "Heart of Texas Ryan," "City of Purple Dreams," "The Smoldering Flame," "The Love of Madge O'Mara," "The Sole Survivor," "The Still Alarm," "Victor of the Plot," "Law North of 65"), Paramount ("Way of a Man with a Maid"), Metro ("Man of Honor"), Vitagraph ("The Usurper").

— F —

FAIR, Elinor; b. Richmond, Va., 1902; educ. private schools and private tuition here and abroad; stage exper., musical comedy at Alcazar Theatre; screen career, Paralta, J. D. Hampton, C. K. Young, Triangle, G. L. Tucker special ("The Miracle Man"), Hodkinson ("End of the Game"); Fox ("Words and Music," "Be a Little Sport," "Married in Haste," "Love Is Love," "The Lost Princess," "Tin Pan Alley"). Hght., 5, 5; wght., 125; brown hair and eyes. Ad., Fox Film Corp., Hollywood, Cal.

FAIRBANKS, Gladys; b. 1889 and educ. Halifax, N. S.; stage career, stock, "Poor Little Rich Girl," "Mrs. Wiggs of the Cabbage Patch," "Redemption," 1918; screen career, Famous Players ("The Poor Little Rich Girl"), Metro ("The Outsider"), Rankin Drew ("Who's Your Neighbor?"), Goldwyn ("Our Little Wife," "The Face in the Dark"). Hght., 5, 8; wght., 135; light brown hair, dark grey eyes. Ad., 421 East 64th st., N. Y. C.; Rhinelander 300.

FARLEY, Dorothea, also scenario writer; b. Chicago; educ. Rockford, Ill., Seminary, Valparaiso Conservatory; stage career, since age of 3, starred in own stk. co for several yrs., in dram. stk. and mus. com.; screen career, Essanay, American, Universal, Keystone, Fox, Sunshine, series of six Century Comedies, now featured in series of Vin Moore Comedies. Home ad., 1731 Bellview, Los Angeles, Cal.; phone 558774; studio, Vin Comedies, 1919 So. Main, Los Angeles, Cal.

FARRAR, Geraldine; b. Melrose, Mass.; educ. Europe and America; stage career, from 1901, debut as Marguerite in "Faust" at Royal Opera House, Berlin, member Royal Opera House, Berlin, and Metropolitan Opera Co., N. Y., has appeared in many operatic roles, one of the greatest living prima donnas; screen career, Lasky ("Carmen," "Joan the Woman," "The Jaguar's Claws"), Artcraft ("The Woman God Forgot"), Goldwyn ("The Stronger Vow," "Shadows," "World and Its Woman," "Flame of the Desert"). Hght., 5, 6; wght., 135; black hair, gray eyes. Permanent ad., Metropolitan Opera House, N. Y. C.; studio, Culver City, Cal.

FARRINGTON, Adele; b. Brooklyn, N. Y.; educ. Lindenwood Coll., St. Charles, Mo.; stage career, comic opera leads with Amelia Bingham, Florence Roberts, 7 yrs. Belasco Stk Co.; screen career, Bosworth, Inc. ("Country Mouse"), Morosco ("Marcillina's Millions," "Roadside Inn"), Lasky ("House of Silence," "Something to Do"), Jesse Hampton ("Fugitive from Matrimony"), Lasky ("Too Much Johnson"). Hght., 5, 5; wght., 150; light hair, gray eyes. Home ad., 1812 Wilcox ave., Hollywood, Cal.

FAZENDA, Louise; b. Lafayette, Ind., 1895; educ. St. Mary's Convent, and L. A. High School, Los Angeles; stage career, short season stock; screen career, Universal, Keystone, Sennett-Paramount ("The Kitchen Lady," "Her First Mistake," "Her Screen Idol," "The Village Chestnut," "The Village Smithy," "The Foolish Age," "Hearts and Flowers," "Treating 'Em Rough," "Back to the Kitchen"). Hght.,

5, 5; wght., 138; light hair, hazel eyes. Ad., 1132 LeMoyne ave., Los Angeles; studio, Mack Sennett Comedies, Los Angeles, Cal.; Wilshire 1222.

FERGUSON, Elsie Louise; b. N. Y. C.; educ. Normal College, N. Y.; stage career, star in "Such a Little Queen," "First Lady of the Land," "The Strange Woman," "Outcast," etc.; 1920, "Sacred and Profane Love"); screen career, Famous Players ("The Danger Mark," "Heart of the Wilds," "Under the Greenwood Tree," "The Parisian Wife," "The Marriage Price," "Salt of the Earth," "Eyes of the Soul," "The Avalanche," "A Society Exile," "The Counterfeit" "His House in Order"). Hght., 5, 6; wght., 125; golden hair, blue eyes. Ad., Famous Players-Lasky Corp., 485 5th ave., N. Y. C.

FERGUSON, Helen; b. Decatur, Ill., 1901; educ. Chicago; screen career, Blackton ("Safe for Democracy"), Metro ("Wilson or the Kaiser"), McManus ("Lost Battalion," "Bruised Humanity"), Vitagraph ("The Gamblers"), Goldwyn ("Going Some"). Hght., 5, 3; wght., 125; brown hair and eyes. Ad., 274. W. 71st st., N. Y. C.; Columbus 10028.

FIELD, Elinor; b. Plymouth, Pa., 1902; educ. L. A. Poly. High; screen career, Sennett Comedies, 18 mos.; Christie Comedies, 7 mos., Strand Comedies, 10 mos. ("Easy Payment," "Dan Cupid," "The Tale of a Hat," "Just Home Maid," "Are Brunettes False?", "For Love or Money"), National ("Hearts and Masks"). Hght., 5, 1; wght., 102; blond hair, hazel eyes. Ad., 827 Glendale ave., Glendale, Cal.; studio, National, Los Angeles.

FIELDING, Margaret; b. Louisville, Ky.; educ. New York; stage career, leading woman in stk. with Keith for 6 yrs. 2 yrs. in vaud. with U. BO., leads in "Double Exposure," "Some Daddy," "The Crowded Hour"; screen career, Fox ("The Moon Sprite," "Every Girl's Dream," "The Mischief Maker," "The Straight Way"), Serico ("The Jeweled Hand"). Hght., 5, 5½; wght., 125; dark brown hair, brown eyes. Ad., Betts & Fowler, 1482 Broadway, N. Y.

FINCH, Flora; b. England; educ. English private school; stage career, began with Ben Greet in England, also in vaud.; screen career, Vitagraph ("A Night Out"), Biograph, Pathe-Thanhouser ("Prudence, the Pirate"), Flora Finch Film, Capellani ("Oh, Boy"), Flagg-Paramount ("The Unwelcome Guest"), Blackton ("Dawn"). Hght., 5, 5; wght., 110; fair complexion, dark hair, blue-gray eyes. Home ad., 253 W. 42nd st., N. Y. C.

FISHER, Margarita; b. Missouri Valley, Iowa; educ. on stage at age of 8; screen career, American ("The Quest," "Miracle of Life"), Equitable ("The Dragon"), Pollard Picture Plays ("Pearl of Paradise," "Miss Jackie of the Navy," "The Little Girl Who Wouldn't Grow Up," "The Butterfly Girl," "The Devil's Assistant"). Hght., 5; wght., 177; copper color hair, gray eyes. Studio ad., American studio, 1811 State st., Santa Barbara, Cal.

FITZ-GERALD, Cissy; stage career, mgmt. Charles Frohman; screen career, Vitagraph ("The Winsome Widow," "How Cissy Made Good," "The Accomplished Mrs. Thompson," "Cissy's Innocent Wink," "Curing Cissy"); now producing series of comedies, "Cissy and Bertie," first release, "Cissy's Funnymoon." Ad., Rothacker Film Co., Chicago, Ill.

FLEMING, Ethel; b. N. Y. C.; educ. Cleveland, O.; stage exper., 2 seasons stk. and road cos.; screen career, Famous Players, Edison, Fox, Triangle ("The Pretender," "Silent Rider," "Tenderfoot Schoolmaster," "Smiles," "Passions Three"), Robertson-Cole ("Modern Husbands"). Hght., 5, 4; wght., 115; blond hair, blue eyes. Home ad., 1001 N. Western Blvd., Hollywood, Cal.

FORDE, Eugenie; b. N. Y. C.; educ. N. Y. C.; stage career, from 1898, with George Munroe, Chauncey Olcott, Wm. Faversham, Blanche Walsh, etc.; screen career, 7 yrs. Christie Comedies, Selig, Universal, American ("Send Him Away with a Smile"), Goldwyn ("Sis Hopkins" with Mabel Normand, "Strictly Confidential"), American ("Fair Enough"). Hght., 5, 6; wght., 139; complexion dark, brown eyes, auburn hair. Home ad., 1600 N. Bronson ave., Hollywood, Cal.; Holly 1167.

FORREST, Ann; b. Denmark, 1897; educ. Denmark; screen career, American, Universal ("The Birth of Patriotism," "The Midnight Man"), Triangle ("The Tar Heel Warrior"), Lasky ("The Grim Game," "The Prince Chap"), Allan Dwan ("A Splendid Hazard"), Goldwyn ("Dangerous Days"). Hght., 5, 2; wght., 104; blond hair, blue eyes. Home ad., 1139 LaBrea, Los Angeles Cal.; Holly 1423.

FORREST, Edith; educ. high sch. and college, Mich.; stage career, 10 yrs. dramatic leads in produs., stock and vaud.; screen career, Selznick ("The Imp"), Vitagraph ("The Golden Shower"), Metro ("The Lifted Veil"), Frohman ("The Invisible Ray"), etc. Hght., 5, 5; wght., 140; red hair, blue eyes. Ad., 270 W. 39th st., N. Y. C.; Greeley 2429.

FREDERICK, Pauline; b. Boston, Mass.; educ. Boston private sch.; stage career, "Roger Brothers" successes, "Princess of Kensington," "Little Gray Lady," "Toddles," "When Knights Were Bold," "Samson" with Gillette, "Joseph and His Brethren," "Innocent" (starred); screen career, Famous Players ("Mrs. Dane's Defense," "A Daughter of the Old South," "Zaza," "La Tosca," "Bedna"), Goldwyn ("Woman on the Index," "Bonds of Love," "Fear Woman," "Peace of Roaring River," "Loves of Letty," "One Week of Life," "The Paliser Case"). Hght., 5, 4; wght., 130; brown hair and blue eyes. Ad., home, 449 Park ave., N. Y.; studio, Goldwyn Culver City Cal.

— G —

GALE, Alice; b. Phila., Pa., 1868; educ. Phila. High Schls.; stage car. with N. S. Co., Leslie Carter, James O'Neil, Marie Doro, Otis Skinner, Billie Burke, Louis Mann, Booth, 5 yrs. at the Grand Opera House Pittsburg, 3 yrs. at Girard Ave. theatre, Phila.; 1 yr. at Proctor's Fifth Ave.; screen career, Fox ("The Darling of Paris," "The New York Peacock," "Camille"), Select Pictures ("Magda"), Para-Artcraft ("L'Apache").

GANE, Vivian; b. Brookville, Kans.; educ. Kansas City; screen career, leading lady in series of Al Jennings' pictures, including "The Outlaw's Alibi," "The Deputy Marshal's Wife," "When Outlaws Meet." Hght., 5, 4; wght., 123; light brown hair, hazel eyes. Home ad., 1224 West 41st stt., Los Angeles Calif.; phone 26332; studio, Capital Film Co., Hollywood, Calif.

GAUNTIER, Gene; b. Wellsville, Mo.; educ. studied drama in Berlin, grad. Kansas City Sch. of Oratory; stage career, stk.; screen career, author, star and co-director of biblical film "From Manger to the Cross," Kalem ("Colleen Baun," "Girl Spy Series," "Tragedy of the Desert," "Down Through the Ages"), Gene Gauntier Feature Players ("In the Form of a Hypnotist," "Daughter of the Confederacy"), 50 Kalem Irish dramas; during 1919, dramatic editor and critic, Kansas City Post; written over 500 produced scenarios; star, scenariost and supervising director Dodge Feature Films. Home ad., 3000 Prospect ave., Kansas City, Mo.

GEORGE, Maud; b. Riverside, Cal., 1890; educ. Los Angeles; stage career, Burbank stock, Los Angeles, 2 seasons with Conrad Le Marie over Orpheum circuit played in "The Sultan's Favorite" for 1 season; screen career, Universal ("Idle Wives," "Shadows of Suspicion," "Even as You and I," "Heart Strings"), Artcraft ("Blue Blazes Rawden"), Ince-Para. ("The Marriage Ring"), Vitagraph ("A Rogue's Romance"), Pathe ("The Midnight Stage"), Rob-Cole ("The Lamb and the Lion"). Hght., 5, 7; stately type, olive complexion, black hair, dark brown eyes. Studio ad., Universal City, Calif.

GERBER, Neva; b. Chicago, Ill.; educ. Immaculate Heart Coll.; screen career, with Edwin August in "The Awakening," Metro ("The Great Secret"), Universal ("The Prodigal Widow," "Like Wildfire," "Caught in the Act," "The Phantom Ship," "The Spindle of Life," "Roped," "The Trail of the Octopus," "The Screaming Shadow"). Hght., 5, 2; wght., 112; light brown hair, brown eyes. Ad. 217 N. Western ave., Los Angeles, Calif.; phone 560576.

GIBSON, Helen; b. Cleveland, Ohio, Aug. 27, 1894; educ. Central High, Cleveland; early career, rodeo rider, holding highest honors for Los Angeles rodeo woman rider 2 yrs.; screen career, Universal ("The Dynamite Special," "Man of God," "The Run of the Yellow Mail," "The Frustrated Holdup," "Fighting Mad"), number of 2-reel releases, Capital Film ("Peril of the Rails," "When Seconds Count," "Border Watch Dogs," "The Ghost of Canyon Diablo," "The Robber of the Golden Star," "Trail of the Rails"). Hght., 5, 6; wght., 142; brown hair, hazel eyes, olive complexion. Ad. Capital Film Co., Hollywood, Calif.

ACTRESSES

GILL, Helen; stage career, "Business Before Pleasure," original "Fair and Warmer," "Experience"; screen career, lead in Selznick Pictures. Hght., 5, 6; wght., 135; dark hair and eyes. Ad., c/o Arthur H. Jacobs, 145 W. 45th st., N. Y. C.; Bryant 4783.

GISH, Dorothy; b. Dayton, O., 1898; stage career from 1902; screen career, Biograph, Reliance-Majestic, Fine Arts ("The Little Yank," "Children of the Feud," "That Colby Girl"), Griffith ("Hearts of the World"), Paramount ("Battling Jane," "The Hope Chest," "The Hun Within," "Boots," "I'll Get Him Yet," "Peppy Polly," "Nugget Nell," "Out of Luck," "Turning the Tables"). Hght., 5; blue eyes, fair hair. Ad., Griffith Studio, Mamaroneck, N. Y.

GISH, Lillian; b. Springfield, O., 1896; educ. finishing schl.; stage career, from 1902; screen career, from 1912 engaged by Griffith for Biograph stock; went with Griffith to Reliance-Majestic and Fine Arts ("Birth of a Nation," "Intolerance," "Souls Triumphant"), Griffith-Artcraft, "Hearts of the World," "The Great Love," "The Greatest Thing in Life," "Romance of Happy Valley," "Broken Blossoms," "True-Heart Susie"), First National ("The Greatest Question"). Studio ad., Griffith studio, Mamaroneck, N. Y.

GLAUM, Louise; b. nr. Baltimore; educ. Maryland; stage career, stk and several prod.; screen career, Thos. H. Ince ("The Wolf Woman," "The Sweetheart of the Doomed," "Love and Justice," "Golden Rule Kate"), Paralta ("Shell 43," "Law Unto Herself"), J. Parker Read, Jr. ("Sahara," "Lone Wolf's Daughter," "Sex"). Hght., 5, 5; wght., 130; brown hair, hazel eyes. Ad. J. Parker Read Jr., Prods., Thos. H. Ince Studio, Los Angeles, Calif.; phone W. 62.

GOLDEN, Ruth Fuller; b. N. Y. C.; educ. Los Angeles; screen career, Vitagraph comedies, "Pegern," "Over the Garden Wall," "Cupid Forecloses." Hght., 5, 7; wght., 128; light brown hazel eyes. Ad., 1729 Winona Blvd., Los Angeles, Calif.; Holly 2216; studio, Vitagraph.

GORDON, Eva; b. Alsace-Lorraine; educ. there; stage career, Berlin with Harry Walden, stock; screen career, Union Film Co. in Berlin, Great Northern Film Co. in Copenhagen, Metro ("Under Suspicion"), World ("The Black Circle"), Hallmark ("The Chains of Evidence"), Jack London Film Co. ("The Star Rover"), Fox ("The White Moll"). Hght., 5, 6; wght., 135; blond hair hazel eyes. Ad., Hotel Ransby, 324 W. 84th st., N. Y. C.; Schuyler 5420.

GORDON, Julia Swayne; b. Columbus, O.; educ. there; stage career, stk., vaud. and prod.; screen career Vitagraph ("The Soul Master," "Son of the Hills," "The Message of the Mouse," "Soldiers of Chance," "The Hillman," "Over the Top," "The Soap Girl," "Love Watches," "The Captain's Captain," "The Girl Problem," "Miss Dulcie from Dixie"), Blackton-Pathe ("The Moonshine Trail"). Hght., 5, 7; wght., 135; brown hair, blue eyes. Ad., 355 W. 51st st., N. Y.

GORDON Maude Turner; b. Franklin, Ind., 1867; educ. Oxford, O., and Franklin Coll. Ind.; stage career, 16 N. Y. prod. including "Nothing But the Truth," "Divorcons," "Melting of Molly"; screen career, Fox, Goldwyn ("The Danger Mark"), Famous, World ("Home," "Bringing Up Betty," "The Oakdale Affair"), Gaumont ("Making Her His Wife"), Selznick ("The Honeymoon"), 3 pictures with Marguerite Clark and 3 with Pauline Frederick. Hght., 5, 1½; wfht., 150; white hair, blue gray eyes. Ad., Flanders Hotel, N. Y. C.

GORDON, Vera; b. Russia; educ. there; stage career, Jacob P. Adler Stk. Co., with Sam Lievert in vaud., "The Land of the Free" with Florence Nash, "Why Worry" with Fannie Brice, "The Gentile Wife" with Emily Stevens; screen career, Universal ("Sorrows of Israel"), International ("Humoresque"). Hght., 5, 5½; wght., 165; black hair and eyes. Ad., Betts & Fowler, 1482 B'way, N. Y.; Bryant 5664.

GREELEY, Evelyn; b. Lexington, Ky.; educ. Frances Shimer Acad. and Univ. School for Girls; stage career, Essanay, Dixie Film Co., World ("The Road to France," "The Allies," "Hit or Miss," "Phil for Short," "Bringing Up Betty," "The Oakdale Affair," "Me and Captain Kidd"). Hght., 5, 3; wght., 115; light hair, brown eyes. Ad., Colonial Studios Bldg., 39 W. 67th st., N. Y. C.

GREEN, Dorothy; b. Petrograd, Russia, 1895; educ. N. Y.; screen career, Lasky ("Country Boy"), World, Fox ("A Parisian Romance"), Metro ("Devil at His Elbow"), International ("Patria") World ("The Rough Neck," "The American Way," "The Praise Agent," "Forest Rivals"), Paramount ("The Dark Star"), Perret-Pathe ("The A B C of Love"). Hght., 5, 6; wght., 125; black hair, green eyes. Ad., home, 828 Seventh ave., N. Y.

GREEN, Helen; b. N. Y. C.; educ. Georgetown Convent, Wash., D. C.; stage exper., 1 yr. played Love in "Experience," 6 mos. stk.; screen career, Famous Players, World, Metro ("The Amazons," "On the Quiet," "In Again, Out Again"). Sub-Deb series ("Woman and Wife," "Honeymoon for Three"), Paramount-Artcraft ("Wanted, a Husband"). Hght., 5, 6; wght., 125; light hair, gray eyes. Ad., 21 W. 46th st., N. Y. C.; Bryant 4194.

GREEN, Margaret; b. N. Y., 1892; educ. there; stage career, "Seven Keys to Baldpate," "Broadway Jones," vaud.; screen career, Pathe ("Nedra"), Mirror, Unity, Ivan ("One Law for Both"), Pathe ("The Angel Factory"), Paramount ("A Sporting Chance").

GREENWOOD, Winifred; b. Oswego, N. Y.; stage career, vaud., stock; headed own co.; screen career, American ("Lying Lips," "Reclamation," "Dust," "The Two Orphans"), Lasky ("The Crystal Gazer"), Universal ("The Deciding Kiss"), Hodkinson ("Come Again Smith"), Paramount ("Maggie Pepper," "Men, Women and Money," "The Lottery Man").

GREY, Olga; b. Budapest, Hungary; educ. Los Angeles and N. Y. C.; early career, concert pianist; screen career, American ("When a Man Rides Alone," "Trixie from Broadway"), Griffith ("Intolerance"), Triangle ("Lure of Wanton Eyes"), Pathe ("Third Eye"). Hght., 5, 7; wght., 141; brown hair and eyes. Home ad., 1488 Sunset Blvd., Los Angeles, Calif.; Main 5284.

GRIFFITH, Cecilia Frances; b. Boston; educ. there; stage career, "Everyman," "Girl From Rector's"; screen career, Metro ("The Yellow Streak," "The Kiss of Hate," "Notorious Gallagher"). Now playing in vaudeville. Hght., 5, 6½; wght., 165; blond complexion, red hair, gray eyes; write scenarios. Ad., home, 19 Adams st., Dorchester, Mass.

GRIFFITH, Corinne; b. Texarkana, Tex.; educ. Sacred Heart Convent, New Orleans; professional dancer 1 yr. before beginning screen career with Western Vitagraph ("The Last Man," "Love Watches," "Miss Ambition"); ingenue leads, later with Earle Williams; Vitagraph ("The Adventure Shop," "Thin Ice," "A Girl at Bay," "The Girl Problem," "The Unknown Quantity," "The Climbers"). Hght., 5, 4; wght., 120; light complexion, light brown hair, blue eyes. Ad., Vitagraph Studio, Brooklyn, N. Y.

GRIFFITH, Katherine; b. San Francisco, Calif.; stage career, 15 yrs.; screen career, Universal ("Snow White," "Talk of the Town"), L-Ko Comedies, Vitagraph ("Irish Princess"), Lasky ("Vicky Van," "Little Princess"), Artcraft "Huckleberry Finn"), Mary Pickford ("Pollyanna"). Hght., 5, 7; wght., 165; black hair, gray eyes. Home ad., 1232 Gower st., Los Angeles, Calif.; Holly 2491.

GUINAN, "Texas"; b. Waco, Texas, 1891; stage career, 6 yrs., Winter Garden Revues, Klaw & Erlanger, Shubert, John Cort, etc., "Hop O' My Thumb" in London; screen career, Triangle, World ("The Gun Woman," "Fuel of Life," "Love Brokers"), Frohman Amuse. ("The She-Wolf"), two-reel pictures for Bull's Eye Film Corp. Hght., 5, 6; wght., 136; light hair, blue eyes. Ad., Bull's Eye Studio, Hollywood, Cal.

— H —

HALL, Ella; b. N. Y., 1897; educ. there; stage career, "Grand Army Man"; screen career, Biograph, Reliance, Universal ("A Jewel in Pawn," "The Little Orphan," "Bitter Sweet," "The Charmer," "The Spotted Lily," "We Are French," "My Little Boy," "Green Magic"), Paralta ("Heart of Rachael"), Bluebird ("Which Woman"), Artcraft ("Under the Top"), Francis Ford Serial ("The Gates of Doom"). Home ad., 1834 El Cerrita Place, Hollywood, Cal.; studio, Francis Ford Studio.

HALL, Lillian; b. Brooklyn, N. Y., 1897; educ. H. S. and business college there; stage exper., stk. in Phil., etc.; screen career, Beth in Wm. A. Brady's "Little Women"; Norma Talmadge ("The Safety Curtain"), Mutual ("Her Second Husband," "Wanted for Murder"), Triangle ("Taxi"), Fox ("My Little Sister"), World

("Coax Me"), Rex Beach ("Going Some"). Hght., 5; wght., 100; blond hair, dark blue eyes. Ad., Hotel Van Nuys, Los Angeles, Cal.

HALLOR, Edith; stage career, Ziegfeld "Follies," "Intoxication" in "Experience"; starred in Comstock & Gest's "Leave It to Jane," co-starred with Wm. Collier in "Nothing But Lies"; screen career, dramatic lead in 6 pictures with Weber Prods., Inc., Selznick. Hght., 5, 6½; wght., 135; auburn hair, hazel eyes. Ad., Wyoming Apts., 853 Seventh ave., N. Y. C.; Circle 3312.

HAMMERSTEIN, Elaine; b. 1897; granddaughter of Oscar Hammerstein, operatic impresario; educ. Armitage Coll., Pa.; stage career, in "The Trap," later lead in "High Jinks"; screen career, Jewell Productions ("The Co-Respondent," "The Battle Cry"), Harry Rapf Prod. ("Wanted for Murder"), Selznick Pict. ("The Country Cousin," "Greater Than Fame," "The Woman Game"). Wght., 120; complexion, fair; brown, wavy hair, gray eyes. Ad., c/o Selznick Pictures Corp., N. Y.

HAMMOND, Virginia; b. Virginia; stage career, debut with E. H. Sothern, "If I Were King," "Our American Cousin," Shakespearian rep., "What's Your Husband Doing?", "The Famous Mrs. Fair"; screen career, World ("The Hand Invisible," "Miss Crusoo"), Select ("The World to Live In"). Hght., 5, 6; wght., 130; light hair, blue eyes. Ad., 105 W. 55th st., N. Y.

HAMPTON, Hope; educ. Dallas, Tex., schools and Sophie Newcomb School, New Orleans, La.; screen career, Hope Hampton Prods., Inc. (lead in "A Modern Salome"). Hght., 5, 3; wght., 118; auburn hair, dark blue eyes. Ad. Hope Hampton Prods., Inc., 1476 Broadway, N. Y.

HANLON, Alma; b. N. Y., 1894; educ. N. Y.; screen career, Kleine, Ivan ("The Faded Flower"), Fox ("Gold and the Woman," etc.), Triumph ("The Libertine"), Apollo ("God of Little Children," "The Mystic Hour," "The Golden God," "When You and I Were Young," "The Public Defender"), U. S. Amusement ("Behind the Mask"), Pioneer Film Corp. ("Sins of the Children"). Ad., Bayside, Long Island, N. Y.

HANSEN, Juanita; b. Des Moines, Ia., 1897; educ. Cal.; screen career, Famous (opp. Jack Pickford), Fine Arts, American (heroine in "Secret of the Submarine"), Keystone, Universal ("The Finishing Touch," "Broadway Love"), Ince-Para. ("Mating of Marcella"), Universal ("The Rough Lover," "The Brass Bullet" serial), First National ("A Midnight Romance"), Artcraft ("The Poppy Girl's Husband"), Fox ("Rough Riding Romance"), Metro ("Lombardi, Ltd."), Selig ("The Lost City" serial). Hght., 5, 3; wght., 130; fair complexion, blond hair, blue eyes.

HARRIS, Marcia; b. Providence; educ. there; stage career, und. Broadhurst, Liebler and Co., Weber and Fields; screen career, Famous, Edison, Fox, Vitagraph ("The Foundling," "The Reformer"), Artcraft ("Poor Little Rich Girl"), Famous Players ("The Little Boy Scout"), Goldwyn ("Day Dreams"), Pathe ("The Bishop's Emeralds"), Fox ("Putting One Over"), Realart ("Anne of the Green Gables"). Hght., 5, 9; wght., 150; dark complexion, dark hair, brown eyes.

HARRIS, Mildred (Mrs. Charlie Chaplin); b. Cheyenne, Wyo., 1901; educ. privately; screen career, Vitagraph, Reliance-Majestic, Fine Arts ("Old Folks at Home," "The Village Prodigal"), Universal ("The Whim," "K.," "The Price of a Good Time," "The Man Who Dared God," "When a Girl Loves," "For Husbands Only," "Home," "Forbidden"), First National ("The Inferior Sex," "Polly of the Storm Country," "Social Mockery"). Hght., 5, 2; wght., 108; blue eyes, brown hair. Ad., Mayer Chaplin Co., 3800 Mission Rd., Los Angeles, Cal.

HARRIS, Winifred; educ. Kew, Richmond, England; stage career, in England, "Madam X," "Sally Bishop," Prince of Wales, "Girl on the Film," Shakespearian prods. with Sir Herbert Tree, Sir Henry Irving; in America, "Taking Chances," "Co-respondent," "Cheating Cheaters," "Royal Vagabond," Cohan and Harris, "Light" in the "Bluebird"; screen career, with Norma Talmadge ("Panthea," "Daughter of Two Worlds"), Authors Films, Inc. ("Crucible of Life"), several pictures with Vitagraph. Hght., 5, 10; wght., 170; light brown hair, dark blue eyes. Ad., 147 W. 44th st., N. Y.; Bryant 3406.

HART, Lallah Rookh; b. and educ. Denver, Col.; screen career, "The Wife," "A la Cabaret," "A Sanatarium Blunder," "Half and Half," "Heart's Strategy," Paramount ("Men, Women and Money"), playing mothers, maiden aunts, eccentric characters. Hght., 5, 4; wght., 120; dark complexion, brown eyes and hair. Ad., home, 427 Olive st., Los Angeles, Cal.

HARTMAN, Greta; b. Chicago, Ill., 1897; educ. private tutors and Sheldon School; stage career, Wilton Lackaye, Wright Lorrimer, created Mary Jane in "Mary Jane's Pa"; screen career, Famous Players, Fox ("The Painted Madonna," "Fantine" in "Les Miserables"), Argus ("The House Without Chillren"), Dietrick Kenyon Co. ("The Bandbox"), Pioneer ("Atonement"). Hght., 5, 5; wght., 135; brown hair and eyes. Ad., 630 W. 135th st., N. Y. C.; Morningside 5060.

HASTINGS, Carey; b. New Orleans; educ. Brooklyn, N. Y.; stage career, in "St. Elmo," "Girl from Rector's," stk. in New York, Norfolk, Richmond, Atlanta, etc.; screen career, Thanhouser, 2 yrs. ("The Vicar of Wakefield," "Her Beloved Enemy," "Her New York," "Under False Colors," "Man Without a Country"), Select ("Heartsease"), Fleur de Lys ("Empty Arms"); 10 weeks Loew's vaud. circuit. Hght., 5, 5; wght., 140; brown hair, hazel eyes. Ad., 2155 Mohegan ave., N. Y.; Fordham, 4781.

HAVER, Phyllis; b. Douglas, Kan., Jan. 6, 1899; educ. Los Angeles; screen career, Lasky, Keystone, Sennett ("Never Too Old," "The Foolish Age," "Hearts and Flowers," "Among Those Present," "Salome vs. Shenandoah," "His Last False Step"). Hght., 5, 6; wght., 126; light complexion, blond hair, blue eyes. Ad., home, 3924 Wisconsin st., Los Angeles, Cal.; studio, Mack Sennett Comedies, Los Angeles, Cal.

HAWLEY, Ormi; b. Holyoke, Mass., 1890; grad. New Eng. Conserv. of Music; stage career, 2 yrs. in stock as leading woman; screen career, starred by Lubin, "The Ragged Earl"; featured by World Film and Popular Players, starred by Mutual and Fox, has played lead in over 250 photoplays ("Where Love Leads"), Ardsley Art Film ("Runaway Romany"), Famous Players ("The Antics of Ann," "Prince Ubaldo"), Betzwood-Goldwyn ("The Road Called Straight"). Hght., 5, 3; wght., 130; fair complexion, blond hair, gray eyes.

HAWLEY, Wanda; b. Scranton, Pa.; educ. Seattle, Wash., and N. Y.; stage career, amateur theatricals in Seattle and concert work in U. S. and Canada; screen career, C. B. DeMille Prod. ("Old Wives for New," "For Better, For Worse"), Famous Players ("Double Speed," "Everywoman," "The Tree of Knowledge," "The Six Best Cellars"). Hght., 5, 3; wght., 110; blond hair, grayish-blue eyes. Ad., Lasky Studio, Hollywood, Cal.

HEMING, Violet; b. Leeds, Yorkshire, Eng.; educ. Malvern House School, Southport, Eng.; stage career, Wendy in "Peter Pan" at 12 yrs., created Rebecca in "Rebecca of Sunnybrook Farm," 2 yrs. leading woman for Geo. Arliss, "The Naughty Wife," 1918 "Three Faces East"; screen career, Goldwyn ("The Turn of the Wheel"), Blackton ("The Judgment House"), Selig ("The Danger Trail"), Para-Artcraft ("Everywoman"). Hght., 5, 4; wght., 118; blond hair, blue eyes. Ad., care of Cohan & Harris, W. 42nd st., N. Y. C.

HENRY, Gale; b. Bear Valley, Cal.; educ. Los Angeles, Cal.; stage career, Temple Opera Co., Century Theatre, Los Angeles, 2 yrs.; screen career, 5 yrs. with Universal, starred in one-reel comedies; commenced production of own comedies February, 1919. Hght., 5, 9; wght., 128; dark hair, brown eyes. Home ad., 1546 Winona Blvd., Los Angeles, Cal.; studio, Bullseye Studio, Santa Monica Blvd., Los Angeles, Cal.

HERNANDEZ, Mrs. George (Anna Dodge); b. River Falls, Wis.; educ. State Normal Schl., River Falls; stage career, with McDonough Stk., Oakland, Cal., and with Walter Bentley Co.; screen career, Selig ("The Rosary"), Edison, Fine Arts, Universal ("The Heritage"), Goldwyn ("Leave It to Susan"), B. B. Features ("Hearts Asleep"), Brentwood ("Where There's a Will"), Humanity ("The Gift Supreme"), Griffith ("Battling Jane"). Hght., 5, 4; wght., 196; brown air, hazel eyes. Home ad., 2228 Duane st., Los Angeles, Cal.

HERRING, Aggie; b. San Francisco; educ. there; stage career, from age of 17, stock cos., vaud.; screen career, Triangle-Ince, Paralta ("Within the Cup"), Vitagraph ("Cupid Forecloses," "A Yankee Princess"), United ("A Man's Fight"),

ACTRESSES

First National ("The Hoodlum"), Hodkinson ("The Lord Loves the Irish"), "The Sage Brusher"). Hght., 5, 4; wght., 165; blond hair, blue eyes. Ad., Federal Photoplay Corp., Los Angeles, Cal.

HICKS, Maxine Elliott; b. Denver, Colo.; educ. private tutor; stage career, "The Things that Count," 8 mos. in Brady's Playhouse, N. Y., "Seven Sisters," "The Little Princess," "Blue Bird"; screen career, Artcraft ("Poor Little Rich Girl"), World ("The Little Duchess," "The Crimson Dove," "Neighbors"), Metro ("The Eternal Mother"), Allen Holubar ("The Right to Happiness"), Tourneur ("The County Fair"), Lasky ("Speed Carr"). Hght., 5; wght., 90; chestnut brown hair, blue eyes. Ad., 1227 So. Hoover st., Los Angeles, Cal.; West 1424.

HILBURN, Betty; educ. Horace Mann Sch., N. Y., St. Elizabeth Convent, Convent Station, N. J.; stage career, "The Betrothal," "Tumble Inn"; screen career, Submarine Film Corp. ("Girl of the Seas"), Fox ("Heart Strings"), Selznick ("Little Red Riding Hood"). Hght., 5, 2; wght., 104; dark brown hair and eyes. Ad., 223 W. 83rd st., N. Y. C.; Schuyler 5793.

HILL, Josephine; b. San Francisco; educ. there; stage career, vaud. with Gus Edwards, featured with "Georgie Price"; screen career, Universal, lead and featured with Edgar Jones Prods. "The Sheriff's Oath," "The Four Bit Man," "At the Point of a Gun," "Love and the Law," "The Fighting Heart," "Shameless Salverson," "The Jack of Hearts," "The Voice on the Wire," "The Bronco and the Bronx"). Hght., 5, 2; wght., 110; light hair, blue eyes. Ad., 6200 De Longpre, Hollywood, Cal.; Holly 2592; studio, Universal City.

HILL, Maud; heavies; b. St. Louis; educ. convent, Chicago; stage career, stk. in West; screen career, with Metro for several years; Fox ("Sister Against Sister," "A Daughter of France," "When Men Desire"), Chas. Miller ("A Dangerous Affair"), Schomer & Ross ("The Sacred Flame"), Edward Griffith ("The End of the Road"). Hght., 5, 7; wght., 135; dark complexion, red brown hair, blue eyes. Ad., home, 6 West 107th st., N. Y. Academy 993.

HOFFMAN, Ruby; b. Phila., Pa.; stage career, stock, Phila.; "Gentleman from Mississippi," and Daniel Frohman's "Detective Keene"; screen career, Pathe, Famous Players ("The Slave Market"), Fox ("The Children of the Ghetto"), Kleine (featured in "The Danger Signal"), World, McClure ("Passion"), Pathe ("The Fatal Ring," "The House of Hate"), Triangle ("Upside Down"). Hght., 5, 6; brown hair and eyes. Ad., home, 206 W. 52nd st., N. Y.; Circle 4652.

HOLLAND, Edna M.; b. 1896; stage career, with Edith W. Mathison, David Belasco, "The Good Little Devil"; screen career, Vitagraph ("Confession of Madam Barrestoff"), Metro ("The Lifted Veil," "Always in the Way"), Famous Players ("World's Great Snare," "Feud Girl"), Wm. Steiner ("The Tenderfoot," "The Masked Rider"). Hght., 5, 9; brunette. Ad., 324 W. 51st st., N. Y. C.; Bryant 3582.

HOLLISTER, Alice; b. Worcester, Mass.; educ. Convent Villa Maria, Montreal; screen career, Mary Magdalene in Kalem's "From the Manger to the Cross," with Sid Olcott in Ireland in ("The Kerry Gow," "Vampire," "Destroyer," "Yellow Sunbonnet," "Lotus Woman"), Famous Players ("Her Better Self"). Ad., 414 32nd st., Woodcliff, N. J.

HOLLOWAY, Carol; b. Williamstown, Mass.; educ. Franklin, Mass.; stage career, Carleton stock and N. Y. prods. Youth in "Everywoman"; screen career, Pilot, Lubin, Lasky, NYMP, American, Fine Arts, Vitagraph ("The Fighting Trail," "The Tenderfoot," "Vengeance and the Woman," "The Iron Test," "Perils of Thunder Mountain"). Ad., 4417 Prospect ave., Hollywood, Cal.; studio, Vitagraph.

HOLMES, Helen; educ. Chicago; early career, artist and artist's model; screen career, Keystone, Kalem, ("Hazards of Helen"), Universal, Railroad stories, Signal-Mutual ("Girl and the Game," "Railroad Raiders," "A Desperate Deed," "The Lost Express," "Medicine Bend," "Whispering Smith"), S. L. K. serial, "The Fatal Fortune." Hght., 5, 6; wght., 135; fair complexion, brown hair and eyes. Ad., Betts & Fowler, 1482 Bway., N. Y.; Bryant 5664.

HOPE, Gloria; b. 1901, Pittsburgh, Pa.; educ. Newark, N. J.; screen career, Ince Triangle, Artcraft ("The Great Love"), Ince-Para. ("Naughty, Naughty"), Paralta ("Heart of Rachael"), Universal ("Outcasts of Poker Flat," "Riders of the Law," "The Day She Paid"), Garson Prod. ("The Hushed Hour"), First National ("Burglar by Proxy"), Goldwyn ("Gay Lord Quex"). Hght., 5, 2; wght., 106; light complexion, auburn hair, blue eyes. Ad., 1423 Curson ave., Hollywood, Cal.

HOPKINS, May F.; b. N. J.; stage exper., "Loyalty," "The Grass Widow," "She's In Again," Ziegfeld Follies; screen career, C. K. Young ("Everybody's Girl," "The Deep Purple"), Capallani ("Virtuous Model," "Easiest Way"), World ("Social Pirate"), Vitagraph, Norma Talmadge ("Two Women"), Mayflower ("Bolshevism on Trial"), Wharton ("Beatrice of Fairfax"), Talmadge ("By Right of Purchase," "Petroleum Prince"). Hght., 5, 5; wght., 123; blond hair, brown eyes. Ad., 243 W. 132nd st., N. Y. C.

HOPPER, Mrs. De Wolf; b. Pittsburgh; educ. there; stage career, with Selwyn, Henry Harris, Shuberts, Arthur Hopkins, "The Quaker Girl," "Be Calm, Camilla"; screen career, Goldwyn, Geo. Cohan ("Seven Keys to Baldpate"), Anita Stewart Prod. ("Virtuous Wives"), Vitagraph ("Third Degree"), Norma Talmadge ("Isle of Conquest"), Wm. Faversham ("Man Who Lost Himself"). Hght., 5, 7; wght., 135; green eyes, brown hair. Ad., Algonquin Hotel, N. Y.

HORTON, Clara Marie; b. Brooklyn, June, 1904; educ. private tuition; stage career, since 4 yrs.; screen career, Eclair 4 yrs., Universal 2 yrs., Triangle 1 yr., Lasky (with Jack Pickford in "Tom Sawyer," "Huck Finn," "The Plow Woman," "The Yellow God," "In Wrong," "Little Shepherd of Kingdom Come," played "Youth" in "Everywoman"), Rex Beach ("Girl from Outside"), Selznick ("Blind Youth"). Golden hair, blue eyes. Home ad., 2660 Magnolia ave., Los Angeles, Cal.

HORTON, Jeanette; b. Horton, N. Y.; educ. Binghamton, N. Y.; stage career, "Seven Keys to Baldpate," "Melting of Molly," "Squab Farm," 4 seasons in stk.; screen career, Kalem ("The Guilt"), Metro ("The Lure of the Heart's Desire," "The Yellow Streak"), also with Emily Wehlen, Mabel Taliaferro, Robert Warwick. Hght., 5, 7½; wght., 138; brown hair and eyes. Ad., Betts & Fowler, 1482 Bway., N. Y. C.

HOTELLING, Louise; b. 1901 and educ. Ithaca, N. Y.; screen career, Arrow ("Profiteers"), Grossman ("Million Dollars Reward"), Wharton ("Great White Trail," "Hun Within Our Gates," "Eagle Eye"). Hght., 5, 1; wght., 105; brown hair and eyes. Ad., 320 N. Tioga st., Ithaca, N. Y.

HOWELL, Alice; b. N. Y., May 5, 1892; educ. N. Y. pub. schs.; stage career, mus. com. in 1907, burlesque for 5 years; Howell & Howell vaud. sketch 3 yrs.; screen career, Keystone since 1914 with L-Ko (leading parts in "The Mother-in-Law," "Balloonatics," "The Honor of the Sawdust," "Neptune's Naughty Daughter"), Century ("Alice of the Sawdust," "Her Horseshoe Obligation"), classic dancing. Medium height, fair complexion, light hair, hazel eyes. Ad., Billy West Comedies, Cropper Dist. Corp., 207 So. Wabash ave., Chicago, Ill.

HOWLAND, Jobyna; b. Indianapolis, Ind.; educ. Denver, Colo.; stage exper. years in B'way prods., "Nancy Lee," "Ruggles," "A Little Journey," etc.; screen career, Norma Talmadge Co. ("Her Only Way," "Way of a Woman"), Select ("What Might Have been"). Hght., 5, 11; wght., 150; red hair, dark eyes. Ad. Hotel Algonquin, N. Y.

HUFF, Louise; b. Columbus, Ga.; educ. there and Horace Mann, N. Y. C.; stage career, "Ben Hur," stock at Utica and N. Y.; screen career, Famous Players ("Seventeen," "Great Expectations," "Freckles," "The Varmint," "What Money Can't Buy," "The Ghost House," "Tom Sawyer," "Jack and Jill," "Bunker Bean"), World ("T'other Dear Charmer," "Sea Waif," "The Crook o' Dreams"), Famous Players ("Oh, You Women"). Hght., 5; wght., 106; fair complexion, blond hair, violet eyes. Ad., home, 64 W. 49th st., N. Y. C.

HULETTE, Gladys; educ. by private tutor; stage career, with De Wolf Hopper, Bertha Kalich, Nazimova, also the original Tyty in New theatre prod. of "Blue Bird"; screen career, Biograph, Edison, Thanhouser ('Her New York," "Pots-and-Pans Peggy," "The Candy Girl," "The Streets of Illusion"), Astra ("The Cigarette Girl," "The Last of the Carnabys," "Miss Nobody," "A Crooked Romance"); swims, rides, draws. Hght., 5, 4; wght., 114; brown hair and gray eyes. Ad., 128 Mt. Jay Place, New Rochelle, N. Y.; New Rochelle 417-J.

HURLEY, Julia; b. Greenwich Village, N. Y.; educ. N. Y.; stage career, 48 yrs. with Charlotte Cushman, under mgmt. E. L. Davenport, with Harrigan and Hart in "Mulligan Guards," "The Gentile Wife" with Emily Stevens; screen career, Famous Players ("Gismonda," "Easy to Get," "The Cost"), Wm. Brady ("Little Women"), World ("Poison Pen"), Warner Bros. ("Beware"). Hght., 5, ½; wght., 134½; silver gray hair, dark hazel eyes. Ad., 306 W. 46th st., N. Y. C.; Bryant 394.

HUTTON, Lucille; b. Indiana, 1901; educ. Sacred Heart Convent, Los Angeles; stage exper., stk.; screen career, Vitagraph, Montgomery & Rock Co., Loane Tucker ("Miracle Man"). Hght., 5, 3; wght., 117; dark hair, brown eyes. Ad., Engstrum Apts., Los Angeles, Cal.

HYLAND, Peggy; b. near Worcestershire, England; educ. Belgium; stage career, in "The Yellow Jacket," and with Cyril Maude's co.; screen career, numerous prods. in England, Famous Players, Vitagraph (in support of E. H. Sothern in the first of his releases on the screen, "The Chattel"), Pathe, Fox ("Other Men's Daughters," "Marriages Are Made," "Bonnie Annie Laurie," "Rebellious Bride," "Merry-Go-Round," "Official Chaperone," "Girl in Bohemia"). Hght., 5, 1; wght., 120; brown hair, green eyes. Now with Samuelson Film Co.

— I —

ILLIAN, Isolde C.; b. Milwaukee, Wis., 1899; educ. Milwaukee Downer Seminary and Collegiate Centenary College, Hackettstown, N. J.; stage career, in stk. in Milwaukee from age of 5; screen career, Thanhouser ("The Mill on the Floss," "The Reunion," "The Crimson Sabre," "Harry's Happy Honeymoon," "Rusty Reggie's Record"), "The Man Hunt." Hght., 5; wght., 108; blond hair, dark blue eyes. Ad., home, 62 Vernon ave., Mt. Vernon, N. Y.

— J —

JANIS, Elsie; b. and educ. Columbus, Ohio; stage career, vaud., "Vanderbilt Cup," "Slim Princess," "The Lady of the Slipper," "Her Gang," 1919; screen career, Selznick ("A Regular Girl," "The Imp"). Hght., 5, 5½; wght., 120; brown hair and eyes. Home ad., Philipse Manor, Tarrytown, N. Y.; studio ad., Selznick Pict. Corp., 729 Seventh ave., N. Y.

JENNINGS, Jane; educ. Brooklyn and N. Y.; early career, teacher of dramatics; screen career, Vitagraph ("Lion and the Mouse," "The Gamblers," "Darkest Hour," "The Climbers," "Girl at Bay," "Out of the Dark"), Triangle ("Taxi," "Woman Under Oath"), American Cinema ("Women Men Forget"), Famous Players ("Lady Rose's Daughter," "The Cost"). Hght., 5, 6; wght., 140; white hair, dark brown eyes. Ad., 661 Prospect place, Brooklyn, N. Y.; Prospect 2270.

JENSEN, Eulalie; b. St. Louis, 1885; educ. Oxford Coll., O., Lorette Acad., St. Louis; stage career, with Bernhardt on tour in U. S.; stk in St. Louis and Chicago, appeared in comic operas, "The Time, the Place and the Girl," "Prince of Pilsen" in U. S. and London, with Maude Adams, vaud., rep.; screen career, Edison, Vitagraph ("Salvation Joan," "The Tarantula," "The Kid," "Mary Jane's Pa," "Tangled Lives," "Strength of the Weak," "Wild Primrose," "The Captain's Captain," "The Girl Problem," "Beating the Odds"), First National ("A Temperamental Wife").

JOHNSON, Edith; b. Rochester, N. Y., 1895; educ. Vassar Coll.; screen career, Lubin, Universal ("Behind the Lines," "The Scarlet Car," "For Love and Gold," "Giant Powder," "The Scarlet Crystal"), Selig ("The Franc Piece," "In the Talons of an Eagle"), Vitagraph ("Smashing Barriers," "Man of Might," serials with Wm. Duncan, "Love and Honor"). Hght., 5, 4; wght., 135; light hair, brown eyes. Ad., home, 1624 Hudson ave., Hollywood; studio, Vitagraph, Hollywood, Cal.

JONES, Jessie; b. Garden City, Kan., 1892; educ. Univ. of Kansas; early career, professional model; screen career, Essanay ("The Unknown," "Strange Case of Mary Page"), Selig "The Crisis," "History of Indiana"), Everett True Comedy Series; characters in "Do the Dead Talk?," Specialty Feature Films and "Within Our Gates," Micheau Films; leads, Superior Film Co. and Castle Film Co. Hght., 5, 6; wght., 128; auburn hair, green eyes. Studio ad., Castle Studios, 2332 N. California ave., Chicago, Ill.

JOY, Leatrice; b. New Orleans, La.; educ. Sacred Heart Acad., New Orleans, La.; stage career, 8 mos. in stk. in San Diego; screen career, Wm. Farnum ("A Man Hunter"), Selznick ("Just a Wife"), Geo. Loane Tucker ("Ladies Must Live"), Bert Lytell ("The Right of Way"), J. Warren Kerrigan ("A Dollar Bid"). Hght., 5, 3; wght., 125; black hair, brown eyes. Home ad., 1626 Vine st., Los Angeles, Cal.; phone 577979.

JOYCE, Alice; b. Kansas City, Mo., 1890; educ. Annandale, Va.; early career, telephone operator in the Gramercy exchange, N. Y. C.; screen career, Kalem, Vitagraph ("The Cambric Mask," "The Lion and the Mouse," "The Song of the Soul," "The Business of Life," "To the Highest Bidder," "The Strength of the Weak," "The Winchester Woman," "Everybody's Girl," "The Captain's Captain," "Third Degree," "Spark Divine," "The Vengeance of Durand," "The Sporting Duchess"). Hght., 5, 7; wght., 120; brown hair, hazel eyes. Ad., Vitagraph, Brooklyn, N. Y.

— K —

KANE, Gail; b. Phila., Pa.; educ. Mt. Mary's, Newburgh, N. Y.; stage career, with many prods., including "The Miracle Man," "The Hyphen"; screen career, All Star, Ariz., Metro, Pathe, World, Mutual ("The Serpent's Tooth," "The Woman in Black," "The Unafraid," "For the Family Name," "Souls in Pawn," "Southern Pride," "The Spectre of Suspicion," "The Bride's Silence," "A Game of Wits"), Graphic ("When Men Betray"), Mutual ("The Daredevil"), Photoplay Libraries ("Empty Arms"). Hght., 5, 7; wght., 142; dark brown hair and eyes. Office ad., 500 Fifth ave., N. Y.

KAYE, Frances Manila; b. Chicago, Ill., 1898; educ. N. Y. C.; stage exper., mus. com., "Rockabye Baby"; screen career, Famous Players ("The Make Believe Wife," "The Golden Bird," "Here Comes the Bride"), Paramount ("Little Miss Hoover," "Come Out of the Kitchen"). Hght., 5, 5; wght., 128; brown hair and eyes.

KEEFE, Zena Virginia; b. San Francisco, 1896; educ. in convent; stage career, vaud., rep. and on tour in "The Fatal Wedding"; screen career, Vitagraph, Ivan ("Enlighten Thy Daughter"), Arden Photoplays ("The Challenge Accepted"), Capellani-Pathe ("Oh, Boy"), Selznick ("Piccadilly Jim," "His Wife's Money," "The Woman That God Sent"). Hght., 5, 3; wght., 120; dark hair, brown eyes. Ad., 219 W. 81st st.; studio, c/o Selznick Pict. Corp., N. Y.

KELLERMANN, Annette; b. Sydney, New South Wales; early career, professional and exhibition swimming and diving in all the principal cities in Australia, England, France, Austria, Germany, U. S., holder of several world's records; stage career, as "Prince Arthur" in Shakespeare's "King John," later at London Hippodrome, on Keith and Orpheum circuits in U. S. with Shuberts; screen career, Universal ("Neptune's Daughter"), Fox ("A Daughter of the Gods," "Queen of the Sea"). Now under contract with Sol Lesser to appear in series of productions. Ad., 498 West End ave., N. Y., or 707 Oak st., South Pasadena, Calif.

KELSO, Mayme; b. Dayton, O.; educ. there and Cincinnati; stage exper., light opera, mus. com., vaud.; screen career, Paramount ("Old Wives for New"), Haworth ("His Birthright"), Lasky ("Men, Women and Money," "Daughter of the Wolf," "Peg o' My Heart," "Don't Change Your Wife," "Jack Straw"), American ("The Week End"), Hampton ("Simple Souls"), Metro ("The Hope"). Hght., 5, 6; wght., 145; blond hair, blue eyes. Ad., home, Stillwell Hotel, Los Angeles, Calif.

KENNEDY, Madge; b. Calif.; educ. there and Art Students' League, N. Y. C.; studied drama and played in amateur theatricals; stage career, Col. stk., Cleveland, 2 yrs., leading comedy role in "Overnight," featured in "Little Miss Brown," "Twin Beds," "Fair and Warmer"; screen career, Goldwyn ("Baby Mine," "Nearly Married," "Friend Husband," "The Kingdom of Youth," "Primrose," "Daughter of Mine," "Day Dreams," "Leave It to Susan," "Through the Wrong Door," "Strictly Confidential"); cartoonist, drew famous patriotic poster. Ad., Goldwyn, N. Y.

ACTRESSES

KENYON, Doris; b. Syracuse, N. Y., Sept. 5, 1897; educ. Packer Coll. Inst. and Columbia Univ.; stage career, in "Princess Pat"; screen career, Famous Players ("The Traveling Salesman"), Essanay ("On Trial"), Pathe ("The Hidden Hand"), Wharton ("The Great White Trail"), De Luxe Pict. ("Street of Seven Stars," "Twilight"), Dietrick-Beck ("The Band Box," "The Harvest Moon"). 1918 season, legitimate prod., "The Girl in the Limousine." Hght., 5, 6; wght., 125; light complexion, brown hair and gray eyes. Home ad., 850 West End ave., N. Y.

KERN, Cecil; b. Portland, Ore., 1892; educ. there and Chicago; stage career, "The Man of the Hour," original co. opp. Douglas Fairbanks, for 2 yrs., "Madame X" for 2 yrs. opp. Wm. Elliott, "Ben Hur," leads in stk.; screen career, Edison ("Girls I Know"), Vitagraph ("Gray Towers Mystery," "Fountain of Jewels"), McManus ("Bruised Humanity"). Hght., 5, 6; wght., 130; fair complexion, blond hair, blue eyes. Home ad., 1 W. 67th st., N. Y. C.

KING, Mollie; b. N. Y., 1898; educ. there; stage career, "Her Own Way," "The Royal Family," vaud., Winter Garden; 1918, Century Roof, "Good Morning, Judge"; screen career, World, Astra-Pathe ("Kick In," "The Double Cross," "Blind Man's Luck," "Seven Pearls," "On-the-Square Girl"), Screencraft ("Suspense"), American Cinema ("Greater Than Love," "Women Men Forget"). Wght., 115; blond hair, hazel eyes. Ad., Hotel Ansonia, N. Y. C.

KINGDON, Dorothy; b. Auburn, N. Y.; educ. N. Y.; stage career, in stock and road productions; screen career, Pathe, Metro ("Romeo and Juliet"), Famous, Ince ("The Belgian," "Her Family's Honor," "Out of the Depths"), Oriental Film Co., Ltd., of India "Sakuntala," featured lead with all Indian cast). Hght., 5, 6; wght, 130; golden brown hair, brown eyes. Ad., 22 Allamount Rd., Cumballa Hill, Bombay, India.

KINGSLEY, Florida; b. 1879, Jacksonville, Fla.; stage career, stk. prods.; screen career, Essanay, Metro ("The Turmoil"), Bluebird ("The Boy Girl"), Pathe ("The Iron Heart," "Mrs. Slacker"), United ("Woman Under Oath"), Selznick ("Love," "Independence, B'Gosh"), Hodkinson ("Made in America"). Hght., 5, 1; wght., 110; gray hair, blue eyes. Ad., 303 West 150th st., N. Y. C.

KINGSTON, Winifred; b. London, Eng.; educ. Scotland and Belgium; stage career, with Henry Miller, Joseph Gaites, Frohman, also stk.; screen career, Lasky, All-Star, Morosco, Fox, opp. Dustin Farnum in "David Garrick," "Davy Crockett," "The Virginian," "The Squaw Man," Farnum-United, "Light of Western Stars," "Corsican Brothers." Hght., 5; wght., 105; gray eyes, reddish hair, fair complexion. Home ad., 1862 Cherokee ave., Hollywood, Calif.; phone 57364.

KIRBY, Ollie; b. Phila.; educ. Bryn Mawr; stage career, vaud.; screen career, Favorite Players, Kalem ("The Tiger's Claws," "The Girl Detective," "Mysteries of the Grand Hotel," "Social Pirates," "Grant, Police Reporter," series). Hght., 5, 3; wght., 120; light hair, blue eyes. Ad., 125 W. 49th st., N. Y. C.; Circle 735.

KIRKHAM, Kathleen; b. Menominee, Mich., 1895; educ. Cummock School there; stage exper., stk. in Los Angeles, with Dustin Farnum in "Virginian," "Squaw Man"; screen career, Lew Cody ("The Beloved Cheater"), First National ("The Beauty Market"), Frank Keenan ("The Master Man"), Univ. ("For Husbands Only"), Artcraft ("Arizona," "He Comes Up Smiling"), Selznick ("Upstairs and Down"), Morosco ("The Third Kiss"). Hght., 5, 8; wght., 150; brown hair, blue eyes. Home ad., 1135 Delaware ave., Los Angeles, Calif.; phone 74802.

KITSON, May; educ. Boston and N. Y.; screen career, Famous Players ("Come Out of the Kitchen," "Firing Line"), World ("Woman of Lies"), "The Burning Question," Pathe ("The Thirteenth Chair"), Hallmark ("The Veiled Marriage"). Hght., 5, 6; wght, 138; gray hair, blue eyes. Ad., 27 W. 67th st., N. Y. C.; Col. 1123.

KNOTT, Lydia; b. 1873; stage career, vaud. stk., Harlem Opera House in "Mrs. Wiggs of the Cabbage Patch"; screen career, World, Ince-Triangle ("Sudden Jim," "The Clodhopper"), Ince-Paramount ("His Mother's Boy"), Universal ("Home," "The Pointing Finger"), Paramount ("Heart of Youth," "What Every Woman Learns"), First National ("In Wrong"), Metro ("Should a Woman Tell"). Hght., 5, 4.

KNOWLAND, Alice; b. Fort Fairfield, Me., 1879; educ. Boston; 10 yrs. legit. stage exper., Keith Stk. Co., "Mrs. Wiggs of the Cabbage Patch," Lew Fields, "The Girl Patsy," etc.; screen career, "Delicious Little Devil" with Mae Murray; Metro ("Satan, Jr."), Hampton ("Parish Priest"), Lasky ("Rustling a Bride"). Hght., 5, 6, wght. 139; gray hair and eyes. Home ad., 1345 Beachwood Dr., Hollywood, Calif.; Holly 1787.

—L—

LA FAYETTE, Ruby; b. July 22, 1844, Augusta, Ky.; educ. Gt. Western Fem. Seminary, Oxford, O.; stage career of fifty yrs., appeared as Lucretia Borgia, Ingomar, Lady Audley; screen career, Universal, playing mothers, in "The Dragnet," "Mother o' Mine," Metro ("In His Brother's Place"), Goldwyn ("Toby's Bow"). Hght., 5, 2; wght., 120; fair complexion, white hair, gray eyes. Ad., home, 680 S. Westlake ave., Universal City, Cal.

LAKE, Alice; b. Brooklyn, 1897; educ. there; stage career, amateur theatricals, pantomime and dancing; screen career, Vitagraph, Mack Sennett, Universal, Roscoe Arbuckle, Christie, Metro, Screen Classics ("Should a Woman Tell?" "Shore Acres"). Hght., 5, 2; wght., 106; light complexion, dark brown hair, brown eyes. Ad., Metro Studio, Hollywood, Calif.

LAMBERT, Dorothy; b. Brooklyn, N. Y.; stage career, understudy with E. H. Sothern, 4 seasons with Viola Allen, understudied "Martha" and "Mary Magdalene" in orig. prod. of "The Holy City," 2 yrs. in U. S. in "The Sign of the Cross," 2 yrs. in Gt. Britain, "Second to None," "Apple of Eden," "Driven From Home," "A Scrap of Paper"; screen career, Herkomer, Neptune, B. & C. Lucoque, Samuelson, Barker, Ideal British Actors. Hght., 5, 4; complexion fair, light brown hair, dark gray eyes. Ad., The Rehearsal Club, 29 Leicester Square, London, England.

LANDIS, Margaret Cullen; b. Nashville, 1896; educ. Ward Seminary; screen career, Balboa (as fancy dancer, "Who Pays"? "Joy and the Dragon," "The Checkmate," "The Martinache Marriage"), "The Confession," "The Parted Curtain," also with Fairbanks and Mary Pickford and other prods. Hght., 5 6½; wght., 123; blond hair, gray-blue eyes. Ad., Garden Court Apts., Los Angeles, Calif.; Holly 3420.

LANGDON, Lillian; b. New Jersey; stage career, comic opera, stk., rep.; screen career, Kalem, Biograph, Reliance-Majestic, Famous Players, Fine Arts ("Diane of the Follies," "Intolerance"), played in Triangle ("Prudence on Broadway," "A Regular Fellow"), Fox ("The Rebellious Bride"), Vitagraph ("The Usurper"), United Artists ("His Majesty, the American"), American ("The Hellion"); wrote, in collaboration, "The Higher Law" and other stage plays; picturized "The Price She Paid."

LARRIMORE, Francine; b. France; stage career, started seven yrs. ago, playing leads from the first, farce, mus. com. and high comedy; screen career, Metro ("Somewhere in America"), Edison ("Royal Pauper"), with Max Linder for Essanay, Fox ("Resurrection"), Gaumont ("Devil's Darling"). At present in "Scandal." Hght., 5, 1; red gold hair, dark blue eyes. Ad., 730 Riverside Drive, N. Y.

LA RUE, Fontaine; b. N. Y. C.; educ. Univ. and N. Y. Schl. of Dramatic Art; stage career, professional toe and Oriental dancing, stk. co. in Chicago, 2 yrs.; screen career, Paramount ("Boots," "Too Many Nieces," "His Precious Life," "Gypsy Joe"), Sennett-Keystone ("His First False Step," "Who Killed Walton?"), Universal ("Wild Cat of Paris," "Playing the Game"), with Sessue Hayakawa in "The Man Beneath," lead in "The White Rat," Paton serial. Hght., 5, 3½; wght., 130; black hair, dark brown eyes. Home ad., 1802 N. Van Ness, Hollywood, Calif.; phone 597623; and care of Willis & Inglis, Los Angeles.

LAUREL, Kay; b. Penn.; private school; stage career, Ziegfeld Follies for 3 seasons; screen career, Goldwyn, "The Brand," with Wally Reid in Famous Players-Lasky's "The Valley of the Giants" and Jack O'Brien's independent production, "Lonely Heart," in which she starred. Now has her own producing company. Hght., 5, 3; wght., 106; hair, light brown; eyes, blue. Ad., Hotel Manhattan, New York City.

LA VARNIE, Laura; b. and educ. Mo.; stage exper., 35 yrs., with Shubert, vaud., stk.; screen career, Biograph, Lasky ("Mickey"), Sennett-Paramount Comedies, Fox Sunshine Comedies ("The Yaller Dog Catcher," "Her First Kiss," and all Fox Sunshine comedies for last 6 mos.). Hght., 5, 4; wght., 150; dark hair and eyes. Ad., 2015 Sunset Blvd., Los Angeles, Calif.; Wilt. 2804.

LAWRENCE, Dakota; b. N. Y. C., 1902; educ. Wadleigh High, Art Students' League; screen career, co-star with John Lowell in Blazed Trail Prods., recent releases, "When Big Dan Rides," "The Hidden Pit," "Danger Patrol," "Across the Line," "Where Peril Lurks," "Code of the North." Hght., 5, 6½; chestnut hair, dark eyes. Ad., Blazed Trail Prods., care of Arrow Film Corp., N. Y. C.

LEDERER, Gretchen; b. Cologne, Germany; educ. Cologne Conservatory of Music; stage career, German musical stock; screen career, Universal ("The House of Gloom," "The Greater Law," "The Little Orphan," "The Rescue," "The Pointed Finger," "The Cruise of the Jolly Roger," "The Silent Lady," "Green Magic"), Universal ("Red, Red Heart," "Kaiser, the Beast of Berlin," "The Model's Confesson," "Kentucky Cinderella"), Triangle ("Wife or Country"). Hght., 5, 7; wght., 140; brown hair and eyes.

LEE, Alberta; b. Akron, O.; educ. Cleveland, O.; stage career, began at age 15, James H. Wallick's "Queens of the Highway," "The Clansman," "The Confession"; screen career, 3½ yrs. Fine Arts; then Triangle, Vitagraph, Mrs. Lincoln in "The Clansman," "Intolerance," "The Lily and the Rose"), Triangle ("Prudence on Broadway"), Vitagraph ("The Wishing Ring Man"), Tyrad ("The Red Viper"), Universal ("Rouge and Riches"). Hght., 5, 3; wght., 135; partially gray hair, dark eyes.

LEE, Carey; b. Louisville, Ky.; stage career, leading woman in stock, featured in vaud.; screen career, Pathe ("Iron Claw"), Reliance, Fox ("The Bondman," featured in "The Darling of Paris," "The Crimson Stain," and many others," author of "The Nigger," "The Bondman," "Samson," "A Gilded Fool"; Cosmopolitan Films, "The Miracle of Love." Hght., 5, 6; wght., 140; fair complexion, blond hair, blue eyes. Home ad., 1808 Marmion ave., N. Y. C.; Tremont 6581.

LEE, Carolyn; educ. Ward's Seminary, Nashville, Tenn.; stage career, many yrs., last 2 yrs. with "The Little Teacher," mngt. Cohan & Harris; screen career, Famous Players, Fox, Pathe, Thanhouser, World, "Anne of the Green Gables," "The Copperhead." Hght., 5, 6; wght., 118; dark hair and eyes. Ad., Actors' Equity, N. Y. C.

LEE, Dixie; educ. St. Francis De Sales Acad., Maysville, Ky.; stage career, Chas. Frohman, Shuberts, Winnipeg Stk. Co., Cal. Stk. Co., Ibsen "Ghosts," "Lavender and Old Lace" and other Bway. successes; 2 yrs. star in vaud.; screen career, Fischer ("The Law of Nature"), Waldorf ("Where Bonds Are Loosed," "Dad's Girl"). Hght., 5, 4½; wght., 120; brown hair, hazel eyes.

LEE, Jennie; b. Sacramento, 1859; stage career, began at 9 with John McCullough, Joseph Jefferson, Edwin Booth, Mme. Modjeska, in stk., vaud.; screen career, Reliance-Majestic, Fine Arts ("Birth of a Nation," "The Children Pay," "Nana, the Flower Girl"), Fox ("One Touch of Sin," "The Innocent Sinner"), Triangle ("Madame Bo-Peep"), Artcraft ("The Little Princess"), Lasky-Paramount ("The Clever Mrs. Carfax," "One Man in a Million"), Universal ("Riders of Vengeance," "Riders of the Law").

LEE, Lila; b. N. Y.; educ. private tutor; stage career, appeared at a very early age under mngt. of Gus Edwards, 10 yrs. in vaud.; screen career, Famous Players ("A Daughter of the Wolf," "Heart of Youth," "Male and Female," "Terror Island," "Hawthorne of the U. S. A."). Hght., 5, 3; wght., 110; black hair and eyes. Ad., Lasky Studio, Hollywood, Calif.

LEE, Virginia; b. Mexico; educ. St. Scholastica's Acad., Covington, La.; screen career, Fox ("Beyond the Law," "Sandy Burke," "Oh, Johnny," "The Whirlpool," "Luck and Pluck"), Southern Fea., Schenck ("Taking the Count"), First National ("A Woman of Two Worlds"). Hght., 5, 4½; wght., 130; fair complexion, blond hair, blue-gray eyes. Ad., home, 705 W. 170th st., N. Y.; St. Nich. 4020.

LEHR, Anna; b. N. Y. C.; educ. St. Catherine's Convent; stage exper., Bway plays; screen career, Triangle, Goldwyn, Fox ("For Freedom," "The Jungle Trail"), Triangle ("Upside Down"), World ("Home Wanted"), Rob-Cole ("The Open Door"), Hallmark ("The Veiled Marriage"). Hght., 5, 8; wght., 112; dark brown hair and eyes. Ad., Algonquin Hotel, N. Y.

LEIGHTON, Lillian Brown; b. Auroraville, Wis.; educ. Wis.; publisher country weekly paper, 12 yrs. legit. stage exper., mostly stk. and vaud.; screen career, 9 yrs., Lasky ("Joan the Woman," "Witchcraft," "Freckles"), Famous Players ("A Lady's Name," "Secret Service," "Louisiana," "All of a Sudden Peggy," "The Devil Stone"), Brentwood ("Poor Relations"). Hght., 5, 3½; wght., 150; dark hair and eyes. Ad., 1962 Cheremoya ave., Los Angeles, Calif.; Holly 429.

LESLIE, Gladys; b. N. Y. C., March 5, 1899; educ. Washington Irving High School and Columbia Univ.; screen career, Edison, Thanhouser, Vitagraph ("The Vicar of Wakefield," "The Beloved Imposter," "Fortune's Child," "Miss Dulcie of Dixie," "Stitch in Time," "Too Many Crooks," "The Girl Woman," "Mystery of Gray Towers," "Golden Showers," "Midnight Bride," "Elsie in New York"). Hght., 5; wght., 95; light hair and complexion, brown eyes. Home ad., 1252 E. 26th st., Brooklyn, N. Y.; Midwood 3915.

LESLIE, Lilie; b. 1892; stage career, stk. prods. Australia, "Experience," with Elliott, Comstock and Gest, Morosco, Belasco, in "The Boomerang"; screen career, 3 yrs., Fox, Lubin, Pathe, Metro ("The Silent Woman," "Man Who Stayed at Home," "Diana Ardway," "Johnny on the Spot," "Satan, Junior"), Universal ("Little Brother of the Rich"). Hght., 5, 5; wght., 135; complexion, fair; red gold hair, brown eyes.

LESLIE, Marguerite; b. Sweden; educ. Sweden and England; stage career, leads with Sir Charles Wyndham, Sir John Hare and in several other Chas. Frohman's London prods.; came to this country to play lead in "The Money Moon," Morosco; "The Secret" with Frances Starr, Belasco; screen career, Famous (in support of John Mason in "Jim the Penman"), World ("The Question"), Emory Film Corp. ("The Chosen Path"). Hght., 5, 8; wght., 146; fair complexion, auburn hair, blue eyes.

LESTER, Kate; b. England; educ. Normal Coll., N. Y.; stage career, with Richard Mansfield, Julia Marlowe, John Drew, Mrs. Fiske; screen career, Famous Players, Edison, World ("The Unbeliever," "Little Women"), Goldwyn ("A Man and His Money," "Heartsease," "Letty," "Bonds of Love," "Cup of Fury," "The Palliser Case," "Woman in Room 13"). Ad., 7131 Lenkill ave., Culver City, Calif.; phone 70150.

LESTER, Louise; b. Milwaukee, Wis.; educ. there; stage career, People's Stock, and Bush Temple, Chicago; screen career, Selig, American ("Calamity Ann," "Mother of the Ranch," "Repaid"), Allan Dwan in "Luck of the Irish." Hght., 5, 4; wght., 140; auburn hair, blue eyes. Ad., 2110 Hollister ave., Santa Barbara, Calif.

LEWIS, Eva; b. St. Louis, Mo.; educ. San Francisco, Cogswell's Coll.; stage career, Ye Liberty Stk. Co., Oakland, Calif., Central and National Stocks, leads for Blaney Attr., N. Y., vaud., Orpheum; screen career, Universal ("Riders of the Range," "Idle Wives," "Jacques of Yukon," "Mother of Mine"), Crescent ("Chosen Prince"), L-Ko ("Wayward Sons"), Francis Ford ("Man of Mystery" serial). Hght., 5, 5½; wght., 140; brown hair, gray eyes. Home ad., 416 Madison ave., Los Angeles, Calif.; Wilshire 5395.

LEWIS, Ida; b. England; educ. Montana; stage career, 30 yrs. in legit., appeared with elder Sothern, with many stk. cos. throughout West, in "Kindling," "East Lynne"; screen career, Horsley, Paralta ("A Man's Man"), Klotz & Streimer ("Whither Thou Goest?" "Patriotism," "Maid o' the Storm," "Heart of Rachael"), Rob-Cole ("Dangerous Waters"). Hght., 5, 5; wght., 160; blond hair, blue eyes. Ad., 147 N. Coronado, Los Angeles, Calif.; Wilshire 1681.

LEWIS, Katharine; b. Newark, N. J., 1899; educ. Manual Training Sch., Brooklyn; screen career, Vitagraph, 18 mos. ("Mr. Jack" series with Frank Daniels, "Walls of Convention," "Kennedy Square," "The Hawk," "The Soul Master"), First National ("Virtuous Wives"). Hght., 5, 6; wght., 120; blond hair, blue eyes.

LEWIS, Vera; b. N. Y.; educ. Normal Coll.; stage career, 1897, rep., vaud. and stk., mgmt. Frohman, Shubert, Belasco; screen career, Fine Arts ("Intolerance"), Fox, Paramount ("Lost in Transit"), Metro ("As the Sun Went Down"), Walthal ("A Still Small Voice," "The Lion and the Lamb"), with Mary Miles Minter in "Nurse Marjory," Madge Kennedy in "The Blooming Angel," Bert Lytell "Lombardi, Ltd.," Gladys

ACTRESSES

Brockwell, "The Devil's Riddle." Ad., home, 6267 Yucca ave., Los Angeles, Cal.

LINDEN, Margaret; b. Australia; educ. there; stage career, "Madam X," "The Fortune Hunter," "Sunday," "Stop Thief," "The Three Bears," "Head Over Heels," "Man Who Came Back"; screen career, World ("The Grouch"), Constance Talmadge ("The Virtuous Vamp"), Famous Players ("Wanted, A Husband," "His House in Order"). Hght., 5, 7½; wght., 142; brown hair, gray eyes. Ad., 236 W. 70th st., N. Y. C.; Columbus 9808 and 9930.

LINDROTH, Helen; educ. America; stage career, 15 yrs. legit.; screen career, Kalem ("From the Manger to the Cross"), Famous Players ("Audrey," "The Spider," "Little Lady Eileen," "Seventeen"), Metro ("The House of Gold," "The Great Romance," "Shadows of Suspicion"), Goldwyn ("The Eternal Magdalene"), McManus Corp. ("The Gray Brother"). Hght., 5, 7½; wght., 160; brown hair and eyes. Ad., 315 W. 51st st., N. Y. C.; Circle 6745.

LITTLE, Ann.; b. Sisson, Calif.; educ. Chicago and Los Angeles; stage career, stock in Los Angeles; screen career, Universal, American, Mutual, Selznick, Metro, Lasky ("Believe Me, Xantippe," "Less Than Kin," "The Squaw Man"), Famous Players ("Rimrock Jones," "Alias, Mike Moran," "The Roaring Road," "Told in the Hills," "The Bear Trap"), National ("Lightning Brice" serial), Hart-Artcraft ("Square Deal Sanderson," "Service Stripes"). Hght., 5, 5; wght., 112; black hair, brown eyes. Ad., Lasky Studio, Hollywood, Calif.; permanent ad., Rex Arms Apts., Orange st., Los Angeles, Calif.

LIVINGSTON, Marguerite; b. Salt Lake City, Utah; educ. there; screen career, Paralta ("Alimony," "Within the Cup"), Pathe ("All Wrong"), Ince ("The Busher," "What's Your Husband Doing?"), Goldwyn ("Billie's Fortune"), J. D. Hampton ("House of a Thousand Candles"). Hght., 5, 3; wght., 120; auburn hair, brown eyes. Ad., 144 So. Virgil, Los Angeles, Calif.; phone 52710; studio, J. D. Hampton Studio.

LORRAINE, Leota; b. Kansas City, Mo., 1893; educ. Univ. of Missouri at Columbia; screen career, Essanay 18 mos., Metro, Triangle, Ince-Para. ("Playing the Game," "The Kaiser's Shadow"), Goldwyn ("The Pest," "The Gay Lord Quex"), Fox ("Be a Little Sport"), Famous Players ("Luck in Pawn"), "The Loves of Letty," with Pauline Frederick, First National ("The Turning Point"). Hght., 5, 5½; wght., 125 blond hair, blue eyes. Home ad., 1765 N. Bronson ave., Los Angeles, Calif.; Holly 2444; studio, MacDonald Film Corp.

LORRAINE, Lillian; b. San Francisco, 1892; stage career; at age of 4 played Eva in "Uncle Tom's Cabin," later stk., "The Great White Way" with Blanche Ring, Ziegfeld Follies of 1909, starred in Follies of 1912; 1919 "Little Blue Devil"; screen career, Kalem, Triangle, Ince ("Playing the Game," "The Kaiser's Shadow"), Goldwyn ("The Pest").

LOVE, Bessie; b. Los Angeles, Cal.; educ. high schl. in Los Angeles; screen career, Triangle-Fine Arts ("A Sister of Six," "Intolerance," "The Heiress of Coffee Dan's," "The Doll's Shop," "Nina, the Flower Girl"), Ince-Triangle ("The Sawdust Ring," "Wee Lady Betty," "Pernickety Polly Ann," "The Dawn of Understanding," "The Enchanted Barn"). With Vitagraph for past year. Ad., home, Hollywood Apts., Hollywood, Calif.

LOVELY, Louise; b. Sydney, Australia, 1896; educ. Switzerland and Sydney; stage career, vaud., mus. com., in Australia, in vaud. for 2½ yrs.; screen career, with Australian Biograph Co., Universal-Bluebird ("Wolves of the North"), Fox ("The Man of Power"), Vitagraph ("The Usurper"), Fox-Farnum ("The Lone Star Ranger," "The Last of the Duanes," "Wolves of the Night," "Wings of the Morning"), Metro ("Johnny on the Spot"), Rob-Cole ("The Butterfly Man"). Hght., 5, 2; wght., 128; fair hair, blue-gray eyes. Ad., home, 1746 Wilcox ave., Hollywood.

LUTHER, Anne; b. Newark, N. J., 1894; screen career, Reliance, Lubin, Selig, Keystone, Fox ("Her Father's Station" "The Island of Destiny"), Ivan ("Moral Suicide"), Triangle ("The Marriage Bubble"), General ("Her Moment"), Pathe ("The Great Gamble"), Fox ("Woman, Woman," "The Jungle Trail"), Western Photoplays, Inc., co-star with Chas. Hutchinson, also Wisteria Prods., Inc. Hght., 5, 5; wght., 129; titian hair, blue eyes.

LYNARD, Lenore; b. Philadelphia; educ. Drexel Inst.; screen career, Jack Pickford ("Burglar by Proxy"), Madlaine Traverse ("What Would You Do"), Geraldine Farrar ("Flame of the Desert"), Goldwyn ("Dangerous Days"), Vitagraph ("The Wolf"). Hght., 5, 6; wght., 130; blond hair, blue eyes. Home ad., Alvarado Apts., Los Angeles, Calif.; Wilshire 5010; studio, Samuelson Films, Universal City, Cal.

LYNNE, Ethel; b. 1896, Longview, Tex.; educ. Carr-Burdette Coll., Sherman, Tex.; stage career, in "Tic Toc Man of Ox," musical comedy; screen career, Universal, Christie ("Local Color," "Nearly a Papa," "Help, Help, Police!" "Are Second Marriages Happy?" "War Gardens," "Efficiency"), Ince-Para. ("Biggest Show on Earth," "He Who Hesitates," "Lobster Dressing," "Reno, All Change"). Hght., 5, 5; wght., 118; brown hair and eyes. Ad., home, 408B S. Alvarado st., Los Angeles, Calif.; phone 44215.

— M —

MacCLEAN, Grace; b. Detroit, Mich.; educ. there; stage career, 7 yrs. permanent stock and prods.; screen career, Ince ("Let's Be Fashionable"), Fox ("Sergeant Tim"), Universal ("Elmo the Mighty," "Blind Husbands"). Hght., 5, 4½; wght., 128; brown hair, dark blue eyes. Home ad., 6511½ Hollywood Blvd., Los Angeles, Cal.; phone 577330 or 577333.

MacDONALD, Katherine Agnew; b. Pittsburgh, Pa.; educ. Blairsville Coll.; screen career, Artcraft, Paramount, Betzwood ("Headin' South," "Shark Monroe," "Riddle Gawne," "Mr. Fixit," "Battling Jane," "Squaw Man," "The Woman Thou Gavest Me"). First National ("The Thunderbolt," "The Beauty Market" "The Turning Point," "The Guest of Hercules," "The Notorious Miss Lisle"). Hght., 5, 8; wght., 134; blond hair, blue eyes. Ad., MacDonald Film Corp., 904 Girard st., Los Angeles, Cal.

MAC LAREN, Mary MacDonald; b. Pittsburgh, Pa.; educ. Greensburg, Pa.; stage career, Winter Garden, N. Y. C., "Passing Show of 1914," "Dancing Around"; screen career, Universal ("Idle Wives," "The Model's Confession," "Vanity Pool," "Bread," "Shoes," "Saving a Family Name," "Petal on the Current," "Unpainted Woman," "Bonnie, Bonnie Lassie," "Rouge and Riches"). Hght., 5, 3; wght., 124; blond hair, blue eyes. Home ad., 127 No. Manhattan Place, Los Angeles, Cal.; phone 560850; studio, Universal.

MADDEN, Golda; b. Denver, 1894; educ. Univ. of Colo.; stage career, stk., William Collier; screen career, Biograph, Lubin, Pathe, Keystone, National, ("Girl of My Dreams"), Brentwood ("Turn in the Road"), Universal ("Fires of Rebellion"), Goldwyn ("Woman in Room 13"), Triangle ("Flying Colors"), American ("Jilted Janet"). Hght., 5, 6; wght., 125; light complexion, blond hair, dark blue eyes. Ad., 1606 McCadden Place, Los Angeles, Cal.

MADISON, Cleo; b. Bloomington, Ill.; educ. Bloomington Normal Univ.; stage career, with James K. Hackett, Virginia Harned, in vaud. on Orpheum circuit, toured with own co.; screen career, Universal, first success in "Trey of Hearts," has headed own co. and directed own prods. for a time ("The Chalice of Sorrow," "Retribution," "Black Orchids," "The Chastening"), Universal ("The Girl Who Lost," "The Web"), National ("Romance of Tarzan," "Girl From Nowhere"). Hght., 5, 2; wght., 125; blue eyes, medium hair with reddish tinge. Ad., 1525 No. Bronson, Los Angeles, Cal.

MALONE, Molly; b. Denver, Colo., 1897; educ. Denver and Los Angeles; screen career, Vitagraph, Lubin, Lasky, Universal ("The Pullman Mystery," "The Range War," "The Marked Man," "Hawaiian Knights," "The Red Stain," "The Scarlet Drop," "A Woman's Fool," "Matching Billy," "Birds of a Feather"), Arbuckle-Para. ("The Desert Hero," "Back Stage," "The Hayseed," "The Garage"), Supreme Comedies ("Molly's Millions," "Molly's Mumps," "Come in the Kitchen," "Her Doctor's Dilemma"). Home ad., 6621 St. Francis Court, Hollywood, Cal.

MANN, Alice; b. Plainfield, N. J., 1900; educ. Boston Girls' Latin Schl.; screen career, Fox ("Help, Help, Police!"), Essanay ("Pair of Sixes"), McClure ("The Yellow Eel"). Hght., 5, 4; wght., 118; light golden hair, blue eyes. Ad., home, 455 Ft. Washington ave., N. Y.; St. Nich. 8812.

MANN, Frankie; b. Mill Hall, Pa., 1892; educ. Boston Girls' Latin Sch.; stage career, 2 yrs. in stk., Orpheum, Phila.; screen career, Lubin, Vitagraph ("Youth"), Pathe ("Ravengar"), Ivan ("The Sex Lure"), A. F. Beck, "The Isle of Jewels. Hght., 5, 4; wght., 120; dark brown hair, brown eyes. Ad., home, 455 Ft. Washington ave., N. Y.; St. Nicholas 8812.

MANNING, Marjorie; stage career, stk. co., and with Oliver Morosco; screen career, Famous Players ("His House in Order," "The Cost," "Miss Antique"), Hess-Ives ("Dismal Swamp"). Hght., 5, 7½; wght., 140; blond hair, blue eyes. Ad., Hotel Grenoble, N. Y.; Circle 909.

MANNING, Mildred; stage career, musical comedy, in Broadway prods. for 8 yrs.; screen career, Biograph ("Charity Ball," "Our Poor Relations," etc.), Vitagraph ("Mary Jane's Pa," "The Princess of Park Row," "Next Door to Nancy," "An Investment in Petticoats"), Hampton-Hodkinson ("The Westerners"), Rob-Cole ("Kitty Kelly, M.D."). Hght., 5, 4; wght., 120; brown hair and eyes, olive complexion.

MANON, Marcia; screen career, Paramount ("Maggie Pepper," "The Test of Honor," "The Lottery Man"), Rob-Cole ("Woman Michael Married"), First National ("In Old Kentucky").

MANSFIELD, Martha; b. Mansfield, O., 1899; educ. there; stage career, Winter Garden, "Century Girl" (Dillingham & Ziegfeld), A. H. Woods' "On With the Dance"; screen career, Essanay (Max Linder comedies), played opposite Montague Love and Eugene O'Brien, played in "Mothers of Men"; opposite John Barrymore in "Dr. Jekyll and Mr. Hyde." Hght., 5, 4; wght., 122; blond hair, gray eyes. Ad., 545 W. 158th st., N. Y. C.

MARCEL, Inez; b. 1899; stage career, stk. prods., with Klaw and Erlanger, Chas. Frohman; screen career, Hobart Henley Prod. ("Gay Old Dog"), Gaumont ("Making Her His Wife"), Catholic Arts Assn. ("The Burning Question," "The Transgression," "The Victim"), Curtis ("Who Is Your Brother?"). Hght., 5, 7; complexion, light. Ad., 174 W. 109th st., N. Y.; Academy 365.

MARINOFF, Fania; b. Odessa, Russia; stage career, "The House Next Door," "Romance of the Underworld," "Within the Law," Arnold Daly's revival of Shaw's "Arms and the Man," Ariel in the tercentenary performance of Shakespeare's "The Tempest," "Karen," "Awakening of Spring," "The Walk-Offs"; screen career, Famous Players ("One of Our Girls"), Kleine ("The Money Master"), Pathe ("Nedra"), World ("Life's Whirlpool"), Artcraft ("Rise of Jennie Cushing"). Black hair and eyes. Home ad., 151 E. 19th st., N. Y. C.

MARKEY, Enid; b. Dillon, Colo., 1896; educ. Denver; stage careeer, Burbank stock, with Nat Goodwin, 1919 Al Woods, "Up in Mabel's Room"; screen career, Ince ("Civilization," "The Devil's Double"), Fox ("The Yankee Way," "Responsibility"), Corona ("The Curse of Eve"), National ("Tarzan of the Apes," "Romance of Tarzan"), Shipman ("Mother, I Need You"). Hght., 5, 4; wght., 125; dark hair, dark eyes. Ad., 245 W. 51st st., N. Y. C., and Eltinge theatre.

MARSH, Mae; b. Madrid, New Mexico, 1897; educ. convents in San Francisco; screen career, Biograph, Reliance-Majestic ("The Birth of a Nation"), Fine Arts ("Intolerance"), Goldwyn ("Polly of the Circus," "The Cinderella Man," "Sunshine Alley," "Fields of Honor," "The Beloved Traitor," "The Face in the Dark," "The Glorious Adventure," "All Woman," "Hidden Fires," "Money Mad," "Spotlight Sadie"). Hght., 5, 3; gray eyes, auburn hair. Ad., mngt. Louis J. Gasnier, Rob-Cole release.

MARSH, Marguerite O.; b. Lawrence, Kansas, 1892; educ. San Francisco and Los Angeles; stage career, two seasons with Raymond Hitchcock; Morosco stock in Los Angeles; screen career, Biograph under Griffith, Essanay, Reliance, Fine Arts ("Mr. Goode, the Samaritan"), Triangle, Goldwyn, Rolfe ("The Master Mystery"), Oliver ("Craig Kennedy" serial), Hallmark ("Phantom Honeymoon"), Fox, Stanton serial. Hght., 5, 2; wght., 120; auburn hair, dark blue eyes, fair complexion. Ad., Hotel Monterey, N. Y. C.

MARSTINI, Rosita; b. France, Sept. 19, 1887; educ. Belgium; screen career, Universal ("The Heart of a Tigress," "On the Trail of the Tigress," "Graft), Fox ("A Tale of Two Cities," "The Innocent Sinner," "Flames of the Flesh"), Lasky-Paramount ("The Clever Mrs. Carfax," "Widow by Proxy." Hght., 5, 6½; wght., 147; light complexion, dark brown hair, dark brown eyes. Home ad., Windsor Apts., Los Angeles, Cal. Now in Belgium.

MARTIN, Florence Evelyn; educ. San Francisco, Cal.; stage career, 3 yrs. with Oliver Morosco prods. playing leads, also one season with Geo. Tyler, playing lead; screen career, Guy Empey Co. ("The Undercurent"). Hght., 5, 3½; wght., 120; dark brown hair, blue eyes. Ad., 208 W. 56th st., N. Y.; Circle 2121.

MARTIN, Vivian; b. near Gr. Rapids, Mich.; stage career, with Richard Mansfield in "Cyrano de Bergerac," in "Officer 666," "Stop Thief," "The Only Son"; screen career, World Film, Fox ("A Modern Thelma"), Morosco-Pallas ("Her Father's Son," "Right Direction," "The Wax Model," "Forbidden Paths," "Little Miss Optimist," "Molly Shawn," "A Kiss for Susie," "The Sunset Trail," "The Trouble Buster," "Mary Gusta," "Molly Entangled"), Para. ("Unclaimed Goods," "Her Country First," "Littlest Scrub Lady," "Mirandy Smiles," "Home Town Girl," "Little Comrade," "Louisiana," "Third Kiss," "His Official Wife"), Gaumont ("Husbands and Wives").

MASON, Shirley; b. Brooklyn, N. Y., 1901; educ. private tutors; stage career, created part of Little Hal in "The Squaw Man," with Wm. Favorsham at the age of 4, "Rip Van Winkle," "Passers-By," also "The Poor Little Rich Girl," etc.; screen career, K. E. S. E. ("Cy Whittaker's Ward"), Edison ("The Apple Tree Girl," "The Wall Invisible"), Famous Players ("Come On In," "Good-Bye Bill," "Gosh Darn the Kaiser"), Paramount ("The Rescuing Angel," "The Final Close-Up," "The Winning Girl"), Fox ("Her Elephant Man"). Hght., 5; wght., 94; brown hair, light gray eyes. Home ad., 1770 Grand Concourse, N. Y. C.; studio, Fox, Los Angeles, Cal.

MATTOX, Martha; b. Natchez, Miss.; educ. East Miss. Coll.; stage career, several years in rep., stk. and prod., playing characters and heavies; screen career, Selig ("Chronicles of Bloom Center"), Universal ("Scarlet Shadow," "Polly Put the Kettle On"), Famous Players ("Huckleberry Finn"), American ("Eve in Exile"), Metro ("Old Lady 31"). Hght., 5, 7; wght., 164; dark brown hair and eyes. Home ad., 2007 Sunset, Los Angeles, Cal.; Wilshire 6851.

MAY, Ann; b. Cincinnati, Ohio, 1901; educ. St. Ursula Acad., grad. Schuster-Martin School of Dramatic Art, 1916, 1 yr. at Little Playhouse, Cincinnati; screen career, Keeney Pict. Corp., Goldwyn, Famous Players, ingenue lead in "A Marriage for Convenience"), Metro ("Lombardi, Ltd."), Univ. ("A Lovely Night"), Ince-Para., opp. Chas. Ray, "Paris Green." Hght., 5, 2½; wght., 103; black hair, brown eyes. Ad., care of Motion Picture News, N. Y. C.

MAY, Doris; b. Seattle, Wash.; educ. French Convent, Seattle; screen career, doubled for Mary Pickford in "The Little American"; Thos. H. Ince, "The Hired Man," "Playing the Game," in "23½ Hours Leave," "What's Your Husband Doing?" "Mary's Ankle," "Let's Be Fashionable," "Green Eyes" (co-star with Douglas MacLean). Hght., 5, 2; wght., 117; golden hair, brown eyes. Ad., Thos. H. Ince Studio, Culver City, Cal.

MAYO, Christine; stage career, in "Excuse Me," "Seven Keys to Baldpate," vaud., stk.; screen career, Metro ("Spell of the Yukon," "Iron Woman," "Fair and Warmer"), Master Drama ("Raffles," with John Barrymore), Metro ("House of Mirth"), World ("The Little Intruder"), Hampton ("A Fugitive from Matrimony"), Goldwyn ("Duds," "Mother's Confession," "A Fool's Paradise," "Two Men and a Woman"); specializes in vampire and emotional leads. Hght., 5, 7; wght., 135; dark hair and eyes. Ad., 1803C Highland, Hollywood, Cal.; home ad., 559 W. 164th st., N. Y.; Aud. 5664.

MAYO, Edna; b. Philadelphia, Pa., 1893; educ. Girls' Coll., Philadelphia; stage career, starred in "Madame X," "Excuse Me," "Help Wanted"; screen career, Essanay since 1915 ("The Woman Hater," "The Little Straw Wife," "The Misleading Lady," "The Strange Case of Mary Page," "The Return of Eve," "The Chaperon"), American ("Hearts of Love"). Hght., 5, 3; wght., 115; fair complexion, light hair, blue eyes.

McAVOY, May; b. N. Y., 1901; educ. N. Y.; screen career, Goldwyn ("Perfect Lady"), United ("Woman Under Oath"), Famous Players ("Mrs. Wiggs of the Cabbage Patch"), World ("Hit or Miss"), H. & H. ("Love Wins"), Blackton ("My Husband's Other Wife"), Vita-

ACTRESSES

graph ("Sporting Duchess"). Hght., 4, 11; wght., 94; dark hair, blue eyes. Ad., home, 217 W. 106th st., N. Y. C.; Acad. 1299.

McCONNELL, Mollie; b. Chicago, 1870; stage career, first with Mrs. Leslie Carter in "Spanish Guide," with Mansfield 2 yrs. in "Old Heidelberg," in England and on Continent with Marie Tempest, Pauline Chase; screen career, with Universal and Balboa in character and grande dame parts, Balboa-Mutual ("Glad Glory"), Ince-Para. ("The Claws of the Hun"), Metro ("The Demon," "No Man's Land," "Fools and Their Money"), Universal ("Bare Fists"), Fox ("Cheating Herself," "The Feud"), Paramount ("His Official Fiancee," "Red Hot Dollars").

McCOY, Gertrude; b. Rome, Ga., 1896; educ. Nassau, Tenn.; stage career, stk. and mus. com., "The Two Orphans"; screen career, 8 yrs. Biograph under Griffith, Pathe, Edison ("Through Turbulent Waters," "On the Stroke of Twelve," "What Could She Do?" "June Friday," "Friend Wilson's Daughter"), Gaumont ("The Isle of Love"), Van Dyke ("The Lash of Destiny"), Authors Film Co.-Mutual ("The Silent Witness," "Madame Sherry"), Artcraft ("The Danger Mark"). Hght., 5, 6½; wght., 135; blond hair, blue-green eyes.

McDOWELL, Claire; b. N. Y.; educ. N. Y.; stage career since babyhood, in "The Clansman," has acted with Faversham, Julie Opp, Marie Dressler; screen career, with Biograph for over 5 yrs., Universal ("The Gates of Doom," "The Storm Woman"), Triangle ("The Strange Weakling," "Everlasting Mercy," "Fighting Back," "The Ship of Doom," "The Follies Girl"), Fox ("Chasing Rainbows," "The Feud"), First National ("Heart o' the Hills"). Hght., 5, 4; wght., 115; brown hair and eyes. Ad., home, Highland ave., Hollywood Park, Hollywood.

McGOWAN, Roxana; b. March 15, 1899, Chicago, Ill., educ. Chicago and Houston, Tex.; screen career, Sennett ("Villa of the Movies," "Her Nature Dance," "A Bedroom Blunder," "Love Loops the Loop," "Summer Girls," "Her Screen Iidol"). On road for 7 mos. with "Yankee Doodle in Berlin" Co. Hght., 5, 4; wght, 120; light complexion, brown hair, gray eyes. Ad., home, 1020 W. 75th St., Los Angeles, Cal.

McQUADE, Mabel; b. Kokomo, Ind., 1897; educ. Darlington Seminary; stage career, dancing; screen career, Vitagraph, Goldwyn, Virginia Pearson Co. ("Impossible Catherine"). Hght. 5, 5; wght., 131; light complexion, blond hair, dark blue eyes. Ad. 126 23rd St., Elmhurst, L. I., N. Y. Newtown 2550.

MERSEREAU, Violet; b. and educ. N. Y.; stage career, child parts in stock, tonred with Margaret Anglin, played Flora in orig. co. of "The Clansman," starred on road as Rebecca in "Rebecca of Sunnybrook Farm"; screen career, Famous Players, Universal ("Little Miss Nobody," "The Girl by the Roadside, "Princess Tatters," "The Wild Cat," "The Raggedy Queen, "Souls United," "Together"); Bluebird ("The Nature Girl"). Hght., 5, 4; wght., 115; blond hair, dark blue eyes. Home ad., Hotel Monterey, N. Y. C.

MIDGLEY, Fannie; b. Cincinnati; stage career, from age of 15, with Henry Miller in "The Great Divide"; screen career, Melies, Biograph, Ince ("The Waifs," "The Apostle of Vengeance," "Civilization," "The Man from Oregon," "Somewhere in France," "Jim Grimsby's Boy"), Paramount ("The Heart of Youth," "The Lottery Man"), United ("The Corsican Brothers").

MILHOLLAND, Helen; b. Kingston, N. Y.; educ. Canada and Paris, France; stage career, stk.; "Why Marry," Selwyn; vaud.; screen career, World Metro, ("The Soul Market"), Famous Players ("The Long Trail"), Creative ("Girl Who Didn't Think"), Arnold Daly ("My Own United States"). Hght., 5; wght., 110; light complexion, brown hair, gray eyes. Home ad., 29 W. 61st St., N. Y. Columbus 8213.

MILTON, Marjorie; educ. Wadleigh High Sch., N. Y.; early career, receptionist in photographic studio; screen career, Vitagraph ("A Woman at Bay"), Pathe ("The Black Secret"), Constance Talmadge ("In Search of a Sinner"). Hght., 5, 8; wght., 140; light brown hair, dark gray eyes. Ad., 15 W. 88th st., N. Y. C., Riverside 7947.

MINEAU, Charlotte; b. Bordeaux, France; educ. Convent de L'Assumption, Louisville, Canada; screen career, Essanay (Geo. Ade Fables, Sweedy Series), 1917, in stk. with Chaplin. Pathe ("Rosemary Climbs the Heights" with Mary Miles Minter, "Carolyn of the Corners" with Bessie Love. Hght., 5, 10; wght., 160; auburn hair, violet eyes. Home ad., Gates Hotel, Los Angeles, Calif.; Bway 826; studio, Mack Sennett.

MINTER, Mary Miles; b. Shreveport, La., April 1, 1902; educ. by private tutors; stage career, child actress supporting Nat Goodwin, Robert Hilliard, Mrs. Fiske, Bertha Kalich, Dustin Farnum, for 4 yrs. appeared in title role in "The Littlest Rebel"; screen career, Metro, American, American-Pathe ("The Eyes of Julia Deep," "Wives and Other Wives," "The Amazing Impostor," "A Bachelor's Wife," "Yvonne from Paris"), American ("Intrusion of Isabel"), Realart ("Anne of Green Gables," "Judy of Rogue's Harbor"). Hght., 5, 2; wght., 112; golden hair, blue eyes. Ad., Realart Pict. Corp., N. Y. Home ad., 56 Fremont place, Los Angeles, Calif.

MITCHELL, Rhea; b. Portland, Oreg.; educ. there; stage career, on Orpheum circuit, stk. at Alcazar, San Francisco; screen career, Lasky ("The Goat"), Metro ("Unexpected Places"), William S. Hart ("The Money Corral"), Burston ("The Hawk's Trail"). Hght., 5, 2; wght., 110; blond hair, dark blue eyes. Home ad., 1742 Northwestern ave., Hollywood, Calif.; phone 599969.

MITCHELL, Yvette; b. San Francisco; educ. Los Angeles; stage career, Orpheum dancing act, "So Long Letty"; screen career, Universal ("The Red Ace," "Flower of Doom," "The Door Between," "Virgin of Stamboul," "The Petal on the Current," "The Wicked Darling"), Mitchell Lewis Prod. ("Last of His People"), Dustin Farnum ("Honor of His Family"), Mayer Prod. Co. ("The Inferior Sex"). Hght., 5, 2; wght., 112; black hair, hazel eyes. Home ad., 6049 Selma ave., Los Angeles, Calif. Holly 348.

MONTROSE, Helene; b. San Francisco; educ. there and Paris; stage career, with Francis Wilson, Frohman Co., operatic exper. in France and Italy; screen career, Famous Players ("Career of Katherine Bush," "Sadie Love," "Counterfeit"), Selznick ("The Country Cousin"), Jose Prod. ("Mothers of Men"). Hght., 5, 6; wght., 135; black hair and dark brown eyes. Ad., Great Northern Hotel, 118 W. 57th St., N. Y.

MOORE, Colleen; b. 1900, Port Huron, Mich.; educ. Convent of Holy Name, Tampa, Fla.; screen career, Triangle, Fine Arts, Ince, Selig (featured in "Little Orphant Annie," "A Hoosier Romance"), Paramount ("The Busher," "The Egg-Crate Wallop"), Fox ("The Wilderness Trail"), Universal ("Common Property," "The Man in the Moonlight"), Christie Comedies (featured in "A Roman Scandal," "Her Bridal Night-Mare"). Hght., 5, 3; wght., 110; brown hair and eyes. Ad., c/o Christie Film Co., Los Angeles, Calif.

MORNE, Maryland; b. England; educ. Convent in Chicago; stage career, "Alice in Wonderland" when 7 yrs. old, Adean stk. in St. Louis; screen career, Allan Dwan ("In the Heart of a Fool"). Hght., 5, 5; wght., 130; blond hair, blue eyes. Home ad., 4736 Franklin ave., Los Angeles, Calif.; Holly 531.

MORRISON, Mrs. Priestly; educ. Missouri State Univ.; stage career, stk. in N. Y. C., Cleveland, Kansas City, Des Moines, Iowa, Los Angeles, etc., covering period of 25 yrs.; screen career, Famous ("Uncle Tom's Cabin," "Misleading Widow," "Wanted, A Husband"), World ("The Steel King," "The Praise Agent"). Hght., 5, 6; wght., 130; brown hair, gray eyes. Ad., 2059 Davidson ave., N. Y. Fordham 533 and 1520.

MOSQUINI, Marie; b. Los Angeles, Calif., 1899; educ. Immaculate Heart Convent; screen career, Rolin Film Co. ("It's a Hard Life"), Harry Pollard Comedies ("Looking for Trouble," "Floor Below"), Harold Lloyd comedies ("His Royal Shyness"). Hght., 5, 4; wght., 125; olive complexion, brown hair, hazel eyes. Home ad., 921 Bernal st., Los Angeles, Calif.; Boyle 3498.

MURRAY, Mae; stage career, mus. com.; screen career, Lasky-Paramount ("To Have and to Hold," "The Dream Girl"), Famous Players ("The Primrose Ring"), Universal ("Princess Virtue," "Face Value"), Lasky ("A Mormon Maid"), Universal ("The Bride's Awakening," "The Scarlet Stain," "What Am I Bid?" "Delicious Little Devil," "Modern Love"), Pathe ("Twin Pawns," "A, B, C of Love"), Paramount-Artcraft ("On With the Dance"). Ad., Famous Players, 485 Fifth ave., N. Y. C.

MYERS, Carmel; b. San Francisco, April 9, 1901; educ. Los Angeles; screen career, Fine Arts, Metro (opposite Harold Lockwood in "The Haunted Pajamas"), Universal ('Sirens of the Sea"), Bluebird ("The Dream Lady," "A Society Sensation"), Universal ("My Unmarried Wife," "Who Will Marry Me?" "The Litttle White Savage." Now playing in "The Magic Melody" at Shubert Theatre.

— N —

NAZIMOVA, Alla; b. Yalta, Crimea, Russia; educ. Zurich, Odessa and dramatic sch. at Moscow; stage career, stock in Kerson, Vilna and Petrograd; first appeared in N. Y. in 1906, presenting "Hedda Gabler," "A Doll's House," "The Master Builder," etc.; screen career, Brenton-Selznick ("War Brides"), Metro ("Revelation," "Toys of Fate," "Eye for Eye," "Out of the Fog," "The Red Lantern," "The Brat," "Stronger Than Death"). Height 5, 3; wght., 116; black hair, violet eyes. Ad., Metro, Hollywood, Calif.

NESBIT, Evelyn; b. Tarentum, Pa.; educ. Shakespeare School at Pittsburgh and private tutors; stage career, 4 yrs. vaud., in Follies, Marigny theatre, Paris; London Hippodrome; screen career, Jos. Schenck ("Her Mistake," "Redemption"), Fox ("The Woman Who Gave," "I Want to Forget," "Thou Shalt Not," "Judge Not," "A Fallen Idol," "My Little Sister," "Woman, Woman"). Hght., 5, 3½; wght., 122; brown hair, hazel eyes. Ad., 201 W. 54th st., N. Y. C.

NIGHTINGALE, Virginia; b. in Vienna of English and French parentage; educ. Los Angeles, San Francisco, Santa Barbara; screen career, 2 yrs. with Mack Sennett, one of the orig. beauties with Mack Sennett studio, Vitagraph ("The Miracle Afternoon" with William Duncan). Hght., 5, 7; wght., 140; black hair, light blue eyes. Home ad., 1308 S. Hill st., Los Angeles, Calif.; phone 60733.

NILSSON, Anna Q.; b. Ystad, Sweden; educ. Sweden; stage career, in Sweden and America; screen career, Famous Players, Goldwyn, Metro ("In Judgment of," "Way of the Strong," "No Man's Land"), Mayflower ("Soldiers of Fortune," "Luck of the Irish," "In the Heart of a Fool"). Hght., 5, 7; wght., 135; fair complexion, blond hair, blue eyes. Home ad., 1901 Wilcox av., Hollywood, Calif.; Holly 3634.

NORMAND, Mabel; b. Boston, Mass.; screen career, Vitagraph, Biograph, Keystone (starred in "Fatty and Mabel," "Mabel's Busy Day," "Fatty and Mabel Adrift," "He Did and He Didn't," "The Bright Lights," etc.), headed Mabel Normand Feature Film Co., star in "Pat," "Mickey," "Mickey Gets Ready," etc., Goldwyn ("Joan of Plattsburgh," "Dodging a Million," "The Venus Model," "Back to the Woods," "Peck's Bad Girl," "A Perfect 36," "Sis Hopkins," "The Pest," "When Doctors Disagree," "Upstairs," "Jinks," "Pinto"). Dark hair and brown eyes. Ad., Goldwyn, Culver City, Cal.

NOVA, Hedda; b. Odessa, Russia; educ. there, Petrograd, Berlin; screen career, Edgar Lewis ("Bar Sinister," "The Barrier"), Vitagraph ("Woman in the Web" serial), Universal ("Spitfire of Seville"), Goldwyn ("The Crimson Gardenia"), Katherine MacDonald ("The Turning Point"), Selig ("The Mask"). Hght., 5, 6; wght., 130; dark hair, brown eyes. Ad., Selig Studio, Los Angeles, Calif.

NOVAK, Jane; b. St. Louis, Mo.; educ. Notre Dame Convent; stage career, vaud., mus. com. stk. 2 yrs.; screen career, Clune Prod. ("Eyes of the World"), Wm. S. Hart ("The Tiger Man," "Selfish Yates"), Ince ("Nine O'clock Town," "String Beans," "Wagon Tracks"), Haworth ("The Temple of Dusk"), Rob-Cole ("His Debt"), Marshall Neilan ("The River's End"). Hght., 5, 7; wght., 135; blond hair, blue eyes. Home ad., 6629½ Hollywood blvd., Los Angeles, Calif.; phone 577769.

NUILLE, Ida; b. Boston, Mass.; stage career, 20 yrs. with all leading productions, under Comstock & Gest in "Chin Chin Chow" for 2 yrs.; screen career, with Norma and Constance Talmadge. Hght., 5; wght., 130; brown hair, blue eyes. Ad., St. Paul Hotel, N. Y.; Columbus 2905.

— O —

O'BRIEN, Gipsy; educ. England; stage career, leads in "I Love You," "Cheating Cheaters," etc.; screen career, Famous Players ("Wanted, A Husband"), Vitagraph ("The Day Resurgent"), etc. Hght., 5, 5; wght., 125; auburn hair, dark blue eyes. Ad., 142 W. 44th st., N. Y. C.; Bryant 1062.

O'BRIEN, Helen; ingenue and comedienne; b. Cedar Rapids, Iowa; screen career, Camel Adv. Film Co., "Pink Nitie," "Bad Bears," Castle Film Co., Emerald Co., "Do the Dead Talk?" Special Feature Films, Billy West comedy series, Alice Howell Comedies. Hght., 5, 5; wght., 128; brown hair, blue eyes. Ad., Emerald Studios, Chicago, Ill.

O'CONNOR, Kathleen; b. Dayton, O., 1897; educ. St. Joseph's Convent and Notre Dame Acad.; screen career, Keystone, Rolin-Pathe, Fox ("Ace High," "Fame and Fortune," "Mr. Logan, U. S. A."), Universal ("Vamping the Vamp," "The Midnight Man," "Gun Fighting Gentleman" with Harry Carey, starring in "The Lion Man"). Hght., 5, 4½; wght., 125; fair complexion, light brown hair, blue eyes. Home ad., 1723 Garfield place, Hollywood, Calif.; studio, Universal.

O'CONNOR, Loyola; b. St. Paul, Minn.; educ. Convent of Holy Name, Portland, Ore.; stage career, Frederick Warde, Frank Mayo, 7 yrs. in "Way Down East," 3 yrs. in "Ben Hur" (mgmt. K. and E.), 3 yrs. in "Rebecca of Sunnybrook Farm"; screen career, since 1913, Vitagraph, Lasky, Famous Players, Fine Arts, Griffith ("True Heart Susie"), Wm. De Mille ("Tree of Knowledge"), Para-Aracraft ("The Love Burglar"), Cecil B. De Mille ("Why Change Your Wife?"). Ad., 7002 Hawthorne ave., Hollywood, Calif.; phone 577527.

O'DARE, Peggy; b. N. Y. C.; educ. there; screen career, leads in L-Ko, 1 yr. Lehrman comedies, Universal ("For Life"), "In the Balance" lead with Eddie Polo, "Vanishing Dagger," "Kentuck's Ward," "Blind Chance" starring in series of two-reel pictures). Hght., 5, 3; wght., 124; blond hair, blue eyes. Home ad., 6615 St. Frances Court, Hollywood, Calif.; Holly 3715; studio, Universal.

O'MADIGAN, Isabel; b. St. Louis; educ. Sacred Heart Convent; stage career, Belasco, "Heart of Wetona," "The Brat," "Common Clay"; screen career, Metro ("Pirate Gold," "Love Defender," "Five Thousand a Minute," "Sylvia Goes on a Spree"), Famous Players ("The Make Believe Wife"), Artcraft ("Suspense"), Hallmark ("Retribution"). Now playing in "Scandal" at 39th St. Theatre. Hght., 5, 7; wght., 139; white hair, green eyes. Ad., 108 Washington place, N. Y.; Spring 1798.

ORTH, Louise; b. Denver, Colo.; educ. Hinshaw Conservatory; stage career, in Blanche Ring's 'Yankee Girl," 2 seasons with Julian Eltinge in "The Fascinating Widow," Morosco stock in Los Angeles, Alcazar stock in "A Modern Eve"; screen career, L-Ko ("Mr. Shoestring in the Hole" and a number of others), Triangle ("Three Black Eyes"). Light hair, blue eyes. Ad., Hotel Monterey, N. Y.

OSTRICHE, Muriel; b. N. Y., 1897; educ. pub. schls., N. Y.; screen career, Eclair, Thanhouser, Vitagraph ("Kennedy Square," "Mortmain"), Equitable ("A Daughter of the Sea," "A Circus Romance," "By Whose Hand?"), World ("The Man She Married," "A Square Deal"), Peerless-World ("Moral Courage," "The Dormant Power," "Leap to Fame," "Tinsel," 'What Love Forgives," "The Bluffer," "The Moral Deadline," "The Hand Invisible"), Schomer-Ross ("The Sacred Flame"). Ad., 141 W. 73d st., N. Y.

OWEN, Seena (Signe Auen); b. Spokane, Wash.; educ. Bruno Hall, there, and in Copenhagen, Denmark; stage career, six weeks in stock, San Francisco; screen career, from 1914, Kalem, Reliance-Majestic, Fine Arts ("Martha's Vindication," "Madame Bo-Peep"), Griffith ("Intolerance," "Fall of Babylon"), Artcraft ("Branding Broadway," "The Sheriff's Son," "Breed of Men," "A Man and His Money," "One of the Finest," "City of Comrades" with Tom Moore, Tourneur ("The Life Line," "Victory"). Ad., 103 N. Manhattan place, Los Angeles, Cal.; phone 560921.

— P —

PAIGE, Jeane; b. Paris, Ill., 1898; screen career, Vitagraph, featured in O. Henry subjects, "The Count and the Wedding Guests," Blue Ribbon Feature ("The Desired Woman"), Vitagraph ("Tangled Lives," "King of Diamonds," "Daring Hearts," "Too Many Crooks," "Beating the Odds," "The Darkest Hour," "The Fortune Hunter"). Hght., 5, 4; wght., 115; dark hair and blue eyes. Ad. Vitagraph Studio, Hollywood, Calif.

ACTRESSES

PALMER, Patricia; b. San Francisco, Calif.; educ. there; stage career, child parts for several yrs.; screen career, 2 yrs., with Vitagraph for one yr., starring in two-reel O. Henry and Wolfville stories, "The Canyon Hold-Up," "The Rose of Wolfville," with W. S. Hart in "The Money Corral," and "Dan Kurrie's Inning," featured in Christie Comedies, in Mitchell Lewis picture, "The Faith of the Strong," now being starred under mgmt. of Cyrus J. Williams in Bradbury Prods. Home ad., Melrose Hotel, 120 S. Grand ave., Los Angeles, Calif.

PALMER, Violet; b. Flint, Mich., 1899; educ. Spokane and Seattle; stage career, in vaud. as child; also stk., mus. com.; screen career, Lasky, Kalem, Fox ("The Blue Streak"), Amer.-Pathe ("Eve in Exile").

PARKS, Frances Craven; b. Dawson, Ga., 1902; educ. Atlanta, Ga.; stage career, Alkahest Lyceum Bureau through southern states; screen career, with D. W. Griffith for 2 yrs. ("The Girl Who Stayed at Home"), now with Wm. De Mille at Lasky, "Jack Straws" with Robert Warwick. Hght., 5, 2; wght 105; dark brown hair, black eyes. Home ad., 4634 Hollywood blvd., Los Angeles, Calif.; Holly 4178.

PARR, Peggy; b. Baltimore, 1890; educ. Notre Dame Convent, Md.; screen career, Essanay ("The Coward," leads in George Ade Fables), Metro ("Sowers and Reapers," "Winning of Beatrice"), Klever Comedies with Victor Moore, Fox ("La Belle Russe," "Lure of Ambition"), Int.-Famous Players ("Cinema Murder"). Hght., 5, 3; wght., 116; dark complexion, dark hair, brown eyes. Ad., 203 W. 85th st., N. Y.; Schuyler 5734.

PAVIS, Yvonne (Marie); b. London, England; educ. Eng. and continent; stage career, dram. stk. and vaud., U. S. A. and Europe; screen career, in Europe and U. S. A., Vitagraph ("Easter Babies"), serial with Universal, Famous Players, Triangle ("High Tide," "Tony America"), Metro ("The Walk-Offs"); writes scenario. Hght., 5, 3½; wght., 110; light complexion, black hair, dark brown eyes. Home ad., 5200 Hollywood blvd., Los Angeles, Calif.; Holly 2230.

PAWN, Doris; b. Norfolk, Neb., 1896; educ. business college; screen career, Universal ("Trey of Hearts"), Fox ("Blue Blood and Red," "The Book Agent," "Some Boy," "The Kid is Clever," Para. ("The City of Dim Faces"), Goldwyn ("Tob's Vow," "Tower of Ivory," "The Strange Boarder"). Studio ad., Goldwyn, Culver City, Calif.

PAYNE, Lila; b. Boston, Mass., 1887; educ. Boston, Mass., pub. schs. and sch. of elocution; early career, directed amateur work in Boston and other Mass. cities for 10 yrs.; stage career, stock in Richmond Stock Co., and Castle Square Stock, Boston; screen career, W. E. M. P. Co. ("The Friend," "Comrades"), Solax ("Littlest Rebel," "The Parting"). Hght., 5, 2; wght., 116; dark brown hair, dark gray eyes. Home ad., 372 Communipaw ave., Jersey City, N. J.; Actors' Equity, N. Y.

PAYSON, Blanche; b. Santa Barbara, Calif.; educ. there; screen career, Keystone ("Wife and Auto Trouble," "Bathhouse Blunder," "Her Circus Knight"), Vitagraph ("His Diplomatic Mission," "Bums and Boarders," "Farms and Fumbles," "Beauties and Barbers"), Sunshine Comedies ("Heart Smasher"). Hght., 6, 3; wght., 215; dark brown hair, brown eyes. Home ad., 317 S. Olive st., Los Angeles, Calif.; phone 10089.

PAYTON, Gloria; b. N. Y. C.; educ. convent; stage career, stock and vaud. for 8 yrs.; screen career, American (played ingenues), Balboa ("The Yellow Bullet," "The Grip of Evil"), Glendale Film Co. ("The Lone Bandit"), Fox ("A Branded Soul"), Mitchell Lewis "Faith of the Strong"). Hght., 5, 3; wght., 118; black hair, brown eyes. Ad., care of Willis and Ingliss, Los Angeles, Calif.

PEARCE, Peggy; b. Long Beach, Calif., 1896; educ. there; screen career, Biograph, "The Mother's Heart"; L-Ko, and Keystone comedies, "The Fisher Johnnie," "Raffles, the Gentleman Burglar," "A Dog Catcher's Love," "Soul of a Plumber," "Won by a Fowl," "The Winning Punch." Hght., 5, 4; wght, 135; blond hair, blue eyes.

PEARSON, Virginia (Mrs. Sheldon Lewis); b. Louisville, Ky., 1888; educ. Louisville; stage career, stk. two seasons as the vampire in Robert Hilliard's "A Fool There Was," followed Mme. Dorsiet in Faversham's orig. prod. "The Hawk"; screen career, Vitagraph, a few mos. in 1910, Famous ("The Aftermath"), Vitagraph 1915 ("The Vital Question"), Fox ("Royal Romance," "When False Tongues Speak," "All for a Husband," "The Bitter Truth," "A Daughter of France," "The Firebrand," "Her Price," "The Liar," "Queen of Hearts," "Buchannon's Wife"), Pearson Prod. ("The Bishop's Emeralds," "Impossible Catherine"). Hght., 5, 7½; wght., 145; dark brown hair and hazel eyes.

PERCY, Eileen; screen career, American, "Some Liar," "Where the West Begins," "Brass Buttons"; Rob.-Cole, "The Gray Horizon," "The Beloved Cheater"; Para-Artcraft, "Told in the Hills," "In Mizzoura"; Hampton-Hodk., "Desert Gold." At present on world tour.

PEREDA, Christina; b. Mexico City; educ. Seville, Spain; stage career, in vaud. as dancer and pantimome and mus. com. in Spain, Cuba and Mexico, came to this country after several yrs. with Molasso's Pantomime Co., with "The Land of Jou," starred on stage when 8 yrs. old; screen career, Goldwyn ("The Woman and the Puppet"), Lew Cody-Gasnier ("The Butterfly Man"). Hght., 5, 5; wght., 125; black hair and eyes. Home ad., Continental Hotel, 626 S. Hill st., Los Angeles, Calif.; phone 10325.

PETROVA, Olga; b. Warsaw, Poland; educ. Brussels, Paris, London; stage career, from age of 20, Shakespearean rep., played Ibsen, Bernstein and Strindberg in Europe, American debut at Folies Bergere, N. Y., under mgmt. Henry B. Harris; starred in "Panthea" and "The Revolt," mgmt. Shuberts; screen career, Lasky-Paramount ("The Undying Flame," "The Law of the Land"), Metro ("The Soul of a Magdalen"), Petrova Pictures ("Daughter of Destiny," "The Life Mask," "Tempered Steel," "The Panther Woman"). Now fulfilling recital tour in vaud. Hght., 5, 5; wght., 130; red hair, green eyes. Ad., 125 W. 40th st., N. Y.

PHILLIPS, Carmen; b. San Francisco, 1895; educ. Univ. of Cal.; stage career, Princess Opera Co. of San Francisco, Hartman and Lombardi's Op. Cos.; screen career, with Universal Vitagraph, Fox, Christie, Universal, Fox Comedies ("Chased in Love," "There's Many a Fool"), Morosco-Paramount ("Forbidden Paths," "The Sunset Trail," "Tyrant Fear," "Unclaimed Goods," "The Home Town Girl"), Bluebird ("The Cabaret Girl"), Fox ("Smiles"), Rob-Cole ("Whitewashed Walls," "The Pagan God," "For a Woman's Honor"). Hght., 5, 5; wght., 130; brunette, black eyes and hair. Ad., home, 6555 Hollywood Blvd., Hollywood. Studio ad., Metro, Hillywood, Calif.

PHILLIPS, Dorothy; b. Baltimore, Md.; educ. there, St. John's Convent; stage career, George Fawcett stk. co. in Baltimore, 2 seasons "Mary Jane's Pa," season with "Everywoman," as "Modesty," Henry W. Savage prod., created title role in "Pilate's Daughter"; screen career, Universal ("Talk of the Town," "Hell Morgan's Girl," "Heart of Humanity," "The Right to Happiness," "Ambition"). Hght., 5, 3½; wght., 123; chestnut hair, dark gray eyes. Ad., 1946 Cahuenga Blvd., Hollywood, Calif.; Holly 3767. Studio, Universal City.

PICKFORD, Lottie; screen career, "Mile-a-Minute Kendall," with Jack Pickford, "The Man from Funeral Range," with Wallace Reid, playing heavies. Ad., Brunton Studio, Hollywood, Calif.

PICKFORD, Mary; b. Toronto, Can., 1893; stage career, in juvenile parts at age of 5, Valentine Stk. Co., Toronto, at age of 9 starred in "The Fatal Wedding," played with Chauncey Olcott in "Edmund Burke," scored success in Belasco's "Warrens of Virginia"; screen career, Biograph, direction Griffith, "The Violin Maker of Cremona," first lead, 1-reeler, Independent M. P. Co., returned to stage for Belasco's "A Good Little Devil," went to Famous Players with entire cast for film version, "Tess of the Storm Country," Artcraft ("The Little Princess," "Romance of the Redwoods," "Poor Little Rich Girl," "Rebecca of Sunnybrook Farm," "M'liss," "Little American," "Amarilly of Clothesline Alley," "Stella Maris," "Johanna Enlists," "Captain Kidd, Jr."), First National ("Daddy Long Legs," "The Hoodlum," "Heart o' the Hills"), United Artists ("Pollyanna"). Hght., 5; wght. 100; golden hair, hazel eyes. Ad., Mary Pickford Co., Los Angeles, Calif.

PITTS, Za Su; b. Parsons, Kan., 1898; educ. Santa Cruz; screen career, has appeared in 15 comedies with La Salle, Universal ("Behind the Footlights," "Why They Left Home"), Famous Players ("The Little Princess," "A Modern Musketeer," "How Could You, Jean"), Metro ("As the Sun Went Down"), Brentwood Prod. ("Better Times"), Paramount ("Men, Women and Money"), Rob-Cole ("The Other Half," "Poor Relations"). Hght., 5, 6; wght., 115; blue eyes, brown hair, light complexion. Ad., 532 S. Fremont ave., Los Angeles. Studio, Brentwood Film Corp.

POWELL, Mabel Alline; b. Dallas, Texas, 1898; educ. Page Seminary, Los Angeles; screen career, Vitagraph, Selig, Rolin. Hght., 5, 6; wght., 165; blond hair, brown eyes. Ad., Hotel Alexandria, Los Angeles.

POWER, Jule (Mrs. Edwards Davis); b. Portland, Ore.; educ. St. Mary's Coll., Portland; stage career, Baker Stk. Co., leads in "The Little Minister," "Her Own Way," "The Little Grey Lady," "The Road to Yesterday," Broadway prods. in support of Kelsey and Shannon, Wilton Lackaye, Grace George; vaud. featured with Edwards Davis in "Found Out," "The Kingdom of Destiny," etc.; screen career, vampire in serial ("Gloria's Romance"), (Kleine), Fox, lead in "Her Mother's Secret." Hght., 5, 6; wght., 140; black hair, blue eyes. Home ad., 44 West 60th st., N. Y., or National Vaud. Artists, 229 West 46th st., N. Y.

PRETTY, Arline; b. Wash., D. C., 1893; educ. Wash. and priv. finishing sch.; stage career, beginning with the Columbia players in Washington playing ingenues and later leads for over 3 yrs.; screen career, began with "The Old Guard," Imp-Universal, Vitagraph ("The Dawn of Freedom," "The Secret Kingdom"), Artcraft ("In Again—Out Again"), Pathe ("The Hidden Hand"), Continental Pic. ("The Challenge of Chance"), Serico Prod. ("The Woman in Gray" serial). Hght., 5, 5½. Ad., care Serico, 220 W. 42nd st., N. Y.

PREVOST, Marie; b. Sarnia, Canada, 1898; educ. Denver; screen career, Mack Sennett Comedies ("Nature Dance," "Sleuths," "East Lynne with Variations," "His Hidden Purpose," "Never Too Old," "Yankee Doodle in Berlin," "Reilly's Wash Day," "When Love is Blind," "Love's False Faces," "The Dentist," "Uncle Tom Without the Cabin," "Salome vs. Shenandoah," "The Speak-Easy"). Hght., 5, 4; wght., 123; dark hair, blue eyes. Ad., 953 West Seventh st., Los Angeles, Cal.; Pico 2111. Studio, Sennett-Paramount.

PRICE, Kate; b. Ireland, 1872; educ. Pawtucket, R. I.; stage career, vaud. with Price and Steel, stk. and rep.; screen career, Vitagraph ("Officer Kate," "Fisherman Kate," "A Night Out"), Keystone ("The Waiter's Ball"), Vim ("Mother's Child," "Fat and Fickle"), Amber Star, Jaxon Film Co. ("Week End Shopping"), Artcraft ("Amarilly of Clothesline Alley"), Fairbanks ("Arizona"), American ("Put Up Your Hands"), Fox ("Tin Pan Alley"). Ad., 1605 N. Kingsley, Los Angeles, Cal.; Holly 3970.

PRUSSING, Louise; educ. Chicago Latin Sch. and Stamford, Conn.; stage career, Athalie in "The Country Cousin," Angela in "The Maid of the Mountains," hostess Blackstone Hotel, Chicago, Vanderbilt Hotel, N. Y. C., Sherry's; screen career, Selznick ("Sealed Hearts," "Out Yonder," "His Wife's Money"). Hght., 5, 6; wght., 130; medium light hair, blue eyes. Ad., 66 W. 49th st., N. Y.; Bryant 418.

PULLIAM, Pauline; b. 1902; educ. Los Angeles; stage career, vaud.; screen career, Pathe ("Carolyn of the Coriers"), Morosco ("Final Close Up"), Fox, Goldwyn ("Sis Hopkins"), Famous Players ("A Girl Named Mary," "All of a Sudden Peggy"), National ("Hall Room Boys" stories). Ad., 1731 N. Mariposa ave., Hollywood, Calif.

PURVIANCE, Edna Olga; b. Reno, Nev.; educ. there and San Francisco; screen career, with Charlie Chaplin at Essanay, Chaplin-First National ("A Dog's Life," "The Adventurer," "Easy Street," "Sunnyside," "Shoulder Arms"). Hght., 5, 4; wght., 130; blond hair, gray eyes. Home ad., 402A Westlake Terrace, Los Angeles, Calif.; phone 55219.

— R —

RAMBEAU, Marjorie; educ. San Francisco, Calif.; stage career, star in "Sadie Love," "Cheating Cheaters," "The Fortune Teller," "The Unknown Woman," "Eyes of Youth"; screen career, Capellani ("The Fortune Teller"). Ad., 305 W. 72nd st., N. Y. C.

RANKIN, Caroline J.; b. Pittsburgh, Pa., Aug. 22, 1889; educ. Chicago; stage career, with "Mrs. Wiggs of the Cabbage Patch," and in stock in Chicago, Cleveland, Cincinnati, Harlem Opera House, N. Y., etc.; screen career, Fox ("Some Boy"), Keystone ("A Seminary Scandal"), Vitagraph ("Quarantined"), Ince-Para. ("A Nine o'Clock Town," "Coals of Fire," "When Do We Eat," "Hard Boiled," "Up in the Air," "Lost in Traffic"). Hght., 5, 7½; wght., 92; light brown hair and gray eyes. Home ad., 1629 Third ave., Los Angeles, Calif.; phone 75609.

REARDON, Mildred; christened by Henry Clive "The Girl with the Brown Eyes," while with Florenz Ziegfeld; screen career, with Pathe, Fox, Cecil De Mille ("Male and Female"), Para.-Artcraft ("Everywoman"). Golden hair, brown eyes, very small. Ad., Hotel Astor, N. Y.

REED, Florence; b. Phila., 1883; educ. Sacrecolus Convent; comes of theatrical parentage; stage career, includes stk. and many prods., with Walker Whiteside; Ramons in "The Painted Woman"; screen career, Pathe ("The Woman's Law"), Brenon ("Lucretia Borgia"), Harry Rapf ("The Struggle Everlasting," "Wives of Men"), United ("Call of the Heart," "Woman Under Oath," "Her Game," "The Eternal Mother, "Her Code of Honor"). Ad., Harry Rapf, 1564 Broadway, N. Y.

REED, Nora; educ. Houston, Texas; screen career, in stock with Famous Players-Lasky Corp., 6 mos.; casting directress for Famous players, 1 yr.; played in "Career of Catherine Bush," "Sinners," "Fear Market." Hght., 5, 7; wght., 120; auburn hair, dark blue eyes. Studio ad., 130 W. 56th st., N. Y.

REEVES, Myrtle; b. Atlanta, Ga., 1897; educ. Washington Seminary, Atlanta; screen career, Vitagraph and Balboa (third episode of "Red Circle" series, "The Grip of Evil," "Dawn of Wisdom"), Universal ("Eternal Love"), Bluebird ("Playthings," "A Kentucky Cinderella"), American ("A Bachelor's Wife"), Vitagraph ("Over the Garden Wall"). Hght., 5, 4; wght., 136; blue eyes, golden hair, and very fair complexion.

RENECK, Ruth; b. Galveston, Texas; educ. Texas and Arizona; stage career, 4 yrs., 1 season in "Secret Service," 1 season "Shenandoah," stock; screen career, Paramount-Artcraft ("Hawthorne of the U. S. A."), Hampton ("The Parish Priest," "The White Dove"). Hght., 5, 2; blond hair, hazel eyes. Home ad., 2320 12th ave., Los Angeles, Calif.; phone 75454.

RENFROE, Vida Estelle von Katz; b. 1900; educ. private schls. and convent; screen career, 3 yrs., starting with the old Amber Star, Metro, James Montgomery Flagg, Geo. M. Cohan, Vim Comedies, Black Diamond Comedies, Sunshine Comedies ("Trial by Jury," "Work and Win 'Em," "Moonshine on the Wabash," "His Caveman Tactics"), Public Health Series ("Cleared for Action"). Hght., 5, 2; wght., 100; dark brown hair and eyes. Ad., 436 E. 3rd st., Jacksonville, Fla.

RHODES, Billie; b. San Francisco; educ. San Francisco; stage career, on Orpheum circuit, soubrette in "Babes in Toyland"; screen career, leads in dramas and comedies, with Kalem, Universal, Christie, Strand-Mutual ("A Two Cylinder Courtship," "Bluffing Father," "Some Nurse," "For Sweet Charity"); Natl. Robertson-Cole ("Girl of My Dreams," "In Search of Arcady," "Lion and the Lamb," "The Love Call," "Hoop-la of the Circus," "Blue Bonnet"). Hght., 5; wght., 106; brown hair and eyes. Ad., home, 1841 Wellington, Hollywood, Calif. Studio, National, Hollywood.

RICE, Fanny; stage career, 25 yrs. appearing in cities in U. S., Canada, also vaud. in Australia and New Zealand; star of own prods.; screen career, Blackton ("Moonshine Trail," "Dawn," "Tinsel's Triumph," "My Husband's Other Wife"). Hght., 5, 5; wght., 140; auburn hair, dark blue eyes. Ad., 340 Lafayette ave., Brooklyn, N. Y.; Prospect 2086.

RICH, Irene; b. Buffalo, N. Y.; educ. St. Margaret's Girls' Sch.; screen career, Paralta ("A Law Unto Herself"), Frank Keenan ("Todd of the Times"), Goldwyn ("The Strange Boarder," "Tough Proposition," "Street Called Straight"), National ("Blue Bonnet"), Fox ("Lone Star Ranger," "Wolves of the Night"). Hght., 5, 5; wght., 138; dark brown hair and eyes. Ad., 703 N. Gramercy Place, Los Angeles, Calif.

RICH, Vivian; b. at sea; educ. Boston; stage career, 1 season with Gus Edwards, vaud.; screen career, American, Selig, Fox ("The Crime of the Hour," "Judgment is Mine," "The Price of Silence," "Beware of Strangers"), Ind. ("Sins of the World"), Mitchell Lewis ("Vengeance is Mine"), J. D. Hampton ("The Mints of Hell"), Fox ("The Last Straw"). Hght., 5, 4½; wght., 115; brown hair, dark brown eyes. Ad., 1323 N. Martel ave., Hollywood, Calif.; phone 577780.

ACTRESSES

RIDGEWAY, Fritzie; b. Butte, Mont., 1898; educ. there and Schl. Fine Arts, Chicago; stage career, stk. in N. Y. C., 2 yrs. vaud.; screen career, Essanay, Triangle ("Up or Down"), Fox ("The Danger Zone"), Universal ("Fire Flingers," featured in "Winning a Bride," "Ranger of Pike's Peak," "Petal on the Current"), Morosco-Lasky ("Judy of Rogues' Harbor"), Sphinx Film Co. (featured in "The Fatal 30" serial). Hght., 5,5; wght., 130; medium complexion, brown hair, dark blue eyes. Ad., Box 813, Laurel Canyon, Hollywood, Calif.

ROBERTS, Edith; b. N. Y. C.; educ. N. Y. C.; stage career, began age 6; also in vaud.; screen career, Nestor ("The Lost Appetite," "Jilted in Jail," "A Burglar by Request," "Her City Beau," "The War Bridegroom," "Five Little Widows," "Seeing Things," "O'Connor's Mag." "Madame Spy," "The Deciding Kiss," "The Love Swindle," "Beans," "Cherries Are Ripe"), Universal ("Lasca," "The Triflers"). Hght., 5, 1; wght., 105; fair complexion, light brown hair, brown eyes. Ad., home, 6122 Selma ave., Hollywood. Studio, Universal City, Calif.

ROBINSON, Daisy; b. N. Y. C.; educ. Ursuline Convent, Quebec, Canada, Holy Cross Acad., N. Y.; stage career, at very early age, played with Joseph Jefferson, Maude Adams, in "Peter Pan," Olga Nethersole; screen career, 1 yr. Reliance-Majestic ("A Bad Man and Others"), Fine Arts ("The Price of Power," "Intolerance"), Morosco ("The Happiness of Three Women"), Lasky ("The Clever Miss Carfax"), Douglas Fairbanks ("When the Clouds Roll By"). Hght., 5, 5; wght., 115; dark brown hair, dark eyes. Home ad., 2652 Beachwood drive, Los Angeles, Calif.; phone 577729.

ROBINSON, Gertrude May; b. N. Y. C., 1895; educ. N. Y. C.; stage career, began as child actress at the age of 4, has appeared in "A Bonnie Briar Bush," "A Midsummer Night's Dream," "Rip Van Winkle" and "Ben-Hur"; screen career, Biograph, Reliance, Victor, Lasky ("The Arab"), Famous ("May Blossom"), Gaumont ("The Haunted Woman," "The Quality of Faith"), Henley-Pathe ("The Gay Old Dog"). Hght., 5, 2; wght., 105; dark brown hair and blue-gray eyes, olive complexion. Home ad., 106 Morningside drive, N. Y. C.

ROBSON, May (Mrs. Stuart Robson); b. Australia; educ. Paris, London, and Brussels; stage career, from 1884, noted character portrayal as Aunt Mary Watkins in "The Rejuvenation of Aunt Mary"; screen career, Vitagraph ("A Night Out"), World ("A Broadway Saint"), Select ("His Bridal Night"), W. H. Prods. ("The Lost Battalion"). Ad., Highlands, N. J.; phone 1249-W.

ROLAND, Ruth; b. San Francisco, Calif.; stage career, since 3 yrs. of age, first appearing in Ed. Holden's "Cinderella" Co. at Columbia theatre, San Francisco; screen career, Kalem, Astra, Pathe ("Hands Up," "Tiger's Trail," "Neglected Wife," "Price of Folly," "Fringe of Society"), Ruth Roland Serials, Inc. ("Adventures of Ruth"). Hght., 5, 4; wght., 122; reddish brown hair, violet eyes. Ad., 901 So. Manhattan Place, L. A., Ruth Roland Studio, Los Angeles.; phone 23955.

ROYCE, Riza; b. Lancaster, Pa.; educ. Wadley High, N. Y. C.; screen career, Selznick, World, Fox ("Sacred Silence," "Checkers," "The Shark"), Guy Empey. Hght., 5, 5½.; wght., 126; dark brown hair, gray-green eyes. Home ad., 155 W. 117th st., N. Y.; phone Harlem 6510.

ROYCE, Ruth; b. Versailles, Mo.; educ. Loretta Acad., Kansas City; stage career, Woodward Stock Co., Lewis Stock Co.; screen career, Universal ("The Beach Combers," "Little Brother of the Rich," "Chris Rube"), Ince, Lasky, Fox ("The Splendid Sin"), with Eddie Polo in Universal serial, "The Vanishing Dagger." Hght., 5, 6; wght., 130; black hair, blue eyes. Home ad., 5222½ Sunset boulevard, Los Angeles, Calif.; phone 597212.

RUBENS, Alma; b. San Francisco; screen career, Triangle ("Reggie Mixes In," "Master of His Home," "The Firefly of Tough Luck," "Blue Blood," "The Passion Flower," "Gown of Destiny," "Regenerates," "The Answer," "Love Brokers," "Judith," "The Ghost Flower"), Ex. Mutual ("Diane of the Green Van"), Rob-Cole ("A Man's Country"), International ("Humoresque"). Hght., 5, 7; wght., 130; black hair, dark eyes. Ad., care International, 729 7th ave., N. Y.

— S —

SAIS, Marin; b. Marin Co., Calif.; educ. Notre Dame Acad., San Jose; screen career, Lasky ("City of Dim Faces"), Haworth ("His Birthright," "Bonds of Honor," "The Golden Hope"), Universal ("The Vanity Pool"), H. B. Warner ("Manya"), 6 yrs. with Kalem Co. as leading woman, also starred in serials "The American Girl," "Girl From Frisco," "Stingaree." Ad., 1325 N. Hobart Blvd., Los Angeles, Calif.

SAMPSON, Teddy; b. N. Y., 1895; stage career, vaud., comic opera, with Gus Edwards, Blanche Ring; screen career, Christie ("Good Morning Judge," "Are Honeymoons Happy?" "Our Little Wife"), Triangle ("Her American Husband," "Fox Woman," "Sympathy Sal," "Child of the Surf," "Big Jim's Heart," "Fencing Master"), Fox "Fighting for Gold"), lead in Capitol Comedies with Smiling Bill Parsons. Hght., 5, 2; wght., 110; black hair, brown eyes. Home ad., 1907 Wilcox Ave., Los Angeles, Calif.; Holly 460.

SAUNDERS, Alice (Mrs. Harry M. O'Connor); b. Holyoke, Mass., 1880; stage exper., stk. in Cal. and N. Y. for 20 yrs.; screen career, Selig, Diando, Kalem, Fox, Lasky, Griffith ("Reconstruction," "The Wolf Faced Man," "The Haunted House," etc.). Hght., 5, 7½; wght., 140; auburn hair, blue eyes. Ad., 161 Date St., Riverside, Calif.

SAUNDERS, Jackie; b. Philadelphia, 1893; educ. St. Joseph's Convent, Phila.; stage career, Dawson's Dancing Dolls; stock; screen career, Biograph, Pathe, Universal, Balboa ("Shrine of Happiness," "Flirting Bride," "Betty Be Good," "The Checkmate"), "Mugsby," "Miracle of Love," Cosmopolitan Film, "Dad's Girl." Author of several scenarios, including "Rose of the Alley." Hght., 5, 3; wght., 115; blond hair, blue eyes.

SAVAGE, Aileen; educ. Madams of the Sacred Heart in Paris and San Francisco; screen career, Buffalo ("The Sport of Kings"), Famous Players, ("The Coat," "Red Head"). Hght., 5, 4½; wght., 119; black hair, dark eyes. Ad., 62 W. 51st St., N. Y.; Circle 3471.

SCHADE, Betty Marie; b. Berlin, 1894; educ. Chicago; stage career, vaud. rep.; screen career, Goldwyn ("Bonds of Love," "The Crimson Gardenia," "Thru the Wrong Door"), Select ("Happiness a la Mode"), "Paris Green" with Chas. Ray, Universal ("Bare Fists"), Leibfreed-Miller ("Deliverance"), Fox ("A Girl in Bohemia," "Shod With Fire"). Hght., 5, 6; wght., 142; light complexion, th.en hair, blue eyes. Ad., home, 7 Carver Court, Los Angeles, Calif.; phone 577112.

SCHAEFER, Anne; b. St. Louis, Mo.; educ. Notre Dame Convent; stage career, 3 yrs. stock cos., 4 yrs. Shakesperian rep. with Louis James, also played "The Green Clad Woman" in "Peer Gynt;" screen career, member of the orginal Vitagraph Co. on West Coast as a feature player, free lancing for 2 yrs., recently returned to Vitagraph stock, playing emotional character leads. Hght., 5, 7½; wght., 160; brown hair and eyes. Ad., 6067 Salem Place, Los Angeles, Calif.; phone 577820.

SCHRAM, Violet; b. San Antonio, Tex., Dec. 1, 1898; educ. Chicago pub. and high schls; early career, professional reader for several yrs.; screen career, Universal, since 1915 ("Shoes," "Saving the Family Name," 15th episode of "Graft," "Two Rebels, "Out of the Darkness," "The Woman with the Parakeets"), Metro ("The Walkoffs"), H. B. Warner ("The Grey Wolf's Ghost"), Tom Moore ("Toby's Bow"). Zane Grey ("The Desert of Wheat"), Fox ("White Lies"). Hght., 5, 3; wght., 120; black hair, dark brown eyes. Home ad., 5674 DeLongpre, Hollywood, Calif.; Holly 4345.

SCOTT, Mabel Juliene; b. Minneapolis, Minn.; educ. there, Stanley Girls' Coll. and Northwestern Conservatory; stage career, dramatic stock at Minneapolis, Omaha, Kansas City and Detroit, leading woman with Fiske O'Hara, starred in "The Intruder" in vaud.; screen career, Rex Beach ("The Barrier"), Edgar Lewis ("The Sign Invisible"), Elk Film Co. ("Reclaimed"), Graphic ("Ashes of Love"), Fox ("Sacred Silence"), Lasky ("The Sea Wolf"). Hght., 5, 6; wght., 128; dark brown hair, brown eyes. Ad., Lasky Studios, Hollywood, Calif.

SEDGWICK, Eileen; b. Galveston, Texas; educ. Ursuline Convent, Galveston; stage career; from childhood, dram. stk., vaud., musical comedy with (5) Sedgwicks Co.; screen career, Universal ("Lure of the Circus", lead with Eddie Polo, "The Radium Mystery," "Man and Beast," "Dropped From the Clouds," "Trail of No Return," "No. 10—West Bound"). Hght., 5, 3; wght., 120; blond hair, dark blue eyes. Home ad., Boulevard Apts., Hollywood Blvd., Los Angeles, Calif.; phone 577332; studio Universal.

SEDGWICK, Josie; b. Galveston Texas; educ. Ursuline Convent, Galveston; stage career, since babyhood, vaud., dram. stk., musical comedy, with (5) Sedgwicks; screen career, Triangle ("Wolves of the Border," "Maternal Spark," "Boss of the Lazy Y," "Paying His Debt," "Beyond the Shadow," "Wild Life"), Fred Stone ("Duke of Chimney Butte"), Goldwyn ("Jubilo"), Fox ("Camouflaged"). Hght., 5, 5; wght., 132; blond hair, grey eyes. Ad., 6511½ Holly. Blvd., Hollywood, Calif.; phone 577332.

SEGER, Lucia Backus; educ. Lake Erie Coll., Painesville, Ohio; stage career, Hoyt comedies, Everett Stk. Co., Teck Theatre Stk. Co.; screen career, Famous Players ("Seven Swans," "Oh! You Women"), Truex-Paramount ("Stick Around"), Blackton ("My Husband's Second Wife"), Jaxon Films ("Awakening of Cecily"), Sunshine Film Co. (Moon Comedies). Hght., 5, 4; wght., 148; brown hair, blue eyes. Ad., 1547 St. Nicholas ave., N. Y.; Wadsworth 3057.

SELBIE, Evelyn; b. Louisville, Ky.; educ. there; stage career, 15 yrs. Proctor's Stk., N. Y., Alcazar Stk., San Francisco, featured in "Human Hearts"; screen career, Universal ("Pay Me," "People vs. John Doe," "Mysterious Mrs. M.," "Hand That Rocks the Cradle"), 3 yrs. leads with Essanay. Hght., 5, 4; wght., 125; black hair, brown eyes. Ad., Auditorium Hotel, Los Angeles, Calif.; Main 3404.

SELBY, Gertrude; b. Phila., 1896; educ. N. Y.; stage career, musical comedy, vaud. and stock, danced with Gertrude Hoffman in vaud.; screen career, Universal, Fox, L-KO, Pathe, Sunshine ("Mongrels," "Son of a Hun," "Who's Your Father," "His Smashing Career," "Damaged No-Goods"), Metro ("Easy to Make Money"). Ad., 5703 Sunset Blvd., Los Angeles, Cal.; phone 599138.

SELWYNNE, Clarissa; b. London, England; educ. there; stage career, 15 yrs. in classical and modern plays, in Eng. and U. S.; screen career, Metro, Universal ("The Bride's Awakening," "Smashing Thru," "The Talk of the Town"), Goldwyn ("Dangerous Days," "Tower of Ivory," "Cup of Fury"), Lois Weber ("Home"), Vitagraph ("Black Gate"). Hght., 5, 7; wght., 135; dark brown hair and eyes. Home ad., Boulevard Apts., Hollywood Blvd., Los Angeles, Cal.; phone 577330.

SEYMOUR, Clarine; b. B'klyn, N. Y.; educ. Mrs. Chase's Finishing School; screen career, Thanhouser, Pathe, Rolin, Christie, Griffith ("True Heart Susie," "Girl Who Stayed at Home," "Scarlet Days"). Hght., 5, 1; wght., 100; black hair and eyes. Ad., Griffith Studio, Mamaroneck, N. Y.

SHAFFER, Marie; b. Hartford, Conn., 1876; educ. N. Y.; screen career, Fox ("The Jungle Trail"), International ("Cinema Murder," with Harry Morey in Vitagraph, Gaumont ("Making Her His Wife"), Abramson ("Some One Must Pay"). Hght., 5, 8½; wght., 155; hair, dark brown tinged with grey; hazel eyes. Ad., 230 W. 101st St., N. Y.; Riverside 1724.

SHANOR, Peggy; b. W. Va., 1896; educ. Winchester School, Pittsburgh, Pa.; stage exper., stk., leads in Middle West; vaud. sketch, legit. with Anderson & Weber, Selwyn & Co., Shuberts; screen career, Pathe ("The House of Hate"), Fox ("The Queen of Hearts"), Famous ("Here Comes the Bride"), Abramson ("The Echo of Youth"), Wisteria Prods. Hght. 5, 5½; wght., 133; dark brown hair, dark grey eyes. Ad., 140 W. 73d St., N. Y. C.; Col. 5786.

SHEPARD, Pearl; educ. N. Y. C.; stage career, concerts as singer; screen career, Selznick ("Break the News to Mother"), Graphic ("Echo of Youth"), Vitagraph comedies, General Film series, Pearl Shepard Comedies; features in over 70 comedies, in features; been in pictures over 5 yrs.; now with Director Frank P. Donovan in special feature comedies for Paramount. Hght., 5, 5; wght., 125; auburn hair, hazel eyes. Ad., Hotel Claridge, N. Y.; studio ad., International Films, N. Y.

SHIPMAN, Edna; educ. Toronto, Canada and Los Angeles, Cal.; screen career, Canadian Photoplays ("Back to God's Country"), Universal-Jewel ("The Trembling Hour"), Goldwyn, Metro, Christie Comedies. Hght., 5; wght., 110; light brown hair, hazel eyes. Ad., 253 W. 100th st., N. Y.; Riverside 4517.

SHIPMAN, Nell; stage career, vaud., "The Piano Fiends," featured in "The Barrier," own co., stock; screen career, Fox, Vitagraph ("The Eighth Great Grand Parent," "Through the Wall"), Lasky, leading woman with Lou-Tellegen ("The Home Trail," "Girl from Beyond," "A Gentleman's Agreement," "Baree Son of Kazan"), Curwood-Carver ("Back to God's Country"). Author of several scenarios. Dark brown hair, brunette complexion. Home ad., 921 E. Wilson st., Glendale, Calif.; Glen 2956-J.

SHORT, Florence; b. Springfield, Mass., 1893; educ. Finch School, N. Y.; stage career, original Passion in "Experience," Hilda in "Sinners," stk., vaud.; screen career, Wharton ("The Eagle's Eye"), Metro ("A Man's World," "Kildare of Storm," "5000 an Hour," "The Outsider," Why Germany Must Pay"), World ("Phil for Short"), Hallmark ("Love, Honor and ?"). Hght., 5, 7; wght., 139; dark brown hair and eyes. Ad., 156 W. 106th St., N. Y.; Acad. 2343.

SHORT, Gertrude; b. Cincinnati, 1900; stage career, at age of 5 yrs. with Nance O'Neil in "Golden Fleece;" with Thos. Jefferson, vaud., Mary Mannering, stock; screen career, Edison, Vitagraph, Universal ("Little Angel of Canon Creek," "Cowboy and the Lady"). Lasky ("The Hostage"), Metro ("Blackie's Redemption"), Paramount ("The Heart of Youth," "In Mizzoura"). Wght., 95; hght., 5, 2; brown hair, blue eyes, light complexion. Ad., home, 6822 Sunset Blvd., Hollywood, Cal.

SHOTWELL, Marie; b. N. Y. C., educ. Mme. Gardiner's Schl., N. Y. C.; stage career, original co. of "Madame Sans Gene," with E. H. Sothern, Frohman stk co., under Henry B. Harris, as Shirley in "The Lion and the Mouse;" screen career, Frohman Amusement Co. ("The Witching Hour"), Acme ("The Thirteenth Chair"), co-starred with Edmund Breeze in Hallmark, ("Chains of Evidence"), Dietrich-Beck ("The Harvest Moon"), Hallmark serial ("The Evil Eye"). Hght. 5, 7½; wght., 154; dark brown eyes, light hair, dark complexion. Home ad., Seymour Hotel, N. Y. C.

SIMPSON, Henrietta; educ. Emma Fullerton Priv. Schl., Phila., Pa.; stage career, with Daly; screen career, World ("Diamonds and Pearls," "Youth," "Phil for Short"), Pathe ("Lightning Raider"), Metro ("Winning of Beatrice"), Blackton ("House Divided"), International ("Cinema Murder"), Famous Players ("Career of Katherine Bush"). Hght., 5, 7½; wght., 155; gray hair, hazel eyes. Ad., 204 W. 70th St., N. Y.; Columbus 1878.

SINCLAIR, Maud B.; b. Cleveland, O.; educ. Detroit and Jackson, Mich.; stage career, Harris & Woods, Chas. Frohman, with stars Joseph Wheelock, Jr., Ethel Barrymore, Charlotte Neilson, 3 seasons with "Old Lady 31;" screen career, Fox, Thanhouser, etc., with Vivian Martin, June Caprice, Alice Joyce. Ad. Rehearsal Club, 220 W. 46th St., N. Y.

SISSON, Vera; b. Salt Lake City, 1895; educ. Denver, Colo.; screen career, joined Universal; played leads opp. J. Warren Kerrigan, with co. 18 mos. ("The Bolted Door," "The Man From Nowhere"); 1915 joined Biograph (in "The Laurel of Tears," "The Trail of the Serpent", Metro ("The Iron Woman," "Paradise Garden"), Lamree Film Corp. ("The Blackmailers"), General ("The Married Virgin", Select ("The Veiled Adventure," "Experimental Marriage"), Paramount ("The Heart of Youth," "His Official Fiancee"), Transatlantic ("The Marriage Blunder"). Hght., 5, 3; wght., 120.

SNOW, Marguerite (Mrs. James Cruze); b. Savannah, 1892; educ. Loretta Heights Acad., Denver; stage career, since 1907, with James O'Neill in "Monte Cristo," H. W. Savage, J. W. Gaites, Delamater and Norris, Walter Lawrence, leads in "Peter Pan," "The College Widow," "Old Heidelberg," "The Christian," "The Devil," "The Road to Yesterday;" screen career, Metro ("The Silent Voice," "The Half-Million Bribe," "Notorious Gallagher", Artcraft ("Broadway Jones"), Pathe ("The Hunting of the Hawk"), with Hale Hamilton "In His Brother's Place." Hght., 5, 5; wght., 105; brown hair, brown eyes. Studio ad., Metro, Hollywood, Calif.

SPAULDING, Nellie Parker; b. Machias, Me.; educ. Emerson Coll. of Expression, Boston; stage career, lyceum platform, vaud., stk.; 20 yrs. stage exper.; screen career 5 yrs.; Select ("Her Great Chance"), Keenan-Pathe ("Ruler of the Road"), Educational ("Business of Life"), Vitagraph ("The Midnight Bride"), Realart ("The Fear Market"), Paramount-Artcraft ("On With the Dance"). Hght., 5, 7; wght., 135; brown hair, blue eyes. Ad., home, 132 22nd St., Elmhurst, L. I., N. Y.; Newtown 2550.

STANWOOD, Rita (Mrs. H. B. Warner); b. Salem, Mass.; educ. there; stage career, "Excuse Me," "When Dreams Come True," "Ghost Breaker," "Pipes of Pan," "Under Cover," etc.; screen career, Jesse D. Hampton ("Gray Wolf's Ghost"), Famous Players ("Ghost Breakers," "Lost Paradise"). Hght., 5, 4½; wght., 122; brown hair and eyes. Home ad., Hollywood Hotel, Hollywood, Calif.

STARK, Pauline; b. Joplin, Mo., 1900; educ. there; screen career, Triangle ("The Shoes That Danced," "Innocents Progress," "Judith," "Alias Mary Brown," "Irish Eyes"), Tourneur ("The Life Line"), Equity ("Eyes of Youth"), Allan Dwan for Mayflower ("Soldiers of Fortune"). Hght., 5, 4; wght., 110; brunette complexion, brown hair, dark grey eyes.

STEADMAN, Vera; b. June 23, 1900, Monterey, Cal., educ. Los Angeles; screen career, 2 yrs. Keystone ("Hula Hula Land," "Tugboat Romeo"), with Sennett-Paramount ("A Bedroom Blunder," "A Pullman Bride," "Are Waitresses Safe?" "That Night," "Why Men Go Wild," "Watch Your Step, Mother," "Oh, Doctor, Doctor," "License Applied For," "Papa By Proxy"). Hght., 5, 2; wght., 118; dark complexion and hair, brown eyes. Studio ad., Christie, Hollywood, Calif.

STEDMAN, Myrtle; b. Chicago; educ. Mrs. Sterrett's Sch., Chicago; stage career, mus. com., light opera, stock, on road; screen career, Selig, Bosworth, Pallas, Morosco, Lasky ("Soul of Kura San"), Vitagraph ("In Honor's Web"), Select "In the Hollow of Her Hand"), Artcraft ("The Teeth of the Tiger"), Beach-Goldwyn ("The Silver Horde"), J. Parker Reed, Jr. ("Sex"), "Bucko McAlister." Blond hair, blue eyes. Personal representative, Regina Kruh, 220 W. 42nd St., N. Y.

STEVENS, Elizabeth; educ. Packer Collegiate Inst., Brooklyn, N. Y.; stage career, 4 yrs.; screen career, society leads, Famous Players, World, Metro, Equitable, Universal. Hght., 5, 7½, wght., 131; blond hair, blue eyes. Ad., c/o J. H. Livingston, 1440 Broadway, N. Y.; Bryant 3805.

STEVENS, Emilly; b. N. Y.; stage career with her aunt, Mrs. Fiske; "Tess," "Divorcons," "Man and Superman," "The Devil;" Broadway star in "The Unchastened Woman;" screen career, Metro ("Wheels of Justice," "The Slacker," "Alias Mrs. Jessup," "Outwitted," "Daybreak," "The Wager," "The Soul of a Woman," "A Man's World," "Kildare of Storm," "Daybreak"), Schomer-Ross Prod. ("The Sacred Flame").

STEVENS, Grace Elizabeth; b. Chicago, 1875; Am. Acad. Drama; stage career, stk., concert; screen career, Thanhauser ("Mill on the Floss"), Metro ("Life's Shadows"), Fox ("A Modern Cinderella"), Goldwyn ("Fair Pretender"), World ("Moral Dead Line," "Power and Glory"), Select ("Break the News to Mother"), Briggs comedies ("Married Life"), "Fall of the Romanoffs" "Third Floor Back." Hght., 5, 7½; wght. 156; dark complexion, gray hair. Home ad., 747 Quincy St., Brooklyn, N. Y.; Bushwick 1692.

STEWART, Anita; b. Brooklyn, 1896; educ. Erasmus Hall; screen career, Vitagraph ("The Girl Philippa," "The Goddess"), First National ("Virtuous Wives," "A Midnight Romance," "In Old Kentucky," "Mary Regan"), Louis Mayer ("Kingdom of Dreams," "Human Desire," "Mind-the-Paint Girl"), First National ("The Fighting Shepherdess," "The Yellow Typhoon"). Light hair, brown eyes. Ad., care Anita Stewart Pict. Corp., 6 W. 48th st., N. Y. C.

STEWART, Katharine; b. Kent, England; educ. Germany; stage career, 22 yrs.; screen career, Empire All-Star Corp. ("Please Keep Smiling"). Hght., 5, 5; wght., 185; dark brown hair, gray eyes. Ad., St. Margaret Hotel, N. Y.

STEWART, Lucille Lee; b. Brooklyn, N. Y.; stage career, vaud.; screen career, Biograph, Vitagraph ("The Conflict," "His Wife's Good Name," "The Ninety and Nine"), Metro ("Five Thousand an Hour" "Our Mrs. McChesney"), Ex-Mutual ("The Eleventh Commandment"), Selznick ("The Perfect Lover," "Sealed Hearts"), Fox ("Eastward Ho!"). Hght., 5, 4; fair complexion, blond hair, dark blue eyes. Home ad., Brightwaters, L. I., N. Y.

STOCKTON, Edith; educ. Rock Island, Ill., and Barrett Inst. Chicago; stage career, dram. stk., Cleveland, Chicago, mus. com. N. Y.; screen career, Fox ("Putting One Over"), Artclass Film ("The Open Door"), Curtiss ("The Little Brother"), Famous Players, supporting Alice Brady. Hght., 5, 4; wght., 128; blond hair, blue eyes. Ad., 418 Central Park West, N. Y.; Riverside 4164.

STONEHOUSE, Ruth; b. Denver, 1894; educ. Monticello Seminary, Godfrey, Ill; early career, professional dancer; screen career, Essanay, Universal, Triangle ("The Phantom Husband"), Universal ("Love Never Dies"), Rolfe ("The Master Mystery"), Arrow ("The Masked Rider"), Metro ("The Four-Flusher," "The Hop"). Hght., 5, 2; wght., 105; olive complexion, light hair, brown eyes. Ad., permanent, 321 Laurel Canyon, Los Angeles, Calif.

STOREY, Edith; screen career, Vitagraph ("An Enemy to the King," "Mr. Aladdin from Broadway"), Metro ("The Legion of Death," "The Silent Woman," "Island of Regeneration," "Tarantula," "The Christian"); been in service driving an ambulance; now with Haworth ("The Price of Folly," "The Claim," "Dust of Egypt"). Ad., 676 Riverside Drive, N. Y.

STUART, Julia; b. Scotland; educ. there; stage career, own co., under Liebler, Booth Tarkington's play, "The Country Cousin"; screen career, Lubin, Eclair, Peerless ("The Flash of an Emerald," "The Master Hand," "The Ballet Girl"), Seiznick ("Common Law"), Famous ("Traveling Salesman"), Fox ("The Painted Madonna"). Ad., 365 W. 45th st., N. Y.

SULLY, Janet Miller; b. Boston, 1876; stage career. from 1885, "Pinafore," 10 yrs. in stk., vaud., mus. com.; screen career, since 1915, Horsley (appeared in all of the 60 Cub comedies), Chaplin ("Easy Street," "A Dog's Life," "The Adventurer," "The Cure"), Universal ("Midnight Madness," "The Petal on the Current"), Metro ("Fair and Warmer"), National ("Hall Room Boys"). Hght., 5, 5½; wght., 160; black hair, hazel eyes. Ad., Rutland Apts., Los Angeles, Calif.

SURTEES, Catherine; b. San Antonio, Texas, 1901; educ. Los Angeles Polytechnic; screen career, 9 months stock with Fox, 6 mos. stk. with Rolin as ingenue lead. Hght 5, 2; wght., 100; Titian hair, green eyes. Home ad., 763 Vine st., Hollywood, Calif.; Holly 2624; studio, Fox.

SWANSON, Gloria; b. Chicago, Ill.; educ. there; screen career, Essanay, Universal, Keystone, Sennett-Paramount ("The Pullman Bride"), Triangle ("Her Decision," "Every Woman's Husband," "Shifting Sands," "Station Content"), Famous Players ("Don't Change Your Husband," "For Better, For Worse," "Male and Female," "Why Change Your Wife?"). Hght., 5, 3; wght., 112; brown hair, blue eyes. Ad., Lasky Studio, Hollywood, Calif.

SWEET, Blanche; b. Chicago; stage career, with Gertrude Hoffman, Chauncey Olcott; screen career, Biograph ("Judith of Bethulia," "Oil and Water"), Griffith ("The Escape"), Lasky ("The Warrens of Virginia," "The Storm"), Independent release ("The Unpardonable Sin," "The Hushed Hour"), J. D. Hampton ("A Woman of Pleasure," "Cressy," "The Deadlier Sex," "Cinderella Jane"). Home ad., 6737 Witley Terrace, Los Angeles, Calif.; phone 577691; studio, J. D. Hampton.

— T —

TALMADGE, Constance; b. Brooklyn, N. Y., Apr. 19, 1900; educ. Erasmus Hall; screen career, Vitagraph, Triangle ("Intolerance"), Selznick ("Scandal," "The Honeymoon"), Select ("Up the Road With Sallie," "A Pair of Blue Stockings," "Mrs. Leffingwell's Boots," "Sauce for the Goose," "Romance and Arabella"), First National ("A Temperamental Wife," "The Virtuous Vamp," "Two Weeks"). Hght., 5, 5, wght., 120; golden hair, brown eyes. Ad., 318 E. 48th st., N. Y.; Vanderbilt 7340.

TALMADGE, Natalie; b. Brooklyn, N. Y.; educ. Brooklyn schs. and Erasmus Hall; screen career, Vitagraph; gave up acting to become assist. gen. mgr. Norma Talmadge Film Corp.; financial mgr. and asst. studio mgr., Comique Film Corp., playing occasional leads; played with Norma Talmadge in "The Isle of Conquest." Hght., 5, 2; wght., 100; brown hair and eyes. Ad., 318 E. 48th st., N. Y.; Vanderbilt 7340.

TALMADGE, Norma; b. Niagara Falls, N. Y., 1897; educ. Brooklyn schls.; entered motion pictures at age of 14 with no previous stage experience; first associated with Vitagraph, later Fine Arts; starred in "The Crown Prince's Double," Triangle, Fine Arts ("The Social Secretary," "Panthea"), Selznick-Select ("The Ghosts of Yesterday," "De Luxe Annie," "Her Only Way," "The Forbidden City," "The Heart of Wetona," "The Probation Wife," "The New Moon," "The Way of a Woman," "The Isle of Conquest," "She Loves and Lies"), First National ("Daughter of Two Worlds"). Hght., 5, 2; wght., 110; dark hair, brown eyes. Ad. Norma Talmadge Film Corp., 318 E. 48th st., N. Y.

TAMS, Irene; educ. Notre Dame Seminary, Newark, N. J.; stage career, vaud. and ingenue lead with "Elixir of Youth"; screen career, 7 yrs., with Biograph and Edison for 2 yrs., World ("Lola"), Milo ("Hired Help," "Entanglement," "Home-Coming," "Fireman's Dream," "The Storm"), Triangle ("Taxi"), Capellani ("Oh, Boy!"). Hght., 5, 1; wght., 112; brown hair, gray eyes. Ad., 66 W. 77th st., N. Y.; Schuyler 3670.

TAPLEY, Rose Elizabeth; b. Petersburg, Va., June 30, 1883; educ. Malden, Mass., and Boston Univ.; stage career, 1900-10, Chauncey Olcott, "Sign of the Cross," "Lion and the Mouse," etc.; screen career, Biograph, Vitagraph, "Money Kings," "Rip Van Winkle," "Memories That Haunt," "Vanity Fair," etc.; 1916-17, toured country for Vitagraph in interest of better pictures; 1917, joined Famous Players for same work; at present mgr. of Club and Social Section of Non-Theatrical Dist. Dept., Famous Players-Lasky Corp. Hght., 5, 6; wght., 137; brown hair, gray eyes. Home ad., 644 Springdale ave., East Orange, N. J.

TAYLOR, Pauline; b. N. Y.; educ. N. Y. C.; stage career, stk., with Eva Taylor in vaud.; screen career, Thanhouser ("Hidden Valley"), Apex ("Couple Wanted," "With All Improvements," "Furnished Complete," "In Bad"). Hght., 5, 7½; wght., 128; light brown hair, dark blue eyes. Ad., Apex Pictures Corp., Indianapolis, Ind.

TELL, Olive; b. N. Y. C.; educ. France; stage career, Sargent School of Acting, N. Y., stk. prods. "Cousin Lucy," "The Intruder," "Romance," "Under Pressure," etc.; screen career, Empire, All-Star-Mutual ("Her Sister," "The Unforeseen," "The Girl and the Judge," "The Smugglers"), Metro ("Secret Strings," "To Hell With the Kaiser"), Universal ("The Trap"), Jans Pict., Inc. ("Love Without Question"). Hght., 5, 5½; wght., 127; brown hair, blue eyes. Ad., care Jans Pictures, Inc., 729 Seventh ave., N. Y.

TENNANT, Barbara; b. and educ. London; stage career, Shakespearean rep.; screen career, featured lead in "The Dollar Mark," "The Marked Woman," "The Price of Malice," "The Closed Road." Retired from screen 1917, returning 1920. Hght., 5, 5½; wght., 124; auburn hair, hazel eyes. Ad., 2307 Holly drive, Hollywood, Calif.

TENNEY, Beth, also scen. writer; b. Manchester, Eng., 1893; educ. Notre Dame Convent, Balt.; stage career, stk., "Oh! Oh! Delphine," "The Love Cure"; screen career, Klever Komedies, double for Ethel Clayton in "Private Pettigrew's Girl"; featured in "The Thirteenth Chair," "Echo of Youth," "Woman, Woman," Gaumont ("Temporary Wife"), Famous ("Oh, You Woman"), McManus ("Lost Battalion"), Triangle ("Three Black Eyes"), Pioneer ("Sins of Children"). Hght., 5, 6; wght., 130; fair complexion, blond hair, dark eyes. Ad., 130 W. 85th st., N. Y. C.; Schuyler 3956.

TERRY, Alice; b. Nashville, Texas, 1896; educ. Washington, D. C.; stage career, "Nobody Home," "Go To It," Washington Square Players; screen career, Crystal ("Strictly Business"), Vitagraph ("The Bottom of the Well," "Love Watches," "The Clarion Call," "Thin Ice"). Hght., 5, 1; wght., 115; fair complexion, blond hair, gray eyes.

TERRY, Ethel; b. 1898; stage exper., mus. com., classical fancy dancing; screen career, leads in Wm. H. Clifford Photoplay Co. ("The Snail," "Denny from Ireland," etc), Egyptian slave girl in "Intolerance." Hght., 5, 1; wght., 117; dark hair and eyes. Home ad., 1012 N. Vermont ave., Los Angeles, Cal.; phone 597046.

TERRY, Ethel Grey; b. Oakland, Calif.; educ. Notre Dame, Boston, Mass.; stage career, with Belasco in "The Lily" two seasons; lead in "The Smouldering Flame," "Search Me," Irving players, Little Theater, Los Angeles, stk.; screen career, Famous ("Sign of the Cross"), Vitagraph ("Arsene Lupin," "Craig Kennedy" serial), Oliver ("Carter Case"), American Cinema ("Greater Than Love"), World ("Phil for Short"), Mayflower ("Mystery of the Yellow Room"), Goldwyn ("Going Some"). Hght., 5, 6; wght., 130; dark complexion, brown hair and gray eyes. Ad., 260 W. 57th st., N. Y., and 1903 Wilcox ave., Hollywood, Cal.

THEBY, Rosemary; b. St. Louis, Mo.; educ. Sargent Dramatic Sch.; screen career, Universal ("Too Much Women," "Boston Blackie's Little Pal," "Unexpected Places," "The Shooting of Sadie Rose"), Artcraft ("The Winged Mystery"), Metro ("The Great Love"), Mayflower ("A Splendid Hazard"). Hght., 5, 5; wght., 124; dark brown hair, hazel eyes. Home ad. 1907 Wilcox ave., Los Angeles, Cal. Holly 460.

THOMAS, Olive Elain; b. Oct. 20, 1898, Charleroi, Pa.; educ. Pittsburgh High; stage career, mus. com. 3 yrs., "Frolic of '14," "Follies of '15," "Frolic of '15"; screen career, Famous Players, Ince-Triangle ("A Girl Like That," "Madcap Madge," "An Even Break," "Frankly Chaste," "Betty Takes a Hand"), Selznick Pict. Corp. ("Upstairs and Down," "The Spite Bride," "The Glorious Lady," "Out Yonder," "Footlights and Shadows"). Hght., 5, 3; wght., 118; light complexion, brown hair, blue eyes. Ad., Selznick Pict. Corp., N. Y. C.

THURMAN, Mary; b. Richfield, Utah; educ. Univ. of Utah; screen career, Fine Arts ("Sunshine Dad"), Keystone ("His First False Step," "The Late Lamented"), Sennett-Paramount ("A Bedroom Blunder," "That Night"), Pathe ("This Hero Stuff," "The House of Betty"), Allan Dwan ("In the Heart of a Fool"). Hght., 5, 3; wght., 123; chestnut hair, gray eyes. Ad., 133 Edgecliff Drive, Los Angeles, Cal.; phone Wilshire 6057.

TINCHER, Fay; b. Topeka, Kan.; educ. there and Chicago; stage career, vaud. one season; screen career, Reliance-Majestic, Fine Arts, Griffith ("Battle of Sexes," "Don Quixote"), Triangle ("Bill, the Office Boy" series), Christie ("Rowdy Ann," "Dangerous Nan McGrew," "Wild and Western," "Go West, Young Woman"). Hght., 5, 2; wght., 110; black hair, brown eyes. Ad., Christie Studio, Los Angeles, Cal.

TITHERIDGE, Madge; b. Melbourne, Australia; educ. England; stage career, 17 yrs. with Cyril Maude, Sir Herbert Tree, Lewis Waller, Coquelin, Sir George Alexander; screen career, Barker (London), ("Brigadier Gerard," "The Woman Who Was Nothing"). Hght., 5, 3; wght., 120; black hair, brown eyes. Home ad., 1565 Third ave., Los Angeles, Cal.; phone 747-89; studio, G. B. Samuelson Film Mfg. Co.

TITUS, Lydia Yeamans; b. Australia; educ. there; stage career, from early age, toured world with husband in own entertainment; screen career, Universal ("High Speed," "The Edge of the Law," "Little Marian's Triumph"), Artcraft ("Romance of Happy Valley"), Paramount ("Happy Though Married"), Vitagraph ("Yankee Princess"), Goldwyn ("Peace of Roaring River," "World and Its Woman," "Strictly Confidential"), Universal ("Gun Fightin' Gentleman"). Hght., 4, 9; wght., 140; brown hair, blue eyes. Home ad., 1515 S. Figueroa st., Los Angeles, Cal.

TONCRAY, Kate; stage career, with Thomas Keene, Alexander Solvini, Nat Goodwin, mgmt. Chas. Frohman, Shubert, Belasco, Brady, etc.; screen career, Biograph, Reliance-Majestic, Fine Arts ("Little Meena's Romance," "The Little Yank," "The Failure"), Artcraft ("Rebecca of Sunnybrook Farm"), Para. ("Battling Jane"), with D. W. Griffith, Old Biograph until he went East, now with Dwan. 5408 Hollywood Blvd. Los Angeles, Cal.; phone 597538.

TRAVERSE, Madlaine; b. Boston, Mass.; educ. Europe; stage career, since 12 yrs. old, vaud., stk. and road, featured at Cohen's Grand opera house, Chicago, and Gaiety, N. Y.; screen career, Artcraft ("The Poor Little Rich Girl"), Ivan ("Sins of Ambition"), Fox ("The Cailliaux Case," "The Danger Zone," "The Love That Dares," "Gambling in Souls," "The Splendid

ACTRESSES

Sin," "The Snares of Paris," "Lost Money," "The Hell Ship," "What Would You Do?" "The Penalty"). Hght., 5, 9; wght., 165; dark brown hair, hazel eyes. Home ad., Hollywood Hotel, Los Angeles, Calif.; Holly 4101; studio, Fox.

TREVELYN, Una; b. English ship; educ. Ward Belmont Sch. for Girls, Nashville, Tenn.; stage career, 4 yrs., 2 seasons with A. H. Woods, N. Y. C., "Common Clay," "Cheating Cheaters," dram. stk.; screen career, old Lubin Co. ("Lost in Mid Ocean"), Goldwyn ("Venus Model"), B. B. Features ("Her Purchase Price"), Universal ("The Woman in the Plot"). Hght., 5, 4½; wght., 128; very fair hair, hazel eyes. Ad., 809 S. Harvard boulevard, Los Angeles, Calif.; Wilshire 910.

TREVOR, Olive; b. New Orleans, La., 1899; educ. Ward-Belmont, Nashville, Tenn.; stage career, dram. reading, vaud., artist's model; screen career, Universal, Gaumont ("The Haunted Manor," etc.), Vitagraph ("Col. Nutt" series, etc.), Fox, Triangle ("Taxi"), Frank Hall ("The Other Man's Wife"). Hght., 5, 5; wght., 118; reddish hair, green eyes.

TURNER, Florence; b. N. Y.; educ. there; stage career, 4 yrs., with Mantell, Grace George, Henry Irving; screen career, Vitagraph, Turner-Trimble-Edwards ("A Welsh Singer"), Mutual ("East Is East," "Doorsteps"), Arrow ("Fool's Gold"). Hght., 4, 10; wght., 102; dark complexion, black hair, dark eyes. Ad., home, Burch House, Walton-on-Thames, Eng. Ad., Hotel Alexandria, Los Angeles, Cal. Studio, Universal Film Co., Universal City, Cal.

— U —

UZZELL, Coreno; b. and educ. Houston, Texas; stage career, with H. W. Savage, Klaw & Erlanger, Al Woods; screen career, Pathe, Famous Players, Mutual, Fox, ("On Trial," "Seven Keys to Baldpate," "Conquered Hearts," "A Woman of Impulse," "Thunderbolts of Fate"), World ("The Oakdale Affair," "The Clouded Name",) San Antonio Pictures Corp. ("Mr. Potter of Texas"), Frohman Amuse. Corp. ("The Invisible Ray" serial). Hght., 5, 6; wght., 134; black hair, brown eyes. Ad., 158 W. 15th st., N. Y.; Watkins. 5383.

— V —

VALE, Vola; stage career, in amateur theatricals in Rochester, N. Y.; screen career, Biograph (stk. member, later played leads for 2 yrs), Universal ("The Adventure of the Last Cigarette," "The Woman He Feared," "The Price of Silence," "Eagle's Wings"), Lasky ("Each to His Kind"), Balboa ("The Secret of Black Mountain"), Paramount ("The Son of His Father"), Ince-Artcraft ("The Silent Man," "The Bloodhound"), Vitagraph ("The Hornet's Nest"), Paramount ("Happy Tho Married"), Rob.-Cole ("Heart in Pawn," "Hearts Asleep"), American ("Six Feet Four").

VALENTINE, Vangie; b. Milwaukee, Wis., 1901; educ. Milwaukee; entered stage work at 5 yrs. did the Fairy in "Blue Bird," Century Roof show, "Miss 1917," leads for Gus Edwards in "Band Box Review," etc.; screen career, "Her Uncle's Wish," "Velvet and Rags," "Measured Steps," Macauley Pict. ("When Bearcat Went Dry"), Bloxbe Film (Young American series); at present with Ziegfeld Midnight Frolic. Hght., 5, 3; wght.; 110; fair complexion, blond hair, blue eyes. Ad., 245 W. 51st st., N. Y. C.

VALERIE, Gladys; b. Wheeling, W. Va.; educ. N. Y. C.; stage career, concert and opera; screen career, Selznick, Mutual, World ("Heart of a Girl"), Famous Players ("Mrs. Wiggs of the Cabbage Patch"), Select ("Marie, Ltd."), Blackton ("Dawn"), First National ("Mind-the Paint-Girl"), Screencraft ("Golden Nugget"). Hght., 5, 5; wght., 125; fair complexion, blond hair, brown eyes. Home ad., Hotel Grampion, 182 St. Nicholas ave., N. Y.; Morningside 3892.

VALLI, Virginia; b. Chicago, 1895; educ. there; stage career, interpretative dancing; screen career, Essanay, World ("His Father's Wife," "The Black Circle," "The Battler"), Dark hair and eyes. Ad., 304 W. 91st st., N. Y. C.

VAN, Beatrice (Beatrice Abbott), also scenario writer; b. Omaha, Neb.; educ. St. Mary's Convent and Lexington Coll.; stage career, in amateur and college productions; screen career, Universal 2½ yrs., American 1 yr. ("The Tiger Lily," "The Dangerous Talent"), author of following stories: "Jackie of the Army," "Molly, Go-Get-'Em," "Ann's Finish," "Paula's Divorce." Ad., 2916 So. Vermont ave., Los Angeles, Calif.

VAN BUREN, Mabel; b. Chicago; educ. there; stage career, stock; screen career, Biograph, Vitagraph, Kinemacolor, Selig, Fox, Clune ("Ramono"), Lasky ("The Sowers," "The Silent Partner," "The Jaguar's Claws," "Unconquered," "The Squaw Man's Son," "Hashimura Togo," "Countess Charming," "The House with the Golden Windows," "The Victoria Cross"), Abrams ("Hearts of Men"). Hght., 5, 3½; wght., 136; dark hair, brown eyes. Ad., home, 4347 Kingswell ave., Hollywood.

VAN NAME, Elsie, also scenario writer; b. Staten Island, N. Y.; educ. N. Y.; stage exper., stk., road shows; screen career, 5 yrs. Universal ("John Ermine of Yellowstone," "The Mystery Ship"), Francis Ford ("Who Was the Other Man," "The Silent Mystery"); wrote "Mystery Ship," "Isle of Intrigue," "Silent Mystery." Francis Ford Studio, 6040 Sunset boulevard, Los Angeles, Calif. Hght., 5, 8; wght., 140; brown hair, blue eyes. Ad., 6210 W. 28th st., Los Angeles, Calif.

VANN, Polly; b. Scranton; educ. Mount St. Mary, Scranton; stage career, vaud., danger; screen career, Universal, Metro ("To the Death"), Mayflower ("Scrap Paper"), Universal ("Hard Lines"), Pathe ("Crooked Daggers"), Selznick ("Regular Girl"), Triangle ("Three Black Eyes"), Hght., 5, 4½; wght., 132; dark complexion, dark brown hair, hazel eyes. Ad., 3544 Broadway, N. Y.

VERNON, Agnes; b. Oregon; educ. Chicago, Ill., Kansas City, Mo.; screen career, Universal-Bluebird (late pictures, "Taking Father Home," "Bringing Home Father," "The Clean-Up," "Sky High"), Keystone ("Dangers of a Bride," "It's Up to You," "A Stormy Knight"), Rob.-Cole ("Bare-Fisted Gallagher"). Hght., 5, 4; wght., 115; light complexion, brown hair, brown eyes. Ad., 1552 Cassil Place, Hollywood, Calif.

VIDOR, Florence; b. Houston, Texas, 1895; educ. convent, high schl. there; screen career, Famous ("The Countess Charming"), Lasky, Artcraft ("The Bravest Way," "New Wives for Old," "Till I Come Back to You," "The Honor of His House," "The White Man's Law"), late pictures ("Turn in the Road," "Poor Relations," "The Other Half," "Better Times." Hght., 5, 4; wght., 120; olive complexion, brown hair and eyes. Home ad., 1514 Sierra Bonita, Los Angeles, Calif.; phone 579306. Studio ad., 6642 Santa Monica boulevard, Hollywood.

— W —

WALCAMP, Marie; screen career, Bluebird ("Hop, the Devil's Brew," "The Flirt," "John Needham's Double"), Gold Seal-Universal ("Onda of the Orient," "Liberty," "The Silent Terror," "The Quest of Virginia," "The Red Ace," "The Indian's Lament"), International ("Patria," "The Lion's Claws," "Tongues of Flame," "The Red Glove" serial), Universal ("The Red Robe"). Ad., Universal City. Now in China.

WALES, Betty; b. Middlebury, Vt., 1900; educ. Castle School, New Rochelle, and Dwight School, Englewood, N. J.; stage exper., ingenue in revival of "Get Rich Quick Wallingford," lead opp. Wm. Collier in "Nothing But the Truth"; screen career, Famous Players ("Oh, You Women"). At present leading ingenue opp. Lewis Stone in Majestic Stk. Co., Los Angeles, Cal. Hght., 5, 4½; wght., 132; brown hair, blue eyes. Home ad., 264 Riverside Drive, N. Y. C.; Riverside 9933.

WALKER, Charlotte; b. Galveston, Tex., 1878; educ. there; stage career from 1895, recent appearances as star or leading woman in "The Wolf," "Just a Wife," "Boots and Saddles," "The Trail of the Lonesome Pine," "The Warrens of Virginia," "Two Virtues"; screen career, Lasky ("Out of Darkness," "The Trail of the Lonesome Pine"), McClure ("Sloth"), Mutual ("Pardners"), Julius Steger ("Just a Woman"), Fox ("Every Mother's Son"), Pathe ("Eve in Exile").

WALKER, Lillian; b. Brooklyn, N. Y.; educ. Brooklyn; early career, photographer's model; stage career, in stk. and vaud.; screen career, Vitagraph ("Princess of Park Row," "The Star Gazer"), Ogden Film Corp. ("The Lust of the Ages," "The Grain of Dust," "Embarrassment of Riches"), Hodkinson ("The Love Hunger,"

"The White Man's Chance," "A Joyous Liar"), Select ("The Better Wife"), Grossman serial ("$1,000,000 Reward"). Hght., 5, 1½; wght., 120; blond hair and blue eyes.

WALLACE, Dorothy; screen career, United ("A Man's Fight," with Dustin Farnum), poster girl for James Montgomery Flagg, appeared in Flagg serials, also supported Gloria Swanson, Olive Thomas, Selznick ("The Spite Bride").

WALTERS, Dorothy; stage career, Belasco, "What's Wrong," Savage, "The Great Name," Frohman, "Lottery Man," "What Ails You?"; screen career, Famous Players ("Misleading Widow," "Little Miss Hoover"), Carl Carlton ("No Children Allowed"), Fox ("Woman, Woman"), World ("Relatives"), Town and Country, Flagg Comedies, Fox with Lee children. At present in "Irene" at Vanderbilt Theatre. Hght., 5, 6; wght., 196; reddish gray hair, gray eyes. Ad., 226 W. 50th st., N. Y.; Circle 4673.

WALTON, Olive; characters; b. Garden City, Kansas; educ. Topeka High Sch.; screen career, Westerns, "Camp-fire Embers," "Do the Dead Talk?". Specialty Feature Films, Castle Films. Hght., 5, 5; wght., 120; red hair, green eyes. Ad., Castle Studios, 2332 N. California Ave., Chicago, Ill.

WARD, Fannie; b. St. Louis, 1875; stage career from 1890, various B'way productions, on tour in "Marriage of William Ashe," "New Lady Bantock," "Madam President," also in vaud.; screen career, Lasky, "The Years of the Locust," "Betty to the Rescue," "Her Strange Wedding," "The Crystal Gazer," "The Sunset Trail," "On the Level," "The Lure of Crooning Waters," "The Winning of Sally Temple," Pathe ("The Yellow Ticket," "The Narrow Path," "Cry of the Weak," "Common Clay," "The Profiteers," "Our Better Selves"). 1919 in England. Hght., 5, 1; wght., 125; fair hair, blue eyes. Ad., Hotel Claridge, N. Y.

WARD, Lucille; b. Dayton, O., 1885; stage career, 15 yrs., name part in "Tillie's Nightmare," also in stk.; screen career, since 1912, in character comedy and leads, with Imp, N. Y., comedy leads with Keystone, with American in Beauty Comedies and Mutual Masterpieces, Morosco ("Happiness of Three Women," "The Road to Love"), American-Mutual ("Annie-For-Spite," "The Frame-up"), Metro ("Amateur Adventuress"), Lasky ("Fires of Faith"), Paramount ("Secret Garden").

WARE, Helen; b. San Francisco; educ. N. Y. Normal Coll.; stage career, from 1899, as understudy, leading woman or star; appeared with Maude Adams, Rose Stahl, Blanche Bates, Robert Edeson, "Within the Law"; screen career, Fine Arts, Bluebird, Selig ("Garden of Allah"), starred in "Third Degree," "The Escape," "The Revolt," "Celebrated Case," "Out There," Crystal ("The Price"), Universal ("Secret Love"), Triangle ("Cross Currents"). Clubs: Twelfth Night, Three Arts Club, Society of Arts and Letters. Ad., 329 Rye Beach ave., Rye, N. Y.

WARNER, Marion; b. Indianapolis, 1893; educ. St. Annis Acad., Victoria, B. C.; screen career, NYMP, 1912-14, Selig (leads in "The Cycle of Fate," "The Far Journey," several Selig animal pictures), Corona ("The Curse of Eve"), Diando ("Very Young Love," "Daddy's Girl," "Daughter of the West," "Old Maid's Baby"); now with King Cole comedies. Hght., 5, 3; wght., 120; blond hair, gray eyes. Ad., Motion Picture Producing Co. of America, 398 Fifth ave., N. Y.; studio ad., Donogan Hills, S. I., N. Y.

WARREN, Mary; b. Phila.; educ. St. Cecelia Acad., Scranton, Pa., 2 yrs. mus. com., Al Jolson; screen career, 5 yrs. Vitagraph, Universal, Triangle, Hampton ("What Every Woman Wants"), Goldwyn ("One of the Finest"), Paramount ("Girls"), Goldwyn ("Heartsease," "City of Comrades"), Universal ("Prince of Avenue A"). Hght., 5, 4; wght., 134; titian hair, violet eyes. Ad., 7059 Jasmine ave., Palms, Los Angeles, Cal.; phone 70002.

WARRENTON, Lule; b. Mich.; educ. Calif.; early career, elocutionist in Notre Dame Univ.; stage career, from age 17, Shakespearian roles, toured British Isles, organized and headed own co., produced children's plays; screen career, 5 yrs. Universal (acted, dir. and wrote scen. "A Bird's Christmas Carol," "Bit o' Heaven," "Star Dust," "The Littlest Fugitive"), Triangle, Goldwyn ("Heart of the Sunset"), Ince ("String Beans"), with Tom Mix in "Whirlwind Trail," Fox ("Be a Little Sport," "Merry-Go-Round"), with George Loane Tucker and H. B. Warner. Ad., 5916 Sunset Blv., Hollywood.

WASHBURN, Hazel; b. Albany, Oct. 25, 1898; educ. Albany, N. Y.; stage career, 2 yrs. with Ziegfeld Follies, 2 yrs. vaud. musical; screen career, Metro ("Revelation"), Select ("Ordeal of Rosetta"), World ("The Wasp"), Pathe. Hght., 5, 6; wght., 125; blond hair, dark eyes. Ad., acre of Betts & Fowler, 1482 Bway, N. Y.; Bryant 5664.

WATERMAN, Ida; stage career; played in "Secret Service" with Wm. Gillette; "The Boomerang"; also with Maude Adams, etc.; screen career, Betzwood-Goldwyn, "A Misfit Earl"; Fox, "Lure of Ambition"; Para.-Artcraft, "The Counterfeit," "Lady Rose's Daughter," "On with the Dance." Hght., 5, 7; wght., 150; gray hair, blue eyes. Ad., 203 West 14th st., N. Y. City; Farragut 2659.

WEER, Helen; b. Anderson, Ind., 1898; educ. in convent St. Joseph's Acad., near Chicago; in "Hitchy Koo" Revue in 1918; screen career, left school to go into motion pictures, 6 mos. with Essanay, World, Frohman, Famous Players, Lubin, Fine Arts ("The Social Secretary," "House Without Children"), Argus Enterprises, Inc. ("A Broadway Saint"). Hght., 5, ½; wght., 99; blond hair. Ad., 687 Madison ave., N. Y.

WEHLEN, Emmy; educ. Vienna and London; stage career, with London Gaiety Co., Daly's, leads in "The Merry Widow," "Dollar Princess," in London, and "Marriage a la Carte," "Tonight's the Night," "The Girl on the Film," etc., in America; screen career, Metro ("The Duchess of Doubt," "The Outsider," "The Shell Game," "House of Gold," "His Bonded Wife," "Sylvia on a Spree," "The Amateur Adventuress," "Fools and Their Money," "A Favor to a Friend"). Hght., 5, 3; wght., 110; blond hair, brown eyes. Ad., Hotel Netherlands, N. Y.

WENDELL, Bunny; b. Boston, 1896; educ. Boston; stage career, in "Follies" of '13, '14, '15, with Castles in "Watch Your Step," and with Raymond Hitchcock in "Beauty Shop," and "Betty," vaud. with Joseph Santley, 3 seasons with "Jack O'Lantern"; screen career, Famous Players, Artcraft ("Less Than Dust"); now rehearsing with "The Night Boat." Hght., 5, 4; wght., 125; brown hair, blue eyes, fair complexion. Ad., home, 812 Lexington ave., or Globe Theatre, N. Y. C.

WEST, Lillian M.; b. N. Y. C.; educ. there and New Jersey; stage career, musical comedy and dramatic; screen career, Fox, Triangle, Selig ("Auction of Souls"), Morosco ("Louisiana"), World ("Woman of Lies"), Sphinx serials ("The Fatal Thirty"). Hght., 5, 5; wght., 130; brown hair and eyes. Home ad., Hotel Glidden, Los Angeles, Cal.

WESTOVER, Winifred; b. San Francisco, Cal.; educ. Dominican Coll. (convent at San Rafael); screen career, 2 yrs. with D. W. Griffith, Fine Arts, playing leads opposite De Wolf Hopper, Wilfred Lucas, Douglas Fairbanks, etc., "Intolerance," with Chas. Ray in "Watch Out William," with Harry Carey in "Gift of the Desert," Para.-Artcraft ("John Petticoats"), Pathe ("This Hero Stuff," "Hobbs in a Hurry," "All the World to Nothing"). Hght., 5, 3; wght., 128; blond hair, dark blue eyes. Home ad., 5120 Hollywood Blvd., Los Angeles, Cal.; phone 597429.

WHIPPLE, Clara Brimmer; b. Missouri; educ. in convent in Germany and finishing schl. in Switzerland; stage career, Pittsburgh stock, Henry Miller's "Dragoon Claw"; screen career, Kalem, Equitable-World ("The Gilded Cage"), Rolfe-Metro ("The Stolen Triumph"), Louis Weber Prod. ("The Man Who Dared God"), Paramount ("Pettigrew's Girl").

WHISTLER, Margaret; b. Louisville, Ky., 1888; educ. Notre Dame Coll., Washington, D. C.; stage career, vaud., stk. and circus throughout Eng. and U. S., with Blanche Bates in "The Girl of Wall Street"; screen career, since 1911, Lubin, Universal ("Behind Life's Stage," "Her Soul's Temptation," "Come Through," "Mary from America"), Selznick ("Poppy"); is painter and designer of gowns for Fox Sunshine comedies. Hght., 5, 3; wght., 134; light brown hair, brown eyes. Ad., Fox Studios, Hollywood, Cal.

WHITCOMB, Mabel; b. Manchester, Eng.; stage career, 15 yrs. with Sir Charles Wyndham, Beerbohm Tree, Drury Lane, Frohman prod.; screen career, 2 yrs. Goldwyn, 3 yrs. World, Mayflower ("Bolshevism on Trial"), Famous Players ("Should a Wife Forgive"), Prisma with Madge Evans, World ("His Father's Wife," "Broadway Saint"), with Jane and Katherine Lee; at present playing in "Three Faces East." Hght., 5, 4; wght., 145; blond hair, brown eyes. Ad., Coytesville, N. J.; Fort Lee 41-R.

WHITE, Pearl; b. Missouri; attracting attention of theatrical man by reciting "Hamlet's Soliloquy," played Little Eva in "Uncle Tom's Cabin"; screen career, first appeared in Wild West pictures, because of her ability to ride, starred with Pathe ("Perils of Pauline," "Elaine" series, "The Iron Claw," "The Fatal Ring," "Pearl of the Army," "Hazel Kirke," "May Blossoms," "New York Lights," "The House of Hate," "The Lightning Raider," "The Black Secret"), Fox ("The White Moll"). Hght., 5, 6; wght., 120; light hair, blue eyes. Ad., care of Fox, N. Y.

WHITMAN, Velma; b. Richmond, Va.; educ. there; screen career, Fox ("East Lynne," "Some Boy," "Melting Millions," "The Book Agent"), 1918-19 with Julian Eltinge, now playing special engagements West Coast Studios. Ad., 2101 Canyon Drive, Los Angeles.

WHITNEY, Claire; b. New York City; educ. N. Y. Wadleigh H. S.; stage career, a one-act vaud. mus. com., also in stock; screen career, from 1909, Biograph, Fox ("The Victim," "The New York Peacock," "When False Tongues Speak," "Thou Shalt Not Steal," "Camille"), Select ("Shirley Kane"), Metro ("The Man Who Stayed at Home"), Para.-Art. ("Career of Katherine Bush"), Ed Jose ("Mothers of Men"), Select ("Isle of Conquest"). Hght., 5, 4; wght., 120; blond hair, brown eyes. Home ad., 50 Morningside ave., N. Y. C.

WIGGIN, Mrs. Margaret A.; b. Indiana; educ. Ill. & Kan.; screen career, Essanay, Selig, Rothacker, Wholesome, Geo. Ade Fables, "Gift of Gab," "The Penny Philanthropist," with Peggy O'Neil. Hght., 5, 6; wght., 150; white hair, blue eyes. Ad., Hotel Grenoble, N. Y. C.

WILKINSON, Mary E.; b. Lafayette, Tenn., 1852; educ. Franklyn, Ky.; early career, teacher, court reporter, proof-reader; screen career, Biograph, Fine Arts ("Bread Line"), D. W. Griffith, Famous Players ("Rose of the Rancho," etc.). Hght., 5, 3; wght., 98; silver hair, hazel eyes. Ad., Imperial Apts., 350 S. Figueroa st., Los Angeles, Cal.; studio, Famous Players.

WILLA, Susanne; b. Los Angeles, Cal.; educ. Paris and San Francisco, Cal.; stage career, Cohan and Harris, musical com. leads, with Emily Stevens, in "Within the Law," playing Aggie, Belasco stk.; screen career, Pathe, Brenon ("Sylvia of the Secret Service," "Kick In," "Arms and the Woman," "Empty Pockets"); at present playing leading feminine role in "Nightie Night." Hght., 5, 2½; wght., 106; blond complexion, golden red hair, green eyes. Ad., 140 W. 55th st., N. Y.

WILLIAMS, Cora; educ. Boston, Mass., and London, Eng.; stage career, 15 yrs. in dramatic companies, stk., etc.; in comic opera as prima donna, soubrette and comedienne; screen career, 2½ yrs. with Edison, Metro ("The Purple Lady"), Famous Players ("The Parisian Wife," "Eyes of the Soul," "Witness for the Defense"), Fisher-Rolfe ("Love Wins"), Cammerait ("Somewhere in Love"), Selznick ("Love"). Hght., 5, 2; wght., 130; grayish hair, brown eyes. Ad., 315 W. 58th st., N. Y.; Columbus 6405.

WILLIAMS, Kathlyn; b. Butte, Montana; educ. Wesleyan Univ. and N. Y. Schl. of Dramatic Art; stage career, "When We Were Twenty-One," "Mrs. Dane's Defense," "The Man of the Hour"; screen career, Morosco-Paramount ("The Highway of Hope," "Big Timber"), Lasky ("Out of the Wreck"), Artcraft ("The Whispering Chorus," "We Can't Have Everything"), Select ("The Better Wife"), Paramount ("A Girl Named Mary," "Tree of Knowledge"). Hght., 5, 5; wght., 138; blond hair, blue-gray eyes. Ad., home, 264 So. Kingsley Drive, Los Angeles, Cal.

WILSON, Edna Mae, b. N. Y., 1903; educ. there; stage career, orig. Dulcie in "The Things That Count," Puck in "Midsummer Night's Dream," "The Prince Chap," etc.; screen career, Fine Arts, World, Edison, Biograph, Universal, Reliance-Majestic, Pathe, National ("Tess of the Mountain Country," "The Fall of a Nation"), Lasky ("Maggie Pepper"), Brunton ("A Man's Country"); fancy, toe and classic dancer. Hght., 5, 3; wght., 98; natural blond, curly hair, dark eyes. Ad., 530 E. Jefferson st., Los Angeles, Cal.

WILSON, Lois; b. Pittsburg, Pa.; educ. Ala. Normal Coll.; screen career, representative of Ala. in Universal's Beauty Contest, Paralta ("A Man's Man," "Turn of a Card," "His Robe of Honor," "One Dollar Bid," "End of the Game"), Lasky ("Love Insurance," "Why Smith Left Home," "It Pays to Advertise," "Too Much Johnson"). Hght., 5, 5½; wght., 120; brown hair, hazel eyes. Ad., Lasky Studio, Hollywood, Cal.

WILSON, Margery; b. Gracey, Ky.; educ. Sandy Valley Seminary; screen career, "Intolerance," Ince-Triangle ("Wolf Lowry," "The Clodhopper," "The Mother Instinct," "The Kentucky School Master"), Triangle ("Mountain Dew," "Wild Sumac," "Lupin Gal," "Bearing Her Cross," "Without Honor," "The Law of the Great North West," "The Finger Print," "The Hand at the Window," "Marked Cards"), Goldwyn ("The Blooming Angel"). Studio ad., Goldwyn, Culver City, Cal.

WOLBERT, Dorothea; b. Philadelphia, Pa.; educ. Mt. Vernon Inst., Baltimore, Md.; stage career, 20 yrs., Chas. Frohman, "The Masqueraders," "Charlie's Aunt," A. L. Willard's "Middleman," "Span of Lift," stock cos.; screen career, New Art Film ("The Solitary Sin"), Fox ("A Man of Sorrow"), Vitagraph ("Sue," "The Enchanted Barn," "Cupid Forecloses," "When Lyn Came Home," "Smashing Barriers," "The Last Man"), Rolin, Lemon, Montgomery & Rock, James Aubrey comedies. Hght., 5; wght., 106; blond hair, blue eyes. Home ad., 123 N. Grand ave., Los Angeles, Cal.; phone 67103.

WOLFE, Jane; b. St. Petersburg, Pa.; educ. Edgehill Inst., Pa.; stage career, with Klaw and Erlanger, in "Buster Brown," "The Ruse," "What Happened to Jones"; screen career, Artcraft ("Rebecca of Sunnybrook Farm," "Under the Top," "Cruise of the Make-Believes," "Mile-a-Minute Kendall," "The Girl Who Came Back," "Thirteenth Commandmant," "The Six Best Cellars"), Famous Players ("Vicky Van," "Men, Women, and Money"), C. B. DeMille ("Why Change Your Wife?"). Hght., 5, 5; wght., 128; brown hair and blue-gray eyes. Ad., Lasky, Hollywood.

WOODWARD, Mrs. Eugenie; b. Cincinnati, O.; stage career, stk. in San Francisco, "Henrietta," with Julia Marlowe in Shakespeare, with Otis Skinner, Wm. Hodge; screen career, World Film ("Bought and Paid For," with Alice Brady), Fox ("East Lynne," "Sporting Blood"), Thanhouser ("Last of the Carnabys"), World ("T'other Dear Charmer"), with Lionel Barrymore in "Copperhead," American Cinema ("Stormy Petrel"), Selznick, with Elaine Hammerstein. Hght., 5, 4; wght., 128; gray hair, brown eyes. Home ad., 70 Morningside Drive, N. Y.; Mngsde 1100.

WORTH, Lillian; educ. N. Y.; stage career, leads and seconds in musical comedy and dramatic stock, small parts in N. Y. prods.; screen career, 2 yrs. with Pathe Freres, B. & C. Film, London, England; S. S. Krellberg (with Helen Holmes in "The Fatal Fortune"), with Constance Talmadge in "In Search of a Sinner." Hght., 5, 8; wght., 139; blond hair, hazel eyes. Ad., 135 Remsen st., Brooklyn, N. Y.; Main 1431.

WRIGHT, Helen; b. St. Paul, Minn., descendant of Scotch and Welsh Royalty; educ. Chicago seminary; stage career, with DeWolf Hopper in "Wang," with Della Fox, Leslie Carter, David Warfield in "The Grand Army Man"; screen career, joined Otis Turner Universal Co., playing character leads ("A Doll's House," "Sirens of the Sea," "The Field of Honor," "The Car of Chance," "The Brass Bullet" serial), Fox ("The Speed Maniac"). Gray hair, brown eyes.

— Y —

YORSKA; stage career, appeared before Leopold II in Belgian Court, adopted by Sarah Bernhardt, toured world with own co. of French Players; screen career, Tyrad ("It Happened in Paris"). Ad., Brunton Studios, Hollywood, Cal.

YOUNG, Clara Kimball; b. Chicago; educ. St. Xavier's Acad., Chicago; stage career, from age of 3, stock, vaud. and prods.; screen career, Vitagraph ("My Official Wife"), World ("Camille," "The Yellow Passport," "The Feast of Life"), at present with own company ("The Foolish Virgin," "The Easiest Way," "The Rise of Susan," "Magda," "Shirley Kaye," "The Savage Woman," "The Marionettes," "The Road Through the Dark," "The Claw," "Cheating Cheaters," "Eyes of Youth," "Forbidden Woman"). Hght., 5, 6; wght., 135; dark hair and eyes. Ad., Garson Studio, Hollywood, Cal., and Aeolian Bldg., N. Y.

YOUNG, Lassie; b. Portland, Ore.; educ. San

Francisco and Brunot Hall, Spokane, Wash.; screen career, in stock with Christie, B. B. Hampton (ingenue lead in "The Dwelling Place of Light"). Hght., 5, 2; wght., 115; blond hair, blue eyes. Studio, B. B. Hampton; home ad., 6019 Yucca ave., Los Angeles, Cal.; Holly 3158.

YOUNGE, Lucille; b. Lyons, France; educ. there and Mich.; stage career, vaud.; screen career, Fox, Fine Arts, Ince ("Fuss and Feathers"), American ("High Play"), Griffith ("The Greatest Thing in Life"), Ince-Para. ("The Virtuous Thief," "Man in the Moon"), Fox ("Fighting for Gold"). Hght., 5, 4; wght., 125; dark brown hair and eyes. Ad., 1337 Waterloo st., Los Angeles, Cal. 1012 N. Vermont, Hollywood, Cal.; phone 597046.

CHILD PLAYERS

—A—

ALEXANDER, Little Ben; b. Goldfield, Nev.; screen career, Griffith ("Hearts of the World"), King Vidor ("Turn in the Road," "Battle of Youth"), Tourneur ("White Heather"), Paralta ("Heart of Rachel"), C. K. Young ("The Better Wife"), Robertson-Cole ("Josselyn's Wife," "Tangled Threads"), Universal ("The Triflers"). Hght., 4; wght., 55; blond hair, dark blue eyes. Ad., 1812 N. Winona Blvd., Los Angeles, Calif.; phone 597485.

ALEXANDER, Lois; b. 1908; educ. private tutor; short stage career; 7 years screen career with parts; Hindoo Princess in "Twenty Thousand Leagues Under the Sea." Ad., home, 640 West 129th St., New York City.

AXZELLE, Violet; b. Feb. 3, 1912, Baltimore; screen career, Universal, Technicolor, World Film, "A Fool's Paradise," "A Wife's Folly," "Behind the Veil," "For the Sake of a Baby," "The Gulf Between" (first m. p. in natural color), "Rasputin the Black Monk," "The Girl from Bohemia"), Schomer-Ross ("The Sacred Flame"). Hght., 3, 4; wght., 53; fair complexion, yellow hair, blue eyes. Ad., home, West Fort Lee, N. J.

—B—

BAKER, Doris; b. Los Angeles, Cal.; educ. priv. school, Los Angeles; stage career, 1 yr. vaud. in own act, 3 yrs. stage, Seattle Stock and Morosco; screen career, 6 yrs., Alkire Co. ("An Ace in the Hole"), Pathe ("I Want to be a Lady"). Hght., 5, 3; wght., 110; blond hair; dk. blue eyes. Home ad., 351½ So. Figueroa St., Los Angeles, Cal. Pico 3046.

BARRY, Wesley; b. Los Angeles, Cal.; educ. there; screen career, Mary Pickford ("Daddy Long Legs"), Blanche Sweet ("The Unpardonable Sin," "A Woman of Pleasure"), Anita Stewart ("Her Kingdom of Dreams"), C. B. DeMille ("Male and Female"). Hght., 4, 6; wght., 84; red hair, blue eyes. Home ad., 1725 Manzanita Ave., Los Angeles, Cal.; studio, Marshall Neilan Productions.

BASKETTE, Lena; b. San Mateo, April 19, 1907; educ. Notre Dame, Redwood City, Cal., studied dancing with Vestoff, former partner of Pavlowa, appeared at Techan Tavern, San Francisco; screen career, Universal ("Brother Jim," "Shoes," "A Romany Rose," "Mysterious Egypt," "The Lonely Little Prince," "A Prince for a Day," "Little Marian's Triumph," "The Caravan," "Dream of Egypt," "Amelita's Friend"). Hght., 4, 7; wght., 75; black hair, brown eyes. Home ad., 1323 Orange Drive, Hollywood, Cal.

BATISTA, Miriam; b. N. Y. City, 1914; played in legitimate prod., "The Whirlwind"; screen prod. International, "Humoresque." Black hair and eyes. Ad. 362 West 45th St., N. Y. City. Bryant 4316.

BELLE, Tula; b. Christiania, Norway, 1909; educ. New Rochelle; screen career, Thanhouser ("Fear of Poverty," "The Vicar of Wakefield," "Through the Open Door"), Metro ("The Brand of Cowardice"), Thanhouser ("Woman and The Beast"), Maurice Tourneur ("The Blue Bird"), Helen Keller ("Deliverance"), George Loane Tucker ("Miracle Man"), Famous Players ("Doll's House"). Hght., 4; brown hair, blue eyes. Ad., 1055 No. St. Andrews Place, Hollywood, Cal.

BUTTERWORTH, Frank; also leads and comedian; b. Lancashire, Eng., 1906; screen career, Ince , Universal ("When You and I Were Young," "The Circus," "When Hearts Were Trumps," "The Children of the Mission," "Amarilly of Clothesline Alley," "The Honorable Algy"), Vitagraph ("The Enchanted Barn"). Hght., 5, 1; wght., 104; fair complexion, brown hair, brown eyes. Ad., home, 6100 Elenor ave., Los Angeles, Cal.

—C—

CARPENTER, Francis Wilburn; b. Glenwood Springs, Col., 1911; screen career, Fine Arts (in juv. co. under Director Franklins, "Children in the House," "Going Straight"), Fox ("Jack and the Beanstalk," "Aladdin and His Wonderful Lamp," "The Girl with the Champagne Eyes," "True Blue," "The Mikado," "The Forbidden Room"), Goldwyn ("Jinx"). Hght., 3, 2; wght., 47; light hair, blue eyes. Ad., home, 1316 Lyman Pl., Los Angeles.

CASWELL, Nancy; b. Los Angeles, 1913; stage exper. with Wm. and Dustin Farnum in "The Littlest Rebel"; screen career, Fox ("Riders of the Purple Sage," "Rainbow Trail," "The Blindness of Divorce"), Paralta ("Within the Cup," "Blue Blood"), Universal ("The End of the Rainbow"), Fox ("Call of the Soul"). Hght., 3, 7; wght., 46; blond hair, blue eyes. Ad., 1544 N. Western, Hollywood, Cal.

CONNELLY, Robert Joseph; b. Brooklyn, 1909; screen career, with Kalem Co. at 3 yrs. old; Vitagraph ("Sonny Jim" series, "A Prince in a Pawnshop," "Bobby, Director," "Bobby, Philanthropist," "Bobby, Pacifist," "Bobby's Bravery," "Just What Bobby Wanted"), O. Henry ("The Discounters of Money," "The Bottom of the Well," "Her Right to Live"), Carson-Neilan ("The Unpardonable Sin"), World ("What Love Forgives"), International ("Humoresque"). Ad., 483 E. 9th st., Brooklyn.

CORBIN, Virginia Lee; b. Prescott, Ariz., 1912; model for artists; screen career, Lasky, with Farrar and Fannie Ward, 8 mos. Universal, with Ben Wilson; played with Allen Holubar in series of pictures written for her; Metro. Balboa, now with Fox ("Jack and the Beanstalk," "The Mikado," "Aladdin and the Wonderful Lamp," "The Babes in the Wood," "Treasure Island," "Ace High," "Six Shooter Andy," "The Forbidden Room"). Hght., 3, 4; wght., 50; light hair, blue eyes. Ad., 1421 Cherokee, Hollywood, Cal.

CRUMPTON, Charles; b. London, England; stage career, "Mother," "Happy Ending," "Rip Van Winkle," "Hansel & Gretel," "Eyes of Youth," "Through the Ages," "Luck of the Navy"; screen career, Universal ("Toy Soldier"), Chapin ("Abraham Lincoln"), Fox ("Green Eyed Monster"), World ("Rasputin"), Artcraft ("Doll's House"), Vitagraph ("Golden Goal"), Canadian ("A World's Shadow"), Famous Players ("Hulda from Holland"). Hght., 4, 7; wght., 80; blond hair, brown eyes. Ad., 108 W. 86th st., N. Y. Schuyler 7314.

—D—

DEAN, Teddy; b. Chicago, 1905; stage career, "Her Own Way," "Little Lord Fauntleroy," "Prince Chap"; screen career, Edison, Fox ("Girl I Left Behind Me"), Frohman ("Then I'll Come Back to You"). Hght., 5, 2; wght., 90; blond hair, blue eyes. Home ad., Chamber st., Bayside, L. I. N. Y.

DE RUE, Carmen; b. Pueblo, Colo., 1908; educ. private tutor; screen career, Lasky ("Squaw Man," "Brewster's Millions," "Master Mind"), Universal (leads for yr. in child co. with Gordon Griffith and Billy Jacobs), Majestic (lead for 1 yr. in child co., dir. Franklins), for one yr. featured as one of Fine Arts "kiddies"; has appeared in more than 100

CHILD PLAYERS

photoplays; Fox ("Jack and the Beanstalk," "Aladdin and the Wonderful Lamp," "Babes in the Woods," "Girl with the Champagne Eyes"). Hght., 4,6; wght., 85; light hair, brown eyes. Home ad., 1627 Hudson ave., Hollywood, Calif.

—E—

EVANS, Madge; b. N. Y. C. 1909; educ. private tuition; stage career, Mimsey in "Peter Ibbetson" with John Barrymore; screen career, child parts in Famous Players ("Zaza," "The Seven Sisters"), Peerless-World ("Seventeen," "Beloved Adventuress," "The Burglar," "Little Patriot," "True Blue," "Web of Desire," "Maternity," "Neighbors," "Wanted, a Mother," "Love Not," "Home Wanted," starred in "Little Duchess," "The Volunteer," "Adventures of Carol," "Gates of Gladness"). Home ad., 50 Cathedral Parkway, N. Y. C.

—G—

GARY, Nadia Louise; b. 1912; Butterfly Baby with Boston Opera Co.; screen career 2 yrs., Goldwyn, Fox, World, Metro, Artcraft, etc. Current releases with Mabel Normand in "The Venus Model"; Wm. Faversham ("The Silver King"), Goldwyn ("Sandy Burke of the U-Bar-U"). Ad., 2 Abbey Court, 4640 B'way, N. Y. C.

GRAUER, Ben; b. N. Y. C. 1910; stage career, Geo. C. Tyler, "Penrod"; J. D. Williams, "Betty at Bay"; Shubert, "Maytime"; screen career, Fox ("Cailleux Case"), World ("Neighbors"), Julius Steger ("Hidden Truth," "Break the News to Mother"), Stage Women's War Relief ("The Mad Woman"), Universal ("His Woman"). Hght. 4, 3; wght., 62; light brown hair, dark brown eyes. Ad., 201 W. 112th st., N. Y. C. Cathedral 8762.

—H—

HORTON, "Little Aida"; b. 1914, Long Island; screen career, Vitagraph (tiniest leading lady Bobby Connelly series, "A Bachelor's Children," "The Desired Woman," "The Mating," "Compliments of the season"), Miller Prod. ("High Speed," "The Romany Call"). Hght., 3, 1; wght., 34; fair complexion, blond hair, blue eyes. Home ad., Aqueduct, Woodhaven P. O., L. I., N. Y.

—I—

IRVING, Mary Jane; b. Columbia, S. C., 1914; screen career, Brunton Studios ("The Temple of Dusk," "Heart of Rachael"), Mastercraft ("The One Woman," "Patriotism"), B. B. Hampton ("The Westerners"), Haworth ("The Gray Horizon"), Goldwyn ("Almost a Husband," "Cup of Fury"), Robt. Brunton ("Live Sparks"). Home ad., 828 So. Burlington, Los Angeles, Cal.

—J—

JOY, Gloria; b. Oct. 16, 1911, Los Angeles; stage career, Little Theatre, Los Angeles, speaking and dancing parts; screen career, leads in "Wanted a Brother," "No Children Wanted," "The Locked Door," "Little Miss Grown Up," "Miss Mischief Maker," "The Midnight Burglar"); with Dorothy Phillips in "The Talk of the Town." Hght., 3, 8; wght., 55; brown hair, hazel eyes. Ad., home, 1133 Lake Shore Ave., Los Angeles, Cal.

—K—

KAY, Honey Beatrice; b. N. Y. C., 1907; specialty characters; screen career, World, with Louise Huff; Fox ("Why I Would Not Marry"), Universal ("Santa and Genii"), Goldwyn, with Mabel Normand; Chas. Miller ("Crowded Hour"), Screen Letter Box. Hght., 4 ft., 2 in., wght., 72; blond hair, blue eyes. Ad., 312 W. 48th St., N. Y. C. Bryant 8560.

—L—

LAWRENCE, Little Adelaide; b Brooklyn, 1905; photographer's model; screen career, Vitagraph ("Easter Babies"), Reliance ("The Barefoot Boy"), Pathe ("Little Keeper of the Light"), Kalem ("Little Wanderer"), Fox ("The High Born Child and the Beggar," "The Queen of Hearts"). Fair complexion, auburn bronze hair, brown eyes. Ad., 274 Rutland Road, Brooklyn, N. Y.

LEE, Master Frankie; b. Gunnison, Colo., 1912; screen career, Mayflower ("The Miracle Man"), Goldwyn ("Bonds of Love"), B. B. Hampton ("The Westerners"), Thos. Ince ("Quicksands," "The Law of Men"), Realart ("Judy of Rogues Harbor," "Nurse Marjorie"), Mary Pickford ("Daddy Long Legs"), Tom Mix ("Rough Riding Romance"). Hght., 3, 9; wght., 42; dark brown hair, dark blue eyes. Home ad., 1460 Vine St., Hollywood, Cal., 'phone 579619.

LEE, Jane; screen career, Fox ("The Clemenceau Case," "The Spider and the Fly," "A Daughter of the Gods," "Patsy," "Two Little Imps," "Trouble Makers," "Love and Hate," "American Buds," "Doing Their Bit," "Swat the Spy," "We Should Worry," "Tell It to the Marines," "Smiles"). Series of 2-reel comedies for Rogers Film Corp., 1639 B'way, N. Y.

LEE, Katherine; b. Glasgow, Scotland; stage career, with Lew Fields; screen career, Fox ("The Clemceau Case," "The Spider and the Fly," "The Daughter of the Gods," "Love and Hate," "The Two Imps," "The Troublemakers," "American Buds," "Doing Their Bit," "Swat the Spy," "We Should Worry," "Tell It to the Marines," "Smiles"); auburn hair. Series of 2-reel comedies for Rogers Film Corp., 1639 B'way, N. Y.

—M—

MESSENGER, Buddie; b. 1909. San Francisco; screen career, Universal, Fox, "Gloriana," "The Street Urchin," "Fighting Joe," "Jack and the Beanstalk," "Treasure Island," "Aladdin," "Babes in the Wood"), First National ("The Hoodlum"); excels as a heavy. Fair complexion, light brown hair, brown eyes. Ad., home, 5423 Sunset Blvd., Hollywood, Cal.

MONAHAN, Janethel; b. N. Y. C., 1907; stage career, understudied Gogo and Mimsey in "Peter Ibbetson," with John Barrymore; screen career, Juvenile Film, "Chip of the Old Block," "Chip's Elopement," "Chip's Rivals," "The World War in Kidland," "For Sale, a Daddy," "Chip's Carmen," "Chip's Movie Co."; Universal ("Me and My Gal"), 10 two-reel comedies by Atlas Film Corp.; Prizma ("May-Days," "Whittier's School Days"). Hght., 4, 6; wght., 79½; chestnut hair, dark blue eyes. Home ad., Center Ave., West Fort Lee, N. J. Post Office Box 155.

MONAHAN, Joseph; b. Brooklyn, N. Y., 1908; stage career, "Peter Ibbetson" with John Barrymore; screen career, 2 yrs. under dir. of Jas. A. FitzPatrick, in "Chip of the Old Block," "Chip's Elopement," "Chip's Rivals," "The World War in Kidland," "For Sale, a Daddy," "Chip's Carmen," "Chip's Movie Co., as Willie Lincoln in "Chapin's Lincoln Cycle," Universal ("Me and My Gal"), 10 two-reel comedies by Atlas Film Corp., Prizma ("May-Days," "Whittier's School Days"). Hght., 4, 6; wght., 77½; dark brown hair, dark blue eyes. Home ad., Center Ave., West Ft. Lee, N. J. P. O. Box 155.

MOORE, Pat; b. England, 1914; screen career, Ince ("Sahara"), Universal ("The Sleeping Lion"), K. MacDonald Pict. ("The Turning Point"), Macarthy ("Out of the Dust"), Mayflower ("A Fool at Heart"). Hght., 3, 8; brown hair and eyes. Home ad., 1739 Vine St., Los Angeles, Cal., 'phone 57427.

—O—

OSBORNE, "Baby" Helen Marie; b. 1911; screen career, Pathe ("Little Mary Sunshine," etc.), Lasalida-Pathe Films ("When Baby Forgot," "Baby Pulls the String," "The Child of M'sieu," "Baby's Diplomacy," "Tears and Smiles"), Diando Films ("The Little Diplomat," "Sawdust Doll," "The Old Maid's Baby," "Dolly's Vacation," "Milady of the Beanstalk," "The Evidence"). Ad., Baby Marie Osborne Prod., Long Beach, Calif.

— R —

RAE, Zoe ("Baby"); b. Chicago, July 13, 1910; screen career, 6 yrs., Biograph and Universal, star of "Gloriana," "Through Baby's Voice," "The Little Pirate," "Danger Within," "Heart Strings," "By Speshul Delivery," "Naked Hearts," "Bobby's Bargain," leading parts in "The Desperado," "The War Waif," "Bettina Loved a Soldier," "We Are French," "The Kaiser the Beast of Berlin," etc. Wght., 72; blond hair, blue eyes. Ad., 1015 Manzanita ave., Los Angeles.

REDDEN, Arthur L.; b. Boston, Mass., July 17, 1908; educ. Los Angeles; screen career, Triangle ("Mayro of Filbert"), New Art Film ("Solitary Sin"), Metro ("Way of the Strong"), Brentwood ("Other Half," "Van Dusen's Home"), Universal ("The Pointing Finger"). Hght., 4, 8; wght., 70; brown hair, dark blue eyes. Home ad., 1324 W. 31st st., Los Angeles, Calif.; West 6459.

REINECKE, Helen; stage career, Winthrop Ames, "The Betrothal," stk. co. in Akron, O., "An Old Sweetheart of Mine," ballet dancer and oriental dancer; screen career, "The Farmer," "The Magician," Selznick ("Sealed Hearts") Hght., 4, 7; wght., 86; light, curly hair, blue eyes. Ad., 158 W. 96th st., N. Y.; Riverside 9891.

— S —

SMITH, Little Bernice; b. Portland, Ore., 1911; stage career, Fisher Circuit, Bert Levy Circuit, featured at the Hippodrome, Portland; screen career, began with Universal at 4 yrs. of age, "The Finest Gold," has played with Murdock MacQuarrie, and also with Helen Holmes in railroad pictures, etc. Now with Gloverio Comedies.

STONE, George; b. 1911, Cleveland, O.; now being educated by tutor; screen career, Biograph, Majestic, Fine Arts; in child parts; has appeared in "Going Straight," "The Little School M'am," etc., Triangle ("An Even Break," "Wild Shumac"), Fox ("Ali Baba and the Forty Thieves"), Artcraft ("Till I Come Back to You," "The Poppy Girl's Husband"), Fox ("The Jungle Trail," "The Speed Maniac"), Hampton-Pathe ("Fighting Cressy"). Hght., 3, 2; wght., 47; blue eyes, brown hair.

— W —

WARD, Baby Ivy; b. London, Eng., 1914; screen career, Metro ("The Great Secret," "The Slacker," "Draft 258," "The Winning of Beatrice," "A Man's World," "Silent Woman"), World ("Neighbors"), Wm. A. Brady ("Little Women"), Leah Baird Co. ("As a Man Thinks"), Charles Richmond Co. ("Everybody's Business"), Artcraft ("Doll's House"), Universal ("Heads Win"), Canadian Co. ("A World's Shadow"). Hght., 3, 6; wght., 34; blond hair, hazel eyes. Ad., 108 W. 86th st., N. Y.; Schuyler 7314.

GEORGE ELWOOD JENKS
Continuity—Reconstruction—Specials
REAL SCREEN PLAYS
The logical result of dramatic ability PLUS six years of thorough studio training.
PAST RELEASES STARRING
William Russell, Olive Thomas, Margery Wilson, Roy Stewart, Pauline Starke, William Desmond, J. Warren Kerrigan, H. B. Warner, Blanche Sweet, etc., etc.
CURRENT RELEASES
"A WOMAN OF PLEASURE"   "THE PARISH PRIEST"
(Blanche Sweet)   (Wm. Desmond)
"BEHIND RED CURTAINS" (H. B. Warner)
JESSE D. HAMPTON PRODS., Hollywood, Calif.

LITTLE BEN ALEXANDER

"Hearts of the World"
"The Turn in the Road"
"The Better Wife"

"Little Ben" in King W. Vidor's initial special production for First National

Permanent address c/o Willis & Inglis

PRODUCERS

—A—

ABRAMSON, Ivan, director and scenario writer; b. Vilna, Russia; educ. Vilna; early exper., impressario of Ivan Abramson Opera Company for 7 years, wrote many plays for Jewish stage, dir. Jacob P. Adler for 15 yrs.; screen career, Ivan ("Enlighten Thy Daughter," "Sins of Ambition," "Babbling Tongues," "When Men Betray," "Ashes of Love," "Moral Suicide," "Someone Must Pay," "One Law for Both," "Echo of Youth"), director general Graphic Film Corp., 729 Seventh ave., N. Y. Home ad., 207 West 110th st., N. Y.

—B—

BEACH, Rex, author; b. Atwood, Mich., 1877; educ. Rollins Coll., Chicago Coll. of Law, Kent Coll. of Law; author of "The Spoilers," "The Barrier," "The Silver Horde," "Going Some," "The Ne'er-Do-Well," "The Net," "The Iron Trail," "The Auction Block," "Heart of the Sunset," "Rainbow's End," "Crimson Gardenia," "The Brand," "The Girl From Outside." Member Players Club, Lambs Club, N. Y. Athletic Club. Home ad., Lake Hopatcong, N. J.

BINNEY, Harold J., producer-director; b. Kansas City, Kans., June 3, 1889; educ. Univ. of Washington; stage career, 3 yrs. vaud., "The Girl I Left Behind Me," "Cigarette," "Shenandoah," etc.; screen career, Biograph, I. M. P., Keystone ("Hash House Fraud," "Court House Crooks," "The Submarine Pirate," "The Snow Cure," etc.); since 1916 independent producer personally directing his own productions, among which were all "Josh Binney" Comedies, and all "Masterpicture" features; late productions are "Her Uncle's Wish," "Velvet and Rags," "Measured Steps." Now operating under name of Canadian Photo-play Productions, Ltd. Ad., Studio, Canadian Photo-play Productions, Ltd., New Toronto, Canada; res., 276 Wright ave., Toronto, Canada.

BLACKTON, J. Stuart, Director General of own company; b. 1875, Sheffield, Eng.; commenced educ. at Eton, Eng., finished in America, C. C. N. Y.; early career, newspaper writer and artist, pioneer in motion picture industry since 1897; organized Vitagraph Co. in 1900; most notable productions, "The Christian," "Island of Regeneration," "The Battle Cry of Peace," "Womanhood," "Missing," "The Common Cause"; founded Motion Picture Magazine 1910; organized Motion Picture Board of Trade of America and was elected its first president in 1915; organized own independent producing co., Blackton Productions, Inc., 1917, merged into J. Stuart Blackton Feature Pictures, Inc., 1919 ("A House Divided," "The Moonshine Trail," "Dawn," "My Husband's Other Wife," "The Blood Barrier," "Passers-by"). Ad., 25 West 45th st., N. Y.

BRENON, Herbert; b. Dublin, Ireland, 1880; educ. St. Paul's and Kings Coll., London; early career, stage dir. and owner of m. p. theatre; screen career, Universal ('Neptune's Daughter"), Fox ("A Daughter of the Gods"), Brenon-Selznick ("War Brides"), Brenon-Select ("The Lone Wolf"), Brenon ("The Fall of the Romanoffs," "Kismet"), independent producer, Herbert Brenon Film Corporation ("The Passing of the Third Floor Back," with Sir Johnston Forbes-Robertson). Propaganda picture for British government; now making a series abroad starring Marie Doro ("Princess Impudence"), Republic ("12-10"). Ad. Lambs Club, N. Y.

BRUCE, Robert Cameron; b. Stowe, Vt., 1887; educ. Univ. of Iowa, Univ. of Minn.; early career, retail lumberman, rancher; screen career, with Katherine F. Carter, Inc. and Educational prod. scenics, including "Me and My Dog," "The World of Dreams," "Wanderer and the Whozitt," "River Gray and the River Green," "Wolf of the Tetons," "Separate Trails," "Frozen Thrills," "Sundown," "An Essay of the Hills." Hght., 6, 2; wght., 150; light hair, blue eyes. Ad., Educational Film Corp., 729 Seventh ave., N. Y.

BRUNTON, Robert A.; b. Glasgow, Scotland; educ. London, at Royal Academy schls.; stage career, scenic artist with Henry Irving at Lyceum theatre, London, made 3 tours of America with Irving as scenic director, 3 yrs. with Shuberts as scenic artist, 3 yrs. with Oliver Morosco; screen career, art director and mgr. of prod., Ince-Triangle; owner and executive head of Robt. Brunton studios, 5341 Melrose ave., Los Angeles, Cal.

—C—

CAPELLANI, Albert; director; b. Paris, 1874; one of pioneers in moving picture art; 17 yrs. moving picture career with Pathe; 5 yrs. in America, World Film, Selznick, Clara K. Young Corp., Metro directing Madame Nazimova in "Eye for Eye," "Out of the Fog," "The Red Lantern"; now at head of own producing corp., starring Marjorie Rambeau, Dolores Cassinelli, June Caprice; personal representative in America and France, Harry Cahane. Ad., Albert Capellani Prods., Inc., 1457 Broadway, N. Y.

CAREWE, Edwin; director; b. Gainsville, Texas; educ. Univ. Missouri and Texas; stage career, 16 yrs.; screen career, Lubin, Rolfe-Metro in "Her Fighting Chance," "The Trail of the Shadow," "The Voice of Conscience," "The Splendid Sinner," "The Trail of Yesterday," "The Snowbird," "House of Tears," "God's Half Acre," "The Final Judgment," "Pals First," "Shades of Suspicion," "The Way of the Strong," "It's Easy to Make Money" now at the head of his own producing company; has made the "Right to Lie," "The Web of Lies." Ad., Brunton Studios, Hollywood, Calif.

CARLETON, Lloyd B.; b. N. Y.; educ. Columbia Coll.; stage career, with Maude Adams, dir. Fawcett Stock Co.; screen career, Thanhouser, Lubin, Fox, Selig, Universal, dir. "Walls of Jericho," "The Idler," "Their Sinful Influence," "Way of the World" (late pictures, "The Unattainable," "The Morals of Hilda," "The Devil's Bondwoman"), Lloyd Carleton Prod. ("The Amazing Woman"). Member M. P. D. A. Home ad., 5846 Carlton Way, Hollywood.

CHAUTARD, Emile, director; b. Paris; educ. France; stage career, leading man at Odeon theatre, Paris, Gymnase theatre, Rayne theatre and Theatre Royal; screen career, with Eclair in Paris, Peerless, Lasky, C. K. Young ("Magda"), Pathe, World, Famous Players-Lasky ("The House of Glass," "The Marionettes," "The Ordeal of Rosetta," "Her Final Reckoning," "The Daughter of the Old South," "Paid in Full," "Under the Greenwood Tree," "The Parisian Wife," "The Marriage Price," "Out of the Shadows," "Eyes of the Soul"), Mayflower Photoplays, Inc. ("Mystery of the Yellow Room"), "The Invisible Foe." Home ad., 790 Riverside drive, N. Y.

CHRISTIE, Al. E., director; b. London, Canada; educ. N. Y.; early career, with Liebler & Co. in productions starring Wilton Lackaye, May Irwin, William C. Hodge and others; screen career, director, producer and author of more than 700 comedies; four years ago organized Christie Film Co., and produced Christie Comedies for independent release, one reel subject weekly and two reel subject monthly. Ad., Christie Film Co., Inc., Hollywood, Cal.

—D—

DeMILLE, Cecil B., director general, **Famous Players-Lasky Corp.;** b. Asheville, Mass.; educ. mil. schl., Amer. Acad. Dram. Arts, N. Y.; stage career, prominent parts in all-star road cos. over the U. S. for 7 yrs., produced number of stage successes, including "Return of Peter

Grim," with David Warfield, wrote and dir. several musical operettas; Famous Players-Lasky Corp., Paramount-Artcraft Pictures ("Joan the Woman," "The Whispering Chorus," "We Can't Have Everything," "The Woman God Forgot," "Old Wives for New," "For Better, For Worse," "Don't Change Your Husband," "Male and Female," "Why Change Your Wife?") Ad., Lasky Corp., Hollywood, Calif.

DWAN, Allan, director; b. Toronto, Can.; educ. Notre Dame, Ind.; screen career, Essanay (scenario writer), American (scen. edit. and dir. for 3 yrs.), Famous Players (dir. "Wildflower," "David Harum"), Selznick ("Panthea"), Goldwyn ("Fighting Odds"), Triangle ("Man Who Made Good"), C. K. Young ("Cheating Cheaters"), Artcraft ("Mr. Fixit," "Bound in Morocco," "He Comes Up Smiling," "Heading South"), Louise Glaum ("Sahara"), Allan Dwan Prod. ("Soldiers of Fortune," "Luck of the Irish," "A Splendid Hazard," "In the Heart of a Fool," "The Scoffer"). Member M.P.D.A. Now producing for Mayflower Photoplays, Inc.

— E —

EMERSON, John, director; b. Sandusky, O., 1874; educ. Oberlin Coll., Heidelberg Univ., Univ. of Chicago; stage career, with Mrs. Fiske, 4 yrs. stage dir., with Shubert, leads with Nazimova, 4 yrs. gen. stage dir. for Chas. Frohman, 2 yrs. starring in "The Conspiracy"; screen career, Famous Players, Fine Arts (produced "Old Heidelberg,") and in collaboration with Anita Loos, "The Americano," "Macbeth," "The Social Secretary"), Artcraft (dir. "Less Than Dust," "In Again, Out Again," "Wild and Wooly"), Paramount ("Oh, You Women"), Constance Talmadge Co. ("A Temperamental Wife," "Virtuous Vamp," "In Search of a Sinner"). Home ad., Lambs Club; studio, 318 E. 48th st., N. Y. C.

EMPEY, Arthur Guy, actor and author; vice-pres. Guy Empey Pict. Corp.; educ. Brooklyn, N. Y.; early career, short story and newspaper writer; stage career, starred with Rose Stahl in "Pack Up Your Troubles," Wagenhalls & Kemper; military career, served in U. S. Army with the regulars and in U. S. Navy before European war; in 1915 went to London and enlisted in British Army, served for eighteen months, discharged in July, 1916, on account of wounds received in Battle of the Somme; author of "Over the Top," "First Call," "Tales From a Dugout"; screen career, "Over the Top," "The Undercurrent," "Oil"; now engaged in producing series of pictures, stories of which are written by himself. Hght., 5, 5; wght., 150; brown hair and eyes. Ad., 220 W. 42d st., N. Y.; Bryant 6492.

— F —

FORD, Francis, director and actor; b. Portland, Me., 1882; stage career, with Amelia Bingham in stock, etc.; screen career, Melise, NYMP, Universal ("Purple Mask," "Good Morning, Judge," "The Unfinished Jewels," "The Puzzle Woman," "The Greatest Sacrifice," "The Chang Fuy Treasure," "The Phantom Ship"), F. Ford Prod. Co. ("Berlin via America," "The Isle of Intrigue"), Ford Miniatures ("The Silent Mystery"), star and director of "The Mystery of 13" and "The Gates of Doom" serials. Hght., 5, 11; wght., 160; fair complexion, black hair, gray eyes. Ad., Ford Studio, 6040 Sunset blvd., Los Angeles, Cal. Home ad., 1210 W. 28th st., Los Angeles.

— G —

GARSON, Harry I., manager and press representative; b. Rochester, N. Y.; educ. there; Broadway Strand theatre, Detroit, Mich., Harry Garson Prod. with Clara Kimball Young and Blanche Sweet; organized Garson Studios, produced "The Eyes of Youth," "The Forbidden Woman"; also directed the latter. Studio ad., 1845 Allesandro st., Los Angeles, Calif.

GASNIER, Louis J.; b. Paris, France; screen career, associated with Pathe Freres 17 yrs., 14 yrs. as Gen. Mgr. and 2 yrs. Vice-Pres.; 1916, organized Astra Film Corp. serving as Pres. and Gen. Mgr. to date; produced Fannie Ward features, Mrs. Vernon Castle features for Pathe; "Hands Up," "The Tiger's Trail," "The Third Eye," serials for Pathe; March 1919, organized Lew Cody Prods.; supervised production of "The Beloved Cheater," "The Butterfly Man"; supervising dir. Dustin Farnum, "Corsican Brothers," "Square Shooting Dan." Home ad., 3847 Hudson Blvd., No. Bergen, N. J.; studio, Verdugo Road, Glendale, Calif.

GRIFFITH, David Wark, gen. mgr. own co.; b. 1880, LaGrange, Ky.; on stage 2 yrs.; screen career, since about 1908, first as actor, then as director for Biograph, where he introduced innovations which changed the whole course of motion picture art; first to use "close-ups" and "cut backs"; trained a large number of screen players who have since become stars, 1914, assumed charge of Reliance-Majestic studios for Mutual; producer of "Judith of Bethulah," "Birth of a Nation," "Intolerance," "Hearts of the World," "The Great Love," "The Greatest Thing in Life," "True Heart Susie," "Romance of Happy Valley," "Girl Who Stayed at Home," "Broken Blossoms," "Scarlet Days." First National ("The Greatest Question"), Griffith Prod., "Romance," "Fires of Youth." Ad., Mamaroneck, N. Y.

— H —

HAMPTON, Jesse D., producer; b. Galesburg, Ill.; educ. Knox College; early career, newspaper, magazine and advertising business several years; screen career, organized Jesse D. Hampton Productions, starring Blanche Sweet, H. B. Warner and Wm. Desmond. Ad., Hollywood, Calif.

HENLEY, Hobart, director; b. Louisville, Ky., 1887; educ. Univ. Cincinnati; stage career, stock in Cincinnati, Cleveland, Buffalo; screen career, from 1913, Universal ("June Madness"), Frank Seng ("Parentage"), Pathe, Goldwyn ("The Face in the Dark," "The Glorious Adventure," "All Woman," "Money Mad," "One Week of Life," "The Peace of Roaring River," "Woman on the Index," "Too Fat to Fight"), Hobart Henley Prod. ("The Gay Old Dog"). Ad., care Pathe Exchange, N. Y.

— I —

INCE, Thomas H., producing director; b. Newport, R. I., 1882; stage career, song and dance artist in "Poets and Puppets" with James A. Herne in "Shore Acres," Edwin Arden in "Ninety and Nine," star in "For Love's Sweet Sake," vaud.; screen career, appointed director general NYMP 1909; director general and one of the three vice-presidents in charge of mfg. Triangle; laid out plants at Inceville, near Santa Monica, Triangle at Culver City, and the new Thomas H. Ince studio at Culver City, Cal. Now producing photoplays featuring Dorothy Dalton, Charles Ray and Enid Bennett for Paramount program. Notable productions, "The Wrath of the Gods," "Civilization," Dorothy Dalton in "Vive la France," "Extravagance," Charles Ray in "String Beans," "Greased Lightning," "The Busher," "Hayfoot, Strawfoot," Enid Bennett in "Happy Tho' Married," "Partners Three," "Nemesis," MacLean and May in "23½ Hours Leave," "What's Your Husband Doing?" "Mary's Ankle," Hobarth Bosworth "Behind the Door," Ince Special. Ad., Culver City, Cal.

INGLIS, Gus, member of Willis and Inglis; early career, actor, stage mgr.; screen career, actor, dir., writer, exhibitor, exchange man; now edits films, manages many well known people, and finances companies. Ad., Los Angeles, Calif.

— J —

JOSE, Edward, director; b. Antwerp, Belgium; educ. Paris Conservatory for Pianists; stage career, for 20 yrs. in France, Belgium, S. America and England, stage director for Antoine and Sarah Bernhardt; screen career, Pathe ("The Light That Failed"), Selznick

ARTHUR GUY EMPEY

IN A SERIES OF

HIS OWN PRODUCTIONS

220 West 42nd Street
New York City

VIVIAN M. MOSES
General Manager

("Poppy," "The Moth"), Artcraft ("La Tosca," "Resurrection," "Fedora"), Artcraft specials, ("My Cousin," "The Beautiful Romance," "Two Brides" and "Fires of Faith"), Anita Stewart Prod. ("The Fighting Shepherdess"), Select ("Isle of Conquest"), Ed. Jose Prod. ("Mothers of Men"). Ad., Friars Club, N. Y.; Hollywood Hotel, Los Angeles, Cal.

— L —

LEHRMAN, Henry; b. Austria; educ. there; screen career, Biograph, Imp, Keystone, helped organized L-KO, organized Lehrman Sunshine Comedies in 1917 with William Fox, organized and president of Henry Lehrman Prods., Inc., producing comedies for First Nat'l release, Sunshine Comedies ("Wild Women and Tame Lions," "Who's Your Father?" "A Tight Squeeze," "A High Diver's Last Kiss," "Mongrels," "The Fatal Marriage"), Lehrman Prods. ("The Twilight Baby"), Ad., 6717 Franklin ave., Los Angeles, Calif.; Holly 2329.

LEWIS, Edgar; b. Holden, Mo., 1872; as a boy was shanghaied and taken to England, later 4 yrs. with circus; stage career, long period of rep. and stock; screen career, Solax, Reliance, Photoplay Prods. Co., Life Photo, 6 yrs. Fox, Lubin ("The Great Divide," "The Barrier"), Edgar Lewis ("The Bar Sinister," "The Sign Invincible," "Calibre 38," "Other Men's Shoes," "Sherry," "Lahoma"). Permanent ad., Edgar Lewis Prods., Inc., 1457 Broadway, N. Y. C., or 201 S. Bonnie Brae st., Los Angeles, Calif.

— M —

MILLER, Charles, director; b. Saginaw, Mich.; educ. Univ. of Mich.; stage career, for 15 yrs. under mgmt. of Chas. Frohman, Henry B. Harris, Klaw & Erlanger, Daniel Frohman, stage dir., stock throughout country, leading man with Clara Bloodgood, Louis Mann, Clara Lipman, etc.; screen career, 1 yr. with Ince, Triangle-Ince ("The Flame of the Yukon"), Select ("The Ghosts of Yesterday"), Metro Screen Classics ("Wilson or the Kaiser," "Why Germany Must Pay"), Goldwyn ("The Service Star"), Mayflower ("Law of the Yukon"). Author of several vaud. acts, has reconstructed many stage plays. Ad., Lambs Club, N. Y.

— N —

NEILAN, Marshall, director; b. 1891; educ. high school; stage career, stk. in San Francisco and Los Angeles, on road with Barney Bernard and others; screen career, Artcraft ("Rebecca of Sunnybrook Farm," "Little Princess," "M'liss," "Stella Maris," "Amarilly of Clothesline Alley," "Hit-the-Trail Holliday," "Hearts of the Wild," "Out of a Clear Sky," "Three Men and a Girl"), Blanche Sweet Co. ("The Unpardonable Sin"), First Nat'l ("Daddy Long Legs," "Her Kingdom of Dreams," "In Old Kentucky"), Marshall Neilan Prods. ("The River's End"). Home ad., Los Angeles Athletic Club; studio, 1723 Allesandro st., Los Angeles; Milshire 5174.

— P —

PERRET, Leonce, director; b. Niort, France, 1880; educ. Paris Univ. and Scola Cantorum; stage career, vaud.; screen career, Gaumont of Paris; formed own corporation, Perret Prods ("Lafayette, We Come," "The Million Dollar Dollies," with Dolly Sisters, "The Unknown Love," "Stars of Glory," "A Soul Adrift," with Dolores Cassinelli, "The Twin Pawns," "A, B, C of Love," with Mae Murray; adapted and directed "The 13th Chair," with all-star cast; special, "A Modern Salome," with Hope Hampton). Coming, "L'Entreinte du Passe," by Henri Ardel and "Koenigsmark," by Pierre Benoit, awarded first prize at Goncourt Academy. Ad., Perret Pictures, Inc., 220 W. 42d st., N. Y.

PHILIPP, Adolf, general director Adolf Philipp Film Corp.; stage career, manager and owner of Adolf Philipp Theatre, N. Y., as star in own plays, author and composer of "Alma, Where Do You Live?" "Adele," "The Midnight Girl," "The Girl Who Smiles," "Mimi," "Two Is Company," etc.; screen career, Adolf Philipp Film Corp. ("The Midnight Girl," "My Girl Suzanne," "Oh! Louise"). Studio ad., 11 E. 14th st., N. Y. Home ad., 1219 Madison ave., N. Y.

— S —

SAMUELSON, George B.; b. Southport, England; educ. there; screen career, founder and managing director of Samuelson Film Mfg. Co., Ltd., of England. ("Milestones," "My Lady's Dress," "Admiral Crichton," "Choosing a Wife," "Quinneys," "The Love Trail," "The Valley of Fear," "Study in Scarlet," "The Sorrows of Satan"). Ad., Samuelson Films, Los Angeles, Calif.

SCHLANK, Morris R.; b. Omaha, Nebr.; educ. there; screen career, Atlas Film Co. ("James Boys in Missouri," "Sapho," "Deadwood Dick," "Secret Service Steve," "The Hidden Hand," "The Dalton Boys," "Sitting Bull," "Ten Nights in a Barroom," "The Police Inspector"), now producing Hank Mann comedies. Ad., 6040 Sunset Blvd., Los Angeles, Calif.

SENNETT, Mack, director-general; screen career, actor with Biograph, where he appeared in many comedies and dramas; 1912 organized Keystone Film Co., with assistance of Ad. and Charles Kessel and Charles Baumann; took his co. to Los Angeles, establishing headquarters there, where he has since been; now supervising production of two-reel comedies for Mack Sennett-Paramount Co. release. "Uncle Tom Without the Cabin," "Back to the Kitchen," "Salome vs. Shenandoah," "His Last False Step," etc., special prods., "Yankee Doodle in Berlin," "Down on the Farm," five parts. Ad., Mack Sennett Comedies, 1712 Allesandro st., Los Angeles, Cal.

SPITZ, Eugene; independent producer, supervising director of Stage Women's War Relief series, owner and manager Estee Studios and Laboratories, Inc., 361 W. 125th St., N. Y. C., Member Green Room Club. Ad., Estee Annex, 210 E. 124th St., N. Y. C.

— T —

TOURNEUR, Maurice, director; b. and educ. Paris, France; stage career, 15 yrs. as producer; screen career, Eclair, World, Paramount, Artcraft, "Jimmy Valentine," "Trilby," "The Whip," "The Poor Little Rich Girl," "The Blue Bird," "Barbary Sheep," "Rose of the World," "Sporting Life," "Prunella," "Woman," "The White Heather," "The Life Line," "Treasure Island," "Victory." Member M. P. D. A. Studios, Triangle, Culver City, Cal., and Paragon, Fort Lee, N. J.

TUCKER, George Loane, director; b. Chicago; stage career, with Cohan & Harris, H. H. Frazee, H. W. Savage, Joe Weber; screen career, producer of the English and European version of "The Christian," "The Prisoner of Zenda" and "Arsene Lupin"; also directed "I Believe," "Traffic in Souls," "Rupert of Hentzau," "The Man Without a Soul," "The Mother," and "The Manx-Man." Anita Stewart in "Virtuous Wives," Para-Art. special ("The Miracle Man"). Now making own productions for Mayflower Photoplay Corp. Ad., Friars' Club, N. Y.

— V —

VIDOR, King W., director; b. Galveston, Texas; educ. southern and eastern colleges; Brentwood ("The Turn in the Road," "Better Times," "The Other Half," "Poor Relations"), First National ("The Family Honor"). Home ad., 1514 Sierra Bonita, Los Angeles, Calif.; phone 579306; studio, King W. Vidor Productions. Releasing thru First Natl. Ex. Circuit, N. Y.

PRODUCERS

— W —

WALSH, Raoul A., director; b. N. Y., 1889; educ. St. Francis Xavier, Seton Hall; screen career, first work under supervision of D. W. Griffith, appeared as John Wilkes Booth in "The Birth of a Nation"; as director for Fox has made "Carmen," "The Honor System," "The Silent Lie," "This Is the Life," "The Pride of N. Y.," "Woman and the Law," "The Prussian Cur," "18-45," "On the Jump," "Every Mother's Son," "Evangeline," "Should a Husband Forgive?" Author of many scenarios. Ad., Great Neck, L. I., N. Y., or care Mayflower Photoplay Corp., N. Y.

WEBER, Lois (Mrs. Phillips Smalley), co-director with Phillips Smalley; b. Pittsburgh; educ. Pittsburgh; early career, concert work; stage career, rep. and stk. with husband; screen career, Gaumont, NYMP, Rex, Bosworth, Universal, Bluebird ("The People vs. John Doe," "Even as You and I," "The Mysterious Mrs. Musselwhite," "The Face Downstairs," "The Hand that Rocks the Cradle"), Lois Weber Prod. ("The Price of a Good Time," "K," "The Man Who Dared God," "For Husbands Only," "Borrowed Clothes," "Forbidden," "There's No Place Like Home"), First Nat'l ("A Midnight Romance," "Mary Regan," "Hypocrites"). Ad., Lois Weber Prod., Hollywood, Cal.; Famous Players Release.

WHARTON, Leopold; b. Manchester, Eng., 1870; educ. Hempstead, Texas.; stage career, associated with Augustin Daly, Olga Nethersole, K. & E.; screen career, since 1909, Pathe (played among other parts, Lincoln in "Abraham Lincoln's Clemency," later dir. comedies, "The Elusive Kiss," etc., then dramas, "Memories," "The Great White Trail"), "The New Adventures of J. Rufus Wallingford," "The Mysteries of Myra," "Patria." Ad., Wharton, Inc., Ithaca, N. Y.

WHARTON, Theodore; b. Milwaukee, Wis., 1875; stage career, has appeared with E. H. Sothern, Augustin Daly, John Drew; screen career, since 1907, first as free lance scen. writer, later scen. ed. and studio supervisor Edison, Kalem, 1908, building first indoor studio, Pathe, 1911, their first dir., later Essanay, Wharton, Inc. ("The New Adventures of Rufus Wallingford," "The Mysteries of Myra," "Patria"). Ad., Wharton, Inc., Ithaca, N. Y.

WILLAT, Irvin V.; b. Stamford, Conn.; educ. De Land, Fla.; screen career, has had experience in every branch of motion picture manufacture; with original Imp as actor, factory supt. NYMP, N. Y., manufactured cameras, first cameraman with Keystone, later with Reliance, All-Star, World Film, in charge of photography for Ince-Triangle, introduced decorated titles to the trade for Ince-Triangle, Ince-Triangle (dir. "In Slumberland"), Ince (dir. "The Guilty Man"), Lasky (Houdini in "The Grim Game"), Ince ("False Faces," "Behind the Door"). Ad., care W. W. Hodkinson, 527 Fifth ave., N. Y.; studio Los Angeles, Calif.

WILLIS, Richard, member Willis and Inglis; early career, actor, screen career, since 1911, acted and wrote scenarios for Nestor, represented and did publicity work for stars, etc.; manages many well known people, has assisted in financing several new companies, is writer of magazine articles of features and interviews with stars, works on the sale of books and stage plays for picture purposes. Ad., Los Angeles, Cal.

Y

YOUNG, Briant S.; also studio executive; b. Salt Lake City, Utah; educ. there and San Francisco; 1903-4 motion picture exhibitor; 1909-10, motion picture producer; 1912-1914, director-general Fiestas; 1914-17, producer motion pictures; 1918-1919, affiliated industries, student of all branches of motion picture industry, including technical, directing, camera efficiency, etc. General Manager Art Unit Studios, Glendale, Calif., Home ad., 2922 So. Flower, Los Angeles, Cal., So. 5537.

HEADQUARTERS
for Cameras, Tripods, Studio Arcs, etc.
Everything for the Production of Film

Pathe Profession Camera

CAMERAS IN STOCK

Pathe

Debrie

Universal

Metal Pathe

New Universal Cameras at Bargain Prices

200 ft. Model Lists $430, our price...... **$330**

200 ft. Model with Automatic dissolving shutter, List $512, our price...... **$405**

400 ft. Model, List $645, our price...... **$510**

400 ft. Model with Automatic dissolving shutter, List $731, our price...... **$585**

New Model Precision Ball-Bearing Tripod.. **$165**

The Right Goods and a Square Deal at

MOTION PICTURE APPARATUS CO., Inc.
110 West 32nd Street   New York City

DIRECTORS

—A—

ABRAMSON, William, assistant director; b. N. Y., 1891; educ. there; screen career ("Enlighten Thy Daughter," "One Law for Both"), Graphic ("Someone Must Pay," "Echo of Youth," "When Men Betray," "Ashes of Love," "Moral Suicide"). Hght., 5, 6; wght., 130; dark complexion, brown hair, blue eyes. Ad., home, 58 E. 113th st.; phone Harlem 8832.

ADOLFI, John G.; b. N. Y.; educ. N. Y. and Philadelphia; stage career, 10 yrs.; screen career, since 1909, leading man for Vitagraph, etc.; recent pictures, "Queen of the Sea" with Annette Kellerman, "The Cavell Case" with Julia Arthur, "Who's Your Brother" with Edith Taliaferro. Ad., Friars' Club, N. Y.

ALGIER, Sidney H., assistant director; b. Shamokin, Pa.; educ. Brooklyn, N. Y.; stage career, 14 yrs. in mus. com. and comic opera, with Shuberts, Klaw & Erlanger, John Cort, etc.; screen career, American (Sequel of "Diamond From the Sky," "Six Feet Four," "The Twinkler," "Some Liar," "Dust," "The Week End," "The Inner Struggle," "A Sporting Chance," "The Reclamation"). Hght., 5, 7; wght., 160; brown hair and eyes. Home ad., 1816 De la Vina st., Los Angeles, Calif.; telephone 2226-W; studio, American Film Co., Santa Barbara, Calif.

ALLEN, Major Jack; educ. Balto., Md.; self producer and distributor of special nature and wild animal pictures; naturalist, traveler, cavalryman in Spanish-American war. Studio ad., Universal, Universal City, Cal.

ALLEY, Alfred Wright, art director; b. Buffalo, N. Y.; educ. there, Calif. and Mexico; early career, civil engineer, architect and interior decorator; screen career, American, Fox, Lois Weber Prod., Universal, Metro. Studio ad., Metro Studios, Hollywood, Calif.; home ad., 1632½ Winona blvd., Hollywood, Calif.; phone 3062.

ALLEY, Y. C.; technical director; productions for J. G. Pictures, Inc., J. M. Shear & Co., Lew Rogers, Supreme Pictures. Ad., home, 232 West 48th st., New York City.

APFEL, Oscar C.; b. and educ. Cleveland, O.; stage career, producer and director Chicago Opera House, Detroit, Cleveland, Pittsburgh, Buffalo; screen career, World ("The Interloper," "Tinsel," "Merely Players," "The Mandarin's Gold"), Lasky ("The Squaw Man," "Cameo Kirby"), Fox ("A Soldier's Oath," "Battle of Hearts," "End of the Trail," "Man of Sorrow"), Paralta ("A Man's Man," "Turn of a Card"), Selig ("Auction of Souls"). Ad., Lambs Club, N. Y.

ARCHAINBAUD, George; b. Paris, France; educ. France; screen career, with Eclair in Paris and U. S. A., Beacon Film, Peerless World, American Cinema Corp., Pathe Freres; producing director for Gail Kane, Ethel Clayton, Kitty Gordon, Alice Brady, Montagu Love, Louise Huff, Creighton Hale and June Caprice "As Man Made Her," "The Brand of Satan," "A Maid of Belgium," "The Cross Bearer," "The Awakening," "The Stormy Petrel," "Love Cheat," "A Damsel in Distress," "Little Mother Hubbard." Ad., home, City Club, 55 W. 44th st., N. Y.; business, Room 809, 1457 Bway, N. Y.

AVERY, Charles; b. Chicago, 1873; educ. Boston; stage career, covering 12 yrs., supporting W. H. Crane, William Faversham, starred in "Charlie's Aunt," original company "The Clansman"; screen career, member of original Biograph, with original Bison, with Keystone since its organization in Cal.; dir. Arbuckle 31 pictures, played in cast 19 pictures with Charles Murray, all "Hogan" series, "Submarine Pirate," "The Last Scent," and others with Sid Chaplin, dir. Ford Sterling, L-Ko Comedies. Hght., 5, 4½; dark complexion, gray hair, eyes. Ad., home, 2028 Sunset Blvd., Hollywood, Cal.; Wil. 6099.

—B—

BADGER, Clarence G., also writer; b. San Francisco, 1880; educ. Boston, Mass.; early career, edit. work "Youth's Companion" and Pacific Coast newspapers; screen career, free lance writer, and on scenario staff of Lubin, Universal, Keystone, became director for Keystone, Oct. 1915; Sennett-Paramount, Goldwyn ("A Perfect Lady," "Daughter of Mine," "Sis Hopkins," "Leave it to Susan," "Through the Wrong Door," "Strictly Confidential," "Almost a Husband," "Jubilo"), "The Strange Boarder," "Water, Water Everywhere," "Kingdom of Youth." Ad., Goldwyn Studio, Culver City, Cal.; home ad., R. F. D. No. 10, Box 890-B, Los Angeles, Cal.; Holly. 2135.

BAKER, George D.; b. Champaign, Ill.; stage career, with Walker Whiteside, David Higgins, McKee Rankin, Nance O'Neil, stock and vaud., also for six yrs. mgr. of own attractions, "Graustark," "In the Bishop's Carriage," "The Goose Girl"; screen career, Vitagraph, three yrs., then "The Dust of Egypt," "The Shop Girl," "A Price for Folly," "Tarantula," etc.), Metro 3 yrs. ("The Wager," "The White Raven," "His Father's Son," "The Shell Game," "Peggy Does Her Darndest," "The Lion's Den," "Toys of Fate," "Revelation," etc.), director general Metro West Coast studios, supervising Lytell and Allison features; author of "Tarantula," "The Wager," "Sowers and Reapers," "In Judgment of ——," "Her Inspiration," "As the Sun Went Down." Now free lancing ("The Cinema Murder," with International, and "The Man Who Lost Himself," with Wm. Faversham). Ad., 130 W. 44th st., N. Y.

BAKER, Le Roy L., technical director, also actor; b. Washington, D. C.; screen career, Pathe, Rolfe, Wharton, Vitagraph, Thanhouser, Universal, Oliver; played in "Perils of Pauline," "The Eagle's Eye," "Exploits of Elaine," "Patria," "Get Rich Quick Wallingford," "Beatrice Fairfax Series," "Mysteries of Myra," "Master Mystery," "Craig Kennedy Serial."

BALLIN, Hugo, Art director; b. N. Y. C. 1880; educ. New York and Europe; member Natl. Inst. Arts and Letters, Natl. Academy of Design; conducted scenic studios in N. Y. and elsewhere; screen career, Goldwyn (directed "Baby Mine"). Author of "Daughter of Mine" and others; "Fields of Honor," "The Stronger Vow"; Geo. Loane Tucker Prod., "The Cinderella Man." Ad., Goldwyn, Culver City, Cal.

BARKER, Reginald; b. Scotland; educ. there; stage career, wrote and staged first play at 16, managed own stock co., Kansas City, prod. director for Henry Miller, Olga Nethersole, Emily Stevens, Robert Hilliard, Walker Whiteside, screen career, Ince ("Golden Rule Kate"), Paralta ("Madame Who?"), Independent ("Carmen of the Klondike"), Mastercraft ("The One Woman"), Goldwyn ("The Turn of the Wheel," "The Stronger Vow," "The Crimson Gardenia"), Rex Beach ("The Brand," "Girl from Outside," "Flame of the Desert," "Bonds of Love," "The Crimson Gardenia"), "Woman and the Puppet," "Dangerous Days." Member M. P. D. A. Ad., home, 122 So. Ardmore, Hollywood, Cal.; studio, Goldwyn.

BARRY, Joseph J.; educ. N. Y.; stage career, 7 yrs. in vaud., stock and musical comedy; screen two years, and director; Nestor, 101 Bison, Universal, Vogue, Fox, Metro, American, Jack London Pictures, Kalem, now with Blazed Trail Prod. Hght., 5, 8; wght., 150; blond hair and gray eyes. Ad., N. V. A. Club, 229 W. 46th st., N. Y.; phone Bryant 4020.

BARTLETT, Charles E.; b. Minneapolis, Minn.; educ. Denver, Colo.; stage career, 10 yrs., started in child parts, played lead in largest stock company in Chicago, Denver, Salt Lake City and Los Angeles; screen career, 9 yrs. as leading man and feature director with Beaver Film Co., Portland, Ore.

BASIL, Joseph, assistant director; b. Brooklyn, N. Y.; educ. there; early career, physical instructor in public schools, swimming teacher and all-around athlete; screen career, Vitagraph ("It Wasn't Him," "Plans and Pajamas," "Puppy Love," "Rough Necks and Roof Tops"), playing comedy roles and as asst. director; now with King Cole Comedies. Home ad., 323 Schermerhorn st., Brooklyn, N. Y.; studio ad., Motion Picture Producing Co. of America, Dongan Hills, S. I., N. Y.

BEAL, Frank; b. Cleveland, 1865; educ. Univ. of Kansas; stage career, with Frohman and W. A. Brady, first as actor then as stage director, 12 yrs. directing stock cos.; 2 yrs. gen. dir. Liebler & Co.; screen career, from 1908, with

DIRECTORS

Selig, American, Pathe, Fox ("The Danger Zone," "The Divorce Trap," "Chasing Rainbows," "Broken Commandments," "Thieves," "Tin Pan Alley"). Author of "Her Moment." President M. P. D. A. 1918. Ad., home, 7106 Hawthorne ave., Los Angeles, Cal.; studio, Fox, Hollywood, Cal.

BEAL, Scott R., assistant director; b. Quinnesec, Mich., 1890; educ. Chicago Univ.; stage career, stage manager and light comedian in stk. and road shows; screen career, Selig, American, Keystone, Universal, National ("The Blue Bonnet," "Hearts and Masks," "The Love Call," "Girl of My Dreams," "A Kentucky Colonel," "Long Lane's Turning." Hght., 5, 6; wght., 135; dark complexion, black hair, brown eyes. Home ad., 1256 N. Kingsley Drive, Los Angeles, Cal.; Hy. 982; studio ad., National Studio, Los Angeles, Cal.

BEAUDINE, William; b. N. Y. C., 1892; educ. N. Y.; screen career, Biograph Comedies, Kalem, Ham & Bud Comedies, Ethel Teare Comedies, Universal, Joker Comedies, Gale Henry & Billy Franey, Triangle, Keystone Comedies, Christie ("Rustic Romeo," "Mixed Drinks," "Pass the Apples, Eve," "Watch Your Step, Mother," "All Jazzed Up"). Ad., 8201 Fountain ave., Los Angeles, Cal.; Holly. 713; studio ad., Christie Studio, Los Angeles, Cal.

BEAUMONT, Harry; b. Abilene, Kan.; educ. St. Joseph, Mo.; stage career, 10 yrs.; screen career, 7 yrs. with Edison as actor, directed 18 mos. for Essanay, Selig, Goldwyn (since July, 1918, "Thirty a Week," "Go West, Young Man," "A Man and His Money," "One of the Finest," "Lord and Lady Algy," "Guy Lord Quex," "Toby's Bow," "Going Some," "Two Cents Worth of Humaneness"). Home ad., 617 Canyon Drive, Beverly Hills, Cal.; studio, Goldwyn.

BERANGER, George A.; b. Sydney, Australia, March 27, 1893; educ. N. S. W., Australia; stage career (Australia), "Sweet Lavender" and Shakespearean rep.; screen career, juvenile Biograph and directing asst. D. W. Griffith all features up to and including "Birth of a Nation"; directed (Griffith-Mutual) 6 productions, leading man Blanche Sweet, Bessie Love, Louise Huff, co-star Constance Talmadge (Reliance), "Flirting with Fate," "Half-Breed," "Manhattan Madness," "Broken Blossoms"; 1917-18 aviator British forces; 1918-19 director staff of D. W. Griffith; 1919 director Fox Film Corp. ("Find the Woman," etc.). Ad., Los Angeles Athletic Club, and New York Athletic Club.

BERTRAM, William; b. Ontario, Can., 1880; stage career, stk. in Spokane and San Francisco, supported Mrs. Leslie Carter; screen career, with Pathe, 1912, in Indian parts; directed "Buck Parvin" series adapted from Chas. Van Loane series, Diando ("A Little Patriot," "Dolly Does Her Bit," "Cupid by Proxy," "Milady of the Beanstalk," "Dolly's Vacation," "Sawdust Doll," "The Old Maid's Baby"), World ("The Arizona Cat Claw"). Ad., care of M. P. D. A., Alexandria Hotel, Los Angeles, Cal.

BEVIS, Ted J., technical director; early career, stage carpenter in New York and Chicago; now at Art Unit Studio, Glendale, Cal. Home ad., 1257 West 53rd st., Los Angeles, Cal.; Ver. 2534.

BINGHAM, E. Douglas, studio manager and technical director; screen career, Wharton, Metro, Rolfe, Oliver ("Patria," "The Eagle's Eyes," "Mysteries of Myra," "Great White Trail," "Master Mystery," "Craig Kennedy," "A Million Dollars Reward"). Ad., 20 E. 48th st., N. Y.

BLACHE, Mme. Alice; b. Paris, 1878; educ. convents in Paris and Geneva; screen career, started as sec. to M. Gaumont in Paris, later in charge of Gau. studio (Paris) 1897, Solax 1910 Co.; producing "The Pit and the Pendulum," "The Rogues of Paris," formed with Herbert Blache U. S. Amusement Co., producing "The Dream Woman," "The Empress," "Sea Waif," "House of Cards," "When You and I Were Young," "Behind the Mask," Bessie Love in "The Great Adventure"; Dolores Cassinelli in "A Soul Adrift."

BLACHE, Herbert; b. London, Eng.; educ. London and Montpelier, France; screen career, Gaumont, Blach Feature, U. S. Amust. Corp., Pathe; dir. Petrova, Florence Reed, Mary Miles Minter, Frank Keenan, Emily Stevens, Edith Storey, Ethel Barrymore, King Baggot, Nazimova ("The Brat," "Stronger Than Death"), Screen Classic (May Allison in "The Walkoffs"). Ad., Friars Club, N. Y.; studio, Metro, Los Angeles, Cal.

BLAKE, Ben; b. 1892; educ. Columbia Univ.; stage career, one year in stock; screen career, started with Imp in 1910; assisted many well-known directors for several years; co-directed with Hobart Henley on "Parentage"; now directing and supervising Universal Educational pictures. Ad., home, 1815 Seventh ave., N. Y.

BLYSTONE, J. G.; b. 1892; screen career, Universal, 3 yrs., directed Joker comedies, wrote many of his own scenarios, joined L-Ko at its formation, directed "Balloonatics"; produced many successful comedies, released on Universal ("A Surf Scandal," "Love Behind Bars," "Soapsuds and Sirens," "Fat and Furious"), now directing Fox Sunshine Comedies ("Virtuous Husbands," "Footlight Maids," "Yellow Dog Catcher," "Her Naughty Wink," "The Quack Duck Hunter"). Studio ad., Fox Sunshine Comedies, Hollywood, Cal.; home ad., 6901 Hawthorne st., Hollywood, Cal.

BORDEAUX, Joe, assistant director; b. Canada, 1886; educ. Cal.; screen career, with Billy West Comedies, Fox "Smiles"; 4 yrs. with Arbuckle ("Fatty and Mabel Adrift," "Waiters' Ball," "His Wife's Mistake"), with Blystone. Ad., 3700 Sunset Blvd., Los Angeles, Cal.

BORZAGE, Frank; b. Salt Lake City, 1893; educ. Salt Lake City; stage career, from age of 14, stock and rep., last stage appearance in "The Prisoner of Zenda"; screen career, Universal, Lubin, American, Mutual, Lasky ("A Mormon Maid"), Triangle ("Flying Colors," "Until They Get Me"), Essanay ("The Curse of Iku"), Macauley Photoplays ("Whom the Gods Would Destroy"), Triangle ("Toton," "Shoes that Danced"), Fred Stone ("Billy Jim," "Duke of Chimney-Butte"), International ("Humoresque"). Member M. P. D. A. Ad., 3974 Wilshire Blvd., Los Angeles, Cal.

BOWMAN, William J.; b. Bakersville, N. C.; educ. Lordsburg Coll., Pomona, Cal.; early career, draftsman; stage career, rep. stock, vaud., with Mantell; toured Orient in Shakespearean rep.; screen career, Thanhouser ("Merchant of Venice"), American, Triangle, Vitagraph ("Master of the Mine," "Inasmuch"), Keystone, Quality ("Second in Command"), "Silent Voice"), Universal ("From Broadway to a Throne"), now independent producer Para-Artcraft ("False Faces"). Ad., Elks' Club, Santa Monica, Cal.

BRABIN, Charles; b. Liverpool, Eng., 1883; educ. Coll. St. Francis Xavier, Mayfield, Sussex, Eng.; stage career, in "Medal and the Maid"; screen career, from 1908, Edison and Vitagraph as dir., with Essanay, 1915 ("The Raven"), Vitagraph ("The Price of Fame," "Mary Jane's Pa," "The Sixteenth Wife"), Metro ("Social Quicksands," "Red, White and Blue Blood," "The Poor Rich Man"), Fox ("Buchanan's Wife," "Thou Shalt Not," "La Belle Russe," "Kathleen Mavourneen," "While New York Sleeps"). Ad., care of Ed Small, Inc., N. Y.

BRACKEN, Bertram; b. Texas; educ. Yale; early career, worked in a bank and was member of 15th U. S. Cavalry for 1½ yrs.; screen career, Melies Co., Lubin, 2 yrs. Fox, 1 yr. direct. Henry B. Walthall; Fox ("The Eternal Sappho," "East Lynne"), Walthall ("Long Arm of Mannister," "The Confession," "The Boomerang"). Studio ad., Selig Studios, 3800 Mission Road, Los Angeles.

BRADBURY, Robert North; b. Walla Walla, Wash.; educ. Baker Sch. and Chicago; stage career, Baker Stk. Co., Portland, Ore., 7 yrs. featured over Orpheum and Pantages circuits; own companies; screen career, Universal, Lasky ("To Have and to Hold"), Kalem ("The Harvest of Gold," "The False Prophet," "The Resurrection of Gold Bar"), Mitchell Lewis ("Faith of the Strong," "Last of His People"), Bradbury Prod. ("Into the Light"). Ad., 418 Mason Bldg., Los Angeles, Calif.

BRADDEN, John D., Art director; b. England; screen career, Fox (9 yrs.), Plunkett and Carroll Co. ("Daughter of the Gods," "Les Miserables," "Edith Cavel," "When Burglars Call"). Home ad., Grantwood, N. J. Studio, Ideal, Hudson Heights, N. J.

BRODSKY, Samuel Richard; educ. Cleveland, Ohio; stage career, stage mgr. for William Postance, Jack Halliday, May Buckley and Vaughn Glazer; also played many parts on legitimate; screen career, directed "The House Without Children," "The Greatest of These," "Men in the Making," "Vanishing Charms," for Argus Co. Hght., 5, 10; wght., 148; brown hair and eyes. Ad., The Argus Enterprises, Cleveland, Ohio; Main 7174.

BROOKE, Van Dyke; b. Detroit, Mich.; stage career, many yrs. in stk., on road in important metropolitan prods.; screen career, from 1908 with Vitagraph, director, scenario writer and actor, directed Norma Talmadge, Anita Stewart, Earle Williams, Mary Fuller, Leah Baird and other stars ("Janet of the Chorus," "The Gods Redeem," "The Primal Instinct"), Thanhouser ("It Happened to Adele"), Vitagraph ("The Fortune Hunter"), Am. Cinema ("The Stormy Petrel"). Member M. P. D. A. Ad., 234 W. 55th St., N. Y.

BROWN, Melville W.; b. Portland, Ore.; stage career, Baker Stk., Portland, Ore.; Columbia theatre, Milwaukee, Wis., Spokane theatre, Spokane, Wash., 4 seasons vaud.; screen career, scenario writer for Triangle, Chaplin, Goldwyn, Universal, Vitagraph now directing Montgomery & Rock, Vitagraph Studio. Home ad., 2045 Pinehurst Road, Hollywood, Cal.; phone 577254; or P. O. Box 142, Hollywood.

BROWNING, Tod; b. Louisville; stage career, toured world at head of "Lizard and Coon" Co., "Mutt and Jeff," "World of Mirth"; screen career, Biograph, Reliance-Majestic, Fine Arts, Metro ("The House in the Mist"), Bluebird ("The Deciding Kiss," "The Brazen Beauty"), Universal ("The Wicked Darling," "An Exquisite Thief," "The Unpainted Woman," "Petal on the Current," "Bonnie, Bonnie Lassie," "The Beautiful Beggar"). Home ad., 1719 Cherokee St., Los Angeles, Cal.; Holly 4142; studio, Universal.

BUCKLAND, Wilfrid, Art director; screen career, technical dir., Lasky. Ad., Famous Players Studio, 1520 Vine St., Los Angeles, Cal.

BUEL, Kenean; originally on legit. stage; joined Kalem shortly after its organization, 7 yrs. there, wrote and produced "Civil War" pictures; joined Fox 1915 ("Blazing Love," "We Should Worry," "Doing Their Bit," "I Want to Forget," "Woman, Woman," "My Little Sister"), Hallmark ("The Veiled Marriage").

BURT, William P., Assistant director; b. St. Peters, Minn.; educ. Denver, Boston; stage career, on legitimate stage for yrs.; screen career, Vitagraph, Thanhouser, Metro, Astra-Pathe; characters, heavies; Pathe (acted in "The Lightning Raider"). Home ad. 393 Central Park West, N. Y. C.

BUTLER, Alexander Beaubien; b. Beamsville, Ont., Canada; educ. Hamilton, Can.; stage career, United States, So. America, So. Africa, Australia Gt. Britain; with Charles Frohman and George Edwards; screen career 1912, produced first feature film, "East Lynne" for London Co., Barker, London (dir. "Five Nights," "The Beetle"), Samuelson ("Just a Girl," "My Lady's Dress," "Damaged Goods," "Sorrows of Satan," "The Admirable Crichton"). Home ad., Alvarado Hotel, Los Angeles, Cal.; studio, Samuelson.

— C —

CABANNE, William Christy; b. St. Louis, 1888; educ. St. Rose Acad., Culver Military Acad.; early career, spent in Navy; stage career, 1908-1910; screen career, since 1910, Fine Arts (dir. Douglas Fairbanks' first pictures, "Double Trouble" and "Reggie Mixes In"), 5 yrs. Griffith's Chief of Staff, author and dir. of "One of Many," "The Slacker," co-author and dir. of "Draft 258," dir. Metro's first serial, "The Great Secret," at head of own company state's rights ("Fighting Through"), W. H. Special ("A Regular Fellow"), Goldwyn ("The Pest"), Lew Cody ("Beloved Cheater"). Ad., 929 So. St. Andrews Pl., Los Angeles, Cal.; studio, Universal.

CAMPBELL, Colin; screen career, Selig (made "The Spoilers," "The Garden of Allah," "The Crisis," "The Still Alarm," "The Law North of 65," "Little Orphan Annie," "A Hoosier Romance"), Universal ("The Yellow Dog," "In the Carquinez Woods"), Mutual ("A Hoosier Romance"), First Natl. ("The Thunderbolt"), United ("The Corsican Brothers"). Member M.P.D.A. Ad., Brunton Studio, Hollywood, Cal.

CAMPBELL, William S.; b. Ashley, Pa.; educ. Ashley High Sch.; early career, 10 yrs. vaud. and motion picture mgr.; screen career, 3½ yrs. with Keystone, directing numerous Sennett-Paramount comedies; Fox Sunshine, Universal, series of Joe Martin, Orang-Outang comedies, now producing series of 26 animal comedies to be released as Campbell comedies. Ad., 1720 Soto St., Los Angeles, Cal.

CARLETON, John T., Assistant director; b. N. Y.; educ. Grad. Columbia Law Sch.; early career, practiced law 15 yrs. pert. mostly to theatrical matters; screen career, associated with brother, Lloyd B. Carleton, as asst. and co-director for past 6 yrs. Vice-pres. Clermont Photoplays Corp. Home ad., 5846 Carlton Way, Hollywood, Cal.; studio, Clermont Photoplay Corp., Los Angeles.

CARPENTER, George Mulford, Art & Technical director; b. Brooklyn, N. Y.; educ. Art Students League, N. Y., and studied abroad; early career, mural painter, assisted Edwin H. Blashfield, decoration Ball Room ceiling, Waldorf-Astoria Hotel, N. Y., decoration Grand Salon, str. "Commonwealth," Fall River Line, etc.; screen career, Metro ("Best of Luck," "Right of Way," designed sets), painted screen and motion picture "Mt. Fuji" for "The Willow Tree," motion picture "Fifth Ave., N. Y.," "Lombardi, Ltd." Home ad., 1440 Stanley ave., Hollywood, Cal.; phone 577371; studio ad., Metro.

CARRE, Ben, Art director; b. Paris, France; educ. Paris; stage career, 6 yrs. on stage; screen career, Gaumont (Paris), Eclair, World, Paramount, Artcraft, Tourneur (Paris), now with Marshall Neilan; "Trilby," "The Whip," "Poor Little Rich Girl," "Undying Flame," "Barbary Sheep," "Blue Bird," "Prunella," "Sporting Life," "Life Line," "In Old Kentucky," "The River's End." Home ad., 6732 Hollywood Blvd., Los Angeles; Holly 3910; studio, Marshall Neilan Prod.

CHAUDET, Louis W.; b. Manhattan, Kan., 1884; early career, photographer; stage career vaud., road shows, Belasco stk.; screen career, Selig, as actor, photographer, asst. dir., Universal (Nestor comedies), Smiling Bill Parsons, 8 comedies, "The Girl of My Dreams," "Merry Andrews" (Rhodes), "Long Lane's Turning" (Walthall), National ("Hoop-La," "The Love Call," "The Blue Bonnet" (Rhodes), Selznick ("Common Sense"). Member M.P.D.A.

CLEMENS, James H., Assistant director; b. England; educ. Pa. and Ky.; stage career, Orpheum Circuit; screen career, 3 yrs. with Universal, 1 yr. Morosco, 2 yrs. Triangle, 1 yr. Keystone-Triangle, 1½ yrs. Christie, now directing Gayety Comedies featuring George Ovey. Home ad., 1216 S. Catalina st., Los Angeles, Cal.; studio, Christie Comedies.

CLEMENTS, Roy; b. Ill., 1877; on stage 22 yrs.; screen career, Essanay ("Snakeville" series), Universal ("Slippery Slim" series, Pat Rooney Features), Sierra Features, Universal ("Fat and Foolish," "A Proxy Elopement," "The Impatient Patient," "The Bright Lights," "Seeing Things," "The Potato Patriot," "Too Much Women"), Triangle ("Crown Jewels"), Hallmark ("When a Woman Strikes," "The Reckoning Day"), Mitchell Lewis ("King Spruce"). Member M.P.D.A. Home ad., 6824 Whiteley Terrace, Hollywood, Cal.

CLIFTON, Elmer; stage career, from 1907, in "The Girl of the Golden West," "The Dollar Mark," mgmt. Belasco when latter was Coast stk. director, two B'way prods. with Richard Bennett; screen career, Reliance-Majestic (Phil. Stoneman in Griffith's "Birth of a Nation," "Intolerance"), Fine Arts, Universal ("Smashing Through," "Kiss or Kill"), Para ("Battling Jane," "The Hope Chest," "Peppy Polly," "Nugget Nell," "Out of Luck," "Turning the Tables"). Ad., Griffith Studio, Mamaroneck, N. Y.

CLINE, Edward Francis; b. Kenosha, Wis., 1892; educ. Lake Forest, Chicago; screen career, Keystone ("The Winning Punch," "His Busted Trust"), Sennett-Paramount ("That Night," "The Kitchen Lady," "Those Athletic Girls," "A Bedroom Blunder," "Sheriff Nell's Comeback," "A School House Scandal," "Training for Husbands"). Member M.P.D.A. Home ad., Alvarado Apts., Los Angeles, Cal.; Wilsh. 5010; studio, Fox Sunshine Studio.

COLLINS, Clifford B., Assistant director; b. McClure, Ohio; educ. Toledo, Ohio; stage career, at Lyceum theatre, Toledo, Ohio as asst. stage director; screen career, from 1914-17, with Thos. H. Ince, as asst. director, 1917-19 with A. E. F. Home ad., 1014 N. Mariposa ave., Hollywood, Cal.; Holly 4080; studio, Brunton Studios.

CONWAY, Jack; b. Graceville, Minn., 1887; educ. there; stage career, from 1907, in stock, melodrama in "Mrs. Temple's Telegram"; screen career since 1911, Selig, Bosworth, Reliance-Majestic, Fine Arts, Universal ("Bitter Sweet," "Judgment of the Guilty"), Triangle ("Doing Her Bit," "Bone of Fear," "Because of a

Woman"), Bluebird ("A Jewel in Pawn"), Triangle ("You Can't Believe Everything," "Restless Souls"), Metro ("Lombardi, Ltd."), Federal ("Desert of Wheat," "The Dwelling Place of Light," "The U. P. Trail"). Member M. P. D. A. Home ad., 2211 Budlong ave., Los Angeles, Cal.; studio ad., Brunton.

COOPER, J. Gordon; educ. St. Francis Xavier College; screen career, Fox, features for Oliver Productions, Inc., starring Herbert Rawlinson, now with Hallmark Prods. Ad., 537 West 149th st., N. Y. C.; Audubon 2040.

COX, George L.; b. Chicago, Ill.; educ. America and Europe; stage career, David Warfield, Nat Goodwin, Mrs. Leslie Carter, stk. and rep.; screen career Selig Polyscope, Advance Motion Picture Co., American, Cox Feature Film Co. Home ad., 1729 Garden st., Los Angeles; phone 1593-J; studio ad., American Film Co., Santa Barbara, Cal.

CRANE, Frank H.; b. San Francisco; stage career, with William Collier, Arnold Daly, James A. Herne; screen career, Pathe ("Stranded in Arcady"), Goldwyn ("Thais"), Petrova ("The Life Mask"), World ("Clarissa," "Neighbors"), Harry Rapf ("Wanted for Murder"), United ("Her Game"). Ad., Friars Club, N. Y.

CRISP, Donald; b. London, Eng.; educ. there; screen career, Biograph, Majestic, Mutual, Clune ("Ramona," "Eyes of the World"), D. W. Griffith ("played role of "Battling Burrows" in "Broken Blossoms"). Famous Players ("Poor Boob," "Love Insurance," "Putting It Over," "Something to Do," "A Very Good Young Man," "Why Smith Left Home," "Too Much Johnson," "The Six Best Cellars"). Ad., Lasky, studio, Hollywood, Cal.

CROSLAND, Frederic Alan; educ. East Orange Preparatory School and Dartmouth College; early career, newspaper game since college, "N. Y. Globe," also short stories various magazines; stage career, with Annie Russell in Sheridan's "Rivals," Goldsmith's "She Stoops to Conquer," Shakespeare stage manager and juvenile parts; screen career, played in pictures with Pathe, Edison, etc., been director for five yrs., starting at age of 21, directed "The Unbeliever," "Kidnapped," for Edison, "The Whirlpool" for Famous Players, "The Country Cousin," "Greater than Fame," "Glorious South" for Selznick; 18 mos. service in France in Signal Corps. Directed the compiling of the Photographic History of the War. Ad., 1 W. 67th st., N. Y.; Columbus 4204.

CRUZE, James; b. Ogden, Utah, 1884; educ. there; stage career, medicine shows, touring country, later formed own co., toured several yrs. in "Heart of Maryland," joined co. playing Shakespeare and stock melodrama; screen career, Metro, Lasky, Paramount ("The City of Dim Faces," "Less than Kin," "Johnny Get Your Gun," "Too Many Millions"), Artcraft (played in "Under the Top," "Johnny Get Your Gun"), Paramount ("You're Fired," "Alias, Mike Moran," "The Roaring Road," "The Love Burglar," "Valley of the Giants," "The Lottery Man," "Hawthorne of the U. S. A."). Black hair, dark eyes. Ad., Lasky Studios, Hollywood, Cal.

CULLISON, Webster; b. Baltimore, Md.; educ. there and Washington; stage career, 19 yrs., owner, actor and stage director; screen career, 9 yrs. producer of pictures, World, Lubin, Equitable, etc., O. Henry stories for Eclair, May Allison with Metro, Juanita Hansen and George Cheseboro with Selig in "The Lost City." Home ad., 5123 Harold Way, Los Angeles, Cal.; Holly. 883.

CUTHBERT, C. E. (Casey), assistant director; b. Michigan; educ. Detroit; stage career, stk., rep. and prod., "Thais" with Constance Collier and Tyrone Power, "Love's Wager" with Fritzie Scheff, "The Enchantress" with Kitty Gordon; screen career, began in 1912, Thos. Ince, Universal, mechanical director with Irene Castle in "Patria," honorably discharged from A. E. F., May, 1919, now with Capital Film Co. Home ad., 4569 Fourth ave., Hollywood, Cal.

— D —

DALY, Wm. Robert; b. Boston, 1872; educ. Boston Latin School; stage career, with Frohman, Liebler, H. B. Harris and Julius Cahn, as actor and director; screen career, began 1910, Imp-Universal, Selig, etc., "The Militant," "Uncle Tom's Cabin," "Miracle Mary," "Calvary's Shadow," "Unto Those Who Sin," "The Making of Crooks," "At Piney Ridge." Member M. P. D. A. Home ad., 1956 Franklin Circle, Hollywood, Cal.

DAVENPORT, Charles E.; b. Easton, Pa., 1884; educ. Pa.; stage career, since childhood, stk., rep. and Shakespearean; training under the late James Booth Roberts and George Bangs; screen career, acting and directing Lubin, Reliance, Majestic ("The Strength of the Weak," "The She Wolf," "Virgin of the Fire," "The Half Wit"), Stage Right and Government prod. "Governor's Boss," "Kavah," "Rule of Reason," "House that Jack Built," "Broken Barriers"), Sholom Aleichem Series in preparation. Ad., Green Room Club, N. Y.

DAVID, Charles Norman, also laboratory expert; b. Chicago, 1889; screen career, 3 yrs. in printing, perforating and laboratories at Essanay, founder of the Active Motion Picture Co. and Interstate Film Producers; cameraman on travelogues for Chicago Herald Land Bureau in Florida, Alabama, Louisiana, Georgia and Texas; director and cameraman of 15 Ebony Comedies; cameraman on "Do the Dead Talk?" produced by Special Feature Production Co.; director "Castle Comedies." Ad., Castle Studios, 2332 N. California ave., Chicago, Ill.

DAVIS, William S.; stage career, staged many Broadway productions for the Frohmans, Harrison Grey Fiske, etc.; screen career, for 6 yrs. Edison, Biograph, Fox ("The Fool's Revenge"), Metro ("Alias Mrs. Jessup," "Under Suspicion," "The Brass Check," "With Neatness and Dispatch," "No Man's Land," "In Judgment Of"), United Pictures, Inc., Supreme Pictures, Inc. Author of many scenarios.

DAWLEY, J. Searle; b. Del Norte; educ. Scott Saxton Coll. of Oratory, Denver; stage career, 4 yrs. stage mgt. for Lewis Morrison Faust Co., 2 yrs. in vaud., 5 yrs. in stk.; screen career, Edison, Famous Players, directed Mary Pickford, H. B. Warner, Billie Burke, Marguerite Clark ("Snow White," "The Seven Swans"), Elsie Ferguson in "The Lie," Doris Kenyon in "Twilight" and "Harvest Moon," wrote and directed "Everybody's Business" for Chas. Richman Co., "The Phantom Honeymoon" for Hallmark. Author of 18 stage plays and several scenarios. Ad., 215 W. 51st st., N. Y.

DAWN, Norman; b. Santa Barbara Rancho, Prov. of Salta, Argentina; scenic cinematographer 7 yrs. Gaumont, Biograph, Ince, Keystone; over 2 yrs. with Universal, producing 2 and 5 reel pictures, "Sinbad the Sailor," "The Eternal Triangle," "Two Men of Tinted Butte," "Lasca," "Down by the Rio Grande," "Hermit Creek," "The Line Runners," etc. Ad., Universal Studio, Hollywood, Cal.; home, 1435 Grand Canal, Venice, Cal.

DEAN, Ralph; educ. N. Y. and Chappaqua; stage career, Chas. Frohman, Liebler & Co., Henry Savage, "Heir to the Hoorah," Cohan and Harris, 5 yrs. dramatic; screen career, Edison, Colonial, Frohman, 2 yrs. directed Geo. Irving; directed "The Rainbow," "The Accomplice," "The Song of Sixpence," "Madam Sherry." Member Lambs Club. Home ad., Chamber st., Bayside, L. I., N. Y.

DE CARLTON, George; assistant director; b. Boston, Mass. June 30, 1867; stage career, in every branch, beginning at early age; screen career, Reliance (asst. to Oscar Apfel), Life Photo ("Northern Lights," "The Lighthouse," "Captain Swift," "The Ordeal"), Fox (asst. to Edgar Lewis, appearing in "The Thief," "The Plunderer," "A Gilded Fool," "Samson," "The Nigger"), Ocean Film, World ("The Rough Neck"). Ad., Friars' Club, N. Y.

DE GRASSE, Joseph; b. France; educ. N. Y.; stage career, from 1883, actor and producer of classic drama, own co.; screen career, from 1909, Pathe (leads and director), Lubin, Universal, from 1913, Argosy ("After the War"), Ince-Para ("Market of Souls"), First Nat'l ("Heart of the Hills"), Para-Art ("L'Apache"), "Wild Cat of Paris," with Priscilla Dean, "My Friend's Wife," Dorothy Dalton, "The Golden Hope," Edith Storey, "The Undertow," Sessue Hayakawa. Member M. P. D. A., Los Angeles, Cal. Ad., 213 W. Windsor Road, Glendale, Cal.; studio, Haworth.

DE LA MOTHE, Leon; b. New Orleans, La.; educ. Mt. St. Mary Acad., Emmittsburg, Md., Notre Dame Univ.; stage career, 10 yrs. exper. as stock director and featured heavy man, also with "Slaves of the Mine," and featured in "Texas"; screen career, director with St. Louis Motion Picture Co. for 2 yrs., Warner's Features 1 yr., Lubin Film Co. 2 yrs., Universal 8 mos., Selig 6 mos. Home ad., 2027 Reservoir st., Los Angeles, Cal.; phone 53289.

DEL RUTH, Hampton, editor and supervising director; b. Venice, Italy, 1888; educ. Oxford Univ., England; screen career, NYMP Co., some successful scenarios are: "The Passer-by," "Old Black Joe," "Count of Monte Cristo," "The Lighted Way," "The Struggle Everlasting," "Ties of Fate," "Love Tales of Hoffman"; 6 yrs. with Keystone and Sennett-Paramount Comedies; at present editor and supervising director of all Wm. Fox Sunshine Comedies. Ad., Los Angeles Athletic Club, Los Angeles, Cal.

DE MILLE, William C.; b. Washington, N. C., 1878; educ. Columbia Univ., A.B., 1900; author of "Strongheart," "The Warrens of Virginia," "The Woman" and other plays and sketches; screen career, Famous Players-Lasky, 1914 ("The Ragamuffin," "The Heir to the Hoorah," "The Clown," "Hashimma Togo," "The Widow's Might," "One More American," "Peg o' My Heart," "The Tree of Knowledge"). Ad., Lasky Studio, Hollywood, Cal.

DILLON, Edward; b. N. Y.; stage career, juv. and com. leads in "The Sporting Duchess," juv. lead and stage mgr. for Otis Skinner, Dustin Farnum, with Rose Melville in "Sis Hopkins"; screen career, Biograph, Reliance-Majestic, Fine Arts ("The Doll Shop," "Might and the Man"), Paramount, Fox ("Luck and Pluck," "Putting One Over," "Never Say Quit," "Help, Help, Police," "The Winning Stroke"). Member M. P. D. A. Ad., 234 West 55th st., N. Y.

DILLON, Jack; b. N. Y., 1886; educ. St. Francis Xavier, N. Y. C.; stage career, stk., "Officer 666," "The Right of Way," "Via Wireless," "The Rosary"; screen career, Kalem, Famous, Nestor, Universal, Lubin, Keystone, First National, Metro, Mary Pickford ("The Right of Way," starring Bert Lytell; wrote original story for Jack Pickford in "A Burglar by Proxy," also wrote for Fox; "An Heiress for a Day" and "Limousine Life," with Olive Thomas; "The Silk-Lined Burglar" and "Wanted—A Husband," starring Priscilla Dean, "Hop o' My Thumb," with Mary Pickford. Ad., Mary Pickford Co., Hollywood, Cal.

DONOVAN, Frank P.; b. Rosendale, N. Y.; stage career, vaud., with Del Henderson in "From Sing Sing to Liberty," etc.; screen career, Manhattan Features, Yankee, Universal, State Right Series ("Bullin the Bullsheviki"), Biograph ("Pardon Me," "Neptune's Stepdaughter," Gertrude Selby Comedies), Vitagraph ("Boobs and Bumbs"), O. Henry's stories; now making feature pictures with Pearl Shepard. Member M. P. D. A. Ad., Green Room Club. N. Y.

DOWLAN, William C.; b. St. Paul; educ. Christian Brothers, St. Paul; stage career, 14 yrs. with Morosco stk., Los Angeles; screen career, Universal (played lead in "Drugged Waters," dir. "The Madcap"), American (dir. "Youth's Endearing Charm"), Metro ("Rose of the Alley," "Nobody," "The Winding Trail," "The Outsider"), Triangle ("Restless Souls"), Fox ("Cowardice Court"), Universal ("Loot," "Under Suspicion"). Home ad., 1642 Shumway ave., Hollywood, Cal.; studio, Universal.

DUNLOP, Scotty; screen career, late releases, Fox ("Vagabond Luck," "The Hell Ship," "The Elephant Man," "Forbidden Trails," "Words and Music," "Be a Little Sport," "Love Is Love"). Ad., Fox Studio, Hollywood, Cal.

—E—

EAGLE, Oscar; b. Gallipolis, Ohio; educ. Chickering Coll., Cincinnati, Ohio; stage career, director and actor, directed "Some Time," "The Melting of Molly," "An Ideal Husband," "A Sleepless Night," "The Little Whopper," "The Little Blue Devil"; screen career, Selig, 2 yrs. Reliance, Famous Players ("The Dictator"), World ("The Cotton King," "Sins of Society," "The Fruits of Desire," with Robert Warwick, "The Little Mademoiselle," with Vivian Martin), American Pict. Asso. Co. ("Home, Sweet Home"). Member M. P. D. A. Permanent ad., Lambs Club, N. Y.

EARLE, William P. S.; b. 1884, N. Y. C.; educ. Barnard School and Columbia Univ. (graduate); early career, writer, playwright and photographer; screen career, Vitagraph producing features only, "Womanhood," "Within the Law," "His Own People," "Mary Jane's Pa," "The Law Decides"), World ("T'Other Dear Charmer"), C. K. Young Co. ("The Better Wife"), Ince ("The Lone Wolf's Daughter"), Selznick ("The Broken Melody," "The Woman's Game"), directing 8 pictures for Selznick. Home ad., 329 W. 57th st., N. Y.; studio ad., Selznick Pictures Corp., N. Y.

EASON, Reaves; b. Prize Point, Miss.; educ. Monrovia and Berkley Coll., Cal.; stage career, 1 yr. drama. stk. with Nielson Stk. Co. and Belasco, Orpheum and Pantages doing character songs; screen career, American ("In Sheep's Clothing," "Poet of the Peaks"), Balboa ("Sirene of the Slums," "Who Wins" series), Mitchell Lewis (author, producer, actor and dir. of "Nine-Tenths of the Law"), Universal ("The Man Hunter" serial, "Jack of Hearts," "Fighting Line," "Tell Tale Wire"). Hght., 6; wght., 158; brown hair, blue eyes. Home ad., 1130 Orange Drive, Hollywood Cal.; Holly 2247.

ECKERLINE, John, technical director; b. N. Y. C.; stage career, Liebler Co., Richard Mansfield; vaud.; long study on costtumes and periods; screen career, Kalem, Pathe, Harold Lockwood, Frohman Amusement Corp., now with Harold J. Binney Prod., Inc. Ad., care of Eaves Co., 110 W. 46th st., N. Y. C.

EDWARDS, Harry; screen career, 5 yrs. director of comedy, Universal, Fox, L-Ko, National; directed 12 pictures for the Hall Room Boys, Flanagan and Edwards. Ad., National studio, Hollywood, Cal.

EDWARDS, J. Gordon; b. Montreal, Can.; educ. Quebec; stage career, rep., toured U. S. and England with Wilton Lackaye, Amelia Bingham, James K. Hackett, stage director and producer for Fox Acad. of Music, producing 250 plays; screen career, "Cleopatra," "Camille," "Salome," "Her Greatest Love," "The Soul of a Buddha," "Under the Yoke," "The Light," "A Woman There Was," "Lone Star Ranger," "When Men Desire," "Wolves of the Night," "Last of the Duanes," "Wings of the Morning"). Ad., Fox, Los Angeles, Cal.

EDWARDS, Walter; b. Michigan; educ. there; stage career, from 1896, starred in "Sherlock Holmes," "Lion and the Mouse," "The Deep Purple"; screen career, Ince ("Ashes of Hope," "The Passion Flower"), Paramount ("Man From Funeral Range," "Viviette," "The Gypsy Trail"), Select ("Pair of Silk Stockings," "Sauce for the Goose," "Mrs. Leffingwell's Boots"), Paramount ("The Final Close-Up," "Girls," "The Rescuing Angel," "Widow By Proxy"), Select ("Who Cares?" "Romance and Arabella," "Happiness a la Mode"). Member M. P. D. A. Studio ad., Lasky, Hollywood; home ad., Culver City, Cal.

ELLIS, Robert du Reel, also actor; b. Brooklyn; educ. Francis Xavier Coll., N. Y.; stage career, mgmt. Shuberts, Klaw & Erlanger; screen career, Kalem, Metro ("In for Thirty Days." "Peggy Does Her Darndest"), Paramount-Artcraft ("Louisiana," "The Third Kiss"), Selznick ("Upstairs and Down." "The Spite Bride"). Ad., care of Selznick Pict. Corp., N. Y.

ESTABROOK, Howard; b. Detroit, 1884; educ. Detroit; stage career, in many N. Y. and London successes, including "Within the Law," "Little Women," etc.; screen career as star. Kleine ("Officer 666"), also World, Metro, Pathe International; as director, Paramount ("Giving Becky a Chance," "The Highway of Hope"), Selznick-Select ("The Wild Girl"). During war filled executive post with Standard Oil. Ad., Lambs Club, N. Y.

—F—

FIELDING, Romaine, also author; b. Corsica; educ. Shattuck Mil. Acad., Univ. of Minn., and Coll. of Physicians and Surgeons (M. D.); early career on N. Y. Herald several yrs.; melodramatic plays; screen career, Lubin (wrote, produced and acted in "The Toll of Fear," "Eagle Nest," "The Garden of the Gods," "The Valley of Lost Hope," "In the Hour of Disaster"), Peerless-Brady ("Moral Courage," "Youth"), Ira Lowry ("For the Freedom of the World"), Romaine Fielding Productions, starring Mabel Taliaferro and Romaine Fielding. Ad., Lambs Club, N. Y.

FISCHER, David G.; educ. Univ. of Virginia; stage career, "Brown of Harvard," "Blue Mouse," for Shuberts, Virginia Harned, Julia Marlowe Bush Temple Stk. Co. Shubert Stk. Co., author of "Lavender and Old Lace," "The Master's Violin," "Immigrants," "John Rawn," "Purchase Price" etc.; screen career, American ("College Chums," "The Battleground," "The Silent Message"), Premier ("Ambition"), Fischer Prod. ("Law of Nature"), Waldorf

("Where Bonds Are Loosed," "Dad's Girl").

FISHBACK, Fred; b. Bucharest, Rumania, 1894; educ. N. Y.; screen career, Mack-Sennett ("Beware of Boarders," "Cactus Nell," "International Spy"), Sunshine Comedies ("Merry Jailbirds," "Money Talks"), Fishback Century Comedies ("A Jungle Gentleman," "Baby Doll Bandit," "Over the Transom"). Member M. P. D. A. Studio ad., L-Ko studio, Hollywood, Cal.

FITCH, George; stage career, stk.; screen career, technical director for all Herbert Brenon prods., also for Warren Producing Co., "Warfare of the Flesh." Now director of British & Colonial Kinematograph Co., Ltd. Ad., 56 Bloomsburg st., London, W. C., England.

FITZGERALD Dallas M.; b. La Grange, Ky.; educ. Louisville, Ky.; "The Open Door," "Chains of Evidence"; now producing Hallmark Prods. Ad., 220 West 42nd st., N. Y. C.

FITZMAURICE, George; b. France; screen career, Kleine (dir. "Stop Thief"), back to Pathe (dir. features, including "Arms and the Woman," "The Iron Heart," "Blind Man's Luck," "Sylvia of the Secret Service," "On-the-Square Girl," "The Recoil," "The Mark of Cain," "Innocent," "Common Clay," "Japanese Nightingale") Famous ("The Avalanche," "The Society Exile," "The Witness for the Defence," "The Counterfeit," "On With the Dance"). Ad., 1 West 67th st., N. Y.; studio ad., Famous Players-Lasky Corp., N. Y.

FITZPATRICK, James A., also scen. writer; b. 1895; Shelton, Conn.; educ. Yale Univ. and Frohman Acad., N. Y. C.; early career, 2 yrs. newspaper work; author of magazine articles and vaud. sketch; stage career, 1 yr. in rep., 1 yr. in vaud.; screen career, Juvenile Film and Cosmofotofilm, author and director of "The World War in Kidland," "Chip of the Old Block," "Chip's Elopement," Jax Film Co. ("Keep Smiling," "Cupid at Work," "Dust Unto Dust," "Uncle Sam's Reason"), Prizma ("May Days," "Memories"). Ad., Prizma, Inc., 71 W. 23rd st., N. Y. C.

FLAVEN, Arthur J.; b. N. Y. C.; educ. N. Y.; screen career, Famous Players and Universal, 5 yrs. asst. dir., "Running Straight," "Call of the Cougar," "Who Wins," with Hoot Gibson. Ad. Universal City, Cal.

FLEMING, Carroll; early career, director on dramatic stage, author of spectacles at N. Y. Hippodrome, wrote "Sis Hopkins" 18 yrs. ago, wrote and directed "The Choir Singer," "The Master Hand," produced "Fancy Free" with Clifton Crawford for Lee Shubert; screen career, Thanhouser ("Song of the Heart," "Rajah's Diamond," "Turn of the Road," etc.), Pathe (early episodes of "The Iron Claw," "The Hidden Hand"). Member M. P. D. A.

FLEMING, Caryl Stacy; b. Cedar Rapids, Ia., 1890; educ. Chicago hgh. schl. and coll.; stage career, 7 yrs. in stk. and vaud.; screen career, Universal, Eclair, Mutual, Federal, Kleine, Terris, Victor Moore comedies. Produced "America Must Conquer" for Liberty Loan; Keeney ("Her Family's Honor"), World ("The Clouded Name"), Physical Culture, Fad and Fancies Comedies, McManus ("Bruised Humanity"). Member Green Room Club, N. Y. Home ad., 276 Riverside Drive, N. Y.

FLYNN, Emmett J.; b. Denver, Colo.; educ. Sacred Heart Coll., Denver; screen career, First National ("Alimony"), Goldwyn ("Racing Strain," "Bondage of Barbara"), American ("A Bachelor's Wife," "Yvonne from Paris," "Other Side of Eden"), Fox ("Eastward Ho," "The Lincoln Highwayman," "Shod wi Fire"). Home ad., 4912 Rosewood ave., Los Angeles, Cal.; phone 567321; studio, Fox Studio, Los Angeles.

FORD, Hugh; b. Wash., D. C.; educ. Univ. of Cal.; stage career, many prods. covering a period of 20 yrs.; staged "Joseph and His Brethren," "The Yellow Ticket," "The Melting Pot," "Garden of Allah," "Bird of Paradise," "Potash and Perlmutter"; screen career, Famous Players ("The Slave Market," "The Crucible," "Prince and the Pauper," "Such a Little Queen," "Sapho"), Artcraft ("Seven Keys to Baldpate," "His House in Order"), Special ("The Woman Thou Gavest Me," "Secret Service"). Member Lambs Club and N. Y. A. C. Studio ad., Famous Players, N. Y.

FORD, Jack; b. Portland, Me., 1895; educ. Univ. of Maine; screen career, from July, 1914, Universal ("The Round Up," "The Range War," "The Secret," "A Marked Man," "A Woman's Fool," "Roped," "Outcasts of Poker Flat," "Fight for Love," "Ace of the Saddle," "Bare Fists," "Rider of the Law," "A Gun Fightin' Gentleman," "Marked Men"). Ad., home, Virginia Apts., Hollywood, Cal.; studio, Universal.

FRAME, Park B.; b. Seattle, Wash.; educ. Juneau, Alaska; screen career, J. D. Hampton (dir. "The White Washed Walls," "The Mints of Hell," "Man Who Turned White," "The Pagan God," "For a Woman's Honor," "The Gray Wolf's Ghost"). Home ad., 1471 Milton ave., Hollywood, Cal.; phone 577648.

FRANKLIN, C. M.; b. San Francisco, 1890; educ. there; early career, cartoonist for San Francisco "Bulletin," "Call," "Examiner"); screen career, Keystone, Majestic, Fine Arts ("A Sister of Six"), Fox ("Jack and the Beanstalk," "The Mikado," "Aladdin and the Wonderful Lamp," "Ali Baba and the Forty Thieves"). Received honorable discharge from the U. S. Army. Ad., L. A. Athletic Club, Los Angeles, Cal.

FRANKLIN, Harry L.; b. 1879; educ. St. Louis and Denver; stage career, 22 yrs. light comedian and juvenile leads with Chas. Frohman, A. H. Woods, etc.; screen career, Metro and International ("The Winning of Beatrice," May Allison, "Kildare of Storm," Emily Stevens, "Sylvia on a Spree," Emmy Wehlen, "Johnny on the Spot"), Metro ("That's Good," "After His Own Heart," "Full of Pep," "In His Brother's Place," "The Fourflusher"), Universal ("Rouge and Riches," Mary MacLaren). Ad., 7952 Norton ave., Hollywood, Cal.

FRANKLIN, S. A.; b. San Francisco, 1893; educ. there; screen career, Selig, Bosworth, Majestic, Fine Arts, Fox ("Ali Baba and the Forty Thieves"), Norma Talmadge Co. ("The Safety Curtain," "Her Only Way," "The Forbidden City," "The Heart of Wetona," "The Probation Wife"), Vitagraph (played in "A Rogue's Romance"), Universal (played in "The Sleeping Lion"), First National ("The Hoodlum," "Heart of the Hills"). Ad., Norma Talmadge Film Corp., N. Y. C.

FRANZ, Joseph J.; b. Utica, N. Y., 1883; educ. Christian Bros. Acad.; stage career, actor and dir. with Elsie De Tourney in Shakespearean rep., on tour in "Lion and the Mouse," "Squaw Man," "Three Weeks"; screen career, Santa Barbara M. P. Co., Universal ("Voice of the Wilderness"), Robertson-Cole ("Life's a Funny Proposition," "Mints of Hell," "A Sage Brush Hamlet," "The Blue Bandanna"), Hodkinson ("End of the Game"), "The Gray Wolf's Ghost" with H. B. Warner. Ad., Hampton Studio, Hollywood, Cal.; home ad., 4389 Sunset Blvd., Hollywood, Cal.

— G —

GAYE, Howard; b. England; educ. there; early career, British diplomatic and Govt. service; special writer for London newspapers; stage career, with Beerbohm Tree, Chas. Hawtrey, Forbes-Robertson; screen career, Reliance-Majestic, Fine Arts ("Diana of the Follies," "Intolerance"), Fox ("The Scarlet Pimpernel," "The Spy"), Mena Film Co. ("By Super Strategy"), Metro ("The Uplifters"), 2 yrs. in English army. Studio ad., Haworth Pictures Corp., Los Angeles, Cal.

GEORGE, Burton; b. Lake Charles, La.; educ. La. State Univ.; stage career, Baldwin-Melville Stock, San Francisco, San Antonio Stock, Denver Stock, Willard Mack Co.; screen career, Biograph, Eclair, Reliance, Lubin, Edison, Universal-Red Feather ("The Isle of Life"), with Fox to direct Geo. Walsh, Amer.-Pathe ("Eve in Exile").

GERRARD, Douglas, also actor; b. Dublin, Ireland, 1885; educ. Univs. of Dublin and Heidelberg, Germany; stage career, Shakespearean rep., Eng. com., classic plays in England and Australia, modern drama under Frohman and others in Eng.; in U. S., leading man with Viola Allen, Ethel Barrymore, Grace George; screen career, Rex, Pathe, Kalem, Famous Players, Universal (dir. "$5,000 Reward," "The Sealed Envelope," "Playthings," "Should a Woman Tell?" "The Velvet Hand," "His Divorced Wife," "The Phantom Melody," "Sins of the Father," "Better Half"). Home ad., L. A. Athletic Club, Los Angeles, Cal. Member M. P. D. A. Studio, Universal City, Cal.

GIBLYN, Charles; b. Watertown, N. Y.; educ. hgh. sch.; stage career, stock, rep, mus. com., as actor and mgr.; with Harrigan and Hart, Wm. Gillette, Sothern, mgmt. Chas. Frohman, H. W. Savage; screen career, 2 yrs. with Universal, Ince ("Honor Thy Name"), Triangle-Ince ("The Vagabond Prince," "Somewhere in

France"), Select ("The Studio Girl"), F. P. Lasky ("Let's Get a Divorce," "Sunshine Nan"), Goldwyn ("Peck's Bad Girl," "Just for Tonight," "A Perfect 36"), Selznick ("Upstairs and Down," "The Spite Bride"). Ad., L. A. Athletic Club.

GILLSTROM, Arvid E.; b. Gotenberg, Sweden, 1889; educ. Sch. of Mines, Colo.; early career, mining eng., leasing and prospector; screen career, asst. dir. Kalem, Keystone ("Hearts and Swords," "Their Social Splash"), King Bee, 26 comedies, Mack Sennett, 4 yrs. ("The Snow Cure," etc.), Fox ("Smiles," "Tell It to the Marines," "Swat the Spy"), Famous Players ("So This Is America," "The Con in Economy"). Ad., home, 1855 Winona Blvd., Hollywood, Cal., and Hotel Astor, N. Y.

GITTENS, Wyndham; b. at sea; educ. W. Indies and Harrow, Eng.; early career, newspaper and magazine writer, also on trade publications; screen career, Biograph, Melies, Universal as screen editor, with Triangle since June, 1917 as director ("The Ship of Doom," "The Second Floor Front," "Me unt Gott," Romayne), Gittens Prod. ("Give and Take"). Ad., home, Wellington Apts., 953 West 7th st., Los Angeles; Pico 2111.

GOLDAINE, Mark S.; b. Hartford, Conn.; educ. there and Pittsburgh W. U.; stage career, 20 yrs., 15 yrs. stage director; screen career, Equitable, Universal, now at National Studio. Author of several plays and sketches. Home ad., 1514 Rodney Drive, Los Angeles, Cal.; phone 597848.

GOULDING, Alf.; b. Melbourne, Australia; educ. there; stage career, 25 yrs. with J. C. Williamson, Australia, Pollar Opera Co., Orpheum Circuit 3 yrs., Morosco 1 yr., Marie Dressler 6 mos.; screen career, 1916, 3 two-reel Fox Comedies, directed Harold Lloyd for 1½ yrs., now with Rolin. Home ad., Glendale, Cal. Glen. 540-J.

GRANDON, Francis J.; b. Chicago; educ. Chicago Univ.; stage career, road and stock; screen career, Biograph, Imp (dir.), also dir. for Lubin, and Griffith-Triangle ("Strathmore," "Cross Currents"), Metro (dir. Mme. Petrova and Edmund Breese), Universal (dir. Violet Mersereau in Bluebird features), Famous ("The Dummy"), Famous Players ("Heart's Desire," "The Little Boy Scout"), Famous Players-Lasky ("The Little Soldier Girl"), Ivan ("Conquered Hearts"), Mutual ("Love's Law," "The Dare Devil"), Sherry ("Wild Honey"), National ("The Lamb and the Lion"). Ad., 532 So. Freemont ave., Los Angeles; studio, Selig Polyscope Co., Los Angeles, Cal.

GRANVILLE, Fred Le Roy, also cinematographer; b. Victoria, Australia; educ. there and New Zealand; early career, naturalist and photographer; screen career, 2 yrs. with Allan Hollubar ("Heart of Humanity," "Ambition"), photographed rescue of Stefansson Arctic expedition, only white man to cross No. Eastern Siberia with camera; lived 15 yrs. in South Sea Islands; directed 2-reel subjects for Universal, now directing "Peggy Hyland" at Brunton Studios, for Samuelson, Ltd., of England. Home ad., Finley ave., Los Angeles, Cal.; Holly. 2880.

GREEN, Al.; b. Perris, Cal.; stage career, 2 seasons in various prods.; screen career, asst. dir. to Marshall Neilan "In Old Kentucky," "Unpardonable Sin," "Daddy Long Legs"; now directing at Garson Studio, Fox ("Right After Brason" with Peggy Hyland), Garson ("Silk Husbands, Calico Wives" with House Peters), now in production picture with Clara K. Young. Ad., home, 831 Bryan st., L. A.; Garson Studio, Los Angeles, Cal.

GRIFFIN, Frank C.; b. Norfolk, Va., 1891; educ. Phila.; early career, drama, stock, vaud.; screen career, Lubin ("Blood Will Tell," "His Wedding Day"), produced for Universal, Lubin and Keystone ("Maggie's False Step"), Fox ("Where Love Leads"), Mack Sennett Comedies, special comedies for Universal, Frank Griffin Prod. ("Three Paces West"), Fox-Sunshine ("Her Private Husband," "A Roaming Bathtub"), Al St. John ("Ship Ahoy," "The Aero-nut"). Author of "Half Angel." Ar., L. A. Athletic Club, Los Angeles, Ca.; studio ad., Al St. John Studio, Los Angeles.

GRIFFITH, Edward Hilaire; b. Bloomington, Ill.; educ. Chicago; early exper., newspaper man, reported for Chicago Tribune, Herald, Journal and Chicago Press Asso., Cleveland Leader; 7 yrs. in reporting, editorial work, special staff corresp., magazine and feature writer; author in collaboration with Francis Trafford Ryall of "The Finish," produced in London, 1910; screen career, Edison, writing orig. stories and reconstruction and adaptations, including works of Wm. J. Locke, Peter B. Kyne, Rex Beach ("Barnaby Lee," "Cupid and Contraband," "The Boy Who Cried Wolf"), Edison ("One Touch of Nature," "The Awakening of Ruth). Directed Corinne Griffith. Ad. Vitagraph Studio, Brooklyn, N. Y.

GRIMMER, Frank; b. N. Y., 1886 educ. N. Y. and New Rochelle; stage career, 5 years; screen career, Thanhouser, 8 yrs. as casting director. Co-director to John B. O'Brien. Ad., 9 Mt. Etna pl., New Rochelle, N. Y.

GRINDE, Nick, assistant director; b. Madison, Wis.; educ. Univ. of Wis., B. A. degree; screen career, B. B. Hampton ("Desert of Wheat," etc.), Home ad., 1837 Morgan Place, Hollywood Cal.; phone 59488; studio, Weber Productions, Inc., Brunton Studios.

GUTTERRES, Moyses H. da Silva, art director, also actor; educ. St. Francis Xavier's Coll. Shanghai, China; stage career, 12 yrs. exp. vaud., operatic, dramatic plays and social entertainments, in Portuguese and English languages; "Quaker Girl," "Balkan Princess," "Expiation," "Gondolier of Death," "Dollar Princess," "Rodolpho de Novaes," "Ici on Parle Francais," "Dairymaids," "The Last Coat," "If I Were King," "The Crusaders"; screen career, art dir. Emerald Motion Picture Co., asst. dir. and art dir. Apex Pictures Corp. Hght., 5, 4; wght., 125; black hair, dark eyes. Ad., Apex Pictures Corp., Indianapolis, Ind.

— H —

HADDOCK, William F.; b. Portsmouth, N. H., 1877; educ. Burdett Coll., Boston; stage career, stk.; screen career, Edison, Melies, Eclair, All-Star, Life Photo, Gotham, Gaumont ("Tempest and Sunshine," "Devil's Darling," "I Accuse," "As a Woman Sows," "The Ace of Death," "The Unsuspected Isle"), Rolfe ("The Master Mystery"), Oliver ("Craig Kennedy" serial). Ad., home, 117 Sherman ave., N. Y. C.; St. Nich. 3200. Member M. P. D. A.

HALE, Albert W.; educ. Bordeaux, France; stage career, producer of spectaculars for Ringling Bro. Circus, musical comedies on Broadway, N. Y.; screen career, Famous Players, "Prisoner of Zenda," Vitagraph, 50 pictures; Pathe Freres, 50 pictures; Thanhouser, 20 pictures; American, 100 pictures. Hght., 5; wght., 205; brown hair and eyes. Ad., Hotel Ansonia, N. Y. C.; Union League Club, Los Angeles, Cal.

HALL, George Edwardes, also scenario writer; b. and educ. Bklyn.; stage career, with Chas. Frohman, Edwin Booth, Stuart Robson, stock; screen career, since 1904, 6 yrs. with Herbert Brenon, Henry Lehrman, Harold J. Binney, author of "War Brides," "Fall of the Romanoffs," "The Lone Wolf." Several yrs. at Imp, now directing for British & Colonial Kinematograph Co., 35 Endell st., Longacre, W. C., 2, London.

HAMILTON, Gilbert P.; b. Chebeaque, Me.; 5 yrs. speaking stage in stock throughout East and Hopkins theatre. Chicago; screen career began in developing dept. Edison, then to Biograph as cameraman, 4½ yrs. with Essanay as supt. of factory and production; directed numerous photoplays, including " Price of Crime," "Peril of the Plains," "Lust of the Red Men," "Even Unto Death," Century ("Inherited Passions"), Triangle 1 yr. ("The Maternal Spark"), "Every Woman's Husband," "The Golden Fleece." World, directing June Elvidge, "The Woman of Lies," "Coax Me," etc. Now directing Helen Holmes in "The Danger Trail." Home ad., Gates Hotel, Los Angeles; studio, 2019 S. Main st., Los Angeles.

HAMILTON, Lloyd Vernon; b. Oakland, Cal., 1892; stage career, Elleford stock, J. F. Hackett, mus. com. and burlesque; screen career, Kalem (originator of Ham comedies, with Bud Duncan, and creator of the character Ham; "Seaside Romeos," "Dudes for a Day"), Sunshine ("Mongrels," "Son of a Hun," "Roaring Lions and Wedding Bells," "A Tight Squeeze," "A Walter's Wasted Life," "The Twilight Baby." Hght., 6, 1; wght., 217; light complexion, blond hair, blue eyes. Ad., home, L. A. Athletic Club; studio, Lehrman Studios, Culver City, Cal.

HANSHAW, Dale; b. Grafton, W. Va.; educ. there, Pittsburgh and N. Y.; early career, 3 yrs. producing vaud. acts; screen career, World, Metro, continuities and scenarios for

Westinghouse Motion Picture Installations

Realizing that the successful operation of electrical equipment of a motion picture studio or theatre depends upon its ability to meet very exacting requirements, Westinghouse has made a special study of these requirements. This places Westinghouse in a position to render valuable engineering service to hundreds of studio and theatre owners.

This service will gladly be given upon request.

Several of the largest studios and theatres are equipped throughout with Westinghouse apparatus. We consider this to be our strongest recommendation, not only for results obtained, but also, for continuity of service.

The following are some of the users and endorsers of Westinghouse apparatus:

Metro. Studios	Grauman's Theatre, Los Angeles
Thos. H. Ince Studios	Strand Theatre, Norfolk, Va.
Robt. Brunton Studios	Pitt Theatre, Pittsburgh, Pa.
Universal Studios	Regent Theatre, Elmira, N. Y.
Clunes Studios	Stanley Theatre, Phila., Pa.
Fox Studios	New Mission Theatre, San Francisco

Write our nearest district office for our new Circular No. 7134.

Westinghouse Electric & Manufacturing Company
East Pittsburgh, Pa.

New York Office Los Angeles Office
165 Broadway 811 Van Nuys Bldg.

Sales Offices in All Large American Cities

Westinghouse

Universal, "The Nature Girl," "The Unfinished House," "Together," produced "Healthograms," "Federation," "Physical Culture Photoplays"; at present producing Transatlantic Boarding School Girls comedies for Transatlantic Film Co. of America, Inc. Ad., Green Room Club, N. Y. C.

HARRISON, Saul E.; b. Brenham, Texas; educ. N. Y. City; stage career, mus. stock, 6 yrs., dram. stock, 3 yrs.; screen career, Universal, Metro, Edison ("The Customary Two Weeks," "One Kind of Wireless," "Edison's Dream Comes True"), 2-reel Flagg-Para. comedies ("Tell That to the Marines," "Independence, B'Gosh!" "Perfectly Fiendish Flanagan"), Grossman Pictures, serial ("One Million Dollars Reward"). Home ad., 2900 Briggs ave., N. Y. C.

HARTFORD, David; b. Rockland, Mich.; educ. Detroit, stage career, 4 yrs. with Barnum's Circus, 10 yrs. actor and prod. dir. under mgmt. E. D. Stair, stk. in Cleveland, Detroit, Omaha, Los Angeles; screen career, dir. for Universal, Famous Players ("Tess of the Storm Country"), Ince ("The Bride of Hate"), Paralta ("Madame Who?" "Inside the Lines," "The Infernal Net," by Sarah Bernhardt), Curwood-First Nat'l ("Back to God's Country," "The Yellow Back"). Home ad., 110 So. Benton Way, Los Angeles, Cal.; studio, Curwood-Carver Prods., Inc., 5341 Melrose ave., Los Angeles.

HARTIGAN, P. C.; b. Cork, Ireland, 1881; educ. Trinity College, Dublin; early career, army officer in South Africa; screen career, began at Western Kalem (3 yrs. as mgr. and director, dir. dramas and reel comedies), 1 yr. with Pathe (dir. "I Love the Nurses" and other comedies), Vitagraph ("The Life of Moses," "Twelfth Night"), Nevada Film ("The Planter"), Fox ("A Fallen Idol").

HARVEY, John ("Jack"); b. Cleveland, O., 1881; educ. pub. sch., Cleveland; early career, baritone in many prods., also in every branch of amusement business from circus to opera; screen career, Vitagraph, Thanhouser, Universal, Imp ("When Thieves Fall Out"), Ernest Truex Comedies, Paramount-Briggs Comedies. Ad., Green Room Club, N. Y.

HAYDON, J. Charles; b. Frederick, Md.; educ. St. John's prep. sch. and Holy Cross Coll., Mass.; stage career, with Chauncey Olcott, "Mistress Nell," about 6 yrs.; screen career, Kinemacolor, Bosworth, Rex. Essanay, directed "The Family Divided," "The Scapegoat," "John Barleycorn," "The Strange Case of Mary Page," "The Sting of Victory," "The Night Workers," and "The Rise and Fall of the Confederacy" for So. Carolina Capital. Ad., Green Room Club, N. Y.

HEARN, Fred G., assistant director; also actor; b. Louisville, Ky.; 20 yrs. on stage; screen career, parts under Griffith, Kirkwood, Nye and others, lately Von Jagow in "My Four Years in Germany," with Marion Davies Film Co., assistant to Julius Steger, Select (played in "The Hidden Truth"), Paramount ("The Dark Star," "The Misleading Widow"). Ad., home, 1372 Ogden ave., N. Y.

HEERMAN, Victor; b. London, England; educ. N. Y.; stage career, with Nat Goodwin in "A Mid-Summer Night's Dream"; screen career, Keystone, Mack Sennett, Fox, "The Two Crooks," "She Loved a Sailor," "Watch Your Neighbor," "Are Waitresses Safe?" 15 mos. U. S. Navy, chief yeoman. Home ad., Los Angeles Athletic Club, Los Angeles, Cal.; B'way 444; studio, 4634 Santa Monica blvd., Los Angeles; Wilshire 655.

HEFFRON, T. N.; b. Virginia City, Nev., 1872; educ. Santa Clara Coll., Cal.; stage career actor and stage director for Cohan and Harris, Wm. A. Brady, Mrs. Fiske, A. H. Woods, Chas. Frohman, heavies in stk.; screen career from 1911, Thanhouser 1 yr., Biograph 1½ yrs., Famous Players, American (dir. Kolb and Dill—"A Peck of Pickles"), Triangle ("The Stainless Barrier," "The Sudden Gentleman," "The Veil," "The Price of Applause"), Rob-Cole ("The Prodigal Liar"), United ("A Man's Fight"), Lasky ("Thou Art the Man," "City of Masks"). Member M. P. D. A. Home ad., 504 So. Hobart Blvd., Los Angeles, Cal.; studio, Lasky, Hollywood.

HENABERY, Joseph; b. Omaha, Neb.; educ. there; early career, architectural drafting and railroading; stage career, San Carlos Opera Co., Geo. W. Lynch Co.; screen career, from 1910, Universal, Reliance-Majestic ("The Green Idol," "Capt. Macklin"), Lincoln in Griffith's "Birth of a Nation," Fine Arts ("Intolerance," "Children of the Feud," "That Colby Girl"), Artcraft ("Fancy Jim Sherwood," "The Man from Painted Post," "Say, Young Fellow"), United Artists ("His Majesty, the American"). Ad., Ince Studio, Culver City, Cal.

HENDERSON, Dell; b. St. Thomas, Ont., Can.; stage career, stk. leads in Chicago, St. Paul, Minneapolis, Omaha; screen career, Biograph, Triangle, Famous Players, Chas. Frohman, World ("Love in a Hurry," "Courage for Two," "Three Green Eyes"). Ad., Lambs' Club, and Hotel Claridge, N. Y. C.

HESSER, Edwin Bower; military director and scenario writer; b. Jersey City, N. J., 1893; early career, reporter, critic and author; stage career, dir. tours of Boston Opera Co.; screen career, Cinema Roma, Rome, Italy; director-in-chief Official Canadian Govt. films ("Canada's Fighting Forces," "In the Fire Trenches with Canada's Army," "Britain at War"), etc., Capt. 213 O. S. B., C. E. F.; Goldwyn, author-dir. Victory Film Co.; served as Capt. Signal Corps, U. S. Army, in Photographic Section; directed following War Dept. prods., "His Best Gift," "The Making of an Aviator," and several training series pictures; wrote scenario "Virtuous Men," released by S. L. Pictures. Ad., Scenario Dept., Anita Stewart Prod., Inc., 6. W. 48th st., N. Y.

HEYWOOD, W. L.; art director; b. England; educ. there; screen career, 18 yrs. author, actor, manager, producer, scenic artist, technical director, art director. Studio ad., Thos H. Ince Studios, Culver City, Cal.

HICKMAN, Howard; b. Columbia, Mo.; educ. San Jose, Calif.; stage career, from 1898, toured with Bernhardt; screen career, Paralta ("The White Lie," "Heart of Rachael," "Two Gun Betty"), B. B. Features ("Trick of Fate," "Josselyn's Wife," "Tangled Threads," "Her Purchase Price," "Beckoning Roads"). Hght., 6; wght., 150; dark hair and eyes. Studio ad., Brunton, 5341 Melrose ave., Los Angeles, Cal.

HILL, Robert J.; b. Port Rohen, Ont., Can.; educ. Detroit, Mich.; stage career, 7 yrs. with Vaughan Glaser in stk. and rep.; screen career, "The Lonely Heart," "The Girl Who Wouldn't Tell," with Violet Mersereau, "Temptation and the Man," "The Crystal's Warning," with Hobart Henley, "The Great Radium Mystery," Pacific Prod. Co. serial. Home ad., 4633 Vermont place, Los Angeles; studio, Pacific Prod. Co., Hollywood, Calif.

HILLYER, Lambert, also scenario writer; b. So. Bend, Ind., 1893; educ. Wilson M. A., Somerville, N. J., Drake Univ., Des Moines, Iowa; early career, newspaper work, short stories, prof. baseball; screen career, American, Mutual, Eastern Film Corp., Triangle, Ince, Artcraft, Hart Prod., as author wrote 17 pictures for Triangle-Ince, including "Sudden Jim," "Son of His Father," "An Even Break," which he also directed; dir. and wrote a series of 16 prod. for Wm. S. Hart in 1917-19, including "The Narrow Trail," "Riddle Gawne," "Square Deal Sanderson," "The Money Corral," "Sand," "By Their Fruits Ye Shall Know Them." Home ad., 914 So. Kingsley drive, Los Angeles, Calif.; studio, W. S. Hart Co., Hollywood, Calif.

HODGE, Rex, assistant director; b. Flint, Mich.; educ. Detroit and Mich. Agricultural Coll.; stage career, with B. C. Whi for a Day," season in "Isle of Spice," season in "Isle of Bong Bong"; screen career, since 1912. asst. prod. mgr. at Universal City until Sept 1918, then asst. dir., "The Millionaire Pirate," "The Sleeping Lion," "His Divorced Wife," "The Phantom Melody," With Monroe Salisbury, "The Fire Flingers" with an all-star cast. Home ad., 6152 De Longpre ave., Los Angeles, Calif.; Holly 1059; studio, Universal City.

HOGAN, Danny ("Kid"); stage manager; b. 1881, Italy; ex-lightweight champion of N. Y.; in vaud. 2 seasons, daredevil acts at Hippodrome; screen career, Universal, asst. dir. and actor, "A Good Little Devil," "Such a Little Queen," with Metro 3 yrs. as art director and actor of under-world parts; stage mgr. with Nazimova, Bert Lytell, May Allison. Ad., Metro Studio.

HOLBROOK, John Knight, also studio mgr.: b. Ripley, Tenn.; educ. National Normal Univ., Lebanon, Ohio; early career, 12 yrs., designing optical instruments, especially for moving pictures; screen career, 6 yrs. chief of photogra-

DIRECTORS

phy, Pathe, Besley South American Expedition, Wharton, Inc., stunts in "Patricia," "Exploits of Elaine," "Mysteries of Myra," also "It Pays to Advertise," "The Profiteer," "Huns Within Our Gates," etc.; writer of scenarios and travel stories, United ("Her Game"). Home ad., 121 E. Mill st., Ithaca, N. Y.

HOLDEN, John K., art director; b. Canada;; educ. Univ. of Calif.; early career, 6 yrs. with Edison Co. in Los Angeles; stage career, 10 yrs. scenic artist and stage manager in theatres and studios in Chicago, N. Y., Boston and Los Angeles; screen career, art director of Clune Film Prod. ("Ramona," "Eyes of the World"), Famous Players ("Rags, Little Pal"), Mary Pickford ("The Foundling"), H. B. Wright Pict. ("Heart of the Hills"), Metro ("Fair and Warmer"). Ad., 745 Cahuenga ave., Los Angeles, Calif.; Holly 1130; studio, Metro Pictures Corp., Los Angeles.

HOLLYWOOD, Edwin L.; b. N. Y.; educ. N. Y.; screen career, Peerless-World, Lasky ("Sweet Kitty Blelairs," "Thousand Dollar Husband"), Pickford ("Less Than Dust," "Pride of the Clan"), Hoffman ("One Hour"), Goldwyn ("Polly of the Circus"), Arden ("The Challenge Accepted" with Zena Keefe); first gov. picture, "The Immigrant," Vitagraph ("Birth of a Soul"). Ad., Green Room Club, N. Y. C.

HOLT, George; b. Fall River, Mass.; educ. there; stage career, with Annie Russell in "The Mysterious Mr. Bugle," played several seasons in vaud., stk., and rd. cos.; screen career, Lubin, Vitagraph ("Billy Smoke," "Mr. Alladin From Broadway"), Lasky-Para ("Sacrifice"), directed Universal ("Kingdom Come," "Four Gun Bandit," "Tempest Cody Turns Detective"), Capital ("Boss of the Flying H"). Home ad., 1144 5th st., Los Angeles, Calif.

HOLUBAR, Allen J.; b. Cal., 1889; stage career, stk., rep., on tour in "Girl of the Golden West," "Man of the Hour," "Everywoman," leading man in Cincinnati, Elmira and Phila. stk. cos.; screen career, from 1914, Universal (lead in "Twenty Thousand Leagues under the Sea," dir. and lead. "Heart Strings"), Bluebird ("Sirens of the Sea," "The Mortgaged Wife"), Jewel ("A Soul for Sale," "Talk of the Town," "Heart of Humanity," "Right to Happiness," "The Gorgeous Canary"); member M. P. D. A. Studio ad., Universal Film Co.; home ad., 1946 Cahuenga st., Los Angeles, Calif.; permanent ad., Friars' Club, N. Y.

HOPPER, E. Mason; b. Vermont; educ. Univ. of Maryland and abroad; stage career, began at 14 yrs., in many branches of theatricals; screen career, directing 8 yrs. for Essanay, Pathe, Famous Players, Goldwyn, producer of more than 300 photoplays, author of over 400 produced scripts, "As the Sun Went Down," "Boston Blackie's Little Pal," "When Bear-Cat Went Dry"; member of M. P. D. A. Home ad., 119 Dwight st., Santa Monica, Calif.; studio, Goldwyn Studio, Culver City, Calif.

HORAN, Charles; b. N. Y.; educ. Fordham, Columbia and Harvard; stage career, grand opera and stock; screen career, played leads at Thanhouser, Metro ("The Quitter"), Goldwyn ("Polly of the Circus"), Triangle ("Three Black Eyes"., Grace Davison in "A Convert of Revenge."

HORNE, James W.; b. San Francisco, 1880; educ. San Francisco; Belasco and Mayer Stk. at Alcazar theatre 9 yrs. in "Brewster's Millions," mgmt. Cohan & Harris; screen career, since 1912 Kalem (scenario ed., became manager when Geo. Melford resigned, "The American Girl"), Universal ("The Bull's Eye"), Pathe ("Hands Up"), Universal ("Midnight Man"), "Hands Up" serial, "The Tiger Trail," "The Midnight Man" with Jas. J. Corbett. Home ad., 1445 Valley View rd., Case Verdugo, Los Angeles, Cal.; studio, Astra Film Corp., Glendale, Calif.

HOURY, Henry; b. and educ. Paris, France; stage exper., leading man Paris theatres, Antoine, Chatelet, Gymnase; screen career, Eclipse, Paris, Vitagraph Co. of America (direct. Corinne Griffith in "Love Watches," "Clutch of Circumstance," "Miss Ambition"), Bushman-Bayne Prod.; for 1920, 10 episodes "When We Love," with Arnold Daly. Ad., 3 Place de la Madelaine, Paris, France.

HOWE, Eliot; b. Boston, Mass.; educ. Harvard Mil. Sch. and Univ. course at Throop Inst. of Tech.; stage career, age of 7 to 12, then finished education as mining engineer; screen career, Selexart ("Blue Blood"), Paralta ("With Hoops of Steel"), Pathe ("Silver Girl," "Todd of the Times"), Frank Keenan Prod. ("Crooked Roads or Straight"). Home ad., 5408 Hollywood blvd., Los Angeles, Calif.; phone 597538; studio, Frank Keenan Productions, Brunton Studio.

HOWELL, W. A.; b. Cincinnati, O., 1877; previous to screen career, dramatic actor, director, producer; since 1910 organizer of own independent picture producing companies; specializes in comedies. Office, 110 West 42d st., N. Y. C.; Bryant 4527.

HOYT, Harry O., also scenario writer; b. Minneapolis, 1885; educ. Univ. of Minnesota, Columbia Univ., Yale Univ.; written short stories and novels for 15 yrs., motion picture plays for 11 yrs.; editor for Fox, Metro, Goldwyn; over one hundred feature picture adaptations; author of following features: "Courage for Two," "Road to France," "Beloved Blackmailer," "By Hook or Crook," "Queen of Hearts," "Just Sylvia," "I Want to Forget," "The Sea Waif"; directed "Hand Invisible," "Thru the Toils," "Broadway Saint," with Montagu Love, "Forest Rivals," With Dorothy Green; directed Catherine Calvert in "That Woman." Ad., Yale Club, N. Y. C.

HUMPHREY, William J.; screen career, Vitagraph ("Tale of Two Cities," "Midnight Bride"), Ivan ("Two Men and a Woman," "Babbling Tongues"), Rialto De Luxe ("The Unchastened Woman"), Humphrey Pictures ("Atonement"). Ad., 152 Parkside ave., Brooklyn, N. Y.

HUNT, Jay, also scenario writer; b. Phila., Pa., 1865; educ. Univ. of Pa.; stage career, character actor and director, author of several plays, including "The Master Workman"; screen career, 1 yr. with Vitagraph, Horsley, Universal, Ince ("His Brother's Keeper," "The Mills of the Gods"), Metro ("The Promise"); member M. P. D. A. Home ad., 260 Convent ave., N. Y.

HUNTER, T. Hayes; b. Philadelphia, 1882; educ. Univ. of Pa.; stage exper., 3 yrs. stage mgr. for David Belasco, produced "The Girl of the Golden West" and others in co-operation with Mr. Belasco; screen career, director general of the Biograph Co., producing Klaw & Erlanger Biograph features; independent producer and sole director of "The Border Legion" featuring Blanche Bates and Hobart Bosworth, "Once to Every Man," with Jack Sherrill and Mabel White; also produced "Fire and Sword," "The Puppet Jury," Goldwyn, "Desert Gold," "The Cup of Fury. Ad., Lambs' Club, N. Y., and care Goldwyn, Culver City, Calif.

HURST, Paul C.; b. Calif.; educ. there; stage career, 5 yrs.; screen career, Universal, Lasky ("Rimrock Jones"), Vitagraph ("Woman in the Web," "Iron Test"), National ("Lightning Brice"), Kalem ("Return of Stingaree"), Pathe ("Tiger's Trail"). Ad., National, Studio Los Angeles, Calif.

HUSTED, Charles Clemens, assistant director; educ. Univ. of Mich.; stage career, season engagements with Stair and Havlin Prods. of "Common Law," "White Sister," "St. Elmo," "Awakening of Helena Ritchie," 4 seasons, associated with following as director and player; stk. cos., Cathrine Countiss, Vaughn Glaser, Mary Servoss, etc., 8 seasons; screen career, educational and industrial pictures, photo-novel series for Screen Letter Box, "Love, Honor and ?," "Heart of a Gypsy," etc. for Chas. Miller Prod. Ad., 120 W. 47th st., N. Y. C.; Bryant 7052.

HUTCHINSON, Craig; b. Austin, Minn., 1892; educ. Mil. School; early career, newspaper work on the Coast; screen career, scenario writer for Keystone, scen. writer and dir. for L-Ko, Universal, 4 mos. dir. comedy; orig. new weekly burlesque "The Weakly Indigestion"; dir. of all New Galety comedies released to date. Home ad., 5403 Romayne st., Hollywood, Cal.; Holly 1475; studio, Gaiety Comedies, Inc.

— I —

INCE, John; b. N. Y., 1879; educ. N. Y.; stage career, from 1888, in many prods., including "Ben Hur," "The Great Divide," etc.; screen career, Lubin, World ("The Struggle"), Equitable ("Sealed Lips," "Secret Strings," "Blind Man's Eyes"), Metro ("Should a Woman Tell," "Please Get Married," "Old Lady 31"), Studio ad., Metro Studio, Los Angeles, Cal.

INCE, Ralph W.; b. Boston, Mass., 1887; stage Career, Richard Mansfield Co., "The College Widow"; screen career, first as actor and then director, Vitagraph (appeared as Lincoln in the "Lincoln" series), directed Jewel Prod. ("The Co-Respondent"), Petrova Pict. and Metro, S-L Pictures ("Virtuous Men"), Selznick Pict. Corp., "The Perfect Lover," Sealed Hearts," "Out Yonder," "His Wife's Money"). Ad., care Selznick Pict. Corp., N. Y.

INGRAHAM, Harrish; b. London Eng., 1881; educ. Bedford Modern School, England; London University; early career, school teacher; came to the United States in 1902 for stage career in stock with Forepaugh Company. Cinn., O.; Dominion Stock Co., Ottawa, Can.; with Adelaide Thurston, leads; own company in vaudeville 2 yrs.; screen career, Pathe (2 yrs.), David Horsley ("The Painted Lie," "Unlucky Jim," "The Single Code," "The Eye of Envy," "Heirs of Hate"), Lasalida-Pathe ("When Baby Forgot," "The Child of M'sieu"), Triangle ("Child of M'sieu"), Ro.-Cole (played in "A Sage Brush Hamlet").

INGRAHAM, Lloyd; b. Rochelle, Ill.; stage career, stock director for Oliver Morosco, Harry Bishop; screen career, Reliance-Majestic, Essanay, Fine Arts, American ("Charity Castles," "Her Country's Call," "Peggy Leads the Way," "A Daughter of Joan," "The Eyes of Julia Deep"), Thos. H. Ince ("What's Your Husband Doing?" "Mary's Ankle," "Let's Be Fashionable"). Member M. P. D. A. Ad., Ince Studio, Culver City, Cal.

INGRAM, Rex; b. Dublin, Ireland, 1892; educ. St. Columba's Coll., Trinity Coll., Dublin and Yale; studied sculpture under Lawrie; stage career, pantomine abroad; screen career, Edison and Vitagraph, scenarist of Fox Prods. ("Blindness of Devotion," "Galley Slave," "Cup of Bitterness," "Song of Hate"); dir. first Bluebirds made in East ("Broken Fetters," "The Great Problem"), wrote and dir. on the Coast, Bluebird ("Chalice of Sorrow," "Flower of Doom"), Paralta ("His Robe of Honor"), was in service in Royal Flying Corps, since returning dir. Universal-special ("The Beach-Comber"), Metro ("Shore Acres"). Ad., Metro Studios, Hollywood, Cal.

IRVING, George; b. N. Y.; educ. N. Y.; stage career, with Chas. Frohman 13 yrs., appearing with William Gillette, Maude Adams, Francis Wilson, and others; screen career, genl. prod. dir. for Frohman ("The Witching Hour"), Petrova Pictures ("Daughter of Destiny"), Metro ("To Hell with the Kaiser"), Goldwyn ("Hidden Fires"), Artco ("As a Man Thinks," "The Capitol"), Select ("A Glorious Lady"), Lawrence Weber ("The Blue Pearl"). President M. P. D. A. Ad., care Atlantic Films, London England; home, Bayside, N. Y.; Bayside 2823-J.

— J —

JACCARD, Jacques; b. near N. Y., 1885; educ. in France; stage career, 4 yrs. as stock producer; screen career, 1910, American, International, Universal, wrote many of the scripts, sometimes appeared as juvenile heavy, adapted and produced "Terrence O'Rourke" series, directed first numbers of "Diamond from the Sky" for American, Anti-Vice M. P. Corp. ("Is Any Girl Safe?", dir. and scen.), Universal ("The Quest of Virginia," "The Red Ace," "Cyclone Smith," Spur and Saddle series and first aerial featurette, "Cassidy of the Air Lanes"). Member M. P. D. A.

JAMES, Harry C.; b. 1896, Ottawa, Canada; stage career, Dominion Stock Co., under Marshall Farnum; screen career, played parts in Majestic-Reliance productions in Hollywood under Wm. C. Cabanne, and in Universal productions with Carter DeHaven and Wallace Beery, asst. director to C. H. Higgin, technical director Lasky Studio, Mae Murray Production Co., with Robert Leonard, making specialty of futurist stage effects. Ad., Box 155, Hollywood, Cal.

JOHNSON, Tefft; b. Wash.; educ. Georgetown Coll.; stage career, mgmt. David Belasco 12 yrs., appearing with Mrs. Leslie Carter and Blanche Bates in "The Heart of Maryland," "Under Two Flags"; screen career, Edison, Vitagraph ("Turn in the Road," "Writing on the Wall"), Tefft Johnson ("Sonny Boy at the Bat," "Sonny Boy in School Days," "Sonny Boy and the Dog Show"), World ("Love Defender," "Love Net," "Love and the Woman," "Home Wanted"). Ad., Green Room Club, N. Y.

JONES, Grover; b. Terre Haute, Ind.; educ. private schools; early career, newspaper reporter; screen career, scenic artist at Universal, scenario editor Morosco Studios; scen. writer for Larry Semon; now directing Milburn Moranti in the Mercury Comedies, released by Bulls-Eye Film Corp. Home ad., Los Angeles, Cal.; studio, Mercury Comedies, Long Beach, Cal.

JONES, Richard, also studio mgr.; b. St. Louis; screen career, with O. T. Crawford in St. Louis 2 yrs., 4 yrs. with Keystone ("Mickey"), Sunshine, Sennett Special (Yankee Doodle in Berlin)," "His Last False Step," "Down on the Farm"). Ad., Los Angeles Athletic Club, Los Angeles; studio ad., Mack Sennett Comedies, Los Angeles, Cal.

JULIAN, Rupert; screen career, "The Kaiser, the Beast of Berlin," Universal (dir. and played in "The Fire Flingers," dir. "The Sleeping Lion"), Bluebird ("The Millionaire Pirate"). Ad., Goldwyn, Culver City, Cal.

— K —

KELLETTE, John William; also scenario writer; b. Lowell, Mass.; screen career, Universal, asst. Dir. Violet Mersereau features; Thanhouser, scen. writer for 2 yrs., Fox Film Corp., co-director and writer on Vivian Martin, June Caprice, Lee Children, George Walsh, Peggy Hyland, Evelyn Nesbit features; now directing Paramount-Briggs comedies ("Saturday," "Burglars," the Circus series, "The Sticky Six," "Burried Gold"); composer of popular songs. Studio ad., Klutho Studio, Jacksonville, Fla.; home ad., Elks Club, 116 W. 43d st., N. Y. C.

KELLEY, Winthrop; b. Portland, Maine; educ. Harvard Univ.; stage career, Castle Sq. stk.; Richard Mansfield. Sothern and Marlowe; screen career, Eclair, Ideal ("The Submarine Eye"), Williamson Bros. Ad., Hotel Somerset, N. Y.

KELSEY, Fred A.; b. Sandusky, O., 1884; educ. high sch.; early career, sailor on Great Lakes; stage career, playing juveniles, comedians, heavies, in "Secret Service," "House of a Thousand Candles"; screen career, Nestor, Reliance-Majestic, Fine Arts, Thanhouser, Universal ("A Slave of Fear," "The Fugitive," "Red Sanders Plays Cupid," "The Outlaw and the Lady," "The Texas Sphinx," "The Honor of an Outlaw," "A 44-Calibre Mystery," "Six Shooter Justice," "The One Way Trail," "Reforming a Reformer"). Member M. P. D. A. Ad., 2209 Fairfield, Hollywood, Cal.; Holly 3340.

KELSON, George; b. England; educ. Univ. of London, stage career 5 yrs. London, 6 yrs. English provinces; screen career, World ("The Way of the Strong," "The Tenth Case," "The Way Out," "The Purple Lily"), Brady ("Stolen Orders," "Little Women"), Mayflower ("Bolshevism on Trial"), Canadian Prod. ("The World Shadow"). Ad., Friars Club, or home, 535 W. 135th st., N. Y.; Mngside 4357.

KENNEDY, Aubrey M.; b. Winnipeg, Man., Canada; educ. St. Mary's Coll., Dayton, O.; early career, author; screen career, 3 yrs. Gen. Mgr. for Essanay, 2 yrs. Gen. Mgr. for American, 3 yrs. Gen. Mgr. of prods. for Universal 2 yrs. Gen. Mgr. of prods. for Goldwyn; author and director of "The Yellow Menace" a serial, "The Masked Rider," serial, 12 2-reel westerns.

KENNEDY, Jack; assistant director; b. Hopkinton, Mass.; educ. Dartmouth Coll.; excelled in college theatricals, author of several scenarios produced by Vitagraph; asst. dir. Mayfair Film Corp. ("Persuasive Peggy"), Vitagraph ("Between Friends," "Bobby Connelly" series kid pictures), Goldwyn-Rex Beach Pictures with Hobart Henley; Famous Players-Lasky Corp., asst. to John Emerson. Home ad., Hotel Grenoble, N. Y. C.

KING, Burton; b. Cincinnati, 1877; stage career, in "Strongheart," "Graustark," "Shot Gun Opera"; screen career, Equitable ("Man and His Angel"), Metro ("Black Butterfly," "A Soul of a Magdalen," "To the Death"), Pathe ("Seven Pears"), Selig ("Out of the Shadow," "The Font of Courage"), International ("Flower of Faith"), Rolfe ("Master Mystery" Houdini serial), Selznick ("Scream in the Night"), McManus ("Lost Battalion"), Wistaria ("Lurking Peril" serial). Ad., M. P. D. A. and 1520 B'way, N. Y.

DIRECTORS

KING, Carleton S.; b. Dec. 15, 1887, St. Louis, Mo.; educ. St. Louis, Chicago and N. Y. C.; stage career, comedian in opera and mus. com., also comedy-drama with Francis Wilson Co., etc.; screen career, 2 yrs. with Edison (played leads and directed "The Way Back," "Breaking the Shackles," "A Child in Judgment," "A Broth of a Boy"), Dixie Films, Vitagraph ("Dry Valley Jackson"), Famous Players ("Uncle Sam, M. D."), Paramount Magazine ("Aint"). Hght., 5, 11; wght., 165; dark complexion, brown hair, gray eyes. Ad., 471 Central Park West, N. Y.

KING, Henry; b. Christiansburg, Va.; educ. Roanoke; 10 yrs. legit. stage exper. as actor, Shakespearean roles in stk.; also "The Lion and the Mouse," "House of a Thousand Candles," "Graustark," etc.; screen career, American ("Mate of Sally Ann," "Beauty and the Rogue," "Six Feet Four"), Ince, Paramount ("23½ Hours' Leave"), Jesse D. Hampton ("Fugitive From Matrimony," "The White Love"). Member M. P. D. A. Studio ad., Jesse D. Hampton Productions, L. A., Calif.

KIRKLAND, David; b. San Francisco; educ. Univ. of Calif.; stage career, with Robert Edeson, Maud Adams; screen career, Essanay ("The Children of the Forest"); member M. P. D. A.; in U. S. service 1917-1919, capt. and adj. 62d Infantry; director, John Emerson, Anita Loos Prods., "A Temperamental Wife," "A Virtuous Vamp." Ad., 318 E. 48th st., N. Y. C.

KNOLES, Harley; b. Rotherham, England, 1880; educ. Cambridge Univ.; stage career, stage mgr. and prod. Liebler & Co.; screen career, World ("Who Is Sylvia?" "The Price of Pride," "The Little Duchess,'"), World ("The Volunteer," "His Brother's Wife," "The Adventures of Carol," "Wanted, a Mother," "Stolen Orders"), Brady Prod. ("Little Women"), Mayflower Photoplay Corp. ("Bolshevism on Trial"), Famous Players, "Half an Hour" with Dorothy Dalton; member Friars' Club and M. P. D. A. Home ad., 490 Riverside drive, N. Y.

KORACH, Milton W., technical director; educ. Cleveland; early career, newspaper specialty man; screen career, Argus ("House Without Children," "Vanishing Charms"), editor Cleveland Plain Dealer Screen Magazine. Ad., Argus Enterprises, Cleveland, Ohio.

— L —

LAMBERT, Capt. Harry; b. Dublin, Ireland; educ. Trinity Coll., Dublin, and Edinburgh Univ.; early career, officer British cavalry for 9 yrs., saw active service in Egypt, India, Basutoland, and Boer War; stage career, light comedy, with Geo. Edwardes, Frank Curzon, Cyril Maude in London, character parts in "Three Faces East," "A Night at an Inn," "The Bluebird"; screen career, director at Vitagraph 1912-15, "An Officer and a Gentleman," "Spirit and the Clay," "The Diver," "The Test," "Ancient Order of Good Fellows," producer of official pictures for New York City at the Panama Pacific Exposition, Author's Film ("The Silent Witness," "The Crucible of Life"), vice-pres. and dir. gen. Lambert Film Corp. and Mirror Films, Inc. Ad., Lambs' Club, N. Y.

LAMBERT, Glen; b. Richmond, Va., 1894; educ. choir school, Cathedral St. John the Divine, N. Y.; stage career, Boston stk. co., vaud. producer; screen career, Florida Photoplays, "Child of the Sea," "The Dream Man" Superior Features, "The Rounder," also with Biograph, Crystal, Eclair, Klutho; author 73 produced scenarios.

LANE, Tamar; educ. Boston, Prince Schl. and Stamford Acad.; has written articles and stories for leading newspapers and magazines; in theatrical and motion picture business for 10 years, serving in various capacities; photoplay editor Boston Evening Record; editor Screen Magazine; author and director of several pictures made by Plaza Film Co.; Gen. Mgr. Character Pictures Corp. Ad., 200 W. 111th st., N. Y. C.

LAVER, H. A. (Jack); educ. Western Reserve Univ.; publicity man, newspaper and magazine writer, publisher of first screen magazine on Pacific coast; screen career, National (asst. dir. on "In Search of Arcady," "The Boomerang," "The Long Arm of Mannister," "The Confession"), dir. comedies for National. Home ad., 6061 Santa Monica blvd., Los Angeles, Calif.; Holly 4276.

LAWRENCE, Edmund; b. Bridgeport, Conn.; educ. Brooklyn, N. Y.; stage career, character actor and comedian, Julia Marlowe, Francis Wilson, E. H. Sothern, Daniel Frohman, Lillian Russell, DeWolf Hopper, the Shuberts; screen career, Fox Film Corp. ("Lure of Ambition," "Queen of Hearts," "The Liar," "Her Price," "The Love Auction," "A Daughter of France," "The Fire Brand," "The Merry-Go-Round," "Lost Money," "What Would You Do?" Home adr 274 Rutland road, Brooklyn, N. Y.; phone Flatbush 5461; studio, Fox, Hollywood, Calif.

LEAVERS, George R. B., technical director; b. Hamilton, Canada; educ. Los Angeles, Throop Acad., Pasadena, Cal., Univ. of Washington; early career, structural engineer, architectural draftsman, designer, supervising engineer of construction for U. S. Gov.; screen career, architect for Art Unit Studios, Glendale, Calif. Home ad., 241 Avenue 25, Los Angeles, Calif.

LEAVITT, Harvey C., technical director; b. Kansas City, Kans.; educ. Colorado Springs, Colo., also Colo. Coll.; early career, general contractor and builder throughout Middle West. Ad., 4261 So. Grand ave., Los Angeles, Calif.; phone So. 3305.

LEONARD, Robert Z.; b. Denver, Colo.; stage career, with Calif. Opera Co., property man, comedian, stage mgr. in comic opera and drama, has sung in over 100 light operas; screen career, Lasky ("A Mormon Maid," "Life's Pendulum"), Famous Players ("The Primrose Ring"), Universal ("Primrose Virtue," "The Bride's Awakening," "Modern Love," "Delicious Little Devil"), Cosmopolitan ("Miracle of Love," "Restless Sex"); member M. P. D. A. Home ad., 1 W. 67th st.; studio ad., Cosmopolitan Film Studios, N. Y. C.

LE SAINT, Edward J.; b. Cincinnati, Ohio; educ. there; stage career, 20 yrs. in stk. and on the road; screen career, Universal ("The Long Chance," "The Three Godfathers"), Fox ("The Devil's Wheel," "The Bird of Prey," "Kultur," "The Strange Woman," "The Call of the Soul," "The Wilderness Trail," "The Speed Maniac"). Home ad., 850 N. Andrews blvd., L. A.; studio, Fox Studio, Los Angeles, Calif.

LE SAINT, Stella Razeto (Mrs. Edward J.); b. San Diego, Calif.; educ. San Francisco; stage career, 10 yrs. in stk. and on the road; screen career, Majestic, Kinemacolor, Selig, Universal, dir. Ed. Le Saint, title role in Universal's "The Three Godfathers," co-director with Mr. Le Saint on everything he makes. Home ad., 80 N. Andrews blvd., Los Angeles, Calif; Wilshire 2931; studio, Fox.

LESSEY, George A.; b.; educ. Amherst, Mass.; educ. Dean Acad., Williston Sem. and Amherst Coll.; stage career, in all branches of theatrical business; screen career, Thanhouser (Romeo in "Romeo and Juliet"), 3 yrs. with Edison (dir. "The Birth of the Star Spangled Banner," etc.), Universal in 1914 (dir. King Baggot), Metro ("The Purple Lady"), Wharton, Inc. ('Patria," "The Eagle's Eye"), De Luxe ("Twilight"). Home ad., 34 W. 75th st., N. Y. C.

LE STRANGE, G. S. (Dick); also Comedian; b. Weisbaden, Germany, 1882; educ. New York Univ.; stage career, stk., vaud., with Savage and Shubert, "Girl of the Golden West" on tour; screen career, Lasky, Fox, Selig, Morosco, Metro leads, Sunset Pict. ("Sundown Slim"), Edison ("Five Dollar Bill," "Whirligig of Life"), directed 20 reel serial featuring Grace Davidson "Bolsheviki of the U. S. A." Hght., 6; wght., 185; blue eyes, blond hair. Home ad., 111 Hollister ave., Ocean Park, Cal.; Sunset studio, San Antonio, Texas.

LEVERING, Joseph; b. Columbus, Ind.; educ. Kansas City, Mo.; screen career, Art Dramas ("Little Miss Fortune," "The Road Between"), Erbograph ("The Little Samaritan" with Marion Swayne, "The Victim," "The Transgressor"), Gaumont ("His Temporary Wife," "Making Her His Wife"); now directing specials for Gaumont Co. Home ad., 518 W. 204th st., N. Y. C.

LEWIS, Charles, also scenario writer; b. Brooklyn; educ. Brooklyn; screen career, Jungle Film Co., Universal, Kinetophoto Corp., Imp, Novelty; produces, directs amateur pictures ("The Dim Light" Lewis Films, directed "Visions," both with full amateur casts). Home ad., 61 Bay 23d st., Brooklyn, N. Y.

LITSON, M. N.; b. N. Y., 1878; educ. Coll. City, N. Y.; stage career, productions, "Sword of the King," "Robin Hood," "Ninety and Nine"; screen career, Paragon ("Paying the Price"), Peerless ("Nathan Hale"), Thanhouser ("Patriot and Spy"), Biograph, Edison, Metro ("The

N. W. ARONSON

Citizens National Bank Building
Los Angeles, California
Phone: Pico 750

MOTION PICTURE EXCHANGE

REPRESENTING

Players—Directors—Authors

ENGAGEMENTS ARRANGED

Largest Collection of Books
for Motion Pictures
on the Pacific Coast

Plays—Adaptations—Publicity

Motion Picture Sales

Eastern Office

CRUSADER SERVICE

1400 Broadway
New York City

Phone: Greeley 6944
Cable: Crusader New York

1400 Broadway
New York City

CRUSADER SERVICE

PURVEYORS OF BIG STORIES FOR BIG PRODUCERS

For Example:

ALLAN DWAN	MAYFLOWER	CHARLES MILLER
"A Splendid Hazard" By Harold MacGrath	PHOTOPLAY CORPORATION	"High Speed" By Clinton H. Stagg
"In the Heart of a Fool" By William Allen White	"The White Mice" By Richard Harding Davis	"Kleath" By Madge Macbeth

MAURICE TOURNEUR
"The Glory of Love," by Pan

and

To C. E. SHURTLEFF Eighty Stories by JACK LONDON

Exclusive Representatives for

ALICE GLENISTER—Motion Picture Rights to Smart Set, Saucy Stories and Parisienne Magazines

VAL CLEVELAND
the latest "Find" in American literature

When ALLAN DWAN bought Val Cleveland's first story "The Scoffer," DWAN said: "This *is* worth ten thousand dollars"

Western Office:

N. W. ARONSON

Citizens National Bank Building
Los Angeles, California

Eternal Question"), Artcraft ("Pride of the Clan," "Poor Little Rich Girl"), production mgr. at Goldwyn Studio. Studio, Goldwyn, Culver City, Calif.

LLOYD, Frank; b. Glasgow, Scotland; stage career, stk., rep., came to America at head of Walker's rep. cos.; also vaud.; screen career (heavy in Rex releases, then dir. own co), Fox ("Les Miserables," "Tale of Two Cities," "Blindness of Divorce," "Riders of the Purple Sage"), Goldwyn ("World and Its Woman," "Loves of Letty," "Silver Horde"), with Pauline Frederick in "Woman in Room 13," "The Roads of Destiny"; member M. P. D. A. Home ad., 1765 N. Vine st., Hollywood, Calif.

LLOYD, Harold Warner, assistant director; b. Long Branch, N. J., 1888; educ. N. Y.; screen career, NYMP, Universal ("Dumb Girl of Portici"), Signal ("Girl and the Game," "Whispering Smith," "Medicine Bend," "Manager of B. and A."), ex-director of Physical Culture, N. Y. Police Dept. Hght., 5, 9½; wght., 160; dark complexion, blue eyes. Ad., Signal, 4560 Pasadena ave., Los Angeles.

LORD, Delmer, assistant director; b. N. Y. C.; screen career, formerly with Mack Sennett, now directing under supervision of Hampton Del Ruth. Home ad., 1022 N. Bonnie Beal, Los Angeles, Calif.; phone 55116; studio, Fox Sunshine Comedies.

LOUIS, Will; b. Woodfield, Md.; stage career, 15 yrs. as stock actor and stage manager; screen career, has directed numerous pictures, specializing in comedies, with Lubin, Edison, Solax, Vim, Goldwyn (played in "Jubilo"). Hght., 5, 6; wght., 150. Home ad., 3651 N. 15th st., Phila.; studio, 750 Riverside ave., Jacksonville.

LOVETT, Shaw; assistant director and actor; b. March 22nd, 1896; N. Y. C.; demobilized from Royal Air Forces as Lieut. in April, 1919; played with Irene Castle in the "Firing Line," and with Billie Burke in the "Misleading Widow," and "Sadie Love." Asst. director with Lawrence Windom in "Darcy," and John S. Robertson in "Sadie Love," "Erstwhile Susan," "Jekyll and Hyde." Studio ad., Famous Players Lasky Corp.

LOWRY, Ira M.; b. Phila., 1888; educ. there; screen career, began 1903, familiar with every branch of the industry through personal experience; designed 400-acre plant now used by Betzwood Film Co., of which he is vice-president and general manager; Betzwood ("The Eyes of Truth," "Sandy Burke," "Oh, Johnny," "Speedy Meade," "A Misfit Earl," "Road Called Straight"). Ad., Betzwood Film Co., Port Kennedy, Pa.

LUDDY, Irving Edward; assistant director; b. Canada; educ. N. Y. C.; early career, manager of the Flatbush and Jefferson Theatres, N. Y. C.; screen career, Vitagraph ("Nights and Nighties," "Cave Men," "Vamps and Varieties," "Rubes and Robbers," "Lovers-Not"). Home ad., Angelno Apts., Los Angeles, Cal.; phone 10815; studio, Vitagraph.

LUND, O. A. C.; also writer; b. Stockholm, Sweden; educ. Upsala Univ.; stage career, Folk Theatre, Stockholm, and Royal Dramatic Theatre; screen career, Eclair, World, Universal, Metro ("The Dollar Mark," "The Marked Woman"), Fox ("The Painted Madonna," "Hearts Revenge," "Peg of the Pirate"), Universal (Violet Mersereau in "Together," "The Unfinished House"), Bluebird ("The Nature Girl"). Ad., Green Room Club, N. Y. C.

— M —

MACDONALD, J. Farrel; b. Waterbury, Conn., 1875; educ. Yale; ex-officer U. S. Army; stage career 18 yrs.; screen career from 1908 with G. M. Anderson, with Griffith (Biograph), Imp as actor and dir.; with Pathe as director produced all 5 and 6 reel Oz features, Keystone-Triangle, Universal ("Roped," "A Fight for Love," played in "Marked Men"), American ("Molly of the Follies," "A Sporting Chance"), Pathe ("This Hero Stuff"). Ad., home, 1443 Martel ave., Los Angeles. Member M. P. D. A.

MACDONALD, Sherwood; b. N. Y. C.; educ. Yale Univ., Ph. B.; early career, lawyer, author; screen career, Republic, Triangle ("What Every Mother Knows," "Muggsy," "Sunny Jane," "Checkmate," "Wildcat," "Bit of Kindling," "Betty Be Good," "Bab the Fixer," "Red Circle" serial). Home ad., 1221 W. 7th st., Los Angeles, Cal.; phone 60121; studio, Becker Macdonald Prods.

MacGREGOR, Norval; b. River Falls, Wis., 1865; stage exper. 20 yrs., lead and manager for Nance O'Neil; 5 yrs. mgr. Janet Waldorf in world tour; screen career, 8 yrs., independent release "100 Years of Mormonism," Selig,,Universal, Calif. Film. Corp., Select ("Children of Banishment" (Mitchell Lewis). Home ad., Sierra Madre, Cal. Member M. P. D. A.

MACKENZIE, Donald; b. Edinburgh, Scotland; educ. Stewart's Coll., Edinburgh; with Augustin Daly Co., Whitney Opera Co., played with Lew Fields in "The June Bride"; screen career, Pathe ("The Perils of Pauline," "The Spender," "The Pardon," "The Shielding Shadow," "The Challenge," "The Seven Pearls," Oliver ("Craig Kennedy" serial), S. L. K. Corp. ("The Fatal Fortune" with Helen Holmes). Ad., Green Room Club, N. Y.

MACQUARRIE, Murdock, also actor; b. and educ. San Francisco; stage career, played the waif in "Lights o' London" at age of 7, in rep., etc., with Henry Miller, W. A. Brady, Joseph Jefferson, E. S. Willard, in leading parts, several seasons in stock; screen career, with Biograph, was first lead with Kinemacolor, to Universal in 1913, Signal ("Stain in the Blood," "Nancy's Birthright"), American ("The Gambler's Last Love"), Selznick ("Panthea"), Bernstein ("Humility," "Loyalty," "Justice"), National ("The Son of Tarzan" serial, Universal ("Twisted Souls," "The Keeper of Hell Gate"). Hght., 5, 8; wght., 150; brown hair, gray eyes. Member M. P. D. A. Home ad., 1967 Beechwood Drive, Hollywood, Cal.

MAIGNE, Charles; b. Richmond, Va., Nov. 11, 1881; educ. Univ. of Notre Dame; early career, newspaper man, war correspondent, magazine writer, officer in U. S. Army; screen career, adapted and directed Famous Players ("The Copperhead"), Artcraft ("The Invisible Bond," "Firing Line"), Select ("Redhead," "World to Live In"), Special ("Quest of the Big 'Un"), now engaged in adapting and directing special productions for Famous Players-Lasky Corp. ("The Copperhead"). Ad., Lambs Club, N. Y.

MARSHALL, George E.; b. Chicago, 1891; educ. St. John's Mil. Acad.; Wisconsin and Univ. of Chicago; screen career, 4 yrs. with Universal "Love's Lariat," "Liberty" serial), dir. "Adventures of Ruth," Ruth Roland Serials. Member M. P. D. A. Ad. 620 W. Moreland, Los Angeles, Cal.

MARSHALL, Roy H.; assistant director; screen career, Lasky, 5 yrs., with Geo. Melford, Wm. C. De Mille, Robert Z. Leonard, Irvin V. Willat, "Rustling a Bride," "A Daughter of the Wolf," "The Grim Game," Brentwood ("The Other Half," "Poor Relations"). Ad., 6433 Dix st., Hollywood, Cal.; phone 577354; studio, Haworth Pictures Corp., Sunset Studio, Los Angeles.

MARSTON, Theodore M.; stage career covering a period of 20 yrs., creating and playing many leading character parts in B'way prods.; with Mary Mannering, H. B. Warner, Wm. H. Crane, etc., appearing in "The Man of the Hour," "The Girl from Rector's," "Quo Vadis," "Alias Jimmy Valentine," "The Squaw Man"; screen career, Pathe, Kinemacolor, Vitagraph, (dir. "Mortmain," "The Secret Kingdom"), McClure ("Greed," "Sloth," "Wrath," of "Seven Deadly Sins" series)' Universal ("The Girl by the Roadside," "The Raggedy Queen"), Vitagraph ("The Black Gate").

MARTIN, E. A.; also scenario writer; stage career, with R. B. Mantell, Frank Mayo, general stage mgr. for David Belasco, author and producer of the play "Wyoming," stk. producer for 6 yrs.; screen career, Selig ("When a Woman's Forty," "The Fighting Fishmaid," "In Tune with the Wild," "The Lost City" serial). Home ad., 3463 Mission road, Los Angeles, Cal.; studio, Selig Zoo.

McCLOSKEY, Justin H.; assistant director; b. Orange, N. J.; educ. St. Johns Parochal Sch., Seton Hall Coll.; stage career, theatre manager and treasurer, New York, Webers, Daly's, Grand Opera House, Casino; screen career, Humanity ("Whom the Gods Would Destroy," "When Bearcat Went Dry," "The Gift Supreme"). Home ad., Boulevard Apts., Los Angeles, Cal.; phone 577332.

DIRECTORS

McGILL, Lawrence B.; b. Courtland, Miss., 1869; educ. Courtland Acad.; stage career, for 20 yrs. directed traveling rep. and stock cos., producing more than 400 plays; screen career, dir., American-Eclair, Reliance-Majestic, All-Star, Metro, Arrow ("Children of St. Anne," "Arizona," "Pierre of the Plains," "The Price He Paid," "The Sealed Valley," "How Molly Made Good," "The Woman's Law," "Crime and Punishment"), Astra Pathe ("The Girl From Bohemia," "The Angel Factory"). Member M. P. D. A.

McGOWAN, John P.; director general; b. S. Australia; educ. Australia; stage career, with Robert Mantell, William Faversham, H. W. Savage, also in stock and vaud.; screen career, with Kalem, making three trips with them to Ireland; later with Lasky and Universal; formed Signal Corp. with S. S. Hutchinson to feature Helen Holmes in railroad films, produced "Girl and the Game," Whispering Smith," "Medicine Bend," "Lass of the Lumberlands," "Diamond Runners," "The Railroad Raiders," "The Lost Express," serial "Lure of the Circus," Universal ("Elmo, the Fearless" serial). Member M. P. D. A. Studio ad., L-Ko Motion Pictures Corp., Hollywood, Cal.

McMACKIN, Archer; b. Lake City, Iowa; educ. Univ. of Chicago and Cornell; early career, magazine and newspaper writer in Chicago, reporter and special writer to Record-Herald; screen career, started writing for Essanay, Biograph and Lubin, later editor, Essanay, also wrote publicity, conducted contest which produced the word "photoplay" now universally used; wrote more than 500 orig. stories and prod. nearly 400 subjects, best pictures, Essanay ("The Final Judgment," "The Right of Way"), American ("In the Purple Hills," "Everyheart"), National ("Nothing But Nerve"), Model-Gale Henry (This Way Out"). Home ad., 205 N. Broadway, Los Angeles, Cal.; Pico 875.

McRAE, Henry Alexander; b. Ontario, Can.; educ. there; stage career, on graduating from school toured with own co. for 2 yrs., later operated stock cos. in Seattle, Portland, Sacramento and San Francisco; took shows to Japan, Hawaii, the Orient; screen career, 1 yr. with Selig, Universal (dir. Bison animal and other features, dir. "The Pirate of Panama"), Bison ("Giant Powder," "A Night with Whispering Smith"). Formerly director-general Universal City, Universal ("Dropped from the Clouds," "Man and Beast," "The Range War"). Now in China for Universal. Ad., L. A. Athletic Club. Member M. P. D. A., Los Angeles, Cal.

MELFORD, George H.; b. Rochester, N. Y.; educ. McGill Univ.; stage career, 7 yrs., in various legit. prods.; screen career, 10 yrs., first with Kalem (as actor and director, produced "The Boer War," "The Invisible Power"), Lasky (dir. "The Hostage," "The Call of the East," "Nan of Music Mountain," "Sandy," "The Bravest Way," "City of Dim Faces," "The Source," "Cruise of the Make Believes," "Everywoman," "The Sea Wolf," "The Round-Up"). Ad., studio, Lasky, Hollywood, Cal.

MENASCO, Milton, art director; b. Los Angeles; educ. St. Vincent's Coll., Los Angeles; studied art with Robert Reid, the mural painter; screen career, 7 pictures for Hayakawa ("Temple of Dusk," "Dragon Painter," etc.), Lew Cody ("Butterfly Man"); now art director with Katherine MacDonald. Home ad., 6511½ Hollywood blvd., Los Angeles, Calif.; phone 577337.

MENESSIER, Henri, assistant director; screen career, Selznick ("The Common Law," "Easiest Way," "Price She Paid"), Nazimova-Metro ("Eye for Eye," "Out of the Fog," "Red Lantern"), asst. director for Chautard Prods., Paragon Studios, Fort Lee, N. J. Home ad., 125 W. 45th st., N. Y. C.

MIDDLETON, Edwin; b. Philadelphia, Pa.; educ. Swarthmore Coll., Pa.; stage career, 30 yrs., 21 yrs. in stk., Phila., supporting Mrs. John Drew, Amelia Bingham, Edward Harrigan, Rose Stahl, etc.; screen career, entered motion pictures in 1906, returning to the legitimate each autumn until 1911, when he joined the Lubin forces, subsequently with Biograph, Gaumont, Frohman Amuse. Corp., and Cissie Fitzgerald Co., directing Thomas Jefferson, Lillian Russell, Lionel Barrymore and Jane Gray; member of Lambs', Players' Club and M. P. D. A. Ad., Cissie Fitzgerald Co., Horsley Studio, Los Angeles, Calif.

MILLARDE, Harry; b. Springfield, O.; stage career, with Walker Whiteside, Robt. Mantell, J. K. Hackett, stock in Cincinnati, O., Wilmington, Del.; screen career, Kalem, Universal, Fox, playing and directing ("Every Girl's Dream," "Miss U. S. A." "Sunshine Maid," "Blue Eyed Mary," "Bonnie Annie Laurie," "Caught in the Act," "Miss Innocence"), Fox ("Gambling in Souls," "Rose of the West," "Sacred Silence," "The White Moll"). Ad., care Fox Film Corp., N. Y., or Hotel Claridge.

MILLER, Ashley; b. Cincinnati, O.; educ. Detroit, Mich.; stage career, with Walker Whiteside, Otis Skinner, Ezra Kendall, Henrietta Crossman, Anna Held; screen career, Edison (7 yrs.), Famous Players, Community Prods.; author of 150 produced photoplays, of "The Seventh Chord," a three-act play with music, of several one-act sketches and one novel, "The Key"; Edison ("Alice's Adventures in Wonderland," "Out of the Ruins"), Pathe ("The King's Game"), Vitagraph ("Princess of Park Row," "The Marriage Speculation"), Ashley Miller Prod. ("Made in America"). Home ad., 4 West 92nd st., N. Y.

MILLS, Thomas R.; b. England; educ. Horsham Coll., Eng.; stage career, with Modjeska, Richard Mansfield, Chas. Frohman, Henry Miller, Louis Mann, covering 16 yrs.; screen career, Reliance 1 yr., Vitagraph 4 yrs. ("The Duplicity of Hargraves," "Cop and the Author," "The Guilty Party," O. Henry series, "A Night in New Arabia," "The Girl in His House"), Goldwyn ("Duds"). Hght., 5, 9½; wght., 175; dark hair, gray eyes. Home ad., 999 E. 5th st., Brooklyn, N. Y.; studio, Goldwyn, Culver City, Calif.

MITCHELL, Claude H.; b. Melbourne, Australia, 1891; educ. Paris, France, Los Angeles, Aberdeen Univ., Scotland; traveled throughout Europe, America, Mexico, etc., in 1914, designed and built the Lone Star Studio, Hollywood, for the Climax Co., including large laboratory, thereafter installing the entire studio equipment, joined the Famous Players-Lasky in 1915 as asst. dir., shortly becoming head of the Asst. Director's Dept., and being in that capacity for 3 yrs., in 1916 published "The Assistant Director's Compendium"; at present writing and directing for Brentwood featuring Zasu Pitts ("Seeing It Thru"). Home ad., 1556 No. Kenmore ave., Hollywood, Calif.; phone 59437; studio, Brentwood.

MITCHELL, Howard M.; b. Pittsburgh, Pa., 1883; educ. there; stage career, stock, rep. and heavies in A. H. Woods prods.; screen career, Lubin (8 yrs. acting and directing), Thanhouser (2 yrs. directing Gladys Hulette and Lottie Briscoe), Balboa (dir. "Petticoats and Pants"), Fox ("The Splendid Sin," "Snares of Paris," "A Girl in Bohemia"). Home ad., Woodward Hotel, 6th and Figueroa, Los Angeles, Calif.

MOODY, Harry G., also scenario writer; b. Sydney, Australia; educ. there; stage career, 16 yrs., stk., vaud., mus. com.; screen career, 1 yr. with Universal, 2 yrs. with Griffith, Doubleday Prod. (The Katterjohns in "Stranded," "Pa's Vacation," "False Faces," "Wild Women," "Pa Steps Out," "Buried Treasure," "Investigating the Count"). Ad., 1745 Allesandro st., Los Angeles, Calif.; Holly 2372; studio, Bronx Studio, Los Angeles; phone 54109.

MOORE, Eugene W.; b. Annapolis Valley, Nova Scotia; educ. Boston, Mass., and N. Y.; stage career, appeared with Edwin Booth, Frederick Warde and Stuart Robson in Shakespearean plays; starred 5 yrs. in "The Burglar," then "Diplomacy"; screen career, since 1912, Thanhouser ("The Candy Girl"), Pathe ("When Baby Forgot"), Universal ("Nancy's Baby," "O'Connor's Mag," "Gene of the Lazy A," "The Girl Who Won Out"), Lasalida-Pathe ("Captain Kiddo"), Eugene Moore Prod., Bluebird ("Sue of the South").

MORRIS, Reggie; b. N. Y., 1890; educ. Newark Acad.; stage career, from 1905, with Richard Carle, with "Johnnie Jones" co., mgmt. Cohan & Harris, also "45 Minutes From Broadway," "Three Twins," with Kitty Gordon in "The Enchantress"; screen career, Edison for 2 yrs., Biograph 3½ in juv. leads, 1914 joined eastern Universal, became member L-KO stock, Keystone ("False to the Finish"), Bluebird ("The Love Swindle"), Sennett ("Back to the Kitchen"). Home ad., 1742½ N. Western, Los Angeles, Calif.; phone 597717; studio, Christie.

MORTIMER, Edmund; b. N. Y. C.; educ. there; stage career, with Mary Mannering, "Thais," all-star, Wm. Faversham; screen career, C. K.

Young ("Savage Woman," "Road Thru the Dark"), Harry Garson ("Hushed Hour"), Tourneur ("County Fair"). Home ad., 1828 Highland ave., Hollywood, Calif.; Holly 2121; studio, Maurice Tourneur Prods., Inc.

MUELLER, Floyd, art director; b. Lafayette, Ind.; educ. Purdue Univ., Art Inst., Chicago; early career, practicing licensed architect, Chicago; screen career, Tourneur ("Victory," "Treasure Island," "Glory of Love"). Home ad., 1316 Fairfax ave., Los Angeles, Calif.; Holly 4495; studio, Maurice Tourneur.

MYLES, Norbert; b. Wheeling, W. Va.; educ. Mount St. Joseph Coll., Baltimore, Md.; stage career, 9 yrs. in stk., Shakespearean rep., vaud., and prod.; screen career, began in 1910 with Pathe as leading man, Kalem, Eclair, Universal, leading man for American, Vitagraph, now directing Helen Gibson in railroad specials. Home ad., 4618 Melbourne ave., Hollywood, Calif.; Holly 4424; studio, Capital Film Company's studio.

— N —

NEILL, R. William; b. Dublin, Ireland; educ. private tutor; stage career, in "Wildfire" with Lillian Russell, starred in "Baby Mine," in London and on American circuits in "O'Reggie"; author of "Prince o' My Dreams," "Heart's Desire," and other plays; screen career, 1½ yrs. with Ince, associated with R. B. West in making of "Civilization"), Paramount ("The Price Mark," "Flare-Up Sal," "Love Me," "Tyrant Fear," "Green Eyes," "Mating of Marcella," "Puppy Love"), Famous Players ("Career of Katherine Bush"), Hodkinson ("The Bandbox"). Member M. P. D. A.

NELSON, J. Arthur, also prod. mgr., author, actor; b. Scranton, Pa., 1877; educ. Princeton Univ.; stage career, director, author and star Stair & Havlin Attr., stk. star and dir. in N. Y., Phila., Boston, etc.; author several plays and books, including "The Photoplay"; screen career, author, star, dir. Universal series of "Slim" comedies; author, dir. "Under Fire in Mexico," "Day of Reckoning," "Lure of the Rose"; member Associated and United Motion Picture Producers; past 3 yrs. dir. gen. Dominion Film Corp., also Federation Film Corp. ("The Boomerang"). Ad., studio, Federation Film Corp., Seattle, Wash.

NIBLO, Fred; b. York, Neb.; educ. there; stage career, 25 yrs., starred and produced own plays in every English speaking country in world; screen career, feature director for Thos. H. Ince, 2 yrs. all Enid Bennett releases, Thos. H. Ince super-special "Dangerous Hours" with all-star cast, J. Parker Read special, "Sex" with Louise Glaum. Ad., Ince Studio, Culver City, Calif.

NIGH, William; b. Berlin, Wis.; educ. Univ. of California, Berkeley, Cal., while in college wrote first play, "Off the Road," afterwards converted into a musical com.; stage career, comedy leads in many mus. prods.; screen career, Reliance (wrote, acted and dir. comedies), California M. P. Corp. ("Salomy Jane"), Metro (dir. "A Yellow Streak"), Fox ("The Slave," dir. "Life's Shadows," "My Four Years in Germany," "The Blue Streak," "Notorious Gallagher"), First National ("The Fighting Roosevelts"), Johnny Dooley comedies.

NOBLE, John W.; b. Albemarle Co., Va., 1880; educ. West Point; early career, Lieut. in U. S. Army for 7½ yrs., in Philippines and China, engineer in Mexico; stage career, 5 yrs. in stk., vaud, and Broadway prods.; screen career, Thanhouser, Biograph, Universal, Mutual, Metro, Goldwyn, Frohman, Selznick. Writer of plays and short stories. Ad., Great Neck Station, L. I., N. Y.

NORTH, Wilfrid; b. London, Eng.; early career, with Mercantile Marine, cattle puncher in Texas, practising lawyer, soldier in N. G. State of Texas; stage career, stage mgr. for Mrs. Fiske 5 yrs., assoc. with Winthrop Ames at the Little Theatre and the New Theatre, also first dir. Harvard Dram. Club and dir. Amateur Comedy Club, N. Y.; screen career, Vitagraph, director late John Bunny, 3 yrs. directed for Vitagraph ("Salvation Joan," "The Ordeal of Elizabeth," "The Kid," "Kitty Mackay," "Mind the Paint Girl"), Select ("The Undercurrent," "Oil"). Home ad., 1270 Allan ave., N. Y. C.; ad., care Guy Empey Prods., 220 W 42nd st., N. Y.

— O —

O'BRIEN, John B.; b. Richmond, Va.; educ. St. John's Coll., Brooklyn, N. Y.; stage career, juv. leads with Augustus Thomas Co.; screen career, Essanay (juv. leads, touring Mexico and Hawaii, also wrote a number of scenarios), Powers, Universal (director), Majestic, Famous Players ("The Foundling," "Hulda From Holland"), Metro ("Vanity"), World ("Maternity"), Triangle ("Souls Triumphant"), Empire All Star ("Queen X," "A Daughter of Maryland," "The Girl and the Judge," "The Richest Girl"), Pathe ("The Bishop's Emeralds," "Impossible Catherine"). Member M. P. D. A.

O'BRIEN, Thomas E., assistant director; b. Grand Rapids, Mich., 1889; educ. Leland Stanford; early career, with Barnum and Bailey's Circus in 1898; stage career, in vaud. and road cos.; screen career, Essanay, Biograph, with D. W. Griffith 2 yrs. as asst. in production of "The Birth of a Nation"; also with Fox and Peerless, played in "The Sage Brusher," Hampton-Hodkinson. Is rough rider and cowboy, 18 mos. with Royal Northwest Mounted Police.

OLCOTT, Sidney; b. Toronto, Can.; educ. Toronto; stage career, for 5 yrs.; screen career, Kalem (first salaried director), Sid Olcott International Prods. (producing abroad). Important productions, "From the Manger to the Cross," "Colleen Bawn," "Mother of Men," "Madame Butterfly," "Seven Sisters," "Poor Little Peppina," "All for Ireland," "The Belgian"), Famous Players ("The Daughter of MacGregor"), Keeney-Sherry ("A Marriage for Convenience"). Hght., 5, 9; wght., 165; iron gray hair, gray eyes. Ad., 315 W. 51st., N. Y., or 229 W. 42nd st., N. Y.

OLIVER, Harold G., art and technical director; b. Hastings, Minn.; stage career, 3 yrs. master of properties, 2 yrs. prop, maker, 2½ yrs. technical director; screen career, Lasky ("Grim Game" with Houdini), Ince ("Behind the Door," "Below the Surface" with Hobart Bosworth"). Home ad., Culver City Hotel, Culver City, Calif.; phone 70386; studio, Ince, Culver City.

O'NEILL, Jack, also scenario writer; b. Philadelphia, Pa.; educ. there; stage career, 3 yrs. vaud.; screen career, Lubin, Pennsylvania, Scarlett, Unicorn, etc., Billy West Comedies, D. L. D. Comedies, Walleene Films, Phila., Pa. Home ad., 3702 Brandywine st., Phila., Pa.

ORMSTON, Frank D., art director; educ. Columbia Univ.; early career, 3 yrs. designer of scenery; screen career, American, Adoliscope, Powers, Universal (prepared sets for "Dumb Girl of Portici," "Hypocrites"), art director for Lois Weber ("For Husbands Only"), Lew Cody ("Beloved Cheater"). Ad., Astra Film Corp., Glendale, Calif.

ORTH, George; b. N. Y. C., March 24, 1894; educ. N. Y. C.; screen career, for 11 yrs., Yankee, Republic, Eclair, Biograph, Gaumont, Atlas, dir. "The Wrong House," "A Reel Romance," "A Wakeful Night," "A Mixed-up Affair," etc., "Millions for a Day," "In Again, Out Again" cameraman in U. S. Signal Corps. Ad., Hotel Monterey, N. Y.

OTTO, Henry; b. St. Louis, Mo.; stage career, 1903-1910; screen career, Metro ("Undine," "Mr. Forty-Four," "River of Romance," "Some Bride," "Fair and Warmer," "The Willow Tree"). Member M. P. D. A. Studio ad., Metro, Hollywood, Calif.; Holly 4485.

— P —

PARKE, William; b. Bethlehem, Pa.; stage director with E. H. Sothern, Richard Mansfield, Arnold Daly, Castle Sq. Theatre, Boston; screen career, Thanhouser, Astra, Educational Films, Goldwyn ("The Shine Gorl," "The Yellow Ticket," "The Key to Power," "Convict 993," "The Paliser Case," "Tower of Ivory"). Ad., 1815 La Brea ave., Hollywood, Calif.

PARKER, Albert; screen career, dir. Douglas Fairbanks in "Arizona," "Knickerbocker Burkaroo," dir. Clara Kimball Young in "The Eyes of Youth." Permanent ad., Lambs' Club, N. Y. C.

PARKER, Max, art director; b. Prescott, Ariz.; educ. there and Los Angeles; early career, 1 yrs. in architecture; screen career, Lasky ("Call of the East," "City of Dim Faces," "Victoria Cross," etc), Mary Pickford ("The Hoodlum," "Heart of the Hills," "Pollyanna"), Douglas Fairbanks ("His Majesty, the America"). Home ad., 919 W. 35th place, Los Angeles, Calif.; West 1279; studio, Mary Pickford Co., Brunton Studio.

DIRECTORS

PARROTT, Charles; b. Balto., 1893; stage career, vaud. 2 yrs., Irish monologue, burlesque; screen career, discovered by Al. Christie at Universal, in Keystone first as actor, then as asst. dir., Fox, 1916 (first release, burlesque on "A Fool There Was," etc.), all Bull's Eye Comedies; now directing the De Havens in "Teasing the Soil." Home ad., 5714 Santa Monica blvd., Los Angeles, Calif.; studio, Sunset.

PATON, Stuart; b. Glasgow, Scotland, 1885; early career, chemist and painter stage career, 6 yrs. in London at Kings Way Theatre, performed before King Edward, King George; screen career, Universal, scenario editor, asst. to Frank Crane, "Twenty Thousand Leagues Under the Sea" ("Peace at Any Price," "Like Wildfire," "The Green Seal," "Beloved Jim"), Universal ("The Gray Ghost"), World ("The Devil's Trail"); also directed Christy Mathewson and Jess Willard in special releases. Member M. P. D. A. Home ad., 1814 Hillcrest rd., Hollywood, Cal.

PECK, Raymond S.; b. Ridgetown, Ont., Can., 1886; educ. Collegiate Inst., Chatham, Ont.; early career, connected with various Canadian and American newspapers in reportorial and editorial capacities; screen career, 1917, joined Universal in Canada as director of publicity for the Dominion and editor of Motion Picture Bulletin, later amalgamated the Bulletin with Canadian Moving Picture Digest, thus launching Canada's first film trade paper, left the Digest to become Montreal branch mgr. of Mutual, in June, 1919, became director of motion pictures for Dept. of Trade and Commerce, Federal Govt. of Canada, Ottawa.

PETERS, Thomas Kimmwood, director, technical engineer, studio manager new Hallmark studios Hunts Point; b. Norfolk, Va.; educ. Los Angeles, Coll. City Mexico; screen career, since 1898; built and managed Co-operative M. P. C. studio, now Griffith Fine Arts; produced and directed for himself in Frisco; directed "Trapped by Wireless," "Saving Mark," "A California Romance," etc.; developed aeroplane camera and manufactured altimeters for Government during war; inventor of cameras, printers and other machinery used in industry; author of "Technique of Cinematography." Ad., 1128 Randall Court, Los Angeles, Cal.

PHILLIPS, R. G., also studio manager; b. South Bend, Ind., 1890; educ. Columbia Univ.; stage career, 1908, business mgr. and press agent, Aitken Shows, Great American Shows, Dan Robinson Co.; screen career, 1911, numerous road attractions, Gaumont Co., Jacksonville studio; asst. dir. "Dead Alive," "Feather-Top," etc.; Serial Film Co., "The Bishop's Secret," 5 reels; 1916, director Superior Film Co.; 1917, director and studio mgr. Ebony Film Corp., Chicago, dir. 18 Ebony comedies, dir. and studio mgr. Castle Studios, 2332 N. California ave., Chicago, Ill.

PHYSIOC, Wray; b. Columbia, S. C., Nov. 22, 1890; educ. Virginia; early career, scenic artist with Walter Burridge and Physioc Studios; screen career, 2 yrs. with Pathe Freres, Eclair, World; organized Hamo Films in 1912; producer of "Hearts of Oak," "Born Again," "Shadows of Doubt"; director American Biograph dramas 3 yrs.; producer of 8-reel feature in natural colors for Technicolor ("The Gulf Between"); now producing a series, "Facts and Follies" in Jacksonville, Fla. Ad., Physioc Studios, 449 First ave., N. Y. C.

POLLARD, Harry A.; b. Republic City, Kan., 1883; stage career, 10 yrs., stock, vaud. and prods.; screen career, director with Universal, American, Goldwyn, National, World-Equitable, Frohman Amuse. Co.; "The Quest," "Miracle of Life," "Girl from His Home Town," "The Devil's Assistant," "The Dragon," "The Danger Game?," "Girl Who Wouldn't Grow Up." Hght., 5, 10; wght., 170; black hair, blue eyes. Ad., Frohman Amuse. Co., Times Square Bldg., or Hotel Claridge, N. Y. C.

POLLOCK, Gabriel L., art and technical director; b. Southern Russia; educ. Russia and Chicago Art Inst.; with Selig Polyscope Co. since 1905. Home ad., 3005 So. Kenwood ave., Los Angeles, Cal.; West 4279; studio, 3800 Mission Road, Los Angeles; East 33.

POWELL, Frank; b. Hamilton, Ont.; educ. Cleveland, O.; stage exper. 12 yrs., stk., actor and stage director with Belasco, Fanny Ward, 2 yrs.; with Ellen Terry in England; screen career, Biograph, Pathe, Fox, Mutual, "A Fool There Was," "Officer 666"; Powell Prods., "The Forfeit," "Heart of the Sunset"; Triangle, "The Unbroken Promise"; World, "You Never Know Your Luck." Ad., Lambs Club, N. Y.

POWELL, Paul; b. Illinois; early career, newspaper man with Chicago "Tribune," Los Angeles "Express"; screen career, from 1912, Lubin, Reliance-Majestic, Fine Arts ("The Marriage of Molly-O," "Hell-to-Pay Austin," "Girl of the Timberlands"), Triangle ("Betsy's Burglar"), Universal ("A Society Sensation," "Who Will Marry Me?" "The Weaker Vessel," "Common Property"), Mary Pickford ("Pollyanna"). Ad., 1957 Lemon st., So. Pasadena, Cal.

PRATT, Gilbert Walker; b. Providence, R. I., 1891; educ. prep. schls. at Tarrytown, N. Y.; screen career, Kalem, NYMP, Rolin (playing heavies and co-directing); Vitagraph ("Boarders and Bums," "Farms and Fumbles"). Home ad., 934 Westmoreland Ave., Hollywood; studio, Vitagraph.

—Q—

QUIRK, William A. ("Billy"), also comedian; b. Jersey City, N. J.; educ. Jersey City High; stage career, stock and vaud., James J. Corbett's Co., Belasco's "The Rose of the Rancho;" screen career, Biograph, Vitagraph, Universal (dir. "Billy Joins the Band"), Metro (dir. Figman Comedies, "Winning an Heiress"), World (played in "The Devil's Trail," "The Arizona Cat Claw"), Pathe ("The Old Maid's Baby," played in "The Sawdust Doll"). Hght., 5, 6½; dark blond hair, dark blue eyes.

—R—

RAYMAKER, Herman C.; b. Fruitvale, Calif.; educ. Petaluma, Calif.; screen career, 3 yrs. with Keystone Comedies, Hank Mann ("Broken Bubbles), Gale Henry "Gas," "Kids," "Chicken a la King"), Mack Sennett ("Soul Mates"), Poppy Comedies ("Diplomatic Ambrose"). Home ad., San Gabriel, Calif.

REED, THEODORE, Technical director; also scenario writer; b. Cincinnati, Ohio; educ. Univ. of Mich., A. B. 1908, M. S. 1909; early career, V. P., Detroit Steering Gear Co.; screen career, Douglas Fairbanks, titles for "Say, Young Fellow," "His Majesty, the American," tech. dir. for "When the Clouds Roll By." Home ad., 7240 Hillside Ave., Hollywood, Calif., phone 57643; studio, Douglas Fairbanks Pictures Corp.

REGAN, THOMAS C.; b. Lowell, Mass.; educ. there; stage career, 5 yrs.; screen career, Pathe, Mittenthal, Univ., World, Jester Comedy Co. as assistant director.

REICHER, Frank; b. Munich, Germany, Dec. 2, 1875; stage career, after 7 yrs. acting in Germany, came to U. S., debut in "Ghosts" in N. Y., has appeared with Julia Marlowe, Mrs. Fiske, Lulu Glaser, Annie Russell, Grace George, etc.; stage director for Henry B. Harris; screen career, Lasky ("Pudd'n-head Wilson," "The Inner Shrine"), Metro, Hayakawa ("Alien Souls"), Fannie Ward ("For the Defense"), Metro ("The Only Road"), Screencraft ("Suspense," "The Prodigal Wife"), World ("The American Way"), Universal ("The Trap"), Photoplay Libraries ("Empty Arms").

REVIER, Harry; b. Phila., 1883; educ. Scranton; stage career, operated chain of theatres in Salt Lake City, Ogden, Vancouver, Los Angeles; screen career, with Gaumont, Universal, Lasky, World, Metro ("The Evil Men Do"), Ogden Pictures ("The Lust of the Ages," "Grain of Dust," "Romance of the Air," "Unconditional Surrender"), Ind. Sales ("The Challenge of Chance"). Ad., Somerset Hotel, N. Y.

REYNOLDS, Lynn Fairfield, also scen. writer; b. Harlem, Iowa, 1889; educ. Denver, Colo.; early career, reporter in Denver; stage career, with Elitch-Long Stock Co., Denver, etc.; screen career, since 1913, Selig, Universal (co-dir. with Gene Gauntier, later dir.), Bluebird ("God's Crucible"), Triangle ("Broadway Arizona"), Fox ("Mr. Logan, U. S. A.," "Western Blood," "Treat 'Em Rough," "Miss Adventure"), Universal special ("Little Brother of the Rich," "The Brute Breaker," "The Overland Red"). Member M. P. D. A. Home ad., 1939 Morgan place, Los Angeles, Calif., studio Universal.

RICKETTS, Thomas; b. London, Eng.; stage career, in Eng. with Sir Henry Irving, wrote and produced "Duvar," 1881, produced and played lead in "Honeymooners," producer for Frohman, K. and E., H. E. Dixey; screen career, from 1907, Essanay, American, Horsley,

Nestor, Universal, American ("The Great Question," "Buzzard's Shadow," "Other Side of the Door"), Centaur-Mutual ("The Single Code," "A Daughter of the Well-dressed Poor," "Forbidden," "The Counterfeit Soul"), United Film Corp. ("The Crime of the Hour"), for State Rights ("Sins of the World"). Member M. P. D. A. Home ad., 1280 Sweetzer ave., Hollywood Blvd., R. F. D. No. 10, Cal.; Holly, 2115.

ROBBINS, Jesse J.; b. Dayton, Ohio; screen career, 7 yrs. with Essanay, as director and general mgr., creator and director "Snakeville" and "Alkali Ike" comedies and many of Broncho Billy Western films, 1915 organized Robbins Photoplays, director and mgr. Chaplin comedies, making Rainbow Comedies past 6 mos. ("Oriental Romeo," "Barnyard Romance," "In Society," "Shimmie Shakers," "On the High Seas"). Ad., Los Angeles Athletic Club, Los Angeles, Calif.

ROBERTSON, John Stuart; b. London, Ont., Canada, June 14, 1878; educ. St. Thomas, Ont., Canada; stage career, stk. co., 2 yrs. with Rose Stahl, with Chas. Frohman, Maude Adams, Henry B. Harris, Rice and Harris, etc.; screen career, Famous Players ("Test of Honor," "Come Out of the Kitchen," "Misleading Widow," "Let's Elope," "Jekyl and Hyde"), Realart ("Erstwhile Susan"). Ad., Famous Players-Lasky Corp., N. Y.

ROSEN, Philip E.; also cameraman; b. Machias, Me.; screen career, Edison, Universal, Fox (photographed "Romeo and Juliet," "The Darling of Paris," "The Greatest Love"), Goldwyn ("Spreading Dawn"), "The Miracle Man," "The Beach Comber," "Little Brother of the Rich," "The Brute Breaker," Universal (dir. "The Double Hold Up," "The Sheriff's Oath"). Home ad., 1010 E. Oxford ave., Hollywood, Cal. Phone 599947. Studio Universal.

ROSSON, Arthur H.; b. Eng.; screen career, Triangle ("Cassidy"), Artcraft ("Headin' South"), Vita., Univ., Norma Talmadge, Liberty Loan picture "100% American" (Mary Pickford), and one for Canadian Victory Loan; J. P. Reed Prod. ("Sahara"), directing Tom Mix for Fox, Mayer-Chaplin ("Polly of the Storm Country," "Social Mockery"). Ad., Los Angeles Athletic Club, and 6091 Salem place, Hollywood, Cal. Studio, Mayer-Chaplin Co., Los Angeles, Cal.

ROSSON, Dick; assistant director; b. New York City, 1894; educ. Newport, R. I.; screen career, Vitagraph, Universal, Famous Players, American, Triangle ("The Haunted House"), Selznick ("Panthea," "The Shoes That Danced," "The Secret Garden." Assisted Arthur Rosson at the Mayer-Chaplin Co., Los Angeles.

RUGGLES, Wesley H.; b. Los Angeles, 1889; stage career, mus. com., stk., rep.; screen career, Keystone (Syd. Chaplin comedies, "Her Painted Hero," Chaplin burlesque of "Carmen"), Vitagraph ("For France," "The Agony Column," "The Winchester Women," O. Henry's Specials, Bobby Connelly Specials), Selznick ("Piccadilly Jim," "Plans of Men"). In U. S. Service 18 mos., mustered out May 15, 1919. Ad., 117 W. 81st St., N. Y.

— S —

SANTELL, Al., also studio executive; b. San Francisco, Cal.; educ. there; early career, architect, short story author; screen career, director of American, Mutual, Master Pictures, Kalem Comedies, World Comedy Features, Smiling Bill Parsons Comedies, Goldwyn Comedies, dir. Kolb & Dill, Fay Tincher, Kathleen O'Connor, Neal Burns, Joan Hill. Now supervising manager comedy prod. at Universal City, personally dir. feature comedies with Joe Martin, the Human Orang-Outang and animals. Home ad., Cordova Hotel, Los Angeles, Cal. Bdwy. 506; studio, Universal.

SARGENT, George L.; b. Phila.; educ. Princeton; stage career, stage director for Dillingham and Cohan & Harris prods.; screen career, Eclair, "Dollars and a Heart"; World, "The Gentleman from Mississippi"; Dra-Ko comedies, Kalem, "The Masked Dancer," American, "The Secret of the Submarine," "The Gilded Youth," "His Brother's Keeper," Univ. "High Speed." Member M. P. D. A. Ad. Green Room Club, N. Y.

SAUM, Clifford P.; b. Columbus, O.; stage career, Wilbur Opera Co., Anna Held, in Ziegfeld's Follies; screen career, Reliance, Biograph, Progress, Thanhouser, Fox, Warner Features ("The Kaiser's Finish"), asst. in "Lest We Forget," now assisting Edgar Lewis, 1919-20. Ad., 606 Candler Bldg., N. Y. C.

SCARDON, Paul; b. Melbourne, Australia, 1878; educ. there; stage career, 12 yrs. in Australia, with Nance O'Neil, Kyrle Bellew, E. H. Sothern and Mrs. Fiske; screen career, Reliance-Majestic, Vitagraph ("Arsene Lupin," "The Game with Fate," "The Golden Goal," "Tangled Lives," "The Green God," "King of Diamonds," "Silent Strength," "Man Who Won," "Fighting Destiny," "The Gamblers," "Beating the Odds," "In Honor's Web"). Ad., Green Room Club, N. Y.

SCHERTZINGER, Victor L.; educ. Univ. Penn.; screen career, N. Y. M. P. Co., Triangle-Ince, Thos. H. Ince, "Ezry," "The Hired Man," "The Family Skeleton," "His Own Home Town," "Nine O'clock Town," "The Sheriff's Son," "Playing the Game," "Coals of Fire," "Claws of the Hun," "String Beans," "Quick Sands"; composed 31 scores for Ince prod., including first original for any picture ("Peggy"). Goldwyn ("Jinx," "Pinto," "The Blooming Angel"). Member M. P. D. A. Home ad., 4891 Hollywood blvd., Hollywood, Cal.; phone 59463; studio, Goldwyn, Culver City, Cal.

SCHULTZ, Carl H.; technical director; 15 yrs. exper. staging prods. and 4 yrs. at Fox Studio, Fort Lee, N. J.; associated with R. A. Walsh, Gordon Edwards, Charles Brabin, Kenean Buel, Wm. Nigh, Dallas Fitzgerald; at present with Hallmark Pictures Corp. Ad., West Norwood, N. J.; phone Closter 143-W.

SCHULZE, Jack; technical director; screen career, Selznick, Pathe, Warner Bros. Ad., 268 W. 84th st., N. Y. C.

SCULLY, Wm. Jos.; assistant director; b. Green Island, N. Y.; screen career, Biograph, prods. in which the following stars appeared: Mary Pickford, John Barrymore, Marguerite, Pauline Frederick, C. K. Young, Enrico Caruso, Elsie Ferguson, Elaine Hammerstein; Famous Players ("The Avalanche," "A Society Exile," "Witness for the Defence"), Selznick ("The Country Cousin," "Greater Than Fame"). Ad., Selznick Pictures, West Fort Lee, N. J.

SEAY, Charles Morgan; b. Atlanta, Ga.; educ. Univ. of the South, Sewanee, Tenn.; stage career, 4 yrs. with road prods., 5 yrs. in vaud. feature act, 6 yrs. in stk. in N. Y. C. and other cities; screen career, directed for Edison, Equitable, Moss, Vitagraph, Local Life, Gray Seal, Div. of Films, C. P. I., U. S. Gov't; at present Community Prods. Ad., Community Prods., Inc., 46 W. 24th st., N. Y. C.

SEITER, William A.; b. N. Y.; educ. Hudson River Mil. Acad.; early career, artist and writer; screen career, Reliance, Universal, Majestic, Crown City, National Film ("Morning After," "Tangled Threads"), 13 comedies for Mr. and Mrs. Carter Dehaven for Goldwyn, National ("Hearts and Masks," "The Kentucky Colonel"). Home ad., St. Francis Court, Hollywood, Cal.; studio, National.

SEITZ, George Brackett, also actor and scenario writer; b. 1883, Mass.; educ. Friends' Schl., Phila.; early career, short story writer and playwright; screen career, joined Pathe in 1912; author of "The Shielding Shadow," "Pearl of the Army," "The Fatal Ring," adapted "The Beloved Vagabond," "Nedra"; Astra ("Fatal Ring," "House of Hate," "Lightning Raider" serials), G. B. Seitz, Inc. ("Black Secret," "Bound and Gagged," "Pirate Gold," "Velvet Hawk" serials). Home ad., 2 West 67th st., N. Y.; studio ad., G. B. Seitz, Inc., 1990 Park ave., N. Y.

SEMON, Lawrence; also comedian; b. West Point, Miss., 1889; educ. Savannah, Ga.; early career, played child parts on stage with Zera Semon, his father; pro. magician, cartoon artist and tumbler in vaud.; screen career, Universal, Palace Players (dir. Frank Daniels Comedies); Vitagraph ("Players and Puppy Love," "Rooftops and Ruffians," "Huns and Hyphens," "Pluck and Plotters," "Traps and Tangles," "Scamps and Scandals," "The Head Waiter"); writes all his own comedies; cartoonist N. Y. Evening Sun, N. Y. Herald and Evening Telegram. Ad., Vitagraph, Hollywood, Cal.

SHAW, William Ray, Technical director; b. Savannah, Ohio; educ. Mansfield, O., Pasadena, Cal., and private sch. in engineering; early career, civil engineering, municipal engineering, designer. Chief Engineer for Art Unit Studios, Glendale, Cal.

DIRECTORS

SHELDON, Roy, also actor; b. Jacksonville, 1885; educ. there; stage career, 8 yrs., stk., vaud., drama; screen career, Sid Olcott, Reliance, Gauntier, Sterling, Champlain, Kalem ("When Man Could Kill," "Mother of Men," "The Taint," "Land of the Lost"), E. I. S. ("Trooper 44"), 2 yrs. with Fox and Creation Films. Hght., 5, 9½; wght., 150; dark complexion, brown hair, dark eyes. Ad., 124 W. 64th st., N. Y.; Col, 9076.

SIDNEY, Scott; stage career, 20 yrs.; screen career, NYMP (produced 80 one- and two-reel subjects), Triangle (dir. "Bullets and Brown Eyes," "The Deserter"), Pallas-Morosco ("The Road to Love," "Her Own People"), National Film Corp. ("Tarzan of the Apes"), Christie special ("Go West, Young Woman," and 26 Christie comedies). Member M. F. D. A. Ad., Christie Studio, Hollywood, Cal.

SIEBEL, Bert E., assistant director; screen career, Universal, National, Pathe, Goldwyn, Thos. Ince. Ad., Thos. Ince Studio, Culver City, Cal

SILSBY, Wilson, art director; b. Chicago, 1883; educ. Chicago, N. Y. and abroad; early career, 17 yrs. designing and building scenery; scenic artist Metropolitan Op.; had own scenic studio, 1912; produced "The Rosary," "The Silver Box," "Justice," "The Pigeon" first time in America; painted mural decorations for Chicago Fed. Bldg.; wrote novel, "Woman with Red Hair"; composed dances for "The Silver Slipper"; screen career, Universal, Pathe, Max Figman, Harry Carey ("Outcasts of Poker Flat"), Rupert Julian ("Millionaire Pirate"), Bradbury Features ("Into the Light"). Ad., Mitchell Lewis Prods., Inc., Bradbury Features, 412 Mason Bldg., Los Angeles, Cal.

SIMONE, Charles, also scenario writer, studio manager, manufacturer and distributor; b. Castellana, Italy, 1874; educ. Europe, America; stage career, stk., rep., playing juvenile and light comedy roles, dramatic coach; screen career, Nestor, Universal, Centaur, Venus, General Film Co., New Haven, Conn., Hallmark Pictures Corp. Albany, N. Y. Ad., 82 Third ave., Albany, N. Y.

SLOMAN, Edward; b. London, 1885; stage career, stock, "Parsifal," "Mummy and Humming Bird," vaud.; screen career, Universal, Lubin, American ("Shackles of Truth," "The Frame Up," "Periwinkle," "The Masked Heart," "The Pagan," "Sands of Sacrifice," "The Sea Master," "A Night in New York," "Snap Judgment," "Aladdin's Night"), Mutual ("The Ghost of Rosey Taylor"), Federal ("The Westerners," "The Sage Brusher"), B. B. Features ("Luck of Geraldine Laire"), Selznick ("Blind Youth"). Member M. P. D. A. Ad., home, 1720 Chapala st., Santa Barbara, Cal.; 608 S. Serrano, Los Angeles, Cal.; phone 560616.

SLOSSER, Ralph J., assistant director; b. N. Y. C.; educ. Los Angeles and U. S. C. College; early career, student; screen career, 2 yrs. property man with Famous Players, 6 mos. asst. tech. dir. with Clara Kimball Young Co., 1 yr. asst. prod. and business mgr. with Goldwyn, at present asst. director at Brentwood Film Co. Home ad., Ellison Apts., Venice, Cal.; phone 5179.

SMALLEY, Phillips; b. Brooklyn, 1870; educ. Balliol College, Oxford, and Harvard Univ.; early career, law, member of N. Y. Bar for 7 yrs.; stage career, Mrs. Fiske, Raymond Hitchcock; screen career, Gaumont, Kalem, NYMP, Rex, Bosworth ("Hypocrites"), Universal ("The Dumb Girl of Portici," "Where Are My Children?" "Shoes," "Saving the Family Name," "Idle Wives," "The Hand That Rocks the Cradle," "The Double Standard," "The Doctor and the Woman"). Member M. P. D. A. Studio, Lois Weber Prod., Hollywood.

SMALLWOOD, Ray C.; b. N. Y., 1888; screen career, Imp, Ince, Universal, dir. "The Best of Luck" for Screen Classics at Metro Studio, Mme. Nazimova in "The Heart of a Child." Ad., Metro Studios.

SMITH, David; b. England; educ. there; early career, business, mechanical draughtsman; stage career, bus. mgr. stock co.; screen career, scenario writer, dir. for Vitagraph, O. Henry-General ("The Enchanted Barn," "Sue," "By the World Forgot," "Baree, Son of Kazan," "A Gentleman's Agreement," "The Wishing Ring Man," "Cupid Forecloses," "A Yankee Princess," "Over the Garden Wall," "A Fighting Colleen"). Ad., home, 4609 Prospect ave., Hollywood, Cal.; studio, Vitagraph.

SMITH, Noel Mason; b. Rockland, Me.; educ. Cal.; screen career, from 1912, L-Ko, Henry Lehrman Sunshine Comedies, Vitagraph ("Tootsies and Tamales," "Healthy and Happy," "Flips and Flops," "Yaps and Yokels," "Mates and Models," "Squabs and Squabbles," "Bungs and Bunglers"), Fox Sunshine ("The Diver's Last Kiss"). Ad., 1355 N. Alvarado st., Los Angeles, Cal.

SNYDER, Jack, assistant director and actor; b. Brooklyn, 1891; educ. Columbia Coll., N. Y.; stage career, vaud.; screen career, Kay Bee-Triangle ("The Food Gamblers," "Cassidy"), Fox ("Les Miserables"), played western roles with Thanhouser and underworld with Metro, Fox and Pathe; in service for 1 yr.; assist. dir. on "Regular Fellers" series; now asst. dir. on making of educationals and short subjects. Home ad., 149 S. 4th st., Brooklyn, N. Y.

SOTHERN, Harry, assistant director; b. London; educ. Rugby; stage career, 7 yrs. in company of E. H. Sothern, his uncle, with Otis Skinner; screen career, Metro ("Romeo and Juliet," and other Bushman and Bayne prods.), Select ("The New Moon").

SPINAK, Leon, Art and technical director and studio executive; b. Paris, France; educ. Ecole des Beaux Arts, Paris; decorated for Czar of Russia, King Emmanuel and Duke of Norfolk, also Franco-British Exposition, London; 5 yrs. with Thos. H. Ince and Robt. Brunton as art director. Home ad., 1432 So. Union ave., Los Angeles, Cal.; West 1377; studio, Art Unit Studios.

STAHL, John; screen career, directed Mildred Harris, Florence Reed in "Wives of Men," "Her Code of Honor," "A Woman Under Oath," Molly King in "Greater Than Love," "Women Men Forget." Ad., Mayer-Chaplin Studio, 3800 Mission Road, Los Angeles, Cal.

STANTON, Richard; b. Phila., educ. there; stage career, stock with Kolb and Dill; screen career, Melies, Ince (produced "Aloha," also played leads), Universal ("Graft" series), Fox (dir. "The Love Thief," "The Scarlet Pimpernel," "The Spy," "The Yankee Way," "Durand of the Bad Lands," "Responsibility," "Rough and Ready," "Why America Will Win," "Eyes of the Soul," "Why I Would Not Marry," "The Jungle Trail," "Checkers"). Member M. P. D. A. Ad., Fox, N. Y.

STARK, Lowell Randall, assistant director; educ. Univ. of Michigan; screen career, 1 yr. writer and asst. dir. Kalem ("Call of the Dance," etc.), 1 yr. comedy scenario editor Metro ("His Wedding," etc.), 2 yrs free lance writer, 6 mos. scen. writer and asst. dir. Johnny Dooley Comedy Co. ("Artificial Art," etc.), asst. dir. Films, Inc. ("That Woman"). Ad., White Plains, N. Y.; White Plains 2531.

STAULCUP, M. P., Art director; b. Amenia, N. Y.; interior decorator and designer, Metro Pictures Corp., Hollywood, Cal.

STEGER, Julius, also playwright; b. Vienna, Austria; educ. there and America; stage career, actor, singer and producer, starring in own prods. and in vaud.; screen career, Rolfe-Metro ("The Stolen Triumph"), for Jos. Schenck ("Redemption," "Just a Woman"), International ("Hidden Truth"), Metro ("Blindness of Love"), State Rights ("The Libertine," "Prima Donna's Husband"), author, singer and musician; associated with Messrs. Shubert in prod. of plays; Select ("Cecilia of the Pink Roses," "Belle of New York"). Ad., Players Club, N. Y.

STEWART, K. C., assistant director; b. Chittenango, N. Y.; educ. Yates High Schl., Williams Coll., Mass.; early career, business and salesman; screen career, 1918, Astra ("The Cry of the Weak," "Our Better Selves"), Universal ("Exquisite Thief," "The Unpainted Woman," "Blind Husbands," 5 comedies with Florence Turner). Home ad., 1835 Argyle st., Hollywood, Cal.; phone 579,957; studio, Universal.

ST. GERMAINE, A., technical director; b. Sherbrooke, Canada; educ. Acad. Sacred Heart, Manchester, N. H.; stage career, since 7 yrs. of age; screen career, Pathe, 6 yrs., Norma Talmadge Co., asst. to Ed. Jose. Home ad., 150 Broadway, Brooklyn, N. Y.; studio ad., Selznick Studios, Fort Lee, N. J.

STORM, Jerome; b. Denver, Colo.; educ. there; stage career, with James O'Neil, Robert Edeson, Olga Nethersole, New York prods., stk.; screen career, Ince-Paramount, directed Charles Ray in "The Girl Dodger," "Greased Lightning," "The Busher," "Bill Henry," "Egg-Crate Wallop," "Paris Green," "Alarm-Clock Andy." Home ad., 1321 Edgecliff Drive, Los Angeles, Cal.; Wilshire 1175; studio, Ince.

STRONG, Jay, assistant director; b. Cleveland, Ohio, 1897; educ. Western Reserve Univ., Cleveland, Ohio; screen career, asst. dir., continuity man for Church Film Corp.; at present asst. dir. for Transatlantic Film Co. of America, Inc., Comedies.

STURGEON, Rollin S.; screen career, free lance scenario writer, member Vitagraph scenario dept., head of producing co.; founded original Western Vitagraph Co. at Santa Monica; new plant constructed under his supervision (dir. "The Chalice of Courage," "God's Country and the Woman," "Through the Wall"), Lasky ("Petticoat Pilot"), Universal ("Destiny," "Pretty Smooth," "Sundown Trail," "Breath of the Gods"). Ad., 723 N. Mariposa, Los Angeles, Cal.

SUTCH, Herbert, assistant director; b. London, Eng., 1882; Technical Coll., South Kensington, London, Wurzburg, Germany, and Vermont Coll.; stage career, Jessie Shirley Stock Co., Spokane; Central Stock Co., San Francisco; Baker Stock Co., Portland; screen career, Fine Arts, both as character actor and as asst. dir.; Arizona Film Corp., Kalem, Mena, Griffith (played in "Scarlet Days"). Ad., home, 4400 Sunset Drive, Hollywood, Cal.

SYMONDS, Henry Roberts; b. Chicago; educ. Univ. of Notre Dame, So. Bend, Ind.; early career, automobile business, Los Angeles and Chicago; 18 mos. in U. S. Army Air Service; screen career, "Milk Fed Vamp," "Twilight Baby," etc., with L-Ko, Sunshine and Henry Lehrman Prod. Ad., Henry Lehrman Prods., Inc., Hollywood, Cal. Home ad., Hotel Glidden, Los Angeles, Cal.; Hollywood, 3910.

—T—

TATE, Cullen, assistant director; b. Paducah, Ky., 1893; educ. Castle Hghts. Sch., Lebanon, Tenn.; screen career, Famous Players ("Joan the Woman," "The Romance of the Redwoods," "The Little American," "The Woman God Forgot," "The Devil Stone," "The Love Burglar," "The Lottery Man," "Hawthorne, U. S. A." Home ad., 1722 Wilcox st., Hollywood, Cal.; phone 577797; studio, Lasky.

TAUSZKY, David Anthony, Art director; b. Cincinnati, Ohio; educ. N. Y. Univ. and Paris, France; early career, portrait painter; screen career, "Eye for Eye," "Please Get Married," all Metro pictures since Feb., 1919. Ad., Salmagundi Club, 47 Fifth ave., N. Y.; studio, Metro, Hollywood, Cal.

TAYLOR, William Desmond; b. Ireland, 1877; educ. Clifton Coll., England; screen career, Ince, Vitagraph, Favorite Players, Morosco, Pallas (dir. "The Parson of Panamint," "Redeeming Love," "The Happiness of Three Women," "The Varmint"), Fox (dir. "North of 53," "The Tale of Two Cities"), Artcraft ("How Could You, Jean," "Johanna Enlists," "Capt. Kidd, Jr."), Paramount ("Mile-a-Minute Kendall"), Artcraft ("Huckleberry Finn"), Realart ("Anne of Green Gables"). Member Los Angeles Athletic, and Town and Country Clubs, M. P. D. A. Studio, Morosco, Los Angeles, Cal.

TERRIS, Tom; b. London, 1877; educ. Christ Coll., Eng.; stage career, actor and actor mgr. in Eng.; screen career, World ("Pursuing Shadow"), Terris ("Woman of the World," "My Country First"), Vitagraph ("Between Friends," "The Business of Life," "Lion and the Mouse," "The Third Degree," "The Climbers," "The Vengeance of Durand," "The Fortune Hunter"). Ad., 676 Riverside Drive, N. Y.; studio, Vitagraph, Brooklyn, N. Y.

TERWILLIGER, George, also author; b. N. Y., 1882; early career, newspaper man on "Dramatic Mirror" and "Telegraph"; screen career, scenario ed. Reliance, then free lance writer, Biograph (wrote "The Battle," "The Mothering Heart"), Lubin (dir. "The Cry of the Blood," "The Nation's Peril"), dir. Star Series for Stage Women's War Relief, "The Sporting Duchess" for Vitagraph. Ad., 875 W. 180th st., N. Y.

THAYER, Otis B.; b. Richland Center, Wis.; educ. Freeport, Ill.; stage career, 15 yrs.; screen career, Selig, Colorado, Pike's Peak, Art-o-Graf Film Co., Independent Prod. ("Awakening of Bess Morton," over 200 shorter releases, "Wolves in Wall Street"). Office, 305 Guardian Trust Bldg., Denver, Colo.; studio, Englewood, Colo.

THOMSON, Frederick A.; b. Montreal, Can.; stage career, 20 yrs.; screen career, Famous ("Sign of the Cross"), Vitagraph ("The Christian," "Wild Beasts at Large," "An Enemy to the King," "Nymph of the Foothills"), Lasky ("The Goose Girl"), Fox ("The Wonderful Adventure"), Pathe ("How Could You, Caroline"), Buffalo ("The Sport of Kings"). Now with Prizma. Ad., Players Club, N. Y.

THORNBY, Robert; b. N. Y. C.; educ. there and Syracuse; stage career, road shows 3 seasons, Keith and Proctor stock 2 seasons; screen career, 10 yrs., started with Vitagraph as actor, then dir. 4 yrs.; Sennett-Keystone 6 mos.; Sterling Kid Comedies 1 yr.; World 1 yr.; Lasky 1 yr.; Pathe 6 mos.; produced for himself; has directed Ethel Clayton, Kitty Gordon, Gail Kane, Sessue Hayakawa, Blanch Sweet, Wm. Desmond; World ("Broken Chains," "Code of the Mountains"), Famous Players ("The Barbarian," "The Hostage"), J. D. Hampton ("The Prince and Betty," "Cressy," "The Deadlier Sex"). Home ad. 2464 Beachwood Drive, Los Angeles, Cal.; Holly, 2019.

TRACY, Bert; b. England; educ. St. Bede's Coll., Eng.; stage career, mus. com.; screen career, Kalem ("The Tiger's Claws"), Vim ("Thirty Days"), Vitagraph ("His Own People"), Sunbeam Comedies ("Hot Sands and Cold Feet," "His Conscience His Guide," "Trial by Jury"); comedian and writer; directing Sunbeam Comedies. Home ad. 587 Riverside Drive, N. Y. C.; studio, Klutho Studio, Jacksonville, Fla.

TRIMBLE, Laurence; b. Robbinston, Me., Feb. 15, 1885; educ. dist. schl., and by private tutor; early career, forming lumbering business, short story writing; screen career, Goldwyn ("The Auction Block," "The Spreading Dawn"), Turner Films, gen. mgr. (dir. "My Old Dutch," "Door Steps," "East Is East," "The Fight Within" (Petrova), "Fools' Gold" (Mitchell Lewis), "The Saintly Show Girl" (Mae Marsh).

TURNER, D. H., also actor; b. N. Y. C., Jan. 12, 1883; educ. Hudson Mil. Acad. and Univ. of Penn.; stage career, 10 yrs. in various prods.; screen career, Edison, Pathe, Henry W. Savage ("Her American Prince," "Revelation," "The Eagle's Eye"), Metro ("Man That Stayed at Home"), San Antonio Pict. ("Mr. Potter of Texas," "Mr. Bingle," "Squire Phin"). Hght., 5, 10½; wght., 175; brown hair, steel-gray eyes. Ad., P. O. Box 872, San Antonio, Texas.

TYROL, Jacques; educ. Austria; stage career, 18 yrs. European stages and U. S., Vienna, Berlin, Petrograd, Moscow; played "Professor Bhaer" in Brady's revival of "Little Women"; screen career, 8 yrs., "The Hand," "Out of the Darkness," "The Face in the Crowd," ("Truth"), Tyrad ("And the Children Pay," "The Red Viper"), decorated by former Emperors of Austria and Germany, Czar of Russia, and reigning heads of German municipalities; with Associated Press, special correspondent Spanish-American War, '98; Boxer uprising, Pekin, China, 1901; massacre Kishineff, 1903; Russian-Japanese War; studied languages and psychology under Ivan Bloch, Metshnikoff and August Forrell. Ad., Green Room Club, Elks or 729 Seventh ave.; Bryant 5426, N. Y.

—V—

VALE, Travers; b. Liverpool, Eng., 1865; educ. Australia, India and U. S.; stage career, produced and plays leads in "Madame X," "Lion and the Mouse"; screen career, Rex, Reliance, Biograph, Universal, World ("A Self-Made Widow," "Betsy Ross," "The Woman Beneath," "The Dormant Power"), Brady-World ("The Dancer's Peril," "Darkest Russia," "Soul Without Windows," "The Witch Woman," "Vengeance," "The Journey's End"). Ad., Pelham, N. Y., or Friars Club, N. Y.

VAN, Wally; supervising director; educ. Cooper Inst.; stage career, director of College Plays; several Thespian stocks and society entertainer; screen career, Vitagraph ("Man Behind the Door," "Love, Luck and Gasoline," and many others; Rothapfel ("False Gods"), "Trail of the Octopus" serial. Ad., 312 Westminster Road, Brooklyn, N. Y.; Flatbush 5983.

VAN DEUSEN, Cortlandt J.; b. Brooklyn, 1890; educ. Polytechnic Coll.; stage career, Shubert and Crescent Stk.; screen career, Kalem, Vitagraph ("Man Behind the Curtain," "In Arcadia," "Mystery of Empty Room"), Jester ("His Golden Romance"), Apex ("Couple Wanted," "Furnished Complete," "All Improvements," "In Bad"); now supervising director Apex. Ad., Apex Pictures Corp., Indianapolis, Ind.

DIRECTORS

VEKROFF, Perry N.; b. Alexandria, Egypt; educ. Robert Coll., Constantinople; early career, studied law and dramatic art at Univ. of Sofia, Bulgaria; stage career, drama, opera, vaud., under Augustin Daly, K. & E., H. W. Savage Thos. Riley; screen career, director, American Kinemacolor, 3½ yrs., Metro, Vitagraph, Bacon-Backer ("Man," "A Woman's Experience"), World ("What Love Forgives," "Dust of Desire"), Arthur Beck serial ("Isle of Jewels"), in preparation "Cynthia of the Minute," with Leah Baird. Ad., Exclusive mgnt, Edward Small, 1493 Broadway, N. Y.

VIGNOLA, Robert G.; b. Italy; educ. Albany; stage career, 7 yrs. Shakespearian rep., melodrama; screen career, Kalem ("The Vampire"), Famous ("The Reward of Patience," "Great Expectations," "The Fortunes of Fifi," "Her Better Self," "The Love That Lives"), Select ("The Claw"), Paramount ("The Girl Who Came Back"), Select ("Experimental Marriage"), Paramount ("Louisiana," "Heart of Youth," "The Third Kiss," "His Official Fiancee," "More Deadly Than the Male"). Ad., International Films, 729 7th ave., N. Y.

VINCENT, James; educ. Springfield, Curry Sch. of Oratory and Dramatic Art; stage career, 15 yrs.; screen career, 12 yrs.; director for Kalem, Pathe, Sterling, Cort, Fox, Pilgrim, Serico, James Vincent Film Corp.; ("The Penalty," "The Atheist," "Land of the Lost," "The Wolf," "The Melting Pot," "Gold and the Woman," "Sins of Men," "Ambition," "The Battle of Life," "Lady from the Sea," "A Royal Romance," "The Hidden Hand," "The Spirit of Lafayette," "The Woman in Gray." Home ad., 215 W. 51st st., N. Y.; office ad., 1465 Broadway, N. Y.; Bryant 7028.

VON STROHEIM, Erich O. H.; b. Austria; educ. Milit. Acad., Austria; early career, army officer, newspaper man and magazine writer in U. S.; stage career, over Orpheum circuit in dramatization of novel by himself, co-author of "The Mask," a stage play; author of "Blind Husbands"; Fine Arts, Selznick ("Panthea"), Mary Pickford ("Less Than the Dust"), Douglas Fairbanks ("In Again, Out Again"), Vitagraph ("For France"), Edison ("The Unbeliever"), Griffith ("Hearts of the World"), Holubar ("Heart of Humanity"), Universal (dir. "Blind Husbands," and "The Devil's Pass Key"). Ad., Universal City, Los Angeles.

VOSHELL, John M., art director; b. Smyrna, Delaware; educ. Phila., Drexel Inst., Sch. of Industrial Art; stage career, 1 yr. stock, Chestnut St. theatre, Phila.; screen career, now with Garson Studios, Los Angeles, Cal. Ad., 2033 Vista Del Mar ave., Los Angeles; phone 7126.

— W —

WALES, R. Ellis, art director; b. Des Moines; screen career, technologist and designer Griffith's Fine Arts Studio 1914-15; personally handled and designed costuming for Babylonian period "Intolerance" and responsible for historical presentation; other personal service, Sir Herbert Beerbohm Tree, John Emerson, Douglas Fairbanks, Norma and Constance Talmadge, Mae Marsh, Elsie Ferguson, Dorothy and Lillian Gish, John Robertson, "Test of Honor" with Barrymore; supervisor technical production and personnel, Famous Players-Lasky Studios, N. Y., 1918-19; at present director production service, W. W. Hodkinson Corp., 527 Fifth ave., N. Y. C.

WARDE, Ernest C.; b. Liverpool, Eng., 1874; son of Frederick Warde, the tragedian; educ. Brooklyn, N. Y.; stage career, 23 yrs., 9 yrs. stage dir. for Richard Mansfield; screen career, Thanhouser ("A Man Without a Country"), Pathe, Paralta ("One Dollar Bid," "A Burglar for a Night," "Three X Gordon"), Farnum-United ("A Man in the Open"), Frank Keenan ("The World Aflame"), J. Warren Kerrigan ("A White Man's Chance," "The Lord Loves the Irish," "Live Sparks," "Thirty Thousand Dollars"). Home ad., Alvarado Hotel, Los Angeles, Cal.; studio, Brunton.

WARREN, Edward; educ. N. Y. C.; stage career, many years' exper. as actor with Charles and Daniel Frohman, Klaw & Erlanger, also stage director; screen career, 8 yrs. director, "Beasts of the Jungle," "Adventure of a Boy Scout," "Divorced," "Warfare of the Flesh," with Walter Hampden, "Thunderbolts of Fate" with House Peters and Anna Lehr, "Weavers of Life," "Beggar Prince of India," etc. Ad., 1482 Broadway, N. Y. C.; Bryant 8757.

WATSON, William H.; b. Montreal, Can.; educ. Los Angeles; early career, printer and developer; 5 yrs. film editor for Keystone; asst. dir. at Sennett Studios; Fox Sunshine Comedies, Century Comedies ("Romeos and Juliets"), Sennett ("Rip and Stitch, Tailors"), at present making super 5-reel comedy "Dad's Forget-Me-Not" for Great Western Prod. Co.

WEBB, Kenneth; b. N. Y. C.; A. B., Columbia Univ.; author of following mus. com. and comic operas: "The Dream Girl," "The Forbidden City," "The Mountaineers," "The Best Sellers,' "The Rainbow Cocktail"; screen career, Select ("Marie, Ltd", "His Bridal Night"), Realart ("Sinners," "The Fear Market"), Vitagraph ("One Thousand Dollars," O. Henry, "Transients in Arcadia," "Springtime a la Carte"). Ad., Lambs Club, N. Y., or care of Famous Players-Lasky, N. Y.

WEBB, Roy, assistant director; educ. Columbia Univ., Art Students League, N. Y. C.; stage career, musical director, musician, composer of operettas and vaud. sketches, "When Dreams Come True," "The Rainbow Cocktail," "The Best Sellers," "Leap Year Land," etc.; now asst. to Kenneth Webb, Famous Players-Lasky Corp. N. Y. ad., Lambs Club, N. Y.

WELLS, Raymond; b. Dodge City, Kan.; stage career, from 1895, rep. melodrama, stk. in Chicago, Portland Ore., Kansas City; screen career Reliance-Majestic, Fine Arts, Universal, Triangle ("The Strange Weakling," "Fanatics," "Fighting Back," "The Man Above the Law," "The Hand at the Window," "Law of the Great Northwest"), 1918-19 producing mgr. stock co. at Camp Kearney; organized Historical Film Corp. of America, producing series pictures depicting stories of the Bible. Ad., Stough Ranch, Burbank, Cal.

WHITE, Gilbert, art director; b. Grand Rapids, Mich.; educ. Columbia Univ., Art Students' League, Julian Acad., Beaux Arts, Paris; early career, mural painter lecturer and decorator. Ad., the Players Club, N. Y.; studio, Goldwyn, Culver City, Cal.

WHITE, Jack; b. N. Y. C. 1897; educ. N. Y., Chicago, Vienna; screen career, N. Y. Motion Picture Co., Keystone ("Damaged No Goods," "Roaring Lions and Wedding Bells"), Sunshine ("A Tight Squeeze," "Mongrels," "A Waiter's Wasted Life"), Lehrman ("A Twilight Baby"). Home ad., 2233 Ewing st., Los Angeles, Cal.

WILLIAMS, Charles J. (C. Jay); b. N. Y. C.; educ. N. Y. C.; stage career, covers 25 yrs., last appearance on stage with Blanche Walsh in "The Test," earlier with Bertha Kalich, Florence Roberts, Digby Bell, "Mr. Pipp" and many other first-class attractions; screen career, 4 yrs. with Edison (dir. "Why Girls Leave Home," "Caste," "The Gilded Kid" and "Wood B. Wed" series), 5 mos. with Universal (with Jeff. De Angelis in "The Funny Side of Life"), 2 yrs. with Vitagraph (dir. Frank Daniels in "Crooky" and "What Happened to Father"). Ad., 102 Riverside Dr., N. Y. C.; Schuyler 9487. Member M. P. D. A.

WINDOM, Lawrence C.; b. N. Y., 1876; educ. there; stage career, with Klaw and Erlanger, Charles Frohman, Henry B. Harris, Richard Mansfield, Joseph Jefferson, Robert Edeson, William Faversham, Elsie Ferguson, road and stk. cos.; screen career, Pathe, Essanay ("Blind Justice," "The Chimney Sweep," "The Way of Patience," "Efficiency Edgar's Courtship," "Fools for Luck"), Triangle ("Taxi," "Upside Down," "It's a Bear"), Para.-Artcraft ("Wanted a Husband").

WITHEY, Chester (Chet); stage career, extensive stock experience; screen career, American, Keystone, Reliance-Majestic, Fine Arts ("The Old Folks at Home," "The Wharf Rat," "Mr. Goode—the Samaritan," "The Village Prodigal," "Madame Bo-Peep"), Vitagraph ("An Alabaster Box"), Artcraft ("The Hun Within"), Para. ("Maggie Pepper," "Little Comrade," "The Teeth of the Tiger"), Norma Talmadge ("The New Moon"). Member M. P. D. A. Author of large number of photoplays. Ad., 750 W. 4th st., Los Angeles, Cal.

WORSLEY, Wallace; b. 1880, Wappingers Falls, N. Y.; educ. Brown Univ. Providence, R. I.; stage career 15 yrs., first N. Y. engagement at Empire theatre under Chas. Frohman, "Notre Dame" with Bertha Galland, juvenile lead William Collier 3 seasons, produced "Checkers"

and was with it 4 seasons, stock several seasons; screen career, Ince ("The Paws of the Bear"), with Paralta since opening ("Wedlock," "A Law Unto Herself," "Shackled," "Intelligence"), Kitty Gordon Co. ("Adele"), Goldwyn ("Street Called Straight," "Little Shepherd of Kingdom Come"). Ad., Lambs Club, N. Y. C., or Los Angeles Athletic Club, L. A., Cal.; studio, Goldwyn, Culver City, Cal.

WORTHINGTON William; b. and educ. Troy, N. Y.; studied grand opera in France and Germany; stage career, grand opera, drama, stock, vaud., "Everywoman," which he directed; screen career, Universal ("Devil's Pay Day"), Pathe ("The Ghost of the Rancho"), Haworth ("His Birthright," "Temple of Dusk," "Bonds of Honor," "Courageous Coward," "Heart in Pawn," "The Debt," "The Grey Horizon"), "The Dragon Painter," "The Illustrious Prince"; prod. for Gibraltar Pict. starring Leah Baird. Member M. P. D. A.

WRIGHT, Fred E.; b. Catskill Mts., N. Y.; educ. Union Coll. and Albany Law Schl.; stage career, Frank Mayo, dir. 15 yrs.; screen career, Columbia, National, Pathe, Essanay (dir. "The Breaker," "The Trufflers," "The Man Who Was Afraid"). Member M. P. D. A.

—Y—

YOUNG, James, also scenario writer; b. Baltimore, 1878; educ. Johns Hopkins Univ.; stage career, Shakespearian rep. with own co., with Sir Henry Irving, Augustin Daly, Viola Allen, Annie Russell, starred in "Brown of Harvard"; screen career, Vitagraph, World, Morosco, Lasky, Haworth, Paralta, Selznick ("A Regular Girl," "Daughter of Two Worlds," "Hearts in Exile," "Goodness Gracious"), directed Norma Talmadge, Mae Murray, Blanch Sweet, C. K. Young, Elsie Janis, Earle Williams, Sessue Hayakawa. Member M. P. D. A. Ad. Lambs Club, N. Y., and L. A. Athletic Club, Los Angeles, Cal.

The all-year-round forum for players, directors, and scenario writers is—

Motion Picture News' "In the Studios" department.

Newspapers use it for their photoplay departments; advertisers use it for results.

SCENARIO WRITERS AND EDITORS

— A —

ACKER, Edward; b. New York City; educ. N. Y. C.; stage career, appeared in "Robespierre" with Sir Henry Irving; early career, wrote special articles and stories for Brooklyn Times, Black Cat, Theatre Magazine, Pearson's, etc.; screen career, as free lance writer for Biograph, Pathe, Kalem, Universal, Essanay, etc.; sold 43 to Biograph, then on their staff for 3 yrs.; author of "A Cry for Help," "What Drink Did," adapted "Lorna Doone," "The Cricket on the Hearth," etc.; contributor of poems and verses to "Judge" and New York Globe. Home ad., 906 East 176th st., New York City.

ADDISON, Smythe, also director; b. Covington, Ky.; scenario dept. Universal Film Co., Keystone; director, David Horsley, Armstrong Comedy series, Alhambra, Criterion, Sydney Grey Comedies, "Heart of California," Independent Features; past year in U. S. Service. Ad., 68 West 68th st., N. Y. C.

ALEXANDER, J. Grubb; b. Scranton, Pa.; educ. Lafayette Coll., Easton, Pa.; early career, civil engineer, author of treatises on bridge construction and bacteriology; screen career, 1913, Universal, Paralta, 1917, to write original photoplays and continuity for Bessie Barriscale and others; First National ("The Thunderbolt," "The Beauty Market" with Katherine Macdonald"), Haworth ("The Under Tow," "The Bleeder" with Sessue Hayakawa), titles and editing of Maurice Tourneur Prod. ("The County Fair," "The Life Line," "The Broken Butterfly"), author of "The Trail of the Octopus," Hallmark Serial. Home ad., 1443 Iowa st., Hollywood, Cal. Holly. 3445.

ANDREWS, Gertrude; b. Toledo, Ohio; educ. Toledo and N. Y., high schl. and Columbia University; stage career, actress, 8 seasons, then dramatist and writer, five plays produced; screen career, Frank Keenan ("Brothers Divided"), Fox ("True Blue"), Universal ("Wheels of Power"). Home ad., 1600 Sierra Bonita ave., Hollywood, Cal.; phone 577721; studio, Brunton Studios, Hollywood, Cal.

ASHTON, Rosalie; b. New Orleans, La.; early career, 2 yrs. reporter for N. Y. Times, magazine writer; screen career, American, Lasky, Goldwyn, World ("Humility," "Rounding Off Corners," "The Brigadier General," "The Chastening"), Vitagraph ("The Wager"), vaudeville sketch and picture, "Proved," now with Who's Who in America, Inc., 35 West 39th st., N. Y.

— B —

BAER, Dr. Berthold A.; educ. Europe; screen career, Lubin, also has written and produced scripts for Selig ("A Modern Cinderella"), Edison, Vitagraph ("Fires of Fate"), Universal Industrial scenarios. Author of plays and short stories. Ad., home, 25 Claremont ave.; bus., 1970 Broadway, N. Y.

BAKER, Charles Graham; early career, newspaper and cartoon work; now picturizing all Vitagraph serials; late releases, "Smashing Barriers," "The Invisible Hand," other adaptations, "The Mightier Strength," "Daring Hearts," "The Fortune Hunter," etc.; director and author of many comedies produced at Vitagraph. Studio ad., Vitagraph, Brooklyn, N. Y.

BAKER, Hettie Grey, production editor; b. Hartford, Conn.; educ. Simmons College; early career, librarian six years, free lance in 1913, screen, Bosworth (scenario editor), Fine Arts (writer), Fox, author of many short stories. Studio ad., care of Fox, N. Y.

BALDWIN, Ruth Ann; b. West Suffield, Conn.; educ. San Diego, Cal.; early career, newspaper and publicity work, commercial art, concert work; screen career, joined Universal in 1913, wrote for Henry McRae, Otis Turner and Frank Lloyd; six mos. as film editor; wrote for William Fox Pictures, Gladys Brockwell and Peggy Hyland; director for 8 mos., making pictures with Cleo Madison, Jack Mulhall, Irene Hunt, Mignon Anderson, Leo Pierson and Donna Drew. Home ad., 3048 W. 12th st., Los Angeles, Cal.; phone 75623.

BALL, Eustace Hale; b. Gallipolis, O., 1881; educ. Univ. of Cincinnati, Art. Acad., Harvard Univ., N. E. Conserv. Music; early career, painter, novelist, Newspaper man, author of novels, "Traffic in Souls," "The Voice on the Wire," also "Love Affairs of a Lonely Woman," "The Art of Photoplay," the Jack Race novels; screen career, scenario ed. and ad. mgr., Eclair, dir. Solax, staff writer All Star, dir. and writer Reliance-Majestic, president Historical Film Co., at present free lance writer and feature editor of the N. Y. Evening Sun. Ad., home, 200 West 95th st., New York.

BARRY, Richard; b. Cal., 1883; early exper., newspaper and magazine writer, novelist and playwright; represented Collier's Weekly, Century Magazine, N. Y. Times; wrote plays ("Brenda of the Woods," "The Love Bird," "Petroleum Prince"); screen career, D. W. Griffith, Equitable, Rolfe-Metro, Universal ("Horns of the Devil"), American ("The Secret of the Submarine"). Ad., care of N. Y. Times Sunday Magazine, N. Y.

BERANGER, Clara; b. Baltimore, Md.; educ. Goucher College; early career, magazine and newspaper work; screen career, began writing as a free lance for Edison, Vitagraph, Kalem, both originals and continuities; staff writer for Fox ("Fedora," "Tale of Two Cities"), Pathe, wrote exclusively for Baby Marie Osborne ("Dolly Does Her Bit," "Winning Grandma," etc.); staff writer for Famous Players ("Come Out of the Kitchen," "Firing Line," "Dr. Jekyll and Mr. Hyde," "Sadie Love," "Girls," "The Cost," "The Fear Market"). Studio ad., Famous Players, 130 W. 56th st., N. Y.; home ad., 267 W. 79th st., N. Y.

BERESFORD, Frank S.; b. 1876, Steubenville, O.; educ. as mining engineer, Cleveland, O.; stage career, with Henry Irving, Maude Adams, stage director Fritzi Scheff for Chas. Dillingham 4 yrs.; screen career, general technical director Universal's eastern studios, tech. mgr. Empire All-Star Corp., script editor Triangle K-Bee studios, special writer and mgr. prod. Pathe-Diando, making Baby Marie Osborne features, scenario editor Virginia Pearson Photoplays, Inc., Paramount ("Paid in Full"), Pathe ("Impossible Catherine"). Ad., home, 1844 N. Winona Blvd., Hollywood, Cal.

BERGMAN, Helmer Walton; b. Sundsvall, Sweden; educ. Univ. of Michigan; stage career, 3 yrs. circus, 1 yr. vaud., 2 yrs. stk. and rep.; screen career, Vitagraph ("Womanhood," "Aladdin from Broadway"), E. H. Sothern ("Enemies of the King"), number of O. Henry stories; entered A. E. F. at outbreak of war, attaining rank of Flight-Commander, discharged June, 1919. Studio ad., Capital Film Co.; home ad., 1914 West 41 Drive, Los Angeles, Cal.; phone 79517.

BINGHAM, Edfrid A.; b. Oak Hill, Ohio; educ. Ohio Univ.; early career, newspaper man in Cincinnati, Denver, Chicago and N. Y.; 7 yrs. on Paris edition of N. Y. Herald, author of 2 novels, "Art Thou the Man?" and "The Heart of Thunder Mountain"; screen career, Rolfe-Metro, Arrow ("Who's Guilty?" series, "The Deemster"), with Goldwyn since May, 1917 ("Lord and Lady Algy," "Gay Lord Quex"). Ad., Young Apts., 1621 Grand ave., Los Angeles; studio, Goldwyn, Culver City, Cal.

BRADLEY, Willard King; educ. N. Y. C.; early career, newspaper and magazine writing; screen career, "Main 4400," "The Little Nomad," "The Burning Rivet," "Empty Arms," "The Street," etc. Ad., 1552 Broadway, N. Y.

BRADY, Jasper Ewing, reader; b. Pittsburgh, Pa.; early career, 14 yrs. commissioned officer in U. S. Army, later Lieut. Col. 32d Regt., N. G. of N. Y.; screen career, Vitagraph ("The Island of Regeneration," "The Island of Surprise," "Surprises of an Empty Hotel," "Little Angel of Canon Creek," "Hero of Submarine D-2"), and many others. Ad., Metro, N. Y. C.

BRET, Tom; b. Bolivar, N. Y.; fought way through parochial school and college; stage career, Snow Stk. Co., Scranton, and road shows; traveled 18,000 miles as lecturer and worked on 18 newspapers in 11 cities; wrote titles for "Wives of Men" (Florence Reed), "Lest We Forget" (Rita Jolivet), "The Master Mystery" (Houdini serial), "Italy on the Firing Line,"

317

"Birth of a Race" (Metropolitan version), rewrote Ibsen's "A Man There Was," "Girl from the Marshcroft," "The Sacred Flame," Paramount Truex Comedies, Cissy Fitzgerald Comedies, "Upstairs and Down," "O, Boy!" titles for "The Trap," Paramount-Drew Comedies. Ad., 220 West 42nd st., N. Y.

BRONSTON, Douglas; b. Richmond, Ky., 1887; educ. Cincinnati, O.; early career, newspaper and magazine writer, press agent, general mgr. for Thomas Dixon's theatrical enterprises, with Liebler, Chas. Dillingham; screen career, Pathe ("Neal of the Navy," "The Grip of Evil," "Ashton Kirke" detective series, "Hazel Kirke," "The Galloper"), Fox ("Thieves"). Member Friars Club, N. Y.

BROWNE, Lewis Allen; educ. pub. schls. N. Hamp., priv. schls. Virginia; early career, city edit. Boston Journal for 10 yrs., asso. ed. N. Y. Sunday American, ed. Wildman Magazine and News Service, asso. ed. Forum Magazine, co-author Morosco farce, "Please Get Married," author several books, magazine writer; screen career, Famous Players ("Miss George Washington" with Marguerite Clark), Vitagraph ("The Soap Girl"), Metro ("Please Get Married"), co-author with Viola Dana, Independent ("Good Dodd"), Goldwyn ("Spotlight Sadie" with Mae Marsh), Selznick ("The Woman Hater" with Owen Moore), comedies produced by Lubin, Christie, etc. Member American Press Humorists' Asso. Home ad., 11 N. Harrison st., East Orange, N. J.

BUCHANAN, Thompson; b. N. Y. C.; educ. Louisville, Ky., Univ. of the South; early career, newspaper man, author, playwright; wrote "Woman's Way," "The Cub," "Life," "Lulu's Husband," "Civilian Clothes"; screen career, author of "Woman's Way," "The Cub" and "The Rack" for World; "World and Its Woman," Goldwyn; author of novels, "The Castle Comedy," "Judith Triumphant"; was private 1st Kentucky Inf. Span.-Amer. War and 1st Lieut. 138 F. A. World War. Ad., 418 So. Kingsley, Hollywood, Calif.; phone 56171.

BUCKLEY, Frederic Robert; b. Ireland; educ. King's Schl. and B'ham Univ. England; early career newspaper work, continuity writer on 5-reel specials, at Vitagraph; pictured Chambers' "Cambric Mask," "By the World Forgot," "The Other Man," etc.; in past year sold play to David Belasco, and twenty-five short stories; in addition, acted principal parts in Vitagraph's "Unknown Quantity," and the Guy Empey superfeature, "The Undercurrent"; n editor "Uncle Sam Magazine" and special publicity man, Empey Pictures Corp. Home ad., 630 W. 135th st., N. Y. C.; studio ad., 220 West 42nd st., N. Y.

BUFFINGTON, Adele; b. St. Louis, Mo., 1900; educ. St. Louis and Univ. of Calif.; stenographer at age of 13 for 2 yrs., treas. of several St. Louis picture houses, came to Calif. 1916 and remained with Miller Amuse. Co., lastly California Theatre until "discovered" by Mr. Ince, began as reader, now doing originals and continuity, Ince ("L'Apache" with Dorothy Dalton, "Meet My Sister," by Lois Zellner, picturized by Adele Buffington). Home ad., Cypress Apts., 2204 Hoover st., Los Angeles, Cal.; West 950; studio ad., Thomas H. Ince Studios, Culver City.

BURNHAM, Julia; b. Trenton, N. J.; author of "The Little Duchess," "The Adventures Carol," "The Volunteer," "The Fires of Youth," "The Glory of Renunciation," "A Soul Without Windows," "The Call of the Soul," "Love, Honor and ?," "The Lure of Ambition." Home ad., 35 W. 75th st.; permanent, Authors' League of America, Inc.

BURTON, G. Marion; b. Stillwater, Minn.; educ. Emerson Coll., Boston, Mass.; early career, dramatic editor of Parisienne and Saucy Stories, short story, publicity and feature writer; screen career, 2yrs. head reader and scenario writer for Vitagraph; later free lance writer for Famous-Lasky, Selznick, Screencraft; now managing editor of scenario dept. of Arthur H. Jacobs, Inc.; late pictures, "The Unknown Quantity," "Thin Ice," "Wishing Ring Man," "Miss Dulcie from Dixie," of Vitagraph; coming releases, Realart, "A Juliet of the Hills," Selznick, "The Woman Game," and "Straight Down the Crooked Lane." Ad., care Arthur H. Jacobs, Inc., 145 W. 45th st., N. Y.

BUSQUET, Leo A.; b. Ogdensburg, N. Y.; educ. Utica Free Academy and Hamilton Coll.; stage career, mus. com., with Shuberts, Klaw & Erlanger, "Oh, Delphine," also newspaper writer; screen career, Universal, Blache ("Prisoner of the Harem"), Balboa ("Nerve," "Jerry in the Park"), "In Haste," "The Edge of the Desert," now scen. ed. Cinema Film Co., "Carry On." Hght., 6; wght., 163. Home ad., 1100 Linwood place, Utica, N. Y.; studio ad., Cinema Film Co., 12 Lafayette st., Utica, N. Y.

—C—

CARLTON, Walter A.; educ. State Univ. Florida; early career, wrote poems and newspaper articles, for 2 yrs. star reporter on "Bradentown Herald"; stage career, 1½ yrs. vaud.; screen career, American ("Out of the Jaws of Death"), Balboa ("Margaret, the Innocent"), Triangle ("Dust of Desire"), "Voice of the Siren," Kay Bee ('Desperate Ambrose'). Hght., 5, 8; wght., 143; auburn hair, gray eyes. Ad., Box 1193, Tampa, Fla.

CARR, Catherine; b. Austin, Tex.; educ. Wash., D. C.; early career, short story writer; screen career, scenarios for Vitagraph, scen. ed. North American Film, Cort, wrote "The Whirl of Life" for Vernon Castle, "The Melting Pot"; Lasky, Triangle ("Blue Blood," "Tar Heel Warrior," "Real Folks"), United ("The Corsican Brothers"). Home ad., 17 Westminster ave., Venice, Cal.

CARSON, Ella Stuart; b. 1880, Hebron, Ind.; educ. Univ. of Chicago, Indiana State Normal; early career, newspaper woman Chicago Tribune and Chronicle, Albuquerque Journal; screen career, scenario writer, "Love Letters," "Mother's Boy," Paramount, Ince-Para., "The Wedding Ring," "The Yellow Back," J. O. Curwood, "His World of Honor," "Keep Him Guessing," Selznick. Studio ad., Selznick Pictures Corp., Fort Lee, N. J.

CHAPIN, Frederic; b. Cleveland, 1875; educ. Chicago; early career, wrote "The Storks," "The Forbidden Hand," "The Woggle Bug," 'Rock and Fulton" sketches; screen career, wrote scenario, "The Argyle Case," "Today," "Heart of the Sunset," "The Venus Model"; author of "Auction of Souls," Selig animal serial, "The Lost City," production mgr. of Pathe. Ad., care Pathe, 25 W. 45th st., N. Y.

CLARK, Violet; b. Omaha, Neb., 1886; educ. Mills Coll., Calif.; 2 yrs. at Univ. of Chicago; screen career, Universal ("Loot," "Bonnie Bonnie Laurie," with Mary MacLaren, "No Experience Required"). Home ad., Hollywood Studio Club, Hollywood, Calif.; Holly 2716; studio, Universal Film Corp.; Holly 2500.

CLAWSON, Elliott J.; b. Salt Lake City; early career, newspaper writer, San Francisco and elsewhere; toured the world; screen career, Universal publicity writer, produced "Hoosier School Master," etc., Morosco, wrote "Mme. La Presidente," "Gentleman from Indiana," etc., Universal ("The Kaiser, the Beast of Berlin," "Fires of Youth," "A Kentucky Cinderella"), Goldwyn ("Little Shepherd of Kingdom Come"). Home ad., 2615 Scott ave., Los Angeles; studio, Goldwyn Studios, Culver City, Calif.

CLIFT, Denison; b. San Francisco, 1885; educ. Stanford Univ.; short story writer, novelist and playwright; author of "Wolves of the Rail" for William S. Hart, "The Midnight Patrol," Ince-Select special; "Wedlock" for Louise Glaum; "And a Still Small Voice" for Henry B. Walthall; "His Birthright" for Sessue Hayakawa; the following original stories and continuities for Madlaine Traverse, "Rose of the West," "The Snares of Paris," "Lost Money," "The Hell Ship," "What Would You Do?" stories for Gladys Brockyell, Tom Mix, Peggy Hyland, etc., formerly feature writer at Lasky, Ince and Paralta studios; now scenario editor of Fox West Coast feature prods. Ad., 1762 Tamarind ave., Hollywood, Calif.

COATES, Franklin B.; b. Springfield, Mass., 1881; educ. New Haven, Conn.; early career, on newspaper; screen career, staff writer for Fox, Goldwyn, Vitagraph; "Romance of the Air," "Tale of Two Nations," "Price of Fame," "Last of the Wares," "Poppy," "Always in the Way," "Amazonian Girl," "The Jungle Man," "The Purple Hour," "Spider and the Fly." Ad., Betts & Fowler, 1482 B'way, N. Y.

COHEN, Bennett Ray; b. Trinidad, Colo.; educ. bus. coll.; early career, newspaper work; screen career, Universal, Vitagraph, Fox "Fame and Fortune," "Pitfalls of a Big City," "The Fallen Angel," "Bride of Fear"), Haworth ("The Greater Profit"). Home ad., 2322 W. 8th st., Los Angeles; Wilshire 320.

COLDEWEY, Anthony W.; b. Louisville, Ky.; educ. Kenyon Coll., Gambier, Ohio; early career, newspaper work; screen career, since 1913; staff writer for Universal, Balboa, Crown City, National, American, Sennett-Keystone, Triangle,

SCENARIO WRITERS AND EDITORS

L-Ko, Vitagraph. Home ad., 214 S. Benton way, Los Angeles; phone 557602.

CONKLIN, Frank Roland; b. Atchison, Kan., 1886; educ. N. Y. C. and Haverford Coll., Pa.; early career, short stories, sketches and plays; screen career, Christie Film Co., author of Christie specials, Christie comedies, Strand Comedies, Supreme Comedies, Gaiety Comedies, etc.; co-author "Wild and Western," "A Roman Scandal," "Passing of Peevish Pete"; author "Kidnapping Caroline," "Mixed Drinks," "Truly Rural," "Nearly Newlyweds." Ad., "The Outpost," 7065 Franklyn ave., Los Angeles; studio, Christie Studios, Los Angeles; Holly 3100.

CONLEY, John J.; b. Boston, Mass., 1884; educ. Boston Latin Schl.; early career, real estate operator in Boston. Home ad., 6713 Yucca st., Hollywood, Cal.; phone 577128; studio, care Metro, Holly 4485.

CONSIDINE, Mildred; b. 1892, Chicago; educ. Acad. of Fine Arts; early career, magazine writer, author vaud. acts; screen career, scenario editor and writer for Monmouth Film Co., adapted 32 reels of the "Jimmie Dale" serial, Essanay, Selznick, Norma Talmadge Co., author of over 100 successful pictures, "Framing Framers," "Ghosts of Yesterday." Ad. home and studio, 321 W. 55th st., N. Y. C.

COOLIDGE, Karl R.; b. Scranton, Pa., 1890; educ. Stanford Univ.; early career, newspaper work and entomological expert, short story writer and author of biological treatises; screen career, scenario ed. Lubin, Keystone, American, staff author Universal; serials, "The Lion Man," "The Moon Riders," western, "The Fighting Line," "A Sagebrush Gentleman," "Striped Shirt Ransom," etc. Ad., Box 12, Hollywood Station, Los Angeles, Calif.

COURTNEY, William B.; b. Dover, N. H.; early career, newspaper work, Passaic, N. J., Washington, D. C., and New England, also in U. S. Army; screen career, free lance, then took staff job with Vitagraph in 1914, commissioned in army; returned to U. S. in May, 1919, and rejoined Vitagraph staff as feature writer, "Defeat of the City," "For France," "Flaming Omen," "Duplicity of Hargraves," and many other features and short subjects of the O. Henry series; several superfeatures now in making. Ad., 148 St. Paul's place, Brooklyn, N. Y.

COWAN, Sada; educ. Europe; stage career, plays produce, "Playing the Game," "The State Forbids," and 14 one-act plays; screen career, Cecil B. De Mille ("Why Change Your Wife?"). Ad., Lasky Studio, Los Angeles, Cal.; Holly 2400.

CUNNINGHAM, Jack; b. Ionia, Iowa; educ. Cornell Coll., Mt. Vernon, Iowa; early career, newspaper man; screen career, Triangle ("The Argument"), Pathe ("Midnight Stage," "Todd of the Times"), Brunton ("Heart of Rachael"), Paralta ("Law Unto Herself"), Hampton ("Burglar for a Night"), Brunton ("$30,000," "The Joyous Liar"), and some 50 or 60 other photoplays; now associated with George Loane Tucker Prod. and Robert Brunton Prod. Home ad., Box 800, R. D. No. 10, Laurel Canyon, Hollywood, Cal.; Holly 3382; studio, Robert Brunton Studio, Inc.

— D —

DAZEY, Charles Turner; b. Lima, Ill.; educ. Harvard Univ. (B. A.); early career, author and playwright, has written verses for Century Magazine and other periodicals, author of several plays, including "In Old Kentucky," co-author of "A Night Out," "The Captain"; screen career, on scenario staff of Metro, author of "The Redemption of Dave Darcey," co-author of "Manhattan Madness," "The Flower of Faith"; American ("The Call to Arms," "A Night in New York"), Metro ("Testing of Mildred Vane"). Member Photodramatists. At present free lance. Ad., Lambs Club, N. Y.

DE CORDOVA, Rudolph; educ. Univ. Coll. Schl., Univ. Coll. and Hospital, London; acted leading parts in Shakespeare and modern drama in London; written many plays in collaboration with Alicia Ramsey (Mrs. De Cordova), produced in London and America; "Monsieur de Paris," "Edmund Kean," "The Password," "As a Man Sows," "Honor," "John Hudson's Wife," "The Mandarin," "Shadow Behind the Throne," "The Quicksands," 7 melodramas produced at London Hippodrome, etc.; wrote scenario for "Romeo and Juliet"; recently engaged on series of important scenarios for Vitagraph. Ad., 45 Beaver st., N. Y. C.

DENCH, Ernest Alfred, also publicity representative; b. London, 1895; educ. London; screen career, author of "The Footballer's Honor" and 20 other produced photoplays; one of vice-presidents of Photoplay Authors' League, author of "Playwriting for the Cinema," "Making the Movies," "Advertising by Motion Pictures," "Motion Picture Education"; former special pub. representative for Lillian Walker, Edward Earle, Eleanor Woodruff and Wilfred North, bus. mgr. for Wheeler Dryden. Home ad., 3052 Emmons ave., Brooklyn, N. Y.

DIX, Beulah Marie (Mrs. George Flebbe); b. Plymouth, Mass.; educ. Radcliffe Coll., A. B. & M. A. degrees, member Phi Beta Kappa; author short stories, books for children, ten novels, including "The Fighting Blade," "Ward Millicent," "Hands Off"; collaborated with E. G. Sutherland in plays, including "The Road to Yesterday," "The Breed of the Freshams," Martin Harvey's great English success, author of "Across the Border," "Moloch"; screen career, Paramount-Artcraft, "Call of the East," "Hidden Pearls," "Squaw Man," "Secret Service," "Woman Thou Gavest Me," "Men, Women and Money," "In Mizzouro." Ad., 2026 Argyle ave., Hollywood, Calif.; Holly 2400; studio, Lasky.

DUNN, Winifred, author and adaptor; b. Rochester, N. Y., daughter of George M. Dunn, private secy. to William Ewart Gladstone and exec. secy. to Labouchere; Selig Polyscope Co., Universal, Edw. Warren Prod., etc.; author of "Friendship," "The Pendulum," "Too Late," "Marianna," "Scratched Locket," "Charity at Home," "Truth," "Wood-witch," "The Hand," "Greater Love," "Prodigal Daughter," "The Coward," "Sinless Child of Sin," "Peg o' the Sea," "Thunderbolt of Fate," "And the Children Pay," "The Red Viper," etc. Member Authors' League of America.

DURANT, Harry R.; b. New Haven, Conn., Yale '94; has written short stories, novels, photoplays and plays; has been managing editor of Biograph, Triangle, Famous Players and Goldwyn, and now manager Play Dept. for Famous Players-Lasky Corp. Ad., Empire Theatre, N. Y. C.

— F —

FAIRFAX, Marion (Mrs. Tully Marshall); b. Richmond, Va., educ. Emerson Coll., Boston, private tutors; author of following plays, all N. Y. Prod., "The Builders," "The Chaperon," "The Talker," "Mrs. Boltay's Daughters," "The Ways and the Means," etc.; screen career, Marshall Neilan and Famous Players-Lasky Co., "The River's End," "Valley of the Giants," "The Clown," "The Widow's Might," "The Blacklist," "Less Than Kin," "Freckles," "The Honor of His House," "The Secret Game," "Hashamura Togo," "Love Insurance," "Vicky Van," "Daughter of the Wolf," "Putting It Over," etc. Ad., 128 N. Ridgewood pl., Los Angeles, Calif.; phone 567430.

FALLON, Thomas F.; b. N. Y., 1885; educ. St. Francis Xavier Coll.; stage career, with Annie Russell, Mme. Kalich, Bertha Galland, Amelia Bingham, Wilton Lackaye, May Irwin; screen career, Famous Players, Biograph, Edison, adaptation and scenario, Fox, Miss Innocence"; in collaboration with Harry Millarde, "Caught in the Act," "Bonnie Annie Laurie," "Blue Eyed Mary," scenario "Sacred Silence" story for Geo. Walsh in preparation. Ad., Fox, N. Y.

FARLEY, Mary Louise; b. Parkersburg, W. Va.; educ. Parkersburg and Chevy Chase, Md.; early career, writing for magazines N. Y.; correspondent for "Cosmos" magazine; screen career, has written over 100 scenarios, "Our Poor Relations," "Dawn of a New Day," "Little Flower Girl," "A Message to Heaven," "Weighed in the Balance," "The Welcome of the Unwelcome," "Father's Hot Toddy," "Little Show," "Perils of a War Messenger"; secry. of the Photodramists, N. Y.; member Authors' League of America. Ad., 600 W. 136th st., N. Y. C.

FOX, Finis; b. Oklahoma; educ. coll. and univ.; early career, sales, newspaper editor, state legislator, gen. mgr. National Mfg. Corp.; screen career, author "The Jury of Fate" (Mabel Taliaferro), "The Voice of Conscience" (Bushman and Bayne), "The Web of Lies" (Dolores Cassinelli); author and scenarioist, "The Great Romance" (Harold Lockwood), "Should a Woman Tell?" scenarioist for Bert Lytell's "Blackie's Redemption," "Easy to Make Money" and "Alias Jimmy Valentine"; Viola Dana's "The Parisian Tigress" and "Please Get Married"; Emmy Wehlen's "Fools and Their Money," etc. Ad., Metro Studio, Hollywood, Cal.

FURTHMAN, Jules; b. Chicago, Ill.; educ. Northwestern Univ., Columbia Univ.; early career, newspaper and magazine work; screen career, writing scenarios since 1910, Fox, Pathe ((Japanese Nightingale" with Farrie Ward, "More Trouble" with Frank Keenan, American ("Brass Buttons," "This Hero Stuff," "Six Feet Four," "Other Side of Eden"), Tourneur (adaptations "Victory," "Treasure Island," "Glory of Love"). Home ad., Alexandria Hotel, Los Angeles, Calif.; studio, Maurice Tourneur Prods.

— G —

GATES, Harvey H.; b. Hawaiian Islands, 1889; Educ. L. D. S. Univ., Utah; early career, newspaper reporter N. Y. Dramatic Mirror, publicity mgr.; screen career, Universal, Lubin, Morosco, National; author of "Love Never Dies," "Sands of Sacrifice" (Wm. Russell), "Broadway Scandal," "Wine Girl," "Hell Morgan's Girl," "Wild Cat of Paris"; adaptations "Exquisite Thief," "Wicked Darling," "Three Godfathers," "The Sealed Envelope," "After the War," "The Midnight Man," "Lightning Brice," "Beckoning Roads," "The Luck of Geraldine Laird," etc. Home ad., 2006 Ivar ave., Hollywood, Calif.; phone 579268.

GERAGHTY, Tom J.; b. Rushville, Ind.; early career, reporter and special writer, contributed to Saturday Evening Post, Munsey's, Pearson's, etc., author of vaud. sketches; screen career, "When the Clouds Roll By" with Douglas Fairbanks, "In Old Kentucky," "Mary Regan," "Her Kingdom of Dreams" for Anita Stewart, "Too Much Johnson" for Bryant Washburn, "A Man's Fight" for Dustin Farnum, "A Heart in Pawn," "The Courageous Coward," "The Bloodhound" for Sessue Hayakawa, "In for Thirty Days," "Her Inspiration" for May Allison, etc.; now writing exclusively for Douglas Fairbanks. Home ad., 2050 El Cerrito place, Hollywood, Calif.; studio, Fairbanks.

GIBSON, Tom, director-author; b. Boston, Mass., 1887; educ. Riverside High Schl.; early career, 1 yr. in vaud., wrote and staged vaud. sketches in San Francisco, newspaper man in Los Angeles, published the Sporting Bulletin; screen career, author of over 250 reels of produced material mostly comedies, Universal, National, Brentwood, etc.; now directing Gale Henry in two-reel comedies, "The Champeen," "The Laundry Lady," etc. Studio ad., Model Comedy Co., Hollywood, Calif.; Willis & Inglis, representatives, ad., P. O. Box G, Hollywood, Calif.

GIBSON, Victor; b. Boston, Mass.; educ. Los Angeles, Calif.; early career, newspaper writer on various coast publications, magazine contributor, novelist; screen career, staff and special writer Brentwood, National, Hampton, Fox, original stories, continuities, subtitles. Ad., P. O. Box G, Hollywood, Calif.

GILLETT, Ethel; b. Calif.; educ. Leland Stanford Univ., Mills Coll., Oakland, Calif.; lectured during war on "Child Welfare," journalish for San Francisco papers; began in pictures 1 yr. ago under supervision of Thos. H. Ince. Home ad., 1835 Argyle, Hollywood, Cal.; phone 579502; studio, Thos. H. Ince Studios, Culver City, Cal.

GLASSMIRE, Albert; b. Phila.; educ. there; early career, stage directing in stk.; author of "The Devil's Workshop," stage play; wrote several scenarios before entering pictures; screen career, Biograph, Universal, Mutual, Triangle-Keystone. Ad., Mack Sennett Studio, Glendale, Cal.

GOLLOMB, Joseph; b. Petrograd, Nov. 15, 1881; educ. Coll. City N. Y., and Columbia; early career, teacher, lecturer, newspaper man N. Y. Evening World, Mail, dramatic critic N. Y. Call, special writer N. Y. Evening Post, Times, Munsey, Harper, etc.; fictionized "Lucille Love" for Evening Mail; screen career, reviewer for New York dailies; scenario writer, Universal, Vitagraph ("A Man's Sacrifice," "The Lonelies," "The City of Romance," "The Surprise Party," "The Shop Girl," "The Man Hunt," etc.); free lance novelist and magazine writer. In 1919, Vitagraph produced "Girl at Bay" with Corinne Griffith, Paramount-Artcraft "The Stained Lily" with Ethel Clayton. Ad., 45 W. 11th st., N. Y. C.

GOULDING, Edmund; educ. England; stage career, commenced at age of 15 in London, later leading man and author, headliner, dramatic sketches, played with Sir Herbert Tree and all principal London theatres; first play "Ellen Young," produced Savoy Theatre, London, 1914; during active service wrote several Famous Players-Lasky features; "The Ordeal of Rosetta" for Select; during 1919, returning from France, adapted and originated a series of pictures for Selznick; adapted "Daughter of Two Worlds" and "Yes or No" with Norma Talmadge. London ad., 166 Shaftsbury ave., London, England; 59 W. 44th st., New York.

GRIFFITH, Raymond; b. Boston, 1890; educ. St. Anselm's Coll., N. H.; stage career, Barnum & Bailey; mus. com., drama, pantomime; screen career, Kalem, L-Ko., Keystone ("The Surf Girl"), Fox ("An Aerial Joy Ride"), Triangle-Keystone ("A Royal Rogue," "His Foothill Folly," "False to the Finish," "Something from the West"), Triangle (played in "The Follies Girl"). Now scenario writer with Mack Sennett Comedies, L. A., Cal.

GUIHAN, Frances; b. St. Louis, Mo.; screen career, Balboa, Metro ("Soul of Kura San," orig., for Hayakawa"), Lasky, adaptations for Hayakawa-Haworth, "His Birthright," "Bonds of Honor," "Courageous Coward," "Heart in Pawn," Pathe, Ruth Roland serial, "Broadway Bab," "The Yellow Typhoon," starring Anita Stewart, "Sherry" for Edgar Lewis, 3 Frohman prods., starring Texas Guinan. Ad., 1707 So. Flower St., Los Angeles, Cal.

— H —

HADLEY, Grace T.; b. Indiana; educ. Stanford Univ.; early career, newspaper and publicity work; screen career, following films made under personal supervision for Society for Electrical Development; Universal ("The House that Runs by Magic," "Santa and the Wonderful Genie," "Table Cookery," "The Heat Chaser," "Which One of These Is YOU?" played leading part in "Current Convenience." Ad., 29 W. 39th st., N. Y. C.

HALL, Emmett Campbell; b. Talbotton, Ga., Nov. 18, 1882; educ. law; served in diplomatic bureau of Dept. of State and other Govt. offices; magazine contributor of short stories, articles and verse; screen author since 1910, associated with Biograph, Kalem, Lubin and Goldwyn companies; seven hundred original photoplays produced, besides adaptations, by fifteen studios. Ad., Delray, Palm Beach County, Fla.

HALL, Walter Richard, also director; b. N. Y. C., May 26, 1887; educ. DeWitt Clinton High and Columbia Law; early career, cartoonist on staff of Success Magazine and various dailies; screen career, has written following serials, "The Fatal Fortune," "The Jeweled Hand," "The Man Without a Face," and "Pirate Gold." Following features, "Hate," "Souls of Men," "The Leech," etc. Short subjects for Vitagraph. Ad., 1203 Candler Bldg., N. Y. C.; Bryant 8446.

HARMER, Frances, reader; b. Brighton, England; educ. there; early career, teacher of College English, librarian in schools, writer for magazines, Hearst's Magazine, Ainslee's, Smith's, Snappy, Woman's Magazine, To-Day's, McCall's, etc.; screen career, Lasky. Home ad., 5956 Hollywood Blvd., Los Angeles, Cal.; phone 579097; studio, Lasky, 1520 Vine st., Los Angeles; Holly. 2400.

HAVEZ, Jean; b. Baltimore, Md.; educ. Johns Hopkins Univ.; stage career, 25 yrs. writing for legitimate stage and vaud. Home ad., 906 Fourth ave., Los Angeles, Cal.; phone 567309; studio, Fatty Arbuckle Comedies.

HAWKS, J. G., also director; b. California; educ. Stanford Univ.; early career, in army; stage career, joined Belasco in 1910; screen career, free lance writer, Monarch (director), Vim (director), Paralta-Artcraft ("Wolves of the Rail," "Blue Blazes Rawden"), Ince-Paralta ("The Sheriff's Son," "Dreamy Dub," "The Kaiser's Shadow," "The Woman Who Dared," "The Desert Wooing," "Partners Three"), for past year editor and mgr. scenario dept. Goldwyn. Studio, Goldwyn's, Culver City, Cal.

HILL, Wycliffe; b. Summerville, La., 1883; early career, 15 yrs. newspaper writer and magazine editor; screen career, Corona Cinema Co. ("The Curse of Eve"), Universal ("Tempest Cody Kidnapper," "Wits and the Woman," "The Counterfeit Trail"). Author of "Ten Million Photoplay Plots" and "Hill's Plot Treatise" for High School dramatic classes. Home ad., 3748 Woodlawn, Los Angeles, Cal.; So. 3102; studio, Universal City, Holly. 2500.

HIVELY, George O.; b. Springfield, Mo., 1889; educ. there, Drury College; early career, sect. to vice-pres. of Santa Fe, stage work 2 yrs., Mo., Okla., Texas; screen career, Keystone, Triangle ("Six-Shooter Justice," "Phantom Riders"), Universal (author of 15 2-reelers, 10 "Cyclone Smith" stories, 10 "Spur and Saddle" stories, "Ace of the Saddle" with Harry Carey,

SCENARIO WRITERS AND EDITORS

"The Lotus Flower," "The Great Air Robbery," "The Rattler's Hiss"). Ad., home, 815 W. Sixth st., Los Angeles; studio, Universal.

HOADLEY, C. B. (Pop); b. Elyria, Ohio; educ. Galion, Ohio; early career, newspaper writer for 20 yrs. on city dailies; screen career, American ("Secret of the Submarine" serial, "Sequel to the "Diamond from the Sky" serial), 100 Lyons and Moran comedies for Universal, Montgomery and Rock comedies for Vitagraph. Home ad., 1518 N. Alexandria ave., Los Angeles, Cal.; Holly. 3132; studio, Vitagraph.

HOADLEY, Harold Wm. ("Hal"); b. Defiance, Ohio, 1893; early career, newspaper reporter at age of 14; author of several produced vaud. sketches; screen career, orig. Imp Co. (1910), Universal, Vitagraph, American, U. S. Air Service, Universal since June, 1919, current releases: continuities for "Gun Fightin' Gentleman" with Harry Casey, "Rouge and Riches" with Mary MacLaren, "The Triflers," "The Day She Paid," "Sins of the Father." Home ad., 1518 N. Alexandria ave., Hollywood, Cal.; Holly. 3132; studio, Universal City, Cal.; Holly. 2500.

HODES, Hal; managing editor Universal New Screen Magazine; early career, operator with Vitagraph 1904-5; subsequently reporter Newark Evening News; advertising and publicity with Kalem 1913-15; sales promotion man Universal, 1915; later asst. general manager of exchanges. Ad., Universal Film Mfg. Co., N. Y.

HOPLEY, Frank Dorrance; b. Portland, Conn.; early career, short story writer; screen career, scen. writer for Kalem ("A Mother's Atonement"), Reliance ("The Ten o'Clock Boat"). Home ad., 116 W. 71st st., N. Y. C. Ad., 1615 Woolworth Bldg., N. Y. C.

HORNER, Bob; b. Spring Valley, Ill., Sept. 14, 1896; educ. Spring Valley and Chicago; screen career, wrote Vitagraph "Whom God Would Destroy," starring Harry Morey and Alice Joyce, "The Bully" for Ebony, "The Millionaire Piker," "The Reckless Rover," "Hell's Valley," "The Uphill Road." Home ad., 4040 Bway, Chicago, Ill.

HOWARD, George Bronson; b. The Relay, Howard Co., Md., 1884; career, in U. S. Government employ, Civil Government, Philippines, Imperial Chinese Service, Canton, China, war cor. for London Chronicle during Russo-Japanese war, author "Norroy, Diplomatic Agent," "Scars on the Southern Seas," "An Enemy to Society," "The Red Light of Mars," "Pages from the Book of Broadway," "God's Man"; screen career, Lasky, Kalem ("Social Pirates"), Universal ("Stronger than Steel," "The Adventure of the Poison Dagger," "The Master Spy"), Moss ("The Power of Evil"), Fox ("Queen of the Sea," "The Spy"). Ad., 654 St. Nicholas ave., N. Y. C.

HUBBARD, Philip; b. London, Eng.; educ. Lancing Coll., Sussex, Eng.; Sandhurst Royal Mil. Coll.; Finsbury Tech. Sch. of Engineering; stage career, Tapping Stk. Co., also with James Welch, Charles Frohman, William Greet, etc., was orig. Capt. Kettle in play of that name at Adelphi theatre, London, in burlesque of Sherlock Holmes, "Sheerluck Jones," etc., played 2 seasons with Jane Cowl, "Captain Paget," "Lilac Time," "Information Please"; screen career, author of scenario of "The Auction Block," Rex Beach Pictures and asst. dir. of production, Dustin Farnum's Liberty Loan picture, etc., Universal, lead with Florence Turner in comedies. Home ad., 2452 Beachwood Drive, Hollywood, Cal.; phone 577786; studio, Universal.

— J —

JAMES, Frederick Henry; b. N. Y. C.; educ. abroad; early career, dramatist, novelist, short story writer; stage career, playwriting, adapting, producing for about 10 yrs.; screen career, free lance writing at first, then staff writing; has several hundred screen prods. of original stories to his credit, "A Pair of Baby Arms," "Memories," "The Man Who Paid," "The Saving Bullet," "Uncle Ben in Paris," "A Kiss for Charity," "His Daughter Pays," "The Danger Zone," reconstructions and adaptations, "Secret Kingdom" (serial), "Jar Stories," "The Violet Widow," etc.; formerly staff writer Vitagraph, Pathe, Fox; later editor Lincoln Picture Classics. Home ad., 2100 Cropsey ave., Brooklyn, N. Y.; Bensonhurst 4100.

JANSEN, Laura; b. Antwerp, Belgium; educ. Belgium, Isle of Wight and London; stage career, in England and America; screen career, since 1917 with Famous Players, and with Directors Capellani and Perret; completed scenario of "A Modern Salome" for Hope Hampton; has been assisting in preparing scripts for the special prods. being made by Emile Chautard. Ad., Coytesville, N. J.

JEFFERSON, L. V.; b. Carthage, Mo., 1874 educ. Kentucky; early career, stock broker, short story writer for Munsey publications, Everybody's, National, etc.; screen career, National ("A Kentucky Colonel," "Son of Tarzon" serial), Federal ("Desert of Wheat"), Haworth ("The Man Beneath," "His Debt"), Art-o-graf ("Last of Open Range"), American ("Put Up Your Hands," "Charge It to Me"), L. S. Stone Pic. ("Man's Desire"), Lasky, Ince, Triangle, World, Universal, Fox, etc., 370 orig. stories and book adaptations produced. Home ad., 3950 S. Hill st., Los Angeles, Cal.; South 964-J.

JENKS, George Elwood; b. Minneapolis, Minn., 1881; educ. there; 12 yrs. varied adventurous career in city society, underworld, West and Canadian wilds; 6 yrs. studio training, tech. dir., cutter, acct. dir., staff writer since days of 1 and 2-reelers; adaptations and original features for many prominent stars. Current releases, "A Woman of Pleasure" (Blanche Sweet), "The Man Who Turned White" and "The Pagan God" (H. B. Warner), "The Parish Priest" (Wm. Desmond), etc., etc., Studio ad., Jesse D. Hampton Prods., Hollywood; home, 22 Linnie ave., Venice, Cal.

JEVNE, Jack; b. Provo, Utah, 1892; educ. Chicago, St. Louis, Salt Lake; stage career, own stk. co., Salt Lake, juvenile leads with Annie Kiskadden (Maude Adams' mother), "Paid in Full," "Little Women," "Within the Law," N. Y. prods., "So Much for So Much," "Alias Santa Claus," "Taking Chances." Home ad., 1820 West 43d Place, Los Angeles, Cal.; phone 79508; studio, Universal City; Holly. 2500.

JOHNSON, Adrian R.; b. Knoxville, Tenn., Jan. 13, 1886; educ. St. Mary's Coll., Belmont, N. C.; early exper., commercial work; screen career, Metro, Fox ("Royal Romance," "Heart and Soul," "Every Girl's Dream," "Camille," "Cleopatra," "Du Barry," "Romeo and Juliet," "Under the Yoke," "Salome," "The Firebrand," "Her Greatest Love," "The Darling of Paris"), Para-Artcraft ("Miracle of Love"). Home ad., 115 West 48th st., N. Y. C.

JOHNSON, Merle; educ. Quincy, Ill., and Univ. of Mich.; early career, newspaper reporter; screen career, actor and asst. director for Essanay, has written following pictures which are in productions: "She Held Her Husband" and "Red Pepper" with Olive Thomas, "Hard Luck O'Day" with Eugene O'Brien, and several two-reel comedies. Ad., Phi Gamma Delta Club, 30 W. 44th st., N. Y.

JOHNSTON, Agnes Christine; b. Swissvale, Pa.; educ. Horace Mann Sch., N. Y., and Workshop Dramatic Course at Harvard Coll.; screen career, 5 yrs. Vitagraph, Thanhouser, Pathe, Mary Pickford, Thos. H. Ince; "Daddy Long-Legs" for Mary Pickford; "23½ House' Leave," MacLean and May; "Carmen," Theda Bara; "Homer Comes Home," Charles Ray; orig. stories, "Alarm Clock Andy," "The Village Sleuth," "Trixie from Broadway," "The Sawdust Doll," "The Old Man's Baby," "The Shine Girl," "Her New York," "Pots-and-Pans-Peggy," "Prudence, the Pirate," "The Amateur Orphan," "Fires of Youth," Sidney Drew Comedies, etc. Home ad., 1911 Pinehurst Road, Hollywood, Cal.; studio, Thos. H. Ince, Culver City, Cal.

JOSEPHSON, Julian; b. Roseburg, Ore.; educ. Stanford Univ.; screen career, Ince-Paramount ("The Hired Man," "Playing the Game," "String Beans," "Fuss and Feathers," "Greased Lightning'," "Hay-Foot, Straw-Foot," "The Egg-Crate Wallop," "Crooked Straight," "Red-Hot Dollars," "Paris Green," "Crossed Wires," "Shakespeare Clancy," "Under the Mask"). Ad., 7212 Lenkill ave., Culver City, Cal.; studio, Thos. H. Ince Studio, Culver City, Cal.

JUSTICE, Maibelle Heickes; b. Indiana; educ. N. Y. C. and Phila.; war work last two yrs., for which has been cited and given honorary rank of Capt., U. S. Regular Army; early career, novelist and short story author; screen career, special original photodramas, "Melissa of the Hills," "The End of the Trail," "Glory of Yolanda," "Intrigue," "Her Husband's Honor," "Friendship of Beaupere," "The Great Game," "The Final Judgment," "A Splendid Sacrifice," and forthcoming new specials. Member Author's League of America, Photodramatists,

Theatre Assembly Club, Drama Comedy Club, etc. Home ad., 41 W. 47th st., N. Y.

— K —

KATTERJOHN, Monte M.; b. Boonville, Ind.; educ. there; early career, newspaper and magazine work, published "Mototopic," pub. first magazine for photoplaywrights; screen career, from 1908, first as free lance, then Universal as scenario ed., then NYMP; Griffith ("Apostle of Vengeance"), Ince ("The Gun Fighter," "The Clodhopper"), Triangle ("Golden Rule Kate"), Paralta ("Madam Who," "Within the Cup," "Carmen of the Klondike," "Puppy Love," "The Fresh Young Thing," "Intelligence"), Paralta ("The Source," "The Man from Funeral Range"), Katterjohn ("Alaska"), Hodkinson ("The Lord Loves the Irish"). Home ad., Waldorf Hotel, Venice, Cal.

KAVANAUGH, Katherine; b. Baltimore, Md.; educ. Notre Dame, Md.; stage career, 2 yrs. stk., 7 yrs. vaud., writer vaud. sketches, "Ambition," to be produced by Valerie Bergere; screen career, Metro (author of "The Wheel of the Law," "The Will o' the Wisp," "The Call of Youth," "The Winding Trail"), Triangle ("Betty Takes a Hand"), Fox ("The Liar"), Metro ("Social Quicksands," "House of Gold," "Impulse of the Moment"), Universal ("Winning His Wife"). Home ad., 3434 Belair Rod., Baltimore, Md.

KELLY, Anthony P.; b. Chicago, 1892; educ. Loyola and Purdue acads.; early career, newspaper reporter in Chicago; screen career, sold first script, a 1-reel, to Vitagraph, later with Balboa, Essanay, Famous Players, Lubin; scenarios of Channing Pollock's "Little Gray Lady" and C. Townsend Brady's "Ring and the Man," Bernstein's "The Thief," Sutro's "Walls of Jericho," recent successes, "The Light at Dusk," Frohman ("My United States," "God's Man," "The Witching Hour," "A Man Without a Country"), Art Dramas ("The Rainbow"), Edgar Lewis ("The Bar Sinister," "The Sign Invisible"), Technicolor ("The Gulf Between"), Moss ("The Sins of the Children"), Empire All Star ("Outcasts"), Legit prod., "Three Faces East" (Cohan and Harris theatre). Ad., 715 Madison ave., N. Y. C.

KENYON, Albert G.; b. San Francisco, 1884; educ. Univ. Cal.; stage exper., actor with Margaret Illington, Sidney Drew, produced own vaud. sketches; screen career, Universal ("The Girl with Green Eyes"), Fox ("Bogus Jimmie," "Bird of Prey," "The Crucible"), Metro ("The Spender"), Paralta ("Ladder of Life"). Ad., 630 N. Gramercy, Los Angeles. Studio, Mayer-Chaplin Co.

KENYON, Charles A.; b. 1880, San Francisco; early career, playwright, "Kindling," "The Claim," and of the vaud. sketches, "We Need the Money," "The Placerville Stage"; screen career, with Lasky, wrote the story, "The Sacrifice" for Margaret Illington, and the story of "On the Level" for Fannie Ward, author of scenario, "The Silent Man," produced by Artcraft, Fox, "The Siren's Song," continuity writer for "Dangerous Days," "The Penalty," Fox, "Wings of the Morning," "Last of the Duanes," "Lone Star Rider" for Farnum, orig. stories, "The Feud," "A Rough Riding Romance" for Tom Mix. Ad., home, 1607 Vista st., Hollywood, Cal.

KRAFT, John W.; b. Indianapolis, Ind., 1888; educ. there; newspaper man; motion picture editor, dramatic critic, newspaper humorist, contributor tod humorous publications, comedy title writer, author of jokes and paragraphs used in The New Screen Magazine" issued by Universal, editor Universal's press books and weekly Bulletin. Ad., 609 W. 191st st., N. Y. C. St. Nich., 3470.

— L —

LAMOTHE, Julian Louis; b. New Orleans, 1893; educ. Tulane Univ., N. O. Coll. of Oratory; early career, wrote scenarios while at college, some newspaper work, author of vaudeville sketches and short stories; screen career, 18 mos. as editor Western Lubin Co., editor Pollard Co., staff writer American ("The Inner Struggle," "Southern Pride," "Dust"), Paralta ("His Robe of Honor," "Humdrum Brown," etc.); student of drama, Psychiatry and Ancient Religions. Home ad., 427 S. Hope st., Los Angeles, Cal.;

LARRIMER, Mary Edna, dramatist and continuity writer; b. Peru, Ind.; educ. classical sch., Chicago Conservatory of Music; editorial writing; author of Belgian play, "Official Bondage," used in war relief work, "Sacrifice," "Lies," "Mercurial Youth," "Elizabeth Ann." Home ad., 718 So. Alvarado, Los Angeles, Cal.; phone 50954.

LAUB, William Barbarin; formerly associated with Chaplin-Lincoln Pict.; cinematographer with Goldwyn, Farrar and Normand prods.; staff writer for Vitagraph; author of "Camera," published by Motion Picture News; co-author with Harry Chandlee and Lawrence McCloskey for the Edgar Jones Prods., supplying all stories produced; editor Universal Industrial prods. Ad., Universal Film Mfg. Co., N. Y. C.

LAWRENCE, Frank, editor-in-chief; b. N. Y. C.; with Vitagraph, Pathe, Universal; "Through the Wall," "Battle Cry of Peace," "The Christian," "The Isle of Regeneration," "The Heart of Humanity," "Right to Happiness," "Blind Husbands," "The Gorgeous Canary," "The Beautiful Beggar," etc. Ad., Universal City, Cal.

LEIBRAND, Lela Owens; b. Council Bluffs, Iowa; educ. Kansas City, Mo.; screen career, Fox, Diando-Pathe, Balboa ("The Climber," Henry King, "A Lady in the Library," Vialo Vale; "The Little Patriot," Baby Marie Osborne; "Marylee Mixes In," Gloria Joy; "The Rose of Blood," Theda Bara; "Bonnie Annie Laurie"). Ad., office, Fox, N. Y. C.

LENGEL, William C.; educ. Kansas City School of Law; director of publicity for Employment Management Section War Industries Board; in charge promotion of Nast Publications, Vogue, Vanity Fair, House and Garden; contributor to Red Book, Ainslee's, All-Story, etc.; author of "The Game," "The Come-Back" in vaud.; "If You Would Write for Vaudeville"; author of "Words and Music By" and "Tin Pan Alley," produced by Fox, among other original photoplays. Member Scenario Staff, Fox Film Corp. Ad., 1356 University ave., N. Y.; Melrose 7600.

LE VINO, Albert Shelby; b. Fredericksburg, Va., 1878; educ. Bucknell Univ.; early career, Wash., D. C., newspaper correspondent N. Y. Times, N. Y. American, fiction and article writer for Collier's, Harper's, Leslie's, author of "Cost in Men and Money of Our Wars"; screen career, "His Bachelor Dinner," "The Other Wife," "The Woman's Law," "Who's Guilty," "Sleeping Memory," "Under Suspicion," "Wilson or the Kaiser," etc. Ad., P. O. Box 123, Hollywood. Studio, Metro, Los Angeles, Cal.

LEWIS, Eugene B.; newspaper ed. and owner in Idaho, newspaper writer on San Francisco Chronicle and Hearst papers, N. Y.; screen career, member of Biograph staff, doing adaptations and originals; ed. Biograph; author of stories and continuities for Universal ("Three Mounted Men," "Roped"), Ince ("What Every Woman Learns"), Hampton ("The Blue Bandanna," "Unchartered Channels"), adaptations for Hampton ("The White Dove," "Mounting Shadows," "The Pink Dove"). Home ad., 1414 N. Benton Way, Hollywood, Cal.

LOCKE, Ashley T.; b. New Albany, Ind.; 5 yrs. general newspaper experience, covering all branches of editorial and reportorial work; 2 yrs. publicity director for Edison; 2 yrs. mgr. motion picture dept., Frank A. Munsey Co.; at present asst. scenario editor, Fox Film Corp. Home ad., 365 St. Johns Place, Brooklyn, N. Y.; studio ad., Fox Film Corp., 130 W. 46th st., N. Y. C.

LONERGAN, Lloyd; b. Chicago; educ. Annapolis Naval Acad.; early exper., magazine and newspaper writer, with Hearst; screen career, Thanhouser (wrote "Million Dollar Mystery," "A Modern Monte Cristo," "Under False Colors," "The Man Without a Country," "The Heart of Ezra Greer"), Chautard ("The Scrap of Paper," "Battle for Billions"), Wistaria ("Lurking Peril"). Home ad., Hotel Richmond, 70 West 46th st., N. Y. C.

LONERGAN, Philip; b. Hackensack, N. J.; educ. Brooklyn, N. Y.; early career, in business, also writer of short stories; screen career, Thanhouser ("The World and the Woman," "King Lear," "The Girl Who Wanted to Live," "The Candy Girl," "Saint, Devil and Woman"), World ("Mandarin's Gold," "Love and the Woman," adapted "Dust of Desire," "His Father's Wife," "Coax Me"). Home ad., 130 Lefferts Place, Brooklyn, N. Y.

LOOS, Anita; b. California; screen career, 6 yrs. with D. W. Griffith in Biograph, Mutual and Triangle Cos., with Douglas Fairbanks in Art-

SCENARIO WRITERS AND EDITORS

craft, Emerson-Loos Co., making Artcraft specials, Paramount-Artcraft ("Oh, You Women," "Come On In"), Douglas Fairbanks ("The Americano," "Wild and Woolly"), Constance Talmadge ("A Temperamental Wife," "The Virtuous Vamp"). Home ad., 103 E. 75th st., N. Y. C.

LORING, Hope; b. Madrid, Spain; educ. convents, boarding schools, private tutors; early career, magazine stories; screen career, Universal ("The Lure of the Circus," "The Society Sensation," "The Cabaret Girl," "The Red Glove," "The 13th Hour," "Vanishing Dagger"), also "Diamond Snake Mystery" for London Co., Ad., 221 S. Wilton Place, Los Angeles, Cal.; Wil. 1158; studio,, Universal.

LOWE, Edward T., Jr.; b. Nashville, Tenn., 1880; educ. there, Fogg High School; screen career, began with Essanay in 1912, 1917-18, editor and asst. supervisor of prods. with that co., Goldwyn ("The World and Its Woman," "Bonds of Love," "Toby's Bow," "Street Called Straight," "Tower of Ivory," "Scratch My Back!" "A Double-Dyed Deceiver"). Ad., 531 So. Mariposa, Los Angeles, Cal.; studio, Goldwyn, Culver City, Cal.

LYNCH, John; b. New York; educ. Cornell and Georgetown Univ.; owner of theatres, writer of fiction and special articles; with Thomas H. Ince for 4 yrs.; now head of scenario dept., Selznick Pictures Corp. Ad., Selznick Studios, Lort Lee, N. J.

— M —

MACPHERSON, Jeanie; b. Boston, Mass.; educ. Paris, France; stage career, in "Strongheart" mgmt. H. B. Harris, and "Havana" mgmt. Shuberts; screen career, acted and directed for Biograph, Edison, Universal, Lasky (has written or adapted "Joan the Woman"), Artcraft "The Little American," "Old Wives for New," "The Whispering Chorus," "Till I Come Back to You," "Don't Change Your Husband," "Male and Female"), personal asst. to C. B. De Mille in all departments pertaining to her stories. Ad., home, 7047 Hawthorne ave., Los Angeles; studio, Lasky, Hollywood.

MARION, Frances; b. San Francisco; educ. San Francisco; early career, artist, designing theatrical posters and illustrating for magazines, newspaper work; screen career, began writing scenarios as a free lance, went with Bosworth to learn the business; wrote "The Foundling" for Mary Pickford, "Daughter of the Sea" for Muriel Ostriche, World, Famous, Artcraft ("Rebecca of Sunnybrook Farm," "Johanna Enlists," "He Comes Up Smiling," "Capt. Kidd, Jr.," "The City of Dim Faces"), Haworth "Temple of Dusk"), Selznick ("A Regular Girl"), Realart ("Anne of Green Gables"), United Artists ("Pollyanna"). Ad., Lasky Studio, Hollywood, Cal.

MATHIS, June; b. Leadville, Colo.; educ. San Francisco and Salt Lake City; stage career, since childhood, leading woman with Cohan and Harris, A. H. Woods, Shuberts, and Liebler; screen career, first free lance scenario writer, now head of scenuario dept. with Metro; recent pictures; "To Hell with the Kaiser," "Toys of Fate," "Eye for Eye," "Out of the Fog," "The Red Lantern," "Lady Frederick," "Five Thousand an Hour," "Kildare of Storm," "The Brass Check," adapted "The Willow Tree," "Right of Way," "Old Lady 31," "Lombardi, Ltd." Ad., 1729 Chuenga ave., Hollywood; 214 West 92nd st., N. Y.; studio, Metro, Hollywood, Cal.

MAXWELL, Ann.; educ. high school, N. Y.; early career, real estate, newspaper and publicity work; screen career, asst. director Vitagraph in Nov., 1915, resigned shortly after to do free lancing, author of "Little Doll's Dressmaker," "Peggy of Fifth Avenue," "On the Turn of a Card," orig. scenario, "The Crossbearer," not orig., "Little Women," " "Way Down East," "Maytime." Home ad., 157 Bridge st., Brooklyn, N. Y.

McCLOSKEY, Lawrence; b. Cincinnati, O., 1886; educ. Cincinnati and Philadelphia; early career, newspaper work; screen career, 3 yrs. scenario editor and special writer, 4 yrs. free lance; author of over 60 screen features in which appeared Madge Kennedy, George Beban, Lionel Barrymore, Louise Glaum, Harry Morey, Elaine Hammerstein, Raymond Hitchcock, Ethel Clayton, Alice Joyce, Doris Kenyon, Gladys Leslie, Kitty Gordon, Louise Huff, etc., Green Room Club, N. Y.

McCONNELL, Guy W., also director; b. Wrightsville, Pa., 1879; early career, journalism, insurance and politics; screen career, Pathe, Frohman, Wholesome Films; produced "Penny Philanthropist"; author "Pearl of the Army" (Pearl White), "Red Snows" (Pathe), "Invisible Ray," "The Northern Lights" (McConnell Films), "True Americanism" (Balmer Films), etc. Ad., Hotel Commodore, N. Y.

McCRORY, John Robert; 1898; educ. high school and commercial college; newspaper artist with Omaha News; screen career, artist and cameraman with K. C. Motion Picture Co., advertising film; animated cartoon, technical drawings and photography with Bray Pictures Corporation. Home ad., 516 West 157th st.; studio ad., 23 East 26th st., N. Y. C.

McGOWAN, Robert F., also director; b. Denver, Colo.; educ. Denver pub. schls.; screen career, scen. Universal ("The Search of a Wife," "Their Only Son," etc.), Christie ("A Blessed Blunder," "Nearly a Papa"). Recreations, swimming, riding. Home ad., 1455 Logan st., Los Angeles, Cal.; studio ad., Christie, Los Angeles, Cal.; Thos. H. Ince, Christie, Universal, National, directed Christie Comedies, has written and produced nearly 100 comedies, also Universal features, now assisting writing and producing with Carter De Haven comedies "After the Ball," "Their Day of Rest," "Hoodooed," "Close to Nature"). Studio, Carter De Haven Studio, 4500 Sunset Blvd., Hollywood, Cal.; home ad., 5343 Lexington ave., Los Angeles, Cal.

McLAUGHLIN, Robert; author of following moving picture productions and plays: "Hidden Charms," "The Eternal Magdalene," "House Without Children," "Fires of Spring," "Decameron Nights," "Pearl of Great Price," "Home Again," "Walk Into My Parlor," "Greatest of These," "Men in the Making." Ad., care of Argus Co., 815 Prospect ave., Cleveland, Ohio.

McNAMARA, Walter; b. Linsmore, Co. Waterford, Ireland, 8176; educ. St. Peter's Sch., Cardiff, S. Wales; early career, editor, novelist, war corresp., actor, director, and comedian; screen career, Universal, began as scen. ed., later wrote and produced "Traffic in Souls," "Ireland a Nation," Goldwyn (played in "Girl from Outside"); author and producer of many orig. photoplays.

McNEIL, Everett; early career, author of eleven published books of fiction and 240 pub. short stories; screen career, with Vitagraph and Edison, author of "The Price Paid," "The Better Success," "The Making of an American," "The Rebellion o' Mandy," "The Martyrdom of Philip Strong," "The Making Over of Geoffrey Manning," and many other produced moving picture scenarios. Home ad., 543 West 49th st., N. Y. C.

MEREDITH, Miriam; chief reader for Thos. H. Ince and J. Parker Read, Jr., prods. for last 2 yrs.; b. Tucson, Ariz.; educ. Cumnock Acad. and Sch. of Expression, Los Angeles, Elesmere Hall, N. Y.; stage career, Burbank Stk. Co., Los Angeles, part of a season with Mrs. Fiske in "Salvation Nell," Wm. Stoermer's Shakespearean Repertory Co., director of pageants for Y. W. C. A. and of Hollywood Children's Theatre Co. Ad., 1848 Morgan Place, Hollywood, Cal.; phone 599728; studio, Ince.

MILLHAUSER, Bertram; b. N. Y.; screen career, Pathe-Astra (continuity "Double Cross," 15 episodes, and co-authorship "The Fatal Ring," "House of Hate," "The Lightning Raider," serials starring Pearl White), G. B. Seitz, Inc. ("The Black Secret," "Velvet Hawk," serials). Studio ad., G. B. Seitz, Inc., 1990 Park ave., N. Y.; home ad., 454 Ft. Washington ave., N. Y. C.

MONTAGNE, Edward Joseph; educ. Brooklyn, N. Y.; early career, newspaper work; screen career, 7 yrs.; wrote and picturized over 100 features for Vitagraph, editor at Bay Shore studios; "The Combat," "Apartment 29," "Lion and the Mouse," "Oil and Water," "Out Yonder," "Beating the Odds," some of most prominent successes; have written and have had produced over 1,000 reels of screen dramas; now associated with Selznick Pictures Corp. Home ad., 799 Gravesend ave., Brooklyn, N. Y.; studio ad., Fort Lee, N. J.

MOSES, Alfred Huger, Jr.; b. Louisville, Ky., 1874; educ. Alabama Polytech., Mass. Inst. of Tech.; early career, 17 yrs. mechanical, electrical and photographic lines; screen career,

Peerless ("The Little Duchess"), Triangle-Fine Art ("The Social Secretary"), Thanhouser, 6 yrs. ("Joseph in the Land of Egypt," etc.), Rolfe-Metro ('Life's Shadows"); Norma Talmadge, Herbert Brenon Prods. Studio ad., British and Colonial Film Co., London, England. Ad., Hoe st., Walthamstow, London, E. C., England.

MOYERS, Bertie Badger; b. Louisville, Ky.; free lance, specializes in refined comedy and comedy drama; has sold to American, Vitagraph, Metro, World, Christie, etc.; Drew comedies ("His First Love," "Joy of Freedom," "Why Henry Left Home," "Too Much Henry," etc.), National ("After the Bawl," "Close to Nature," "Why Divorce?" "Forget Me Not"), Christie ("Who's With the Baby?"). Ad., 215 Verne st., Tampa, Fla.

MULLIN, Eugene; b. Brooklyn, N. Y.; educ. Sacred Heart Acad.; early career, mining and railroad business; screen career, 7 yrs. with Vitagraph as writer, director and editor, 6 mos. with Universal as editor-in-chief, adapted features for Vitagraph, ("The Christian," "Within the Law," "The Cambric Mask," "The Third Degree"); written 50 orig. stories, 75 adaptations; now with Goldwyn as managing editor. Ad., 71 Cumberland st., Brooklyn, N. Y., Prospect 7135; studio, Goldwyn, N. Y.

MURILLO, Mary; b. Bradford, Yorkshire, Eng.; educ. Sacred Heart Convent, London; screen career, wrote for Lois Weber, Philip Smalley, Herbert Brenon and Edgar Lewis. Chief writer for Fox, having written or adapted fifty Fox productions until 1918, for Theda Bara, William Farnum, etc. Since 1918 free lancing, writing for Norma Talmadge "The Forbidden City," "The Secret of the Storm Country," "The Heart of Wetona." Wrote for Metro, Emily Stevens, Ethel Barrymore, Madame Nazimova, Harold Lockwood, also for Clara Kimball Young and the "Panther Woman" for Petrova, Frank Hall "The Other Man's Wife"). Ad., Hotel Algonquin.

MURPHEY, Will C.; b. Camden, N. J., 1878; early career, newspaper man, Herald, Sun, American, former secretary N. J. Senate; wrote "Why Women Sin," "For Her Daily Bread," "Why He Divorced Her," "The Double Life" for stage; screen career, "Coax Me" (World), "Far East" (World), "Why Women Sin" (Wistaria). Ad., New York Press Club, 21 Spruce st., N. Y. C.; 3505 Beekman.

MYTON, Fred; b. Garden City, Kan.; educ. Penn. Mil. Coll., Chester, Pa.; screen career, since 1913, with Kalem, Universal, Lasky, Paralta and Brunton, continuities in the past year include "Desert Gold," "A Man in the Open," for Dustin Farnum, "Burglar by Proxy," with Jack Pickford, "A Trick of Fate" and others for Bessie Barriscale," "The Prince and Betty" with William Desmond, "A Fugitive from Matrimony" with H. B. Warner," "Cressy," "The Deadlier Sex," "Simple Souls" with Blanche Sweet; at present with J. D. Hampton Prods. Ad., 2511 Beverly ave., Ocean Park, Cal.; Ocean Park 4768.

— N —

NATTEFORD, J. F.; court reporter, general business man with barn-storming repertory co., Newspaper writer, executive positions in automobile industry; screen career, publicity writer, film editor and title writer; now scenario editor and title writer for Screencraft Pictures. Member A. M. P. A., and author of published stories and articles. Ad., care of Screencraft Pictures, 1476 Broadway, N. Y.; Bryant 772.

NEITZ, Alvin J.; b. Washington, D. C.; educ. Wentworth Milit. Acad., Lexington, Mo.; stage career, stage mgr. 3 seasons Riley and Woods's Casino Girls; screen career, asst. director 2 yrs. Thos. H. Ince, director and scenario editor 2 yrs. Horsley, author of scenarios, "The Good for Nothin' Brat," "Star of India," "Fighting Back," "Hell Cat," "The Gun Woman," "The Learnin' of Jim Benton." Ad., home, 33 Westminster ave., Venice, Cal.; studio, Capital Film Co.

— O —

O'CONNOR, Mary H., scenario and film editor; b. St. Paul, Minn.; early career, newspaper, magazine and novel writer; screen career, 1 yr. with Vitagraph, 3 yrs. Griffith, 3 yrs. Famous Players. Ad., 7002 Hawthorne ave., Hollywood, Cal.; phone 577-527; studio, Famous Players-Lasky corp., Hollywood, Cal.

OLMSTEAD, E. Stanley; scenario editor for Blackton Prods.; b. Cherokee Co., N. C.; educ. Washington, D. C., and Europe; journalist career on Evening Mail, McClure's Magazine, Musical America, Morning Telegraph; novelist and short story writer; screen career, Vitagraph ("One Thousand Dollars," "The Buyer from Cactus City"), Blackton ("My Husband's Other Wife," "Dawn," "The Wife and the Girl," "The Blood Barrier," "The Moonshine Trail," written in collaboration with J. S. Blackton. Ad., Friars' Club, N. Y.; studio ad., Blackton Prod., Inc., 25 W. 45th st., N. Y.; Bryant 8513.

OSMUN, Leighton Graves; b. 1880, Newark, N. J.; educ. Newark Acad. and Univ. of Penna.; early career, fiction writer, "The Clutch of Circumstance" (novel); screen career, Lasky 2 yrs., author of "The Devil Stone" for Geraldine Farrar, "The Jaguar's Claws" for Sessue Hayakawa, "Castles for Two" for Marie Doro, "Heir to the Hoorah" for Anita King, "Bettie to the Rescue" for Fannie Ward. Ad., Selznick Studio, Fort Lee, N. J.

— P —

PAGET, Francis; b. 1861; educ. Wellington College, completed France and Germany, graduate of Sandhurst, service in India, lieut., famous march to Kandahar; toured world, prospected in Klondike; in Boer War with Ian Hamilton's column; connected with moving picture theatre in Montana; there wrote Miss Glaum's play, "A Law Unto Herself," continuity writer for Robert Brunton Studios, 5341 Melrose ave., Los Angeles, Cal.

PALMER, Frederick; b. Belmont, N. Y., 1881; educ. Cornell Univ.; early career, newspaper man, editor, actor; screen career, since 1914, Selig, Nestor, Keystone, Vogue, Universal, Triangle, Wm. Fox. At present, president Palmer Photoplay Corp., 570-599 I. W. Hellman Bldg., Los Angeles. Home ad., 1317 Liberty st., Los Angeles, Calif.

PARK, Ida May (Mrs. Joseph De Grasse), also director; b. Los Angeles, Cal.; educ. San Francisco, Cal.; stage career, 12 yrs. leading woman in support of well-known stars; screen career, Pathe and Universal ("Fires of Rebellion," "Bondage," "Model's Confession," "Bread," "Vanity Pool," "The Amazing Wife"), Lew Cody special ("The Butterfly Man"), now own producing company, Park-De Grasse special prods. Home ad., 213 W. Windsor Rd., Glendale, Cal.

PARKER, William; b. Walla Walla, Wash., Sept. 17, 1886; early career, newspaper reporter, editorial writer and editor; screen career, American, Universal, Ince, Fox, J. D. Hampton; recent stories and continuities "Money Isn't Everything," "What Every Woman Wants," "Bare-Fisted Gallagher," "The Third Eye," Pathe serial, Universal special, "The Virgin of Stamboul," etc.; now associated with King W. Vidor. Home ad., 1146 Arapahoe st., Los Angeles, Cal.

PARSONS, Agnes, scenario writer and film editor; b. Burlington, Iowa; screen career, scenario writer for Fox ("Melting Millions"), Triangle ("Wild Sumac"), Educational Films ("Citizens in the Making"). Ad., 812 Majestic Bldg., Los Angeles, Cal.; phone 61245.

PHILIPPS, Henry Albert; b. Brooklyn, N. Y., Jan. 28, 1880; early career, assoc. ed. Metropolitan Magazine, lecturer, Brooklyn Inst. of Arts, assoc. ed. Motion Picture Magazine, etc., author of "The Plot of the Short Story," "The Photodrama," "Art in Short Story Narration," "The Universal Plot Catalogue," "The Feature Photoplay," "A Complete Course in Short Story Writing," and other books; original photoplays, "Heiress for a Day," "The Primitive Woman," "The Self-Made Widow," "The Mate of the Sally Ann," "Bonnie Annie Laurie," "The Love Burglar," "Bolshevism," "Pierre Le Grand." Ad., Larchmont, N. Y.

PIGGOTT, William; b. Liverpool, Eng., 1876; educ. Liverpool Coll.; early career, ranching in Canada, business in Winnipeg; screen career, free lance writer, Vitagraph, 1913, with American, 1914, author of "Daddy's Soldier Boy," "Tainted Money" (Vitagraph), adapted Van Loan series, "Buck-Parvin," 'End of the Road' (American), Fox ("The Price of Silence"). Now with Universal, continuity editor. Home ad., 2260 Beechwood Drive, Hollywood, Cal.

SCENARIO WRITERS AND EDITORS

PLYMPTON, George Holcombe; b. Brooklyn, N. Y., 1889; educ. Brooklyn Boys' High, Cooper Union; early career, business and magazine work; screen career, Vitagraph (for 2½ yrs., writing many orig. one-reel comedies and five-reel picturizations, including "Soldiers of Chance," "Dead Shot Baker," "The Tenderfoot," "The Home Trail"); wrote and prod. "The Making of Good Citizens" and "Fire Fighters" for 'Frisco Exposition; Metro-Drew comedies and adaptations for Lasky; 1919, 1st Lieut. Q. M. C., U. S. A. Ad., 2100 Highland ave., Hollywood, Cal.

POLAND, Joseph F.; b. Waterbury, Conn., Sept. 4, 1892; educ. St. John's Coll. and Erasmus Hall, Brooklyn, N. Y.; screen career, Kalem (adapted and in part wrote orig. "Stingaree" series), Vitagraph (wrote "Hesper of the Mountains," etc.), Art Drama ("The Cloud"), Fox ("Patsy"), Pathe ("Miss Nobody"), Universal ("The Spitfire of Sevilla"), author over 100 photoplays. Hght., 5, 11; wght., 145; hair dark, eyes gray. Studio, Universal City, Cal.

POWELL, A. Van Buren; b. Macon, Ga., Mar. 31, 1886; educ. Macon and N. Y. C. pub. and high schls.; early career, writer of special articles; screen career, Biograph, Kalem, Colonial, Vitagraph and free lance; author of "Everybody's Girl," "The Girl Woman," etc.; now editor "Scripts and Scribes" dept., the Billboard. Ad., 130 St. Paul's Place, Brooklyn, N. Y.

PRINTZLAU, Olga; b. Phila., 1893; educ. there and Los Angeles; screen career, Edison, Majestic, American, Universal, Ince, Lasky ("Believe Me, Xantippe," "One More American," "Why Change Your Wife?" "Jack Straw," "Prince Chap," "Peg o' My Heart"), Fox ("Lawless Love"), Blue Bird ("City of Tears"), Brentwood ("Turn in the Road"). Ad., Lasky Film Co., 6265 de Longpre ave., Hollywood, Cal.; home ad., 5846 Harold Way, Los Angeles, Cal.

PROCTOR, George DuBois; educ. Andover and Yale; motion picture editor of The Morning Telegraph; editor Motion Picture News; newspaper man and writer; Capellani Prod. ("The Fortune Teller," "Held in Trust," "Little Mother Hubbard"), Edgar Lewis Prod. ("Other Men's Shoes"), 10 Lasky prods., 6 for Triangle and 8 for World. Ad., Green Room Club, N. Y.

— R —

RAMSEY, Alicia; educ. at Orford Coll., London, and Leipsig; has written short stories pub. in chief magazines in England and America; two novels, "Mortimer Dixon" and "Miss Elizabeth Gibbs"; many plays alone or in collaboration with husband, Rudolph de Cordova, produced in London and U. S., among them are "Monsieur de Paris," "Edmund Kean," "As a Man Sows," "Isla, the Chosen," "Honor," "Bridge," "John Hudson's Wife," "The Mandarin," "The Shadow Behind the Throne," "The Quicksands"; 7 melodramas produced at London Hippodrome; many original scenarios produced by Famous Players, Metro, Vitagraph, etc., in which Line Cavalieri, Alice Joyce, Billie Burke, etc., have appeared. Ad., 45 Beaver st., N. Y.

REARDON, Mark S., 3d; b. Brooklyn, N. Y.; educ. Columbia Univ., Adelphi Coll., St. Francis Xavier Coll., N. Y. Law Schl.; early career, lawyer and author, wrote "The Last Laugh," "Trapped," "Romance of a Day," etc.; screen career, author of "In Wolf's Clothing," "Her Husband's Friend," "New Love and the Old," etc., 1st lieut. adj. A. E. F. 1918-19, now gov. atty. War Dept.; latest literary work "The Family Album." Home ad., 170 Keap st., Brooklyn, N. Y.; bus. ad., War Dept., Washington. D. C.

REED, Katharine Speer; early career, magazine writer and special newspaper work in Boston, Phila. and N. Y.; also advertising exper.; screen career, has written O. Henry stories, original and adapted comedies, "Let's Elope" with Marguerite Clark, "Greater Than Fame" and "Just a Wife" for Selznick, and about 40 others. Now with Harry Rapf's Selznick prods., Los Angeles. Home ad., 143 W. 69th st., N. Y. C.; Columbus 7963.

REED, Luther A.; b. Berlin, Wis., 1888; educ. Columbia Univ., Mo.; early career, 5½ yrs. with N. Y. Herald, 2d lieut. infantry, U. S. A. 8 mos.; 2 yrs. Universal and Metro (wrote "In for Thirty Days," "A Favor to a Friend," "The Ameteur Adventuress"), Fox, Ince ("Behind the Door," "Under the Surface," "Let's Be Fashionable"); co-author stage comedy "The Wonderful Workshop," produced by Erlanger & Golden. Ad., 29 Claremont ave., N. Y. C.; studio, Thos. H. Ince, Culver City, Calif.

REID, Donald Gordon; b Tarrytown, N. Y.; screen career, Vitagraph, World, U. S. Division of Films, Pathe, Arden ("The Immigrant," "The Challenge Accepted," "The Ordeal," "The Leavening"). Home ad., 365 E. 209th st., N. Y.

REID, James Halleck; b. Homer, Ind.; screen career, editor scenario dept. Universal, Vitagraph ("The Seventh Son," "The Victoria Cross"), Reliance ("Father Beauclaire," "Before the White Man Came," "Cripple Creek"), Paramount (played in "The Two Brides"), National ("The Confession"). Home ad., Coytesville, N. J.; office, 1600 Broadway, N. Y.

REYNOLDS, Stephen Allen; b. Boston, Mass.; educ. private sch.; early career, adventurer, soldier of fortune, governmental inspector, author; screen career, Reliance ("The Master Cracksman"), etc. Ad., Fox Film Corp., Hollywood, Calif.

RICE, Elmer L.; b. N. Y.; graduate N. Y. Law Sch. '12; member N. Y. Bar, author of "On Trial," "For the Defense," "The Iron Cross," and other plays. Ad., 1732 Grenshaw blvd., Los Angeles, Calif.; prone 75084; studio, Goldwyn, Culver City, Calif.

RICH, H. Thompson; educ. grad. Dartmouth Coll.; early career, teacher, newspaper man, magazine writer; later editor-in-chief The Forum Magazine; left magazine field to serve in war; screen career, writer of original stories and continuity; American Cinema Corp. ("A Woman Strays"); with Metro Pictures Corp.' scenario dept., Hollywood, Calif. Permanent ad., 43 Donaldson ave., Rutherford. N. J.

RIPLEY, Arthur D., also cutter; b. Townshend, Vt.; educ. Morris High, N. Y.; screen career, film editor for Kalem, Vitagraph, Fox ("Salome," "Cleopatra"), Metro ("The Spender," "Peggy Does Her Darndest"), under supervision of Geo. D. Baker, now assisting Henry Kolker with development of his scripts and editing his productions. Ad., 770 Hollywood blvd., Hollywood, Calif.

RITCHEY, Will M.; b. Evansville, Ind.; educ. Univ. of Wooster, Ohio; early career, newspaper editor for 12 yrs.; screen career, Selig, Lubin, Vitagraph, Balboa, Astra, Famous Players ("Everywoman," "Told in the Hills," "The Dub," "Alias Mike Moran," "Something to Do," "The Winning Girl," "Pettigrew's Girl," ("Rose o' the River," "A Sporting Chance"). Ad., 929 Galena ave., Pasadena, Calif.; Colo. 1273; studio, Famous Players-Lasky.

ROLANDS, George K., also director and film editor; educ. Baltimore City Coll.; stage career, actor with Frohman Cos., including "Peter Pan," "Samson," "Flag Lieut.," "Mons. Beaucaire," with Maude Adams in "Chanticleer," Jas. K. Hackett Co., Marie Doro, etc.; screen career, N. Y. Producing Co., author and director ("Trapped," "Lure of New York"), ("Web of Life" featuring James Cruze), associate dir. Schomer Film Co. ("Ruling Passions"), Emily Stevens in "The Sacred Flame," also special editor for all Exclusive Features and Canyon Pictures Corp. Ad., 1001 Faile st., N. Y.; Intervale 1465.

RUSSELL, L. Case; b. Yankton, S. D.; writer of verse, stories, etc.; special writer Motion Picture Magazine; author of over 100 produced photoplays, "The Light Within," "Black Butterfly," "To the Death," "Soul of a Magdalene," "Merely Players," "Two-Edged Sword," several Sydney Drew comedies; recent releases, "Water Lily," "Fruits of Passion," "Root of Evil"; at present writing and supervising 12 Blazed Trail Prods., featuring John Lowell, those released being "When Big Dan Rides," "Hidden Pit," "Danger Patrol," "Across the Line," "Tell Tale Tracks," "Where Peril Lurks," "Code of the North." Ad., Blazed Trail Prods., Green Lake P. O., Fulton Co., N. Y.

— S —

SCHROCK, Raymond L.; b. Goshen, Ind., 1892; educ. Univ. of Ill.; stage career, director for stk.; screen career, Gauntier, ed. and dir. ("Twilight"), Universal, scen. ed. ("The Man Inside," "Elusive Isabel," "Code of His Ancestors," "The Finer Metal"), World ("Her Hour," "A Leap to Fame," "His Royal Highness"), Fox ("Caught in the Act," "Splendid

Malefactor," "Way to Happiness," "The Winning Stroke"), Frohman ("The She Wolf"). Home ad., 601 W. 139th st.; Aud. 2320.

SCHROEDER, Doris; b. Long Island, N. Y.; educ. Brooklyn Girls High Sch.; screen career, 9 yrs. motion picture work, adaptations, "My Fighting Gentleman," "Charity Castle," for American, "Price of Applause," "Love's Pay Day," for Triangle, "The Little Boss," for Vitagraph, "My Unmarried Wife," "The Trembling Hour," "Under Suspicion," "Pals," "Jewel" for Universal. Ad., 4515 Russell ave., Los Angeles, Calif.; Holly 737; studio, Universal.

SCOTT, Leroy; b. Fairmount, Ind., 1875; A. B., Ind. Univ. 1897; newspaper work, asst. editor Woman's Home Companion 1900-1; has devoted entire time to writing since 1904; written novels, short stories, stage dramatization of own fiction; feature prods. made with Norma Talmadge, Anita Stewart, etc.; member Eminent Authors Pictures, Inc., producing and releasing through Goldwyn; pictures made under own personal supervision, to be released as Leroy Scott Features; member The Players, West Side Tennis. Ad., 49 W. 85th st., N. Y.

SERPICO, James; b. Napoli, Italy, 1896; educ. there and Rossi private coll., N. Y. C.; early career, 4 yrs. asst. mgr. Electric and Savoy theatres, Madison, N. J.; screen career, adapted "The Great Sacrifice," "The Fluffy Philly," "Hounds of the Underworld," "The Better Road," "The Home Brand," "The Paved Road," for Star Pictures, Marquette Film Corp., Purity Pictures, Madison Film Corp., Paragon Art Pictures, etc. Served in U. S. Army, mustered out May, 1919. Ad., 23 Central ave., Madison, N. J.

SHAW, Stanley; b. Boston, Mass.; newspaper writer and editor, advertising, author many short stories, novelettes and magazine serials, "Jungle Heart," Vitagraph, "Fighting Destiny," Harry Morey, "That Quiet Night," Truart Pictures. Ad., Camp Wildwood, South Hanson, Mass.

SHERWIN, Louis; scenario writer, editor of scripts, films and titles; b. London; educ. Charterhouse, England, and privately on the continent; early career, 8 yrs. dramatic critic N. Y. Evening Globe, contributor to American, Metropolitan, Vanity Fair, etc. Ad., Goldwyn Studio, Culver City, Calif.

SLOANE, Paul H.; educ. N. Y. Univ., B. S., also N. Y. U. Sch. of Journalism; screen career, started with Edison studios in 1914, film editor, scenario editor and director; scenario writer with Pathe; wrote Rainbow Comedies; was in U. S. A. service; Vitagraph, now writing original stories for Fox. Ad., 783 Beck st., N. Y. C.; Melrose 4950.

SLOCUM, Daisy Mayer; b. Cleveland, O.; educ. there; stage career, traveled through the British Isles, S. Africa, Australia and Continent in vaud.; in drama, light opera, vaud. in U. S.; screen career, wrote for Selig, Vitagraph, Frontier, American. Home ad., The Parkview, Ansel road, Cleveland, Ohio., or care J. Allen Boone, N. Y.

SMITH, R. Cecil; b. 1880, Parkersburg, W. Va.; educ. Univ. of Chicago; stage career, juveniles and characters in several stk. cos., mgr. Chutes Park, Denver, Colo., mgr. Tuileries Park, Denver; screen career, played character roles in Ince prods. for 2 yrs.; Ince-Triangle scenario dept., "Master of His Home," "Madcap Madge," "Claws of the Hun," "The Busher," "Home Breaker," "Out of the Night," "L'Apache," "His Wife's Money." Home ad., Culver City, Cal.; studio ad., Selznick Studios, Fort Lee, N. J.

SOMERVILLE, Roy; b. New Orleans, La.; educ. Trinity Coll.; early career, 12 yrs. newspaper experience, wrote number of vaud. sketches, author of "The Prairie Waifs," originator of "Kid Ryan" series, etc.; screen career, Fine Arts ("The Little Yank," "An Innocent Magdalene," "Acquitted," "Reggie Mixes In," "Children in the House," "The Devil's Needle," "Hitting the Trail," "Embarrassment of Riches," "The Danger Games," "Pursuit of Polly," "What Shall We Do With It?"), Hodkinson ("The Bandbox"), Fox ("Eastward Ho!"). Home ad., 320 St. Nicholas ave., N. Y. C.; tel. Morningside 5310.

SPENCE, Ralph H.; b. Houston, Texas, 1889; formerly vice-pres. and gen. mgr. Houston Daily Telegram, correspondent with Pershing on Mexican border; screen career, Mack Sennett, Sunshine Comedies, Fox ("The Yankee Way," "This Is the Life," "The Kid Is Clever," "I'll Say So"), for Geo. Walsh ("A Camouflage Kiss"), for June Caprice ("Smiles") for Lee children; also director, writes "Newsettes" for Fox News. Ad., Fox Films Corp., N. Y., or Hotel Astor.

STARR, Helen; b. New Milford, Conn.; educ. Stanford Univ., Calif.; stage career, stock in Worcester, Mass., Mt. Vernon, N. Y., Lawrence, Mass., Waterbury, Conn.; toured Keith circuit with Marie Doro, De Wolf Hopper, "Within the Law"; screen career, publicity dept. Mutual, N. Y. Script editor Universal 1 yr., scenario writer Universal 1 yr., American, U. S. Secret Service during war; now Goldwyn scenario dept. Ad., 1340 Douglas st., Los Angeles, Calif.; Pico 2254; studio, Goldwyn, Culver City, Calif.

STATTER, Arthur F.; b. Carlisle, England; educ. England and Cornell Coll., Mt. Vernon, Iowa; newspaper man, asst. secretary U. S. Treasury in Roosevelt administration, scenario writer Universal, Triangle, Ince; now with Jesse D. Hampton Prod.

STEARNS, Myron Morris; b. Hartford, Conn., 1884; educ. Stanford Univ. (grad. 1906); early career, 9 yrs. newspaper work; largely with Los Angeles Times, 3 yrs. magazine work, fiction, articles and verse, Colliers, Century, Harper's, and many others; screen career, American Film Co.; recently scenario writer Sunset Studios; now scenario editor Griffith Studios. Home ad., West st., Mamaroneck, N. Y.; bus. ad., 720 Longacre Bldg., N. Y.

STECK, H. Tipton; b. Chicago, Ill.; educ. business coll. in Chicago; early career, 2 yrs. reporter and press agent on Chicago newspapers; wrote for magazines; screen career, 10 yrs. with Essanay as scenario editor, manager of production and feature writer; Essanay ("Graustark"), Universal ("Outcasts of Poker Flat," "Riders of the Law," "Gift of the Desert" with Harry Carey, "The Incorrigible" with Priscilla Dean), Tourneur ("Broken Butterfly"), First National ("Duke of Chimmey Butte," "The Turning Point"), author of over 500 produced photoplays. Ad., 1741 N. Cherokee ave., Hollywood, Calif.; Holly 4428.

STERNBERG, Jo; screen career, 3 yrs. World Film in charge of all film, asst. dir. to Emile Chautard; connected with General Staff, U. S. A., for 2 yrs. in charge of "Training of the Soldier" film series; film editor and laboratory supervisor for Wm. A. Brady. Ad., care of Wm. A. Brady, The Playhouse, W. 48th st., N. Y.

STEWART, Charles Conger; b. N. Y. C.; supervisor and improver of picture shows in Chicago; lecturer on pictures and fiction; writer of picture and short stories; most of fiction pub. in Munsey and Street and Smith publications; chief reader and analytical expert for Fox. Home ad., Ditmas ave., E. Elmhurst, L. I., N. Y.; studio ad., Fox Film Corp., N. Y.

STONE, Le Roy; film editor; b. San Francisco, 1894; educ. Univ. of California; m. p. career, associated with Thomas H. Ince since 1913. Experience covers practically all lines of production. Recently toured East in behalf of Ince Productions, making study of presentations in theatres, inspecting exchanges and making exhaustive investigations of laboratories of New York and New Jersey. Personally edits all Wm. S. Hart Productions. Home ad., 2207 West 11th st., Los Angeles, Calif.; studio, Hart Prods., Hollywood, Cal.

STUART, Kathryne; educ. Columbia Univ.; early career, publicity and journalistic exper. for a yr.; Famous Players ("Erstwhile Susan," "His Bridal Night," "Career of Katherine Bush," "His House in Order," etc.). Home ad., 34 W. 51st st., N. Y. C.; studio, Famous Players-Lasky Corp., N. Y.

SULLIVAN, C. Gardner; b. Stillwater, Minn., 1886; educ. Univ. Minnesota; early career, newspaper man; screen career, Edison, Ince ("A Corner in Colleens," "The Thoroughbred," "Civilization"), Triangle-Ince ("Happiness"), ("The Girl Glory"), Ince ("Civilization"), Triangle ("Peggy," "Hell's Hinges," "Those Who Pay"), Artcraft ("Selfish Yates," "Shark Monroe," "Branding Broadway"), Ince-Paralta ("Love Me," "Naughty, Naughty," "The Vamp," "The Accursed Town"), Paramount ("The Haunted Bedroom," "Market of Souls," "Virtuous Thief," "Stepping Out"), Artcraft ("Poppy Girl's Husband"). Ad., Ince, Culver City, Cal.

SUTTON, T. Shelley; b. Hanford, Calif., 1877; educ. Univ. of Ill.; early career, 18 yrs. newspaper experience; author of many short sto-

ries and more than 30 vaud. successes; screen career, 6 yrs. writing for Pathe, Lubin, Essanay, Selig and Universal; 2 yrs. staff writer for Universal, writing Westerns for Harry Carey, Neal Hart, etc.; "The Grudge," "The Cougar," "A Texas Sphinx," "Fighting Blood," "Girl From Guthrie," "Forbidden Soil," "The Taint," "Phantom Gold," "Betty's Bandit," "The Straggler," etc. Home ad., 901 West 58th st., Los Angeles, Calif.; Vermont 925; studio, scenario editor, Coburn Prods., Inc., Hollywood, Calif.

—T—

TAYLOR, Rex; b. Des Moines, Iowa; educ. Hamilton Inst. and Iowa State Coll.; early career, mining engineering, life insurance; stage career, rep., vaud.; screen career, Goldwyn ("Leave It to Susan," orig. and continuity, "Strictly Condential," "The Wrong Door," adaptations), Universal ("The Love Swindle," "Beans," "She Hired a Husband," original), Vitagraph ("Miss Ambition," "Nymph of the Foothills," originals). Ad., 1916 Vista Del Mar, Hollywood, Calif.; phone 579363.

TAYLOR, Sam; b. N. Y. C., Aug. 13, 1894; educ. Fordham Univ., 1915; film editor of Kalem 1916, in 1917 for Universal; in charge of scenario and film editing depts. of motion picture division of Medical Corps, U. S. A. 1918; feature continuity writer on Vitagraph scenario staff 1919, adapted "The Gamblers," "In Honor's Web," "Over the Garden Wall," etc. Ad., 14 Butler pl., Brooklyn, N. Y.

TERHUNE, Albert Payson; b. Newark, N. J., 1872; educ. Columbia Univ., Paris, Geneva and Florence; early career, explorer, newspaper and magazine writer, novelist, editor, etc.; screen career, Famous Players, Pathe, Gaumont, etc.; author of "Dollars and the Woman," "The Years of the Locust," novelized "Red Circle" for Pathe, "Crimson Stain" for Consolidated; 1919, author of "Once a Mason," "The Amateur Liar," "The Night of the Dub," for the Sidney Drews and Ernest True; "The Wildcat" for Frank Keenan; "Driftwood" for Roland West; "The Lotus Eater" for Hearst's International; played character role in World's "The Love Defender." Ad., Sunny Bank, Pompton Lakes, N. J.

THEW, Harvey F.; b. Mankato, Minn., 1883; educ. Univ. of Minn.; early career, newspaper man; screen career, Famous Players ("Seventeen," "Plow Girl," "The Shuttle," "Jules of the Strong Heart"), Universal ("Delicious Little Devil," "Beach Comber"), George Beban ("Hearts of Men"), Jack Pickford ("Bill Apperson's Boy"), Goldwyn ("Duds," "Man in Lower Ten"), etc. Home ad., 1768 Las Palmas, Hollywood, Calif.; studio, Goldwyn.

THOMPSON, Hamilton; b. Conn.; early career, newspaper man and magazine editor; managed fir Alaska magazine; screen career, Fox Film Corp., publicity and adv. dept., at present scenario editor ("Bonnie Annie Laurie," "When They Come Back," "Swat the Spy," "The Brain Master" (serial), "Me and Capt. Kidd"). Ad., 905 Seventh ave., N. Y.

TODD, Robert Lee; b. Springfield, Ill., 1895; educ. Hot Springs, Ark., stage expert with Howard Thurston, magician; screen career, Keystone, L-Ko, Ince, Paralta, Dougles Fairbanks ("He Comes Up Smiling"). Home ad., 8475 Francisco st., Los Angeles, Cal.

TYLER, G. Vere; b. Richmond, Va., educ. Richmond and Europe; early career, novelist, dramatist, essayist and psychological fictionist; scen. writer; has written several vaud. successes, society novelettes and short stories for Smart Set magazine; contributor to Town Topics, also editorial columns of New York American and other Hearst papers; screen career, "A Huntress of Men" (Universal), "The Wax Model" (Pallas-Paramount), engaged by Joseph M. Schenck (Selznick) to write script, several photoplays forthcoming. Home ad., 105 E. 15th st., N. Y.; Stuyvesant 120.

—U—

UNSELL, Eve; educ. Emerson Coll., Boston; early career, newspaper work; screen career, free lance scenario writer, "Are You a Mason?" Famous Players ("Eyes of the Soul," "The Parisian Wife," "Out of the Shadow"), Goldwyn ("Cup of Fury"), Realart ("Sinners"), Adnac ("The Great Shadow"); organized scenario dept. Famous Players-Lasky British producers, London, England. Ad., 272 Lincoln road, Brooklyn, N. Y.; Flatbush 304.

—V—

VAN LOAN, H. H.; b. Athens, N. Y., 1885; educ. Yale prep. and Columbia Univ.; early career, 3 yrs. publicity mgr. for Univ.; started first moving picture column in N. Y. C., 1914, "Flashes in the Screen" in N. Y. Globe, also in 200 other newspapers; screen career, author of "Vive La France," Universal ("The Beautiful Beggar"), Select ("The New Moon"), Vitagraph ("The Highest Trump," "A Rogue's Romance"), Pathe ("The Third Eye" serial), Fox ("The Speed Maniac," "The Last Night," "Three Gold Coins," "The Red Terror"), Anita Stewart ("Danger"), Maurice Tourneur ("The Great Redeemer"). Ad., 121 West Eulalia st., Glendale, Calif.

VAN PETTEN, Stacey A.; b. Dec. 11, 1883, Peoria, Ill.; educ. Grinnell, Iowa, 2 yrs. at Iowa Coll.; early career, 10 yrs. exper. as court reporter in criminal and civil courts of Chicago; author of numerous short stories. magazine articles, adv. booklets, etc.; for past several yrs. specialized in scenario writing, and in capacity of scenario editor or as free lance has written many orig. stories and continuities for leading producers; at present scenario editor of Atlas Educational Film Co., Chicago, Ill. Home ad., 1516 Hood ave., Chicago, Ill.

—W—

WALLACE C. R.; screen career, Keystone, Universal, Triangle, Robertson-Cole, Fox. Home ad., Clark Hotel, Los Angeles, Calif.; Bway 7200; studio, Fox, Hollywood, Cal.

WEADOCK, Louis; b. Saginaw, Mich.; educ. Notre Dame Univ.; early career, newspaper business in N. Y., Cnicago, Boston, Phila., San Francisco, Los Angeles and Grand Rapids, Mich. Home ad., 1821 N. Normandie ave., Hollywood, Calif.; studio, Douglas Fairbanks.

WHITCOMB, Daniel Frederick; b. Louisville, Ky., 1880; educ. private school, Boston; early career, fiction writer, reporter; screen career, scenario writer since 1910, free lance and on staff of Universal, Keystone, Fox, Balboa, American, Ince and Goldwyn; author of more than 200 original features, "Little Mary Sunshine," "Shadows and Sunshine," "Told at Tyilight," American, "Game of Wits" and "Bride's Silence," Gail Kane; Mission, "Send Him Away With a Smile," and "What Every Mother Knows," Gloria Joy. Permanent home address, 1611 McCadden place, Hollywood, Cal.

WHITTAKER, Charles Everard; b. Dublin, Ireland, 1878; educ. Owens Coll., Manchester, and New Coll., Oxford; early career, journalism, traveled in Africa, Asia and all over Europe; screen career, adapted "The Whip," "The Pride of the Clan" (Mary Pickford), "Arms and the Girl" ((Billie Burke), "On the Quiet," "Here Comes the Bride" (John Barrymore), "La Tosca," "Resurrection," "Fedora," "Her Final Reckoning" (Pauline Frederick), "The House of Glass," "The Claw," "Eyes of Youth" (Clara Kimball Young), "Partners of the Night" (Eminent Authors, Inc.), "Mothers of Men" (Edward Jose), "The White Heather," "The Life Line," "The Broken Butterfly" (Maurice Tourneur), author of "Woman" and "Fires of Faith." Ad., Garson Studio, Los Angeles.

WILKINSON, Jas.; b. Los Angeles, Cal.; educ. there; opr. in Los Angeles theatres; 2 yrs. with Mutual Film Co.; five serials and five features with J. P. McGowan and Helen Holmes, 2 serials with Eddy Polo at Universal, asst. dir. to Polo on European trip, at present with Christy Cabanne. Ad., Universal Film Mfg. Co., Universal City, Cal.

WILLETS, Gilson; b. N. Y. C.; educ. there; author; 20 yrs. globe-trotter in quest of special stories, Russia, Egypt and Arabia; special sled journey to Arctic Circle, north of Finland and Sweden; 3 mos. trip to India for story of plague; member Harriman Expedition in Mexico, etc.; screen career, author of first moving picture serial, "The Adventures of Kathleen," also author of "Hands Up," "Tiger's Trail," "Adventures of Ruth," "The Double Cross," Pathe serials; "The First Fair," Pathe feature. Home ad., Algonquin Hotel, N. Y. C.; studio, Pathe, N. Y.

SCENARIO WRITERS AND EDITORS

WILLIAMS, Harry H.; b. Minnesota; educ. there; author, actor and song writer for 20 yrs., also motion picture director for Mack Sennett, Triangle, etc. Home ad., Hotel Waldorf, Venice, Cal.; studio, Fatty Arbuckle, Culver City, Cal.

WILLIS, F. McGrew; b. Iowa, 1890; stage career, rep.; screen career, free lance writer, then Pathe, Mutual, Balboa, Universal ("The Bride's Awakening" with Mae Murray, "The Phantom Melody"). Head of F. McGrew Willis Institute, 418 Wright and Callender Bldg., Los Angeles, Cal.

WILSON, Chas. Jerome, Jr.; b. N. Y. C.; author of first juvenile feature released through World ("Jess of the Mountain Country"), Triangle ("The Greater Law," "Her Decision," "Those Restless Ones"), Goldwyn ("Spotlight Sadie"), Fox ("White Lies"), Universal ("Breath of the Gods," "Prince of Avenue A," "Outdone," "Yellow Orchid"). Home ad., 35 W. Mountain st., Pasadena, Cal.; studio, Universal.

WING, William E., scenario writer and editor; b. Maine; educ. Maine and Minn. and Univ. of So. California; screen career, Biograph, Fine Arts ("Casey at the Bat," "Sold for Marriage," "The Microscope Mystery"), Vitagraph ("Little Miss Adventure," "The Spirit of the Range"), National ("Tarzan of the Apes"), "Lure of the Circus," Polo serial; "Elmo the Mighty" serial; "Trails of Doom," Franklyn Farnum serial. Ad., 1543 Council st., Los Angeles, Cal.; Main 8550.

WOODS, Frank E.; early career, on staff of N. Y. Dramatic Mirror as "Spectator," published first review of motion pictures, afterward chief editor Mirror; screen career, Kinemacolor, Biograph, Reliance-Majestic, Fine Arts, wrote ("The Children Pay," "The Bad Boy," "Betsy's Burglar"), author of "The Little School Ma'am," prod. mgr. for Lasky for past 3 yrs. Ad., Lasky, Hollywood.

WOODS, Walter; mgr. and director of stock cos. at St. Louis, Cincinnati, Richmond, Brockton, Lowell, Waltham and Salem, Mass., and St. John, N. B., author of plays, including "Billy, the Kid," "Girl of Eagle Ranch," "Within Four Walls," "The Sunset Gun," "The Reformers," etc. Ad., Famous Players-Lasky Co., Hollywood, Cal.

— Y —

YOHALEM, George M.; b. N. Y. C.; screen career, 5 yrs. in scenario and title departments of Famous Players, now writing scenarios for Selznick Pictures. Ad., care of Selznick, N. Y.

YOUNG, Harold; b. Salt Lake City, Utah; educ. there; early career, short-story writer, essayist, etc.; screen career, wrote "The Gringo" for Overland Feature Film Corp. Studio ad., Art Unit Studios, Los Angeles, Cal.; home ad., 2922 So. Flower st., Los Angeles, Cal.; So. 5537.

YOUNG, Howard Irving; educ. N. Y. Univ. and Sorbonne Univ. of Paris; screen career, scen. ed. Crystal, ed. Reliance; staff writer, Kalem, Pathe, Metro; author of "Hearts in Exile," "The Mission of Morrison," "The Apaches of Paris," "The Lotos Woman," "Sacred Silence," Fox ("The Steel King"), World; now editor Paramount Screen Magazine, Famous Players-Lasky Corp., 1st Lieut. Inf., A. E. F., January, 1918, to July, 1919. Clubs: Secretary Green Room Club, Dramatic Committee of Authors' League, Photodramatists, Transportation, Psi Upsilon Club, Cercle Interallie (Paris). Ad., Green Room Club, N. Y.

YOUNG, Waldemar; educ. Stanford Univ., Cal.; early career, sporting editor San Francisco Chronicle, dramatic critic S. F. Examiner and S. F. Chronicle, mgr. on tour with Frank Fogarty, advance agent Gertrude Hoffman, played Orpheum Circuit in "When Caesar Ran a Paper"; screen career, Universal as scenario editor and writer, "The Man Trap," "Flirting with Death," "The Show Down," "The Clean Up," "The Car of Chance," "The Light of Victory," "Cherries Are Ripe," "Pirate Gold," "Fire Flingers," "Spitfire of Seville," "Sundown Trail"). Ad., home, 1552 Cassil Pl., Los Angeles.

YOUNGER, A. P.; b. Sacramento, Cal.; educ. San Francisco; screen career, "Fair and Warmer," "The Walk-Offs" for May Alison, "Eliza Comes to Stay" for Viola Dana. Home ad., 1723 W. 9th st., Los Angeles, Cal.; Wil. 497; studio, Metro.

— Z —

ZELLNER, Arthur J., scenario writer and film editor; b. Memphis, Tenn.; educ. Louisiana State Univ.; early career, magazine and newspaper writer; at present with Metro Specials. Ad., 1762 Ivar ave., Hollywood, Cal.; phone 57170.

ZELLNER, Lois; b. Macon, Ga.; educ. private schools and tutors; screen career, free lance writer, groundwork on one-reel comedies, two yrs. writing features, Paramount ("The Innocent Lie," "As Men Love," "Giving Becky a Chance"), Thos. H. Ince ("The Little Brother"), Pathe ("Over the Hill"), Astra ("The Girl from Bohemia," special feature for Mrs. Vernon Castle), Bluebird ("Lady Eldone's Daughter"), Goldwyn ("The Odd Pearl"). Ad., 1762½ Ivar, Los Angeles, Cal.; phone 57170.

CINEMATOGRAPHERS

— A —

ABEL, David; b. Russia, 1884; educ. Russia; screen career, American, Fine Arts, Goldwyn ("Thais," "The Splendid Sinner"), Special Artcraft ("The Hun Within"), Talmadge Co. ("The Heart of Wetona," "The Probation Wife," "Nancy Lee"). Home ad., Hotel Theresa, N. Y.; studio, 318 East 48th st., N. Y. C.

ABOUSSLEMAN, Charles; b. Mount Lebanon, Syria, 1888; educ. French Coll. of the Lazarist Fathers in Syria; screen career, Eclair, Pathe, Gaumont and Universal; specialized in outside and scenic photography; made official Industrial Films for Bolivian Govt. in S. America; speaks French, English, Spanish, Turkish and Arabic. Member Cinema Camera Club. Ad., home, 620 54th st., Brooklyn.

ADAMS, William S.; b. N. Y.; educ. there; screen career, Vitagraph ("The Juggernaut," "Shadows of the East," "The Wreck," featuring Anita Stewart), Blackton ("Moonshine Trail," "Dawn," "Tinsel Triumphs," featuring Sylvia Breamer). Ad. home, 1645 East 9th st., Brooklyn, N. Y.; phone Midwood 6612.

ALDER, William F.; b. Oil City, Pa.; educ. Lewis Inst. Technology, grad. from Illinois State Univ. as registered engineer; screen career, with Bell and Howell, camera makers, installed first Gaumont chronophone for Herbert Blache, in 1907, organized Chicago Scenic Stage Lighting Co., with American as cameraman, then to Universal, Sterling, Quality and Ince, successfully experimented with stereoptic and 3-color effects. Over the Rhine Co. with Julian Eltinge; in Orient taking scenic for Universal. Member Cinema Camera Club. Home ad., 1340 Mariposa st., Los Angeles, Cal.

ALEXANDER, Frank Nesbitt; educ. Shawville High Sch. and Acad.; Cowling & Willis Business Coll., Ottawa, Inst. of Languages, Ottawa; asst. law clerk, Inland Revenue Service; road manager, Enterprise Amuse. Co.; free lance news cameraman for Universal, Pathe, International, British-Canadian Gazette. Now staff cameraman for Fox News. Permanent ad., Ottawa, Can.; Sherwood 3203.

ALEXANDER, J. Melrose; educ. Shawville Acad., Shawville, Que., Canada; official photographer for Dept. of Trade and Commerce, Government of Canada. Ad., 638 Gladstone ave., Ottawa, Can.; Sherwood 3203.

ALLEN, Albert C.; b. Nashville, Tenn., 1875; screen career, Gaumont, photographer "Crater Lake National Park," Pathe; "Pear Growing in Oregon," contributed to Gaumont's "Reel Life," News, etc.; specialist in educational, scenic, topical, wild life and scientific pictures, also Universal Screen Magazine and Fox News. Home ad., Medford, Ore.

ALLER, Joseph (Altschuler); b. Russia; educ. there and tech. schl. in N. Y. C.; screen career, professional photographer in N. Y. and Europe;

took up motion picture photography in 1904. Biograph, Mutoscope, organized Aller Laboratories at former Griffith Studios; now with D. W. Griffith as laboratory superintendent; inventor of Eastman Negative Keyed stock and film devices. Ad., 4500 Sunset Blvd., Los Angeles, Cal.

ANDRIOT, Lucien; b. Paris, France; educ. there; early exper., photographer; screen career, Pathe, Gaumont, Eclair, Peerless ("Silver Fox," "Two Lives," "The Price," "The Marked Woman," "M'liss," "The Face in the Moonlight," "Impostors," "Camille"), Paragon ("Feast of Life," "La Boheme," "Almighty Dollar"), Artcraft ("Pride of the Clan"), Select ("The Mad Lover"), Capellani Prod. ("Oh! Boy," "Virtuous Model," "The Right to Lie"), Faversham and Elliot ("The Man Who Lost Himself"). Ad., home, 7 E. 45th st., New York City.

ARNOLD, John; b. N. Y. C.; 1883; educ. U. S. A.; screen career, World, Life, Metro ("Some Bride," "Please Get Married"). Ad., Metro Studio, Hollywood, Cal.

AUGUST, Joe; b. Idaho Springs, Colo.; educ. Colo. Sch. of Mines; screen career, 6 yrs. with Ince ("Truthful Tulliver"), Para.-Artcraft ("John Petticoats"). Ad., Metro Studio, Hollywood, Cal.

— B —

BADARACCO, Jacob A.; b. 1883, Hoboken, N. J.; screen career, Universal, World, Famous Players, Pathe ("Hidden Hands" serial), at present with Taylor Holmes Prod. Co. at Biograph Studio. Member Local 557, I. A. T. S. E. Ad., 254 Manhattan ave., N. Y.; Cathedral 8540.

BAKER, Friend F.; b. Hamburg, Ia.; educ. Tabor Coll.; early career, commercial photography, also school teacher; screen career, Universal 1 yr., Ince 1 yr., back to Universal ("Love Never Dies," "The Car of Chance," "The Clean-Up"), Fox ("The Wilderness Trail," "Thieves"). Member Amer. Soc. of Cine.; home ad., 1538 Morningside Ct., Hollywood, Cal.

BARLATIER, Andre; b. France; educ. there; screen career, Eclipse, Paris, Universal, Fox, Ralph Ince, charge of Universal factory, photographed "Daughter of the Gods", Metro ("The Black Butterfly"), World ("The Burglar"), Schomer-Rose ("The Sacred Flame"). Home ad., 701 W. 178th st., N. Y. C.; studio, Goldwyn, Culver City, Cal.

BECK, Frederick; b. Budapest; photographed Willard and Johnson fight at Havana, took full charge three cameras, Astor Cup Race for Paramount, ten camera men, "The Three Musketeers," "House of Bondage," Lottie Pickford, Fulton and Dempsey fight. Ad., home, 203 W. 103rd st.; bus., Candler Bldg., N. Y.

BELL, Walter W.; b. Baldwin, Kan.; educ. Baker Univ.; screen career, now photographing Capitol Comedies. Home ad., 1868 Allesandro st., Los Angeles, Cal.; studio, National Film Corp.

BENOIT, George; screen career, Fox ("Regeneration," "The Serpent," "Carmen," "The Honor System," "The Scarlet Letter"), Quiroga Benoit Film (Argentina), ("Juan Sin Ropa"). Member I. A. E. T. S. E., local 557, 220 W. 42nd st., N. Y.; home ad., 114 W. 47th st., N. Y.; Bryant 4541.

BITZER, George W.; b. Boston, Mass.; screen career, Biograph ("Judith of Bethulia," "The Battle of Elder Bush Gulch," "The Battle"), Reliance-Majestic ("The Battle of the Sexes," "Home, Sweet Home," "The Escape"), chief cameraman for "The Birth of a Nation" and "Intolerance" made first Mutoscope in 1895; "Hearts of the World," "Scarlet Days," and other Griffith subjects. Ad., Griffith Studio, Mamaroneck, N. Y.

BITZER, J. C.; b. Boston, Mass.; Biograph, N. Y. and Cal.; Triangle, D. W. Griffith ("Intolerance"), Keystone, Screencraft, Goldwyn ("Face in the Dark," "Back to the Woods," "The Glorious Adventure"), All Good ("The Whirlwind"). Ad., Room 1603, Candler Bldg., N. Y.

BIZEUL, Jacques; b. Nantes, France; photographer for last 3 yrs. for Emile Chautard. Ad., home, West Fort Lee, N. J.; studio, Mayflower Photoplays, Inc.

BLACKELY, Walter W.; b. Boston, Mass., 1892; screen career, George Kleine Co., N. Y., and Chicago, 3 yrs., Fairmount Film Co., Gaumont ("Love Thy Neighbor"), Benjamin Chapin's Lincoln Cycle, Pathe. In service in Navy at photo. work. Home ad., 102 Congress st., N. J.

BLOUNT, Frank M.; b. Tampa, Fla.; educ. there and N. Y. C.; screen career, Lasky ("The Grim Game"), Ince ("Behind the Door," "Beneath the Surface"). Studio ad., Irvin V. Willat Co., Ince Studio, Culver City, Cal.; home ad., Box 165, Culver City, Cal.; phone West 62.

BLYTHE, Sydney C. W.; b. London, Eng.; educ. Archbishop Tennysons, London; screen career, 5 yrs. works mgr. and head photographer of Samuelson Film Co., Ltd., of England; "My Lady's Dress," "Admirable Crichton," "Valley of Peal," "Just a Girl," "Choose a Wife," "Sorrows," "Husband Hunter"; with G. B. Samuelson, Cal.

BOYLE, John William; b. Memphis, Tenn., 1892; educ. pub. schls., New Orleans, La.; screen career, organized and operated the "Item Animated Weekly," special work for Mutual Weekly, cameraman with Nola, New Orleans ("The Man Who Lost"), Metro ("Her Great Match"), Astra-Pathe ("Kick In"), Thomas Dixon's "Fall of a Nation," Fox ("Cleopatra," "Wings of the Morning"). Home ad., 5536 De Longpre ave., Hollywood, Cal.

BRAUTIGAM, Otto; b. Manchester, Eng., 1877; educ. Municipal Tech. Sch., Manchester; early career, mechanical engineer, semi-prof. photographer; specialized on lantern slides; screen career, 5 yrs. with Edison; toured Europe with Charles Brabin and players in 1913; joined Thanhouser in 1915 ("The Flight of the Duchess"), Victory Film ("The Triumph of Venus"), Blackton Prod. Member I. A. T. S. E., local 557, 220 W. 42nd st., N. Y. Ad., 310 Claremont ave., Jersey City, N. J.

BREDESEN, Henry; cameraman since 1909; educ. Beloit, Wis.; formerly with Thos. A. Edison, Inc., now with Mack Sennett. Ad., 1476 Sunset Blvd., Los Angeles, Cal.

BROENING, Henry Lyman; b. Baltimore, Md.; educ. Balto. Polytech. and Johns Hopkins Univ.; early career, lecture illustrating, stereopticon slides and photography; screen career, Monopole Film ("Carmen," "The Seat of the Fathers"), Famous Players ("Helene of the North," "Still Waters," "Silks and Satins," "Miss George Washington," etc.), Famous Players-Paramount ("The Mysterious Miss Terry"), Allan Dwan ("Soldiers of Fortune," "Luck of the Irish"). Ad., Allan Dwan Prod., Cal.

BROTHERTON, James, Long Beach, Cal.; studio, National Film Corp.

BROTHERTON, Robert, Diando Film Corp.; now Crosby Laboratory, Hollywood, Cal.

BROWN, John Webster; b. Aberdeen, Scotland, 1888; educ. there and Chicago; early career, portrait studios; screen career, American, Universal ("The Other Train," "The Divinity of Motherhood"), Universal ("Roped," "Rider of Vengeance," "Outcasts of Poker Flat," "Three Wise Men"), Empey Prod. ("Undercurrent"). Member local 557, I. A. T. S. E. Home ad., 1980 65th st., Brooklyn, N. Y.

BROWNELL, Hobart H., also director; b. Burlington, Vt.; educ. Oregon City, Ore.; started as news weekly cameraman, met manager of Mutual Film Corp. Exch. at Portland, Ore., and Seattle, Wash.; Adventure Scenics Corp. ("Just Over Yonder," "Waters of Destiny," "Flaming Ice," "The Tempest"). Home ad., 2723½ Sunset Blvd., Los Angeles, Cal.; studio ad., Adventure Scenics Corp., Los Angeles, Cal.

BROWNING, Irving; educ. N. Y. C.; screen career, 10 yrs. in motion pictures; played comedies for four years, studied portrait photography; last year has been photographing and directing High pictures and Educational subjects for Universal Screen Magazine and Health Associations; at present making single reel travels. Ad., 66 East 196th st., N. Y.

BUCHANAN, James B.; b. Monongahela, Pa.; educ. Carnegie Inst.; screen career, Sun, Clarion Features, Universal Animated Weekly, Hudson Film, Hearst-Pathe News, International Film Service; served 11 mos. in France, received 1st Lieut. commission in Photographic Division of Signal Corps. Home ad., 314 Fourth st., Monongahela, Pa.; studio ad., care of Fox Film Corp., N. Y. C.

BUFFUM, J. H.; b. Boston, Mass., 1881; trained printer, proofreader, writer, editor; A. P. representative; special writer metropolitan dailies; investigator for trade publications; entered moving picture production in 1911, laboratory expert, cameraman, ind. producer of specialties; from 1913-1919 staff cameraman for News Weeklies for Pathe, Selig-Tribune, one yr. contribution producer for Gaumont's "Reel Life," Screen Telegram and Kinograms; now director of art title production at Universal. Ad., 514 Union League Bldg., Los Angeles, Cal.

CINEMATOGRAPHERS

BULL, Clarence S., cinematographer and director of still photography; b. Montana; educ. Univ. of Michigan; photographing, traveling from Canadian Rockies to Hudson Bay with geographical expeditions, through mountains, spent 1 yr. making bird studies in So. America; started making photographic studies when 7 yrs. of age; was engaged in motion picture prod. along scientific and travel lines while at Univ. of Michigan. Ad., Goldwyn Film Corp., Los Angeles, Cal.

— C —

CABOT, Harry; b. Scranton, Pa.; educ. Scranton and Toronto, Canada; screen career, Kinemacolor, 2 yrs., Triangle Eastern 1916-17, Yorke Metro 1917; Wm. Fox 1918-19, Oliver Films 1919, series of 20 two-reel Chief Flynn detective stories. Home ad., 243 Riverdale ave., Yonkers, N. Y.

CALCAGNI, David; educ. Italy; screen career, Pathe, Fox, Brenon ("The Eternal Sin"), Goldwyn ("Auction Block," by Rex Beach), Mutual, now with Metro. Home ad., 367 14th st., Brooklyn, N. Y.

CANADY, D. R.; chief cameraman; b. 1894, Paris, France; early career, aviator, motordrome rider before 1908; screen career, photographed and directed foremost industrial pictures in U. S.; latest production "The Greatest of These"; inventor of attachment for ultra speed photography, which fits any camera; first to use soft focus borders; chief cameraman for Argus Motion Picture Co., Cleveland, Ohio.

CANN, Bert; b. N. Y. C.; educ. N. Y., Paris, Vienna, Budapest; early career, portrait photographer; stereoscopic expert for Dr. Trenkler Co., Leipzig; screen career, Pathe Freres and others, Ince ("23½ Hours' Leave," "Mary's Ankle," "Playing with Fires"). Ad., Thos. H. Ince Studios, Culver City, Cal.

CARLETON, Herbert Oswald; b. Rochester, N.Y.; educ. N. Y.; early career, mech. and inventor, working m. p. mach.; has patented Duplex Printing Machine; screen career, Vitagraph, Renfax, Singing Pictures, Dramascope, Crystal, Dyer (industrial), Rolfe-Metro ("The High Road," "Satan Sanderson," "The Bridge"). Ad., home, 1133 75th st., Brooklyn.

CAWOOD, Al; b. Moberly, Mo., 1880; educ. N. Y.; screen career, Kalem Co. 7 yrs. 6 mos., making educational picture in Alaska for Herald Film Co., 5 yrs with Universal and Lyons-Moran, made 250 pictures for Lyons & Moran, now with Ruth Roland Serial Co. Home ad., 1226 June st., Hollywood, Cal.; Holly. 3126; studio, Ruth Roland Studio.

CEDERBERG, Eric J.; b. Sweden, 1890; educ. Sweden; screen career, Swedish Bioscope, Columbia, Melies, Rex, Imp, Mohawk, Hector, American Biograph ("Difference of Opinion," "Mister Paganini"), Kinemacolor ("House on the Plains"). Photographing specials. Member I. A. T. S. E., 220 W. 42nd st., N. Y.

CHASTON, Fred.; b. London, 1871; educ. Liverpool; early career, U. S. Army, Alaskan service as photog. and master mechanic; screen career, Lubin ("The Lion and the Mouse," "The Third Degree," "The Great Ruby," "The Rights of Man," "A Man's Making," "Those Who Toil"). Charter member I. A. T. S. E., secy. and treas. local 557. Member Green Room Club, N. Y. C.

CHOCKLETT, A. Luther; b. Taylor's Store, Va.; educ. Roanoke pub. schls. and high schl.; early career, motion picture machine operator; screen career, Mutual Weekly Dept. of Gaumont, Universal, Animated Weekly, Stone Specialty Films ("A Modern Cola Plant," "Elks' National Home," "Valley of Virginia," "Historic Virginia," "Under the Protection of the W. O. W." Home ad., 1014 7th ave., S. E., Roanoke, Va.

CLARKE, Frederic Colburn; b. Wyoming, O.; educ. Ohio; screen career, All-Red Feature Co. (Canada), W. H. Clifford Photoplay Co., 1917, head of Still Dept. for Goldwyn, also special photographer to Mary Garden in 1918, to Florence Turner and 1919 to Nazimova. Home ad., 7616 Norton ave., Hollywood, Cal.

CLAWSON, Dal.; screen career, Bosworth, Universal, Morosco, Ince ("Hypocrites," "The Rosary," "The Merchant of Venice," "The Dumb Girl of Portici," "Honor Thy Name"), Lois Weber ("For Husbands Only," "Forbidden"), Hayakawa ("Bonds of Honor"), United ("The Corsican Brothers"). Member Cinema Camera Club. Home ad., 6128 Selma ave., Los Angeles; studio, Lois Weber Studio, Hollywood, Cal.

COOK, Clyde; b. Brockwayville, Pa.; screen career, "The Show-Down," "Southern Justice," "The Greater Law," Triangle ("Up or Down"), with Alan Dwan ("Soldiers of Fortune"). Member Cinema Camera Club, L. A. Ad., 604 N. Belmont ave., Los Angeles, Cal.

COOPER, William S.; b. Phila.; educ. there; early career, photographer; screen career, Lubin, photographed for Frank Brandon and George Terwilliger, Peerless-World ("Youth"), J. M. Lowry Photo. ("For Freedom of the World"). Ad., home, 1043 N. College ave., Phila. Member local 557, I. A. T. S. E., 220 W. 42nd st., N. Y.

COUDERT, George C.; b. Montbelard, France, 1884; educ. Newark, N. J.; early career, photographer in own studio in Newark; also mfr. raw film, Newark Celluloid Co.; screen career, Pathe, Reliance, Italian-American, Metro, International, Charter Features, Moss, Kleine, Equitable, Fairmount Film Corp. ("Hate"); Y. M. C. A. Prod. ("Round the Clock with the Rookie," "White Hairs"), and activities of Y. M. C. A. at Camp Dix, Devens, Pelham Bay, Springfield; serial at Wilkesbarre, Pa. Member I. A. T. S. E., local 557. Ad., 291 Market st., Newark, N. J.

CRAFT, William James; b. N. Y. C.; educ. there; stage career, 5 yrs. stk., rep. and prod.; screen career, began in 1910, Kalem ("Hazards of Helen"), 3 yrs. official photographer Pathe with Canadian Exped. Forces in Canada, Gt. Britain and France; Universal ("The Great Radial Mystery"). Home ad., 2120 Santa Monica Blvd., Santa Monica, Cal.; studio, Universal.

CROLLY, William S.; b. N. Y.; educ. there; early career, pianist, church organist and choir director; screen career, cameraman for Reliance-Majestic, Kalem, Universal, Pathe ("The Gay Old Dog").

CRONJAGER, Henry; b. Germany; educ. Germany; early career, photographer to the profession; screen career, Edison ("The Battle of Trafalgar"), Biograph ("The Road to Yesterday," "Lord Chumley"), Thanhouser, Vitagraph ("The Combat," "Ninety and Nine," "For France"). Now on Coast with Mary Pickford. Studio ad., Marshall Neilan Prod., Los Angeles.

— D —

DAVIS, Charles John; b. N. Y. C., 1891; educ. Brooklyn, N. Y.; early career, professional cycle rider; screen career, Vitagraph, pictures taken in front line trenches of France and Italy with E. M. Newman, Warner Bros. ("Fighting Roosevelts"), Vitagraph ("Pride," "Sporting Duchess"). Hght., 5, 4; wght., 154; dark complexion, brown hair, blue eyes. Home ad., 322 Albemarle Road, Brooklyn, N. Y.; studio ad., Vitagraph, Brooklyn, N. Y.

DEAN, Faxon M.; b. Guyten, Ga., 1882; educ. Georgetown Univ.; early career, newspaper photographer, 3 yrs. theatrical electrician; screen career, for 11 yrs. with Pathe, Universal and American (filmed "The Light," "Life's Staircase," "Pastures Green," "Tangled Skeins," "The Counterfeit Earl," "Mountain Mary," "The Wasp"), Pallas-Paramount ("Lost in Transit"), Lasky-Paramount ("Countess Charming"). Member Cinema Camera Club. Home ad., 260 Valentine Lane, Yonkers, N. Y.; Yonkers 567.

DELAVAN, Fred M., Jr.; b. Chicago, 1886; educ. Chicago; early career, chemist with Eastman, press photographer Chicago Herald, expert Paget & Autchrom color photographer; screen career, Selig (news and commercial pictures); foreign camera correspondent for Selig-Tribune and later asst. editor; with Gaumont News & Graphic 1917-19; asst. news editor, Fox News. Home ad., 19 State st., Flushing, N. Y.; office, 3 West 61st st., N. Y. C.

DEPEW, Ernest; b. Brushton, N. Y.; educ. Calif.; screen career, 4 yrs. cameraman, with Thos. H. Ince 6 mos.; Chaplin ("Dog's Life," "Shoulder Arms"), Fox Sunshine ("Bell Boy's Millions," "Wild Waves and Women," "Dabbling in Society"), Ruth Roland ("Adventures of Ruth"), Sphinx Serial Co. ("The Fatal Thirty"). Member Amer. Soc. Cinematographers. Home ad., 1357 McCadden Place, Hollywood, Cal.; phone 577244; studio ad., Campbell Comedies.

DE VINNA, Clyde; b. Akinsville, Mo.; early career, newspaper photographer; screen career, since 1914, with Ince ("Whither Thou Goest," "A Corner in Colleens"), Para. to ("Rose o' Paradise," "Madame Who"), Fox ("The Lincoln

Highwayman"). Ad., Brunton Studios, Hollywood, Cal.
DU BRAY, J. A.; screen career, Lew Cody Productions, Astra Film Co. Home ad., 103½ Brand Blvd., Glendale, Cal.
DUHEM, Raymond A.; b. San Francisco; screen career, Mutual, International; filmed Panama Canal from aeroplanes, Yellowstone Nat. Park, Canadian Pacific R. R., Universal Current Events Animated Weekly, Screen Telegram, Hearst-Pathe, Gaumont, etc., expert camera work, trick photography; now owner and manager Duhem M. P. Mfg. Co. Ad., 700 Hayes st., San Francisco, Cal.; Market 4432.
DUNMYRE, Louis H.; b. Butler, Pa.; early career, exhibitor for 8 yrs.; screen career, Lubin ("When Youth Was Ambitious," "A Romance of a Beanery," "The Bigamist," "Dollars and the Woman"). Member local 557, I. A. T. S. E. With Burton King Serial, Mirror Studio, Glendale, L. I. Ad., 875 W. 180th st., N. Y.
DUPREZ, Charles J.; publicity photographer; with Denver Post, Brown Bros., World Film, Lawrence Weber Prod. ("Blue Pearl," "Oakdale Affair," "Steel King," "Heart of Gold," "His Father's Wife," "Bringing Up Betty"). Ad., 164 Ivy st., Elmhurst, L. I., N. Y.

— E —

EAGLER, Paul; b. Newman, Ill., 1889; screen career, Kay-Bee, Triangle ("The Millionaire Vagrant," "The Bond of Fear"), Ince-Paramount ("The Son of His Father"), Chas. Ray Prods. ("False Faces"); now in charge dept. of photography. Studio ad., Ince, Culver City, Cal.
EDESON, Arthur; educ. N. C. C. Coll., 2 yrs. at Chemistry Labr.; early career, worked 8 yrs. in leading portrait studios in N. Y. as portrait photographer; screen career, World ("Dollar Mark," "Hearts in Exile," "Bought and Paid For"), Goldwyn ("Baby Mine," "Nearly Married"), Garson ("Hushed Hour"), C. K. Young ("Cheating Cheaters," "Eyes of Youth"). Hght., 5, 4½; wght., 148; brown hair, blue eyes. Home ad., 1741 N. Cherokee ave., Los Angeles, Cal.; Holly. 4428.
EDMOND, William M., also actor; b. Pa.; stage career, vaud. under Frohman, Brady in "Frenzied Finance"; screen career, Pathe ("Perils of Pauline," "The Idol of Paris"), Eclair, Balboa, Universal ("Joker" comedies, played in "The Light of Victory"). Member Cinema Camera Club. Home ad., 901½ So. Vermont ave., Los Angeles, Cal.
EVERETTS, Allen; b. Kaelskrona, Sweden; Thos. A. Edison, Pathe Freres, 3 yrs.; at the war fronts in Russia, Balkan States and Turkey. Member local 557, I. A. T. S. E. Ad., 603 Academy st., N. Y. C.

— F —

FETTY, Charles C.; b. Indianapolis, Ind., 1890; early career, commercial and portrait photographer; screen career, cameraman for Universal Weekly, Coburn Photo-Film Co., featured races at famous Indianapolis speedway, later with Emerald Motion Picture Co., Ebony Film Co. Ad., Ebony Film Co., 2332 N. California ave., Chicago, Ill.
FISHER, Ross G.; b. Springfield, Mo., 1886; educ. St. Louis; early career, Gene Gauntier, Olcott International Players series of Irish plays, Marion Leonard ("Romany Rye"), Horsley Cub comedies, 2 yrs. with Christie Film Co., Natl. Film Corp. ("The Love Call"), George Loane Tucker ("Ladies Must Live"), George Beban ("One Man in a Million"). Ad., George Beban Studio, 904 Girard st., Los Angeles; home ad., 6313 Fountain ave., Hollywood, Cal.
FLEMING, Victor L., cameraman; b. Los Angeles; worked with Alan Dwan at Fine Arts; Artcraft ("A Regular Guy," "Wild and Woolly," "Down to Earth," "The Man from Painted Post"); now dir. Douglas Fairbanks ("When the Clouds Roll By"). Home ad., 1618 Crenshaw Blvd., Los Angeles, Cal.
FOSTER, William C.; b. Bushnell, Ill., 1880; early career, vaud. and circus; screen career, Selig, Universal, Equitable, Metro, Chaplin, Fox ("Sins of the Parents," "Price of Silence," "Tale of Two Cities," "Les Miserables," "Riders of the Purple Sage," "Rainbow Trail"), Jesse D. Hampton ("Man Who Turned White," "Woman of Pleasure"), Beach-Goldwyn ("The Silver Horde"), Dustin Farnum Prod. ("Corsican Brothers"). Member A. S. of C. Home ad., 5615 La Marada st., Hollywood, Cal.
FRAWLEY, Jack; b. N. Y. C., 1866; educ. there; early career, photographer; screen career, with Lubin, Philadelphia, 20 yrs. as studio manager, director, etc.; making educational films, special M. P. work at Camp Dix, N. J. Home ad., 2241 West Somerset st., Philadelphia, Pa.
FRENCH, Eugene De Tousard; b. Phila., Pa., May 18, 1887; stage career, 8 yrs. stk. and vaud.; screen career, Pathe, Lubin, Regent, Regal, Victor ("Snow White"), "What Becomes of the Children?" "The Legend of the Everglades." Member local 557, I. A. T. S. E.
FRIED, A.; machine designer and camera mechanic; b. Austria, 1886; educ. Vienna, Budapest and N. Y.; screen career, connected with motion picture industry for past 6 yrs.; present position with Fox Film Co. Home ad., 5947 Willoughby ave., Los Angeles, Cal.; studio, Fox Film Corp.
FROMMER, Henry G.; b. Poughkeepsie, N. Y.; Crystal Film Co. Comedies, Western Photoplays, Inc. "Wolves of Kultur"), Triumph ("Master of the House," "Man and His Angel," "The Senator," "The Price"), Ivan ("Conquered Hearts"). Home ad., 73 State st., Ossining. N. Y. Member local 557, I. A. T. S. E.
FUQUA, John W.; b. Macon, Mo., 1884; educ. Burns, Ore.; early career, rancher, theatre manager, exhibitor; screen career, Bunny Films, Active M. P. Co., has made industrial and educational films, Chicago Herald Travelogues, Northwestern Film Corp. ("Before the White Man Came"), all Indian feature 7-reels. Home ad., 101 So. Oxford st., Los Angeles, Cal.

— G —

GANDOLFI, Alfred E.; b. Italy; screen career, Cines at Rome, Italia at Torino, Pathe, Lasky, Morosco-Pallas, Fox ("The Little Minister," and all other William Farnum pictures); first man to use a foreground reflector in Cal., inventor of double exposure, sunshade, etc.; Lasky, Dustin Farnum; Morosco, Cyril Maude; World, Montagu Love; 6 yrs. with Oscar Apfel; Selig ("The Market of Souls"), World ("The Grouch," "The Pirate's Gold," "The Little Intruder"), Mac-Donald ("The Thunderbolt"), now with Goldwyn, N. Y. Home ad., 630 Palisade ave., West New York, N. J.
GARMES, Lee; b. Peoria, Ill., 1898; educ. Denver, Colo.; early career, printing; screen career, Dorothy Gish Prods. ("The Hope Chest," "Nugget Nell," "I'll Get Him Yet," "Nobody Home"), Model Comedy Co. (Gale Henry in "Don't Chase Your Wife," "Chicken a la King," "Sweet Cookie"). Home ad., 1338 Beechwood Drive, Los Angeles, Cal.; studio, 5821 Santa Monica Blvd., Los Angeles; Holly. 157.
GAUDIO, Eugene; b. Italy; educ. there; screen career, Imp, Universal, chief photographer for "Twenty Thousand Leagues Under the Sea," Metro ("Toys of Fate," "Eye for Eye," "Out of the Fog," "The Red Lantern"), B. B. Features ("Kitty Kelly, M.D.," "The Lock of Geraldine"). Home ad., 1401 Spaulding ave., Hollywood, Cal.; studio, B. B. Features, Brunton Studios.
GAUDIO, Gaetano, "Tony"; b. Italy; educ. Univ. of Rome; screen career, Vitagraph 1 yr., Universal, head cameraman 4 yrs., Biograph 3 yrs., Yorke-Metro ("The Hidden Spring," "Under Handicap," "Big Tremaine," "Pidgin Island," "Mister Forty-Four"). Ad., studio, Meyer Chaplin Co., 3800 Mission Rd., Los Angeles, Cal.
GELENG, Louis A. J.; b. London, England, July 24, 1880; educ. common schls.; in photographic business since 15 years old, first with father, then worked for well-known society photographers in Chicago, later in business for himself making pictures on porcelain, glass, leather, ivory, etc.; screen career, since 1903, took pictures of the Panama Canal for Govt., Vitagraph ("Youth Gone to the Dogs," etc.), 1 year each with Selig and Lubin. Member local 557, I. A. T. S. E. Now with Fox, N. Y.
GILSON, Charles; b. Brooklyn, N. Y.; educ. Brooklyn and Mt. Vernon; screen career, Paramount, Edison ("Star Spangled Banner," "The Law of the North," "The Telltale Step"), McClure ("The Seven Deadly Sins"), U. S. Government picture; U. S. Motion Pict. Co., Rainbow Releases, Russian Kinetophone Co., St. Petersburg, Russia. Ad., 109 W. Sidney st., Mt. Vernon, N. Y.
GLENNON, Bert Lawrence; b. Anaconda, Mont.,

CINEMATOGRAPHERS

1893; educ. Stanford Univ., '12; stage career, stage mgr. for Oliver Morosco 1 yr., "Tick Tok Man"; screen career, Keystone, Famous Players, Clune Film Corp., Kalem Co., ("Ramona," "Eyes of the World," "Stingaree" series, 26 pictures), National ("Lightning Brice" serial, 15 episodes). Home ad., 1718 Vine st., Los Angeles, Cal.; phone 57685; studio, National, Santa Monica and Gower, Los Angeles; Holly, 4470.

GOBBETT, David William; b. and educ. England; screen career, with Urban, Pathe, Gaumont, Reliance, Biograph, Lubin, Buffalo Jones Big Game film. Ad., Green Room Club, N. Y. C.

GOODFRIEND, Pliny, also asst. director; b. Drayton, N. Dak., 1891; educ. pub. and high schls.; screen career, Vitagraph, Lasky, Marshall Neilan, Mayflower, Louis B. Mayer, Goldwyn. Home ad., 1532 3rd st., Santa Monica, Cal.; phone 217-J; studio, Brunton Studio.

GOSDEN, Alfred; b. London, England; educ. St. Paul's School, London; screen career, "The Durbar" at Delhi, India, for Kinemacolor, Biograph, Reliance-Majestic, Fine Arts ("Don Quixote"), Lubin, Universal ("The Spitfire of Seville" with Hedda Bova, "The Breath of the Gods" with Tsuru Aaki, "Pretty Smooth" with Priscilla Dean). Home ad., 4549 Kingswell ave., Los Angeles, Cal.; Holly. 1859.

GRAY, King D.; b. Virginia, 1886; educ. there; first to start lighting effects at Universal; screen career, New Art ("Solitary Sin"), Fox ("Cowardice Court"), Universal ("Paid in Advance," "Hearts of Humanity"), Ben Wilson Prods. ("The Octopus," "The Screaming Shadow"). Member Amer. Soc. Cinematographers. Home ad., 6674 Selma ave., Hollywood. Cal.; Holly. 3279.

GREGORY, Carl Louis; 1st Lieut. S. C.; b. Kansas; educ. Ohio State Univ.; early exper., scenario writer, dir., author, photographer, lecturer; screen career, Edison, Metro, Williamson Submarine expedition ("Thirty Leagues Under the Sea," motion pictures underneath the ocean in the West Indies); member Royal Photographic Society of Great Britain, Amer. Chemical Society, N. Y., Fox (Annette Kellermann in "Queen of the Sea"). Now chief instructor of cinematography in photographic section of Signal Corps, U. S. A. Member local 557, I. A. T. S. E. Ad., 76 Echo ave., New Rochelle, N. Y.

GREINER, Arthur Leroy; b. Denver, Colo., 1894; educ. Colo. Agriculture College; screen career, New York Motion Picture Co., Vitagraph Co., Universal Film Co. Home ad., Vine Apts., Hollywood, Cal.; phone 579839; studio, Universal City, Cal.

GUISSART, Rene; b. Paris, France; educ. Paris; screen career, Eclair, France; then Eclair in U. S. as chief cameraman, Climax, superintended building of studio and laboratory at Los Angeles; Griffith, direction of Alan Dwan; came east to join Fox; now with World in Madge Evans features; Tournier (latest prod., "Woman," "My Lady's Garter"); now with Maurice Tourneur.

— H —

HARDE, Harry D.; b. 1894; educ. Jersey City, N. J.; with Pathe since their advent in this country; features, "Go Get 'Em, Garringer" serials, "Hands Up," "Tiger's Trail," features, "Twin Pawns," "A, B, C of Love"), Hope Hampton Co. ("Modern Salome"); now working on feature for Pathe. Home ad., 535 Palisade ave., Jersey City, N. J.

HATKIN, Philip; b. Riga, Russia; educ. Russia; early career, 11 years a photographer; screen career, Kinemacolor, Kleine ("Bondwoman," "Crimson Path," etc.), World Film ("Yellow Passport," "Social Highwayman," "Perils of Divorce," "The Summer Girl," "The Men She Married," "The Man Who Forgot," etc.), Peerless Brady ("Moral Courage," "Yankee Pluck," "Brand of Satan," "The Iron Ring," "The Maid of Belgium"). Member local 557, I. A. T. S. E. Ad., Friars' Club, N. Y. C.

HILBURN, Percy; screen career, several years with Vitagraph, Lasky, Fanny Ward-Pathe ("Japanese Nightingale," "The Narrow Path"), Farrar-Goldwyn ("Turn of a Wheel," "Shadows"), Normand-Goldwyn ("Sis Hopkins"), "Dangerous Days," with Geraldine Farrar in "Flame of the Desert," "World and Its Woman," "Woman and the Puppet." Ad., 1910 Pinehurst Rd., Hollywood, Cal.; studio, Goldwyn.

HOFFMAN, Charles Wilbur; b. N. Y. C.; educ. Chase School of Art, International School of Design; early exper., photographer, artist, portrait painter; screen career, Thanhouser, Edison, Paragon, World, Famous Players, Lyman H. Howe, Inc., Royal Cinema-War-News Corp., Pathe. Home ad., 395 E. 197th st. Member Cinema Camera Club, N. Y.

HOLLISTER, Geo. K.; b. N. Y. C.; early career, official war correspondent and photographer; cinematograph experience since its earliest inception; camera man for the following motion picture stars, Ethel Barrymore, Emily Stevens, Edith Story, Bessie Love, Helen Holmes, Alice Hollister, Marjorie Rambeau, Nance O'Neil, Alice Joyce, Ruth Roland, etc. Ad., Union Local 557, 220 W. 42nd st., N. Y. C.

HORN, Edward; b. N. Y., 1881; cameraman 11 yrs.; Pathe, Geo. Kleine ("Officer 666," "Stop Thief," "Who's Who"), Biograph-World ("As in a Looking-Glass"), etc. Member local 557, I. A. T. S. E.; now with Edgar Lewis Prod. Ad., 70 Lincoln ave., Hastings-on-Hudson, N. Y.

HORNE, Pliny W.; b. Wallingford, Conn., 1891; educ. Conn. and Calif.; screen career, Peerless, Universal, Triangle ("Fighting Back," "The Spindle of Life," "The Hero of the Hour," "The Shoes that Danced," "Innocent's Progress," "The Secret Code," "Society for Sale"), Universal ("The Fireflingers"); specialist in lighting effects; now in Africa with the Smithsonian African Expedition in conjunction with Universal Film Co. Ad., 2004 Cahuenga ave., Los Angeles, Cal.; Holly. 2780.

HUNT, J. Roy; b. Carperton, W. Va., 1884; screen career, Milo, Gaumont, Fox ("The Daughter of the Gods"), Charter Feature, Herbert Brenon, ("War Brides," "The Eternal Sin"), Select ("The Lone Wolf"); 9 mos. with British Govt. as official cinematographer; during 1919 experimented on moving pictures in natural colors. Ad., 2129 35th ave., Birmingham, Ala.

— I —

IRISH, Roy; 10 yrs. exper. as cameraman with Essanay, Universal, Fox, Vitagraph, Triangle, American; now with Mary Miles Minter Co., under direction Lloyd Ingraham. Ad., American Film Co., Santa Barbara, Cal.

— J —

JACKMAN, Fred J.; b. Toledo, Iowa, 1881; educ. engineering course, Calif. Sch. of Mechanical Art; screen career, Pathe, Essanay, Rolin, Keystone, 4 yrs. supervising cinematographer for Mack Sennett. Home ad., 5336 Virginia ave., Los Angeles, Cal.; studio, Mack Sennett Comedies, 1712 Allesandro st., Los Angeles.

JENNINGS, Dev.; screen career, Fox ("Miss Adventure," "The Feud"). Ad., 1409 Maltman st., Los Angeles, Cal.

JOHNSON, Jugo C.; educ. N. Y. C.; screen career, Geo. Kleine ("Wild Oats," "The Scarlet Road," "Gloria's Romance," starring Billie Burke); at present with Selznick. Ad., 501 W. 123rd st., N. Y.; Mngsde. 4542.

— K —

KEEPERS, Harry Leslie; b. Newark, N. J., 1882; educ. Newark; practical stage electrician; operated one of first projectors in N. Y. C. at Tony Pastor's, installed machines for Keith and Proctor, using and making first two-wing shutter; screen career, Vitagraph, globe trotter with Clara Kimball Young and Maurice Costello, Edison, Wanamaker Expedition, making "Life of American Indian," first prize Panama Expos., Universal (feature productions), inventor of Focalplanograph Camera, author of course in Cinematography, Empire All-Star ("Outcast"), Curtiss Prod. ("Who's Your Brother"), Fleur De Lys ("Empty Arms"), Metro ("Legion of Death"). Charter member I. A. T. S. E., local 557. Ad., 534 W. 159th st., N. Y. C.; Audubon 4771.

KIRBY, Frank G.; b. Bremen, Germany; educ. Bremen; early career, art photographer; screen career, Edison as director, Life Photo, Fox ("The Bitter Truth," "She"); controls patents on mechanical developments on cameras; specialist in photography and laboratory work; now with Wm. Farnum with Fox; charter member I. A. T. S. E., local 557, N. Y.

— L —

LANCASTER, L. L., supt. of photography; b. Lafayette, Ind., 1888; early career, commercial photographer; screen career, 7 yrs. laboratory work at Universal City, past 2 yrs. head cameraman and laboratory supt. West Coast Universal Studios. Ad., Universal City, Cal. Home ad., Lankershim, Cal.

LATHEM, Alfred H.; b. Birmingham, Ala.; educ. Univ. of Alabama; screen career, organized Southern M. P. Corp., laboratory man at Lasky Laboratories; "The Right to Happiness," starring Dorothy Phillips, "The Girl of 1,000 Faces," "Oh! It's Easy," "The $10,000 Reward," "Country Maid," "Some Girl," "Matrimonial Bliss," "Old Dials for New," featuring Florence Turner, "The Little Green Devil," "In the Dark," "The Man Hunter." Hght., 5, 10; wght., 150; dark hair, hazel eyes. Ad., 1815 Cahuenga ave., Hollywood, Cal; phone 57674; studio, Universal Film Co.

LAWRENCE, George W.; b. St. Paul, Minn.; educ. Univ. Calif., Berkeley, Cal.; early career, civil and electrical engineer, scenic photographer; screen career, Universal ("The Nature Man," "War of the Tongs," "Chalice of Sorrow," "Upper Three and Lower Four"), Paramount ("Rule G"), Mutual ("Death Lock," "The Planter"). Specialize on Light Effects. Ad., Universal City, Cal.

LEACH, Henry Anderson; b. Toronto, Can., 1878; educ. U. A. A.; early career, photographer; screen career, Powers Co., Universal, Fox ("Miss U. S. A," "The Lure of Ambition"). Home ad., 109 Sherman ave., N. Y. C.; studio, Fox, N. Y.

LE PICARD, Marcel A.; b. Le Havre, France; screen career, Pathe, Reliance-Majestic, Mutual, Universal, Fox, Ivan, Goldwyn, last year prods. include all the "Madge Kennedy" pictures, also all the "Will Rogers" prods., "Almost a Husband," "Jubilo." Ad., Goldwyn Pict. Corp., Los Angeles, Cal.

LEWIS, Atwood Lloyd; b. Philadelphia; 30 yrs. photographer, 10 yrs. at motion pictures, Lubins, Universal, Thanhouser, Fox, Ogden ("Birth of the Race"), Goldwyn and others. Charter member I. A. T. S. E., local 557, 220 W. 42nd st., N. Y. C.

LIGUORI, Alfonso; b. Salerno, Italy, 1885; educ. Brooklyn; early career, commercial photographer; screen career, Famous Players ("An Innocent Lie," "The Smugglers," "A Daughter of MacGregor"), Olcott Players, Inc. ("The Belgian"). Member Cinema Camera Club. Ad. home, 761 E. 133d st., N. Y.; Melrose 1038.

LINDEN, Edwin G.; b. Lake Geneva, Wis.; educ. there; screen career, photographer, motion picture operator for 7 years, feature cinematographer for Selig 6 yrs. Home ad., 225 N. Kenwood st., Glendale, Cal.; studio ad., Selig Polyscope Co., 3800 Mission Road., Los Angeles, Cal.; phone, East 33.

LISSACK, William; b. Glasgow, Scotland; 5 yrs. news photo., London News Agency, London, Eng.; Inter. News Agency, N. Y.; screen career, Mutual Crystal, Fox, Wharton Bros., E. I. S. Film Corp.

LYONS, Chester; b. Westfield, N. Y.; screen career, Reliance, Eclair, Ince-Triangle, Ince-Para., all Charles Ray Para. productions to date, Paramount ("The Egg Crate Wallop," "Red Hot Dollars"). Home ad., 7056 Clarington ave., Culver City, Cal.; studio, Ince.

LYONS, Reginald Edgar; b. N. Y. C.; educ. Brooklyn, N. Y.; screen career, 6 yrs. Eastern Vitagraph, Christie, La Salle, Vitagraph ("Wheels of Justice," "Mortmain," "Hearts of Flame"). 1 yr. chief photographer for 79th Div., A. E. F., Argonne and Meuse sectors; returned to Vitagraph in May, 1919, photographing Montgomery and Rock, Big V. Comedies. Member A. S. of C. Home ad., 4603 Melbourn, Hollywood, Cal.; Holly. 1666; studio, Vitagraph.

— M —

MacWILLIAMS, Glen; b. San Francisco; educ. Los Angeles; screen career, 2 yrs. with Griffith, 3 yrs. with Douglas Fairbanks. 14 pictures, among which was "Say, Young Fellow."

MAEDLER, Richard W.; b. N. Y. C.; screen career, photographed titles and inserts of following Fox pictures: "Last of the Duanes," "Lure of Ambition," "Wings of the Morning," "Should a Husband Forgive?" "Checkers," "Sacred Silence," "Eastward Ho!" "Evangeline," "Kathleen Mavourneen." Home ad., Lemoine ave., Fort Lee, N. J.; studio ad., Fox Film Corp., N. Y.

MARSHALL, William C.; b. 1883, Houston, Tex.; educ. Horace Mann Schl., N. Y.; screen career, Yankee, Pathe, Ocean-Fox, Famous Players, pictures, "Great Expectations," "Amazons," "Arms and the Girl," "Land of Promise." Now on West Coast with Famous-Paramount Co.; studio ad., Lasky Studio, Hollywood, Cal.

McCARTHY, J. P.; screen career, several yrs. cameraman for D. W. Griffith; organized McCarthy Pictures Corp.; produced "Out of the Dust." Office, 609 Homer Laughlin Bldg., Los Angeles, Cal.

McCLAIN, A.; b. Louisville, Ky.; screen career, began in 1915, Universal ("Hearts of Humanity," "Elmo the Mighty"), number of features with Allan Holubar. Home ad., 205 Grand Oaks, Pasadena, Cal.; studio, Universal.

McCLUNG, Hugh C.; b. Brenham, Texas; educ. high schls. Texas; early career, navigator and press photographer; screen career, Artcraft ("Say, Young Fellow," "Mr. Fix-It," "Bound in Morocco," "He Comes Up Smiling," "A Modern Musketeer," "Headin' South," "A Knickerbocker Buckaroo"), Universal ("Overland Red"). Photographed "The Wonderful Schools of Los Angeles," winning first prize at the Panama-Pacific Exposition. Member Am. Soc. of Cinematographers. Studio ad., Universal City, Cal.; home ad., 4280 Brighton ave., Hollywood, Cal.

McCOY, William H.; b. Brooklyn, N. Y.; educ. Brooklyn pub. schls.; screen career, photographer for Reliance, Universal, now with Vitagraph, filmed "The Tale of Two Cities," "The Man Who Couldn't Beat God," "The Ruse." Member I. A. T. S. E., local 557. Home ad., 724 Chauncey st., Brooklyn, N. Y.; studio, Vitagraph, Brooklyn.

McGANN, William M.; b. Pittsburgh, Pa.; educ. St. Vincent's Coll. and La Salle Acad.; early career, telephone company in Los Angeles; screen career, 1 yr. with Hobart Bosworth, 6 mos. American, 2½ yrs. Fox, 6 mos. George Beban features, 6 mos. Lewis Stone features. Home ad., 1249 W. 6th st., Los Angeles, Cal.; phone 556615.

MESCALL, John J.; b. Litchfield, Ill.; educ. Indianapolis; early career, portrait and press photographer; screen career, news cameraman for Gaumont, Goldwyn, making Booth Tarkington-Edgar pictures. Home ad., 2468 W. Washington st., Los Angeles, Cal.; phone 73903; studio, Goldwyn.

MILLER, Harold Louis (Henry); b. London, England; educ. London; screen career, with Robert W. Paul, London, in 1905, in 1906 with Kinemacolor, London, in 1912 sent to American Kinemacolor from London co., also photographer for B. S. Moss ("Three Weeks"), Astra ("The Romantic Journey"). Member I. A. T. S. E., local 557; studio ad., Post Talking Picture Co., N. Y.; home ad., 29 No. 7th ave., Whitestone, L. I., N. Y.

MILNER, Victor; educ. N. Y. C.; screen career, Pathe Freres, Selig, Giants and White Sox World Tour, Belgian Congo, Wm. S. Hart, all Artcraft prods., in charge of laboratory of Eberhard Schneider, N. Y. C.; last big feature "Out of the Dust"; at present with J. D. Hampton photographing H. B. Warner ("Fugitive from Matrimony," "House of a Thousand Candles," "The White Dove"). Secretary Amer. Soc. of Cinematographers.

MINNERLY, Nelson Harvey; educ. N. Y. and N. J., Englewood High Schl., Englewood, N. J.; screen career, asst. cameraman World ("Price of Pride," "Phil for Short"), Adanac Prod. ("World Shadow"), asst. dir. World ("Gates of Gladness," "Carol of Subway," "Little Patriot," "Stolen Orders"). photographer, Serico ("The Jewelled Hand"). Ad., 128 Convent ave., N. Y.; Morningside 6689.

MITCHELL, Pell, editor "Fox News"; b. Fulton, Ky.; educ. Vanderbilt Univ.; early career, expert in still photography, later a newspaper man, special writer and advertising mgr.; screen career, Mutual as editor of "The Mutual Weekly," later "The Gaumont News," joined Fox to organize "Fox News" August, 1919. Home ad., 219 W. 34th st., N. Y.; studio ad., Fox News, 3 West 61st st., N. Y.

MOLLOY, Thos. F.; b. Wellesley, Mass.; educ. Brooklyn, N. Y.; early career, photographer; screen career, with Vitagraph ("The Blue En-

CINEMATOGRAPHERS

envelope," "The Walls of Convention," "Indiscretion," "Over the Top," "The Climbers," "The Fortune Hunter"). Home ad., 301 East 23d st., Brooklyn, N. Y.; studio, Vitagraph, Brooklyn.

MORGAN, Lieut. Ira H.; screen career, Essanay, Eclair, Liberty Film Co. Member Cinema Camera Club. Studio, Brentwood Film Co., Los Angeles.

MOSS, Stewart Belfield; educ. Fort St. Model High Schl., Sydney, Aus.; early career, photographing and editing for A. R. C.; screen career, photographed educational scenics, news and special subjects for Universal, International Film Service; now with American Red Cross. Ad., 17 Manhattan ave., N. Y. C.; Bryant 3151.

— N —

NAGY, Anthony U.; b. Hungary; educ. Europe; early career, portrait photographer, screen career, Universal, now with Christie Comedy Co. Home ad., 1258 Beechwood drive, Los Angeles, Calif.

NELSON, Frederick; b. 1889, Chicago; educ. there; screen career, chemist and negative developer for Selig 8 yrs., then cameraman "Brown of Harvard," "Pearl of Great Price"; cameraman, chemist and negative developer for Ebony Film Corp. ("The One Dollar Bill," "Cool Heads and Hot Feet," "The Bully," "Spooks," "The Milk-Fed Hero," "The Devil for a Day"). Ad., 4925 N. Tripp ave., Chicago, Ill.

NICKERSON, Clark R.; b. N. Y. C.; screen career, Vitagraph ("The Law Decides," "The Courage of Silence," "Within the Law," "Womanhood," "The Sixteenth Wife"). Ad., home. In U. S. service. Member Cinema Camera Club, N. Y.

NORTON, Stephen S.; b. Palmyra, N. Y.; educ. Buffalo, N. Y.; screen career, entered field as cameraman in 1912; has photographed over 140 pictures, from one to six reels, worked for directors, Robert Leonard, Lois Weber, Phillips Smalley, Henry Otto, Douglas Girrard, Allen Holubar, Jack Dillon, etc.; has photographed Olive Thomas, Alma Rubens, Mary MacLaren, Tyrone Power, Wm. Desmond, Ella Hall, Cleo Madison, etc. Ad., Hotel Northern, 429 W. 2nd st., Los Angeles, Calif.

— O —

ORTLIEB, Alfred; b. Ivry-Sur-Seine, France; educ. Paris; early career, in business as salesman; screen career, photographer for Gaumont, Selig, Metro ("The Shooting of Dan McGrew," "Greater Love Hath No Man"), Perret Prod., Inc. ("Lafayette We Come," "Stars of Glory"), Pathe ("Twin Pawns," "The A B C of Love").

— P —

PERRY, Paul P.; b. Denver, Colo.; educ. there; stage career, 4 yrs. theatrical stage electrician; screen career, Famous Players ("Everywoman," "The Sea Wolf," "The Round-Up," "Told in the Hills," "Pettigrew's Girl," "A Sporting Chance," "Money, Men and Women," "Good Gracious Annabelle," "City of Dim Faces"). Home ad., 6070 Selma, Hollywood, Calif.; Holly 2713; studio, Famous Players-Lasky Co.

PERUGINI, Francis; b. N. Y.; educ. N. Y. Psychiatric Inst.; early career, studied medicine; screen career, Imperial, Pathe, Eastern, Kineticartoon, Klever, with Ernst Truax. Ad., Green Room Club, N. Y. Home ad., 2218 Cropsey ave., Brooklyn, N. Y.

PETERSON, Gus; b. San Francisco, Calif.; educ. Los Angeles; screen career, Biograph, Bosworth ("Smoke Bellew," "Beach Combers"), Fred Stone ("Billy Jim"), B. B. Features ("Her Purchase Price"), Universal ("Rouge and Riches"), Triangle ("I Love You"), 7 yr. Photographic Section of Signal Corps of U. S. Army, 10 mos. spent in France taking pictures of different engagements. Ad., 626 S. Bonnie Brae st., Los Angeles, Calif.; Wilshire 4254.

PHYSIOC, Lewis W., manager Goldwyn Laboratories; b. Columbia, S. C.; educ. Coll of Agricultural and Mechanical Arts, Raleigh, N. C.; screen career, 12 yrs. scenic artist, 2 yrs. tech. dir. for Cameraphone, tech. dir. and producer Edison Kinetoscope, 2 yrs. tech. dir. for Pathe Freres, 2½ yrs. cameraman Famous Players ("Bab's Diary," "Seven Keys to Baldpate,"

"The Knife," "Rolling Stones," "A Girl Like That"), C. K. Young ("The Reason Why"), Goldwyn ("Peck's Bad Girl," "Perfect 36"), Selznick ("Upstairs and Down," "The Spite Bride"). Ad., 1326 Milton ave., Hollywood, Cal.

POLITO, Sol; b. Palermo, Sicily; educ. Italy and N. Y.; early career, still photographer, m. p. developer and licensed projector; screen career, Biograph, Metro ("Rip Van Winkle"), Walter Miller Features, Universal, Kismet, Features, Peerless-World ("Sins of Society," "The World Against Him"); now with Allan Dwan-Mayflower. Member Cinema Camera Club, L. A. Home ad., 4351 Kingsland ave., Los Angeles; studio, Brunton Studio; phone Holly 4080.

PORTER, Hector A.; b. Ellendale, N. Dak., 1896; educ. State Normal Industrial Schl.; early career, Manual Training Teacher, Agricultural Schl., Park River, N. D., and High Schl., Shreveport, La.; screen career, asst. cameraman for 6 mos. at Lasky Studio, Hollywood, with Bryant Washburn, now second cameraman at Goldwyn Studio, Culver City, Calif. Ad., 1634 Vine st., Hollywood, Calif.; Holly 1191.

POWELL, Ernest; screen career, Thanhouser ("Her Dream Mother"), B. S. Moss ("One Day," "Girl from Rectors"), Rothacker ("Trooper 44"); now with King Cole Comedies. Home ad., Woodcliffe, N. J.; studio ad., Motion Picture Producing Co. of America, Dongan Hills, S. I., N. Y.

POWERS, Len; b. Rodney, Iowa, 1894; educ. Portland, Ore.; screen career, as cameraman has been connected with Reliance, Fox ("The Honor System"), Mack Sennett ("Beware of Boarders"), Hank Mann Co. ("Broken Bubbies"), Fox ("Back to Nature Girls," "The Yellow Dog-Catcher," "Virtuous Husband"). Home ad., 1426 N. Serrano ave., Los Angeles, Calif.

— Q —

QUINN, Arthur T.; b. N. Y.; educ. St. Francis Xavier Coll., N. Y.; screen career, Vitagraph ("The Girl Philippa," "The Suspect," "Thou Art the Man," "Kennedy Square"). Ad., 1389 Bedford ave., Brooklyn, N. Y.

— R —

RAMSAY, R. L.; b. Beaver Falls, Pa., 1887; educ. Pittsburgh; screen career, Fox. Home ad., 1163 N. Western ave., Los Angeles, Cal.; studio, Fox.

RAYMOND, Jack O.; educ. Berne, Switzerland, and Paris; made pictures of Hamburg-American Trip around the world in 1916; makes scenics and travelogues; Pathe Freres, Paris; International, Universal. Ad., 540 W. 165th st., N. Y.; Audubon 2832.

REA, Thomas H.; b. Nebraska; educ. there; screen career, Universal ("Lasca," "Two Men of Tinted Butte," "Sinbad, the Sailor," "The Eternal Triangle," "The Girl in the Gang"). Home ad., 756 East 22nd st., Los Angeles, Calif.; studio, Universal.

REED, Arthur; b. Houston, Texas; screen career, Lasky Studios, Hollywood, Calif. Home ad., 250 Riverside drive, N. Y.; studio ad., Famous Players-Lasky Corp., 130 W. 56th st., N. Y.

REID, Wm. W.; b. Concordia, Kan., 1887; Pathe correspondent for Northern Kansas. Home ad., 1123 Van Buren st., Topeka, Kan.; studio, Orpheum Theatre Bldg., Topeka.

REINHART, William A.; educ. Cincinnati, Ohio; early career, portrait photographer; screen career, Famous Players, Fox ("Ace High"), Triangle ("Gown of Destiny"), Frohman ("Witching Hour"), Rolfe (Houdini Serial), Gaumont ("Isle of Love"). Ad., 714 8th ave., N. Y.

REYNOLDS, B. F.; b. and educ. Grand Rapids, Mich.; screen career, Essanay, Universal ("Blind Husbands"). Member Cinema Camera Club. Home ad., 244 So. Olive st., Los Angeles; studio, Universal City, Cal.

REYNOLDS, Ernest M.; educ. Cleveland, Ohio, and technical schls.; 1911 began career in laboratory and still camera work, began cinematographic end of trade in 1913; latest pictures, "The House Without Children," "Hidden Charms."

RICARDO, Arnold; educ. Antwerp, Belgium, Amsterdam, Holland; Brooklyn, N. Y.; screen career, 5 yrs. exper. with Kansas M. P. Co., Southern Educational, National Pictures Corp., McHenry Film Co., Fleur-de-Lys Co., Goldwyn, making news, scenic, educational, industrial prods. as second cameraman and stills. Member I. A. T. S. E., local 557. Ad., 145 Prospect Park West, Brooklyn, N. Y.

RIES, Irving G.; b. Akron, Ohio; screen career, Rothacker, Chicago, Educational, Selig Tribune Weekly; spent 1½ yrs. in Germany, Russia and Belgium making "Fighting With the Germans" and 6 mos. in Mexico making "Barbarous Mexico"; Model Comedy Co. ("A Wild Woman," "Cash"), Vitagraph ("Flips and Flops," "Healthy and Happy," "Mates and Models," "Squabs and Squabbies," "Bungs and Bunglers," "Yaps and Yokels"). Member Cinema Camera Club. Ad., 6132 De Longpre ave., Hollywood, Calif.

RIES, Park J.; b. Akron, O., 1897; screen career, began at age of 13 in Akron as photoplay operator, with Universal two seasons as cinematographer, L-Ko ("As Fate Decides," "Where Is My Husband?"), Fox ("Oh, What a Knight," "Money Talks," "Jail Birds"), Poppy Comedies ("Daddy Ambrose," "Heroic Ambrose," "Foxy Ambrose," "Diplomatic Ambrose"), Vitagraph ("The Invisible Hand" serial). Member Cinema Camera Club. Home ad., 1314 Beechwood drive, Hollywood.

RIZARD, George; b. Paris, France; in U. S. since 1895; early career, portrait and miniature photographer; screen career, 6 yrs. with Pathe, American and Balboa. Speaks English, French, Spanish; is familiar with all branches of photography. Ad., Woodward Hotel, Los Angeles, Calif.; American Studio, Santa Barbara, Calif.

ROOS, Charles G., also director; b. Canada, 1882; educ. Galt High Cchl., Chemistry and still photography; with Pathescope of Canada, Ltd., making educational subjects for Ontario Gov't and Committee of Pub. Information, Ottawa, Ont. Home ad., 1457 Dundas st., West, Toronto, Ont., Canada; studio ad., Pathescope of Canada, Ltd., 156 King st., West, Toronto, Ont., Canada.

ROOS, Leonard H.; b. 1896, Galt, Ont.; educ. Galt and Toronto; screen career, specializes in news photography, Atlas Motion Pict. Co., Detroit, Strand Star Weekly Review, Canadian Topical Review, All-Canada Weekly, Hearst Pathe News, film editor Detroit Free Press; Canadian editor Fox News. Home ad., 48 Brant road North, Galt, Ont., Canada; studio ad., Dominion Laboratories, 120 University ave., Toronto, Ont., Canada.

ROSE, Jackson J.; b. Chicago, 1886; early career, news and com. photographer; screen career, with Essanay, Selig, Rothacker, International, Commonwealth, Apex; 10 yrs. exper. as cameraman; filmed "Graustark," "The Slim Princess," "Prince of Graustark," "The Breaker," "The Alster Case," "Skinner's Dress Suit," "Skinner's Baby"; associated with over 26 directors photographing over 275 prods.; inventor of many camera devices; owns complete Bell and Howell outfit with every known attachment. Studio ad., Apex Co., 223 N. New Jersey st., Indianapolis, Ind.

ROSHER, Charles G.; studied technical and artistic photography abroad; early career, Messrs. Speaight, Ltd., Court photographers, London; screen career, Nestor, Gene Gautier, Pathe, Victory Co., Mutual (filmed the battle of Ojinaga with General Villa in Mexico), Lasky (photographed all of of William C. De Mille's prods., including "Anton, the Terrible," "The Plow Girl," also "The Primrose Ring," "The Secret Game," "One More American," "Johanna Enlists," "Captain Kidd, Jr."); chief cameraman for "Daddy Long Legs," "Hoodlum," "Heart of the Hills," "Pollyanna." Member Cinema Camera Club. Studio, Mary Pickford Co., Los Angeles, Calif.

ROSSMAN, Earl W.; b. Scotland, S. D.; educ. Dakota Wesleyan Univ. as civil engineer; early career, newspaper man and photographer; stage career, mgr. of N. Y. theatre and McKinley Sq. theatre, N. Y. C.; screen career, Kinemacolor, Shubert, Mississippi Film; now on expedition in So. Africa for Prizma, Inc. Studio, 71 W. 23d st., N. Y.

ROTH, Charles A.; educ. Columbia Coll. and Cornell Univ.; early career, research chemist, Brooklyn Polytechnic Inst.; screen career, chief cameraman Brewster Film Co.; cameraman of color work Power Reproduction Co.; cameraman Iconocrone Co.; cameraman and research chemist Prizma; X-Ray photographer in A. E. F. in France; now with Prizma. Ad., 2106 Amsterdam ave., N. Y.

RUBINSTEIN, Irving B. ("Ruby"); b. N. Y. C., 1892; educ. U. S. Military Schl.; screen career, with Doc Willat, built studio for Carl Laemmle at Havana, Cuba, also Ruby Twinplex Studio, several laboratories in U. S. and Canada; camera work for Universal, American Films, Paramount, Frohman Amuse., World, and many independent features; mustered out of U. S. Army Feb., 1919, with rank of sergt.-major, Engineers; Zion Films ("Broken Barriers"); now working with Chas. E. Davenport; one of first to use Bell & Howell Camera in East and now owns a $2,400.00 outfit. Ad., 100 W. 119th st., N. Y. C.

RUCKER, Joseph T.; b. Atlanta; educ. there; early career, laboratory film work; screen career, Universal, Pathe, covering Middle West for Pathe News. Member I. A. T. S. E., local 557. Home ad., 5824 Broadway, N. Y.

RUTTENBERG, Joseph; b. Russia; educ. Boston, Mass.; early career, toured Europe with Joseph Urban as cameraman; screen career, Fox ("Doing Their Bit," "The Woman Who Gave," "Women, Women," "Fallen Idol," "My Little Sister," "From Now On"). Home ad., 945 Fox st., N. Y. C.; studio ad., Fox, N. Y.

— S —

SCHEIBE, Geo. H.; b. Plymouth, Wis., 1880; photographer and chemist since 1896; expert developer of negatives and positives, toning and tinting, managed negative laboratory for Triangle Keystone, also cameraman for Thos. H. Ince and Mack Sennett Comedies, inventor of Scheibe's Monotone Filter. Ad., 342 S. Broadway, Suite 400, Los Angeles, Calif.

SCHELLINGER, Rial B.; screen career, Fox ("The Mischief Maker," "Camille," "Cleopatra," "A Modern Cinderella"). Member local 557, I. A. T. S. E. Ad., 52 Rhodes st., New Rochelle, N. Y.

SCHNEIDER, Max; b. Egen, Bohemia; educ. there; grad. Royal Imperial Art Schl. of Bohemia; screen career, Kalem, Reliance, Keystone, World, Thos. Ince, photographed features of Alice Brady, Ethel Clayton, Holbrook Blynn, etc. Member local 557, I. A. T. S. E. Ad., 220 Candler Bldg., N. Y.

SCHOENBAUM, Charles Edgar; b. California; educ. there, Poly High Schl.; early career, photo-engraver; screen career, Lasky ("Vicky Van," "Love Insurance," "Why Smith Left Home," "It Pays to Advertise," "Too Much Johnson"), J. D. Hampton ("The Best Man"). Ad., 1528 Morningside, Los Angeles, Calif.; Holly 2955.

SEELING, Charles R.; b. Perth Amboy, N. J.; educ. Phila., Pa.; screen career, photographed Nell Shipman, Bessie Love, Monroe Salisbury, Mahlon Hamilton, Betty Blythe; Vitagraph ("Baree, Son of Kazan," "A Gentleman's Agreement," "A Girl from Beyond," "Pegeen," "The Dawn of Understanding," "The Enchanted Barn," "The Wishing Ring Man"), Universal ("That Devil Bateze"). Home ad., 1868 Allesandro st., Los Angeles, Calif.; Wilshire 5235.

SEIDMAN, I. Sy.; b. and educ. N. Y. C.; photographer, Goerz lens salesman, newspaper man, head cameraman Educational Films, N. Y., 1911, camera work and editor Physical Culture Screen Mag.; specialized in scientific, educational and commercial films and news weeklies. Ad., Room 1104, 110 West 40th st., N. Y. City; Bryant 738.

SEITZ, John F.; b. Chicago; educ. there; screen career, Essanay, American, St. Louis M. P. Co. ("Ranger of Lonesome Gulch," "The Quagmire," "Whose Wife?" "Edged Tools"), American-Mutual ("A Soul for Pawn"), Hampton-Hodkinson ("The Sage Brusher"), chemist. Home ad., 1625 State st., Santa Barbara; studio, American, Santa Barbara.

SHELDERFER, Joseph; b. Brooklyn; early career, m. p. operator; screen career, Vitagraph ("Dust of Egypt," "A Price for Folly," "A Two-Edged Sword"), Lasky ("The Ghost House"). Member local 557, I. A. T. S. E. Ad., 300 Chauncey st., Brooklyn, N. Y.

SHELTON, Byron J.; b. St. Louis, Mo.; educ. there; now at Gale Henry Studio. Ad., Glidden Hotel, Hollywood, Calif.; Holly 3910.

SINTZENICH, Hal; educ. Bedford Coll., England; screen career, Williamson Bros. Submarine Films ("Girl of the Sea"), Lady Mackenzie's African Big Game Hunt, Kinemacolor World Tours, Tourneur ("White Heather").

CINEMATOGRAPHERS

Ad., 906 Longacre Bldg., N. Y.; Bryant 6057; Williamson Bros. ("Submarine Eye"), Selznick ("Out Yonder"), World's Tours, Tourneur ("White Heather"). Ad., 906 Longacre Bldg., N. Y.; Bryant 6057; studio ad., Selznick Studios, Fort Lee, N. J.

SMITH, Al Ira; b. Memphis, Tenn., Oct. 15, 1887; educ. Chicago Art Institute and Univ. of Tenn.; early career, cartoonist; screen career, Selig, Pathe, Gaumont and Smith Films ("Timothy," "Jitneyed," "See America First," "Alaska Wonders in Motion," etc.). Home ad., 131 S. Grand ave., Los Angeles, Cal.; studio ad., 303 S. Hill st., Los Angeles, Cal.

SMITH, Leonard; screen career, Vitagraph ("Battle Cry of Peace"), Larry Seamon comedies, "Between Friends"; General Pershing's personal staff photographer during the war; now with King Cole Comedies. Home ad., 1011 Ocean ave., Brooklyn, N. Y.; studio ad., Motion Picture Producing Co. of America, Dongan Hills, S. I., N. Y.

SONNTAG, Emil B.; b. and educ. Chicago; screen career, cameraman Selig Polyscope Co. 8 yrs.; Rothacker Film Co. 2½ yrs., Amazon Film Co., 2½ yrs., as laboratory mgr.; cameraman for Northwestern Film Corp. ("Before the White Man Came"). Home ad., 1706 Augusta st., Chicago, Ill.

SQUIRE, Harry E.; b. N. Y.; educ. Trinity Schl. and Mechanics Inst.; screen career, Paramount Pictograph, Edison, Paramount-Flagg comedies ("One Every Minute," "Pride and Pork Chops," "Beresford of the Baboons," "The Last Bottle," "Welcome Little Stranger," "The Con in Economy"), chief cinematographer for Educational Dept. of Famous Players-Lasky Corp., Long Island City, N. Y. Home ad., 2679 Briggs ave., N. Y. C.; Fordham 1908.

STEENE, E. Burton, also technical director; b. Philadelphia, 1879; educ. Univ. of Pa.; early career, cavalry officer in Spanish war, special cor. and photographer in army corps; N. Y. Telephone Co. 5 yrs.; screen career, began in 1909 with Pathe as asst. ed. Pathe Weekly, covered world making scenics; now chief photographer and tech. dir. Pathe industrial dept., with Educational Film. Member local 557, I. A. T. S. E. Ad., 220 Candler Bldg., N. Y. Elks, Spanish War Vets.

STUART, Robert A.; b. Sheffield, Eng.; educ. N. Y.; screen career, Imp-Universal, Vitagraph ("Rose of the South," "The Enemy," "Soldiers of Chance," "Her Right to Live"). Member local 55 M, A. T. S. E. Home ad., 1019 E. 15th st., Brooklyn, N. Y.

STUMAR, Charles; b. Budapest, Hungary, 1890; screen career, since 1916 with Ince, photographer of the Louise Glaum specials. Home ad., 7023 Watseka ave., Culver City, Calif.; phone 70002.

STUMAR, John Stuart; screen career, chief photographer of Dorothy Dalton prod., "Vive La France," "Quicksand," "Extravagance," etc., Enid Bennett, "The Marriage Ring," etc., Ince-Paramount ("Market of Souls," "L'Aache"). Ad., Ince Studio, Culver City, Calif.

STURGIS, F. H.; b. Michigan; educ. Calif.; screen career, laboratory work for 2 yrs.; motion picture camera 1 yr.; 20 yrs. photographic exper.; Monrovia Feature Film Co., Hearst-Pathe, Clune Producing Co., Federal Photoplays. Home ad., 6059 Holly blvd., Hollywood, Calif.; studio, Federal Photo Plays, Hollywood.

— T —

TAINGUY, Lucien b. Paris, France; educ. Paris; screen career, with George Melies in Paris ("The Trip Around the Moon"), in America with Vitagraph, All-Star, Eclair, Peerless-World ("All Man," "The Beloved Adventuress," "The Man Who Forgot"). Home ad., 601 W. 127th st., N. Y. C.; Mngside. 3085. Member local 557, I. A. T. S. E., N. Y.

TANNURA, Philip; b. N. Y. C., 1897; educ. N. Y. C.; screen career, Reliance, Biograph, Majestic, Kinemacolor, Famous Players, Edison ("The Little Chevalier," "Knights of the Square Table," "Story the Key Told," "Apple Tree Girl," "The Unbeliever"); athletics; played character parts. Hght., 5, 4; wght., 120; dark complexion, black hair, brown eyes. Home ad., 2737 Decatur ave., N. Y.

THORNLEY, William H.; b. Cincinnati, Ohio; educ. there; early career, photographer; screen career, Brentwood ("Better Times," "Turn of the Road"), Pathe ("Terror of the Range" serial, "Border Raiders," "The Devil's Trail"), Stuart Paton Prod. ("The Fatal Sign" serial). Home ad., 5322 Lexington ave., Los Angeles, Calif.; Holly 3319; studio, Stuart Paton Studio, Ocean Park, Calif.

THORPE, Harry; b. St. Paul, Minn.; educ. there and Los Angeles, Calif.; screen career, Douglas Fairbanks ("Down to Earth," "Man From Painted Post," "Reaching for the Moon," "A Modern Musketeer," "When the Clouds Roll By"), 18 mos. in France. Ad., Douglass Fairbanks Studio, Hollywood, Calif.

THORPE, William Harris; b. St. Paul; general photographic work, for 3 yrs. half-tone operator Thorpe Engraving Co.; screen career, Kalem, cameraman Hollywood studios; Artcraft ("Headin' South"). Member Cinema Camera Club. U. S. Expeditionary Forces, France.

TODD, Arthur Lyle; b. and educ. N. Y. C.; screen career, Gaumont, Kalem, Reserve Photoplays Co., World, Perry Pictures, Film D'Art, late pictures "The Whip," "Betsy Ross," "Auntie," Brunton-Hodkinson ("The Lord Loves the Irish"). Home ad., 721 West Lake, Los Angeles; studio, Brunton.

TOTHEROH, Roland; b. San Francisco, Cal., 1890; educ. Alameda; early career, cartoonist; screen career, Essanay, Lone Star and Mutual. Head cameraman Charlie Chaplin Film Co. Member Cinema Camera Club. Studio, 1416 La Brea ave., Los Angeles, Cal. Home ad., 1222 Highland ave., Hollywood, Calif.

TRAVIS, Norton C.; b. Brooklyn, N. Y.; educ. there; screen career, Pathe, Fox, engaged in making moving pictures in first line trenches on Russian western front; now developing speed camera at work. Member local 557, I. A. T. S. E., 220 W. 42nd st., N. Y.

TROFFEY, Alex., film cutter; b. Long Island; educ. there; 8 yrs. cutting; Universal, Vitagraph, Monmouth ("Jimmie Dale" serial 32 reels); Frohman Amuse. ("Once to Every Man"), T. Hayes Hunter ("Border Legion"); with Goldwyn since its inception. Ad., Goldwyn Pictures Corp., 469 Fifth Ave., N. Y.

TUERS, William H.; b. N. Y. C.; educ. Trinity Schl.; screen career, Baumer Films, Metro, Oliver Films, Rolfe Prods., MacManus Corp. Home ad., 1499 E. 10th st., Brooklyn, N. Y., or Green Room Club, N. Y.

— U —

ULLMAN, Edward; b. Natchez, Miss., 1874; educ. there; early career, wide range photographic work; screen career, Reliance, Majestic, Universal, supt. of photography dept. and chief cameraman ("Father and the Boys," "The Wild Cat of Paris," "Blinding Trail," "Little White Savage," "Broadway Scandal"), Christie ("Two A. M."). Ad., 1107 So. Western ave., Los Angeles, Calif.; studio, Christie.

— V —

VALLEJO, Enrique Juan (or Harry); b. Mexico City; educ. there and Los Angeles; screen career, Keystone, photographed first Chas. Chaplin picture, Universal, Pathe, Clune Films ("Ramona," "Eyes of the World"), International ("Patria"), Pathe ("Twenty-one," "Kidder & Ko."), National ("Romance of Tarzan," "Tarzan of the Apes," 7 comedies of "Hall Room Boys" series, one Billy Parsons comedy), Federal ("Desert of Wheat," "Dwelling Place of Light"). Home ad., 1611 Curson ave., West Hollywood, Calif.; phone 2374; studio, Federal Photoplays Co., Brunton Studio.

VAN BUREN, Ned; b. Gouverneur, N. Y., 1882; educ. there; early exper. photography; screen career, Mittenthal, NYMP ("The Alien"); Gaumont Weekly, Conness Till Co., Edison ("Children of Eve"), Universal ("Thread of Life"), Vitagraph, Famous ("Nanette of the Wilds," "Her Better Self," "Double Crossed," "The Slave Market"), Artcraft ("Seven Keys to Baldpate"), with Buffalo Film Co at present. Member local 557, I. A. T. S. E. Ad., 147 W. 55th st., N. Y.

VAN DER VEER, Willard; b. Brooklyn, 1894; stage career, since age of 10, "Polly of the Circus," Sign of the Four"; screen career, 1916-17, Gaumont, West Indian series, tours around the world; Sept. 1917, to June 25, 1919, Photographic Div., Signal Corps., U. S. Army, A. E. F.; Outing Chester series, "Foolish Fish of Sawback," "Hippity, Hoppity, Wapiti." Ad., care Motion Picture News, N. Y.

VAUGHAN, Roy V.; b. 1893; educ. Los Angeles, Cal.; early career, learned manufacture of surveying instruments; screen career, built motion picture cameras, operating them later for Triangle, Selznick, Goldwyn ("Her Excellency the Governor," "The Food Gamblers," "The Haunted House," "The Man Hater"). Member 557, I. A. T. S. E. Ad., 206 W. 106th st., N. Y.

— W —

WAGNER, William F.; b. N. Y., 1893; educ. N. Y.; screen career, Pathe, Famous Players, Metro ("The Pretenders"), Mutual ("Mary Moreland"). Now with Selznick, N. Y. Home ad., 142 W. 77th st., N. Y.

WALES, Claude Henry ("Bud"); b. Indianapolis, Ind.; educ. Univ. of Wash.; screen career, Universal, Keystone, Triangle, Beaver Films, Fine Arts, National ("Fall of a Nation"), Lenox Prod. Co. ("The Betrayal," 8 reels), "Madam Sphinx," "Tony America," "Headin' North," "The Painted Lily," etc., photographed 2 yrs. in Alaska, traveled around the world. Home ad., 159 W. 45th st., Los Angeles, Calif.

WALKER, Vernon L.; screen exper., for Edwin Bower Hesser ("On Secret Service," "The White Coat," five-reel dramas), Starline Company ("You Can Never Tell," "State of Georgia," 12-reel historic pageant, "Alaska Today," 5-reel travelogue in the making of which every foot of Alaska was covered), staff photographer Selig-Tribune Weekly; National Film Corp., Denver ("Where the Sun Sets Red," "The Mating of Meg Malloy," "In the Shadows of the Rockies," "The Bandit of Lonesome Gap," "The Bridge Across," etc., etc.; now head cameraman for The Art-O-Graf Film Co., Denver, Colo.; enlisted in Photo Section Signal Corps, U. S. A. Home ad., 2858 Race st., Denver, Colo.

WARREN, Dwight W.; b. 1888, Los Angeles; early career, 8 yrs. in still photography; screen career, 2 seasons with Ince, Kay-Bee Triangle ("In Slumberland"). Home ad., 14 N. El Molino st., Alhambra, Los Angeles, Calif.; studio, Hart Studio, Los Angeles.

WARRENTON, Gilbert; b. Paterson, N. J.; screen career, Univ. Fine Arts, Triangle, American ("Law of the Great Northwest," "Hard Rock Breed," "High Tide," "The Golden Fleece," "Fair Enough," "Put Up Your Hands"), Mary Pickford Co. and International. Member Cinema Camera Club, Los Angeles. Home ad., 1525 Bronson ave., Los Angeles, Calif.

WEBBER, George; b. Kingston, Ont.; educ. C. C. N. Y.; screen career, Lubin, World, Biograph, Thanhouser; photographed "The Million Dollar Mystery," "Tillie's Tomato Surprise," Metro ("The Eternal Mother"), Goldwyn (Tom Moore in "Go West, Young Man," Man and His Money," "One of the Finest," "City of Comrades," "Lord and Lady Algy," Mabel Normand in "Upstairs," "The Jinks," "Pinto," Madge Kennedy in "The Blooming Angel").

WHITMAN, Philip H.; b. N. Y.; screen career, formerly with Universal, Keystone and Sennett companies, now doing special productions with Hampton Del Ruth. Home ad., 1748½ N. Western ave., Los Angeles, Calif.; Holly 2623; studio, Fox.

WILKY, L. Guy; b. Phoenix, Ariz.; educ. Univ. Ariz.; screen career, Lubin, American, Ince-Triangle, Paralta; specialist in artificial lighting and special effects for artistic prod.; student of art and composition with its relation to cinematography; with Bessie Barriscale for 1 yr., Famous Players 6 mos., affiliated with Wm. C DeMille, photographed "Tangled Threads," "Two-Gun Betty," "The Woman Michael Married," "The Tree of Knowledge." Member A. S. of C. Home ad., 5517 Sierra Vista ave., Hollywood, Calif.; phone 599514; studio, Lasky.

WILLIAMS, Frank D.; b. Nashville, Mo., 1893; educ. Pittsburg; screen career, Essanay, Keystone, chief cameraman with Sennett 4½ yrs., photographer Charlie Chaplin, Mabel Normand in "Mickey," Annette Kellerman in "Queen of the Sea," owns tank patents on this picture; Roscoe Arbuckle, Metro, Bushman & Bayne, "The Dragon Painter," "The Gray Horizon," "The Tong Man" and other Sessue Hayakawa pictures; head of photograph dept. for Haworth Pictures Corp.; owns patent for putting characters into action on photographic background. Member Cinema Camera Club, Los Angeles. Ad., 1710 W. 6th st., Los Angeles, Calif.

WILLIAMS, Lawrence E.; screen career, Thanhouser, Reliance, Famous Players, Harry Rapf, Frank A. Keeney Prods., Artcraft, Virginia Pearson Co. ("The Bishops Emeralds," "Impossible Catherine"), Shear & Co. ("Lonely Heart"). Is familiar with every branch of photography. Ad., 540 S. 6th ave., Mt. Vernon, N. Y.

WILLIAMS, Walter E.; b. Indiana, 1891; educ. there; screen career, Fine Arts, Reliance, Majestic, Fox ("Jack and the Bean Stalk," "The Splendid Sin," "The Snares of Paris," "Lost Money," "What Would You Do?" with Madlaine Traverse, "In the Days of Auld Lang Syne" with Peggy Hyland. Is familiar with every branch of photography. Ad., 5723 La Mirada ave., Los Angeles, Calif. Member Cinema Camera Club.

WINTHER, Carl Pagh; b. Denmark; screen career, cinematographer for Majestic-Reliance, Fine Arts Studio; directing of Higganie pictures, Alaska wilds, California wild life, Mexico birds and game, life in India and the West Indies for Dr. Salisbury and Rex Beach.

WYCKOFF, Alvin; director of photography; b. Elmira, N. Y.; educ. Detroit Univ., Detroit, Mich.; stage career, William Owen 2 seasons, eastern dram. stock 5 seasons; screen career, Artcraft, Selig ("Monte Cristo," "The Spoilers," "Wizard of Oz"), Lasky ("Joan of Arc," "The Cheat"), Famous Players ("Male and Female," "Girl of the Golden West," "Squaw Man," "The Virginian"); supervised erection of new Lasky laboratory; is also inventor of numerous appliances; familiar with every branch of photography. Member Cinema Camera Club. Ad., Famous Players-Lasky Studio, Hollywood, Calif.

WYNARD, Edward; b. N. Y. C.; screen career, Imp 5½ yrs., Roland West Film Co., 12 pictures for Norma Talmadge Film Corp., Fox, Ray Emory Prod. Co. "The Chosen Path"), National Film Co., Dietrich and Beck ("The Band Box"), Tyrad ("The Red Viper"), Norma Talmadge ("The Forbidden City"). Hallmark. Ad., 536 Dean st., Brooklyn, N. Y.

— Y —

YOUNG, Hal.; b. Australia; screen career, Sid Olcott Irish productions, Famous, World ("The Dark Silence"), Metro, Selznick ("The Foolish Virgin," "The Easiest Way," "The Common Law"), Para-Art ("Witness for the Defense"), Realart ("Anne of Green Gables"). Member Cinema Camera Club. Ad., 1043 Boston rd., N. Y.; Intervale 5590.

YOUNG, Jack R.; b. N. Y. C., 1896 (claims to be youngest professional cameraman); stage experience, with Blanch Ring in "When Claudia Smiles"; screen career, D. W. Griffith, M. Sennett, Reliance, cameraman with Fox, National Drama, Bluebird Prod. ("The Nature Girl," "The Great Cause"), Edgar Jones Prod. ("Quicksand," "Border River," "Beloved Brute"), on expedition to Grand Fall, Labrador for Mills Bros. Ad., Edgar Jones Prod., Inc., Augusta, Maine.

— Z —

ZALIBRA, George C. ("Duke"); b. Pittsburg, Pa., Feb. 9, 1887; educ. St. Joseph's Acad., Pittsburg, Pa.; early career, stage mgr.; screen career, Pathe, Keystone and Mutual ("A Trip Through Africa," "Through the Alps," "Trip to the North Pole," etc.), Goldwyn ("The Scrub Lady"). Member Cinema Camera Club, Los Angeles. Home ad., 132 Edmund st., Pittsburg, Pa.

ZANGRILLI, Orestes A.; b. Italy, 1881; educ. N. Y.; screen career, Kalem Co. 9 yrs., Universal Film Co. 1 yr. Ad., 52 Sherman st., Montclair, N. J.

ZOLLINGER, William M.; b. Brooklyn, 1874; educ. there; screen career, Vitagraph ("War"), Thanhouser ("Silas Marner," "War and the Woman," "King Lear"); is familiar with every branch of photography. Member local 577 I. A. T. S. E., 220 W. 42nd st., N. Y.

MOTION PICTURE ORGANIZATIONS

THE NATIONAL BOARD OF REVIEW—ITS HISTORY, ORGANIZATION AND POLICIES

The National Board of Review was organized in March, 1919, by the People's Institute at the request of the theatres exhibiting motion pictures in New York City. The work of the Board became national in scope in June of the same year at the request of the manufacturers of motion-picture films. Since that date, the Board has gained an increasing control over the films exhibited in America.

The Board is composed as follows: a general committee of thirty representatives from various civic agencies located in New York, together with certain disinterested, public-spirited individuals; an executive committee chosen from this membership; and a review committee of 100 members. This last unit, divided into sub-committees, is at work at least five days each week. The general committee was called together by the People's Institute at the beginning of the Board's existence, and elects its own members. The review committee is selected by the general committee, the tenure of office being three months. No member of the Board is engaged in any branch of the motion-picture business, and no voting member is salaried directly or indirectly for his services.

The Board is self-governing in all particulars, establishes its own standards, elects its own officers and executive staff, and controls its own finances. The money to defray expenses is raised wholly from three sources: By voluntary subscriptions from persons interested in and benefited by its work; by subscriptions to its weekly bulletin service; and by a charge to all producing companies for a review of their product at a flat rate per reel.

The general committee, as presently constituted, is presided over by Everett Dean Martin. The executive staff, with headquarters at 70 Fifth Avenue, is composed as follows:

Executive Staff

W. D. McGuire, Jr.........Executive Secretary
Orrin G. Cocks..............Advisory Secretary
W. M. Covill..............Membership Secretary
W. A. Barrett................Review Secretary
Alice B. Evans..........Corresponding Secretary

Besides the committees given above, a national advisory committee with representatives in all of the larger cities of the Union co-operates with the National Board of Review in furnishing information and promoting the Board's plans. The advisory committee for New York City, which consists of thirty-five members, includes such names as Percy Mackaye, William H. Maxwell, Jacob H. Schiff, Oscar S. Straus and Stephen S. Wise. The representatives of the national advisory committee for other cities are listed as follows:

D. Hiden Ramsay, Asheville, N. C.; W. A. Percy, Atlanta, Ga.; Hon. H. W. Adams, Beloit, Wis.; John M. Casey, Boston, Mass.; S. Parkes Cadman and Dr. J. P. Warbasse, Brooklyn, N. Y.; John L. Alexander and Shailer Mathews, Chicago, Ill.; George A. Bellamy, Mrs. George Crile and Miss Charlotte Rumbold, Cleveland, Ohio; D. G. Johnson, Colorado Springs, Colo.; A. W. Taylor, Columbia, Mo.; Elmer Scott, Dallas, Tex.; Mrs. Helen Ring Robinson and Mrs. Margaret D. Conway, Denver, Colo.; Dr. Harris F. Rall, Evanston, Ill.; A. G. Arvold, Fargo, No. Dak.; Dan C. Beard, Flushing, N. Y.; Miss Mary Gray Peck, Geneva, N. Y.; Harry C. Hurd, Indianapolis, Ind.; L. A. Halbert, Kansas City, Mo.; R. H. Edwards, Lisle, N. Y.; Everett C. Beach and S. M. Cooper, Los Angeles, Calif.; Mrs. Fred Levy, Louisville, Ky.; Charles Stelzle, Maplewood, N. J.; John M. Dean, Memphis, Tenn.; G. R. Radley, Milwaukee, Wis.

M. L. Burton, Mrs. Charles W. Cartwright and Robins Gilman, Minneapolis, Minn.; J. E. McCulloch and Hamilton Love, Nashville, Tenn.; Anson Phelps Stokes, New Haven, Conn.; Mrs. Paul Getzchman and T. T. Sturgess, Omaha, Nebr.; Ernest A. Batchelder and Vernon O. Whitcomb, Pasadena, Calif.; Miss Helen L. Coe, Portland, Me.; W. G. Eliot, Jr., William T. Foster and Mrs. Millie Trumbull, Portland, Oreg.; Sergeant Richard Gamble, Providence, R. I.; Edward C. Fellows, Randolph, N. Y.; R. Andrew Hamilton, Rochester, N. Y.; Charles DeY. Elkus and Mrs. Bert Schlesinger, San Francisco, Calif.; Dr. Sarah Kendall, Seattle, Wash.; U. G. Manning, South Bend, Ind.; C. A. Fleming and S. Glasgow, Spokane, Wash.; Rev. James Boyd Coxe and Horace M. Swope, St. Louis, Mo.; Walter W. Nicholson and Miss Minnie E. Paddock, Syracuse, N. Y.; Festus Foster, Topeka, Kan.; Burdette G. Lewis, Trenton, N. J.; Samuel Gompers, Washington, D. C., and Dr. Frank Oliver Hall, Winchester, Mass.

In criticizing productions, the members of a reviewing committee are required to bring to the picture the judgment of the typical audience and must endeavor to reflect what the people of the United States would think about any given production were they sitting en masse to view the picture. In other words, the standard of judgment must be public opinion and not personal prejudice or views.

The decisions of the National Board of Review are enforced by public officials and other agencies, which are kept acquainted with the criticisms and accomplishments of the Board, principally by the publication of a weekly official Bulletin. This publication is furnished free of charge to officials in the principal cities of thirty-eight states. It gives a list of all pictures reviewed during each current week, with notes and decisions thereon. Accordingly, though the Board is a voluntary, extra-legal body, having no legal power resident in itself, its decisions have the effect of legal verdicts through the co-operation of mayors, license-bureaus, police departments and boards of public welfare in cities throughout the country, where the official correspondents enforce the judgments of the National Board.

That the National Board of Review is an active body is evidenced by the following excerpt from a recent publication of the organization: "The National Board sits at the gateway through which all motion pictures must pass before they reach the American public. During a single year a ceaseless stream of five thousand subjects flows past it. Since 1909 the National Board has daily inspected and passed upon films, until now it views 10,000 reels or 10,000,000 feet a year, which are copied from 20 to 150 times each and circulated in all parts of the United States."

NATIONAL ASSOCIATION OF THE MOTION PICTURE INDUSTRY, INC.

The information compiled and submitted below gives the officers and directors of the National Association of the Motion Picture Industry, who were elected at the third annual meeting, held at Rochester, N. Y., on Aug. 5th, 1919. The personnel of the executive committee follows. There are also included the other principal committees of the association, together with their respective chairmen. The headquarters of the National Association is located in Room 806, Times Building, New York.

Officers and Directors for 1919-1920

President: William A. Brady, Wm. A. Brady Picture Plays, Inc.
Vice Presidents: Adolph Zukor, Famous Players-Lasky Corporation; Samuel Goldwyn, Goldwyn Pictures Corporation; Will C. Smith, Nicholas Power Company; E. M. Porter, Precision Machine Company; P. A. Powers, Universal Film Mfg. Company; Paul H. Cromelin, Inter-Ocean Film Corporation.
Treasurer: J. E. Brulatour, Eastman Film.
Executive Secretary: Frederick H. Elliott, 806 Times Building.

Producers' Division, Class No. 1

Adolph Zukor, Famous Players-Lasky Corporation.
J. Stuart Blackton, J. Stuart Blackton Feature Pictures, Inc.
William A. Brady, Wm. A. Brady Picture Plays, Inc.
Paul Brunet, Pathe Exchange, Inc.
William Fox, Fox Film Corporation.
Samuel Goldwyn, Goldwyn Pictures Corporation.
D. W. Griffith, D. W. Griffith Enterprises.
Carl Laemmle, Universal Film Mfg. Company.
Richard A. Rowland, Metro Pictures Corporation.
Joseph M. Schenck, Norma Talmadge Picture Corporation.
Lewis J. Selznick, Select Pictures Corporation.
Albert E. Smith, Vitagraph Company of America.

Supply & Equipment Division, Class No. 3

J. E. Brulatour, Eastman Films.
Harry H. Allen, Wyanoak Publishing Company.
Willard B. Cook, Pathescope Company of America.

STUDIO DIRECTORY

Joseph F. Coufal, Standard Slide Company.
Walter J. Moore, H. C. Miner Lithographing Company.
E. M. Porter, Precision Machine Company.
B. F. Porter.
Will C. Smith, Nicholas Power Company.
L. P. Weber, Acme Lithographing Company.

Distributors' Division, Class No. 4

Walter W. Irwin, Famous Players-Lasky Corporation.
W. E. Atkinson, Metro Pictures Corporation.
William J. Clark, Exhibitors Mutual Distributing Corporation.
Arthur S. Friend, Famous Players-Lasky Corporation.
Ricord Gradwell, World Film Corporation.
Gabriel L. Hess, Goldwyn Distributing Corporation.
Lewis Innerarity, Pathe Exchange, Inc.
P. A. Powers, Universal Film Mfg. Company.
John M. Quinn, Vitagraph, Inc.
W. R. Sheehan, Fox Film Corporation.
Percy L. Waters, Triangle Distributing Corporation.
J. D. Williams, First National Exhibitors Circuit.

General Division, Class No. 5

John C. Flinn, 485 Fifth Ave.
Fred J. Beecroft, 729 Seventh Ave.
George Blaisdell, 516 Fifth Ave.
Paul H. Cromelin, 218 West 42nd St.
Paul Gulick, 1600 Broadway.
Lesly Mason, 1587 Broadway.
J. Robert Rubin, 165 Broadway.
Julian M. Solomon, Jr., 141 East 25th St.
Thomas G. Wiley, 209 West 48th St.

Executive Committee

Walter W. Irwin, Chairman; William A. Brady, ex-officio; Jack G. Leo, Fox Film Corp.; Louis J. Selznick, Select Pictures; Paul H. Cromelin, John M. Quinn, J. E. Brulatour, Gabriel L. Hess, John C. Flinn, W. E. Atkinson, Lewis Innerarity, Arthur S. Friend.

Censorship Committee, Gabriel L. Hess; Fire Prevention Committee, J. E. Brulatour; Legal and Legislative Committee, Nathan Vidaver; Transportation Committee, P. H. Stilson.

In the following are submitted the various classes of membership in the National Association of the Motion Picture Industry and the entrance fees and annual dues for each class.

Producer, Class No. 1.

	Entrance Fee.	Annual Dues.
Class A to comprise features released through distributing companies	$250	$100
Class B to comprise those who produce for State right sales and serials	150	50
Class C to comprise those producing for a program of one, two and three reels, producers of industrial pictures, and film developers and printers	75	25

Exhibitors, Class No. 2

Class.	Seating Capacity.	Annual Dues.
A	3001 or over	$50
B	2001 to 3000	36
C	1001 to 2000	24
D	501 to 1000	19
E	301 to 500	12
F	300 or under	6

Supply and Equipment, Class No. 3

	Entrance Fee.	Annual Dues.
Banner and Photograph Manufacturers	$50	$25
Camera, Studio and Laboratory Equipment Dealers	100	50
Camera, Studio and Laboratory Equipment Manufacturers and Importers	250	100
Carbon Manufacturers and Importers	250	100
Chairs, Exclusive Dealers in	100	25
Chairs, Manufacturers and Importers	250	100
Chemical Manufacturers, Importers and Dealers:		
Class A, Manufacturers and Importers	250	100
Class B	100	25
Costumes, Props and Furnishing Manufacturers	150	50
Electric Sign Dealers	50	25
Electric Sign Manufacturers	100	50
Electric Light, Heat and Power Companies:		
In Cities up to 100,000	50	10
In Cities up to 500,000	75	25
In Cities up to 1,000,000	150	75
In Cities over 1,000,000	250	100
Electric Light Plant Manufacturers	50	25
Film Renovators	25	10
Film Cleaning Machine Manufacturers	50	25
Lens for Cameras and Projectors, Manufacturers and Importers of	100	50
Lithograph and Poster Manufacturers	250	100
Lobby Display Manufacturers	50	25
Motion Picture Machine Dealers	50	25
Motion Picture Machine Distributors	100	50
Motor Generator, Rotary Converter, Rectifier, Transformer, Arc Controller and Rheostat Manufacturers	75	25
Musical Instrument Manufacturers	150	100
Operating Booth Manufacturers (asbestos or metal)	100	50
Printers of Tickets, Folders, Heralds, Small Work	50	25
Projection Machine Manufacturers and Importers:		
Class A, Standard Machines	250	100
Class B, Home Machines (including Importers)	100	50
Raw Film Manufacturers, Importers and Agents	500	250
Screen Manufacturers and Importers	150	50
Slide and Novelty Manufacturers	50	25
Stage Lighting Equipment Manufacturers	150	50
Stage and Studio Scenery Manufacturers	150	50
Ticket Selling Machine and Device Manufacturers	75	25
Ventilating Equipment Manufacturers	75	25
Engravers and Electrotypers	100	50

Distributor and Exchange, Class No. 4

	Entrance Fee.	Annual Dues.
Motion Picture Film Distributors	$500	$250
Exchanges (Each)	50	25

General Division, Class No. 5

	Entrance Fee.	Annual Dues.
Advertising Agents	$250	$100
Architects and Builders and Sub-Contractors:		
In Cities up to 100,000	25	10
In Cities up to 500,000	50	25
In Cities up to 1,000,000	150	75
In Cities over 1,000,000	250	100
Bill Posting Companies:		
In Cities up to 100,000	50	10
In Cities up to 500,000	75	25
In Cities up to 1,000,000	150	75
In Cities over 1,000,000	250	100
Banks and Trust Companies	75	25
Camera Men	10	5
Employes of Establishments and Plants in any way connected with the Motion Picture Industry	2	2
Employment Agents	50	25
Exhibition Halls:		
Up to 2500 Capacity	50	25
Over 2500 Capacity	100	50
Insurance Companies	250	100
Motion Picture Actors and Actresses other than Stars	10	5
Motion Picture Stars	150	75
Newspapers, Daily and Sunday:		
In Cities up to 100,000	50	10
In Cities up to 500,000	75	25
In Cities up to 1,000,000	150	75
In Cities over 1,000,000	250	100
Program Publishers	50	25
Projection Engineers	25	10
Publications Devoted Exclusively to Motion Pictures	250	100
Publications with Motion Picture Department	150	100
Studio Directors	50	25
Studio Managers	25	10
Transportation and Express Companies	250	100
Film Exporters and Forwarders	100	50
State Rights Buyers	10	5

WHO'S AT THE HELM

MACKLYN ARBUCKLE
President of San Antonio Pictures Corporation

Mr. Arbuckle has been a prominent figure in the theatrical world for a good many years. Taking up the stage as his profession at an early age, he worked his way to stardom because of his talent and personality. He was starred in George Ade's drama, "The County Chairman," and also starred in "The Round-Up" and other plays. Mr. Arbuckle is now identified with pictures and holds the office of President of San Antonio Pictures Corporation and is also a member of the Board of Directors. The capital stock of this concern is $150,000.00. The Company started producing the first of July, 1919, under the direction of Leopold D. Wharton, and Mr. Arbuckle is featured exclusively in photoplay comedy-dramas. The first six subjects are from the pens of Holman F. Day, Irvin S. Cobb, George Barr McCutcheon, Archibald Clavering Gunter, George V. Hobart and Fred Jackson. For further information see "Actors."

GERALD F. BACON
Gerald F. Bacon Productions

Gerald Bacon has been prominently identified with both stage and screen for many years, beginning his theatrical career with Sanger & Jordan, play-brokers, following a short time as mining engineer in the West. Mr. Bacon, in addition to his work as play-broker and producer for the stage, has produced more than half a dozen photodramas, including "A Woman's Experience," "Men," "The Melting Pot," and "The Whirl of Life." Mr. Bacon's business address is the Fulton theatre, N. Y. C.

JOHN RANDOLPH BRAY
President and General Manager

Mr. Bray was born in Michigan. He became a newspaper artist and cartoonist with the Brooklyn Eagle and the Detroit Free Press. He was a pioneer in the development of animated cartoon processes. Became president of Bray Studios, 1915-1919, president of Bray Pictures Corporation in 1919. The address of this concern is 23 East 26th st., N. Y. C.

JAMISON HANDY
Vice-President

Mr. Handy was born in Chicago and educated in the University of Michigan. Trained himself as a newspaper writer and executive with the Chicago Tribune under Medill McCormick. Later became asscociated with Harrington Emerson, efficiency expert. Then with Herbert Kaufman in sales and advertising business. In 1916-1918 became president of Keeley-Handy Syndicate with Chicago Herald. He is a writer of well-known motion picture serials. Specialist in production of Industrial Pictures.

J. F. LEVENTHAL
Vice-President

Mr. Leventhal was born in Tennessee and educated himself as an architect. In 1916-1919 became identified with Teknagraph Films. In 1918 originated animated technical drawings, called "Keknagraphs." Produced "Training of Soldier Films" for U. S. Army. Originator of "Gasoline Engine Films." In 1919 he became vice-president of Bray Pictures Corporation.

PAUL BRUNET
Vice-President and General Manager of Pathe Exchange, Inc.

Paul Brunet, in addition to being vice-president and general manager of Pathe Exchange, Inc., has the signal honor of being an administrator of Pathe Cinema, Ltd., of Paris, the international motion picture organization. He is the only vice-president of Pathe Exchange, Inc., who has been paid this high tribute. Mr. Brunet was elected vice-president and general manager of Pathe Exchange, Inc., on March 7, 1918. Under him the organization has grown into one of the most influential in the film industry. Mr. Brunet recently was honored by an appointment as one of the board of governors of the Franco-American Board of Commerce and Industry, along with such well known New Yorkers as Albert Breton, Joseph T. Cosby, Paul Fuller, Jr., Ernest Iselin, Arthur B. Leach, H. Michelin, Jean Revillon, and J. R. Munoz, all of whom are identified with big enterprises. Before assuming his present offices with Pathe Mr. Brunet was its comptroller. Under his administration and his power for organization the department gained vastly in its effectiveness. Before coming to this country from France five years ago to join the Eclectic Film Company, which at that time distributed Pathe's product, Mr. Brunet was prominent in the banking circles of Paris. All his business life has been devoted to the handling of big financial institutions, and the rapid growth of Pathe Exchange, Inc., is a monument to his ability.

ROBERT BRUNTON
Producer
See "Producers"

C. L. CHESTER
President C. L. Chester Productions, Inc., 120 West 41st St., N. Y. C.

Mr. Chester is one of the pioneer producers in the motion picture industry. He has been a picture man all his adult life, starting in still photography and entering the motion picture business almost as soon as motion pictures were invented. He has supervised the filming of many notable travel features and himself has taken subjects on trips into the wilds. C. L. Chester's Productions, Inc., produce Chester Outings, weekly, one reel travel pictures, and screenics, weekly, one reel combination animal life and Famous Wits release.

AL E. CHRISTIE
President Christie Film Company
See "Producers"

WILLIAM J. CLARK
President

Mr. Clark, in addition to being President of the Clark-Cornelius Corporation, is President of Exhibitors' Mutual Distributing Corporation, Consolidated Theatres, Inc., Grand Rapids. Mich.; an officer of and director in various industrial and financial corporations in Grand Rapids, Mich., and Little Rock, Ark.

H. G. CORNELIUS
Treasurer

Mr. Cornelius is also secretary and treasurer of the Wolverine Brass Works, Grand Rapids, Mich.; vice-president of Exhibitors' Mutual Distributing Corporation and vice-president of the Consolidated Theatres, Inc., of Grand Rapids.

S. J. ROLLO
Secretary

Mr. Rollo was formerly director of sales and exchanges for Exhibitors' Mutual Distributing Corporation; was sales manager of the Mutual Film Corporation, prior to which he was connected in an executive capacity with the sales department of Montgomery Ward Company, Chicago, and the National Biscuit Company.

WALTER K. PLUMB
General Manager

Mr. Plumb was treasurer of the Exhibitors' Mutual Distributing Corporation, which position he took upon the completion of war work as executive secretary to the Tanners' Council; he has extensive interests in Grand Rapids, Mich., and was for some years connected with the sales department of the National Biscuit Company and the Loose-Wiles Biscuit Company in an executive capacity.

COLVIN W. BROWN
Assistant Treasurer

Mr. Brown was director of publicity of Exhibitors' Mutual Distributing Corporation, prior to which he was advertising manager of the Mutual Film Corporation. His first connection with the film industry was as Western representative of the Exhibitors' Trade Review, prior to which he was sales manager of the New York Evening Mail Syndicate and editorial executive on a Mid-West newspaper.

JACK COHN
Jack and Harry Cohn

Jack Cohn's early career was identified with newspaper work. His screen career began with Universal Film Manufacturing Company, where he had charge of special exploitation. He is at present president of the Hall Room Boys Photoplays, Inc., with offices at 1600 Broadway. He distributes with his brother, Harry, the Hall Room Boys' comedies and series of educational and industrial pictures.

THEODORE C. DEITRICH
President of Deitrich-Beck, Inc., and De Luxe Pictures, Inc.

Theodore C. Deitrich was born in New Brighton, Pa., and until he entered the motion picture industry four years ago had spent practically his entire life in newspaper and magazine work, having been managing editor and editorial and dramatic writer in New York, Chicago, and San Francisco. Four years ago he was transferred by William Randolph Hearst from the New York American to the International Film Service, where he remained until November, 1917, when he organized the De Luxe Pictures, Inc., and since then Deitrich-Beck, Inc.

MARK M. DINTENFASS
Owner and Producer of Cuckoo Comedies

Mr. Dintenfass has been in the motion picture business for a great many years. He bought the Jacksonville studios, which include laboratories, from Lubin and there he produces the Cuckoo comedies which are released through United Picture Theatres. He is owner and producer of the Lee Kid comedies, vice-president of Tribune Productions, Inc., president of Stellar Laboratories, secretary and treasurer of "My Four Years in Germany" Company, and owner of the Vim Film Corporation.

A. H. FISCHER
President of A. H. Fischer Features, Inc., and Vice-President and Treasurer of Octagon Films, Inc.

A. H. Fischer, president and treasurer of A. H. Fischer Features, Inc., with studios and laboratory at 46 Main st., New Rochelle, N. Y., entered the film business in August, 1918, when in association with B. A. Rolfe, who produced the Houdini serial, "The Master Mystery." Since then he has produced, also with Mr. Rolfe, "A Scream in the Night," by Charles A. Logue. Organized in June, 1919, with B. A. Rolfe and Charles A. Logue, A. H. Fischer Features, Inc., for the production of special features. Bought the former Thanhouser studios in New Rochelle. Now producing a series of pictures based on stories written by Robert W. Chambers, and a series of pictures based on stories by Charles A. Logue. Completed productions: "The Amazing Lovers," from "The Shining Band," by Robert W. Chambers;fl "The Red Virgin," by Charles A. Logue. Besides his film activities Mr. Fischer is engaged in extensive glove and leather manufacturing.

B. A. ROLFE
Vice-President A. H. Fischer Features, Inc., and President of Octagon Films, Inc.

Mr. Rolfe was producer of vaudeville acts in association with Jesse L. Lasky and C. B. Maddock. Entered film business as the head of Rolfe Photoplays, Inc., which he organized, and which produced Metro releases from the inception of Metro until 1918. One of the organizers of Octagon Films, Inc., which produced the Houdini serial, "The Master Mystery," as a B. A. Rolfe production. With A. H. Fischer and Charles A. Logue formed in June, 1919, A. H. Fischer Features, Inc., now producing Chambers and Logue stories.

CHARLES A. LOGUE
Secretary A. H. Fischer Features, Inc.

Mr. Logue is writer of all scripts, both adaptations and originals, picturized by the company. Former newspaper man on New York World and New York Tribune; also contributor to Munsey's and other magazines. Wrote first script about three years ago—"The White Raven," produced by Metro. Since then wrote the following original stories: "My Lady Incog" and "The Feud Girl" (Famous Players), "A Wife by Proxy" (Metro), "The Duchess of Doubt" (Metro), "Outwitted" (Metro), "The Compact" (Metro), "The Service Star" (Goldwyn), "Just for Tonight" (Goldwyn), "The Kingdom of Youth" (Goldwyn), "On Record" (Lasky), "Treason" (Empire), "Ashes of Embers" (Famous Players), "The Lost Battalion" (MacManus), "A Scream in the Night" (Rolfe-Selznick), "The Flame of the Desert" (Goldwyn), "The Red Virgin" (A. H. Fischer Features, Inc.) His adaptations are: "The Heir to the Hoorah" (Lasky), "My Four Years in Germany" (Gerard), "Laughing Bill Hyde" (Rex Beach-Goldwyn), "Too Fat to Fight" (Rex Beach-Goldwyn), "The Brand" (Rex Beach-Goldwyn), "The Amazing Lovers" (Fischer Features). His serials are: "The House of Hate," "The Hidden Hand," and "The Tiger's Trail" (Pathe), and "The Master Mystery" (B. A. Rolfe).

CHARLES G. STEWART
General Manager of A. H. Fischer Features, Inc. and Octagon Films, Inc.

Mr. Stewart, manager, the Princess theatre, New York, for three years; manager, the Knickerbocker theatre, New York, under Triangle regime; manager, the Rialto and Rivoli theatres, New York, from the time of opening until January 1, 1919. Theatrical producer under the firm name of Stewart and Morrison, Inc., which produced "Our Pleasant Sins" at the Belmont theatre, New York, season 1918-19; "Betty Behave," season 1919-20. General manager of A. H. Fischer Features, Inc., and Octagon Films, Inc., since January 1, 1919.

WILLIAM FOX
President Fox Film Corporation

William Fox got into the motion picture industry of his own volition because he had been cheated in the purchase of a penny arcade and wished to recoup in some amusement enterprise. That was several years ago, and now he is the head of his own motion picture concern. Fifteen years ago William Fox was in the cloth-sponging business on the lower East Side of New York City. He soon progressed to foreman, manager, and eventually owner of the establishment. Soon after he ventured with his penny arcade with the zeal consummated, Mr. Fox found that the business was wholly fictitious. He set about the task of building up the business of the arcade, and in a few weeks was rewarded by a lucrative patronage. Encouraged, he branched out and took over two other similar enterprises, operating them successfully. From an arcade owner, Mr. Fox became a theatre owner. He leased the Dewey theatre in 14th street and the Gotham theatre in 125th street, New York. This was fourteen years ago, when the film business was beginning to attract attention. His start as a film man was humble enough. He formed the Greater New York Film Rental Company with offices at 116 East 14th street, and thus set himself up in business as a film distributor for the New York territory. The concern gradually branched out and established branch offices through the East. Mr. Fox then organized the Box Office Attraction Company. He formed a selling organization that covered twenty-two cities and made preparations to produce his own plays, continuing the meanwhile the distribution of other companies' films. In 1914 Fox Film Corporation absorbed the Box Office Attraction Company. The Eclair studio was purchased, companies were organized and productions started. He established a film printing plant at Fort Lee, N. J., in 1915, together with laboratories for handling the entire output of the organization. Branch offices were established in the United States, Canada, South America, Australia, New Zealand and Cuba. In 1916 the studios at Hollywood were completed. In 1919 construction was started on the $2,500,000 William Fox building at 10th avenue, from 55th to 56th streets, Manhattan. This building was constructed to house the administration offices, the eastern studios and the laboratory, and will accommodate nearly 5,000 employees. It includes room for twenty companies to work simultaneously.

EDWIN FRAZEE
President Frazee Film Productions, Inc.

Edwin Frazee will be remembered as a director of comedies formerly with Mack Sennett's Keystone Company. He was the creator of the comedy successes "Crooked to the End," "Bath-Tub Perils," also Fox Film comedy "Social Pirates." Mr. Frazee is the originator of trick photography as applied to moving picture comedies and has reserved innumerable ideas to be used now that he has acquired his own company and can consequently secure a free field to produce his effects. The Frazee Comedies feature humor attached to a rush of novel situations. Riverside, California, has been chosen as the studio site, because of its natural setting, having a background of hills and vegetation with a reliable climate. Mr. Frazee has always developed his own plots for scenarios and directs without any script, although he is open to suggestion and has a staff of assistants with that aim.

WILLIAM L. SHERRILL
President Frohman Amusement Corp.

Mr. Sherrill was born in Dadeville, Ala. Previous to his connection with the motion picture industry he was identified with various life insurance companies in an executive capacity. Was the first film executive to recognize the screen value of legitimate stage attractions and popular novels and was the first in the industry to acquire the screen rights to certain works of Booth Tarkington, Lionel Sutro, Augustus Thomas, George Ade, Edward Locke and other literary celebrities. One of the pioneers in independent productions and state right distribution. Mr. Sherrill is a director in several commercial enterprises. City residence, Hotel Commodore, New York; country residence, Rye, N. Y.

JESSE JAMES GOLDBURG
General Manager Frohman

Mr. Goldburg was born in New York City. Educated Dwight School, New York Preparatory School, and New York Law School. Organized Life Photo Film Corporation, the first independent producing organization in the United States. Created and established the state right method of distribution of productions and devised the territorial division of state rights and the percentages originally allotted to each territory. Thereafter organized and was vice-president of Ocean Film Corporation and the Rialto Film Corporation. Has occupied several positions of supervising director, sales manager, advertising and publicity manager. At present engaged as general manager of the Frohman Amusement Corporation, Times Building, New York City.

JOSEPH A. GOLDEN
President Crystal Film Company and Stockholder of Allgood Pictures Corporation

Joseph A. Golden has been identified with the motion picture business for several years, acting principally in the capacity of director. He has handled the megaphone for twelve years and introduced the first stage star in pictures, namely, Blanche Walsh, in "Resurrection." He has directed Norma Talmadge, Lenore Ulric, Cyril Scott, Holbrook Blinn, Julia Dean, Helen Ware, Jane Grey, James O'Neill and many others. Mr. Golden is now directing a fifteen-episode serial called "The Whirlwind," starring Charles Hutchison, who is the star of "The Great Gamble," a serial distributed by Pathe and directed by Mr. Golden.

SAMUEL GOLDWYN
President Goldwyn Pictures Corporation

Samuel Goldwyn began his business career at the age of thirteen in New York. He pursued a career along mercantile lines until the motion picture started to make inroads into American social development. In 1912 he induced Cecil DeMille to enter the picture field and a $20,000 corporation was formed with Jesse Lasky. In 1916 Mr. Goldwyn retired as chairman of the Board of Directors of the Lasky Corporation, and in 1916 he formed the Goldwyn Pictures Corporation, which started to produce pictures in 1917. He secured the services of many of the foremost stars, and in 1919 he directed the reorganization of the Goldwyn Company, with F. F. Godsol, the Shuberts, A. H. Woods and the Selwyns on the directorate and a capitalization of $20,000,000. In 1919 he formed the Eminent Authors Pictures, Inc., with Rex Beach as president and with Rupert Hughes, Leroy Scott, Basil King, Gouverneur Morris, Gertrude Atherton and Mary Roberts Rinehart under exclusive contract. Under his direction the Goldwyn Company purchased the Triangle Studios at Culver City, California. In December, 1919, a merger of new interests was effected which brought H. F. Du Pont, Eugene E. Du Pont, W. W. Laird, R. R. M. Carpenter, C. C. Kurtz, E. V. R. Thayer, Duncan A. Holmes, William Topkins, George T. Bissel, G. W. Davison, Macmillan Hoopes and Abbott M. Wittenberg into the Goldwyn Pictures Corporation.

RALPH BLOCK

Mr. Block was born in Cherokee, Iowa, June 21, 1889. He was educated in public schools and traveled abroad. Graduated from University of Michigan in 1911. Became a member of the editorial staffs of Louisville Courier-Journal and Detroit News. Later dramatic critic of Kansas City Star and New York Tribune. Mr. Block left the latter newspaper to become associated with Goldwyn Pictures Corporation. Now abroad for Goldwyn Pictures Corporation.

JOHN W. GREY
President Supreme Pictures, Inc.

John W. Grey entered the motion picture business as advertising manager of Universal Film Manufacturing Company where he continued for a year and a half. While acting in that capacity he realized the value of merchandizing methods in the industry and in the sale of film. He planned the second serial ever released and really the first syndicate serial, "Lucille Love the Girl of Mystery," handled "The Trey of Hearts," and started the "Black Box" campaign—exploited and assisted in establishing the feature, "Traffic in Souls." Mr. Grey left Universal to become assistant to the president of Mutual Film Company, supervising advertising and publicity, and handled and promoted the sales plans for "The Escape," "The Avenging Conscience," and other Griffith productions. He personally wrote and directed single reel productions for Norma Phillips and handled all costs for the Reliance studio in New York and Yonkers. Mr. Grey left Mutual to join Vitagraph as assistant to the president, A. E. Smith. While there he had supervision of sales, publicity, exploitation and productions; handled "The Battle Cry of Peace," and all features. When International was formed Mr. Hearst sent for Mr. Grey and appointed him head of the exploitation department. He next became head of the scenario department and titling and editing department of Pathe and had personal supervision of all production; worked on many serials and personally wrote stories for Baby Marie Osborne—series for Bryant Washburn, series for Astra, and continuity for many leading features. Mr. Grey then left Pathe to go in business with Arthur B. Reeve and collaborated with him in writing the "Houdini" serial, "Carter Case" serial, "One Million Dollars Reward" serial, "Grim Game" serial, "The Isle of Hate" feature, "White Lights" serial and "Whispering Walls" serial.

DAVID W. GRIFFITH
D. W. Griffith Attractions; The Wark Producing Corporation; D. W. Griffith Service

David W. Griffith is one of the shining lights of the motion picture industry. More than any other factor in the picture world he is responsible for putting the photoplay upon an artistic plane. This director and producer was formerly identified with the stage where he earned a salary of $15 a week. When the motion picture was launched as a form of entertainment he was quick to realize its tremendous possibilities and he joined the Biograph Company as an "extra" at an insignificant salary. He soon showed his worth and advanced to a position which commanded a princely stipulation for those days—some years ago. He is now recognized as the highest paid director in the picture field. David W. Griffith was the first to see the advantages of the multiple reel picture as a means of entertainment. He was the guiding genius of that masterpice "The Birth of a Nation," the first big picture ever produced in America. Where others used a mere handful of actors, Mr. Griffith used thousands. This picture was followed by another tremendous photoplay, "Intolerance." He went to England, where he was commissioned by the English Government with the taking of pictures for the war archives. The creation of his efforts on the other side was "Hearts of the World." Then followed "Broken Blossoms." Mr. Griffith has made dozens of photoplays of shorter length than the above mentioned. He is not only responsible for introducing such technical inventions as the "flashback" and "fade-out" and visualizing stories on a tremendous and lavish scale, but he is also responsible for bringing out many of our most brilliant screen stars. See also " Producers."

HARRY GROSSMAN
President of Grossman Pictures, Inc.

Harry Grossman, producer and supervising director of "$1,000,000 Reward," has forced his way to the front among producers of episode pictures, maintaining from the first a determination and produce serials on the highest plane possible. In his more recent activities in the production of serials, Mr. Grossman, in association with Octagon Films, Inc., was responsible for the serial production "The Master Mystery," with Harry Houdini. Following this he produced the Oliver Films, Inc., feature serial production "The Carter Case," with Herbert Rawlinson and Margaret Marsh as the featured players. He has now produced "$1,000,000 Reward," with Lillian Walker. Grossman Pictures, Inc., is located at Ithaca, N. Y.

SAMUEL H. HADLEY
President of Classical Motion Picture Company, Inc.

Hopp Hadley first exhibited motion pictures in 1908 in an 800 capacity tent. He graduated from New York University in 1901. Was an actor and theatrical manager until entrance into picture business as scenario editor of Majestic Company. Was advertising manager of Reliance and Mutual. Is identified with Frank G. Hall enterprises.

FRANK G. HALL
President of Hallmark Pictures Corporation

Mr. Hall entered the picture business as exhibitor, operating a chain of theatres in New Jersey. Later entered distributing branch of the independent field, buying and distributing independent productions. Mr. Hall founded the Independent Sales Corporation and later merged his interests in Hallmark Pictures Corporation. He has five producing companies working. Also a serial company on the Pacific Coast under the supervision of Ben Wilson. He has more than thirty-five special productions on the market.

JESSE D. HAMPTON
Producer
See " Producers "

HOBART HENLEY
President Hobart Henley Productions
See " Producers "

W. W. HODKINSON
President W. W. Hodkinson Corporation

W. W. Hodkinson has been identified with the film industry for over twelve years, being one of the pioneers in the field. He entered motion pictures in Ogden, Utah, in 1907, in order to prove to himself that the nickel store-show was not the limit of the motion picture field. Seeing after a time that he would have to insure his product, he opened a film exchange as representative of a Chicago concern. His salary was $15 a week. Then he and a partner bought one of the town's nickel shows, established a policy of changing films weekly and charged 10 cents admission. Within two years he had bought both his competitors out. He had also established a protective ruling for his territory and would rent his films only to houses charging 10 cents admission. He returned subsequently to Ogden, took over the exchange for that territory, and opened a newer and larger theatre. Later he took over a theatre in Salt Lake City and in 1911 went to Los Angeles and then to San Francisco as representative of General Film Company. In Los Angeles he put on a greatly improved basis in less than six weeks' time, but San Francisco was a hard nut to crack. Mr. Hodkinson saw that rulings were necessary, and being in full charge of the territory, announced that he would require large houses to charge 10 cents, with two changes a week, and that the small houses could run three reels only, limited to three changes a week. Later he took charge of the entire Pacific coast. Hodkinson established his concern in 1913. In 1914 he saw that to perpetuate his units on the coast he would have to apply these selective principles nationally. He got the Bosworth Company, the Famous Players Company and the Lasky Company as his units. He organized Paramount and made it a distributing organization. In 1916, resigned from Paramount and in 1917 began the labor of organizing a new distributing company and this became eventually the W. W. Hodkinson Corporation. In 1919 he offered his product to the exhibitors on an open booking sales plan.

SAMUEL S. HUTCHINSON
President American Film Company, Inc.

Samuel S. Hutchinson was born in Cheyenne Wyoming, in 1869. Moved to Green County Illinois, in 1871, where boyhood days were spent. Educated at Illinois Wesleyan University, Bloomington, Ill., receiving a degree of Bachelor of Science. Member of Sigma Chi Fraternity. Was president of the Interstate Oratorical Association in 1893. Started business career in Chicago bank. Sixteen years ago was president and general manager of the Theatre Film Service Company, Chicago. Three years later was president and manager of the H. & H. Film Service. Since 1909, the founding of the American Film Company, has been its president continuously; also president of the American Company, London, Limited, a British corporation, established in 1911, to handle the English and Continental activities of the American Film Company. President of the American Projecting Company, manufacturers of the American Projectoscope, a portable motion picture machine. Mr. Hutchinson has two sons, J. Hobart Hutchinson, assistant manager of the American Film Company, and Winston S. Hutchinson, connected with the sales and distribution division of the American Film Company. Home address, 6231 Sheridan road, Chicago, Ill.

VICTOR KREMER
President of Victor Kremer Film Features, Inc.

Mr. Kremer has had a varied career in the amusement business. Prior to entering the motion picture field he was one of the biggest publishers of popular music in the United States. During his career in the publishing business he maintained offices in New York, Chicago and San Diego, and handled many of the biggest song successes of the period. He entered the motion picture business as a producer and was responsible for the promotion of a series of Shorty Hamilton feature dramas and a series of pictures starring Margarita Fisher. During the past year he has become one of the factors in the distributing on a territorial basis, five of the most important Chaplin pictures, made during the comedian's contract with Essanay. Mr. Kremer maintains offices in New York, Chicago and San Diego, and in addition to the Chaplin features he handles many of the Essanay productions starring Henry B. Walthall, Jack Gardner, Richard Travers, Bryant Washburn and others. He maintains residences in New York and San Diego, and is also largely interested in several clay mines situated on the west coast.

WHO'S AT THE HELM

CARL LAEMMLE
President Universal Film Manufacturing Company

From the partnership of a little clothing store to the presidency of one of the biggest moving picture concerns in a few years' time is the story of the meteoric rise of Carl Laemmle, the guiding genius of the Universal Film Manufacturing Company. After Laemmle had accumulated the magnificent fortune of $4,000 from the profits of the sale of all wool creations to the populace of Oshkosh, Wis., he became struck with the idea of getting into a "ten cent" business. The crowds in front of a moving picture theatre in Chicago decided him—moving pictures it was. He started a moving picture theatre in Chicago, and with his usual foresight, realizing the need of a distributing organization, created the first exchange. In 1909 he organized the independent film producers into the Imp Company, as a first step in the fight against the General Film Company, then known as the "trust." In 1910 he organized the Motion Picture Sales Company, still fighting the trust, which was now giving ground. His purchase of 12,000 acres in the San Fernando Valley, late in 1912, was the beginning of the Universal City of today. The Universal Company sailed to the shores of rapid success with Laemmle at the helm. Practically every known screen star of today has at one time or another appeared in Universal pictures. Many of them owe their careers to Carl Laemmle's far-sightedness.

HENRY LEHRMAN
President Henry Lehrman Productions, Inc.
See " Producers "

SOL LESSER
Sol Lesser Enterprises

Sol Lesser has been identified with the motion picture industry since 1909, and at the present time the largest individual state right operator handling such films as "Hearts of the World," "Intolerance," "Mickey," "Yankee Doodle in Berlin," and the Sennett "Bathing Girl Act," "Sky-Eye," and many others. Mr. Lesser has just opened the Sol Lesser Film Exchange at 729 Seventh ave., N. Y. C. The exchange will handle all the films Mr. Lesser buys for Greater New York. Branches are conducted in Cleveland, Chicago, Los Angeles, San Francisco, and Seattle.

EDWARD A. MacMANUS
President of MacManus Corporation

Mr. MacManus was born in Fishkill Landing, N. Y., and educated at Newburgh High School, Spencerian Business College, and Cornell University. Early career, printer, correspondent for New York papers, reporter for New York World, circulation manager Collier's Weekly, advertising representative Hampton's Agency, promotion manager for Ladies' World and McClure's Magazine. Motion picture career, originated screen serials, developed idea which resulted in combination of Ladies' World and Edison and first serial, "What Happened to Mary?" He became general manager with Hearst service, organized serial combination with Pathe and Vitagraph ("Perils of Pauline," "Exploits of Elaine," "Goddess," "Wallingford," "Mysteries of Myra," and "Patria" (produced by Wharton, Inc.). Became manager with Paramount Pictures Corporation, produced independently "The Lost Battalion" with survivors and "The Gray Brother," with Thomas Mott Osborne. Mr. MacManus was a member of 71st Regiment, N. G. N. Y. in Spanish War; on athletic teams of 71st Regiment and Irish-American Athletic Club. He is a member of the Metropolitan Museum, New York Athletic Club, 71st Regiment Veterans' Club. Home address, 206 West 92d st., N. Y. C.

MAXWELL KARGER
Director General Metro Pictures Corporation and Screen Classics, Inc.

Mr. Karger was born in Cincinnati January 17, 1879. Was educated in Cincinnati schools. On reaching maturity became first violinist with orchestra of Metropolitan Opera House, New York City. He remained with this institution for seven years. Entered the motion picture business several years ago as a scenario writer. Has been with Metro Pictures Corporation as director general for the past three years. Supervises all productions. Mr. Karger is 5 feet 10 inches in height and weighs 174 pounds. Home address, Hollywood Hotel, Hollywood, Cal. Studio address, Metro Studio, Hollywood, Cal.

K. HODDY MILLIGAN
President Creation Films, Inc.

K. Hoddy Milligan was former president of the Franklin Oil and Gas Company, and has been connected with the theatrical business for the last fifteen years.

MARSHALL NEILAN
Director of Marshall Neilan Productions
See " Producers "

ADOLF PHILIPP
President Adolf Philipp Film Corporation
See " Producers "

C. B. PRICE
President C. B. Price Co., Inc.

Mr. Price has been associated with the motion picture industry for several years. He has been identified with the most prominent distributors and producers in the United States, always being a leader in the establishment of the business of the concerns whom he represented. He has been special representative and manager of the New York exchange for the Triangle Distributing Corporation, coast manager of the V. L. S. E., the Mutual, and western representative of the McClure Motion Picture Corporation. He resigned on January 1, 1919, as eastern representative of the Fox Film Corporation and organized the business of C. B. Price Co., Inc., which has grown to such magnitude within the year that he has decided to move from the Times Building, New York, to more spacious quarters, equipped with new and improved ideas, furnishing every convenience for state rights and foreign buyers. There will be private projection rooms, vaults and special editing rooms, together with private offices and reception rooms.

ROBERT W. PRIEST
President The Film Market, Inc.

Robert W. Priest was first identified with the dry goods business, and soon after became associated with a theatrical company which he successfully piloted throughout the country. He became manager eventually for DeWolf Hopper, William Faversham, Pavlowa and Mordkin (the imperial Russian ballet), etc., afterward joining the Messrs. Shubert, where he handled the Winter Garden attractions, the Hippodrome and musical comedies. While associated with Lee Shubert, Mr. Priest became interested in the motion picture business through the Captain Scott Antarctic films, which he edited and introduced in this country. Through this connection Mr. Priest became the American manager of Gaumont, Ltd., of London. He exploited Pathe's "The Life of Our Saviour" and Paul J. Rainey African hunt pictures. Then followed a period in which Mr. Priest acted in various capacities with several distributing companies to round out a thorough education in the picture industry. He joined Thos. H. Ince as publicity director for "Civilization." From the Ince affiliation he took charge of the defunct Patriot Film Corporation and revived interest in the British Government pictures, which later became the Allied War Pictures. About this time Mr. Priest entered the state right field and as general manager of Arrow Film Corporation sold "The Deemster" on the open market. This exploitation resulted in the partnership of Shallenberger & Priest, the former being the president of Arrow. This firm handled independent productions for W. H. Clune, Harry Rapf, L. Lawrence Weber and others. At the height of this association he became associated with Robertson-Cole. When he sold his interest to this concern he organized the Film Market, Inc., for the purpose of handling films for independent producers.

GEORGE KLEINE
Producer

Mr. Kleine was born in New York in 1863. Attended New York schools and College of the City of New York. Received degree A. B., class of 1882. Started in business in Chicago in 1893, general optical business, special projection apparatus. Took up motion pictures in 1896. Introduced the Magniscope to this market. Specialized in projection apparatus and moving picture films from this period. Established Kleine Optical Company in 1897. Closed out general optical business in 1900, confining operations to moving picture machines and films. From 1900 to 1906 supplied the general demand for machines and films, at that time largely confined to traveling lecturers, circus men, tent showmen, etc. Began importing films about 1903. Sold American and European made films to the early picture theatres and exchange men. Established selling and renting branches in the United States and Canada in 1906. In 1907 Mr. Kleine founded the Kalem Company, together with Messrs. Long and Marion. The name of the company was founded on the initials—K-L-M. Was president of the Kalem Company during its first year of operation. He gradually acquired exclusive control for the United States and Canada of the output of foreign producers as new manufacturers opened up, and by 1908 controlled the French factories Gaumont, Urban-Eclipse, Lux, Raleign and Roberts, Theophile, Pathe; English factories Gaumont, Urban-Eclipse, Warwick, Walturdaw, Clarendon Film Co.; Italian factories Aquila-Ottolenghi, Itala Films (Rossi), Ambrosio. In combination with the Biograph Company opposed the Edison Licenses in 1908. Settled quarrels in December and accepted licenses from Motion Picture Patents Company in January, 1909, sold his distributing exchanges to the General Film Company in April, 1910. Distributed his products through General Film Company thereafter. Vice-president of General Film Company 1910 to 1913, president 1916. In 1913 opened up various distributing offices to take care of super-features, such as "Quo Vadis," "Cleopatra," "Spartacus," etc. Stopped European importations in 1914 and produced in America during the following years; 1915 to 1916 his exchanges distributed his own productions and in addition to those of Edison, Essanay, and Selig. Closed branch exchanges in December, 1918. Since 1919 Mr. Kleine's film business has been conducted in his own name as an individual. At present time he has in addition, various interests in other film corporations.

MORRIS KOHN
President of Realart Pictures

Morris Kohn was for many years a well known figure in motion picture theatres. In the past three years he has become widely acquainted in producing and distributing circles. A pioneer in the motion picture theatre, Mr. Kohn about twelve years ago established the Automatic Vaudeville Company, opening the Unique theatre at 14th street and 6th avenue, and later opened and started theatres in many cities throughout the country, the most important of which were located in Boston, Chicago, Milwaukee and Kansas City. He became treasurer of Select Pictures Corporation at the time of the incorporation of that concern, but later resigned his office to become treasurer of Realart Pictures Corporation.

J. S. WOODY
General Manager Realart Pictures

J. S. Woody's connection with the film world dates from 1908 with O. T. Crawford Film Exchange, St. Louis. In 1913 he became associated with the General Film Exchange, in a special capacity, covering all territory west of Denver. He stayed with this company until 1914, when he joined Mutual to handle the Pacific Northwest district. Two years later he became affiliated with Triangle in New York, where he attracted the attention of Arthur S. Kane, then general manager of Select, with the result that Mr. Woody became field manager for Select. He was later promoted to general sales manager, and when Mr. Kane organized Realart Mr. Woody went with him in the same position he held with Select. Since then he has been promoted to general manager, the position he holds at present.

H. Y. ROMAYNE
Treasurer Romayne Co.

Mr. Romayne is a member of the Oregon, California, and Washington bars, and up to three years ago was practising law.

E. D. ULRICH
General Manager Romayne Co.

Mr. Ulrich is a member of the Oregon, California and Washington bars, and up to three years ago was president of the Auto Funding Company of America, and assisted in various enterprises, such as Pacific Tool and Steel Company of Portland, Ore., the Fulton Ship Yards of Los Angeles, etc.

THOMAS A. BAKER
Treasurer Romayne Co.

Mr. Baker was formerly deputy and sheriff of Kern County, California, for twenty years, and is a son of the founder of Bakersfield.

WATTERSON R. ROTHACKER
President Rothacker Film Manufacturing Company

Mr. Rothacker was born in Chicago May 6, 1885. The Idaho Thunder Mountain gold rush in 1901 drew him from the Lewis Technical High School, where at the age of 16 he sank all his available wealth in the Terror Mine. Then he went to work as editor-porter-business manager of the Wiener, Idaho, Signal. In order to support the Signal he hustled freight afternoons at the local railroad depot. But the Signal's appetite for printer's ink and white paper eventually proved too much for its 17-year-old editor's freight trucking capacity, and Mr. Rothacker went to work for a year on the Mule Shoe Bar Ranch in Colorado, learning how to rope steers and getting the price of a ticket back to Chicago. He was western manager of the Billboard in Chicago when he succumbed to the movie fever in May, 1910. He was the pioneer in the industrial films branch of the motion picture industry. Carl Laemmle, Robert H. Cochrane, and Mr. Rothacker were the stockholders in the Industrial Moving Picture Company, the latter being general manager. In 1913 Mr. Rothacker bought out Messrs. Laemmle and Cochrane, and in 1916 a new corporation was formed and the firm name changed to the Rothacker Film Manufacturing Company. About five years ago he began doing laboratory work for others and developed this side of his business, until today large producers feature "Rothacker Prints" in their advertising. In the last few years the Rothacker Film Manufacturing Company has put out a number of outdoor industrial and educational releases. The address of the company is 1339-1351 Diversey Parkway, Chicago, Ill.

C. C. PETTIJOHN
Assistant to the President Select Pictures Corp.

Mr. Pettijohn was born in Indianapolis May 5, 1881. Graduated from Indianapolis High School in 1900, and from Indiana University, Department of Law, in 1903. Practised law in Indianapolis 1903 to 1916. First, became identified with the picture industry an general counsel for American Exhibitors' Association. Was one of the first persons in the industry to talk exhibitor co-operation. Mr. Pettijohn has always been a firm believer that co-operative exhibitor producing and distributing organizations will eventually control the industry. Organized the Affiliated Distributors' Corporation, one of the few ventures which paid one hundred cents on the dollar before withdrawing from the field. Is an active supporter and worker in the National Association of the Motion Picture Industry. Signed a long-time contract with Lewis J. Selznick on October 20, 1919. Familiarly known in the industry as "Selznick's right bower."

CHARLES R. ROGERS
Director of Sales, Select Pictures Corporation

After leaving the English High School, Boston, Mass., at the age of 17, Mr. Rogers was employed as a representative for a haberdashery shop in Boston, visiting colleges, "prep" schools and a university, taking orders for haberdashery and clothing. After three years, resigned to accept a position as representative for a clothing specialty house and traveling throughout New England and New York State. Was with this concern for three years. Resigned to accept a position as special representative for Mayer & Lowerstein, one of the largest manufacturers of varnish in the country, calling upon the manufacturers of pianos, motor cars, furniture, etc. Covered New England and New York States. Was with them eight years. Upon getting married, he resigned from this concern, as he did not wish to do any more traveling. Mr. Rogers then built the first moving picture theatre in East Buffalo, called the Eastern Star. Also dabbled with a few state right productions such as "Three Weeks," "Neptune's Daughter" and some of the B. S. Moss releases. Six months after having built this theatre Mr. Rogers made application to Mr. Selznick for a position as branch manager of his Buffalo exchange, and was accepted. This was the first position he held with any film company. After having met with success at the Buffalo office, a year later was given the Boston office. After having been in the Boston office for ten months, placing that exchange among the successful branches, Mr. Selznick at that time bought out Mr. Zukor's interest in the Select Pictures Corporation and offered him a position as director of sales—a position which he accepted.

S. E. MORRIS
Vice-President and General Manager Select Pictures Corp.

A few years ago when Lewis J. Selznick was vice-president and general manager of World Film Corporation, Mr. Morris worked his way to the position of manager of World's Cleveland exchange. Later, when Mr. Selznick left the World Corporation and founded his own company, he installed him as treasurer of Selznick enterprises. Shortly after, Mr. Morris, retaining his position as treasurer, became general manager. In this position he remained until Select Pictures Corporation was formed, at which time Mr. Morris was selected to handle the important sales territory lying in the rich heart of the central states, and given the title of East Central general manager, having jurisdiction over Select's Detroit, Cincinnati and Cleveland branches, with headquarters established in the latter city. Mr. Morris knows the film business thoroughly. He has been an exhibitor in Cleveland before entering World Film Corporation's exchange in that city, and therefore is able to approach sales propositions from the theatre owner's angle. Sam Morris is a native of Oil City, Pa. In April, 1919, he was recalled to the home office to assume the position of vice-president and general manager, which position he now holds.

DAVID SELZNICK
Assistant Secretary and Assistant Treasurer Select Pictures Corporation

Mr. Selznick was born in Pittsburgh, Pa., and educated in the New York City public schools, Hamilton Institute and Columbia University. His business career started in 1916 when he became secretary of Film Advertising Service, Inc. In 1918 he became secretary of Selznick Pictures Corporation, and in 1919 the assistant treasurer of Select Pictures Corporation.

W. E. SHALLENBERGER
President Arrow Film Corporation

W. E. Shallenberger hails from Ohio. He was a boyhood chum of the late Charles J. Hite, and when the latter made his entry into pictures in the days of the H. & H. Film Exchange of Chicago, Mr. Shallenberger, his brother and Samuel Hutchinson were Hite's partners and financial backers. Later he assisted in the promotion of the American Film Company of Chicago, of which he was one of the largest stockholders. This led to the purchase of the Thanhouser plant of Edwin Thanhouser, effected by Hite, Shallenberger and associates, and later the formation of the Mutual Film Corporation by the above, in which later venture they were joined by H. E. Aitken, J. R. Freuler, and other men who have since become large operators in the film business. He later joined the above in financing the N. Y. Motion Picture Company, Reliance and Majestic. Then followed the Syndicate Film Corporation which made every one a fortune with its one release, "The Million Dollar Mystery." Mr. Shallenberger then started the Arrow Film Corporation, which concern produced for some time for Pathe and the State Rights Market. Connection with the latter field convinced Mr. Shallenberger that here was a real opportunity for his endeavors and the operation of a brokerage office to take care of the requirements of the state right buyer. This has been accomplished after a couple of years of hard work. The Arrow is known as an independent film concern. It is at present handling three serials, starring Ruth Stonehouse, Anne Luther, George Larkin, Ann Little and Jack Hoxie. In addition to their serial progress, it is releasing a big variety of short reel comedy and dramatic subjects as well as a feature program of large proportions.

HERBERT K. SOMBORN
President Equity Pictures Corporation

Mr. Somborn began his moving picture career in 1907 in Pittsburgh, Pa., associated with Clark and Rowland. As the firm expanded, he opened up branch offices throughout the United States, and was general manager of these offices. In 1909 he went into partnership with J. M. Mullen under the firm name of Mullen Film Service, this being the first film company to break into "independent" distribution of pictures. He established offices in Syracuse, Kansas City, Minneapolis, and other points. In 1911 he opened the first Feature Film Exchange in the United States at Rochester, N. Y. Later became connected with the original Majestic Motion Picture Corporation, starring for their first production Mary Pickford and Owen Moore. He later spent several years in California, becoming financially interested in numerous independent productions, among which was "The Unpardonable Sin." Mr. Somborn is now president of the Equity Pictures Corporation and actively engaged in its management.

H. A. SPANUTH,
President Commonwealth Pictures Company, 1333 Argyle St., Chicago, Ill.

Mr. Spanuth is a pioneer in motion pictures and is recognized as one of the first men to make a film using a legitimate star, and probably the first to employ the idea of state rights buying, and the first to utilize motion photography for political campaign purposes. He was general manager of Miles Bros. Film Exchange of New York, organized and operated Carl Laemmle's Film Exchange in the same city, afterward becoming advertising manager for the company distributing Universal and Mutual products. In 1912 he produced the five-reel drama "Oliver Twist," with Nat C. Goodwin as the star. Also covered Col. Theodore Roosevelt's tour of the country for motion pictures. He developed the Celebrated Players' Co., and organized and acted as managing director of the Central Film Co. Mr. Spanuth was instrumental in forming the F. I. L. M. Club of Chicago, the first of such associations of exchange men for greater efficiency and correction of untoward conditions in their work. Mr. Spanuth is producing the "Vod-a-Vil Movies," which consist of four to six vaudeville acts, released in lengths of one thousand feet, every other week. "Spanuth's Sermonettes" is his latest achievement. It portrays ethical ideals in pictures of one-reel length released twice each month.

MAURICE TOURNEUR
President Maurice Tourneur Productions, Inc.
See "Producers"

LEWIS ROACH
President Transatlantic Film Corp.

Mr. Roach was born in England and was educated at Harrow, Cambridge and Paris universities. Formerly special correspondent to the Daily Mail of London and subsequently airplane manufacturer. Entered the motion picture business in 1910 as European publicity director for Rex, Imp and Solex Films. Director of the Histrionic Film Company, which was the first to present

Sarah Bernhardt in moving pictures. Later publicity and continental manager for Transatlantic Film Company, London. Then produced films in England and Denmark. Four years in Intelligence Department of British Army.

CHARLES YALE HARRISON
American Sales Manager Transatlantic Corp.

Mr. Harrison was born in 1893 in Philadelphia, Pa., and educated in Montreal, Quebec, and London, England. Screen career, exhibitor in Montreal two years, publicity, Broadway theatre, New York City. American Sales Director of Transatlantic Film Company of America, Inc.

MATTHIAS RADIN
President and General Manager Tyrad Pictures

Mr. Radin was born in Sweden, migrated to the United States when he was eight years old and attended the public schools of New York City. He graduated from New York University and in 1904 was admitted to the bar of New York, having received the degrees of A. B. and LL.B. He then conducted a chain of theatres in Long Island in Rockville Centre, Lynbrook, Hempstead and Mineola, known as the O'Connor-Radin circuit. Mr. Radin also conducted a number of theatres on the lower East Side of New York. He then went into the employ of the Universal Film Manufacturing Company as salesman. He was thereafter promoted to take charge of the Jewel productions in New York City, which he launched. He then became manager of that institution and supervised certain territory on behalf of the Universal Film Manufacturing Company. He became president and general manager of Tyrad Pictures, Inc., in February, 1919. Mr. Radin is married, has a family, a son and daughter, and resides in this city.

AMEDEE J. VAN BEUREN
President Timely Films, Inc., AyVeeBee Corporation and V. B. K. Corporation

Mr. Van Beuren became a producer of motion pictures when he brought Mr. and Mrs. Sidney Drew back to the screen in two-reel comedies. His preceding interests in the amusement line include the ownership and management of the Moorish Gardens and the Van Kelton Stadium Airdomes, the Notlek Tennis Courts and Ice Skating Rinks in New York City. For many years he was vice-president of the Van Beuren Billposting Company. Mr. Van Beuren still retains his interests in all these concerns. Timely Films, Inc., produce "Topics of the Day," selected from the press of the world by The Literary Digest and distributed by Pathe. The AyVeeBee Corporation produce the Paramount-Ernest Truex Comedies. V. B. K. Corporation produce the Paramount-Drew Comedies.

L. LAWRENCE WEBER
President of Apollo Trading Corporation and L. Lawrence Weber Photo Dramas, Inc.

Mr. Weber has been identified with amusements for several years. With Bobby North he organized the Popular Plays and Players, Inc., which exploited Mme. Petrova. When Metro "bought in" its producing companies, Popular Plays and Players was dissolved. The same two men have had years of experience in theatrical producing as well, Mr. Weber being manager of the Longacre theatre, N. Y. C. When Popular Plays and Players was dissolved Messrs. Weber and North organized the L. Lawrence Weber Photo Dramas, Inc., which produced for its initial venture "Raffles, the Amateur Cracksman," with John Barrymore. This corporation consists of Mr. Weber, Mr. North and Lee Shubert—and has just completed making the stage play, "The Blue Pearl," and will make a number of other productions during the year.

JACK WEINBERG
President Canyon Pictures Corporation

Mr. Weinberg entered the motion picture business in 1905, opening an exchange at 27 E. 21st st., N. Y. C. He became interested in a moving picture theatre at 129 E. Houston st., N. Y. C., and a theatre at 1759 Pitkin ave., Brooklyn, N. Y. Mr. Weinberg first began producing in 1912; at that time also became associated with Exclusive Features, Inc., conducting a film exchange. He has always been an advocate for pictures with thrills produced with technical details and proper direction, maintaining that people are ready to admire red-blooded action. He is also a firm believer in the heart interest story.

CLARENCE WOLF
President Betzwood Film Company

Mr. Wolf, president of Betzwood Film Company, is a member of the banking firm of Wolf Brothers & Company, Philadelphia, who have large and varied interests throughout the country.

ADOLPH ZUKOR
President Famous Players-Lasky Corporation

Adolph Zukor, son of Jacob and Hannah Zukor, was born on January 7, 1874, and at the age of 16 came to America. His first position in this country was as a sweeper in a fur store. The boy worked hard and advanced rapidly—an advance hastened financially by the invention of a patent snap in furs. In 1894 Mr. Zukor left for Chicago, where he entered the fur trade and it was there he met his future wife, whom he married in 1897. Returning to New York in 1903, he ventured with Marcus Loew in the Penny Arcade, a feature then in vogue. This was the foundation of the Marcus Loew Enterprises, of which Mr. Loew became president and Adolph Zukor treasurer, extending soon to a chain of theatres all over the East. Shortly after the beginning in the exhibiting end of the moving picture business, the photoplay began to lose its first novelty because of the crude pictures which the producers of those days turned out. Mr. Zukor soon realized that unless the standard of the screen was raised the industry was doomed to perish, and he wrote to the various producing companies begging them to raise their standards. Mr. Zukor stated that if they didn't give him better pictures he would make them himself. This decision resulted, in 1912, in the formation of the Famous Players Film Company, for which Mr. Zukor secured the services of Daniel Frohman. In September, 1913, the success of the first features attracted into the field other concerns which adopted the policy of the Famous Players, among which were the Jesse L. Lasky Feature Play Company and Bosworth, Inc., who combined their distributing sources in order to give exhibitors a more extended service, for which purpose the Paramount Pictures Corporation was launched. On July 1, 1916, the Famous Players Film Company and the Jesse L. Lasky Feature Play Company combined under the name of Famous Players-Lasky Corporation. On September 1, 1916, the Famous Players-Lasky Corporation absorbed the Oliver Morosco Photoplay Company and Bosworth, Inc. The latter was producing under the title of Pallas Pictures. In October, 1916, the Artcraft Pictures Corporation was created to distribute productions of Mary Pickford and other stars and producers. On January 1, 1917, Paramount Pictures Corporation was absorbed by Famous Players-Lasky Corporation. On April 15, 1917, Artcraft Pictures Corporation was absorbed by the Famous Players-Corporation, and Paramount and Artcraft Pictures was placed on the open market by the Star Series plan, beginning August 5, 1917. In January, 1918, the sales and executive departments of Artcraft and Paramount were coordinated and the corporate names of these concerns were discontinued, but retaining the trademarks and making all sales through Famous Players-Lasky Corporation.

JOHN C. FLINN

Born in Evanston, Ill., and educated there. Entered the newspaper business as a reporter on the Chicago Inter-Ocean. Later joined the staff of the New York Herald, serving nine years as reporter and dramatic editor. Five years ago became publicity manager of the Jesse Lasky Feature Play Company, and on the formation of the Famous Players-Lasky Corporation became its Director of Advertising and Publicity. In February, 1920, assumed high executive position as head of the corporation's Exhibition Department.

List of Film Companies

—A—

Acme Motion Picture Company, Austin ave., Chicago, Ill. Oscar Holmes.

Acme Pictures Corporation, 220 West 42d st., N. Y. C. Leonce Perret, director.

Adventure Scenics Corporation, c/o Robertson-Cole Company, 1600 Broadway, N. Y. C. Jesse G. Sill, H. H. Brownell, John Rantz.

Alexander Film Corporation, 126 West 46th st., N. Y. C. William Alexander, president.

Alkire Company, Wright-Callender Building, Los Angeles, Cal. Walter H. Alkire, president; Philip H. White, production manager.

Aller Laboratories, 4500 Sunset Boulevard, Hollywood, Cal. Joseph (Altschuler) Aller, proprietor, 500,000 weekly equipment. Laboratory did negative and print work for all Griffith subjects past five years. Also "The Miracle Man," "Daddy Longlegs," "The Unpardonable Sin."

Allgood Pictures Corporation, 815 Longacre Bldg., N. Y. C. Philip Bernstein, president; Louis F. Orenstein, vice-president; Amiel Alperstein, treasurer and general manager; Joseph A. Holden.

Allied Film Corporation, Washington and First sts., Spokane, Wash. Charles Dreyer, manager.

Alpha Pictures, Inc., 126 West 46th st., N. Y. C. M. Rothfleish, president; B. Kerzner, treasurer; B. H. Mills, sales manager.

American Cinema Corporation, 411 Fifth ave., N. Y. C. Walter Niebuhr, president; James S. Sheehan, studio manager.

American Film Company, Inc., 6227-6235 Broadway, Chicago, Ill. Samuel S. Hutchinson, president; John R. Freuler, secretary and treasurer. Department heads—R. R. Nehls, general manager; J. Hobart Hutchinson, assistant manager; C. A. Stimson, general sales manager; L. M. Belfield, publicity director; A. L. Thompson, western studio, manager, Branches—American Company (London), Ltd., 89-91 Wardour st., London, W. I., England; all Pathe exchanges in the United States. Studios and laboratories—Santa Barbara, Cal.; Chicago, Ill., and Croydon, Eng. (See also American Projecting Company and Signal Film Corporation.)

American Projecting Company, 6229 Broadway, Chicago, Ill. Samuel S. Hutchinson, John R. Freuler, officers. Department heads—R. R. Nehls, general manager; J. Hobart Hutchinson, assistant manager; Arthur McMillan, sales manager; Bruno Stechbart, superintendent. Factory, 11-17 South Desplaines st., Chicago, Ill. See also American Film Company, Inc.)

G. M. Anderson Photoplay Company, Longacre Bldg., N. Y. C. G. M. Anderson. (See Golden West Productions.)

Apollo Pictures Company, 1402 Broadway, N. Y. C. (See Harry Raver.)

Apollo Trading Corporation, 220 West 48th st., N. Y. C. L. Lawrence Weber, president; Benjamin Hicks, vice-president; Bobby North, treasurer; Ben A. Boyar, office manager. Branch—28 Denmark st., London, Eng. (See also L. Lawrence Weber Photo Dramas, Inc.)

Roscoe Arbuckle Comedies, Culver City, Cal. (See Comique Film Company.) Released through Famous Players-Lasky Corporation, 485 Fifth ave., N. Y. C.

The Argus Motion Picture Company, Inc., 815-823 Prospect ave., Cleveland, Ohio. H. H. Cudmore, general manager.

Arrow Film Corporation, Candler Bldg., N. Y. C. W. E. Shallenberger, president; W. Ray Johnston, vice-president and treasurer; P. B. Dana, sales manager; M. Cohen, London office.

Artclass Pictures Corporation, Longacre Bldg., N. Y. C. Adolph Weiss, president; George M. Merrick, supervisor of productions. Studios, Yonkers, N. Y. (See also Numa Pictures Corporation.)

Artco Productions, Inc., 135 West 44th st., N. Y. C. Arthur Beck, president; Leah Baird, secretary and treasurer. Studio, Leah Baird Studios, Cliffside, N. J. (See also Arthur Beck Serial Productions, Inc., and Gibraltar Pictures.)

Artcolor Pictures Co., Inc., 126 West 46th st., N. Y. C. Louis J. Dittmar, president; Ed. H. Phillippi, vice-president; C. Lang Cobb, general manager.

Art-O-Graf Film Company, Inc., Guardian Trust Bldg., Denver, Col. O. B. Thayer, president and production director; Tom Gibson, managing editor; David W. Townsend, secretary and treasurer; Vernon L. Walker. Studio, Englewood, Col.

Astra Film Corporation, Glendale, Cal. L. J. Gasnier, president; Mrs. Emma Gasnier, vice-president; G. Bardet, secretary; Frank Ormston, art director; Opal Craig, film editor; Al. Sprague, stage manager; S. E. Schlager, publicity manager; Ethel Wood, chief clerk; Kenneth O'Hara, studio manager; James Horne, director. Studios, Glendale, Cal., and 1 Congress st., Jersey City, N. J. Productions released through Pathe Exchange, Inc.

Atlas Educational Film Company, 63 E. Adams st., Chicago, Ill. I. R. Rehm, president; L. Palmer Bowman, studio director; Charles W. Hitchcock. Studio, Diamond studio, 2624 Milwaukee ave., Chicago, Ill.

Atlas Film Corporation, Newton, Mass. Frank J. Howard, president; L. E. Dadmun, vice-president and general manager; Herbert L. McClearn, treasurer; Ida Harrison, general representative. Studio, Newton, Mass.

Attractions Distributing Corporation, 1482 Broadway, N. Y. C. Bernard P. Fineman, president. Controls the Katherine MacDonald Pictures and the Paramount-Burlingham Travel Pictures.

Aywon Film Corporation, 729 Seventh ave., N. Y. C. Nathan Hirsh, president.

AyVeeBee Corporation, Palace Theatre Annex, 1562 Broadway, N. Y. C. Amedee J. Van Beuren, president; Edward J. Shalvey, treasurer; Clayton J. Heermance, secretary; Mann Page, scenario editor; Rutgers Neilson, director of publicity and advertising. Producers of Paramount-Ernest Truex Comedies. (See also V. B. K. Film Corporation and Timely Films, Inc.)

—B—

B. B. Features, Brunton Studios, 5341 Melrose ave., Los Angeles, Cal. Franklyn L. Hutton, president; Howard C. Hickman, vice-president; Lynden Bowring, secretary; J. L. Frothingham, treasurer and general manager.

Gerald F. Bacon Productions, Fulton Theatre Bldg., 46th st. and Broadway, N. Y. C. Gerald F. Bacon and Oliver D. Bailey, directors of company.

Leah Baird Studios, Cliffside, N. J. Arthur F. Beck, president.

Reginald Barker Productions, c/o Goldwyn Studios, Culver City, Cal.

Baumer Films, Inc., 6-8 West 48th st., N. Y. C. N. J. Baumer, president; W. J. Casey, vice-president; Emile Levy, secretary and treasurer. Department heads—E. H. Philippi, sales manager; J. L. Barnard, supervisor of production; Carl Bender, publicity. Branches—Boston, 44 Bromfield st.; Chicago, 1714 Tribune Bldg. Exchanges—Principal cities throughout the United States.

Bay State Film Company, 10 High st., Boston, Mass. Chester M. Coram, president and manager.

Rex Beach Pictures Co., Inc., 469 Fifth ave., N. Y. C. Samuel Goldwyn, president; Rex Beach, vice-president; Gabriel L. Hess, secretary and treasurer. (See also Goldwyn Pic-

FILM COMPANIES

tures Corporation and Eminent Authors Pictures, Inc.)

George Beban Company, Hollywood, Cal. George Stout, manager.

Arthur F. Beck Serial Productions, Inc., 135 West 44th st., N. Y. C. Arthur F. Beck, president and treasurer. Studio, Leah Baird Studios, Cliffside, N. J. (See also Artco Productions, Inc., and Gibraltar Pictures.)

Betzwood Film Company, The, Empire Bldg., 13th and Walnut sts., Phila., Pa.; Clarence Wolf, president; Ira M. Lowry, vice-president and general manager; F. C. Wagner, Jr., treasurer; Norman Jefferies, scenario, publicity, advertising sales, etc. Studios, Betzwood, Montgomery County, Pa.; P. O. address, Port Kennedy, Pa.

Big Productions Film Company, care of Arrow Film Corporation, 220 West 42nd st., N. Y. C. W. Ray Johnston, president.

Big V Comedies, care of Vitagraph Company of America, 1600 Broadway, N. Y. C.

Biograph Studios and Laboratories, 807 East 175th st., N. Y. C. H. H. Bruenner; Thomas A. Persons.

J. Stuart Blackton Feature Pictures, Inc., 25 West 45th st., N. Y. C. J. Stuart Blackton, president and director general; J. Stuart Blackton, vice-president; Sanford Samuel, treasurer; Stanley Olmsted, scenario editor. For Department Heads see Pathe Exchange, Inc. Studio, 423 Classon ave., Brooklyn, N. Y.

Carlyle Blackwell Productions, Hollywood, Cal. New York office, 1457 Broadway. Studio, Hollywood Studios, Santa Monica Blvd. and Seward st., Hollywood, Cal.

Blazed Trail Productions, Inc., care of Arrow Film Corporation, 220 West 42nd st., N. Y. C.

Bloxbe Pictures Corporation, 130 West 46th st., N. Y. C. E. Schwalbe, president and general manager.

Bloom Film Laboratory, 7520 Sunset Boulevard, Hollywood, Hollywood, Cal. John M. Lackamira Bloom, proprietor and manager. Present capacity, negatives, 40,000 daily; positives, 130,000 daily.

Boston Art Film Studios, Inc., 146 Stuart st., Trinity Court, Boston, Mass. Edward A. Meysenburg.

William A. Brady, The Playhouse, 48th st., N. Y. C.

Bray Pictures Corporation, The, 23 East 26th st., N. Y. C. J. R. Bray, president; J. F. Leventhal, vice-president; Jamison Handy, vice-president; Watson B. Robinson, secretary and treasurer; E. D. Parmelee, assistant secretary and treasurer; Rowland Rogers, assistant secretary and treasurer. Department heads—Mrs. Marguerite Gove, scenario; Rowland Rogers, educational; Max Fleischer, cartoon; F. Lyle Goldman, technical art; J. F. Leventhal, experimental and research; E. Dean Parmelee, head of Chicago office; Jamison Handy, sales. Branch office, 208 So. La Salle st., Chicago, Ill.

Brentwood Film Corporation, 4811 Fountain ave., Hollywood, Cal. Lloyd C. Haynes, president; W. H. Rimmer, vice-president; Willard Barrows, treasurer; H. M. Brandel, assistant treasurer; S. P. Trood, secretary; H. L. Maynes, assistant secretary; Sarah Y. Mason, A. D. Ripley, scenarios; R. B. Putney, supt. laboratory; Henry Kolker, Claude Mitchell, directors. Studio, 4811 Fountain ave., Hollywood, Cal.

Briggs Pictures, Inc., 30 East 42nd st., N. Y. C. C. A. Briggs, president; Mr. Yokel, vice-president; J. S. Gillespie, treasurer; John William Kellette, director; Lew Taylor, cameraman; Edward Becker, assistant cameraman; Doty Hobart, scenario editor; Alex Yokel, general manager. Studios, Eastern, Hudson Heights, N. J.; Southern headquarters, Briggs Studio, 9th and Main sts., Jacksonville, Fla. Pictures released through Famous Players-Lasky Corp.

British-American Finance Corporation, 126 West 46th st., N. Y. C. Nancibelle Grant, president.

J. Frank Brockliss, 729 Seventh ave., N. Y. C. Sidney Garrett, president. Branch—167 Wardour St., London, Eng. Five branches throughout Great Britain, Dublin, Paris, Turin, Moscow, Barcelona, Brussels, Copenhagen, Sydney, Cape Town, Bombay, Tokio.

Robert Brunton Productions, 5301-5601 Melrose ave., Los Angeles, Cal. Studio, Robert Brunton Studios, 5301-5601 Melrose ave., Los Angeles, Cal. (Care W. W. Hodkinson Corporation, 516 Fifth ave., N. Y. C.

Brunton Studios, 5341 Melrose ave., Los Angeles, Cal. Robert Brunton, president and general manager; M. C. Levee, vice-president and business manager; J. S. Frothingham, treasurer; J. C. Okey, technical director; R. B. Kidd, scenario editor; M. P. Havez, Irene Rivierre, Florence Parks, scenarios; Ernest C. Warde, Howard Hickman, directors.

Buffalo Motion Picture Corporation, s. e. cor. 6th ave. and 48th st., N. Y. C. Frank L. Talbot, president; Frank B. Caldwell, vice-president; J. William Prouse, second vice-president; James M. Sparks, secretary. Peter Ernst, Andrew J. Keller, Louis J. Moschell, Edward A. Jones, William Atkinson constitute the board of directors. Buffalo office, 338 Ellicott Square.

Bulls Eye Film Corporation, 729 Seventh ave., N. Y. C. Milton L. Cohen, president and treasurer; Wm. Moore, vice-president; Nat. H. Spitzer, studio manager. Studio, 5821 Santa Monica Boulevard, Hollywood, Cal.; Long Beach, Cal.

Burrud (Sunset) Scenics, c/o Bulls Eye Film Corporation, 729 Seventh ave., N. Y. C.

Burston Films, Inc., Longacre Bldg., N. Y. C. Louis Burston, president; M. C. Kenny, secretary; M. T. Benjamin, treasurer; James Calwell, publicity; W. S. Van Dyke, director. Studio, 6050 Sunset Blvd., Hollywood, Cal.

Byoir & Hart, 6 West 48th st., N. Y. C. Charles S. Hart.

—C—

William Christy Cabanne Producing Company, 1745 Allesandro st., Los Angeles, Cal.

Campbell Comedies, 1720 N. Soto st., Los Angeles, Cal. Wm. S. Campbell, Edna Schley, John Grey, Al McKinnon and S. W. Wallace. Using E. & R. Jungle Film animals. Wm. S. Campbell, director, producing series of animal comedies for release through C. L. Chester Productions, Inc.

Canadian Photoplays, Ltd., Calgary, Can. New York office, First Nat. Ex. Cir., 6 West 48th st.

Canadian Photoplay Productions, Ltd., Toronto, Can. Harold J. Binney, director general. Studio, Toronto, Can.

Canyon Pictures Corporation, 126 West 46th st., N. Y. C. Jack Weinberg, president; Joseph M. Goldstein, treasurer. Studio address, 3800 Mission Road, Los Angeles, Cal. Producing Western pictures starring Franklyn Farnum.

Albert Capellani Productions, Inc., 1457 Broadway, N. Y. C. Albert Capellani, president; Harry Cahane, treasurer; Louis M. Jerowski, secretary. Department heads, Solito Solano, director of publicity. Studios, Solax Studio, Fort Lee, N. J., and Brunton Studio, Hollywood, Cal.

Capital Film Company, Consumers Bldg., Chicago, Ill. S. L. Barnhard, president; D. A. Coulter, vice-president; B. Herbert Milligan, treasurer; J. R. Lorain, publicity manager; C. E. Eckels, general manager; Carl H. Pafenbach, studio manager; John Powers, production manager; Christeen H. Warnack, scenario; Milton Baker, technical director; Roy A. Eiler, supt. laboratory; M. Fahrney, director. Studio, Hollywood, Cal.

Capital Pictures Corporation, Inc., Fairfax, Va. Marshall Hartman, president and director general.

Capitol Comedies, care of Goldwyn Distributing Corporation, 469 Fifth ave., N. Y. C.

Lloyd Carleton Productions, 430 So. Broadway, Los Angeles, Cal. Lloyd B. Carleton.

Edwin Carewe Productions, Inc., 1457 Broadway, N. Y. C. Edwin Carewe, president; Harry C. Cahane, treasurer; Abraham L. Feinstein, secretary. Department heads, Solita Solano, director of publicity. Studios, Solax Studio, Fort Lee, N. J., and Brunton Studio, Hollywood, Cal.

Celebrated Players Film Corporation, 207 So. Wabash ave., Chicago, Ill. J. L. Friedman, president.

Century Comedies, 1600 Broadway, N. Y. C. (See Universal Film Manufacturing Company.) Studios, Hollywood, Cal.

Charles Chaplin Film Corporation, 1420 La Brea ave., Hollywood, Cal. Alfred Reeves, studio manager; Charles Chaplin, scenario editor; Douglas Tuck, technical director; Charles Levin, supt. laboratory; Charles Chaplin, director.

Sydney Chaplin Company, 6642 Santa Monica Blvd., Hollywood, Cal. Sydney Chaplin, production manager; Henry Clive, art director; Cliff Elfeldt, Reggie Lyons, directors; John Meighan, master of properties.

Chaplin-Mayer Pictures Company, 2 West 45th st., N. Y. C. Louis B. Mayer, president; Bennie Ziedman, vice-president; J. Robert Rubin, secretary and treasurer; Arthur H. Rosson, director; A. G. Kenyon, George Hall, directors; William Shay, film editor; Jack Neville, publicity; George Hopkins, art director; Antonio Gaudio, Hal Rosson, cameramen. Studio, 3800 Mission road, Los Angeles, Cal.

Character Pictures Corporation, 17 West 42nd st., N. Y. C. Albert W. Plummer; Charles W. Buck; David Shapiro.

Emil Chautard Pictures Corporation, Fort Lee, N. J. Emil Chautard. Studio, Fort Lee, N. J.

C. L. Chester Productions, Inc., 120 West 41st st., N. Y. C. C. L. Chester, president; H. H. Caldwell, vice-president; Katherine Hilliker, secretary; Raymond S. Harris, sales manager and advertising; Katherine Hilliker, editor of productions. (See also Outing-Chester Pictures.)

Christie Film Company, 6101 Sunset Blvd., Los Angeles, Cal. Al E. Christie, president; C. H. Christie, treasurer and general manager; Fred L. Porter, vice-president and secretary. Department heads, Al E. Christie, director of pictures; Scott Sidney, director of pictures; William Beaudine, director of pictures; W. Scott Darling, editor of scenario dept.; Frank R. Conklin, Keene Compson, Jack Jevue, Nan Blair, Harry Loos, scenarios; Pat Dowling, publicity and advertising. Studio, 6101 Sunset Blvd., Los Angeles, Cal. Christie Comedies are released through the following independent exchanges—Peerless Film Service Co., San Francisco; Peerless Film Service Co., Los Angeles; The Greater Features, Inc., Seattle; Celebrated Players Film Corp., Chicago; First National Exchange, Inc., New York; First National Exchange, Inc., Buffalo; Quality Film Co., Inc., Pittsburgh; Electric Theatre Supply Co., Philadelphia; E. & H. Film Distributing Co., Atlanta; American Feature Film Co., Boston; American Feature Film Co., New Haven; R. D. Lewis Film Co., Oklahoma City, Okla.; R. D. Lewis Film Co., Dallas; Standard Film Service Co., Cleveland; Capital Film Service, Inc., Washington; Standard Film Service Co., Detroit; Standard Film Service Co., Cincinnati; Standard Film Corp., St. Louis; Supreme System, Inc., Minneapolis; First National Exchange, Vancouver, B. C.; Crescent Film Co., Kansas City; A. H. Blank Enterprises, Omaha; Mid-West Distributing Co., Milwaukee; Famous Players Film Service, Toronto; Arrow Photoplays Co., Denver; Reginald Warde, New York; S. A. Lynch Enterprises, Atlanta; Enterprise Distributing Corp., New Orleans; Enterprise Distributing Corp., Dallas; Capital Film Service, Inc., Baltimore.

Cinema Classics, Inc., 32 West 47th st., N. Y. C. H. C. K. Mattison, president; Joel F. Seedoff, vice-president and treasurer; M. L. Fulton, secretary.

Cinema Distributing Corporation, 220 West 42nd st., N. Y. C. Paul H. Cromelin, president.

Clark-Cornelius Corporation, The, 1600 Broadway, N. Y. C. William J. Clark, president; L. A. Cornelius, vice-president; S. J. Rollo, secretary; H. C. Cornelius, treasurer; Walter K. Plumb, general manager; Colvin W. Brown, assistant treasurer. (See also Exhibitors Mutual Distributing Corporation.)

Classical Motion Picture Co., Inc., 130 West 46th st., N. Y. C. Hopp Hadley, president; W. L. Russell, treasurer; Lynn S. Card, secretary.

Cloverio Film Company, Lents, Portland, Ore. Hector Cloverio, sole owner and supervisor. Department heads—Joseph Grant Kelly, Jr., publicity; Louis Hodes, scenario editor; George Speer, photography department. Studio, Lents, Portland, Ore.

Clune Film Producing Company, 547 So. Broadway, Los Angeles, Cal. I. M. Newman, president; A. S. Brown, vice-president; O. K. Evans, president and treasurer.

Lew Cody Film Corporation, Glendale, Cal. L. J. Gasnier, president and general manager; Lew Cody, vice-president; Sydney Cohan, treasurer and sales manager; G. Bardet, secretary; Kenneth A. O'Hara, studio manager. Studios, Astra Studios, Glendale, Cal., and 1 Congress st., Jersey City, N. J. (See also Astra Film Corporation.)

Jack and Harry Cohan, 1600 Broadway, N. Y. C. (See also Hall Room Boys Photoplays, Inc.)

Columbus Photoplays Company, Exchange Bldg., Columbus, Ga. Col. H. Hamilton, director general; R. E. L. Golden, treasurer; Mrs. J. B. Smith, manager.

Comique Film Corporation, 1493 Broadway, N. Y. C. Joseph M. Schenck, president and treasurer; Lou Anger, general manager; Jean Havez, Harry Williams, scenarios. Studio and western offices, Culver City, Cal. (See Roscoe Arbuckle Comedies.)

Commonwealth Film Corporation, 1600 Broadway, N. Y. C. Sam Zierler, president and general manager.

Commonwealth Pictures Company, 220 So. State st., Chicago, Ill. H. A. Spanuth, president; John Keane, vice-president; Dana Spanuth, secretary and treasurer. Department heads—Henrietta Burr, booker; Edith Conrad Beale, editor. Studio, 1333 Argyle st., Chicago, Ill.

Community Productions, The, Hastings-on-Hudson, N. Y. Christine A. Bowles; Mary W. Fry; Elizabeth Miller; Warren D. Foster; William H. Foster; Ernest H. Smith; Forrest Izard.

Consolidated Film Corporation, 738 So. Olive st., Los Angeles, Cal., and 90 Golden Gate ave., San Francisco, Cal. Marion H. Kohn, president.

Continental Pictures Corporation, 1482 Broadway, N. Y. C. Fred L. Wilke, president; E. Lanning Masters, special representative. Chicago office, Suite 922, 208 So. La Salle st.

Corona Cinema Company, 901-903 Baker-Detwiler Bldg., Los Angeles, Cal. F. E. Keeler, president; I. W. Keerl, vice-president.

Cosmofotofilm Company, 220 West 42nd st., N. Y. C. E. H. Cromelin, president; E. C. Wallace, treasurer and general manager.

Cosmopolitan Films, Willemsen & Company, 428 Camp st., New Orleans, La.

Cosmopolitan Productions, International Film Service, 729 Seventh ave., N. Y. C.

Creation Films, Inc., Cliffside, N. J. K. Hoddy Milligan, president; B. D. Biggerstaff, vice-president; C. C. Shively, treasurer; C. R. Konig, secretary. Department heads—K. Hoddy Milligan, general manager; B. D. Biggerstaff, scenario; Frank C. Beetle, publicity; B. H. Milligan, sales. Pictures distributed through Capital Films Co., Consumers Bldg., Chicago, Ill.

Crest Picture Corporation, Times Bldg., N. Y. C. Carle Carlton, general manager.

Cromlow Film Laboratories, Inc., 220 West 42nd st., N. Y. C. Paul H. Cromelin, president; Allan A. Lownes, treasurer and general manager. Laboratory, 62 Standish ave., West Orange, N. J.

Cropper Distributing Corporation, The, 207 So. Wabash ave., Chicago, Ill. Ross C. Cropper, president; George West.

Crystal Film Company, Longacre Bldg., Room 815, and 430 Claremont Parkway, N. Y. C. Joseph A. Golden, president; A. Alperstein, treasurer. (Also Allgood Pictures Corporation.)

Cuckoo Comedies, care of Mark Dintenfass, 1600 Broadway, N. Y. C.

Cathrine Curtis Corporation, Los Angeles, Cal. Cathrine Curtis, president; George M. Taylor, vice-president; Dorman T. Connet, secretary and treasurer. Cathrine Curtis, Albert L. Judson, Reese Llewellyn, William Dewey Loucks, E. R. Pirtle, Malcolm McLellan, Robert N. Simpson, Arthur F. Spaulding, George M. Taylor and George J. Whalen compose board of directors. Loucks & Alexander, counsel, New York office, 120 Broadway.

Curtiss Pictures Corporation, 33-35 West 42nd st., Aeolian Hall, N. Y. C. L. Roy Curtiss, president; Henry C. Rahe, general manager.

Curwood-Carver Productions, Inc., 6 West 48th st., N. Y. C. R. C. Thomas, president; Ernest Shipman, manager; James Oliver Curwood, director; H. P. Carver, managing director; care of First National Exhibitors Circuit.

Grace Davison Productions, c/o Pioneer Film Corporation, 130 West 46th st., N. Y. C.

Carter DeHaven Comedies, Hollywood, Cal. Carter DeHaven, c/o Famous Players-Lasky Corporation, 485 Fifth ave., N. Y. C.

Deitrich-Beck, Inc., 135 West 44th st., N. Y. C. Theodore C. Deitrich, president; Arthur F. Beck, treasurer; Thomas F. Macmahon, secretary. Studio, Leah Baird Studio, Cliffside, N. J. (See also De Luxe Pictures, Inc.)

Delcah Photoplay Company, L. A. Investment Bldg., Los Angeles, Cal. Joseph Montrose, general manager.

De Luxe Pictures, Inc., 135 West 44th st., N. Y. C. Theodore C. Deitrich, president; Doris Kenyon, treasurer; William Chilvers, vice-president and

FILM COMPANIES

secretary. Studio, Leah Baird Studio, Cliffside, N. J. (See also Deitrich-Beck, Inc.)

De Luxe Victor Moore Productions, Candler Bldg., N. Y. C. A. E. Riskin, R. R. Riskin.

Diamond Film Company, Audobon Bldg., New Orleans, La. R. M. Chisholm, president; W. J. Hannon, vice-president and general manager; Arthur J. Leopold, attorney.

Mark M. Dintenfass, 1600 Broadway, N. Y. C. Owner and producer of Cuckoo Comedies. Studio, Riverside ave., Jacksonville, Fla. Will Lewis, Jr., studio manager.

Diva Pictures, Inc., 469 Fifth ave., N. Y. C. Jacob Hilder, president; Moritz Hilder, secretary and treasurer. (See also Goldwyn Pictures Corporation.)

Johnny Dooley Film Comedies, Longacre Bldg., N. Y. C. Clarence L. Bach, president; Lawrence Wolf, vice-president; Harry Hochheimer, secretary and treasurer.

Doubleday Production Company, Bronz Studio, on Allesandro st., Hollywood, Cal. Ovid Doubleday, president; L. S. McKee, secretary; Charles Mack, manager; H. M. Owens, western representative.

Douglass Natural Color Film Co., Ltd., San Rafael, Cal. Leon F. Douglass, president; Thomas J. Lennon, vice-president; Thomas P. Boyd, second vice-president and general manager; Henry A. Melvin, chairman board of directors; Frank H. Kerrigan, treasurer; Peter Bacigalupi, Jr., secretary.

Allan Dwan Productions, c/o Mayflower Photoplay Corporation.

— E —

E. & R. Jungle Film Company, 1720 No. Soto st., Los Angeles, Cal. Edwards & Rounan, owners.

Eagle Film Corporation, 211 W. Saratoga st., Baltimore, Md. Alfred Waldeck, president; John Waldeck, treasurer; Raymund Hechinger, secretary; Sam Phillips, director. Studio, 211 W. Saratoga st., Baltimore, Md.

Educational Films Corporation of America, 729 Seventh ave., N. Y. C. G. A. Skinner, president; E. V. Hammons, vice-president and general manager. Producing Robert Bruce scenics; Hudson's Bay Party scenics; Indian Expedition scenics; Mediterranean Expedition scenics; handling Photoplay Magazine Screen Supplement; the Red Cross Travel Series; De Luxe Hand Colored scenics; Black-and-White Cartoon Comedies, and Ditmars' "Living Book of Nature." Exchange Centers in the United States—Denver, Atlanta, Dallas, St. Louis, Chicago, Kansas City, Cincinnati, Baltimore, Cleveland, Boston, Philadelphia, New York, San Francisco, Los Angeles, Seattle. Canada—Vancouver, Toronto, Montreal, Skagway. Mexico—Mexico City. Sales Cities in Foreign Lands—Valparaiso, Buenos Aires, Rio de Janeiro, Panama, South America; Johannesburg, Capetown, Cairo, Africa; Lisbon, Madrid, Rome, Paris, Berlin, Warsaw, London, Brussels, Prague, Petrograd, Christiania, Stockholm, Budapest, Bucharest, Europe. Red Cross Cameramen in the Field—Warsaw, Belgrade, Bucharest, Budapest, Paris, Archangel, Petrograd, Constantinople, Prague, Siberia. Sales Cities and Red Cross Cameramen—Vladivostok. Sales Cities, China, Peking; Japan, Tokio. Subsidiary Company—Far East Film Corporation, 729 Seventh ave., N. Y. C.; Reginald Warde, president; E. W. Hammons, vice-president. London Branch, The Educational Film Company, Ltd., 71 Wardour st., W. I; H. Holford Bottomly, A. J. Davidson. General laboratory—Wilkes-Barre, Pa. Production Studio—Providence, R. I. Educational Exchanges—Celebrated Players Film Corporation, Chicago, Indianapolis, Milwaukee; Electric Theatre Supply Company, Philadelphia; Federal Feature Film Corporation, Boston; Baltimore Booking Company, Baltimore; First National Exhibitors' Exchange, Pittsburg; Standard Film Service Company, Cincinnati, Cleveland, Detroit; Standard Film Corporation, Kansas City, Mo.; Consolidated Film Corporation, San Francisco, Los Angeles; Greater Features, Inc., Seattle; Arrow Photo Plays Company, Denver, and Monarch Film Company, Ltd., Toronto and Montreal, Canada. Subsidiary Companies affiliated with Educational Films Corporation of America—The Alliance Film Securities Corporation, 729 Seventh ave., N. Y. C., c/o Educational; E. W. Hammons, president; G. A. Skinner, vice-president. Coronet Film Corporation, 729 Seventh ave., N. Y. C., c/o Educational; G. A. Skinner, president.

Educator's Cinematograph Company, 70 Fifth ave., N. Y. C. Alfred H. Saunders, governor of education.

Eff & Eff Productions, Inc., 145 West 45th st., N. Y. C. Joseph Finger, president; Frank P. Donavan, director.

Elk Photoplays, Inc., The, 126 West 46th st., N. Y. C. Jacob Berjowitz, president and general manager; E. Berman, treasurer; B. H. Mills, secretary and sales manager.

Emerald Motion Picture Corporation, 1717 No. Wells st., Chicago, Ill. Frederick J. Ireland, president; M. E. Oberdorfer, secretary and treasurer; J. W. Martin, business manager. Studio, Chicago, Ill.

Eminent Authors Pictures, Inc., 469 Fifth ave., N. Y. C. Rex Beach, president; Samuel Goldwyn, chairman board of directors; P. W. Haberman, treasurer; Gabriel L. Hess, secretary. (See also Goldwyn Pictures Corporation.)

Guy Empey Pictures Corporation, 220 West 42nd st., N. Y. C. James F. Shaw, president; Arthur Guy Empey, vice-president; F. C. Richardson, secretary and treasurer.

Entente Film Corporation, 247 No. 11th st., Philadelphia, Pa. Benjamin Primavera, manager; Morton Z. Paul, president.

Enwood Feature Picture Company, Denver, Colo. O. D. Woodward, president, care of Republic Distributing Corporation, 729 Seventh ave., N. Y. C.

Equity Pictures Corporation, 33 West 42nd st., N. Y. C. H. K. Somborn, president; Joseph I. Schnitzer, treasurer. Department heads—Harry L. Reichenbach, publicity; A. B. Williamson, assistant publicity; Nat. G. Rothstein, advertising; John N. Weber, auditor. Studio, Garson Studios, Inc., 1845 Allesandro st., Los Angeles, Cal.

Erbograph Studios, 203 West 146th st., N. Y. C. Ludwig G. B. Erb, president; Benjamin Goetz, secretary and treasurer.

Essanay Film Manufacturing Company, 1333 Argyle st., Chicago, Ill. George K. Spoor, president. Studios, 1333 Argyle st., Chicago, Ill. (See also Spoor-Thompson Machine Company.)

Exclusive Features, Inc., 126 West 46th st., N. Y. C. Joseph Goldstein, J. Weinberg. (See also Canyon Pictures Corporation.)

Exhibitors Mutual Distributing Corporation, 1600 Broadway, N. Y. C. William J. Clark, president; H. C. Cornelius, vice-president; L. A. Cornelius, secretary; Walter K. Plumb, treasurer. (See also Clark-Cornelius Corporation.)

Export & Import Film Company, 729 Seventh ave., N. Y. C. Ben Blumenthal.

— F —

Facts and Follies, Inc., c/o Pioneer Film Corporation, 130 West 46th st., N. Y. C. Bernard Macfadden.

Douglas Fairbanks Pictures Corporation, Hollywood, Cal., and 1482 Broadway, N. Y. C. Douglas Fairbanks, president; John Fairbanks, treasurer; Dennis O'Brien, secretary and treasurer. Department heads—John Fairbanks, general manager; Robert Fairbanks, manager of productions; Leeds Baxter, auditor; Victor Fleming, director; Tom Geraghty, scenario editor; Joan Boison, scenario reader; Albert MacQuarrie, casting director; J. Theodore Reed, technical director; Edward M. Langley, art director; William McGann, Harry Thorpe, cinematographers; Charles Warrington, still department; Frank England, custodian of properties; William Nolan, cutting department; A. J. Coe, location agent; Paul Burns, properties; Carlyle R. Robinson, director of publicity. Studio, Melrose and Bronson aves., Los Angeles, Cal.

Famous Players-Lasky Corporation, 485 Fifth ave., N. Y. C. Adolph Zukor, president; Jesse L. Lasky, vice-president; Arthur S. Friend, treasurer; Emil E. Shauer, assistant treasurer; Eugene J. Zukor, assistant treasurer; Elek John Ludvigh, secretary; Ralph A. Kohn, assistant secretary; L. S. Wicker, assistant secretary; Frank Mayer, assistant secretary; John Flinn, associate executive. Department heads: Production Department—Cecil B. De Mille, director general; Whitman Bennett, production manager; Robert A. MacAlarney, scenario editor; Charles Eyton, general manager, West coast studios; J. N. Naulty, general manager,

Eastern studios; Frank E. Woods, supervising director, West coast studios; Nathan Friend, general manager Educational Department. Department of Distribution—Al Lichtman, general manager; Fred C. Chamberlain, assistant general manager; Sidney R. Kent, sales manager. Publicity—Jerome Beatty, director of publicity and advertising. Studios, Long Island City, N. Y.; 130 West 56th st., N. Y. C.; Fort Lee, N. J.; Hollywood, Cal. (two). Special representatives to Exchanges—J. W. Allen, headquarters at Chicago; M. H. Lewis, headquarters at Kansas City; W. J. Pratt, headquarters at Atlanta; L. L. Dent, headquarters at Dallas. District managers—Harry Asher, Boston district; W. E. Smith, Philadelphia district; C. E. Holcomb, Southern district (Atlanta); Louis Marcus, Salt Lake City; Norman Webber, San Francisco. Exchanges—Boston, Portland (Me.), New Haven, New York, Buffalo, Philadelphia, Washington, Pittsburgh, Cincinnati, Cleveland, Chicago, Minneapolis, Detroit, Kansas City, St. Louis, Des Moines, Omaha, Atlanta, New Orleans, Dallas, Oklahoma City, Charlotte, Salt Lake City, Denver, San Francisco, Los Angeles, Seattle, Portland (Ore.). Canadian organization—Famous Lasky Film Service, Ltd., George W. Weeks, general manager, supervising branch exchanges at Toronto (home office), Montreal, St. John, Winnipeg, Calgary and Vancouver.

Fay Film Corporation, 1739 No. Campbell ave., Chicago, Ill. R. F. Fry, president; Frank S. Watterson, general manager.

Federal Photoplays, Inc., 25 West 45th st., N. Y. C. Benjamin B. Hampton, president; C. A. Weeks, secretary and treasurer; E. F. Warner, assistant secretary and assistant treasurer. Department heads—Wm. Clifford, scenario; J. B. Chapman, publicity; J. G. Fater, advertising. Studio, Brunton Studios, 5341 Melrose st., Los Angeles, Cal. (See also Federal Photoplays of California, Zane Grey Pictures, Inc., and Great Authors Pictures, Inc.)

Federal Photoplays of California, 5341 Melrose st., Los Angeles, Cal. Benjamin B. Hampton, president; Hewlings Mumper, secretary and treasurer; Norris N. Mumper, assistant secretary and assistant treasurer. Department heads—Wm. Clifford, scenario; J. B. Chapman, publicity; J. G. Fater, advertising. Branch office, 25 West 45th st., N. Y. Studio, Brunton studio, 5341 Melrose st., Los Angeles, Cal. See also Zane Grey Pictures, Inc., Great Authors Pictures, Inc., and Federal Photoplays, Inc.)

Ferndale Film Studios, Inc., The, Ferndale, L. I. C. F. K. Andrews; Miss L. Minnie Kirmmse; E. G. W. Dietrich.

Films Incorporated, 1482 Broadway, N. Y. C. William W. Young, president; S. Kantrowich, vice-president; Joseph J. Macdonald, secretary and treasurer; Edward Marshall, chairman committee on production. These officers with J. J. Flannery constitute the board of directors.

Film Market, Inc., The, Times Bldg., N. Y. C. Robert W. Priest, president.

Film Novelties, Inc., 145 West 45th st., N. Y. C. J. Finger, president; A. J. Danziger, general manager.

Film Specials, Inc., 130 West 46th st., N. Y. C. Joseph M. Schenck; W. S. Epstein, general manager.

First National Exhibitors' Circuit, Inc., The, 6-8 West 48th st., N. Y. C. Robert Lieber, president; T. L. Tally, vice-president; H. Schwalbe, secretary and treasurer; J. D. Williams, manager. Directors—T. L. Tally, R. H. Clark, H. Schwalbe, Aaron Jones, E. H. Hulsey, J. G. Von Herberg, Robert Lieber. Department heads—J. D. Williams, general manager; W. J. Morgan, manager contract department; C. L. Yearsley, director of publicity and advertising; E. J. Hudson, publicity representative; George R. Grant, auditor. Exchanges—Atlanta, Ga., First Nat. Exhibitors' Cir. of Va., 146 Marietta st.; Boston, Mass., Gordon-Mayer Film Corp., 35 Piedmont st.; Buffalo, N. Y., First Nat. Exch., 215 Franklin st.; Chicago, Ill., First Nat. Ex. Exch., 110 So. State st.; Cleveland, Ohio, First Nat. Ex. Cir. of Ohio, 402 Sloan Bldg.; Dallas, Tex., First Nat. Ex. Cir. of Texas, 1924 Main st.; Denver, Colo., First Nat. Ex. Cir. of Colo., 1518 Welton st.; Des Moines, Iowa, A. H. Blank, 326 Iowa Bldg.; Detroit, Mich., First Nat. Exch. of Mich., 63 E. Elizabeth st.; Indianapolis, Ind., The H. Lieber Co., 24 W. Washington st.; Kansas City, Mo., A. H. Blank Enterprises, 317 Floyd Bldg.; Kansas City, Mo., Richards & Flynn, 12th Street theatre; Los Angeles, Cal., First Nat. Ex. Exch., 633 So. Bway.; Louisville, Ky., First Nat. Exch. of Ky. and Tenn., Nat. Theatre Bldg.; Milwaukee, Wis., First Nat. Ex. Exch., 408 Toy Bldg.; Minneapolis, Minn., First Nat. Ex. Cir. of N. W., 408-18 Loeb Arcade Bldg.; New Haven, Conn., First Nat. Ex. Exch., 126 Meadow st.; New York City, First Nat. Ex., Inc., 509 Fifth ave.; Oklahoma City, Okla., First Nat. Ex. Exch., 127 So. Hudson st.; Omaha, Neb., A. H. Blank Enterprises, 314 So. 13th st.; Ottawa, Can., H. Brouse, Dom. Amuse. Co.; Imperial theatre; Phila., Pa., Peerless Feature Film Exch., 1339 Vine st.; Pittsburgh, Pa., First Nat. Ex. Exch., 414 Ferry st.; Richmond, Va., First Nat. Ex. Cir. of Va., 904 E. Broad st.; St. Louis, Mo., Grand Cent. Film Co., New Grand Cent. theatre; Salt Lake City, Utah, First Nat. Ex. Cir. of Colo., 136 E. 2nd So. st.; San Francisco, Cal., Turner & Dahnken, 134 Golden Gate ave.; Seattle, Wash., Ex. Film Exch., Inc., 2023 3rd ave.; Toronto, Can., Regal Films, Temple Bldg.; Toronto, Can., Allen Bros., Allen Theatre Bldg.; Vancouver, B. C., First Nat. Ex. Cir., Ltd., 1318 Standard Bank Bldg.; Washington, D. C., First Nat. Ex. Exch., 916 "G" st., N. W.

A. H. Fischer Features, Inc., 46 Main st., New Rochelle, N. Y. A. H. Fischer, president and treasurer; B. A. Rolfe, vice-president; Charles A. Logue, secretary. Department heads—Charles G. Stewart, general manager; Charles A. Logue, scenario; Carey Wilson, sales; Harry H. Poppe, advertising and publicity. Studio, A. H. Fischer Studios and Laboratory, 46 Main st., New Rochelle, N. Y. (See also Octagon Films, Inc.)

Cissy Fitzgerald Comedies, care of United Picture Theatres of America, Inc., 1600 Broadway, N. Y. C.

Florida Film Corporation, 22 West Ninth st., Jacksonville, Fla. H. J. Klutho, president; Fay Smith, vice-president; Harland Smith, secretary; Virgil MacKenzie, general manager; Glen Lambert and Bert Tracy, picture directors. Studios, Klutho studios, 22 West Ninth st., Jacksonville, Fla.

Francis Ford Producing Company, 6040 Sunset Blvd., Hollywood, Cal. Francis Ford, director; Harry Ellis Dean, studio manager; Nell Dean, publicity; Elsie Van Name, scenario.

Forward Film Distributors, Inc., 110 West 40th st., N. Y. C. J. Joseph Sameth, president; M. Warschauer, vice-president; Harry Roth, secretary and treasurer. London office, 17 Shaftsbury ave., care of J. A. Barkey & Co.

Foundation Film Corporation, 1600 Broadway, N. Y. C. Murray W. Garsson, president. Laboratories, Hudson Heights, N. J.

Fox Film Corporation, 10th ave., 55th to 56th sts., 130 West 46th st., N. Y. C. William Fox, president; Winfield R. Sheehan, general manager. Department heads—Arthur James, advertising and publicity; Merritt Crawford, director of publicity; Hamilton Thompson, Denison Clift, Hampton Del Ruth, scenario editors. Studios: Western, 1401 North Western ave., Los Angeles, Cal.; Eastern, 10th ave., 55th to 56th sts., College Pt., L. I., and Fort Lee, N. J. United States Exchanges — Atlanta, Boston, Buffalo, Chicago, Cincinnati, Cleveland, Dallas, Denver, Detroit, Kansas City, Los Angeles, Minneapolis, Indianapolis, New Haven, New Orleans, New York, Omaha, Philadelphia, Pittsburgh, Salt Lake City, San Francisco, Seattle, St. Louis, Washington. Foreign exchanges—Great Britain: London, Liverpool, Manchester, Newcastle, Glasgow, Leeds, Cardiff, Birmingham, Dublin. Australia: Sydney, Melbourne, Brisbane, Adelaide, Wellington, N. Z. South America: Rio de Janeiro, Sao Paulo, Buenos Aires, Rosario, Montevideo, Lima, Peru. Canada: Montreal, Toronto, St. John, Vancouver, Calgary, Winnipeg. Agencies: Paris, France; Rome, Italy; Barcelona, Spain; Copenhagen, Denmark; Stockholm, Sweden; Christiania, Norway; Moscow, Russia; Johannesburg, South Africa; Bombay, India; Batavia, Java; Hong Kong, China; Yokohama, Japan; and Manila, Philippine Islands.

Fox Studios (Western), 1417 N. Western ave., Los Angeles, Cal. Sol M. Wurtzel, studio manager; George Teffeau, studio supt.; Denison Clift, scenario editor; Frank Burns, laboratory supt.; E. A. Yerby Smith, technical director; J. Anthony Roach, H. H. Van Loan, Gus Meins, scenarios; Hampton Del Ruth, scenario editor; E. J. LeSaint, Scott Dunlap, Howard Mitchell, Cliff Smith, Eddie Cline, J. G. Blystone, Roy Del Ruth, Delmar Lord, directors; Louis Seiler, production manager; Fay Dur-

FILM COMPANIES

ham, Frank Good, Walter Williams, George Schneiderman, Earl Ellis, Irving Rosenbern, Bud Courcier, Frank Heisler, G. F. Schoedsack, P. D. Whitman, E. B. DuPar, cameramen.

Frazee Comedies, Riverside, Cal. (See Frazee Film Productions, Inc.)

Frazee Film Productions, Inc., Magnolia and Jurupa aves., Riverside, Cal. Edwin Frazee, president and general manager; Joe Murphy, assistant manager; M. J. Twogood, secretary and treasurer; Florence Gottlieb, publicity and scenario department. New York office, 17 West 44th st.; London office, 90 Fleet st. Frazee Comedies released through Clune Exchange in United States and England.

Frohman Amusement Corporation, The, Times Bldg., N. Y. C. William L. Sherrill, president; Jesse L. Goldberg, secretary and general manager; Joseph Schwartz, acting treasurer. Studios, New York City and Los Angeles, Cal.

—G—

Garson Studios, Inc., 1845 Allesandro st., Los Angeles, Cal. Harry Garson, president and general manager; E. W. Butcher, vice-president and studio manager; R. M. Yost, publicity; John M. Voshell, technical director; C. B. Edington, auditor.

L. J. Gasnier Productions, Verdugo Road, Glendale, Cal. L. J. Gasnier, director general. (See Astra Film Corporation and Lew Cody Productions.)

Gaumont Company, Flushing, L. I. F. G. Bradford, manager.

Gayety Comedies, Inc., 1501 Gower st., Los Angeles, Cal. Craig Hutchinson, production manager, scenario editor and director; Claude Hill, studio manager; James Clemens, technical director.

Gibraltar Pictures, 135 West 44th st., N. Y. C. Arthur F. Beck; Charles C. Burr.

Dorothy Gish Productions, New Art Film Co. (D. W. Griffith), Longacre Bldg., N. Y. C.

Wyndham Gittens Productions, 926 Investment Bldg., Los Angeles, Cal.

Golden West Productions, 209 W. 9th st., Glendale, Cal. G. M. Anderson.

Goldwitt Film Sales Company, 145 West 45th st., N. Y. C. Mortimer D. Sikawitt, president; Samuel Goldstein.

Goldwyn Pictures Corporation, 469 Fifth ave., N. Y. C. Samuel Goldwyn, president; F. J. Godsol, Moritz Hilder, Lee Shubert, Edgar Selwyn, Abraham Lehr, vice-presidents; P. W. Haberman, treasurer; Gabriel L. Hess, secretary; F. J. Godsol, chairman of executive committee. Also connected in the directorate of the corporation are H. F. du Pont, Eugene E. du Pont, W. W. Laird, R. R. M. Carpenter, G. C. Kurtz, E. V. R. Thayer, Duncan A. Holmes; William Topkis, George T. Bissell, G. W. Davison, Macmillan Hoopes, Abbot M. Wittenberg. Department heads—Ralph Block, director of publicity and advertising; Howard Dietz, manager of publicity; Eugene Mullin, head of scenario department in East; J. G. Hawkes, head of scenario department in West; Felix Feist, sales; Geoffrey Nye, Far East representative. Studio, Culver City, Cal. Branches —Atlanta, Ga., 111 Walton st.; Boston, Mass., 42 Piedmont st.; Buffalo, N. Y., 200 Pearl st.; Chicago, Ill., 207 So. Wabash ave.; Cincinnati, O., 216 East 5th st.; Cleveland, O., 403 Standard Theatre Bldg.; Dallas, Tex., 1922 Main st.; Denver, Colo., 1440 Walton st.; Detroit, Mich., Film Exchange Bldg.; Kansas City, Mo., 1120 Walnut st.; Los Angeles, Cal., 912 So. Olive st.; Minneapolis, Minn., 16 No. 4th st.; New York City, 509 Fifth ave.; Philadelphia, Pa., s. e. cor. 13th and Vine sts.; Pittsburgh, Pa., 1201 Liberty ave.; San Francisco, Cal., 985 Market st.; St. Louis, Mo., 3312 Lindell Blvd.; Seattle, Wash., 2018 Third ave.; Washington, D. C., 714 11th st., N. W.; New Orleans, La., 714 Poydras st.; Omaha, Neb., 1508 Howard st.; Salt Lake City, U., 135 East 2nd South st.

Goldwyn Distributing Corporation, 469 Fifth ave., N. Y. C. Samuel Goldwyn, president; Felix F. Feist and Alfred Weiss, vice-presidents; Gabriel L. Hess, secretary and treasurer. (See also Goldwyn Pictures Corporation.)

Goldwyn Studios, Culver City, Cal. Abraham Lehr, general manager; Milton Gardner, secretary; Mason N. Litson, production manager; J. G. Hawks, scenario editor; Gilbert White, technical director; Lewis Physioc, supt. of laboratory; Thompson Buchanan, E. A. Bingham, Rex Taylor, Edward T. Lowe, E. Richard Schayer, Gerald C. Duffy, Harvey Thew, Charles Kenyon, Bess E. Haas, Elliot Clawson, Elmer L. Rice, Louis Sherwin, J. E. Nash, Jean Hollingsworth, Elanor Flori, H. Schrieber, Margaret Minning, scenarios; Harry Beaumont, Victor L. Schertzinger, T. Hays Hunter, Wallace Worsley, Reginald Barker, Clarence Badger, Frank Lloyd, directors; J. S. Woodhouse, Clarke Irvine, Helen Starr, C. S. Bull, Eugene Richee, Lloyd J. Roby, J. C. Gault, Hal White, Sue McNamara, R. E. Dawson, publicity. (See also Goldwyn Pictures Corporation.)

Graphic Film Corporation, 729 Seventh ave., N. Y. C. Ivan Abramson, president. Exchanges handling product—Eastern Feature Film Exchange, 57 Church st., Boston, Mass.; Hygrade Feature Film Co., Charlotte, N. C.; Southeastern Pictures Corp., 61 Walton st., Atlanta, Ga.; Major Film Co., 10 Piedmont st., Boston, Mass.; Joseph Horowitz, Detroit, Mich.; First Nat'l Ex. Cir., St. Louis, Mo.; Superb Productions, Omaha, Neb., and Des Moines, Ia.; Frank Gersten, Inc., 130 West 46th st., New York; Screen Art Pictures Co., 1315 Vine st., Phila., Pa.; Special Feature Film Co., Atlanta, Ga.; First Nat'l Ex. Cir., 35 Piedmont st., Boston, Mass.; Unity Photoplay Corp., 207 So. Wabash ave., Chicago, Ill.; First Nat'l Ex. Cir., Minneapolis, Minn.; First Nat'l Ex. Cir., Kansas City, Mo.; M & R Feature Film Co., San Francisco, Cal.; N. J. Metro Film Co., 729 Seventh ave., New York.

Great Authors Pictures, Inc., 5341 Melrose st., Los Angeles, Cal. Benjamin B. Hampton, president; E. F. Warner, C. A. Weeks, vice-presidents; Hewlings Mumper, secretary and treasurer. Department heads—Wm. Clifford, scenario; J. B. Chapman, publicity; J. G. Fater, advertising; Edward Sloman, director. Branch—New York office, 25 West 45th st. Studio, Brinton Studio, 5341 Melrose st., Los Angeles, Cal. (See also Zane Grey Pictures, Inc., Federal Photoplay of California, and Federal Photoplays, Inc.)

Great Western Producing Company, 1600 Broadway, N. Y. C. (See Universal Film Manufacturing Company.) Studios, Hollywood, Cal. Julius Stern, president; A. Stern, vice-president; Louis Jacobs, general manager.

Great Western Pictures Corporation, Longacre Bldg., N. Y. C. Emmett Dalton, president.

Greiver Distributing Corporation, 207 So. Wabash ave., Chicago, Ill.

Zane Grey Pictures, Inc., 5341 Melrose st., Los Angeles, Cal. Benjamin B. Hampton, president; E. F. Warner, vice-president; Hewlings Mumper, secretary and treasurer. Department heads—Wm. Clifford, scenario; J. B. Chapman, publicity; J. G. Fater, advertising; Jack Conway, director. Branch office, 25 West 45th st., New York. Studio, Brunton Studio, 5341 Melrose st., Los Angeles, Cal. (See also Great Authors Pictures, Inc., Federal Photoplays of California, and Federal Photoplays, Inc.)

David Wark Griffith Attractions, Longacre Bldg., N. Y. C. D. W. Griffith, owner and producer. Executive Department—Albert L. Grey, general manager; John Lloyd, personal representative; Robert Edgar Long, publicity; Agnes Wiener, executive secretary. Studio Department—J. C. Epping, studio manager; Myron M. Stearns, scenario editor; G. W. Bitzer, chief photographer; Frank Wortman, technical director; Samuel Thompson, chief electrician; Albert H. A. Banzhaf, counsel. Studio, Orienta Point, Mamaroneck, N. Y.

D. W. Griffith Service, 720 Longacre Bldg., N. Y. C. Albert L. Grey, general manager. (See D. W. Griffith Attractions.)

Grossman Pictures, Ithaca, N. Y. Harry Grossman, president, general manager and supervising director; Abel Cary Thomas, secretary; E. D. Bingham, technical director; George Littman, sales manager; T. D. Bonneville, publicity and advertising. Branches—Business, publicity, advertising offices, 110 West 42nd st., N. Y. C. Studio, Ithaca, N. Y.

—H—

Hallmark Pictures Corporation, 130 West 46th st., N. Y. C. Frank G. Hall, president. Department heads—John Glavey, C. Clarkson Miller, and Olga Jaffe, scenario; Joseph L. Kelley, publicity; Hopp Hadley, advertising; W. F. Rodger, sales; J. L. Burke, business manager; Harry P. Diggs, exploitation; Leon D. Britton, productions manager. Studios, 230 West 38th st. and 517 West 54th st., New York City.

Hall Room Boys Photoplays, Inc., 1600 Broadway, N. Y. C. Jack Cohn, president; Harry Cohn, secretary and treasurer.

Hope Hampton Productions, Inc., Longacre Bldg., N. Y. C.

Jesse D. Hampton Productions, 1425 Fleming st., Hollywood, Cal. Jesse D. Hampton, owner and general manager; E. L. Smith, studio manager; Fred Gabourie, production manager; A. F. Statter, scenario editor; Henry King, Robert Thornby, Joseph Franz, directors.

Benjamin B. Hampton Productions, Los Angeles, Cal. See Zane Grey Pictures, Inc., and Great Authors Pictures, Inc.)

Calvert Harrison Feature Film Corporation, 115 N. Pennsylvania ave., Indianapolis, Ind. C. Hanford Harrison, business manager.

William S. Hart Productions, 1215 Bates st., Los Angeles, Cal. E. M. Allen, manager; Lambert Hillyer, director; Paul H. Conlon, publicity; Bennett Musson, scenario editor; Thomas Brierly, technical director; Le Roy Stone, film editor; H. J. Howard, casting director.

J. Frank Hatch Enterprises, Inc., 729 Seventh ave., N. Y. C. J. Frank Hatch.

Haworth Pictures 5341 Melrose ave., Los Angeles, Cal. George W. Stout, general manager; Wm. J. Connery, vice-president; Wm. Worthington, Joseph DeGrasse, directors; Eddie Scott, film editor; Charles Greenberg, general counsel and secretary.

Hobart Henley Productions, 363 West 125th st., N. Y. C. Hobart Henley, president; Benjamin P. Schoenfein, studio manager; Warren V. Fromme, assistant director; Richard L. Fryer, cameraman; Hadley Waters, publicist; Hulda Salat, casting department; Jules W. Redston, technical department; Felix Larson, scenic department; Edward Quinn, property department. Studio, 361-363 West 125th st., N. Y. C. Home office, 25 West 45th st., N. Y. C. Branch, Los Angeles, Cal.

Gale Henry Comedies, c/o Model Comedy Company, 5821 Santa Monica Blvd., Hollywood, Cal. Released through Bulls Eye Film Corporation, 729 Seventh ave., N. Y. C.

L. I. Hiller, Longacre Bldg., N. Y. C.

Historical Film Company of America, The, Burbank, Cal. J. A. McGill, president; Raymond Welt, director of productions.

W. W. Hodkinson Corporation, 527 Fifth ave., N. Y. C. W. W. Hodkinson, president; Raymond Pawley, vice-president and treasurer; Mary A. Bell, secretary; F. B. Warren, vice-president in charge of distribution and advertising. Department heads—P. N. Brinch, assistant to the president and manager of foreign department; C. E. Hopkins, auditor. Branches — Distributing through Pathe Exchange, Inc., with sales force in each office.

Hollywood Studios, Inc., Santa Monica Blvd. and Seward st., Hollywood, Cal. John Jasper, general manager.

Burton Holmes Travel Pictures, Aeolian Bldg., 33 West 42nd st., N. Y. C. Burton Holmes, c/o Famous Players-Lasky Corporation.

Taylor Holmes Productions, Inc., c/o Metro Pictures Corporation, Longacre Bldg., N. Y. C. Taylor Holmes, president; Paul Turner, vice-president; H. H. Bruenner, treasurer; Thomas A. Persons, supervising director in charge of productions; Gus Mohme, director of sales. Studio, Biograph studio, 175th st. and Southern Boulevard, the Bronx, N. Y. C.

Wm. Horsley Film Laboratories, 6060 Sunset Boulevard, Hollywood, Cal. William Horsley, sole owner. Arthur T. Horsley, laboratory expert. Wm. C. Horsley, laboratory superintendent. Capacity, 150,000 ft. negative per week, 400,000 ft. positive per week.

Humanity Producing Company, Brunton Studios, 5341 Melrose ave., Los Angeles, Cal.

Humphrey Pictures, Inc., c/o Pioneer Film Corporation, 130 West 46th st., N. Y. C.

Arthur S. Hyman Attractions, Consumers Bldg., Chicago, Ill. W. G. McCoy, manager, Film Bldg., Detroit, Mich.

Hyperion Productions, Inc., George H. Wiley, president; Walter Richard Hall; Joseph W. Farnham; James Vincent.

— I —

Thomas M. Ince Productions, Culver City, Cal. Thomas M. Ince, president; J. Parker Reed, Jr., general manager; Clark Thomas, production manager; W. J. Gilmour, supt. of studio; Fred Fralick, casting director; Harvey Leavitt, technical director; W. P. Heywood, art director; Spencer Valentine, purchasing dept.; Alfred Brandt, laboratory dept.; Paul Eagler, head cameraman; C. Garner Sullivan, Julien Josephson, E. Magnus Ingleton, Luther Reed, Helen Badgley, Bernard McElroy, Ethel C. Thorp, Adele Buffington, F. Ely Paget, John B. Ritchie, Miriam Meredith, Miss Lorimer, scenarios. Companies—Enid Bennett Company, Fred Niblo, director; Charles Ray Company, Jerome Storm, director; MacLean-May Company, Lloyd Ingraham, director; Bosworth Company, Irvin Willat, director.

International Film Service, 729 Seventh ave., N. Y. C. William R. Hearst, president; Morril Goddard, treasurer; R. V. Anderson, general sales manager; E. B. Hetrick, general news manager; Leslie Jordan, advertising manager.

Inter-Ocean Film Corporation, 220 West 42d st., N. Y. C. Paul H. Cromelin, president and general manager.

Ivan Film Productions, Inc., 126 West 46th st., N. Y. C. I. E. Chadwick, general manager. (See Merit Film Corporation.)

Ivy Films Corporation, Lincoln Studio, Grantwood, N. J. Henry L. Keats, president.

— J —

Louis Jacobson Enterprises, Inc., 110 West 42nd st., N. Y. C. Louis Jacobson, president and treasurer.

Jans Distributing Corporation, 729 Seventh ave., N. Y. C. H. F. Jans, president and treasurer; F. E. Backer, general manager.

Jans Productions, Inc., 729 Seventh ave., N. Y. C. Herman F. Jans, president and treasurer; F. E. Backer, general manager; B. A. Rolfe, director general. See also Jans Distributing Corporation.) Studio, Peerless Studio, Fort Lee, N. J.

Jaxon Film Company, Commercial Trust Bldg., N. Y. C. F. A. Tichenor, president; Walter Young, secretary.

Al Jennings Photoplay Company, Hollywood, Cal. H. M. Owens, general manager. Studio, Hollywood, Cal.

Jester Comedy Company, 220 West 42nd st., N. Y. C. William Steiner, president. (See also William Steiner Productions, The Photo Drama Co and The Tex Pictures, Inc.)

Jewel Productions, Incorporated, 1600 Broadway, N. Y. C. (See Universal Manufacturing Company.)

Johnson & Hopkins Company, 398 Fifth ave., N. Y. C. Walter L. Johnson; Earle H. Hopkins. (See Motion Picture Producing Company of America.)

Jolly Comedies, care of Film Specials, Inc., 126 West 46th st., N. Y. C.

Juvenile Photoplay Distributors, Inc., 729 Seventh ave., N. Y. C. A. D. V. Storey, president; Jack Cohn, production manager; Bernard Miller.

— K —

S. L. K. Film Corporation, 112 West 42nd st., N. Y. C. S. Krellberg.

Arthur S. Kane Pictures Corporation, 452 Fifth ave., N. Y. C. Arthur S. Kane, president.

James Keane Feature Photoplay Productions, 220 West 42nd st., N. Y. C. James Keant, director; E. A. Keant, general manager; Florence Vincent, chief of scenario staff.

Frank Keenan Productions, Inc., Robert Brunton Studios, 5341 Melrose ave., Los Angeles, Cal. Frank Keenan, president; Robert Brunton, vice-president and general manager; Fred G. Andrews, business manager; Carlos Huntington, publicity; Gertrude Andrews, scenarios; Elliot Howe, director; Robert Newhardt, cameraman.

J. Warren Kerrigan Pictures, Inc., Brunton Studios, 5341 Melrose ave., Los Angeles, Cal., care of W. W. Hodkinson Corporation, 516 Fifth ave., N. Y. C.

FILM COMPANIES

King Cole Comedies, care of Motion Picture Producing Company of America, 398 Fifth ave., N. Y.

Kinogram Publishing Corporation (Kinograms), 71 West 23rd st., N. Y. C. Dennis J. Sullivan, general manager; Terry Ramsaye.

George Kleine, 63 East Adams st., Chicago, Ill. New York office, 110 West 46th st. Merrill Smith, general manager.

Victor Kremer Film Features, 105 West 40th st., N. Y. C. Victor Kremer, president; J. Shenfield, secretary. Branches—Chicago office, 1345 Argyle st.; Pacific coast office, 728 Broadway, San Diego, Cal.

— L —

L-Ko Pictures Kompany, 1600 Broadway, N. Y. C. Julius Stern, president; Abe Stern, vice-president and secretary; Louis Jacobs, business manager; Ed. Haas, technical director; Fred Fishback, Robert Hill, J. P. McGowan, William Watson, Jesse Robbins, directors. Studios, 6100 Sunset Blvd., Hollywood, Cal. (See also Universal Film Manufacturing Company.)

LaSalle Film Company, The, 1450 Dayton st., Chicago, Ill. B. F. Lewis, general manager; Phil Grau, secretary; F. J. Seng, treasurer. Studio, Sunset and Gower sts., Los Angeles, Cal.

Lasky Studios, 1520 Vine st., Los Angeles, Cal. Charles Eyton, general manager; Fred Kley, studio manager; Cecil B. De Mille, director general; Donald Crisp, Wm. De Mille, George Melford, Sam Wood, Thomas Heffron, Charles Maigne, directors; Alvin Wyckoff, director of photography; L. M. Goodstadt, casting director; Al Palm, supt. of laboratory; Wilfred Buckland, art director; Henry Kotani, Paul Perry, C. E. Schoenbaum, Guy Wilky, Victor Ackland, Al Gilks, William Marshall, cameramen; Loren Taylor, title dept.; W. E. Sender, auditing dept.; Edmund Mitchell, purchasing dept.; Elizabeth Mcgaffey, research dept.; Howard Wells, property dept.; Clare West, designer; Roy Diem, costumes; Beulah Marie Dix, Frances Harmer, Clara Kennedy, Mary H. O'Connor, Will M. Ritchey, Frank E. Woods, Walter Woods, Olga Printzlau, Elmer Harris, Frank Finnegan, Margaret Turnbull, scenarios. (See also Famous Players-Lasky Corporation.)

Henry Lohrman Productions, Inc., Culver City, Cal. Henry Lohrman, president; Edward L. Symonds, studio manager; Mr. Sarber, technical director; Norman Taurog, director; George Meehan, Charles Selby, cameramen.

Sol Lesser Enterprises, Longacre Bldg., N. Y. C. Sol Lesser, president; Maurie Meyers, publicity. Branches—Cleveland, Chicago, Los Angeles, San Francisco, Seattle. Exchange, Sol Lesser Film Exchange, 729 Seventh ave.

Edgar Lewis Productions, Inc., 1457 Broadway, N. Y. C. Edgar Lewis, president; Harry Cahane, treasurer; Abraham L Feinstein, secretary. Department head, Solita Solano, director of publicity. Studios, Solax Studio, Fort Lee, N. J., and Brunton Studios, Hollywood, Cal.

Liberty Feature Films Company, San Francisco, Cal. Studio, Niles, Cal.

Life-Grams, Inc., 825 Longacre Bldg., N. Y. C., care of Wilk & Wilk.

Harold Lloyd Comedies (See Rolin Film Company.)

— M —

C. R. Macauley Photoplays, Inc., 516 Fifth ave., N. Y. C. Charles R. Macauley, president; Fred H. Albert, vice-president; Hy. Butterfield, treasurer; Donald Woodruff, business manager.

Katherine MacDonald Picture Corporation, Girard and Georgia sts., Los Angeles, Cal. Chas. E. Evans, president and treasurer; Sam Rork, production manager; H. W. Rork, secretary; Fred Bagley, business manager; Ursula March, casting director; E. C. Largey, studio manager; Milton Monasco, technical director; Colin Campbell, J. A. Barry, directors; Joseph Brotherton, cameraman.

MacManus Corporation, 2 West 47th st., N. Y. C. Edward A. MacManus, president and treasurer; Marion Sanger, secretary; H. A. Palmer, business manager; Charles Philipps, publicity director; Burton King and Sidney Olcott, producing directors.

Hank Mann Comedies, care of Arrow Film Corporation, 220 West 42nd st., N. Y. C. Morris Schlank, producer. Studio, Francis Ford studio, 6040 Sunset Blvd., Hollywood, Cal.

Mastercraft Photoplay Corporation, Brunton Studios, Los Angeles, Cal. Dr. F. Eugene Farnsworth, president and director general; E. R. Sherburne, treasurer.

Master Films, Incorporated, 1214 Aeolian Bldg., 33 West 42nd st., N. Y. C. Charles C. Burr, president and general manager; E. J. Clode, vice-president.

McCarthy Picture Productions, 609 Laughlin Bldg., Los Angeles, Cal. John P. McCarthy, supervisor and director; John F. Powers, manager.

Mayflower Photoplay Corporation, 1465 Broadway, N. Y. C. Isaac Wolper, president and general manager; B. A. Prager, treasurer; A. W. Sampson, assistant treasurer; J. C. Bills, Jr., secretary and clerk. Branches—68 Devonshire st., Boston, Mass.; 5341 Melrose ave., Los Angeles, Cal. Studios—West Fort Lee, N. J., and Hollywood, Cal. Producers associated with Mayflower—George Loane Tucker, Allan Dwan, Emile Chautard, R. A. Walsh, Charles Miller.

Stella Mayhew Productions, The, New Rochelle, N. Y. Stella Mayhew Taylor; William B. Taylor; Jacob S. Ruskin.

Melies Manufacturing Company, 110 West 40th st., N. Y. C. Paul C. Melies.

Mena Film Company, Fountain and Berando sts., Hollywood, Cal. E. W. Kuehn, president; G. C. Driscoll; R. R. Hollister.

Mento Motion Picture Company, 220 West 42nd st., N. Y. C. S. Samson.

Mercury Comedy Company, Balboa Studios, Long Beach, Cal. Milburn Moranti, general manager; Grover Jones, director; Al Moranti, technical director; Miles Burns, cameraman. (See also Moranti Comedies.)

Merit Film Corporation, 130 West 46th st., N. Y. C. I. E. Chadwick, vice-president. Branches—680 Broadway, Albany, N. Y.; M. F. Tobias, 327 Main st., Buffalo, N. Y.; N. I. Filkins, Belmont Bldg., Cleveland, Ohio; George Stockton, 130 West 46th st., New York; F. J. Willis.

Metropolitan Film Company, 1482 Broadway, N. Y. C. C. Milton Morrison.

Metro Pictures Corporation, 1476 Broadway, N. Y. C. Richard A. Rowland, president; William E. Atkinson, general manager; Maxwell Karger, director general of productions; Joseph W. Engel, treasurer; J. E. D. Meador, director of advertising and publicity; E. M. Saunders, general sales manager; Charles K. Stern, assistant treasurer; Harry J. Cohen, manager of foreign department; Col. Jasper E. Brady, scenario editor, eastern studio; June Mathis, scenario editor, western studio. Studios—61st st. and Broadway, New York; Hollywood, Cal. Exchanges—Atlanta, Ga., 146 Marietta st.; Boston, Mass. 60 Church st.; Buffalo, N. Y., 327 Main st.; Chicago, Ill., 5 So. Wabash ave.; Cincinnati, O., 7th and Main sts.; Cleveland, O., 404 Sincere Bldg.; Dallas, Tex., 1924 Main st. (2); Denver, Colo., 1721 California st.; Detroit, Mich., 51 East Elizabeth st.; Kansas City, Mo., 928 Main st.; Los Angeles, Cal., 820 So. Olive st. (2); Little Rock, Ark., 106 So. Cross st.; Minneapolis, Minn., Produce Exchange Bldg.; New Haven, Conn., 126 Meadow st.; New York (2), 729 Seventh ave.; New Orleans, La., Saenger Amus. Co. Bldg., Liberty st. and Tulane ave.; Oklahoma City, Okla., 127 So. Hudson st.; Omaha, Neb., 211 So. 13th st.; Philadelphia, Pa., 1321 Vine st.; Pittsburgh, Pa., 1018 Forbes st.; Salt Lake City, U., 20 Post Office Place; San Francisco, Cal., 55 Jones st.; St. Louis, Mo., 3313 A Olive st.; Seattle, Wash., 2002 Third ave.; Toronto, Can., 21 Adelaide st., W.; Washington, D. C., 916 G st. N. W. (See also Screen Classics, Inc. and Nazimova Productions.)

Metro Studios, Hollywood, Cal. Maxwell Karger, director-general; Herbert Blache, Jack Dillon, John E. Ince, Henry Otto, Ray C. Smallwood, Arthur D. Ripley, W. A. Howell, directors; Clifford P. Butler, business manager; David H. Thompson, studio manager; Horace Williams, casting director; William Swigart, cashier; Eva Roth, wardrobe mistress; June Mathis, head scenario dept.; Finis Fox, Albert S. LeVino, A. P. Younger, Lois Zellner, Arthur Zellner, scenarios; Ted Taylor, publicity director; Howard Strickling, publicity; George A. McGuire, supt. of laboratories; John J. Arnold, Rudolph Bergquist, Robert Kurrle, Sol Polito, Harold Wenstrom, William Edmunds, John Sykes,

Mickey Whalen, cameramen. (See also Metro Pictures Corporation.)

Charles Miller Productions, care of Mayflower Photoplay Corporation, 1465 Broadway, N. Y. C. Charles Miller. Studio, 230 West 38th st., N. Y. C.

Mission Productions, 902 Baker-Detwiler Bldg., Los Angeles, Cal. I. W. Keerl, general manager.

Model Comedy Company, 5821 Santa Monica Blvd., Hollywood, Cal. Bruno J. Becker, general manager; Gale Henry, director; Al Risley, publicity. (Also Gale Henry Comedies.)

Monopol Pictures Company, 1476 Broadway, N. Y. C. Max Cohen, director of sales and exploitation. Distributors of State Right films.

Moranti Comedies, care of Bulls Eye Film Corporation, 729 Seventh ave., N. Y. C. (See also Mercury Comedy Company.)

B. S. Moss Motion Picture Corporation, 729 Seventh ave., N. Y. C. B. S. Moss, president; Myron Sulzberger, secretary and treasurer; Arthur McQue, publicity.

Motion Picture Producing Company of America, 398 Fifth ave., N. Y. C. Walter L. Johnson, president; Earle H. Hopkins, secretary and treasurer. Marc Connelly, director of publicity and advertising. Studio, Dongan Hills, Staten Island. Affiliated Companies—Sterospeed Productions, Inc.; Vivilite Products Corporation. Producers of King Cole Comedies.

Multnomah Film Corporation, 33rd and Halsey sts., Portland, Ore. Raymond Wells.

—N—

National Film Company, Tuilleries Park, Englewood, Denver, Colo. George A. Levy, general manager; J. W. Boot, treasurer; J. H. Hine, secretary; W. H. Ender, W. E. Morris.

National Film Corporation of America, 1116 Lodi st., Hollywood, Cal., and 1600 Broadway, New York. Harry M. Rubey, president; Isador Bernstein, vice-president; William LaPlante, treasurer; Joe Brandt, general representative. Studio, Santa Monica Boulevard, Gower to Lodi sts., Hollywood, Cal.

National Picture Theatres Incorporated, 729 Seventh ave., N. Y. C. Lewis J. Selznick, president; Harry Crandall, Charles Olson, Hector Pasmezoglu, Ike Libson, John Harris, Jake Wells, vice-presidents; Lee Kugel, director of advertising, publicity, exploitation and service. (See also Select Pictures Corporation, Republic Distributing Corporation, and Selznick Pictures Corporation.)

National Studios, 1116 Lodi st., Hollywood, Cal. Isadore Bernstein, production manager; Martin Doner, art director; Bertram Bracken, Mark Goldaine, Paul Hurst, Harry Edwards, William Seiter, directors; Franklyn Hall, L. V. Jefferson, Everett Maxwell, Harvey Oates, scenarios; Lenwood Abbot, laboratory. (See also National Film Corporation of America.)

Nazimova Productions, The, 1476 Broadway, N. Y. C. (See also Metro Pictures Corporation.)

Marshall Neilan Productions, 1723 Allesandro st., Los Angeles, Cal. Marshall Neilan, director; Victor Heerman, director; Tom Held, assistant director; H. I. Peyton, assistant director; Henry Cronjager, head cameraman; Sam Landers, cameraman; Foster Leonard, assistant cameraman; Ben Carre, art director; Howard M. Ewing, electrical expert; Wellington Wales, business manager; William Bomb, studio manager; Marion Fairfax, scenario editor; J. R. Grainger, eastern representative; Peter Gridley Smith, publicity director; Eddie O'Hara, studio publicity manager; Naida Carle, publicity writer; Lucita Squier, eastern auditor. Studio, 1723 Allesandro st., Los Angeles, Cal. Eastern offices, Capitol Theatre Bldg., N. Y. C.

Northwestern Film Corporation, Sheridan, Wyo. John E. Maple, general manager.

Novagraph Company, c/o Pathe Exchange, Inc., 25 West 45th st., N. Y. C. Charles Watson, president.

Numa Pictures Corporation, Longacre Bldg., N. Y. C. Adolph Weiss, president; George M. Merrick, supervisor of productions. Studios, Yonkers, N. Y. (See Artclass Pictures Corp.)

—O—

Oakley Super Quality Productions, Inc., 529 West 8th st., Los Angeles, Cal.

Octagon Films, Inc., 46 Main st., New Rochelle, N. Y. Headquarters A. H. Fischer Studio and Laboratory. B. A. Rolfe, president; A. H. Fischer, vice-president; Charles G. Stewart, general manager; Harry H. Poppe, advertising and publicity manager. (See also A. M. Fischer Features, Inc.)

Oliver Films, Inc., 308 East 48th st., N. Y. C. I. Oliver, president; J. W. Grey, Arthur B. Reeve, T. D. Bonneville, publicity.

Outing-Chester Pictures, 120 West 41st st., N. Y. C. (See C. L. Chester Productions, Inc.)

—P—

Pacific Producing Company, 1600 Broadway, N. Y. C. (See also Universal Film Manufacturing Company.) Studios, Hollywood, Cal.

Palmer Photoplay Corporation, 571-591 I. W. Hellman Bldg., Los Angeles, Cal. Frederick Palmer, president; H. E. Teter, vice-president; S. M. Warmbath, secretary and treasurer; Roy L. Manker, general manager. Following departments are maintained—Department of education; continuity department; photoplay sales department; research and technical department. Educational department supervised by Cecil B. DeMille, Thomas H. Ince, Lois Weber and Rab Wagner. Dorothy Yost, head of continuity; Adeline Alvord, director of research department; Kate Corbaley, head of photoplay sales department. Organization is engaged exclusively in the handling of stories for motion picture production.

Paramount-Artcraft Pictures, 485 Fifth ave., N. Y. C. (See Famous Players-Lasky Corporation.)

Paramount Pictures Corporation, 485 Fifth ave., N. Y. C. (See Famous Players-Lasky Corporation.)

Parex Film Corporation, 729 Seventh ave., N. Y. C. William L. Sherry, president; M. V. Sherry, vice-president; N. J. Sennott, secretary. (See also Wm. L. Sherry Service.)

Pathe Exchange, Inc., 25 West 45th st., N. Y. C. Charles Pathe, president; Paul Brunet, vice-president and general manager; Lewis Innerarity, secretary; Louis Landry, treasurer; Fred C. Quimby, director of exchanges. Charles Pathe, Paul Fuller, Leon Madieu, Louis Landry, Paul Brunet, Edmund G. Lynch, Lewis Innerarity, Fred C. Quimby and Gaston Chanier constitute the board of directors. Studio, 1 Congress st., Jersey City, N. J. Branches—Atlanta, Ga., 111 Walton st.; Dallas, Tex., 1715 Commerce st.; Chicago, Ill., 220 So. State st.; Minneapolis, Minn., 608 First ave. North; New York City, 1600 Broadway; Boston, Mass., 7 Isabella st.; Los Angeles, Cal., 732 So. Olive st.; St. Louis, Mo., 3308 Lindell ave.; San Francisco, Cal., 985 Market st.; Albany, N. Y., 35-37 Orange st.; Pittsburg, Pa., 1018 Forbes st.; Cincinnati, O., 124 East 7th st.; Cleveland, O., 750 Prospect ave., S. E.; Oklahoma City, Okla., 119 So. Hudson st.; Phila., Pa., 211 No. 13th st.; New Orleans, La., 229 Dauphine st.; Washington, D. C., 916 G st., N. W.; Kansas City, Mo., 928 Main st.; Denver, Colo., 1436 Welton st.; Omaha, Neb., 1417 Harney st.; Seattle, Wash., 2133 Third ave.; Salt Lake City, U., 64 Exchange pl.; Indianapolis, Ind., 66 W. New York st.; Detroit, Mich., 63 E. Elizabeth st.; Des Moines, Ia., 100½ E. Locust st.; Newark, N. J., 6 Mechanic st.; Charlotte, N. C., 235 So. Tryon st.; Buffalo, N. Y., 218 Franklin st.; Milwaukee, Wis., 174 Second st.; Spokane, Wash., 408 First ave.; Little Rock, Ark., 1116 W. Markham st.; Portland, Ore., 392 Burnside st.

Paton Films, Inc., Nat Goodwin Pier, Hollister ave. and Ocean Front, Santa Monica, Cal. Stuart Paton, director general; Dr. Henry Noel Potter, general manager. Studio, Nat Goodwin Pier, Santa Monica, Cal.

Leonce Perret Productions, 220 West 42nd st., N. Y. C. Also Acme Pictures Corporation, 220 West 42nd st., N. Y. C. Leonce Perret, director.)

Adolf Philipp Film Corporation, 11 East 14th st., N. Y. C. Adolf Philipp, president; Paul Philipp, treasurer and business representative; Maurice Weissman, secretary. Department heads—J. H. Dreher, sales manager; Tom Bret, title editor. Studio, 11 East 14th st., New York.

Photoplay Libraries, Inc., 500 Fifth ave., N. Y. C. Lester Park; Edward Whiteside.

Photoplay Magazine Screen Supplement, 350 N. Clark st., Chicago, Ill. James R. Quirk, publisher.

FILM COMPANIES

Photo Drama Co., The, 220 W. 42nd st., N. Y. C. William Steiner, president; Studio, Cliffside, N. J. (See also Wm. Steiner Productions, The Tex Pictures, Inc., and Jester Comedy Company.)

Physical Culture Photoplays, Inc., c/o Pioneer Film Corporation, 130 West 46th st., N. Y. C. Bernarr MacFadden. (See also Facts and Follies, Inc.)

Mary Pickford Company, Hollywood Cal. Mary Pickford, president. Department heads—F. E. Benson, studio manager; E. D. Shanks, auditor; Mark Larkin, publicity director; Mrs. Elizabeth Cameron, secretary to Miss Pickford; Marion B. Jackson, scenario; Paul Powell, director for "Pollyanna"; Max Parker, technical director; Charles Rosher, cameraman; Mrs. Adele Chinley, head of wardrobe. Studio, Hollywood, Cal.

Pioneer Film Corporation, 130 West 46th st., N. Y. C. Morris Rose, president; Louis Haas, vice-president and treasurer; M. H. Hoffman, secretary and general manager. Department heads—W. F. Hurst, comptroller; Southard Brown, director of publicity. Branches, Buffalo, N. Y., 145 Franklin st.; New York City, 130 West 46th st.; Cleveland, Ohio, 812 Prospect ave.; Detroit, Mich., 53 East Elizabeth st. Exchanges affiliated with Pioneer, Eastern Features Film Co., 57 Church st., Boston, Mass.; Masterpiece Film Attractions, 1235 Vine st., Phila., Pa.; Criterion Film Service, 67 Walton st., Atlanta, Ga.; Greater Stars Productions, 716 Consumers Bldg., Chicago, Ill.; M & R Exchange, 107 Golden Gate ave., San Francisco, Cal.; M & R Exchange, 730 So. Olive st., Los Angeles, Cal.; Screen Art Pictures, Inc., Washington, D. C. Producing organizations affiliated with Pioneer, Grace Davison Productions, Humphrey Pictures, Inc., Physical Culture Photoplays, Inc., National Film Corporation of America; Atlas Film Corporation.

Playter Photoplayers, Inc., The, Minnehaha Park, Spokane, Wash. Wellington Playter, president.

Plymouth Film Corporation, 786 Broad st., Newark, N. J. James K. Shields, president; B. F. Jones, vice-president; Dr. Yarrow, secretary; Mr. Macauley, treasurer.

Snub Pollard Comedies. (See Rolin Film Company.)

Poppy Comedies, Times Bldg., c/o Frohman Amusement Corporation.

Post Pictures Corporation, 527 Fifth ave., N. Y. C. Albert Redfield, president and treasurer; Clyde E. Elliot, vice-president and general director; Germaine De Maria, director of publicity; Marie Post, editor scenario department; Horace C. Shimeld, chief cameraman.

C. B. Price Co., Inc., Times Bldg., N. Y. C. C. B. Price, president; F. H Price, vice-president; Asa B. Kellogg, secretary; C. A. Meade.

Prizma, Incorporated, 71 West 23rd st., N. Y. C. H. Wilson Saulsbury, president; Carroll H. Dunning, Frances T. Homer and C. H. D. Walsh, vice-presidents; William V. D. Kelley, technical adviser; S. C. Strock, treasurer; George P. Kelley, secretary. Department head, Howard G. Stokes, assistant general manager, in charge of production, advertising, publicity and service. Laboratory, 3193 Boulevard, Jersey City, N. J. Pictures distributed by Republic Distributing Corporation, 130 West 46th st., N. Y. C.

Producers Security Corporation, 516 Fifth ave., N. Y. C. Ricord Gradwell, president and general manager; F. J. Hawkins, secretary; Nathan Vidaver, general counsel; Campbell McCulloch, director of advertising and publicity; Ricord Gradwell, John Maynard Harlan, F. J. Hawkins and Nathan Vidaver, directors of corporation.

— Q —

Quality Film Company, 208 Iowa st., Davenport, Ill. C. B. Holman and Ivan L. Swanson, managers.

— R —

Rainbow Comedies, care of Universal Film Company, 1600 Broadway, N. Y. C.

Harry Raver, Inc., 1402 Broadway, N. Y. C. (See Apollo Pictures Company.)

J. Parker Read, Jr., Productions, Robert Brunton Studios, 5341 Melrose ave., Los Angeles, Cal. (Care of W. W. Hodkinson Corporation, 516 Fifth ave., N. Y. C.)

Realart Pictures Corporation, 469 Fifth ave., N. Y. C. Morris Kohn, president and treasurer. Department heads—J. S. Woody, general manager; J. C. Ragland, general sales manager; Ben F. Simpson, field manager; E. S. Flynn, special representative; John Pond Fritts, publicity and advertising; Dario L. Farella, controller; Lewis Kinskern, contract manager; Jay A. Gove, associate director of publicity; C. Alfred Karpen, advertising accessories; Bert Adler, exploitation; Harry Day, exploitation; Edna S. Michaels, feature writer; Mrs. Patience Bevier Cole, feature writer; Ben Davis, exploitation; E. L. Massie, Pacific coast exploitation; James Cuniff, chief traveling auditor. Branches—Atlanta, Ga., 146 Marietta st.; Boston, Mass., 5 Isabella st.; Buffalo, N. Y., 221 Franklin st.; Chicago, Ill., 207 So. Wabash ave.; Cincinnati, O., Mercantile Library Bldg.; Cleveland, O., 942 E. Prospect ave.; Dallas, Tex., 1905 Commerce st.; Denver, Colo., 1742 Glenarm st.; Detroit, Mich., 306 Joseph Mack Bldg.; Kansas City, Mo., 509-10 Republic Bldg.; Los Angeles, Cal., 643 So. Olive st.; Minneapolis, Minn., 801 Produce Exchange Bldg.; New York, 729 Seventh ave.; New Orleans, La Saenger Bldg., Tulane and Liberty sts.; Omaha, Neb., 1216 Farnam st.; Philadelphia, Pa., 1237 Vine st.; Pittsburgh, Pa., 1018 Forbes st.; San Francisco, Cal., 1006-1008 David Howe Bldg., 995 Market st.; Seattle, Wash., 2012 Third ave.; St. Louis, Mo., 3626 Olive st.; Washington, D. C. Rooms 806-820 Mather Bldg., 916 G st., N. W.

Renco Film Company, National Life Bldg., Chicago, Ill. Mr. Reynolds, manager; Harry Earl, advertising.

Republic Distributing Corporation, 130 West 46th st., N. Y. C. Berton N. Busch, president and general manager; Lewis J. Selznick, advisory director and treasurer; C. C. Pettijohn, secretary; Lee Kugel, publicity; S. B. Van Horn, advertising; G. R. Meeker, sales manager. Branches—Mrs. A. H. Sessions, 148 Marietta st., Atlanta, Ga.; Geo. M. A. Fecke, 78 Broadway, Boston, Mass.; J. E. Kimberley, 269 Main st., Buffalo, N. Y.; L. A. Rozelle, 207 S. Wabash ave., Chicago, Ill.; R. E. Flagler, N. W corner 7th and Main sts, Cincinnati, Ohio; C. A. Thompson, Belmont Bldg., Cleveland, Ohio; Tom N. Parker, 1905 Commerce st., Dallas, Tex.; John Child, 1753 Welton st., Denver, Colo.; G. F. Weaver, 63 E. Elizabeth st., Detroit, Mich.; W. E. Truog, 1612 Main st., Kansas City, Mo.; T. E. Hancock, 818 S. Olive st., Los Angeles, Cal.; Robert Cotton, 6th and 1st ave., Minneapolis, Minn.; Norman Moray, 130 West 46th st., New York; W. R. Priest, 1315 Vine st., Phila., Pa.; Fred Salinger, 1201 Liberty ave., Pittsburgh, Pa.; W. G. Carter, 3617 Washington ave., St. Louis, Mo.; Floyd St. John, 104 Golden Gate ave., San Francisco, Cal.; Jack Weil, 1301 5th ave., Seattle, Wash.; R. B. Smeltzer, 916 "G" st., N. W., Washington, D. C. (See also Select Pictures Corp.)

Robertson-Cole Company, 1600 Broadway, N. Y. C. Rufus Cole, Lieut. Robertson, Alexander Beyfuss; A. S. Kirkpatrick, vice-president and general manager. Branches—Los Angeles, Cal.; San Francisco, Cal.; London, Eng.; Sydney, Australia; Calcutta, Ind.; Bombay, Ind.; Singapore and Rangoon. Exchanges in all the principal cities of the United States. (See also Robertson-Cole Distributing Corporation.)

Robertson-Cole Distributing Corporation, 1600 Broadway, N. Y. C. (See Robertson-Cole Company.)

Rogers Film Corporation, Capitol Theatre Bldg., N. Y. C. Louis T. Rogers.

Ruth Roland Film Company, 1919 Main st., Los Angeles, Cal. Ruth Roland, president; L. E. Kent, studio manager; Gilson Willets, scenario; Charlie Gee, technical director; D. C. Harrison, film editor; George Marshall, director; Al Cawood, camera man. (Also Ruth Roland Serials, Inc.) Pictures released through Pathe Exchange, Inc., 25 West 45th st., N. Y. C.

Rolin Film Company, Culver City, Cal. Mal Roach, president; C. M. Roach, secretary and treasurer; E. L. Wisdom, vice-president; Mal Roach, Fred Newmayer, Al Goulding, Frank Terry, directors; Walter Lundin, cameraman; W. D. McCary, technical director.

Roma-New York Pictures Corporation, 1400 Broadway, N. Y. C. P. A. Powers, president; Gen. Giuseppe Garibaldi, vice-president; Anne Feinman, secretary; Capt. Ezio Garibaldi, assistant secretary; R. H. Cochrane, treasurer. The board of directors consist of the above named persons in addition to Tarkington Baker and Dan B. Lederman. Studio—Italy. (See also Universal Film Mfg. Co.)

Romayne Super-Film Company, Culver City, Cal. H. Y. Romayne, president; E. D. Ulrich, general manager; Thomas A. Baker, treasurer; J. E. Kelly, production manager; Walter McNamara, scenario department; Otto M. Steiger, publicity and advertising department; Frank P. Hamilton, sales department; Vin Moore and Charles Avery, scenario and comedy directors. Studio—Culver City, Cal.

Rothacker Film Manufacturing Company, 1339-1351 Diversey Parkway, Chicago, Ill. Watterson R. Rothacker, president; David Beaton, Jr, vice-president; H. J. Aldous, secretary and treasurer; J. G. Hahn, assistant secretary; J. G. Mammoser, assistant treasurer. Laboratory—1339 Diversey Parkway, Chicago, Ill.

— S —

S. L. Pictures, 1476 Broadway, N. Y. C. Herbert Lubin, president; Arthur H. Sawyer, treasurer and general manager; Bert Ennis, director of publicity; Bert Lubin, sales manager.

San Antonio Pictures Corporation, 416-417 Central Office Bldg., San Antonio, Tex.; Macklyn Arbuckle, president; Charles Schreiner, Jr., vice-president; L. P. Hart, vice-president; L. D. Wharton, vice-president and general manager; T. W. Wharton, supervising director; R. D. Barclay, treasurer; William H. Furlong, secretary; W. C. Hogg, assistant secretary; R. J. Boyle, counsel. These officers, together with F. M. Lewis, Ike T. Pryor, and J. E. Jarratt, constitute the board of directors. Studio—5700 S. Press st., San Antonio, Tex.

Sanborn Laboratories, Inc., Culver City, Cal. P. M. Burke, president; O. D. Bennett, vice-president. Daily capacity, 100,000 ft. positive, 30,000 ft. negative.

P. D. Sargent Productions, 753 South Boyle ave., Los Angeles, Cal. Clyde C. Westover, general manager; Park B. Frame, producing director.

Schomer-Ross Productions, Inc., 1440 Broadway (temporary office until Feb. 1, 1920), 126 West 46th st. (after Feb. 1, 1920), N. Y. C. S. Schomer, director-general; Sidney L. Ross, president and treasurer; Leon Rosen, secretary; E. S. Manheimer, general manager; Agnes Eagen Cobb, sales manager; Nat Rothstein, publicity manager.

Screencraft Pictures, Inc., Longacre Bldg., N. Y. C. Maurice Fleckles, president; Joseph Pollak, vice-president; Akiba Weinberg, treasurer.

Screen Classics, Inc., 1476 Broadway, N. Y. C. (See Metro Pictures Corporation.)

Screen Follies, Inc., 220 West 42d st., N. Y. C. F. A. A. Dahme, president; Luis Seel, secretary and treasurer; F. A. A. Dahme, title illustrations and titles; Luis Seel, animated films, announcers, trailers, and cartoons.

Screen Letter Box, Strand Theatre Bldg., N. Y. C. Morris Kashin.

George B. Seitz, Inc., c/o Pathe Exchange, Inc., 25 West 45th st., N. Y. C.

Select Pictures Corporation, 729 Seventh ave., N. Y. C. Lewis J. Selznick, president; C. C. Pettijohn, assistant to the president; S. E. Morris, vice-president and general manager; F. A. Selznick, treasurer and secretary; David Selznick, assistant secretary and treasurer. Department heads—M. C. Howard, comptroller; C. R. Rogers, sales manager; C. C. Ryan, purchasing; Lee Kugel, advertising, publicity, and exploitation; Louis Brock, export. Branches, see Republic Distributing Corporation, also 66 New York st., Indianapolis, Ind.; 19 Portsca st., New Haven, Conn.; 718 Poydras st., New Orleans, La.; 1512 Howard st., Omaha, Neb.; 160 Regent st., Salt Lake City, Utah; 501 Excelsior Life Bldg., Toronto, Ont.; 679 Broadway, Albany, N. Y.; 69 Church st., Boston, Mass.; 178 Franklin st., Buffalo, N. Y.; 220 S. State st., Chicago, Ill.; 402 Strand Theatre Bldg., Cincinnati, Ohio; 315 Prospect ave., Cleveland, Ohio; 1917 Main st., Dallas, Tex.; 1728 Walton st., Denver, Col.; 920 Main st., Kansas City, Mo.; 736 S. Olive st., Los Angeles, Cal.; 16 No. 4th st., Minneapolis, Minn.; 729 Seventh ave., N. Y. C.; 1308 Vine st., Phila., Pa.; 3313 Olive st., St. Louis, Mo.; 985 Market st., San Francisco, Cal.; 308 Virginia st., Seattle, Wash.; 525 13th st., N. W., Washington, D. C.; Select Pictures Corporation, 43 Rue la Bruyere, Paris, France, Lewis J. Selznick, president; Select Pictures Corporation, Sydney, N. S. W., Australia, Lewis J. Selznick, president; Select Pictures Corporation, Ltd., 289 St. Catherine st., W., Montreal, Canada, Lewis J. Selznick, president. (See also Selznick Pictures Corporation.)

Selig Polyscope Company, Inc., Garland Bldg., Chicago, Ill. Studio, 3800 Mission Road, Los Angeles, Cal. Col. Wm. H. Selig, president; Thomas S. McGee, studio manager; William E. Wing, E. A. Martin, scenarios; Webster Cullison, Francis Grandon, Leon de la Mothe, directors; Harry Neuman, Eddie Lindon, Gerald MacKenzie, cameramen; Frank Prucha, supt. of laboratory.

Selznick Pictures Corporation, 729 Seventh ave., N. Y. C. Myron Selznick, president; F. A. Selznick, treasurer. Department heads—John Lynch, scenario; Lee Kugel, publicity; Randolph Maller, purchasing; Frank Hampton, studio manager; James Dent, business manager; Mr. Raphe, art director. Studios, West Fort Lee, N. J., and 507 East 175th st., N. Y. C. Branches (See also Select Pictures Corporation, Republic Distributing Corporation, National Picture Theatres, Inc.)

Larry Semon Comedies, care Vitagraph Company, 1600 Broadway, N. Y. C.

Mack Sennett Comedies, 1712 Allesandro st., Los Angeles, Cal. Mack Sennett, president; J. A. Waldron, general manager; Ray Griffith, Albert Glassmare, scenarios; Richard Jones, Reggie Morris, directors; Fred Jackman, cameraman. Studio, 1712 Allesandro st., Los Angeles, Cal.

Serico Producing Company, Candler Bldg., N. Y. C. George H. Wiley, president.

Wm. L. Sherry Service, 729 Seventh ave., N. Y. C. (See Parex Film Corporation.)

Ernest Shipman, 6 West 48th st., N. Y. C.

C. E. Shurtleff, Inc., 729 Fifth ave., N. Y. C. Mitchell Lewis Productions for Metro.

Signal Film Corporation, 6235 Broadway, Chicago, Ill. Samuel S. Hutchinson, president; John R. Freuler, secretary and treasurer. (See also American Film Company, Inc.)

Spoor-Thompson Machine Company, 1345 Argyle st., Chicago, Ill. George K. Spoor, president. (See also Essanay Film Manufacturing Company.)

State Rights Distributors, Inc., 729 Seventh ave., N. Y. C. Louis Weinberg, general manager; Ira H. Simmons, general sales manager.

William Steiner Productions, 220 West 42nd st., N. Y. C. William Steiner, president. Studios, Cliffside, N. J., and San Jose, Tex. (See also Photo Drama Co., The Tex Pictures, Inc., and Jester Comedy Company).

Sterling Films, Ltd., 166 Bay st., Toronto, Can. I. Soskin, president; M. Volansky, secretary and treasurer. Offices in Montreal, Can.

Anita Stewart Productions, Inc., 2 West 45th st., N. Y. C. Louis B. Mayer, president; Rudolph Cameron, vice-president and general manager; E. B. Hesser, advertising and publicity manager; Wm. H. Leahy, publicity manager.

Stereospeed Productions, Inc., care Johnson & Hopkins Company, 398 Fifth ave., N. Y. C.

Al St. John Comedies, Burston Studios, 6059 Sunset blvd., Hollywood, Cal. New York Office, 220 West 42nd st., care Warner Bros. J. L. Warner, president; James P. Taylor, secretary and treasurer; Al St. John, vice-president; Jack Froliech, technical director; Frank C. Griffith, director; Harry Brand, publicity; Frank McGee, Frank Zukor, George Crocker, cameramen. (Released through Famous Players-Lasky Corporation.)

Submarine Film Corporation, The, Longacre Bldg., N. Y. C. J. E. Williamson, general manager. (Also Williamson Bros.)

Success Pictures Company, 905 Haas Bldg., Los Angeles, Cal. Leonard J. Meyberg, distributor.

Sun Films, Inc., 730 So. Olive st., Los Angeles, Cal. Branches, 114 Golden Gate ave., San Francisco, Cal.; 2016 Third ave., Seattle, Wash.; territory, seven western states, Hawaiian Islands and Alaska.

Sunbeam Comedies. (See also Florida Film Corporation.)

Sunshine Comedies, care Fox Film Corporation, 130 West 46th st., N. Y. C.

Supreme Comedies, care Robertson-Cole Company, 1600 Broadway, N. Y. C.

Supreme Pictures, Inc., 101-103 West 42nd st., N. Y. C. John W. Grey, president; Arthur B.

WHO'S WHO

Reeve, vice-president; J. F. Cleaveland, secretary; J. A. Forney, treasurer; H. Sumnich, assistant secretary. Studio, Flushing, L. I.

Sylvanite Productions, Balboa Studios, Long Beach, Cal. Alvin J. Neitz, director; Robert Sullivan, general manager.

Syndicate Superfeatures, Inc., care George Kleine, 63 East Adams st., Chicago, Ill.

— T —

Norma Talmadge Film Corporation, 318 East 48th st., N. Y. C. Joseph M. Schenck, president; Edward J. Mannix, general manager. Studio, 318 East 48th st.

Charles A. Taylor Studios, Inc., 1745 Allesandro st., Los Angeles, Cal. James Tynan, publicity and advertising manager.

Territorial Sales Corporation, 1600 Broadway, N. Y. C.

Tex Pictures, Inc., The, 220 West 42nd st., N. Y. C. William Steiner, president. Studios, Cliffside, N. J., and San Antonio, Tex. (See also William Steiner Productions, The Photo Drama Co., and Jester Comedy Company.)

Timely Films, Inc., Palace Theatre Annex, 1562 Broadway, N. Y. C. Amedee J. Van Beuren, president; A. E. Siegel, treasurer; Clayton J. Heermance, secretary; Rutgers Neilson, director of publicity and advertising. Producers of "Topics of the Day," selected from the press of the world by the Literary Digest. (See also V. B. K. Film Corporation and Ay-Vee-Bee Corporation.)

Titan Feature Photoplay Company, Sherwood Bldg., Spokane, Wash. J. Don Alexander, president; R. E. Musser, secretary and treasurer; C. L. Mayo, vice-president; J. G. Sullivan, field manager.

Titan Pictures Corporation, 301 Garrick Bldg., 58 Randolph st., Chicago, Ill. Frederick Russell Clark.

Topical Tips, 220 West 42nd st., N. Y. C. Tom Bret.

Maurice Tourneur Productions, Inc., Culver City, Cal. Maurice Tourneur, president; J. E. Brulatour, treasurer; Sam Mayer, secretary; Jules Furthman (Stephen Fox), scenario; John S. Dunham, publicity; Johnny Gray, film editor; Floyd Mueller, art director; Ed Mortimer, casting director; Charles Van Enger, Rene Guissart, cameramen. Advertising through Famous Players-Lasky Corporation.

Tower Film Corporation, 71 West 23rd st., N. Y. C.

Transatlantic Film Company of America., Inc., 729 Seventh ave., N. Y. C. Lewis Roach, president; Jacques Cibrario, vice-president; Charles Yale Harrison, American sales manager. Agencies, Russia, England, France, Italy, Belgium, Holland, Scandinavia, Finland, Spain, Portugal, Balkan States, Egypt, Japan, China, India, Australia, South Africa, and South America.

Triangle Distributing Corporation, 1459 Broadway, N. Y. C. Exchanges in principal cities of United States.

Triangle Film Corporation, 1459 Broadway, N. Y. C. (Also Triangle Distributing Corporation.)

Tribune Productions, Inc., care of Mark M. Dinterfass, 1600 Broadway, N. Y. C.

Triumph Film Corporation, Longacre Bldg., N. Y. C. Joseph A. Golden, president.

Truart Pictures, Inc., 1457 Broadway, N. Y. C. Charles H. France, director general; Bory Osso, vice-president and general manager.

George Loane Tucker Productions, care Brunton Studios, 5341 Melrose ave., Los Angeles, Cal. (Also Mayflower Photoplay Corporation, 1465 Broadway, N. Y. C.)

Tyrad Pictures, Inc., 729 Seventh ave., N. Y. C. Matthias Radin, president and general manager; Jacques Tyrol, secretary, treasurer, and general director; Matthias Radin, sales manager; Jacques Tyrol, technical director; Winifred Dunn, scenario. Branches, Pittsburgh, Pa., 100 Fourth ave., Buffalo, N. Y., Palace Theatre Bldg.

— U —

United Artists Corporation, 729 Seventh ave., N. Y. C. Oscar A. Price, president; Hiram Abrams, general manager; Paul N. Lazarus, advertising and publicity manager. Home office, 729 Seventh ave., New York. Branch offices, Atlanta, Ga., 111 Walton st.; Boston, Mass., 41-43 Winchester st.; Toronto, Can., Stair Bldg., 123 Bay st.; Chicago, Ill., 17 N. Wabash ave.; Dallas, Tex., 1930 Main st.; Cleveland, Ohio, Plymouth Bldg., 2143 Prospect ave.; Denver, Colo., 617 19th st.; Detroit, Mich., 605 Joseph Mack Bldg.; Kansas City, Mo., 922 Oak st.; Los Angeles, Cal., 643 S. Olive st.; Minneapolis, Minn., 402 Film Exchange Bldg.; New York City, 729 Seventh ave.; New Orleans, La., 1401 Tulane ave.; Phila., Pa., 314 Bulletin Bldg.; Pittsburgh, Pa., 412 Ferry st.; San Francisco, Cal., 100 Golden Gate ave.; Seattle, Wash., 1200 Fourth ave.; Washington, D. C., 801 Mather Bldg.

United Picture Theatres of America, Inc., 1600 Broadway, N. Y. C. J. A. Berst, president; C. C. Johnson, secretary; Milton M. Goldsmith, treasurer; Lloyd Willis, assistant to president; Theodore L. Liebler, Jr., manager scenario dept.; Leon J. Bamberger, manager contract dept.; R. W. Baremore, publicity and advertising; William Lord Wright, western studio representative.

United States Photoplay Corporation, 922-923 Munsey Bldg., Washington, D. C. Frederick F. Stoll, president; Dr. George L. Carder, vice-president; Dr. H. H. Prentice, director; Capt. L. S. Flavin, director; William P. Doing, director; C. L. Wakeman, secretary. Studio, E. K. Lincoln Studio, Grantwood, N. J.

Unity Photoplays Company, 207 S. Wabash ave., Chicago, Ill. Frank Zambreno, president.

Universal Film Manufacturing Company, 1600 Broadway, N. Y. C. Carl Laemmle, president; R. H. Cochrane, vice-president; Siegfried Hartman, secretary; P. A. Powers, treasurer; Tarkington Baker, general manager and supervisor of Universal City. Department heads, H. M. Berman, general manager of exchanges and sales manager; E. H. Goldstein, assistant sales manager; Edward Moffat, advertising manager; Albert Tuchman, purchasing agent; Harry Levey, general manager industrial department; Percy Heath, scenario department; Paul Gulick, editor-in-chief of Moving Picture Weekly; P. D. Cochrane, manager of poster department; Sidney Singerman, assistant manager of poster department; Edward Roskam, manager program department; Harry Rice, director of publicity; John W. Krafft, press book editor; Joseph H. Mayer, special exploitation representative; Lee Reiner, still department. Studios, Universal City, Cal. Branches, Atlanta, Ga., 111 Walton st.; Baltimore, Md., 412 E. Balt., st.; Boston, Mass., 13 Stanhope st.; Boston, Mass., 60 Church st.; Boston, Mass., 20 Winchester st.; Buffalo, N. Y., 35 Church st.; Butte, Mont., 52 E. B'way; Calgary, Alta., 407 W. 8th ave.; Charlotte, N. C., 307 W. Trade; Chicago, Ill., Consumers Bldg.; Cincinnati, Ohio, 501 Strand st.; Cleveland, Ohio, Prospect ave., and Huron st.; Charleston, W. Va., 607 Deydoh st.; Columbus, O., 294½ N. High st.; Dallas, Tex., 1900 Commerce; Denver, Colo., 1422 Welton st.; Des Moines, Ia., 918 Locust st.; Detroit, Mich., 63 E. Elizabeth st.; El Paso, Tex., 110 E. Franklin st.; Evansville, Ind.; Ft. Smith, Ark., 307 Garrison st.; Indianapolis, Ind., 113 W. Georgia st.; Jacksonville, Fla., 330 W. Forsythe st.; Kansas City Mo., 214 E. 12th st.; Los Angeles, Cal., 822 S. Olive st.; Louisville, Ky., 407 Walker Bldg.; Memphis, Tenn., 226 Union ave.; Milwaukee, Wis., 133 Second st.; Minneapolis, Minn., 719 Hennepin ave.; Montreal, Que., 295 St. Catherine st., W.; Newark, N. J., 25 Branford pl.; New Haven, Conn., 126 Meadow st.; New Orleans, La., 914 Gravier st.; New York City, 1600 B'way; Okla. City, Okla., 116 W. 2d st.; Omaha, Neb., 1304 Farnam st.; Phoenix, Ariz., 117 N. 2d st.; Phila., Pa., 1304 Vine st.; Pittsburgh, Pa., 938 Penn ave.; Portland, Ore., 405 Davis st.; St. Louis, Mo., 2116 Locust st.; Salt Lake City, Utah, 56 Exchange pl.; San Francisco, Cal., 121 Golden Gate ave.; Seattle, Wash., 215 Virginia st.; Spokane, Wash., 16 S. Wash. st.; Sioux Falls, S. D., Colonial Theatre Bldg.; St. John, N. B., Can., 87 Union st.; Toronto, Can., 106 Rich. st. W.; Vancouver, B. C., 711 Dunsmuir st.; Washington, D. C., 307 9th st., N. W.; Wichita, Kan., 209 E. 1st st.; Wilkesbarre, Pa.; Winnipeg, Can., 40 Aikens Bldg.

Universal Studios, Universal City, Cal. Merrill Montgomery, production manager; Tarkington Baker, general manager; Monroe Bennett, film editor; Harry Williams, technical director; Frank Lawrence, film editor; Bert King, head property man; Ray Rockett, purchasing dept.; Percy Heath, scenario editor; Karl L. Coolidge,

Arthur Gooden, Wycliffe A. Hill, George Hively, Hal Hoadley, Phillip Hubbard, Hope Loring, William Piggott, J. F. Poland, Doris Schroeder, Chas. J. Wilson, scenarios; Tod Browning, Wm. Christie Cabayne, Norman Dawn, Wm. C. Dowlan, Reeve Eason, Jack Ford, Harry Franklin, Douglas Gerrard, Allen Holubar, Eddie Kull, Lynn Reynolds, Phillip E. Rosen, Albert Russell, Al Santell, R. S. Sturgeon, Eric Von Stroheim, Arthur Flaven, Edward Sawders, John West, directors; Alfred Lathem, Friend Baker, Sidney Blythe, John Brown, Wm. James Craft, Wm. Edmunds, Fred Leroy Granville, King D. Gray, Arthur Greiner, Harold Jones, Roy Klaffki, R. H. Kline, J. Kull, George Lawrence, Milton Loryea, A. McLain, Hugh McClung, Virgil Miller, Milton Moore, Cecil Myers, Stephen Norton, Harold Oswald, Gus Peterson, B. F. Reynolds, cameramen. (See also Universal Film Manufacturing Company.)

— V —

V. B. K. Film Corporation, Palace Theatre Annex, 1562 Broadway, N. Y. C. Amedee J. Van Beuren, president; Harry J. Kelton, treasurer; Clayton J. Heermance, secretary; William H. Rice, scenario editor; Rutgers Neilson, director of advertising and publicity. Producers of Paramount-Drew Comedies. (See also AyVeeBee Corporation and Timely Films, Inc.)
Amedee J. Van Beuren Enterprises, Palace Theatre Annex, 1562 Broadway, N. Y. C. Amedee J. Van Beuren, president. (See also Timely Films, Inc., AvVeeBee Corporation, V. B. K. Film Corporation.)
King Vidor Productions, Hollywood Studios, 6642 Sunset Blvd., Hollywood, Cal. King Vidor.
Vim Film Corporation, care of Mark M. Dintenfass, 1600 Broadway, N. Y. C.
Vitagraph Company of America, 1600 Broadway, N. Y. C. Albert E. Smith, president; A. Victor Smith, assistant to the president; John M. Quinn, general manager; A. W. Goff, assistant general manager. Department heads, George Randolph Chester, scenario and production editor; B. W. Conlon, publicity and advertising director; W. S. Smith, western studio manager; R. A. Reader, eastern studio manager; Frank Loomis, casting director. Studios—Eastern studio, Brooklyn, N. Y., Locust ave. and East 15th st.; western studio, 1708 Talmadge st., Hollywood, Cal. Exchanges, Albany, N. Y.; Atlanta, Ga.; Boston, Mass.; Buffalo, N. Y.; Chicago, Ill.; Cincinnati, O.; Cleveland, O.; Dallas, Tex.; Denver, Colo.; Detroit, Mich.; Kansas City, Mo.; Los Angeles, Cal.; Minneapolis, Minn.; New Orleans, La.; New York City; Omaha, Neb.; Phila., Pa.; St. Louis, Mo.; Salt Lake City, Utah; San Francisco, Cal.; Seattle, Wash.; Spokane, Wash.; Washington, D. C.; Montreal, Can.; Toronto, Can.; St. John, N. B.; Winnipeg, Can.
Vitagraph Studios (Western), 1708 Talmadge st., Hollywood, Cal. William S. Smith, studio and production manager; Roy McCray, technical director; Samuel Liffon, laboratory supt.; Chas. Giegrich, publicity; William Duncan, Wm. S. Bauman, David Smith, Gilbert Pratt, Noel Smith, Larry Semon, Chester Bennett, directors; Stephen Smith, I. G. Ries, Park J. Ries, William Grow, cameramen.

— W —

W. H. Productions Company, 71 West 23d st., N. Y. C. Joseph Simmonds, president; H. J. Shepard, advertising manager; H. Winick, Carl Lothrop.
Waldorf Photoplays, Inc., 220 West 42d st., N. Y. C.
R. A. Walsh Productions, care of Mayflower Photoplay Corporation, 146 Broadway, N. Y. C.
Wark Producing Corporation, Longacre Bldg., N. Y. C. (See also David Wark Griffith.)
Warner Brothers, 220 West 42d st., N. Y. C. Company consists of H. M. Warner, Albert Warner, S. L. Warner and J. L. Warner.
Edward Warren Productions, 1482 Broadway, N. Y. C.
L. Lawrence Weber Photo Dramas, Inc., 220 West 48th st., N. Y. C. L. Lawrence Weber, president; Bobby North, treasurer; Ben A. Boyar, manager; Lee Shubert, director. Branches, 28 Denmark st., London, Eng. (See also Apollo Trading Corporation.)
Lois Weber Productions, 4634 Santa Monica blvd., Hollywood, Cal. Lois Weber.
Billy West Comedies, care of Bulls Eye Film Corporation, 729 Seventh ave., N. Y. C.
Western Photoplays, Inc. A. Alperstein, care of Pathe Exchange, Inc., 25 West 45th st., N. Y. C.
Wharton Studios, 623 W. State st., Ithaca, N. Y.
Wholesome Films Corporation, 17 N. Wabash ave., Chicago, Ill. Milton Daily, president; A. M. Allen, vice-president; M. Feldstein, general manager; P. W. Stanhope, secretary and treasurer. New York office, 220 West 42d st.
Williamson Bros., Longacre Bldg., N. Y. C. (See Submarine Film Corporation.)
Jacob Wilk, care of Wilk & Wilk, Longacre Bldg., N. Y. C.
Wilk & Wilk, 825 Longacre Bldg., N. Y. C.
Wistaria Productions, Inc., 1520 Broadway, N. Y. C. Burton King, vice-president and director-general.
Harold Bell Wright Story Pictures Corporation, Los Angeles, Cal.; E. W. Reynolds, president and general manager; Charles M. Stone, tresurer; George L. Belcher, secretary; Harold Bell Wright, director general.

— Z —

Zion Films, Inc, 116 West 39th st., N. Y. C. L. Kehlmann, president and treasurer; M. Kehlmann, vice-president and manager; R. Walitzky, secretary.

FOREIGN MARKET FILM DUTIES

FOREWORD
The credit for the figures presented hereafter goes to the Department of Commerce, Bureau of Foreign and Domestic Commerce, Washington, D. C., which prepared them expressly for Motion Picture News. Conversion equivalents of weights and moneys are given for the convenience of the reader. The figures presented are the latest available.

EXPLANATORY NOTES.
Notice.—In making use of the accompanying statement, the fact should be kept in mind that authoritative information in regard to rates of duty can be obtained only from the customs authorities of the country concerned. While every care has been taken to insure accuracy, the Bureau of Foreign and Domestic Commerce is **unable to guarantee** that the rates given in the statement will be applied to the articles concerning which inquiry is made. To test the rates, small **trial shipments** are advisable. Authoritative **decisions** in regard to the customs classification of articles not specified in the tariff may be obtained in advance in a number of countries. More detailed information in regard to this matter will be given by the Bureau upon application. The statements should be filed for reference, but, in view of the **frequent changes** in the customs tariffs of foreign countries, should not be used in future without confirmation by this Bureau.

When two or more rates of duty are shown for the same article, products of the United States as a rule are admitted at the lowest rate ("conventional" or "minimum"), except: (1) Into France and French colonies, where (in the case of most articles) the "general" rate is applied; (2) into Canada, where the "general" rate is applied; and (3) into other British colonies, where the "preferential" rates (if any) are withheld from all non-British imports. Other exceptions are noted in the statement.

An asterisk (*) indicates that the article is not specified in the tariff, but has been classified by customs decision. Figures preceded by (‡) are inserted merely to facilitate the verification of the statement, and may be ignored by the reader.

BASIS OF WEIGHT.
Unless otherwise specially set forth in the statement, the basis of weight for the assessment

FOREIGN MARKET

of specific customs duties is as shown below. For colonies, the basis may be taken to be the same as in the mother country.

Gross Weight.—Austria-Hungary (articles dutiable at not more than 7.50 crowns per 100 kilos), Bulgaria (articles dutiable at not more than 10 leva per 100 kilos), Colombia, Costa Rica, Ecuador (classes 3-12, 14-17, 19-21, 23, 24, 26, 27, 29-31, 34, 36, 39, 42, 43, and 45), France (articles dutiable at not more than 10 francs per 100 kilos), Germany (articles dutiable at not more than 6 marks per 100 kilos), Honduras, Italy (articles dutiable at not more than 20 lire per 100 kilos), Nicaragua, Portugal (articles dutiable at not more than 0.005 milreis per kilo), Salvador, Serbia (articles dutiable at not more than 10 dinars per 100 kilos), Switzerland and Venezuela.

Net Weight (actual or legal).—Austria-Hungary (articles dutiable at more than 7.50 crowns per 100 kilos), Belgium, British Possessions, Bulgaria (articles dutiable at more than 10 leva per 100 kilos), China, Denmark (including immediate packing), Ecuador (classes 13, 18, 22, 25, 28, 32, 33, 35, 37, 38, 40, 41, 44, and 46-58, including immediate packing), Finland, France (articles dutiable at more than 10 francs per 100 kilos), Germany (articles dutiable at more than 6 marks per 100 kilos), Greece, Italy (articles dutiable at more than 20 lire per 100 kilos), Japan, Netherlands, Norway, Persia, Portugal (articles dutiable at more than 0.005 milreis per kilo), Russia, Serbia (articles dutiable at more than 10 dinars per 100 kilos), Sweden and the United Kingdom.

Legal Weight.—By "legal weight," which is the basis for duty on many articles in some countries of Latin America, is meant the weight of the articles and their immediate containers or packing. In most other countries legal weight is calculated upon the gross weight with certain tare allowances.

DUTIABLE VALUE.

Import Price (C.I.F.).—In most countries the value used as a basis for calculating ad valorem rates of duty is theoretically the value of goods at the port of importation, but the methods of determining the value at such port are far from uniform. In some cases the value is arrived at by adding a certain percentage to the invoice value, when such value does not include freight, insurance, etc.; in other cases—for example, in the absence of an invoice or when the correctness of the invoice is questioned—it is determined by making a deduction from the wholesale (duty-paid) price at the port of entry. In Australia, New Zealand and Haiti, 10 per cent. is added to the invoice value or fair market value at the place of exportation.

Export Price (F.O.B.).—In the following countries the value taken as a basis for ad valorem rates of duty is the value at the place of exportation, usually including the cost of packing and other expenses incidental to preparing the goods for shipment: Cuba, Dominican Republic, Newfoundland and Panama. In Canada and the Union of South Africa the dutiable value must not be less than the current value for home consumption at the place of purchase.

Official Value.—Ad valorem duties are based on the official valuations prescribed (for most articles) by Argentina, Bolivia, Paraguay, and Uruguay.

CONVERSION EQUIVALENTS.

Currency.

Balboa		$1.00
Bolivar		.193
Boliviana		.389
Colon		.465
Crown (Austria-Hungary)	(a)	.203
Crown (Denmark, Norway, Sweden)	(a)	.268
Dinar (same as franc)		.193
Dollar (Straits Settlements)		.5678
Dollar (elsewhere)		1.00
Drachma (same as franc)		.193
Florin	(a)	.402
Franc	(a)	.193
Gourde	(b)	1.00
Kran—20 shahis	(a)	.1332
Leu (same as franc)	(a)	.193
Lev (same as franc)	(a)	.193
Lira (same as franc)	(a)	.193
Mark (Finland, same as franc)		.193
Mark (Germany)	(a)	.238
Milreis (Brazil, paper)	(c)	.257
Milreis (Portugal, paper)		.68
Peseta (same as franc)	(a)	.193
Peso (Argentina, Paraguay, gold)		.965
Peso (Chile, gold)	(a)	.365
Peso (Guatemala, most articles)	(b)	.51
Peso (Honduras)	(c)	.55
Peso (Mexico)	(a)	.498
Peso (Salvador)		1.00
Peso (Uruguay)	(a)	1.034
Pound (Egyptian)		4.943
Pound (sterling)		4.8665
Pound (Turkish)	(a)	4.40
Ruble	(a)	.515
Rupee	(a)	.3244
Sol	(a)	.4867
Sucre		.4867
Tael (customs)	(c)	1.207
Tical		.3709
Yen		.498

WEIGHTS.

	Pounds.
Batman	6.548
Catty (see Picul)	
Central	100
Cwt. (see Hundredweight)	
Funt (see Pood)	
Hundredweight (Canada)	100
Hundredweight (d.)	112
Kilogram (Kilo) 1,000 grams	2.2046
Kin	1.3228
Oke (Greece)	2.822
Picul (China, British colonies), 100 catties,	133.33
Picul (Japan), 100 kin	132.28
Pood, 40 funt	36.1123
Pound (Haiti), ½ kilo	1.1023
Quintal (Latin America)	101.4
Ton (Canada, Union of South Africa)	2,000
Ton (metric), 1,000 kilos	2,204.6
Ton (d.)	2,240

MEASURES.

Bushel (imperial), (d.)	bushels 1.0315
Gallon (imperial) (d.)	gallons 1.2009
Gallon (imperial proof) (d.)	U. S. proof gals 1.374
Hectoliter, 100 liters	gallons 26.417
Liter	quarts 1.0568
Meter, 100 centimeters, 1,000 millimeters,	inches 39.37

(a) Normal value: actual rate of exchange variable.
(b) For customs purposes, account being taken of proportionate payment in gold (if any) required.
(c) Fluctuating currency, quotation from estimate of the Director of the Mint for April 1, 1919.
(d) Current in the United Kingdom and most British colonies. In Canada, the bushel of weight is the legal unit for grain and certain other products.

SURTAXES.

The surtaxes accompanied by date are affected by fluctuations in the currency (paper or silver). Certain charges (warehousing, customs handling, local taxes, revenue stamps, etc.) are not included; the rates of duty shown, increased by the surtaxes, should therefore be regarded as the minimum. Surtaxes marked "most articles" apply to the articles concerning which inquiry was made, unless the contrary is noted in the statement of rates of duty. The surtaxes (which include certain requirements increasing the duties) **are to be added to the rates** in the statement.

Argentina: When the regular duty is
  not less than 10% ad valorem nor
  more than 20% ....(a) 2% ad val.
  When dutiable at more than 20%.(a) 7% ad val.
Bahamas ....10% of duty
Bermuda ....10% of duty
Bolivia:
  Most dutiable articles.........15% of duty
  Most free articles............(a) 2% ad val.
Brazil:
  The "actual duties" in the attached statement include 2% gold surtax and increase due to proportion of duty payable on a gold basis. The calculations are based on a value of 12½ pence (25 cents) to the paper milreis and are subject to change in accordance with variations in its value for customs purposes as fixed by the Brazilian Government.
British Guiana:
  Articles subject to ad valorem rates.10% of duty
  Articles subject to specific rates
    (except matches)............. 5% of duty

Bulgaria:
  Most dutiable articles (octroi).....20% of duty
  Free articles........................0.5% ad val.
Colombia ....7% of duty
Costa Rica:
  Imports intended for the province
    of Limon.............................5% of duty
  Imports for interior provinces........2% of duty
Egypt: At Alexandria (wharfage and
  paving)...............................0.5% ad val.
Finland: Dutiable articles...............3% of duty
Haiti: (January 1, 1919)................11.6% of duty
Honduras: (January 1, 1919).............9.1% of duty
Newfoundland: Dutiable articles (except coal)..........................10% of duty
New Zealand.............................1% ad val.
Nicaragua..............................12½% of duty
Paraguay: Dutiable articles......(a) 1.5% ad val.
Peru:
  Callao, Salaverry, Mollendo, Ilo,
    Paita, and Pisco...................10% of duty
  Other ports...........................8% of duty
Portugal ....40% of duty
Salvador ....1.5% of duty
St. Lucia: Most dutiable articles......10% of duty
Uruguay:
  Most articles subject to specific duties or dutiable at more than 12%
    ad valorem ....(a) 14% ad val.
  Articles dutiable at 9-12% ad valorem.........................(a) 9% ad val.
  Other (including free) articles..(a) 4% ad val.
Venezuela ....56.55% of duty

Statement of Rates of Duty on CINEMATOGRAPH FILMS

	Rate for all countries	Rate for all countries
SOUTH AFRICA	L. s. d.	
Films for bioscopes and cinematographs per 100 feet.	50	
STRAITS SETTLEMENTS		
All goods other than certain beverages.	free	
	Rubles per pood	
RUSSIA		
Magic lanterns and other projecting lanterns and photographic apparatus, including developed cinematograph films.	13.20	
Articles of all kinds not specified of celluloid (French treaty), including undeveloped cinematograph films.	0.82½	
	1st Tariff Persetas per kilo	2nd Tariff Persetas per kilo
SPAIN		
Instruments and apparatus not specified for arts and sciences, including developed cinematograph films, net weight.	3.00	3.00
Celluloid manufactures, other than articles for personal adornment including undeveloped cinematograph films, net weight.	2.00	2.00
	Dollars per kilo General	Dollars per kilo U. S.
CUBA		
Celluloid manufactured into cinematograph films and similar articles, whatever may be the purpose for or conditions under which imported, net weight.	5.20	4.16
	Rate of Duty General	Rate of Duty Conventional
	Marks per 100 kilos	Marks per 100 kilos
GERMANY		
Manufactures of celluloid not specified.	200.00	
	General Lire per 100 kilos	Conventional Lire per 100 kilos
ITALY		
Manufactures of celluloid not specified.	100	80
JAPAN		
Films, not specified..ad valorem..	40%	
	General Crowns per kilo	Minimum Crowns per kilo
NORWAY		
Manufactures of celluloid not specified, including inner packing.	1.50	1.20
NETHERLANDS		
Articles not specified.	Free	Free
	Francs per 100 kilos	Francs per 100 kilos
FRANCE (a)		
Cinematograph films:		
Merely sensitized, net weight.	480.00	320.00

(a) Including the increased rates of July 8, 1919.

	Rate of Duty	Rate of Duty Dollars 100 lbs.
ARGENTINA		
Films for cinematographs, exposed Valuation 5.00 pesos per kilo.	25%	70.03
BOLIVIA		
Cinematograph films, including weight of packing, valuation 4 Bolivianos per kilo.	30%	$21.17
	Milreis per kilo Actual	
BRAZIL		
Films for cinematographs, exposed (No. 15), nominally 25 milreis per kilo.	48.150	547.10
BRITISH GUIANA		
Cinematograph films.	Free	Free
	Pesos per kilo	
CHILE		
Photographs on celluloid films, legal weight.	6.00	99.34
COLOMBIA		
Cinematograph films, exposed.	5.00	242.68
DUTCH GUIANA		
Optical instruments.	Free	Free
Articles not otherwise specified ad valorem	10%	10%
ECUADOR		
Films for cinematographs.	Free	Free
PARAGUAY		
Films for cinematographs Valuation, 5.00 pesos per kilo.	42%	95.20
PERU		
Photographs on paper and cardboard.		
	Nominal Rate of Duty	Actual Rate of Duty
ARGENTINA		
Optical and other instruments, not specified, ad valorem.		25%
	Milreis per kilo	Milreis per kilo
BRAZIL		
Films for cinematographs, blank (No. 15).	10.000	19.260
	Pesos per kilo	
CHILE		
Films prepared for photography, gross weight.	0.30	
COLOMBIA	per kilo	
Films for cinematographs, blank..	0.10	

Temporary Admission of Motion Picture Films in South American Countries.

In Bolivia Motion Picture films are entitled to free admission under bond. To cancel the bond a certificate should be secured from the Bolivian customs agent at Mollendo or Antofagasta or from a Bolivian consul in the country to which exported, as stated in Tariff Series 34, page 112.

The laws of Colombia provide for the free temporary admission of the property of theatrical or dramatic companies, but there is nothing in the law itself to indicate whether this provision is extended to motion picture films or not. Inasmuch as other laws granting exemptions in Columbia are rather strictly construed it is probable that no refund would be granted to films upon re-exportation.

According to a report of October 24, 1914, from Consul S. H. Wiley at Asuncion, films entered in Paraguay for temporary exhibition and to be re-exported are not subject to duty. No information has been received as to procedure necessary to secure this exemption, but it probably consists in the requirement that a bond equal to the duties be deposited.

It has been held in Peru, by a resolution of January 5, 1910, that motion picture films are not subject to temporary free importation. It was held at the same time, however, that scientific institutions might import films free of duty upon guaranteeing their re-exportation. It appears probable that a similar exemption might be secured for films intended for educational or similar purposes. A Peruvian resolution of February 22, 1914, subjected films to the same conditions as inflammable and explosive articles, as regards transportation. Packages containing such articles should be marked "Peligrose." They are also excluded from baggage unless marked as indicated.

A law of Uruguay, enacted in October, 1912, authorized the temporary free admission of all articles imported to be re-exported in any form. No information has been received as to its application to cinematograph films, but in view of its general terms it appears reasonable to suppose that it would be held to include motion picture films.

FOREIGN MARKET

No information is available as to the treatment of motion picture films in Venezuela, and under the circumstances it is probable that they would be dutiable as ordinary imports. There appears to be no general provision for temporary free admission of articles.

	Rate of Duty	Rate of Duty Dollars per 100 lbs.
ARGENTINA		
Films for cinematographs, exposed Valuation 5.00 pesos per kilo....	25%	70.03
BOLIVIA		
Cinematographs and their accessories, ad valorem.............	30% Milreis per kilo Actual	34.5%
BRAZIL		
Films for cinematographs, exposed (No. 15), nominally 25 milreis per kilo..................................	48.150	547.10
BRITISH GUIANA		
Cinematograph Films.............	Free Pesos per kilo	Free
CHILE		
Photographs on celluloid films, legal weight.....................	6.00	99.34
COLOMBIA		
Cinematograph films exposed......	5.00	242.68
Cinematograph films sensitized....	.10	
DUTCH GUIANA		
Optical Instruments...............	Free	Free
Articles not otherwise specified, ad valorem.........................	10%	10%
ECUADOR		
Films for cinematographs.........	Free	Free
PARAGUAY		
Films for cinematographs Valuation 5.00 pesos per kilo....	42%	95.20
PERU		
Photographs on paper and cardboard...........................		

	Rate of Duty Soles per kilo	Rate of Duty Dollars per 100 lbs.
PERU		
Pictures known as cinematographs, legal weight.....................	1.00	24.28
Manufactures of celluloid and gelatin not otherwise specified, legal weight...........................	4.00	97.09
URUGUAY		
Cinematograph Films, ad valorem..	31%	45%
Official valuation fixed at 3.50 pesos per kilo...................		74.87
Reduction of 50% on used films		
	Bolivars per kilo	
VENEZUELA		
Films for cinematographs.........	1.25	17.13
	Francs per 100 kilos	
FRENCH GUIANA		
Cinematograph films:		
With impressions..............	165.00	14.44
Merely sensitized..............	300.00	26.26
	Per 100 ft.	Per 100 ft.
TRINIDAD		
Cinematograph films.............	5d.	0.10

	Rate of Duty General Ad Valorem	Rate of Duty Preferential Ad Valorem
NEW ZEALAND		
Magic lanterns, bioscopes, cinematographs, kinetoscopes..........	30%	20%
	Per Lb.	Per Lb.
Printed posters..................	3 3-5d.	3d
Films for bioscopes, cinematographs and kinetoscopes................	Free	Free
BRITISH NORTH BORNEO		
Traveling shows, such as cinematograph and other similar equipment imported temporarily for public entertainment............	Free	
Articles not specified..ad valorem	5%	
JAPAN		
Chromolithographic prints (in relief and cut); printed pictures for advertising purposes............	Free	
Magic lanterns, cinematographs and kinetoscopes, and parts thereof ad valorem	50%	
Manufactures of celluloid not specified................ad valorem	40%	
Films not specified....ad valorem	40%	
Articles imported for use in theatrical and other performances are exempt from import duty if they are to be reexported within one year from date of importation and if security for the full duty is deposited.		

CHINA		
Articles not specified....ad valorem (No provision for temporary admission.)	5%	
Advertising matter, if declared for free distribution................	Free	
CEYLON		
Advertising matter...............	Free	
Articles not specified...ad valorem (No provision for temporary admission.)	7½%	

	Rate of Duty	Rate of Duty
BAHAMAS		
Articles not specified...ad valorem	20%	
Note—Any animal or thing imported into the colony for some temporary purpose approved by the Governor-in-Council if satisfactory bond be given for the reexportation thereof within ninety days and for the payment of a duty of customs of one and one-half per centum ad valorem..................	1½%	
	General	Preferential
BARBADOS		
Articles not specified...ad valorem	10%	10%
Note—There is no provision in the tariff regarding temporary free importation of theatrical accessories, etc.		
JAMAICA		
Articles not specified...ad valorem	16 2-3%	
Note—Professional implements, instruments, and tools of trade, etc., in the possession of persons not coming to the island as settlers.......................	Free	
Philosophical and scientific apparatus and appliances brought by professional artists, lecturers, or scientists for use by themselves temporarily for exhibition, etc., and not for sale..............	Free	
Used theatrical effects to be reexported.....................	Free	

SOME OF THE LEADING ENGLISH PRODUCING CONCERNS.

With closer coordination of the foreign and local markets now more a matter of present moment than of future probability, a strong interest is manifest in American film circles of the competitive strength of foreign companies and the advances in film production, stories of which are brought over by those who have had opportunity to observe conditions on the other side.

The fact that English film companies have thrown down the gauntlet of competition to American producers is well known. A number of these concerns are patterning their product to appeal to the American public, and are more and more strongly pushing their output in this market.

The better known English corporations, whose productions are best suited to American consumption, together with their addresses, and a few of their best productions as listed by Bioscope, the English trade publication, are presented below:

Hepworth Picture Plays, Ltd., 2 Denman Street, Piccadilly Circus, London, W. 1. ("David Copperfield," "Coming Thro' the Rye," "Sheba," "Possession," "City of Beautiful Nonsense," "Sweet Lavender," etc.)

British Actors' Film Co., Ltd., Melbourne Road, Bushey, Herts. ("The Usurper," "Lady Clare," etc.)

Gaumont Co., Ltd., 6 Denman Street, Piccadilly Circus, London, W. 1. ("First Men in the Moon," "The Fall of a Saint.")

British & Colonial Kinematograph Co., Ltd., 33-35 Endell Street, Long Acre, London, W. C. 2. ("Twelve Ten," "Nobody's Child," "The Temptress.")

Samuelson Film Co., Ltd., Worton Hall, Isleworth, Middlesex. ("Milestones," "Elder Miss Blossom," "Tinker, Tailer, Soldier, Sailor.")

George Clark Productions, 41 Ebury Street, Victoria, London. ("Garden of Resurrection," "March Hare.")

Ideal Film Co., Ltd., 76-78 Wardour Street, London, W. 1. ("Masks and Faces," "His Greatest Performance," "Chinese Puzzle.")

Broadwest Film Co., Ltd., Wood Street, Walthamstow, E. 17. ("A Great Coup," "Her Son," "Crucifixion.")

London Film Co., Ltd., St. Margarets, Twickenham. ("The House of Temperley," "The Prisoner of Zenda," "The Christian," "The Manxman.")

AN ANNOUNCEMENT

After an association covering a period of 12 consecutive years with D. W. Griffith, serving in the capacity of Laboratory Superintendent, I have decided to remain on the West Coast and continue the activities of the Aller Laboratories commencing January 1, 1920.

The Laboratory work of all Griffith Releases up to now, as well as the following subjects, was done under my personal supervision: Special town releases of "The Miracle Man," "Daddy Long Legs," "The Unpardonable Sin," and negatives and sample prints of all prominent producers.

JOSEPH (ALTSCHULER) ALLER
Laboratories: 4500 Sunset Blvd.

Holly 2800 LOS ANGELES

SANBORN QUALITY

No alibis—
we stand on
our service
and work

Sanborn Laboratories

CULVER CITY, CAL.

PHONE, 70099

STUDIO DIRECTORY

Seventh Motion Picture News Chart of

City or Exchange Center	A—General Trade Conditions Since Jan. 1, 1919 B—Outlook for the Future	Number of Theatres A—Opened B—Closed Since Jan. 1, 1919	In What Degree Have Admission Prices Been Raised
Buffalo, N. Y.	A—Good B—Excellent	A—None B—None	Slightly
Springfield, Ill.	A—Excellent B—Very Good	A—None B—One	General Raise From 15c to 20c and 25c
Toledo, O.	A—Uncertain B—Good	A—35 B—None	Slightly
Milwaukee, Wis.	A—Good B—Very Bright	A—None B—None	About 40%
Dallas, Tex.	A—Excellent B—Excellent	A—9 B—2	45%
Montreal, Quebec	A—Good B—Good	A—None B—2	Average of 5c
Ottawa, Ont.	A—Fair B—Fair	A—None B—One	Average of 5c
Toronto, Ont.	A—Flourishing B—Excellent	A—8 B—None	40%
Rochester, N. Y.	A—Excellent B—Bright	A—29 B—None	90%
Salt Lake City, Utah	A—Fine B—Dubious	A—2 B—None	40%
Richmond, Va.	A—Fine B—Exceptionally Good	A—None B—None	50%
San Francisco, Cal.	A—Very Good B—Most Excellent	A—Unknown B—None	25%
Providence, R. I.	A—Good B—Bright	A—2 B—1	30%
Spokane, Wash.	A—Above Average A—Fair	A—9 B—None	10%
Los Angeles, Cal.	A—Greatly Improved B—Exceptionally Bright	A—None B—None	40%
Baltimore, Md.	A—Excellent B—Most Promising	A—None B—None	50%
Chicago, Ill.	A—Best Ever Experienced B—Very Bright	A—Not known B—Not known	100%
Butte, Mont.	A—Good B—Very Bright	A—8 B—7	No Raise
Cincinnati, O.	A—Excellent B—Excellent	A—Not known B—Not known	10%

STUDIO DIRECTORY

National Film Trade Conditions—1920

What is the Average Length of Runs	Are Exhibitors Tending Toward Booking Combinations?	Number of Theatres in Course of Construction?	Strength of Exhibitors' Organizations?	Is There Too Much Theatre Competition in Your Territory?
Four Days	Talked of but nothing done	Five	All Large Houses Organized	Yes
Three to Seven Days	No	Two	No Local Organization	No
One Week	No	None	Good—40 Members in Manager's Asso.	No
A Week Downtown Two Days in Suburbs	Yes	One	Powerful	In Suburbs, Yes
Two Days	Yes	75 (in the State)	Good	No
Three Days	No	One	Weak	No
1-2 Weeks Large Houses 3 Days Small Houses	No	One	Negative	No
3 to 7 Days	Slightly	Two	Good	No
3 Days	No	None	Powerful	No
2½ Days	No	Two	Nil	Yes
3 to 7 Days	No	None	Very Strong	No
One Week	No	Six	Good	No
One Week	No	None	No Local Organization	No
4 Days	Yes	None	Good	Yes
3 to 7 Days	No	Two	Powerful	No
1-2 Weeks Largest Houses 3 Days Small Houses	Yes	Two	Claimed Strongest in Country	No
3 Days	No	Nine	Very Strong	No
3 Days	Yes	Five	No Organization	Yes
3 to 7 Days	Yes	One	Good	No

INDEX TO FEATURE RELEASES OF THE YEAR 1919

A. B. C. of Love (Acme-Perret-Pathe), Mae Murray............................Dec. 13
Ace of the Saddle (Universal), Harry Carey...................................July 19
Adele (United Picture Theatres), Kitty Gordon................................Feb. 1
Adventure Shop, The (Vitagraph), Corinne Griffith............................Jan. 11
After His Own Heart (Metro), Hale Hamilton...................................May 10
After the War (Argosy), Grace Cunard...Jan. 11
Alias Mike Moran (Paramount), Wallace Reid...................................Mar. 29
All Wrong (Pathe), Bryant Washburn...May 24
Almost a Husband (Goldwyn), Will Rogers......................................Oct. 25
Almost Married (Metro), May Allison..June 14
Amateur Adventuress, The (Metro), Emmy Wehlen................................May 17
Amateur Widow, An (World), Zena Keefe..May 24
Amazing Imposter, The (American-Pathe), Mary Miles Minter....................Feb. 1-8
Amazing Wife, The (Universal), Mary MacLaren.................................Mar. 16-29
American Way, The (World), Arthur Ashley-Dorothy Green.......................July 12
Anne of Green Gables (Realart), Mary Miles Minter............................Nov. 29
Are You Legally Married? (Elk Photoplays, Inc.), Lew Cody-
 Rosemary Theby...Oct. 4
Arizona Cat Claw, The (World), Edythe Sterling...............................Nov. 1
As a Man Thinks (Raver-Hodkinson), Leah Baird................................May 3
As the Sun Went Down (Metro), Edith Story....................................Feb. 22
Avalanche, The (Artcraft), Elsie Ferguson....................................July 12

Bachelor's Wife, A (American-Pathe), Mary Miles Minter.......................May 24
Bandbox, The (Hodkinson), Doris Kenyon.......................................Nov. 22
Bare-Fisted Gallagher (Robertson-Cole), William Desmond......................June 28
Bare Fists (Universal), Harry Carey..Apr. 26
Be a Little Sport (Fox), Albert Ray-Elinor Fair..............................July 12
Beating the Odds (Vitagraph), Harry T. Morey.................................May 10
Beauty Proof (Vitagraph), Harry T. Morey.....................................June 7
Beloved Cheater, The (Robertson-Cole), Lew Cody..............................Dec. 6
Best Man, The (Hampton-Hodkinson), J. Warren Kerrigan........................May 10
Better 'Ole, The (World), Special Cast.......................................Mar. 8
Better Times (Robertson-Cole), Zasu Pitts-David Butler.......................June 21
Better Wife, The (Select), Clara Kimball Young...............................July 19
Bill Apperson's Boy (First National), Jack Pickford..........................July 26
Bill Henry (Ince-Paramount), Charles Ray.....................................Aug. 30
Birth of a Race, The (Russell), Special Cast.................................May 3
Bishop's Emeralds, The (Pathe), Virginia Pearson-Virginia Valli..............June 7
Black Circle, The (World), Creighton Hale-Virginia Valli.....................Nov. 1
Black Gate, The (Vitagraph), Earle Williams..................................Dec. 13
Blackie's Redemption (Metro), Bert Lytell....................................Apr. 26
Blind Husbands (Universal), Eric Von Stroheim................................Oct. 18
Blind Man's Eyes (Metro), Bert Lytell..Mar. 22
Blinding Trail, The (Universal), Monroe Salisbury............................Apr. 26-May 3
Blue Bandanna, The (Robertson-Cole), William Desmond.........................Dec. 6
Bluffer, The (World), June Elvidge...Jan. 18
Bolshevism on Trial (Select), Special Cast...................................Apr. 19
Bonds of Honor (Exhibitors Mutual), Sessue Hayakawa..........................Feb. 1
Bonds of Love (Goldwyn), Pauline Frederick...................................Nov. 15
Bonnie, Bonnie Lassie (Universal), Mary MacLaren.............................Nov. 8
Boomerang, The (Pioneer), Henry B. Walthall..................................May 10-17
Boots (Paramount), Dorothy Gish..Mar. 15
Brand, The (Goldwyn), Kay Laurell-Russell Simpson............................Mar. 8
Brass Buttons (American-Pathe), William Russell..............................Mar. 22
Brat, The (Nazimova-Metro), Nazimova...Sept. 6
Break the News to Mother (Select), Special Cast..............................June 7

Breed of Men (Artcraft), William S. Hart.....................................Feb. 15
Breezy Jim (Triangle), Crane Wilbur..Feb. 22
Bringing Up Betty (World), Evelyn Greeley....................................Aug. 22
Broadway Saint, A (World), Montague Love.....................................July 26
Broken Blossoms (D. W. Griffith), Lillian Gish-Richard Barthelmess...........May 24
Broken Butterfly, The (Robertson-Cole), Lew Cody-Pauline Starke..............Sept. 28
Broken Commandments (Fox), Gladys Brockwell..................................Sept. 13
Brothers Divided (Pathe), Frank Keenan.......................................Dec. 13
Burglar by Proxy (First National), Jack Pickford.............................Sept. 6
Busher, The (Paramount), Charles Ray...June 7

Cabaret Girl, The (Bluebird), Ruth Clifford..................................Jan. 4
Calibre 38 (Edgar Lewis-Sherry), Mitchell Lewis-Hedda Nova...................Apr. 5
Call of the Soul, The (Fox), Gladys Brockwell................................Jan. 18
Cambric Mask, The (Vitagraph), Alice Joyce...................................Apr. 5
Captain Kidd, Jr. (Artcraft), Mary Pickford..................................Apr. 5-May 4
Captain's Captain, The (Vitagraph), Alice Joyce..............................Jan. 4
Career of Katherine Bush (Paramount-Artcraft), Catherine Calvert.............Aug. 16
Carolyn of the Corners (Pathe), Bessie Love..................................Mar. 1
Castles in the Air (Metro), May Allison......................................May 24
Challenge of Chance, The (Hallmark), Jess Willard............................July 5
Charge It to Me (American-Pathe), Margarita Fisher...........................May 3
Chasing Rainbows (Fox), Gladys Brockwell.....................................Aug. 20
Cheating Cheaters (Select), Clara Kimball Young..............................Feb. 8
Cheating Herself (Fox), Peggy Hyland...Aug. 16
Checkers (Fox), Special Cast...Aug. 9
Child of M'sieu (Triangle), Baby Marie Osborn................................Feb. 22
Choosing a Wife (First National), Special Cast...............................July 23
City of Comrades, The (Goldwyn), Tom Moore...................................May 26
Climbers, The (Vitagraph), Corinne Griffith..................................Nov. 8
Clouded Name, The (World), John Lowell.......................................Aug. 30
Coax Me (World), June Elvidge..Aug. 9
Colonel Bridau (Entente Film Corp.), Special Cast............................July 13
Come Again Smith (Hodkinson), J. Warren Kerrigan.............................Feb. 1
Come Out of the Kitchen (Paramount), Marguerite Clark........................May 24
Coming of the Law, The (Fox), Tom Mix..May 24
Common Clay (Pathe), Fannie Ward...Oct. 8
Common Property (Universal), Robert Anderson.................................Nov. 29
Counterfeit, The (Paramount-Artcraft), Elsie Ferguson........................Nov. 29
Country Cousin, The (Selznick-Select), Elaine Hammerstein....................Nov. 15
Courage for Two (World), Carlyle Blackwell-Evelyn Greeley....................Feb. 15
Courageous Coward, The (Robertson-Cole), Sessue Hayakawa.....................Apr. 26
Cowardice Court (Fox), Peggy Hyland..Jan. 28
Craving, The (Bluebird), Francis Ford..Jan. 18
Creaking Stairs (Universal), Mary MacLaren...................................Feb. 8
Crimson Gardenia, The (Beach-Goldwyn), Owen Moore-Hedda Nova.................June 28
Crimson Shoals (Monopol), Francis Ford.......................................Nov. 1
Crook of Dreams (World), Louise Huff...Nov. 1
Crooked Straight (Paramount-Artcraft), Charles Ray...........................Jan. 1
Crown Jewels (Triangle), Claire Anderson-Joe Bennett.........................Apr. 26
Cry of the Weak, The (Pathe), Fannie Ward....................................Apr. 26
Cupid Forecloses (Vitagraph), Bessie Love....................................July 12

Daddy Long Legs (Pickford-First National), Mary Pickford.....................May 24
Damsel in Distress, A (Pathe), Creighton Hale-June Caprice...................Oct. 25
Danger Zone, The (Fox), Madlaine Traverse....................................Jan. 18
Dangerous Waters (Robertson-Cole), William Desmond...........................Sept. 27

STUDIO DIRECTORY

Daring Hearts (Vitagraph), Bushman-Bayne..................Aug. 9
Dark Star, The (Paramount-Artcraft), Marion Davies-Norman Kerry..Aug. 16
Daughter of Mine (Goldwyn), Madge Kennedy................May 17
Dawn (Blackton-Pathe), Sylvia Breamer-Robert Gordon.......Dec. 16
Day Dreams (Goldwyn), Madge Kennedy.......................Jan. 25
Day She Paid, The (Universal), Francelia Billington, Barney Sherry..Dec. 20
Dead Line, The (Robertson-Cole), Sessue Hayakawa..........Aug. 16
Delicious Little Devil, The (Universal), Mae Murray.......May 3
Deliverance (Liebfreed-Miller), Helen Keller..............Aug. 30
Desert Gold (Hampton-Hodkinson), Special Cast.............Nov. 15
Destiny (Jewel-Universal), Dorothy Phillips...............Aug. 23
Devil's Trail, The (World), Betty Compson-George Larkin...June 21
Divorce Trap, The (Fox), Gladys Brockwell.................Jan. 25
Divorcee, The (Metro), Ethel Barrymore....................Feb. 8
Don't Change Your Husband (Artcraft), Cecil De Mille-Special Cast..Oct. 4
Dragon Painter, The (Robertson-Cole), Sessue Hayakawa.....Jan. 25
Dub, The (Paramount), Wallace Reid

Eastward, Ho (Fox), William Russell.......................Nov. 29
Easy to Make Money (Metro), Bert Lytell...................July 26
Echo of Youth, The (Graphic), Charles Richmond-Leah Baird..Feb. 15-Mar. 8
Egg Crate Wallop, The (Ince-Paramount-Artcraft), Charles Ray..Oct. 11
Enchanted Barn, The (Vitagraph), Bessie Love..............Jan. 25
End of the Game, The (Hodkinson), J. Warren Kerrigan......Mar. 29
Erstwhile Susan (Realart), Constance Binney...............Nov. 22
Eternal Magdalene, The (Goldwyn), Marsh-Dalton-Elliott....May
Evangeline (Fox), Special Cast............................Aug. 23
Eve in Exile (American-Pathe), Charlotte Walker...........Dec. 20
Every Mother's Son (Fox), Charlotte Walker................Jan. 4
Everywoman (Paramount-Artcraft), Special Cast.............Dec. 27
Experimental Marriage (Select), Constance Talmadge........Apr. 5
Exquisite Thief, The (Universal), Priscilla Dean..........Apr. 19
Extravagance (Paramount), Dorothy Dalton..................Apr. 12
Eyes of the Soul (Artcraft), Elsie Ferguson...............May 3
Eyes of Youth (Equity), Clara Kimball Young...............Nov. 15

Fair and Warmer (Metro), May Allison......................Nov. 1
Fair Enough (American)(Margarita Fisher).................Jan. 4
Faith (Metro), Bert Lytell................................Feb. 8
Faith of the Strong, The (Select), Mitchell Lewis.........Sept. 20
Fall of Babylon, The (D. W. Griffith), Special Cast.......Aug.
Fallen Idol, A (Fox), Evelyn Nesbit.......................Aug. 31
False Code, The (Keenan-Pathe), Frank Keenan..............Oct. 4
False Evidence (Metro), Viola Dana........................May 3
False Faces, The (Paramount-Artcraft), Henry B. Walthall..Feb. 22-Mar. 1
Favor to a Friend, A (Metro), Emmy Wehlen.................Aug. 23
Fear Woman, The (Goldwyn), Pauline Frederick..............July 19
Feud, The (Fox), Tom Mix..................................Dec. 20
Fight for Love, A (Universal), Harry Carey................Mar. 15-22
Fighting Colleen, A (Vitagraph), Bessie Love..............Nov. 22
Fighting Cressy (J. D. Hampton-Pathe), Blanche Sweet......Dec. 6
Fighting Destiny (Vitagraph), Harry T. Morey..............Mar. 29
Fighting for Gold (Fox), Tom Mix..........................Apr. 12
Fighting Roosevelts, The (First National), Special Cast...Feb. 1
Fighting Through (Hodkinson), E. K. Lincoln...............Feb. 1
Final Close-Up, The (Paramount), Shirley Mason............June 7-14
Fire Flingers, The (Universal), Rupert Julian.............Apr. 12
Fires of Faith (Famous Players-Lasky), Eugene O'Brien-
  Catherine Calvert
Firing Line, The (Paramount-Artcraft), Irene Castle.......May 17
Fit to Win (Public Health Films), Special Cast............July 19
Flame of the Desert, The (Goldwyn), Geraldine Farrar......Apr. 12
Follies Girl, The (Triangle), Olive Thomas................Nov. 15
Fools and Their Money (Metro), Emmy Wehlen................Apr. 26
Fools' Gold (Arrow), Mitchell Lewis.......................June 21

Fools' Gold (Arrow), Mitchell Lewis.......................May 17
For a Woman's Honor (Robertson-Cole), H. B. Warner........Sept. 27
For Better, For Worse (Artcraft), Cecil B. De Mille.......May 10
For Freedom (Fox), William Farnum.........................Jan. 11
For Freedom of the East (Goldwyn-Betzwood), Lady Tsen Mei..Jan. 25
Forbidden (Jewel-Universal), Mildred Harris...............Sept. 6
Forbidden Fire (J. Parker Read, Jr.), Louise Glaum........Mar. 29
Forbidden Room, The (Fox), Gladys Brockwell...............Mar. 15
Forest Rivals (World), Dorothy Green-Arthur Ashley........Sept. 20
Forfeit, The (Hodkinson), House Peters-Jane Miller........Mar. 22
Fortune's Child (Vitagraph), Gladys Leslie................Feb. 8
Four Flusher, The (Metro), Hale Hamilton..................Aug. 30
Fugitive from Matrimony, A (Robertson-Cole), H. B. Warner..Dec. 13
Full of Pep (Metro), Hale Hamilton........................June 7

Gamblers, The (Vitagraph), Harry T. Morey.................Aug. 2
Gambling in Souls (Fox), Madlaine Traverse................Mar. 22
Game Is Up, The (Bluebird), Ruth Clifford.................Jan. 18-25
Gates of Brass (Keenan-Pathe), Frank Keenan...............July
Gay Lord Quex, The (Goldwyn), Tom Moore...................Dec. 27
Gay Old Dog, The (Henley-Pathe), John Cumberland..........Nov. 22
Gentleman of Quality, A (Vitagraph), Earle Williams.......Mar. 15
Getting Mary Married (Select), Marion Davies..............Apr. 19
Ginger (World), Garreth Hughes............................May 3
Girl Alaska, The (World), Lottie Kruse....................Aug. 23
Girl Dodger, The (Paramount), Charles Ray.................Mar. 8
Girl at Bay, A (Vitagraph), Corinne Griffith..............June 28
Girl in Bohemia, A (Fox), Peggy Hyland....................Nov. 15
Girl From Outside (Goldwyn), Special Cast.................Nov. 22
Girl Problem, The (Vitagraph), Corinne Griffith...........Mar. 1
Girl Who Stayed at Home, The (Artcraft), D. W. Griffith...Apr. 5
Girl With No Regrets, The (Fox), Peggy Hyland.............Feb. 8
Girl-Woman, The (Vitagraph), Gladys Leslie................Aug. 9
Girls (Paramount), Marguerite Clark.......................July 12
Glorious Lady, The (Selznick-Select), Olive Thomas........Nov. 15
Go Get 'Em Garringer (Astra-Pathe), Helen Chadwick-
  Franklyn Farnum...Mar. 15-22
Go West, Young Man (Goldwyn), Tom Moore...................Feb.
God and the Man (Cosmofotofilm), Special Cast.............May 17
Gold Cure, The (Metro), Viola Dana........................Jan. 18
Golden Shower, The (Vitagraph), Gladys Leslie.............Dec. 27
Good Gracious Annabelle (Paramount), Billie Burke.........Apr.
Gray Towers Mystery (Vitagraph), Gladys Leslie............Oct. 25
Greased Lightning (Paramount), Charles Ray................May 10
Great Romance, The (Screen Classics), Harold Lockwood.....Jan. 25
Great Victory, The (Screen Classics), Special Cast........Jan. 4
Greatest Thing in Life, The (Artcraft), Lillian Gish......Jan. 4
Grim Game, The (Paramount-Artcraft), Houdini..............Sept. 13
Gun Fightin' Gentleman, A (Universal), Harry Carey........Dec. 6

Hand Invisible, The (World), Montagu Love.................Mar. 15
Happy Though Married (Paramount-Ince), Enid Bennett.......Feb. 22-Mar. 1
Happiness a la Mode (Select), Constance Talmadge..........June 28
Hard Boiled (Paramount), Dorothy Dalton...................Feb. 15
Haunted Bedroom, The (Paramount), Enid Bennett............June 21
Hawthorne of the U. S. A. (Paramount-Artcraft), Wallace Reid..Nov. 29
Hay-Foot, Straw-Foot (Ince-Paramount), Charles Ray........July 5
Heart in Pawn, A (Haworth-Robertson-Cole), Sessue Hayakawa..Mar. 8-15
Heart o' the Hills (First National), Mary Pickford........Dec. 13
Heart of a Gypsy, The (Hallmark), Special Cast............Dec. 13
Heart of Gold (World), Louise Huff........................Jan. 25
Heart of Humanity, The (Jewel-Universal), Dorothy Phillips..Jan. 11-25
Heart of Wetona, The (Select), Norma Talmadge.............Jan. 4
Heart of Youth, The (Paramount), Lila Lee.................Sept. 20

STUDIO DIRECTORY

Hearts Asleep (Robertson-Cole), Bessie Barriscale..............Apr. 5
His Divorced Wife (Universal), Monroe Salisbury................Nov. 15
His Father's Wife (World), June Elvidge........................Sept. 13
His Majesty, The American (United Artists), Douglas Fairbanks..Sept. 27
His Official Fiancee (Paramount-Artcraft), Vivian Martin.......Oct. 18
His Parisian Wife (Artcraft), Elsie Ferguson...................Feb. 8
Home (Jewel-Universal), Mildred Harris.........................Aug. 30
Home Breaker, The (Paramount), Dorothy Dalton..................May 17
Home Town Girl, The (Paramount), Vivian Martin.................June 7
Home Wanted (World), Madge Evans...............................July 5
Hoodlum, The (First National), Mary Pickford...................Sept. 13
Hoop-La (National Film-Robertson-Cole), Billie Rhodes..........Feb. 15-22
Hope Chest, The (Paramount), Dorothy Gish......................Jan. 4
Hornet's Nest, The (Vitagraph), Earle Williams.................July 19
House Divided, A (Blackton-Hallmark), Sylvia Breamer...........May 23
House of Intrigue, The (Robertson-Cole), Special Cast..........Sept. 27
House Without Children, The (Film Market, Inc., State Rights),
 Special Cast..Aug. 23
Hushed Hour, The (Carson Productions), Blanche Sweet...........Aug. 23
Hearts of Men (Hiram Abrams), George Beban.....................Apr. 19
Hearts of the World (D. W. Griffith), Lillian and Dorothy Gish.Aug. 30
Heartsease (Goldwyn), Tom Moore................................Sept. 6
Hell Roarin' Reform (Fox), Tom Mix.............................May 31
Help! Help! Police! (Fox), George Walsh........................May 10
Her Code of Honor (United), Florence Reed......................Mar. 15
Her Game (United Pictures), Florence Reed......................Oct. 25
Her Greatest Performance (Triangle), Ellen Terry...............Aug. 16
Her Inspiration (Metro), May Allison....................Jan. 18-Feb. 1
Her Purchase Price (Robertson-Cole), Bessie Barriscale.........Sept. 6
Here Comes the Bride (Paramount), John Barrymore...............Feb. 1
Hidden Truth, The (Select), Ann Chase..........................Feb. 1
Highest Trump, The (Vitagraph), Earl Williams..................Aug. 9
His Bridal Night (Select), Alice Brady.........................May 31
His Debt (Robertson-Cole), Sessue Hayakawa.....................

I Want to Forget (Fox) Evelyn Nesbit...........................Jan. 4
I'll Get Him Yet (Paramount), Dorothy Gish.....................May 31
Illustrious Prince, The (Robertson-Cole), Sessue Hayakawa......Nov. 22
Impossible Catherine (Pearson-Pathe), Virginia Pearson.........Oct. 18
Indestructable Wife, The (Select), Alice Brady.................Mar. 1
In for Thirty Days (Metro), May Allison........................Jan. 25
In His Brother's Place (Metro), Hale Hamilton..................July 26
In Honor's Web (Vitagraph), Harry T. Morey.....................Nov. 15
In Mizzoura (Paramount-Artcraft), Robert Warwick...............Jan. 25
In the Hollow of Her Hand (Select), Alice Brady................Oct. 25
In Wrong (First National), Jack Pickford.......................Oct. 25
Intrusion of Isabel (American-Pathe), Mary Miles Minter........Apr. 12
Island of Intrigue, The (Metro), May Allison...................Apr. 19
Isles of Conquest, The (Select) Norma Talmadge.................Nov. 8
It Happened in Paris (Tyrad Pictures), Mme. Yorska-W. Lawson Butt.Nov. 22
It Pays to Advertise (Paramount-Artcraft), Bryant Washburn.....Nov. 22
It's a Bear (Triangle), Taylor Holmes..........................Mar. 15

Jacques of the Silver North (Select), Mitchell Lewis...........June 14
Jane Goes A-Wooing (Paramount), Vivian Martin..................Jan. 18
Jinx (Goldwyn), Mabel Normand..................................Dec. 27
John Petticoats (Paramount-Artcraft), William S. Hart..........Nov. 15
Johnny-Get-Your-Gun (Artcraft), Fred Stone.....................Nov. 29
Joselyn's Wife (Robertson-Cole), Bessie Barriscale.............Mar. 1
Joyous Liar, A (Brunton-Hodkinson), J. Warren Kerrigan.........May 17
Jubilo (Goldwyn), Will Rogers..................................Dec. 20
Jungle Trail, The (Fox), William Farnum........................Apr. 26
Just Squaw (Robertson-Cole), Beatriz Machelena.................May 10

Kathleen Mavourneen (Fox), Theda Bara..........................Sept. 6
Khavah (Zion Films), Alice Hastings............................May 24
Kiddies in the Ruins, The (Cosmofotofilm), Special Cast........May 17
Kitty Kelly, M. D. (Robertson-Cole), Bessie Barriscale.........Oct. 18
Knickerbocker Buckaroo, The (Artcraft), Douglas Fairbanks......June 7

L'Apache (Paramount-Artcraft), Dorothy Dalton..................Dec. 20
La Belle Russe (Fox), Theda Bara...............................Sept. 20
Lady of Red Butte, The (Paramount), Dorothy Dalton.............June 7
Lamb and the Lion, The (Robertson-Cole), Billie Rhodes.........Mar. 22
Lasca (Universal), Frank Mayo..................................Nov. 29
Last of His People, The (Select), Mitchell Lewis...............Dec. 27
Last of the Duanes, The (Fox), William Farnum..................Sept. 27
Law of Men, The (Paramount), Enid Bennett......................Mar. 24
Law of Nature, The (Fischer Prods.), Bessie Kennedy............Jan. 25-Feb. 1
Leave It to Susan (Goldwyn), Madge Kennedy.....................June 7
Life Line, The (Tourneur-Paramount-Artcraft), Special Cast.....Oct. 11
Life's a Funny Proposition (Robertson-Cole), William Desmond...Feb. 22
Light, The (Fox), Theda Bara...................................Jan. 25
Lightning Raider, The (Pathe), Pearl White.....................Mar. 15
Lion and the Mouse, The (Vitagraph), Alice Joyce...............Jan. 4
Lion's Den, The (Metro), Bert Lytell...........................Feb. 22
Little Brother of the Rich, A (Universal), Special Cast........May 31
Little Comrade, The (Paramount), Vivian Martin.............Apr. 26-May 3
Little Diplomat, The (Pathe), Baby Marie Osborne...............May 31
Little Intruder, The (World), Louise Huff......................Apr. 5
Little Miss Hoover (Paramount), Marguerite Clark...............Jan. 4
Little Rowdy, The (Triangle), Hazel Daly.......................Mar. 22
Little White Savage, A (Bluebird), Carmel Myers................Mar. 1
Lone Star Ranger, The (Fox), William Farnum....................Oct. 4
Lone Wolf's Daughter, The (J. Parker Reed, Jr.-Hodkinson),
 Louise Glaum...Dec. 20
Long Arm of Mannister (National Film), Henry B. Walthall.......Nov. 8
Long Lane's Turning, The (Robertson-Cole), Henry B. Walthall...Feb. 22
Loot (Universal) Ora Carew.....................................Sept. 27
Lord and Lady Algy (Goldwyn), Tom Moore........................Oct. 11
Lord Loves the Irish, The (Brunton-Hodkinson), J. Warren Kerrigan.Dec. 27
Lost Battalion, The (W. H. Productions), Special Cast.....July 19-Sept. 20
Lost Money (Fix), Madlaine Traverse............................Dec. 13
Lost Princess, The (Fox), Albert Ray-Elinor Fair...............Nov. 8
Lottery Man, The (Paramount-Artcraft), Wallace Reid............Oct. 25
Louisiana (Paramount), Vivian Martin...........................Aug. 2
Love and the Woman (World), June Elvidge.......................June 28
Love Auction, The (Fox), Virginia Pearson......................Feb. 22
Love Burglar, The (Paramount), Wallace Reid....................Aug. 9
Love Call, The (Robertson-Cole), Billie Rhodes.................May 3
Love Cheat, The (Pathe), June Caprice-Creighton Hale...........Aug. 16
Love Defender, The (World), June Elvidge.......................Mar. 29
Love, Honor and ? (Miller-Hallmark), Stuart Holmes-Ellen Cassidy.Oct. 18
Love Hunger, The (Hodkinson), Lillian Walker...................Mar. 8
Love in a Hurry (World) Carlyle Blackwell-Evelyn Greeley.......Jan. 11
Love Is Love (Fox), Albert Ray-Elinor Fair.....................Aug. 23
Love That Dares, The (Fox), Madlaine Traverse..................May 23
Love's Prisoner (Triangle), Olive Thomas.......................June 7
Luck and Pluck (Fox), George Walsh.............................Feb. 15
Lure of Ambition (Fox), Theda Bara.............................Nov. 22
Lyons Mail, The (Triangle), H. B. Irving.......................Aug. 2
Made in America (Hodkinson), Special Cast......................Mar. 1
Maggie Pepper (Paramount-Artcraft), Ethel Clayton..............Feb. 22
Male and Female (Paramount-Artcraft), Special Cast.............Dec. 6
Man and His Money, A (Goldwyn), Tom Moore......................Apr. 26
Man Beneath, The (Robertson-Cole), Sessue Hayakawa.............July 5

SUN-LIGHT ARC
THIS IS IT →

"The Light That Never Fails"

Sun-light Arc can be used for General Flood Lighting, for Spot Lighting, or Several Spots, for Wonderful Effect Lighting.

Always there when needed.

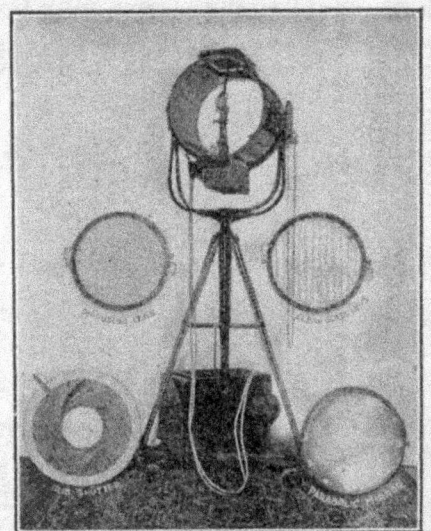

SUN-LIGHT ARC LAMPS
CAN BE BOUGHT
OR
RENTED BY DAY, WEEK OR YEAR

SUN-LIGHT ARC CORPORATION
218 West 48th Street, N. Y. C., U. S. A.

J. JUSTICE HARMER, President

BRANCH OFFICES

1735 Highland Ave., Hollywood, Cal.
FRANK ELLIOTT, Manager

ADOLPHE OSSO

Representative for France, Italy Belgium and Switzerland

416 rue St. Honore, Paris (8e)
Tel. Central 08-50

WILLIAM SANDOZ
Brazil

FOREIGN MARKET

Man Hunter, The (Fox), William Farnum..................................Mar. 8
Man in the Open, A (United), Dustin Farnum..............................Feb. 15
Man of Honor, A (Screen Classics), Harold Lockwood......................Apr. 26
Man Who Stayed at Home (Screen Classics-Metro), King Baggott-
  Claire Whitney...June 28
Mandarin's Gold (World), Kitty Gordon....................................Feb. 8
Man's Country, A (Robertson-Cole), Alma Rubens...........................July 12
Man's Desire (Robertson-Cole), Lewis S. Stone............................July 19
Man's Fight, A (United), Dustin Farnum...................................Aug. 2
Man Who Won, The (Vitagraph), Harry T. Morey.............................Aug. 23
Man Who Turned White, The (Robertson-Cole), H. B. Warner.......May 17-24
Marie, Ltd. (Select), Alice Brady..Apr. 5
Marked Men (Universal), Harry Carey......................................Dec. 27
Market of Souls, The (Ince-Paramount-Artcraft), Dorothy Dalton...........Sept. 20
Marriage for Convenience, A (Keeney-Sherry), Catherine Calvert...........Mar. 8
Marriage Price, The (Artcraft), Elsie Ferguson...........................Apr. 19
Married in Haste (Fox), Albert Ray-Elinor Fair...........................Apr. 19
Mary Regan (First National), Anita Stewart...............................May 17
Master Man, The (Pathe), Frank Keenan....................................May 17
Master of Men (Harma Productions), Mary Pettingay.......................Apr. 12
Mayor of Filbert, The (Triangle), Jack Richardson........................May 24
Me and Capt. Kidd (World), Evelyn Greeley................................Nov. 15
Men, Women and Money (Paramount), Ethel Clayton..........................July 5
Merry Go Round, The (Metro), (Fox), Viola Dana...........................Sept. 27
Microbe, The (Metro), Viola Dana...Aug. 2
Midnight Patrol, The (Thomas Ince-Select), Special Cast............Feb. 15-22
Midnight Romance, A (First National), Anita Stewart......................Jan. 11
Midnight Stage, The (Pathe), Frank Keenan................................Apr. 12
Millionaire Pirate, The (Bluebird), Monroe Salisbury.....................Feb. 15
Mind the Paint Girl (First National), Anita Stewart......................Dec. 6
Miracle Man, The (Paramount-Artcraft), Special Cast......................Sept. 6
Misfit Earl, A (Betzwood-Goldwyn), Louis Bennison........................Nov. 22
Misleading Widow, The (Paramount-Artcraft), Billie Burke.................Sept. 13
Miss Adventure (Fox), Peggy Hyland.......................................May 10
Miss Dulcie from Dixie (Vitagraph), Gladys Leslie........................Mar. 22
Modern Husbands (Robertson-Cole), Henry B. Walthall......................June 7
Molly of the Follies (American-Pathe), Margarita Fischer.................Feb. 15
Money Corral, The (Artcraft), William S. Hart............................May 3
Moonshine Trial, The (Blackton-Pathe), Sylvia Breamer....................Nov. 1
Moral Deadline, The (World), June Elvidge................................Feb. 22
More Deadly Than the Male (Paramount-Artcraft), Ethel Clayton............Feb. 20
Mother and the Law, The (D. W. Griffith), Mae Marsh-Robert Harron.......Aug. 30
Mrs. Wiggs of the Cabbage Patch (Paramount), Marguerite Clark............Mar. 1
My Husband's Other Wife (Blackton-Pathe), Breamer-Gordon.................Dec. 27
My Little Sister (Fox), Evelyn Nesbit....................................June 28
Mystery of the Yellow Room, The (Realart), Special Cast..................Nov. 4
Nature Girl, The (Bluebird), Violet Mersereau............................Jan. 4
Never Say Quit (Fox), George Walsh.......................................Mar. 29
New Moon, The (Select), Norma Talmadge...................................May 24
Nugget Nell (Paramount), Dorothy Gish....................................Aug. 9
Oh! Boy (Capellani-Pathe), June Caprice..................................June 21
Oh, Johnny (Goldwyn), Louis Bennison.....................................Feb. 1
Old Maid's Baby, The (Pathe), Baby Marie Osborne.........................Feb. 15
One of the Finest (Goldwyn), Tom Moore...................................June 14
One-Thing-at-Time-O'Day (Metro), Bert Lytell.............................July 5
One Week of Life (Goldwyn), Pauline Frederick............................May 31
Open Door, The (Robertson-Cole), John P. Wade-Same Ryan..................Oct. 25
Open Your Eyes (Warner Brothers), Special Cast...........................July 12
Other Man's Wife, The (Frank Hall-Hallmark), Stuart Holmes...............Aug. 23
Other Men's Wives (Ince-Paramount), Dorothy Dalton.......................June 21
Our Better Selves (Pathe), Fannie Ward...................................July 19

Out of Luck (Paramount), Dorothy Gish....................................Sept. 6
Out of the Fog (Nazimova-Metro), Nazimova................................Feb. 15
Out of the Shadow (Paramount), Pauline Frederick.........................Jan. 25
Outcasts of Poker Flat, The (Universal), Harry Carey.....................June 28
Over the Garden Wall (Vitagraph), Bessie Love............................Sept. 27

Pagan God, The (Robertson-Cole), H. B. Warner............................Aug. 16
Paid in Advance (Jewel-Universal), Dorothy Phillips......................July 12
Paid in Full (Paramount), Pauline Frederick..............................Mar. 8
Parisian Tigress, The (Metro), Viola Dana................................Apr. 12
Peace of Roaring River, The (Goldwyn), May Allison.......................Aug. 23
Peggy Does Her Darndest (Metro), May Allison.............................Mar. 1
Peppy Polly (Paramount), Dorothy Gish....................................Apr. 19
Perfect Lover, The (Selznick), Eugene O'Brien............................Sept. 20
Pest, The (Goldwyn), Mabel Normand.......................................May 3
Petal on the Current, A (Universal), Mary MacLaren.......................Aug. 9
Petigrew's Girl (Paramount), Ethel Clayton...............................Apr. 19
Phantom Honeymoon (Hallmark), Marguerite Marsh-Vernon Steel..............Oct. 25
Phil for Short (World), Evelyn Greeley...................................June 7
Place in the Sun, A (Triangle), Special Cast.............................May 10
Playthings of Passion (United), Kitty Gordon.............................June
Please Get Married (Metro), Viola Dana...................................Oct. 25
Pitfalls of a Big City (Fox), Gladys Brockwell...........................Apr. 19
Pointing Finger, The (Universal), Mary MacLaren..........................Dec. 13
Poison Pen, The (World), June Elvidge....................................Nov. 22
Poor Boob, The (Paramount), Bryant Washburn..............................Apr. 5
Poor Relations (Robertson-Cole), Florence Vidor..........................Nov. 1
Poor Rich Man, The (Metro), Bushman-Bayne................................Jan. 4
Poppy Girl's Husband, The (Artcraft), William S. Hart....................Apr. 5
Praise Agent, The (World), Arthur Ashley-Dorothy Green...................Aug. 16
Pretty Smooth (Universal), Priscilla Dean................................May 31-June 7
Prince of Innocence, The (Buffalo M. P. Corp.), Stella K. Talbot.........May 3
Probation Wife, The (Jesse Hampton-Pathe), William Desmond...............Dec. 20
Prodigal Liar, The (Robertson-Cole), William Desmond.....................Mar. 22
Profiteers, The (Pathe), Fannie Ward.....................................June 28
Prudence on Broadway (Triangle), Olive Thomas............................July 12
Puppy Love (Paramount), Lila Lee...Mar. 29
Put Up Your Hands (American-Pathe), Margarita Fischer....................Mar. 15
Putting One Over (Fox), George Walsh.....................................July 12
Quickening Flame, The (World), Montagu Love-June Elvidge.................Apr. 26

Rebellious Bride, The (Fox), Peggy Hyland................................Mar. 22
Red Lantern, The (Nazimova-Metro), Nazimova..............................May 10
Red Viper, The (Tyrad Pictures), Special Cast............................Sept. 6
Redhead (Select), Alice Brady..May 31
Regular Fellow, A (Triangle), Taylor Holmes..............................Apr. 19
Regular Girl, A (Selznick-Select), Elsie Janis...........................Nov. 29
Rescuing Angel, The (Paramount), Shirley Mason...........................Apr. 26
Restless Souls (Triangle), Alma Rubens-Jack Conway.......................May 3-Apr. 5
Rider of the Law (Universal), Harry Carey................................Oct. 25
Riders of Vengeance (Universal), Harry Carey.............................May 31
Right to Happiness, The (Jewel-Universal), Dorothy Phillips..............Aug. 30
Right to Lie, The (Pathe), Dolores Cassinelli............................Nov. 22
Road Called Straight, The (Betzwood-Goldwyn), Louis Bennison.............May 10
Roaring Road, The (Paramount), Wallace Reid..............................Apr. 16
Rogue's Romance, A (Vitagraph), Earle Williams...........................May 31
Romance and Arabella (Select), Constance Talmadge........................Feb. 15
Romance of Happy Valley, A (Artcraft), D. W. Griffith....................Feb. 8
Romany Lass (Harma Productions), Special Cast............................Apr. 19
Roped (Universal), Harry Carey...Jan. 4
Rose of the West (Fox), Madelaine Traverse...............................July 26
Rothapfel's First Unit Program (Hallmark), Special Cast..................May 1
Rough Neck, The (World), Montagu Love....................................May 24
Rough Riding Romance (Fox), Tom Mix......................................Aug. 9

STUDIO DIRECTORY

Rustling a Bride (Paramount), Lila Lee................May 24

Sacred Flame (Schomer-Ross), Emily Stevens....................Nov. 8
Sacred Silence (Fox), William Russell........................Oct. 25
Sage Brush Hamlet, A (Robertson-Cole), William Desmond........Aug. 9
Sahara (Hodkinson), Louise Glaum..............................July 12
Sandy Burk of the U-Bar-U (Goldwyn), Louis Bennison...........Feb. 1
Satan Junior (Metro), Viola Dana..............................Mar. 15
Sawdust Doll, The (Pathe), Baby Marie Osborne.................Apr. 5
Scarlet Days (Griffith-Paramount-Artcraft), Special Cast......Nov. 22
Scarlet Shadow, The (Universal), Mae Murray...................Mar. 1-15
Scarlet Trail, The (B. S. Moss), Special Cast.................Jan. 4
Scream in the Night, A (Select), Fritzi Brunette..............Oct. 25
Sealed Envelope, The (Bluebird), Fritzi Brunette..............Mar. 8
Sealed Hearts (Selznick-Select), Eugene O'Brien...............Nov. 15
Secret Garden, The (Paramount), Lila Lee......................Jan. 25
Secret Service (Paramount-Artcraft), Robert Warwick...........July 6
Shadows (Goldwyn), Geraldine Farrar...........................Mar. 1
Shadows of Suspicion (Screen Classics), Harold Lockwood.......Feb. 15-Mar. 1
She Wolf, The (Frohman), Texas Guinan.........................June 14-21
Sheriff's Son, The (Paramount), Charles Ray...................Apr. 12
Should a Husband Forgive? (Fox), Miriam Cooper................Nov. 1
Silent Strength (Vitagraph), Harry T. Morey...................Feb. 15
Silk Lined Burglar, The (Universal), Priscilla Dean...........Apr. 5-Mar. 22
Silver Girl, The (Pathe), Frank Keenan........................Jan. 18
Silver King, The (Paramount-Artcraft), William Faversham......May 17
Siren's Son, The (Fox), Theda Bara............................Sept. 15
Six Hopkins (Goldwyn), Mabel Normand..........................Nov. 1
Six Feet Four (American-Pathe), William Russell...............June 7-14
Sleeping Lion, The (Universal), Monroe Salisbury..............
Smiles (Fox), Jane and Katherine Lee..........................Oct. 18
Snares of Paris (Fox), Madlaine Traverse......................June 21
Sneak, The (Fox), Gladys Brockwell............................Aug. 30
Society Exile, A (Paramount-Artcraft), Elsie Ferguson.........Nov. 22
Soldiers of Fortune (Realart), Special Cast...................July 12
Solitary Sin, The (Solitary Sin Corp.-State Rights), Special Cast..June 21
Some Bride (Metro), Viola Dana................................May 17
Some Liar (American-Pathe), William Russell...................Oct.
Someone Must Pay (Abramson-Graphic), Gail Kane................May 10
Something to Do (Paramount), Bryant Washburn..................June 21
Spark Divine, The (Vitagraph), Alice Joyce....................Oct. 4
Speed Maniac, The (Fox), Tom Mix..............................Apr. 19
Speedy Meade (Goldwyn), Louis Bennison........................Jan. 4
Spender, The (Metro), Bert Lytell.............................July 25
Spite Bride, The (Selznick-Select), Olive Thomas..............Sept.
Spitfire of Seville, The (Universal), Hedda Nova..............June 28
Splendid Sin, The (Fox), Madlaine Traverse....................July 26
Sporting Chance, A (American-Pathe), Ethel Clayton............May
Sporting Chance, A (Paramount), Ethel Clayton.................June 28
Spotlight Sadie (Goldwyn), Mae Marsh..........................Dec.
Square Deal Sanderson (Artcraft), William S. Hart.............Oct. 4
Stepping Out (Paramount-Artcraft), Enid Bennett...............May 3
Stitch in Time, A (Vitagraph), Gladys Leslie..................Nov. 1
Stream of Life, The (Plymouth Film Corp.), Special Cast.......Oct. 13
Strictly Confidential (Goldwyn), Madge Kennedy................Sept. 13
Stripped for a Million (Victor Kremer), Crane Wilbur..........May 10
Stronger Vow, The (Goldwyn), Geraldine Farrar.................Feb. 22
Sue of the South (Bluebird), Edith Roberts....................Sept. 20
Sundown Trail, The (Universal), Monroe Salisbury..............Jan. 11
Suspicion (M. H. Hoffman-State Rights), Grace Davidson........

Tangled Threads (Robertson-Cole), Bessie Barriscale...........June 14
Taste of Life, A (Bluebird), Edith Roberts....................Mar. 15

Taxi (Triangle), Taylor Holmes................................May 17
Teeth of the Tiger (Paramount-Artcraft), Special Cast.........Dec. 20
Temperamental Wife, A (First National), Constance Talmadge....Sept. 27
Test of Honor, The (Paramount), John Barrymore................Apr. 5
That's Good (Metro), Hale Hamilton............................Nov. 8
Thieves (Fox), Gladys Brockwell...............................May 24
Thin Ice (Vitagraph), Corinne Griffith........................May 17
Third Degree, The (Vitagraph), Alice Joyce....................Sept. 27
Third Kiss, The (Paramount-Artcraft), Vivian Martin...........Aug. 23
Thirteenth Chair, The (Pathe), Yvonne Delva-Creighton Hale....Aug.
Thou Shalt Not (Fox), Evelyn Nesbit...........................Apr. 5
Three Black Eyes (Triangle), Taylor Holmes....................Sept.
Three Green Eyes (World), Carlyle Blackwell-Evelyn Greeley-Montagu Love....Apr. 26
Through the Wrong Door (Goldwyn), Madge Kennedy...............Aug. 2
Thunderbolt, The (First National), Katherine MacDonald........Aug. 2
Thunderbolts of Fate (Edward Warren-Hodkinson), House Peters-Anna Lehr......Apr. 19
Tiger Lily, The (American-Pathe), Margarita Fisher............July 26
Toby's Bow (Goldwyn), Tom Moore...............................Dec. 27
Todd of the Times (Pathe), Frank Keenan.......................Feb. 1
Told in the Hills (Paramount-Artcraft), Robert Warwick........Sept. 20
Tong Man, The (Haworth-Robertson-Cole), Sessue Hayakawa.......Dec. 20
Too Many Crooks (Vitagraph), Gladys Leslie....................June 14
Toton (Triangle), Olive Thomas................................Mar. 29
Trap, The (Universal), Olive Tell.............................Aug. 30
Trembling Hour, The (Universal), Special Cast.................Nov. 1
Trick of Fate, A (Robertson-Cole), Bessie Barriscale..........Mar. 1
Trixie From Broadway (American-Pathe), Margarita Fisher.......June 14
True Heart Susie (Griffith-Artcraft), Lillian Gish............Mar. 29
Turn in the Road, The (Robertson-Cole), Special Cast..........Mar. 15
Turning the Tables (Paramount-Artcraft), Dorothy Gish.........Nov.
23½ Hours Leave (Paramount-Artcraft), Douglas MacLean-Doris May.....May 8
Twilight (De Luxe), Doris Kenyon..............................Oct. 11
Twin Pawns (Pathe), Mae Murray................................
Two Brides, The (Paramount), Lina Cavalieri...................Mar. 1-15

Unbroken Promise, The (Triangle), Jane Miller.................July 26
Under Suspicion (Universal), Ora Carew-Forrest Stanley........Nov. 22
Under the Top (Artcraft), Fred Stone..........................Jan. 18
Undercurrent, The (Select), Guy Empey.........................Nov. 29
Unknown Love, The (Pathe), Dolores Cassinelli-E. K. Lincoln...Apr. 19
Unknown Quantity, The (Vitagraph), Corinne Griffith...........Apr. 12
Unpainted Woman, The (Universal), Mary MacLaren...............May 10-17
Unpardonable Sin, The (Garson-Neilan), Blanche Sweet..........May 17
Unveiling Hand, The (World), Kitty Gordon.....................Mar. 8
Unwritten Code, The (Metro), May Allison......................May 17
Uplifters, The (Metro), Taylor Holmes.........................July 12
Upside Down (Triangle), Taylor Holmes.........................June 28
Upstairs (Goldwyn), Mabel Normand.............................Aug. 30
Upstairs and Down (Selznick), Olive Thomas....................June 21
Usurper, The (Vitagraph), Earle Williams......................Apr. 26

Vagabond Luck (Fox), Albert Ray-Elinor Fair...................Nov. 29
Vagabond of France, A (Pathe), Henri Krauss...................Jan. 18
Valley of the Giants, The (Paramount-Artcraft), Wallace Reid..Sept. 13
Veiled Adventure, The (Select), Constance Talmadge............May 24
Vengeance of Durand, The (Vitagraph), Alice Joyce.............Nov. 16
Venus in the East (Paramount-Artcraft), Bryant Washburn.......Feb. 8
Victory (Paramount-Artcraft), Special Cast....................Dec. 6
Virtuous Men (S-L Pictures), E. K. Lincoln....................Apr. 19-26
Virtuous Model, The (Pathe), Dolores Cassinelli...............Sept. 27

376 STUDIO DIRECTORY

Virtuous Sinners (Pioneer), Wanda Hawley-Norman Kerry....May 24
Virtuous Thief, The (Ince-Paramount), Enid Bennett....Sept. 20
Virtuous Vamp, A (First National), Constance Talmadge....Nov. 29
Virtuous Wives (First National), Anita Stewart....Jan. 11
Volcano, The (Raver-Hodkinson), Leah Baird....Aug. 23

Wit Wins (Burton King-Hallmark), Florence Billings-Hugh Thompson Oct. 11
Witness for the Defense (Paramount-Artcraft), Elsie Ferguson....Sept. 27
Wolf, The (Vitagraph), Earle Williams....Aug. 16
Wolves of the Night (Fox), William Farnum....Aug. 9
Woman He Chose, The (Mickey Film Corp., Chicago, State Rights), Special Cast....Nov. 22
Woman Michael Married (Robertson-Cole), Bessie Barriscale....Aug. 2
Woman Next Door, The (Paramount), Ethel Clayton....May 31
Woman of Lies, A (World), June Elvidge....Oct. 25
Woman of Pleasure, A (Hampton-Pathe), Blanche Sweet....Nov. 22
Woman on the Index, The (Goldwyn), Pauline Frederick....Apr. 25
Woman There Was, A (Fox), Theda Bara....June 14
Woman Thou Gavest Me (Paramount-Artcraft), Special Cast....June 21
Woman Under Cover, The (Universal), Fritzi Brunette....Sept. 13
Woman Under Oath, The (United), Florence Reed....June 28
Woman, Woman (Fox), Evelyn Nesbit....Feb. 8
Words and Music By (Fox), Albert Ray-Elinor Fair....May 31-June 7
World Aflame, The (Pathe), Frank Keenan....Aug. 2
World and His Woman, The (Goldwyn), Geraldine Farrar....Sept. 13
World to Live In, The (Select), Alice Brady....Mar. 8
Wagon Tracks (Artcraft), William S. Hart....Aug. 23
Wanted, a Husband (Paramount-Artcraft), Billie Burke....Dec. 27
Wanted for Murder (Harry Rapf Prods.-Film Clearing House), Elaine Hammerstein....Feb. 8

Way of a Man with a Maid, The (Paramount), Bryant Washburn....Jan. 11
Way of a Woman, The (Select), Norma Talmadge....Aug. 29
Way of the Strong, The (Metro), Anna Q. Nilsson....Mar. 29
Web of Chance, The (Fox), Peggy Hyland....Dec. 27
Westerners, The (B. B. Hampton-Hodkinson), Special Cast....Aug. 16
What Am I Bid? (Universal), Mae Murray....Apr. 5

What Every Woman Learns (Paramount-Artcraft), Enid Bennett....Nov. 1
What Every Woman Wants (Robertson-Cole), Grace Darmond....Mar. 8
What Love Forgives (World), Barbara Castleton-Johnny Hines....Jan. 4
What's Your Husband Doing? (Ince-Paramount-Artcraft), Douglas MacLean-Doris May....Nov. 22
When a Girl Loves (Jewel-Universal), Mildred Harris....Mar. 29
When a Man Rides Alone (American), William Russell....Jan. 4-11
When Bearcat Went Dry (World), Special Cast....Oct. 25
When Fate Decides (Fox), Madlaine Traverse....June 7
When Men Desire (Fox), Theda Bara....Mar. 22
When My Ship Comes In (Independent Sales), Jane Grey....Apr. 5
Where Bonds Are Loosed (Waldorf Photo Plays), Special Cast....Aug. 9
Where the West Begins (American Pathe), William Russell....Mar. 1
White Heather, The (Maurice Tourneur-Hiller and Wilke), Special Cast.May 17
Whitewashed Walls (Robertson-Cole), William Desmond....Apr. 12
Who Cares? (Select), Constance Talmadge....Jan. 25
Who Will Marry Me? (Bluebird), Carmel Myers....Feb. 1-8
Who's Your Brother? (Curtiss Pictures Corporation), Special Cast....Nov.
Why Germany Must Pay (Screen Classics), Creighton Hale-Helen Ferguson....Jan. 25
Why Smith Left Home (Paramount-Artcraft), Bryant Washburn....Oct. 25
Wicked Darling, The (Universal), Priscilla Dean....Feb. 8-22
Widow By Proxy (Paramount-Artcraft), Marguerite Clark....Oct. 4
Wife or Country (Triangle) Harry Mestayer-Gretchen Lederer....Jan. 4-11
Wilderness Trail, The (Fox), Tom Mix....July 19
Winchester Woman, The (Vitagraph), Alice Joyce....Nov.
Wings of the Morning (Fox), William Farnum....Dec. 6
Winning Girl, The (Paramount), Shirley Mason....Mar. 22
Winning Stroke, The (Fox), George Walsh....Oct. 11
Wishing Ring Man, The (Vitagraph), Bessie Love....Mar. 8

Yankee Doodle in Berlin (Lesser-Sennett), Special Cast....July 12
Yankee Princess, A (Vitagraph), Bessie Love....Apr. 19
You Never Know Your Luck (World), House Peters....Nov. 29
You're Fired (Paramount), Wallace Reid....June 28-July 5

Yvonne from Paris (American-Pathe), Mary Miles Minter....July 12

¶ For latest up-to-date news of Releases, Reviews, and Exploitation Aid

READ

MOTION PICTURE NEWS—

IT COVERS THE FIELD

Kathleen Kirkham

Leads and Heavies with

DOUGLAS FAIRBANKS
FRANK KEENAN
LEW CODY
KATHARINE MACDONALD

UNIVERSAL, MOROSCO,
CLUNE, ETC.

Representatives:
Willis & Inglis
Los Angeles

HENRY MORTIMER

LEADING MAN

CURRENT RELEASES

"The Road Called Straight"
Betzwood Film Co.

"His Wife's Friend"
Thos. H. Ince Co.

"The Fear Market"
Realart Co.

Mary MacLaren

Yours sincerely, Frank Losee

Beatrice Burnham

Leads

Peggy O'Dare

Universal Leading Woman...

CHARLES K. FRENCH
Character Leads and Heavies

LATE PICTURES:

"Stronger Than Death"
from Book,
"Hermit Doctor of Gaya"
with Nazimova *(Metro)*

"Jubilo," with Will Rogers
(Goldwyn)

"What Would You Do?"
with Madlaine Traverse *(Fox)*

"Flames of the Flesh" and
"The White Lie"
with Gladys Brockwell *(Fox)*

2217 Ewing St., Los Angeles.
Phone: Wil. 2847

JAMES FARLEY

Heavy Leads and Heavies
with

Gale Kane
Mme. Yorska
Dorothy Gish
Kathlyn Williams
Dorothy Phillips
Constance Talmadge
Vivian Martin and others

Business Address:

c/o Mabel Condon Exchange
Hollywood

Helen Ferguson

Margaret Linden

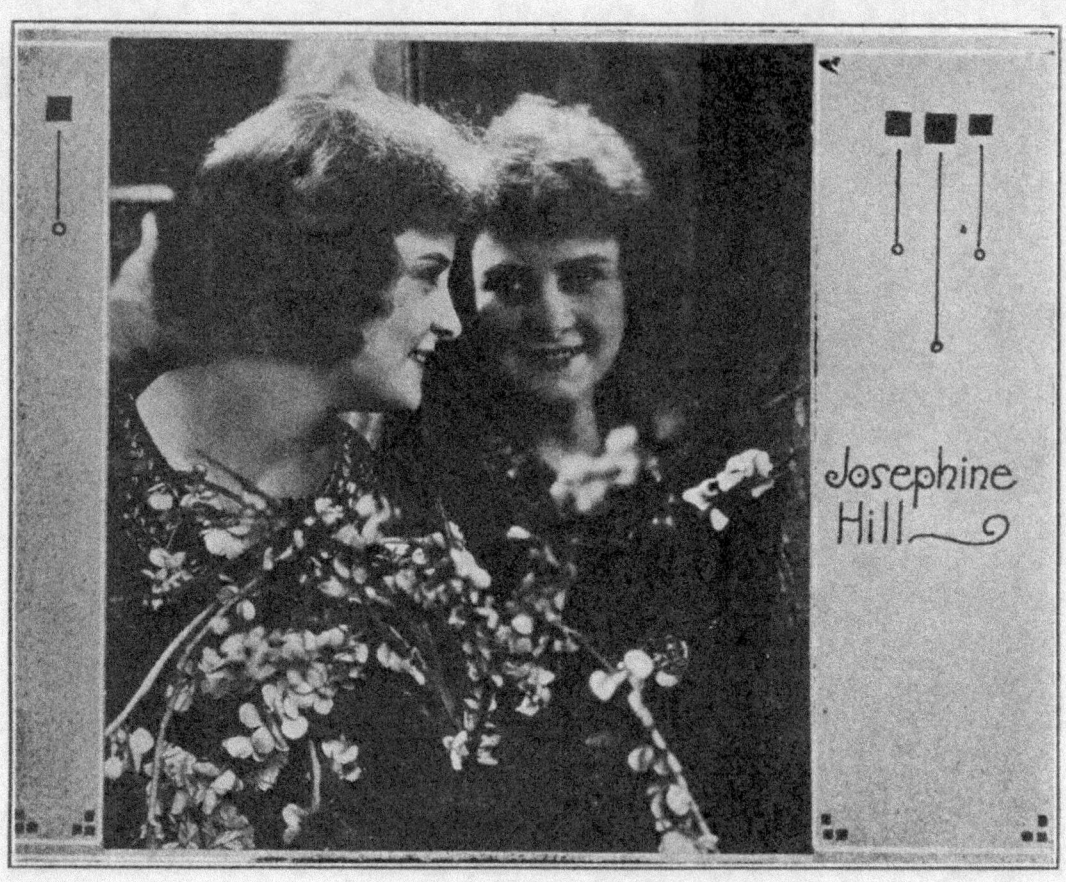

Josephine Hill

Neva Gerber

Co-Starring in the Ben Wilson Productions

Webster Cullison

Producer

The greatest feature serial ever made -
"The Lost City -"

Leon de LaMothe

directing

THE BIG WESTERN SERIAL DRAMA
—o—
"THE VANISHING TRAILS"
for

The Selig Polyscope Company

Best wishes to all of my old friends and — I still remain — the same old "Kent" —

"HOOT" GIBSON

Universal Western Star

Current Releases:

- "The Crow"
- "Runnin' Straight"
- "The Sheriff's Oath"
- "Winning a Home"
- "The Lone Hand"
- "Trail of the Holdup Man"
- "Double Holdup"
- "Roarin' Dan"
- "The Voice on the Wire"
- "Harmony Ranch"
- "Shameless Salvason"

Winner of Gold Belt Pendleton, Oregon, 1912, at age of 19, for the best all around cowboy in this world.

WALTER HIERS

The Fat Juvenile

"It Pays to Advertise"—Bryant Washburn
"What's Your Husband Doing?"—MacLean & May
"Going Some"—Rex Beach Story
"The Turning Point"—Katherine MacDonald
"Mrs. Temple's Telegram"—Bryant Washburn
"Hard Boiled"—Dorothy Dalton
"Bill Henry"—Charles Ray
"When Doctors Disagree"—Mabel Normand
"The Fear Woman"—Pauline Frederick
"Spotlight Sadie"—Mae Marsh
"Our Little Wife"—Madge Kennedy
"An Experimental Marriage"—Constance Talmadge
"Seventeen"—Jack Pickford
"Mysterious Miss Terry"—Billie Burke
"A Man's World"—Emily Stevens
"The End of the Tour"—Lionel Barrymore
"God's Man"—H. B. Warner

Now under long term contract with Famous Players-Lasky Corp.

Address:
Lasky Studios, Hollywood, Calif.

MAY McAVOY

*Management of
Edward Small*

"Perfect Lady," Goldwyn

"Mrs. Wiggs of the Cabbage Patch," Famous

"Hit or Miss," World

"Love Wins," H. & H.

"My Husband's Other Wife," Blackton

"Sporting Duchess," Vitagraph

FREDERIC STARR

Heavies
"The Desert of Wheat"
Zane Grey Story
Produced by B. B. Hampton

"The Poppy Girl's Husband"
Wm. S. Hart Production

Playing the Heavy
in
Jack Dempsey Serial
now in production

CLARA HORTON

Starred in
"The Girl from the Outside"
Rex Beach Story

RECENT PRODUCTIONS:

"Every Woman"—*Lasky*
"The Little Shepherd of Kingdom Come"—*Goldwyn*

GLADYS HULETTE

MANAGEMENT
EDWARD SMALL

Riley Hatch

MANAGEMENT OF EDWARD SMALL

J. Herbert Frank

MANAGEMENT EDWARD SMALL

O'CONNOR

MARY

Famous Players-Lasky Corp.

Editor

of

Scenarios and Films

LOYOLA

Characters

CURRENT RELEASES:

"True Heart Susie"—*Griffith*
"Tree of Knowledge"—*W. C. deMille*
"Why Change Your Wife"—*C. B. deMille*
"The Love Burglar"—*Paramount-Artcraft*

7002 Hawthorne Avenue, Hollywood, Calif.   Phone: 577927

EDDIE POLO

Serial Leads with Universal

FIRST 1920 PRODUCTION

"THE VANISHING DAGGER"

Serial in 18 Episodes

PELL TRENTON

CURRENT RELEASES:

"THE UPLIFTERS"
May Allison—Metro

"FAIR AND WARMER"
May Allison—Metro

"THE WILLOW TREE"
Viola Dana—Metro

"THE BETTER PROFIT"
Edith Storey

"CRESSY"
Blanche Sweet

Jack Gilbert

"The White Heather"
"Heart o' the Hills"
"Ladies Must Live"
"The Glory of Love"

Under Contract to

Maurice Tourneur

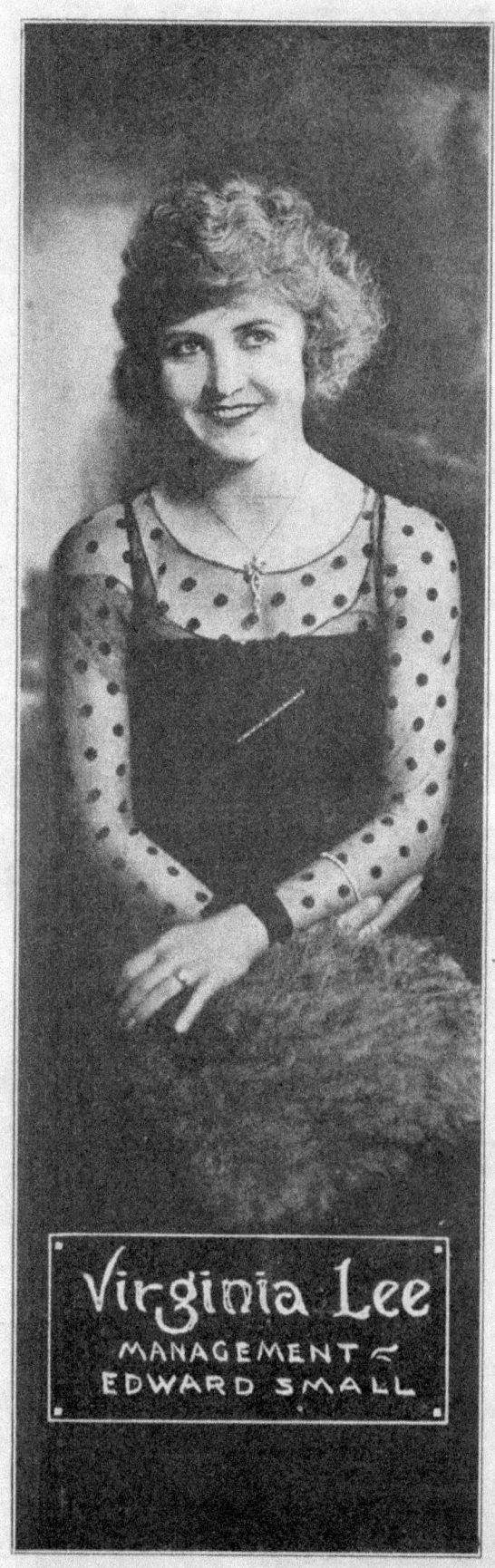

Norman Kerry

in

Alan Dwan Feature Productions.

Lenore Lynard

Alvarado Apartments
Phone Wil. 5010.

Art Acord

Featured Western Leads

ROY STEWART

Star of

"The Westerner"
Stuart Edward White

"Desert of Wheat"
Zane Grey

"The Sage Brusher"
Emerson Hough

"Just a Wife"
Eugene Walters

Ruth Stonehouse

Appearing in "THE HOPE"

Directed by Herbert Blache
Metro Production

Joseph Anthony Roach

Scenarios
Originals and Continuity
for
William Fox Productions

Pearl Shepard

Management - Edward Small

Ivo Dawson

Management - Edward Small

Jack Made A Hit With Royalty

FILM UPSETS ROYAL DIGNITY

Prince of Wales Slaps Thighs Over Comedy at Academy of Music in New York

By Universal Service
NEW YORK, Nov. 19.—Edward Albert, Prince of Wales, smiled his way

JACK COOPER
Featured

Money Talks
Virtuous Husbands
Merry Jail Birds
Big Yellow Dog Catcher
His Footlight Maids
The School House Scandal
Hungry Lions and Tender Hearts
The Heart Snatchers
The Light Weight Lover

FOX SUNSHINE COMEDIES

Supervision
HAMPTON DEL RUTH

Raymond McKee
MANAGEMENT OF EDWARD SMALL

George Howard

MANAGEMENT OF EDWARD SMALL

WM. HORSLEY FILM LABORATORIES

Capacity 300,000 feet weekly

Equipment: Bell & Howell, Printers and Perforators, William Horsley Sprocket Movement Printers, Three Powers 6-B Projectors, polishers, Bell & Howell Patchers, Separate positive and negative developing rooms, private projection rooms for editors and theatres for reviewers, and other conveniences not found at other laboratories.

Accommodations for producing companies include magazine refilling dark rooms, cameraman's editing rooms, inspecting projection room, preview theatre, still photograph studio and laboratory, and other features.

We do negative developing and make prints for Christie Comedies, National, Mr. and Mrs. Carter DeHaven Comedies, Francis Ford Serials, Louis Burston, King Baggot Serials, and list of our other patrons include Mitchell Lewis Company, Frohman Amusement Company, Continental Producing Companies, Gold Star Company and others.

WM. HORSLEY FILM LABORATORIES AND COMMERCIAL STUDIOS

6060 Sunset Blvd.   *Hollywood 3693*   Los Angeles, California

PAULINE TAYLOR

Leads

APEX PICTURES CORP.

INDIANAPOLIS, IND.

Producer of

MAN BEHIND THE CURTAIN
IN ARCADIA
HIS GOLDEN ROMANCE
THE STAR PRINCE

Recent Productions

COUPLE WANTED
WITH ALL IMPROVEMENTS
FURNISHED COMPLETE
IN BAD

COURTLAND J. VAN DEUSEN

Supervising Director

APEX PICTURES CORPORATION
Indianapolis, Ind.

Douglas Gerrard
Producing Universal Special
Attractions and Super Features

Melville W. Brown
Director
Willis & Inglis, Representatives

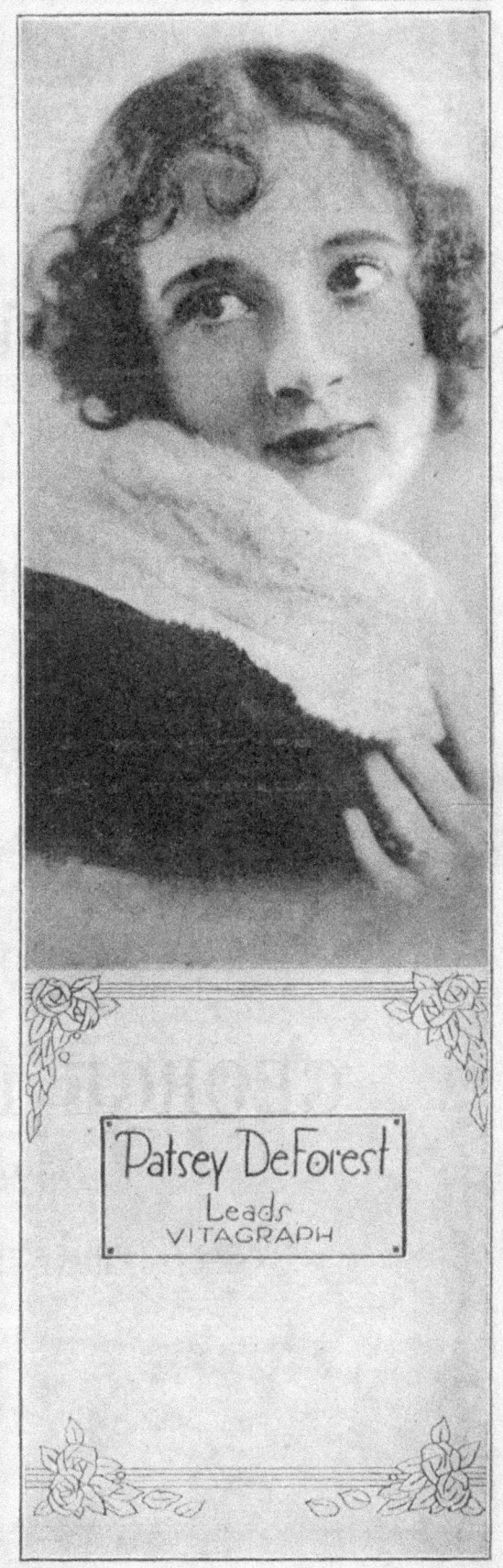

Patsey DeForest
Leads
VITAGRAPH

Frank D. Ormston

Art Director

GASNIER PRODUCTIONS

GEORGE FAWCETT

Director

MANAGEMENT EDWARD SMALL

Colin Campbell
and
"Colin Campbell Directed Pictures"

LATEST	JUST COMPLETED
The Thunderbolt / The Beauty Market — First National The Corsican Brothers with Dustin Farnum	When Dawn Came for Hugh E Dierker Photoplays Co

NOW DIRECTING
Edith Storey in "Moon Madness"

William C. Foster

Member of

American Society of Cinematographers
Hollywood · Calif

PHOTOGRAPHER

of

"The Silver Horde" —— Goldwyn
"Corsican Brothers" —— Dustin Farnum – United
and Special Feature of
Dierker Photo Drama Co.....

Ben Carre —
Art Director
Marshall Neilan Productions.

Charles Parrott
M.P.D.A.

Directing
Mr. & Mrs. Carter DeHaven
PARAMOUNT-ARTCRAFT PICTURES.

Rollin S. Sturgeon
Director
"God's Country and the Woman"
"A Petticoat Pilot"
"Destiny" "Pretty Smooth"
"Sundown Trail"
Current Release:
"Breath of the Gods"

CLAUDE H. MITCHELL
Writing & directing
five-reel features
for Brentwood

JACQUES TYROL

Producer and Director

"Truth"
"The Face in the Crowd"
"The Pendulum"
"The Red Viper"
"Friendship"
"And the Children Pay"
"Broken Hearts"

ADOLF PHILIPP

Director General of

The ADOLF PHILIPP FILM
CORPORATION

Offices and Studios
11 E. 14th St., New York City

Author and Composer of Famous
Broadway Successes

"ALMA, WHERE DO YOU LIVE?"
"ADELE"
"THE MIDNIGHT GIRL"
"AUCTION PINOCHLE"
"TWO IS COMPANY"
"THE GIRL WHO SMILES"
"MIMI" AND OTHER BROADWAY SUCCESSES

NOW PRODUCING MUSICAL FILM COMEDIES
"THE MIDNIGHT GIRL" "OH LOUISE" "MY GIRL SUZANNE"
By ADOLF PHILIPP

BURTON KING

Vice-President

and

Director-General

of the

WISTARIA PRODUCTIONS, Inc.

Edwin L. Hollywood
Director

Fred L. Granville

Now directing
PEGGY HYLAND
for
G. B. SAMUELSON
FILM MFG. CO.

Alexander B. Butler ~

Director

with

G. B. Samuelson ...

Universal City . —

GEORGE LLOYD SARGENT

Feature Director

M. P. D. A.

THE GREEN ROOM CLUB

NEW YORK CITY

ARCHER McMACKIN

Director

Comedies and Comedy Dramas

See These Two SPECIAL Comedies
Now Showing

"NOTHING BUT NERVE"　　**"THIS WAY OUT"**
Flanagan & Edwards　　　　　Gale Henry
National Film Corp'n　　　　　Model Comedy Co.

BERTRAM BRACKEN

Director of the Master Drama

"The Confession"

Now making the stupendous production

"The Mask"

with a series of well-known novels to follow

EDMUND LAWRENCE
Director

Productions with *Virginia Pearson, Theda Bara* and *Mme. Petrova*

Current Releases:

"LURE OF AMBITION"   "THE MERRY-GO-ROUND"
Theda Bara   Peggy Hyland

"LOST MONEY"
Madlaine Traverse

Permanent Address: 274 Rutland Road, Brooklyn, N. Y.

Edward Griffith
DIRECTOR

Management
Edward Small

GEORGE L. COX, *Director*—American Film Co.

Santa Barbara, Cal.

Recent Releases and Coming:

"The Rose of Hell"
"The Week End"
"The Thirteenth Piece of Silver"
"The Hellion"
"Payment Guaranteed"
"The Golden Gift"
"Their Mutual Child"
"The Blue Moon"

Member: Motion Picture Directors Association

Lynn F. Reynolds
M.P.D.A.
Adapted and Directed
"A LITTLE BROTHER OF THE RICH"
"THE BRUTE BREAKER"
"OVERLAND RED"

Jess Robbins
— DIRECTOR —
Los Angeles Athletic Club

Watch 'em go past!!

(William E.)
WING

SERIALS!!

LURE OF THE CIRCUS
Eddie Polo

ELMO THE MIGHTY
Elmo Lincoln

TRAILS OF DOOM
Franklyn Farnum
(in production)

BUT THE OLD PSYCHOLOGY STILL IS WORKING

"VENGEANCE AND THE GIRL" — "PUNCHER AND THE PUP" — "LONESOME" — "TROUBLOUS TRAILS" — "'KID PINK' TRANSMIGRATES"

Just Coming Into the Market

Four new, six-reel features coming up.

Now playing around as editor of the Selig Polyscope Company

CHARLES KENYON

Original Stories

The Fued........Tom Mix
The Devil's Wheel.......
    Gladys Brockwell
The Scarlet Road.......
    Gladys Brockwell
The Bird of Prey.......
    Gladys Brockwell
The Siren Song..Theda Bara
Sacrifice..Margaret Illington
On the Level..Fannie Ward

Adaptations

Dangerous Days...Goldwyn
The Penalty.......Goldwyn
The Light......Theda Bara
Hell Roarin' Reform.....
    Tom Mix
The Last of the Duanes..
    William Farnum
The Lone Star Ranger...
    William Farnum
The Rainbow Trail......
    William Farnum
The Wings of the Morning.
    William Farnum

Author of the following New York Stage Productions:

Kindling ....
    Produced by
    Margaret Illington
Husband and Wife......
    Produced by
    Arthur Hopkins
The Claim.............
    Produced by
    Henry Harris Estate
The Operator..In Vaudeville

At Present With
GOLDWYN....Culver City

EMMETT J. FLYNN

Now Directing

WILLIAM RUSSELL

For

WILLIAM FOX

CURRENT RELEASES:
"Eastward Ho"
"The Lincoln Highwayman"

COMING:
"Shod with Fire"
"The Other Side of Eden"

PAST SUCCESSES:
Alimony—First National Exhibitors
Bondage of Barbara—Mae Marsh
The Racing Strain—Mae Marsh
A Bachelor's Wife—Mary Miles Minter
Yvonne from Paris—Mary Miles Minter

William C. Dowlan

Director

~Metro

KATHRYNE STUART

Scenario Writer

Famous Players-Lasky Eastern Studio

"Erstwhile Susan"
"His Bridal Night"
"Career of Catherine Bush"
"His House in Order"
"Probation Wife"

JUNE MATHIS

Head of Scenario Department

METRO

ADAPTED:

"Out of the Fog."
"Lombardi, Ltd."
"Fair and Warmer."
"Eye for Eye."—Nazimova

~Eliot~ Howe

Director

Frank Keenan
PRODUCTIONS

Address
5408 Hollywood Blvd.
Hollywood, Calif.

~Percy~ Hilburn

Chief Cameraman
Goldwyn

(See Biography)

WILL M. RITCHEY

Photoplaywright

With

Famous Players-Lasky Corporation

Notable Releases of Past Year

Everywoman	Told in the Hills
Pettigrew's Girl	A Sporting Chance
Alias Mike Moran	The Winning Girl
The Dub	Something to Do
The Sea Wolf	Rose o' the River

Arthur J. Zellner   Lois Zellner

THE ZELLNERS

On the Metro Staff
Writing Specials

METRO STUDIOS   ::   Hollywood

LOUIS SHERWIN

Continuity   *Editing*   *Titling*

Assistant to J. G. HAWKS
Supervisor of Production at Goldwyn Studios
Editor of Goldwyn Titles for past year

Eight years dramatic critic, N. Y. Globe. Contributor to American, Metropolitan, Vanity Fair, Smart Set and other magazines.

This Space Is Hopefully Dedicated

By Stephen Fox, The Well Known

Scribe, To Inspire Replies To That

Very Pertinent Question

Should Authors Advertise?

LEWIS ALLEN BROWNE

Writing Originals and Continuities for Selznick Pictures

Author of

"MISS GEORGE WASHINGTON," Marguerite Clark
"THE SOAP GIRL," Gladys Leslie
"GOOD DODD," Walter Hiers
"GAS LOGIC," Mr. and Mrs. Sidney Drew
"SOONER OR LATER," Owen Moore
"THE LAND OF OPPORTUNITY," Ralph Ince
Etc., Etc., Etc.

Co-author

"SPOTLIGHT SADIE," Mae Marsh
"PLEASE GET MARRIED," Viola Dana

Selznick Studio, West Fort Lee, N. J.

J. GRUBB ALEXANDER

Originals   Continuities   Titles

"THE THUNDERBOLT"—Katherine MacDonald's first First National. *The picture that is breaking all house records.*
"THE BEAUTY MARKET"—Katherine MacDonald First National.
"EAST OR WEST"—Carlyle Blackwell Productions.
"THE TRAIL OF THE OCTOPUS"—Frank G. Hall's record-breaking serial with Ben Wilson.

Titles and editing for the Maurice Tourneur successes
"THE LIFE LINE" and "THE BROKEN BUTTERFLY."
"THE COUNTY FAIR"—Maurice Tourneur Productions.

In production:

"THE UNDERTOW"   —Hayakawa Haworth Production.
"THE BLEEDER"   —Hayakawa's next Haworth Production.
"THE BETTER HALF"—Universal Mary MacLaren Special.

Address: Hollywood, California   Phone Holly 3445

WINIFRED DUNN

Author of
"Friendship"
"The Pendulum"
"Too Late"
"Marianna"
"Scratched Locket"
"Charity at Home"
"Truth"
"Wood-witch"
"The Hand"
"Greater Love"
"The Prodigal Daughter"
"The Face in the Crowd"
"Out of the Darkness"
"The Coward"
"The Sinless Child of Sin"
"Peg o' the Sea"
"The Thunderbolt of Fate"
"And the Children Pay"
"The Red Viper"
etc., etc.

(See Biography)

AMEDEE J. VAN BEUREN ENTERPRISES

Palace Theatre Annex
1562 Broadway, New York City

TIMELY FILMS, *Incorporated*
Producing

"TOPICS OF THE DAY"

SELECTED FROM THE PRESS OF THE WORLD BY

The Literary Digest

AyVeeBee Corporation
Producing
PARAMOUNT-ERNEST TRUEX COMEDIES

V. B. K. Film Corporation
Producers of
PARAMOUNT-DREW COMEDIES

Gaudio Brothers
CINEMATOGRAPHERS

Tony
with
Anita Stewart Productions

Gene
with
Bessie Barriscale Features

JACKSON J. ROSE

Frank Sullivan   E. J. Vallejo   F. H. Sturgis

Cinema and Still Photography
—unexcelled—

Photographing Douglas Fairbanks

HARRY THORPE

WILLIAM McGANN

Assistant Richard Holahan

Fairbanks Studios
Hollywood

Announcing

The Buffum Process of Art Title Making

A logical outgrowth of the best art of the industry at large—

—discovered and perfected by the head of one of the best Art Title departments in the business.

AN INVENTION THAT WILL REVOLUTIONIZE THIS GROWINGLY-IMPORTANT BRANCH OF THE INDUSTRY

For Players   For Producers

SERVICE

LICHTIG (HARRY)

MARKHAM BUILDING

Phone 577450

Hollywood, Calif.

REPRESENTING PLAYERS OF NOTE

ENGAGEMENTS   **PUBLICITY**

MEADOW BROOK NURSERIES, INC.
275 Grand Avenue
Englewood, New Jersey

MOTION PICTURE STUDIO DEPARTMENT

Among the more common articles which we supply for studios are

Palms	Cut Flowers
Ferns	Bouquets
Bay Trees	Smilax
Tropical Plants	Boxwood Trees

Our service, however, covers a much wider scope

If the set calls for a garden in flower, growing hedges and trees, paths, walks or driveways, we have the material and the organization to supply you at the shortest possible moment. Our proximity to the Dyckman, Fort Lee, and Forty-second Street ferries assures you getting your goods when you want them.

Our plant being located in the country where land and rents are low, our prices are correspondingly low.

Phone Englewood 1707-1708
We will have what you want

MABEL CONDON   M. E. M. GIBSONE

The Mabel Condon Exchange

Hollywood, Calif.

CASTING	BOOKS	PUBLICITY
Directors	Plays	Continuities
Leads	Magazine Stories	Editing
Supporting Casts	Authors	Studio Rentals

NEW YORK PRODUCERS AND TALENT REPRESENTED

PUBLICITY   BOOKS
    ORIGINAL STORIES   PLAYS
        CONTINUITY   ADAPTATIONS

BETTS & FOWLER

REPRESENTING

PRODUCES, DIRECTORS, PLAYERS, AUTHORS

EDWIN CRANE FOWLER   ORA FLETCHER
General Manager   Motion Picture Department

CHARLOTTE CARTER   CHARLES REED JONES
Literary Department   Publicity

FITZGERALD BUILDING   Telephone
1482 Broadway, New York   Bryant 5664

Fontaine La Rue

Leads and Heavy Leads

c/o Willis & Inglis
Los Angeles

Colin Kenny
Leading Business — U.S.A.

Arthur N. Millett
Actors Association Hollywood, Calif.

WILLIAM V. MONG

HAMMERHEAD, MAURICE TOURNEUR'S "THE COUNTY FAIR"

MAX, IN GEORGE LOANE TUCKER'S "LADIES MUST LIVE"

MR. RIVETT IN KATHERINE MACDONALD'S "THE TURNING POINT"

OLD LEO IN BESSIE BARRISCALE'S "THE LUCK OF GERALDINE LAIRD."

ADDRESS
MONG RANCH—WHITTIER, CALIFORNIA
PHONE WHITTIER 5151

Roy Del Ruth

Directing

Fox Sunshine Comedies

under the supervision

of

Hampton Del Ruth

Fred Fishback

Producer

Century Comedies

Ann Forrest

Wanda Hawley

"Little Miss Booker"

Vivian Rich

PERCY MARMONT

Harry S. Northrup

Edward Cecil
Leads

RICHARD R. NEIL

DWIGHT CRITTENDEN
As the Schoolmaster in
"The Little Shepherd of Kingdom Come"

GLADDEN JAMES
as
HOWARD JEFFRIES, JR.
in
"THE THIRD DEGREE"
Address all communications to
REGINA B. KRUH
Personal Representative
Bryant 4060   220 W. 42nd St., N. Y.

Capt. Philip Hubbard
(see biography)

Clyde Benson

George Hackathorn
Juvenile Leads
Personally engaged by Lois Weber for her first Paramount-Artcraft Special.
Lois Weber Studios   Hollywood

ALBERT McQUARRIE
with
Douglas Fairbanks Company

FRITZI RIDGEWAY
Featured Character Leads

Milton Sills

JACK CURTIS
Character Leads & Heavies

Henry C. Hicks
Phone West 1680
Address: 2440 W. Pico St. Los Angeles

CHARLES CRUMPTON
English Boy Actor

Schuyler 7314 108 W. 86th St., New York

BABY IVY WARD
Five year old emotional actress
108 W. 86th St. New York City
Schuyler 7314

May Kitson
27 W. 67TH ST., N.Y.
COLUMBUS 1123

Yours While
Martha Mattox

EDWARD J. PEIL

Leading Business
Supporting such stars as

Vivian Martin	William Russell
Dorothy Gish	H. B. Warner
Lillian Gish	William Desmond
Gail Kane	Margarita Fisher
Blanche Sweet	Mary Miles Minter
Mary MacLaren	Sessue Hayakawa

Joseph Granby

Heavies

518 W. 134th St., New York
Morningside 9798

or

Green Room Club

WM. F. MORAN

Characters

Character Leads—Character Heavies
Eccentric Characters

Address:
Actors Association of Los Angeles
6408 Hollywood Blvd.   Holly 1946

WALLACE MacDONALD
Leading Man

Current Releases:
Madge Kennedy—"*Leave It To Susan*"
Marguerite Clark—"*A Girl Named Mary*"
Frank Keenan—"*Brothers Divided*"
Mary MacLaren—"*Rouge and Riches*"
Anita Stewart—"*The Fighting Shepherdess*"
Address: Los Angeles Athletic Club

FREDERIC M. MALATESTA

Heavies

Ten Pictures with Metro
Selig Studio
Current Production

"The Mask"

KATHLEEN O'CONNOR

Being Starred In
"The Lion Man"
Taken from "The Strange Case of Cavendish"
By Randolf Parish

(Photo by Campbell)

WHEELER DRYDEN
(SON OF LEO DRYDEN)

Starring in Film Comedies after seven years' tour of India, Burma, Federated Malay States, Straits Settlements, China, Philippine Islands, and Japan.

Fred W. Huntly

Characters and Director

2017 Ivanhoe Avenue

Phone: Wilshire 4376

HENRY G. SELL
Leads
58 W. 36th St.   New York City
Greeley 6372

SIDNEY MASON
Leads
Address:
3657 Broadway, N. Y. C.,   Telephone: Audubon 8110
or Green Room Club

EARL SCHENCK
Leads, Heavies and Character Leads
Management EDWARD SMALL
1493 Broadway, N. Y.

WILLIAM ANKER
339 W. 58th St.   N. Y. C.
Phone: Columbus 9998

Florence Deshon
—Goldwyn—

LEADING CHARACTERS

THUMA JADEE BAXTER
520 N. Meridian St.
Apt.—26
Indianapolis, Ind.

LUCIA BACKUS SEGER
1547 St. Nicholas Ave., N. Y. C.
(Phone: 3057 Wadsworth)
Characters

HEDDA NOVA

Just Completing

"THE MASK"

for Selig

HENRY
KOLKER

And

ARTHUR D.
RIPLEY

BRENTWOOD FILM
CORPORATION

4811 Fountain Avenue
Los Angeles   California

James Harrison
Leading Juvenile in Christie Comedies

EDDIE BARRY

in

CHRISTIE
Two-Reel Specials

Ogden Crane
Address: Actors Association
Hollywood, Calif.
(See Biography)

Charles Clary
Current Releases
"The Street called Straight"
"The Woman in Room 13" } Goldwyn
Address: 1774 North Vine, Phone 577025
Hollywood

Maud Cooling

Dean Raymond

Grace Stevens

J. Ray Avery
Juvenile Leads
Alpin Hotel - Los Angeles

WEDGWOOD NOWELL

RECENT RELEASES

Heavy Leads and Principal Supporting Roles With

H. B. WARNER in "The Man Who Turned White" (Robertson-Cole)
BESSIE BARRISCALE in "Kitty Kelly, M. D." (Robertson-Cole)
DUSTIN FARNUM in "A Man's Fight" (United Picture Theatres)
KATHERINE MACDONALD in "The Beauty Market" (First National)
J. WARREN KERRIGAN in "The Lord Loves the Irish" (Brunton-Hodkinson)
BESSIE BARRISCALE in "Her Purchase Price" (Robertson-Cole)
ALMA RUBENS in "Diane of the Green Van" (Robertson-Cole)
KITTY GORDON in "Adele" (United Picture Theatres)
J. WARREN KERRIGAN in "The Dream Cheater" (Brunton-Hodkinson) and
as MONSIEUR CHATEAU RENAUD, opposite DUSTIN FARNUM in United Picture Theatres Superb Production of "THE CORSICAN BROTHERS"

(C) *Shirley Blanc L. A.*

JACK CONNOLLY

Perry Woods with Charles Ray in "The Egg Crate Wallop"

Motorcycle officer with William Russell in "The Lincoln Highwayman"

Now doing Tommy Cleary with William Russell in "Ruth of Circle A"

991 N. Virgil   Phone: Wilshire 584

Hector V. Sarno

Current Releases:

"The Silver Horde"
    by Rex Beach
"The Right to Happiness" with
    Dorothy Phillips
"Rio Grande"
    by Augustus Thomas

GIBSON GOWLAND

Leading Character Role in

"WHITE HEATHER"
"BLIND HUSBANDS"

First 1920 George Loane Tucker Production

"THE RIGHT OF WAY"
"THE FIGHTING SHEPHERDESS"

CAROL HOLLOWAY
Feature Player

American Lithograph Co.
Portland, Ore.

HELEN MILHOLLAND

ROSCOE KARNS
"Dal"
In King W. Vidor's initial Production for First National

Permanent Address:
King W. Vidor Productions
Hollywood, Cal.

CHARLES ARLING
"In Old Kentucky"
"Back to God's Country"
"Snares of Paris"
"One Week's End"

ART FLAVEN

Directing

" Hoot " Gibson

for

UNIVERSAL FILM MFG. CO.

Address: Universal City

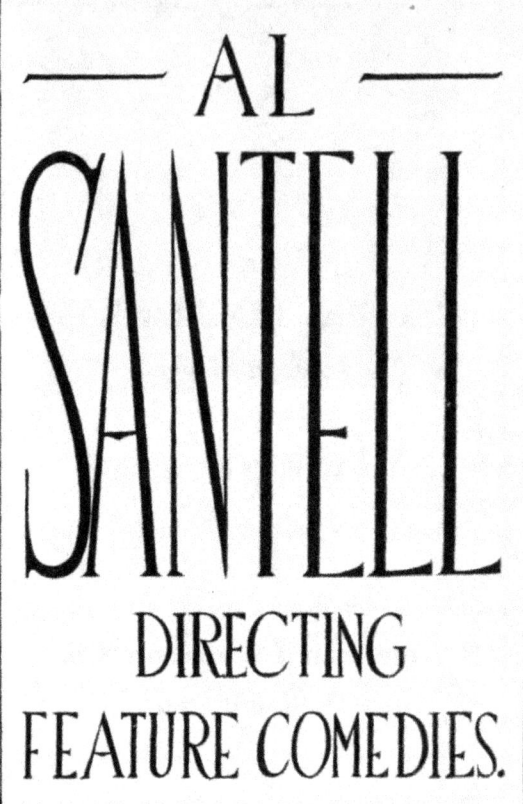

AL SANTELL

DIRECTING FEATURE COMEDIES.

CLARENCE G. BADGER
Director

Recent Productions

JUBILO
with Will Rogers

THE STRANGE BOARDER
with Will Rogers

STRICTLY CONFIDENTIAL
with Madge Kennedy

WATER, WATER EVERYWHERE
with Will Rogers

SEVEN OAKS
with Will Rogers

THROUGH THE WRONG DOOR
with Madge Kennedy

THE KINGDOM OF YOUTH
with Madge Kennedy

SIS HOPKINS
with Mabel Normand

LEAVE IT TO SUSAN
with Madge Kennedy

NORMAN DAWN

DIRECTOR

UNIVERSAL

James Clemens
Directing
George Ovey in Gayety Comedies

GILBERT PRATT
Director

Craig Hutchinson
Director
—
The New Gayety Comedies

DALLAS M. FITZGERALD
Director
220 W. 42nd Street, New York City
Bryant 7392

Charles E. Bartlett

Director General

Beaver Film Co.
Portland, Ore.

Just finished
"Headin' North"
in 7 reels

EDWIN MIDDLETON

Member of

M. P. D. A.
The Lambs
The Players

Address:
c/o Motion Picture News

---

* * * *

PAUL POWELL

DIRECTOR OF

Mary Pickford's

"POLLYANNA"

* * * *

Harry Beaumont

Director

Goldwyn
West Coast Studios

JEAN HERSHOLT

Director

"The Golden Trail"
featuring JANE NOVAK

Just finishing
"Men of Today and Tomorrow"
with CAROL HOLLOWAY
and all star cast

WILLIAM J. HUMPHREY

Director

A Tale of Two Cities—*Vitagraph Co.*
Two Men and a Woman—*Ivan Co.*
Babbling Tongues—*Ivan Co.*
The Unchastened Woman—*Rialto De Luxe Co.*
Atonement—*Humphrey Pictures, Inc.*
The Midnight Bride—*Vitagraph Co.*

GEORGE K. ROLANDS

Director

Author and Film Editor

1001 Faile St.   New York

Intervale 1465

GEORGE IRVING
Director
M. P. D. A.

"RAFFLES"
First Nat. Ex. Cir.

"THE SILVER KING"
Paramount-Artcraft

"AS A MAN THINKS"
Artco

"BLUE PEARL"
J. Laurence Weber
Alliance Film, Ltd.
London, Eng.
Through Ed. Small, Inc.

TOD BROWNING
Directing
Special Features

TOM GIBSON
Author of over two hundred reels of produced comedy

NOW
DIRECTING
HANK MANN
GALE HENRY
ETC., ETC.

Willis & Inglis
Representatives

J. G. Blystone
Director
William Fox
Sunshine Comedies

Agnes Parsons

Consulting Editor
Continuity Expert

Titling
Film Editing

---

812 Majestic Bldg.
Los Angeles
Phone: 61245

J. ROY HUNT

Works for You

ERNEST M. REYNOLDS

Cinematographer

Latest Work:
"Hidden Charms"

FREDERICK H. JAMES

resting after his 22 mile swim—Battery to Sandy Hook.

When not writing photoplays, Mr. James devotes his time to water sports.

Albert Shelby LeVino

— for three years Staff Writer —

Metro Pictures Corporation

Gabriel L. Pollock

Art Director

Selig Polyscope Company
Los Angeles

Home Address:
3005 South Kenwood Ave.
Phone: West 4279

Nick Grindé

Assistant Director

with

Lawrence Weber

C. R. Wallace

Film Editor
to
Director Emmett J. Flynn
of

William Fox Productions

Starring
William Russell

Jacques Jaccard
Author—Producer—Director
Now Directing Tom Mix for Wm. Fox

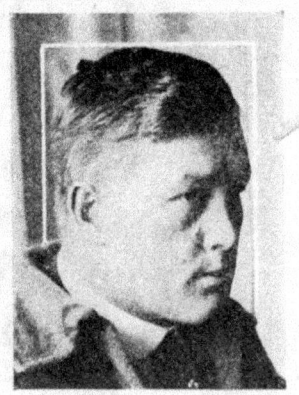

HARVEY GATES
Photoplaywright
"The Wild Cat of Paris"—*Original*

ADAPTATIONS:
"The Exquisite Thief"
"The Wicked Darling"

CURRENT RELEASES:
"The Beckoning Road"—
  Bessie Barriscale
"The Luck of Geraldine Laird"—
  Bessie Barriscale

MARION FAIRFAX
Writer and Editor
of
Marshall Neilan Productions

DORIS SCHROEDER
Adaptations and Continuity
Universal

CURRENT PRODUCTIONS:
"The Trembling Hour"
"Under Suspicion"
"Kentucky Jim"
"Jewel"

BENNETT RAY COHEN
Now Writing For
Haworth Film Corporation

Current Releases:
"Fame and Fortune"—Tom Mix
"Pitfalls of a Big City"—Gladys Brockwell
"The Greater Profit"—Edith Storey

OLGA PRINTZLAU
Scenario Writer—Lasky Company
With Wm. de Mille Specials
RECENT PRODUCTIONS:
Peg o' My Heart
Why Change Your Wife?
      with Wm. de Mille
Jack Straw
The Prince Chap
Turn of the Road

LAURA JANSEN
SCENARIO WRITER

Agnes Christine Johnston
Writing for Thomas H. Ince Productions.
Current Releases: "Daddy Long Legs" "23½ Hours Leave" & Charles Ray Stories.

Karl R. Coolidge
Serial Author Universal
Complete Continuity:
"The Lion Man"
Co-author:
"The Moon Riders"

JACK CUNNINGHAM

Associated with

George Loane Tucker
Productions

and

Robert Brunton Productions

Address:

Brunton Studios
Hollywood, Calif.

A. P. "BILL" YOUNGER

Metro Staff Writer

Now Doing Specials

HOLLYWOOD STUDIOS

HOPE LORING

Originals
Adaptations
Continuities

221 S. WILTON PLACE

Victor Gibson

Writer

Originals—Subtitles
Continuities

ASK

DENISON CLIFT
KING VIDOR
CHARLES SWICKARD
LEW CODY
ETC., ETC.

EDNA SCHLEY, Markham Bldg.
Hollywood, Representative

THIS SPACE RESERVED AS A MEDIUM

through which to express to the entire Motion Picture profession my sincerest appreciation and my heartiest endorsement of

"THE MOTION PICTURE NEWS"

for its splendid efficiency, its proven honesty, its unprejudiced poise and its "wide-awake" progressiveness, and more especially of

Mr. J. C. JESSEN

its Western Representative, to whom much credit is due for this splendid reputation.

L. V. JEFFERSON
Scenario Writer

3950 So. Hill St.   Phone: South 964-J

HARVEY THEW

Writer of Stories and Continuity

The record for 1919 includes Scripts produced with Mae Murray, Jack Pickford, Bessie Barriscale, Tom Moore, William Desmond, Elmo Lincoln, Lew Cody, Texas Guinan, Priscilla Dean

UNDER THE DIRECTION OF:

James Kirkwood, Robert Leonard, Rex Ingram, Tom Mills, Howard Hickman, Harry Beaumont, George Fitzmaurice, Cliff Smith.

Now on the Goldwyn Staff

Charles E. Whittaker

Scenario Writer for

John Barrymore

Billie Burke

Pauline Frederick

Clara Kimball Young

also for

Maurice Tourneur

Eminent Authors, Inc.

The Famous Players-Lasky Corp.

The Salvation Army, *and*

The United States Government

Author of — "WOMAN,"
"FIRES OF FAITH,"
and others

T. SHELLEY SUTTON
Photo-Playwright

Specializing in Westerns
Author of More Than 100 Stage and Screen Successes
"The West That Was"
Cowboy, Desert, Indian and Alaskan Features
Lubin, Pathe, Selig, Essanay and Triangle

Two yrs. staff writer with Universal; 25 yrs. newspaper experience, police reporter and news editor, with Chicago Chronicle, Portland Oregonian, S. F. Call, L. A. Times, Herald, Express and Examiner. Wrote recent Orpheum hit, "The Actress and the Critic," starring Constance Crawley two seasons; also "Pickles," "The Chink," "The Shyster," "Painless Dentist" and other vaudeville tabloids. Screen productions include "Phantom Gold," "The Taint," "The Grudge," "The Trail of No Return," "A Texas Sphinx," "The Taming of Bill Magee," "The Girl From Guthrie," "The Straggler," "The Story of a Kiss," etc., etc.

At present Scenario Editor and author of all productions featuring Wallace Coburn, COBURN PRODUCTIONS, Inc., Hollywood, Calif. Residence: 901 West 58th St., Los Angeles, *Phone: Vermont 925*

R. Ellis Wales

Complete staging,
designing
and effects,
including executive
supervision
of
Feature photoplays

Two years each with
D. W. Griffith
and
Famous Players-Lasky

Present affiliation:
W. W. Hodkinson Corporation
527 Fifth Avenue,
New York, N. Y.

MARTIN G. COHN
Formerly Film Editor

Inter-Ocean Film Corporation

Now in conjunction with

TOM BRET

Cutting and Editing

Just Completed

THE ETERNAL UNION OF THE SEAS
BIRTH OF A RACE
CARMEN OF THE NORTH
AYWON FILM CO. RELEASES
CISSY FITZ-GERALD COMEDIES
JOHNNY DOOLEY COMEDIES
AL JOY COMEDIES

EDWARD SEDGWICK
Original Stories and Continuities
For William Fox Film Corp.

—— IN THE PAST ——

THE YANKEE WAY
with George Walsh

CHEATING THE PUBLIC
with All Star Cast

ROUGH AND READY
with William Farnum

STOLEN HONOR
with Virginia Pearson

DIVORCE
with All Star Cast

OPEN YOUR EYES
with All Star Cast (Special)

THE WINNING STROKE
with George Walsh

THE SEA BEAST
with George Walsh

AND
THE THIRTEENTH BRIDE!
Fox's All Star Serial

—— IN PREPARATION ——
Friendship and Pillage!

Address FOX FILM CORP.
130 W. 46th Street   New York City

CONTINUITY   ADAPTATIONS
TOM BRET
SCENARIOS   SUBTITLES

Editor
Topical Tips
and
Motion Picture Press Association

> The most successful film editor in the world.—Dramatic Mirror.
> A master of art captioning.
> —Zit, in N. Y. Journal.
> Bret has written the titles for more motion picture subjects than any other man in the world.—Robert Priest, Pres., Film Market, Inc.

Tom Bret was formerly subtitle editor, Vitagraph, and scenario editor, Rolfe-Metro Studios.
Just finished Metropolitan version, "Birth of a Race," "Blind Love," featuring Lucy Cotton, and "The Sacred Flame," featuring Emily Stevens.
Pathe-Drew Comedies
    Paramount-Truex Comedies
Suite 2003-11 Candler Bldg.
220 West 42nd Street
Phone Bryant 9120

EUGENE B. LEWIS

Author of Originals

Enid Bennett
in
"What Every Woman Learns"
Harry Carey
in
"Three Mounted Men"
and
"Roped"
H. B. Warner
in
"Unchartered Channels"

ADAPTATIONS:
"The White Dove" with H. B. Warner from novel by Wm. J. Locke and "Haunting Shadows" from the Meredith Nicholson novel, "The House of a Thousand Candles."

With Jesse D. Hampton Productions

Permanent Address:
1414 North Benton Way
Hollywood, Calif.

Reaves (Breezy) Eason

Author—Actor and Producer
in

NINE-TENTHS OF THE LAW

with
Mitchel Lewis—Jimsy May
and "Breezy" Reaves

Now Under Contract at the
BIG "U"
Making Them Wild and Woolly
with
ART ACORD

PAUL H. SLOANE

*Now Writing
Original Stories
for*

FOX FILMS

W. C. L.

A writer of magazine fiction, stage plays and motion pictures. Member Fox Scenario Staff. See Lengel, W. C., biographical section.

THOMPSON BUCHANAN

Associate Editor

Goldwyn Pictures
Corporation
of New York

STUDIOS
Culver City, California

AUTHOR OF PLAYS:
"Civilian Clothes"
"A Woman's Way"
"Life"
"The Cub"

PICTURES:
"Thirty a Week"
"The World and Its Woman"
"The Rack"
"A Woman's Way"

KING D. GRAY

Member American Society of Cinematographers

Cinematographer for
Ben Wilson Productions
"The Trail of the Octopus"

In Production:
"The Screaming Shadow"

Current Features
"The Solitary Sin"
Robertson-Cole

"Cowardice Court"—Fox

WILLARD VANDER VEER

CINEMATOGRAPHER

Formerly photographer of Chester Outings and Screenics, released by

C. L. Chester Productions, Inc.

Now with Universal

BERT LAWRENCE GLENNON

Cinematographer

"Lightning Bryce," Serial

"The Kentucky Colonel"

with
NATIONAL FILM CORP.

ALFRED GOSDEN
Cinematographer
Universal City, Calif.

Priscilla Dean
in
"THE BRAZEN BEAUTY"
"THE WICKED DARLING"
"THE EXQUISITE THIEF"
and
"PRETTY SMOOTH"

Hedda Nova
in
"THE SPITFIRE OF SEVILLE"

Helen Jerome Eddy
in
"THE TREMBLING HOUR"

Tsuru Aoki
in
"THE BREATH OF THE GODS"

Rene Guissart

Photographing
Anita Stewart

L. L. LANCASTER

Cameraman
for
Universal Film Mfg. Co.
and
Chief Photographic Department
Universal City for past two years

Stephen S. Norton

· PHOTOGRAPHING ·
· FEATURES ·
for
Metro

D. R. CANADY

Chief Cinematographer

Argus Motion Picture Co.
Cleveland, Ohio

Park J. Ries

Cinematographer

Now Photographing Antonio Moreno

Vitagraph Co.

Thomas Buckingham

Cameraman

Glidden Hotel   Hollywood

Hugh C. McClung
Member of
AMERICAN SOCIETY of CINEMATOGRAPHERS
428 Brighton Ave.
Los Angeles, Cal.

ALFRED H. LATHEM
Cinematographer
Universal Film Co.
Recent Features:
Dorothy Phillips in
"The Right to Happiness"
and all
Florence Turner Productions
also
"The Moon Riders"
18 Episode Serial
featuring
ART ACORD

A. FRIED
Camera Master Mechanic
Designer and Builder of Motion Picture Machinery

3 years with William Fox West Coast Studios
Owner of a Complete Camera Repair Shop

Address:
William Fox Film Corp.
5947 Willoughby Avenue, Hollywood
Los Angeles

ALEX TROFFEY
Film Cutter

Also Laboratory Expert

With GOLDWYN since its inception. Formerly with Universal, Vitagraph, Monmouth, Frohman Amusement Corp. and T. Hayes Hunter. Address: Goldwyn Pictures Corporation, 469 Fifth Avenue, New York City.

C. SHARPE-MINOR
FILM SCORE

music set to

FEATURES and COMEDIES

by

C. SHARPE-MINOR

The music fits the picture as he makes it fit when he plays at

GRAUMAN'S
319 Ferguson Bldg.
Phone 13926
Los Angeles, Calif.

"Art Titles by Buffum"

—implies, to both exhibitor and public, the highest achievement in animated art backgrounds.

---

now with
UNIVERSAL
J. H. BUFFUM
DIRECTOR
Art Title Department

MARIE SHORES

With
Films, Incorporated

Publicity Director
Scenario Editor

Starring
Catherine Calvert

TOM NASH

Business and Production Manager of
Franklyn Farnum Serial Co.

SELIG POLYSCOPE CO.
Los Angeles, Calif.

LILLIAN R. GALE
Publicity
M. P. D. A. Press Representative
234 W. 55th St.   N. Y. C.
Circle 1844

Bernard F. McElroy

Personal Representative for
Thos. H. Ince

Ince Studios—Culver City, Cal.

IRVING E. LUDDY
Asst. Director
for
Montgomery & Rock Co.
Vitagraph Studios—Hollywood

Rex E. Hodge
Assistant Director
Past year at Universal
Now with Vitagraph

M. H. GUTTERRES
Assistant Director to
C. J. VAN DEUSEN
Apex Pictures Corporation
INDIANAPOLIS, IND.

C. E. CUTHBERT

Better known as

"CASEY"

Associated with
Syd Chaplin
Hollywood Studio
Los Angeles, Calif.

Spencer Valentine

Season:

1905 Valentine Four
1906 Valentine Four
1907 Valentine Four
1908 Valentine & Valentine
1909 Valentine & Valentine
1910 Stock
1911 Stock
1912 Thos. H. Ince
1913 Thos. H. Ince
1914 Thos. H. Ince
1915 Thos. H. Ince
1916 Thos. H. Ince
1917 Thos. H. Ince
1918 Thos. H. Ince
1919 Thos. H. Ince
1920 Thos. H. Ince

Victor Milner

SECRETARY
American Society of Cinematographers

PHOTOGRAPHING
H·B·WARNER
RELEASES

"Out of the Dust"
(McCarty Pictures Corp. Special)
"A Fugitive from Matrimony"
"House of a Thousand Candles"
"The White Dove"
"Unchartered Channels"
(With Jesse D. Hampton)

Address
American Society of Cinematographers
Markham Bldg., Hollywood
California

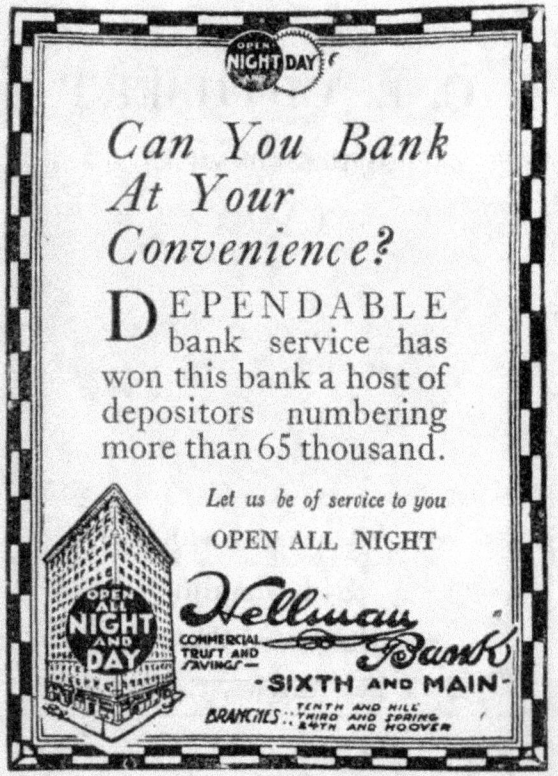

Can You Bank At Your Convenience?

DEPENDABLE bank service has won this bank a host of depositors numbering more than 65 thousand.

Let us be of service to you
OPEN ALL NIGHT

Hellman Bank
COMMERCIAL TRUST AND SAVINGS
—SIXTH AND MAIN—
BRANCHES: TENTH AND HILL
THIRD AND SPRING
24TH AND HOOVER

LENSES

The Largest Variety in Stock

High Luminosity—Flat Field Special Lenses

Made to order in our factory in France

New Rochelle Optical Exchange

10 Drake Avenue
New Rochelle
N. Y., U. S. A.

Presenting the First Annual Newspaper and Theater Directory

Following investigation and statistical work covering a period of a year, MOTION PICTURE NEWS was able to present the first newspaper and theatre census of the principal cities of the United States and Canada. The facts as given below are compiled from a questionnaire sent to all newspapers in cities of over twelve thousand population. The questionnaire was backed by repeated follow-ups, with the understanding that any paper failing to reply was in a measure "not interested in motion pictures."

The directory as re-published herewith is the latest step in a constant effort to increase cooperation between the motion picture industry and the daily newspaper. Its value to producers, distributors and others placing advertising and publicity through newspapers is evident; likewise, its presence in the offices of the newspapers listed will be of year-round service, both through making available a knowledge of what other papers are doing regarding motion pictures, and through the presence of the producers' annual announcements in these pages.

The name of the newspaper appears first in the table, then the time of publication, the circulation, the name of the photoplay editor, and the amusement advertising rate. The quoted matter following is a resume of the answers to various questions. Where the managing editor or some other executive is listed in the place given to the photoplay editor's name it is an indication that the person so listed is the one attending to photoplay news.

An additional index by States is given at the end of the directory.

ABERDEEN, SOUTH DAKOTA—Population 11,846

AMERICAN—Morn., Sun.—5,300—J. H. McKeever—50 cts. inch
"Six theatres, all downtown, no advertising daily or Sunday. No special editorial co-operation. Would use cuts or mats. Sunday circulation 5,600. Agitation favoring state censorship prompted a boycott and theaters are still peeved."

DAILY NEWS—Aft.—4,127—J. G. Sanders, Mg. Ed.—25 cts. inch
"Six theatres, all downtown, six advertise daily. No special editorial co-operation but co-operates considerably in preparation of advertising. Would appreciate any copy for ads and any new ideas."

ABERDEEN, WASHINGTON—Population 18,220

WORLD—Aft.—6,189—Leonard Hinton—40 cts. inch.
"Nine theatres, five downtown houses. Gives advertising reading notices, photoplay department daily. Will co-operate with exhibitors in preparing advertising to any extent they request."

ABILENE, TEXAS—Population 12,806

DAILY REPORTER—Aft. & Sun.—3,638—Geo. S. Anderson, Mg. Ed.—33 cts. inch. Sunday circulation 3,900. Three theatres, all downtown, three advertise daily and Sunday. Editorial co-operation. Helps exhibitors by suggesting layouts of display, etc."

ADRIAN, MICHIGAN—Population 11,284

TELEGRAM—Aft.—10,404—J. S. Gray, Mg Ed.—Rates not mentioned
"Three theatres, all downtown, three advertise daily. Editorial co-operation. Theatres given all the co-operation required. Appreciate ad-mats received in time to solicit copy."

AKRON, OHIO—Population 80,291

BEACON JOURNAL—Aft.—29,755—H. Eaton, Photo Ed.—75 cts. inch
"Twenty-eight theatres, nine downtown houses. Daily notices, publicity cuts on Saturday. Editorial co-operation. Assists exhibitors in preparation of advertising. Cuts and mats used on Saturday. Seventeen theatres advertise daily."

TIMES—Aft. & Sun.—21,000—Mary Ley, Photo Ed.—75 cts. inch.
"Sunday circulation, 20,000. Saturday and Sunday photoplay department. Editorial co-operation. Press matter and news concerning plays and players used. Prefer good action pictures. Twenty-two theatres advertise daily and ten Sunday."

PRESS—Aft.—19,567—M. L. Felber—Rates not given
"Twenty-five theatres, nine downtown houses, twenty-two advertise daily. Runs 'movie page' practically every day. Co-operates with exhibitor in preparation of advertising. Cuts and mats are used if they are good."

STUDIO DIRECTORY

ALBANY, NEW YORK—Population 107,979

TIMES-UNION—Aft. 36,000—James T. Glynn, Mg. E.—$2.10 per inch
"Sixteen theatres, 6 downtown houses, sixteen advertise daily. Reviews given but news is printed according to its value. Cuts and mats used but prefers matter a week or two ahead of Albany bookings."

KNICKERBOCKER PRESS—Morn. & Sun.—34,592—Lynn J. Arnold, Jr., Mg. Ed.—65 cts. inch
"Fifteen theatres, seven downtown houses, eight advertise daily and three Sunday. Editorial co-operation, provided advertising reading notices and news is of value. News of productions and players printed. Efficient copy department and good engraving plant assists exhibitors in preparation of advertising.

JOURNAL—Aft.—17,000—James H. Gaylor—Rates not given
"Fifteen theatres, nine downtown houses, eight advertise daily. All advertisers are played up. Advertising reading notices made a specialty of Saturdays. Prints a little news but thinks most of it overdrawn. Co-operates with exhibitor in preparation of advertising."

ALBUQUERQUE, NEW MEXICO—Population 13,507

EVENING HERALD—Aft.—4,261—Mrs. Alida F. Sims—Rates not given
"Four theatres, all downtown, four advertise daily. Cuts used when space permits. Reviews of productions and news of players used. Co-operates with exhibitors in advertising."

ALLENTOWN, PENNSYLVANIA—Population 60,297

MORNING CALL—Morn.—23,535—Eugene J. Hazard, Photo Ed.—Rates not given
"No special editorial co-operation. Cuts and mats used."

EVENING ITEM—Aft.—8,613—Chas. W. Weiser, Mg. Ed.—Rates not given
MORNING DEMOCRAT—Morn.—Under same management
"No special editorial co-operation. Advertising reading notices given under each theatre. Appreciate ad mats and designs."

CHRONICLE & NEWS—Aft.—5,132—Fred T. Willenbacher—30 cts. inch
"No special editorial co-operation. Mats and cuts used if good."

LEADER—Aft.—6,125—Geo. R. Roth, Mg. Ed.—25 cts. inch
"Fifteen theatres, five downtown houses, five advertise daily. No special editorial co-operation."

ALTOONA, PENNSYLVANIA—Population 60,000

TRIBUNE—Morn.—9,000—J. V. Taylor—25 cts. inch
"Gives liberal reading notices daily, on current bills, and gives exhibitors assistance in preparing advertising. Twelve theatres, four downtown houses, four advertised daily."

AMARILLO, TEXAS—Population 13,505

DAILY NEWS—Morn. & Sun.—4,610, incl. Sun.—R. B. McCorkel, Mg. Ed.—32 & 37 cts. inch
"Three theatres, all downtown, three advertise daily. Notices given with ads. No special editorial co-operation."

AMSTERDAM, NEW YORK—Population 34,319

EVENING RECORD—Aft.—5,873—E. O. Stowitts, Photo Ed.—35 cts. inch
"Five theatres, all downtown, five advertise daily. Gives reading notices on change of bill. Co-operates with theatres in preparing advertising."

ANACONDA, MONTANA—Population 14,000

ANACONDA STANDARD—Morn. & Sun.—17,707—Ed.'s name not given—55 daily, 60 Sun.
"Anaconda, three theatres, Butte 8 theatres. All Anaconda theatres advertise; three-Butte. Reading notices given occasionally. No special editorial co-operation."

ANDERSON, INDIANA—Population 23,453

HERALD—Aft. & Sun.—6,800—M. Walker—25 cts. inch
"Sunday circulation 8,200. Although exhibitors are helped in advertising copy there is no special editorial co-operation."

ANDERSON, SOUTH CAROLINA—Population 11,424

DAILY MAIL—Aft.—4,693—G. Paul Brown—20 cts. inch
"Six theatres, all downtown, two advertise daily, one Sunday. No special editorial co-operation. Cuts and mats used in moderation."

ANNISTON, ALABAMA—Population 13,686

STAR—Aft. & Sun.—6,514—H. P. Prater—50 cts. inch
"Sunday circulation 6,514. Five theatres, two downtown, four advertise daily and four Sunday. No special editorial co-operation. Attractive cuts of women, etc., used."

ANSONIA, CONNECTICUT—Population 16,204

EVENING SENTINEL—Aft.—6,579—H. F. Emerson, Adv. Mgr.—50 cts. inch
"No special editorial co-operation. Liberal amount of reading notices given. Cuts and mats used." Six theatres, all downtown, all advertise daily.

ASHLAND, WISCONSIN—Population 11,594

PRESS—Aft.—2,850—John C. Chapple, Mg. Ed.—Rates not mentioned
"Three theatres, all downtown, two advertise daily. No special editorial co-operation. Cuts and mats used if sufficient advertising connected with it. Would like producers to advertise."

ASHEVILLE, NORTH CAROLINA—Population 20,157

CITIZEN—Morn. & Sun.—11,711—C. B. Taylor—50 cts. inch
"Sunday circulation 10,003. Four theatres, all downtown, three advertise daily and Sunday. Reading notices given every day on each picture. News of pictures and players printed on Sunday. Cuts and mats used on Sunday."

ASTORIA, OREGON—Population 10,117

EVENING BUDGET—Aft.—2,200—J. E. Gratke, Mg. Ed.—30 cts. inch
"Four theatres, all downtown, advertise spasmodically. No special editorial co-operation. Copy prepared for exhibitors."

ATHENS, GEORGIA—Population 16,900

BANNER—Morn & Sun.—3,500—H. J. Rown—18 to 40 cts. inch
"Sunday circulation 3,552. Two theatres, one downtown, two advertise daily, two Sunday. Editorial co-operation. Prepared advertising for theatres. Mats used with copy of story."

ATLANTA, GEORGIA—Population 179,292

ATLANTA JOURNAL—Aft. & Sun.—60,787—Robert Haverty—10 cts. per line
"Sunday circulation 71,653. Twenty-two theatres, 15 downtown houses; ten theatres advertise daily, 11 Sunday. Editorial co-operation."

GEORGIAN—Morn.-AMERICAN—Sun.—65,000—C. A. Carroll—$1.40 inch
"Sunday circulation 100,000. Eight theatres advertise daily, nine Sunday. No special co-operation."

Other Atlanta daily: CONSTITUTION—Morn. & Sun.

ATLANTIC CITY, NEW JERSEY—Population 51,667

PRESS & UNION—Morn. & Aft.—14,871—F. E. Croasdale, Mg. Ed.—12 cts. line 3,500 lines
"Sixteen theatres, all downtown, all but one advertise daily. Reading notices with advertising. No special editorial co-operation."

Other Atlantic City daily: GAZETTE-REVIEW.

STUDIO DIRECTORY

ATTLEBORO, MASSACHUSETTS—Population 18,480
DAILY SUN—Aft.—5,000—C. C. Cain, Jr., Photo Ed.—Rates not mentioned. "Two theatres, all downtown, one advertises daily. Special editorial co-operation. Cuts and mats used. Prints column of news each week."

AUBURN, NEW YORK—Population 32,468
ADVERTISER JOURNAL—4,921—Victor J. Callanan, Mg. Ed.—60 cts. inch. "Four theatres, four downtown, three advertise daily. Special editorial co-operation. Co-operates with theatres in preparing advertising if requested."
CITIZEN—Aft.—7,474—Wm. O. Dapping, Mg. Ed.—60 cts. inch. "Four theatres, four downtown houses, all advertise daily. No special editorial co-operation. Assist theatres with advertising copy if requested."

AUGUSTA, MAINE—Population 13,860
AUGUSTA DAILY-KENNEBEC JOURNAL—Morn.—10,633—G. R. Chadbourne, Mg. Ed.—40 cts. inch. "Two theatres, one downtown, one advertises daily, one occasionally. No special editorial co-operation."

AUGUSTA, GEORGIA—Population 49,451
CHRONICLE—Morn. & Sun.—12,110—Bradley Chester, Photo Ed.—70 cts. inch. "Ten theatres, seven downtown houses, seven advertise regularly, three occasionally. No special editorial co-operation. Paper too small to use many cuts or mats."

AURORA, ILLINOIS—Population 33,022
BEACON NEWS—Aft. & Sun.—16,000—Ed's name not given—Rates not given. "Sunday circulation 16,000. Five theatres, all downtown, all advertise. No special editorial co-operation, but news of pictures and players is occasionally printed."

AUSTIN, TEXAS—Population 23,218
AMERICAN—Morn. & Sun.—7,000—Bytelle, Mg. Ed.—Rates not given. Sunday circulation 9,000. "Six theatres, all downtown, five advertise daily, five Sunday. No special editorial co-operation, but news of features and players is printed occasionally."
STATESMAN—Aft. & Sun.—F. Ray Carpenter, Photo Ed.—98 cts. inch. "Circulation not given. Five theatres, all downtown, four advertise daily, none Sundays. No special editorial co-operation. Cuts and mats used."

BAKERSFIELD, CALIFORNIA—Population 15,538
BAKERSFIELD CALIFORNIAN—Aft.—6,230—R. C. Miller, Mg. Ed.—Rates not given. "Five theatres, three downtown, four advertise daily. No special editorial co-operation. Does not use cuts or mats."
ECHO—Morn. & Sun.—Cir. not given—A. W. Mason, Mg. Ed.—Rates not given. "No reading notices given. No editorial co-operation unless paid for. Advertising prepared if requested. Nine theatres, one downtown, three advertise daily, five Sunday."

BALTIMORE, MARYLAND—Population 579,590
AMERICAN—Morn. & Sun.—No cir. given—W. B. Clarke, Mg. Ed.—37½ cts. line. Sunday circulation 92,406. "110 theatres, 15 downtown, 42 advertise Sunday. Editorial co-operation given. Reviews printed of pictures and players as space permits."
STAR—Aft.—Cir. not given. Twenty-eight daily theatres advertise daily. Same management as AMERICAN.
NEWS—Aft. & Sun.—105,416—Henry Ehrman—15-30 cts. line. "Nine theatres advertise daily, 44 Sunday. Special editorial co-operation daily. Special attention is given to advertising copy."
STAR—Aft.—40,000—J. R. Evans—25 cts. line. "Thirty-two theatres advertise Monday. Special editorial co-operation. All advertising copy prepared and designs gotten up."
SUN—Morn, Aft. & Sun.—73,159 (Eve.); 95,443 (Morn.)—J. M. Shellman—$1.00 per line. Sunday circulation 123,701. Thirteen theatres advertise daily and Sunday. Special editorial co-operation. All advertising prepared for theatres, layouts, cuts, copy, etc."

BANGOR, MAINE—Population 26,061
DAILY NEWS—Morn.—18,341—Lawrence T. Smyth—50 cts. inch. "Four theatres, all downtown houses, all advertise daily. No special editorial co-operation. Reviews given."

BARRE, VERMONT—Population 11,706
TIMES—Aft.—6,765—F. E. Langby, Adv. Mg.—20 cts. inch. No editorial co-operation. "Four theatres, two downtown houses, two advertise daily. Try to make advertising attractive."

BATAVIA, NEW YORK—Population 13,278
NEWS—Aft.—8,458—Ralph Young, Photo Ed.—35 cts. inch. "No special editorial co-operation. Reading notices given as attraction or ad."

BATTLE CREEK, MICHIGAN—Population 28,122
ENQUIRER AND NEWS—Morn., Aft. & Sun.—11,500 Fred Evans, Photo Ed.—37½ and 45 cts. inch. "Eight theatres, eight downtown houses, six advertise daily, seven Sunday. Editorial co-operation given."

BAY CITY, MICHIGAN—Population 47,047
BAY CITY TIMES—Aft.—16,765—W. H. Gustin, Mg. Ed.—Rates not given. "Ten theatres, five downtown houses, six advertise daily. No special editorial co-operation. Layouts sometimes printed."

BAYONNE, NEW JERSEY—Population 64,461
BAYONNE TIMES—Aft.—9,600—H. L. Martin, Mg. Ed.—45 cts. inch. "Nine picture theatres, three downtown houses. Seven advertise daily. Special editorial co-operation. Can use cuts."
BAYONNE REVIEW—Aft.—5,000—L. Vultre, Mg. Ed.—35 cts. inch. "Six theatres advertise daily. No special editorial co-operation. Appreciate ad-mats."

BEACON, NEW YORK—Population 10,165
JOURNAL—Aft.—1,350—J. F. Cronin, Mg. Ed.—10 cts. inch. "Three theatres, all downtown, all advertise daily. Special editorial co-operation given. Cuts used, not mats."

BEAUMONT, TEXAS—Population 33,000
BEAUMONT ENTERPRISE—Morn. & Sun.—19,547—Alfred Jones—No rates given. "Five theatres, all downtown, four advertise daily. Sunday circulation 23,786. No special editorial co-operation. Prepare advertising copy."
JOURNAL—Aft. & Sun.—6,424—C. E. Marsh, Mg. Ed.—56 cts. inch. Sunday circulation 5,292. "No special editorial co-operation. Reviews given. Cuts and mats used if of current interest."

BELLAIRE, OHIO—Population 13,896
LEADER—Aft.—3,480—M. Aldredge, Mg. Ed.—No rates given. "Five theatres, four downtown; three advertise daily. No special editorial co-operation."

BELLEVILLE, ILLINOIS—Population 21,139
NEWS-DEMOCRAT—Aft.—5,000—A. E. Kern—Rates not given. "Nine theatres, two downtown; two advertise daily. Special editorial co-operation given."

BELOIT, WISCONSIN—Population 17,122
DAILY NEWS—Aft.—Circ. not given—Mrs. M. M. Wallace—35 cts. inch "Two theatres, both downtown; both advertise daily. No special editorial co-operation. Good advertising copy service given daily."

BEVERLEY, MASSACHUSETTS—Population 22,959
EVENING TIMES—Aft.—4,500—Photo Ed. not given—50 cts. inch "Two theatres, both neighbor houses; both advertise. No special editorial co-operation. Cuts used at times."

BIDDEFORD, MAINE—Population 17,475
RECORD—Aft.—2,378—A. H. Milliken—30 cts. inch "Two theatres, one downtown; one advertises daily. No special editorial co-operation. No co-operation in preparing advertising."

BILLINGS, MONTANA—13,020
GAZETTE—Morn., Aft. & Sun.—14,000—Joe L. Markham—No rates given "Three theatres, all downtown; all advertise in the daily. No special editorial co-operation given."

BINGHAMTON, NEW YORK—Population 55,901
PRESS AND LEADER—Aft.—Circ. not given—Pierce Weller—$2.50 inch "Twenty-two theatres, six downtown houses; eight advertise daily. Advertising rates, $2.50 per inch, first insertion, $1.25 subsequent. No special editorial co-operation."
REPUBLICAN HERALD—Morn.—11,000—John Schanz—$1.00 and $1.50 inch "Twenty theatres, six downtown, six advertise daily. No special editorial co-operation. Assists exhibitors in preparation of advertising."

BIRMINGHAM, ALABAMA—Population 132,685
AGE HERALD—Morn. & Sun.—23,974—W. M. Hulsey—$1.75 per inch "Sunday circulation, 30,340; rates, $2.10 inch. Special editorial co-operation. Twelve theatres, eight downtown houses (three colored); four advertise daily, five Sundays."
LEDGER—Aft.—38,022—Hyman Leader—$1.00 per inch "Thirteen theatres, eleven downtown houses; eight advertise daily. Special editorial co-operation. Could use mats. Copy department at exhibitors' disposal."
NEWS—Aft. & Sun.—50,000—Herbert Porter—Rates not given "Fifteen theatres, ten downtown houses; six advertise daily, six Sunday. Special editorial co-operation. Reviews given and news of features and players printed."

BLOOMINGTON, ILLINOIS—Population 26,850
PANTAGRAPH—Morn.—17,254—H. O. Davis, Mg. Ed.—40 cts. inch "No special editorial co-operation. Four theatres, four downtown houses; two advertise daily. Could use ad mats if sent several days ahead of showing of picture."
DAILY BULLETIN—Aft. & Sun.—7,547—Editor's name not mentioned—Rates not given "Five theatres, four downtown houses; three advertise daily, four Sunday. No special editorial co-operation."

BOISE, IDAHO—Population 29,637
STATESMAN—Morn. & Sun.—Circ. not given—H. E. Abend, Mg. Ed.—Rates not given "Four theatres, all downtown; all advertise daily and Sunday. Special editorial co-operation given."
CAPITAL NEWS—Aft. & Sun.—12,682—H. A. Lawson, Photo Ed.—40 cts. inch "Four theatres, three downtown; two advertise daily, two Sunday. Special editorial co-operation. Sunday circulation, 11,894."

BOSTON, MASSACHUSETTS—Population 767,589
ADVERTISER-AMERICAN—Sun.—365,000—E. F. Harkins—40 cts. line "Forty theatres, sixteen downtown houses; thirty advertise. Editorial co-operation given. Reviews given."
AMERICAN—Aft.—300,000—F. J. McIsaac—40 cts. city, 20 cts. suburban "One hundred and fifty theatres, twenty-five downtown houses; fifty advertise daily, twenty Sundays. Editorial co-operation in editorial and advertising matter."
RECORD—Aft. & Sun.—41,855—F. H. Cushman—25 cts. line "Eighty-three theatres, twelve downtown houses; twenty-six advertise daily and twenty-three Sunday. Special editorial co-operation and assistance given in preparing advertising copy."
BOSTON GLOBE—Morn., Aft. & Sun.—289,447—Chas. S. Howard—30 cts. per line "Metropolitan Boston, eighty-four theatres; thirty downtown houses; twenty-five advertise daily. Of eighty-four Metropolitan Boston theatres, many use the suburban papers once a week."
POST—Morn. & Sun.—459,603—Harold Crosby—40 cts. daily and Sun. "Eighty-five theatres in greater Boston, eighteen downtown houses; thirty advertise daily and thirty Sundays. Editorial co-operation given. Other papers: Herald; Journal; Transcript.

BRADDOCK, PENNSYLVANIA—Population 20,935
DAILY NEWS HERALD—Aft.—2,100—Clark W. Kelly, Mg. Ed.—15 cts. inch "Eight theatres, all downtown; four advertise daily. No special editorial co-operation. Daily program published."

BRADFORD, PENNSYLVANIA—14,544
BRADFORD ERA—Morn.—3,623—D. W. Dean, Mg. Ed.—30 cts. per inch "Three picture theatres, all downtown; all advertise daily. No special editorial co-operation."

BRANDON, MANITOBA, CANADA—Population 17,177
SUN—Aft.—4,664—W. S. Harris, Mg. Ed.—28 cts. inch "Transient rate for advertising, 50 cents per inch. Three theatres, all downtown; all three advertise. No special editorial co-operation."

BRANTFORD, ONTARIO—Population 23,132
EXPOSITOR—Aft.—10,200—A. T. Whitaker—50 cts. inch "Three theatres, three downtown; three advertise daily. Editorial co-operation. Readers usually prepared by editorial staff.

BRIDGEPORT, CONNECTICUT—Population 115,289
TIMES—Morn. & Aft.—12,214—D. J. Lustig—35 cts. inch "Reading notices given according to size of advertising. No special editorial co-operation. Assists exhibitors with advertising copy. Thirty-five theatres, ten downtown houses; ten advertise daily."
POST—Aft. & Sun.—45,000 combined cir.—Elida Bedell—98 cts. inch "Sunday circulation, 18,000. Special editorial co-operation. Reading notices weekly. Fifteen theatres, seven downtown; nine advertise daily, nine Sundays."
STANDARD TELEGRAM—Morn.—(Under same management as above)—45,000 combined circulation

BRIDGETON, NEW JERSEY—Population 14,335
EVENING NEWS—Aft.—6,027—Wm. B. Kirby—Rates not given "Three theatres, three downtown; advertise about three times a week. No special editorial co-operation."

BROCKTON, MASSACHUSETTS—Population 62,288
ENTERPRISE—Aft.—16,868—L. E. Rich—75 cts. inch "No special editorial co-operation. Eight theatres, four downtown; all advertise daily."

STUDIO DIRECTORY

BROOKLYN, NEW YORK—Population 1,634,351

TIMES—Aft.—10,625—Pauline Brady—80 cts. inch "Nine theatres, five downtown houses; all advertise daily. No special editorial co-operation."

CITIZEN—Aft. & Sun.—36,000—C. H. Albrecht—Rates not given "Sunday circulation, 38,000. Over one hundred theatres, 30 downtown; 40 advertise daily, 60 Sunday. Editorial co-operation given."

EAGLE—Aft. & Sun.—46,000—Arthur Pollock—Rates not given "Sunday circulation, 68,000. Editorial co-operation given. Thirty-one theatres advertise daily, 37 Sundays."

TIMES—Aft. & Sun.—Combined circ. 41,289—W. M. Oestreiche, Mg. Ed.—25 cts. agate line "Special editorial co-operation. Reading notices and reviews given." Additional paper: Standard-Union

BROWNSVILLE, TEXAS—Population 12,310

HERALD—Aft. & Sun.—2,013—J. M. Stein, Mg. Ed.—Rates not mentioned "Three theatres, all downtown; all advertise. Daily reading notices given but no special editorial co-operation."

BUFFALO, NEW YORK—Population 480,000

COURIER—Morn.—48,000—William Martin, Photo Ed.—Rates not given "Sunday circulation, 117,000. Special editorial co-operation. One hundred and fifty theatres, eleven downtown; ten advertise daily and Sunday."

ENQUIRER—Aft.—37,000—William Martin—Rates not given "Special editorial co-operation. One hundred and fifty theatres, eleven downtown; ten advertise daily, ten Sunday."

EVE. NEWS—Aft.—Circ. not given—J. D. Wells, Mg. Ed.—20 cts. line "Special editorial co-operation. Reviews and news of pictures given. Ninety-five theatres, eight downtown houses; seventeen advertise daily."

TIMES—Aft. & Sun.—56,861—J. S. Brown—$3.50 inch Sun.—$2.25 daily "Sunday circulation, 71,435. Special editorial co-operation. About fifteen theatres advertise daily and Sunday. Reading notices given Sundays and Thursdays."

EXPRESS—Morn. & Sun.—37,507—Marion De Forest—$2.10 & $3.80 inch "Fifty-eight theatres, ten downtown houses; seven advertise daily, seven Sunday. Special editorial co-operation. Reviews given." Other Buffalo papers: Commercial.

BURLINGTON, IOWA—Population 24,324

GAZETTE—Aft.—10,382—Geo. A. Stivers, Mg. Ed.—Rates not given "Four picture houses, four downtown; all advertise daily. Reading notices at regular line rate. No special editorial co-operation."

HAWK EYE MORNING EXPRESS—Morn. & Sun.—10,908—W. E. Morgan—Rates not given "Sunday circulation, 12,264. No special editorial co-operation given. Three theatres, all downtown; all advertise daily and Sunday."

BURLINGTON, VERMONT—21,247

FREE PRESS—Morn.—Circ. not given—Mg. Ed.'s name omitted—35 cts. inch "No editorial co-operation. Four theatres, three downtown; all advertise daily."

BUTLER, PENNSYLVANIA—Population 25,545

CITIZEN—Morn.—Circ. not given—N. A. Geyer, Mg. Ed.—16 cts. per inch "No special editorial co-operation. Six theatres, five downtown; four advertise daily."

TIMES—Aft.—2,300—C. B. Henninan, Mg. Ed.—10 cts. inch "No special editorial co-operation. Five theatres, four downtown; three advertise daily."

BUTTE, MONTANA—41,781

DAILY POST—Aft.—14,188—J. Cummings—48 cts. inch "No special editorial co-operation. Twelve theatres, eight downtown; seven advertise daily."

CAIRO, ILLINOIS—Population 15,392

EVENING CITIZEN—Aft.—2,689—J. C. Fisher, Mg. Ed.—Rates not given "No special editorial co-operation. Five theatres, three downtown; two advertise daily."

BULLETIN—Morn. & Sun.—1,910—E. U. Myrick—Rates not given "No special editorial co-operation. Five theatres, three downtown; four advertise daily."

CALGARY, CANADA—Population 81,000

CALGARY HERALD—Aft.—Circ. not given—H. Kelly—84 cts. inch "Six theatres, six downtown; all advertise daily. Reading notices daily, with spread on Saturday. No special editorial co-operation."

CAMDEN, NEW JERSEY—Population 102,465

COURIER—Aft.—11,691—A. L. Ingram—36 cts. inch "Movie reader column. Mondays and Thursdays. No special editorial co-operation. Twenty-six theatres, six downtown houses; twelve advertise daily.

POST-TELEGRAM—Aft.—12,170—T. N. Patterson, Ad. Mg.—3 cts. line "About twenty-five or thirty theatres, ten downtown houses; fifteen advertise daily. No editorial co-operation."

CANTON, ILLINOIS—Population 12,438

DAILY LEDGER—Aft.—6,555—H. L. Owen—20 cts. inch "Editorial co-operation. Four theatres, three downtown; three advertise daily. Reviews given, news of players and features printed.

CANTON, OHIO—Population 50,426

DAILY NEWS—Aft. & Sun.—13,810—J. V. McCann—40 cts. to $1.00 inch "Sunday circulation, 11,907. Editorial co-operation given. Ten theatres, seven downtown; seven advertise daily, other three occasionally.

REPOSITORY—Aft. & Sun.—24,000—Clifford Grass—50 cts. inch "Sunday circulation, 18,000. Special editorial co-operation. Seven theatres, six downtown; five advertise daily, seven Sunday.

CARBONDALE, PENNSYLVANIA—Population 18,532

CARBONDALE LEADER—Aft.—5,400—G. W. Smithing, Mg. Ed.—35 cts. inch "Four theatres, four downtown houses; three advertise daily. No special editorial co-operation. Reading notices depend on size of ads.

CEDAR RAPIDS, IOWA—Population 35,858

MORNING TIMES—Morn.—3,216—Walter Bechtel, Adv. Mgr.—Rates not given "Ten theatres, six downtown; four advertise daily. No special editorial co-operation. Assist in preparing advertising when necessary.

REPUBLICAN—Sun.—(Under same management)—11,809—Rates not given "Runs one to two pages for all theatres on Sunday, using cuts."

CHAMBERSBURG, PENNSYLVANIA—Population 12,192

REPOSITORY—Aft.—4,561—Shirley J. Zarges—10 cts. inch "No special editorial co-operation. Two theatres, two downtown; both advertise daily. Give notices on each show."

CHAMPAIGN, ILLINOIS—Population 13,835

DAILY GAZETTE—Aft.—4,605—O. L. Davis, Mg. Ed.—25 cts. inch
"No editorial co-operation. Four theatres, four downtown; all advertise daily."

NEWS—Aft. & Sun.—7,610—Shirley Kre San—35 to 50 cts. inch
"Editorial co-operation. Reviews and news printed. Assist in preparing advertising when necessary. Five theatres, five downtown houses; all advertise daily. Sunday circulation 7,641."

CHARLESTON, SOUTH CAROLINA—Population 60,121

AMERICAN—Morn. & Sun.—Circ. not given—Mary Hughes—Rates not given
"Special editorial co-operation. Seven theatres, all downtown; five advertise daily and Sunday."

EVE. POST—12,903—F. O. Emerson—$1.50 per inch
"No special editorial co-operation. Six theatres, four downtown; four advertise daily."

CHARLESTON, WEST VIRGINIA—Population 35,000

MAIL—Aft.—9,336—Thos. D. Mags—Rates not given
"No special editorial co-operation. Fourteen theatres, seven downtown; four advertise daily."

GAZETTE—Morn. & Sun.—11,400—H. H. Pfahler—Rates not given
"Sunday circulation 12,000. Ten theatres, eight downtown; five advertise daily. Do not advertise on Sunday."

CHARLOTTE, NORTH CAROLINA—Population 37,951

NEWS—Aft. & Sun.—11,598—W. M. Bell—Rates not given
"No special editorial co-operation. Sunday circulation not given. Seven theatres, all downtown, six advertise in daily and Sunday. Gives each theatre notice of day's program and week's program on Sundays."

OBSERVER—Morn. & Sun.—18,500—T. J. Pierson—Rates not given
"Sunday circulation 20,000. Six theatres, all downtown; five advertise daily. No special editorial co-operation."

CHATTANOOGA, TENNESSEE—Population 57,077

TIMES—Morn. & Sun.—Combined circ. 29,164—Mg. Ed's name not given—$1.00 per inch
"Twelve theatres, five downtown houses; five advertise daily and five Sunday. No editorial co-operation given."

CHESTER, PENNSYLVANIA—Population 40,474

TIMES—Eve.—Combined circ. 14,500—E. M. Orowitz—Rates not given
"No special editorial co-operation. Forty theatres, six downtown; six advertise daily. Would prefer mats."

REPUBLICAN—Morn.—(Under same management)—Photoplay notices Tuesdays and Thursdays

CHICAGO, ILLINOIS—Population 2,521,822

EVENING AMERICAN—Aft.—F. W. McQuigg—55 cts. inch
"Editorial co-operation. Number of theatres not given. Seventy-five to eighty-five advertise daily. Make own news cuts. Reviews given."

EVENING JOURNAL—Aft.—116,000—Virginia Dale—15 cts. line
"Three hundred theatres, twelve downtown; forty-seven advertise daily. Editorial co-operation. Publicity in the way of news notes and leads."
Other papers: Calumet; Examiner; Herald; Post.

CINCINNATI, OHIO—Population 402,175

POST—Aft.—192,964—Chas. O'Neill—Photo Ed.—35 cts. line
"One hundred and twenty-five theatres, twenty-five downtown; fifteen advertise daily. Motion picture page run every Saturday with art layout. Special editorial co-operation."

COMMERCIAL TRIBUNE—Morn. & Sun.—40,915—Wade Mountfort, Mg. Ed.—10 to 16 cts. line daily; 25 cts. Sun.
"Eighty-three theatres, twenty downtown; seven advertise daily and Sunday. Reading notices given on Mondays, Thursdays and Sunday. Editorial co-operation."

TIMES-STAR—Aft.—16,066—Oscar Doob—30 cts. line
"One hundred and ten theatres, twenty downtown houses; ten advertise daily. Editorial co-operation. About two columns of reading notices given Saturdays."
Additional paper: Enquirer.

CLARKSBURG, WEST VIRGINIA—Population 25,000

TELEGRAM—Aft. & Sun.—7,934—Mg. Ed's name not given—35 to 50 cts. inch
"Sunday circulation 8,531. Six theatres, five downtown houses; five advertise daily and Sunday. No special editorial co-operation."

CLEVELAND, OHIO—Population 750,000

PLAIN DEALER—Morn. & Sun.—168,440—Harlowe Hoyt—Rates not given
"Special editorial co-operation. About 130 theatres, sixteen downtown houses; sixty-seven advertise daily and Sunday."

PRESS—Aft.—180,724—Fred W. Meier—30 cts. line
"One hundred and forty theatres, fifteen downtown houses; eighty advertise daily and eighty Sunday. Editorial co-operation. Reviews and news printed."
Additional paper: News.

CLINTON, IOWA—Population 26,802

CLINTON HERALD—Aft.—7,675—J. J. O'Connor, Adv. Mg.—Rates not given
"No special editorial co-operation. Five theatres, all downtown; five advertise daily. Free reading notices given Saturday."

COATESVILLE, PENNSYLVANIA—Population 13,369

RECORD—5,285—Fred Manship—Rates not given
"Two theatres; both advertise daily. Editorial co-operation. Reviews printed."

COFFEYVILLE, KANSAS—Population 15,982

MORNING NEWS—Morn. & Sun.—2,100—A. J. Valentine—Rates not given
"Sunday circulation, 2,500. Four theatres, four downtown; two advertise except Sunday. No special editorial co-operation."

JOURNAL—Aft.—5,000—Mg. Ed's name not given—Rates not given
"Four theatres, all downtown; four advertise daily. Editorial co-operation. Write most of exhibitors' copy, which consists largely of reading notices."

COHOES, NEW YORK—Population 23,477

REPUBLICAN—Aft.—3,496—F. V. Kennedy, Mg. Ed.—35 cts. inch
"Three theatres, two downtown houses; two advertise daily. No special editorial co-operation."

COLORADO SPRINGS, COLORADO—Population 31,717

GAZETTE—Morn. & Sun.—4,641—M. A. Ege—Rates not given
"Sunday circulation, 7,005. Six theatres, four downtown; five advertise daily, five Sunday. Editorial co-operation. Page of news printed in Sunday issue."

TELEGRAPH—Aft.—5,789—T. W. Ross—50 cts. inch
"No special editorial co-operation. Seven theatres, five downtown; five advertise daily."

COLUMBIA, SOUTH CAROLINA—Population 33,506

RECORD—Aft. & Sun.—13,000—Jack Young—Rates not given
"Sunday circulation, 13,000. Editorial co-operation. Four theatres, all downtown; four advertise daily, four Sunday. Picture section Sundays."

STUDIO DIRECTORY 493

DAILY SPY—2,309—H. B. Ceepher—10 cts. per inch. No special editorial. "Three theatres, none downtown; three advertise daily. No co-operation."

COLUMBUS, GEORGIA—Population 21,805

ENQUIRER-SUN—Morn. & Sun.—5,080—W. J. Baldwin—25 cts. inch. "Sunday circulation, 5,096. Nine theatres, seven downtown; four advertise daily, one Sunday. Free photoplay page daily, double page Sunday. Editorial co-operation."

LEDGER—Aft. & Sun.—7,425—F. G. Storey—Rates not given. "Sunday circulation, 7,425. Nine theatres, seven downtown; five advertise daily, one Sunday. No special editorial co-operation."

COLUMBUS, OHIO—Population 204,567

DISPATCH—Aft. & Sun.—76,605—H. E. Cherrington—17½ cts. line. "Editorial co-operation. Sunday circulation, 75,542. Forty-six theatres, eight downtown; eight advertise daily, two Sundays. Reviews printed."

OHIO STATE JOURNAL—Morn. & Sun.—53,155—Daisy Krier—17½ cts. per line. "Sunday circulation, 27,147. Fifty-five theatres fifteen downtown; ten advertise daily. Editorial Co-operation. Make cuts and assist in preparing copy."

CITIZEN—Aft.—74,174—Dale Frazier—12½ cts. per line. "Editorial co-operation. Forty-five theatres, ten downtown houses; five advertise daily."

CONCORD, NEW HAMPSHIRE—Population 22,291

DAILY PATRIOT—Morn. & Aft.—3,074—Combined circ.—30 cts. inch. "Editorial co-operation. Four theatres, all downtown; four advertise daily. News of pictures and players printed."

CONNELLSVILLE, PENNSYLVANIA—Population 12,845

COURIER—Aft.—6,880—W. S. Stimmel—Rates not given. "Nine theatres, four downtown houses; three advertise daily. No special editorial co-operation."

DAILY NEWS—Aft.—4,654—M. B. Pryce—15 cts. per inch. "No special editorial co-operation. Could use several columns of news every week. Can use all sizes. Three theatres, three downtown; three advertise daily."

CORNING, NEW YORK—Population 13,459

LEADER—Aft.—7,191—Mg. Ed's name not given—Rates not given. "No editorial co-operation given. Five theatres; four advertise daily."

COUNCIL BLUFFS, IOWA—Population 30,778

NONPAREIL—Morn. Aft. & Sun.—16,211—J. L. Boeshans, Ad. Mg.—Rates not given. "Sunday circulation, 15,692. Six theatres; four advertise three times a week. No special editorial co-operation."

COVINGTON, KENTUCKY—Population 55,896

KENTUCKY POST—Aft.—17,263—Elmer Dressman—50 cts. to 22 cts. according to space. "Editorial co-operation. Seven theatres; three advertise, two twice a week."

DALLAS, TEXAS—Population 111,986

DISPATCH—Aft.—P. M. Sarazan—$1.47 per inch. "No special editorial co-operation. Thirteen theatres, ten downtown houses; nine advertise daily."

EVENING JOURNAL—Eve.—40,000—E. M. Dealey—Rates not given. "Fifteen theatres, ten theatres downtown; six advertise daily. No special editorial co-operation."

MORNING NEWS—Morn. & Sun.—68,339—E. M. Dealey—Rates not given. "Fifteen theatres, ten downtown; six advertise daily, none Sunday. No special editorial co-operation. Sunday circulation, 101,654."

TIMES-HERALD—Aft. & Sun.—45,000—Sky Mead—Rates not given. "Sunday circulation, 48,000. Nineteen theatres, fourteen downtown; eight advertise daily, eight Sunday. Editorial co-operation."

DANVILLE, ILLINOIS—Population 30,847

PRESS—Morn. & Sun.—9,000—Mg. Ed's name not given—30 cts. inch. "Sunday circulation, 9,000. No special editorial co-operation. Six theatres, five downtown houses; four advertise daily, four Sunday."

DANVILLE, VIRGINIA—Population 19,697

REGISTER and BEE—Morn., Aft. & Sun.—Combined circ. 10,365—50 cts. inch. "No special editorial co-operation. Four theatres, four downtown; three advertise daily, none Sunday. Reviews printed."

DAVENPORT, IOWA—Population 46,340

DEMOCRAT—Morn. Aft. & Sun.—18,161—J. F. Gordon—70 cts. inch. "Sixteen theatres, eight downtown; five advertise daily, five Sunday. Several pages of picture news printed on Sunday. No special editorial co-operation."

DAILY TIMES—Aft.—27,000—J. Rachman—56 cts. inch. "Twenty-five theatres, eight downtown; twelve advertise daily. Photoplay department has two and sometimes three pages Saturday afternoon. Daily department one column."

DAYTON, OHIO—Population 123,794

JOURNAL—Morn. & Sun.—27,000—W. K. Matthews—75 cts. inch. "Editorial co-operation. Forty theatres, eight downtown; five advertise daily, two Sunday. Sunday circulation, 33,500."

NEWS—Aft. & Sun.—38,395—James Muir—$1.00 per inch. "Twenty-six theatres, nine downtown; six advertise daily, none Sunday. No special editorial co-operation. Reviews printed occasionally."

DECATUR, ILLINOIS—Population 37,565

HERALD—Morn. & Sun.—Circ. not given—Ruth Cade—Rates not given. "No special editorial co-operation. Eight theatres, five downtown; three advertise daily, four Sunday. Only print news on Sunday."

REVIEW—Aft. & Sun.—17,282—R. V. Price—Rates not given. "Sunday circulation, 15,658. Photoplay department in Sunday issue. Editorial co-operation. Eight theatres, five downtown houses; seven advertise daily."

DENVER, COLORADO—Population 245,523

POST—Aft. & Sun.—113,261—F. E. White—20 cts. line. "Sunday circulation, 141,662. Editorial co-operation. About fifty theatres, ten downtown houses; nine advertise daily, none Sunday."

EXPRESS—Aft.—15,400—Mrs. Leonora Fishel—70 to 80 cts. inch. "Editorial co-operation. About fifty theatres, eight downtown houses; twelve advertise daily. Reviews and news printed."

Other papers: Rocky Mountain News; Times.

DES MOINES, IOWA—Population 96,691

CAPITAL—Aft. & Sun.—60,000—J. Shipley—$1.19 Daily; $1.26 Sunday. "Editorial co-operation. Fifteen theatres, ten downtown houses; six advertise daily, six Sunday. Reviews and news printed."

NEWS—Aft. & Sun.—47,043—J. A. Day, Mg. Ed.—No rates given. "Sunday circulation, 47,043. Eighteen theatres, ten downtown houses; eight advertise daily, two Sunday. Editorial co-operation."

REGISTER & TRIBUNE—Morn. Aft. & Sun.—111,517—Rates not given. "Sunday circulation, 70,745. Editorial co-operation. Eighteen theatres, six downtown; six advertise daily. Reviews and news printed."

STUDIO DIRECTORY

DETROIT, MICHIGAN—Population 825,000

JOURNAL—Aft.—Circ. not given—C. G. Reed—Rates not given. "Special editorial co-operation. One hundred and twenty theatres, thirty downtown houses; twenty-five advertise daily and Sunday. Reviews and news printed. Mats of stars can be used often."

DETROIT NEWS—Aft.—218,589—H. Heffernon—$4.20 per inch; $2.80 Sun. Sunday circulation 182,203. About 180 theatres, twenty-five downtown; ten advertise daily, ten Sunday. Reviews given; liberal number of stories used Sunday.

FREE PRESS—Morn.—Circ. not given—Mary Humphrey—$4.90 daily; $5.60 Sun. "Sunday picture department, which devotes several columns to 'Specials,' and also a column called 'Screen Chat.' Special editorial co-operation. One hundred and fifty theatres, twenty-five downtown; twenty-five advertise Sunday, twenty-five daily."

TIMES—Aft.—18,000—R. E. Marcotte—$2.10 inch. "Theatres advertise in Detroit Times-Journal daily and Detroit News and Free Press Saturday night. Liberal amount of reading notices given. Editorial co-operation."

DU BOIS, PENNSYLVANIA—Population 14,007

COURIER—Morn.—Circ. not given—H. B. Lindsay—Rates not given. "Reviews and news printed. Editorial co-operation. Three theatres; one ad advertises daily. Circulation not given."

DAILY EXPRESS—Aft. 3,300—Howard Hasbrook—Rates not given. "No special editorial co-operation. No reading notices given. News of players and features given. Four theatres, four downtown; two advertise daily."

DUBUQUE, IOWA—Population 39,428

TIMES-JOURNAL—Morn., Aft. & Sun.—5,858—A. C. Bordeaux—42 cts. inch. Sunday circulation 11,632. Reviews given, but news of players and features printed only occasionally. Editorial co-operation. Eight theatres, five downtown; eight advertise Sunday, eight daily."

DULUTH, MINNESOTA—Population 89,331

DULUTH NEWS-TRIBUNE—Morn., Aft. & Sun.—22,000—J. E. Rice—$1.50 inch. Sunday circulation 30,000. Twelve theatres, seven downtown; six advertise daily, eight Sunday. Editorial co-operation. Picture column daily for past two years."

DURHAM, NORTH CAROLINA—Population 22,863

MORNING HERALD—Morn. & Sun.—5,966—W. N. Keener, Mg. Ed.—22½ cts. inch. Sunday circulation 5,966. Editorial co-operation. Five theatres, four downtown; three advertise daily. News and reviews printed. Assist in preparing advertising."

EASTON, PENNSYLVANIA—Population 29,882

EXPRESS—Aft.—11,481—Katherine McGrath—37½ cts. inch. "No special editorial co-operation. Eight theatres, four downtown houses; eight advertise daily. Prepares advertising copy if requested."

FREE PRESS—Aft.—15,445—C. N. Anderson—29 cts. inch. "No special editorial co-operation. Eight theatres, four downtown; eight advertise daily. News printed but no reviews."

EAST ST. LOUIS, ILLINOIS—Population 69,502

DAILY JOURNAL—Aft. & Sun.—10,000—J. W. Reid—Rates not given. Sunday circulation 10,000. Eight theatres, three downtown; three advertise daily. No special editorial co-operation. Two columns of reading notices given daily."

EAST LIVERPOOL, OHIO—Population 21,577

REVIEW—Aft.—6,214—F. A. O'Hanlon—Rates not given. "Editorial co-operation. Five theatres, all downtown; five advertise daily. Runs Monday amusement page."

MORNING TRIBUNE—Morn.—J. R. Meek, Mg. Ed.—15 cts. inch. "Eight theatres, five downtown; four advertise daily. No special editorial co-operation. Would like designs of ads that the exhibitors don't get."

EAU CLAIRE, WISCONSIN—Population 18,647

LEADER & TELEGRAM—Morn. & Aft.—9,200—Editor's name not given—30 cts. inch. "Sunday circulation 9,200. No special editorial co-operation. Four theatres, all downtown; four advertise daily. News and reviews printed occasionally."

BULLETIN—Morn. & Aft.—Circ. not given—Rates not given. Editorial co-operation. "Ten theatres, eight downtown; eight advertise daily. Editorial co-operation. Reviews and news printed. Reading notices printed to considerable extent."

EDMONTON, ALBERTA, CANADA—Population 70,000

JOURNAL—Aft.—21,782—F. H. McPherson—70 cts. inch. "Reading notices printed on same ratio as display space. No special editorial co-operation. News printed on Saturday only. Six theatres, all downtown; five advertise daily."

ELGIN, ILLINOIS—Population 27,485

NEWS—Aft.—7,284—J. E. Thompson—Four downtown; four advertise daily. Editorial co-operation. "Sixteen theatres, four downtown; four advertise daily. Editorial co-operation. Prints reading notices freely on Saturday. Reviews and news printed."

ELIZABETH, NEW JERSEY—Population 82,411

ELIZABETH DAILY JOURNAL—Aft.—Circ. not given—57 cts. inch. "No special editorial co-operation. Thirteen theatres, five downtown; four advertise daily. Reviews printed."

PUBLIC OPINION—Morn.—4,740—Ross K. Gilbert, Mg. Ed.—19 cts. inch. "No special editorial co-operation. Two theatres, both downtown; both advertise daily. Mats used, which are deemed best by local exhibitors."

VALLEY SPIRIT—Aft.—1,070—Robt. Sellers, Adv. Mg.—25 cts. inch. Editorial co-operation. News of motion picture stars printed regularly. Two theatres, two downtown; both advertise daily."

ELKHART, INDIANA—Population 21,028

REVIEW—Aft.—3,500—Paul Shafer—Rates not given. "No special editorial co-operation. Five theatres, all downtown; four advertise daily. Gives reasonable amount of daily reading notices. News printed once a week."

ELMIRA, NEW YORK—Population 41,809

STAR-GAZETTE—Aft.—25,889—M. D. Richardson—75 cts. inch. "No special editorial co-operation. Four theatres, all downtown; four advertise daily. News printed on special or unusual features."

ELMIRA HERALD—10,316—Mary Connelly—30 cts. inch. "Reviews and news printed. Cuts of recognized stars used with sketches of same. Editorial co-operation. Five theatres, four downtown; five advertise daily."

EL PASO, TEXAS—Population 49,505

HERALD—Aft. & Sun.—25,000—G. A. Martin—Rates not given. Sunday circulation 30,000. Eighteen theatres, ten downtown; six advertise daily. Feature articles with cuts printed regularly. Programs for following week run every Saturday."

STUDIO DIRECTORY

ELYRIA, OHIO—Population 17,396

CHRONICLE-TELEGRAM—Aft.—7,500—J. F. Burke, Mg. Ed.—Rates not given "Four theatres, all downtown; four advertise daily. No special editorial co-operation. Reading notices printed occasionally."

ENID, OKLAHOMA—Population 18,209

DAILY EAGLE—Aft. & Sun.—4,798—W. M. Taylor—Rates not given "Sunday circulation 5,009. No special editorial co-operation. Four theatres, all downtown; four advertise daily."

ERIE, PENNSYLVANIA—Population 72,401

HERALD—Aft. & Sun.—8,955—Frank Dillon—42 cts. inch "Sunday circulation 9,500. Fifteen theatres, five downtown; five advertise daily, five Sunday. Editorial co-operation. Reading notices daily."

EUGENE, OREGON—Population—12,083

REGISTER—Morn. & Sun.—4,548—Otto Gilstrap, Photo. Ed.—25 cts. inch. "Sunday circulation 4,733. Four theatres, three downtown; three advertise daily; one Sunday. No special editorial co-operation."

EUREKA, CALIFORNIA—Population—13,768

STANDARD—Aft.—5,073—E. S. Ballard, Photo. Ed.—28 cts. inch. "Editorial co-operation. Four theatres, all downtown; four advertise daily. Gives generous allowance of space each day for reading notices."

EVANSTON, ILLINOIS—Population—27,724

THE EVANSTON NEWS-INDEX—Aft.—4,600—A. H. Bowman, Mg. Ed.—50 cts. to $1.00 contract. Three theatres, two downtown; three advertise daily. Reading notices printed occasionally when requested."

EVANSVILLE, INDIANA—Population—71,284

COURIER—Morn. & Sun.—24,194—Miss Sursa, Photo. Ed.—Rate omitted. "Sunday circulation 21,177. No special editorial co-operation. News printed. Reviews of pictures and players given."

PRESS—Aft. Circ. omitted—May Cameron, Photo. Ed.—98 cts. inch. Editorial co-operation. "Ten theatres, three downtown houses; four advertise daily. News and reviews printed."

EVERETT, WASHINGTON—Population—32,848

HERALD—Aft.—12,452—Chas. Coleman, Mg. Ed.—75 cts. inch. "No special editorial co-operation. Layouts printed. Seven theatres, all downtown; seven advertise daily."

TRIBUNE—Morn. & Sun.—3,174—A. R. Fenwick, Mg. Ed.—20 cts inch "Editorial co-operation. Reasonable amount of reading notices printed gratis. Four theatres, all downtown; three advertise daily. News of features printed."

FARGO, NORTH DAKOTA—Population—16,351

CURIER-NEWS—Morn.—13,629—R. M. McClintock, Photo. Ed.—50 cts. inch. "Eight theatres, all downtown; three advertise daily. Editorial co-operation. Reviews and news printed."

FARGO FORUM—Aft.—11,559—H. P. Paulson, Mg. Ed.—Rate omitted "No special editorial co-operation. Seven theatres, all downtown; seven advertise daily. Limited amount of news printed; reviews occasionally."

FITCHBURG, MASSACHUSETTS—Population—40,507

SENTINEL—Aft.—6,912—Henry O'Keefe, Photo. Ed.—35 cts. inch. "Amusement notices used Wednesday and Saturday. Liberal reading notices on Saturday. No special editorial co-operation. Five theatres, four downtown; four advertise daily."

FLINT, MICHIGAN—Population—49,546

JOURNAL—Aft.—24,829—C. H. McKinley, Photo. Ed.—Rate omitted. "Twenty theatres, nine downtown; seven advertise daily. Editorial co-operation. Reviews for theatres having both amusement and commercial rates."

FOND DU LAC, WISCONSIN—Population 20,367

COMMONWEALTH—Aft.—5,755—E. M. Jenison, Photo. Ed.—Rate omitted. "Four theatres, all downtown; four advertise daily. Reviews given. No special editorial co-operation."

THE DAILY REPORTER—Aft.—Circ. omitted—Rate omitted "If news is news it is printed, if advertising it is not. Use cuts and mats with advertising contract. No special editorial co-operation."

FORT WAYNE, INDIANA—Population—72,322

JOURNAL GAZETTE—Morn. & Sun.—28,629—E. R. Lewis, Photo. Ed.—50 cts. in. "Sunday circulation 24,500. Fifteen theatres, ten downtown; ten advertise daily, five Sunday. One double column cut of fair size with story. No special editorial co-operation."

NEWS & SENTINEL—Aft.—32,566—C. L. Schroeder, Photo. Ed.—Rate omitted. "No readers except calendar on Saturday showing all attractions for coming week. News printed according to value. No special editorial co-operation. Ten theatres, five downtown houses, seven advertise daily."

FORT WORTH, TEXAS—Population—94,494

RECORD—Morn. & Sun.—Combined circ. 25,000—Miss Kimble, Photo. Ed.—$2.50 in. "Layout Sunday with readers; editorial co-operation. Eight downtown houses, six advertise daily and Sunday. Reading notices and news printed liberally."

FORT WORTH STAR-TELEGRAM—Aft. & Sun.—62,123—Mary B. Leffler, Photo. Ed.—$2.50 inch. "Sunday circulation 65,000. No special editorial co-operation. Twelve theatres, ten downtown houses; five advertise daily, five Sunday."

FRESNO, CALIFORNIA—Population—29,809

HERALD—Aft.—8,972—Roy Garman, Photo. Ed.—Rate omitted. "Six theatres, all downtown; all advertise daily. No special editorial co-operation. Assist in preparation of advertising."

GADSDEN, ALABAMA—Population—13,326

JOURNAL—Aft.—4,722—C. A. Ver Beck, Mg. Ed.—Rate omitted. "No special editorial co-operation. Gives notices on special attractions. All vertising prepared for two theatres. Three theatres; two advertise daily."

GALVESTON, TEXAS—Population—40,289

THE NEWS—Morn. & Sun.—combined circ, 11,722—L. C. Elbert, Mg. Ed.—Rate omitted. "Eight theatres, seven downtown; two advertise regularly, others periodically. No special editorial co-operation."

TRIBUNE—Aft.—9,275—Circ. omitted—Ed. omitted—Rate omitted "Eight theatres, seven downtown; two advertise daily. No special editorial co-operation."

GARDNER, MASSACHUSETTS—Population—16,353

THE NEWS—3,327—S. W. Rogers, Mg. Ed.—25 cts. inch. "One theatre; advertises daily. Use readers furnished by theatre. News printed at request of theatre managers."

GARY, INDIANA—Population—16,802

POST—Aft.—5,010—A. M. Harris, Photo. Ed.—35 cts. inch. "Eleven theatres, ten downtown; eight advertise daily. No special editorial co-operation. Cuts and mats used when possible."

496   STUDIO DIRECTORY

HACKENSACK, NEW JERSEY—Population 16,011

RECORD—Aft.—5,000—J. Smith, Photo. Ed.—25 cts. inch. "Six theatres; four advertise daily. Readers are run daily. Items submitted in plates or mat form are sometimes run as fillers. Prefer 60-line cuts."

HALIFAX, NOVA SCOTIA—Population 46,619

DAILY ECHO—Aft.—10,002—J. Gowen, Mg. Ed.—50 cts. inch. "Ten theatres; eight advertise daily. Each theatre has a free reading notice every day. Runs full page of picture items daily and two pages on Saturday."

ECHO—Aft.—11,000—H. Jones, Ed.—50 cts. inch. "Runs photoplay department on Saturday. Runs daily reading notices. Conducts its own reviews."

HAMILTON, ONTARIO—Population 81,969

SPECTATOR—Aft.—31,000—G. McKenty, Photo. Ed.—10 cts. line. "Thirteen theatres. All advertise; some daily and some three times a week. Runs reading notices occasionally, in proportion to the advertising. Runs cuts for the local houses when the ad space bought warrants this practice."

HAMILTON, OHIO—Population 81,969

JOURNAL—Aft.—7,435—H. Gard, Photo. Ed.—45 cts. inch. "Six theatres, four of which advertise daily. Runs reading notices every day."
DAILY REPUBLICAN-NEWS—Aft.—6,299—C. Greenawalt, Photo. Ed.—40 cts. inch. "Runs daily reading notices with the advertising. Reviews more important pictures by member of the staff."

HAMMOND, INDIANA—Population 24,481

TIMES—Aft.—10,000—P. Parry, Photo. Ed.—40 cts. inch. "Four theatres; all advertise daily. Has a photoplay section in the Saturday issue occasionally. Runs daily reading notices."

HARTFORD, CONNECTICUT—Population 107,038

POST—Aft.—10,658—C. Hemenway, Mg. Ed.—$1.40 inch. "Eight theatres advertise daily of the eleven in the location. Reading notices in the daily picture section which is given special attention in the Saturday issue. Would use mats."

TIMES—Aft.—36,055—R. Andrews, Mg. Ed.—$1.54 inch. "Gives daily reading notices to those carrying ads at $1.54 an inch. Would use cuts if not too large." Additional paper: Courant.

HATTIESBURG, MISSISSIPPI—Population 14,952

AMERICAN—Aft.—4,020—G. Butler, Photo. Ed.—50 cts. inch. "Three theatres; two advertise daily. Runs reading notices daily. Would use cuts."

HAVERHILL, MASSACHUSETTS—Population 47,071

GAZETTE—Aft.—13,716—R. Wright, Mg. Ed.—50 cts. inch. "Four theatres, all of which advertise daily. Runs daily reading notices."

HAZELTON, PENNSYLVANIA—Population 27,511

PLAIN SPEAKER—Aft.—7,684—W. Dershuck, Ed.—25 cts. inch. "Ten theatres; seven advertise daily. Runs a special page on Saturday in which is included a weekly review."
STANDARD-SENTINEL—Morn.—7,900—Henry Walser, Mg. Ed.—25 cts. inch. "Runs a theatre page on Saturday, including from one-half to one column of reading notices."

TRIBUNE—Aft.—4,792—A. G. Perry, Photo. Ed.—35 cts. inch. "No special editorial co-operation. Fourteen theatres, seven downtown; seven advertise daily."

GLENS FALLS, NEW YORK—Population 16,313

POST-STAR—Morn.—8,045—R. E. Fairman, Mg. Ed.—30 cts. inch. "Three theatres; all advertise daily. No special editorial co-operation. News and readers printed occasionally."

TIMES—Aft.—6,250—C. V. Furness, Mg. Ed.—35 cts. inch. "Five theatres, five downtown theatres; all advertise daily. No special editorial co-operation. News printed occasionally."

GRAND FORKS, NORTH DAKOTA—Population 14,827

HERALD—Morn, Aft. & Sun.—16,000—G. Benson, Mg. Ed.—40 cts. inch. "Six theatres; all advertise daily. Sunday circulation 11,582. Runs reading notices daily in proportion to advertising. Has Sunday picture section."

GRAND RAPIDS, MICHIGAN—Population 123,227

HERALD—Morn, & Sun.—32,417—C. Saunders, Photo. Ed.—$1.75 inch. "Thirty-nine theatres; two advertise daily and six on Sunday. Runs reading notices daily and on Sunday publishes a picture page. Prefer photographs."

NEWS—Aft.—16,582—L. Parcell, Photo. Ed.—$1.40 inch. "Saturday issue has amusement section covering all theatrical news. Runs daily reading notices. Conducts its own reviews." Additional paper: Press.

GREAT FALLS, MONTANA—Population 13,948

LEADER—Aft.—4,043—O. DeSchou, Photo. Ed.—Rate omitted. "Five theatres; three advertise daily. Would be willing to run Saturday photoplay section if managers supplied the material. Would use mats."

DAILY TRIBUNE—Morn. & Sun.—12,551—L. Diehl, Ad. Mgr.—Rate omitted. "Weekly reviews are given free; daily readers are run at 5 cts. per line. Would use pictures of well-known artists."

GREENSBORO, NORTH CAROLINA—Population 18,391

DAILY RECORD—Aft.—3,481—J. Watkins, Mg. Ed.—25 cts. inch. "Runs theatre page Saturday. Gives daily reading notices. Three theatres; all advertise daily."

GREENSBURG, PENNSYLVANIA—Population 14,687

RECORD—Aft.—4,200—E. Laughlin, Mg. Ed.—15 cts. inch. "Three theatres; two advertise daily. Runs daily reading notices pertaining to current shows. Prefers mats."

TRIBUNE—Aft.—Circ. Omitted—S. Morgan, Jr., Mg. Ed.—8-12 cts. inch. "Runs daily reading notices. Would run mats when possible."

GREENVILLE, SOUTH CAROLINA—Population 17,395

DAILY PIEDMONT—Aft.—Circ. Omitted—F. Challen, Photo. Ed.—30 cts. inch. "Runs readers every day. Six theatres, four of which advertise daily. Would use mats."

DAILY NEWS—Morn. & Sun.—10,376—B. Peace, Mg. Ed.—42 cts. inch. "Sunday circulation 8,895. Runs an amusement page on Sunday. Runs daily reading notices on about 50% basis."

GUELPH, ONTARIO—Population 15,175

HERALD—Aft.—3,240—A. Smith, Mg. Ed.—56 cts. inch. "Three theatres, two of which advertise daily. Runs daily reading notices. Conducts its own reviews."

GUTHRIE, OKLAHOMA—Population 11,911

LEADER—Aft.—12,800—Ed. Omitted—Rate omitted. "Three theatres, two of which advertise daily. Has Saturday picture page and runs daily reading notices."

STUDIO DIRECTORY

HELENA, MONTANA—Population 13,258

INDEPENDENT—Morn. & Sun.—4,855—B. Haralson, Photo. Ed.—35 cts. inch. "Sunday circulation 5,600. Four theatres, all of which advertise daily. On Sunday has a photoplay department. Conducts its own reviews. Prints daily reading notices."

RECORD-HERALD—Aft.—Circ. omitted—G. Roberts, Mg. Ed.—35 cts. inch. "Publishes a daily 'Movie Column,' including the reading notices of the current attractions. On Saturday runs one to two pages of theatrical and picture news, including cuts and calendar of attractions."

HOLYOKE, MASSACHUSETTS—Population 62,852

TELEGRAM—Aft.—8,600—W. Rathbun, Photo. Ed.—25 cts. inch "Six theatres; three advertise daily. Runs readers every day from three to ten inches per house. Would use mats or cuts of clean, interesting, newsy matter."

TRANSCRIPT—Aft.—12,500—A. Anders, Photo. Ed.—40 cts. inch "Runs a photoplay section two or three times a week. Liberal space given two or three times a week with free illustrations, depending on the size of the advertisement."

HOUSTON, TEXAS (Cont.)—Population 93,122

PRESS—Aft.—Circ. omitted—J. Elfenbein, Photo Ed.—Rate omitted "Runs daily reading notices which are considered to be of news value. Has photoplay department in the Saturday issue. Conducts reviews on Monday."

HUTCHINSON, KANSAS—Population 19,339

GAZETTE—Morn. & Sun.—8,433—M. Rose, Photo. Ed.—40-65 cts. inch. "Sunday circulation 8,675. Six theatres, five of which advertise daily. Runs daily reading notices in proportion to the advertising bought."

NEWS—Aft.—11,471—G. Gwinn, Photo. Ed.—35 cts. inch "In the Saturday issue reviews of the coming week's attractions are printed from the reading notices submitted. Occasionally an amusement page and special features are run."

INDEPENDENCE, KANSAS—Population—13,296

REPORTER—Aft.—2,613—C. Knox, Mg. Ed.—Rate omitted. "Runs daily reading notices. Prints reviews conducted by members of the staff."

INDIANAPOLIS, INDIANA—Population—259,413

NEWS—Aft.—118,639—R. Smith, Mg. Ed.—17 cts. line. "Runs photoplay section on Wednesday and Saturday. In these issues, includes the reading notices. Prints reviews conducted by member of staff."

STAR—Morn. & Sun.—93,170—C. Kelly, Photo. Ed.—15 cts. line. "Fifty-two theatres; twenty advertise daily. Runs Sunday photoplay department and a column of reading notices each day during the week. Conducts its own reviews. Sunday circulation 106,647."

DAILY TIMES—Aft.—47,856—M. Mercer, Photo. Ed.—12 cts. line. "Publishes reading notices to liberal extent every day and conducts photoplay department on Sunday. Prefers photographs."

ITHACA, NEW YORK—Population—16,759

DAILY NEWS—Aft.—Circ. omitted—C. Platt, Mg. Ed.—25 cts. inch. "Five theatres; all advertise daily. Runs reading notices every day. Would use mats."

JOURNAL—Aft.—6,668—G. Stover, Photo. Ed.—50 cts. inch. "Runs daily reading notices. Occasionally prints reviews of pictures conducted by member of staff."

JACKSON, MISSISSIPPI—Population—26,790

DAILY NEWS—Aft. & Sun.—5,695—H. Bricknell, Mg. Ed.—35 cts. inch. "Sunday circulation 5,695. Three houses; two advertise daily. Runs photoplay department on Sunday and gives liberal space to readers and cuts during the week."

JACKSON, TENNESSEE—Population—16,318

SUN—Aft. & Sun.—4,161—C. Brown, Mg. Ed.—Rate omitted. "In Sunday issue runs reading notices. Would use mats and proofs."

JACKSONVILLE, FLORIDA—Population—70,173

TIMES-UNION—Morn. & Sun.—30,000—Ed. omitted—Rate omitted. "Sunday circulation 35,000. Eight theatres; five advertise daily. Runs four pages or more in picture section on Sunday. Also gives brief reading notices each day during the week."

JAMESTOWN, NEW YORK—Population—37,839

JOURNAL—Aft.—7,570—J. Clary, Mg. Ed.—Rate omitted. "Seven theatres; four of these advertise daily. No special publicity service rendered."

JANESVILLE, WISCONSIN—Population—14,195

GAZETTE—Aft.—8,200—A. HELMS, Mg. Ed.—Rate omitted. "Four theatres all advertise daily. Publishes a daily photoplay feature. Conducts its own reviews."

JERSEY CITY, NEW JERSEY—Population—293,921

JERSEY JOURNAL—Aft.—37,151—J. MacKenzie, Photo. Ed.—15 cts. line. "About forty theatres; eighteen advertise daily. On Saturday runs reading notices according to the amount of advertising space bought."

JOHNSTOWN, PENNSYLVANIA—Population—54,542

DEMOCRAT—Morn.—10,700—J. Blough, Photo. Ed.—Rate omitted. "Eight theatres; four advertise daily. Reading notices are carried occasionally. Conducts its own reviews."

LEADER—Aft.—8,500—F. Church, Mg. Ed.—25 cts. inch. "Would use mats of two or three-column size, if of general interest. Runs reading notices daily."

TRIBUNE—Aft.—24,434—H. Hesselbein, Mg. Ed.—Rate omitted. (No information of publicity activities submitted in questionnaire.)

JOPLIN, MISSOURI—Population—32,848

NEWS-HERALD—Aft. & Sun.—16,594—M. McGilveney, Photo. Ed.—Rate omitted. "Four theatres; three advertise daily. Sunday issue has photoplay department. No special publicity service rendered during the week."

KALAMAZOO, MICHIGAN—Population—45,842

GAZETTE—Aft. & Sun.—23,197—J. Walsh, Mg. Ed.—Rate omitted. "Sunday circulation 22,475. Eight theatres; six advertise daily. Runs daily reading notices. On Sunday publishes amusement department."

KANKAKEE, ILLINOIS—Population 14,150

GAZETTE—Aft.—2,200—H. F. Schmidt, Mg. Ed.—Rate 15 cts. inch "Six theatres. One neighborhood. Gives no reading notices but would. Exhibitors not aroused to need of publicity. Exhibitors advertise on big attractions only."

EVENING DEMOCRAT—3,612—J. O. Smith, Mg. Ed.—Rate omitted "Amusement and commercial rate the same. Gives reading notices frequently. Would use cuts of prominent actors. Reviews productions showing in the city."

KANSAS CITY, MISSOURI—Population 281,911

STAR—Morn., Aft. & Sun.—225,000—R. E. Stout, Mg. Ed.—Amus. rate 50-60 cts. "About 80 theatres. Downtown, 5. Prints photoplay section. Gives short advance notice and reviews features. Regards picture news of interest. Prefers own matter to producers' material." Other papers: Journal; Post; Times.

KINGSTON, ONTARIO, CANADA—Population 18,874

BRITISH WHIG—Aft.—D. 6,424—W. 4,152—L. A. Guild, Mg. Ed.—Rate 70 cts. inch "Give free readers to advertisers inch for inch. Reviews features. Prefers mats. Exhibitors prepare copy. Displays usually small."

KINGSTON, NEW YORK—Population 26,549

EXPRESS AND ACCORDIAN—D. and W.—Cir. and rate omitted—J. G. Sullivan, Mg. Ed. "Two theatres. Neither use the paper's columns. All of other questions not answered."

KITCHENER, ONTARIO, CANADA—Population 15,196

NEWS RECORD—Aft.—3,950—W. V. Uttley, Mg. Ed.—Rate 50 cts. inch "Three theatres, all central. Gives reading notices Saturday. Theatres prepare copy. All theatres advertise daily."

KOKOMO, INDIANA—Population 19,694

DISPATCH—Morn.—5,180—Sunday—5,500—G. Armstrong—Rate 25 cts. inch "All theatres advertise daily. Gives free reading notices. Does not print layouts. Devotes page to pictures in Sunday edition. Would use good producers' material."

DAILY TRIBUNE—Eve.—8,491—C. E. Walk—30 cts. inch "Gives free reading notices on big productions only. Prints layouts—which are charged. Would use producers' material if good, especially mats and cuts."

LACKAWANNA, NEW YORK—Population 16,346

JOURNAL—Aft.—900—Harriet Ellis—Rate 30 cts. inch "Use some picture matter. Gives reading notices in exchange for house courtesies. Would use producers' material. Five theatres. None advertise extensively."

LA CROSSE, WISCONSIN—Population 31,367

TRIBUNE AND LEADER PRESS—13,502—Aft. & Sun.—N. D. Tvis—Rate 50 cts. inch "Eight theatres. Five downtown. Gives every picture free reading notice. Regards motion picture matter of limited public interest. Theatres use ready written copy."

LAFAYETTE, INDIANA—Population 20,896

JOURNAL—Morn.—10,415—W. H. Robertson—Rate omitted "Gives Monday reading notices. Six theatres, one neighborhood. Would use good producers' material. All theatres buy small space daily."

LANCASTER, OHIO—Population 14,840

GAZETTE—Morn. & Aft.—3,650—C. J. Beach, Adv. Ed.—Rate omitted "Four theatres, all downtown. Gives small free reading notices with displays. Would use some producers' material. Exhibitors object to commercial rate."

LANCASTER, PENNSYLVANIA—Population 49,685

DAILY NEW ERA—Aft.—10,962—C. B. Hollinger—Rate 35 cts. inch "Four theatres. One neighborhood. Gives free reading notices. Prints layouts complimentary occasionally. Exhibitors prepare own copy. Exhibitors allowed to furnish reviews."

LANSING, MICHIGAN—Population 37,512

STATE JOURNAL—26,315—Aft.—F. A. Van Fleet, Mg. Ed.—Rate omitted "Gives some free reading notices. Seven theatres in city. Four advertise daily. Reviews better productions. Would use some producers' material. Exhibitors prepare all copy."

LAFAYETTE, INDIANA—Population 20,896

COURIER—Aft.—8,994—Milton Pottitzer—Rate 40 cts. inch "Six theatres. Does not give free reading notices. Prints no reviews. Would use mats and cuts under conditions. Assists exhibitors in preparing copy. Exhibitors liberal advertisers."

LA PORTE, INDIANA—Population 12,533

ARGUS—Aft.—2,250—J. A. Chanley, Mg. Ed.—Rate omitted "Three theatres. Reviews bigger productions. Regards motion picture news as of public interest. Would use cuts and mats from producers showing locally."

HERALD—Aft.—3,376—V. G. Root—Rate omitted "Three theatres. All advertise daily. Gives reading notices—and layouts occasionally—both complimentary. Theatres furnish all copy. Would use mats and cuts if gratis."

LAWRENCE, MASSACHUSETTS—Population 95,834

EAGLE-TRIBUNE—Morn., two neighborhood & Aft.—14,058—Grace Murphy—Rate 60 cts. inch "Nine theatres, two neighborhood. Six advertise daily. Gives free readers daily. Runs motion picture page weekly gratis. Uses cuts and mats."

LAWRENCE, KANSAS—Population 13,018

JOURNAL WORLD—Aft.—4,509—E. D. Keilmann, Mg. Ed.—Rate omitted "Three theatres. Two advertise daily. Gives weekly free reading notice. Regards picture news as advertising. Theatres furnish all copy."

GAZETTE—Aft.—2,390—R. Delvattville, Adv. Mgr.—Rate omitted "Three theatres. Two advertise daily. Gives weekly free readers. Regards picture news of public interest. Might use mats and cuts. Co-operates with advertisers."

LEAVENWORTH, KANSAS—Population 19,363

POST—Aft. & Sun.—D. 6,017—S. 64,417—W. Wallace—Rate 35 cts. inch "Ten theatres. Seven are neighborhood houses. Prints photoplay section in Sunday issue. Gives daily reading notices. Reviews features. Regards picture news of public interest. Uses mats and cuts. Writes most of picture theatre copy."

LEBANON, PENNSYLVANIA—Population 19,926

NEWS—Aft.—8,349—J. H. Manbeck—Rate 50 cts. inch "Three theatres. Gives daily reading notices. Aids exhibitors with copy. All theatres advertise daily. Seldom uses producers' material as news."

LEOMINSTER, MASSACHUSETTS—Population 19,789

ENTERPRISE—Aft.—3,991—W. N. Howe, Mg. Ed.—Rate 25 cts. inch "Two theatres. Gives no free reading notices, or free movie news. Would use good producers' material, including cuts. Advertisers use daily display."

LETHBRIDGE, ALBERTA, CANADA—Population 14,500

DAILY HERALD—Morn. & Aft.—D. 5,678—H. G. Long, Mg. Ed.—Rate 35 cts. inch "Three theatres. Free reading notices at discretion of the editor. Prints no layouts. Motion picture news of some public interest. Advertisers are liberal."

STUDIO DIRECTORY

LEXINGTON, KENTUCKY—Population 38,819

HERALD—Morn. D. & Sun.—11,579—E. Gehan—Rate 40 cts. inch
"Four theatres. All use display columns daily. Has no photoplay section. Gives no free reading notices. Reviews big productions. Regards photoplay news of public interest."

LEADER—Aft. & Sun.—13,400—J. M. Ross—Rate 35 cts. inch
"Four theatres. Give small readers daily. Reviews productions occasionally. Might use some producers' material, especially mats and cuts. Theatres prepare all copy."

LEWISTON, MAINE—Population 27,305

SUN—Morn.—9,259—L. B. Mills—Rate 50 cts. inch
"Four theatres. Gives some free readers. Has no photoplay section. Would use producers' material to some extent. All theatres advertise and prepare own copy."

LIMA, OHIO—Population 33,904

NEWS—Aft. & Sun.—12,500—Marshall Harrison—Rate 50 cts. inch
"Eight theatres. One neighborhood. Prints photoplay section in Sunday issue. Gives free readers Sunday only. Regards pictures of news interest. Would use cuts and mats."

TIMES-DEMOCRAT—Aft.—7,125—W. J. Galvin—Rate 30 cts. inch
"Eight theatres. Five advertise daily. Gives free readers daily. Reviews pictures. Regards pictures of news interest. Would use cuts and mats. Advertisers buy liberal space."

LINCOLN, NEBRASKA—Population 45,643

DAILY STAR—Aft. & Sun.—D. 31,267—Mrs. R. Hilton—Rate omitted
"Seven theatres. Two neighborhood. Five advertise daily. Run readers but are charged at regular rates. Has photoplay section. Would use mats and cuts."

LITTLE FALLS, NEW YORK—Population 13,045

TIMES—Aft.—3,100—John Crowley, Mg. Ed.—Rate 25 cts. inch
"Three theatres. All advertise daily. Gives short free readers to advertisers. Co-operates with theatres. Does not regard M. P. news of public interest."

LITTLE ROCK, ARKANSAS—Population 53,811

DEMOCRAT—Aft.—23,342—J. W. Enochs—Rate 70 cts. inch
"Six theatres; five advertise daily. Reading notices given on Saturday. Prints movie news occasionally. Would use good mats and cuts. Co-operates with advertisers."

DAILY NEWS—Aft.—11,200—R. P. Ronnins, Mg. Ed.—Rate 40 cts. inch
"Seven theatres; all advertise. Publishes page devoted to theatres in Saturday edition. No free daily reading notices. All exhibitors buy small space."

LOGANSPORT, INDIANA—Population 20,262

TRIBUNE—Morn & Sun.—5,450—L. P. Demier—Rate omitted
"Five theatres; all advertise daily. Gives free daily reading notices and prints layouts frequently. Prints movie news, and uses mats and cuts."

PHARAS REPORTER—Aft.—6,621—A. J. West—Rate 35 cts. inch
"Five theatres; four advertise. Gives daily reading notices. Regards picture news of interest to public. Can use mats and cuts."

LONDON, ONTARIO, CANADA—Population 46,300

ADVERTISER—Noon—43,000—A. E. Wigle—Rate omitted
"Seven theatres; five advertise daily. Gives daily reading notices. Regards movie news as interesting to public. Assists exhibitors with copy."

FREE PRESS—Morn. & Aft.—41,610—Grace Blackburn—Rate $2.30 inch
"Six theatres; four advertise daily. Gives free readers line for line with display purchased. Gives complete reviews. Regards picture news of value to public."

LONG BEACH, CALIFORNIA—Population 24,437

PRESS—Aft.—7,000—C. Cutshaw, Mg. Ed.—Rate 75 cts. inch
"Eight theatres; four advertise daily. Optional commercial rate of 28c. offered without reading notices. Contemplates using layouts. Considers movie news good copy."

DAILY TELEGRAM—Aft.—6,576—W. H. Case, Mg. Ed.—Rate 75 cts.
"Seven theatres. Three advertise daily. No photoplay section. No free reading notices. Prints no movie news free. Regards movie news interesting to public."

LORAIN, OHIO—Population 34,360

TIMES-HERALD—Aft.—8,500—Ed. not stated—Rate omitted
"Nine theatres; six advertise daily. Reading notices given every day. Prints no movie news."

LOS ANGELES, CALIFORNIA—Population 600,000

EXAMINER—Morn & Sun.—Cir. omitted—Florence Lawrence—Rate omitted
"About 80 theatres. Twenty located downtown. Fifteen advertise in daily and Sunday issue. Gives reading notices in turn. Prints reviews. Regards movie news of interest to public. Producers furnish newspapers with copy."

EXPRESS—Aft.—55,957—M. Lathrop—Rate $2.38 inch
"About 80 theatres. Nineteen located downtown. Twenty advertise in daily and Sunday issues. Prints photoplay section. Does not give free reading notices. Layouts used are complimentary. Movie news of great interest. Producers' press staff furnish copy."

EVENING HERALD—Aft.—139,000—Guy Price—Rate $3.08 inch
"About 80 theatres. Twenty located downtown. Twenty advertise daily. In addition to weekly photoplay page, reading notices are given. Paper specializes in the field. Exhibitors buy big space."

RECORD—Aft.—42,000—W. P. Campbell, P. Ed.—Rate $1.25 inch
Other papers: Herald; Times; Tribune.

LOUISVILLE, KENTUCKY—Population—235,114

EVENING POST—Aft.—42,425—P. Marshall, Photo. Ed.—16 cts. line.
"Thirty-one theatres; nine advertise daily. Runs a photoplay section daily, including reading notices. Would use mats and electros."

TIMES—Aft.—63,043—M. Aronhime, Photo. Ed.—17 cts. line.
"Runs photoplay section in the Saturday issue. Prints daily reading notices. Would use photos of leading artists."

COURIER-JOURNAL—Sun.—Circ. omitted—(Same management as the Times).
"Runs full page of picture news, including reviews conducted by member of the staff."
Additional paper: Herald.

LOWELL, MASSACHUSETTS—Population—111,004

COURIER-CITIZEN—Morn. & Aft.—16,780—S. Fleet, Photo. Ed.—49 cts. inch.
"Ten theatres; eight advertise daily. Gives reading notices every day, allowing four lines of reader material to one inch of display."

LYNN, MASSACHUSETTS—Population—98,207

ITEM—Aft.—15,121—H. Valpey, Photo. Ed.—80 cts. inch.
"Eleven theatres, six advertise daily. In the Saturday issue publishes a photoplay department, including the reading notices."

TELEGRAM-NEWS—Aft. & Sun.—15,311—A. Erwin, Photo. Ed.
"Runs daily reading notices in proportion to the advertising. Would use cuts or mats if they concern the artists themselves."

STUDIO DIRECTORY

McKEESPORT, PENNSYLVANIA—Population—45,965
DAILY NEWS—Aft.—11,310—J. Long, Mg. Ed.—Rate omitted.
"Seven theatres; all advertise daily. Reading notices are given in proportion to the paid advertising and depending on the quality of the picture."

MACON, GEORGIA—Population—41,992
NEWS—Aft. & Sun.—19,547—T. Simmons, Mg. Ed.—$1.00 inch.
"Five theatres; four advertise daily. Photoplay department occupies about ten or twelve inches on week-days and a full page on Sunday. The photoplay department is carried on in close co-operation with the show management. Sunday circulation 17,429."
TELEGRAPH—Morn. & Sun.—21,589—G. Long, Mg. Ed.—$1.00 inch.
"Sunday circulation 19,986. No special publicity service rendered."

MADISON, WISCONSIN—Population—29,469
CAPITAL TIMES—Aft.—10,800—W. Evjue, Mg. Ed.—25 cts. inch.
"Six theatres; five advertise daily. Runs daily reading notices. Would use 65-line half-tone cuts. Conducts its own reviews."
DEMOCRAT—Morn. & Sun.—5,861—H. Noll, Mg. Ed.—22 cts. inch.
"Runs daily reading notices. Publishes Sunday stage page. Sunday circulation 5,975."

MAHANOY CITY, PENNSYLVANIA—Population—16,951
AMERICAN-TRIBUNE—Aft.—2,590—J. Kirchner, Ad. Mgr.—Rate omitted.
"Two theatres; both advertise daily. Runs daily reading notices."

MANCHESTER, CONNECTICUT—Population—13,641
HERALD—Aft.—3,177—W. Asimus, Photo. Ed.—50 cts. inch.
"Two theatres; both advertise daily. Runs daily reading notices, allowing one-quarter column for each theatre."

MANCHESTER, NEW HAMPSHIRE—Population—76,635
UNION—Morn.—25,554—F. Frisselle, Photo. Ed.—$1.00 inch.
"Ten theatres; four advertise daily. Publishes a reader for each house on the day that the program changes. On Saturday runs two or three columns covering all theatres and includes program for the coming week."
LEADER—Aft.—(Same management as the Union).
MIRROR—Aft.—5,172—R. Blood, Mg. Ed.—5 cts. line.
"On Saturday usually carries a page of picture news and on other days a column or two. Conducts its own reviews. Would use cuts or mats."

MANISTEE, MICHIGAN—Population—12,381
NEWS-ADVOCATE—Aft.—2,912—R. Anderson, Photo. Ed.—25 cts. inch.
"Runs reading notices daily, the extent depending on the quality of the pictures shown. Reviews its own pictures."

MANSFIELD, OHIO—Population—22,100
SHIELD—Morn. & Sun.—3,557—W. Angle, Photo. Ed.—12 cts. inch.
"Six theatres; all advertise daily. Runs reading notices daily from one to two columns. Reviews its own reviews."

MARIETTA, OHIO—Population—12,923
JOURNAL—Aft.—4,123—L. Harness, Mg. Ed.—15 cts. inch.
"Three theatres; all advertise daily. Runs cuts and readers daily. Can use unmounted cuts or mats."
DAILY TIMES—Aft.—4,924—F. McKinney, Mg. Ed.—15 cts. inch.
"Runs daily from twenty to twenty-five lines of readers, depending on the amount of advertising carried. Would use mats or cuts but not over the two-column size."
REGISTER-LEADER—Aft.—3,137—T. O'Donnell, Photo. Ed.—15 cts. inch.
"Runs reading notices daily. Would use 65-line screen mats."

MARINETTE, WISCONSIN—Population—14,610
EAGLE-STAR—Aft. Circ. omitted—F. Noyes, Mgr.—Rate omitted.
"Four theatres; three advertise daily. Runs reading notices occasionally. Sometimes reviews pictures by member of staff."

MARION, INDIANA—Population—19,656
CHRONICLE—Aft.—6,830—E. Moss, Ad. Mgr.—Rate omitted.
"Five theatres; all advertise daily. Carries Saturday photoplay department. Runs readers to extent of 50% of paid advertising."

MARION, OHIO—Population—22,032
TRIBUNE—Aft.—5,500—L. Lamborn, Mg. Ed.—35 cts. inch.
"Five houses; four of which advertise daily. Runs reading notices about three times a week."
STAR—Aft.—10,086—G. Van Fleet, Mg. Ed.—Rate omitted.
"On Saturday runs a 300-line review of the coming week's program."

MARQUETTE, MICHIGAN—Population—12,117
MINING JOURNAL—Morn.—5,240—F. Russell, Mg. Ed.—20 cts. inch.
"Six theatres; all advertise daily. Reading notices are run daily. Synopsis of pictures advertised for the day are printed on the same date."

MARLBORO, MASSACHUSETTS—Population—14,991
ENTERPRISE—Aft.—2,900—E. Merriman, Mg. Ed.—Rate omitted.
"Three theatres, two of which advertise daily. No special publicity service rendered."

MARSHALL, TEXAS—Population—12,984
MESSENGER—Aft.—1,250—H. Henderson, Mg. Ed.—20 cts. inch.
"Two theatres, both of which advertise daily. Runs daily reading notices."
SENTINEL—Morn. & Sun.—2,300—H. Price, Mg. Ed.—15 cts. inch.
"Runs reading notices of brief length every day."

MARSHALLTOWN, IOWA—Population—16,025
TIMES-REPUBLICAN—Aft.—15,000—J. Whitacre, Photo. Ed.—40 cts. inch.
"Gives review only of the pictures played. Will use cuts or mats at regular advertising rates."

MARTINSBURG, WEST VIRGINIA—Population—12,032
JOURNAL—Aft.—3,319—M. von Schlegell, Mg. Ed.—Rate omitted.
"Three theatres; all advertise daily. Reading notices are run daily. Would use mats or cuts."
WORLD—Aft.—2,879—G. McKown, Mg. Ed.—Rate omitted.
"Give reading notices nearly every day, printing reviews of best pictures."

MASON CITY, IOWA—Population—13,495
GLOBE GAZETTE—Aft.—9,602—W. Muse, Mg. Ed.—35 cts. inch.
"Four theatres; all advertise daily. Runs photoplay department on Saturday. Conducts its own reviews."

MATTOON, ILLINOIS—Population—12,218
JOURNAL-GAZETTE—Aft.—3,214—Ed. omitted—Rate omitted.
"Three houses, all of which advertise daily. No special publicity service rendered."

MEMPHIS, TENNESSEE—Population—143,231
PRESS—Aft.—27,352—R. Roddy, Photo. Ed.—$1.00 inch.
"Fifteen houses, five of which advertise daily; all advertise on Saturday. Runs photoplay department on Saturday, extending liberal space to the reading notices."
Other papers: Commercial Appeal; News; Scimitar.

STUDIO DIRECTORY

MERIDIAN, MISSISSIPPI—Population—21,806
DISPATCH—Morn. & Sun.—4,000—P. Smith, Mg. Ed.—28 cts. inch. "Sunday circulation 4,000. Photoplay department is printed every day. Reading notices are published at 5 cts. per line."

MERIDEN, CONNECTICUT—Population—28,528
JOURNAL—Aft.—5,166—W. Allen, Photo. Ed.—Rate omitted. "Two houses, both of which advertise daily. Give daily reading notices."
MORNING RECORD—Morn.—Circ. omitted—Ed. omitted—90 cts. inch. "No special publicity service rendered."

MIAMI, FLORIDA—Population—16,027
HERALD—Morn. & Sun.—6,455—E. Taylor, Gen. Mgr.—50 cts. inch. "Sunday circulation 7,524. Five theatres, all of which advertise. Gives reading notices nearly every day. Would use mats or cuts."
DAILY METROPOLIS—Aft.—6,711—Ed. omitted—50 cts. inch. "Five theatres, four of which advertise daily. Gives daily reading notices."

MEADVILLE, PENNSYLVANIA—Population—13,472
MESSENGER—Morn.—Circ. omitted—Ed. and Rate omitted. "Three theatres; two advertise daily. Gives daily reading notices. Would use mats or cuts."

MICHIGAN CITY, INDIANA—Population—20,710
NEWS—Aft.—3,418—Ed. omitted. Rate omitted. "Five theatres; three advertise daily. Prints reading notices but not regularly every day."

MIDDLETOWN, OHIO—Population—14,827
NEWS-SIGNAL—Aft.—4,800—H. Spears, Mg. Ed.—20 cts. inch. "Six theatres; one advertises every other day. Gives reading notices when ads are run."

MILLVILLE, NEW JERSEY—Population—13,246
REPUBLICAN—Aft.—1,800—M. Haukins, Ad. Mgr.—30 cts. inch. "Two theatres; none advertises daily. Give one reading notice of an important picture."

MILWAUKEE, WISCONSIN—Population—417,054
JOURNAL—Aft. & Sun.—113,683—W. Rowland, Photo. Ed.—Rate omitted. "Sixty theatres; nine advertise daily. Every day reviews are run together with any other matter of interest. Sunday issue has regular photoplay department."
SENTINEL—Morn.—81,752—G. Joy, Photo. Ed.—15 cts. line. "Every Thursday a picture layout is printed. Every day reading notices and a directory are published. Photographs are preferred."
EVENING SENTINEL—Aft.—(Same management as the Sentinel).
SUNDAY SENTINEL—Sun.—67,162—(Same management as foregoing). "On Sunday a full page is devoted to all amusements." Other papers: Free Press; Leader; News; Wisconsin.

MINNEAPOLIS, MINNESOTA—Population—353,460
JOURNAL—Aft. & Sun.—99,010—C. Miles, Photo. Ed.—$3.50 inch. "Sunday circulation 90,777. Theatres number sixty-two; four advertise daily; seven on Sunday. Motion picture reviews are run every day. An announcement of the attractions at all theatres runs in box-form on Wednesday. Sunday issue carries an amusement section of from three to four pages."
DAILY NEWS—Aft.—72,127—A. Altrawitz, Photo. Ed.—$3.50 inch. "Reading notices are run daily Sunday issue carries photoplay section. Conducts its own reviews. Would use mats."

TRIBUNE—Morn, Aft. & Sun.—124,074—H. Wise, Photo. Ed.—$3.50 inch. "Sunday issue carries a photoplay department. Reviews appear on Monday. Daily reading notices are given in connection with display advertising. Sunday circulation 132,842."

MISSOULA, MONTANA—Population—16,492
MISSOULIAN—Morn. & Sun.—4,450—D. Batchelor, Photo. Ed.—35 cts. inch. "Four theatres; all advertise daily. Gives daily readers. Sunday issue extends space to picture news as liberally as circumstances will permit. Sunday circulation 5,600."

MOLINE, ILLINOIS—Population—26,403
DISPATCH—Aft.—10,800—C. Lucas, Photo. Ed.—42 cts. inch. "Saturday issue carries two pages of picture news. Gives daily reading notices. Conducts its own reviews."

MONESSEN, PENNSYLVANIA—Population—18,752
INDEPENDENT—Aft.—2,700—F. Lane, Photo. Ed.—15 cts. inch. "Two theatres; both advertise daily. Reading notices are given gratis in proportion to the amount of advertising."

MONTGOMERY, ALABAMA—Population—41,777
JOURNAL—Aft. & Sun.—22,000—J. DeMoth, Ad. Mgr.—45 cts. inch. "Five theatres; three advertise daily. Sunday issue carries photoplay department. Print reviews of features. Sunday circulation 22,000."

MONROE, LOUISIANA—Population—12,246
NEWS-STAR—Aft.—2,400—J. Smith, Mg. Ed.—20 cts. inch. "Two theatres; both advertise daily. In Saturday issue gives about four inches of reading notices."

MONTREAL, PROVINCE OF QUEBEC, CANADA—Population—473,712
GAZETTE—Morn.—40,000—T. Frazier, Photo. Ed.—7 cts. line. "About sixty-five theatres; twelve theatres advertise daily. Reading notices are printed Tuesday, Thursday and Saturdays. Prefer photographs.
DAILY STAR—Aft. Circ. omitted—S. Powell, Photo. Ed.—20 cts. line. "Carries photoplay department daily. Reading notices are run entirely dependent upon their news value. Conducts its own reviews." Other papers: Herald; Mail; News.

MOOSE JAW, SASKATCHEWAN—Population—23,000
EVENING TIMES—Aft. Circ. omitted—Ed. omitted—Rate omitted. "Two theatres; both advertise daily. Readers are printed at rate of 10 cents per line."

MORGANTOWN, WEST VIRGINIA—Population—12,239
NEW DOMINION—Morn.—2,507—R. Reid, Mg. Ed.—20 cts. inch. "Four theatres; all advertise daily. Runs daily reading notices."
POST—Aft.—3,500—C. Tucker, Photo. Ed.—10 cts. inch. "Gives daily reading notices and conducts its own reviews. Would use cuts or mats of stars."

MORRISTOWN, NEW JERSEY—Population—13,033
DAILY RECORD—Aft.—3,709—W. Tomlinson, Mg. Ed.—30 cts. inch. "Two theatres; both advertise daily. Gives the theatres one reader a week."

MOUNT CARMEL, PENNSYLVANIA—Population—19,386
ITEM—Aft.—3,500—E. Kemble, Ad. Mgr.—25 cts. inch. "Six theatres; two advertise daily. No special publicity service rendered."

MOUNT VERNON, NEW YORK—Population—37,623
DAILY ARGUS—Aft.—7,193—M. Porter, Mg. Ed.—35 cts. inch. "Four theatres; all advertise daily. Runs daily reading notices. Can use mats or cuts if backed up by advertising."

STUDIO DIRECTORY

MUNCIE, INDIANA—Population—24,969

PRESS—Aft.—9,998—W. Sutton, Mg. Ed.—25 cts. inch. "Nine theatres; five advertise daily. Makes a feature of the theatre page on Saturday. Devotes space daily to reading notices. Conducts its own reviews."

STAR—Morn. & Sun.—26,858—F. Harrold, Mg. Ed.—70 cts. inch. "Sunday circulation 16,318. Runs daily reading notices and has a regular Sunday photoplay department. Conducts reviews by member of staff."

CHRONICLE—Aft.—12,900—A. McCrea, Mg. Ed.—60 cts. inch. "Six theatres; five advertise daily. A page is devoted on Saturday to theatrical write-ups of those houses advertising. Reading notices are given daily; ad rate with free notices is 75 cts. an inch."

MUSKOGEE, OKLAHOMA—Population—38,309

TIMES-DEMOCRAT—Aft.—12,400—B. Budgewater, Mg. Ed.—Rate omitted. "Five theatres; four advertise daily. No special publicity service given. Would use mats of stars."

PHOENIX—Morn. & Sun.—12,053—G. McGee, Photo. Ed.—40-42 cts. inch. "Sunday circulation 12,959. Sunday ad rate is from 45 to 47 cts. an inch. Sunday issue carries photoplay department. Prints reviews conducted by member of staff. Would use photographs and attractive layouts."

NASHUA, N. H.—Population 26,901

TELEGRAPH—Aft.—4300—G. Parkhurst, Mg. Ed.—Rate not given. "Four downtown theatres. Two first-run houses. Four advertise daily except Sunday. Has special editorial co-operation in connection with ads, reviews and reading notes. Would use cuts."

NATCHEZ, MISSISSIPPI—Population 17,500

DEMOCRAT—Morn. & Sun.—3,200—R. Smith—25-30 cts. inch. "Three theatres, all downtown. Three advertise daily. Prefer single and double column cuts. Sunday circulation 3,500."

NEWARK, OHIO—Population 28,271

ADVOCATE—Aft.—6,043—F. Woolson, Mg. Ed.—30 cts. inch. "Five theatres, all downtown. Furnishes liberal reading notices with ads. Prints reading notices daily."

AMER. TRIBUNE—Aft.—6,217—F. Neighbor, Gen. Mgr.—30 cts. inch. "Five theatres, all downtown. Liberal ad reading notices daily. Have reviews occasionally. Would use mats."

NEWARK, NEW JERSEY—Population 366,721

EVE. NEWS—Aft.—96,119—W. Flanigan—30 cts. inch. "Sixty-three theatres; fifteen downtown, 25 neighborhood. Sixteen advertise daily. Run Amusement Section on Saturday. Special editorial co-operation in connection with news matter, theatrical notices and reviews. Would use mats." Other papers: Star-Eagle; Sunday Call.

TIMES—Aft. & Sun.—4,447—E. Myers—50 cts. inch. "Furnishes ad notices and has reading matter in connection with houses that advertise. Twelve theatres, two downtown. Would use mats but not of scenes from pictures." Other papers: Mercury; Standard.

NEW BRITAIN, CONNECTICUT—Population 50,612

HERALD—Aft.—6,024—H. Jones—60 cts. inch. "Five theatres, four downtown, three advertise daily. Render news service in way of notices and ad reading material. Occasional reviews contained."

RECORD—Aft—Circulation omitted—J. Cone.—Rate omitted when "Three theatres advertise regularly. Limited news service extended to the interest of the exhibitors and the paper."

NEW BRUNSWICK, NEW JERSEY—Population 30,019

DAILY NEWS—Aft.—8,400—E. Boyd, Mg. Ed.—40-45 cts. inch. "Four theatres, all downtown. Limited news service extended in way of reviews and reading notices."

SUNDAY TIMES—Sun.—Same management as Daily News. "Full page department on Sunday for pictures and legitimate stage news and notices."

NEWBURGH, NEW YORK—Population 27,876

NEWBURGH NEWS—Aft. 11,150—Ed. not given—Rate omitted "Three theatres, all downtown. Three advertise daily. Limited reading notices. Editorial co-operation given on request for the same."

NEWBURYPORT, MASSACHUSETTS—Population 15,311

DAILY NEWS—Aft.—5,946—J. Mannix, Mg. Ed.—35 cts. inch. "Two theatres downtown. One advertises daily. No special news service rendered. Would use cuts."

NEW CASTLE, PENNSYLVANIA—Population 39,569

HERALD—Aft.—8,200—W. DuPre—30 cts. inch "Four theatres; three of the neighborhood type, and one downtown. All advertise daily. Liberal news service and editorial co-operation given. Would use cuts and mats."

NEW HAVEN, CONNECTICUT—Population 144,505

TIMES-LEADER—Aft.—15,661—C. Hendrick, Ad. Mgr.—$1.50 inch. "Twenty-five theatres. Extends liberal service in the way of notices, news items and reviews. Would use cuts and mats in limited way."

UNION—Aft & Sun.—12,927—E. Sullivan—$1.50 inch. "Five downtown theatres; one neighborhood house. Five advertise daily. Prints layouts and notices. Sunday circulation 7,796."

REGISTER—Aft. & Sun.—26,957—H. Kennedy—$1.50 inch "Eight downtown theatres. Three theatres advertise every day. Prints notices when advertising space is made use of. Necessary editorial co-operation rendered." Other papers: Journal-Courier; Yale Daily News.

NEW LONDON, CONNECTICUT—Population 20,557

TELEGRAPH—Morn.—4,860—J. Connell, Mg. Ed.—40 cts. inch "Four theatres. Give advertising reading notices daily."

THE DAY—Aft.—10,636—W. Slocum, Mg. Ed.—75-$1.00 inch "Ad reading notices inserted in proportion to advertising. Would print items of real news value."

NEW ORLEANS, LOUISIANA—Population 361,221

THE ITEM—Aft. & Sun.—75,000—L. Newmeyer, Gen. Mgr.—Rate omitted "Sixty theatres. Runs magazine section weekly and a feature page on Sunday. Reviews on request."

TIMES-PICAYUNE—Morn. & Sun.—75,692—N. Thatcher—20 cts. line "Fifty-eight theatres; fourteen downtown, forty-four neighborhood. Six advertise daily. Sunday section made a magazine feature. Extensive service rendered." Other papers: Spokesman; States.

STUDIO DIRECTORY

NEWPORT NEWS, VIRGINIA—Population 20,446

DAILY PRESS—Morn. & Sun.—7,359—L. Jester—$1.00 inch.
"Thirteen theatres. Seven advertise daily. Prints press matter and gives reading notices to the theatres with advertising. Sunday circulation 9,409."

TIMES-HERALD—Aft.—12,579—Same management as Daily Press

NEW YORK, NEW YORK—Population 5,047,221

GLOBE—Aft.—183,010—F. Taintor—60 cts. line
"Extensive service given in connection with publishing of notices, reviews and news matter. Runs daily 'On the Screen' column."

HERALD—Morn. & Sun.—125,000—J. Logan—60 cts. line
"Runs daily notices to theatres and extend full editorial co-operation. Sunday circulation 212,209."

EVE. MAIL—Aft.—102,204—T. Oliphant—60 cts. line
"Runs daily department devoted to the news of the picture field with special reviews on Broadway films on Monday and Tuesday."

TIMES—Morn. & Sun.—393,178—J. Spearing—Rate omitted
"Prints reviews of important productions by one of the newspaper's staff. No special service given on reading notices for theatres."

TRIBUNE—Morn. & Sun.—110,000—H. Underhill—Rate omitted
"Reading notices and publicity run daily in 'On the Screen' department. On Sunday full page is devoted to motion picture section. Reviews conducted and printed. Other New York papers: American; Evening Journal; Mail; World; Telegram; Post.

NIAGARA FALLS, NEW YORK—Population 42,257

GAZETTE—Aft.—12,759—G. Blight—40-65 cts. inch
"Ten theatres; four downtown, six neighborhood houses. Runs reading notices in proportion to advertising."

IN THE MIST—Aft.—1,890—W. Tuttle, Mg. Ed.—Rate omitted
"No special service rendered except reading notices to Buffalo theatres."

NORFOLK, VIRGINIA—Population 86,540

LEDGER DISPATCH—Aft.—46,143—H. Perkins, Mg. Ed.—$1.50-$2.50 inch
"Fourteen theatres; two neighborhood, and twelve downtown. Press matter is given in proportion to display advertising, and press material in excess of this advertising is included with charges."

NORTH ADAMS, MASSACHUSETTS—Population 22,019

HERALD—Circulation omitted—T. Haggerty, Mg. Ed.—20-30 cts. inch
"Reading notices are run every day. News items, if good stuff, are printed. Would use cuts and mats."

TRANSCRIPT—Aft.—7,866—J. Hardman, Mg. Ed.—50 cts. inch
"On Saturday prints notices of attractions for advance week. Would use mats and cuts furnished by theatres advertising."

NORTHAMPTON, MASSACHUSETTS—Population 19,776

DAILY HAMPSHIRE GAZETTE—Aft.—5,848—J. Best—25 cts. inch
"Includes write-up of picture events every Saturday."

HERALD—Aft.—3,600—G. Knoll, Jr., Mg. Ed.—25 cts. inch
"Two theatres, both of which advertise. Makes use of considerable number of 'readers'. Would prefer cuts."

NORTH TONAWANDA, NEW YORK—Population 13,508

NEWS—Aft.—3,212—E. Hewitt—20 cts. inch
"Three downtown theatres, all of which advertise. Prints reading notices and news items."

NORWALK, CONNECTICUT—Population 26,000

HOUR—Aft.—3,306—Mg. Ed. omitted—40 cts. inch
"Print five-inch 'readers' for local theatres. Would use mats."

NORWICH, CONNECTICUT—Population 20,932

BULLETIN—Morn.—9,998—H. Briggs, Mg. Ed.—Rate omitted
"Prints five lines of ad reading notices for every line of paid space."

OAKLAND, CALIFORNIA—Population 183,002

ENQUIRER—Aft.—27,030—M. Smith—$1.50 inch
"Five theatres advertise daily. Allow 25% of paid space in free reading notices. Runs feature page on Saturday."

POST—Aft.—24,000—W. McPherson—Rate omitted
"Includes photoplay departments on Monday and Thursday. Runs reading notices tri-weekly."

OGDEN, UTAH—Population 29,528

EXAMINER—Morn. & Sun.—Circ. omitted—J. Eldredge, Adv. Mgr.—35 cts. inch
"Six theatres, all of which advertise. Runs ad reading notices. Would use mats of artists' heads."

OGDENSBURG, NEW YORK—Population 16,375

REPUBLICAN JOURNAL—Morn.—4,112—H. Belgard—20 cts. inch
"Three theatres; all advertise daily. Would use mats."

OIL CITY, PENNSYLVANIA—Population 18,645

THE BLIZZARD—Aft.—3,107—S. Rosenthal, Mg. Ed.—15-25 cts. inch
"Runs daily photoplay section and gives reading matter accompanying advertisements. Cuts are preferred."

OIL CITY DERRICK—Morn.—6,201—J. Orr—Mg. Ed.—25 cts. inch
"The three theatres in the city advertise daily. Runs a column of publicity daily. Full co-operation in preparation of ads and copy material."

OKLAHOMA CITY, OKLAHOMA—Population 83,559

OKLAHOMAN—Morn. & Sun.—51,456—E. Dyer—Rate omitted
"Nine theatres, all of which advertise. Devotes almost a page to picture stories on Sunday. Sunday circulation 62,169."

NEWS—Aft.—26,616—R. Bailey—75 cts. inch
"Runs picture section on Saturday. Has reviews occasionally. Would use mats with preference for human interest material."

TIMES—Aft.—38,639—F. Sutton—Rate omitted
"Runs a picture section and prints reviews conducted by member of staff. Would use cuts and mats, attractive and of suitable size."

OLEAN, NEW YORK—Population 17,981

HERALD—Aft.—4,035—W. Ostrom, Mg. Ed.—Rate omitted
"Three theatres, all of which advertise daily except Sunday. Reading notice space allotted to the theatres but not every day."

EVE. TIMES—Aft.—5,031—H. McCaul, Ad. Mgr.—Rate omitted
"Gives daily reading notices to the theatres, of which there are three."

OMAHA, NEBRASKA—Population 133,274

BEE—Morn., Aft. & Sun.—69,000—S. Gould, Mg. Ed.—$1.40 inch
"Thirty-two theatres; eleven advertise daily, three on Sunday. Runs a column each day covering news shows. Have two-page section in Sunday issue. Sunday circulation 64,000."

DAILY NEWS—Aft. & Sun.—86,817—Wilson—$2.50 inch
"Gives daily reading notices to theatres and runs full-page section on Sunday. Prints reviews conducted by member of staff."

WORLD-HERALD—Aft. & Sun.—80,120—W. Watson, Mg. Ed.—$1.54-$1.82 inch
"Runs Sunday features and gives daily reading notices to theatres. Would use cuts of general interest."

OSHKOSH, WISCONSIN—Population 35,097

DAILY NORTHWESTERN—Aft.—14,216—E. Kennedy, Mg. Ed.—Rate omitted
"Publishes daily write-ups on features in local houses. Runs a Sunday 'Amusement' page."

OSWEGO, NEW YORK—Population 25,364

TIMES—Aft.—3,250—J. Slattery—30-50 cts. inch
"Five theatres, all of which advertise daily except on Sunday. Can use cuts only."

OTTAWA, ONTARIO—Population 87,062

CITIZEN—Morn. & Aft.—28,129—E. Green—5 cts. line
"Runs two-page picture feature Saturday afternoon and Monday morning, in proportion to ad space purchased."

JOURNAL—Morn. & Aft.—30,000—W. McLaughlin—5 cts. line
"Publishes a photoplay department on each Saturday and gives advance write-ups on coming attractions without mentioning name of theatre."

COURIER—Aft.—13,606—E. Canney—Rate omitted
"Six theatres; all advertise. Runs photoplay department on Saturday. Uses cuts and mats as supplied by local theatres."

OWENSBORO, KENTUCKY—Population 17,212

MESSENGER—Morn. & Sun.—5,943—M. Brown, Mg. Ed.—25 cts. inch
"Runs page of reading notices on Sunday. Conducts reviews on good pictures. Picture and player news items printed from time to time as fillers."

INQUIRER—Aft. & Sun.—4,500—V. Duncan—25 cts. inch
"On Sunday makes up theatre page containing several columns of ad reading notices. Prints readers daily."

PADUCAH, KENTUCKY—Population 24,170

NEWS-DEMOCRAT—Morn. & Sun.—6,986—N. Berry, Mg. Ed.—40 cts. inch
"Sunday circulation 7,154. Three theatres; two advertise. Run daily reading notices for theatres, and utilize mats in proportion to advertising contracted for."

SUN—Aft.—Circ., Ed., and Rate Omitted
"Two theatres, both of which advertise. No special publicity service rendered."

PARIS, TEXAS—Population 12,081

NEWS—Morn. & Sun.—4,260—A. Neville, Mg. Ed.—25 cts. inch
"Sunday circulation 4,310. Three theatres which advertise occasionally. No special service given."

PARSONS, KANSAS—Population 14,500

REPUBLICAN—Morn. & Sun.—4,500—L. Meadows, Mg. Ed.—24 cts. inch
"Three theatres, two of which advertise. Give daily reading notices. Sunday photoplay section. Conducts reviews."

THE SUN—Aft.—3,250—A. Murlin, Mg. Ed.—20 cts. inch
"Gives daily reading notices and conducts reviews." Would use mats.

PASSAIC, NEW JERSEY—Population 66,276

DAILY NEWS—Aft.—8,595—W. Clearwater—50 cts. inch
"Seven theatres, six of which advertise daily. Give reading notices to theatres every day."

HERALD—Aft.—8,535—W. McBride, Mg. Ed.—7 cts. line
"Give daily reading notices to theatres. Would use single and double-column cuts."

PATERSON, NEW JERSEY—Population 134,305

EVE. NEWS—Aft.—11,221—J. Levine—90 cts. inch
"Ten theatres, five of which advertise daily. Gives reading notices to theatres three times a week. Prints lay-outs if paid for." Additional paper: Call; Press-Guardian.

PAWTUCKET, RHODE ISLAND—Population 55,335

TIMES—Aft.—23,752—A. Adam, Mg. Ed.—4-8 cts. inch
"Seven houses, four of which advertise daily. Uses cuts of current local attractions. Prints combination dramatic department."

PEEKSKILL, NEW YORK—Population 15,491

DAILY UNION—Aft.—2,000—C. Gardner, Jr.—Rate omitted.
"Prints a reader every day. No special publicity service rendered except this."

EVE. NEWS—Aft.—2,178—E. Lowe—25 cts. inch
"Small photoplay section daily. Gives daily reading notices. Could use cuts preferably; mats also acceptable."

PENSACOLA, FLORIDA—Population 25,212

JOURNAL—Morn. & Sun.—6,000—H. Watkins, Mg. Ed.—50 cts. inch
"Sunday circulation 8,500. Give theatres daily reading notices as much as possible. Would use cuts and mats of stars."

PEORIA, ILLINOIS—Population 70,006

STAR—Aft. & Sun.—23,501—C. Smith—75 cts. inch
"Gives reading notices with advertising. Prints picture and player items that are of news value. Sunday circulation 15,255."

PERTH AMBOY, NEW JERSEY—Population 38,265

EVE. NEWS—Aft.—8,425—J. Clevenger, Mg. Ed.—Rate omitted
"Gives reading notice every day. Treats cuts as advertising and are sold at space."

PETERSBURG, VIRGINIA—Population 25,112

EVE. PROGRESS—Aft.—7,130—B. Oliver, Photo. Ed.—25 cts. inch
"Runs daily notices of reading material. Reviews occasionally. Picture and player items if they are of local interest."

PHILADELPHIA, PENNSYLVANIA—Population 1,750,000

INQUIRER—Morn. & Sun.—Circ. omitted—H. Knapp—Rate omitted
"Approximately 200 theatres; 22 advertising during week-days, and 30 on Sundays. Give reading notices on Sunday and Tuesday only. Include picture and player items if they have news value."

THE PRESS—Morn. & Sun.—39,816—J. Duffy—30-35 cts. line
"Sunday circulation 104,118. Photoplay news is incorporated in the dramatic department on Sunday. Reviews are covered by regular assignments."

EVE. BULLETIN—Aft.—Circ. omitted—W. Simpson, Ad. Mg.—45 cts. line
"Picture news included in 'Review of Theatres' section. No complimentary publicity service rendered."

PUBLIC LEDGER—Morn. & Sun.—197,428—C. Bonte—22½ cts. line
"Runs daily reading notices. Prints reviews conducted by members of staff. Sunday circulation 134,710."

EVE. PUBLIC LEDGER—Aft.—A. Plough—(Same management as foregoing)
Other papers: Record; Star; Telegraph, North American.

PITTSBURG, KANSAS—Population 16,845

DAILY HEADLIGHT—Circ. omitted—F. Brinkerhoff, Mg. Ed.—Rate omitted
"Four theatres, all of which advertise. No special publicity service given in way of publishing notices."

MORNING SUN—Morn. & Sun.—4,320—A. Bascom—20 cts. inch
"Runs readers at display rates. No special complimentary publicity service rendered. Reviews conducted and printed at space rates. Sunday circulation 4,433."

PITTSBURGH, PENNSYLVANIA—Population 590,000

DISPATCH—Morn. & Sun.—58,131—J. McDonnell—$3.50 inch
"Runs photoplay department on Sunday. Gives reading notices to advertisers. Conducts reviews at theatres furnishing advertising. Sunday circulation 56,932; advertising rate, $4.00 an inch."

CHRONICLE TELEGRAPH—Aft.—93,043—W. Lewis, Ed.—Rate omitted
"Runs a photoplay section on Sunday. Gives reading notices on Tuesday after first performance. Conducts its own reviews. Sunday circulation 142,042."

STUDIO DIRECTORY

PORTLAND, MAINE—Population 62,161

PRESS—Morn. & Sun.—F. Owen, 75 cts. inch "Six theatres, all of which advertise. Devotes full pages to pictures on Sunday and week-days. Give reading notices inch for inch."

EVE. EXPRESS—Aft.—25,260—G. Norton, Mg. Ed.—Rate omitted "Regular amusement page printed every day. Runs reading notices inch for inch of advertising. Eight theatres, six of which advertise."

TELEGRAM—Sun.—21,546—T. Flaherty, Mg. Ed.—Rate omitted "Amusement page published in Sunday issue. Reading notices run, inch for inch of advertising."

PORTSMOUTH, OHIO—Population 27,511

DAILY TIMES—Aft. & Sun.—12,000—E. Schusky—22-35 cts. inch "Sunday circulation 8,000. Gives daily reading notices. On Sunday devote full page to notices and cuts for local theatres."

PORTSMOUTH, VIRGINIA—Population 37,569

STAR—Aft. & Sun.—3,800—Ed. omitted—Rate omitted "Five theatres; three advertise. Gives daily reading notices."

POTTSVILLE, PENNSYLVANIA—Population 21,684

CHRONICLE—Aft.—2,500—C. Sterner—18 cts. inch "Four theatres; three advertise daily. Run daily reading notices. Would use mats."

DAILY REPUBLICAN—Aft.—Circ. omitted—H. Zerbey, Mg. Ed.—50 cts. inch "No special publicity service rendered. Prints picture and player news at times when the same is of general interest."

POUGHKEEPSIE, NEW YORK—Population 32,281

STAR ENTERPRISE—Aft.—9,920—R. Brown, Ad Ed.—Rate omitted "Six theatres; five advertise daily. No special publicity service rendered."

EAGLE NEWS—Morn.—6,000—E. Moore—Rate omitted "Gives daily reading notices and runs a picture department in the publication. Prints reviews conducted by member of staff."

PROVIDENCE, RHODE ISLAND—Population 247,600

NEWS—Aft.—25,000—J. Lucas, Photo Ed.—6 cts. line "Twelve theatres; seven advertise daily and nine on Saturday afternoon. Runs reading notices on Wednesday and Saturday. Prints review on Tuesday."

DAILY JOURNAL—Morn. & Sun.—29,875—E. Kirby, Mg. Ed.—7½ cts. line "Sunday circulation 45,322. Prints reviews furnished by theatres after re-editing. Allows one photograph for every $100 worth of business during the current week and on Sunday an ad of 200 lines."

EVE. BULLETIN—Aft.—55,300 (Same management as foregoing)

JOURNAL & BULLETIN—Morn., Aft. & Sun.—W. Ball, Mg. Ed.—Rate omitted "Photoplay department printed on Sunday and advance notices and reviews during the week."

TRIBUNE—Aft. & Sun.—26,725—J. Minkins—Rate omitted "Runs reading notices on Sunday and three times a week. Conducts its own reviews."

PUEBLO, COLORADO—Population 51,218

CHIEFTAIN—Morn. & Sun.—8,352—W. Parker—50 cts. inch "Sunday circulation 9,721. Liberal in publishing reading notices for local theatres. Eight theatres; seven advertise."

QUEBEC CANADA—Population 78,190

CHRONICLE—Morn.—14,600—A. Penny—75 cts. inch "Seven theatres; four advertise daily. Carries a special page on Saturday and from two two three columns daily of items appertaining to pictures."

POST—Morn. & Sun.—76,068—A. Mittelhauser—$3.50 inch "Sunday circulation 105,164; ad rate for Sunday $4.00 an inch. Conducts its own reviews. Gives reading notices to theatres. Has Sunday photoplay department. Would use cuts of artists."

PRESS—Aft. & Sun.—123,559—P. Mansfield—$2.00 inch "Runs Sunday picture section and on week-days includes reviews and gossip items. Sunday circulation 121,919; ad rate on Sunday for pictures $2.67 per inch."

SUN—Aft.—74,501—A. Mittelhauser—$1.40 inch "Runs daily reading notices, according to amount of advertising. Would use cuts of picture artists. Conducts reviews."

Other papers: Leader; Gazette-Times.

PITTSFIELD, MASSACHUSETTS—Population 36,531

BERKSHIRE EVE. EAGLE—Aft.—14,482—F. Couch—40 cts. inch "Five theatres, all of which advertise daily. In Saturday issue publish page of news and cuts of coming attractions in 'Behind the Screen News.' Conducts reviews of special interest."

THE RECORD—Morn. & Sun.—124,283—H. Goldberg, Photo. Ed.—30 cts. inch "Runs a photoplay section on Sunday. Gives reading notices on Tuesday after first performance. Conducts its own reviews. Sunday circulation 142,042."

PHOENIX, ARIZONA—Population 16,870

GAZETTE—Aft.—8,244—J. Ingram, Photo. Ed.—50 cts. inch "Special two-page theatrical spread on Saturday. Gives daily reading notices. Conducts reviews."

PINE BLUFF, ARK.—Population 16,743

COMMERCIAL—Aft.—4,930—J. Wiley, Ed.—25 cts. inch "Give some reading matter each day with somewhat greater space on Saturday. Have occasional reviews. Three houses, all of which advertise daily."

GRAPHIC—Morn. & Sun.—3,421—A. Whidden, Mg. Ed.—Rate omitted "Runs daily reading notices as space permits. Would use mats and cuts of pictures in local houses. Sunday circulation 3,421."

POMONA, CALIFORNIA—Population 12,202

BULLETIN—Morn. & Sun.—2,421—R. Driscoll, Mg. Ed.—Rate omitted "Three theatres, all of which advertise. Give reading notices in proportion to advertising."

PORT CHESTER, NEW YORK—Population 15,129

DAILY ITEM—Aft.—3,928—T. Blain, Mg. Ed.—21 cts. inch "Three houses, all of which advertise regularly. Allows 5 inches for readers in daily issue. Also allows space to theatres for one cut daily on complimentary basis."

PORT HURON, MICHIGAN—Population 18,863

TIMES-HERALD—Aft.—11,556—E. Ottaway, Mg. Ed.—40 cts. inch "Five theatres, all of which advertise daily. Print readers if 55 cents rate is paid on advertising instead of 40 cents. Runs general picture news a few times a week."

PORTLAND, OREGON—Population 260,601

OREGONIAN—75,000—Morn. & Sun.—L. Allen—$1.33-$1.75 cts. inch "Sunday circulation 100,000. About fifty theatres, eight of which advertise daily. Runs a picture page on Sunday. Prints about 400 advance reading notices for main advertisers and have column for picture news of local interest."

OREGON JOURNAL—Morn., Aft. & Sun.—Circ. omitted—S. Raddon, Jr.—Rate omitted "Twenty-four theatres, sixteen of which advertise daily. Regular department with layout and notices on Sunday. Give daily reading notices."

Other papers: News; Telegram.

506 STUDIO DIRECTORY

TELEGRAPH—Aft.—11,427—Trumble—$1.00 inch
"Nine theatres; all advertise daily except Sunday. Runs reading notices at charge of 2 cents per line. Conducts and prints reviews."

QUINCY, ILLINOIS—Population 36,730

JOURNAL—Aft.—8,314—E. Meyer—30 cts. inch
"Nine theatres, five of which advertise daily. Gives daily reading notices and conducts reviews."
WHIG—Morn. & Sun.—8,170—R. McNeal—Rate omitted
"Gives daily reading notices and endeavors to make up interesting theatrical page without referring to the picture advertised. Would use good mats of general interest."

RACINE, WISCONSIN—Population 44,528

JOURNAL NEWS—Aft.—7,666—T. Starluck, Adv. Mgr.—35 cts. inch
"Seven theatres; five advertise. No special publicity service rendered."
TIMES-CALL—Aft.—6,232—H. Haight—50-75 cts. inch
"Conducts reviews and allows no free ad reading notices."

RALEIGH, N. C.—Population 19,833

NEWS-OBSERVER—Morn. & Sun.—21,209—D. Haywood, Mgr. Ed.—Rate omitted
"Three theatres; all advertise. Runs ad reading notices in proportion to the display service purchased. Sunday circulation 21,209."
TIMES—Aft.—5,296—J. Park, Mgr. Ed.—25 cts. inch
"Runs photoplay department on Monday, usually announcing program and special features."

READING, PENNSYLVANIA—Population 103,361

EAGLE—Aft. & Sun.—31,531—R. Gellers—10 cts. line
"Runs ad reading notices on Sunday and Wednesday. Conducts its own reviews. About fifteen theatres, nearly all of which advertise."
NEWS-TIMES—Morn.—12,410—P. Glass—56 cts. inch
"Runs daily Theatrical Guide stating the principal features and star at each theatre. Gives reading notices in proportion to the advertising."
TELEGRAM—Aft.—(Same management as the News-Times)

REDLANDS, CALIFORNIA—Population 12,856

DAILY FACTS—Aft.—2,180—C. Arthur—Rate omitted
"Gives five inches every day for reading notices and two cuts each week, both gratis."

RENO, NEVADA—Population 13,579

EVE. GAZETTE—Aft.—4,532—Ed. omitted—30 cts. inch
"On Saturday runs a picture page giving programs of all local houses and synopsis of pictures shown following week. Prints daily reading notices if 50 cents rate is paid on advertisements instead of the 30 cents."

RICHMOND, INDIANA—Population 23,932

PALLADIUM—Aft.—11,096—J. Hansell, 37 cts. inch
"Five theatres; four advertise. Print daily picture news but enlarge on the same on Saturday."
ITEM—Morn. & Sun.—8,225—C. Clay, Mg. Ed.—35 cts. inch
"Give daily reading notices and print picture layouts. Conduct reviews. Sunday circulation 8,600."

RICHMOND, VIRGINIA—Population 134,917

NEWS-LEADER—Aft.—Circ. omitted—R. Hess—70 cts. inch
"Runs ad reading notices at space rates. Eleven theatres; eight advertise."
TIMES-DISPATCH—Morn. & Sun.—30,082—Ed. omitted—$1.00-$1.25 inch
"Picture news each Sunday with illustrations. News during the week for the changes only. Conducts its own reviews."

VIRGINIAN—Morn. & Sun.—11,395—T. Eaton—50 cts. inch
"Sunday circulation 11,395. Thirteen theatres; nine advertise. In Sunday issue publishes publicity for the current week."
EVE. JOURNAL—Aft.—21,600—Z. Woodall—50 cts. inch
"Gives reading notice on any day that film merits notice. Runs a special photoplay page on Monday. Prefers single-column mats of stars." Other Richmond papers.

RIVERSIDE, CALIFORNIA—Population 18,297

PRESS—Morn.—4,875—W. Leamon—25 cts. inch
"Prints picture items that are of real news value. Gives reading notices to a limited extent. Conducts its own reviews."

ROANOKE, VIRGINIA—Population 40,574

TIMES—Morn. & Sun.—Circ. omitted—P. Chapmen—50 cts. inch
"Runs reading notices when space is paid for. Five theatres, all of which advertise."
WORLD-NEWS—Aft.—(Same management as the Times)

ROCHESTER, NEW YORK—Population 254,035

DEMOCRAT & CHRONICLE—Morn. & Sun.—64,000—M. Adams, City Ed.—12½ cts. line
"Sixteen theatres; ten advertise regularly. Ad reading notices are given to theatres in proportion to advertising done."
HERALD—Morn. & Sun.—35,000—H. Southgate—10 cts. line
"Sunday circulation 24,000. Gives daily reading notices. Have dramatic department in Sunday issue combining theatrical and picture news."
TIMES-UNION—Aft.—67,121—A. Warner—12½ cts. line
"Gives daily reading notices. Motion picture houses are covered in separate section under heading 'Motion Pictures.'"
Other papers: Post Express; Record; Union and Advertiser.

ROCKFORD, ILLINOIS—Population 52,337

REGISTER GAZETTE—Aft.—13,477—P. Edmeson—50 cts. inch
"Runs photoplay department in Saturday issue. Gives limited ad reading notices to theatres. Prefer mats."
MORNING STAR—Morn. & Sun.—11,500—J. Riley, Mg. Ed.—50 cts. inch
"Sunday circulation 13,000. Eight theatres; four advertise daily and two on Sunday only. Runs daily reading notices depending on the size of ad copy."

ROCK ISLAND, ILLINOIS—Population 26,945

DAILY UNION—Sun.—5,000—J. Watts, Mg. Ed.—Rate omitted
"Seven houses, all of which advertise. Runs ad reading notices daily and on Sunday devotes five columns to the same sort of material. Would use mats. Sunday circulation 7,500."

ROME, GEORGIA—Population 14,146

TRIBUNE-HERALD—Morn. & Sun.—3,135—J. McCartney, Mg. Ed.—15 cts. inch
"Three theatres, all of which advertise. No special publicity service. Might use cuts mounted. Conducts its own reviews. Sunday circulation 3,135."

ROME, NEW YORK—Population 23,868

SENTINEL—Aft.—5,353—Ed. omitted—75 cts. inch
"Every evening runs free readers for the houses advertising in the paper."

RUTLAND, VERMONT—Population 14,417

HERALD—Morn.—Circ. omitted—Ed. omitted—25 cts. inch
"Three houses, all of which advertise daily. Conducts reviews by member of paper staff."

STUDIO DIRECTORY

ST. CATHERINES, ONTARIO—Population 12,487

STANDARD—Aft.—8,066—W. Moore, Mg. Ed.—35¼ cts. inch
"Runs a special theatre page on Saturday. Gives daily reading notices to theatres. Conducts reviews by member of staff."

ST. JOHN, NEW BRUNSWICK—Population 42,511

GLOBE—Aft.—6,000—F. Ellis, Mg. Ed.—2 cts. line
"On Wednesday page is devoted to news of the stage and picture activities. Prints one free reader each week for each amusement house. Amusements are charged 2 cents a line for a contract using 5,000 lines or more."

ST. JOHNS, NEWFOUNDLAND—Population 25,700

DAILY NEWS—Morn.—7,500—J. Currie, Lit. Ed.—10-15 cts. inch
"Five houses, all of which advertise daily. Runs daily reading notices."

DAILY STAR—Aft.—7,628—R. Dowden—8 cts. inch
"Average one-sixth column daily for reading notices, sometimes using, cuts also (column). Would use mats or cuts suitable for Hoe rotary press."

ST. JOSEPH, MO.—Population 82,712

GAZETTE—Morn. & Sun.—17,648—W. Ladd, Mg. Ed.—8 cts. line
"Runs daily reading notices and on Sunday prints a column or more of picture news. Would use mats preferably of beauty interest. Sunday circulation 14,216."

NEWS-PRESS—Aft.—39,636—C. Calvert—10-15 cts. line
"Runs criticisms and advance notices and prints a list of pictures shown during the week."

ST. LOUIS, MISSOURI—Population 734,667

STAR—Aft.—100,600—A. Kaye—16-25 cts. line
"Gives readers on Friday and Monday and on other days at special request. Would use close-up photographs and individuals; would also use mats of pictures sent before their release."

GLOBE-DEMOCRAT—Morn. & Sun.—170,000—J. McAuliffe, Mg. Ed.—22-30 cts. line
"Sunday circulation 170,000. Theatres number 126. Sixteen to twenty-two advertise daily. Runs a photoplay department on Sunday and print reading notices only on Monday and in the Sunday department."

POST-DISPATCH—Aft. & Sun.—170,000—H. James—25-30 cts. line
"On Saturday gives advance news and notes; on Monday prints reviews of first runs. Three houses; all advertise." Additional paper: Times.

ST. PAUL, MINNESOTA—Population 236,766

DAILY NEWS—Aft. & Sun.—70,184—F. Boardman—$3.50 inch
"Sunday circulation 45,000. Theatres number thirty-five; of these nine advertise daily. Regular photoplay department run on Sunday. Conducts reviews and gives daily reading notices to the larger theatres." Additional paper: Dispatch.

ST. THOMAS, ONTARIO—Population 14,054

TIMES-JOURNAL—Aft.—Circ. omitted—L. Dingman, Mg. Ed.—42 cts. inch
"Runs theatrical section on Saturday. No special publicity service outside of this section. Three houses; all advertise."

SAGINAW, MICHIGAN—Population 53,988

NEWS-COURIER—Aft. & Sun.—22,854—M. Gorman, Mg. Ed.—84 cts. inch
"Four theatres; all advertise. Runs picture department on Saturday and Sunday, including the programs for the week. Sunday circulation 21,839."

SALEM, OREGON—Population 18,286

OREGON STATESMAN—Morn. & Sun.—4,160—R. Hendricks, Mg. Ed.—20-30 cts. inch
"Has Sunday picture department. Gives daily reading notices. Conducts reviews. Would use mats or cuts."

SALT LAKE, UTAH—Population 109,530

DESERET NEWS—Aft.—20,066—Bennett—$1.00 inch
"Ten theatres, five of which advertise. Runs Saturday picture department and a midweek review. Also prints a daily Amusement Box."

HERALD—Morn. & Sun.—Circ. omitted—A. Winton—$1.25 inch
"Conducts and prints reviews. Runs Sunday picture page. Prints advance notices. Co-operates with regards to suggesting features and layouts." Other papers: Telegram; Tribune.

SAN ANTONIO, TEXAS—Population 115,063

EXPRESS—Morn. & Sun.—35,884—G. Witting—98 cts. inch
"Sunday circulation 47,550. Nine theatres, all of which advertise. Runs photoplay department in Sunday issue."

EVENING NEWS—Aft.—18,533—(Same management as Express)
"Runs picture section in Saturday issue."

SAN BERNARDINO, CALIFORNIA—Population 15,603

INDEX—Aft. & Sun.—2,600—A. Wood—30 cts. inch
"Gives daily reading notices and runs photoplay section in Sunday issue. Seven theatres, three of which advertise daily. Sunday circulation 2625."

THE SUN—Morn. & Sun.—4,649—G. Haven—Rate omitted
"Sunday circulation 4,740. Have photoplay department on Sunday, including layouts. Runs short readers every day."

SAN DIEGO, CALIFORNIA—Population 48,900

SUN—Aft.—16,591—F. Fiske, Mg. Ed.—65 cts. inch
"Runs photoplay department in Saturday issue, including layouts of attractions. Gives daily reading notices. Eighteen theatres, six of which advertise daily."

UNION-TRIBUNE—Morn., Aft. & Sun.—30,939—E. Parmelu—75 cts.-$1.00 inch
"Gives daily reading notices to advertisers or at charge of 48 cents per inch."

SANDUSKY, OHIO—Population 20,127

REGISTER—Morn. & Sun.—5,324—E. Walrath—Rate omitted
"Sunday circulation 5,843. Four theatres, three of which advertise daily. No special publicity service rendered except that occasionally layout of attractions are printed gratis."

STAR JOURNAL—Aft.—6,466—C. Abbey—20 cts. inch
"No special publicity service given. Layout on attractions are printed gratis. Picture items are printed as fillers on off days."

SAN FRANCISCO, CALIFORNIA—Population 530,000

BULLETIN—Aft.—96,000—W. Bodin—$2.80 inch
"Eighty theatres; eleven advertise daily. Three page section on Saturday with layouts. Has a midweek page every Wednesday. Gives daily reading notices to houses. Special ad rate for 40 inches per week is 2.80 cents an inch; season rate, 4.20 cents per inch."

CALL-POST—Aft.—95,595—C. Swint—$4.20 inch
"Eleven theatres advertise. Saturday picture section in combination with stage news. Review on Monday; midweek on Wednesday, Thursday or Friday with picture. Occasional special feature run."

DAILY NEWS—Aft.—51,000—G. Warren—$2.75 inch
"Notices are given Monday, Wednesday and Saturday with an occasional special story. Might use mats."

CHRONICLE—Morn. & Sun.—99,917—T. Bailey—Rate omitted
"Sunday circulation 141,036. Photoplay department run on Sunday and Monday, which includes reading notices. Also print complimentary layouts."
EXAMINER—Morn. & Sun.—124,500—T. Nunan, Photo. Ed.—Rate omitted.
"Sunday circulation 265,321. Two pages are given to amusements on Sunday and a regular picture page is run on Monday. Publishes daily reading notices. Presents player and picture articles as news of interest to the public when it is felt that articles have real news value."

SAN JOSE, CALIFORNIA—Population 37,086
MERCURY-HERALD—Morn. & Sun.—14,500—F. Baker—$1.25 inch
"Give daily reading notices to the theatres when they use enough advertising. Three houses, all of which advertise daily. Sunday circulation 15,000."

SANTA BARBARA, CALIFORNIA—Population 13,818
MORNING PRESS—Morn.—3,294—A. Pettersen, Mg. Ed.—Rate omitted
"Five houses, all of which advertise daily. Runs theatre page daily. Reading notices are governed by the amount of advertising."

SARATOGA SPRINGS, NEW YORK—Population 13,763
SARATOGA SUN—Aft.—2,150—R. Durant, Mg. Ed.—Rate omitted
"Gives daily reading notices as requested. Three theatres, two of which advertise daily."

SASKATOON, SASKATCHEWAN—Population 28,000
THE PHOENIX—Morn.—9,000—F. Coucher—6 cts. inch
"Three houses; two advertise daily. Give reading notices to houses advertising daily. Runs special page in Saturday edition."
DAILY STAR—Aft.—25,500—R. Patton—6 cts. inch
"Prints one full-page of theatre news on Saturday. Gives daily reading notices and conducts its own reviews occasionally."

SAULT STE. MARIE, MICHIGAN—Population 14,499
EVENING NEWS—Aft.—4,187—J. Chandler, Cy. Ed.—Rate omitted
"Endeavoring to get co-operation of local theatres to an extent that will justify special department."

SAVANNAH, GEORGIA—Population 67,917
MORNING NEWS—Morn. & Sun.—20,100—J. Miller, Mg. Ed.—Rate omitted.
"Five theatres, four of which advertise daily. Give reading notices on Sunday in proportion to the ad space bought. Sunday circulation 24,000."
PRESS—Aft.—16,465—W. Sutlive, Mg. Ed.—Rate omitted.
"Every Saturday gives a photoplay department and prints daily reading notices. Would use mats."

SCHENECTADY, NEW YORK—Population 80,386
GAZETTE—Morn.—21,957—R. Hall, Photo. Ed.—$1.50 inch.
"Twelve theatres; ten advertise daily. Gives daily reading notices and from time to time prints a column of 'Movie Gossip.' Conducts reviews occasionally."
UNION-STAR—Aft.—17,660—W. Marlette, Photo. Ed.—$1.50 inch
"Gives daily reading notices in connection with ads. On Saturday allows 10 lines of reading notices with each inch of Amusement column."

SCRANTON, PENNSYLVANIA—Population 141,351
REPUBLICAN—Morn.—27,130—J. Mitchell, Mg. Ed.—$1.50 inch.
"Reviews plays and gives advance notices once a week for those that advertise. Prints reading notices on Saturday in proportion to the ad space bought."
TIMES—Aft.—36,861—J. Keator, Mg. Ed.—$1.68-$1.96 inch Prints a combination amusement department daily consisting of reading notices, cuts, etc. Readers are printed in proportion to the ad space used."

SEATTLE, WASHINGTON—Population 313,029
STAR—Aft.—65,246—D. Henry—Rate omitted
"There are forty-eight theatres, nine of which are regular advertisers. Prints Saturday photoplay department and gives daily reading notices."
TIMES—Aft. & Sun.—72,541—G. Bellman—Rate omitted
"Prints one picture page daily and on Sunday runs a department from six to ten pages long. Reviews pictures occasionally. Sunday circulation 94,665."
Other papers: Bulletin; Post-Intelligencer.

SEDALIA, MISSOURI—Population 18,925
CAPITAL—Aft. & Sun.—3,500—R. Burrowes—15 cts. inch
"Gives daily reading notices to theatre in location. On Sunday runs at least a column. Stories of players or pictures are run whenever they seem to have sufficient news value. Sunday circulation 3,500."

SELMA, ALABAMA—Population 14,988
JOURNAL—Aft. & Sun.—1,600—D. Kincey, Mg. Ed.—25 cts. inch
"Sunday circulation 1,600. Runs Sunday picture page and prints daily readers. Would use cuts."

SHAMOKIN, PENNSYLVANIA—Population 20,841
HERALD—Aft.—1,840—W. Steel—12 cts. inch
"No special publicity service rendered except that readers are printed occasionally."

SHARON, PENNSYLVANIA—Population 17,538
HERALD—Aft.—4,505—W. Ramsay, Mg. Ed.—Rate omitted
"Renders no special publicity service now, but is ready to co-operate with theatres in publication of picture news."
TELEGRAPH—Aft.—6,500—J. Evans, Mg. Ed.—23 cts. inch
"Runs daily calendar allowing about 80 words for each theatre. Conducts reviews of more important productions. Would use mats."

SHAWNEE, OKLAHOMA—Population 16,312
NEWS-HERALD—Morn. & Sun.—4,000—H. Spaulding, Mg. Ed.—Rate omitted
"Four theatres; all advertise daily. Has Sunday photoplay section. Gives reading notices but not every day. Would use cuts that would increase advertising of the paper."

SHEBOYGAN, WISCONSIN—Population 27,863
PRESS—Morn.—6,742—C. Broughton, Mg. Ed.—Rate omitted
"Eight theatres five of which advertise daily. Gives daily reading notices to those houses which are not allowed cuts of pictures."

SHENANDOAH, PENNSYLVANIA—Population 28,097
HERALD—Aft.—4,034—T. Davies, Mg. Ed.—Rate omitted
"Would use mats of leading actors. No special publicity service rendered. Four of the six houses in the location advertise daily."

SHREVEPORT, LOUISIANA—Population 32,906
JOURNAL—Aft.—10,000—J. Howe—40 cts. inch
"Gives daily reading notices and publishes photoplay section in Saturday issue. Conducts reviews and would use mats. Six of eight theatres in location advertise daily."
NEWS-AMERICAN—Aft. & Sun.—6,408—W. Ingram, Mg. Ed.—50 cts. inch.
"Eight theatres; one advertises in News-American. Runs daily reading notices for the Grand Opera House. Would use mats of general interest."
TIMES—Morn. & Sun.—17,100—A. Israel, Mg. Ed.—75 cts inch.
"Gives daily reading notices and publishes Sunday photoplay section. Runs picture and player stories occasionally. Conducts reviews."

STUDIO DIRECTORY

SIOUX CITY, IOWA—Population 54,098

JOURNAL—Morn., Aft. & Sun.—56,302—L. Prince, Photo. Ed.—$1.50 inch. "Sunday circulation 28,200. Ten theatres; four advertise daily. Runs Sunday photoplay section. Gives reading notices on Thursday and Sunday. Would use 65 line cuts. Conducts its own reviews at times."

TRIBUNE—Aft.—50,659—J. Kelly, Mg. Ed.—$1.50 inch. "Runs special page in Saturday issue. No special daily publicity service rendered."

SOUTH BEND, INDIANA—Population 65,114

TRIBUNE—Aft.—17,432—R. Horst, Mg. Ed.—42 cts. inch. "Five theatres, four of which advertise daily. Runs an amusement page in Saturday issue and gives daily reading notices. Conducts its own reviews."

NEWS-TIMES—Morn., Aft. & Sun.—16,431—I. Dolk, Photo. Ed.—Rate omitted. "Devotes one page on Sunday and gives daily reading notices. Would use 2 or 3 column mats on theatrical page as fillers. Sunday circulation 17,474."

SPOKANE, WASHINGTON—Population 135,657

CHRONICLE—Aft.—41,651—W. Holden—$1.03-$1.20 inch. "Runs special theatrical page on Friday. Reading notices are run frequently during the week. Ten theatres; seven advertise daily. Use cuts and mats of films and stars appearing in the local houses."

PRESS—Aft.—11,840—W. Gardner—30-75 cts. inch. "Advertising rate is more specifically as follows: 75c. for two inches daily, 5 days a week; 30c. for all additional matter. Runs daily reading notices and in Saturday issue prints full-page of photoplay news."

SPOKESMAN-REVIEW—Morn. & Sun.—45,991—M. Glendenning, Cy. Ed.—$2.75 inch. "Sunday circulation 45,991. Maintains dramatic department on Sunday. Gives daily account in brief form of what the managers say. Publishes player and picture news."

SPRINGFIELD, ILLINOIS—Population 57,972

ILLINOIS STATE JOURNAL—Morn. & Sun.—25,000—W. Dagon—90 cts. inch. "Sunday circulation 16,000. Gives daily reading notices in proportion to advertising. Devotes large space in Sunday issue to motion pictures. Would use cuts of stars and directors of a good coarse screen type."

STATE REGISTER—Aft. & Sun.—29,000—W. Sine—90 cts. inch. "Sunday circulation 29,000. Eleven theatres, four of which advertise daily. Gives daily reading notices. Would use mats of stars."

SPRINGFIELD, MISSOURI—Population 38,685

LEADER—Aft. & Sun.—14,767—J. Acuff, Photo Ed—42-75 cts. inch "Five theatres; four advertise daily. On Sunday publishes a picture column about one and a half columns long. This embodies the reading notices. Cuts used only as paid matter. Sunday circulation 12,848."

REPUBLICAN—Morn. & Sun.—11,650—C. Robertson, Bus. Mgr.—Rate omitted. "No special publicity service rendered."

SPRINGFIELD, MASSACHUSETTS—Population—100,375

REPUBLICAN—Morn. & Sun.—44,854—J. Carroll—Rate omitted. "Sunday circulation 19,624. Fifty theatres; six advertise daily. Has Sunday photoplay department and gives daily reading notices. Runs picture and player news on Sunday."

DAILY NEWS—Aft.—G. Doyle, Photo. Ed. (Same management as Republican.) "Runs picture and player news as matter of public interest in Saturday issue."

UNION—Morn., Aft. & Sun.—42,883—A. Wood—$1.80 inch. "Sunday circulation 28,976. Rate for Sunday $1.26 per inch. Prints photoplay department on Sunday including the complete bill for the week. Gives daily reading notices except Wednesday and Saturday."

SPRINGFIELD, OHIO—Population—50,058

SUN—Morn. & Sun.—12,500—L. Johnson—30 cts. inch. "Sunday circulation 11,600. Runs special photoplay department on Sunday. Notices are run for exceptional plays at especial request. Conducts reviews by member of the paper staff."

NEWS—Aft. & Sun.—15,337—A. Tennant—35 cts. inch. "Sunday circulation 11,741. Eight theatres; six advertise daily. Motion picture section on Sunday with layout of stars or scenes from play. Gives reading notices on Sunday, gratis; one for each ad. Prefer cuts."

STAMFORD, CONNECTICUT—Population—29,032

DAILY ADVOCATE—Aft.—7,438—R. Whittaker, Mg. Ed.—Rate omitted. "Five theatres; all advertise. Gives daily reading notices."

STEUBENVILLE, OHIO—Population—22,391

HERALD-STAR—Aft.—6,676—C. Simeral, Mg. Ed.—Rate omitted. "Three theatres; two advertise daily. No special publicity service rendered."

STOCKTON, CALIFORNIA—Population—25,702

DAILY INDEPENDENT—Morn. & Sun.—4,785—J. O'Keefe—Rate omitted. "Sunday circulation 4,910. Five theatres; four advertise daily. Makes up a page of picture news on Wednesday and Sunday. Gives reading notices every day."

RECORD—Aft.—13,485—G. Keitle—56 cts. inch. "On Wednesday and Saturday publicity and cuts are published. On other days the reading notices alone are printed."

STRATFORD, ONTARIO—Population—12,946

DAILY BEACON—Aft.—3,450—K. Beirne, Mg. Ed.—20 cts. inch. "During fall and winter months a Saturday theatre page is printed. Prints news features about well-known artists. Reviews pictures by member of the staff."

STREATOR, ILLINOIS—Population—14,287

FREE PRESS—Aft.—3,464—J. Fornof, Mg. Ed.—Rate omitted. "Two theatres, both of which advertise daily. No special publicity service rendered."

INDEPENDENT-TIMES—Aft.—2,925—V. LeRoy, Mg. Ed.—18 cts. inch. "Ad rates is more specifically: 10 cts. a line in 7 pt. type for readers; 18 cts. an inch for display and 13 cts. if repeated. No free publicity service rendered except in case of extraordinary feature."

SUPERIOR, WISCONSIN—Population—44,344

TELEGRAM—Aft.—15,380—A. Dod, Mg. Ed.—$1.00 inch. "Five theatres; three advertise daily and one other three times a week. Have a daily department with greater spread on Saturday."

SYDNEY, NOVA SCOTIA, CANADA—Population—24,000

POST—Morn. & Aft.—7,236—J. Fergusson—21 cts. inch "Eleven theatres; four advertise daily. Gives readers on Tuesday, gratis. Publishes reading notices on other days if paid for. Prints Saturday photoplay department."

SYRACUSE, NEW YORK—Population 146,587

JOURNAL—Aft.—45,030—F. Chase—Rate omitted "Thirty-five theatres; eight advertise daily. Gives daily reading notices to houses. On Saturday prints from one to two pages of stage and picture news."

POST-STANDARD—Morn. & Sun.—52,324—B. York—Rate omitted "Sunday circulation 50,000. Runs photoplay section on Sunday. Gives daily reading notices to the theatres. In the matter of co-operation, gives suggestions as to layouts and special ads." Additional paper: Herald.

509

TRINIDAD, COLORADO—Population 12,274

PICKETWIRE—Aft.—1,575—F. Rose, Mg. Ed.—Rate omitted. "Five theatres, all of which advertise daily. Runs daily reading notices. Would use one and two-column cuts. Conducts it own reviews."

TROY, NEW YORK—Population 73,302

RECORD—Morn. & Aft.—25,537—D. Marvin, Mg. Ed.—$1.80 inch. "Twenty theatres; six advertise daily. No special publicity service rendered."
TIMES—Aft.—16,118—E. Paul—$2.10 inch. "Gives reading notices only with amusement ads. Two-column cuts of stars are run with reference to attractions in which they appear, as material of interest to the public."

TUCSON, ARIZONA—Population 15,604

CITIZEN—Aft.—4,187—J. Hall—30 cts. inch. "Three houses, all of which advertise daily. On each Saturday there are published the programs and publicity articles appertaining to the bills for the coming week. Conducts its own reviews."
ARIZONA DAILY STAR—Morn. & Sun.—3,318—W. Upshaw—Rate omitted. Sunday circulation 3,862. Prints Sunday photoplay section and gives daily reading notices. Aids houses in the preparation of advertising copy."

TULSA, OKLAHOMA—Population 28,240

DEMOCRAT—Aft. & Sun.—22,262—V. Smith, Mg. Ed.—Rate omitted. "Twelve theatres, ten of which advertise daily. Sunday circulation 22,262. Prints cuts and stories desired by managers at regular rates."
TIMES—Morn.—17,116—V. Smith, Mg. Ed.—Rate omitted. "Prints cuts and stories desired by managers at regular rates. Would use portraits of players and scenes from plays."
WORLD—Morn., Aft. & Sun.—21,509—F. Steenrod, Mg. Ed.—Rate omitted. "No special publicity service rendered." Sunday circulation 21,509."

UNION HILL, NEW JERSEY—Population 23,000

HUDSON DISPATCH—Aft.—12,224—F. Galland—4 cts. line. "Theatres number 15; all advertise daily. Picture section every day on full page. Conducts its own reviews. Would use single-column cuts."

UNIONTOWN PENNSYLVANIA—Population 19,140

HERALD—Morn.—9,767—J. Shean, Mg. Ed.—Rate omitted. "Three theatres; all advertise daily except Sunday. Daily publication averages two columns of local readers and film gossip. Conducts its own reviews."
GENIUS—Morn.—6,495—(Same management as the HERALD)

UTICA, NEW YORK—Population 82,434

OBSERVER—Aft.—17,797—M. Sammons—$1.50 inch. "Sixteen theatres, seven of which advertise daily. Each inch of amusement advertising space carries a definite amount of reading notices regardless of the day of the week."
DAILY PRESS—Morn.—22,052—H. Hughes, Mg. Ed.—$1.50 inch. "Prints daily reading notices for those theatres carrying advertising." On Saturday carries all commercial notices and local theatrical notices on the one page."
HERALD-DISPATCH—Aft.—20,428—A. Foote—$1.50 inch. "Prints reading notices to theatres daily. Conducts its own reviews."
SUNDAY TRIBUNE—Sun.—12,500—(Same management as HERALD-DISPATCH) "Runs theatrical pages with special illustrations and notices."

VANCOUVER, WASHINGTON—Population—11,930

COLUMBIAN—Aft.—1,700—S. Hopkins, Photo. Ed.—20 cts. inch. "Three theatres; all advertise daily. Have a daily theatrical column. Prints reading notices every day in proportion to the ad space used. Prefer cuts."

VANCOUVER, BRITISH COLUMBIA—Population—114,220

DAILY PROVINCE—Aft.—58,674—R. Brown, Mg. Ed.—98 cts. inch. "Legitimate theatres pay an ad rate of $2.10 per inch. Twenty-four theatres, ten of which advertise daily. No special publicity service rendered. Publishes dispatches, organization changes and notices of new theatres, under construction or renovation, as news of public interest."
DAILY SUN—Morn. & Sun.—Circ. omitted—R. Jamieson, Photo. Ed.—Rate omitted. "Sixteen picture theatres, nine of which advertise daily. Each Sunday devotes from four to eight pages exclusively to pictures. Conducts mid-week reviews. Would prefer two and three-column mats of stars."
WORLD—Aft.—20,000—C. Abraham, Photo. Ed.—70 cts. inch. "Runs photoplay section on Saturday embodying reading notices, which are allowed to a reasonable extent. Would use one or two-column 65-screeen cuts. Conducts its own reviews."

VICKSBURG, MISSISSIPPI—Population—22,090

EVENING POST—Aft.—3,240—L. Cashman, Ad. Mgr.—25 cts. inch. "Two theatres; both advertise daily. Prints reading notices daily and conducts reviews by members of the staff. Would use cuts of prominent screen artists."

VICTORIA, BRITISH COLUMBIA—Population—60,000

DAILY TIMES—Aft.—10,422—W. Wilson, Photo. Ed.—3 cts. line. "Five theatres, all of which advertise daily. Prints reading notices daily in proportion to the advertising space used. Publishes reviews conducted by member of staff."

VINCENNES, INDIANA—Population—16,759

SUN—Aft.—3,066—G. Purcell, Mg. Ed.—9 cts. inch. "Six theatres, all of which advertise daily. Runs reading notices only when space is paid for."
COMMERCIAL—Morn. & Sun.—3,983—C. Adams, Ad. Mgr.—Rate omitted. "No publicity or ad service rendered."

VIRGINIA, MINNESOTA—Population—13,671

ENTERPRISE—Aft.—2,473—E. Smith, Mg. Ed.—22 cts. inch. "Five theatres, four of which advertise daily. Devotes about one column daily to free readers and picture events of interest."
VIRGINIAN—Aft.—3,400—Ed. omitted—20 cts. inch. "Publishes daily reading notices for the theatres."

WASHINGTON, PENNSYLVANIA—Population—20,702

DAILY NEWS—Aft. & Sun.—4,500—J. Hammer, Mg. Ed.—Rate omitted. "Six theatres; all advertise daily. Allows each theatre a reasonable length of free readers every week-day and Sunday. Special attention is given to the Sunday picture page."

WACO, TEXAS—Population—28,707

TIMES-HERALD—Aft. & Sun.—C. Glover, Jr., Photo. Ed.—Rate omitted. "Eight theatres, four of which advertise daily. Gives reading notices to the theatres daily and on Sunday runs an amusement section of three or four pages."

WAKEFIELD, MASSACHUSETTS—Population—12,305

DAILY ITEM—Aft.—2,545—G. Campbell, Mg. Ed.—Rate omitted. "Runs reading notices of brief length but not regularly. Two theatres, both of which advertise daily when open."

WALLA WALLA, WASHINGTON—Population—23,275

UNION—Morn. & Sun.—3,600—R. Fisher, Photo. Ed.—Rate omitted. "Four theatres, all of which advertise daily. Reading notices are printed every day when paid for. Considerable space is devoted to the pictures in the Sunday issue. Sunday circulation 3,875.

STUDIO DIRECTORY

BULLETIN—Aft. & Sun.—5,013—C. Garfield, Photo. Ed.—35 cts. inch.
"No special publicity service is rendered. Occasionally on Sunday some space is devoted to picture and player articles as matter of interest to the public. Sunday circulation 5,013."

WALTHAM, MASSACHUSETTS—Population—29,688

EVENING NEWS—Aft.—2,725—C. Burgess, Mg. Ed.—20 cts. inch.
"Four theatres, all of which advertise daily. Brief reading notices are given daily to the theatres. Would use cuts if they brought advertising."

WARREN, OHIO—Population—12,074

CHRONICLE—Aft.—5,022—G. Marvin, Photo. Ed.—22 cts. inch.
"Four theatres; three advertise daily. Runs a daily theatrical department covering the local houses. Gives daily reading notices. Conducts its own reviews."

TRIBUNE—Aft.—6,050—T. Deming, Mg. Ed.—25 cts. inch.
"Publishes a 'Movie Page' every day, including reading notices for the theatres. Would use cuts and mats of artists preferably, suitable for 12½ em column."

WARREN, PENNSYLVANIA—Population—14,045

MIRROR—Morn.—3,583—C. Berger, Photo. Ed.—25 cts. inch.
"Three theatres, all of which advertise daily. Runs a photoplay department in the Saturday issue. Gives one three-inch reader daily. Prints player and picture items often as matter of public interest because of the demand for such news. Would use mats of human interest."

TIMES—Aft.—4,174—E. Lowey, Photo. Ed.—20 cts. inch.
"Reading notices are run gratis every day. Would use mats. Conducts its own reviews."

CHRONICLE—Morn. & Sun.—3,400—C. Johnston, Mg. Ed.—18 cts. inch.
"Sunday circulation 5,000. Running reading notices to any reasonable extent. Conducts regular Sunday department of one to two pages. Would appreciate regular supply of mats."

WASHINGTON, DISTRICT OF COLUMBIA—Population—353,378

POST—Morn. & Sun.—61,848—F. Morse, Photo. Ed.—30 cts. per line
"Sunday circulation 80,105. Eighteen downtown theatres; forty neighborhood houses. Reading notices, printed on Monday, Tuesday, Thursday and Sunday. Has photoplay section on Sunday. Prefers 6 x 10 glazed photos."

STAR—Aft. & Sun.—101,643—W. Lanvorigt, Photo. Ed.—22 cts. line.
"Sunday circulation 82,119. Monday and Tuesday reviews; Wednesday advance notices. On Sunday, one page is devoted to the news of the photoplays. Conducts its own reviews."

HERALD—Morn. & Sun.—41,887—E. Dorsey, Photo. Ed.—15 cts. line.
"Sunday circulation 34,200. Ad rate 10 cts. per line in the Thursday issue week amusement section. Runs a photoplay department in the Sunday issue. Runs reading notices three times a week. Conducts reviews when requested. Additional paper: Times."

WATERBURY, CONNECTICUT—Population—82,517

DEMOCRAT—Aft.—7,214—E. Maloney, Mg. Ed.—75 cts. inch.
"About twenty houses, six of which advertise daily. Runs daily reading notices, allowing one-inch reader for every inch of display. Reviews specials."

WATERLOO, IOWA—Population—32,703

EVENING COURIER—Aft.—14,484—A. Peterson, Mg. Ed.—42 cts. inch.
"Six theatres; four advertise daily. Runs Saturday photoplay department. Publishes theatre news every day. Would use 65-screen half-tone cuts or mats."

TIMES-TRIBUNE—Morn. & Sun.—11,148—F. Hanlon, Mg. Ed.—75 cts. inch.
"Gives regular run of readers every day with a feature cut free on Sunday. Sunday circulation 12,376."

WAUKEGAN, ILLINOIS—Population—18,898

DAILY SUN—Aft.—3,750—W. Smith, Mg. Ed.—20 cts. inch.
"Four theatres; all advertise daily. Runs daily reading notices."

GAZETTE—Aft.—3,000—J. Woodman, Mg. Ed.—20 cts. inch.
"Gives daily reading notices to the theatres. Would use two or three-column mats."

WAUSAU, WISCONSIN—Population—18,352

RECORD-HERALD—Aft.—5,353—Ed. omitted—Rate omitted.
"Three theatres; all advertise daily. No special editorial co-operation cited in the questionnaire."

WAY CROSS, GEORGIA—Population—18,134

JOURNAL-HERALD—Aft.—1,800—J. WILLIAMS, Mg. Ed.—20 cts. inch.
"Gives a special rate for reader notices and runs one for each theatre every day during the week. Two houses, both of which advertise daily."

WEST CHESTER, PENNSYLVANIA—Population—12,722

DAILY LOCAL NEWS—Aft.—11,926—W. Thomson, Mg. Ed.—42 cts. inch.
"Three houses, all of which advertise daily. No special publicity service rendered."

WHEELING, WEST VIRGINIA—Population—42,817

NEWS—Aft. & Sun.—15,395—L. Crow, Mg. Ed.—Rate omitted.
"Thirteen theatres, three of which advertise daily. Gives liberal reading notices daily. Sunday photoplay and theatre matter is combined on the theatrical pages."

REGISTER—Morn. & Sun.—15,595—J. Plummer, Photo. Ed.—75 cts. inch.
"Sunday circulation 16,233. Sunday ad rate 90 cts inch. Publishes a Sunday photoplay department and runs daily reading notices. Prints reviews conducted by member of the staff."

WICHITA, KANSAS—Population—54,972

THE BEACON—Aft.—39,322—N. Conner, Photo. Ed.—Rate omitted.
"Nine theatres; five advertise daily. Runs Saturday photoplay department. Reading notices included only when the editor sees fit to comment on new pictures."

EAGLE—Morn. & Sun.—55,018—F Parsons, Photo. Ed.—$1.20 inch.
"Sunday ad rate is $1.40 per inch. On Sunday prints two pages of feature stories and photo layouts. Runs special feature daily, containing advance reviews and news stories."

WILKES-BARRE, PENNSYLVANIA—Population—73,660

RECORD—Morn.—16,923—R. Goodwin, Photo. Ed.—$1.00 inch.
"Ten theatres; six advertise daily. Runs daily reading notices. Would use cuts."

TIMES-LEADER—Aft.—20,292—J. Forestal, Mg. Ed.—$1.00 inch.
"Runs daily reading notices. Conducts its own reviews."

EVENING NEWS—Aft.—11,537—J. McKewon, Ad. Mgr.—60 cts inch.
"Free reading notices are given every day, varying in size from two to ten inches in size. Would use single-column electros. Conducts its own reviews."

WILLIAMSPORT, PENNSYLVANIA—Population—33,181

GAZETTE AND BULLETIN—Morn.—11,748—Ed. omitted—25-40 cts. inch.
"Five theatres, three of which advertise daily. No special publicity service rendered."

512 STUDIO DIRECTORY

WILLIMANTIC, CONNECTICUT—Population—12,206
SUN—Aft.—16,110—J. Person, Mg. Ed.—Rate omitted.
 "Runs photoplay department on Friday. Publishes reading notices regularly, according as they seem justified by their news value."
CHRONICLE—Aft.—3,463—A. Cunningham, Mg. Ed.—Rate omitted.
 "Three theatres; all advertise daily. Runs daily reading notices and sometimes conducts its own reviews."

WILMINGTON, DELAWARE—Population—92,057
EVERY EVENING—Aft.—13,200—F. Reybred, Mg. Ed.—60 cts. inch.
 "About ten theatres; five advertise. Gives daily reading notices of from ten to twenty lines. Would probably use 60-screen single-column cuts."

WILMINGTON, NORTH CAROLINA—Population—27,781
STAR—Morn. & Sun.—6,002—D. Bain, Photo. Ed.—30 cts. inch.
 "Four theatres; all advertise. Runs daily reading notices. On Sunday runs theatre columns submitted by press agents of the local houses."

WINDSOR, ONTARIO—Population—17,829
BORDER CITIES STAR—Aft.—12,402—A. Baxter, Photo. Ed.—3½ cts line.
 "Eight theatres; five advertise daily. On Saturday runs reading notices to extent of one-half the ad space used."

WINNIPEG, MANITOBA—Population—203,255
EVENING TRIBUNE—Aft.—36,423—M. Allen, Photo. Ed.—6 cts. line.
 "Twenty-five theatres; eighteen advertise daily. Runs daily reading notices. Publishes photoplay department in the Saturday issue of two or three columns, including a lot of special photoplay news features."
FREE PRESS—Morn. & Aft.—80,282—J. Conklin, Photo. Ed.—10 cts. line.
 "Runs Saturday photoplay section of from four to five pages. Conducts its own reviews. Gives liberal space daily to reading notices to theatres."

WINONA, MINNESOTA—Population—18,583
REPUBLICAN-HERALD—Aft.—Circ. omitted—F. Rucker, Ad. Mgr.—35 cts. inch.
 "Six theatres; four advertise daily. No special publicity service rendered."

WINSTON-SALEM, NORTH CAROLINA—Population—29,034
JOURNAL—Morn. & Sun.—6,447—E. James, Photo. Ed.—30 cts. inch.
 "Eight theatres; five advertise daily. Has photoplay department in the Sunday issue and gives reading notices daily to the theatres. Prefers mats. Sunday circulation 7,365."
SENTINEL—Aft.—7,800—H. Aitchison, Photo. Ed.—30 cts. inch.
 "Photoplay department on Saturday. In the Saturday issue reading notices are printed to an extent equivalent to that of the advertising space paid for. Would use mats of pictures booked for this city."

WOBURN, MASSACHUSETTS—Population—15,308
DAILY TIMES—Aft.—3,400—J. Haggerty, Mg. Ed.—Rate omitted.
 "One theatre and a hall fully equipped. The theatre advertises daily. Gives reading notices occasionally. Uses cuts supplied by house advertising with paper only."

WOONSOCKET, RHODE ISLAND—Population—40,075
CALL—Aft.—11,888—T. Walsh, Photo. Ed.—$1.00 inch.
 "Five theatres; four advertise daily. Gives reading notices in connection with the advertising."

WORCESTER, MASSACHUSETTS—Population—145,986
GAZETTE—Aft.—Circ. omitted.—N. Skerritt, Photo. Ed.—$1.50 inch.
 "Twenty-one theatres; six advertise daily. Runs reading notices daily but in proportion to the paid advertising. Publishes a theatre page on Saturday. Conducts its own reviews."
TELEGRAM—Morn. & Sun.—31,573—Herbert, Photo. Ed.—$1.50 inch.
 "Runs reading notices only at the option of the paper. Publishes advance notices of current productions as a matter of local news interest only. Would use mats."
Additional paper: Post.

YAKIMA, WASHINGTON—Population—18,737
HERALD—Aft. & Sun.—4,652—J. Ellis, Jr.—Rate omitted.
 "Two theatres; both advertise daily. Runs photoplay department on Sunday containing reading notices. Sunday circulation 5,507."
REPUBLIC—Aft.—4,758—S. Anthon, Photo. Ed.—Rate omitted.
 "Has photoplay section in the Tuesday issue if conditions permit; otherwise later on in the week."

YONKERS, NEW YORK—Population—90,886
NEWS—Aft.—3,640—T. Tunnard, Photo. Ed.—25 cts. inch.
 "The ad rate of 25 cts. per inch holds if over 300 inches be used. Prints a daily film page, including free reading notices. Nine theatres; four advertise daily. Cuts are preferred."
THE GAZETTE AND DAILY—Morn.—14,555—S. Elsesser, Mg. Ed.—50 cts. inch.
 "Fourteen theatres; three advertise daily. Has photoplay section every day, containing reading notices."

YOUNGSTOWN, OHIO—Population—93,341
TELEGRAM—Aft.—21,000—C. Leedy, Photo. Ed.—75 cts. inch
 "Twelve theatres, all of which advertise daily. Prints daily feature and publishes reading notices according to their news value each day. Conducts its own reviews."
VINDICATOR—Aft. & Sun.—W. Rook, Photo. Ed.—75 cts. inch.
 "Runs reading notices daily. Each day, including Sunday, a special section is devoted to the motion pictures. Conducts its own reviews.

ZANESVILLE, OHIO—Population—29,949
SIGNAL—Aft.—11,044—J. Downs, Mg. Ed.—75 cts. inch.
 "Four theatres, all of which advertise daily except Sunday. Publishes reading notices daily to a reasonable extent. Puts out a photoplay section daily. Would use mats of principal stars and brief stories with the same when possible."
TIMES-READER—Morn.—21,015—W. Litteck, Photo. Ed.—75 cts. inch.
 "Gives daily reading notices to the theatres. Prints to some extent player and picture articles as news of interest to the public. Four theatres, all of which advertise daily."

YORK, PENNSYLVANIA—Population—49,430

State Rights Percentages

THE proper percentages to be charged for each district have now become stabilized. After many changes during the past three years the percentages finally adopted by the First National Exhibitors' Circuit are most generally accepted. The State Rights buyers are expected to pay their stipulated percentage of the gross price set for the United States and its possessions, including also the Dominion of Canada.

First National percentages can be found in the following list supplied by the circuit to Motion Picture Studio Directory and Trade Annual.

PERCENTAGES FOR TERRITORIES

FRANCHISE HOLDER	ADDRESS	TERRITORY	%
Sol. Lesser and Gore Bros.	Broadway Theatre Los Angeles, Cal.	Counties of San Luis Obispo, Santa Barbara, Kern, Ventura, Los Angeles, San Bernardino, Riverside, Orange, San Diego and Imperial in California & Arizona.	2 27/56
Turner & Dahnken	134 Golden Gate Ave. San Francisco, Cal.	Nevada, Territory of Hawaii and all counties in California except those above mentioned.	3 2/14
Exhibitors Film Ex.	1200–4th Ave., Seattle, Wash.	Alaska, Washington, Oregon, Montana, and all counties in Idaho north of and including Idaho county.	3 5/8
First National Ex. Circuit of Colo.	1744 Curtis St., Denver, Colo.	Colorado, New Mexico, Utah, Wyoming and all counties in Idaho south of Idaho county.	1 3/4
Western Theatre Co.	Rex Theatre, Vancouver, B. C.	All Canada West of and including Fort William and Port Arthur.	2
First National Ex. Exchange	110 So. State St., Chicago, Ill.	Illinois.	8 1/4
H. Lieber Co.	24 W. Washington St., Indianapolis, Ind.	Indiana.	3 1/8
A. H. Blank	Garden Theatre, Des Moines, Iowa	Kansas, Iowa & Nebraska.	4 3/4
First National Film Ex. of Michigan	Film Building, Detroit, Mich.	Michigan.	4 1/4
First National Ex. Circ. of N. W.	Film Exchange Bldg., Minneapolis, Minn.	Minnesota, Wisconsin, N. & S. Dakota.	5
Skouras Bros.	New Grand Central St. Louis.	Missouri.	3 1/4
First Natl. Ex. Cir. Co. of Ohio	Sloan Bldg., Cleveland, Ohio.	Ohio.	7

STUDIO DIRECTORY

FRANCHISE HOLDER	ADDRESS	TERRITORY	%
Gordon-Mayer Film Co.	35 Piedmont St., Boston, Mass.	New England States.	8
First National Ex. Exchange.	916 G St. N.W., Washington, D. C.	Maryland, Dist. of Col. and Del.	2 1/4
First National Ex. Exchange of N. J.	729–7th Ave., New York City	New Jersey.	3 5/8
First National Ex.	509–5th Ave., New York City	New York	14 1/2
First National Ex. Exchange.	414 Ferry St., Pittsburgh, Pa.	West Va. & Western Penna. consisting of all counties west of and including Fulton, Huntingdon, Center, Clinton & Potter.	4 1/8
Peerless Feature Film Exch.	13th & Vine Sts., Philadelphia, Pa.	Eastern Pa., consisting of all counties east of those above mentioned.	4 3/4
H. Brouse	Imperial Theatre, Ottawa, Canada	All Canada East of, but not including Fort William & Port Arthur.	3 1/8
First National Ex. Circ. of Va.	904 E. Broad St., Richmond, Va.	Georgia, Fla., Ala., Va., N. & S. Carolina.	3 1/4
First National Ex. of New Orleans	712 Poydras St., New Orleans, La.	Louisiana & Mississippi.	1 3/8
First National Ex. Circ. of Texas	Old Mill Theatre, Dallas, Texas	Texas, Oklahoma & Arkansas.	4 1/2
Big Feature Rts. Corporation	Rex Theatre Bldg., Louisville, Ky.	Kentucky & Tennessee.	1 7/8

MOTION PICTURE NEWS and MOTION PICTURE STUDIO DIRECTORY have led in efforts towards securing newspaper cooperation with the motion picture industry.

The STUDIO DIRECTORY works for you all the year round — MOTION PICTURE NEWS with an every week punch.

What Can We Do For You?

From its very beginning MOTION PICTURE NEWS has sincerely aimed to be of help to all genuinely connected with this industry. If we can give you information, advice, or assistance of any kind—just

Call Bryant 9360

or write to

MOTION PICTURE NEWS

729 7th Ave., New York

MOTION PICTURE NEWS COVERS THE FIELD

WINFIELD-KERNER COMPANY

Established 1905

325-27 East 6th Street, Los Angeles

ARC LAMPS
Suitable for Motion Picture Photography

Winfield-Kerner
Lamps
and
Equipment
Used in
Every Studio
on the
West Coast

A Lamp for Every Studio Need

WEST COAST STUDIOS AND COMPANIES

American Film Co., Santa Barbara.

Astra Film Corporation, Verdugo Road, Glendale.

Beban, Geo., Productions, 434 H. W. Hellman Bldg., Los Angeles.

Brentwood Film Corporation, 4811 Fountain Ave., Hollywood.

Bringing Up Father Comedies, 6100 Sunset Blvd., Hollywood.

Bull's Eye Film Corporation, 5823 Santa Monica Blvd., Hollywood.

Burston Films, 6050 Sunset Blvd., Hollywood.

Capital Film Co., 1025 Lillian Way, Hollywood.

Carpess Film Co., 626 Homer Laughlin Bldg., Los Angeles.

Chaplin, Charles, Studio, 1420 LaBrea Ave., Hollywood.

Chaplin, Mildred Harris Co., 3900 Mission Road, Los Angeles.

Chaplin, Syd., Productions, 6642 Santa Monica Blvd., Hollywood.

Christie Film Co., 6101 Sunset Blvd., Hollywood.

Clermont Photoplay Corp., 323 Title Insurance Bldg., Los Angeles.

Cohn, Marion H., Productions, 1116 Lodi Street, Hollywood.

Comique Film Corporation (Roscoe Arbuckle), Culver City.

DeHaven Comedy Co., 4500 Sunset Blvd., Hollywood.

Dierker Film Co., 1023 Van Nuys Bldg., Los Angeles.

E. & R. Jungle Film Co., 1720 N. Soto St., Los Angeles.

Fairbanks, Douglas, Co., 5320 Melrose Ave., Hollywood.

Famous Players-Lasky Corporation, 1520 Vine St., Hollywood.

Ford, Francis, Studios, 6040 Sunset Blvd., Hollywood.

Fox, William, Film Corporation, 1417 N. Western Ave., Hollywood.

Fox, William, Studio (Ranch), 2450 Teviot, Los Angeles.

Gaiety Comedies, Inc., 1501 Gower St., Hollywood.

Garson Studios, 1845 Allesandro St., Los Angeles.

Gasnier, L. J., Productions, Verdugo Road, Glendale.

Goldwyn Film Corporation Studios, Culver City.

Great Western Film Co., 6100 Sunset Blvd., Hollywood.

Hampton, J. D., Productions, Sunset and LaBrea Blvds., Hollywood.

Hart, Wm. S., Studio, 1215 Bates St., Los Angeles.

Haworth Pictures Corp., 4500 Sunset Blvd., Hollywood.

Historical Film Corporation of America, Burbank.

Horsley, David, Studios, 1919 So. Main St., Los Angeles.

Ince, Thomas H., Studios, Inc., Culver City.

Lehrman, Henry, Studios, Culver City.

Lesser, Sol, Enterprises, 434 H. W. Hellman Bldg., Los Angeles.

Lewis, Edgar, Productions, Universal City.

L.-Ko Motion Picture Corporation, 6100 Sunset Blvd., Los Angeles.

Mayer, Louis B., Productions, 3900 Mission Road, Los Angeles.

McCarthy Pictures Corporation, 609 Laughlin Bldg., Los Angeles.

MacDonald, Katherine, Studios, 904 Girard St., Los Angeles.

Mann, Hank, Comedies, 1919 S. Main St., Los Angeles.

Metro Pictures Corporation, 6300 Romayne, Hollywood.

Model Comedy Co., 5821 Santa Monica Blvd., Hollywood.

Moranti Comedies, Inc., Long Beach.

Morosco Studios, 201 N. Occidental Blvd., Los Angeles.

National Film Corporation of America 1116 Lodi St., Hollywood.

Ray, Chas., Productions, Inc., 1425 Fleming St., Hollywood.

Reed, J. Parker, Jr., Productions, care Ince Studios, Culver City.

Rolin Film Co., Culver City.

Romayne Studio, Washington Blvd., Culver City.

Samuelson, G. B., Productions, Universal City.

Selig, W. H., Pictures, 3800 Mission Road, Los Angeles.

Sennett, Mack, Comedies, 1712 Allesandro, Los Angeles.

Shurtleff, C. E., Inc., 6300 Romayne St., Hollywood.

Special Pictures Corporation, 634 H. W. Hellman Bldg., Los Angeles.

Special Pictures Corp. Studios, Long Beach.

St. John, Al., Comedies, 5823 Santa Monica Blvd., Hollywood.

Stewart, Anita, Productions, 3900 Mission Road, Los Angeles.

Sylvanite Productions, 239 So. Van Ness St., Los Angeles.

Tourneur, Maurice, Productions, Universal City.

Triangle Film Corporation, 405 Currier Bldg., Los Angeles.

Universal Film Mfg. Co., Universal City.

Vitagraph Co., 1708 Talmadge St., Hollywood.

Wade Productions, 6050 Sunset Blvd., Hollywood.

Warner Brothers, 1919 So. Main St., Los Angeles.

Weber, Lois, Productions, 4634 Santa Monica Blvd., Los Angeles.

Willatt, Irving, Productions, Culver City.

Wilson, Ben, Productions, 5823 Santa Monica Blvd., Hollywood.

Young, Clara Kimball, Co., 1845 Allesandro St., Los Angeles.

STUDIO DIRECTORY

Companies Working at Jasper Hollywood Studios
6642 Santa Monica Blvd., Hollywood

Callaghan Andrew J., Productions, Inc. (Bessie Love Co.)
Neilan, Marshall, Productions.
Phillips-Holubar Productions.
Schwab, D. N., Productions, Inc.
Vidor, King, Productions, Inc.

Companies Working at Robert Brunton Studios
5341 Melrose Ave., Hollywood

Jack Dempsey—Pathe Serial.
Annette Kellerman Company.
Betty Compson Productions.
B. B. Hampton-Great Authors Productions.
Selznick Pictures.
United Theatre Productions.
Republic Pictures.
L. Lawrence Weber Productions.
Mayflower Pictures Corporation.
Mary Pickford Film Co.
Mae Marsh Pictures.
James Oliver Curwood Productions.
Bessie Barriscale Productions.
J. Warren Kerrigan Productions.

EASTERN STUDIOS
NEW YORK CITY

Adolf Philipp Film Corp., 11 East 14th St., Stuyvesant 6787.
Bacon-Backer, 230 West 38th St., Greeley 2486.
Biograph, 807 East 175th St., Tremont 5100.
Columbia-Metro, 3 West 61st St., Columbus 8181.
Crystal, 430 Claremont Parkway, Tremont 3766.
Edison, Decatur Ave. & Oliver Pl., Fordham 8330.
Erbograph, 203 West 146th St., Audubon 3716.
Estee's, 361 West 125th St., Morningside 4985.
Famous Players, 130 West 56th St., Circle 500.
Fifty-fourth St., 517 West 54th St., Columbus 6498.
Filmart, 69 West 90th St. (used for school of acting), Riverside 1315.
Fox, West 55th St., Circle 6800.
International, 127th & Second Ave., Harlem 6298.
Norma Talmadge, 318 East 48th St., Vanderbilt 4338.
Oliver, 308 East 48th St., Murray Hill 6276.
Pathe, 134th St. & Park Ave., Acad. 4730.
Victor, 645 West 43rd St., Longacre 20.

BROOKLYN AND LONG ISLAND

J. Stuart Blackton, 423 Classon Ave., Brooklyn, N. Y., Prospect 9683.
Famous Players, Long Island City, N. Y.
Frohman Amuse. Corp., 140 Amity St., Flushing, L. I., Flushing 3994.
Mirror, Glendale, L. I., Rich Hill 3545.
Gaumont, Flushing, L. I., laboratory, Flushing 2211.
Hal Benedict, College Point, Flushing, L. I., Flushing 3142.
Vitagraph, E. 15th St. & Locust Ave., Midwood 6100.

NEW JERSEY

Charter Film (Benj. Chapin), Ridgefield Park, N. J. (used as laboratory at present), Hackensack 583.
Eclair-Fox, Fort Lee, N. J., Fort Lee 120.
Ideal (Briggs), Hudson Heights, N. J., Union 5067.
Kalem, Cliffside, N. J., Cliffside 789.
Lincoln, Grantwood, N. J., Morsmere 649.
Paragon (Chautard), Fort Lee, N. J., Fort Lee 329.
Pathe-Astra, 1 Congress St., Jersey City, N. J., Webster 4675.
Peerless, Fort Lee, N. J., Fort Lee 290.
Solax, Fort Lee, N. J., Fort Lee 166.
Universal-Selznick, Leonia, N. J., Fort Lee 350.

MISCELLANEOUS

Beaver, Dongan Hills, Staten Island, N. Y., New Dorp 535.
A. H. Fisher, New Rochelle, N. Y., New Rochelle, 2277.
Griffith, Orienta Point, Mamaroneck, N. Y., Mamaroneck 1191.
Plimpton, 965 Yonkers Ave., East Yonkers, N. Y., Mt. Vernon 3884.
Reliance, 537 Riverdale Ave., Kingsbridge, near Yonkers, N. Y. C., Kingsbridge 270.
Unexcelled, 120 School St., Yonkers N. Y. Yonkers 4600.

STUDIO DIRECTORY

ALPHABETICAL INDEX TO BIOGRAPHIES AND PORTRAITS

A

	Biography	Portrait
Abbe, Jack	203	
Abel, David	329	
Abraham, Jake	203	
Abramson, Ivan	289	
Abramson, William	294	
Abroussleman, Charles	329	
Acker, Edward	317	
Acker, Eugene	203	
Acord, Art	203	401
Adams, Claire	257	
Adams, Dora Mills	257	
Adams, Kathryn	257	
Adams, Lionel	203	
Adams, William S.	329	
Addison, Smythe	317	
Adolfi, John G.	294	
Aiken, Alma	257	
Ainsworth, Charles Sydney	203	
Aitken, Spottiswoode	203	
Albertson, Arthur	203	
Albertson, E. Cort	203	
Alden, Mary	257	
Alder, William F.	329	
Alexander, Ben	286	288
Alexander, Claire	257	
Alexander, Clifford	203	
Alexander, Edward	203	
Alexander, Frank D.	203	
Alexander, Frank Nesbitt	329	
Alexander, Gus	203	
Alexander, J. Grubb	317	428
Alexander, J. Melrose	329	
Alexander, Lois	286	
Alexander, Sara	257	
Algier, Sidney H.	294	
Allardt, Arthur	203	
Allen, Albert C.	329	
Allen, Alfred	203	
Allen, Beatrice	257	
Allen, Diana	257	
Allen, Major Jack	294	
Allen, Phyllis	257	
Allen, Ray	257	
Allen, Ricca	257	455
Alier, Joseph	329	
Alley, Alfred Wright	294	
Alley, Y. C.	294	
Allison, May	257	80
Alter, Lottie	257	
Amador, Charles Edward	203	
American Society of Cinematographers		173
Anderson, Claire	257	
Anderson, Helen Relyea	257	
Anderson, Mary	257	66
Anderson, Mignon	257	445
Anderson, Robert	204	
Andrews, Frank	204	
Andrews, Gertrude	317	
Andriot, Lucien	320	
Anker, William	204	454
Aoki, Tsuru	258	
Aoyama, Yukio	204	
Apfel, Oscar C.	294	
Arbuckle, Andrew	204	
Arbuckle, Maclyn	204	341
Arbuckle, Roscoe	204	10
Archainbaud, George	294	95
Ardizoni, John	204	
Arey, Wayne	204	
Arling, Charles	204	465
Arnold, Edward	204	
Arnold, John	330	
Aronson, N. W.		306
Arthur, Julia	258	
Artigue, Pierre		473
Asher, Max	204	
Ashley, Arthur H	204	
Ashton, Iris	258	441
Ashton, Rosalie	317	
Ashton, Sylvia	258	
Atwill, Lionel	204	
Aubrey, James	204	
Aucker, William	204	
August, Edwin	204	
August, Joe	330	
Austen, Leslie	204	
Austin, Albert	204	
Austin, Jere	205	438
Avery, Charles	294	
Avery, J. Ray	205	458
Axzelle, Violet	286	
Ayres, Agnes	258	89

B

	Biography	Portrait
Bacon, Gerald F.	341	
Bacon, Lloyd Francis	205	
Badaracco, Jacob A.	330	
Badger, Clarence G.	294	466
Baer, Berthold A.	317	
Baggot, King	205	67
Bailey, Bill	205	439
Bailey, Mildred E.	258	
Bainbridge, Wm. Herbert	205	
Baird, Leah	258	
Baird, Stewart	205	
Baker, Charles Graham	317	
Baker, Doris	286	463
Baker, Edwin King	205	
Baker, Friend F.	330	
Baker, George D.	294	105
Baker, Hettie Grey	317	
Baker, LeRoy L.	294	
Baker, Thomas A.	346	
Baldwin, Ruth Ann	317	
Ball, Eustace Hale	317	
Ballin, Hugo	294	
Ballin, Mabel	258	
Banks, Mrs. Estar	258	
Banks, Perry	205	
Bara, Theda	258	26
Barker, Bradley	205	
Barker, Corinne	258	76
Barker, Reginald	294	
Barlatier, Andre	330	
Barnett, Chester	205	
Barney, Marion	258	
Barrett, Thomas A.		
Barrie, Nigel	205	83
Barrington, Herbert	205	
Barriscale, Bessie	258	
Barrows, Henry A.	205	
Barry, Eddie	205	457
Barry, Joseph J.	294	
Barry, Richard	317	
Barry, Wesley	286	
Barrymore, Ethel	258	
Barrymore, John	205	
Barrymore, Lionel	205	
Barthelmess, Richard	206	
Bartlett, Charles E.	294	468
Bartlett, Harry	206	
Barton, Grace	258	
Basil, Joseph	294	
Baskette, Lena	286	
Batista, Miriam	286	
Baxter, Thuma Jadee	258	455
Bayne, Beverly	258	
Beach, Rex	289	
Beal, Frank	294	
Beal, Scott Rathbone	295	
Beamish, Frank	206	
Beaudine, William	295	
Beaumont, Harry	295	468
Beban, George	206	
Bechter, William A.	206	
Beck, Frederick	330	
Beck, Lillian	258	
Beery, Noah, Jr.	206	
Belasco, Jay	206	
Bell, Walter W.	330	
Belle, Tula	286	
Belmont, Joseph	205	
Belmore, Daisy	258	
Benedict, Hal—Studios		185
Benedict, Kingsley	206	
Benham, Harry	206	
Benner, Yale Despine	206	
Bennett, Belle	259	
Bennett, Enid	259	
Bennett, Joseph	206	
Bennett, Richard	206	
Bennison, Louis	206	
Benoit, George	330	
Benson, Clyde	206	449
Benton, Curtis	206	
Beranger, Clara S.	317	170
Beranger, George A.	295	469
Beresford, Frank S.	317	
Bergen, Thurlow	206	
Bergman, Helmer Wilhelm	317	
Bergman, Henry	206	
Berkeley, Gertrude	259	

ALPHABETICAL INDEX

Name	Biography	Portrait
Bernard, Dorothy	259	
Berrell, George	206	
Bertram, William	295	79
Besserer, Eugenie	259	
Betts & Fowler		434
Bevan, William	207	
Bevis, Ted J.	295	
Biala, Sara	259	
Billings, Florence	259	
Billington, Francelia	259	385
Bingham, Edfrid A.	317	
Bingham, E. Douglas	295	
Binney, Constance	259	
Binney, Faire	259	
Binney, Harold J.	289	131
Biron, Lillian	259	448
Bitzer, George W.	330	
Bitzer, J. C.	330	
Bizeul, Jacques	330	
Blache, Mme. Alice	295	155
Blache, Herbert	295	155
Black, Fritzie	259	
Black, W. W.	207	
Blackton, J. Stuart	289	2
Blackwell, Carlyle	207	
Blackwell, Irene	259	85
Blake, Ben	295	
Blakely, Walter W.	330	
Blinn, Genevieve	259	
Blinn, Holbrook	207	
Block, Ralph	343	
Bloom, J. M.		433
Bloomer, Raymond	207	
Blount, Frank M.	330	
Blue, G. Monte	207	
Blystone, J. G.	295	470
Blythe, Betty	259	383
Blythe, Sydney C. W.	330	
Boland, Eddie	207	
Boland, Mary	259	
Bolder, Robert	207	
Booker, Beula	259	442
Boone, Dell	259	
Bordeaux, Joe	295	
Borzage, Frank	295	
Bosworth, Hobart	207	
Boteler, Wade	207	
Botter, Henry P.	207	
Bouton, Betty	259	
Bowers, John	207	
Bowes, Clifford W.	207	
Bowman, William J.	295	
Boyle, Irene	259	
Boyle, John Wm.	330	
Brabin, Charles	295	
Bracken, Bertram	295	419
Bracy, Sidney	207	
Bradbury, Robert North	295	
Bradbury, Ronald	207	
Bradley, Willard King	317	
Brady, Alice	260	
Brady, Edwin J.	207	
Brady, Jasper Ewing	317	
Brammall, John Gardiner	207	
Brautigam, Otto	330	
Bray, John Randolph	341	
Breamer, Sylvia	260	36
Bredeson, Henry	330	
Breese, Edmund	208	463
Brenon, Herbert	289	
Brent, Evelyn	260	
Bret, Tom	317	478
Brinley, Charles E.	208	
Brockwell, Gladys	260	
Brodsky, Samuel	295	
Brody, Anne G.	260	
Broening, Henry Lyman	330	
Bronston, Douglas	318	
Brooke, Myra	260	
Brooke, Van Dyke	296	
Brooks, Joe	208	
Brooks, Sam	208	
Brotherton, James	330	
Brotherton, Robert	330	
Broughton, Lewis	208	
Brown, Anita	260	
Brown, Chamberlain		181
Brown, Colvin W.	342	
Brown, Iva	260	
Brown, J. Edwin	208	
Brown, John W.	330	
Brown, Melville W.	296	409
Brown, William H.	208	
Browne, Bothwell	208	
Browne, Lewis Allen	318	428
Brownell, Hobart H.	330	
Browning, Irving	330	
Browning, Tod	296	470
Bruce, Beverly	260	
Bruce, Robert Cameron	289	
Bruce, Kate	260	
Brundage, Mathilde	260	
Brunet, Paul	341	
Brunette, Fritzi	260	
Brunton, Robert A.	289	184
Brunton, William	208	
Bryant, Charles	208	
Buchanan, James B.	330	
Buchanan, Thompson	318	479
Buckingham, Thomas		482
Buckland, Wilfrid	296	
Buckley, Floyd Thomas	208	
Buckley, Frederick Robert	318	
Buckley, William	208	
Buel, Kenean	296	
Buffington, Adele	318	
Buffum, Jesse H.	330	{432, 483}
Bull, Clarence S.	331	
Bunker, Ralph	208	
Bunny, George	208	
Burke, Billie	260	
Burke, Joseph	208	
Burke, Olive	260	
Burnham, Beatrice	260	381
Burnham, Julia	318	
Burns, Ed. J.	208	
Burns, Fred	208	
Burns, Neal	208	
Burns, Robert Paul	208	
Burns, Sammy	209	
Burress, William	209	
Burston Films		186
Burt, William P.	296	
Burton, Clarence F.	209	
Burton, G. Marion	318	
Burton, Ned	209	
Busch, Mae	260	
Bushman, Francis X.	209	
Busquet, Leo A.	318	
Butler, Alexander B.	296	416
Butler, "Babs"	260	
Butler, David	209	
Butterworth, Ernest	209	
Butt, Lawson W.	209	
Butterworth, Frank	286	
Byram, Ronald	209	
Byron, Nina	260	

C

Name	Biography	Portrait
Cabanne, Wm. Christy	296	121
Cabot, Harry	331	
Cain, Robert	209	
Calcagni, David	331	
Caldwell, Virginia	260	
Calhoun, Alice B.	260	
Calhoun, Jean	261	
Calvert, Catherine	261	38
Cameron, Rudolph	209	
Cameron, Tom	209	
Campbell, Colin	296	411
Campbell, William S.	296	
Campeau, Frank	209	383
Canady, D. R.	331	481
Cann, Berthold	331	
Cannon, Pomeroy	209	
Capellani, Albert	289	106
Caprice, June	261	
Carew, Ora	261	
Carewe, Edwin	289	147
Carey, Harry	209	
Carleton, Herbert Oswald	331	
Carleton, John T.	296	
Carleton, Lloyd B.	289	151
Carleton, William T.	209	
Carlton, Walter A.	318	
Carlyle, J. Montgomery	209	
Carlyle, Richard	209	
Carmen, Jewel	261	
Carpenter, Francis W.	286	
Carpenter, George Mulford	296	
Carr, Catherine	318	
Carre, Ben	296	412
Carrigan, Thomas J.	209	
Carrington, Evelyn Carter	261	
Carroll, Marcelle	261	
Carroll, Wm. Arthur	210	
Carson, Ella Stuart	318	216
Carter, Harry	210	
Caruso, Enrico	210	
Cassinelli, Dolores	261	64
Cassity, Ellen	261	
Castle, Irene	261	

STUDIO DIRECTORY

Name	Biography	Portrait
Castleton, Barbara	261	
Caswell, Nancy	286	
Cavelleri, Lina	261	
Cavender, Glen	210	
Cawood, Albert E.	331	
Cecil, Edward E.	210	443
Cecil, Nora	261	
Cederberg, Eric J.	331	
Chadwick, Helene	261	
Chambers, Marie	261	
Chandler, Warren	210	
Chaney, Lon	210	
Chapin, Frederic	318	
Chaplin, Charles Spencer	210	
Chaplin, Mildred Harris	268	18
Chaplin, Sydney	210	37
Chapman, Audrey Emily	261	447
Chapman, Edythe	261	
Charleson, Mary	261	
Chase, Colin	210	
Chaston, Fred	331	
Chaudet, Louis W.	296	
Chautard, Emile	289	104
Cheseboro, George	210	
Chester, C. L.	341	
Childers, Naomi	261	42
Chocklett, A. Luther	331	
Christie, Al E.	289	118
Christman, Pat	210	
Claire, Gertrude	261	
Clapham, Leonard T.	210	
Clark, Frank	210	
Clark, Harvey	210	
Clark, Marguerite	262	
Clark, Violet	318	
Clark, Wm. J.	341	
Clarke, Betty Ross	262	30
Clarke, Frederic Colburn	231	
Clary, Charles	221	457
Clawson, Dal	331	174
Clawson, Elliott J.	318	
Clay, Velma Louise	262	
Clayton, Ethel	262	14
Clayton, Marguerite	262	
Clemens, James H.	296	467
Clement, Eloise May	262	
Clements, Roy	296	
Cliffe, Henry Cooper	221	
Clifford, Kathleen	262	71
Clifford, Ruth	262	
Clifford, William	221	
Clift, Denison	318	161
Clifton, Elmer	296	
Cline, Edward Francis	296	72
Coates, Franklin B.	318	
Cobb, Edmund	221	
Cody, Albert R.	221	460
Cody, Lewis J.	221	
Cogley, Nick	221	
Cohen, Bennett Ray	318	474
Cohill, Wm. Wright	221	
Cohn, Jack	342	
Cohn, Martin G.		478
Coldeway, Anthony Weller	318	
Coleman, Frank	221	
Coleman, Vincent	221	460
Coleson, Robert	221	
Collins, Clifford B.	296	
Collins, May	262	
Colwell, Goldie	262	
Compson, Betty	262	
Concord, Lillian	262	
Condon, Mabel, Exchange		434
Conklin, Charles J.	221	
Conklin, Chester Cooper	221	
Conklin, Frank Roland	319	
Conklin, William	221	
Conley, Effie	221	
Conley, John J.	319	
Connelly, Edward J.	221	
Connelly, Robert Joseph	286	
Conness, Robert	221	
Connolly, Jack	221	
Considine, Mildred	319	464
Conway, Jack	296	417
Cook, Clyde	331	
Cook, Warren	221	
Cooley, Hallum	222	
Coolidge, Karl R.	319	475
Cooling, Maud	262	458
Coombs, Guy	222	
Cooper, Claude Hamilton	222	
Cooper, Edna Mae	262	448
Cooper, George	222	
Cooper, Hewitt		377
Cooper, Jack	222	405
Cooper, J. Gordon	297	152
Cooper, Miriam	262	
Cooper, William S.	331	
Corbett, James J.	222	
Corbin, Virginia Lee	286	
Corey, Eugene	222	
Cornelius, H. G.	341	
Cornwall, Anne	262	
Cortes, Armand F.	222	416
Cosmopolitan Productions		22
Cossar, John Hay	222	
Costello, Maurice	222	
Cotton, Lucy	262	24
Coudert, George C.	331	
Courtney, Wm. Basil	319	
Courtot, Marguerite	262	
Cowan, Sada	319	
Cowell, George	222	
Cox, George L.	297	
Coxen, Edward	222	420
Craft, Wm. James	331	
Craig, Blanche	262	
Craig, Charles	222	
Crane, Frank H.	297	
Crane, James L.	222	
Crane, Ogden	222	
Crane, Ward	222	457
Crimans, W. W.	222	
Crimmins, Daniel	222	
Crisp, Donald	297	
Crittenden, Dwight	223	448
Crolly, William S.	331	
Cronjager, Henry	331	
Cronk, Olga	263	
Crosland, Frederic Alan	297	
Crowell, Josephine	263	
Crumpton, Charles	286	451
Crusader Service		307
Crute, Sally	263	
Cruze, James	297	
Cullington, Margaret	263	
Cullison, Webster	297	389
Cumming, Dorothy	263	
Cummings, Irving	223	
Cummings, Robert	223	
Cuneo, Lester	223	
Cunningham, Jack	319	476
Curley, Pauline	263	378
Curran, Thomas A.	223	
Currier, Frank	223	
Curtis, Jack	223	450
Cuthbert, C. E.	297	485

D

Name	Biography	Portrait
D'Albrook, Sidney	223	
Dalton, Dorothy	263	
Daly, Arnold	223	
Daly, Hazel	223	
Daly, Wm. Robert	297	
Dana, Margaret	263	
Dana, Viola	263	80
Daniels, Bebe	263	
Daniels, Frank	223	
Darclay, Louis	223	
Darling, Grace	263	
Darling, Helen	263	
Darling, Ida	263	
Darmond, Grace	263	
Davenport, Alice	263	
Davenport, Blanche	263	
Davenport, Charles E.	297	
David, Charles N.	297	
Davidson, John	223	
Davidson, Max	223	
Davidson, Wm. Beatman	223	
Davies, Howard	223	
Davies, Marion	263	23
Davis, Charles John	331	
Davis, Edwards	223	461
Davis, J. Gunnis	223	
Davis, Mildred	263	
Davis, William S.	297	
Davison, Grace	263	35
Daw, Marjorie	264	196
Dawley, J. Searle	297	
Dawn, Hazel	264	
Dawn, Norman	297	466
Dawson, Ivo	224	404
Dazey, Charles Turner	319	
Dean, Faxon M.	331	
Dean, Jack	224	
Dean, Julia	264	
Dean, Louis	224	

ALPHABETICAL INDEX

Name	Biography	Portrait
Dean, Priscilla	264	
Dean, Ralph	297	
Dean, Ted	286	
Deane, Hazel	264	
Dearholt, Ashton	324	
Dearing, Ann	264	
DeCarlton, George	297	
DeConde, Syn M.	324	
De Cordoba, Mercedes	264	
De Cordoba, Pedro	324	
de Cordova, Leander	324	
De Cordova, Rudolph	319	
De Forest, Patsey	261	409
De Grasse, Joseph	297	
De Grasse, Samuel A.	324	
De Haven, Carter	324	
De Haven, Flora Parker	264	
Deitrich, Theodore C.	342	
De Lacy, John V.	324	
De Lacy, May	264	
de La Mothe, Leon	297	389
de la Motte, Marguerite	264	
Delaney, Bert	324	
Delaney, Leo	324	
Delaro, Hattie	264	
Delavan, Frederick M., Jr.	331	
Del Ruth, Hampton	298	137
Del Ruth, Roy		436
De Mille, Cecil B	289	
De Mille, Wm. Churchill	298	
Dempster, Carol	264	
Dench, Ernest Alfred	319	
Dent, Vernon	324	
Depew, Ernest	331	
Depp, Harry	324	
De Remer, Rubye	264	385
De Rue, Carmen	286	
Deshon, Florence	264	455
Desmond, William	324	
De Vaull, Wm. P.	324	
Devere, Harry T.	324	
De Vinna, Clyde	331	
De Vore, Dorothy	264	
Dexter, Elliott	324	
Dillon, John Webb	324	
Dillon, Edward	298	
Dillon, Jack	298	
Dintenfass, Mark M.	342	
Dix, Beulah Marie	319	
Dominguez, Beatrice	264	
Donaldson, Arthur	324	
Donnelly, James A.	324	
Donovan, Frank P.	298	
Dooley, John	325	
Dorety, Charles	325	
Dorian, Charles W.	325	
Doro, Marie	264	
Dowlan, William C.	298	423
Dowling, J. Joseph	325	
Dressler, Marie	264	
Drew, Cora	264	
Drew, Mrs. Sidney	265	
Druce, Hubert	225	
Drumier, Jack	225	
Dryden, Wheeler	225	153
Dubray, J. A.	332	
Dubray, Clare	265	
Ducrow, Tote G.	225	
Dudley, Charles	225	
Duffy, Jack	225	
Duhem, Raymond A.	332	
Dumont, Gordon	225	
Dunbar, Helen	265	
Dunbar, Robert N.	225	
Duncan, Albert Edward	225	
Duncan, William	225	52
Dunham, Maudie	265	
Dunkinson, Harry Leopold	225	
Dunlap, Scott	298	
Dunmyre, Louis H.	332	
Dunn, Bobby	226	
Dunn, Edward Frank	226	
Dunn, J. Malcolm	226	
Dunn, William R.	226	
Dunn, Winifred	319	429
Dupre, Louise	265	
Dupee, George	226	
Duprez, Charles J.	332	
Durant, Harry R.	319	
Durfee, Minta	265	
Durham, Lewis	226	
Durning, Bernard J.	226	
Dwan, Alan	290	
Dwyer, Ruth	265	86

E

Name	Biography	Portrait
Eagle, Oscar	298	
Eagler, Paul	332	
Earle, Edward	226	
Earle, William P. S.	298	
Eason, Reeves	298	479
Eckerline, John	298	
Eddy, Helen Jerome	265	460
Edeson, Arthur	332	
Edeson, Robert	226	
Edgington, Ida	265	
Edmond, William M.	332	
Edwards, Charles	226	
Edwards, Harry	298	
Edwards, J. Gordon	298	
Edwards, Walter	298	109
Eldridge, Charles	226	459
Elkas, Edward	226	
Elliott, Frank	226	
Elliott, Robert	226	446
Ellis, Robert du Reel	298	220
Elmer, William	226	
Eltinge, Julian	226	
Elvidge, June	265	94
Emerson, John	290	127
Empey, Arthur Guy	290	291
Entwistle, Harold	226	
Esmonde, Merceita	265	
Estabrook, Howard	298	
Evans, Herbert D.	226	
Evans, Madge	287	
Everetts, Allen	332	
Eyton, Bessie	265	

F

Name	Biography	Portrait
Fair, Elinor	265	
Fairbanks, Douglas	227	
Fairbanks, Gladys	265	
Fairfax, Marion	319	474
Fallon, Thomas F.	319	164
Famous Players-Lasky	3, 4, 5, 6, 7, 8, 9, 10	
Farley, Dorothea	265	463
Farley, James	227	384
Farley, Mary Louise	319	
Farnum, Dustin	227	
Farnum, Franklyn	227	
Farnum, William	227	
Farrar, Geraldine	265	
Farrington, Adele	265	
Faulkner, Ralph C.	227	
Faversham, William	227	
Fawcett, George	227	410
Fay, Hugh	227	
Fazenda, Louise	265	
Fellowes, Rockcliffe Rockcliffe	227	
Fenton, Mark	227	
Ferguson, Casson	227	
Ferguson, Elsie Louise	266	13
Ferguson, Helen	266	387
Fetty, Charles C.	332	
Field, Eliner	266	
Field, George	227	
Fielding, Margaret	266	
Fielding, Romaine	298	154
Fillmore, Clyde	227	
Finch, Flora	266	
First National		198
Fischer, A. H.	342	
Fischer, David G	298	
Fishback, Fred	299	436
Fisher, George	227	
Fisher, Margarita	266	
Fisher, Ross G.	332	
Fitch, George	299	
Fitz-Gerald, Cissy	266	
Fitz Gerald, Dallas M.	299	467
Fitzmaurice, George	299	
FitzPatrick, James A.	299	124
Fitzroy, Louis	227	
Flanagan, D. J.	227	
Flaven, Arthur J.	299	466
Fleming, Carroll	299	
Fleming, Caryl Stacy	299	
Fleming, Ethel	266	
Fleming, Victor L.	332	120
Flinn, John	348	
Flynn, Emmett J.	299	423
Foote, Courtenay	228	
Ford, Francis	290	158
Ford, Harrison	228	

	Biography	Portrait
Ford, Hugh	299	
Ford, Jack	299	
Forde, Eugenie	266	
Forman, Tom	228	
Formes, Carl, Jr	228	
Forrest, Alan	228	
Forrest, Ann	266	442
Forrest, Edith	266	
Forth, George J.	228	
Foshay, Harold	228	
Foss, Darrell Burton	228	
Foster, J. Morris	228	445
Foster, William C.	332	411
Fox, Finis	319	163
Fox, Stephen		427
Fox, William	342	
Foxe, Earle A.	228	
Frame, Park	299	
Francis, Alec Budd	228	
Franck, John L.	228	
Frank J. Herbert	228	393
Franklin, C. M.	299	
Franklin, Harry L.	299	
Franklin, S. A.	299	
Franz, Joseph J	299	
Fraunholz, Fraunie	228	
Frawley, Jack	332	
Frazee, Edwin	343	
Frederick, Pauline	266	202
French, Charles K.	228	384
French, Eugene De Tousard	332	
French, George B.	228	
Fried, A.	332	483
Frohman Amusement Corp		188
Frommer, Henry G.	332	
Fuqua, John W.	332	
Furey, James A.	228	
Furthman, Jules	320	

G

	Biography	Portrait
Gaden, Alexander	228	
Gaillard, Robert	228	
Gale, Alice	266	
Gale, Lillian		484
Gallagher, Raymond	229	
Gamble, Warburton	229	461
Gandolfi, Alfredo	332	
Gane, Vivian	266	78
Garmes, Lee	332	
Garson, Harry I.	290	
Gary, Nadia Louise	387	
Gasnier, Louis	290	
Gates, Harvey H.	320	474
Gaudio, Eugene	332	430
Gaudio, Gaetano	332	430
Gauntier, Gene	266	
Gaye, Howard	299	
Geldert, Clarence H.	229	
Geleng, Louis A. J.	332	
George, Burton	299	
George, Maud	266	
Geraghty, Tom J.	320	166
Gerald, Pete	229	
Gerard, Charles	229	
Gerber, Neva	266	388
Gerrard, Douglas	299	409
Gibbs, Robert Paton	229	
Giblyn, Charles	299	
Gibson, Ed ("Hoot")	229	390
Gibson, Helen	266	
Gibson, Tom	320	470
Gibson, Victor	320	476
Gilbert, John C.	229	395
Giles, Corliss	229	
Gill, Helen	267	440
Gillett, Ethel	320	
Gillstrom, Arvid E.	300	
Gilson, Charles	332	
Girard, Joseph W.	229	460
Gish, Dorothy	267	
Gish, Lillian	267	
Gittens, Wyndham	300	
Glass, Gaston	229	
Glassmire, Albert	320	
Glaum, Louise	267	
Glendon, J. Frank	229	
Glennon, Bert Lawrence	332	480
Golden, Ruth Fuller	267	
Gobbett, David Wm.	333	
Goldaine, M. S.	300	
Goldburg, Jesse James	343	
Golden, James A.	343	
Golden, Ruth Fuller	267	
Goldsmith, Frank	229	

	Biography	Portrait
Goldsworthy, John	229	
Goldwyn Pictures Corp.	43, 44, 45, 46, 47, 48	
Goldwyn, Samuel	343	
Gollomb, Joseph	320	
Goodfriend, Pliny	333	
Goodwins, Fred	229	
Gordon, Eva	267	
Gordon, Harris	229	
Gordon, Huntley	229	397
Gordon, James	229	
Gordon, Julia Swayne	267	
Gordon, Maude Turner	267	
Gordon, Robert	230	65
Gordon, Vera	267	
Gosden, Alfred	333	480
Goulding, Alf	300	
Goulding, Edmund	320	168
Gowland, Gibson	230	464
Granby, Joseph	230	452
Grandon, Francis J	300	
Grant, Edwin J.	230	
Granville, Fred Le Roy	300	416
Grassby, Bertram	230	
Grattan, Stephen	230	
Grauer, Ben	287	
Graves, Ralph	230	
Gray, Clifford	230	
Gray, King D.	333	480
Greeley, Evelyn	267	11
Green, Al	300	
Green, Dorothy	267	
Green, Helen	267	
Green, Margaret	267	
Greene, Kempton	230	
Greenleaf, Chas. L.	230	
Greenwood, Winifred	267	
Gregory, Carl Louis	333	
Greiner, Arthur Leroy	333	
Grey, John W.	343	
Grey, Olga	267	
Gribbon, Harry	230	
Griffin, Frank C.	300	
Griffith, Cecelia Frances	267	
Griffith, Corinne	267	
Griffith, David Wark	299, 343	102
Griffith, Edward H.	300	420
Griffith, Katherine	267	
Griffith, Raymond	320	
Grimmer, Frank	300	
Grimwood, Herbert	230	461
Grinde, Nick	300	472
Grisel, Louis R.	230	
Grossman, Harry	344	
Grossmith, Lawrence	230	
Guihan, Frances	320	171
Guinan, "Texas"	267	
Guise, Thomas Sheldon	230	
Guissart, Rene	333	481
Gullan, Campbell		60
Gutterres, Moyses	300	485

H

	Biography	Portrait
Hackathorn George H.	230	449
Hackett, Albert	230	
Haddock, William F.	300	
Hadley, Grace T.	320	
Hadley, Hopp	344	
Haines, Robert Terrell	230	
Hale, Alan	231	
Hale, Albert W.	300	
Hale, Creighton	231	
Hall, Al	231	
Hall, Ben	231	
Hall, Donald	231	
Hall, Ella	267	
Hall, Emmett Campbell	320	
Hall, Frank G.	344	
Hall, George Edwards	300	
Hall, Howard	231	
Hall, Lillian	267	411
Hall, Thurston	231	
Hall, Walter Richard	320	167
Hall, Winter	231	444
Hallam, Henry	231	
Hallard, C. M.	231	61
Halliday, John		439
Hallor, Edith	268	
Ham, Harry	231	
Hamer, Fred	231	456
Hamilton, Gilbert P.	300	141
Hamilton, Hale	231	
Hamilton, Lloyd Vernon	300	97
Hamilton, Mahlon	231	41

ALPHABETICAL INDEX

Name	Biography	Portrait
Hammerstein, Elaine	268	
Hammond, Virginia	268	
Hampton, Hope	268	74
Hampton, Jesse D.	290	119
Handy, Jamison	341	
Hanlon, Alma	268	
Hanna, Franklyn	231	
Hansen, Juanita	268	
Hanshaw, Dale	300	
Harde, Harry D.	333	
Hardin, Neil Cameron	231	
Hare, Francis Lumsden	231	440
Harkness, Carter B.	232	
Harlam, Macey	232	
Harlan, Kenneth	232	
Harlan, Otis	232	
Harmer, Frances	320	
Harmon, "Pat"	232	
Harris, Marcia	268	
Harris, Mildred	268	18
Harris, Winifred	268	
Harrison, Chas. Yale	348	
Harrison, James	232	457
Harrison, Saul E.	302	
Harron, Robert	232	
Hart, Albert	232	
Hart, Lallah Rookh	268	
Hart, Neal	232	68
Hart, William S.	232	
Hartford, David M.	302	417
Hartigan, P. C.	302	
Hartman, Greta	268	
Harvey, John	302	
Harvey, Lew	232	
Hastings, Carey	268	
Hatch, Wm. Riley	232	393
Hatkin, Philip	333	
Hatteras, Richard	232	
Hatton, Edward	232	
Hatton, Raymond	232	
Haver, Phillis	268	
Havez, Jean	320	
Hawks, J. G.	268	
Hawley, Ormi	268	
Hawley, Wanda	268	442
Hayakawa, Sessue	232	
Haydon, J Charles	302	
Hayes, Frank	232	
Hays, Wm. T.	232	
Hearn, Edward	232	
Hearn, Fred G.	302	
Hebert, Henry J.	233	
Heerman, Victor	302	
Heffron, T. N.	302	
Hellman Bank		486
Heming, Violet	268	
Henabery, Joseph	302	
Henderson, Dell	302	
Henley, Hobart	290	138
Henry, Gale	268	
Henry, George	233	
Herbert, A. J.	233	
Herbert, Holmes Edward	233	
Hernandez, George F.	233	446
Hernandez, Mrs. George	268	
Herring, Aggie	268	
Hersholt, Jean R.	233	469
Hesser, Edwin Bower	302	
Heyes, Herbert H.	233	
Heywood, W. L.	302	
Hickman, Alfred	233	
Hickman, Howard	302	
Hicks, Henry C.	233	450
Hicks, Maxine Elliot	269	
Hiers, Walter	233	390
Higby, Wilbur	233	
Hilburn, Betty	269	
Hilburn, Percy	333	425
Hill, Josephine	269	388
Hill, Maud	269	40
Hill, Robert F.	302	189
Hill, Rollo Lee	233	
Hill, Wycliff A.	320	
Hilliard, Harry S.	233	
Hillyer, Lambert	302	159
Hines, John	233	
Hively, George O.	320	
Hoadley, C. B.	321	
Hoadley, Harold Wm.	321	
Hodes, Hal	321	
Hodge, Rex E.	302	485
Hodkinson, W. W.	344	
Hoffman, Charles Wilbur	333	
Hoffman, Otto F.	233	
Hoffman, Ruby	269	
Hogan, Danny	302	
Holbrook, John Knight	302	
Holden, John K.	303	
Holding, Thomas	233	
Holland, Cecil C.	234	
Holland, Edna M.	269	
Hollingsworth, Alfred	234	
Hollister, Alice	269	
Hollister, George K.	333	
Holloway, Carol	269	465
Hollywood, Edwin L.	303	415
Holmes, Helen	269	
Holmes, Stuart	234	87
Holmes, Taylor	234	
Holt, George	303	
Holt, Jack	234	
Holubar, Allen J.	303	
Hoose, Ralph R.	234	
Hoover, Billy		397
Hope, Gloria	269	
Hopkins, May F.	269	
Hopley, Frank Dorrance	321	
Hopper, Mrs. De Wolf	269	
Hopper, E. Mason	303	143
Horan, Charles	303	
Horn, Edward	333	
Horne, James W.	303	
Horne, Pliny A.	333	
Horne, Wm. T.	234	
Horner, Bob	321	
Horsley Film Laboratories		406
Horton, Aida	287	
Horton, Clara Marie	269	392
Horton, Jeanette	269	
Hotelling, Louise	269	
Houdini, Harry	234	
Houry, Henry	303	
Housman, Arthur	234	
Howard, Chas. Ray	234	
Howard, George	234	406
Howard, George Bronson	321	
Howe, Eliot	303	425
Howell, Alice	269	
Howell, W. A.	303	
Howland, Jobyna	269	
Hoxie, Hart	234	
Hoxie, Jack	234	
Hoyt, Arthur	234	
Hoyt, Edward N.	234	
Hoyt, Harry O.	303	160
Hubbard, Philip	321	449
Huff, Louise	269	32
Hughes, Gareth	234	
Hughes, Lloyd	234	
Hulette, Gladys	269	392
Human, Billy	234	
Humphrey, William J	303	469
Hunt, Jay	303	
Hunt, J. Roy	303	471
Hunt, Leslie M.	234	
Hunter, T. Hayes	303	132
Huntley, Hugh	234	439
Huntly, Fred W.	235	453
Hurley, Julia	270	
Hurst, Paul C.	303	
Husted, Chas. Clemens	303	
Hutchinson, Charles A.	235	
Hutchinson, Craig	303	467
Hutchinson, Samuel S.	344	
Hutton, Lucille	270	
Hyland, Peggy	270	59

I

Name	Biography	Portrait
Illian, Isolde C.	270	
Ince, John	303	
Ince, Ralph	303	
Ince, Thomas H.	290	8, 9
Inglis, Gus	290	178
Ingraham, Harrish	304	
Ingraham, Lloyd	304	
Ingram, Rex	304	115
Irish, Roy	333	
Irving, George	304	470
Irving, Mary Jane	287	
Irwin, Boyd	235	

J

Name	Biography	Portrait
Jaccard, Jacques	304	473
Jackman, Fred J.	333	
Jamelson, Wm. Edward	235	
James, Frederick Henry	321	471
James, Gladden	235	440, 448
James, Harry C.	304	
James, James Wharton	235	
Janis, Elsie	270	

STUDIO DIRECTORY

	Biography	Portrait
Jansen, Laura	321	475
Jasmine, Arthur	235	
Jefferson, L. V.	321	477
Jefferson, Thomas	235	
Jeffrey, Hugh S.	235	
Jenks, George Elwood	321	288
Jennings, Al	235	78
Jennings, Dev	333	
Jennings, Jane	270	83
Jensen, Eulalie	270	
Jevne, Jack	321	
Jobson, Edward	235	
Joby, Hans	235	
Johnson, Adrian R.	321	
Johnson, Edith	270	53
Johnson, Emory	235	
Johnson, Hugo C.	333	
Johnson, Merle	321	220
Johnson, Noble	235	
Johnson, Tefft	304	
Johnston, Agnes Christine	321	475
Johnston, J. W.	235	
Jones, Buck	235	382
Jones, Jessie	270	
Jones, Grover	304	
Jones, Richard	304	
Jordan, Sid	235	
Jose, Edward	290	135
Josephson, Julian	321	
Joy, Ernest C.	235	
Joy, Gloria	287	
Joy, Leatrice	270	
Joyce, Alice	270	
Joyner, Francis	235	
Julian, Rupert	304	
Junior, John		440
Justice, Maibelle Heikes	321	

K

	Biography	Portrait
Kane, Gail	270	
Kann, Marvin	236	
Karger, Maxwell	345	
Karns, Roscoe	236	465
Karr, Hillard Sinclair	236	
Katterjohn, Monte M.	322	
Kavanaugh, Katherine	322	
Kay, Beatrice	287	
Kaye, Frances Manila	270	
Keaton, "Buster"	236	
Keefe, Zena Virginia	270	
Keeling, Robert Lee	236	
Keenan, Frank	236	
Keepers, Harry Lester	333	
Kellard, Ralph	236	
Kellermann, Annette	270	
Kellette, John Wm.	304	
Kelley, Winthrop	304	
Kelly, Anthony Paul	322	
Kelly, Paul	236	
Kelsey, Fred A.	304	
Kelso, Mayme	270	
Kelson, George	304	
Kennedy, Aubrey M.	304	
Kennedy, Ed	236	
Kennedy, Jack	304	
Kennedy, Madge	270	
Kenny, Colin	236	435
Kent, Charles	236	
Kent, Cranfurd	236	77
Kenyon, Albert G.	322	
Kenyon, Charles A.	322	422
Kenyon, Doris	271	
Kepler, Edward	236	
Kern, Cecil	271	
Kerrigan, Jack Warren	236	70
Kerry, Norman	236	399
Kessel, Nicholas, Laboratories		534
Kilgour, Joseph	236	
Kim, Sam	236	
Kimball, Edward Marshall	236	
King, Burton	304	415
King, Carleton S.	305	
King, Emmett C.	237	
King, Henry	305	
King, Mollie	271	
Kingdon, Dorothy	271	
Kingsley, Florida	271	
Kingston, Winifred	271	
Kirby, Frank Gordon	333	
Kirkby, Ollie	271	
Kirkham, Kathleen	271	379
Kirkland, David	305	
Kirkland, Hardee	237	
Kirkwood, James	237	
Kitson, May	271	451

	Biography	Portrait
Klein, Robert	237	
Kleine, George	346	
Knoles, Harley	305	
Knott, Lydia	271	
Knowland, Alice	271	
Kohn, Morris	346	
Kolker, Henry	237	456
Korach, Milton W.	305	
Kortman, Robert	237	462
Koupal, T. Morse	237	
Krafft, John W.	322	
Kremer, Victor	344	

L

	Biography	Portrait
La Croix, Emile	237	
Laemmle, Carl	345	
La Fayette, Ruby	271	
Laidlaw, Roy	237	
Lake, Alice	271	
Lambart, Henry	305	
Lambert, Dorothy	271	
Lambert, Glen	305	
Lamothe, Julian Louis	322	
Lancaster, Leland L.	334	481
Landis, Cullen	237	
Landis, Margaret Cullen	271	
Lane, Charles	237	
Lane, Tamar	305	
Langdon, Lillian	271	
Lanning, Frank	237	
Lanoe, J. Jiquel	237	382
La Reno, Dick	237	
Larkin, George Alan	237	
La Rocque, Rodney	237	
Larrimer, Mary Edna	322	
Larrimore, Francine	271	
Larson, Oscar M.	237	
La Rue, Fontaine	271	435
Lathem, Alfred H.	334	482
Laub, William B.	322	
Laurel, Kay	271	
La Varnie, Laura	271	
Laver, Jack	305	
Law, Burton	237	
Law, Walter	237	
Lawrence, Adelaide	287	
Lawrence, Dakota	272	
Lawrence, Edmund	305	419
Lawrence, Frank	322	327
Lawrence, George W.	334	
Lawrence, W. E.	237	
Leach, Henry A.	334	
Leavers, George R. B.	305	
Leavitt, Harvey C.	305	
Lederer, Gretchen	272	
Lederer, Otto	238	
Lee, Alberta	272	
Lee, Carey	272	
Lee, Carolyn	272	
Lee, Dixie	272	
Lee, Frankie	287	
Lee, Harry	238	
Lee, Jane	287	
Lee, Jennie	272	
Lee, Katherine	287	
Lee, Lila	272	
Lee, Virginia	272	398
Le Guere, George	238	
Lehr, Anna	272	
Lehrman, Henry	290	
Leiber, Fritz	238	
Leighton, Lillian	272	
Leibrand, Lela Owens	322	
Lengel, Wm. C.	322	479
Leonard, Robert Z.	305	112
Le Picard, Marcel A.	334	
Le Saint, Edward J.	305	
Le Saint, Stella Razetto	305	
Leslie, Gladys	272	
Leslie, Lilie	272	
Leslie, Marguerite	272	
Lesser, Sol	345	187
Lessey, George A.	305	
Lester, Kate	272	
Lester, Louise	272	
Le Strange, Dick	305	
Leventhal, J. F.	341	
Levering, James	238	
Levering, Joseph	305	
Le Vino, Albert Shelby	322	472
Lewis, Atwood Lloyd	334	
Lewis, B. A.	238	
Lewis, Charles	305	
Lewis, Edgar	292	

ALPHABETICAL INDEX

Name	Biography	Portrait
Lewis, Eugene B.	322	479
Lewis, Eva	272	
Lewis, Ida	272	
Lewis, Katherine	272	
Lewis, Mitchell	238	
Lewis, Ralph	238	
Lewis, Sheldon	238	
Lewis, Vera	272	
Lewis, Walter P.	238	
Lichtig, Harry		432
Liguori, Alfonso	334	
Lincoln, E. K.	238	49
Lincoln, Elmo	238	
Linden, Edwin G.	334	
Linden, Margaret	273	387
Linder, Max	238	69
Lindroth, Helen	273	
Lingham, Thomas Glessing	238	
Lissack, William	334	
Litson, M. N.	305	
Little, Anne	273	
Littlefield, Lucien L.	238	
Livingston, Jack	238	437
Livingston, John J.		180
Livingston, Marguerite	273	
Lloyd, Frank	308	110
Lloyd, Harold C.	238	193
Lloyd, Harold Warner	308	
Locke, Ashley T.	322	
Lockney, J. P.	238	
Logue, Charles A.	342	
Lonergan, Lloyd	322	
Lonergan, Philip	322	
Long, Walter	238	
Lonsdale, Harry G.	239	
Loos, Anita	322	127
Lord, Delmer	308	
Loring, Hope	323	476
Lorraine, Leota	273	
Lorraine, Lillian	273	
Los Angeles Exchange		183
Losee, Frank	239	380
Louis, Will	308	
Louis, Willard	239	
Love, Bessie	273	
Love, Montagu	239	
Lovely, Louise	273	
Lovett, Shaw	308	
Lowe, Edmund		88
Lowe, Edward T., Jr.	322	
Lowell, John	239	
Lowry, Ira M.	308	
Lucas, Wilfred	239	
Lucy, Arnold	239	
Luddy, Irving Edward	308	485
Lund, Oscar A. C.	308	
Luther, Anne	273	
Lynard, Lenore	273	399
Lynch, John	323	215
Lynne, Ethel	273	
Lyon, Ben	239	
Lyons, Chester	334	
Lyons, Eddie	239	73
Lyons, Reginald Edgar	334	
Lytell, Bert	239	80
Lytell, Wilfred	239	396
Lytton, Roger	239	28

M

Name	Biography	Portrait
Mac Clean, Grace	273	
Mac Dermott, Marc	239	386
Mac Donald, Donald	239	
Mac Donald, J. Farrel	308	
Mac Donald, Katherine Agnew	273	15
Mac Donald, Sherwood	308	126
Mac Donald, Wallace	239	452
Mac Dowell, Melbourne	239	
Mac Gregor, Norval	308	
Mack, Hayward	239	
Mack, Joseph P.	239	
Mackay, Charles	240	
Mackay, Edward	240	
Mackenzie, Donald	308	
Mac Laren, Mary	273	380
Mac Lean, Douglas	240	
Mac Lean, R. D.	240	
Mac Manus, Edward A.	345	
Mac Pherson, Jeanie	323	
MacQuarrie, Frank	240	
MacQuarrie, Murdock	308	
MacWilliams, Glen	334	
Madden, Golda	273	
Madison, Cleo	273	
Maedler, Richard W.	334	
Maigne, Charles	308	
Mailes, Charles Hill	240	
Malatesta, Fred	240	453
Malone, Molly	273	
Maloney, Leo D.	240	
Mann, Alice	273	
Mann, Frankie	274	
Mann, Hank	240	90
Manning, Marjorie	274	
Manning, Mildred	274	
Manon, Marcia	274	
Mansfield, Martha	274	
Marburgh, Bertram	240	
Marcel, Inez	274	
Marcus, James A.	240	
Marinoff, Fania	274	
Marion, Frances	323	
Markey, Enid	274	
Marks, Willis	240	
Marmont, Percy	240	443
Marquis, Joseph Phillip	240	
Marr, Gordon	240	
Marsh, Mae	274	
Marsh, Marguerite C.	274	
Marshall, George E.	308	
Marshall, Roy Howard	308	
Marshall, Tully	240	
Marshall, William C.	334	
Marstini, Rosita	274	
Marston, Theodore M.	308	
Martin, E. A.	308	
Martin, Florence Evelyn	274	92
Martin, Vivian	274	
Mason, "Smiling" Billy	240	
Mason, Charles E.	240	
Mason, Dan	241	
Mason, Shirley	274	
Mason, Sidney L.	241	454
Mathis, June	323	424
Mattox, Martha	274	451
Maxwell, Ann	323	
May, Ann	274	21
May, Doris	274	
Mayall, Hershall	241	437
Mayflower Photoplay Corp.		195
Mayo, Christine	274	
Mayo, Edna	274	
Mayo, Frank	241	
McAvoy, May	274	391
McCall, Billy	241	
McCarthy, J. P.	334	
McCarthy, Myles	241	
McClain, A.	334	
McCloskey, Justin H.	308	
McCloskey, Lawrence	323	
McClung, Hugh C.	334	482
McConnell, Guy W.	323	
McConnell, Mollie	275	
McCoy, Gertrude	275	
McCoy, Harry H.	241	
McCoy, William H.	334	
McCrory, John Robert	323	
McCullough, Philo	241	
McDaniel, George A.	241	
McDonald, Francis J.	241	103
McDowell, Claire	275	
McDowell, Nelson	241	462
McElroy, Bernard		484
McEwen, Walter	241	
McGann, William M.	334	431
McGarry, Garry	241	
McGill, Lawrence B.	309	
McGowan, John P.	309	
McGowan, John W.	241	
McGowan, Robert F.	323	
McGowan, Roxana	275	
McGrail, Walter	241	438
McGregor, Gordon	241	
McIntosh, Burr	241	
McKee, Raymond	241	405
McKim, Robert	241	
McLaughlin, Robert	323	
McLean, Jack	242	
McMackin, Archer	309	418
McNamara, Walter	323	
McNeil, Everett	323	
McQuade, Mabel	275	
McQuarrie, Albert	242	449
McRae, Harry Alexander	309	
Meadowbrook Nurseries, Inc.		433
Meighan, Thomas	242	
Melford, George H.	309	
Menasco, Milton	309	
Menessier, Henri	309	
Meredith, Miriam	323	
Merlo, Anthony	242	
Mersereau, Violet	275	
Mescal, John J.	334	
Messenger, Buddie	287	

STUDIO DIRECTORY

	Biography	Portrait
Mestayer, Harry	242	
Metcalfe, Earl Keeney	242	
Middleton, Edwin	309	468
Midgley, Fannie	275	
Migel Silk		12
Milash, Robert E.	242	
Milholland, Helen	275	465
Millarde, Harry	309	
Miller, Ashley	309	
Miller, Charles	292	
Miller, Harold Atchinson	242	
Miller, Harold Louis	334	
Miller, Walter	242	99
Millett, Arthur Nelson	242	435
Millhauser, Bertram	323	
Milligan, K. Hoddy	345	
Mills, Frank	242	
Mills, Thomas R.	309	
Milner, Victor	334	486
Milton, Margery	275	
Mineau, Charlotte	275	
Minnerly, Nelson Harvey	334	
Minor, C. Sharpe		483
Minter, Mary Miles	275	
Mitchell, Claude H.	309	413
Mitchell, Howard M.	309	136
Mitchell, Pell	334	
Mitchell, Rhea	275	447
Mitchell, Yvette	275	
Mix, Tom	242	
Molloy, Thomas F.	334	
Monahan, Janethel	287	
Monahan, Joseph	287	
Mong, William V.	242	436
Montagne, Edward Joseph	323	218
Montague, Frederick	242	
Montgomery, Earl	242	54
Montrose, Helene	275	
Moody, Harry	309	
Moore, Coleen Noylan	275	
Moore, Eugene W.	309	
Moore, Matt	242	75
Moore, Owen	242	
Moore, Pat	287	
Moore, Tom	243	
Moore, Victor	243	
Moran, Lee	243	73
Moran, William F.	243	452
Moranti, Milburn M.	243	
Mordant, Edwin	243	
Moreno, Antonio	243	378
Morey, Harry T.	243	
Morgan, Frank	243	296
Morgan, Ira H.	335	
Morley, Jay	243	
Morne, Maryland	275	
Morris, Reggie	309	
Morris, S. E.	347	
Morrison, Arthur	243	444
Morrison, James Woods	243	400
Morrison, Mrs. Priestly	275	
Mortimer, Edmund	309	
Mortimer, Henry	243	379
Moses, Alfred Huger, Jr.	323	
Mosquini, Marie	275	
Moss, Stewart Belfield	335	
Motion Picture Art Directors' Ass'n		100
Motion Picture Art Directors' Ass'n		101
Motion Picture Apparatus Co.		293
Mower, Jack	243	
Moyers, Bertie Badger	324	
Mueller, Floyd	310	
Mulhall, Jack	243	
Mullen, Gordon Douglass	243	
Mullin, Eugene	324	162
Murillo, Mary	324	
Murphy, Will C.	324	
Murray, Charles	243	
Murray, Mae	275	25
Musgrave, Billy	243	
Mussette, Charles	244	
Myers, Carmel	276	
Myles, Norbert	310	
Myton, Fred	324	

N

Nagel, Conrad	244	
Nagy, Anthony	335	
Nash, Thomas S.		484
Natteford, J. F.	324	
Nazimova, Alla	276	
Neilan, Marshall	292	197
Neill, James	244	
Neill, Richard R.	244	443
Neill, R. William	310	134

	Biography	Portrait
Neitz, Alvin J.	324	
Nelson, Frederick	335	
Nelson, Jack	244	
Nelson, J. Arthur	310	
Nesbit, Evelyn	276	
New Rochelle Optical Exchange		486
Niblo, Fred	310	
Nichols, George O.	244	
Nickerson, Clark R.	335	
Nigh, William	310	
Nightingale, Virginia B.	276	50
Nilsson, Anna Q.	276	441
Noble, John W.	310	133
Norcross, Frank M.	244	
Normand, Mabel	276	
North, Wilfrid	310	145
Northrup, Harry S.	244	443
Norton, Stephen S.	335	481
Nova, Hedda	276	456
Novak, Jane	276	
Nowell, Wedgwood	244	464
Nuille, Ida	276	
Nye, G. Raymond	244	459

O

Oaker, John	244	
Oakman, Wheeler	244	
O'Brien, Eugene	244	
O'Brien, Gypsy	276	
O'Brien, Helen	276	
O'Brien, John B.	310	
O'Brien, Thomas E.	310	
O'Connor, Edward	244	
O'Connor, Harry M.	244	
O'Connor, Kathleen	276	453
O'Connor, Louis J.	244	
O'Connor, Loyola	276	394
O'Connor, Mary H.	324	394
O'Dare, Peggy	276	381
Ogle, Charles	244	
Oland, Warner	245	
Olcott, Sidney	310	
Oliver, Guy	245	
Oliver, Harold G.	310	
Olivo, Valerio	245	
Olmsted, E. Stanley	324	
O'Madigan, Isabel	276	
O'Malley, Patrick H.	245	462
O'Neill, Jack	310	
O'Neill, James	245	
O'Reilly, J. Francis	245	
Ormonde, Eugene	245	
Ormston, Frank D.	310	410
Orth, Louise	276	
Orth, George	310	
Ortlieh, Alfred	335	
Osborne, Helen Marie	287	
Osmun, Leighton-Graves	324	
Ostriche, Muriel	276	
Otto, Henry	310	
Overton, Evart Emerson	245	
Ovey, George	245	461
Owen, Seena	276	

P

Paget, Alfred	245	
Paget, Francis	324	
Paige, Jean	276	
Paisley, G. Charles	245	
Pallette, Eugene	245	
Palmer, Frederick	324	
Palmer, Patricia	277	444
Palmer Photoplay Corp.		{176, 177}
Palmer, Violet	277	
Pape, Edward Lionel	245	
Park, Ida May	324	
Parke, William	310	
Parke, William, Jr.	245	
Parker, Albert	310	
Parker, Max	310	
Parker, William	324	122
Parks, Frances Craven	277	
Parr, Peggy	277	
Parrott, Charles	311	412
Parsons, Agnes	324	471
Pathe Films		194
Paton, Stuart	311	
Pattee, Herbert Horton	245	
Pauncefort, George	245	
Pavis, Yvonne Marie	277	
Pawn, Doris	277	
Payne, Lila	277	

ALPHABETICAL INDEX

Name	Biography	Portrait
Payson, Blanche	277	
Payton, Gloria	277	
Pearce, George C.	245	
Pearce, Peggy	277	459
Pearson, Virginia	277	
Peck, Raymond S.	311	
Pegg, Vester	245	
Peil, Edward	246	452
Penill, Richard	246	
Percy, Eileen	277	
Percyval, T. Wigney	246	
Pereda, Christina	277	
Periolat, George E.	246	
Perret, Leonce	292	146
Perry, Paul	335	
Perry, Walter	246	
Perugini, Francis	335	
Peters, T. Kimmwood	311	
Peterson, Gus	335	
Petrova, Olga	277	
Pettie, Graham	246	
Pettijohn, C. C.	246	
Philipp, Adolf	292	414
Phillips, Augustus	246	
Phillips, Carmen	277	
Phillips, Dorothy	277	29
Phillips, Henry Albert	324	
Phillips, R. G.	311	
Physioc, Lewis W.	335	
Physioc, Wray	311	
Pickford, Jack	246	
Pickford, Lottie	277	
Pickford, Mary	277	
Pierce, Ben	246	
Pierson, Leo	246	444
Pigott, William	324	
Pike, William	246	
Pitts, Za Su	277	
Playter, Wellington	246	
Plumb, Walter K.	341	
Plympton, George Holcombe	325	
Poland, Joseph F.	325	
Polito, Sol	335	
Pollar, Gene	246	98
Pollard, Harry	246	
Pollard, Harry A	311	
Pollock, Gabriel	311	472
Pole, Eddie	246	394
Porter, Hector A.	335	
Potel, Victor	246	
Powell, A. Van Buren	325	
Powell, David	246	
Powell, Ernest	335	
Powell, Frank	311	
Powell, Mabel Alline	278	
Powell, Paul	311	468
Powell, Russ	246	
Power, Jule	278	
Power, Nicholas, Company		519
Powers, Len	335	
Pratt, Gilbert Walker	311	467
Pretty, Arline	278	
Prevost, Marie	278	
Price Co., C. B.	345	191
Price, Kate	278	
Priest, Robert W.	345	
Printzlau, Olga	325	475
Prior, Herbert	246	
Prizma		200
Proctor, George Dubois	325	219
Prussing, Louise	278	
Pulliam, Pauline	278	
Purves, Jack H.	246	
Purviance, Edna Olga	278	

Q

Name	Biography	Portrait
Quinn, Arthur T.	335	
Quirk, William A.	311	

R

Name	Biography	Portrait
Radin, Matthias	348	
Rae, Zoe	288	
Rambeau, Marjorie	278	
Ramsey, Alicia	325	
Ramsay, R. L.	335	
Randall, Bernard	247	96
Randolf, Anders	247	
Rankin, Caroline J.	278	
Rattenberry, Harry L.	247	
Rawlinson, Herbert	247	
Ray, Albert	247	
Ray, Charles	247	20
Raymaker, Herman C.	311	
Raymond, Dean	247	458
Raymond, Jack	335	
Raymond, Pete	247	
Rea, Thomas H.	335	
Reardon, Mark S.	325	
Reardon, Mildred	278	
Redden, Arthur L.	288	
Reed, Arthur	335	
Reed, Florence	278	
Reed, Katherine Speer	325	
Reed, Luther A.	325	
Reed, Nora	278	
Reed, Theodore	311	
Reeves, Myrtle	278	
Reeves, Bob	247	189
Regan, Thomas C	311	
Reicher, Frank	311	149
Reid, Donald Gordon	325	
Reid, James Halleck	325	
Reid, Wallace	247	
Reid, William W.	335	
Reinecke, Helen	288	
Reinhart, William A.	335	
Rene, Alex W.	247	
Reneck, Ruth	278	
Renfroe, James Lige	247	
Renfroe, Vida Estelle	278	
Revier, Harry	311	
Reynolds, B. F.	335	
Reynolds, Ernest M.	335	471
Reynolds, Lynn Fairfield	311	421
Reynolds, Stephen Allen	325	
Rhodes, Billie	278	
Ricardo, Arnold	335	
Rice, Elmer L.	325	
Rice, Fanny	278	
Rich, Charles G.	247	
Rich, H. Thompson	325	169
Rich, Irene	278	
Rich, Vivian	278	442
Richardson, Jack	247	
Richman, Charles	247	
Richmond, Warner Paul	247	
Ricketts, Thomas	311	
Rigeway, Fritzie	279	450
Ridgway, John H.	247	
Ries, Irving G.	336	
Ries, Park J.	336	482
Riesner, C. Francis	248	
Ripley, Arthur D.	325	456
Ritchey, Will M.	325	426
Ritchie, Billie	248	
Rizard, George	336	
Roach, Bert	248	
Roach, Hal.		192
Roach, Joseph Anthony		402
Roach, Lewis	347	
Robbins, Jesse X.	312	421
Robbins, Marc.	248	
Roberts, Edith	279	
Roberts, Theodore	248	81, 82
Robertson-Cole	335	
Robertson, John Stuart	312	
Robinson, Daisy	279	
Robinson, Gertrude May	279	
Robson, Andrew	248	
Robson, May	279	
Rock, Charles	248	
Rock, Joseph P	248	55
Rodney, Earl	248	
Rogers, Charles R	336	
Rogers, Will	248	
Roland, Ruth	279	
Rolands, George K.	325	469
Rolfe, B. A.	342	
Rollo, S. J.	341	
Romayne, H. Y.	346	
Rooney, Gilbert G.	248	
Roos, Charles G.	336	
Roos, Leonard H.	336	
Roscoe, Albert	248	
Rose, Jackson J.	336	430
Roseman, Edward	248	
Rosen, Philip E.	312	
Rosher, Charles G.	336	
Ross, George	248	
Ross, Milton	248	
Rossman, Earl W.	336	
Rosson, Arthur H.	312	125
Rosson, Dick	312	
Roth, Charles A.	336	
Rothacker, Watterson R.	346	
Royce, Riza	279	
Royce, Ruth	279	447
Rubens, Alma	279	
Rubinstein, Irving B.	336	
Rucker, Joseph T	336	
Ruggles, Wesley	312	

STUDIO DIRECTORY

Name	Biography	Portrait
Russell, L. Case	325	
Russell, William	248	27
Ruttenberg, Joseph	336	

S

Name	Biography	Portrait
Sack, Nathaniel	248	
Sackville, Gordon	248	
Sage, Stuart	249	
Sais, Marin	279	
Salisbury, Monroe	249	84
Sampson, Teddy	279	
Samuelson Films		58
Samuelson, George B.	292	
Sanford, Philip	249	
San Francisco Exchange		182
Santell, Al	312	466
Santschi, Thomas	249	
Sargent, George L.	312	418
Sarno, Hector V.	249	464
Saum, Clifford P.	310	
Saunders, Alice	279	
Saunders, Jackie	279	441
Savage, Aileen	279	
Sawyer, Donald	249	
Saxe, Templer	249	
Saxon, Hugh A.	249	
Seardon, Paul	312	
Schade, Betty	279	445
Schable, Robert	249	
Schaefer, Anne	279	
Schlebe, George H.	336	
Schellinger, Rial B.	336	
Schenck, Earl		454
Schertzinger, Victor L.	312	113
Schlank, Morris R.	292	91
Schneider, Max	336	
Schoenbaum, Charles Edgar	336	
Schram, Violet	279	
Schrock, Raymond L.	325	
Schroeder, Doris	326	474
Schultz, Carl H.	312	
Schulze, Jack	312	
Schumm, Harry W.	249	
Scott, Leroy	326	
Scott, Mabel Juliene	279	
Scott, William	249	
Scully, Wm. Joseph	312	
Sears, Allan	249	
Seay, Charles Morgan	312	
Sedgwick, Edward	249	478
Sedgwick, Eileen	279	189
Sedgwick, Josie	280	
Sedley, Henry	249	
Seeling, Chas. Richard	336	
Seger, Lucia Backus	280	455
Seidman, I. Sy	336	
Seigmann, George	249	
Seiter, William A.	312	403
Seitz, George B.	312	144
Seitz, John F.	336	
Selbie, Evelyn	280	
Selby, Gertrude	280	
Selby, Norman	249	
Sell, Henry G	249	454
Selwynne, Clarissa	280	
Selznick, David	347	
Selznick Pictures	211, 212, 213, 214	
Semon, Lawrence	312	
Sennett, Mack	292	7, 114
Serpico, James	326	
Seymour, Clarine	280	
Shaffer, Marie	280	
Shallenberger, W. E.	347	
Shanor, Peggy	280	
Shaw, Brinsley	250	
Shaw, Stanley	326	
Shaw, William Ray	312	
Sheer, William A.	250	
Shelderfer, Joseph	336	
Sheldon, Roy	313	
Shelton, Byron J.	336	
Shepard, Pearl	280	404
Sheridan, Frank	250	
Sherrill, Jack	250	
Sherrill, William L.	343	
Sherry, J. Barney	250	
Sherwin, Louis	326	427
Shield, Ernest W.	250	445
Shields, Wilbert	250	
Shipman, Edna	280	
Shipman, Nell	280	
Shirley, Arthur	250	
Shores, Marie		484
Short, Antrim	250	
Short, Florence	280	400
Short, Gertrude	280	
Shotwell, Marie	280	408
Shumway, Leonard C.	250	
Sidney, Scott	313	
Siebel, Bert E.	313	
Siegel, Bernard	250	
Sills, Milton	250	450
Silsby, Wilson	313	
Simone, Charles	313	
Simpson, Allan Hart	250	
Simpson, Henrietta	280	
Simpson, Russell	250	456
Sinclair, Maud	280	
Singleton, Joseph E.	250	
Sintzenich, Hal	336	
Sisson, Vera	280	
Sloane, Paul H.	326	479
Slocum, Daisy Mayer	326	
Sloman, Edward	313	
Slosser, Ralph J.	313	
Small, Edward		179
Smalley, Phillips	313	
Smallwood, Ray	313	
Smiley, Joseph W.	250	
Smiley, Robert W.	250	
Smith, Al Ira	337	
Smith, Bernice	288	
Smith, David	313	
Smith, Leonard M.	337	
Smith, Noel Mason	313	
Smith, R. Cecil	326, 216, 217	
Snow, Marguerite	280	
Snyder, Jack	313	
Somborn, Herbert K.	347	
Somerville, George J.	250	
Somerville, Roy	326	
Sonntag, Emil B.	337	
Sothern, Harry	313	
Sothern, Sam	250	
Spanuth, H A.	347	
Spaulding, Nellie Parker	281	
Spence, Ralph H.	326	
Spere, Charles	251	
Spinak, Leon	313	
Spingler, Harry	251	
Spitz, Eugene	292	148
Spottswood, James Carlisle	251	446
Sprotte, Bert	251	
Squire, Harry E.	337	
Stahl, John M.	313	130
Standing, Gordon	251	
Standing, Herbert	251	
Standing, Herbert, Jr.	251	438
Standing, Wyndham	251	39
Stanley, Edwin	251	
Stanley, Forrest	251	
Stanton, Richard	313	
Stanwood, Rita	281	
Stark, Lowell Randall	313	
Starke, Pauline	281	
Starkey, Bert	251	
Starr, Frederick	251	391
Starr, Helen	326	
Statter, Arthur F.	326	
Staulcup, M. P.	313	
Steadman, Vera	281	
Stearns, Louis	251	
Stearns, Myron Morris	326	
Steck, H. Tipton	326	
Stedman, Myrtle	281	
Steel, Vernon	251	439
Steene, E. Burton	337	
Steers, Larry	251	462
Steger, Julius	313	
Steppling, John	251	
Sterling, Ford	251	
Sternberg, Jo	326	
Stevens, Edwin	251	
Stevens, Elizabeth	281	
Stevens, Emily	281	
Stevens, George	251	
Stevens, Grace Elizabeth	281	458
Stevenson, Charles E.	251	
Stewart, Anita	281	19
Stewart, Charles Conger	326	
Stewart, Charles G.	342	
Stewart, Katherine	281	
Stewart, K. C.	313	
Stewart, Lucille Lee	281	
Stewart, Roy	252	401
Stewart, Victor A.	252	
St. Germain, A.	313	
St. John, Al	252	
Stockdale, Carl	252	
Stockton, Edith	281	

ALPHABETICAL INDEX

	Biography	Portrait
Stoll, Frederick		172
Stone, George	288	
Stone, Le Roy	326	159
Stone, Lewis S.	252	
Stonehouse, Ruth	281	402
Storey, Edith	281	
Storm, Jerome	313	111
Stowe, Leslie	252	
Stowell, William H.	252	
Strong, Eugene	252	
Strong, Jay	314	
Stuart, Julia	281	
Stuart, Kathryne	326	
Stuart, Robert A.	337	424
Stumar, Charles	337	
Stumar, John Stuart	337	
Sturgeon, Rollin S.	314	413
Sturgis, F. H.	337	431
Sullivan, C. Gardiner	326	
Sullivan, Danny	252	
Sullivan, Frank		431
Sullivan, William A.	252	
Sully, Janet Miller	281	
Sunlight Arc		373
Surtees, Catherine	281	447
Sutch, Herbert	314	
Sutherland, John	252	
Sutherland, Victor	252	
Sutton, T. Shelley	326	477
Swain, Mack	252	
Swanson, Gloria	281	
Sweet, Blanche	281	
Swickard, Charles	252	
Swickard, Joseph	252	62
Sylvanite Prods.		190
Symonds, Henry Roberts	314	

T

	Biography	Portrait
Taber, Richard	252	
Tainguy, Lucien	337	
Talmadge, Constance	281	17
Talmadge, Natalie	281	
Talmadge, Norma	282	16
Tams, Irene	282	93
Tannura, Philip	337	
Tapley, Rose Elizabeth	282	
Tate, Cullen B.	314	
Tauszky, David Anthony	314	
Taylor, Pauline	282	407
Taylor, Rex	328	
Taylor, Sam	328	473
Taylor, William Desmond	314	108
Tead, Phillips	252	
Tearle, Conway	252	31
Tell, Olive	282	63
Tellegen, Lou	252	
Tennant, Barbara	282	
Tenney, Beth	282	
Terhune, Albert Payson	328	
Terriss, Tom	314	117
Terry, Alice	282	
Terry, Ethel	282	
Terry, Ethel Grey	282	
Terwilliger, George	314	
Thayer, Otis B.	314	
Theby, Rosemary	282	
Thew, Harvey F.	328	477
Thomas, Al Franklyn	252	
Thomas, Olive Elain	282	
Thompson, Hamilton	328	
Thompson, Hugh	253	34
Thomson, Frederick A.	314	
Thornby, Robert	314	128
Thornley, William H.	337	
Thorpe, Harry	337	431
Thorpe, Wm. Harris	337	
Thurman, Mary	282	
Tilton, Edwin Booth	253	
Tincher, Fay	282	
Titheridge, Madge	282	
Titus, Lydia Yeamans	282	
Todd, Arthur Lyle	337	
Todd, Harry	253	
Todd, Robert Lee	328	
Toncray, Kate	282	
Tooker, William H.	253	
Totheroh, Roland	337	
Tourneur, Maurice	292	107
Tower, Halsey	253	
Tracy, Bert	314	
Travers, Richard C.	253	
Traverse, Madlaine	282	57
Travis, Norton C.	337	
Trenton, Pell	253	395
Trevelyn, Una	283	398

	Biography	Portrait
Trevor, Olive	283	
Trimble, George S.	253	
Trimble, Laurence	314	
Troffey, Alex	337	483
Truesdell, Fred C.	253	
Truex, Ernest	253	
Tucker, George Loane	292	
Tuers, William H.	337	
Turner, Bowd M.	253	
Turner, D. H.	314	
Turner, F. A.	253	
Turner, Florence	283	
Turner, William H.	253	
Turpin, Ben	253	
Tyler, G. Vere	328	
Tyrol, Jacques	314	414

U

	Biography	Portrait
Ullman, Edward	337	473
Ulrich, E. D.	346	
U. S. Photoplay Corp.		172
Unsell, Eve	328	165
Uzzell, Corene	283	

V

	Biography	Portrait
Vale, Travers	314	
Vale, Vola	283	
Valentine, Spencer		486
Valentine, Vangie	283	
Valentino, Rudolph	253	
Valerie, Gladys	283	
Vallejo, Enrique Juan	337	431
Valli, Virginia	283	
Van, Beatrice	283	
Van, Wally	314	139
Van Beuren, Amedee J.	348	429
Van Buren, Mabel	283	
Van Buren, Ned	337	
Van Der Veer, Willard	337	480
Van Deusen, Cortlandt J.	314	407
Van Dyke, Truman	253	
Vane, Denton	253	
Van Loan, H. H.	328	
Van Loan, Philip	254	
Van Meter, Harry L.	254	
Van Name, Elsie	283	
Vann, Polly	283	
Van Petten, Stacey A.	328	
Vaughan, Roy V.	338	
Vekroff, Perry N.	315	153
Vernon, Agnes	283	
Vernon, Bobbie	254	
Vidor, Florence	283	
Vidor, King W.	292	123
Vignola, Robert G.	315	
Vincent, James	315	140
Vitagraph Company		51
Vitagraph Big V Comedies		56
Vivian, Robert	254	
Von Stroheim, Erich	315	
Voshell, John M.	315	

W

	Biography	Portrait
Wade, John P.	254	
Wagner, William F.	338	
Walcamp, Marie	283	
Wales, Betty	283	
Wales, Claude Henry	338	
Wales, R. Ellis	315	478
Walker, Charlotte	283	
Walker, Lillian	283	
Walker, Robert Donald	254	
Walker, Vernon L.	338	
Wallace, C. R.	328	472
Wallace, Dorothy	284	
Wallock, Edwin N.	254	
Walpole, Stanley	254	
Walsh, George	254	
Walsh, Raoul A.	292	
Waltemeyer, Jack	254	
Walters, Dorothy	284	
Walthall, Henry B.	254	
Walton, Olive	284	
Ward, Chance E.	254	
Ward, Fannie	284	
Ward, Freddie Fay	254	
Ward, Hap	254	
Ward, Ivy	288	451
Ward, Lucille	284	

STUDIO DIRECTORY

	Biography	Portrait
Warde, Ernest C.	315	129
Warde, Frederick B.	254	
Ware, Helen	284	
Warner, H. B.	254	
Warner, Marion	284	
Warren, Dwight W.	338	
Warren, Edward	315	
Warren, Fred	254	
Warren, Mary	284	
Warrenton, Gilbert	338	
Warrenton, Lule	284	
Warwick, Robert	254	
Washburn, Bryant	255	
Washburn, Hazel	284	
Waterman, Ida	284	
Watson, William H.	315	
Weadock, Louis	328	
Webb, George	255	
Webb, Kenneth	315	116
Webb, Roy	315	
Webber, George F.	338	
Weber, L. Lawrence	348	
Weber, Lois	292	
Weer, Helen	284	
Wehlen, Emmy	284	
Weigel, Paul	255	437
Weinberg, Jack	348	
Welch, Niles	255	
Welden, Jess C.	255	
Wells, Raymond	315	
Welsh, William J.	255	
Wendell, Bunny	284	
West, Billy	255	
Westinghouse Electric		301
West, Charles H.	255	386
West, Lillian Mildred	284	
Westover, Winifred	284	
Wharton, Leopold	293	
Wharton, Theodore	293	142
Wheatcroft, Stanhope	255	
Whipple, Clara Brimmer	284	
Whistler, Margaret	284	
Whitcomb, Barry	255	
Whitcomb, Daniel Frederick	328	
Whitcomb, Mabel	284	
White, Billy	255	
White, George	255	
White, Gilbert	315	
White, Jack	315	
White, Pearl	285	
Whitlock, T. Lloyd	255	
Whitman, Alfred	255	
Whitman, Philip H.	338	
Whitman, Velma	285	
Whitman, Walt	255	
Whitney, Claire	285	
Whitson, Frank	255	
Whittaker, Charles Everard	328	477
Wilkinson, James	328	
Wiggin, Margaret A.	285	
Wilbur, Crane	255	
Wilkinson, Mary E.	285	
Wilky, L. Guy	338	
Willa, Susanne	285	
Wiliat, Irvin V.	293	{156, 157}
Willets, Gilson	328	
Williams, C. Jay	315	
Williams, Cora	285	
Williams, Earle Rafael	255	
Williams, Frank D.	338	175
Williams, Harry H.	329	
Williams, Kathlyn	285	
Williams, Lawrence E.	338	
Williams, Walter E.	338	
Willis, F. McGrew	329	
Willis, Richard	293	178
Wilson, Ben	256	150
Wilson, Charles Jerome, Jr.	329	
Wilson, Edna Mae	285	
Wilson, Hal	256	
Wilson, Lois	285	
Wilson, Margery	285	
Wilson, Tom	256	
Windemer, Fred C.	256	
Windom, Lawrence C.	315	
Winfield-Kerner Company		516
Wing, Ward	256	
Wing, William E.	329	422
Winther, Carl Pagh	338	
Wise, Harry	256	
Withey, Chet	315	103
Wolbert, Dorothea	285	
Wolf, Clarence	348	
Wolfe, Jane	285	
Woods, Frank E.	329	
Woods, Walter	329	
Woodward, Eugenie	285	
Woodward, Henry F.	256	
Woody, J. S.	346	
Worsley, Wallace	315	
Worth, Lillian	285	
Worthington, William	316	408
Wright, Fred E.	316	
Wright, Helen	285	
Wyckoff, Alvin	338	
Wynard, Edward	338	
Wynne, Hugh	256	

Y

	Biography	Portrait
Yohalem, George M.	329	
Yorska	285	
Young, Briant S.	293	
Young, Clara Kimball	285	
Young, Hal	338	
Young, Harold	329	
Young, Howard Irving	329	
Young, Jack R.	338	
Young, James	315	
Young, Lassie	285	459
Young, Tammany	256	463
Young, Waldemar	329	
Younge, Lucille	286	
Younger, A. P.	329	476

Z

	Biography	Portrait
Zallbra, George C.	338	
Zangrilli, Orestes A.	338	
Zellner, Arthur	329	426
Zellner, Lois	329	426
Zellinger, William M.	338	
Zukor, Adolph	348	

¶ For service when you need it
¶ Use the "In The Studios" Section of MOTION PICTURE NEWS
¶ For players, directors and writers.

PRODUCERS
DIRECTORS
ARTISTS

who wish to obtain stories for use in future productions should avail themselves of the services of the

FILM FICTION MART

This service is rendered absolutely without charge to all Producers, Directors and Artists. Investigations are made and negotiations carried on with the utmost care; the stories being chosen especially for the individual and not submitted in a hit or miss manner in the hope that something will be found suitable.

SYNOPSES

of any books desired will be submitted at any time upon request.

WHY NOT AVAIL YOURSELF OF THIS SERVICE?

FILM   FICTION   MART
MOTION PICTURE NEWS
729 Seventh Avenue
New York City

Robert J. Shores
Manager

PRINTING

COMMERCIAL — RELEASES

NEGATIVE DEVELOPING

ASK US ABOUT THE LOWEST
NEGATIVE INSURANCE RATES
OF ANY LABORATORY

NICHOLAS KESSEL LABORATORIES, Inc.
FORT LEE, N. J.

Phone, Fort Lee 221

THE PRODUCERS SECURITY CORPORATION

RICORD GRADWELL, President

(*An Organization of Service*)

General Offices: 516 Fifth Avenue, New York City
Branch: 404 Citizens Natl. Bank Bldg., Los Angeles, Cal.

───o───

The Object of this Corporation is to adequately safeguard and protect the interests of the

INDEPENDENT PRODUCERS

by rendering them a *guaranteed service* covering

SALES	DISTRIBUTION	AUDITING
PUBLICITY	ADVERTISING	LEGAL SERVICE

Booklet on Application

The Silver Creek Press
PO Box 334
Random Lake WI 53075
Rschroeter@SilentReels.com

Publisher's Note

I don't remember the name of the auction house I bought it from, but sometime in the mid-to-late 1990s, I was top bidder on a collection of books and magazines related to movies and TV. They were from the collection of Frank Buxton (1930-2018), and came in six large, heavy boxes.

Over the years, I have sold many of these items, but I held onto The Motion Picture Studio Directory and Trade Annual 1920. Believing it had special interest to early film enthusiasts, I was reluctant to let it go to just one buyer. So I decided to publish it in the form you now hold. Pages are reproduced here just slightly larger than originally published. I adjusted some pages in Photoshop, so print from the other side of the page wouldn't show through the white spaces. Pages face each other as originally published.

The image below appears with an article on Frank Buxton on Wikipedia, which says this 1966 photo is in the public domain, and has it captioned:

"Photo of Frank Buxton from the [ABC] television program *Discovery*."

Dear Post Office official:

If you have opened this package, looking for content that disqualifies it from being sent via Media Mail, don't celebrate quite yet.

Please be informed that what follows on the next page is
not an advertisement.
It is, rather, a
Public Service Announcement.

Looking for *Silent Films*
and other great movies & classic TV shows?
Check out

GRAPEVINE VIDEO
www.grapevinevideo.com
4021 W. San Juan Ave • Phoenix AZ 85019
All silents have musical accompaniment!